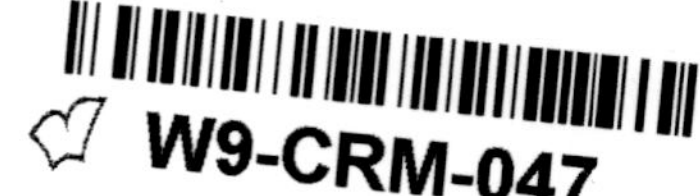

'BILL HARRY KNOWS MORE ABOUT THE BEATLES THAN THE BEATLES KNOW THEMSELVES'

MIKE READ

The Ultimate Beatles Encyclopedia is the most comprehensive book on the Fab Four ever produced. With over 1500 entries and 300 rare and unseen photos, this A-Z of Beatledom will clarify any query, settle any argument, inform and entertain. Every detail of the Beatles' amazing careers is here: every record released, every song written, every gig played ...

But *The Ultimate Beatles Encyclopedia* is much more than a reference book. Biographies of over 500 people associated with the group reveal stories of love affairs, drugs, court cases and internal disputes. Myths are shattered on touring days, early girlfriends and rock rivalries, and the record put straight on the deaths of Brian Epstein and Stuart Sutcliffe. No date is omitted, no crucial figure is overlooked, no incident left out. From the Abbey Road studios to the Zodiac club, *The Ultimate Beatles Encyclopedia* has them all – everything you ever wanted to know about the world's greatest band.

BILL HARRY is the world's leading authority on the Beatles. He attended the Liverpool College of Art with John Lennon, and founded the seminal music paper *Mersey Beat* which helped launch the band in the early sixties. He is the author of a number of books on the *Beatles*, including *Beatlemania, The McCartney File, Sergeant Pepper's Lonely Hearts Club Band* and *The Book of Lennon*. The book is drawn from his own massive archive, spanning over thirty years, and contains many exclusive photos and clippings.

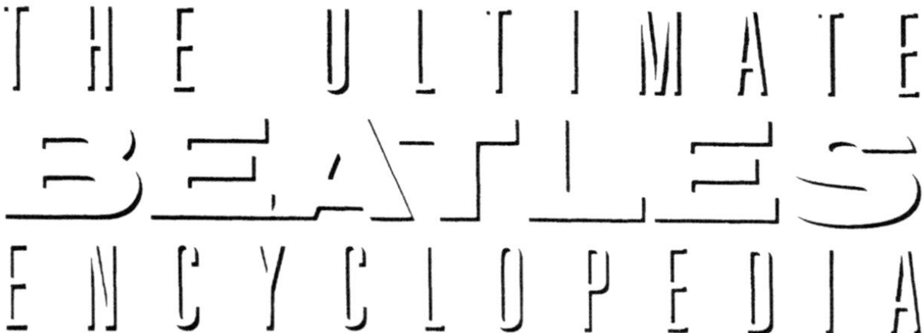
THE ULTIMATE
BEATLES
ENCYCLOPEDIA

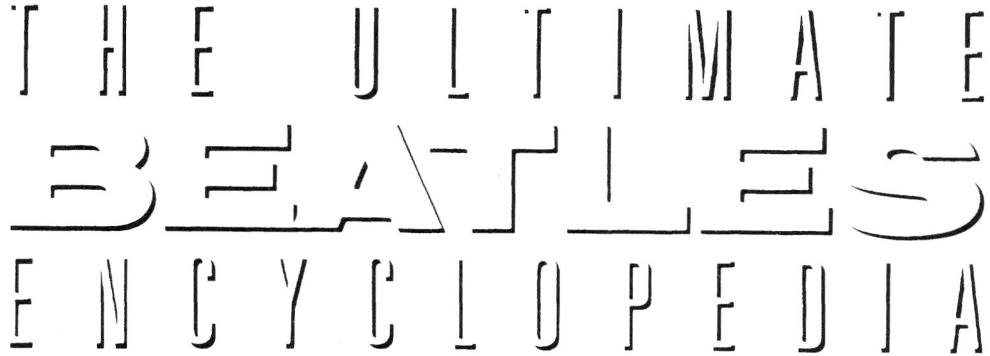

Bill Harry

NEW YORK

First published in Great Britain in 1992 by Virgin Books

Library of Congress Cataloging-in-Publication Data
Harry, Bill.
The ultimate Beatles encyclopedia / Bill Harry. — 1st American ed.
p. cm.
ISBN 0-7868-8071-6
1. Beatles—Encyclopedias. I. Title.
ML421.B4H45 1993
782.421660922—dc20 93-26933
CIP
MN

First Paperback Edition
1 0 9 8 7 6 5 4 3 2 1

I dedicate this book to my two lost friends, John Lennon and Stuart Sutcliffe, remembering the days when we vowed to make Liverpool famous. John and I were to see that happen, but Stuart never did. John's work will always live – but I am especially pleased to see that Stuart's work is at last receiving recognition.

ACKNOWLEDGEMENTS

Material in this book began to be gathered in 1961 when I launched the *Mersey Beat* newspaper in Liverpool and became the first person to write about the Beatles on a regular basis. I have used quotes and background material from interviews and conversations I have conducted personally with John Lennon, Paul McCartney, George Harrison, Ringo Starr, Pete Best, Stuart Sutcliffe, Brian Epstein, Bob Wooler, Allan Williams, Ray McFall, Rory Storm, Millie Sutcliffe, Brian Casser, Johnny Hutchinson, Johnny 'Guitar' Byrne, Pat Delaney, Brian Kelly, Sam Leach, Joe Flannery, Neil Aspinall, Mal Evans, Clive Epstein, Alistair Taylor, Derek Taylor, Gerry Marsden, Jackie Lomax, Cilla Black, Kingsize Taylor, Jim McCartney, Mike McCartney, Billy J. Kramer, Elsie Greaves, Iris Caldwell, Jonathan Hague, Les Chadwick, Cynthia Lennon, Pete Shotton, Mike Evans, Tony Bramwell, Peter Brown, Beryl Marsden, Ray Connolly, Ray Coleman, Mike Berry, Steve Aldo, Mitch Murray, Arthur Ballard, Cliff Bennett, Freda Kelly, Howie Casey, the Chants, the Beach Boys, Terry Doran, Bob Dylan, Manfred Weissleder, Horst Fascher, the Fourmost, Jim Gretty, Johnny Hamp, Dezo Hoffman, the Hollies, Peter Jones, Bert Kaempfert, Rod Murray, Alun Owen, P. J. Proby, Little Richard, Norman Rossington, Dick Rowe, Tony Sheridan, Mimi Smith, Brian Sommerville, Tony Barrow, Sounds Incorporated, Alvin Stardust, the Swinging Bluejeans, Lu Walters, Mary Wells, Kenny Lynch and many others.

I have also researched from my vast library of over 250 Beatles books and 500 fan magazines, and my collection of newspaper clippings and numerous magazines. In addition, I have corresponded with dozens of other contacts associated with the Beatles story and used research I have compiled in the hundreds of Beatles articles I have written over the last 30 years in newspapers, magazines and Beatles fanzines.

I'd also like to thank the many Beatles fans who contact me with items of useful information and the excellent fan magazines such as *Beatlefan*, *Beatles Now*, *Beatles Unlimited*, *Strawberry Fields* and *Instant Karma*.

A large number of photographs come from my personal Mersey Beat files and from the photographers I commissioned in the early days of the paper — Les Chadwick, Peter Kaye, Graham Spencer and Dick Mathews. Among the many people who have allowed me to use photographs I must mention Jan Olaffson, Sam Leach, Liz and Jim Hughes, the late Clive Epstein, EMI Records, the National Film Archives, the late Dick James, the Rocket Record Company, Polydor Records, Merseyside Tourism Office, Ron Jones, Philip Nevitski, Sotheby's, Virgin Records, Warner Bros Video, Edsel Records, Flying Music Co, Mitch Murray, Johnny Hamp, Granada Television and United Artists.

Thanks to everyone at Virgin Publishing who helped to put the book together: Rob Shreeve, Emma Worth, Sally Holloway, Guy Lloyd, Paul Forty, Riona MacNamara and designer Adrian Morris.

I must also acknowledge the help and support of my wife Virginia, who was as much a part of the whole scene as I was myself, from the time in 1960 when she began to aid me in the planning of *Mersey Beat*. Her constant companionship through those years led people to call us 'Mr & Mrs Mersey Beat'. Incredibly, songwriter John Schroeder wanted to write a musical about the two of us! He was intrigued as to how an impecunious young couple, with hardly any experience of the world, helped to keep a whole scene going — and one which was eventually to change the entire international music industry.

Bill Harry. London, 1992.

• Abbey Road *(Album)*

The Beatles' twelfth British album and the last one that the group recorded in the studio – *Let It Be* had been recorded earlier, when sessions had been organized using the title 'Get Back'.

Abbey Road was issued in Britain on Parlophone PCS 7088 on 26 September, 1969 and went straight to No. 1 in Britain within a week. It was issued in America on SO 383 on 1 October 1969, where it also topped the charts.

Originally, there was some conflict as to the approach to the album. John wanted a rock 'n' roll style album and Paul plumped for a pop symphony, or pop opera, with the songs segued into each other to produce one long medley. A compromise was achieved with Side One following along the lines of John's wish for individual tracks and Side Two satisfied Paul with tracks so close together they basically formed a sixteen-minute medley.

Abbey Road became the best-selling Beatles album with sales of approximately ten million during the decade after release. It was also the first Beatles album to be issued solely in stereo and it won a **Grammy Award** as Best Engineered Non-Classical Recording.

The tracks were: Side One: 'Something', 'Maxwell's Silver Hammer', 'Oh Darling', 'Octopus's Garden', 'I Want You (He's So Heavy)'. Side Two: 'Here Comes The Sun', 'Because', 'You Never Give Me Your Money', 'Sun King', 'Mean Mr Mustard', 'Polythene Pam', 'She Came In Through The Bathroom Window', 'Golden Slumbers', 'Carry That Weight', 'The End', 'Her Majesty'.

The cover was striking and comprised a colour photograph, bled off on all sides, with no title or text. The photograph was taken by **Iain Macmillan** at 10.00 a.m. on 8 August, 1969. He was given ten minutes to take the shot outside the **Abbey Road Studios**. He balanced on a stepladder and took six shots of the four walking across the zebra crossing. It was Paul who selected the cover shot from the pictures taken by Macmillan. Paul had, in fact, come up with the original idea for the sleeve and had presented Macmillan with a sketch for it. Many people can see Paul's hand in *Abbey Road* and the individual tracks written by him were: 'Maxwell's Silver Hammer', 'Oh Darling', 'You Never Give Me Your Money', 'She Came In Through The Bathroom Window', 'Golden Slumbers', 'Carry That Weight', 'The End' and 'Her Majesty'.

A bizarre affair grew from the photograph. From America, a few weeks after *Abbey Road* was issued, a 'Paul Is Dead!' movement got underway. Disc jockey Russ Gibbs, on the Detroit radio station WKNR-FM, suggested that Paul had an argument with the other members of the Beatles at Abbey Road Studios on 9 (or 10) November 1966 and had stormed out of the session, driven away in his Aston-Martin and been decapitated in a crash. Brian Epstein had hushed up the death and replaced Paul with a lookalike. Gibbs said clues could be found on subsequent Beatles albums, including *Abbey Road*. It was pointed out that Paul was barefoot in the picture, which indicated a Mafia (or Grecian) sign of death. A Michigan journalist, Fred LaBour, reviewing the album, claimed that the group was leaving a cemetery and that John was dressed as a minister, Ringo as an undertaker and George as a gravedigger, and pointed out that Paul was out of step with the others, which apparently meant that it was in fact either his corpse, or, more popularly, a substitute who'd had plastic surgery. According to the rumours, proof positive of the imposter theory was the fact that Paul was holding a cigarette in his right hand and everyone knew the real Paul McCartney was left-handed.

Photographer Iain Macmillan pointed out, 'Paul turned up in his Oxfam suit and sandals and because it was a hot day he decided to do some shots with sandals on and some with sandals off. Paul checked all the pictures with a magnifying glass. I don't think the other three were particularly bothered. He chose the nearest shot with the legs stretched in almost uniform style and it was pure coincidence that it happened to be the one with his sandals off. I got the job through John but it was Paul's idea and I was given ten minutes around lunchtime to do it.'

Paul himself told disc jockey Paul Gambaccini, 'I just turned up at the photo session. It was a really nice hot day and I think I wore sandals. I only had to walk around the corner to the crossing because I lived pretty nearby. I had me sandals off and on for the session. Of course, when it comes out people start looking at it and they say, "Why has he got no shoes on? He's never done that before." Okay, you've never seen me do it before but in actual fact it's just me with me shoes off. Turns out to be some old Mafia sign of death or something.'

But 'Paul Is Dead!' fanatics were not deterred. In the course of their study of the *Abbey Road* cover they discovered that the registration number – 28IF – of a Volkswagen car in the background, indicated that Paul would have been 28 IF he had lived.

In fact, Paul was 27. Macmillan had been aware of the car, which belonged to a man who lived in the block of flats next door to the studios, and had tried to get the car moved for the photo session but the police pick-up truck was not able to get there in time. For years afterwards the man's number plates were stolen on numerous occasions and the car, with the plates (LMW 28IF) was eventually sold at auction at Sotheby's in 1986.

A photograph on the reverse of the sleeve shows the Abbey Road street sign. There is a crack in it – which theorists claimed was a mystical omen of the split in the group following Paul's death!

● Abbey Road Studios, *3 Abbey Road, St John's Wood, London NW8*

Due to its association with the Beatles, Abbey Road is recognized as the most famous recording studio in the world; but in fact this **EMI** recording complex has always

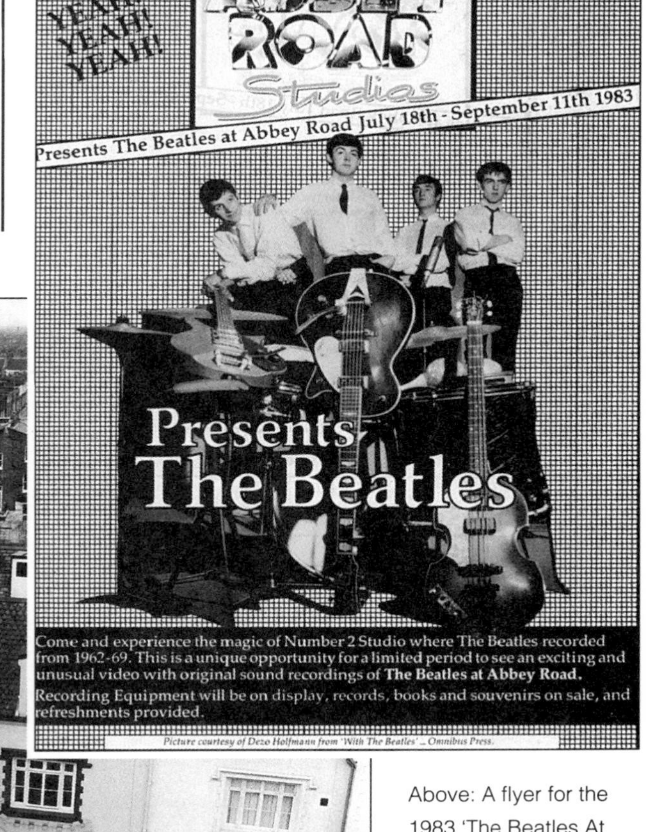

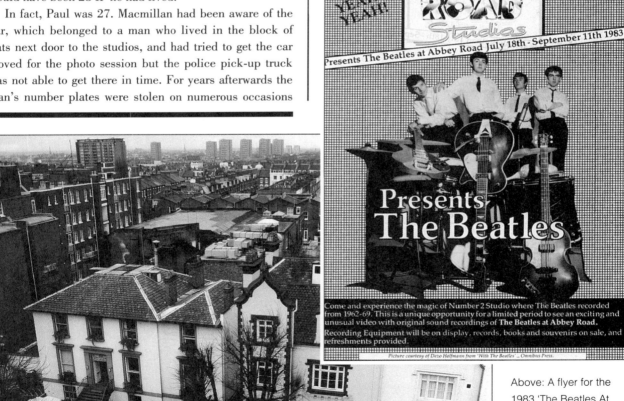

Above: A flyer for the 1983 'The Beatles At Abbey Road'.
Left: The world-famous Abbey Road Studios (Abbey Road Studios)

been the home of hit records, producing a stream of No. 1 recordings since charts first appeared in 1952. In fact, in the first 30 years of the charts, between 1952 and 1982, Abbey Road Studios accounted for a total of 74 No. 1 records, fifteen of them by the Beatles.

The building was first erected as a detached residence in 1830 with nine bedrooms, five reception rooms, two servants' rooms, a wine cellar and a large garden area.

It was purchased by the Gramophone Company Limited in December 1929 for £16,500 and converted into recording studios. By the time it was officially opened on 12 November 1931, the Gramophone Company had merged with Columbia Records to become EMI.

The studio complex has four Studios known as One, Two, Three and Four. The largest is Studio One, which is mainly used for orchestral and opera recording. The Beatles mainly used Studio Two, which was generally referred to as the 'pop studio', although they did use some of the other studios from time to time.

The Beatles first entered Abbey Road Studios for their original recording audition on Wednesday, 6 June 1962, and became regular users over a period of seven years. The Beatles were half an hour late for their recording audition and George Martin and Ron Richards were producing, with **Norman Smith** as engineer, Chris Neal as second engineer. Another member of the Abbey Road staff who decided to stay behind that summer's evening to work on the audition was **Ken Townsend**, later to become general manager of the studios.

Reports from some of those present indicate that it was the personalities of the individual Beatles and not the numbers they recorded which really convinced George Martin to sign them up. **Pete Best** was the band's drummer, but had been replaced by Ringo Starr by the time the group next arrived at the studios on Tuesday, 4 September 1962, to record 'Love Me Do' and 'How Do You Do It' in Studio Two, which was to become almost a second home for them.

As time went by the Beatles' productions became more intricate and many musicians, orchestras and choirs were eventually to appear on their records. Almost all of their Abbey Road sessions were produced by George Martin and among the host of people at Abbey Road who participated in Beatles recordings, mainly as engineers, or second engineers, at one time or another were: Norman Smith, Chris Neal, Richard Langham, Stuart Eltham, **Geoff Emerick**, Jacques Esmenjaud, David Lloyd, Ken Scott, Ron Pender, Hugh Davies, Mike Stone, Jerry Boys, Malcolm Davies, Vic Gann, Phil McDonald, Pete Abbott, Graham Platt, Richard Lush, Peter Vince, Graham Kirkby, Mike Sheady, Peter Bown, **John Smith**, Dave Harries, Jeff Jarratt, **Glyn Johns**, Tony Clark, Alan Parsons, Martin Benge, Nick Webb, Chris Black, Neil Richmond and John Kurlander.

Abbey Road is a busy recording studio and does not offer access to visitors. Beatles enthusiasts have to make do with taking photographs of the exterior, while a few yards from the studio gates is the most photographed zebra-crossing in the world, as immortalized on the cover of the *Abbey Road* album. However, between 18 July and 11 September 1983, Abbey Road Studios were opened to the public at a special multi-media event called 'The Beatles At Abbey Road', which took place in Studio Two, and during this time presented a special compilation video of the Beatles' recording career and provided visitors with souvenirs.

Interestingly enough, one of the first Beatles-related auctions took place at the studios. The auctioneers Phillips, Son & Neale presented their 'Sale Of The Century' at Abbey Road Studios on Thursday, 16 October 1980. Among the items for sale were: a pair of Studer J37 4-track tape recorders used by the Beatles on *Sgt Pepper*; the loudspeaker used on the Beatles EMI audition by Paul McCartney; a Mellotron tape organ used by the Beatles on various recordings, with original tapes; metal positive ('silver disc') with original Beatles signatures; a standing brass ashtray used by Ringo Starr on EMI sessions and a roll of loo paper stamped 'EMI Ltd', the last one of a batch rejected by the Beatles.

The entire history of the studio has been documented in *Abbey Road* by Brian Southall (Patrick Stephens Ltd).

● Abbotsfield Park, Chassen Road, Urmston, Lancashire

Site which hosted the annual 'Urmston Show'. During the 1963 Urmston Show, Kennedy Street Enterprises, a Manchester-based agency, promoted a special music carnival in a marquee on Monday, 5 August. The show itself commenced at 11.30 a.m., but the 'Pop Carnival' actually started at 7.30 p.m.

Advertised as a 'Twist & Shout Dance', it starred the Beatles, with **Brian Poole & the Tremeloes**, the

Dennisons and Johnny Martin & the Tremors in support. Compere for the event was **David Hamilton**, who was paid a fee of ten guineas.

The Dennisons had their new single 'Be My Girl' approaching the Top 30 – and the audience that night were entertained with two versions of 'Twist And Shout', one by Brian Poole & the Tremeloes, the other by the Beatles.

When the Beatles were due to go on, Ringo's drum kit had already been set up. A van arrived at the back of the tent and the boys got out, carrying their guitars, with Ringo carrying drumsticks. They went straight on stage, dressed in their collarless Pierre Cardin suits, and the crowd rushed forward – there were no seats provided; the inside of the marquee was in a dance hall format. After their performance they rushed back into their van and were driven away.

● ABC T*heatre, Blackpool, Lancashire*

The Beatles made their debut at this venue on 14 July 1963 and next appeared there the following month on 11 August and 25 August. Their final appearance in 1963 took place on Sunday, 8 September when the Sons of the Piltdown Men, Terry Young, Jack Douglas, Lee Leslie, the Countrymen and Chas McDevitt and Shirley Douglas were also on the bill.

Their 19 July 1964 appearance at the venue was for a live broadcast of ABC TV's 'Blackpool Night Out'. ***Mersey Beat*** covered the event and their report read:

> 'When we arrived at the ABC Theatre, Blackpool, at the invitation of **Nems Enterprises** recently, the Beatles were in the middle of rehearsals on stage and Paul was belting out "Long Tall Sally" – in fine form.
>
> 'Seated around in the vast, luxurious theatre were members of the cast – **Mike and Bernie Winters**, Jimmy Edwards, **Lionel Blair** and also Brian Epstein, **Neil Aspinall, Mal Evans** and Johnny Hackett.
>
> 'For almost an hour the boys were on stage performing – "I wish we could have mimed during rehearsals," John told us later – and soon after they joined us they were called back on stage.
>
> '"We've been rehearsing for hours," John said,

Virginia Harry, John Lennon and Bill Harry at the ABC, Blackpool. (*Mersey Beat* Archives)

when he rejoined us, and in another half hour he was on stage again.

'During the whole time, on stage or off, the boys were clowning around and having quite a laugh.

'When one of the production team called for silence and gave instructions to the cast he was greeted with applause from John, George, Paul and Ringo, and when there was a delay during dress rehearsals George was shouting "Come 'ead" and John, "I'm going home!"

'The rehearsals for the TV show "Blackpool Night Out" were proving to be even more hilarious than the programme that was screened, as Jimmy Edwards and Frank Berry kept coming out with jokes that weren't in the script.

'"They'll use different jokes on the actual programme because they want to keep the musicians in the pit laughing," John explained.

'Apart from singing several numbers including "A Hard Day's Night" and "Long Tall Sally", the Beatles appeared in several sketches.

'Ringo really looked picturesque as a patient in a brightly coloured smock and patterned pyjamas during the first sketch and all four were certainly dressed for the part when they took the stage as dustmen.

'The boys are certainly branching out, having emerged as personalities and comedians and we look forward to seeing them on a similar variety programme.'

In fact, the four were back at the ABC for another 'Blackpool Night Out' show hosted by Mike and Bernie on 1 August 1965. Also on the bill were Teddy Johnson and Pearl Carr, Johnny Hart and the Lionel Blair Dancers.

● ABC Cinema, *Warwick Road, Carlisle, Cumberland*

The Beatles first appeared at this venue as part of the **Helen Shapiro** tour on 8 February 1963. An unfortunate incident at their hotel, the **Crown and Mitre**, later that night during which they were refused entrance to a function because of their leather jackets, resulted in an anti-Beatle report in the *Daily Express*.

Their second and final appearance at the cinema took place on the group's autumn tour of Britain on 21 November 1963. John Lennon was quite delighted with the reception the Beatles received at this gig and said, 'There was even a bit of screaming for us. We'd had that in clubs, but in a big hall like the ABC, there it was a memorable experience.'

● ABC, *London Road, West Croydon, Surrey*

The Beatles appeared at this venue only once, during the **Tommy Roe/Chris Montez** Tour, on 21 March 1963.

● ABC, *Lothian Road, Edinburgh, Scotland*

The Beatles' debut appearance at this cinema on 29 April 1964 was jointly promoted by Brian Epstein and Albert Bonici. They next appeared at the cinema on 19 October 1964.

● ABC, *London Inn Square, Exeter, Devon*

The Beatles made their debut here on 28 March 1963 as part of the **Tommy Roe/Chris Montez** Tour. They returned to the venue later the same year during their Autumn Tour on 14 November and their final appearance at the cinema took place on 28 October 1964.

● ABC, *Great Yarmouth, Suffolk*

The Beatles appeared at this cinema in the seaside resort of Great Yarmouth only once. The occasion was a concert on 28 July 1963.

● ABC, *Market Street, Huddersfield, Yorkshire*

The Beatles appeared at this venue only once at a concert which took place on 29 November 1963.

● ABC, *Ferensway, Hull, Yorkshire*

The Beatles made their debut at this venue on 24 November 1963. Their second and final appearance at the cinema took place on 16 October 1964.

● ABC, *Saltergate, Lincoln*

The Beatles appeared here once, on 28 November 1963. At a press conference before the show Ringo developed earache. A doctor was called and, being female, was delayed by guards and it took her twenty minutes to get by them and examine her patient. They went to the local hospital for a further examination and one of the nurses

For light relief, John dances with George. (*Mersey Beat* Archives)

commented that it was an occupational hazard for a Beatle with the hair getting into their ears.

Ringo was rushed back in time for the show and as soon as they finished their performance they whizzed away to the nearest police station, still in their stage clothes and make-up. After they'd changed and were ready to leave in their car, which had been surrounded by twenty policemen, the police chief insisted that they sign autographs for his daughters.

● ABC, *Abington Square, Northampton*

Both appearances by the Beatles at this cinema took place in 1963. The first was as part of the **Tommy Roe/Chris Montez** Tour on 27 March and the second was during their own Autumn Tour on 6 November.

● ABC, *George Street, Plymouth, Devon*

The Beatles appeared in concert twice at this venue. The first appearance took place on 13 November 1963, and the second on 29 October 1964.

● ABC, *South Street, Romford, Essex*

The Beatles only appeared at this venue once, as part of the **Tommy Roe/Chris Montez** Tour on 20 March 1963.

● ABC, *Station Road, Wigan, Lancashire*

The Beatles made a single appearance at this venue on their only British tour of 1964 on Tuesday, 13 October.

The ABC manager Neville Ward had been making arrangements for some weeks and in addition to the 40 members of the St John Ambulance Brigade who were on call, his six members of staff were aided by six volunteers from the Wigan Amateur Operatic Society.

There was a capacity audience of 2,000 and the acts who preceded the Beatles were the **Rustiks**, **Michael Haslam**, **Sounds Incorporated, Mary Wells** and **Tommy Quickly**. Compere for the show was **Bob Bain**.

● Abergavenny Town Hall Ballroom, *Abergavenny, Monmouthshire, Wales*

The Beatles appeared here on 22 June 1963. Paul, George, Ringo and **Neil Aspinall** travelled to the gig in the group van, while John remained in London to record a **'Juke Box Jury'** appearance. Brian Epstein booked a helicopter to fly John to Wales at a cost of £100. He landed at Peny Pound football ground and rushed to the Town Hall where the show was to start at 9.50 p.m.

There were approximately 500 people at the gig, and afterwards the Beatles were invited to a small reception by Lord Mayor Jack Thurston. A local singer Bryn Yemm was one of the selected guests and since everyone seemed to know him, Paul asked: 'Who are you?' 'I'm only a local kid,' he replied and Paul laughed and said, 'I like that.' Later, Brian Epstein had a chat with Bryn and asked him to come up and see him in London. 'But I didn't have any money, so I couldn't do it,' he said. However, Bryn Yemm and the Yemmen recorded for EMI Columbia and their first single was called 'Black Is The Night'. Bryn was later to team up with his wife Ann and promote his own career, which resulted in four albums in the British charts in a single year and an entry in *The Guinness Book of Records*.

● Abrams, Steve

In 1967 Steve Abrams was a PhD student at Oxford. The young American was eager to study the effects of marijuana on people to determine whether it was harmless.

As it was illegal, he couldn't carry out his research without permission from the Home Office, who referred him to the Chief Constable of Oxford, who refused his request.

Steve, nevertheless, went to Chichester to report on the **Rolling Stones** drug bust trial for *International Times*. When Judge Black sentenced Keith Richard to a year in prison with £500 costs and Mick Jagger to three months with £100 costs, there was a certain amount of sympathy from the public and the national press, both feeling that the Stones had been treated too harshly.

An appeal was lodged and Steve decided to galvanize public opinion even further. Within a matter of hours of the Chichester verdict being given he put into operation an idea he'd had for some time – a full-page advertisement in *The Times* newspaper bearing the signatures of a number of respected people who had an enlightened attitude towards marijuana.

He discussed the idea with Miles (of *International Times* and the **Indica Gallery**) and mentioned the difficulty of obtaining the necessary finance. Miles approached Paul McCartney and talked him into putting up the money. As it turned out, the bill was paid from the Beatles' advertising account.

The advertisement appeared in *The Times* of 24 July 1967 and began:

> The signatories to this petition suggest to the Home Secretary that he implement a five-point programme of cannabis law reform:
>
> 1. The government should permit and encourage research into all aspects of cannabis use, including its medical applications.
>
> 2. Allowing the smoking of cannabis on private premises should no longer constitute an offence.
>
> 3. Cannabis should be taken off the dangerous drugs list and controlled, rather than prohibited, by a new *ad hoc* instrument.
>
> 4. Possession of cannabis should either be legally permitted or at most considered a misdemeanour punishable by a fine of not more than £10 for a first offence and not more than £25 for any subsequent offence.
>
> 5. All persons now imprisoned for possession of cannabis or for allowing cannabis to be smoked on private premises should have their sentences commuted.

There were 64 signatories within the advertisement in support of the proposal. They included Brian Epstein, John Lennon, Paul McCartney, Ringo Starr, George Harrison, George Melly, David Hockney, David Bailey, David Dimbleby, Kenneth Tynan, Jonathan Miller, R. D. Laing, painters John Piper and Patrick Procktor, publishers Anthony Blond and Tom Maschler, and Tom Driberg, the MP.

● Academy Of Meditation, *Shankaracharya Nagar, India*

The **Maharishi Mahesh Yogi**'s ashram in the Himalayas. He invited the Beatles and their party to take part in a three-month course of Transcendental Meditation with him at the ashram (a holy place where people study and meditate), set on a plateau 150 feet above the River Ganges, half a mile south of the mountain town of Rishikesh.

On Friday, 15 February 1968 John and **Cynthia Lennon**, George and **Pattie Harrison**, **Jennie Boyd** and a number of friends flew out from London airport to Delhi. Also on the flight were some representatives of the press, including **Don Short** of the *Daily Mirror* and Robin Turner of the *Daily Express*. After a 20-hour flight they arrived at Delhi at 8.15 a.m. **Mia Farrow** was at the airport to meet them. Three cars were needed to drive them to Rishikesh, 150 miles away. It was a cold, wet day and when they arrived they were met by the Maharishi, had some tea, then went to bed.

Paul McCartney and **Jane Asher** and Ringo and **Maureen Starkey** flew out from London on 19 February.

There were approximately 70 students at the ashram for the course, ranging from the young to the old and from America, Britain, Finland, Denmark, Sweden and Germany. They included a German Lufthansa pilot, a British Rail signalman with his mother, a Hollywood actor named Tom, a hairdresser from Canada and a German physicist. Among the friends of the Beatles were Mia and **Prudence Farrow**, **Donovan** and Gypsy Dave, **Mike Love** of the **Beach Boys**, **Neil Aspinall**, **Mal Evans**, **Alexis Mardas** and jazz musician Paul Horn.

The Academy was extremely luxurious for an ashram. There was a lecture hall and two dining halls. One dining room was covered, the other had no roof. A new swimming pool was being built beside the lecture hall. The accommodation was very comfortable and comprised five-room stone-built cottages, newly furnished, which had twin beds or four-poster beds, new rugs on the walls and floors, dressing tables, shelves and cupboards and a bathroom, toilet and shower, plus electric heating. The ashram employed a full-time staff of 40, which included cooks, cleaning staff and printers at the Academy's printing works.

Breakfast was served outdoors at 7.00 a.m. It consisted of cornflakes, puffed wheat or porridge, fruit juice, tea or coffee, toast, marmalade or jam. The students then meditated before they had a vegetarian lunch and dinner, which comprised soup, lots of salads, rice and potatoes, which they ate from long, plastic-covered tables. For the Beatles and their party, Mal Evans often travelled all the way to Delhi to obtain eggs. The Maharishi didn't take meals with his students.

There were two 90-minute lectures each day at 3.30 p.m. and 8.30 p.m. The students meditated alone and had notices for their rooms which read: 'Meditating: Do Not Disturb'. George and John were most enthusiastic students and meditated between seven and nine hours a day.

During the party's stay, there were celebrations for three birthdays. George was 25 on 25 February and was presented with a cake with white icing and pink flowers which had the greeting 'Jai Guru Deva' in gold letters. Pattie was 23 on 17 March. A boy from Lancaster, called Mike, who with his mate Paul had hitch-hiked to India on their way to Australia and were paying for their course by working in the kitchens, celebrated his 21st birthday.

Ringo, who had been troubled so much by stomach ailments since he was a child, couldn't adapt to the food and Maureen couldn't stand the insects, so the couple decided to leave Rishikesh much earlier than planned, on 1 March. On their return, Ringo compared the ashram to a Butlins holiday camp. Paul and Jane managed to remain for six weeks, but left before the three-month course was over on 26 March. When asked if they were disillusioned, Paul replied, 'No, just a little homesick.'

On 31 March, there was an announcement by the Beach Boys that they would embark on a concert tour with the Maharishi called 'World Peace I' and they hinted that the Beatles would be involved.

Alexis Mardas didn't like the ashram because be felt that it was too materialistic and not spiritual enough. The Academy was surrounded by barbed wire, there was a helicopter pad, and he was appalled at the idea of an ashram with four-poster beds, masseurs and servants bringing water – and accountants. He suspected that the presence of full-time accountants indicated an overriding interest in money. He discovered that some of the Swedish ladies on the course had left all their money to the Maharishi and he also heard that the Maharishi expected the Beatles to donate 10–25 per cent of their annual income to a Swiss account in his name.

An example of the Maharishi's business sense occurred during discussions about **Apple** financing a film about the Maharishi with the proceeds going to a Transcendental Meditation University in London. The Maharishi kept haggling over the finances and Neil Aspinall made a special trip to discuss the film with him – the Maharishi had an accountant at his side throughout the meeting and kept insisting that he be paid an additional 2.5 per cent.

Magic Alex decided to discover if he could expose the Maharishi to the Beatles. He began to smuggle wine into the compound to give to some of the women, particularly a blonde nurse from California. She revealed that she'd had several private meetings in the Maharishi's cottage, during which he'd provided her with chicken for dinner, despite the fact that it was a vegetarian community. The girl also alleged that at one of her private consultations, the Maharishi had made sexual advances. Alex set a trap for the Maharishi and then confronted John and George with what he'd discovered. George didn't believe it at first and was angry with Alex. Then they began to discuss it and decided to leave the next morning. When morning came, John told the Maharishi that they were leaving. When he asked why, John told him, 'You're the cosmic one, you should know.'

The Maharishi was a powerful figure in the area and the group began to worry about how they were going to get home. Alex sent to Deradoon to fetch taxis, but the word was out and they couldn't hire any. Eventually they rented two old cars and paid the drivers to take them to Delhi. The cars broke down and the party had to flag down a saloon car and hitch a lift to their destination.

Despite the disappointing conclusion to their adventure, the period at the ashram had done them well, particularly in the case of John. There were no drugs or alcohol allowed at the ashram and as a result John was weaned off the drugs he had been taking. Both he and Paul wrote a large number of songs, approximately fifteen each, and Cynthia was to comment: 'He [John] went so deeply within himself through meditation that he separated himself from everything.'

● Across The Universe

The inspiration for the song came when John woke up at 7 o'clock one morning with the words 'pools of sorrow, waves of joy' spinning around in his head. He couldn't get back to sleep and began writing the number.

Evidence of the influence of the **Maharishi Mahesh Yogi** is contained in the chorus phrase *'Jai Guru De Va Om'* which refers to the Maharishi's teacher Guru Deva. The first version of the song was produced by George Martin on 4 February 1968.

During the session it was decided that some female voices were needed to sing the line, 'Nothing's going to change my world'.

Paul found two girls standing in the rain outside the studio and brought them in on the session. There was sixteen-year-old **Lizzie Bravo** from Brazil, who was staying in nearby Maida Vale and had ambitions of becoming an actress, and seventeen-year-old Gayleen Pease from Stoke Newington, London N16 who was studying for her 'A' levels.

The two were asked to sing the line over and over again.

The number was originally considered as the 'A' side of a Beatles' single, but 'Lady Madonna' was chosen instead and the track lay on the shelf for some time.

Comedian **Spike Milligan** had suggested to the World Wildlife Fund that they issue an album, with the proceeds going to their charity, and 'Across The Universe' was donated by the Beatles.

The album was called *No One's Gonna Change Our World* and it was issued on **EMI** Star Line SRS 5013 (LP) on 12 December 1969. Other artists featured on the album included **Cilla Black**; **Rolf Harris**; the **Hollies**; **Spike Milligan**; the Bee Gees; Lulu: Dave Dee, Dozy, Beaky, Mick and Tich; Cliff Richard & the **Shadows**; Bruce Forsyth and Harry Secombe.

When **Phil Spector** was called in to work on a number of Beatles tapes, he completely altered 'Across The Universe', removing the vocals by Paul and the two girls and introducing his 'wall of sound' and the famous 'Spector overkill'. This was the version which wound up on the *Let It Be* album.

The number also appeared on *The Beatles 1967-1970* and the *Rarities* compilations and in the boxed set of albums *The Beatles Box*.

David Bowie featured the number on his *Young Americans* album and John played on the track with him. The song was also performed by the Beatles in the film *Let It Be*.

● Act Naturally

Country music fan Ringo Starr got a chance to air his vocals on live shows and on record with this song, composed by Johnny Russell and Voni Morrison, which was a hit for Buck Owens in 1963. Ringo performed it on the group's American and British tours in 1965.

The number appears on the British *Help!* album and the American *Yesterday... And Today* LP. It is also found on the British EP *Yesterday* and was issued in the States as the flipside to 'Yesterday' on **Capitol** 5498 on 13

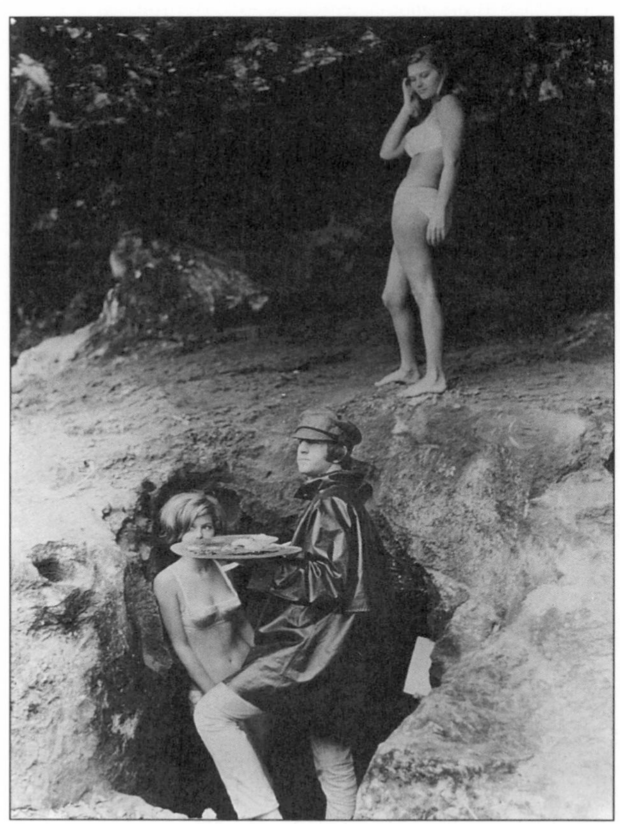

'Act Naturally' provided Ringo with his vocal highlight in *'Help'*. (©Apple/Walter Shenson Films)

September 1965. It's also to be found on *The Beatles Box* and *The Beatles Collection* sets.

It was also a TV highlight for Ringo and he played the number on 'The **Ed Sullivan** Show' in 1965, the '**Cilla**' show in 1965 and his own 'Ringo' TV special in 1978. In 1989 he re-recorded the number at **Abbey Road Studios** with Buck Owens.

● Adams, Beryl

Brian Epstein's original secretary, who was 26 years old when she began to work for him following his transference to the Whitechapel branch of **NEMS.** When Brian began to manage the Beatles, she also had to deal with a number of their affairs, including preparing their weekly pay packets.

When Brian moved to London she remained in Liverpool and married disc jockey **Bob Wooler**. For a time she managed the local band the Kirkbys, then divorced Bob and later remarried.

● Adams, Bob

A British road manager who was reputed to have been the first 'roadie' in the business. He retired in 1981 after 21 years working as a road manager for numerous bands including Cliff Richard & the **Shadows**, the Everly Brothers and Bo Diddley. He was hired for a time by the Beatles, who called him 'Old Bob'. John Lennon presented him with a signed photograph from 'The Beaters' as initially he could never remember their name. Before he retired he also worked for Paul McCartney and **Wings**.

● Adelphi Cinema, *Middle Abbey Street, Dublin, Eire*

Venue where the Beatles made their first-ever appearance in Ireland on 7 November 1963. On landing at Dublin Airport they were interviewed by Frank Hall of Radio Telefis Eireann, the television station, during which there was mention of their Irish backgrounds. Paul commented, 'I think we've all got a bit, except "limey" on the end here' – pointing to Ringo. John, Paul and George all had Irish ancestry and George's mother Louise was at the airport, having come over to Ireland to visit her numerous relations. Paul was to bring up the link again at their show when he told the audience, 'It's nice to be back home.'

Compere for the concert was Frank Barry and the Beatles opened with 'I Saw Her Standing There' and finished with 'Twist and Shout'. They were hustled out of the stage door into an *Evening Herald* van and on to the Gresham Hotel, where they were staying.

When the concert ended there was a riot by a mob of screaming teenagers during which windows were smashed, cars overturned, a hundred people injured and twelve of the rioters arrested.

● Adelphi Hotel, *Ranelagh Street, Liverpool 1*

The most famous hotel in Liverpool. Extremely popular in the days when the luxury liners ploughed their way across the Atlantic and headed for the seaport, it was once described as 'a great Cunard liner stuck in the middle of the city'.

Before setting off for the registry office to get married, **Freddie Lennon** and **Julia Stanley** met on the Adelphi steps on 3 December 1938, and after the ceremony were treated to lunch by Fred's brother Stanley at the large public house, nicknamed 'the big house', at the side of the Adelphi.

On 6 March 1964 the hotel was the setting for the annual ball organized by the Hospital Wing Aid Committee of the Home for Aged Jews. The dinner was in honour of Brian Epstein, who attended, along with **Alma Cogan**, Lionel Bart, Gerry Marsden and **Bernard Delfont**.

The hotel, now known as the Britannia Adelphi, has become the venue for the annual Beatles convention held in Liverpool each August bank holiday.

● Adelphi Theatre, *Bath Road, Slough, Berkshire*

Venue where the Beatles commenced their third British tour on 18 May 1963 on a bill with **Roy Orbison** and **Gerry & the Pacemakers**. Initially, Roy Orbison topped the bill of the show, but within a short time the Beatles were officially announced as headliners.

Their repertoire comprised: 'Some Other Guy', 'Do You Want To Know A Secret', 'Love Me Do', 'From Me To You', 'Please Please Me', 'I Saw Her Standing There' and 'Twist And Shout'.

Prior to the actual show on the opening night, Gerry Marsden, leader of Gerry & the Pacemakers, presented them with a silver disc for 'From Me To You'.

The group also appeared at the theatre on their

following tour on 5 November 1963 with the **Brook Brothers** and the **Kestrels.**

On 16 November 1965 Paul McCartney visited the cinema to see the Gene Pitney package show, primarily to watch Peter and Gordon, who were on the bill. From behind the curtain he made an announcement over the microphone: '**Arthur Howes** presents...the Gene Pitney Show! And to start the show in swinging style – the Mike Cotton Sound!' The audience, of course, had no idea that a member of the Beatles was making the announcement.

● Adelphi Ballroom, *New Street, West Bromwich, Birmingham*

The Beatles appeared at this venue only once, on the evening of 19 November 1962, following an earlier lunchtime session at the **Cavern.**

● Ad Lib Club, *Leicester Street, London WC2*

A trendy club and one of London's first discotheques, which boasted an exclusive celebrity membership list and was a watering hole for the stars of the swinging sixties such as the Beatles, the **Rolling Stones**, **Twiggy**, **Marianne Faithfull**, Lulu and **Alma Cogan**. It was managed by Brian Morris.

John, **Cynthia Lennon**, George and **Pattie Harrison** experienced their first psychedelic trip one night at the club. Earlier that evening they had attended a dinner party in Bayswater, hosted by the Beatles' London dentist. He lined up four sugar cubes on his mantel and then put them in their coffee. After they'd drunk their coffee he informed them that the cubes contained LSD.

Cynthia and Pattie were frightened. The four made their excuses and left, first stopping at the Pickwick club to look in on their friends, the group **Paddy, Klaus & Gibson.** They then arrived at the Ad Lib club. John was to say that they were out of their heads. The club was on the fourth floor of the building and had to be reached by a lift. John said, 'When we finally got in the lift we all thought there was a fire, but it was just a little red light. We were all hot and hysterical, and when we arrived on the floor, the lift stopped and the door opened, and we were all screaming.'

Rock artist Guy Peellaert executed a painting of the Ad Lib club which was featured in his 1974 book *Rock Dreams*. In the painting the Beatles are seen holding court and other Ad Lib regulars in the painting are Keith Richard, Anita Pallenberg, **Brian Jones**, Jeff Beck, Keith Relf, Scott Walker, Alan Price, Eric Burton, **Keith Moon**, Charlie Watts, Mick Jagger, Marianne Faithfull, **P. J. Proby**, **Sandie Shaw**, Zoot Money and Georgie Fame.

● Aintree Institute, *Longmoor Lane, Aintree, Liverpool 9*

In August 1961 **Bob Wooler** noticed two girls dancing in rhythm at the Aintree Institute. He considered them so good he invited them to dance on stage and suggested they form an act. Bob coined the name 'Shimmy Shimmy Queens' for them and with specially made dresses and the addition of another girl dancer, they made their debut at **Litherland Town Hall**. Further appearances followed at venues such as the Aintree Institute and **Hambleton Hall**. The girls' names were Marie Williams, Joan Pratt and Maureen O'Donnell. They appeared on the same bill as the Beatles at the Aintree Institute on 19 August 1961.

WE GUARANTEE A GREAT SHOW
Every FRIDAY and SATURDAY at . . . .

AINTREE INSTITUTE

Buses 20, 21, 30, 61, 91, 92, 93, 95, 96, 500 to the Black Bull—we're next door

LOOK! This Friday— DOMINOES With their new Kingsize sound
LEE EDDIE 5 Liverpool's Livesome Fivesome

LOOK! LOOK! This Saturday— GREAT BOPPIN' BEATLES!! This Saturday
plus Johnny Sandon and the Searchers

IT'S ALWAYS AI AT THE AI——YOUR WEEKEND DANCES

The Beatles made a total of 31 appearances at the venue after making their debut there on 7 January 1961. All but one of their appearances, their last, took place in 1961. They were: 13, 14, 18, 21, 27, 28 January; 8, 10, 15, 18, 22 February; 1, 4, 8, 11 March; 21, 28 July; 4, 12, 18, 19, 26 August; 2, 9, 16, 23, 28 October; and 11 November.

When they appeared there on 27 January 1962, **Brian Kelly** paid their fifteen pounds fee in coins. Brian Epstein was furious and described the incident in *A Cellarful of Noise* when they were paid '... in sixpences and florins and even halfpennies and I kicked up an awful fuss, not because £15 isn't £15 in any currency, but because I thought it was disrespectful to the Beatles.' Epstein ensured that they never appeared at the Aintree Institute again.

The venue featured non-stop jiving every Thursday, Friday and Saturday and posters announced 'Take a bus to the Black Bull – we're next door.'

The promotions by **Brian Kelly** were usually compered by Bob Wooler and generally featured three bands a night. The promotions ceased early in 1962 when the building was sold to a local church and it became a church social club.

● Ain't She Sweet

A number originally penned in the twenties by Jack Yellen and Milton Ager. A rock 'n' roll interpretation of the song was recorded by **Gene Vincent** in 1956 and included on his album *Bluejean Bop*.

It was the only number recorded during the May 1961 recording sessions in Hamburg on which John Lennon sang lead vocals. From that session this was a pure Beatle track, with no **Tony Sheridan** participation.

Strangely enough, it wasn't the first of the Polydor numbers to be issued as a single in either Britain or the United States, though it must have been the most obvious track from the entire recordings to capitalize on the Beatles' success. Which is how it turned out when it was issued in Britain on Polydor NH 52-317 on 29 May 1964 with 'If You Love Me Baby' on the flipside. The previous Polydor releases by the Beatles, 'My Bonnie', 'Sweet Georgia Brown' and 'Why' had all failed to chart, but 'Ain't She Sweet' reached No. 24 in the *New Musical Express* charts. The same pattern followed in America. Atco had a flop with 'Sweet Georgia Brown' but when 'Ain't She Sweet' was issued on ATCO 6308 on 6 July 1964 with 'Nobody's Child' on the flip it reached No. 19 in *Billboard*, No. 14 in *Cash Box* and No. 13 in *Record World*.

Ain't She Sweet was also the title of an album issued by Atco on Atco SD 33-169 on 5 October 1964, in an attempt to cash in on the Top Twenty success of the 'Ain't She Sweet' single. It contained the title track, plus three other numbers recorded by Tony Sheridan and the Beatles in Hamburg in 1961: 'Sweet Georgia Brown', 'Take Out Some Insurance On Me Baby' and 'Nobody's Child'. The sleeve featured the caption: 'Ain't She Sweet. The Beatles & Other Great Group Sounds From England'. The 'other great group sounds from England' were by an unknown group called the Swallows, who were unlikely to be an English group. The Swallows performed eight numbers: 'I Wanna Be Your Man', 'She Loves You', 'How Do You Do It', 'Please Please Me', 'I'll Keep You Satisfied', 'I'm Telling You Now', 'I Want To Hold Your Hand' and 'From Me To You'.

The American record buyers were now cottoning on to the fact that old tracks were being recycled and this was reflected in poor sales and the lack of any chart position.

This album, minus the tracks 'How Do You Do It' and 'I'll Keep You Satisfied', was re-released on Clarion 601 on 17 October 1966 under the title *The Amazing Beatles And Other Great English Group Sounds*.

● Akustik Studio, 57 Kirchenallee, Hamburg, Germany

A small recording booth to the rear of Hamburg's main railway station.

On Saturday, 15 October 1960, **Allan Williams** decided to have a record cut in what was basically a record-your-voice booth for sending greetings to relatives and such. Williams had two groups appearing in Hamburg at the time – the Beatles and **Rory Storm & the Hurricanes**. He was particularly impressed by the voice of **Lu Walters** of the Hurricanes and wanted to record him with the Beatles providing backing. **Pete Best** didn't accompany them to the booth, so the Hurricanes' drummer Ringo Starr took his place – making it the first time that John, Paul, George and Ringo played together. They backed Lu on a version of Gershwin's 'Summertime'. Two other members of the Hurricanes, Ty Brien and Johnny 'Guitar' Byrne, then joined Lu and Ringo on two further tracks, 'Fever' and 'September Song'.

The Beatles asked Williams if they could cut a record, but he wasn't willing to pay the extra money.

Lu Walters was to recall that nine copies of the disc were cut. No one seems to know what happened to them. Rory Storm had one, Lu gave one to his ex-wife and Williams left his copy behind him in a London pub several years later.

● Albany Cinema, *Northway, Maghull, Liverpool 31*

A three-hour charity variety show to raise funds for an ambulance for the local St John Ambulance Brigade, organized by **Jim Gretty**, saw comedian **Ken Dodd** topping the bill on 15 October 1961. The Beatles were an odd choice for this Sunday afternoon concert which featured light operatic arias, songs from *Carousel*, trad jazz and country music. Other acts on the bill were Les Arnold, Joe Cordova, Dave Dunn, Jim Markey, Lennie Rens, Bert King and the Eltones, Denis Smerdon, Edna Bell and Jackie Owen and the Joe Royal Trio. Country music was performed by Hank Walters & the Dusty Road Ramblers and Walters was to say, many years later, that Lennon had come up to him and said, 'I don't go much on your music, lad, but give us your hat.' Walters told Lennon that he didn't think much of the Beatles' music and they'd never get anywhere unless they got with it and played country music.

Ken Dodd also thought their music was terrible and made a complaint to the organizers. When one of them came into his dressing room and said they'd been told that if they gave him their card he might be able to get them some bookings, he threw the card away. He was reminded of it years later when Paul McCartney mentioned that they'd worked with him before. 'No, you've never worked with me, lad,' Dodd told him. When Paul mentioned it had been at the Albany, Dodd said, 'That noise wasn't you, was it?' 'Yeah, we were rubbish, weren't we?' 'You certainly were,' said Dodd. 'I had you thrown off.'

The Beatles closed the show with a ten-minute spot.

● Album Sleeves

The cover of *Sgt Pepper's Lonely Hearts Club Band* is arguably the most famous album cover of all time and the *Abbey Road* sleeve the most parodied, although these feats shouldn't conceal the fact that the entire series of Beatles album covers was innovative for their time and changed the entire approach to album sleeve presentation and design.

Prior to the consideration, care and creativity which went into the design of a Beatles album cover, the covers of albums were usually very basic and static, generally consisting of a photograph of the artist/artists concerned and a piece of lettering with the album title and artist's name. The field of album cover design was never the same after the release of *Sgt Pepper's Lonely Hearts Club Band*.

The Beatles' first album was at one time to be called 'Off The Beatle Track' and Paul McCartney designed a cover for it – a head-and-shoulders sketch of each of the four members of the band, two on top, two below, with the lettering in between, and the 'B' in 'Beatle' sporting antennae. This plan was abandoned and the album was called *Please Please Me* while the cover featured a photograph by veteran theatrical/film photographer **Angus McBean** of the Beatles looking down from the stairwell at **EMI House**. An interesting shot, although the sleeve wasn't particularly trendsetting. The sleeve notes were by Beatles Press Officer **Tony Barrow**.

The next album cover was taken by photographer **Robert Freeman**. Called *With The Beatles*, the sleeve featured a black and white shot of the heads of the four Beatles, wearing turtleneck sweaters, presenting the faces in a half-light, a technique pioneered by American photographer **Richard Avedon** and used to effect by **Astrid Kirchherr** in her Hamburg photographs of the Beatles. It was Freeman who conceived the idea of a black and white photograph, and although **EMI** initially resisted the idea, Brian Epstein and George Martin pressed for its use. The image has since become one of the most potent images of the Beatles and has been utilized by artists in paintings (e.g. David Oxtoby's *Yesterdays*) and parodied by other bands (e.g. the 1974 EP *With The Roogalator*). Sleeve notes were by Tony Barrow.

Robert Freeman was also responsible for the cover of the *A Hard Day's Night* album, which was done in the style of a photostrip, Polyphoto or photo kiosk strip – five square shaped head shots of each member of the group stretched across the cover in a total of twenty images, similar to the images Freeman designed for the *A Hard Day's Night* film, also displaying the half-light technique.

Brian Epstein and the Beatles were using Freeman regularly and he was once again commissioned to produce an album sleeve, this time for *Beatles For Sale*, for which he featured a colour portrait of the group, in the open air, unsmiling. It was a gatefold sleeve and an inner photograph consists of a collage of the group standing against a background of photographs of film stills – including images of Albert Finney, **Jayne Mansfield**, Ian Carmichael and Victor Mature – perhaps a hint at the *Sgt Pepper* sleeve to come? The back cover featured another colour shot of the four by Freeman (which was used as the cover of the American *The Early Beatles* album) and sleeve notes were by **Derek Taylor**.

The cover of *Help!* shows the four in their costumes from the Alpine sequences in the film, against a stark white background. Each of the four is posed miming a letter in semaphore. This is said to spell out the name of the film H-E-L-P. On the American album, which is more like the cover of the film poster, the figures of John and Paul have been transposed, which would make any planned semaphore message gobbledegook.

The photograph on the cover of *Rubber Soul* was the last album cover to be taken by Robert Freeman. The shot was taken in the garden of John's house in Weybridge, Surrey, and an intriguing distorted effect has been produced. Freeman explained it by saying, 'The distorted effect in the photo was a reflection of the changing shape of their lives. They had begun their careers as musicians, but the wide range of people and ideas they had encountered, their financial success, and the new privacy of their homes encouraged them to take up more varied and personal interests.' There is also a selection of seven black and white Freeman shots on the back cover.

The Beatles asked their friend **Klaus Voormann** to design the cover of their *Revolver* album. It comprises some fine line drawings of the heads of the individual Beatles surrounding a collage of photographs. The impressive image, with its delicate draughtsmanship, brought Voorman a **Grammy Award**.

A cover painting by David Christian was displayed on the cover of the compilation album *A Collection of Beatles' Oldies (But Goldies)*, which was a colourful and decorous design of a male dressed in 'Swinging London' fashions sitting on a drum-like shape with a drawing of the Beatles surrounding a vintage car in the background. The back cover featured a photograph by **Robert Whitaker**. This was probably put together by EMI without consultation with the Beatles, as it was not an album of new material.

The cover of *Sgt Pepper's Lonely Hearts Club Band* was the most expensive and elaborate front cover design ever produced up to that time and the first to print the complete song lyrics contained in the album.

In stark contrast to the intricate detail of the *Sgt Pepper* sleeve, the cover of *The Beatles* double album was in plain white, with the name 'The Beatles' written in small letters on it. This was a concept by artist **Richard Hamilton** and the sleeve package also contained some poster collages and a set of colour prints of photographs taken by **John Kelly**. As with the *Sgt Pepper* album, the Beatles had sought advice on the cover design from Robert Fraser, who'd recommended artist Peter Blake for *Sgt Pepper* and suggested Hamilton for the double album which, because of its design, has come to be known as the 'white' album. It is indicative of the fact that the Beatles approached seriously the subject of their album covers – apart from ones they were not really involved in, such as the compilations and *Yellow Submarine* – and their interest in the appearance of their album covers led to other groups taking an active part in how theirs were designed.

The *Yellow Submarine* cover was an illustration of the cartoon Beatles as featured in the animated cartoon.

The cover of *Abbey Road* is, next to *Sgt Pepper*, their most famous cover and the most imitated – how many album sleeves have since featured artists traversing a zebra crossing? The cover photograph was taken on the morning of 8 August 1969 by **Iain Macmillan** and the actual design of the sleeve was simple with only two photographs used and no title on the front cover – a bold move in itself.

Originally, the cover of the next sleeve, initially called 'Get Back', was to be taken on the same spot on the EMI stairwell as the *Please Please Me* album cover and taken by the same photographer, **Angus McBean** (a reference to them 'getting back' to their roots). This shot was taken, but not used until the double-album compilations *The Beatles 1962-1966* and *The Beatles 1967-1970*. The *Let It Be* (as the album was re-titled) sleeve featured four close-up shots of the individual members of the band, taken by **Ethan Russell** during the filming, placed in a square on a black background.

The Beatles had no real say in further sleeves. John Lennon's request to design the cover of their *Rock 'n' Roll* compilation was turned down by EMI and a cover painting by Roy Kohara, which the Beatles hated, was used.

It was **Capitol Records** who generally controlled the look of their American sleeves, which didn't display the imagination of the British releases in which the Beatles were involved. The one sleeve in which they took active participation, for *Yesterday... And Today*, was actually withdrawn by **Capitol** and a different cover pasted over it.

However, in the field of album cover design the Beatles, once again, had proved to be innovators, and the covers of albums of popular music have benefited and evolved into an art form in their own right as a result.

● Aldo, Steve

Liverpool singer who appeared on the Beatles' final tour of Britain at the close of 1966.

Aldo first started singing at the age of thirteen in *The Backyard Kids* at the Pavilion, Liverpool. He later sang with **Howie Casey** & the Seniors before moving to Cardiff to become a ladies' hairdresser.

He worked at Raymonde's (Mr Teasy Weasy) in London before going to sea for a year, then returned to Liverpool, joined the Challengers, moved to Hamburg and sang occasionally with the Dominoes. He joined the Nocturnes for a short time before becoming a member of the Griff-Parry Five.

Shortly after the Beatles tour he ceased singing and became a publican.

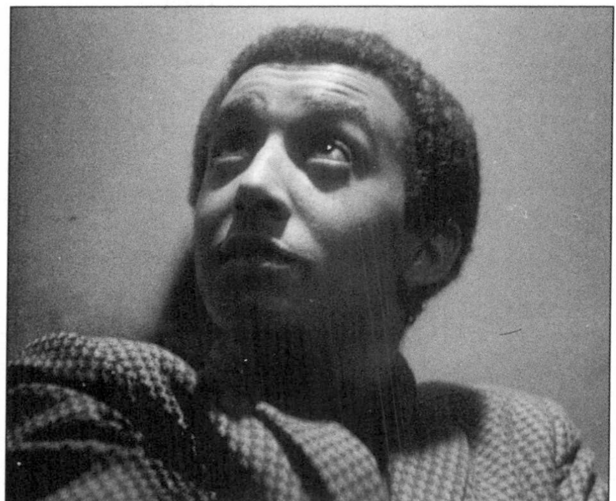

Steve Aldo – a Liverpool singer who appeared with the Beatles.

● Alexander, Arthur

Rhythm and blues singer, born on 10 May 1940 in Florence, Alabama. Alexander first made an impact in 1961/2 with songs such as 'Anna', 'Soldier Of Love', 'A Shot Of Rhythm And Blues', 'You Better Move On', and 'Go Home Girl'. In fact, his use of the word 'girl' in his songs became common lyric parlance and had an influence on John Lennon's lyrics.

In 1962 John introduced four songs popularized by Alexander into the Beatles act, and sang lead vocals on all

A flyer for the ill-fated Beatles Convention at the Alexandra Palace.

of them: 'Anna (Go To Him)', 'A Shot Of Rhythm And Blues', 'Soldier Of Love (Lay Down Your Arms)' and 'Where Have You Been All My Life?'

The Beatles recorded 'Anna', which was included on their debut album *Please Please Me*, and 'Where Have You Been All My Life?' is to be found on the **Star Club** albums. They performed 'A Shot Of Rhythm And Blues' and 'Soldier Of Love' on their BBC radio appearances.

The **Rolling Stones** recorded 'You Better Move On'.

● Alexandra Hall, *College Road, Crosby, Liverpool L23*

A hall where promoter **Brian Kelly** ran promotions. He booked the Beatles here only once, on 19 January 1961.

It was at halls like this where rock 'n' roll prospered and thrived on Merseyside, in the days when the events were referred to as 'jive' and lots of the venues were called 'jive hives'.

Brian Kelly was one of the handful of promoters who provided work for the growing army of Mersey bands after launching his first jive session in May 1959. Apart from Alexandra Hall he ran promotions at **Lathom Hall, Litherland Town Hall** and the **Aintree Institute**.

● Alexandra Palace, *London N22*

A notable London building which has housed various exhibitions and shows. The large structure was severely damaged by fire at the onset of the eighties.

The Palace was the venue for London's *Art Spectrum* from 11-31 August 1971, which was held in the Great Hall. The exhibition featured five of John and Yoko's films: *Cold Turkey*, *Ballad of John and Yoko*, *Give Peace A Chance*, *Instant Karma* and *Up Your Legs*. On 18 and 19 December 1976 it was the site of the first European Beatles Convention. Guests included **Cavern** disc jockey **Bob Wooler** and **Allan Williams** and there was also an exhibition of paintings by **Stuart Sutcliffe**.

● Ali, Muhammad *(Cassius Clay)*

When the Beatles travelled to Miami in February 1964 to stay at the **Deauville Hotel** to record 'The **Ed Sullivan** Show', they were asked to visit the training camp of Cassius Clay on 18 February.

Harold Conrad, who was promoting the World Heavyweight Championship bout between Sonny Liston and Clay, had asked Brian Epstein if the Beatles would like to visit Clay's camp, but the offer was rejected. Following their televised show at the Mau Mau Lounge, Conrad asked Ed Sullivan if he could meet the Beatles and Sullivan took him to their room and introduced him. Paul said, 'I think Clay is going to win.' Conrad mentioned that the visit to Clay's camp had been turned down, but they said they'd go and John commented, 'Don't worry about Brian, we'll handle him.'

The boxer and the Beatles clowned it up for the assembled photographers, with shots of Clay standing over a supine group of Beatles on the canvas. The 'Louisville Lip' told the press that although the Beatles were the prettiest, he was the greatest. He also commented, 'They were regular, friendly, everyday fellows. Success hasn't gone to their heads.' A few days later he won the Heavyweight title for the first time.

Clay was to change his name to Muhammad Ali and he won the World Heavyweight Champion title three times.

On hearing Ringo play drums, he joked, 'My dog plays better drums!'

Muhammad Ali – the Beatles visited his training camp when he was known as Cassius Clay. (Columbia Pictures)

● Allen, Dave

Popular Irish comedian who has enjoyed success for many years with his own series of comedy shows on BBC

Television. In 1963 he appeared with the Beatles on the **Helen Shapiro** tour and the following year he also joined them on the bill when they toured Australia.

He was one of the judges, together with **Derek Taylor** and the editor of the Sydney *Sunday Mirror*, of a competition organized by that paper offering the winners an invitation to Paul's 22nd birthday party at the Sheraton Hotel. There were over 10,000 entrants and seventeen girls won the opportunity of meeting the Beatles at the party.

Dave and his wife Judith are neighbours of the Harrisons in Henley.

Dave was also on the bill with the Beatles when they appeared for the second time on TV's Val Parnell's 'Sunday Night At The London Palladium' on 12 January 1964.

● All I've Got To Do

A John Lennon composition featured on the *With The Beatles* album. The group recorded the song on Wednesday, 11 September 1963. It was also included on **Capitol**'s American album, *Meet The Beatles*.

● All My Loving

A song which first appeared on the *With The Beatles* album in November 1963.

Paul originally conceived the number one day while he was having a shave. He said of it, 'I wrote "All My Loving" like a piece of poetry and then, I think, I put a song to it later.'

In February 1964 the number was the title track of an EP release (GEP 8891) and reached No. 13 in the British charts.

The other numbers on the EP were 'Ask Me Why', 'Money (That's What I Want)' and 'P.S. I Love You'. It was also featured on the **Capitol Records** EP *Four By The Beatles*, issued in America in May 1964.

The song has been featured on several albums, including the American *Meet The Beatles*, *The Beatles 1962-1966* compilation, the live *The Beatles At The Hollywood Bowl* in 1977, *The Beatles Collection* in 1978 and the mammoth World Records' *The Beatles Box* and *The Beatles' Ballads* in 1980.

The group also featured the number on various TV shows including 'Sunday Night At The London Palladium', 'The **Ed Sullivan** Show' and '**With The Beatles**' and on two of their '**Saturday Club**' and two of their '**From Us To You**' radio recordings.

'All My Loving' has been recorded by almost 100 different artists including the Trends, Count Basie, the **Chipmunks**, Herb Alpert and the George Martin Orchestra. On the version by the George Martin Orchestra, Beatles publisher **Dick James** sang part of the number. Foreign language versions included *'Toi l'ami'*, the French version by Richard Anthony, *'Con todo mi amor'*, a Spanish version by the Sandpipers, *'Feche os olhos'*, a Portuguese version by Renato & his Blue Caps and *'Gyts a gras'*, a Welsh version by Beti Williams.

● All My Loving (EP)

The Beatles' fourth EP. As usual, Parlophone took two tracks from the latest Beatles album release, *With The Beatles*, together with two tracks from their *Please Please Me* album, which had previously been released as the flip-sides of the group's first two singles.

All My Loving was issued on Parlophone GEP 8891 on 7 February 1964 and contained the tracks 'All My Loving', 'Ask Me Why', 'Money (That's What I Want)' and 'P.S. I Love You'. The EP reached No. 13 in the British charts.

● All Shook Up

Elvis Presley's first British No. 1 hit. It was also his only No. 1 on the HMV label when it reached the charts in July 1957, and the composition was credited to Otis Blackwell/Elvis Presley.

The **Quarry Men** included it in their repertoire soon after the Presley record hit the charts, with Paul on lead vocals.

● All Systems Freeman

A BBC Television show on which the promotional film for 'Lady Madonna' was premiered on 15 March 1968.

● All Things Must Pass

Tuesday, 25 February 1969, was George Harrison's 26th birthday and he went to **Abbey Road** and, in the absence of the other members of the Beatles, recorded three of his own compositions: 'Old Brown Shoe', 'Something' and 'All Things Must Pass'.

'All Things Must Pass' had been inspired by American group the Band and George had considered it might be suitable for the *Let It Be* album. It wasn't included on that release and George recorded it again with a set of musicians, including **Eric Clapton,** at **Trident Studios** and it was issued as the title track of his *All Things Must Pass* album.

● All This And World War II

An unusual film, based on Lennon & McCartney compositions, which was conceived by Lou Reizner who died soon after it was completed.

The publicity blurb proclaimed: 'Six years in the making with an original cast of more than fifty million, *All This And World War II* consists of a priceless collection of documentary footage recorded during the war by dozens of teams of Fox Movietone News cameramen in every theatre of operation. The assembled footage is projected against a backdrop of contemporary rock music written by John Lennon and Paul McCartney and performed by the world's leading exponents of today's sound. The effect is remarkable in that it tends to lift the footage from the shadows of some 31 years, making it contemporary.'

The movie was produced by Sandy Leiberson and Martin J. Machet, directed by Susan Winslow and released by 20th Century-Fox in 1976.

Reizner's brightest idea was to have a number of other artists perform the Lennon & McCartney material and the interpretations include: 'Lucy In The Sky With Diamonds', **Elton John**; 'Golden Slumbers'/'Carry That Weight', the Bee Gees (who also perform 'Sun King' and 'She Came In Through The Bathroom Window'); 'Polythene Pam', Roy Wood; 'We Can Work It Out', the Four Seasons; 'Hey Jude', the Brothers Johnson; 'Getting Better', Status Quo; 'Get Back', Rod Stewart; 'When I'm Sixty-Four', **Keith Moon**; 'Come Together', Tina Turner; 'I Am The Walrus'/'The Long And Winding Road', Leo Sayer; 'Because', Lynsey De Paul; 'Strawberry Fields Forever', Peter Gabriel; 'She's Leaving Home', Brian Ferry; 'Yesterday', David Essex; 'Nowhere Man', Jeff Lynne; and 'Help!', Henry Gross. Other numbers were performed by Frankie Valli, Richard Cocciante, Frankie Laine, Helen Reddy, the London Symphony Orchestra and the Royal Philharmonic Orchestra.

The soundtrack was issued as a double album package with an illustrated booklet on 20th Century 2T-522 on 25 October 1976 in the US. It was issued in Britain on Riva RVLP 2 on 5 November 1976. The American album was reissued on 16 June 1977.

Rod Stewart's version of 'Get Back' was issued as a single in Britain on Riva 6 and reached No. 2.

● All Together Now

This song was recorded on Friday, 12 May 1967 for the *Yellow Submarine* album. The number was mainly written by Paul, with a little help from John. All four Beatles come in to repeat 'All Together Now' approximately 50 times and the sequence of the Beatles singing the number was used in the live footage at the end of the *Yellow Submarine* film.

● All You Need Is Love

The song which John and Paul wrote specially for the **'Our World'** programme, beamed to 400 million viewers on Sunday, 25 June 1967.

They only had a short time to write a number which was suitable for the occasion and recording for the backing track began at **Olympic Sound Studios** on Wednesday, 14 June, and continued at **Abbey Road** in the large Number One studio, where the orchestra began recording on Friday, 23 June. The following day the Beatles attended a press call at the studio and on Sunday, 25 June performed the number live before the satellite audience on five continents.

Only 25 hours before it went on the air, the decision was taken to issue 'All You Need Is Love' as the group's fifteenth single.

The single was issued in Britain on Friday, 7 July on Parlophone R 5620 and went straight to the No. 1 position where it remained for four weeks. It was issued in America on **Capitol** 5964 on 17 July, where it also went to No. 1. The flipside was 'Baby You're A Rich Man'.

'All You Need Is Love' was also used as the title of the television documentary series by **Tony Palmer** and an album of that title was issued by Theatre Projects Records (9199 995) in February 1978 with the Beatles number as the first track. The song was also included on the *Yellow Submarine* album in January 1969, *The Beatles 1967-1970* in April 1973; the *Magical Mystery Tour* album in November 1976 and *Reel Music* in March 1982.

● All You Need Is Love: A Story Of Popular Music

The title album to the television documentary series, produced by **Tony Palmer**, which was also called 'All

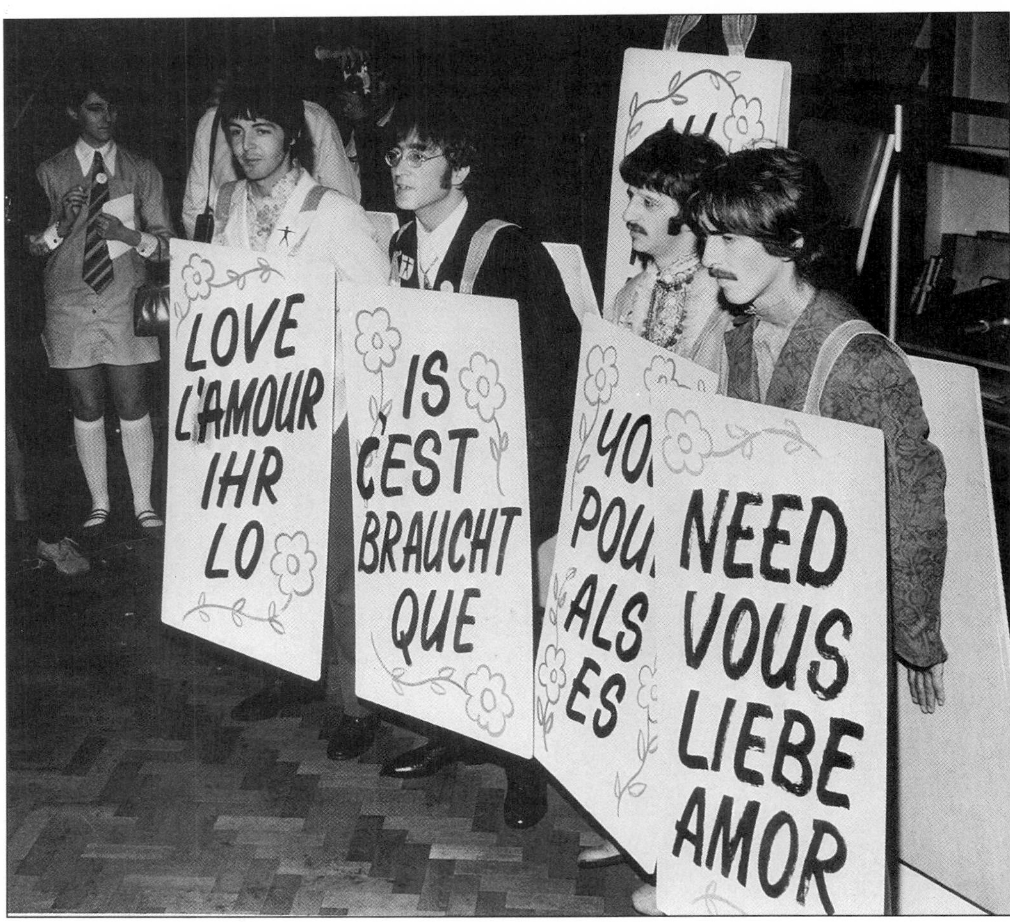

The Beatles act as sandwich men to promote 'All You Need Is Love'. (EMI)

You Need Is Love'. Considering the special nature of the *No One's Gonna Change Our World* album, and putting that aside, this became the first album compilation to receive permission to include a Beatles track. It was issued in February 1978 on Theatre Projects Records 9199 995.

There were twenty tracks on the album and the opening track was the Beatles version of 'All You Need Is Love'.

American Bandstand

An ABC Television show in the United States which first interviewed the Beatles by telephone on 15 February 1964 and also on 18 April. An entire edition of the show was devoted to the Beatles on 25 July 1964. It included a short, behind-the-scenes film of the making of *A Hard Day's Night*, in addition to clips from the film itself. Another programme with a Beatles theme was broadcast on 10 October and included a filmed interview with the group. In May 1965 the programme screened excerpts of the Beatles performing at the ***New Musical Express*** Poll Winner's Concert at Wembley, although there was no soundtrack to the clip.

● And I Love Her

Jane Asher was the inspiration for this ballad by Paul, although John gave him a hand with the lyrics.

It first appeared on the *A Hard Day's Night* album in August 1964, followed by the British EP *Extracts From The Film 'A Hard Day's Night'* and the American **Capitol** EP *Four By The Beatles*. The track was also included on the American album *Something New*, the compilations *The Beatles 1962-1966*, *Love Songs* and *The Beatles' Ballads*, and the American *The Beatles Rarities* in 1980 and *Reel Music* in 1982.

The group also performed the number on their **'Top Gear'** radio show on 16 July 1964.

One of the most popular of the Beatles' love ballads, it has been recorded by over 300 different artists, covering a range of styles and moods, including Ray Davies, Julie London, Smokey Robinson, Georgie Fame and Connie Francis.

● And Your Bird Can Sing

A John Lennon composition recorded in April 1965 and featured on the *Revolver* album.

● Anello and Davide

Specialist shoemakers, based in Charing Cross Road, London WC2, who made footwear for the entertainment fraternity, ranging from ballet shoes to boots for movies, dancers and show business personalities.

When John and Paul returned from a fortnight's holiday in Paris in October 1961, they passed through London and saw some footwear which impressed them in the window of the shop. The black boots were of a narrow-toed, high-Cuban-heeled, elastic-sided, ankle-length Flamenco style. They went into the store and bought a pair each. When they returned to Liverpool, George and Pete were also struck by the boots and both ordered a pair for themselves from Anello and Davide.

This company was later to make the special 'Beatle boots' for the group, including those worn on the American tour of 1964.

● Anglican Cathedral, St James Road, Liverpool 1

The largest Anglican Cathedral in Europe, which was designed by Sir Giles Gilbert Scott. One side of the Cathedral spreads along Hope Street, opposite Gambier Terrace and with the **Liverpool Institute** and Art College to its side. Surprisingly, at the other end of Hope Street is the Catholic Cathedral.

Construction of the Anglican Cathedral began earlier this century and wasn't completed until the sixties.

In 1953, the eleven-year-old Paul McCartney auditioned here for a place in the choir, but was unsuccessful.

On Sunday, 29 March 1981 there was a capacity congregation at a special memorial service to John Lennon during which a selection of Lennon & McCartney songs were played on the Cathedral organ.

To celebrate the 150th anniversary of the Royal Liverpool Philharmonic Orchestra, Paul McCartney wrote a partly autobiographical 'Liverpool Oratorio' in collaboration with Liverpool-based composer Carl Davies which was given its world premier at the Anglican Cathedral in June 1991.

● Anna (Go To Him)

Number composed by **Arthur Alexander** and released by him on the Dot label on 17 September 1962. It was a particular favourite with John Lennon who sang lead vocal on the Beatles' interpretation.

The group recorded it for their *Please Please Me* album and on two BBC radio **'Pop Go The Beatles'** shows. It was included on their *The Beatles (No. 1)* EP and on *The Beatles Collection*. In America it was issued on the EP *Souvenir of Their Visit: The Beatles* and on the albums *Introducing The Beatles*, *The Beatles Versus The Four Seasons*, *Songs, Pictures and Stories Of The Fabulous Beatles* and *The Early Beatles*.

● Annabel's, Berkeley Square, London W1

An exclusive London club.

On the evening of 31 December 1966, George, **Pattie Harrison** and Brian Epstein, together with a few friends, decided to have supper at the club. As George was wearing a sweater at the time he was told that he would have to put a tie over the sweater or be refused admission. The party decided to give Annabel's a miss and retired to the nearby Lyon's Corner House in Coventry Street.

● Ann-Margret

Glamorous actress/singer, born in Stockholm, who went to America at the age of five and became a major star, making her film debut in *A Pocketful Of Miracles*. She starred in *Bye Bye Birdie* and co-starred with **Elvis Presley** in *Viva Las Vegas*. Ann-Margret was called 'the female Elvis'.

In 1961 the Beatles introduced her current hit 'I Just Don't Understand' into their repertoire, with John on lead vocal.

Ringo Starr's name was romantically linked with the actress and he had to deny that there was an actual romance during press interviews on the Beatles' second American tour. The Hollywood scandal magazine *Confidential* was among the periodicals which hinted at romance, commenting that Ringo had 'bent her shell-pink ears with an hour of long-distance oogly-googling, all in a special type of Teddy Boy lingo that left little Annie limp'.

Ann-Margret – subject of a rumoured romance with Ringo. (National Film Archive)

● Another Girl

Number penned by Paul and recorded on Monday, 15 February 1965 for inclusion on the *Help!* album.

● Another Hard Day's Night

Title of one of the orchestral tracks performed by the George Martin Orchestra on the soundtrack of the film *Help!* The instrumental version of 'A Hard Day's Night' is heard in the background of a scene set in an Indian restaurant.

Although the track wasn't included on the British *Help!* album, **Capitol** included it among six orchestral tracks on the American album version of *Help!* issued in August 1965.

● Anthony, Les

A former Welsh guardsman hired by John Lennon as a chauffeur-cum-bodyguard. A tall, imposing figure, Anthony was part of the staff at John's home in **Kenwood,** Weybridge, Surrey.

He was later to sell his account of his days as John's chauffeur to the newspapers.

● Antrobus Arms, *Amesbury, Wiltshire*

A public house where the Beatles lodged for three days from 3 May 1965, during the filming of the Salisbury Plain sequences in *Help!* During the evening they were able to relax in the pub's lounge where, on several occasions, Paul and Ringo played poker with actor Leo McKern.

● Any Time At All

A number penned by John Lennon and recorded in June 1964 for the *A Hard Day's Night* album. It was also included on the *Extracts From The Album 'A Hard Day's Night'* EP, the *Rock 'n' Roll Music* compilation and the **Capitol** album *Something New*.

● Apache

A British No. 1 and a million-seller for the **Shadows** in 1960. Britain's leading group at the time, they were also the backing band for Cliff Richard and during their March 1960 tour, Jerry Lordan, a singer on the bill, played them an instrumental he had written called 'Apache'. It became the group's first hit. The Beatles included it in their repertoire in 1960, although they dropped it by the following year.

● Apollo Theatre, *Stockport Road, Ardwick Green, Ardwick, Manchester*

Also known as the ABC Cinema. The Beatles appeared at this venue three times.

Their Apollo debut took place on 20 November 1963, when three of the numbers they performed were filmed by Pathe News, and, together with backstage scenes, released as an eight-minute colour short for cinema release for the week of 22 December.

The film was called *The Beatles Come To Town* and the three numbers were 'From Me To You', 'She Loves You' and 'Twist And Shout'.

Their second appearance at the venue, on 14 October 1964, received the following report in ***Mersey Beat***:

> 'The audience went completely wild when the Beatles took the stage at Ardwick's Apollo Theatre last

The Beatles on stage at the Apollo Theatre, Ardwick, Manchester. (National Film Archives)

week, and although the screams, yells and shrieks continued almost unabated throughout the whole of their 28-minute spot, the boys could still be heard above the din. Attendants tried to keep the audience seated, but virtually everyone in the theatre was standing on a seat seeking a better view of the four lads who, with this tour, have proved once and for all that they remain the biggest and most talented show-biz phenomenon this country has ever produced.

'The show opened with the **Rustiks**, who also backed the second act on the bill, Bolton vocalist **Michael Haslam**, who received a great ovation.

'**Sounds Incorporated** were the next to take the stage and their act has improved tremendously during the last few months. Stage presentation is original and entertaining and their choice of material (ranging from "Maria" to the "William Tell Overture") was greeted with wholesale enthusiastic response.

'Sounds remained on stage to back **Mary Wells**, who was accompanied by her own guitarist Melvin Turrell. Looking exceptionally glamorous in a full-length silver dress, Mary sang many of her big hits, including "Two Lovers" and "My Guy". Although her performances proved she is one of the world's leading songstresses, the young audience didn't seem to appreciate her talents, although her reception was warm. Her rendition of "Time After Time", although excellent, would have been more suitable in cabaret.

'The **Remo Four** opened the second half of the show and were joined by **Tommy Quickly** who had the girls in the audience screaming continually as he strode, walked, pranced and danced across the stage, full of bounce and verve. Despite the fact that he was directly before the Beatles' act, no one seemed impatient and he made quite an impact. Perhaps this tour can help to sell Tommy's current release, "The Wild Side of Life".

'When the Beatles appeared to perform their old favourites, including "Money", "Twist And Shout" and many others – that was it!

'Brian Epstein, who was standing at the side of the stage, could well be proud of the best value-for-money tour of the year.'

Their last appearance at the venue took place on 7 December 1965.

● Apple Boutique, *94 Baker Street, London W1*

In the nineteenth century when it had been built, it was a four-storey house. Over the years it evolved into a shop and offices in a busy shopping area of the capital. Situated at the corner of Baker Street and Paddington Street, it became the first of the Beatles' Apple ventures to open.

Three Dutch designers, one male (Simon Posthuma) and two female (Josje Leeger and Marijke Koger), had set up a fashionable boutique called the Trend in Amsterdam, which, after an apparently successful start, soon developed financial troubles and had to close. Simon and Marijke wandered around Europe for a time and then settled in London where they met Simon Hayes and Barry Finch, partners in a public relations firm. Hayes became their business manager, Josje joined them from Amsterdam and Finch became the fourth member of the **Fool**.

They created a number of psychedelic-style designs for the Beatles, painting a Rolls-Royce for John, a fireplace for George and sundry other colourful tasks. Suddenly, it seemed they had talked the Beatles into launching a boutique. **Pattie Harrison**, who wore some of their designs, was to comment: 'I don't know how we met them. They just appeared one day.' And **Neil Aspinall** said: 'They crept up on us.'

Whatever the case, the Beatles gave the Fool £100,000 in September 1967 to design and stock the boutique. They immediately engaged a few dozen art students to paint a huge psychedelic mural across the entire front and side of the building. It was an exciting visual display but brought a torrent of complaints from local traders. Eventually, the complaints were so vociferous that the mural had to be erased.

The idea for the Apple Boutique was to be, as Paul was to comment, 'A beautiful place where you could buy beautiful things'. **Pete Shotton** was called down from his Hayling Island Supermarket to manage the store and among the shop assistants was Pattie Harrison's sister **Jennie.**

Invitations to the Gala party on 5 December 1967 read: 'Come at 7.46. Fashion Show at 8.16.' and the star-studded assembly discovered that the single drink available was apple juice. John and George were in attendance, but Ringo was filming in Rome and Paul had retreated to his farm in Scotland.

The venture lasted barely eight months. It was a financial disaster with a great amount of pilfering, together with overspending by the Fool. Pete Shotton wanted out and **John Lydon** was brought in as head of Apple Retail, but couldn't sort out the problems. It was decided to close down the venture.

On Tuesday morning, 30 July 1968, the staff were told they could give everything away. The Beatles and their girlfriends had been around the previous evening, selecting their pick of the stock. Paul commented: 'We went along, chose all the stock we wanted – I got a smashing overcoat – then told our friends. Now everything that's left is for the public.' Ringo was to say, 'I couldn't find anything that fitted me.'

Their first customer that morning was actor Michael J. Pollard who, when he'd completed his shopping, was told to keep his wallet in his pocket.

Not much publicity had been given to the fact that Apple were to give away the entire £10,000 worth of stock because Paul didn't want traders from Carnaby Street to turn up and take it away in handcarts. It was a gift to the ordinary punter and by word of mouth, telephone calls, and the staff going onto the street to bring passers-by into the store, the stock began to go, people began to gather and the police were called in to handle the crowds.

Paul, with the help of **Derek Taylor**, prepared a press statement, which read:

'We decided to close down our Baker Street shop yesterday and instead of putting up a sign saying "Business will be resumed as soon as possible" and then auction off the goods, we decided to give them away. The shops were doing fine and making a nice profit on turnover. So far, the biggest loss is in giving the things away but we did that deliberately... We're giving them away – rather than selling them to barrow boys – because we wanted to give rather than sell.

'We came into shops by the tradesman's entrance but we're leaving by the front door. Originally, the shops were intended to be something else, but they just became like all the boutiques in London. They just weren't our thingy. The staff will get three weeks' pay but if they wish they'll be absorbed into the rest of Apple. Everyone will be cared for. The Kings Road shop, which is known as Apple Tailoring, isn't going to be part of Apple anymore but it isn't closing down and we are leaving our investment there because we have a moral and personal obligation to our partner **John Crittle** who is now in sole control. All that's happened is that we've closed our shop in which we feel we shouldn't, in the first place, have been involved.

'Our main business is entertainment – communication. Apple is mainly concerned with fun not with frocks. We want to devote all our energies to records, films and our electronics adventures. We had to re-focus. We had to zoom in on what we really enjoy, and we enjoy being alive, and we enjoy being Beatles.

'It's 1968: already, it's 1968. Time is short. I suppose really what we're doing is spring cleaning in mid-summer. The amazing thing is our giving things away. Well, the answer is that it was much funnier to give things away.

'Well, it's just that the Beatles are the Beatles are the mop tops are the Beatles are the mop tops... are whatever you see them to be, whatever you see us to be. Create and preserve the image of your choice. We are yours with love.'

● Appleby, Ron

A promoter from Southport, Lancashire, who also acted as compere for jive hives on Merseyside. He was a compere for promoter **Brian Kelly** at **Litherland Town Hall** and claimed that he was the first person to have announced the group on stage as the Beatles, after they'd shortened their name from the Silver Beatles. This caused a great deal of amusement in Liverpool at the time as **Bob Wooler** also claimed the honour and the two of them were often seen arguing about it.

The group were known in Liverpool as the Silver Beatles immediately prior to their first trip to Hamburg in August 1960. They returned to Liverpool in December and appeared at the **Casbah Club** on 17 December, the **Grosvenor Ballroom** on 25 December and Litherland Town Hall on 27 December. If they weren't introduced on stage as the Beatles at the Casbah and Grosvenor, then Appleby's claim would seem to be true – and it is unlikely that there would have been a compere at the Casbah, for instance, because it was such a small club.

● Apple Corps

By 1967 the Beatles were advised that they were in a financial position in which any further money they earned could be instantly taken in tax – and that they had £2 million to play around with which, if they didn't invest, would be taken by the taxman. They decided to create a company with a number of divisions and in January 1968 changed their company Beatles Ltd to Apple Corps Ltd. Paul McCartney commented: 'It's a pun – apple core – see?'

All four Beatles became company Presidents. **Neil Aspinall** was appointed Managing Director, **Alistair Taylor**, General Manager, and **Peter Brown** and Harry Pinsker (head of the accountancy firm **Bryce Hanmer**) became Directors. As the company grew **Peter Asher** became A&R man, **Malcolm Evans** was made assistant Managing Director, **Derek Taylor** became Director of Public Relations, **Alexis Mardas** became their electronics ace, **Dennis O'Dell**, manager of films, **Ron Kass**, Head of the Record Division, **Jeremy Banks**, Art Director, and **Tony Bramwell**, Assistant to the Film Division and record plugger to **Apple Records**. The actual divisions were **Apple Electronics**, **Apple Films Ltd**, Apple Music Publishing, Apple Wholesale, Apple Retail, Apple Television and Apple Records. Arrangements were made for **Capitol Records** to be the distributor for America, Canada and Mexico, while **EMI** handled the rest of the world.

Offices were found at 95 Wigmore Street, London W1 and then at 3 **Savile Row, London W1**. The first venture was the television presentation of **Magical Mystery Tour**, followed by the **Apple Boutique** at 94 Baker Street, London W1.

Initially, there was great euphoria over the Apple concept, which was to provide an opportunity for creative people without 'the men in suits' inhibiting them.

Paul said, 'We want to help other people but without doing it like charity and without seeming like patrons of the arts. We always had to go to the big man on our knees, touch our forelocks and say, "Please can we do so and so?" And most of those companies are so big, and so out of touch with people like us who just want to sing or make films, that everyone has a bad time. We are just trying to set up a good organization, not some great fat institution that doesn't care. We don't want people to say yessir, nossir.'

John Lennon commented, 'The aim of the company isn't a stack of gold teeth in the bank. We've done that bit. It's more of a trick to see if we can get artistic freedom within a business structure; to see if we can create things and sell them without charging three times our cost.'

Unfortunately, it didn't take long for the dream to go sour and the Apple Boutique closed within ten months. The only division which seemed to be making money was

Apple Records, primarily because of the Beatles' releases. The staff indulged in extravagances – with orders of champagne and caviare among the daily supplies ordered; office furniture and equipment regularly disappeared; company expenses were used to buy cars, while lavish expense accounts soon began to cause financial problems. Their accountant warned the Beatles that they would encounter severe problems unless they brought someone in to sort out the mess.

They discussed hiring various business experts, such as Lord Beeching, and Paul suggested that they hire the New York law firm, Eastman And Eastman, to run their business affairs. Although the other members of the group were aware that the company was run by the relatives of Paul's girlfriend **Linda**, they were brought in as financial advisers. The group were also approached by **Allen Klein** and with John, George and Ringo voting for him, he was appointed to take charge of Apple. He immediately began sacking people and put an end to the extravagances. The experienced Ron Kass went and an inexperienced **Jack Oliver** was appointed to take his place. The tea ladies were sacked – and no one could get a cup of tea!

Apart from personnel sacked by Klein, others resigned and the Beatles' original dream faded until, by 1970, the only function of the company seemed to be the collection of Beatles royalties.

● Apple Electronics

A division of **Apple Corps** set up specially for **Alexis Mardas** to develop and market the various electronic gadgets he created.

Mardas had been introduced to John Lennon who was intrigued by the series of electronic gadgets which Mardas, who became known as 'Magic Alex', had shown him. The previous 'electronics genius' in the life of the Beatles had been **Adrian Barber** who had designed the 'coffins' (amplifiers) for them and the sound system for the **Star Club**. In Liverpool, Adrian had also made gadgets before their time, putting radios inside coke cans and such.

Magic Alex dazzled the Beatles with his claims, some of which were quite extraordinary, yet the Beatles provided him with the finance and told him to develop the gadgets and market them for Apple.

The major brief he had was to build a studio for the Beatles at Apple, and he told them he would construct a 72-track studio.

Alexis filed one hundred patent applications – but none of them was accepted. Not a single item was completed or marketed for Apple Electronics, a division which actually didn't produce anything, and when **Allen Klein** appeared on the horizon, Apple Electronics ceased to exist.

● Apple Films Limited

One of the several companies formed in 1968 by **Apple Corps**. **Dennis O'Dell** was appointed to run the company and Tony Bramwell assisted. The company was involved in the production of a handful of films, including *Yellow Submarine* and *Let It Be*.

● Applejacks, The

A group from Solihull in Birmingham who comprised Al Jackson (vocals), Martin Baggott (lead guitar), Phil Cash (rhythm guitar), Don Gould (organ), Megan Davies (bass guitar) and Gary Freeman (drums).

Their first single 'Tell Me When' reached No. 7 in the British charts and their follow-up was the Lennon & McCartney composition 'Like Dreamers Do', which was issued in Britain on **Decca** FII916 on 5 June 1964, and in America on London 9681 on 6 July. Paul McCartney wrote the number for the group.

The record reached No. 20 in the British charts.

● Apple Records

Of the several different companies launched by the Beatles' **Apple Corps**, Apple Records seemed to be the one with the most potential, particularly as an agreement was made for future Beatles products to be issued on the Apple label. However, **EMI**'s Parlophone label still maintained its catalogue numbers and continued to handle distribution.

The company was launched in August 1968, with 33-year-old American **Ron Kass**, former head of Liberty's International Division, as Managing Director; 23-year-old **Peter Asher** as the company's A&R man and 23-year-old **Tony Bramwell** in charge of promoting the products.

Advertisements and posters announcing the venture had brought in hundreds of tapes to Apple's HQ, but most were left unheard and the main signings came from personal preferences of the individual directors.

The very first artist signed to Apple was **James**

Taylor, discovered by Peter Asher. He only found fame after leaving the label. He cited the main complaint made by the artists about Apple – that they felt that the company did not handle the promotion of their signings very well. The artists also complained that they found themselves being neglected due to the internal financial disputes at Apple.

'Our First Four' was a specially promoted package conceived by an advertising agency, Wolff Olins, to promote the first four releases by the Beatles, **Mary Hopkin**, **Jackie Lomax** and the **Black Dyke Mills Band**.

Apple Records basically lasted from August 1968 to May 1976 and, apart from the success of records by the Beatles as a group and individually, the company did not do very well commercially and only achieved two non-Beatles Gold Discs.

When Apple Records was being wound down late in 1975 there was consideration given to the idea of releasing a double album of the best of the non-Beatle Apple artists, but it went the way of other Apple Records ideas – nowhere.

Despite the lack of success of the Apple artists, apart from the initial chart action of acts such as **Mary Hopkin** and **Badfinger**, there were some excellent artists and releases. Over the years there has grown a keen collector's market for Apple products and in 1991, the first Apple CDs were eventually released.

APPLE DISCOGRAPHY – SINGLES (in chronologicial order)

'HEY JUDE' C/W 'REVOLUTION', THE BEATLES.

Released in Britain on Apple R 5722 on 30 August 1968 and in America on Apple 2276 on 26 August 1968.

'THOSE WERE THE DAYS' C/W 'TURN, TURN, TURN', MARY HOPKIN.

Released in Britain on Apple 2 on 30 August 1968 and in America on 26 August 1968. The number was an old song, penned by Gene Raskin, which Paul McCartney had discovered and liked and had once tried to interest the **Moody Blues** in recording. The single was also produced by Paul and the same instrumental backing track was used while Mary sang new vocal tracks for the Italian, French, German and Spanish markets. A multi-million seller internationally and a No. 1 hit in Britain and No. 2 in America.

'SOUR MILK SEA' C/W 'THE EAGLE LAUGHS AT YOU', JACKIE LOMAX.

Released in Britain on Apple 3 on 6 September 1968 and in America on Apple 1802 on 26 August 1968. Produced by George Harrison, this single failed to register, even though the musicians playing on the track included George Harrison and **Jackie Lomax** on rhythm guitars, Paul McCartney on bass, **Eric Clapton** on lead guitar, Ringo Starr on drums and Nicky Hopkins on piano.

'THINGUMYBOB' 'YELLOW SUBMARINE', BLACK DYKE MILLS BRASS BAND.

Issued in Britain on Apple 4 on 6 September 1968 and in America on Apple 1800 on 26 August 1968. Paul McCartney produced this record of the instrumental theme he composed for the television series 'Thingumybob'. Unfortunately, the record wasn't a hit and the Brass Band didn't record for Apple again.

'*QUELLI ERAND GIORNI*' C/W 'TURN, TURN, TURN', MARY HOPKIN.

Issued in Europe on Apple 2 on 25 October 1968.

'MAYBE TOMORROW' C/W 'AND HER DADDY'S A MILLIONAIRE', THE IVEYS.

Issued in Britain on Apple 5 on 15 November 1968 and in America on Apple 1803 on 27 January 1969.

'ROAD TO NOWHERE' C/W 'ILLUSIONS', TRASH.

Issued in Britain on Apple 6 on 24 January 1969 and in America on Apple 1804 on 3 March 1969. Originally a group from Glasgow called the Pathfinders, discovered by **Tony Meehan** who brought them to Apple's attention. They changed their name to White Trash, which proved to be a burden – the name was banned by the BBC – and shortened it to Trash. Their next projected album wasn't released, they had one more single from Apple and were then dropped from the label.

'*LONTANO DAGLI OCCHI*' C/W 'THE GAME', MARY HOPKIN.

Issued in Italy on Apple 7 on 7 March 1969.

'*PRINCE EN AVIGNON*' C/W 'THE GAME', MARY HOPKIN.

Issued in France on Apple 9 on 7 March 1969.

'CAROLINA ON MY MIND' C/W 'TAKING IT IN', JAMES TAYLOR.

Issued in America on Apple 1805 on 17 March 1969. The single was produced by **Peter Asher** and Paul McCartney played bass on the title track, but the single failed to register in the charts.

'GOODBYE' C/W 'SPARROW', MARY HOPKIN.

Issued in Britain on Apple 10 on 28 March 1969 and in

America on Apple 1806 on 7 April 1969. The record reached the No. 2 position in the British charts and No. 13 in the American.

'GET BACK' C/W 'DON'T LET ME DOWN', THE BEATLES WITH BILLY PRESTON.

Issued in Britain on Apple R 5777 on 11 April 1969 and in America on Apple 2490 on 5 May 1969.

'NEW DAY' C/W 'I FALL INSIDE YOUR EYES', JACKIE LOMAX.

Issued in Britain on Apple 11 on 9 May 1969. The 'A' side was produced by Jackie Lomax and **Mal Evans** and the flipside by George Harrison. None of Jackie's Apple records made any impact on the charts.

'KING OF FUH' C/W 'NOBODY KNOWS', BRUTE FORCE.

Issued in Britain on Apple 8 on 16 May 1969. Brute Force was the pseudonym of a 20-year-old New York songwriter, Steven Friedland, who penned and produced this fantasy story. **EMI** refused to press or distribute the record, so Apple tried to take on the task themselves, but the record received no airplay, poor distribution – and vanished. The single was eventually issued in America in 1971 on Brute Force Records.

'THE BALLAD OF JOHN AND YOKO' C/W 'OLD BROWN SHOE', THE BEATLES.

Issued in Britain on Apple R 5786 on 30 May 1969 and in America on Apple 2531 on 7 June 1969.

'NEW DAY' C/W 'THUMBIN' A RIDE', JACKIE LOMAX.

Issued in America on Apple 1807 on 2 June 1969. The flipside of this single, a Jerry Leiber/Mike Stoller composition, was produced by Paul McCartney on the eve of his wedding to **Linda**.

THAT'S THE WAY GOD PLANNED IT' C/W 'WHAT ABOUT YOU', BILLY PRESTON.

Issued in Britain on Apple 12 on 27 June 1969 and in America on Apple 1808 on 7 July 1969. The Beatles bought Preston's contract from **Vee Jay Records** in America and he was with Apple for three years. This single achieved a No. 11 position in the British charts.

'GIVE PEACE A CHANCE' C/W 'REMEMBER LOVE', THE PLASTIC ONO BAND.

Issued in Britain on Apple 13 on 4 July 1969 and in America on Apple 1809 on 7 July 1969. The number which has become a peace anthem was recorded at John and **Yoko**'s second 'Bed In' at the Queen Elizabeth Hotel in Montreal, Canada, with backing vocals provided by a number of their celebrity visitors. John and Yoko had embarked on their recording partnership and used the name **Plastic Ono Band** and its variations. The flipside was a Yoko composition, also recorded at the hotel. The single reached No. 2 in the British charts and No. 14 in the American.

'NO ESCAPING YOUR LOVE' C/W 'DEAR ANGIE', THE IVEYS.

Issued in Europe on Apple 14 on 18 July 1969.

'STORM IN A TEACUP', THE IVEYS. 'SOMETHING'S WRONG', JAMES TAYLOR. 'LITTLE YELLOW PILLS', JACKIE LOMAX. 'HAPPINESS RUNS', MARY HOPKIN.

Issued on CT2 on 18 July 1969. This was a special promotional EP produced by Apple for Wall's Ice Cream and available only for a limited period of time at various outlets in London's West End which sold Wall's Ice Cream.

'*HARE KRISHNA MANTRA*' C/W 'PRAYER TO THE SPIRITUAL MASTERS', RADHA KRISHNA TEMPLE.

Issued in Britain on Apple 15 on 29 August 1969 and in America on Apple 1810 on 22 August 1969. The record reached No. 12 in the British charts, but failed to make the American charts.

'*QUE SERA SERA*' C/W 'FIELDS OF ST ETIENNE', MARY HOPKIN.

Issued in Britain on Apple 16 on 19 September 1969 and in America on Apple 1823 on 15 June 1970.

'GOLDEN SLUMBERS'/'CARRY THAT WEIGHT' C/W 'TRASH CAN', TRASH.

Issued in Britain on Apple 17 on 3 October 1969 and in America on Apple 1811 on 15 October 1969. A modest hit which only reached No. 35 in the British charts. It was the last release on Apple for Trash.

'GIVE PEACE A CHANCE' C/W 'LIVING WITHOUT TOMORROW', HOT CHOCOLATE BAND.

Issued in Britain on Apple 18 on 10 October 1969 and in America on 17 October 1969. Errol Brown and Tony Wilson approached Apple for permission to change the lyrics of 'Give Peace A Chance' for a reggae version they wanted to record. John Lennon liked the idea and they recorded it for Apple, with Tony Meehan producing. It failed to register and they didn't make another Apple single, but went on to be one of the most successful chart artists in Britain for the next two decades.

'EVERYTHING'S ALL RIGHT' C/W 'I WANT TO THANK YOU', BILLY PRESTON.

Issued on Apple 19 on 17 October 1969 and in America on Apple 1814 on 20 October 1969. The 'A' side was produced by George Harrison.

'COLD TURKEY' C/W 'DON'T WORRY KYOKO', THE PLASTIC ONO BAND.

Issued in Britain on Apple R 1001 on 24 October 1969 and in America on Apple 1813 on 20 October 1969. Paul McCartney refused to record this song as a Beatles single, so John decided to collect together some musicians in another incarnation of the Plastic Ono Band. They included himself on guitar/vocals, Eric Clapton on lead guitar, **Klaus Voormann** on bass guitar, Ringo Starr on drums and Yoko Ono on backing vocals. John also decided to dispense with the Lennon & McCartney composing credit and the song is simply credited to John Lennon. The flipside is a song Yoko wrote to her daughter Kyoko. The single reached No. 13 in the British charts and No. 30 in the American.

'SOMETHING' C/W 'COME TOGETHER', THE BEATLES.

Issued in Britain on Apple R 5814 on 31 October 1969 and in America on Apple 2654 on 6 October 1969.

'YOU KNOW MY NAME' C/W 'WHAT'S THE NEWS MARY JANE', THE PLASTIC ONO BAND.

This was an Apple single scheduled to be issued on Apple 1002 on 5 December 1969, but it was never released.

'COME AND GET IT' C/W 'ROCK OF ALL AGES', BADFINGER.

Issued in Britain on Apple 20 on 5 December 1969 and in America on Apple 1816 on 29 January 1970. The first of three British hit singles for **Badfinger**. This title track of Ringo Starr's movie ***The Magic Christian*** was penned by Paul McCartney and reached No. 4 in the charts. It did even better in America where it topped the charts.

'TEMMA HARBOUR' C/W '*LONTANO DAGLI OCCHI*', MARY HOPKIN.

Issued in Britain on Apple 22 on 16 January 1970 and in America on Apple 1816 on 29 January 1970. A No. 6 chart hit in Britain which reached the position of No. 39 in America. Mickie Most produced the 'A' side, Paul McCartney the flipside.

'ALL THAT I'VE GOT' C/W 'AS I GET OLDER', BILLY PRESTON.

Issued in Britain on Apple 21 on 30 January 1970 and in America on Apple 1817 on 16 February 1970.

'HOW THE WEB WAS WOVEN' C/W 'THUMBIN' A RIDE', JACKIE LOMAX.

Issued in Britain on Apple 23 on 6 February 1970. The single was produced by George Harrison, but Jackie's career with Apple was coming to a close.

'INSTANT KARMA' C/W 'WHO HAS SEEN THE WIND', JOHN/YOKO WITH THE PLASTIC ONO BAND.

Issued in Britain on Apple R 1003 on 6 February 1970 and in America on Apple 1818 on 20 February 1970. John wrote this number, **Phil Spector** produced and the Plastic Ono line-up this time was John Lennon (vocals/guitar/electric piano), George Harrison (guitar/grand piano), Klaus Voorman (bass guitar/electric piano), **Alan White** (drums/grand piano), **Billy Preston** (organ), Mal Evans (chimes), Yoko Ono (vocals). The chanting was provided by a group of people who were brought in from a nearby late-night club, Hatchetts in Piccadilly. John produced the flipside which was written and sung by Yoko. The single reached No. 5 in Britain and No. 3 in America.

'AIN'T THAT CUTE' C/W '*VAYA CON DIOS*', DORIS TROY.

Issued in Britain on Apple 24 on 13 February 1970 and in America on Apple 1820 on 16 March 1970. R&B singer Doris signed with Apple in 1970 after recording and co-writing some songs with Billy Preston. George Harrison produced the title track.

'GOVINDA' C/W '*GOVINDA JAI JAI*', RADHA KRISHNA TEMPLE.

Issued in Britain on Apple 25 on 6 March 1970 and in America on Apple 1821 on 24 March 1970. The second and last single on Apple by this vocal/instrumental assembly who reached No. 23 in the British charts with this track, produced by George Harrison.

'LET IT BE' C/W 'YOU KNOW MY NAME', THE BEATLES.

Issued in Britain on Apple R 5833 on 6 March 1970 and in America on Apple 2764 on 11 March 1970.

'HOW THE WEB WAS WOVEN' C/W 'I FALL INSIDE YOUR EYES', JACKIE LOMAX.

Issued in America on Apple 1819 on 9 March 1970.

'KNOCK KNOCK WHO'S THERE' C/W 'I'M GOING TO FALL IN LOVE AGAIN', MARY HOPKIN.

Issued in Britain on Apple 26 on 20 March 1970. A No. 2 chart hit for Mary in Britain.

'THE LONG AND WINDING ROAD' C/W 'FOR YOU BLUE', THE BEATLES.

Issued in America on Apple R 2832 on 11 May 1970.

'JACOB'S LADDER' C/W 'GET BACK', DORIS TROY.

Issued in Britain on Apple 28 on 28 August 1970 and in America on Apple 1824 on 21 September 1970. Although she'd had some chart hits on Atlantic early in the sixties, Doris wasn't to find any chart success with her Apple releases.

'My Sweet Lord' c/w 'Long As I Got My Baby', Billy Preston.

Issued in Britain on Apple 29 on 4 September 1970. The George Harrison composition, co-produced by George and Billy.

'Beaucoups Of Blues' c/w 'Coochy-Coochy', Ringo Starr.

Issued in America on Apple R 2969 on 5 October 1970. No British release for this single, which reached No. 87 in the American charts.

'No Matter What' c/w 'Carry On Till Tomorrow', Badfinger.

Issued in America on Apple 1822 on 10 December 1970, where it reached No. 8 in the charts.

'Think About Your Children' c/w 'Heritage', Mary Hopkin.

Issued in Britain on Apple 30 on 16 October 1970 and in America on Apple 1825 on 18 October, 1970. Written by Errol Brown and Tony Wilson, who had recorded for Apple as the Hot Chocolate Band. Mary reached No. 19 in the British charts with the number.

'Carolina On My Mind' c/w 'Something's Wrong', James Taylor.

Issued in Britain on Apple 32 on 6 November 1970 and in America on Apple 1805 on 26 October 1970.

'No Matter What' c/w 'Better Days', Badfinger.

Issued in Britain on Apple 31 on 6 November 1970. A No. 5 hit in the British charts.

'My Sweet Lord' c/w 'Isn't It A Pity', George Harrison.

Issued in America on Apple 2995 on 23 November 1970. A No. 1 hit in America.

'My Sweet Lord' c/w 'Little Girl', Billy Preston.

Issued in America on Apple 1826 on 3 December 1970.

'Mother' c/w 'Why', John/Yoko with the Plastic Ono Band.

Issued in America on Apple 1827 on 28 December 1970.

'My Sweet Lord' c/w 'What Is Life', George Harrison.

Issued in Britain on Apple R 5884 on 15 January 1971. It was George's first solo single and gave him a No. 1 hit. Apart from topping the British charts, the single was No. 1 in various countries around the world, including Australia, Austria, Brazil, France, Germany, Mexico, Norway, Singapore, Spain, Sweden and Switzerland. Among the backing musicians were Ringo Starr on drums, Klaus Voorman on bass guitar, Gary Wright on piano, George Harrison and Badfinger on guitars, Peter Drake on steel guitar. The number also proved controversial when George was sued for plagiarizing the **Chiffons**' hit 'He's So Fine', and he paid compensation a few years later.

'What Is Life' c/w 'Apple Scruffs', George Harrison.

Issued in America on Apple 1828 on 15 February 1971. Another track from the *All Things Must Pass* album, released only in America and reaching No. 10 in the charts.

'Another Day' c/w 'Oh Woman Oh Why', Paul McCartney.

Issued in Britain on Apple R 5889 on 19 February 1971 and in America on Apple 1829 on 22 February 1971. First solo single from Paul, which brought him a No. 1 in Britain and a No. 5 position in the American charts. This was the song credited to Paul and Linda McCartney, which caused **Sir Lew Grade** to sue – but the dispute was settled when Paul agreed to appear in a TV special for Grade.

'Power To The People' c/w 'Open Your Box', John/Yoko with the Plastic Ono Band.

Issued in Britain on Apple R 5892 on 12 March 1971. John and Yoko produced both tracks with Phil Spector. Another political message from John which reached No. 6 in the British charts.

'Power To The People' c/w 'Touch Me', John/Yoko with the Plastic Ono Band.

Issued in America on Apple 1830 on 22 March 1971 where it reached the No. 11 position. **Capitol** insisted on changing the flipside as they were concerned about the lyrics to 'Open Your Box'.

'It Don't Come Easy' c/w 'Early 1970', Ringo Starr.

Issued in Britain on Apple R 5898 on 9 April 1971 and in America on Apple 1831 on 19 April 1971. Ringo's first solo single which reached No. 5 in the British charts. It was his second American single and reached No. 4 in the charts there. Ringo penned the number himself and George Harrison and Steve Stills are featured on guitars, Klaus Voorman on bass guitar and Ron Cattermole on saxophone and trumpet. The flipside, also written by Ringo, was a tribute to his fellow Beatles.

'Try Some, Buy Some' c/w 'Tandoori Chicken', Ronnie Spector.

Issued in Britain on Apple 33 on 16 April 1971 and in America on Apple 1832 on 19 April 1971. George Harrison and Phil Spector got together on this single to try to find a hit for Spector's wife. George also wrote the song, which only reached No. 77 in the American charts.

'Let My Name Be Sorrow' c/w 'Kew Gardens', Mary Hopkin.

Issued in Britain on Apple 34 on 18 June 1971. This single was produced by Tony Visconti, whom she married. After their divorce, Visconti married John Lennon's former lover May Pang. The single reached No. 46 in the British charts.

'Sour Milk Sea' c/w 'I Fall Inside Your Eyes', Jackie Lomax.

Issued in America on Apple 1834 on 21 June 1934.

'God Save Us' c/w 'Do The Oz', Bill Elliott and the Elastic Oz Band.

Issued in Britain on Apple 36 on 16 July 1971 and in America on Apple 1836 on 7 July 1971. When the alternative magazine *Oz* was taken to court over its notorious 'Schoolkids' issue, John decided to record this number to raise money for the defence. It was written by Yoko, recorded at their studio in Tittenhurst Park and produced by John, Yoko, Phil Spector and Mal Evans. Newcastle vocalist Bill Elliott was featured, while John Lennon provided lead vocals on the flipside of the record. It had no chart success.

'Bangladesh' c/w 'Deep Blue', George Harrison.

Issued in Britain on Apple R 5912 on 30 July 1971 and in America on Apple 1836 on 28 July 1971. The title song was written as part of George's efforts to bring relief to the troubled country of Bangladesh. The flipside was composed immediately after George's mother Louise had died of a terminal illness. The number reached No. 10 in the British charts and No. 23 in the American.

'Uncle Albert/Admiral Halsey' c/w 'Too Many People', Paul and Linda McCartney.

Issued in America on Apple 1837 on 2 August 1971. The single reached No. 1 in the American charts and received a **Grammy Award**.

'Back Seat Of My Car' c/w 'Heart Of The Country', Paul and Linda McCartney.

Issued in Britain on Apple R 5914 on 13 August 1971. A track from the *Ram* album which eventually reached No. 39 in the British charts.

'Joi Bangla/Oh Bhaugowan' c/w 'Raga Mishra-Jhinjhoti', Ravi Shankar and Chorus.

Issued in Britain on Apple 37 on 27 August 1971 and in America on 9 August 1971. Produced by George Harrison.

'Mrs Lennon' c/w 'Midsummer New York', Yoko Ono with the Plastic Ono Band.

Issued in Britain on Apple 38 on 29 October 1971 and in America on Apple 1839 on 29 September 1971. The first solo single from Yoko, comprising two numbers from her forthcoming album *Fly*.

'Imagine' c/w 'It's So Hard', John Lennon with the Plastic Ono Band.

Issued in America on Apple 1840 on 11 October 1971. The number reached No. 3 in the American charts.

'Day After Day' c/w 'Money', Badfinger.

Issued in America on Apple 1841 on 10 November 1971, where it reached No. 4 in the charts.

'Happy Xmas (War Is Over)' c/w 'Listen, The Snow Is Falling', John/Yoko with the Plastic Ono Band and the Harlem Community Choir.

Issued in Britain on Apple R 5970 on 24 November 1972 and in America on Apple 1842 on 1 December 1971. The single reached No. 2 in Britain. It had been released in America the year previously, but didn't chart, although it has since become a Christmas classic and is regularly re-released. John did not feature the Apple logo on the single.

'Water Paper and Clay' c/w 'Jefferson', Mary Hopkin.

Issued in Britain on Apple 39 on 3 December 1971. The record didn't register in the charts.

'Day After Day' c/w 'Sweet Tuesday Morning', Badfinger.

Issued in Britain on Apple 40 on 14 January 1972. Third and final British chart hit for Badfinger – it reached the No. 5 position.

'Mind Train' c/w 'Listen, The Snow Is Falling', Yoko Ono with the Plastic Ono Band.

Issued in Britain on Apple 41 on 21 January 1972.

'Give Ireland Back To The Irish' c/w 'Give Ireland Back To The Irish (instrumental version)', Wings.

Issued in Britain on Apple R 5936 on 25 February 1972 and in America on Apple 1847 on 28 February 1972. The single reached No. 13 in the British charts and No. 21 in the American. Paul and Linda wrote the song regarding the Bloody Sunday incident in Ireland on 3 January 1972. Due to the political nature of the song it was banned in Britain by both the BBC and the IBA.

'Sweet Music' c/w 'Song of Songs', Lon and Derrek Van Eaton.

Issued in America on Apple 1845 on 6 March 1972. A

tape of these two brothers performing was sent to several record companies. Apple A&R man Tony King liked their tape and took it to George Harrison. George liked it, and so did Ringo and John, so the group were signed to Apple and flew to London to record their debut album. The 'A' side of this single was produced by George Harrison and Ringo Starr was one of the drummers on the track. The flipside was produced by Klaus Voorman.

'Baby Blue' c/w 'Flying', Badfinger.

Issued in Britain on Apple 42 on 10 March 1972 and in America on Apple 1844 on 6 March 1972. It was their final American hit, reaching No. 14 in the charts.

'Back Off Boogaloo' c/w 'Blindman', Ringo Starr.

Issued in Britain on Apple R 5944 on 17 March 1972 and in America on Apple 1849 on 20 March 1972. The single reached No. 2 in Britain and No. 9 in America. Ringo wrote the song and George Harrison produced the session. The backing musicians included George Harrison on guitar, Klaus Voorman on bass guitar, Ringo on drums and vocals, Gary Wright on keyboards and Lesley Duncan, Madeline Bell and Jean Gilbert on backing vocals.

'F Is Not A Dirty Word' c/w 'The Ballad Of New York City/John Lennon-Yoko Ono', David Peel and the Lower East Side.

Originally scheduled for release in America on Apple 6498/6499 on 20 April 1972, but only promotional copies were sent out to disc jockeys. John and Yoko discovered this controversial singer in New York in 1971.

'Woman Is The Nigger Of The World' c/w 'Sisters O Sisters', John/Yoko with Elephant's Memory.

Issued in Britain on Apple 5953 on 12 May 1972 and in America on Apple 1848 on 24 April 1972.

'Mary Had A Little Lamb' c/w 'Little Woman Love', Wings.

Issued in Britain on Apple R 5949 on 12 May 1972 and in America on Apple 1851 on 29 May 1972. Number penned by Paul and Linda for their daughter Mary which reached No. 6 in the British charts and No. 28 in the American.

'We're On Our Way' c/w 'Supersoul', Chris Hodge.

Issued in Britain on Apple 43 on 9 June 1972 and in America on Apple 1850 on 3 May 1972. This first Apple single by Hodge reached No. 44 in the American charts. His second single failed to register and he moved to RCA Records.

'Hippy From New York City' c/w 'The Ballad Of New York City/John Lennon-Yoko Ono', David Peel and the Lower East Side.

Originally scheduled for release in America on Apple 6545/6546 on 16 June 1972, but only promotional copies were sent out to disc jockeys.

'Knock Knock Who's There' c/w 'International', Mary Hopkin.

Issued in America on Apple 1855 on 8 November 1972.

'Now Or Never' c/w 'Move On Fast', Yoko Ono with Elephant's Memory.

Issued in America on Apple 1853 on 13 November 1972. Two tracks from Yoko's *Approximate Infinite Universe* album.

'Saturday Night Special' c/w 'Valse De Soleil Coucher', Sundown Playboys.

Issued in Britain on Apple 44 on 24 November 1972 and in America on Apple 1852 on 26 September 1972. The only Apple release for this group of Cajun-style players.

'Hi, Hi, Hi' c/w 'C Moon', Wings.

Issued in Britain on Apple 5972 on 1 December 1972 and in America on Apple 1857 on 4 December 1972. Paul produced the single which became the second Wings single to be banned by the BBC – they cited suggestive lyrics. It reached No. 3 in the British charts and No.10 in the American.

'Water Paper and Clay' c/w 'Streets Of London', Mary Hopkin.

Issued in America on Apple 1843 on 1 December 1972.

'Power Boogie' c/w 'Liberation Special', Elephant's Memory.

Issued in Britain on Apple 45 on 8 December 1972 and in America on Apple 1854 on 4 December 1972. A group John Lennon and Yoko Ono discovered in New York and hired to provide backing on some records and gigs.

'Goodbye Sweet Lorraine' c/w 'Contact Love', Chris Hodge.

Issued in America on Apple 1858 on 22 January 1973. This second and final release on Apple for Hodge was unsuccessful and he left the label.

'Death of Samantha' c/w 'Yang Yang', Yoko Ono with Elephant's Memory.

Issued in Britain on Apple 47 on 4 May 1973 and in America on Apple 1859 on 26 February 1973.

'Warm Woman' c/w 'More Than Words', Lon and Derrek Van Eaton.

Issued in Britain on Apple 46 on 9 March 1973. Last Apple single from the brothers. By this time it was obvious that the majority of artists signed to Apple weren't achieving chart success, despite the fact that there had been some talented acts, such as Jackie Lomax, Doris Troy and James Taylor; and the hits by artists such as Mary Hopkin and Badfinger seemed to have dried up. From then on, the Apple singles were basically solo releases from the individual Beatles and Yoko Ono.

'MY LOVE' C/W 'THE MESS', PAUL MCCARTNEY AND WINGS.

Issued in Britain on Apple R 5985 on 23 March 1973 and in America on Apple 1861 on 9 April 1973. The 'A' side was recorded during the *Red Rose Speedway* album sessions and the flipside was recorded during a Wings concert in Holland. The single reached No. 7 in Britain and hit the No. 1 spot in America.

'GIVE ME LOVE' C/W 'MISS O'DELL', GEORGE HARRISON.

Issued in Britain on Apple 5988 on 25 May 1973 and in America on Apple 1862 on 7 May 1973. George's last hit single for some time, it reached No. 8 in the British charts and No. 1 in the American.

'LIVE AND LET DIE' C/W 'I LIE AROUND', WINGS.

Issued in Britain on Apple R 5987 on 1 June 1973 and in America on Apple 1863 on 18 June 1973. The number which Paul composed for the eighth Bond film, although he insisted that he record the number himself. On the flipside, Denny Laine takes over on lead vocal for the first and only time on a Wings single. The number reached No. 7 in the British charts and No. 2 in the American.

'PHOTOGRAPH' C/W 'DOWN AND OUT', RINGO STARR.

Issued in Britain on Apple R 5992 on 10 October 1973 and in America on Apple 1865 on 24 September 1973. Ringo co-wrote the title number with George Harrison. The musicians include Ringo and Jim Keltner on drums, George Harrison on twelve-string guitar, Nicky Hopkins on piano, Klaus Voorman on bass guitar, Vini Poncia and Jimmy Calvert on acoustic guitars, Lon and Derrek Van Eaton on percussion and Bobby Keyes on tenor sax. The single reached No. 4 in the British charts and No. 1 in the American.

'WOMAN POWER' C/W 'MEN, MEN, MEN', YOKO ONO.

Issued in America on Apple 1867 on 24 September 1973.

'HELEN WHEELS' C/W 'COUNTRY DREAMER', PAUL MCCARTNEY AND WINGS.

Issued in Britain on Apple R 5993 on 26 October 1973 and in America on Apple 1869 on 12 November 1973. The name in the title refers to Paul's Land-Rover. The single reached No. 12 in Britain and No. 10 in America.

'RUN, RUN, RUN' C/W 'MEN, MEN, MEN', YOKO ONO.

Issued in Britain on Apple 48 on 9 November 1973.

'MIND GAMES' C/W 'MEAT CITY', JOHN LENNON.

Issued in Britain on Apple R 5994 on 16 November 1973 and in America on Apple 1868 on 29 October 1973. John dropped the Plastic Ono credit and began recording again under his own name – he also finished his producing collaboration with Phil Spector and only worked with him again on the *Rock 'n' Roll* album. The single reached No. 19 in the British charts and No. 9 in the American.

'JET' C/W 'MAMUNIA', PAUL MCCARTNEY AND WINGS.

Issued in America on Apple 1871 on 28 January 1974. A few weeks after this American release, Capitol Records changed the flipside to 'Jet' and reissued it on 18 February, with the same catalogue number. It reached No. 7 in the American charts.

'YOU'RE SIXTEEN' C/W 'DEVIL WOMAN', RINGO STARR.

Issued in Britain on Apple R 5995 on 8 February 1974 and in America on Apple 1870 on 3 December 1973. Another American No. 1 single for Ringo and a No. 4 position in Britain.

'OH MY MY' C/W 'STEP LIGHTLY', RINGO STARR.

Issued in America on Apple 1872 on 18 February 1974. Ringo's fifth American Top Ten hit, reaching No. 5 in the charts.

'APPLE OF MY EYE' C/W 'BLIND OWL', BADFINGER.

Issued in Britain on Apple 49 on 8 March 1974 and in America on Apple 1864 on 17 December 1973.

'BAND ON THE RUN' C/W 'NINETEEN HUNDRED EIGHTY FIVE', PAUL MCCARTNEY AND WINGS.

Issued in America on Apple 1873 on 8 April 1974. The single reached No. 1 in the American charts and won a Grammy Award.

'WHATEVER GETS YOU THRU THE NIGHT' C/W 'BEEF JERKY', JOHN LENNON.

Issued in Britain on Apple R 5998 on 4 October 1974 and in America on Apple 1874 on 23 September 1974. Among the musicians backing John on this single are Elton John (organ/piano), Jim Keltner (drums), Eddie Mottau (acoustic guitar), Jessie Ed Davis (guitar), Ken Ascher (clarinet), Klaus Voorman (bass guitar), Arthur Jenkins (percussion) and Bobby Keyes (tenor saxophone). John uses the pseudonym the Hon. John St John Johnson for his guitar credit. The single reached No. 24 in the British charts and provided him with his first No. 1 in America as a solo artist. Elton John had predicted he'd top the charts with the number and, following a promise, he appeared on stage at Elton's Madison Square Garden concert.

'JUNIOR'S FARM' C/W 'SALLY G', PAUL MCCARTNEY AND WINGS.

Issued in Britain on Apple R 5999 on 25 October 1974 and in America on Apple 1875 on 4 November 1974. More tracks from the *Band On The Run* album. The single reached No. 16 in the British charts and No. 3 in the American. It was Paul's last single for Apple.

'ONLY YOU' C/W 'CALL ME', RINGO STARR.

Issued in Britain on Apple R 6000 on 15 November 1974 and in America on Apple 1876 on 11 November 1974. John Lennon suggested that Ringo should cover this old Platters song and he also played acoustic guitar on the session. Ringo shared drumming honours with Jim Keltner, Billy Preston played electric piano, Jesse Ed Davis and Steve Cropper were on electric guitars and **Harry Nilsson** provided backing vocal support. The single reached No. 25 in the British charts and No. 6 in the American.

'DARK HORSE' C/W 'I DON'T CARE ANYMORE', GEORGE HARRISON.

Was due to be issued in Britain on Apple 6001 on 22 November 1974, but wasn't. It was issued in America on Apple 1877 on 18 November 1974. It reached No. 15 in the American charts.

'DING DONG DING DONG' C/W 'I DON'T CARE ANYMORE', GEORGE HARRISON.

Issued in Britain on Apple R 6002 on 6 December 1974. It only managed to scrape into the British charts at No. 38. The song is said to have been inspired by the engravings on the walls of George's home, **Friar Park**.

'DING DONG DING DONG' C/W 'HARI'S ON TOUR (EXPRESS)', GEORGE HARRISON.

Issued in America on Apple 1879 on 23 December 1974. The single only reached No. 36 in the American charts.

'NO NO SONG' C/W 'SNOOKEROO', RINGO STARR.

Issued in America on Apple 1880 on 27 January 1975. The flipside was an Elton John/Bernie Taupin composition. The single wasn't a chart success for Ringo.

'NO. 9 DREAM' C/W 'WHAT YOU GOT', JOHN LENNON.

Issued in Britain on Apple R 6003 on 31 January 1975 and in America on Apple 1878 on 16 December 1974. Another track from *Walls and Bridges*, which only reached No. 23 in the British charts and No. 9 in the American.

'SNOOKEROO' C/W 'OO-WEE', RINGO STARR.

Issued in Britain on Apple R 6004 on 21 February 1975. Ringo's run of chart success seemed to have ended – and so did his releases on Apple. This was his last British Apple single.

'DARK HORSE' C/W 'HARI'S ON TOUR (EXPRESS)', GEORGE HARRISON.

Issued in Britain on Apple R 6001 on 28 February 1975. Not a chart entry.

'STAND BY ME' C/W 'MOVE OVER MS L', JOHN LENNON.

Issued in Britain on Apple R 6005 on 18 April 1975 and in America on Apple 1881 on 10 March 1975. A track from the *Rock 'n' Roll* album which reached No. 27 in the British charts and No. 20 in the American. John had originally written the flipside for **Keith Moon**'s album *Two Sides Of The Moon*.

'IT'S ALL DOWN TO GOODNIGHT VIENNA' C/W 'OW-WEE', RINGO STARR.

Issued in America on Apple 1882 on 2 June 1975. Another track from the *Goodnight Vienna* album which achieved a modest position of No. 31 in the American charts – this was Ringo's first single not to reach the Top 30.

'SLIPPIN' AND SLIDIN'' C/W 'AIN'T THAT A SHAME', JOHN LENNON.

Plans were in preparation for this second single from the *Rock 'n' Roll* album to be issued in America on Apple 1883 on 2 June 1975, but the plan was dropped.

'YOU' C/W 'WORLD OF STONE', GEORGE HARRISON.

Issued in Britain on Apple R 6007 on 12 September 1975, and in America on Apple 1884 on 15 September 1975. Taken from the *Extra Texture* album, it only reached No. 38 in the British charts, and No. 20 in the American charts.

'IMAGINE' C/W 'WORKING CLASS HERO', JOHN LENNON.

Issued in Britain on Apple 6009 on 24 October 1975.

'THIS GUITAR' C/W 'MAYA LOVE', GEORGE HARRISON.

Issued in America on Apple 1885 on 8 December 1975 and in Britain on Apple 6012 on 6 February 1976. George Harrison's last single on the Apple label and also the last solo Beatle single to be issued on Apple. It did not reach either the British or American charts.

APPLE DISCOGRAPHY – ALBUMS

WONDERWALL MUSIC, GEORGE HARRISON.

Issued in Britain on SAPCOR 1 on 1 November 1968 and in America on Apple ST 3350 on 2 December 1968.

THE BEATLES, THE BEATLES.

Issued in Britain on Apple PCS 7067/8 on 22 November 1968 and in America on Apple SWBO 101 on 25 November 1968.

TWO VIRGINS, JOHN LENNON AND YOKO ONO.

Issued in Britain on SAPCOR 2 on 29 November 1968 and in America on Apple T 5001 on 11 November 1968.

JAMES TAYLOR, JAMES TAYLOR.

Issued in Britain on SAPCOR 3 on 6 December 1968 and in America on Apple SKAO 3352 on 17 February 1969. The tracks were, Side One: 'Don't Talk Now', 'Something's Wrong', 'Knocking 'Round The Zoo', 'Sunshine Sunshine', 'Taking It In', 'Something In The Way She Moves'. Side Two: 'Carolina On My Mind', 'Brighten Your Night With My Day', 'Night Owl', 'Rainy Day Man', 'Circle 'Round The Sun', 'Blues Is Just A Bad Dream'. Taylor was discovered by Peter Asher and moved to England to record for Apple. He had no success with the label and felt that he was not being given adequate promotion. He left Apple in 1969 and later found success with Warner Brothers Records, while retaining Peter Asher as his producer. Taylor later married Carly Simon and both Paul and Linda McCartney have contributed vocals to albums by both singers.

UNDER THE JASMINE TREE, THE MODERN JAZZ QUARTET.

Issued in Britain on SAPCOR 4 on 6 December 1968 and in America on Apple ST 3353 on 17 February 1969. The tracks were, Side One: 'Blue Necklace', 'Three Little Feelings'. Side Two: 'Exposure', 'Jasmine Tree'. This well-established jazz outfit only signed with Apple for a specifically limited period, during which they issued two albums.

YELLOW SUBMARINE, THE BEATLES.

Issued in Britain on Apple PCS 7070 on 17 January 1969 and in America on Apple SW 153 on 13 January 1969.

POST CARD, MARY HOPKIN.

Issued in Britain on SAPCOR 5 on 21 February 1969 and in America on Apple ST 3351 on 3 March 1969. Paul McCartney produced this album which contained a selection of songs from various songwriters including **Donovan**, Nilsson, Gershwin and Irving Berlin. The tracks were, Side One: 'Lord Of The Reedy River', 'Happiness Runs (Pebble And The Man)', 'Love Is The Sweetest Thing', 'Y Blodwyn Gwyn', 'The Honeymoon Song', 'The Puppy Song', 'Inchworm'. Side Two: 'Voyage Of The Moon', 'Lullaby Of The Leaves', 'Young Love', 'Someone To Watch Over Me', 'Prince En Avignon', 'The Game', 'There's No Business Like Show Business'. For the American release, 'Those Were The Days' replaced 'Someone To Watch Over Me'. The album reached the No. 3 position in Britain.

IS THIS WHAT YOU WANT, JACKIE LOMAX.

Issued in Britain on SAPCOR 6 on 21 March 1969 and in America on Apple ST 3354 on 19 May 1969. Lomax's only album for Apple, produced by George Harrison. The tracks were, Side One: 'Speak To Me', 'Is This What You Want', 'How Can You Say Goodbye', 'Sunset', 'Sour Milk Sea', 'I Fall Inside Your Eyes'. Side Two: 'Little Yellow Pills', 'Take My Word', 'The Eagle Laughs At You', 'Baby You're A Lover', 'You've Got Me Thinking', 'I Just Don't Know'. For the American release 'How Can You Say Goodbye' was replaced by 'New Day'.

LIFE WITH THE LIONS, JOHN LENNON AND YOKO ONO.

Issued in Britain on Zapple 01 on 9 May 1969 and in America on Zapple ST 3357 on 26 May 1969.

ELECTRONIC SOUND, GEORGE HARRISON.

Issued in Britain on Zapple 02 on 9 May 1969 and in America on Zapple ST 3358 on 26 May 1969.

LISTENING TO RICHARD BRAUTIGAN, RICHARD BRAUTIGAN.

Originally scheduled to become Zapple 03 and to be issued on 23 May 1969, but the project was dropped.

ACCEPT NO SUBSTITUTE, DELANEY AND BONNIE.

Originally due to be issued in Britain on SAPCOR 7 on 30 May 1969, but the project was dropped and the LP was issued on the Elektra label the following month.

WHITE TRASH, TRASH.

The debut album by Trash was given the catalogue number SAPCOR 7 and the release date in Britain on 20 June 1969, but it was never issued.

MAYBE TOMORROW, THE IVEYS.

Issued in Europe (but not Britain) on SAPCOR 8 on 4 July 1969 while a projected American release on Apple ST 3355 on 14 July 1969 was withdrawn. The album, produced by Tony Visconti and Mal Evans, was also available in Japan. At the time of this release the Iveys comprised Tom Evans (rhythm guitar), Pete Ham (lead guitar), Ron Griffith (bass guitar) and Mike Gibbons (drums). They later decided to drop the name Iveys and call themselves Badfinger. The tracks were, Side One: 'Maybe Tomorrow', 'See-Saw Grampa', 'Beautiful And Blue', 'Dear Angie', 'Think About The Good Times', 'Yesterday Ain't Coming Back'. Side Two: 'Fisherman', 'Sali Bloo', 'Angelique', 'I'm In Love', 'Knocking Down

Our Home', 'I've Been Waiting'.

THAT'S THE WAY GOD PLANNED IT, BILLY PRESTON.

Issued in Britain on SAPCOR 9 on 22 August 1969 and in America on 10 September 1969. The tracks were, Side One: 'Do What You Want', 'I Want To Thank You', 'Everything's All Right', 'She Belongs To Me', 'It Doesn't Matter', 'Morning Star'. Side Two: 'Hey Brother', 'What About You', 'Let Us Get Together Right Now', 'This Is It', 'Keep To Yourself', 'That's The Way God Planned It'.

ABBEY ROAD, THE BEATLES.

Issued in Britain on PCS 7088 on 26 September 1969 and in America on Apple SO 383 on 1 October 1969.

WEDDING ALBUM, JOHN LENNON AND YOKO ONO.

Issued in Britain on SAPCOR 11 on 24 October 1969 and in America on Apple SMAX 3361.

SPACE, THE MODERN JAZZ QUARTET.

Issued in Britain on SAPCOR 10 on 24 October 1969 and in America on 10 November 1969. The tracks were, Side One: 'Visitor From Venus', 'Visitor From Mars', 'Here's That Rainy Day'. Side Two: 'Dilemma', 'Adagio From Concierto De Aranjuez'.

LIVE PEACE IN TORONTO, PLASTIC ONO BAND.

Issued in Britain on Apple CORE 2001 on 12 December 1969 and in America on Apple SW 3362 on 12 December 1969. The tracks were, Side One: 'Blue Suede Shoes', 'Money', 'Dizzy Miss Lizzy', 'Yer Blues', 'Cold Turkey', 'Give Peace A Chance'. Side Two: 'Don't Worry Kyoko (Mummy's Only Looking For A Hand In The Snow)', 'John John (Let's Hope For Peace)'. An appearance at the Toronto Rock 'n' Roll Revival Concert in September 1969 resulted in this album with John backed by Eric Clapton on guitar, Alan White on drums and Klaus Voorman on bass guitar. The second side of the album featured two numbers written by Yoko. The album didn't chart in Britain, but it reached No. 10 in America.

MAGIC CHRISTIAN MUSIC, BADFINGER.

Issued in Britain on SAPCOR 12 on 9 January 1970 and in America on Apple ST 3364 on 16 February 1970. The tracks were, Side One: 'Come And Get It', 'Crimson Ship', 'Dear Angie', 'Fisherman', 'Midnight Sun', 'Beautiful And Blue', 'Rock Of All Ages'. Side Two: 'Carry On 'Til Tomorrow', 'I'm In Love', 'Walk Out In The Rain', 'Angelique', 'Knocking Down Our Home', 'Give It A Try', 'Maybe Tomorrow'. For the American release, the tracks 'Angelique' and 'Give It A Try' were not included.

MCCARTNEY, PAUL MCCARTNEY.

Issued in Britain on Apple PCS 7102 on 17 April 1970 and in America on Apple STAO 3363 on 20 April 1970. Paul's first solo album, produced by himself, on which he also plays all the instruments. The tracks were, Side One: 'The Lovely Linda', 'That Would Be Something', 'Valentine Day', 'Every Night', 'Hot As Sun', 'Glasses', 'Junk', 'Man We Was Lonely'. Side Two: 'Op You', 'Momma Miss America', 'Teddy Boy', Singalong Junk', 'Maybe I'm Amazed', 'Kreen-Akrore'. The album reached No. 2 in Britain and No. 1 in America.

LET IT BE, THE BEATLES.

Issued in Britain on Apple PXS 1 on 8 May 1970 and in America on Apple AR 34001 on 18 May 1970.

DORIS TROY, DORIS TROY.

Issued in Britain on SAPCOR 13 on 11 September 1970 and in America on Apple ST 3370 on 9 November 1970. The singer produced this album herself and among the artists performing on it are George Harrison, Ringo Starr, Jackie Lomax, Klaus Voorman and Steve Stills. The tracks were, Side One: 'Ain't That Cute', 'Give Me Back My Dynamite', 'You Tore Me Up Inside', 'Games People Play', 'Gonna Get My Baby Back', 'I've Got To Be Strong'. Side Two: 'Hurry', 'So Far', 'Exactly Like You', 'You Give Me Joy Joy', 'Don't Call Me No More', 'Jacob's Ladder'.

ENCOURAGING WORDS, BILLY PRESTON.

Issued in Britain on SAPCOR 14 on 11 September 1970 and in America on Apple ST 3370 on 9 November 1970. Billy's second and final album for Apple, produced by himself and George Harrison. The tracks were, Side One: 'Right Now', 'Little Girl', 'Use What You Got', 'My Sweet Lord', 'Let The Music Play', 'The Same Thing Again'. Side Two: 'I've Got A Feeling', 'Sing One For The Lord', 'When You Are Mine', 'I Don't Want You To Pretend', 'Encouraging Words', 'All Things Must Pass', 'You've Been Acting Strange'.

THE WHALE, JOHN TAVENER.

Issued in Britain on SAPCOR 15 on 25 September 1970 and in America on Apple SMAS 3369 on 9 November, 1970. The tracks were, Side One: 'The Whale' (Part One). Side Two: 'The Whale' (Concluded). Tavener was a British classical composer/conductor who had studied at the Royal Academy of Music. His composition *The Whale* was first performed in 1966. The Apple recording was made at the Church of St John the Evangelist in London with a host of musicians, including the London Sinfonietta and Chorus, with Tavener playing Hammond organ.

BEAUCOUPS OF BLUES, RINGO STARR.

Issued in Britain on Apple PAS 10002 on 25 September 1970 and in America on Apple SMAS 3368 on 28 September 1970. Recorded in Nashville. The tracks were, Side One: 'Beaucoups Of Blues', 'Love Don't Last Long', 'Fastest Growing Heartache In The West', 'Without Her', 'Woman Of The Night', 'I'd Be Talking All The Time'. Side Two: '$15 Draw', 'Wine, Women And Loud Happy Songs', 'I Wouldn't Have You Any Other Way', 'Loser's Lounge', 'Waiting', 'Silent Homecoming'. The album reached No. 65 in America.

NO DICE, BADFINGER.

Issued in Britain on SAPCOR 16 on 27 November 1970 and in America on Apple ST 3367 on 9 November 1970. The tracks were, Side One: 'I Can't Take It', 'I Don't Mind', 'Love Me Do', 'Midnight Caller', 'No Matter What', 'Without You'. Side Two: 'Blodwyn', 'Better Days', 'It Had To Be', 'Waterford John', 'Believe Me', 'We're For The Dark'.

ALL THINGS MUST PASS, GEORGE HARRISON.

Issued in Britain on Apple STCH 639 on 30 November 1970 and in America on Apple STCH 639 on 27 November 1970. The tracks were, Side One: 'I'd Have You Anytime', 'My Sweet Lord', 'Wah-Wah', 'Isn't It A Pity'. Side Two: 'What Is Life', 'If Not For You', 'Behind That Locked Door', 'Let It Down', 'Run Of The Mill'. Side Three: 'Beware Of Darkness', 'Apple Scruffs', 'Ballad of Sir Frankie Crisp (Let It Roll)', 'Awaiting On You All', 'All Things Must Pass'. Side Four: 'I Dig Love', 'Art Of Dying', 'Isn't It A Pity' (second version), 'Hear Me Lord'. Side Five: 'Out Of The Blue', 'It's Johnny's Birthday', 'Plug Me In'. Side Six: 'I Remember Jeep', 'Thanks For The Pepperoni'. The album rose to No. 1 in both the British and American charts.

PLASTIC ONO BAND, JOHN LENNON.

Issued in Britain on Apple PCS 7124 on 11 December 1970 and in America on Apple SW 3372 on 11 December 1970. Often nicknamed 'The Primal Scream' album. The tracks were, Side One: 'Mother', 'Hold On', 'I Found Out', 'Working Class Hero', 'Isolation'. Side Two: 'Remember', 'Love', 'Well Well Well', 'Look At Me', 'God', 'Mummy's Dead'. The album reached No. 13 in the British charts and No. 6 in the American.

PLASTIC ONO BAND, YOKO ONO.

Issued in Britain on SAPCOR 17 on 11 December 1970 and in America on Apple SW 3373 on 11 December 1970. A six-track album, with all songs composed by Yoko. As this was her first real solo album, John does not receive the usual co-credit. The tracks were, Side One: 'Why', 'Why Not', 'Greenfield Morning I Pushed An Empty Baby Carriage All Over The City'. Side Two: 'AOS', 'Touch Me', 'Paper Shoes'.

FROM THEN TO US; THE BEATLES CHRISTMAS ALBUM, THE BEATLES.

Issued in Britain on LYN 2154 on 18 December 1970 and in America on SBC 100 on 18 December 1970 – although only to members of the Beatles' fan clubs in both countries and not to the general public.

RAM, PAUL AND LINDA McCARTNEY.

Issued in Britain on Apple PAS 10003 on 28 May 1971 and in America on Apple SMAS 3375 on 17 May 1971. The tracks were, Side One: 'Too Many People', '3 Legs', 'Ram On', 'Dear Boy', 'Uncle Albert/Admiral Halsey', 'Smile Away'. Side Two: 'Heart Of The Country', 'Monkberry Moon Delight', 'Eat At Home', 'Long Haired Lady', 'Ram On', 'The Back Seat Of My Car'. The album reached No. 1 in the UK and No. 2 in America.

RADHA KRISHNA TEMPLE, RADHA KRISHNA TEMPLE.

Issued in Britain on SAPCOR 18 on 28 May 1971 and in America on Apple SKAO 3376 on 21 May 1971. Members of the London branch of the Radha Krishna Temple, whom George Harrison took into the **Apple studios**. He produced this album, which came in a package with the lyrics to the chants, a biography of Krsna and other material relevant to the temple. The tracks were, Side One: 'Govinda', 'Sri Gurvastakam', 'Bhaja Bhakata/Arati', 'Hare Krishna Mantra'. Side Two: 'Sri Isopanisad', 'Bhaja Hunre Mana', 'Govinda Jaya Jaya'.

CELTIC REQUIEM, JOHN TAVENER.

Issued in Britain on SAPCOR 20 on 2 July 1971. The tracks were, Side One: 'Celtic Requiem'. Side Two: 'Coplas', 'Nomine Jesu'. The final Apple album from this classical composer. All three compositions were recorded at the Church of St John the Evangelist in London.

COME TOGETHER, STELVIO CIPRIONI.

Issued in America on Apple SW 3377 on 17 September 1971. The tracks were, Side One: 'Games People Play', 'Come Together (Arrival in Rome)', 'Love Is Blue', 'Fascinum', 'Monument To Love', 'Love Is Blue'. Side Two: 'Love Is Blue' 'I Can Sing A Rainbow', 'Come Together', 'Love Is Blue'/'Bas Vibrations', 'Come Together'/'Get Together'. A soundtrack album for the film, which **Allen Klein** added to the Apple catalogue.

FLY, YOKO ONO.

Issued in Britain on SAPCOR 21 on 1 October 1971 and in America on Apple SVBB 3380 on 20 September 1971. The full album credit was: By Yoko Ono and the Plastic Ono Band with Joe Jones Tone Deaf Music Co. The tracks were, Side One: 'Midsummer New York', 'Mind Train'. Side Two: 'Mind Holes', 'Don't Worry Kyoko', 'Mrs Lennon', 'Hirake', 'Toiler Piece'/'Unknown', 'O 'Wind (Body Is The Scar Of Your Mind)'. Side Three: 'Airmale', 'Don't Count The Waves', 'You'. Side Four: 'Fly', 'Telephone Piece'.

EARTH SONG – OCEAN SONG, MARY HOPKIN.

Issued in Britain on SAPCOR 21 on 1 October 1971 and in America on Apple SMAS 3381 on 3 November 1971. The tracks were, Side One: 'Earth Song', 'Ocean Song', 'International', 'How Come The Sun', 'There's Got To Be More'. Side Two: 'Silver Birch And Weeping Willow', 'Martha', 'Streets Of London', 'Wind, Water, Paper And Clay'.

IMAGINE, JOHN LENNON AND THE PLASTIC ONO BAND, WITH THE FLUX FIDDLERS.

Issued in Britain on Apple PAS 10004 on 8 October 1971 and in America on Apple SW 3379 on 9 September 1971. The tracks were, Side One: 'Imagine', 'Crippled Inside', 'Jealous Guy', 'It's So Hard', 'I Don't Want To Be A Soldier Mama, I Don't Want To Die'. Side Two: 'Give Me Some Truth', 'Oh My Love', 'How Do You Sleep?', 'How?', 'Oh Yoko'. The album reached No. 1 in both the British and American charts.

RAGA, RAVI SHANKAR.

Issued in America on SWAO 3384 on 7 December 1971. The tracks were, Side One: 'Dawn To Dust', 'Vedic Hymns', 'Baba Teaching', 'Birth To Death', 'Vinus House', 'Gurur Bramha', 'United Nations'. Side Two: (Medley) 'Raga Parameshwari'/'Rangeswhart', 'Banaras Ghat', 'Bombay Studio', 'Kinnara School', 'Frenzy And Distortion', 'Raga Desh'. This was the soundtrack album to the film *Raga*.

WILD LIFE, WINGS.

Issued in Britain on PCS 7142 on 7 December 1971 and in America on Apple SW 3386 on 7 December 1971. First album from Paul and Linda McCartney's new band, Wings, which reached No. 11 in the British charts and No. 10 in the American. The tracks were, Side One: 'Mumbo', 'Bip Bop', 'Love Is Strange', 'Wild Life'. Side Two: 'Some People Never Know', 'I Am Your Singer', 'Tomorrow', 'Dear Friend'.

EL TOPO, ALEXANDRO JODOROWSKY.

Issued in America on SWAO 3388 on 27 December 1971. The tracks were, Side One: 'Entiero Del Primer Juguete', 'Bajo Tierra', 'La Cathedral De Los Puerlos', 'Los Mendigos Sagrados', 'La Muerte Es Un Nacimiento', 'Curios Mexicano', 'Valas Fatasma'. Side Two: 'El Alma Nace En La Sangre', 'Topo Triste', 'Los Dioses De Azucar', 'Las Flores Nacen En El Barro', 'El Infierno De Las Angeleses Prostitutos', 'Marcha De Los O Jos En El Trianqulos', 'La Mieldel Dolor', '300 Conejos', 'Conocimiento A Traves De La Musica', 'La Primera Flor Despues Del Diluvio'. An unusual release for Apple – the soundtrack for a metaphysical Western movie produced by cult director Jodorowsky.

THE CONCERT FOR BANGLADESH, GEORGE HARRISON AND FRIENDS.

Issued in Britain on STCX 3385 on 10 January 1972 and in America on STCX 3385 on 20 December 1971.

STRAIGHT UP, BADFINGER.

Issued in Britain on SAPCOR 19 on 11 February 1972 and in America on Apple SW 3387 on 13 December 1971. The tracks were, Side One: 'Take It All', 'Baby Blue', 'Money', 'Flying', 'I'd Die, Babe', 'Name Of The Game'. Side Two: 'Suitcase', 'Sweet Tuesday Morning', 'Day After Day', 'Sometimes', 'Perfection', 'It's Over'. Album produced by Todd Rundgren, excepting four tracks produced by George Harrison: 'I'd Die, Babe', 'Name Of The Game', 'Suitcase' and 'Day After Day'.

THE POPE SMOKES DOPE, DAVID PEEL.

Issued in America on SW 3391 on 28 April 1972. The tracks were, Side One: 'I'm A Runaway', 'Everybody's Smoking Marijuana', 'F Is Not A Dirty Word', 'The Hippie From New York City', 'McDonald's Farm', 'The Ballad Of New York City'. Side Two: 'The Ballad Of Bob Dylan', 'The Chicago Conspiracy', 'The Hip Generation', 'I'm Gonna Start Another Riot', 'The Birth Control Blues', 'The Pope Smokes Dope'. The album was produced by John Lennon and Yoko Ono.

SOME TIME IN NEW YORK CITY, JOHN LENNON AND YOKO ONO AND THE PLASTIC ONO BAND WITH ELEPHANT'S MEMORY PLUS INVISIBLE STRINGS.

Issued in Britain on Apple PCSP 716 on 15 September 1972 and in America on Apple SVBB 3392 on 12 June 1972. The tracks were, Side One: 'Woman Is The Nigger

Of The World', 'Sisters, O Sisters', 'Attica State', 'Born In A Prison', 'New York City'. Side Two: 'Sunday Bloody Sunday', 'The Luck Of The Irish', 'John Sinclair', 'Angela', 'We're All Water'. The album reached No. 19 in the British charts and No. 48 in the American.

ELEPHANT'S MEMORY, ELEPHANT'S MEMORY.

Issued in Britain on SAPCOR 22 on 10 November 1972 and in America on SMAS 3389 on 18 September 1972. The band who backed John Lennon and Yoko Ono on some American gigs. They were originally going to tour with John, but he cancelled it. However, he agreed to produce an album with the band, together with Yoko. The tracks were, Side One: 'Liberation Special', 'Baddest Of The Mean', 'Cryin' Blacksheep Blues', 'Chuck 'n' Bo'. Side Two: 'Gypsy Wolf', 'Madness', 'Wind Ridge', 'Power Boogie', 'Local Plastic Ono Band'.

THOSE WERE THE DAYS, MARY HOPKIN.

Issued in Britain on SAPCOR 23 on 24 November 1972 and in America on SW 3395 on 25 September 1972. The tracks were, Side One: 'Those Were The Days', 'Que Sera Sera', 'Fields Of St Etienne', 'Kew Gardens', 'Temma Harbour', 'Think About Your Children'. Side Two: 'Knock Knock, Who's There', 'Heritage', 'Sparrow', 'Lontano Dagli Occhi', 'Goodbye'.

PHIL SPECTOR'S CHRISTMAS ALBUM, VARIOUS ARTISTS.

Issued in Britain on SAPCOR 24 on 8 December 1972 and in America on SW 3400 on 11 December 1972. The tracks were, Side One: 'White Christmas', 'Frosty The Snowman', 'Bells Of St Mary', 'Santa Claus Is Coming To Town'. 'Sleigh Ride', 'It's A Marshmallow World'. Side Two: 'I Saw Mommy Kissing Santa Claus', 'Rudolph, The Red Nosed Reindeer', 'Winter Wonderland', 'Parade Of The Wooden Soldiers', 'Christmas (Baby Please Come Home)', 'Here Comes Santa Claus', 'Silent Night'. An album which Spector had originally produced several years earlier with a range of artists from his original Phillies record label: Darlene Love, the **Ronettes** and Bob B Soxx & the Blue Jeans.

BROTHER, LON AND DERREK VAN EATON.

Issued in Britain on SAPCOR 25 on 9 February 1973 and in America on SMAS 3390 on 22 September 1972. The tracks were, Side One: 'Warm Woman', 'Sun Song', 'More Than Words', 'Hear My Cry', 'Without The Lord', 'Sweet Music'. Side Two: 'Help Us All', 'Maybe There's Another', 'Ring', 'Sunshine', 'Another Thought'. The only Apple album from the brothers. It was produced by Klaus Voorman with the exception of 'Sweet Music', which was produced by George Harrison.

APPROXIMATELY INFINITE UNIVERSE, YOKO ONO.

Issued in Britain on SAPDO 1001 on 16 February 1973 and in America on SVBB 3399 on 8 January 1973, with the credit: By Yoko Ono and the Plastic Ono Band with Elephant's Memory, Endless Strings and Choir Boys. Yoko's second double album. The tracks were, Side One: 'Yang Yang', 'Death Of Samantha', 'I Want My Love To Rest Tonight', 'What Did I Do!', 'Have You Seen A Horizon Lately'. Side Two: 'Approximately Infinite Universe', 'Peter The Dealer', 'Song For John', 'Catman (The Roses Are Coming)', 'What A Bastard The World Is', 'Waiting For The Sunrise'. Side Three: 'I Felt Like Smashing My Face In A Clear Glass Window', 'Winter Song', 'Kite Song', 'What A Mess', 'Shiranakatta (I Didn't Know)', 'Air Talk'. Side Four: 'I Have a Woman Inside My Soul', 'Move On Fast', 'Now Or Never', 'Is Winter Here To Stay?', 'Looking Over From My Hotel Window'.

IN CONCERT 1972, RAVI SHANKAR AND ALI AKBAR KHAN.

Issued in Britain on SAPDO 1002 on 13 April 1973 and in America on SVBB 3396 on 22 January 1973. The tracks were, Side One: 'Raga – Hem Bihag'. Side Two: 'Raga – Manj Khamaj (Part One)'. Side Three: 'Raga – Manj Khamaj (Part Two)'. Side Four: 'Raga – Sindhi Bhairabi'. The album was produced by George Harrison, Zakir Hussein and Phil McDonald.

THE BEATLES 1962–1966, THE BEATLES.

Issued in Britain on PCSP 717 on 20 April 1973 and in America on SKBO 3403 on 2 April 1973.

THE BEATLES 1967–1970, THE BEATLES.

Issued in Britain on PCSP 718 on 20 April 1973 and in America on SKBO 3404 on 2 April 1973*RED ROSE SPEEDWAY*, PAUL MCCARTNEY AND WINGS.

Issued in Britain on Apple PCTC 251 on 4 May 1973 and in America on Apple SMAL 3409 on 30 April 1973. The tracks were, Side One: 'Big Barn Bed', 'My Love', 'Get On The Right Thing', 'One More Kiss', 'Little Lamb Dragonfly'. Side Two: 'Single Pigeon', 'When The Night', 'Loup (1st Indian On The Moon)', 'Hold Me Tight', 'Lazy Dynamite', 'Hands Of Love', 'Power Cut'. The album reached No. 4 in Britain and No. 1 in America.

LIVING IN THE MATERIAL WORLD, GEORGE HARRISON.

Issued in Britain on Apple PAS 10006 on 22 June 1973 and in America on Apple SMAS 3410 on 30 May 1973. The tracks were, Side One: 'Give Me Love (Give Me Peace

On Earth)', 'Sue Me Sue You Blues', 'The Light That Has Lighted The World', 'Don't Let Me Wait Too Long', 'Who Can See It', 'Living In The Material World'. Side Two: 'The Lord Loves The One (That Loves The Lord)', 'Be Here Now', 'Try Some Buy Some', 'The Day The World Gets Round', 'That Is All'. The album reached No. 3 in Britain and No. 1 in America.

RINGO, RINGO STARR.

Issued in Britain on Apple PCTC 252 on 9 November 1973 and in America on Apple SWAL 3413 on 2 November 1973. The tracks were, Side One: 'I'm The Greatest', 'Have You Seen My Baby', 'Photograph', 'Sunshine Life For Me (Sail Away Raymond)', 'You're Sixteen'. Side Two: 'Oh My My', 'Step Lightly', 'Six O'Clock', 'Devil Woman', 'You And Me (Babe)'. The album reached No. 6 in the British charts and No. 2 in the American.

MIND GAMES, JOHN LENNON WITH THE PLASTIC U.F. ONO BAND.

Issued in Britain on Apple PCS 7165 on 16 November 1973 and in America on Apple SW 3414 on 2 November 1973. The tracks were, Side One: 'Mind Games', 'Tight A$', 'One Day (At A Time)', 'Bring On The Lucie (Freda Peeple)', 'Nutopian International Anthem'. Side Two: 'Intuition', 'Out Of The Blue', 'Only People', 'I Know (I Know)', 'You Are Here', 'Meat City'. The album reached No. 9 in the British charts and No. 18 in the American.

FEELING THE SPACE, YOKO ONO.

Issued in Britain on SAPCOR 26 on 23 November 1973 and in America on SW 3412 on 2 November 1973. The tracks were, Side One: 'Growing Pain', 'Yellow Girl (Stand By For Life)', 'Coffin Car', 'Woman Of Salem', 'Run, Run, Run', 'If Only'. Side Two: 'A Thousand Times Yes', 'Straight Talk', 'Angry Young Woman', 'She Hits Back', 'Woman Power', 'Men, Men, Men'.

BAND ON THE RUN, PAUL MCCARTNEY AND WINGS.

Issued in Britain on Apple PAS 10007 on 30 November 1973 and in America on Apple SO 3415 on 5 December 1973. The tracks were, Side One: 'Band On The Run', 'Jet', 'Bluebird', 'Mrs Vandebilt', 'Let Me Roll It'. Side Two: 'Mamunia', 'No Words', 'Picasso's Last Words (Drink To Me)', 'Nineteen Hundred And Eighty Five'. The album reached No. 1 in both Britain and America.

ASS, BADFINGER.

Issued in Britain on SAPCOR 27 on 8 March 1974 and in America on 26 November 1973. The tracks were, Side One: 'Apple Of My Eye', 'Get Away', 'Icicles', 'The Winner', 'Blind Owl'. Side Two: 'Constitution', 'When I Say', 'Cowboy', 'I Can Love You', 'Timeless'.

WALLS AND BRIDGES, JOHN LENNON WITH THE PLASTIC ONO NUCLEAR BAND.

Issued in Britain on Apple PCTC 253 on 4 October 1974 and in America on Apple SW 3416 on 26 September 1974. The tracks were, Side One: 'Going Down On Love', 'Whatever Gets You Thru The Night', 'Old Dirt Road', 'What You Got', 'Bless You', 'Scared'. Side Two: 'No. 9 Dream', 'Surprise Surprise (Sweet Bird Of Paradox)', 'Steel And Glass', 'Beef Jerky', 'Nobody Loves You (When You're Down And Out)'. The album reached No. 5 in the British charts and reached No. 1 in America.

GOODNIGHT VIENNA, RINGO STARR.

Issued in Britain on Apple PCS 7168 on 15 November 1974 and in America on Apple SW 3417 on 18 November 1974. The tracks were, Side One: 'Goodnight Vienna', 'Occapella', 'Oo-Wee', 'Husbands And Wives', 'Snookeroo'. Side Two: 'All By Myself', 'Call Me', 'No No Song', 'Only You', 'Easy For Me', 'Goodnight Vienna'. The album reached No. 24 in Britain and No. 8 in America.

DARK HORSE, GEORGE HARRISON.

Issued in Britain on Apple PAS 10008 on 20 December 1974 and in America on Apple SMAS 3418 on 9 December 1974. The tracks were, Side One: 'Hari's On Tour (Express)', 'Simply Shady', 'So Sad', 'Bye Bye Love', 'Maya Love'. Side Two: 'Ding Dong Ding Dong', 'Dark Horse', 'Far East Man', 'It Is "He"'. The album didn't reach the British charts but reached No. 4 in America.

ROCK 'N' ROLL, JOHN LENNON.

Issued in Britain on Apple PCS 7169 on 21 February 1975 and in America on Apple SMAS 3418 on 17 February 1975. The tracks were, Side One: 'Be-Bop-A-Lula', 'Stand By Me', 'Rip It Up'/'Ready Teddy', 'You Can't Catch Me', 'Ain't That A Shame', 'Do You Wanna Dance', 'Sweet Little Sixteen'. Side Two: 'Slippin' And Slidin'', 'Peggy Sue', 'Bring It On Home To Me'/'Send Me Some Lovin'', 'Bony Moronie', 'Ya Ya', 'Just Because'. The album reached No. 10 in the British charts and No. 6 in the American.

EXTRA TEXTURE, GEORGE HARRISON.

Issued in Britain on Apple PAS 10009 on 3 October 1975 and in America on Apple SW 3420 on 22 September 1975. The tracks were, Side One: 'You', 'The Answer's At The End', 'The Guitar (Can't Keep From Crying)', 'Ooh

Baby (I Know That I Love You)', 'World Of Stone'. Side Two: 'A Bit More Of You', 'Can't Stop Thinking About You', 'Tired Of Midnight Blue', 'Grey Cloudy Lies', 'His Name Is Legs (Ladies And Gentlemen)'. The album reached No. 22 in the British charts and No. 8 in the American.

SHAVED FISH, JOHN LENNON.

Issued in Britain on Apple PCS 7173 on 24 October 1975 and in America on Apple SW 3421 on 24 October 1975. The tracks were, Side One: 'Give Peace A Chance', 'Cold Turkey', 'Instant Karma', 'Power To The People', 'Mother', 'Woman Is The Nigger Of The World'. Side Two: 'Imagine', 'Whatever Gets You Thru The Night', 'Mind Games', 'No. 9 Dream', 'Happy Xmas (War Is Over)', 'Give Peace A Chance'. It reached No. 6 in the British charts and reached No. 12 in the American.

BLAST FROM YOUR PAST, RINGO STARR.

Issued in Britain on Apple PCS 7170 on 12 December 1975 and in America on Apple SW 3422 on 20 November 1975. The tracks were, Side One: 'You're Sixteen', 'No No Song', 'It Don't Come Easy', 'Photograph', 'Back Off Boogaloo'. Side Two: 'Only You (And You Alone)', '*Beaucoups* Of Blues', 'Oh My My', 'Early 1970', 'I'm The Greatest'.

In 1975 Paul McCartney's releases began to be issued by EMI in Britain and Capitol in America. In 1976 George Harrison's records began to be issued by his own label, Dark Horse. Although Ringo Starr also formed his own record label, Ring O' Records, his own releases were issued by different labels, including Atlantic, Portrait, Capitol and Boardwalk. John Lennon moved to Capitol and then to Geffen Records.

● Apple School

In 1968 it was decided to establish an Apple School in which **Julian Lennon**, **Zak Starkey** and the children of Apple employees such as **Derek Taylor**, could be educated. There were to be between fifteen to twenty children, including any children of friends such as **Bob Dylan,** and the school would introduce some exciting new educational ideas – which is why Ivor Cutler, who appeared as Buster Bloodvessel in *Magical Mystery Tour*, was hired as consultant – he had some interesting theories on what could be achieved. The head of the school was to be **Ivan Vaughan**, the friend who had introduced John and Paul to each other.

These are the minutes of a meeting held at Apple to discuss the school on 9 May 1968. Those present were John Lennon, Ringo Starr, **Ivan Vaughan**, **Alexis Mardas** and **Derek Taylor**:

Administration.

1. (Ministry of Education) regulations concerning required amenities e.g. lavatories, fire escape, open space, size of accommodation, concerning quality of staff, if aim is to get the school approved by the Ministry at a future date.

It was decided to leave the regulations for the school in the hands of Ivan who would be aided by Professor Doris M. Lee.

2. Accommodation: Suitability in terms of proximity to the homes of the prospective pupils.

A decision cannot yet be made concerning a suitable site for the school until new homes have been found by the people concerned.

(Note 1. Full account to be taken of proposed moves in the near future on the part of a number of the interested families).

Suitability in terms of ease of conversion to meet both the [Ministry's] regulations and also to meet requirements on educational grounds.

Finance.

Immediate: A. Initial funds required to pay for the time of professional people engaged in a consultative capacity during the initial planning stages.

It was agreed to discuss the matter of finance with Stephen Maltz who would advise which would be the best company to supply the funds necessary.

B. Salary of Ivan Vaughan – to begin investigations and consultations as soon as possible.

As from today Ivan will receive £50 per week, being the average wage for a Headmaster.

Future: A. Accommodation: Cost of initial purchase
Cost of conversion
Cost of equipment and books

Ivan promises to set out a list for the above requirements listing prices.

B. Salary of permanent staff

C. Funds for professional and other visitors invited to contribute to the school in one way or another.

4. What overall policy to adopt with regard to payment of fees.

No decision was finalized with regard to future finance, and a further meeting in approximately three weeks time was decided upon.

Appointment of Staff

A. Ivan Vaughan

B. Two additional members of staff on a permanent basis (both female, male or one male and one female?)

C. One secretary on a permanent/part-time basis.

John stressed the need for a permanent secretary.

D. Other contributions to the school to be invited as necessary on a casual basis.

Enrolment of Pupils.

What overall policy with regard to their number and to their background

John stated there should be no discrimination regarding background.

Questions for discussion at a future date. Interested people are invited to give thought to them during the coming weeks.

Curriculum: What examinations, if any, to be allowed to influence the curriculum:? A flexible approach to be the guideline to follow in all respects. At the same time, how far should content of traditional state schools be taught? i.e. Reading, writing, mathematics, science, etc. What importance to be attached to other activities? i.e. music, astrology, art, history, archaeology, drama, one foreign language (French?) electronics, etc.

John requested that all arts including music, dancing, theatre, films should be in the school timetable. The art of propaganda in the advertising field must also be taught.

With regard to religious teaching, all aspects must be dealt with e.g. gods of other countries.

Games and physical exercises will be encouraged but not enforced. Aids to learning: T.V. tape, film, programmed learning.

Discipline:

No physical discipline of any kind.

Every attempt will be made to deal with any difficulties of a disciplinary nature during school time. If necessary, consultations will be held with the parents concerned. The aim of the school is for the children concerned to enjoy it so much they would prefer it to home.

Duration of school times:

Terms to follow (strictly?) those already adopted by state schools. Length of the school day? Normal school times were decided upon.

The school will accommodate children from the age of 2 to 40 which means they will remain at one school.

John stated that all attempts should be made to open the school by September.

As it turned out, the venture never got off the ground. **Pete Shotton** pointed out that the original idea for the school had been John's. John had wanted the children of Beatles and Apple employees to have an alternative to the traditional system of education that he had hated as a

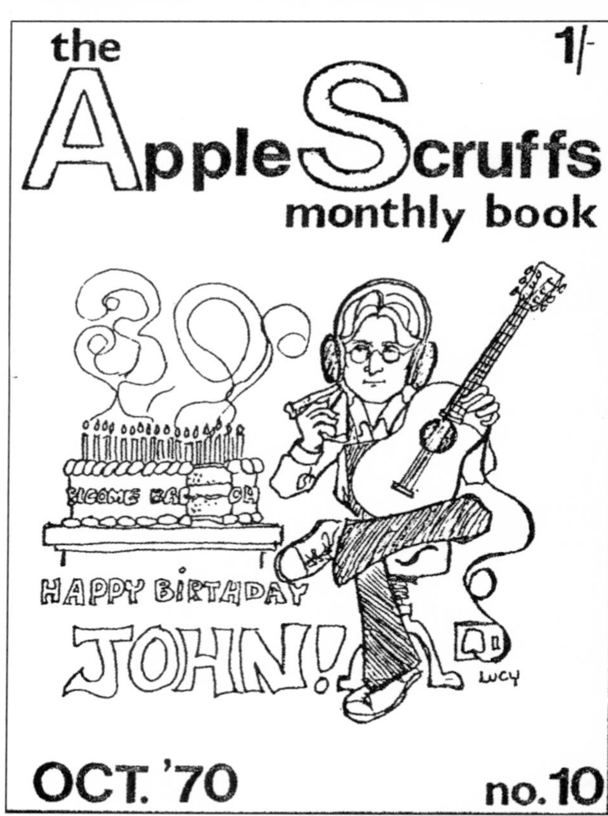

The dedicated Apple Scruffs even produced their own fan magazine.

child and thought that a more enlightened, alternative system could be developed. He felt that with enlightened teachers such as Ivan Vaughan, the right atmosphere could be created for the children, so that they could really enjoy learning.

Ivan was persuaded to leave his studies in educational psychiatry to join the project, although he was sensible enough to request a guarantee – and £10,000 was deposited in his account.

It was **Neil Aspinall** and Pete Shotton who finally persuaded John that the project was too ambitious and costly to undertake until the other Apple subsidiaries began showing a profit.

● Apple Scruffs

The name a group of the Beatles' most dedicated fans began to call themselves.

A number of the girls, mainly from Britain and America, left their homes to move to London in order to follow the Beatles around, spending endless hours waiting outside recording studios, houses and the Apple building itself, hoping for a glimpse of their idols.

What made this act of dedication so unusual was that the girls didn't just hang around for a few days or weeks or months, but spent a few years devoting their time to Beatle-watching.

They regarded themselves as an extra-special group and included Margo, Sue-John, Chris, Di, Kathy, Virginia, Dani, Wendy, Jill, Lucy, Carol, Tommy and Jimmy.

After they'd got to know each other from sitting around on the steps of 3 **Savile Row**, the girls decided to officially call themselves Apple Scruffs. Tommy was the only boy they would allow to join the group at the time, although later they admitted Jimmy. The Scruffs came mainly from America – Houston, New York, Chicago and Cleveland.

Margo Stevens was the leader of the Scruffs and in 1970 they launched their own *Apple Scruffs* magazine. This contained so much information about Beatle activities that even members of the Apple staff read it to find out what was going on and the Beatles themselves also received copies.

A group of Apple Scruffs broke into Paul McCartney's house in Cavendish Avenue one day by climbing up a ladder and entering through an open bathroom window. They stole clothes and photographs. Some of the photographs were important to Paul and he told Margo about them, and she managed to get them back for him. As a result, Paul wrote the song 'She Came In Through the Bathroom Window'.

When the girls were waiting outside the recording studios one night where George had been recording, he suddenly came out and invited them into the studio where he played them a song he'd written specially for them, 'Apple Scruffs', which was included on his *All Things Must Pass* album.

The Apple Scruffs eventually disbanded in December 1973, after the Savile Row building was no longer occupied, and as the members of the Beatles had gone their separate ways. They occasionally gathered together for reunions. One of the girls, Carol Bedford, wrote a book about the Scruffs and called it *Waiting For The Beatles*. One of the boys, Jimmy Lyford, died of an AIDS-related disease in San Francisco in October 1988.

● Apple Studios, *3 Savile Row, London W1*

The Beatles' own recording studio in the basement of the Apple building. The entire story of the studio was something of a fiasco. Naturally, since they had such a building, the Beatles felt they should have a studio of their own and they turned to 'Magic' **Alex Mardas**, head of **Apple Electronics**, who promised them that he would not only build them a studio but construct the most modern recording studio in the world. While Abbey Road had been using a four-track machine and had recently acquired an eight-track, Alex promised the Beatles that he would provide them with a 72-track, built by himself. He would also erect a sonic screen, an invisible wall of ultra-high-frequency beams which would surround Ringo in place of the usual heavy screens which blocked his view of what was going on.

When the Beatles were becoming disenchanted with working on the 'Get Back' project at **Twickenham Film Studios**, they decided to continue filming and recording at their own studios and on 20 January 1969, moved to the Apple Studios. It was impossible to record there.

The mixing console Alex had been building was a crude affair which didn't work – and was sold to an electronics shop in Edgware Road for five pounds. Alex had even forgotten to install an intercom system between the studio and the control booth. The basement also contained the heating and ventilation units for the entire building and was continually making hissing sounds.

The Beatles appealed to George Martin who arranged for two four-track machines to be sent down from the **Abbey Road Studios** and brought in some engineers and staff to set up the mobile unit and prepare the basement for recording.

Two days later, on 22 January, the Beatles were able to return and continued recording for the rest of that month with George Martin producing, assisted by **Glyn Johns** and Alan Parsons.

● Archer, Jeffrey

A former MP and best-selling author of blockbuster novels such as *Kane And Abel*.

When Archer was an undergraduate student at Oxford's Brasenose College he helped to organize a Beatles charity performance, in aid of the NSPCC at the **Grafton Ballrooms**, Liverpool on 12 June 1963.

On 5 March 1964 Archer organized a dinner at Brasenose College, Oxford, at which the Beatles were the guests of honour. The occasion was to celebrate their fund-raising efforts for Oxfam in 1963. Prior to the dinner, Archer met the group for drinks at Vincents, an Oxford club.

● Arlanda Airport

Airport situated 25 miles from Stockholm. The Beatles landed there on 24 October 1963 at the beginning of their short tour of Sweden. There was a press reception at which John confused the reporters by calling himself John Jagger while George referred to himself as George Chakiris.

John, George and Paul in costume during their 'Around The Beatles' appearance.

12 Arnold Grove, *Wavertree, Liverpool 17*

Birthplace of George Harrison. In common with terraced houses of its type, it had no bathroom and no indoor toilet. The outdoor toilet was situated in a paved backyard. Thirty-three-year-old **Louise Harrison** (nee French) gave birth to her fourth and final child at 12.10 p.m. on 25 February 1943.

His father, George **Harold Harrison**, was to say, 'I vaguely remember tiptoeing up the stairs to see him after he was born. A tiny, squalling, miniature replica of myself.' The new arrival, a boy, was named George after King George VI.

George spent the first six years of his life at Arnold Grove and as a baby was bathed in the kitchen sink and later, like the rest of the family, graduated to a zinc tub which was brought in from the backyard at bathtime. George was to recall that the downstairs rooms were extremely cold in the winter, with the only heating consisting of a single coal fire.

The Harrisons had spent eighteen years on the Council Housing List and were finally allocated a brand new Council house in Speke, Liverpool. As soon as they heard, they packed their belongings and moved from Arnold Grove on 2 January 1950.

During the six years that George lived in the Arnold Grove two-up, two-down house, the rent was ten shillings (50p) a week.

● Around The Beatles

The British television company Rediffusion had expressed interest in a Beatles television special and when Brian Epstein was in New York with the Beatles in February 1964, he had a meeting with producer Jack Good and suggested that he produce the show.

During negotiations with **Vyvienne Moynihan** of Rediffusion, Epstein insisted that Good be the producer. He also demanded that his own artists **Cilla Black** and **Sounds Incorporated** be included in the show, that **Murray The K** be hired as compere, that **NEMS** would retain world distribution rights and that he would be credited as co-producer. Incidentally, John Lennon talked Brian out of having Murray The K in the show.

Rediffusion agreed to all his terms and the one-hour special, originally called 'John, Paul, George and Ringo', but changed to 'Around The Beatles', was filmed over a two-day period on 27 and 28 April 1964, and networked a week later on 6 May. It was repeated the following month on 8 June and excerpts from the show were screened by ABC TV in America on 24 May.

The Beatles performed 'She Loves You', 'I Want To Hold Your Hand', 'Can't Buy Me Love', 'Twist And Shout', **'Roll Over Beethoven'**, 'I Wanna Be Your Man', 'Long Tall Sally' and 'Shout'. They also sang a medley of 'Love Me Do', 'Please Please Me' and 'From Me To You' and presented an excerpt from Shakespeare's *A Midsummer Night's Dream*. This amusing sketch, in which the group appeared in costume, featured John as Thisbe, Paul as Pyramus, George as Moonshine and Ringo as the Lion, although the group were at first reluctant to appear in the sketch.

In addition to Cilla and Sounds Incorporated, the show also featured **Long John Baldry**, **P. J. Proby** and Millie.

● Art Of The Beatles

The major exhibition of visual arts inspired by the Beatles. The vast tribute was the brainchild of Ron Jones, who was Merseyside Tourism Development Officer for Merseyside County Council at the time. The County Council commissioned **Mike Evans** to prepare a feasibility study and then the exhibition was given the go-ahead.

It opened at the **Walker Art Gallery** in Liverpool from 4 May to 30 September 1984.

The Art Of the Beatles was an attempt to display the influence of the Beatles on the visual culture of the sixties , to establish how the group influenced numerous fashion styles – in clothes, graphics, painting, advertising, illustration and sculpture.

In his introduction to the lavish eighty-page exhibition catalogue, Evans points out that art loomed largely in the origins of the Beatles. After all, John Lennon was an art student, not a truck driver like **Elvis Presley**. Evans says, 'One-time Beatle (and Lennon's mentor in many ways) **Stuart Sutcliffe** was also at **Liverpool College of Art**, and ended his brief life in his chosen role as a painter. Fellow students of the two included Lennon's wife-to-be **Cynthia Powell** and the founder of the influential ***Mersey Beat*** paper Bill Harry. George Harrison and Paul McCartney meanwhile were pupils at the Liverpool Institute grammar school, next door to the art college. Their earliest gigs together included the deliberately "arty" **Jacaranda** coffee bar. . . As soon as they established themselves on the Hamburg club scene, they were taken up by an "existentialist" crowd of art students and such. In all, the Beatles' early environment was a peculiar mix of the tatty glitter of rock 'n' roll clubland and the fringes of big city Bohemia.'

Evans was to expand his text and pictorial content in a more detailed exploration of the Beatles and their relationship with art in a book, *The Art of The Beatles*,

Left: The poster and advertising promotion for the 'Art Of The Beatles' exhibition featured a painting by David Oxtoby. Above: Mike Evans and Ron Jones, organisers of the 'Art Of The Beatles' exhibition. (Merseyside Tourism Office)

published by Anthony Blond.

The exhibition design was carried out by Colin Wilson and Jim Donahue, graphic design was by the Alphabet Design Partnership and the exhibition was constructed by Beck and Pollitzer Ltd.

The first room of the exhibition was called 'Liverpool' and contained material relating to the Liverpool days, including **Cynthia Lennon** illustrations, paintings by **Stuart Sutcliffe**, Adrian Henri, Sam Walsh and Maurice Cockrill and photographs by **Astrid Kirchherr**, **Peter Kaye**, **Mike McCartney** and Graham Spencer. The next section, headed 'Memorabilia' included Beatle wallpaper, bedspreads, ashtrays, skirts, trays, postcards and posters. This was followed by artwork in the section on 'Record Sleeves' and, in the same room, a section 'Illustration/Posters' which included work by Alan Aldridge, **Richard Avedon**, Andy Warhol and several others.

The next section 'Animation' featured designs from *Yellow Submarine* and the 'Film/Theatre' section included posters and photographs from films and plays such as *A Hard Day's Night, Let It Be, In His Own Write, John, Paul, George, Ringo . . . And Bert* and *Lennon*. The next section on 'Painting' included works by John Bratby, **Peter Blake**, David Oxtoby, James Marsh and Cynthia Lennon. 'Drawings/Cartoons' included comic strips and work by John Lennon, **Gerald Scarfe**, Hirschfeld, Paul McCartney and Max Ernst. 'Photography' included a bumper display of photographs by a large range of exponents, including **Dezo Hoffman**, **Robert Freeman**, **Linda McCartney** and Iain Macmillan. The final section of the exhibition was categorized 'Sculpture' and included work by **David Wynne**, **Arthur Dooley**, John Doubleday and Gerald Scarfe.

The exhibition drew the largest response in the history of the gallery.

Later in the eighties, Mike Evans collated further 'Art Of the Beatles' exhibitions for Tokyo, Japan and Cologne, Germany.

● Ashcroft & Daw, *Charing Cross Road, London WC2*

The first paperback bookstore to open in London.

Brian Epstein worked in the store for a short time in the fifties. The book section was situated on the ground floor, where Marty Feldman (who was later to become a famous comedian) worked, and the record department was in the basement where Brian worked.

Those were the days of cubicles where potential purchasers could select their choice and hear the record played in a listening booth. Brian used to spend a great deal of time in the centre cubicle listening to classical records.

● Ashcroft, Ken

Merseyside disc jockey who originally acted as DJ for the **Majestic Ballroom, Birkenhead,** and then the **Iron Door Club**, Liverpool. In 1963, Brian Epstein offered him a position in **NEMS Enterprises**, which he accepted and was then appointed personal assistant to **Billy J. Kramer**. For a short time he became Epstein's personal assistant and was then made personal assistant to **Alistair Taylor**. He was later appointed manager of the **Remo Four**.

● Asher, Jane

Titian-haired British actress, born on 5 April 1946.

Her father, Dr Richard Asher, was a consultant in blood and mental diseases at Central Middlesex Hospital in Acton, her mother was a professor of classical music at the Guildhall School of Music and Drama and had taught George Martin to play the oboe. She had a brother **Peter** and a younger sister, Clare.

Jane Asher – a fairytale romance with Paul McCartney. (Maran/Kettledrum/Bavaria Atelier)

Jane began her film career at the age of five in *Mandy*. Her interest in acting began when her parents took their three children to a theatrical agency, thinking it would be fun for them to learn to act.

Peter was two years older than Jane and Clare was two years younger. All three children had striking red hair. Apart from *Mandy*, she appeared in *The Quatermass Experiment*. Her stage debut was at the Oxford Playhouse in *Alice in Wonderland* when she was twelve and two years later she became the youngest actress ever to play Wendy in the London production of *Peter Pan*. Throughout her teens she appeared in television dramas such as 'The Cold Equations', and in films such as *The Greengage Summer* and Walt Disney's *The Prince And The Pauper*. During the sixties she appeared regularly on stage, television and films. Her stage roles included the Broadway production of *The Philanthropist* and many appearances with the Bristol Old Vic.

She first met the Beatles on 18 April 1963. The group were having a snack in the Royal Court Hotel in Sloane Square, where they were staying, when Jane approached them. She mentioned that she'd been asked to write an article about the group for *Radio Times*. They were aware of her as she'd been a guest panellist on **'Juke Box Jury'** and they were all charmed by her, although it was George who seemed to engage most of her attention as she joined them on a trip to journalist Chris Hutchins' flat in the Kings Road. During the course of the next few hours Paul began to show his interest in Jane and the others left him to talk to her alone. Later he escorted her home and arranged to meet her again. The romance became public when they were snapped by a photographer as they left the Prince of Wales Theatre after attending Neil Simon's play *Never Too Late*.

Jane lived with her parents and her mother invited Paul to use a spare room in their home whenever he was in London, an offer he took up between 1963 and 1966. The couple were continually in the public eye. Jane encouraged Paul's appreciation of the arts and they visited theatres and art galleries and took holidays in Portugal, Switzerland, Kenya, Scotland and America together. During their relationship she continued her career as an actress appearing in films such as *Alfie*, *Masque Of The Red Death*, *The Deep End* and in TV dramas such as 'The Stone Tape'.

She helped Paul to find a five-storey Victorian house in Cavendish Avenue, St John's Wood, London NW8, in 1966 and aided him in furnishing and decorating it. She also had her own key. It was Jane who encouraged Paul to buy **High Park Farm** in Scotland as a retreat for them both.

They had one basic problem: Jane was adamant about pursuing her career as an actress while Paul wanted her to give it all up if they were married. His idea of a wife was a person who would become a housewife and devote her time to rearing the children. When Jane went to Bristol to appear with the Old Vic Company, Paul was furious and wrote 'I'm Looking Through You'. However, he couldn't keep away and went to Bristol to see her. It was while he was in Bristol that he conceived the song 'Eleanor Rigby'. Jane, in fact, was the inspiration for many of his love songs, including 'Here, There and Everywhere' and 'And I Love Her'.

The press kept urging them to announce a wedding date and Jane would say, 'I certainly would be most surprised if I married anyone else but Paul', while Paul kept denying engagement plans, even publicly, such as on one of the group's **'Ready, Steady, Go!'** appearances in March 1964.

In 1967 Jane left for a three-month tour of America with the Bristol Old Vic Company, and while there she celebrated her 21st birthday. Paul flew over to attend her birthday party and eight months later, on Christmas Day, he proposed and gave Jane an emerald and diamond engagement ring.

On 1 January 1968 she visited his family and the couple announced that they intended to get married later in the year. In June they attended the wedding of Paul's brother **Mike** to Angela Fishwick. The next month the romance was over.

During the absences when Jane was acting, Paul had been dating other girls, including folk singer Julie Felix. It was his affair with an American girl, **Francie Schwartz**, which brought the romance to an end. Jane arrived at Cavendish Road unexpectedly one night when Paul was in bed with Schwartz. One of the **Apple Scruffs** outside the house, Margo Stevens, attempted to warn Paul by intercom, but he didn't answer. When Jane went upstairs she knocked on the bedroom door, realizing what was going on, then drove off in a fury. Later that evening her mother arrived to collect all her belongings.

On 20 July 1968, Jane announced on BBC TV's **'Dee Time'** that the engagement was off. The couple did meet one or two times after the announcement and Jane was to say, 'I know it sounds corny, but we still see each other and love each other, but it hasn't worked out. Perhaps we'll be childhood sweethearts and meet again and get married when we're about seventy.'

Tragically, on 26 April 1969, the body of Jane's father was discovered in the **Wimpole Street** house– he'd died of an overdose of barbiturates and alcohol.

Peter Asher and Gordon Waller, with girlfriends, attending a London film premiere. (National Film Archives)

Jane met cartoonist **Gerald Scarfe** and the two became lovers, resulting in Jane giving birth to her first child, Kate, on 17 April 1974. They had two more children and then decided to get married in 1981. She returned to acting and has since appeared in many film, TV and stage productions, in addition to becoming a successful writer of books on subjects ranging from decorative cakes to making fancy dress costumes.

● Asher, Peter

Jane Asher's younger brother, who got to know Paul McCartney very well when Paul lived at the Asher family house in **Wimpole Street, London W1.**

Peter was one half of the folk duo **Peter & Gordon** and he asked Paul if he could provide them with a number to record. He gave them 'World Without Love', which took Peter & Gordon to the top of the British charts and established them in America. They had several further hits before they decided to disband in 1967.

Peter then joined **Apple Records** as head of A&R and his first discovery was the American singer/songwriter **James Taylor**.

On 21 July 1968, following Jane Asher's declaration the previous night on the TV show **'Dee Time'** that her romance with Paul was over, Paul stormed into Apple and demanded that Peter be sacked. **Ron Kass** talked him out of this course of action, although Asher's productions were no longer to receive any priority or strong promotion.

James Taylor became disenchanted with Apple because of the lack of promotion for his products and returned to America. He asked Peter to be his manager and continue to produce his records. He left for America where he had great success with Taylor and also became manager of Linda Ronstadt.

In 1969 Tony King replaced him at Apple Records as head of A&R.

● Askey, Arthur

One of Liverpool's most famous comedians who was successful on music hall, had his own radio and television shows and starred in films for decades before his death in 1981.

Rita Grade Freeman, **Sir Lew Grade**'s sister, related an anecdote about Askey and the Beatles. She said, 'Arthur Askey met them before they became famous when he was rehearsing one of his "silly songs" in a recording studio in Liverpool. They were making their first demo disc there, and he stayed to listen to them. After they'd finished playing he went over to them and said, "You're not bad, you know. What do you call yourselves?" One of them replied, "The Beatles." "My God!" said Arthur, "you'll never get anywhere with a name like that!" '

Another source reports that Askey told Paul that they'd never get anywhere with a name like the Beatles after he'd met him at a concert. This seems more likely as they were known as the **Quarry Men** when they made their only demo disc in Liverpool.

The Beatles and Askey met on a number of occasions and there was a photograph of him with the group featured in the first issue of *Beatles Monthly*.

On 26 October 1966, Askey commented on the Beatles receiving their **MBEs**, 'I'm not saying it's given them swollen heads, but now the boys think the initials on our pillar boxes stand for Eleanor Rigby.'

● Ask Me Why

A Lennon & McCartney composition, on which John performs lead vocals, which was issued as the 'B' side of their 'Please Please Me' single on 11 January 1963. It was also one of the tracks on their debut album *Please Please Me*, issued in March of that year, and was also included on the *All My Loving* EP in February 1964.

Vee Jay Records in the States utilized it on their re-release of the *Introducing The Beatles*, *Beatles Vs The Four Seasons* and *Songs, Pictures And Stories Of The Fabulous Beatles* albums and *Souvenir Of Their Visit To America (The Beatles)* EP. **Capitol Records** also issued it as a track on their *The Early Beatles* album. The group performed it live on stage at Hamburg's **Star Club** and it is included on *The Beatles Live At The Star Club in Hamburg, Germany, 1962* album.

The Beatles performed the number during their Parlophone recording audition on 6 June 1962, but recorded the song on 26 November 1962, when there was a dispute about how the compositions should be credited on release, to McCartney–Lennon or Lennon–McCartney. The credit was finally resolved, some months later, in John's favour.

● Aspinall, Neil

The person closest to the Beatles throughout their career.

Neil was born in Prestatyn, North Wales, on 13 October 1942. His family moved to Liverpool where he attended West Derby School before enrolling at the **Liverpool Institute**, where he shared the same class as Paul McCartney for Art and English lessons. George Harrison also attended the school but was in the class one year behind Paul and Neil. Neil was to comment, 'My first encounter with George was behind the school's air-raid shelters. This great mass of shaggy hair loomed up and an out-of-breath voice requested a quick drag of my Woodbine.'

With nine GCEs under his belt, Neil left the Institute in July, 1959 to study accountancy and remained with a local firm for two years, receiving a wage of fifty shillings (£2.50) per week as a trainee accountant. At the time he was living as a lodger in **Pete Best**'s house and it was through the Best connection that he became involved with the Beatles. Pete had joined the group and travelled to Germany with them. On their return they were booked at the **Casbah Club** and **Mona Best** asked Neil to make some posters announcing 'The Return Of The Beatles'.

The group had relied on public transport to get them to local gigs, but by February 1961 it was obvious that they could no longer rely on that method of rushing from hall to hall. They'd tried a spell hiring **Frank Garner** to drive them to gigs, but he was the bouncer at the Casbah club and found he couldn't keep the two jobs going at the same time. Pete decided to approach Neil and ask him to drive them to their gigs. Pete suggested that he buy a van and commented, 'He bought a battered old grey and maroon model for fifteen pounds (other sources say he bought a second-hand van for £80), but at least it went, which was the main consideration. So Neil entered enthusiastically the world of showbusiness as our first roadie.' He charged each of them five shillings (25p) per man, per gig.

By July 1962, on the group's return from their second trip to Germany, Neil decided to take the plunge and become their official road manager as he was now earning more money driving them around than as an accountant and he also helped Mrs Best to run the Casbah Club.

Neil and Pete Best were the closest of friends and when Brian Epstein called Pete in for a meeting and then announced that he had been sacked, Neil was waiting for him downstairs in the **NEMS** shop. Neil was furious when he heard. He called Mona to tell her what had happened, then joined Pete for a few beers at the Grapes pub. Disgusted with the situation, Neil told Pete he'd quit – but Pete told him he must stay, that the Beatles were going places.

When Neil turned up at the group's next gig, Brian Epstein asked him why Pete hadn't turned up. 'Well, what did you expect,' he told him. Neil asked Paul and John what had happened and was told, 'It's got nothing to do with you. You're only the driver.'

Pete's prediction that the Beatles were going places was exceeded beyond expectations . . . and wherever the Beatles went, Neil was with them. **Mal Evans** was brought in to help out as Assistant Road Manager and Neil became much more of a personal assistant to the group. Paul McCartney dubbed him 'Nell', and the Beatles always called him Nell, rather than Neil.

When the Beatles launched their **Apple Corps** company, they appointed Neil as Managing Director.

On 30 August 1968, he married Suzy Ornstein at Chelsea Registry Office and Paul McCartney attended.

Neil survived the appearance of **Allen Klein** in the Beatles' affairs and after the Apple building in **Savile Row** was sold, he continued to administer their affairs from offices in Mayfair, a post he still holds.

There has probably been no one closer to the Beatles than Nell and no one privy to the most private aspects of their lives. He has always been discreet, utterly loyal, and would keep everything in complete confidence. If ever he wrote a book about his experiences, he has mused, he would arrange for it to be published after his death.

● Assembly Hall, *Mold, Flintshire, Wales*

The Beatles only appeared at this venue once, on 24 January 1963.

● Assembly Rooms, *Corporation Street, Tamworth, Staffordshire*

This gig took place on 1 February 1963, on the eve of their first major British tour with **Helen Shapiro**. It was a double booking and they also appeared in nearby Sutton Coldfield.

● Astoria Ballroom, *Oldham, Greater Manchester*

The Beatles only appeared at this venue once, on 12 February 1963. They'd previously appeared in Sheffield, Yorkshire, earlier the same evening.

● Astoria Ballroom, *Wilson Street, Middlesbrough, Yorkshire*

The Beatles only appeared at this venue once, on 25 June 1963. The group had originally been provisionally booked to appear there on 29 January 1963, but the booking had not been confirmed and Eden Kane appeared that night.

● Astoria Cinema, *232–6 Seven Sisters Road, Finsbury Park, London N4*

Site of *The Beatles Christmas Show* which ran for sixteen

nights from 24 December 1963–11 January 1964. There were two performances each evening, with the exception of 24 and 31 December. There were also no performances on 25 and 29 December.

Brian Epstein engaged **Peter Yolland** to produce the show on the recommendation of agent Joe Collins (father of Joan and Jackie). Peter, who had been producing traditional pantomimes for several years, devised a spectacular opening.

The houselights were dimmed and the theatre was in semi-darkness when two spotlights trained on the curtain, which opened to display a small screen, which flickered images of a silent movie car chase, a channel swimmer and an ancient aircraft as a commentator was announcing, 'By land . . . by sea . . . by air . . . Yes, by land, by sea, and by air come the stars of Brian Epstein's fabulous Beatles Christmas Show.'

A dummy helicopter landed. 'And here's your pilot for the evening, **Rolf Harris**' introduced the voice, and Rolf came down the steps, holding his clipboard with the passenger list. One by one the guest artists appeared and after **Cilla Black** had been introduced, Rolf said that the entire cast had been assembled. In pantomime style the audience contradicted him and he had to call back the helicopter and say, 'And now ladies and gentlemen, boys and girls . . .' but the 'copter began to move away again. He called it to land and the Beatles emerged to a raucous welcome from the audience. A backcloth then hid them as the **Barron Knights** rostrum drew them onto the stage as they played 'Big Girls Don't Cry'. When the Barron Knights finished their set the rostrum moved back and **Tommy Quickly** emerged from the wings. As he finished his set with 'Kiss Me Now', there was no sign of another act. A small screen appeared with the words 'Three out of four doctors . . . ' and a spotlight picked out the Beatles, huddle together in conversation, dressed in white coats like doctors. 'Yes, three out of four doctors . . . ' came the words on the screen, to be replaced by ' . . . leaves one doctor'. Ringo, Paul and George had moved away and the lone John suddenly disappeared as the spotlight turned off. The **Fourmost** were on stage and began playing 'Hello Little Girl'. After their performance the small screen appeared with the announcement, 'Beatlerama Productions present, in breathtakingly colourful black and white Beatlescope, "What A Night".'

The Beatles then appeared in a sketch with John as Sir John Jasper, Paul as the Signalman, Ringo as a snowman and George as Ermyntrude.

The comedy melodrama over, **Billy J. Kramer** & the Dakotas next appeared. There was a ten-minute interval and then the Barron Knights opened the second half, followed by Cilla Black, who had an eight-minute spot which ended with her singing 'Love Of The Loved'. She was followed by Rolf Harris, who had altered the lyrics to his two hits 'Tie Me Kangaroo Down Sport' and 'English Country Garden' to fit the spirit of the occasion. Then the Beatles appeared to perform 'Roll Over Beethoven', 'All My Loving', 'This Boy', 'I Wanna Hold Your Hand', 'Money' and 'Twist And Shout'.

The Astoria could seat over 3,000 per show and 100,000 tickets for the 30 shows were sold in advance.

The Beatles were to appear at the venue two further times as part of their UK concert tours. They performed there on 1 November 1964 as part of their only British concert tour that year and their final appearance at the venue took place on 11 December 1965.

The cinema was later transformed into the Rainbow Theatre, a venue exclusively for rock concerts.

● ATC Club, *Birkdale, Lancashire*

A venue where the Beatles appeared only once, early in 1961. The club was close to the seaside resort of Southport, and they were said to have received only one pound and ten shillings between them for their appearance.

● *Atlanta Stadium, Atlanta, Georgia*

Almost 36,000 fans turned out to see the Beatles at this 55,000-seater baseball stadium, newly built for the Braves, on Wednesday, 18 August 1965.

The group arrived at the airport in a private Lockheed Electra at around 2.00 p.m. and they and their entourage were transported in three limousines which took them to the stadium. Their 5.00 p.m. press conference at the venue began ten minutes late and they were introduced by local DJ Paul Drew who acted as master of ceremonies to the assembly of 150 journalists, the majority of them editors of high school papers. The *Atlanta Journal* had called Drew 'the fifth Beatle', because the DJ from the local radio station WQXI had visited the Beatles in London and travelled with them in the US in 1964. He'd also visited them in Nassau and New York. Apart from acting as master of ceremonies at the press conference, he was to introduce the group on stage at the stadium. Drew had also written a piece called 'How to get along with the Beatles' in the local paper. Members of the 457-strong local fan club were at the conference to present the Beatles with gifts and Mayor Ivan Allen Jr. attended and presented the group with the key to the city. The Mayor had said that their appearance in Atlanta had stirred up as much excitement as the *Gone With The Wind* premiere in 1939. The press conference took fifteeen minutes and was held in a locker room of the stadium.

The show was preceded at 7.30 by 'London Look', a fashion show, with a local group the Atlanta Vibrations providing background music, having won the honour in a 'Battle of Beatle Bands' competition.

The show itself began at 8.15 with King Curtis, the Discotheque Dancers, **Cannibal & the Headhunters**, Brenda Holloway and **Sounds Incorporated**. The Beatles appeared on stage at 9.37 p.m. wearing dark blue suits. They performed 'Twist And Shout', 'She's A Woman', during which Paul's mike fell over, 'I Feel Fine', 'Dizzy Miss Lizzy', 'Ticket To Ride', 'Everybody's Trying To Be My Baby', in which George performed lead vocal, 'Can't Buy Me Love', 'Baby's In Black', 'I Wanna Be Your Man', with Ringo performing lead vocal, 'A Hard Day's Night', 'Help!' and 'I'm Down'.

The group were then driven directly to Atlanta Airport.

Auctions

Ten years after the Beatles disbanded, a market in Beatles memorabilia had grown to such an extent that major auction houses began to introduce special rock 'n' roll memorabilia auctions, with Beatles items the main attraction on the agenda.

Beatles material first went under the hammer at Sotheby's in June 1979, producing such interest that the annual Rock 'n' Roll Memorabilia auctions were launched in 1981 at Sotheby's, the major auction house situated at 34–35 New Bond Street, London W1A 2AA.

Hilary Kay, director of Sotheby's Collectors' Department, originally suggested to the Musical Instrument Department at the company that a Steinway piano they had on offer was worth more than their assessment because it had once belonged to John Lennon. Her instinct was justified. The piano, together with another that had previously belonged to Paul McCartney, brought in far more money than had been anticipated. The Music Department had valued John's piano at £1,000 – it went for £7,500. Paul's piano, which had been considered of even less worth because of its dilapidated condition, went for £9,000!

Hilary took over the organization of the Rock auctions from then on, also acting as auctioneer.

The material sold at the auctions includes musical instruments, photographs, posters, gold discs, telegrams, drawings, letters, Apple souvenirs and memorabilia, drawings and paintings by **Stuart Sutcliffe**, bubblegum machines, **Dezo Hoffman** and Jurgen Vollmer photographs, *Yellow Submarine* celluloids and Christmas fan club records.

All the items are documented in a lavish catalogue. Here are two sample entries from the 1984 catalogue:

> Lot 208: Letter from George Harrison to Stuart Sutcliffe, in blue ballpoint pen, concerning Harrison's journey back to Liverpool, informing Stuart of bookings for the Beatles and asking him to 'come home sooner, as if we get a new bass player for the time being, it will be crumby, as he will have to learn everything'; talking about Paul McCartney, 'it's no good with Paul playing bass, we've decided, that is if he had some kind of bass and amp to play on!'; requesting Stuart to send some money to **Frank Hessy** because he wanted 'to get an echo for Christmas £34, or £6 down, the rest when Frank catches me'; discussing his playing, 'I am learning everything I can get my hands on now!' Two pages with envelope, dated 16 December 1960.
>
> This item sold for £500.
>
> Lot 260: Telegram from John Lennon to **Bob Wooler** dated '20 June '63' apologizing for an incident between Lennon and Wooler, in original envelope. Message reads: 'Really sorry Bob terribly worried to realize what I had done Stop what more can I say John Lennon'. The incident referred to in the telegram was a physical fight between **Bob Wooler** and John Lennon resulting in Lennon being sued for injuries. This matter was settled for £200 and an apology from Lennon.

This item fetched £550. Ironic that the telegram brought Bob almost three times the amount of his original compensation!

Vendors contact Hilary either by letter or telephone to discuss items they wish to offer for sale. When the item is sent by registered post, Hilary will phone the client to voice an opinion as to its value and to suggest a reserve price if the item is worth more than £100. Sotheby's do not charge for a verbal estimate; if a person makes an appointment to take along memorabilia, they will receive an assessment of the object's value without being committed.

When an item is put forward for sale there is an insurance premium of one per cent of the price it fetches. Items above £500 are subject to ten per cent commission, those below to 15 per cent. VAT is also charged. If a person bids successfully for an item, they are liable for the price they have bid, together with ten per cent commission.

The success of the London auctions led to the New York branch of Sotheby's launching its own Rock 'n' Roll Memorabilia sales in 1983. These have been generally dominated by John Lennon material. At the second Rock 'n' Roll Memorabilia sale in June, 1984, **Yoko Ono** offered 117 items for sale. The auctioneer was Pamela Brown Sherer.

With the success of the Sotheby's pop auctions, other London auction houses entered the music memorabilia market, with, once again, the most desirable items relating to the Beatles.

Christie's of South Kensington, based at 85 Old Brompton Road, London SW7 3LD, has auctioned many items of extreme interest to Beatles enthusiasts. As with the Sotheby's items, many add an insight into the Beatles story. Here is an example of two lots from the August 1988 sale:

> Lot 292: Costume accessories used by John Lennon in the role of Ugly Sister in a performance of *Cinderella* held at **Liverpool College of Art**, 1959, comprising: two hats, one of straw trimmed with blue and pink feathers, the other of cream 'silk' trimmed with a bow; with a pair of ladies corsets of pink cotton fastened with hooks and lacing; and six pieces of sheet music; accompanied by an affidavit from **June Furlong**, Lennon's friend and artist's model at Liverpool College of Art; and a letter of authenticity from **Rod Murray**, a contemporary student, and fellow performer in the production.

The catalogue included some further information about the item:

> John Lennon wrote a version of *Cinderella*, with Rod Murray for the Liverpool College of Art in 1959. These garments were loaned to Lennon by a friend, June Furlong, who had met Lennon in the life class where she was a model. The performance of *Cinderella* was held in the canteen basement at the college, the other ugly sister was played by Geoff Mohammed, Rod Murray appeared as Dandini, June Harry as Cinderella, and John Chase as Prince Charming.

> Lot 370: An interesting and rare collection of *Yellow Submarine* material comprising: a) an original working script for *Yellow Submarine*, January 1968, revised as shot, 142 xeroxed pages and one typescript page, annotated throughout in red biro and pencil by various directors of animation the title page inscribed 'For Max Wilk'; b) King features/Suba Film *Yellow Submarine* original film script, 1968, mimeographed typescript, 146 found pages; c) a xerox copy of a letter, 31 January 1968, from Peter Gruenthal, the New American Library to Bert Gray New English Library Ltd, concerning Max Wilk's commission to write a book as a tie in with the *Yellow Submarine* movie. 2pp; d) working notes and a manuscript draft, Max Wilk 'Log Of The Yellow Submarine', February–March 1968. 88 xeroxed pp, some annotations; e) Max Wilk 'Here Come The British' November 1965, typescript draft for a screen comedy commissioned by **Walter Shenson**; f) an original annotated progressive sketch for 'The Running Indian Monster' in full headdress, ink and pencil preliminary sketch for the Indian chase in the 'Sea Of Monsters' sequence; and related material.

A footnote added further information:

> Accompanying letter from Max Wilk outlines his connection with the Beatles and the *Yellow Submarine* project. By 1966 the Beatles had starred in *A Hard Day's Night* and *Help!*, the original United Artists commitment was for three films and film producer

An original John Lennon illustration, sold at Sotheby's auction in 1983. (Sotheby's)

Walter Shenson asked Wilk to write a possible screen comedy for them, which he did 'Here Come The British' however, this was eventually passed on, and in 1967 the *Yellow Submarine* project had begun. In December 1967 Max Wilk was approached by the New American Library to write a book based on *Yellow Submarine*, he agreed and when requesting to see the script was told that the script ' . . . wouldn't be available. Seemed it was being written by writers as the film was being animated . . . ' Wilk went to the studio in Soho Square and was shown around by Abe Goodman, when he asked for the script Goodman replied 'I'll have to put one together for you . . . there's so much rewriting going on each day – in every sequence. I'll gather up as much as I can from each unit, and run it through the xerox machine page by page . . . ' this was done until there was finally one working screenplay for *Yellow Submarine*. From this the storyline for 'The Log Of The Yellow Submarine' was written, and on February 12th with the cels to be used in the book, dummy manuscript, notes, and a pencil drawing given to Wilk by one of the animators, he returned to New York, and after refining the story line, and collaborating with Erich Segal over footnotes, the *Yellow Submarine* book was published in London and New York and was a great success.

The other major London auction house is Phillips West Two, situated at 10 Salem Road, Bayswater, London W2 4DL.

An example from their April 1991 catalogue reads:

> Lot 658: An interesting interview with John Lennon, dating from Autumn 1969, contained on two BASF reel to reel tapes. The interview with John and **Yoko** was conducted by the Australian disc jockey Tony MacArthur and reviews the Beatles' *Abbey Road* album track by track. The interview was never broadcast. On the tape Lennon describes 'Maxwell's Silver Hammer' as 'A typical McCartney singalong . . . ' and 'I think Paul drove George and Ringo into the ground when they were recording it . . . ' Ringo's 'Octopus's Garden', 'It will be a few years before his production is going as fast as ours, it took George a few years . . . ' On 'Because', ' . . . Yoko plays classical piano . . . she was playing and I said give me the chorus backwards, I wrote on top of it, " 'Because' is 'Moonlight Sonata' backwards. . ." ' On 'Sun King', 'that's where we pretended to be Fleetwood Mac for a few minutes. . .' He describes the **Plastic Ono Band**'s 'Rock And Roll Revival' concert in Toronto, the forthcoming release of *The Wedding Album*, White Trash's 'Golden Slumbers' single and on the chance of the Beatles playing live again, Lennon says 'there's always a chance. . .' The interview is SOLD WITHOUT COPYRIGHT

Invitation to a rock and pop auction, held by Phillips West Two. (Phillips West Two)

and lasts 2 ½ hours.

On a smaller scale, annual Beatles auctions commenced in Liverpool at Eldon E. Worrall & Co of Seel Street, L1. Examples of the type of material to be sold at these auctions is found in some of the typical lots of their 1985 auction:

Lot 29: A scrapbook containing various cuttings relating to the Beatles, including an early photograph of Paul McCartney seated in an antique chair; a commercial photocopy of the group; and two letters from Paul McCartney, sent from 20 Forthlin Road, Allerton, Liverpool 18 with original envelopes bearing the postmarks 7 April 1963 and 27 May 1963 respectively.

Lot 105: An original school photograph of 1956 from the **Liverpool Institute** High School, showing Paul McCartney, his brother **Mike**, Les Chadwick who was bass player for **Gerry & the Pacemakers**, Don Andrew and Colin Manley of the **Remo Four**, Len Garry of the **Quarry Men** and **Neil Aspinall**.

The auctions have been taking place for over a decade, but there seems to be no dearth of material. In addition to the usual material found at most of the auctions each year – Apple watches, gold discs, autographed albums, *Yellow Submarine* cels – unique items pop up regularly, placed in sales by former Beatle associates such as Tony Barrow, **Derek Taylor**, Tony Bramwell and **Pete Best**. A highlight of the 1991 sale at Christie's was an entire collection of John Lennon memorabilia belonging to **Cynthia Lennon**. She had finally decided to shed her mementoes, including personal address books, birth certificates, postcards and Christmas cards illustrated by John, and furniture and household items from **Kenwood**, together with items such as the **Ivor Novello Award** which John received in 1963 for 'She Loves You'.

Over the years, the items have increased in value to the extent that few genuine fans can afford the items and the sales attract investors and major companies. The Hard Rock Cafe has been a regular bidder and the Beatles souvenirs decorate several of their restaurants. Other major buyers have ranged from Japanese department stores to radio stations.

● Australia House, *The Strand, London WC2*

Prior to their trip to Australia, the Beatles were invited to a special reception at Australia House during the last week in April 1964. They were the guests of the Rt Hon. Sir Eric Harrison, the Australian High Commissioner, who had left a reception at Downing Street hosted by Prime Minister Alec Douglas-Home, to preside at the function.

The Strand was crowded with fans and inside the building the Beatles held a press reception. Among the 700 guests were celebrities such as actress Jessie Matthews and actors Dick Van Dyke and **Wilfred Brambell**.

Sir Eric told the press, 'There has never been a reception quite like this in Australia House and I hope there will never be another one. I guess I am what you would call a square but those photographers were just too much. They climbed all over the chairs and then when we went inside an enclosed office they were thrusting their cameras through the windows and rapping on the glass. I threatened to draw the blinds unless they could comport themselves.'

● Avedon, Richard

Noted American photographer whose innovations proved influential. **Astrid Kirchherr** originally used an Avedon technique of having a subject's face in half-shadow when she took some portraits of members of the Beatles in Hamburg – and this technique was also used by **Robert Freeman** for his *With The Beatles* album cover.

In 1967 Avedon was commissioned by *Look* magazine to photograph the Beatles for their front cover. The photograph was also published as a poster the same year and was later to be used on the cover and gatefold of the 1977 compilation *Love Songs*, although the positions of Paul and Ringo were changed on the LP sleeve.

● Azena Ballroom, *White Lane, Gleadless, Sheffield, South Yorkshire*

During a break in their tour with **Helen Shapiro**, the Beatles appeared at this venue on 12 February 1963. The promoter who had booked the group was Peter Stringfellow. Originally, he'd booked them to appear at St Aidan's Church Hall, where he usually held his dances. However, due to the growing popularity of the Beatles, the police advised Stringfellow to alter the venue and select larger premises so he transferred the dance to the Azena.

• Baby, The

Nickname which the **'Exis'** (Existentialists) gave to Paul McCartney during the Beatles' first trip to Hamburg. The 'Exis' were the students who attended their gigs and included **Astrid Kirchherr**. They called George 'The Beautiful One' and John 'The Sidie Man'.

• Baby It's You

A composition by Mack David, Burt Bacharach and Barney Williams, which provided the Shirelles with a Top Ten hit in America following its release in December 1961. The Beatles immediately included it in their repertoire, with John Lennon on lead vocals, and continued to perform it until late in 1963.

They recorded the number on Monday, 11 February 1963 during their marathon recording session for the *Please Please Me* album. The number was also included on **Vee Jay**'s American albums *Introducing The Beatles* and *Songs, Pictures And Stories Of the Fabulous Beatles*. It was also included on **Capitol**'s *The Early Beatles* album.

The Beatles performed 'Baby It's You' on two of their BBC radio programmes – **'Side By Side'** and **'Pop Go The Beatles'**.

• Baby's In Black

Some sources have claimed that this number was penned solely by John, others claim that it was a true Lennon & McCartney collaboration in a room during one songwriting bout.

Neither mentioned who inspired them to write the song, but the speculation in Liverpool at the time was that it had been inspired by **Astrid Kirchherr**, who had been mourning the death of **Stuart Sutcliffe**.

The number was the first song recorded for the *Beatles For Sale* album on Tuesday, 11 August 1964.

The track was also included on the *Beatles For Sale* (No. 2) EP and the *Beatles '65* album in America.

It was one of the songs which the Beatles performed regularly in concert and they included it in their 1964 Christmas show, on their European and British tours in 1965 and on their world tour in the summer of 1966.

• Baby You're A Rich Man

Recorded at **Olympic Sound Studios** in Barnes, London SW13, a studio which the **Rolling Stones** had been using. In fact, Mick Jagger was present at this session and it was rumoured that he joined in on backing vocals. **Brian Jones** of the Rolling Stones played oboe on the track. At the beginning of the song John played a clavioline and both he and Paul played pianos. Keith Grant was the engineer for the session and the second engineer, Eddie Kramer, played vibraphone.

As the number was also mixed at Olympic it became the first Beatles record to be recorded and mixed outside of **Abbey Road** since they began recording with **EMI**.

The song was the amalgamation of two songs, one written by Paul, the other by John, and the original title had been 'One Of The Beautiful People'. They'd recorded the song specially for the animated film *Yellow Submarine*, but it was used as the 'B' side of 'All You Need Is Love'. Although the number wasn't used on the *Yellow Submarine* soundtrack album, it was used in the actual film.

The recording session took place on Thursday, 11 May 1967.

• Bach, Barbara

Ringo Starr's second wife. Barbara was born in New York City in 1951. She shortened her surname from Goldbach and became a leading American model. She married and moved to Rome where her European origins (Rumanian grandmother, Irish mother, Austrian father) helped her secure roles in several international films.

While in Rome she divorced her first husband. Her most famous role was opposite Roger Moore in the James Bond spectacular *The Spy Who Loved Me*, and other movies included *The Humanoid*, *Force Ten At Navarone*,

Barbara Bach with Ringo in a scene from *Caveman*. (United Artists)

The Jaguar Lives, *The Volcanic Island* and *The Unseeen*.

She first met Ringo when she co-starred with him as Lana, a prehistoric beauty, in the film *Caveman*.

The couple were married on Monday, 27 April 1981 at **Marylebone Register Office** in London.

● Back In The USSR

A parody of the **Beach Boys** style and one of the many compositions which Paul McCartney wrote during his sojourn at Rishikesh. Beach Boy **Mike Love** was also at the ashram and it has been suggested that he helped Paul on some of the verses. Paul's brother **Mike** even suggested that the Beatles should get the Beach Boys to sing the middle section of the song on the record, but they didn't.

Twiggy, a friend of Paul's, claims that Paul wrote the song specially for a projected documentary of a visit she was making to Russia, but the trip was cancelled.

When the group began recording the number in August 1968, they were experiencing tensions during their recording sessions and Ringo became so fed up that he walked out of the recording. Paul took over on drums and 'Back In The USSR' became one of the few Beatles records on which Ringo was absent. A few days later h returned – and found the studio festooned with flowers including lots of flowers around his drum kit, with th message, 'Welcome Back Ringo'.

The number was included on *The Beatles* double albun and was also featured on the compilation *The Beatle 1967-1970*.

In 1976, when it was included on a double album, *Roc 'n' Roll Music*, it was decided to issue the number as single to help to promote the album. 'Back In The USSR coupled with 'Twist And Shout' was issued in Britain o Parlophone R 6016 on 25 June 1976.

● Bad Boy

On Monday, 10 May 1965, during their sessions for *Help* the Beatles recorded two Larry Williams numbers, 'Dizz Miss Lizzy' and 'Bad Boy'. 'Bad Boy' had been released b Williams in 1959, although it hadn't been a big hit f him, and the Beatles had included it in their repertoire i 1960, with John on lead vocals.

The day after the session the tapes were sent to **Capit Records** in America and 'Bad Boy' was used on th

Beatles VI release in June 1965. 'Dizzy Miss Lizzy' turned up on the *Help!* album.

'Bad Boy' wasn't issued in Britain until it appeared on the compilation album *A Collection Of Beatles Oldies (But Goldies)*, although it hadn't been a goldie or an oldie for them. It was also to be included on the *Rock 'n' Roll Music* and *Rarities* compilations.

● Badfinger

Aside from the Beatles, they were the most successful group on the Apple label.

As the Liverpool/Welsh group the Iveys, they were discovered by Liverpudlian **Bill Collins**, who was a friend of **Mal Evans**. When Bill and the group moved to London, Bill arranged a booking at the Marquee Club. The personnel of the band at that time comprised Pete Ham (lead), Tom Evans (rhythm), Mike Gibbons (bass) and Rob Griffiths (drums). Mal Evans brought **Peter Asher** along to hear the band, but Asher wasn't particularly interested. Mal asked Bill for some tapes of the band, which he played for Paul McCartney. Mal then played further tapes to John Lennon, George Harrison and **Derek Taylor** and they said the group should be signed to Apple. The Iveys signed with Apple Publishing in April 1968, and **Apple Records** in July 1968. The group made their recording debut with 'Maybe Tomorrow' in November 1968.

Mike Gibbons left the band and Tom Evans took over on bass guitar while Joey Molland, a guitarist from Liverpool, took over on rhythm. Their big hit came with 'Come And Get It', a number written by Paul McCartney, who also produced their single. Their name was also changed to Badfinger ('Badfinger Boogie' was the working title Paul had for his number 'With A Little Help From My Friends'). 'Come And Get It' was the soundtrack tune from Ringo Starr's movie ***The Magic Christian*** and it was issued in Britain on 5 December 1969 on Apple 20 and in America on 12 January 1970 on Apple 1815. It reached No. 4 in the British charts and No. 7 in the American. Their other British hits were 'No Matter What', which reached No. 5, and 'Day After Day', which reached No. 10. Their other American hits were 'No Matter What', which reached No. 8, 'Day After Day', which reached No. 4, and 'Baby Blue', which reached No. 14.

Their number 'Without You', became a No. 1 hit internationally for **Harry Nilsson**.

The group appeared on *The Concert For Bangladesh* and the different members played on John Lennon's *Imagine* album and George Harrison's *All Things Must Pass*.

Due to the problems at Apple, Badfinger eventually signed with Warner Bros in 1973, but they had no further hits. There had been a change of management and they eventually appointed an American manager to look after their affairs.

Things began to go seriously wrong when they found themselves penniless, their songwriting royalties tied up by legal wrangles with Apple and their Warner Bros recording advances seeming to have disappeared before they reached the group, with Warner initially thinking that the group had something to do with it. When it was found that the group knew nothing of the financial discrepancies, Warner settled some extra money on them. However, things were financially dire and in April 1975 Peter Ham hanged himself and left a suicide note blaming the music business and the group's American manager. For a couple of years Joey Molland and Tom Evans worked as labourers and then reformed the group. On 18 November 1983, Evans hanged himself. His suicide note to Molland read 'You're next'. Despite this, Molland remains a member of a revamped Badfinger, who are currently based in America.

● Badge

A number George Harrison co-wrote with **Eric Clapton**. It was recorded by Cream and entered the British Top Twenty following its release in April 1969. It reached No. 60 in the American charts. An instrumental section of the number is to be found in the middle of Harrison's number 'Here Comes The Sun'.

George and Eric performed the number on stage together during a concert at London's Rainbow Theatre in 1971.

● Bad To Me

A song John Lennon penned while on holiday in Spain. It was written for **Billy J. Kramer** as a follow-up to his debut disc 'Do You Want To Know A Secret!' and was issued in Britain on Parlophone R 5049 on 26 July 1963, and in the States on Liberty 55626 on 23 September 1963. The single provided Billy with his second British chart topper, reached No. 9 in the American charts and eventually sold more than a million copies.

Although John made a demo disc of the song for George

Martin to work from, the Beatles themselves never recorded the number.

● Bain, Bob

British comedian/compere, popular on the cabaret circuit, who appeared with the Beatles on their autumn tour of Britain from 9 October until 10 November 1964.

● Ballad Of John And Yoko, The

The 'Get Back' single was still No. 1 in the charts when 'The Ballad Of John And Yoko' was issued on Parlophone R 5786 on 30 May 1969. John had considered holding up the release until 'Get Back' had started to slip down the charts, but felt that the single might date as it was a 'newsy' tale of John's recent marriage to **Yoko Ono** and their trips to Paris and Amsterdam, with references to his 'Bigger Than Christ' newspaper story and the attitude of journalists to the couple.

When the number was recorded on 14 April 1969, only John and Paul performed on the session as George was out of the country and Ringo was filming ***The Magic Christian***. Paul played piano, bass and drums on the track.

When the single was issued in America on Apple 2531 on 4 June 1969, 'Get Back' was also in the No. 1 position. Although 'The Ballad Of John And Yoko' reached No. 1 in Britain, it only reached No. 8 in the American charts. This is probably due to the reaction in America against John's use of the name 'Christ' in the lyrics. There was initially a deal of pressure exerted to have the word bleeped out, but Apple refused. Some radio stations censored the record themselves, others played the flipside, George Harrison's 'Old Brown Shoe', others simply banned it.

John once referred to the track as 'Johnny B. Paperback Writer'.

The record reached No. 1 in Germany, Austria, Holland, Norway, Spain, Belgium, Denmark and Malaysia.

The track was included on *The Beatles 1967-1970* compilation, the *Hey Jude* album and the 1982 compilation *20 Greatest Hits*.

● Ballard, Arthur

A Liverpool-born artist who attended the Liverpool College of Art and then spent most of the time until his retirement in 1981 teaching at the college.

At one time he displayed a great potential and was part of what almost seemed to be a Liverpool renaissance in art in the fifties. There was some controversy in 1956 when one of his abstract works was hung upside down at an exhibition in the **Walker Art Gallery**, but it resulted in several sales for him.

Arthur Ballard – tutor to John Lennon and Stuart Sutcliffe at art college.

In 1957 he left for Paris for a short time to paint and study, and in 1958 had an exhibition at the New Shakespeare Gallery in Liverpool. His work was exhibited in the John Moore exhibitions at the Walker Art Gallery in 1959 and 1961. He also had a metal relief, one of his best works, fitted on the door to Johnson's TV shop in Lord Street.

Commenting about Arthur in his book *Art In A City*, art critic John Willett wrote: 'He has great faith in Liverpool's individuality, which he thinks will assert itself in art sooner or later: we'll see something "better than the Beatles". He's proud of the efforts he's made to support individualists in the college, e.g. precisely, Lennon of the Beatles, whom the graphic design department were reluctant to accept. "The boy was no good as an artist," he claims, "and an intolerable, rebellious nuisance. But he had character." '

Arthur was particularly struck by the talent of **Stuart Sutcliffe** and used to visit Stuart in his **Percy Street** flat, close to the college, as Stu was reluctant to attend the lessons at the college. It was through his belief in Stu's talent that Arthur championed John, who was a student continually on the verge of being expelled, due to his raucous behaviour and unsatisfactory work. Arthur also used to meet students in the local pub **Ye Cracke** in Rice Street.

He did prevent John from being expelled at one point but was unsuccessful in obtaining a place for him in the graphic design department.

On his retirement, Arthur moved to London for a while before settling in Wales.

● Balmoral Club, The, *Bahamas, West Indies*

A luxurious holiday complex near to Cable Beach in the Bahamas. The Beatles stayed in a house on the grounds of the Balmoral Club for several days from 22 February 1965 while they were filming sequences for *Help!*

● Baltimore Civic Centre, *Baltimore, Maryland*

There were two performances at the Civic Centre, each one drawing more than 13,000 people. Seventy-one police were stationed in the auditorium. There was the obligatory press conference and when Ringo was asked what he thought of American television, he replied, 'It's great – you get eighteen stations, but you can't get a good picture on any of them.'

● Bambi Kino, *33 Paul-Roosen Strasse, St Pauli, Hamburg, Germany*

The Bambi Filmkunsttheatre was a cinema run by **Bruno Koschmider**. When the Beatles first arrived in Hamburg on 17 August 1960 they were taken to the Bambi Kino (as it was more popularly known) and told that they were to sleep there. Along a gloomy little hallway were some small, windowless rooms, which Paul was to call 'dungeons'. They were next to the Bambi's toilets, where the Beatles were expected to wash and shave, using cold water from the urinals.

The first room they were taken to had one light bulb, two beds and an old sofa. John and **Stuart Sutcliffe** immediately commandeered the beds and George took over the sofa. There were only two other rooms, so tiny, measuring 5 ft x 6 ft, that there was only space to fit in a bed. Paul and Pete took one each.

These were their uncomfortable quarters for the next four months, although there was some respite at night due to the number of girls who came to share their beds with them, some buying tickets to the cinema and making their way to their rooms through a connecting door.

Some weeks later they made friends with a group of students; one of them, **Astrid Kirchherr**, arranged for Stuart to move out and stay in the attic room of her parents' home. George took his bed over.

Due to complaints about noise the **Indra** was closed and the Beatles were moved to the **Kaiserkeller** club on 4 October, although they were to remain billeted in the Bambi. By this time the boys were acutely aware of their low pay and approached Koschmider for a rise. He refused. They received an offer from a rival club, the **Top Ten**, and agreed to take it up when their Kaiserkeller contract lapsed in December. Koschmider's spies reported their intentions to him and he threatened them and then reported to the police that George was only seventeen and under-age for the St Pauli area. He was deported. The group decided to continue at the Top Ten Club as a quartet and John Lennon was the first to remove his personal belongings to the new club, where they were to share a large top-floor room with **Tony Sheridan**. When Paul and Pete went to the Bambi to collect their possessions, the absence of light in their rooms caused them to take an unusual step in providing light of their own. They attached four rubber contraceptives to some old tapestry covering on the wall and lit them. By the time they'd burned out, Pete and Paul had gathered their belongings and left, the contraceptives having left some scorch marks on the wall.

They were settled in at their new billet when, in the middle of the night, the police arrived and took Pete and Paul away to the local police station where they were charged with attempting to cause a fire at the Bambi Kino. Their explanations were ignored and they were taken to prison and put in cells. A few hours later the police took them to the airport and deported them, having obtained their passports from their belongings – but leaving the rest of their possessions in Hamburg.

● Banks, Jeremy

Silver-haired photographic coordinator at **Apple**, who joined the Beatles' employ in 1968. He was 33 years old at the time and was also engaged as photographic coordinator for the Beatles and worked with **Derek Taylor** in the Apple press office.

Taylor had first met Jeremy on 3 November 1966 in

Arthur Howes' office. Taylor had brought his clients, the **Beach Boys**, there and Banks was handling special features for the *Daily Star* newspaper and covered the Beach Boys story with photographer **John Kelly**.

He joined Apple and was part of the organization until December 1969. He would arrange photographic sessions, deal directly with photo agencies to obtain a commission for Apple, advise on sleeve design and think up publicity gimmicks – one of which was to send Apple's first four releases to Her Majesty The Queen, which resulted in a thank-you letter from Buckingham Palace.

Adrian Barber – he recorded the Beatles at Hamburg's Star Club. (Cavern Mecca)

● Barber, Adrian

A Yorkshire musician who was based in Liverpool in the late fifties and early sixties. He was guitarist with Cass & the Cassanovas who, when **Brian Casser** left, became the Big Three. Regarded as one of the top local musicians, he was also renowned for being an electronics wizard. Among his unique gadgets were huge black amplifiers which he designed and constructed, nicknamed 'coffins'. He made them for several Mersey bands, including the Beatles.

He refused to sign with Brian Epstein and left the Big Three to become stage manager at the **Star Club** in Hamburg, building a complete PA and recording system for the club. During his sound testing he recorded various bands, including the Beatles. **Kingsize Taylor**, leader of a Mersey band, asked Adrian for the tapes and he gave them to him. They were released many years later in 1977 as *The Beatles Live! At The Star Club in Hamburg, Germany, 1962*, although Adrian wasn't credited – and Taylor even tried to intimate that he'd recorded the performances himself!

Joey Dee was so impressed with the sound system Adrian had built for the Star Club that he hired him to build a similar system for the **Peppermint Lounge** in New York. Adrian remained in America, became a successful recording manager and DJ, and now lives in Brighton, Massachusetts.

● Barron Knights, The

A comedy/rock group from Leighton Buzzard comprising Duke D'mond, vocals; Paul Longford, guitar; Butch Baker, guitar; Barron Anthony, bass; and Dave Balinger, drums. The group had a series of record hits with comic medleys of hits by other groups, including 'Call Up The Groups', 'Come To The Dance', 'Pop Go The Workers' and 'Merry Guitar Pops'.

The group were booked to appear on the *Beatles Christmas Show* in December 1963/January 1964 at the **Gaumont, Bradford**, the **Liverpool Empire** and the **Finsbury Park Astoria**, London.

In those days there were high jinks between the groups. The Beatles' act on the *Christmas Show* began when they stood on a blacked-out stage and a small spotlight picked out each of their heads in turn, ending with John Lennon's. One night some members of the **Barron Knights** grabbed John in the wings and held him so that when the spotlight turned to where John should have been, there was nothing there.

● Barrow, Tony

At the age of seventeen, when he was still a sixth form student at Merchant Taylor's College in Crosby Merseyside, Tony Barrow was appointed record reviewer for the ***Liverpool Echo***. Under the name 'Disker', he reviewed the latest record releases and also included a small local chart of the top-selling singles.

He moved to London in 1954 to work at **Decca Records** where he became the only full-time writer of album sleeve notes in Britain, while still retaining his *Echo* column.

Brian Epstein sent a letter to Disker requesting a mention of the Beatles. The letter was passed on to Barrow who contacted Epstein and told him that he only wrote about actual recording acts. He suggested that Epstein contact a colleague on the *Echo*, columnist George Harrison. Having discovered that Tony worked for Decca, Brian once again contacted him requesting help with contacts at Decca. Barrow passed over the message and the Beatles auditioned for the company. When Barrow asked **Mike Smith** how the audition went, Smith was very

Former Beatles press officer Tony Barrow (left), with Brian O'Hara of the Fourmost.

positive and in his Disker column, Barrow wrote: 'Latest episode in the success story of Liverpool's instrumental group the Beatles. Commenting upon the outfit's recent recording test, Decca disc producer Mike Smith tells me that he thinks the Beatles are great. He has a tape of their audition which runs over thirty minutes and is convinced his label will be able to put the Beatles to good use. I'll keep you posted.'

However, Decca gave the Beatles the thumbs down. After Brian succeeded in gaining a Parlophone contract for the band, he approached Barrow for advice again. Tony pointed out that it would be sensible if he paid for independent public relations to plug the record and Brian offered him twenty pounds to produce a publicity kit for 'Love Me Do'. As he couldn't send out all the kits from his office at Decca, Tony noted that **Tony Calder**, who used to work in the same office at Decca, had left to set up a PR company with **Andrew Loog Oldham**. He contacted them and they were hired by Epstein to send out the press releases and arrange press interviews.

With the release of 'Love Me Do', Barrow wrote in his Disker column: 'John Lennon and Paul McCartney chant out their self-written lyrics of "Love Me Do", an infectious medium-paced ballad with an exceptionally haunting harmonica accompaniment. There's nothing startlingly distinguished about the simple, repetitive lyrics but "Love Me Do" relies more upon punchy ear-catching presentation. There's a refreshing do-it-yourself approach to the single.'

Epstein had offered the Beatles' PR account to Oldham, who turned it down. He asked Barrow if he would take on the task. Barrow also turned it down. He had a secure job at Decca and a steady girlfriend, Corinne, whom he married. He didn't want to take the chance of giving it all up for what seemed a risky venture. Brian then took him to lunch at the popular seafood restaurant Wheelers and offered him £32 per week, twice the amount he was getting at Decca – and he took up the offer.

Epstein asked him to find a London office for **NEMS** where he could handle the press work and he found premises at **Service House**, 13 Monmouth Street. Eventually hiring an assistant, Jo Berman, and a secretary, Valerie Sumpter.

As the organization grew he graduated to plush offices in Argyll Street, next to the **London Palladium**, and as the Beatles were more or less a full-time account, he concentrated on the other NEMS artists while Brian employed various people such as **Brian Sommerville** and **Derek Taylor** to look after the Beatles' press personally, although Tony did continue to handle their press activities from time to time.

He also managed to write prolifically: a series of

souvenir magazines about the Beatles, the **Cavern** and other beat artists, record sleeve notes for the early Beatles albums and regular features about the Beatles' activities for *Beatles Monthly*. In many cases he had to use a pseudonym. Although he wasn't earning a fortune from **NEMS Enterprises**, his contract stated that any proceeds from freelance writing under his own name would have to be shared with the company, therefore Tony used the name Alistair Griffin for his books and Frederick James for his *Beatles Monthly* articles.

It was Tony who came up with the suggestion for the Beatles' Christmas records for fan club members.

After Brian Epstein's death he set up his own PR company, Tony Barrow International, retaining artists such as **Cilla Black** and expanding his activities until he had a roster of star names. Unfortunately, ill health caused him to retire in the late seventies and he moved to Morecambe on the north-west coast.

In 1980 he had recovered sufficiently to begin freelance writing and by 1981 had become prolific in his output with regular features in *Beatles Monthly* (this time under his own name) and syndicated columns in provincial publications, in addition to numerous commissions for record sleeves. He also sought out personalities with former Beatles associations in order to ghost their 'stories' for the national press. Angie McCartney was the subject of one of his series in the *Daily Star*, her daughter Ruth was another (in *19* magazine). In 1982 he penned *P.S. We Love You* for Mirror Books.

Tony's features for *Beatles Monthly* are of tremendous interest to readers due to the fact that Tony travelled quite extensively with the group. He was present on their American trips, their trip to the far east (and the harrowing experience in Manila), attended their meeting with **Elvis Presley** and, at the request of Paul, taped their final concert at **Candlestick Park**.

● Bassey, Shirley

Internationally renowned British singer, born in Cardiff, Wales, on 8 January 1937.

Shirley visited the Beatles backstage during their **Carnegie Hall** appearance in February 1964 – she was appearing in concert there the following week.

She recorded 'Something' in 1970, which reached No. 4 in the British charts, and she followed up with 'Fool On The Hill', which only reached the position of No. 48.

● Bayerischer Hof Hotel, Munich, Germany

Hotel where the Beatles stayed on Thursday, 23 June, 1966 during their short German tour. They arrived late in the afternoon and moved into their fifth floor suite. Later, on their way to a press conference at the hotel, they were jammed in a lift for ten minutes as there were fifteen people crammed inside. Once freed, they attended their conference, during which they were presented with a Golden Otto Award by *Bravo* magazine. They returned to their rooms where they carried out preliminary rehearsals for their concert the following day as they hadn't performed for several weeks. During the following evening they relaxed by taking a dip in the hotel pool.

● Beach Ballroom, Sea Beach, Aberdeen, Aberdeenshire, Scotland

Setting for the Beatles' final appearance of their short Scottish tour, on Sunday, 6 January 1963.

● Beach Boys, The

Californian group famous for their 'surf sound', who were one of the leading American bands when the Beatles first arrived in the States in February 1964. That was the month in which the group reached No. 5 in the charts with 'Fun, Fun, Fun' and later the same year they topped the American charts for the first time with 'I Get Around'. They shared the same record label as the Beatles in America, **Capitol Records**, and because both their names began with 'Beat', they were bedfellows in the record bins at record stores.

The following year they appeared in the film *The Girls On The Beach*, with the Crickets and Leslie Gore. The plot concerned kids at a school hop who think they have booked the Beatles, but get the Beach Boys instead.

In fact, a fierce competitiveness was generated when the Beatles became successful in America, particularly in the mind of Brian Wilson. Brian was the creative fire behind the group, which also comprised his brothers Car and Dennis, his cousin **Mike Love** and friend A Jardine.

Brian's output following the appearance of the Beatles was so stimulated that the group had a huge string of hits and became the biggest-selling band on Capitol Records next to the Beatles. Brian, at times, seemed obsessed with the Beatles' success and once, when the Beach Boys were stranded at Shannon Airport in Ireland on their way to London, they shared the VIP lounge with Brian Epstein. Brian Wilson was keen to ask him when the Beatles were next appearing in America and when Brian told him it would be in almost a year's time, Brian seemed visibly relieved.

Brian Wilson turned his concentration increasingly to the production and writing of music, and ceased touring. He was replaced for a while on the road by Glenn Campbell and then by Bruce Johnson.

After hearing the *Rubber Soul* album in 1965, Brian was so impressed that he was determined to outshine it and said, 'I was sitting around a table with friends, making a joint when we heard "Rubber Soul" for the first time, and I'm smoking and I'm getting high, and the album blew my mind because it was a whole album with all good stuff.' He then stated that he would produce the greatest rock 'n' roll album ever made and set to work on *Pet Sounds*. It was well received critically in Britain, but was something of a failure in America where Capitol rush-released *The Best Of The Beach Boys* compilation several weeks later, which sold better and went Gold.

Still determined to outshine the Beatles, Brian invited lyricist Van Dyke Parks to join him in producing a rock 'n' roll album which would be his masterpiece, initially to be called *Dumb Angel*, then *Smiley Smile*.

During the making of the album, the Beatles' *Sgt Pepper's Lonely Hearts Club Band* was released and it was suggested that this had such an effect on Brian that he scrapped his project and merely issued a few of the tracks on an album called *Smile*.

Later, when the Beach Boys decided not to appear at the Monterey Rock Festival, Jan Wenner, editor of *Rolling Stone*, was to write in his publication: 'The Beach Boys are just one prominent example of a group that has gotten hung up in trying to catch the Beatles.'

The Beatles and the Beach Boys actually became quite good friends. Carl Wilson and Mike Love visited the Beatles backstage at their Portland Coliseum concert on 22 August 1965, and when the Beach Boys toured England, the Beatles rang them up at their hotel, individually.

Paul McCartney also attended a Beach Boys recording session on 10 April 1967. Rumours were spread that Paul either produced or sang on one of the numbers recorded, 'Vegetables', although it seems unlikely.

The Beatles also praised the Beach Boys back home in England, which helped to increase the group's popularity.

The Beach Boys, the popular American group who became friends of the Beatles.

(Capitol Records)

In fact, the Beach Boys employed **Derek Taylor**, the Beatles' former press officer, as their own publicist.

He was to comment: 'I lived in Hollywood then but my British links were strong and with *Pet Sounds* out and the Beatles increasingly flattering about the Beach Boys and with *Good Vibrations* on the way, we started to pump information into England about this tremendous band,'

In fact, Paul said at the time that he regarded 'God Only Knows' as the best song ever written.

In 1967 Mike Love and Bruce Johnson performed at the Beatles party held to celebrate their *Magical Mystery Tour* film. Mike Love was also to join the Beatles at the Maharishi's ashram in Rishikesh in India where it was rumoured that he helped Paul in composing 'Back In The USSR'.

Paul and **Linda McCartney** attended the group's concert at Anaheim, California, in 1976.

● Beat Brothers, The

The Beatles recorded for producer **Bert Kaempfert** at an infants' school in Hamburg in May 1961, as backing band to **Tony Sheridan**. During the sessions they cut some numbers supporting Sheridan: 'My Bonnie', 'The Saints', 'Why (Can't You Love Me Again)', 'Sweet Georgia Brown', 'Nobody's Child' and 'If You Love Me Baby' (aka 'Take Out Some Insurance On Me, Baby'). They also recorded two numbers on their own, 'Ain't She Sweet', with John Lennon on lead vocals, and an instrumental called 'Cry For a Shadow'.

When Polydor released two of the songs in Germany in August 1961, they were credited to Tony Sheridan and the Beat Brothers. Kaempfert had decided that the name 'Beatles' was not suitable for use on the record as, according to rumour, he felt that it sounded too much like the north German slang word 'Peedles', denoting the male sex organ. So he came up with the name the Beat Brothers. He also used the name to cover the backing musicians on other Tony Sheridan recordings he made. The musicians included bass guitarist Colin Milander, drummer Johnny Watson, organist Roy Young and tenor saxophonist Rikki Barnes. Among the titles this line-up of the Beat Brothers recorded were 'Let's Dance', 'Ya Ya' and 'What'd I Say'. As some of these titles have been issued on releases along with the Beatles tracks, this has led to some confusion with fans mistakenly believing that the Beatles were featured on the other songs.

● Beatlemania! (Film)

A 95-minute movie version (although an edited 86-minute version has also been shown) of the hit Broadway show, released for a limited screening in America, but not released in Britain.

It's basically a film of the successful Broadway stage show. Ely Landau and his wife Edie co-produced it with Steve Leber and David Krens. Joe Manduke directed the movie which featured 30 Lennon & McCartney songs.

Mitch Weissman (Paul), Ralph Castelli (Ringo), David Leon (John) and Tom Teeley (George) portrayed the Beatles. The number 'Please Please Me', which wasn't in the original stage production, was added to the film's soundtrack.

Landau explained why he wanted to make a film version of his profitable show: 'It is a phenomenon when you see 3,000 kids in Hartford, Connecticut, knowing the first note of each song and giving standing ovations to four very talented kids at the end of each song, knowing they are not the Beatles, but truly an incredible simulation. It is something that Edie and I feel should be brought to a wider audience than just that of the live theatre.'

Filming began on 23 March 1981 at the Long Beach Convention Centre in California. Four performances of the stage show were filmed before a live audience, then the production company moved into a Hollywood sound and special effects studio. The movie's publicity read: 'In the studios *Beatlemania!*'s famed audio-visual effects involving some 4,000 visual images including slides, original drawings and film clips, will be joined with newly created graphics, special effects and film footage of the 60s.'

● Beatlemania! (Stage Musical)

Title of a multi-media musical based on the Beatles' career, which was produced by Steve Leber and David Krens at a cost of one million dollars. It was staged by Jules Fisher who conceived the multi-media approach, using slides and projectors to create visual images of the Beatles while four actors portrayed the group on stage with seven off-stage musicians in support. Following a trial run in Boston, the show opened at the Winter Gardens Theatre, Broadway, New York, on 31 May 1977. The actors were Joe Pecorrino as John, Mitch Weissman as Paul, Leslie Fradkin as George and Justin McNeal as Ringo.

The Beatles considered legal action and their representative **John Eastman** commented: 'I'm representing all four and they are very angry at this show. They have been ripped off. These guys have just taken someone else's act and recreated it completely.'

Beatlemania! proved to be very successful and there was a film version, a touring show and presentations in several countries including Japan, the UK and South America.

● Beatlemania (Term)

A term which came into existence following the Beatles' appearance on 'Sunday Night At The London Palladium', on 13 October 1963. The group appeared live before an audience of 15,000,000 viewers nationwide that evening, performing a twelve-minute act. For the first time ever, the stars of the show were seen briefly at the beginning of the evening, albeit only for a few seconds. Compere Bruce Forsyth announced, 'If you want to see them again, they'll be back in 42 minutes.' The crowds of fans had begun to build up during the day and when the Beatles attempted to escape the theatre via the front entrance in Argyle Street, they were swamped by fans – and the cameras of the national newspapers. Despite Philip Norman in *Shout!* implying that there were only a handful of fans and photographer **Dezo Hoffman** saying that there were only about eight fans, photographs and eye witnesses disprove their claims. The headlines of the national newspapers were full of reports of the group's spectacular success and the *Daily Mirror* coined the phrase 'Beatlemania!' which was taken up by all the other newspapers. It then became an established term throughout the world, which is still in use today.

The group's press officer **Tony Barrow** was to tell **Hunter Davies**, 'From that day on, everything changed. My job was never the same again. From spending six months ringing up newspapers and getting "No", I now had every national reporter and feature writer chasing me.'

With tedious regularity ever since, any new pop group who creates a sensation is generally labelled to be 'as big as the Beatles' and a variation of the word is used – Monkeemania, Rollermania, and so on.

The word 'Beatlemania' was once considered as the title of their debut film and it was eventually used as the title of a Broadway show, based on the Beatles, which opened in 1977.

● Beatles, The

Inspired by the skiffle boom, a pupil at **Quarry Bank School** in Liverpool named John Lennon decided to form a skiffle group in 1957 and laid the foundation of what was to become the most famous rock band of all time. His initial name the **Blackjacks** only lasted a week and the school became the inspiration for the new name when John dubbed the group the **Quarry Men** in March 1957. John sang and played guitar and he was accompanied by **Colin Hanton** on drums, **Eric Griffiths** on guitar, **Pete Shotton** on washboard, **Rod Davis** on banjo and Bill

(Sotheby's)

Smith on tea-chest bass; the latter was soon replaced by **Ivan Vaughan**, who alternated on the instrument with **Nigel Whalley**.

The band's main inspiration was skiffle music, as performed by artists such as **Lonnie Donegan** and bands such as the Vipers. Numbers in their repertoire included: 'Freight Train', 'Maggie May', 'Midnight Special', 'Railroad Bill', 'Come Go With Me' and 'Worried Man Blues'. Such a repertoire was appropriate for the type of cheap instruments they could afford. One of the advantages of skiffle music was that the basic instruments were not costly, enabling thousands of youngsters throughout Britain to emulate the skiffle sounds of the hit artists.

At the same time, John, inspired by 'Heartbreak Hotel', was a fan of American rock 'n' roll music and continued to introduce numbers into their repertoire which had been hits for **Buddy Holly**, **Carl Perkins**, the Coasters, **Elvis**, **Jerry Lee Lewis** and **Gene Vincent**. Between June and July 1957, there was a six-man line-up for the group with Len Garry on tea-chest bass.

On 6 July 1957, Ivan Vaughan invited Paul McCartney, one of his friends from the **Liverpool Institute**, along to their gig at Woolton Parish Church. The fifteen-year-old McCartney and the sixteen-year-old Lennon were introduced and a unique songwriting partnership was to flourish.

The line-up of the Quarry Men increased to seven with the inclusion of Paul on guitar and vocals, **John Lowe** on piano and George Harrison on guitar and vocals from February 1958. Harrison was a friend of Paul's from the Liverpool Institute whom he'd met on the bus journeys to school. By the middle of 1958 Garry and Griffiths had left, leaving a five-man outfit.

The group appeared in several local talent contests, but had few gigs. By January 1959 they weren't operating as a group, although John and Paul kept in touch with their mutual interest in songwriting. George joined a group called the **Les Stewart Quartet**.

That might have been the end of the Quarry Men saga, but for a stroke of good fortune. The Les Stewart Quartet had been booked as a resident band at a new cellar club in Liverpool called the **Casbah**. Situated in the West Derby area of Liverpool, it was run by **Mrs Mona Best**, primarily for the benefit of her sons **Pete** and Rory. Stewart, upset because of the time his guitarist **Ken Brown** had spent on decorating the club, refused to play there. George Harrison and Brown walked out of the group, George contacted his friends John and Paul and the Quarry Men were reunited as a quartet. After seven gigs at the club Ken Brown left the group following a disagreement about money and he encouraged Pete Best to form a group with him called the Blackjacks. Between October 1959 and January 1960 John, Paul and George continued as a trio, calling themselves **Johnny & the Moondogs** for some Carroll Levis audition.

John Lennon was, by this time, a student at **Liverpool College of Art**. Conscious of their need for a bass guitarist, he approached two other students, independently of each other, and offered them the job if they could obtain a guitar. The two were **Stuart Sutcliffe** and **Rod Murray**. Both were unable to afford a guitar, so Rod began to make one by hand. Then Stuart sold a painting at an exhibition and he was able to buy a bass guitar and joined the group in January 1960, when they called themselves the Beatals. The quartet continued together until May, when they were joined by drummer **Tommy Moore** and called themselves the Silver Beetles. The 36-year-old Moore was only with them for a short time, during which they auditioned for pop impresario **Larry Parnes** and appeared on a short tour of Scotland backing singer **Johnny Gentle**. In July 1960 they had another drummer, **Norman Chapman**, but his tenure lasted barely weeks.

Chapman was called up for National Service and the group urgently needed another drummer. They had been booked for a short season in Hamburg. The gig had come about via a local coffee bar owner, **Allan Williams**, who had already sent another band, Derry & the Seniors to Hamburg. He'd used the respelled Silver Beatles at his **Jacaranda Club**, a short-lived strip club, and the **New Cabaret Artistes Club** and had obtained a few local bookings for them at venues such as the **Grosvenor Ballroom**. By his own admission, he only used them because they were cheap and he did not reckon them to be in the same class as many of the other local bands.

Liverpool, by this time, was literally swarming with rock 'n' roll groups who, like the Silver Beatles, had continued playing music long after the skiffle boom had faded.

McCartney contacted **Pete Best** and offered him the drum seat. He took it. The group decided to call themselves the Beatles as from August 1960 and their first trip to Hamburg. When Sutcliffe joined, and they'd briefly used the name Beatals, they strove for a better title. As their main rock 'n' roll inspiration at the time was Buddy Holly, Stuart thought they should have a name similar to that of Holly's backing band the Crickets and thought up Beetles. This was changed to the Silver Beetles, but then it was truncated again, John Lennon added the 'a', making it Beatles, George Harrison's assumption that the name might have been inspired by a motorcycle gang called the Beetles in the film *The Wild One* is wrong; the film was barred from British screens until the late sixties and they

The Beatles on stage at the Cavern shortly after Ringo replaced Pete Best. (©Apple/Peter Kaye Collection)

couldn't possibly have seen the film at the time of their name change.

When the Beatles left for Hamburg in 1960, they weren't regarded as a leading band in Liverpool and, in some cases, were looked down on by some of the other groups. It was their stint in Hamburg which pulled the band together musically, a 'baptism of fire' which transformed them from an average band into a dynamic outfit. This was caused by the fact that they had to play such long hours and were bullied by the clubowner **Bruno Koschmider** to 'make a show', which resulted in their act becoming much tighter musically. Oddly, this transformation didn't seem to happen to the many other Liverpool acts who appeared in Hamburg.

However, it wasn't Hamburg alone which made the Beatles something special. The fact that Liverpool had so many venues for local acts to play at, coupled with the rivalry between more than 300 Merseyside groups, continued to forge the Beatles until they were to be regarded as Liverpool's top band, a fact confirmed by the poll published by the music paper ***Mersey Beat*** on 4 January 1962.

At the time Pete Best was regarded as the most potent symbol in the band. Following their stint in Hamburg, bass guitarist Stuart Sutcliffe had left them and they were a four-man outfit. John Lennon, Paul McCartney and George Harrison were the three front-line guitarists and they alternated as lead singers and also performed vocal harmony with either Paul and John or all three. Pete Best played drums and occasionally sang one song, although he had developed a distinctive drum sound during his spell in Hamburg which became known as 'the atom beat', which was copied by other drummers.

Intrigued by the growing interest in the Beatles, a local

record retailer, Brian Epstein, signed them up and they initially auditioned for **Decca Records** on New Year's Day, 1962. They weren't successful, but Epstein managed to secure a contract with Parlophone Records and George Martin became their A&R Man. In August of that year Pete Best was sacked and replaced by Ringo Starr, a drummer from Liverpool group **Rory Storm & the Hurricanes**, whom the Beatles had appeared with in Hamburg.

Their first single 'Love Me Do' was issued on 5 October 1962, and was a modest hit.

1963 and 1964 proved to be the most important years in their careers. During 1963 they created a sensation in Britain and **'Beatlemania'** was born. Within months they had graduated from being a support act at concerts to starring in the Royal Variety Show and the highest rating TV show 'Sunday Night At The London Palladium'.

There were various reasons for their success. National Service in Britain had ended and young men no longer had their lives disrupted for two years while they were seconded for compulsory army training. The post-war bulge (later known as the 'baby boom'), in which an unprecedented number of babies were born immediately at the end of the war as returning servicemen were reunited with their wives, caused the largest explosion in the birth rate up to that time and those babies were now teenagers – the largest number of teenagers Britain had ever known. In addition, these teenagers had money to spend. The youngsters were also demanding more freedom than their parents had experienced in their youth and were eager to create their own sounds and fashions. The media had also developed to the extent that it was possible to create an overnight sensation – with television, radio and the proliferation of newspapers and magazines, it no longer required years performing at theatres throughout the country to achieve fame.

1964 was the most important year of all for it was the year in which the Beatles conquered the biggest record market in the world – America.

It took a combination of talent and luck – and the group also became symbols. America was mourning the death of President John F. Kennedy and the Beatles appeared on the scene to bring them fun and excitement and end their mourning. They also brought rock 'n' roll back to its homeland. Rock 'n' roll had been created in America in the fifties, but had waned to an extent because the major rock artists had faded from the public eye. After Elvis Presley's army service, he lost much of his early rebelliousness. Jerry Lee Lewis and **Chuck Berry** had been the subject of scandals and their careers had suffered, Buddy Holly, the Big Bopper and Ritchie Valens had been killed in an air crash, and the American media had promoted music of a more sanitized nature, performed by good-looking young singers who were acceptable to the parents of teenagers – Frankie Avalon, Tab Hunter, Ricky Nelson, Bobby Vee, James Darren and so on.

Being in the right place at the right time seemed to favour the Beatles. They were hanging around the Jacaranda when Allan Williams was seeking a group to go to Hamburg. **Ed Sullivan** happened to be at London Airport when the Beatles arrived back from Sweden to a tumultuous welcome, which resulted in them appearing on the top-rating 'Ed Sullivan Show'. Lucky instances were frequent in their career. If Brian Epstein hadn't dropped into the HMV store in London to have some acetates cut they might never have secured a recording contract.

At some contrast to the luck was the fact that they initially weren't regarded highly in various quarters. Derry & the Seniors didn't want them to go to Hamburg as they believed the Beatles would ruin the scene for other groups. When they appeared at **Litherland Town Hall** in Liverpool, part of the audience believed they were a German group. All three pop labels of **EMI** turned them down and didn't think they had anything new to offer. Several parties approached by Epstein wouldn't invest in the group because they believed the Beatles didn't have a future. **Capitol Records** rejected them on three occasions and their initial record releases in America in 1963 only sold in the hundreds of copies.

During the sixties, the Beatles not only became a musical phenomenon, they affected the styles and fashions of the decade. Apart from being musically innovative, they changed almost every aspect of the record industry, from bringing about the restructure of royalties for artists and producers to influencing the designs of album sleeves. They revolutionized music tours, popularized the Pop promo and transformed studio recording.

The Beatles officially split on 31 December 1970, when Paul McCartney took out a lawsuit in the High Court to dissolve their partnership, resulting in an official receiver being appointed to handle the group's affairs.

After more than a decade together, they were like four

young men ready to leave the family nest. All four were married, although it was the wives of John and Paul who were most active in their husbands' careers. John had become more interested in his collaborations with **Yoko Ono** than with Paul and the other Beatles, and Paul was ready to embark on solo ventures with his wife **Linda**. George was also loath to continue being a Beatle. They had abandoned touring in 1966 and the succeeding years were known as their 'studio years', when they mainly gathered together to record. George had developed as a songwriter in his own right and his recorded efforts with the Beatles were almost George Harrison solo works.

It was Paul who had mainly kept the group together after Brian Epstein had died, egging them on to make *Magical Mystery Tour* and constantly eager for the Beatles to go on the road again. They had been drifting apart for some time, but the main bone of contention seemed to be when John, George and Ringo officially appointed **Allen Klein** to represent them. Paul insisted on John Eastman as his representative and the scene was set for the dissolution of the group.

On Tuesday, 27 April 1971 John, George and Ringo decided to drop their appeal against the High Court order placing their affairs in the hands of a receiver. They faced legal costs of £100,000. Mr James Douglas Spooner was immediately appointed as receiver and manager of the group's business and the saga of the Beatles had finally come to an end.

Beatles, The (Album)

The Beatles was the simple title of the group's first double album which, when released, became the biggest-selling double album of all time, reaching the No. 1 position in various international charts, including those in Britain and America, and selling more than six and a half million copies within the first two years of issue.

The cover of *The Beatles* was in marked contrast to the elaborate sleeve of *Sgt Pepper's Lonely Hearts Club Band*. **Richard Hamilton**, the artist who was brought in to advise the Beatles on the sleeve design by **Robert Fraser**, suggested a plain white cover, individually numbered in the style of a limited edition. He also suggested a collage of images of the Beatles should be enclosed on a poster. His ideas were adopted, with Gordon House designing the package which included four colour prints of portraits of the individual Beatles by **John Kelly**, together with a poster montage of shots of the Beatles which also contained the lyrics to the songs on the reverse side.

The montage of photographs for the poster was assembled by **Jeremy Banks**, **Neil Aspinall** and **Mal Evans** and there was some controversy because they included a 'nude' shot of Paul. Oddly enough, there was a larger photograph of John Lennon in the nude which passed without comment.

Due to the starkness of the sleeve, the album became commonly known as 'The White Album'. Incidentally, it had originally gone by the working title 'A Doll's House', but it was pointed out that another band had recently used that same title.

The Beatles was the first Beatles album to be issued on **Apple**'s own label and Paul McCartney asked **Derek Taylor** to arrange for an advertising agency to develop a major publicity and advertising campaign for the release. A meeting was arranged between a senior director of J. Walter Thompson, the advertising agency, and after a preliminary discussion, a second meeting was held a week later with several representatives from J. Walter Thompson, plus Paul McCartney, Derek Taylor, **Ron Kass**, Jeremy Banks, **Peter Asher**, Neil Aspinall and **Jack Oliver**. The agency suggested that there be television adverts, with Paul McCartney appearing in them – the cost of the TV commercials would be £56,000. Thompson's also suggested six London buses be painted white with 'Beatles Bus' written on the side of the windows. Paul didn't like the idea and the proposed massive campaign was dropped.

The album took five months to record and the sessions began on Thursday, 30 May 1968 at **Abbey Road Studios** and ended on Thursday, 17 October 1968, during which time a staggering 32 tracks had been recorded, 30 of which found their way onto the double album. One of the tracks recorded but not issued was 'What's The New Mary Jane', which remains unreleased, another was the George Harrison composition 'Not Guilty'.

The sessions had not been entirely happy ones and at one period, Ringo walked out following a criticism by Paul, and didn't return for two weeks. John Lennon had become disillusioned with the group and wanted to leave. Since they'd recorded their last album there had been other changes, apart from the creation of Apple – the death of Brian Epstein and the emergence of **Yoko Ono**.

The majority of the 30 tracks had been written while

the Beatles were studying at the ashram in Rishikesh.

The tracks were, Side One: 'Back In The USSR', 'Dear Prudence', 'Glass Onion', 'Ob-La-Di Ob-La-Da', 'Wild Honey Pie', 'The Continuing Story Of Bungalow Bill', 'While My Guitar Gently Weeps', 'Happiness Is A Warm Gun'. Side Two: 'Martha My Dear', 'I'm So Tired', 'Blackbird', 'Piggies', 'Rocky Raccoon', 'Don't Pass Me By', 'Why Don't We Do It In The Road', 'I Will', 'Julia'. Side Three: 'Birthday', 'Yer Blues', 'Mother Nature's Son', 'Everybody's Got Something To Hide Except Me And My Monkey', 'Sexy Sadie', 'Helter Skelter', 'Long Long Long'. Side Four: 'Revolution 1', 'Honey Pie', 'Savoy Truffle', 'Cry Baby Cry', 'Revolution 9', 'Goodnight'.

Although this was the first Beatles album on the Apple label, EMI still retained the Beatles and the releases went out using the Parlophone catalogue numbers. *The Beatles* was issued in Britain on Parlophone 7067-8 on 22 November 1968, and went straight to No. 1 in the charts.

The album was issued in America on **Capitol** SWBO 101 on 25 November 1968 with advance orders of almost two million and went to No. 1 in the charts.

● Beatles Abroad, The

A 45-minute radio programme transmitted on the Light Programme on 30 August 1965. The show was hosted by **Brian Matthew** who had recorded interviews with the group which were included in the broadcast.

● Beatles At Shea Stadium, The

A documentary of the concert, also known as 'Live at Shea Stadium'. This one-hour TV special was filmed at **Shea Stadium** in Flushing, New York, on 15 August 1965, when the Beatles appeared before an audience of 55,600 fans.

There were lots of behind-the-scenes incidents in the film: George chatting with Brian Epstein; images of the four preparing for their entrance; shots of some of the other bands, such as **Sounds Incorporated**, performing; Brian Epstein proudly watching from the wings, with introductions by **Ed Sullivan** and **Murray the K**.

The group performed: 'I'm Down', 'Twist And Shout', 'I Feel Fine', 'Dizzy Miss Lizzie', 'Ticket To Ride', 'Act Naturally', 'Can't Buy Me Love', 'Baby's In Black' and 'A Hard Day's Night'.

The show was first screened in Britain on BBC TV on 1 March 1966, and in America on 10 January 1967.

● Beatles At The Beeb

A BBC radio programme which compiled the various numbers the Beatles performed live on radio in the early sixties. The show was originally broadcast by the BBC on 7 March 1982. A much larger compilation was assembled into a three-part series which was syndicated to radio stations throughout the US and broadcast in three parts from 29–31 May 1982. A revised version of the British broadcast was transmitted in the UK on 27 December 1982. For America, each of the three parts opened with excerpts from the theme songs from the **'Pop Go The Beatles'** and **'From Us To You'** programmes.

The line-up of songs featured in the three-part series was, Part One: 'The Hippy Hippy Shake', 'Memphis, Tennessee', 'Dream Baby', 'Please Mr Postman', 'Some Other Guy', 'Too Much Monkey Business', 'Do You Want To Know A Secret', 'I'll Be On My Way', 'Crying, Waiting, Hoping', 'Pop Go The Beatles', 'To Know Her Is To Love Her', 'Don't Ever Change', 'That's All Right, Mama', 'Carol', 'Soldier Of Love', 'Lend Me Your Comb', 'Clarabella' and 'A Shot Of Rhythm & Blues'. Part Two: 'Matchbox', 'Sure To Fall', 'Lonesome Tears In My Eyes', 'Sweet Little Sixteen', 'Nothin' Shakin' (But The Leaves On The Trees)', 'I Just Don't Understand', 'So How Come (No One Loves Me)', 'I Got A Woman', 'I Got To Find My Baby', 'The Honeymoon Song', 'From Us To You', 'All My Loving', 'Roll Over Beethoven', 'Till There Was You', 'I Wanna Be Your Man', 'Can't Buy Me Love', 'Happy Birthday Saturday Club', 'This Boy'. Part Three: 'Long Tall Sally', 'Rock And Roll Music', 'And I Love Her', 'A Hard Day's Night', 'Things We Said Today', 'I'll Follow The Sun', 'I'm A Loser', 'She's A Woman', 'I Feel Fine', 'Johnny B. Goode', 'Kansas City/Hey Hey Hey', 'Everybody's Trying To Be My Baby', 'Honey Don't', 'Dizzy Miss Lizzy', 'Ticket To Ride'. A book of the same title was published by BBC Books, written by Kevin Howlett.

● Beatles At The Hollywood Bowl

The Beatles concerts at the Hollywood Bowl were both recorded by Capitol Records and produced by Voyle Gilmore. The engineer on the 1964 concert was Hugh Davies, and Pete Abbott engineered the concert the following year.

It was decided that the tapes were not of sufficiently high standard to release. Over twelve years later Capitol asked George Martin to use the latest technical advances to enhance the original tapes and, together with engineer Geoff Emerick, he succeeded.

The Beatles At The Hollywood Bowl was issued in Britain on EMTV 4 on 6 May 1977 and reached No. 1; Capitol issued it on SMAS 11638 on 4 May 1977 and the album reached No. 2.

The tracks were: Side One, 'Twist And Shout', 'She's A Woman', 'Dizzy Miss Lizzy', 'Ticket To Ride', 'Can't Buy Me Love', 'Things We Said Today', 'Roll Over Beethoven'. Side Two, 'Boys', 'A Hard Day's Night', 'Help!', 'All My Loving', 'She Loves You', 'Long Tall Sally'.

● Beatles Ballads – *The 20 Original Tracks*

An **EMI** compilation issued on PCS 7214 on 20 October 1980. This first Beatles album of the eighties was also the first twenty-track album of Beatles music, although ten of the tracks had already been contained on a previous compilation, *Love Songs*. The album was released without promotion or advertising and initially didn't warrant enough sales to enter the charts. Then came the tragic death of John Lennon and sales increased, with the result that it reached No. 21 in the ***New Musical Express*** charts.

The cover featured a painting by John Patrick Byrne which had previously been featured in the book *The Beatles Illustrated Lyrics*. In a style not unlike that of the French primitive painter Henri Rousseau, it depicted the Beatles in a garden surrounded by animals.

The tracks on the album were, Side One: 'Yesterday', 'Norwegian Wood (This Bird Has Flown)', 'Do You Want To Know A Secret?', 'For No One', 'Michelle', 'Nowhere Man', 'You've Got To Hide Your Love Away', 'Across The Universe', 'All My Loving', 'Hey Jude'. Side Two: 'Something', 'The Fool On The Hill', 'Till There Was You', 'The Long And Winding Road', 'Here Comes The Sun', 'Blackbird', 'And I Love Her', 'She's Leaving Home', 'Here, There And Everywhere', 'Let It Be'.

● Beatles Box, The

A boxed set of eight Beatles albums which first became available via World Records, the mail-order arm of **EMI** Records in December 1980 on SM 701–SM 708. Although packaged for the UK market only, import copies found their way to various record stores in America the following year.

The albums comprised variations of songs which were different from the original releases and each album had a completely new sleeve design by Frank Watkin. Sleeve notes were compiled by Hugh Marshall and the selection of 125 tracks in chronological order was compiled by Simon Sinclair.

The set comprised:

Album One, Side One: 'Love Me Do', 'P.S. I Love You', 'I Saw Her Standing There', 'Please Please Me', 'Misery', 'Do You Want To Know A Secret?', 'A Taste Of Honey', 'Twist And Shout'. Side Two: 'From Me To You', 'Thank You Girl', 'She Loves You', 'It Won't Be Long', 'Please Mr Postman', 'All My Loving', 'Roll Over Beethoven', 'Money (That's What I Want)'.

Album Two, Side One: 'I Want To Hold Your Hand', 'This Boy', 'Can't Buy Me Love', 'You Can't Do That', 'A Hard Day's Night', 'I Should Have Known Better', 'If I Fell', 'And I Love Her'. Side Two: 'Things We Said Today', 'I'll Be Back', 'Long Tall Sally', 'I Call Your Name', 'Matchbox', 'Slow Down', 'She's A Woman', 'I Feel Fine'.

Album Three, Side One: 'Eight Days A Week', 'No Reply', 'I'm A Loser', 'I'll Follow The Sun', 'Mr Moonlight', 'Every Little Thing', 'I Don't Want To Spoil The Party', 'Kansas City/Hey Hey Hey'. Side Two: 'Ticket To Ride', 'I'm Down', 'Help!', 'The Night Before', 'You've Got To Hide Your Love Away', 'I Need You', 'Another Girl', 'You're Going To Lose That Girl'.

Album Four, Side One: 'Yesterday', 'Act Naturally', 'Tell Me What You See', 'It's Only Love', 'You Like Me Too Much', 'I've Just Seen A Face', 'Day Tripper', 'We Can Work It Out'. Side Two: 'Michelle', 'Drive My Car', 'Norwegian Wood (This Bird Has Flown)', 'You Won't See Me', 'Nowhere Man', 'Girl', 'I'm Looking Through You', 'In My life'.

Album Five, Side One: 'Paperback Writer', 'Rain', 'Here, There And Everywhere', 'Taxman', 'I'm Only Sleeping', 'Good Day Sunshine', 'Yellow Submarine'. Side Two: 'Eleanor Rigby', 'And Your Bird Can Sing', 'For No One', 'Dr Robert', 'Got To Get You Into My Life', 'Penny Lane', 'Strawberry Fields Forever'.

Album Six, Side One: 'Sgt Pepper's Lonely Hearts Club Band', 'With A Little Help From My Friends', 'Lucy In The Sky With Diamonds', 'Fixing A Hole', 'She's Leaving Home', 'Being For The Benefit Of Mr Kite', 'A Day In The

Life'. Side Two: 'When I'm Sixty-four', 'Lovely Rita', 'All You Need Is Love', 'Baby You're A Rich Man', 'Magical Mystery Tour', 'Your Mother Should Know', 'The Fool On The Hill', 'I Am The Walrus'.

Album Seven, Side One: 'Hello Goodbye', 'Lady Madonna', 'Hey Jude', 'Revolution', 'Back In The USSR', 'Ob-La-Di Ob-La-Da', 'While My Guitar Gently Weeps'. Side Two: 'The Continuing Story of Bungalow Bill', 'Happiness Is A Warm Gun', 'Martha My Dear', 'I'm So Tired', 'Piggies', 'Don't Pass Me By', 'Julia', 'All Together Now'.

Album Eight, Side One: 'Get Back', 'Don't Let Me Down', 'The Ballad Of John And Yoko', 'Across The Universe', 'For You Blue', 'Two Of Us', 'The Long And Winding Road', 'Let It Be'. Side Two: 'Come Together', 'Something', 'Maxwell's Silver Hammer', 'Octopus's Garden', 'Here Comes The Sun', 'Because', 'Golden Slumbers', 'Golden Slumbers/Carry That Weight', 'The End', 'Her Majesty'.

● Beatles Cartoon Series, The

King Features, the major American agency for cartoon strips in newspapers and animated shorts for television, obtained the rights to make a series of cartoon films featuring the Beatles and their songs.

Al Brodax, who later became involved in the Beatles' animated feature film *Yellow Submarine*, was the executive producer of the series.

The majority of the shorts were animated abroad by Canawest of Vancouver, Canada, and the Artransa Studio in Sydney, Australia. Twenty-six were also commissioned from a British company, George Dunning's TV Cartoons Studio.

Paul Frees, an American 'voice-over' professional, who had worked on 'voices' for several Hollywood firms, was contracted to provide the voices of John Lennon and George Harrison. The English actor who dubbed the voices of Paul McCartney and Ringo Starr preferred to remain anonymous, although it was later suggested that Lance Percival provided the voice-overs. The voices were quite unlike those of the Beatles themselves and no attempt was made to mimic a 'Scouse' accent as it was considered to be too difficult for American youngsters to understand.

The basic idea of the series was that the Beatles would always be harassed by a group of fans, the novelty being that the fans could materialize in all manner of inventive disguises.

The 67-episode series was first screened on ABC TV in the US on 25 September 1965. The weekly half-hour series was screened by ABC TV each Saturday from 10.30–11.00 a.m. until 7 September 1969. It has since appeared in syndication in the latter part of the seventies. The series was shown in England on Granada Television, but not networked.

The series was stylistically typical of American children's cartoons and owed nothing to either the Beatles' real personalities or their lives, though an attempt was made to capture their visual appearance.

There were no Liverpool-based adventures – even the 'Penny Lane' episode was set in London. The group became involved in adventures with various characters, including vampires, leprechauns, mad scientists and bullfighters in locations ranging from Africa, Mexico and Hawaii to Spain, London and Hollywood. Each episode used a title from a well-known Beatles recording and they ranged from 'A Hard Day's Night' to 'You've Really Got A Hold On Me'.

● Beatles Christmas Records, The

Beatles press officer **Tony Barrow** first came up with the idea of a special Beatles recorded message for their fans in 1963. He was a bit concerned that due to the swelling membership of the official fan club, there had been inevitable delays in the processing of the large number of membership applications and Barrow considered a bonus gift would act as a sweetener. The Beatles agreed and promptly insisted that he write the script of their personal message. It was decided to issue a 33⅓ rpm flexidisc, manufactured by Lyntone Recordings.

The record was posted out with the fan club's second national newsletter, dated Christmas 1963, part of which read:

> Dear Beatle People,
>
> With this Newsletter comes your own special Christmas gift from John, Paul, George and Ringo – a copy of THE BEATLES' CHRISTMAS RECORD. This record is exclusive to our Club and will not be made available elsewhere – it has exceptional souvenir value too because only 25,000 copies of the disc have been pressed. Just enough to supply every existing Club member with a free copy in time for Christmas. We hope you enjoy it and that you'll be able to make your

non-member friends just a little bit jealous by playing it to them over the holiday!

The recording had been made at Studio Two in **Abbey Road** on 17 October, following the sessions for 'I Want To Hold Your Hand' and 'This Boy'. George Martin produced and the single-sided flexidisc lasted for five minutes and ten seconds, issued on LYN 492 on 6 December 1963.

The order of tracks was: 'Good King Wenceslas', 'John Talking', 'Paul Talking', 'Good King Wenceslas, Ringo', 'George Talking', 'Good King Wenceslas, George' and 'Rudolph The Red Nosed Ringo'.

The Christmas record proved to be such a success that it was decided to make it an annual gift to fan club members and the second disc was recorded with George Martin between 26–28 October 1964 at Studio Two in Abbey Road. Membership had now increased to a massive 65,000 and the flexidisc, called 'Another Beatles Christmas Record', was issued on LYN 757 on 18 December 1964. It was four minutes and five seconds long and comprised: 'Jingle Bells', 'Paul Talking', 'John Talking', 'George Talking', 'Ringo Talking', 'Can You Wash Your Father's Shirts?' and 'Happy Christmas'.

'The Beatles Third Christmas Record' was recorded in October 1965 at Abbey Road's Studio Two with George Martin after they'd completed some *Rubber Soul* recordings. The cover was a photograph which Roger Whitaker had taken at Granada Studios in Manchester during the filming of 'The Music Of Lennon & McCartney' special. It was issued on 17 December 1965, on LYN 948. It was six minutes and twenty-six seconds long and comprised: 'Yesterday', sung out of tune; 'All Talking'; 'Happy Christmas', John; 'Auld Lang Syne'; 'All Talking'; 'Same Old Song', John; 'All Talking'; 'Auld Lang Syne'; and 'All Talking'.

The 1966 fan club release was a more structured production because, possibly on a suggestion by Paul, it was decided to make it into a mini-pantomime and was called 'The Beatles Fourth Christmas Record – Pantomime: Everywhere It's Christmas'. George Martin produced, as usual, but this year the disc was recorded in the basement studios of **Dick James** Music at Dick James House, 71/75 New Oxford Street, London WC1, on Friday, 25 November 1966. It was also the Beatles' first double-sided Christmas record. It was issued on LYN 1145 on 16 December 1966, was six minutes and thirty-eight seconds long and comprised, A Side: 'Everywhere It's Christmas', all singing; 'Orowanyna', intro by Paul, all singing; 'A Rare Cheese', intro by Ringo; George and John; 'The Feast', all; 'The Loyal Toast', intro by George; 'Toast', Ringo. B Side: 'Podgy The Bear & Jasper', intro by Paul; 'Podgy' by John; 'Jasper' by George; 'Felpin Mansions' with John as the Count and Ringo as the Butler; 'Please Don't Bring Your Banjo Back', Paul, all singing; 'Everywhere It's Christmas', all singing.

Their next flexi, 'The Beatles Fifth Christmas Record – Christmas Time (Is Here Again)', was another pantomime. It was recorded on Tuesday, 28 November 1967 at EMI's Studio Two and was the last time George Martin presided over the recordings. It was also the last time the Beatles recorded a Christmas message together. The applause used was recorded on location in Dublin. The front cover was designed by John and Ringo and there was a back-cover painting by **Julian Lennon**. The Beatles wrote a song specially for the disc, 'Christmas Time (Is Here Again)', which was attributed to Lennon/McCartney/Harrison/Starr. The group also brought in a guest artist, Victor Spinetti. The single-sided flexidisc was issued on LYN 1369 on 15 December 1967. It was six minutes and nine seconds long and the tracks were: 'Christmas Time (Is Here Again)', intro by John, with all singing; 'The Boys Arrive At BBC House', Victor Spinetti as the BBC Wise One; 'An Audition', John; 'Tap Dancing', Ringo and Victor Spinetti; 'Are you 13 Amp', **Mal Evans**; 'Get One Of Those For Your Trousers', John; 'Sir Gerald', Paul; 'Sir Gerald', John; 'Christmas Time (Is Here Again), Onto The Next Round And Introduction', by George; 'Plenty Of Jam Jars'; 'Quiz Show', John as Quizmaster; 'Prizewinner', George; 'Get One Of Those For Your Trousers'; 'Theatre Hour', Ringo; 'Christmas Time (Is Here Again)'; 'They'd Like To Thank You . . .', George Martin and all; 'When Christmas Time Is O'er', George Martin on organ, John as Scottish Poet.

The next release, 'The Beatles Sixth Christmas Record', was recorded separately in November 1968. John and Paul were recorded at their London homes and Ringo in Surrey. George recorded his excerpt in America with Mal Evans and Tiny Tim and some of the musical links were made during rehearsals for *The Beatles* white album at George's home in Esher. Disc jockey **Kenny Everett** became involved in the recording and editing of the flexi, on which each of the four gave separate Christmas greetings. The disc was issued on LYN 1743/1744 on 20 December 1968. It was another double-sided flexi, lasting a total of seven minutes and fifty-five seconds. The track listings were: A Side: 'Ob-La-Di', Ringo; 'Happy Christmas, Happy New Year', Paul; 'Helter Skelter'; 'Yok And Jono', a poem by John; 'George from America', with Mal Evans. B Side: 'Ringo Starr'; introduction by Ringo Starr; 'Happy Christmas, Happy New Year', Paul; 'Once Upon A Pool Table', poem by John; 'George and Tiny Tim'; 'Nowhere Man', Tiny Tim; Ending.

The final release, 'The Beatles Seventh Christmas Record', was recorded separately during the autumn of 1969 with John and **Yoko** recording their pieces at Tittenhurst Park, Ringo from his home in Surrey, Paul from his Cavendish Avenue house and George at Apple in **Savile Row**.

Once again, Kenny Everett was in charge of producing the record and he receives credit under his real name of Maurice Cole.

Ringo took the photograph used on the cover of the record and the back cover sported a drawing by Ringo's son, Zak. The flexidisc was issued on LYN 1970/1 on 19 December 1969. The double-sided record lasted seven minutes and forty seconds. The track listings were, A Side: 'Happy Christmas', Ringo; 'John and Yoko Talking'; 'Wonderful Christmas', George; 'Ringo Talking'; 'John and Yoko Talking'; 'This Is To Wish You All A Merry, Merry Christmas', Paul; 'Paul Talking'; 'This Is To Wish You A Merry, Merry Christmas', reprise. B Side: 'John and Yoko Talking'; 'Happy Christmas', John and Yoko; 'Happy Christmas'/'Magic Christian', Ringo; 'Ringo Talking'; 'John and Yoko Talking'.

As there was no specially recorded Christmas disc the following year, the fan club decided to issue a twelve-inch album containing all seven previous Christmas messages. This was issued on Apple LYN 2154 on 18 December 1970 under the title *From Then To You – The Beatles Christmas Record 1970*.

The album was also issued in America. As the flexidiscs hadn't been previously released there, the American album was issued with a different sleeve than the British one, which had pictures of all the previous covers of the Christmas flexis. The album was issued in America on Apple SBC 100 on 18 December 1970, and was simply called *The Beatles Christmas Album*.

● Beatles Collection, The

To capitalize on the Christmas market, **EMI** decided to issue a special de luxe limited edition boxed set of Beatles albums. The package was called *The Beatles Collection* and it was issued on Parlophone/Apple BC 13 on 2 December 1978.

A set of twelve British Beatles albums, previously released between the years 1962 and 1970 was issued in a dark blue box which had the title and individual signatures of the Beatles printed in gold on the front. The package also contained a bonus album called *Rarities*, which had seventeen tracks considered 'rare', which were a combination of 'B' sides of records, foreign releases and EP tracks. It was announced that the *Rarities* album would

(Picture Music International)

only be available with the boxed set and would not be issued separately – however, this was not to be the case.

The albums contained in the boxed set were: *Please Please Me*, *With The Beatles*, *A Hard Day's Night*, *Beatles For Sale*, *Help!*, *Rubber Soul*, *Sgt Pepper's Lonely Hearts Club Band*, *The Beatles*, *Yellow Submarine*, *Abbey Road*, *Let It Be* and *Rarities*. This was not actually a 'complete' collection of all recordings between 1962–1970 as a number of albums such as *A Collection of Beatles Oldies (But Goldies)*, *Magical Mystery Tour*, *Hey Jude* and *The Beatles At the Hollywood Bowl* were excluded.

The Beatles Collection was also issued in America on **Capitol** BC 14 on 1 December 1978. The American set, however, was to become much more of a collector's item because Capitol only produced 3,000 sets – and they were all numbered. It was said that 3,050 sets had actually been pressed with the first 50 sets going to Capitol executives and prominent record industry figures. The American *Rarities* album was also slightly different from the British one. With the catalogue number Capitol SPRO 8969, *Rarities* substituted the English versions of 'She Loves You' and 'I Want To Hold Your Hand' for the German language versions which were on the British release. The set was of obvious interest to American collectors as it comprised the original British versions of the albums, which differed from the individual Capitol album releases which generally included fewer tracks.

● Beatles Come To Town, The

An eight-minute film of the Beatles, screened in British cinemas during the week commencing 22 December 1963 as an item of Pathe News.

This was a weekly cinema newsreel which ran for decades, but finally succumbed to the competition from television news in the mid-sixties.

The news team filmed the Beatles performing three numbers at the **Apollo Theatre, Ardwick**, Manchester on 20 November 1963. The newsreel showed them performing two of the numbers, 'She Loves You' and 'Twist And Shout', amid much audience hysteria.

Pathe shot the film in both black and white and colour and the performance was also used in the film ***Pop Gear*** in 1965.

● Beatles EPs Collection, The

After **EMI** had released collections of Beatles singles and albums, they decided to release the EP collection, presented in a matching box to that of *The Beatles Collection* of albums, with the title and Beatles' autographs in gold on the cover of the box.

The collection comprised the original twelve British Beatles EPs, together with the *Magical Mystery Tour* double EP and a special bonus EP of four songs, previously unavailable in stereo.

This bonus EP was simply called *The Beatles* and it featured the same picture sleeve as that used on the cover of the 'Penny Lane' single, issued in 1967. The tracks were: 'The Inner Light', 'Baby You're A Rich Man', 'She's A Woman' and 'This Boy'.

The Beatles EPs Collection was issued on Parlophone BEP 14 on 7 December 1971, once again aimed at the Christmas market and comprised: *The Beatles' Hits*, *Twist And Shout*, *The Beatles No. 1*, *All My Loving*, *Long Tall Sally*, *Extracts From The Film A Hard Day's Night*, *Extracts From The Album A Hard Day's Night*, *Beatles For Sale*, *Beatles For Sale No. 2*, *The Beatles' Million Sellers*, *Yesterday*, *Nowhere Man*, *Magical Mystery Tour* and *The Beatles*.

● Beatles For Sale (EP)

An EP with the same title as that of their most recent album release. Three of the four titles had once been considered as possible singles. The EP was issued on Parlophone GEP 8931 on 6 April 1965 and contained the tracks: 'No Reply', 'I'm A Loser', 'Rock And Roll Music' and 'Eight Days A Week'. The cover of the EP was the same **Bob Freeman** shot used on the cover of the album.

● Beatles For Sale (No. 2)

The second collection of tracks from the *Beatles For Sale* album to be issued on an EP in Britain. This was the Beatles' ninth EP release in the UK and was issued on Parlophone GEP 8938 on 4 June 1965. The tracks were: 'I'll Follow The Sun', 'Baby's In Black', 'Words Of Love' and 'I Don't Want To Spoil The Party'.

● Beatles' Hits, The

The second Beatles EP to be issued by Parlophone. *The Beatles' Hits* featured a front cover photograph by **Angus McBean** and, as with the first EP, sleeve notes by Beatles Press Officer **Tony Barrow**. It was issued on Parlophone GEP 8882 on 6 September 1963 and reached the position of No. 17 in the British charts. The tracks were the first three Beatles singles, together with one former 'B' side. They were: 'From Me To You', 'Thank You Girl', 'Please Please Me' and 'Love Me Do'.

● Beatles Invite You To Take A Ticket To Ride, The

A Bank Holiday radio special which took place on Monday, 7 June 1965, between 10.00 a.m. and 12.00 noon. Produced by Keith Bateson and presented by Denny Piercey, it had been recorded on 26 May at the Piccadilly Theatre studios in London.

All previous Bank Holiday specials had been called

'From Us To You', but this title had been dropped. The BBC radio programme was the very last appearance by the Beatles in which they performed songs on the radio. Times were changing with the appearance of the pirate ship Radio Caroline, to be followed by other ships such as Radio London which brought competition. The system of groups performing live or recording specially for radio had arisen because of restrictions on the number of records which could be played. A wind of change was blowing through the world of British radio which was to provide a wider range and much wider choice for listeners.

On this, their final BBC radio recording, they performed 'Everybody's Trying To Be My Baby', 'I'm A Loser', 'Honey Don't', 'She's A Woman', 'Ticket To Ride', 'The Night Before' and 'Dizzy Miss Lizzy'. Their special guests were the **Hollies** and the Ivy League. The Ivy League comprised John Carter on vocals and bass guitar, Ken Lewis on vocals and keyboards and Perry Ford on vocals, keyboards and alto. Under their previous name of Carter-Lewis & the Southerners, they had been special guests on two of the **'Pop Go The Beatles'** programmes.

● Beatles Live! The, *At The Star Club In Hamburg, Germany, 1962*

When **Adrian Barber** left the Big Three to become stage manager of the **Star Club** in Hamburg, he developed a completely new sound system for the club. Initially, testing the sound, he decided to record the various bands who performed there. Adrian used a tape recorder and strapped a mike to the centre mike stand on stage – there were three stage mikes at the time.

Over a period of time he recorded numerous bands and some of the recordings, including ones of **Jerry Lee Lewis** and **Cliff Bennett & the Rebel Rousers**, were released in Hamburg on the Hanseatic label.

In December 1962 he recorded the Beatles. One of the Liverpool bands appearing at the club at the time were **Kingsize Taylor** & the Dominoes and leader Ted Taylor asked Adrian if he could have the tapes. Adrian gave them to him and they were forgotten about for ten years, until there was a Mersey Beat revival show in Liverpool promoted by **Allan Williams** and Ted Taylor was on the bill. He mentioned the tapes to Williams, who eagerly told him they could make a fortune from them. Taylor remembered he'd given them to a local recording engineeer years previously and they set off to find him. Fortunately, they were able to obtain the tapes.

Williams contacted Bill Harry in London and asked him if he could sell them to a record company. Harry took a number of record executives on trips to Taylor's butcher shop in Southport, but they weren't enthusiastic. One main problem was that 'bootleg' records were now outlawed in Britain by an act of Parliament and since **EMI** had signed the group at the time of the recordings, the tapes would be illegal. Williams insisted that the recordings had taken place before they'd signed with EMI, but Harry pointed out to him that Ringo was on drums and therefore the tapes were recorded in December 1962 when the EMI contract had been in force for months. Williams suggested that they concoct a story that it was an earlier gig when **Pete Best** was a member, that at the time of the recordings he was ill and replaced by Ringo. Harry rejected this suggestion.

Most record companies were concerned about the legal can of worms which could be opened by such a release. However, one entrepreneur introduced to Williams by Harry did arrange a deal with a major record company who were willing to spend a great deal of money enhancing the quality of the tapes and were prepared to advertise the album on television. Their lawyers had concluded that they might be able to fight off an injunction by a defence based on the recordings being of historical interest. This deal would probably have made Williams and Taylor wealthy men.

They suddenly announced they'd done a deal with **Paul Murphy** of Buk Records. Murphy was a former singer from Liverpool who had worked as a recording manager for Polydor in Hamburg. The tapes were cleaned and enhanced and initially issued in Germany on the Bellaphon label on 8 April 1977 as a double album. The Beatles' lawyers attempted to prevent the release in Britain, but the judge concluded that they were of historic interest – the lawyers did not point out to him that the recent law in Parliament relating to bootlegs made release of the record illegal. These recordings have been released throughout the world on a number of occasions and a great deal of money has been made – but certainly not by Williams and Taylor. Adrian Barber, who made the original recordings in the first place, has never received a cent.

The British release on Lingasong LNL 1 on 25 May 1977 reached No. 27 in the ***New Musical Express*** album chart. It was issued in America on

Atlantic/Lingasong LS-2-7001 on 13 June 1977. It reached No. 111 in *Billboard*, No. 183 in *Cash Box* and No. 165 in *Record World*. It has since been issued on a variety of different labels every few years.

The tracks on the album are: 'I Saw Her Standing There', 'Roll Over Beethoven', 'Hippy Hippy Shake', 'Sweet Little Sixteen', 'Lend Me Your Comb', 'Your Feet's Too Big', 'Twist And Shout', 'Mr Moonlight', 'A Taste Of Honey', 'Besame Mucho', 'Reminiscing', 'Kansas City/Hey Hey Hey', 'Nothin' Shakin' (But The Leaves On The Trees)', 'To Know Her Is To Love Her', 'Little Queenie', 'Falling In Love Again', 'Ask Me Why', 'Be-Bop-A-Lula', 'Hallelujah, I Love Her So', 'Red Sails In The Sunset', 'Everybody's Trying To Be My Baby', 'Matchbox', 'I'm Talking About You', 'Shimmy Shimmy', 'Long Tall Sally' and 'I Remember You'.

The original tapes and the albums included dialogue between the numbers when the Beatles made announcements and the audience responded. When Paul announced 'a request for the Scottish lady', he was referring to Scots singer Isabelle Bond, who was appearing at the **Top Ten Club** at the time and whose favourite number performed by the Beatles was 'A Taste Of Honey'. **Horst Fascher** can also be heard making an introduction and the mention of Bettina refers to Bettina Derlin, the 23-stone Star Club bierfrau who was one of Lennon's many German girlfriends.

● Beatles' Million Sellers, The

At the time of the Beatles' tenth British EP release, the group had achieved a total of five million-selling singles and **EMI** decided to include four of them on this EP and issue it in time to capitalize on the Christmas market.

It was issued on Parlophone GEP 8946 on 6 December 1965 and the tracks were: 'She Loves You', 'I Want To Hold Your Hand', 'Can't Buy Me Love' and 'I Feel Fine'.

● Beatles' Movie Medley, The

In 1981 a medley of Beatles songs by a number of session musicians from Holland was issued as a single called 'Stars On 45'. It topped the American charts and reached No. 2 in the British charts in 1981.

As a result, **Capitol Records** in the US decided to issue something similar – a medley of songs by the Beatles themselves. John Palladino edited together seven tracks and segued them together, using extracts from 'Magical Mystery Tour', 'All You Need Is Love', 'You've Got To Hide Your Love Away', 'I Should Have Known Better', 'A Hard Day's Night', 'Ticket To Ride' and 'Get Back'. Consideration was given to including a 'B' side which would feature a Beatles interview called 'Fab Four On Film' which had been recorded during the filming of *A Hard Day's Night*. This was dropped in favour of the track 'I'm Happy Just To Dance With You'.

The single was issued in America on Capitol B-5107 on 15 March 1982, but didn't fare as well as the Dutch medley and only reached No. 12 in the *Billboard* charts. **EMI Records** in Britain did not want to issue the single, but due to demand and the fact that imports of the American single began to trickle over, they issued it two months later on Parlophone R6055 on 24 May 1982 and the record reached the position of No. 10 in the charts.

In some way, the medley single acted as a promotional booster to *Reel Music*, an album of Beatles film tracks, issued the week following the single's release in America.

● Beatles 1962–1966, The

The release of a four-album bootleg Beatles set in America called *The Beatles Alpha Omega* is said to have inspired **EMI** to release two double albums of Beatles material, *The Beatles 1962–1966* and *The Beatles 1967–1970*.

The two double albums were issued on the same day in America, 2 April 1973, and in Britain on 19 April 1973. The British album was released on Parlophone PCSP 717 and reached No. 1 in the charts. The American album was released on **Capitol** SKBO 3403 and reached No. 3 in the charts.

In both countries the covers were the same. The front cover sported a photograph of the Beatles on the **EMI House** stairwell, taken at the *Please Please Me* photo session, and the reverse featured a photograph taken in the same place and position a few years later.

The tracks on the album are, Record One/Side One: 'Love Me Do', 'Please Please Me', 'From Me To You', 'She Loves You', 'I Want To Hold Your Hand', 'All My Loving', 'Can't Buy Me Love'. Record One/Side Two: 'A Hard Day's Night', 'And I Love Her', 'Eight Days A Week', 'I Feel Fine', 'Ticket To Ride', 'Yesterday'. Record Two/Side One: 'Help!', 'You've Got To Hide Your Love Away', 'We Can Work It Out', 'Day Tripper', 'Drive My Car', 'Norwegian Wood (This Bird Has Flown)'. Record Two/Side Two: 'Nowhere Man', 'Michelle', 'In My Life',

'Girl', 'Paperback Writer', 'Eleanor Rigby', 'Yellow Submarine'.

● Beatles *1967–1970*, The

A double album issued in Britain on Parlophone PCSP 718 on 19 April 1973 where it reached No. 1 in the charts for one week. It was issued in America on **Capitol** SKBO 3404 on 2 April 1973 where it was No. 1 for one week.

The sleeves on the British and American releases were identical: a photograph of the Beatles looking down from a stairwell at **EMI House** in a similar style to the shot on the cover of the *Please Please Me* album, but taken a few years later.

The album was issued simultaneously with *The Beatles 1962–1966* and the cover of that double album is featured on the reverse side of this.

The tracks on the album are, Record One/Side One: 'Strawberry Fields Forever', 'Sgt Pepper's Lonely Hearts Club Band', 'With A Little Help From My Friends', 'Lucy In The Sky With Diamonds', 'A Day In The Life', 'All You Need Is Love'. Record One/Side Two: 'I Am The Walrus', 'Hello Goodbye', 'The Fool On The Hill', 'Magical Mystery Tour', 'Lady Madonna', 'Hey Jude', 'Revolution'. Record Two/Side One: 'Back In The USSR', 'While My Guitar Gently Weeps', 'Ob-La-Di Ob-La-Da', 'Get Back', 'Don't Let Me Down', 'The Ballad Of John And Yoko', 'Old Brown Shoe'. Record Two/Side Two: 'Here Comes The Sun', 'Come Together', 'Something', 'Octopus's Garden', 'Let It Be', 'Across The Universe', 'The Long And Winding Road'.

● Beatles *'65*

An American album issued on **Capitol** ST 2228 on 15 December 1964.

It is the US version of the *Beatles For Sale* album and includes eight of the tracks from the British LP, plus 'I'll Be Back', a track from the British album *A Hard Day's Night*, and two tracks from a single release, 'I Feel Fine' and 'She's A Woman'.

Beatles '65 sold over three million copies within six weeks and was the fastest-selling American album of the year, rushing into the No. 1 spot less than ten days after its release.

The tracks on the album are, Side One: 'No Reply', 'I'm A Loser', 'Baby's In Black', 'Rock And Roll Music', 'I'll Follow The Sun', 'Mr Moonlight'. Side Two: 'Honey Don't', 'I'll Be Back', 'She's A Woman', 'I Feel Fine', 'Everybody's Trying To Be My Baby'.

● Beatles (No. *1*), The

The third Beatles EP which only reached the No. 24 position in the charts, although it entered the charts on four different occasions.

The EP was issued on Parlophone GEP 8883 on 1 November 1963 and contained four tracks from the *Please Please Me* album, which was still No. 1 in the charts. The EP cover was the **EMI** stairwell shot by **Angus McBean** and sleeve notes were by **Tony Barrow**. The tracks were: 'I Saw Her Standing There', 'Misery', 'Anna (Go To Him)' and 'Chains'.

● Beatles Official Fan Club

The first Beatles fan club was formed by a Liverpool fan, **Bernard Boyle**, in September 1961 prior to Brian Epstein managing the group and several months before an official fan club was sanctioned.

Bernard was president, Jennifer Dawes treasurer and Maureen O'Shea secretary.

In 1962 the first official club was run by Roberta **'Bobbie' Brown** from her house in Buchanan Road, Wallasey. Shortly after forming the club she was aided by a friend, **Freda Kelly**, and when she became engaged to be married the club was placed in Freda's capable hands. By that time she was working at **NEMS** and funds were provided by Brian Epstein on behalf of the Beatles.

It was Beatles' press agent **Tony Barrow** who, in June 1963, proposed that the club should have a National Secretary and be run from London. The official club was now run from 13 Monmouth Street, London, while Freda continued as its Northern Secretary, operating from Liverpool.

Barrow created a fictitious name for the head of the London office, **Anne Collingham**. Due to the vast amount of mail which had to be dealt with, several full-time workers were employed: Michael Crowther-Smith, Tony Catchpole, Yvonne Sainsbury, Monica Stringer and Mary Cockram.

Sean O'Mahony agreed to an official fan club section each month in the *Beatles Book* and NEMS employees Maureen Payne and Valerie Sumpter posed for the photographs which 'identified' them as Bettina Rose and Anne Collingham.

The fan club thrived with 80,000 paid-up members in 965, one of the largest fan clubs ever. Despite ubscriptions, it was not a profitable venture and had to be ubsidized throughout its existence.

Apart from the membership cards, newsletters and pecial offers, members of the club were given a unique reat – a series of special Beatles Christmas records, nade specially for the club. This was an idea originated y Tony Barrow, which the Beatles were enthusiastic bout.

In October 1966 Freda was appointed Joint National ecretary and later the London office was closed and reda was running the entire operation again from iverpool, which she continued to do until the club was fficially closed in March 1972.

Beatles Second Album, The

With a montage of photographs on the cover and the ubtitle *Electrifying big-beat performances by England's aul McCartney, John Lennon, George Harrison and Ringo tarr*, **Capitol Records**' second Beatles album was issued n Capitol ST 2080 on 10 April 1964.

The album contained the five tracks from the British *Vith The Beatles* album which weren't included on *Meet he Beatles*, together with four tracks from singles already eleased in America and two previously unreleased tracks rom *Long Tall Sally*, the British EP.

The album became Capitol Records' fastest-selling lbum ever, up to that date, with over 250,000 copies sold n the first day of release. It swiftly reached No. 1 in the harts and sold over a million copies.

The tracks were, Side One: 'Long Tall Sally', 'I Call 'our Name', 'Please Mr Postman', 'I'll Get You', 'She oves You'. Side Two: 'Roll Over Beethoven', 'Thank You Girl', 'You Really Got A Hold On Me', 'Devil In Her leart', 'Money (That's What I Want)', 'You Can't Do 'hat'.

On 2 May 1964 *The Beatles Second Album* was No. 1 in he charts, followed by *Meet The Beatles* at No. 2 and *ntroducing The Beatles* at No. 4.

Beatles Sing For Shell, The

film of the Beatles' performance at the opening night of heir concerts at the **Festival Hall, Melbourne** on Monday, 15 June 1964.

The concerts were filmed by the Nine Television network and edited into a film called ***The Beatles Sing For Shell***, which was televised throughout Australia.

● Beatles VI

Issued on Capitol ST 2358 on 14 June 1965, *Beatles VI* contained the six tracks from *Beatles For Sale* which weren't used on the *Beatles '65* album, together with three tracks from the forthcoming British album *Help!* and two further tracks.

The tracks were, Side One: 'Kansas City' 'Hey! Hey! Hey!', 'Eight Days A Week', 'You Like Me Too Much', 'Bad Boy', 'I Don't Want To Spoil The Party', 'Words Of Love'. Side Two, 'What You're Doing', 'Yes It Is', 'Dizzy Miss Lizzy', 'Tell Me What You See', 'Every Little Thing'.

The album topped the charts in *Billboard*, *Cash Box* and *Record World*.

● Beatles Story, The

A double-album issued in America on **Capitol** STBO 2222 on 23 November 1964 to celebrate the first anniversary of the label issuing 'I Want To Hold Your Hand'.

The album included a medley of Beatles numbers, a brief excerpt from a concert and various interviews in what was a musical biography of the group's career. It sold a million copies and reached No. 7 in the American charts. Written and narrated by John Babcock, Al Wiman and Roger Christian, the album contained interviews with all the Beatles, plus Brian Epstein and George Martin.

The tracks were, Side One: 'On Stage With The Beatles', 'How Beatlemania Began', 'Beatlemania In Action', 'Man Behind The Beatles – Brian Epstein' and 'John Lennon – Who's A Millionaire?' Side Two: 'Beatles Will Be Beatles', 'Man Behind Their Music – George Martin' and 'George Harrison'. Side Three: 'A Hard Day's Night – Their First Movie', 'Paul McCartney' and 'Sneaky Haircuts And More About Paul'. Side Four: A live performance of 'Twist And Shout' from the 23 August 1964 performance at the Hollywood Bowl, 'The Beatles Look At Life', 'A Beatles Medley', 'Things We Said Today', 'I'm Happy Just To Dance with You', 'Little Child', 'Long Tall Sally', 'She Loves You', 'Ringo Starr' and 'Liverpool And All The World'.

● Beatles Today, The

An hour-long BBC Radio One special, transmitted on 30 March 1970, which included music from the ***Get Back*** (before the name was changed to *Let It Be*) album sessions. George Harrison was interviewed for the programme on 11 March.

● Beatles Vs The Four Seasons, The

After **Capitol Records** had secured the rights to issue all further Beatles product in America, **Vee Jay Records** continued to exploit the limited material they had, using various repackaging ideas. One of these was a two-album set *The Beatles vs The Four Seasons*, containing all the tracks Vee Jay had previously issued on the *Introducing The Beatles* album, together with a set of twelve numbers from a Four Seasons album. Despite its subtitle *The International Battle Of The Century*, the album failed to register in either the *Cash Box* or *Record World* charts and only reached No. 142 in *Billboard* after it was issued on Vee Jay DX-30 on 1 October 1964.

The album came with: 'Scorecards, biographies, pictures, stories of all the contestants plus: free bonus 8" x 15" full colour Beatles picture suitable for framing'.

The Beatles tracks were: 'I Saw Her Standing There' 'Misery', 'Anna', 'Chains', 'Boys', 'Ask Me Why', 'Please Please Me', 'Baby It's You', 'Do You Want To Know A Secret?', 'A Taste Of Honey', 'There's A Place' and 'Twist And Shout'.

The Four Seasons numbers were: 'Sherry', 'I've Cried Before', 'Marlena', 'Soon', 'Ain't That A Shame', 'Walk Like A Man', 'Connie-O', 'Big Girls Don't Cry', 'Sta Maker', 'Candy Girl', 'Silver Wings' and 'Peanuts'.

The Four Seasons comprised Frankie Valli (vocals), Gerry Polci (vocals/drums), Don Ciccone (bass), Lee Shapiro (keyboards) and John Paiva (guitar).

This basic idea was heavily exploited by a series of bootleg albums in the States, several of them lampooning *The Beatles vs The Four Seasons* album cover. Among the numerous bootleg LPs in this vein were *Beatles vs Chuck Berry*, *Beatles vs Don Ho*, *Beatles vs Buddy Holly And The Isley Brothers*, *Beatles vs Little Richard And Larry Williams* and *Beatles vs Carl Perkins*.

Paul, Ringo and George horse around with Faron of Faron's Flamingos. (Cavern Mecca)

Beatle Talk: Red Robinson Interviews The Beatles

nterview album, issued in America by Great Northwest Music Co. on GWC 4007 on 15 November 1978.

The album contained excerpts from interviews with the eatles taken at press conferences in Vancouver, Canada, 1 1964 and Seattle in 1966, and ran for approximately wenty minutes, with narration from disc jockey Red obinson. It failed to make the charts.

With a different cover and title, it was issued in Britain s *The Beatle Interviews* on Everest Records CBR 1008 on 5 June 1982, with the adddition of further material ncluding John Lennon's comments about 'the Beatles are igger than Jesus' remarks.

Beatmakers, The

he Beatles and **Gerry & the Pacemakers** combined to rm the Beatmakers who made a single appearance as a roup at **Litherland Town Hall** on 19 October 1961.

Gerry Marsden wore George Harrison's leather outfit nd George, who played lead, wore a hood. Paul played ass and wore a nightie and Freddie Marsden and **Pete est** played one drum each. It was so much fun that Karl erry, leader of Karl Terry & the Cruisers, who were on e bill that night, joined them on stage to sing.

The numbers performed by the Beatmakers that vening were 'Whole Lotta Shakin' ', 'What'd I Say?', 'Red ails' and 'Hit The Road, Jack'.

Beat Show, The

BBC radio programme, broadcast from Manchester. The ow was presented by Gay Byrne, produced by Geoff awrence and featured the Northern Dance Orchestra. 'he Beat Show' was broadcast from 1.00 to 1.30 p.m. ach Thursday and the Beatles made a single appearance n 4 July 1963 when they performed 'From Me To You', 'A aste Of Honey' and 'Twist And Shout'.

Beautiful Dreamer

song originally written by Stephen Foster at the end of e last century, but very popular in this one. A number hich had been recorded over the years by many major rtists, including Al Jolson and Bing Crosby. Slim 'hitman recorded a popular version in 1954 and at the eginning of the sixties several Liverpool bands began to erform it at gigs, including the **Searchers**, **Rory Storm & the Hurricanes** and **Billy J. Kramer**. The Beatles included it in their repertoire in 1962 and performed it on BBC radio's **'Saturday Club'** on 26 January 1963.

● Be-Bop-A-Lula

A rock classic which provided **Gene Vincent** with his first million-seller in 1956. Penned by Vincent and Tex Davis, Vincent and the Blue Caps performed it in the film *The Girl Can't Help It.* The film influenced the **Quarry Men** who included the number in their repertoire. The group still performed the song, with John as lead vocalist, when they became the Beatles and it was one of the numbers they performed at Hamburg's **Star Club** and is subsequently to be found on the Star Club album releases.

● Because

John Lennon composition featured on the *Abbey Road* album. John was writing a number about himself and **Yoko** one day when he heard Yoko at the piano playing some Beethoven chords. It was the 'Moonlight Sonata' (Beethoven's piano sonata in C sharp minor, opus 27 No. 2). John was inspired to reverse the chords and then wrote 'Because' around them. John, Paul and George are featured on the track performing three-part vocal harmony.

● Beecher-Stevens, Sydney A.

In 1961 when he was marketing manager at **Decca Records**, he received a call from **Tony Barrow** who informed him that an influential record retailer, Brian Epstein, was seeking a record company for his group. Epstein talked to Beecher-Stevens and a meeting was arranged, supposedly to discuss retail percentages. When Beecher-Stevens and his assistant Colin Borland invited Epstein up for lunch in the executive club at Decca's embankment offices, the topic soon turned to the Beatles. Brian showed them a copy of ***Mersey Beat*** in which the group were prominently featured and later they listened to 'My Bonnie'. Beecher-Stevens contacted **Dick Rowe** who arranged for his assistant Mike Smith to see the group in Liverpool.

Beecher-Stevens and Dick Rowe met Epstein for lunch in the executive club once again on 6 February 1962, but this time to say that Decca was not interested in his band.

Beecher-Stevens died at his home in Hove, Sussex, in 1987 at the age of 79.

● Begin The Beguine

Famous Cole Porter composition. The Beatles introduced the number into their repertoire for a short time during 1960.

● Being For The Benefit Of Mr Kite

A John Lennon composition from the *Sgt Pepper* album. John was to comment, 'It was from this old poster I'd bought at an antique shop. We'd been down to Surrey, or somewhere, filming a TV piece to go with "Strawberry Fields Forever". There was a break and I went into this shop and bought an old poster advertising a variety show which starred Mister Kite. It said the Hendersons would also be there, late of Pablois Fanques Fair. There were hoops and horses and someone going through a hogshead of real fire. Then there was Henry the Horse. The band would start at ten to six. All at Bishopsgate.

'I hardly made up a word, just connecting lines together word for word really. I wasn't very proud of that. There was no real work. I was just going through the motions because we needed a new song for *Sgt Pepper* at that time.'

The antique shop where John purchased the poster on 31 January 1967 was actually located in Sevenoaks, Kent, and it referred to a fair which took place near Rochdale in Lancashire in February 1843.

In 1980, John was to add: 'The whole song is from a Victorian poster which I bought in a junk shop. It is so cosmically beautiful. It's a poster for a fair that must have happened in the 1880s. Everything in the song is from that poster, except the horse wasn't called Henry.'

The sound effects on the record were quite elaborate. John had told George Martin that he wanted to capture the genuine sensation of a circus and Martin suggested that they use a calliope, an instrument of steam whistles played through a keyboard. They weren't able to hire such an instrument but Martin managed to obtain a tape of a calliope playing Sousa marches. The tape was cut up into pieces and thrown into the air, so that the pieces could all be mixed up and reassembled. More effects were included on overdubs with Ringo, George, **Mal Evans** and **Neil Aspinall** playing harmonicas, George Martin playing Wurlitzer organ and John playing Hammond organ.

● 2850 Benedict Canyon, *Bel Air, California*

The Beatles rented a house at this address for nine days in August 1965 when they were on the West Coast. Rented on Monday, 23 August, it had a mountainside view and swimming pool. While they relaxed at the house they had several visitors. On Tuesday 24 August, **Eleanor Bron** was one of the first of their guests and sat talking to John by the swimming pool. Other visitors included Joan Baez, members of the **Byrds** and Maureen Payne, a former **NEMS Enterprises** receptionist who was now living in LA.

The house was guarded by a dozen policemen and members of the Burns Agency, and was protected by a five-bar wooden gate. On Wednesday, 25 August, a group of four fans, Paula, Mikki, Sue and Kay hired a single-seater helicopter and each of them in turn flew over the house to wave at the Beatles.

The Beatles' presence in the area was well publicized and local radio stations broadcast the address. There were lots of sightseers and fans gathering on hillsides with binoculars.

It was during this sojourn that they were hosted to a **Capitol Records** party on Tuesday, 24 August, whose guests included Julie Andrews, Gene Barry, Tony Bennett, Jack Benny, Richard Chamberlain, Eddie Fisher, Jane Fonda, Rock Hudson, Gene Kelly, Henry Mancini, Groucho Marx, Steve McQueen, **Hayley** and Juliet Mills, Edward G. Robinson, James Stewart and Dick Van Dyke. On Friday, 27 August they visited **Elvis Presley**. George and Paul also dropped into the recording studios to see the Byrds, who were recording 'The Times They Are A-Changing'.

During their stay the temperature soared over 90 degrees and they made full use of the pool.

On Monday, 30 August, the group held a farewell party at the poolside for the media.

● Bennett, Kim

A publisher at Ardmore and Beechwood, **EMI**'s publishing arm.

Bennett was assistant to **Sid Coleman** who was enthusiastic about the Beatles and wanted to publish their material at a time when no one else in the industry was interested. Even the individual pop labels of EMI had turned Epstein down. After Coleman had arranged the meeting between Epstein and George Martin, his company was to promote the Beatles' first release, 'Love Me Do'.

With the amount of new records released each week, the number of established artists with new products and e rigid attitudes of people in the industry, the promotion f this unusual record by an unknown northern group was ot an easy task. Yet Kim Bennett was enthusiastic and egan approaching the various disc jockeys. He didn't ave much success. Jack Jackson, a prominent disc ockey, was to say, 'I've seen pictures of them [the Beatles] nd my first reaction was that there was something wrong ith my eyesight.' This was a typical attitude.

Bennett managed to get 'Love Me Do' its first BBC adio play on 'Twelve O'Clock Spin'. The man who gave e record its first BBC plug was an ex-**Radio uxembourg** disc jockey, Ted King, who commented on is meeting with Bennett: 'We met one lunchtime in a Tin an Alley pub. I knew a little about the Beatles, of course, ut wasn't mad about the disc. But Kim was so nthusiastic over it all that I decided if you can't beat 'em, en you have to join 'em. And I must say now that I'm ighty glad I did so.'

Bennett, Peter

n independent American record promotions man, hired by e Beatles to promote **Apple Records** in the States from 967. This included promotion of the Beatles' records, cluding a number of their solo releases and discs by **ames Taylor**, **Mary Hopkin** and **Billy Preston**.

Bennett worked hard on promoting all the discs, cluding ones he was unhappy about, such as John and oko's 'Woman Is The Nigger Of The World'. He set up a levision coup by arranging for John and **Yoko** to co-host e 'Mike Douglas Show' on TV for a week and he also ok George Harrison backstage at Madison Square arden to meet **Elvis Presley** and renew their quaintanceship. He was with John during his 'long eekend' in Los Angeles, following the break-up with oko. Bennett, who also worked for **Allen Klein**, became government witness against Klein in a tax-evasion trial 1978.

Bernstein, Sid

1963 Sid Bernstein, a former student at Columbia niversity and an ex-ballroom manager who had also ted as an independent promoter/agent, was 38 years old d earning $200 a week working for General Artists orporation (GAC), the largest theatrical agency in merica.

During the evenings, Sid was taking a night-school course under Dr Max Lerner at the New School for Social Research in New York. He'd begun the course in 1962 and in October of that year, as part of the course, he was required to read English newspapers each week. By the time his course had finished in February 1963 he had noted the rise of an obscure group from Liverpool who had begun to dominate the British press with headlines of **'Beatlemania'**.

He had a hunch that the Beatles were unique, but couldn't convince anyone at GAC, so he decided to strike out on his own.

He sought out and found Brian Epstein's phone number in Liverpool and called him in February 1963. Sid had decided on promoting them independently in New York and suggested to Epstein that he would like to book them to appear at **Carnegie Hall**. Epstein was impressed with the idea of such a prestigious venue, but was still cautious. Bernstein was thinking of a booking in four months' time, but Epstein pointed out that they didn't have an American audience and there was no airplay in the States and so such a concert would be premature.

Sid asked Brian how much the Beatles were being paid for an appearance. It was the equivalent of $2,000 a night. Bernstein offered him $6,500 for two concerts on the one day at Carnegie Hall. He suggested that the appearance should take place the following year on Lincoln's Birthday, 12 February 1964. Epstein agreed on the condition that the deal would become null and void if the Beatles didn't have a hit in the American charts by the end of 1963.

Fortunately for Bernstein, his gamble paid off when it was announced that **Ed Sullivan** had booked them for his TV show shortly prior to the Carnegie Hall appearance.

Booking the Beatles for Carnegie Hall was no simple matter. No pop group had ever appeared at the world-famous concert hall and Bernstein knew he'd be turned down if it was discovered exactly who the Beatles were. When he phoned to make the booking, a Polish lady asked him who the Beatles were. He told her they were a phenomenon. 'Oh, that's all right, then,' she said. Bernstein, who came from the East Bronx and only had a low income, had to borrow the $500 required for the deposit. He'd taken a gamble on his hunch because he had booked them without ever hearing one of their records and he had no idea what they sounded like.

The shows at Carnegie Hall were presented at 2.30 and 7.30 p.m. on Wednesday, 12 February 1964, and there were 20,000 people milling about outside, trying to get a glimpse of the 'phenomenon'. All 2,870 seats at each show had been sold out in advance and Bernstein had to obtain permission to place 150 chairs on the stage.

After the second show, Bernstein walked with Epstein across to the 17,000-seater Madison Square Garden and told him that the huge venue wanted to present the Beatles and he could have the tickets printed up and on sale within 24 hours. He offered Epstein $25,000 for the booking and said he would also pay an additional $5,000 to the British Cancer Fund. Brian pondered for a moment, then said, 'Sid, let's save it for the next time.'

As it turned out, 'the next time' became an even bigger event – the largest-ever live entertainment presentation up to that time. The box office manager of Carnegie Hall told Sid that they could have sold 250,000 tickets if they had had them – Bernstein then lost interest in Madison Square Garden and began to think in terms of the biggest venue in New York – **Shea Stadium**, the 55,600-seater baseball park.

He phoned Brian Epstein with the proposal. Epstein demurred. Bernstein told him that he was so convinced it would be a success that he'd pay Brian for every empty seat. 'Let's do it, Sid,' said Epstein.

As with the Carnegie Hall gig and all dealings between Bernstein and Epstein, there were no written contracts. Everything was settled by gentleman's agreement over the phone. Bernstein offered $100,000 in advance against 60 per cent of gross receipts. Epstein told him to send $50,000 immediately and pay the balance before the concert. Bernstein didn't have the money; in fact he had lost everything on a recent stage tour of 'Shindig'. He told Brian that his money was tied up and asked if he could be given a few months' grace. Brian said that he'd be in New York in two months' time, on 10 April at the Waldorf Towers, and Sid could give him the deposit then and pay the balance on 10 June. Sid asked him if he could begin to advertise the event and Epstein said 'no'. He asked if he could mention the fact that he was presenting the show, without actually advertising the fact, and Epstein said he had no objection to Sid talking about it.

Bernstein was in financial straits at the time. His wife Gerry had just given birth to Adam, the first of their six children, they owed rent on their home in the East Bronx, money on grocery bills and had no way of raising a loan. Sid began to tell friends that he was promoting the Beatles at Shea Stadium in August 1965 and that deposits fo tickets should be sent to him at PO Box 21. Sid had hope to get 30 or 40 deposits in advance which could help hi perilous financial state. When he went to the post offic three weeks later there were more than three sacks of mai The concert had sold out within three weeks. When Si went to see Brian at the Waldorf, he was able to give him cheque for $100,000.

The Shea Stadium concert proved to be a sensatior although it cost Sid a lot of money to stage. He brought i a team of detectives and hundreds of security men an paid Lloyds of London $25,000 for insurance cover. Th receipts totalled more than $300,000. He was able to giv the Beatles a cheque for a further $80,000 for their 28 minute performance, but his costs had been such that h only made a profit of $6,500. However, his associatio with the Beatles transformed his life and he becam manager of the Rascals, Laura Nyro and numerous othe acts over the years and even launched his ow independent record label.

He set up a deal for another Shea Stadium appearanc for 23 August 1965, with the Beatles receiving 65 per cer of the gate. The concert grossed $282,000 and the Beatle received $183,000. It wasn't as successful as the firs concert as there were 11,000 seats unsold and tickets ha to be given away free.

Bernstein travelled to Britain with the Rascals i October 1966 and met Brian Epstein over dinner. H offered him one million pounds for the Beatles to appear a Shea Stadium in 1967, to include world television rights Brian told him that he couldn't make any plans for liv appearances by the group at that time.

The last time that Bernstein saw Brian Epstein was i April 1967. Brian had called him to a meeting at th Waldorf Astoria in New York, together with **Nat Weiss** Epstein proposed that Sid should join himself and Weis in a management partnership. Bernstein would bring in hi groups the Rascals and the Blues Project and Epstei would offer all of his artists with the exception of th Beatles. Bernstein and Weiss would run the America operation and Epstein and **Robert Stigwood** would ru the London end of the business. As the Bee Gees an Cream were still relatively unknown and as **Cilla Blac** had failed to penetrate the American market, Bernstei turned the offer down.

In 1979, Bernstein wanted the Beatles to reunite for

special concert in aid of the Vietnamese Boat People. He believed that the Beatles name and the concert, recording and television rights of the event could raise $500 million around the world. However, as he was always closer to Epstein than the Beatles and because Brian was now dead, he just couldn't reach any of the former members of the Beatles individually. He decided to go over the heads of their advisors, agents, lawyers and so on by reaching them through advertising. He took out a full-page advertisement in the *New York Times* outlining his plan for a benefit in aid of the Boat People. The only response was an enquiry on behalf of John. Bernstein placed all the information in writing and took it over to the Dakota Building where the doorman took the package. That was the last Sid heard of the matter, apart from a comment from George Harrison who told a journalist, 'It was cute the way the ad in the [*New York*] *Times* tried to put the responsibility for saving

Chuck Berry – one of the Beatles' rock 'n' roll idols. (National Film Archives)

the world on our shoulders.'

Sid was to admit that he'd tried to do something similar a few years earlier, in 1976. He placed an ad in the *European Herald Tribune* and the *Sunday Times* in England suggesting that the Beatles get together for a concert in aid of either the victims of a recent major earthquake in Italy or the homeless and parentless children of Biafra. He received no response, but noticed that Paul McCartney later held a benefit concert to raise money to save the city of Venice from sinking.

In 1981, Sid teamed up with **Clive Epstein** to manage a Liverpool band called Motion Pictures. Unfortunately, Clive died before they could develop their partnership. Later on, with the help of his wife Gerry, Sid began to write his memoirs.

● Berry, Chuck

The legendary American rock 'n' roll star, born in St Louis, Missouri, in 1931, who was one of the Beatles' seminal influences.

When they used to perform his songs on stage at the **Cavern**, John would introduce the number by saying, 'This is a record by Chuck Berry, a Liverpool-born white singer with bandy legs and no hair!'

The group were impressed by the vitality of the songs he wrote and recorded his 'Rock & Roll Music' for their *Beatles For Sale* album and 'Roll Over Beethoven' for their *With The Beatles* LP.

His 'Little Queenie' and 'I'm Talkin' About You' were recorded at Hamburg's **Star Club** and are featured on the Star Club album packages.

John performed two Chuck Berry titles on his *Rock And Roll* album, 'You Can't Catch Me' and 'Sweet Little Sixteen', following a tribute to Berry he'd included on 'Come Together', which led to him being accused of plagiarizing Berry's 'You Can't Catch Me', which resulted in him agreeing to record some Berry numbers on an album.

In 1972 John achieved an ambition and actually performed with Chuck Berry. This occurred when John and **Yoko** were given a week's residency as hosts on the American TV programme 'The Mike Douglas Show'. John picked Berry as a guest and performed with him on 'Johnny B. Goode' and 'Memphis'.

● Berry, Mike *(Publisher)*

A music publisher who formerly worked for Sparta Music before joining the Beatles' publishing company, Apple Music, as professional manager in January 1968.

When Berry was at Sparta he was interested in signing a group called the Iveys, who were managed by **Bill**

Collins. Bill, a Liverpudlian, was the father of Lou Collins, who had worked with Paul's brother **Mike** at Andre Bernard's. **Mal Evans** obtained tapes of the group to play for Paul McCartney and **Apple** was to sign up the group. Apple then offered Berry the job of heading the Apple Publishing division.

He is not to be mistaken for **Mike Berry** the singer, who toured with the Beatles.

Mike Berry. (*Mersey Beat* Archives)

● Berry, Mike (Singer)

In 1962 Mike Berry was leader of the London band Mike Berry & the Outlaws, who had hit the charts with 'Tribute To Buddy Holly', produced by Joe Meek. They began touring the north of England, particularly around the Merseyside area, and were booked into the **Cavern** for an entire week. The Beatles appeared on some of their shows at the club and **Bob Wooler** introduced Brian Epstein to Berry. Epstein had been impressed at seeing Berry on **'Thank Your Lucky Stars'** the previous week plugging his latest release 'Don't You Think It's Time' and invited the nineteen-year-old singer back to his flat in Falkner Street to hear a demo tape of the Beatles. Berry was accompanied by a member of his group, Chas Hodges, who was later to become famous as one half of hit duo Chas and Dave. Epstein played the tape and told him that if he could get the group on television he'd give Berry's group a lot of work in the Merseyside area.

Epstein also invited Berry to **NEMS**' store and arranged for Paul McCartney to give him a lift home from the Cavern one night.

Mike renewed his friendship with the Beatles when he was booked to appear with them on a mini-tour in September/October 1963 which opened at the **Gaumont Worcester** on 4 September and ended at the **Music Hall, Shrewsbury** on 18 October. Berry then joined them on their five-concert tour of Sweden from 24 to 29 October.

A few years later Mike didn't have a manager, having left **Robert Stigwood**, and asked his brother, actor Peter Bourne (who was one of Epstein's boyfriends), if he'd mention to Epstein that he was looking for a manager. Brian said that he couldn't do anything for Mike at the time and Mike thought he'd be on the scrap heap at the age of 22.

Berry's last hit was 'My Little Baby' in April 1963 and he vanished from the pop scene for more than a decade, to reappear much later as a television actor in series such as 'Are You Being Served?' and 'Wurzel Gummidge'. He also returned to the charts with a series of hits at the beginning of the eighties with 'The Sunshine Of Your Smile', 'If I Could Only Make You Care', and 'Memories'.

With the growth of the 'nostalgia' circuit in Britain in the late eighties, Mike reformed the Outlaws and began appearing live on stage once again.

● Besame Mucho

A song written in 1943 by Consuelo Valazquez and Selig Shaftel which has been recorded by over a hundred different artists, ranging from Mario Lanza to the Coasters. It was the Coasters' version in 1960 which led to it being added to the repertoire of rock groups and the Beatles began performing it in 1962. Paul took the lead vocal honours and the group can be heard performing the number on *The Beatles Live! At The Star Club In Hamburg, Germany, 1962* album. They also recorded it during their **Decca audition** on 1 January 1962 and on the BBC radio show **'Here We Go'**, transmitted on 14 June 1962. The group are also seen performing the number in their *Let It Be* movie.

● Best, Mona

Arguably the first promoter to give the Beatles regular support.

Mona Best, affectionately called 'Mo' by her family and friends, was born of English parents in Delhi, India, where she worked for the Red Cross and met and married John Best, a commissioned officer. The couple had two sons 'eter and Rory, and returned to England at the end of the var, in 1945.

For two years they lived in a flat in Casey Street, .iverpool, before moving into a large Victorian House at 8 Iaymans Green in the West Derby area of Liverpool. The uge house had a large complex of cellars and when Pete vas sixteen, Mona had noticed the number of young riends visiting him at the house and decided to turn part f the cellar area into his own private club. But word got ut and more ambitious plans developed, which resulted in club for young people with live groups, which proved opular in the area and was one of the first cellar clubs in .iverpool to present rock 'n' roll groups exclusively, as pposed to the strict policy of jazz for venues such as the **:avern** and the Cat A Coombs. The **Casbah** opened in .ugust 1959 and the resident group were the **Quarry Ien** – John Lennon, Paul McCartney, George Harrison nd **Ken Brown**. After several appearances they brought ieir own residency to an end after a dispute. This ccurred when guitarist Ken Brown turned up for the gig ut was obviously suffering from a heavy cold and the fair-inded Mrs Best decided he was too ill to play, but let im help out at the club. At the end of the evening when ie divided up the group's money, she paid Brown his iare. John, Paul and George were furious and left the ub, ending both their residency and their association ith Ken Brown.

The Casbah continued to be successful and the new residents were the **Blackjacks**, a group which Brown encouraged Pete Best to form. Mo bought her son a new set of drums and the group began to build up a following. In August 1960, Paul McCartney phoned up and asked Pete to become a member of the Beatles.

On the group's return from Germany they appeared at the Casbah and since **Stuart Sutcliffe** had remained in Hamburg, Pete arranged for a friend of his, **Chas Newby**, to deputize on four gigs.

Since their association with **Allan Williams** had been terminated, Pete took over the role of manager, arranging all the gigs, hustling for higher fees and collecting the money. When Mona began a series of independent promotions at St John's Hall, Tuebrook, she booked the Beatles for eleven gigs there and on the first of their bookings for Mrs Best she paid them £20 – a 200% increase on the £5 she used to pay for the Casbah bookings. These gigs, plus the Casbah appearances and the gigs Pete was lining up, proved a lifeline for the Beatles during the early months of 1961.

Mrs Best was championing the group, obviously because of her son's part in it, but she was determined to help them to success and even wrote off to Granada Television in an attempt to get them on television. Producer David Plowright wrote back to her on 21 September 1961:

> 'Dear Mrs Best,
>
> 'Thank you for your letter telling me about "The Beatles". I will certainly bear them in mind and will contact you again if it is possible to invite them to take part in our programme PEOPLE AND PLACES at any time.'

Ironically, the Beatles were to make their television debut on that very show.

In August 1962 Pete was sacked from the Beatles. Mrs Best was furious at what she regarded as disgraceful treatment after Pete had worked so hard for the success of the group over the two most important formative years. She was to tell Beatles biographer **Hunter Davies**: 'He'd [Pete] been their manager before Brian [Epstein] arrived, did the bookings and collected the money. I'd looked upon them as friends. I'd helped them so much, got them bookings, lending them money. I fed them when they were hungry. I was far more interested in them than their own parents.'

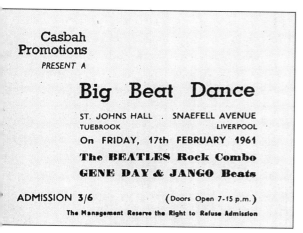

Casbah Promotions
PRESENT A

Big Beat Dance

ST. JOHNS HALL . SNAEFELL AVENUE
TUEBROOK LIVERPOOL

On FRIDAY, 17th FEBRUARY 1961

The BEATLES Rock Combo

GENE DAY & JANGO Beats

ADMISSION 3/6 (Doors Open 7-15 p.m.)

The Management Reserve the Right to Refuse Admission

ecial promotion organised by Mona Best to provide regular rk for the Beatles. (*Mersey Beat* Archives)

No satisfactory answer that made sense was ever given for Pete's sacking – as the theory that his drumming ability wasn't up to scratch crumbles under analysis of the facts. There was a theory that the other members were jealous because Pete had become the most popular member of the group in Liverpool. Another theory was that John, Paul and George felt Mona wanted to manage them, that she was a strong character, had Pete's interest in mind and might cause problems once Epstein took over. Certainly, she had to be strong to provide the necessary discipline for the Beatles, who were tardy at times; if they were to become successful they had to be professional and their attitudes had to change. Perhaps they resented her efforts to help them and regarded it as 'interference'.

Mona died on 9 September 1988 at a Liverpool hospital following a heart attack after a long illness.

● Best Of George Harrison, The

An **EMI** compilation which was issued in Britain on Parlophone PAS 10011 on 20 November 1976 and in America on Capitol ST 11578 on 8 November 1976.

Since George's contract with Parlophone had expired, EMI were free to re-release previous products by the Beatles and the individual members. George suggested a title for the album to EMI and also a song selection which he would have preferred on the release. EMI completely ignored him and when they issued the album he was annoyed because the first half of the album comprised tracks from Beatles recordings. EMI had already issued compilations by John Lennon and Ringo Starr, but all the tracks on their releases were relevant to their solo careers.

Due to his frustration at the EMI snub, George refused to promote the album and it received no chart placing.

A completely different sleeve was used for the American release, which reached No. 31 in the charts and qualified for a Gold Disc.

The tracks were, Side One: 'Something', 'If I Needed Someone', 'Here Comes The Sun', 'Taxman', 'Think For Yourself', 'For You Blue', 'While My Guitar Gently Weeps'. Side Two: 'My Sweet Lord', 'Give Me Love (Give Me Peace On Earth)', 'You', 'Bangladesh', 'Dark Horse', 'What Is Life'.

● Best On Record, The

Title of the annual **'Grammy Awards'** shows presented on American television by NBC TV.

The Beatles received many awards and th presentations were featured in several video clips. Th segment screened on 18 May 1965 showed a film of **Pete Sellers** presenting the Beatles with their Grammy award on the set of *Help!* Also screened was a scene from *A Har Day's Night* and film of the boys performing 'I'm Happ Just To Dance With You'.

On 24 May 1967, Liberace introduced an excerpt fro their 'Strawberry Fields' promotional film. They wer featured again on the show on 5 May 1969. John Lenno appeared as a guest presenter on 1 March 1975 and Ring Starr and **Harry Nilsson** were guest presenters on 1 February 1977.

● Best, Pete

The original fifth Beatle, who joined the group in Augu 1960 prior to their first trip to Hamburg.

Born Peter Randolph Best in Madras, India on 2 November 1941 to English parents: **Mona**, who was a Re Cross nurse, and John Best, an army physical traini instructor. His brother Rory was born in 1944 and th following year the family sailed to England and settled Liverpool, living in Casey Street for two years befo moving to a large house at 8 Haymans Green in the We Derby district.

He passed the 11-plus examination at Blackmoor Pa primary school in West Derby and moved into th Collegiate Grammar School in Shaw Street where he was achieve five 'O' levels.

Mona Best converted Haymans Green into a club call the **Casbah** and the **Quarry Men** initially became t resident band there in August 1959. Several weeks lat there was a dispute within the group when John, Paul a George disagreed with their guitarist **Ken Brown** bei paid for a gig he did not perform due to an illness. As result they walked out on their residency. Brown talk Pete into forming a group with him called the **Blackjac** to take up the Casbah residency. Mona bought Pete a dr kit from the music department at Blackler's store and t band began to build up a loyal following with a rock roll repertoire of numbers by **Chuck Berry**, **Litt Richard**, **Jerry Lee Lewis** and **Carl Perkins**.

In the meantime, the Quarry Men had changed th name to the **Silver Beetles** and comprised John, Geor Paul, **Stuart Sutcliffe** and **Tommy Moore**. Moore the group soon after they'd auditioned for **Larry Parnes** at the **Wyvern Club** and when **Allan Williams** had arranged for them to appear for a season in Hamburg, they urgently needed a regular drummer.

They had begun to drift back to the Casbah Club and noted the smart effect of Pete's new blue mother-of-pearl drum kit. One afternoon there was a phone call from Paul McCartney, 'How'd you like to come to Hamburg with the Beatles?' As it looked as if the Blackjacks were about to disband and with the offer of travelling to another country, Pete was only too pleased to accept and successfully auditioned for the group at Allan Williams' club.

The trip to Hamburg completely galvanized the Beatles and the intensely long hours of playing and the encouragement to actually 'make a show' for the paying customers resulted in a new dynamism in the group's act. They initially played at a small club called the **Indra**, then moved to the **Kaiserkeller** where they were second on the bill to **Rory Storm & the Hurricanes**.

During this time Pete had become firmly installed as a member of the group, not only on stage, but joining the others in their drinking bouts and in picking up girls – or rather, being picked up by girls – and Pete seemed to be particularly popular with the girls who attended the Kaiserkeller. Apart from his abilities as a drummer – and o one ever queried his skills – he was particularly good ooking and because he sat concentrating on his drums ith his head down, developed a somewhat moody image.

The group were about to continue their Hamburg eason by appearing at a rival club to the Kaiserkeller, the **Top Ten**, when Pete and Paul were accused of trying to et fire to the **Bambi Kino**, where their clothes and elongings had been stored, and both were deported. **Peter Eckhorn**, who ran the Top Ten Club, was able to end Pete's kit back to Liverpool in a crate.

Stuart Sutcliffe had remained in Hamburg for a time, Pete had to arrange for a temporary bassist for their four gs in Liverpool in December. Beginning with their ppearance at the Casbah on 17 December.

When they performed in Liverpool, both audiences and llow musicians were able to see the difference their aptism of fire' in Hamburg had caused. They had all nproved beyond recognition. Pete was to tell Beatles ographer **Hunter Davies**, 'When we came back from ermany I was playing using my bass drum very loud and ying down a very solid beat. This was unheard of at the time in Liverpool as all the groups were playing the **Shadows**' style. Even Ringo in Rory Storm's group copied our beat and it wasn't long before most drummers in Liverpool were playing the same style. This way of drumming had a great deal to do with the big sound we were producing.'

For the next year, Pete and his mother Mona were acting managers and agents for the group and arranged all the gigs and negotiated and collected the fees. During this period the local disc jockey **Bob Wooler** considered that Pete Best was the Beatles' biggest asset and said that at the **Aintree Institute** and **Litherland Town Hall** gigs, it was principally Best who was the attraction. Pete was encouraged to include a singing spot in the act, 'Peppermint Twist', and his popularity grew to the extent that it was decided to place him in front of the other three at their performance at a St Valentine's Dance on 14 February 1961. The idea of placing a drummer in front of the line-up was unprecedented. However, it only occurred once, the stage was mobbed and the girls surged forward and almost pulled him off it. Southport promoter Ron Appleby, who compered the group at Litherland Town Hall, commented on Pete's appeal by saying, 'He was definitely the big attraction with the group, and did much to establish their popularity during their early career.' In 1963, **Pat Delaney**, the **Cavern** doorman, was to say, 'Before the Beatles recorded, Pete was inclined to be more popular with the girls than any other member of the group. There were several reasons why I believe he was so popular. Girls were attracted by the fact that he wouldn't smile, even though they tried to make him. They also tried to attract his attention on stage, but he wouldn't look at them. When he left the Beatles there were exclamations of surprise. "The Beatles will never be the same without him" . . . "He was the Beatles" . . . "They've taken away the vital part", were comments I heard.'

It was Mona Best who originally made the first approach to the Cavern on behalf of the Beatles. She contacted **Ray McFall** and discussed the group with him. He said he'd think about it. It was Pete who then rang Peter Eckhorn and fixed them up with their Top Ten, Hamburg season in April 1961. It was also via the Bests that **Neil Aspinall**, who was a lodger at 8 Haymans Green, became the Beatles' road manager. During 1961 Mona Best also contacted Granada Television in an attempt to secure them a spot on the programme **'People And**

Places'.

When Brian Epstein took over the reins, he discussed their gigs and fees with Pete and the relationship between them seemed to be quite an amicable one. When the group auditioned for **Decca** they were originally turned down. There was no comment of any sort regarding Best's ability as a drummer.

On 7 March 1962, following the group's appearance at the **Playhouse Theatre in Manchester** recording the BBC radio show **'Teenager's Turn'**, it was Pete who was mobbed by the Manchester girls and he was almost prevented from catching the coach with the other members of the group. It was during that month that Pete first discovered that they had been turned down by Decca. The others all knew about it, but no one had bothered to inform him. 'I was hurt because I was the last to know about it,' he said. 'The others knew a couple of weeks earlier. They let it slip out in a casual conversation one day.'

The same thing happened regarding the Parlophone contract. They just didn't bother to inform him. Yet his popularity locally was stronger than ever. The cover of ***Mersey Beat*** which ran the story of their Parlophone recording featured a large photograph of Pete Best, and items inside told how girls had taken to sleeping in the garden of Haymans Green, just to be near him.

Pete was chatting with Paul McCartney and told him that he was considering buying a Ford Capri. Paul told him, 'If you take my advice you won't buy it, that's all. You'd better be saving your money.' This was an obvious warning sign, but the penny didn't drop. Pete didn't even suspect what was happening on Wednesday 15 August when, following their Cavern lunchtime session, Pete asked John at what time he and Neil should give him the customary lift in his car the next day. John said, 'Don't bother' and rushed away.

Epstein called him to arrange for a meeting at 11.30

Former Beatle Pete Best with his band the Pete Best Five, shortly after signing with Decca Records. (Decca Records)

he next morning. Pete arrived at the **NEMS** store, driven y Neil, and went to see Brian, presuming it would be the usual discussion about the forthcoming gigs. He was completely flabbergasted when Brian told him, 'The boys want you out of the group. They don't think you're a good enough drummer.' While he was in the office the phone ang – it was Paul, asking if Pete had been given the news. Brian told Pete that he'd been replaced by Ringo but asked if he could perform at the next gig at Chester prior o Ringo taking his place. Pete left the office and he and Neil went to the Grapes pub to discuss the shocking news. Neil phoned Mona Best who immediately tried to contact Epstein by phone, without success.

The events which led to the sacking have always been hrouded in mystery. Brian Epstein did not want the task f sacking Pete, so the decision had originally come from ohn, Paul and George. The reasons remain unclear. There was an attempt to push the responsibility onto George Martin because he had used a session drummer at the recording audition. Mona Best phoned Martin and he told her, 'I never suggested that Pete Best must go. All I said was that for the purposes of the Beatles' first record I would rather use a session man. I never thought that Brian Epstein would let him go. He seemed to be the most saleable commodity as far as looks went. It was a surprise when I learned that they had dropped Pete. The drums were important to me for a record, but they didn't matter much otherwise. Fans don't pay particular attention to the quality of the drumming.'

It was not uncommon for A&R men to use session drummers at the time and exactly the same thing was to happen to Ringo Starr. When he arrived at the recording studios on 11 September 1962, a session drummer, Andy White, was present. White also played drums on 'P.S. I Love You', while Ringo was handed a pair of maracas. Martin told Beatles biographer Hunter Davies, 'He [Ringo]

ete sits behind George, Paul and John on the Cavern stage. (Cavern Mecca)

couldn't do a roll – and still can't – though he's improved a lot since. Andy was the kind of drummer I needed. Ringo was only used to ballrooms. It was obviously best to use someone with experience.' Ringo himself was to tell Davies how shocked he was to arrive at the session and find another drummer there. 'I thought that's the end,' he said, 'they're doing a Pete Best on me.'

Since no one had ever criticized Best's drumming before and in the light of what happened with Ringo, it's obvious that Martin's use of a session drummer at the original audition was used as an excuse to conceal the real reason why he was sacked.

There have been a number of theories regarding this. One is that he simply did not fit in with the group because of his moodiness. In the famous **Bob Wooler** article in *Mersey Beat*, the only Beatle mentioned by name was Pete, who was described as 'mean, moody and magnificent'. Yet this image was one which seemed to work in the Beatles' favour and Pete has said that in the two years he was with the group, they got along together fine. Another reason put forward was that Pete was shy and hardly spoke to anyone, yet John Lennon was to write a letter to *Mersey Beat* the following year saying, 'I would also like to point out to the people who say that Ringo is always kept in the background – this is not deliberate. Paul, George and I think that Ringo is gear and have been trying to bring him forward in the act. However, Ringo is still rather shy and it will take a bit of time. In six months Ringo will really be playing a major part in the act.'

It seems unlikely that the reason stemmed purely from George Martin's remark about Pete's drumming ability as the other members of the group had already begun to build a barrier between themselves and Pete as is evidenced by the fact that they didn't even bother to tell him about the Decca rejection. The most common theory, apart from the aspersions about Pete's drumming ability, was that the other members of the Beatles were jealous of him. Since a lot of people in Liverpool were calling the group Pete Best and the Beatles, this is a possibility – and Mona Best was convinced that this was the real reason for the sacking.

Mona told Hunter Davies, 'They were jealous and wanted him out. Pete hadn't realized what a following he had till he left. He was always so very shy and quiet, never shot his mouth off, like some people I could mention.

'He'd been their manager before Brian arrived, did the bookings and collected the money. I'd looked upon them as friends. I'd helped them so much, got them bookings, lending them money. I fed them when they were hungry. I was far more interested in them than their own parents.'

Another theory which went around Liverpool at the time was that John, Paul and George felt there would be conflict with Mrs Best. She was a formidable woman with great strength of character and it was rumoured that she had wanted to become the group's manager. She had been acting as such prior to the appearance of Epstein, yet it is felt that the three would have resented being officially managed by her. After Brian had signed the group, the others still felt that Mona might continue to make her presence felt on behalf of her son.

Whatever the reason the only two people who can really divulge the truth are Paul McCartney and George Harrison.

Many people, in fact, blamed George for the sacking which is probably why he received a black eye from fans the first time the group appeared at the Cavern with Ringo. George also wrote to one of their fans, 'Ringo is a much better drummer and he can smile – which is a bit more than Pete could do. It will seem different for a few weeks but I think that the majority of our fans will soon be taking Ringo for granted.'

Epstein was very upset about the turn of events and prior to telling Pete the unfortunate news, had a sleepless night. He told Pete he wanted to continue to manage him and would place him with another band – the **Merseybeats**. Pete didn't want to remain with Epstein after what had happened and certainly didn't want to start up again with an unknown group. Behind the scenes Epstein had his friend **Joe Flannery** approach Pete about joining **Lee Curtis** & the All Stars. Pete agreed as the group were receiving a lot of publicity in *Mersey Beat* and seemed to have a strong manager in Joe.

In the meantime, there was a furore in Liverpool over the sacking. *Mersey Beat* hadn't been given the true reason for the sacking, but had accepted a statement which had been given to Bill Harry by Epstein. It appeared under the heading 'Beatles Change Drummer!'

'Ringo Starr (former drummer with Rory Storm & the Hurricanes) has joined the Beatles, replacing Pete Best on drums. Ringo has admired the Beatles for years and is delighted with his new engagement. Naturally he is tremendously excited about the future.

'The Beatles commented: "Pete left the group by mutu

greement. There were no arguments or difficulties, and his has been an entirely amicable decision." '

Hundreds of letters and petitions of protest were sent to *Mersey Beat* and when the Beatles were due to appear at he Cavern with Ringo on 19 August 1962, the Best fans vere out in force. Ray McFall arranged for Brian Epstein o have a bodyguard and during scuffles, George Harrison vas given a black eye. Fans were chanting 'Pete For Ever, Ringo Never', and 'Pete Is Best', although by the end of he set Ringo appeared to be well received by the fans.

Naturally, due to Pete's popularity on Merseyside, ffers began to arrive from several groups. He decided to oin Lee Curtis & the All Stars and he made his debut with he band at the **Majestic Ballroom, Birkenhead** on Monday, 10 September. On 24 November, Pete was again ppearing at the Majestic with the All Stars and was also elebrating his 21st birthday. Compering the show, Bob Wooler read out a telegram that had arrived for Pete: Congratulations, many happy returns, all the best – John, aul, George, Ringo and Brian'.

Pete travelled to Hamburg to appear at the **Star Club** ith the All Stars and the following year, in August 1963, e married his girlfriend Kathy.

During the same year Lee Curtis parted company with e All Stars. The singer had signed a solo recording ontract and was appearing on TV shows without the roup, so they became the Pete Best All Stars. The other embers were Wayne Bickerton, Tony Waddington and rank Bowen. Mrs Best took over as the group's manager.

Mo went to see **Dick Rowe** and **Mike Smith** at Decca nd secured a recording contract. Their debut single 'I'm onna Knock On Your Door', issued in June 1964, wasn't success and Decca dropped the group.

On 30 March 1964 Pete appeared as a guest on the merican TV programme 'I've Got A Secret'.

Pete was to say, 'Magazines both in Britain and across e Atlantic had been printing far-fetched stories that I ad quit the Beatles because of illness and that Ringo was lled in only because I was too sick to play.' In fact, this rt of falsification of the facts came to a head when a eatles interview in *Playboy* magazine in February 1965 ad a quote from John saying, 'Ringo used to fill in metimes if our drummer was ill, with his periodic ness.' And Ringo commented: 'He took little pills to ake him ill.' Pete sued and an out-of-court settlement as eventually made a few years later.

Pete and his wife Kathy were living at Haymans Green, but one night when Kathy was visiting her mother, Pete became terribly depressed and attempted to gas himself. His brother Rory smelt the gas and battered down the door and, together with Mo, spent several hours reviving him.

He decided to continue to attempt to find success as a musician and during 1965 the Pete Best All Stars were touring Canada and were asked to make a record in New York for an independent company, Mr Maestro. By this time Tommy McGurk, who had replaced Frank Bowen, had left the group and two saxes were added and the name of the band changed to the Pete Best Combo. An album *Best Of The Beatles* was issued on Savage 71 which contained six rock standards and six original compositions by Tony Waddington and Wayne Bickerton. The tracks were: 'Last Night', 'Why Did You Leave Me Baby', 'Shimmy Like My Sister Kate', 'I Need Your Lovin'', 'Nobody But You', 'I Can't Do Without You Now', 'Casting My Spell', 'Wait And See', 'Some Other Guy', 'I'm Blue', 'She's Alright' and 'Keys To My Heart'.

The record didn't chart and the group had to leave the

States due to Musicians' Union regulations. The rules would have allowed Pete to remain in America by himself, but he didn't want to desert the group. However, it was becoming obvious that success in the music business was eluding him and in 1968 he decided to give it all up. He initially went to work in a local bakery and then joined the civil service in 1969, where he has been ever since.

There have been occasional returns to the entertainment business. In 1978 Dick Clark invited him to appear on a television reunion with various other veteran musicians. Then Clark invited him to be technical adviser on a TV movie called *The Birth Of The Beatles*, although the advice of Pete and other Mersey veterans such as Bob Wooler was reportedly ignored by the producers.

Although he remains a civil servant, Pete is given time off occasionally to appear at various American conventions where he has proved very popular. He also records in Liverpool with Billy Kinsley, former founder member of the **Merseybeats**.

● Bibliography

There have been more books published about the Beatles than any other 20th Century icons. There is such an extensive bibliography of Beatles books that, treated in any detail, they would need to be contained in a separate volume. In fact, there have been two books published on the subject – *Paperback Writers: The History of The Beatles in Print* (Virgin, 1984) and *Here, There And Everywhere: The First International Beatles Bibliography:* 1962-1982 (Pierian Press, 1985).

Two companies in particular have taken pride in publishing books on the Beatles. Pierian Press of Ann Arbor, Michigan, has specialized in volumes of a scholarly appeal, which are available on mail order only, and Genesis Publications of Guildford, Surrey, produce high quality limited editions.

The complete list is as follows. Titles within each year are listed chronologically.

1964

Here Are The Beatles, Charles Hamblett, Four Square Books. 128 pages of trivia. It was the first book about the group to be issued.

The True Story Of The Beatles, Billy Shepherd, Beat Publications. First Beatle biography, a paperback, issued by the publishers of Beatles Monthly. The American edition was published by Bantam Books.

All About The Beatles, Edward De Blasio, MacFadden-Bartell. One of the first American paperbacks on the market. A slim volume containing a selection of photographs of the group.

The Beatles Up To Date, uncredited, Lancer Books. American paperback which features photos by Dezo Hoffman.

The Beatle Book, Dezo Hoffmann, Lancer Books. Another American paperback with almost 100 photographs.

Out of the Mouths of Beatles, Adam Blessing, Dell Books. A 64-page book of Beatle photographs.

Beatles Ltd, Robert Freeman, George Newnes.

Ringo's Photo Album, Ringo Starr, Jamie Publishers.

Die Beatles Kommen, Dennis Bow, Fahrplan Eine Weltsensation.

Love Me Do: The Beatles Progress, Michael Braun, Penguin Books. Penned by a New York journalist, th atmosphere of the Beatles' life on the road has probabl never been more accurately conveyed.

A Hard Day's Night, John Burke, Pan Books. A straight forward novelization of the Beatles' debut film. It wa published in the United States by Dell Books.

A Cellarful Of Noise, Brian Epstein, Souvenir Press Autobiography of the Beatles' manager, ghosted by Dere Taylor. It was published in America by Doubleday and i paperback by Pyramid Books.

The Beatles, Norman Parkinson and Maureen Cleav Hutchinson. A 32-page book of photographs.

The Beatles Quiz Book, Jack House, William Collins.

Love Letters To The Beatles, selected by Bill Adler, Putna & Sons. Hardback with drawings by the artist Osborn.

Dear Beatles, selected by Bill Adler, Grosset & Dunla The British edition was published by Blond and Briggs.

In His Own Write, John Lennon, Jonathan Cape. A selection of John's versatile cartoons, stories and poem with an introduction by Paul McCartney. It was publishe in America by Simon & Schuster in 1985.

Grapefruit, Yoko Ono, Wunternaum. Yoko Ono's book conceptual minimalisms. This was a limited edition of 5C copies.

1965

Help!, Random House. Book of the film.

Help!, Al Hine, Dell Books. Novelization of the Beatle second film was published in Britain as a paperback Mayflower Books.

Communism, Hypnotism And The Beatles, The Reverer David A Noebel, Christian Crusade. Odd book accusi the Beatles of subverting American youth.

A Spaniard In The Works, John Lennon, Jonathan Cap The second volume of John's writings, published America by Simon & Schuster.

Die Beatles: Fabelwesen Unserer Zeit, Christine Ehrhar Wolf Frhr Von Tucker.

The Beatles Diary, Beat Publications. Beatles events 1965.

1966

Jp The Beatles' Family Tree, Cecil R Humphrey-Smith, Michael G Heenan and Jennifer Mount, Achievements Ltd. One of the rarest of the Beatle books.

The Penguin John Lennon, John Lennon, Penguin. Paperback collection of John's two books in one volume.

Murray The K Tells It Like It Is, Baby, Murray Kaufman, Holt, Rinehart & Winston. Autobiography of the New York disc jockey Murray the K, who gained international fame when he took advantage of Beatlemania at the time of the group's first visit to America in February 1964.

1967

ohn Lennon: In His Own Write & A Spaniard In The Works, John Lennon, Signet Books. American paperback ollection of John's two books, also republished in 1981.

he Golden Beatles, Northern Songs. The first book of Beatle lyrics, covering 50 songs and illustrated with hotographs.

he Writing Beatles, John Lennon, Signet Books. Another ignet paperback of John's two books, the American quivalent of *The Penguin John Lennon*.

rt And The City, John Willett, Methuen & Co Ltd. An ntriguing exploration of the Merseyside renaissance in nusic and art which began in the fifties. The Liverpool rtists include Stuart Sutcliffe.

968

he Beatles: The Authorised Biography, Hunter Davies, leinemann. Published in America by McGraw-Hill. A evised edition was published by Heinemann and IcGraw-Hill in 1978. A paperback was published in merica by Dell and in England by Mayflower in 1969. his was the first Beatles book to become a best-seller.

he Beatles: The Real Story, Julius Fast, G. Putnam & ons. Unauthorised American biography.

he Beatles, Anthony Scaduto, Signet Books.

he Beatles: A Study In Sex, Drugs, And Revolution. The everend David A. Noebel, Christian Crusade.

ie Beatles In Yellow Submarine, Max Wilt, Signet. Based the movie, with lots of coloured illustrations. Published Britain by Four-Square Books.

ie Yellow Submarine Gift Book, World Distributors. A rge-sized, hardbound book of lavish colour illustrations om the film.

ie Beatles Book, edited by Edward E Davis, Cowles lucational Corporation. Fourteen articles and essays by ch eminent contributors as William F. Buckley, **Timothy Leary** and Ned Rorem, hardcover only.

The Beatles: Words Without Music, Rick Friedman, Grosset & Dunlap. In this paperback edition, editor Friedman has collected numerous quotes by and about the Beatles.

In His Own Write: The Lennon Play, Adrienne Kennedy, Victor Spinetti, John Lennon, Jonathan Cape. Script of the play based on John's two books. Published in America by Simon & Schuster.

Beatles & Co, Juan Carlos Kreimer, Editorial Galerma. An Argentinian book outlining the Beatles' history in the Spanish language.

1969

The Beatles Illustrated Lyrics, edited by Alan Aldridge, Macdonald Unit. It was published in America by Delacorte in 1969, Dell in 1972 and Delta in 1980.

1970

The Beatles Get Back, Jonathan Cott and David Dalton, photographs by Ethan Russell, Apple Publishing. Yet another Beatle innovation – a luxuriously printed souvenir book, contained in the same package as the Let It Be album.

1971

The Girl Who Sang With The Beatles, Robert Hemenway, Alfred A. Knopf. The first example of published fiction about the Beatles.

We Love You Beatles, Margaret Sutton, Doubleday. A 48-page children's book.

The Beatles Illustrated Lyrics Vol II, Alan Aldridge, BCI Publishing. Published in America by Delta/Seymour Lawrence the same year. Macdonald republished it in 1990.

The Beatles, Aram Saroyan, Barn Dream Press. A curiosity item. A four-page book containing eight words, and selling for only five cents.

Lennon Remembers, Jann Wenner, Straight Arrow. The first gritty no-holds-barred book about the life of a Beatle. It was issued in Britain in 1972 by Talmy, Franklin. Penguin Books brought out a paperback version in 1972 containing 60 photographs and a cover painting by Philip Castle.

1972

Apple To The Core, Peter McCabe and Robert D. Schonfeld, Pocket Books. Hardbound and paperback editions were published in Britain by Martin Brian and O'Keefe. Sphere produced a paperback edition in 1973.

The Lennon Factor, Paul Young, Stein and Day.
The Beatles Years, edited by Ray Connolly, Macmillan. Basically a collection of Beatles lyrics.
The Longest Cocktail Party, Richard DiLello, Charisma Books.
Published in the United States by Playboy Books. DiLello's account of his days as an Apple employee. Reprinted by Pierian Press in 1984.
Body Count, Francie Schwartz, Straight Arrow. This was the first of the kiss-and-tell books.

1973

As Time Goes By, Derek Taylor, Straight Arrow. Derek Taylor's autobiography. It was published in Britain in 1972 in hardback by Davis Poynter Ltd and in 1974 in paperback by Abacus. In 1983 it was reprinted in a hardbound edition, complete with a new index by Pierian Press.
Twilight Of The Gods: The Beatles In Retrospect, Wilfred Mellors, Viking Press. The Beatles' music dissected and analysed by a leading British Professor of Music.

1974

The Beatles: Yesterday...Today...Tomorrow, Rochelle Larkin, Scholastic Book Services. A slim volume, written by a fan, but well illustrated with more than 85 photographs.
The Beatles, Patricia Pirmangton, Creative Education. Another outline of the Beatles' story for young readers.

1975

The Paul McCartney Story, George Tremlett, Futura. It was republished in London the following year by White Lion and in America in 1977 by Popular Library.
The Beatles: The Fabulous Story Of John, Paul, George & Ringo, compiled by Robert Burt, edited by Jeremy Pascall, Octopus Books/Orbis Publishing. Large format, *illustrated* book comprising 13 unrelated Beatles articles.
The Beatles Story, Edited by Rob Burt. Phoebus. A paperback version of *The Beatles: The Fabulous Story of John, Paul, George and Ringo*.
The Beatles Lyrics Complete, Futura Books. Reissued the following year as *The Beatles Lyrics*.
The Beatles Lyrics Illustrated, Dell. An American paperback.
The Beatles Illustrated Record, Roy Carr and Tony Tyler, New English Library. A copiously illustrated, lavishly produced best-seller also published in the United States by Harmony Books. It was reissued in Britain by New English Library and in America by Harmony Books i 1978 and 1981.
The Beatles Collection, City of Liverpool Public Relation Department. A large, album-shaped fold-out, with 1 colour shots of Beatle albums.
The Beatles, Dezo Hoffmann, Shinko Music. A collection o black-and-white photographs.
The Beatles, Shinko Music. Another illustrated book.
The Man Who Gave The Beatles Away, Allan Williams an William Marshall, Elm Tree Books. The story of Alla Williams, who inaccurately claimed 'I was the Beatles first manager.' It was published in America by Macmilla in 1975 and a paperback version was issued in the State by Ballantine Books in 1977. The British paperback wa published by Coronet in 1976.
The John Lennon Story, George Tremlett, Futura Books.
The Complete Beatles Quiz Book, Edwin Goodgold and Da Carlinsky, Warner Books.

1976

Linda's Pictures, Linda McCartney, Alfred A. Knopf. collection of 148 plates. Ballantine produced a softbac version of the book in the same year.
Los Beatles, Alistair Simms, Ediciones Technical Press. 96-page rendition of the Beatles' story.
All Together Now, Harry Castleman & Walter J. Podrazi Pierian Press. The first Beatles project issued by Pieria Press. Also issued in paperback by Ballantine.
Beatles Discography, Arno Guzek, privately printed. Danish fan who published his own 75-page paperback.
Paul McCartney In His Own Words, Paul Gambaccin Omnibus Press.
All You Need Is Love, Tony Palmer, Weidenfeld Nicolson/Chappell & Company. Published to tie in wi the seventeen-part London Weekend Television series. paperback version from Futura Books was published th following year.
Beatles A-Z, John Neville Leppert, privately printe Published by a fan from the Crosby area of Liverpool.
Growing Up With The Beatles, Ron Shaumburg, Pyrami Books. A Beatles' fan from Kansas traces his own li between the years 1964 and 1976. It was republished America in 1980 by Perigee Books.
John Lennon: One Day at a Time, Anthony Fawcett, Gro Press. An illustrated hardcover by the man who becan John and Yoko's personal assistant for two years. The bo was published in Britain the following year by Ne

English Library.

On Stage: The Beatles, Debra Keenan, Creative Education. A 46-page children's book.

The Beatles, George Zanderbergen, Crestwood House. A 48-page illustrated children's book.

1977

The Facts About a Pop Group Featuring Wings, Dave Gelly, Andre Deutsch. Aimed at young readers, with over 50 photographs. Issued in America by Harmony Books.

Paul McCartney & Wings, Tony Jasper, Octopus Books. Published in America by Chartwell Books.

Paul McCartney & Wings, Jeremy Pascall, Hamlyn. Published in America by Chartwell Books.

George Harrison: Yesterday & Today, Ross Michaels, Flash Books. Published in Britain by Music Sales.

Paul McCartney: A Biography In Words and Pictures, John Mendelsohn, Sire Books/Chappell Music Ltd.

Wings, Rock Fun. A Japanese photo-book.

A Hard Day's Night, edited by Philip DiFranco, Chelsea House. A visual record of the Beatles' first film. Published in Britain by Penguin.

Yesterday Seems So Far Away: The Beatles Yesterday And Today, John Swenson, Zebra Books.

The Beatles Again?, Harry Castleman and Walter Podrazik, Pierian Press. The companion volume to *All Together Now*.

1,000 Beatles Facts (And a Little Hearsay), Ed Nibbervoll and Evan Thorburn, J. Albert.

Mersey Beat: The Beginning of The Beatles, Bill Harry, Omnibus Press. Issued in America by Quick Fox.

1978

The Beatles: The Authorized Biography, Hunter Davies, William Heinemann. Updated edition, published in America by McGraw-Hill, and as a British paperback by Granada in 1979.

The Beatles: An Illustrated Record, Roy Carr and Tony Tyler, New English Library.

Behind The Beatles Songs, Philip Cowan, Polyantric Press. Slim volume of stories behind 62 numbers.

Paperback Writer, Mark Shipper, Grosset & Dunlap. A humorous, lampooning novel. Published in Britain by the New English Library. Ace Books issued a paperback version in America in 1980.

The Beatles In Their Own Words, Miles, Omnibus Press. Issued in America by Quick Fox and republished in Britain by WH Allen in 1981.

Hands Across The Water: Wings Tour USA, Hipgnosis/Paper Tiger. A handsome, illustrated souvenir. Published in America by Reed Books.

26 Days That Rocked The World, uncredited O'Brien Publishing. This large format 64-page book takes a nostalgic look at the Beatles' 1964 American tour.

Beatle Madness, Martin A. Grove, Manor Books.

Paul McCartney: Beatle With Wings, Martin A. Grove, Manor Books.

The Beatles Trivia Quiz Book, Helen Rosenbaum, New American Library.

The Official Sgt Pepper's Lonely Hearts Club Band Scrapbook, Robert Stigwood and Dee Anthony, Guild & Western.

Sgt Pepper's Lonely Hearts Club Band, Henry Edwards, Pocket Books. A paperback novelization of **Robert Stigwood**'s movie.

A Twist Of Lennon, Cynthia Lennon, WH Allen. Cynthia relates her life from her birth until the end of her marriage to John.

The Beatles Forever, Nicholas Schaffner, McGraw-Hill. A detailed history of the group from 1964 to 1977.

1979

Pocket Beatles Complete, Wise Publications.

The Beatles Concert-ed Efforts, Jan Van de Bunt & Friends, Beatles Unlimited. A slim volume published by the Dutch fan magazine Beatles Unlimited.

Every Little Thing: The Beatles On Record, Mitchell McGeary and William McCoy, Ticket To Ryde Ltd. 18-page booklet containing information on 400 records.

Beatles Movie Catalog. Toru Matahira. A 256-page Japanese paperback.

Up Against It: A Screenplay For The Beatles, Joe Orton, Eyre Methuen. Screenplay for a proposed Beatles film called 'Up Against It'. It was published in America by Grove Press.

Elvis Presley – The Beatles, Stella H. Alicio, Pendulum Press. A 64-page children's book.

Il Viaggio Dei Cuori Solitari: Un Libro Sui Beatles, Roberto Antoni, Il Formichiere. The first Beatles biography penned by an Italian.

All You Need Is Ears, George Martin, Macmillan.

1980

Things We Said Today, Colin Campbell and Allan Murphy, Pierian Press. A large-format, handbound limited edition.

The Beatles: A Day In The Life, Tom Schultheiss, Pierian Press. The first major chronology of the Beatles' life and career, a day-by-day diary of the years from 1960-1970. It was published as a paperback in Britain in 1981 by Omnibus Press, and in America by Quick Fox, and was also issued in America by Perigee/Putnam's in 1982.

Strawberry Fields Forever: John Lennon Remembered, Vic Garbarini, Brian Cullman, Barbara Graustark, Delilah/Bantam.

Across The Universe, Arno Guzek, privately published. 27 pages.

The Boys From Liverpool: John, Paul, George, Ringo. Nicholas Schaffner, Methuen.

The Beatles Illustrated Lyrics, Volumes One And Two, edited by Alan Aldridge, Macdonald Futura. A reissue of both books, sold as a two-volume set and published in America by Delacorte Press.

John Lennon 1940-80: One Day At A Time, Anthony Fawcett, New English Library. Republished after John's death.

John Lennon: Death Of A Dream, George Carpozi Jr., Manor Books.

I, Me, Mine, George Harrison, Genesis Publications. Later published by Simon & Schuster in the United States and W H Allen in Britain.

The Beatles A To Z, Goldie Friede, Robin Titone, Sue Weiner, Eyre Methuen. This first Beatles encyclopaedia is a large format book with more than 3,000 separate entries and over 100 photographs.

The Writings Of John Lennon, Simon & Schuster. Their two Lennon books, *In His Own Write* and *A Spaniard In The Works* in one volume.

Lennon: What Happened! edited by Timothy Green Beckley, Sunshine Publications.

Lennon: Up Close and Personal, edited by Timothy Green Beckley, Sunshine Publications. The companion volume to *Lennon: What Happened!*

1981

The Beatles, Geoffrey Stokes, Rolling Stone/WH Allen/Omnibus Press. The best Beatles 'coffee table' book, with 236 duotones and 86 colour photographs.

John Lennon In His Own Words, compiled by Miles, Omnibus Press.

In The Footsteps Of The Beatles, Mike Evans and Ron Jones, Merseyside County Council. A Beatle Trail around the centre of Liverpool.

Paul McCartney Und Wings, Dewes, Klaus and Rudie Oertel, Bastei/Luebbe.

I, Me, Mine, George Harrison, WH Allen. George discusses his life as a composer.

Rock 'N' Roll Times, Jurgen Vollmer, Google Plex Books. A selection of Jurgen Vollmer photographs.

In His Own Write/A Spaniard In The Works, John Lennon New American Library.

The Compleat Beatles, Delilah/ATV/Bantam. Two books totalling 1,024 pages with over 100 photographs, and the complete sheet music and lyrics to 211 songs.

Paul McCartney Composer/Artist, Paul McCartney Pavilion Books. American edition by Simon & Schuster.

All You Needed Was Love: The Beatles After The Beatles John Blake, Hamlyn. American edition published b Putnam's/Perigee Books.

Shout! The True Story Of The Beatles, Philip Norman, Elm Tree Books. An American paperback version wa published by Warner Books in 1982.

Lennon & McCartney, Malcolm Doney, Midas Books Published in America by Hippocrene Books and as paperback by Omnibus Press in Britain the following year.

The Beatles Apart, Bob Woofinden, Proteus Books Illustrated with 60 black-and-white and 17 colour shots.

John Lennon & The Beatles Forever, Ed Naha, Towe Books.

You Can't Do That: Beatles Bootlegs & Novelty Discs Charles Reinhart, Pierian Press. 1,394 entries, coverin over 1,000 song titles.

John Lennon 4 Ever, Conrad Snell, Crown Summit Books.

The John Lennon Story, John Swenson, Leisure Books.

John Lennon: A Personal Pictorial Diary, Warren Tabatch Sportomatic Ltd. A small 110-page illustrated booklet.

The Beatles, Alan Clark, Alan Clark Productions. A 60 page special limited collector's edition.

Lennon '69: Search For Liberation, edited by Jeff Long The Bhaktivedanta Book Trust. Conversations the Swam Bhaktivedanta had with John, Yoko and George.

A Tribute To John Lennon 1940–1980, edited by Ly Belanger, Michael Brecher, Jo Kearns, Nicolas Locke an Mike Statzkin, Proteus Books.

A Cellarful Of Noise, Brian Epstein, New English Library Slim paperback reprint of the 1964 book.

The Beatles For The Record, Stafford Pemberto Publishing. Large format, illustrated book. Published i America in 1982 by Totem Books.

The Lennon Tapes, Andy Peebles, BBC Publications. An 88-page transcript of John's last interview, on 6 December 1980.

John Lennon: 1940–1980, compiled by Ernest E Schworck, ESE. A large-size 90-page paperback.

John Lennon: 1940–1980, Ray Connolly, Fontana.

Thank U Very Much, Mike McCartney, Arthur Baker. Published in America by Delilah Books under the title *The Macs*. A paperback edition was published in Britain by Granada Books in 1982.

Pour John Lennon, Maurice Achard, Alain Moreau.

1982

The Beatles At The Beeb, Kevin Howlett, BBC Publications. Pierian Press published a hardbound edition in America in 1983.

Liverpool 8, John Cornelius, John Murray.

The Beatles Forever, Helen Spence, Colour Library Book. Another picture book with 210 colour shots. Published in America by Crescent Books as *The Beatles*.

Das Album Der Beatles, Michael Jurgs and Hans Heinrich Ziemann, Willi Braam. A 384-page German language book with 300 photographs.

The Beatles Album File And Complete Discography, Jeff Russell, Blandford Press. Published in the US by Scribner's under the title *The Beatles On Record*. It has since been reprinted by Blandford Press.

The Beatles On Record, Mark Wallgren, Simon & Schuster.

The Long And Winding Road, Neville Stannard, Virgin Books. It contains details of every Beatles' release. Published in America by Avon Books.

Lots Of Liverpool, a Beatles Unlimited special. A guide book for Beatles fans visiting Merseyside.

The Beatles' England, David Bacon and Norman Maslow, 910 Press.

John Lennon's Secret, David Stuart Ryan, Kosmik Press.

The Legacy Of John Lennon, David A. Noebel, Thomas Nelson Publishers.

As I Write This Letter, Marc A. Catone, Greenfield Books.

The Beatles: A Collection, Robert and Cindy DelBuno. Robcin Associates.

Collecting The Beatles, Barb Fenick, Pierian Press. The essential guide to memorabilia.

The Complete Beatles Lyrics, Omnibus Press.

The 1975 John Lennon Interview, Lavinia Van Driver, privately printed.

The Playboy Interviews With John Lennon & Yoko Ono, David Sheff, Berkley Books.

The Ballad Of John & Yoko, Rolling Stone Press. Published in Britain by Michael Joseph.

Photographs, Linda McCartney, MPL Communications.

Abbey Road, Brian Southall, Patrick Stephens Ltd. A history of the studios.

The Beatles Down Under, Glenn A. Baker, Wild & Woolley Press.

The Beatles Who's Who, Bill Harry, Aurum Press. Biographies of over 300 people associated with the Beatles.

With The Beatles, Dezo Hoffmann, Omnibus Press. Over 300 photographs.

1983

The Ocean View, Humphrey Ocean, MPL Communications/Plexus Books. Book of the Wings tour of America.

Stardust Memories, Ray Connolly, Pavilion Books.

The Love You Make, Peter Brown and Steven Gaines, McGraw Hill. Another kiss-and-tell book. The British edition was published by Macmillan.

Loving John, May Pang and Henry Edwards, Warner Books. A kiss-and-tell book. The British edition was published by Corgi Books.

Dakota Days, John Green, St Martin's Press. Another 'kiss-and-tell' book. Published in Britain by Comet Books in 1984.

John Lennon: Summer Of 1980, Perigee Books. The British edition, published by Chatto & Windus in 1984, includes all 78 photographs, together with a bonus poster.

The Beatles: 24 Posters, Colour Library Books.

John Lennon: A Family Album, Nishi F. Saimuru, Kadokawa Shoten.

The Complete Beatles U.S. Record Price Guide, Perry Cox and Joe Lindsay, O'Sullivan Woodside & Co.

Let's Go Down The Cavern, Spencer Leigh, Royal Life Insurance.

Working Class Heroes, Neville Stannard, Virgin Books.

Yesterday: Photographs Of The Beatles, Robert Freeman, Weidenfeld & Nicolson. Published in America by Holt, Rinehart, Winston.

Paul McCartney, Alan Hamilton, Hamish Hamilton.

The Literary Lennon, Dr James Sauceda, Pierian Press.

The Beatles: An Illustrated Diary, Har van Fulpen, Plexus Books.

Follow The Merseybeat Road, Sam Leach, Eden

Publications.
John Lennon: In My Life, Pete Shotton and Nicholas Schaffner, Stein & Day.
The Beatles Records In Australia, Bruce Hamlin, privately published.
Give Peace A Chance: Music And The Struggle For Peace, Marianne Philbin, Chicago Review Press.
The Beatles: The Fab Four Who Dominated Pop Music For A Decade, Robert Burt and Jeremy Pascall, Treasure Press. A 92-page hardbound reworking of the 1975 book.
The Beatles, Colour Library Books. A reprint of 1982 publication *The Beatles Forever*.
Liverpool – The 60s, Brunning's. Subtitled *A Photographic Celebration*.
The Mersey Sound, Adrian Henri, Roger McGough, Brian Patten, Penguin. A bestselling volume of the work of the Mersey poets.
New Volume, Adrian Henri, Roger McGough, Brian Patten, Penguin.
The Beatles: A Musical Evolution, Terence O'Grady, Twayne Publishers. An analysis of the Beatles' music.

1984

The Beatles' Labels, Howard Kramer, privately published.
The Beatles, John Tobler, WH Smith. Coffee table book. Published in America by Exeter Books.
The Music Of The Beatles, Martin E. Horn, Big Eye Publications.
Beatlemania: A History Of The Beatles On Film, Bill Harry, Virgin Books.
The Beatles Reader: A Selection Of Contemporary Views, News & Reviews of The Beatles in Their Heyday, edited by Charles P. Meises, Pierian Press.
A Cellarful Of Noise, Brian Epstein, Pierian Press.
John Lennon: For The Record, Peter McCabe and Robert D. Schonfeld, Bantam.
The Longest Cocktail Party, Richard DiLello, Pierian Press.
Waiting For The Beatles, Carol Bedford, Blandford Press.
The Beatles: Here, There (And Everywhere), Mathias Wiaschek and Wilfried Pelz, Modern music.
The Book Of Lennon, Bill Harry, Aurum Press.
The Beatles, Bill Harry, Beatle City. A large-size booklet.
Give My Regards To Broad Street, Andrew Harvey with George Perry, Pavilion Books. Book of the film.
Paperback Writers: An Illustrated Bibliography, Bill Harry, Virgin Books.
The Beatles Conquer America, Dezo Hoffman, Virgin Books. A photographic record. Published the following year in America by Avon Books.
Lennon: A Liverpool Echo Tribute, The Liverpool Echo. A 48-page large-size paperback.
The Art Of The Beatles, Mike Evans, Anthony Blond. Published in America by William Morrow & Co.
Paul McCartney: The Definitive Biography, Chris Welch, Proteus Books.
John Winston Lennon 1940–1966, Ray Coleman, Sidgwick & Jackson. The first volume of Coleman's biography.
John Ono Lennon (1967–1980), Ray Coleman, Sidgwick & Jackson. The second volume of the biography. Both volumes were published as one paperback by Futura the following year. In 1985, McGraw-Hill published a hardcover version of both volumes in one book called *Lennon*, comprising 672 pages.
Beatles, Musketeers And Supermen: The Films Of Richard Lester, Neil Sinyard, Croom Helm.
Fifty Years Adrift (In An Open-Necked Shirt), Derek Taylor, Genesis Books. A treasure-chest of memorabilia.
Come Together: John Lennon In His Time, Jon Wiener, Random House.
John Lennon: An Illustrated Biography, Richard Wootton, Hodder and Stoughton.

1985

Beatle! Pete Best with Pat Doncaster, Plexus. Published in America by Dell.
The Beatles, Orbis. A pop-up book.
Dear Mr Fantasy, Ethan Russell, Houghton Mifflin Co. A selection of Russell's photographs.
The Beatles Authorized Biography: Second Revised Edition, Hunter Davies, McGraw-Hill.
The Book Of Beatle Lists, Bill Harry, Javelin Books.
The Book Of Beatles Lists, Charles Reinhart, Contemporary Books. 230-page paperback.
John Lennon Conversations, Linda Deer Domnitz, Coleman Publishing. A Spiritualist communicates with John and describes his life in the spirit world.
Ask Me Why: The Beatles Quizbook, Bill Harry, Javelin Books.
Listen To These Pictures: Photographs of John Lennon, Bob Gruen, Sidgwick & Jackson.
Step Inside, Cilla Black, J. M. Dent.
Here There And Everywhere: The First International Beatle Bibliography 1962–1982, Carol D. Terry, Pierian Press.

The Beatles: Untold Tales, Howard A. DeWitt, Horizon Books. Anecdotes about the group's early days.

Yesterday . . . Came Suddenly, Bob Cepicon and Waleed Ali, Timbre Books/Arbor House. A Beatles biography.

Collecting The Beatles: Volume 2, Barbara Fenick, Pierian Press. Second volume on Beatles memorabilia.

Beatles For Sale: The Beatles Merchandising Guide, Bill Harry, Virgin Books.

John Lennon, Dezo Hoffmann, Columbus Press. A photographic portfolio of shots taken between 1962-1970.

Beatlefan Volumes One And Two, Pierian Press.

The Beatles: Their Greatest Hits, edited by Joyce Robins, St Michael.

Julian Lennon, Yolanda Flesch, Running Press.

1986

The Faces Of John Lennon, Dezo Hoffmann, McGraw-Hill.

The Beatles Live!, Mark Lewisohn, Pavilion Books.

Julian Lennon, Kalia Lulow, Ballantine.

John Lennon/Julian Lennon, Nancie S. Martin, Avon Superstars.

Songs Of George Harrison, Genesis Publications.

Mike Mac's White And Blacks Plus One Colour, Mike McCartney, Aurum Press. Published in America by Viking Penguin.

Skywriting By Word Of Mouth, John Lennon, Harper & Row. Published in Britain by Pan Books.

The Beatles Price And Reference Guide For American Records, Perry Cox and Michael Miller, Cox-Miller Publications.

Beatlefan: Vols 3 & 4, Pierian Press.

McCartney – Songwriter, Howard Elson, Comet Books.

The McCartney File, Bill Harry, Virgin Books.

Four Ever – 25 Jahre Beatles, Peter Schuster, Belser Verlag.

In His Own Youth. In My Own Words, Julia Baird, River Women Press. Julia Baird was one of John Lennon's halfsisters.

The Beatles: A Celebration, Geoffrey Giuliano, St Martin's Press.

McCartney: The Definitive Biography, Chris Salewicz, St Martin's Press. Published the following year in Britain by Macdonald/Queen Anne Press, where it underwent a title change to *McCartney: The Biography*.

The Beatles Down Under: The 1964 Australia and New Zealand Tour, Glenn A. Baker, Roger Dilernia, Pierian Press.

The Beatles In Tokyo, Jam Publishing Co.

The Beatles: A Recording History, Allen J. Wiener, McFarland & Co. Published in Britain by Bailey Brothers and Swinfen.

1987

Come Together: John Lennon In His Time, Jon Wiener, Faber.

Sgt Pepper's Lonely Hearts Club Band, Bill Harry, Atalanta Press.

Yoko Ono, Jerry Hopkins, Macmillan. Unauthorized.

Alles Was du Brauchst Ist Liebe, Andreas Peglau, Zentralhaus Publikation.

Bob Dylan and The Beatles, Tino Markworth, Hobo Press.

The Beatles' Last Concert, Eric Lefcowitz, Terra Firma Press.

The Beatles Book, Omnibus Press.

Music And Maiden Overs: My Showbusiness Life, Vic Lewis, Chatto & Windus. Autobiography of the Managing Director of NEMS.

The Lennon Companion, edited by Elizabeth Thomson and David Gutman, Macmillan. Published in softback by Papermac in 1988 and in America by Schirmer Books.

McCartney, Chet Flippo, Sidgwick & Jackson. Published in America by Doubleday.

Lennon, Carole Lynn Corbin, Franklin Watts Ltd.

It Was Twenty Years Ago Today, Derek Taylor, Bantam.

30 Years of Beatles Music – A Chronicle, Kurt Erlemann, Er-Ro Publications.

The Beatles In Liverpool, Peter Kaye, Starlit Liverpool Ltd. A photographic portfolio.

Les Beatles, Pierre Merle and Jacques Volcouve, Solar.

Paul Ist Schuld, Corinne Ullrich Crox, Phantom Verlag. A German novel about two Beatle fans.

John Lennon, Alan Posener, Rowohlt Taschenbuch Verlag CmbH. A German language biography.

Beatle People: In Words and Pictures, The Walrus, privately published.

1988

Yesterday, The Beatles Remembered, Alistair Taylor, with Martin Roberts, Sidgwick & Jackson.

All My Loving, Carolyn Lee Mitchell with Michael Munn, Robson Books. Memoirs of a fan.

Tell Me Why: A Beatles Commentary, Tim Riley, Alfred A. Knopf Inc. Published in Britain by the Bodley Head.

The Lives Of John Lennon, Albert Goldman, Bantam.

John Lennon, My Brother, Julia Baird with Geoffrey Giuliano, Grafton Books.

Do You Want To Know A Secret? Making Sense Of The Beatles' Unreleased Recordings, L. R. E. King, Storyteller Productions.

Imagine: John Lennon, Andrew Solt and Sam Egan, Bloomsbury. Companion to the Warner Bros film.

The Complete Beatles Recording Sessions, Mark Lewisohn, EMI/Hamlyn.

The Official Price Guide To Memorabilia Of Elvis Presley And The Beatles, Jerry Osborne, Perry Cox, Joe Linday, House of Collectibles/Ballantine.

1989

The Beatles Album File And Discography, Jeff Russell, Blandford Press. A revised, updated edition.

The Beatles In Holland, Henk Van Gelder with Lucas Ligtenberg, Loeb Uitgevers.

Fixing A Hole: A Second Look At The Beatles' Unauthorized Recordings, L. R. E. King.

Help! A Companion To 'The Beatles' Recording Sessions', L. R. E. King. Limited edition booklet.

Beatles '64: A Hard Day's Night In America, Carl Gunther and A. J. S. Rayl, Doubleday. A photographic record. Published in the UK by Sidgwick & Jackson.

The Beatles: A Private View, Robert Freeman, Octopus. Published in America by Mallard Press.

The Beatles, Bill Yenne, Magna Books. A basic history.

The Beatles: A Bio-Biography, William McKeen, Greenwood Press. Another basic re-telling.

Dark Horse: The Secret Life Of George Harrison, Geoffrey Giuliano, Stoddart Publishing, Canada. Published in Britain by Bloomsbury. The American edition published by E. P. Dutton in 1990, was retitled *Dark Horse: The Private Life Of George Harrison.*

Blinds & Shutters, Michael Cooper, Genesis Publications. Limited to 5,000 numbered and signed copies, it features more than 600 photographs.

Brian Epstein: The Man Who Made The Beatles, Ray Coleman, Viking. Published in America by McGraw-Hill as *The Man Who Made The Beatles: An Intimate Biography Of Brian Epstein.*

The Murder Of John Lennon, Fenton Bresler, Doubleday. Published in the UK by Sidgwick & Jackson.

Paul McCartney Solo 1970–1990, Rob van den Berg, Loeb. First Dutch language story of Paul's solo career.

Baby, You Can Drive My Car, Alf Bicknell and Garry Marsh, No 9 Books. Diary of the Beatles' chauffeur.

1990

The Art And Music Of John Lennon, John Robertson, Omnibus Press. Published in America by Birch Lane Press in 1991.

Apple Log IV: A Guide For The U.S. & Canadian Apple Records Collector, Jeffrey Levy, MonHudProd Media Group.

How They Became The Beatles: A Definitive History of the Early Years 1960–1964, Gareth L. Powlowski, Dutton. Published in Britain by Macdonald.

Nothing Is Beatleproof (Advanced Trivia for Fab Four Fanciers), Michael J. Hockinson, Popular Culture Ink.

The Beatles Price Guide For American Records, Perry Cox and Joe Lindsay, Perry Cox Ent/BIOdisc.

Ticket To Ride, Kevin Gunn, Denny Somach, Kathleen Somach, William Morrow. 48 previously unpublished interviews. Published in Britain by Macmillan.

Warp And Woof! Dawn L. Searcy, Number 9 Books. Slim volume of fiction by a Californian Beatle fan.

Unfinished Music No 1: An Unauthorized Companion To Year One Of The Lost Lennon Tapes. L. R. E. King, Storyteller Productions.

Listening To The Beatles, David Schwartz, Popular Culture Ink.

The John Lennon Family Album, Nishi F. Saimaru, Chronicle Books.

Daddy, Come Home: The True Story Of John Lennon And His Father, Pauline Lennon, Angus & Robertson.

McCartney, Jacques Volcouve and Michael Dubreuil.

The Beatles Day To Day: A Chronology 1962–1989, Mark Lewisohn, Harmony Books.

Paul McCartney: 20 Years On His Own, Edward Gross, Pioneer Books.

Beatlesongs, William J. Dowlding, Fireside.

Sweet Beatle Dreams: The Diary of Mary Mack Conger, Mary Mack Conger, Andrews and McMeel.

The Beatles Memorabilia Price Guide, Jeff Augsburger, Marty Eck and Rick Rann, Branyan Press.

The Official Price Guide To Memorabilia Of Elvis Presley And The Beatles, Jerry Osborne, Perry Cox and Joe Linday, Ballantine.

Every Little Thing: The Definitive Guide To Beatles Recording Rarities, Rare Mixes and Other Musical Oddities, 1958–1986, William McCoy and Mitchell McGeary, Pierian Press.

The Beatles: Life And The Songs, G. Schmidel, Muzyka.
The Other Side Of Lennon, Sandra Shevey, Sidgwick & Jackson.
The Classic Poster Book: The Beatles, Pyramid Books.
Linda McCartney's Home Cooking, Linda McCartney and Peter Cox, Bloomsbury.
Days In The Life: John Lennon Remembered, Philip Norman, Century. Mainly a pictorial record.
The Quiet One: A Life Of George Harrison, Alan Clayson, Sidgwick & Jackson.

1991

Fab Films Of The Beatles, Edward Gross, Pioneer Books.
Blackbird: The Life And Times Of Paul McCartney, Geoffrey Giuliano, E. P. Dutton.
The Beatles Album, Geoffrey Giuliano, Viking Studio Books. Items from his vast memorabilia collection.
Yoko Ono, Arias and Objects, Barbara Haskell and John Hanhardt, Peregrine Smith Books.
The Last Days Of John Lennon: An Intimate Memoir, Fred Seaman, Birch Lane Press. Published in Britain by Xanadu as *Living On Borrowed Time*.
The Unseen Beatles, Bob Whitaker, Collins.
Speaking Words Of Wisdom: Reflections On The Beatles, Spencer Leigh, Cavern City Tours.
The Beatles After The Break-Up: In Their Own Words, Omnibus Press.
John Lennon: His Life & Legend, Richard Buskin, PIL (Publications International Limited) and Omnibus Press.
Ringo Starr: Straight Man Or Joker? Alan Clayston, Sidgwick & Jackson.
Tomorrow Never Knows: 30 Years Of Beatles Music And Memorabilia, Geoffrey Giuliano, Dutton. Published in the UK by Dragon's World and in America by Viking Studio under the title *The Beatles Album: Thirty Years Of Music And Memorabilia*.
The Rolling Stones Rock And Roll Circus, Mike Randolph, Chronicle Books.
The Beatles Album, Julia Delano, Grange Books. Lavishly illustrated. Published in America by Smithmark.
Yesterday: My Life With The Beatles, Alistair Taylor, Pioneer Books.
The Beatles' Merseyside, Ian Forsyth, S. B. Publications.
Bob Gruen's Works: John Lennon.
Illegal Beatles: Archival Back Issues 1986–1988, edited by Doug Sulpy, Storyteller Productions.
The Revolver Sessions: Photographs by Robert Freeman, UFO Books.
The Beatles' Liverpool, Ron Jones, Merseyside County Council.
The Beatles, Mike Clifford, Smithmark. Coffee-table book.
Beatle Poems, Howard DeWitt, privately published.

● Bicknell, Alf

Chauffeur to the Beatles whose memoirs, *Baby, You Can Drive My Car*, were published in 1989.

Born on 28 October 1928, Alf spent most of his working life as chauffeur to a host of famous names. He joined the Beatles team during their British tour, late in 1964, and it was while he was driving the group to Salisbury Plain during the filming of *Help!* that John Lennon asked him if he'd like to travel to America with them.

While in the States he recalls, 'I remember attending a party with the Beatles, thrown by **Capitol Records** boss **Alan Livingston**. The guest list was incredible: there was Gene Barry, Tony Bennett, Richard Chamberlain, Jane Fonda, Rock Hudson, Dean Martin, Groucho Marx, **Hayley** and Juliet Mills and James Stewart. I knew James Stewart from before, and him and his missus invited me back, but Brian [Epstein] wouldn't let me go.'

Alf also joined the Beatles on Friday, 27 August 1965, when they met **Elvis Presley**. 'He shook my hand and called me "Sir",' he recalls.

He also accompanied the group on their trips to Germany, the Philippines and Tokyo and during the recording of 'Yellow Submarine' he even joined in the singing on the chorus.

He was present at their last concert at **Candlestick Park** in San Francisco and, with their touring days over, Alf found himself returning to his old job, but with unique and exciting memories of four years of travelling with the Beatles.

In 1989, No. 9 Books in Britain published Alf's memoirs, *Baby, You Can Drive My Car*, which was co-written by Garry Marsh and included an introduction by George Harrison.

Also in 1989, Alf, who had settled down in Ruthin, North Wales, put up five Beatles tapes for auction at Sotheby's in London. The tapes had been given to him by John Lennon when Alf was still the group's driver. One tape has John making several attempts at a demo recording of 'If I Fell'. In the recording he experiments with different keys and guitar patterns.

Acker Bilk – a leading exponent of the trad jazz craze. (Acker Bilk)

Another tape has George Harrison composing his first song, while a third has the Beatles assuming comic voices to read passages from the Bible and sing their favourite hymns.

Alf had expected to raise £60,000 at the auction, but three of the tapes unfortunately failed to reach their reserve price, although he did sell two of them for a total of £12,000.

● Bilk, Acker – and his Paramount Jazz Band

Somerset-born Bernard Stanley Bilk ('Acker' is slang for 'mate') was the first British artist to go to No. 1 in the American charts – twenty months before the Beatles led the 'British Invasion' – with his single 'Stranger On The Shore', which also reached No. 2 in Britain.

Bilk was one of Britain's leading proponents of 'trad jazz', which became a popular fad in the late fifties and early sixties.

He appeared a number of times at the **Cavern Club** in Liverpool and shared the bill with the Beatles on a 'Riverboat Shuffle' on the **MV *Royal Iris*** on Friday, 25 August 1961. The ferry boat left Liverpool landing stage at 7.45 p.m. and sailed along the Mersey providing entertainment for the fans, before returning to the pier head at 11.00 p.m.

The Beatles were once again teamed up with Acker and his Paramount Jazz Band when the two attractions appeared at the **Queens Hall, Leeds** on 28 June 1963.

● Bill Black Combo, The

One of the acts who were booked to appear on the Beatles' first tour of America, which comprised 31 shows in 24 cities. The Bill Black Combo was paid $1,500 per week for the tour, although their leader, Bill Black, wasn't actually in the tour line-up.

Black was a Memphis-born bass player who appeared on many of **Elvis Presley**'s early recordings. He was also one of Presley's backing musicians but quit when Presley hit the big-time as he only paid his band $100 a week each. Black then formed his Bill Black Combo, which had six Top Twenty entries in the American charts, including 'Smokie Part 2', 'White Silver Sands', 'Don't Be Cruel' and 'Josephine'.

Black died of a brain tumour during an operation on 21 October 1965.

● Birch, Norman

One of John Lennon's uncles, the husband of Harriet, one of **Julia Lennon**'s sisters.

John had bought the original family home in Wavertree where Norman and Harriet lived. In 1991 there was some controversy when **Yoko Ono** instructed her lawyers to evict them from their house, which was now Yoko's property. When the newspapers discovered what was happening there was a great deal of coverage in the press, which caused Yoko to cancel her previous instructions to her lawyers.

Norman died on 30 October 1991 when he was killed in a car accident near his home (just as Julia Lennon and **John Dykin** were). He was 77 years old.

● Birthday

Song recorded for *The Beatles* white album on Wednesday, 18 September 1968. That evening BBC 2 were screening a

1956 rock 'n' roll film *The Girl Can't Help It* for the first time on British TV and the Beatles wanted to nip around to Paul's nearby house to see the movie in between their session.

Paul arrived in the studio early and had almost completed writing when the others arrived. With a little help from his friends, mainly John, the song was completed and the backing track recorded in time for them to see the film.

They then returned to **Abbey Road** and completed the recording.

Yoko Ono and **Pattie Harrison** were in the studio and joined in the singing of the 'Birthday' chorus, while **Mal Evans** helped out with handclaps. Paul sang lead vocals, with John joining in, and Paul also played piano on the track, although the instrument had been adjusted to sound like an electric harpsichord.

● Birth Of The Beatles, The

A 104-minute made-for-TV movie, produced by Dick Clark in 1979. The film was directed by Richard Marquand with a screenplay by John Kurland and Jacob Eskender.

The film was a dramatization of the Beatles' career, with music provided by Beatles-soundalike group **Rain**, who hailed from Southern California and recorded the soundtrack with the numbers: 'Dizzy Miss Lizzy', 'Don't Bother Me', 'Johnny B Goode', 'Roll Over Beethoven', 'Ask Me Why', 'Love Me Tender', 'Twist And Shout', 'P.S. I Love You', 'Please Please Me', 'Thank You Girl' and 'I Want To Hold Your Hand'.

The cast included: Stephen Mackenna as John Lennon, Rod Culbertson as Paul, John Altman as George, Ray Ashcroft as Ringo, Ryan Michael as **Pete Best**, David Wilkinson as **Stuart Sutcliffe** and Brian Jameson as **Brian Epstein**.

Filming on the $2.5 million production began in Liverpool on 11 June 1979 and the completed movie made its American debut as the *ABC Friday Night Movie* at 8.00 p.m. on 23 November 1979.

It was first screened in Britain on BBC 1 on New Year's Eve, 1980.

The story opens as the Beatles set off for their first appearance on the **'Ed Sullivan** Show'. We then witness their early career in flashback. They audition for **Larry Parnes** at the **Wyvern Club**, ask Pete Best to join them and set off for **Hamburg** in 1960. **Astrid Kirchherr** takes photographs of the group and John has high jinks at the gigs, putting a toilet seat around his neck. George is deported and the group return to Liverpool. They appear at **Litherland Town Hall**, then set off for Hamburg once more. Astrid develops the Beatle-style haircut with **Stuart Sutcliffe**. Stu dies. In 1961 the group meet Brian Epstein and sign with **NEMS**. We see Brian after he's received a beating and discover he's a homosexual. John gets married. The group become successful and set off for America.

During the June filming in Liverpool, accurate locations weren't actually used and as the **Cavern** had been knocked down, interiors were filmed in a London studio. The team then moved to Hamburg, completing their locations on 30 July.

● Blackbird

Song written, sung and recorded by Paul for *The Beatles* double album. Paul originally recorded the song solo in Studio Two at **Abbey Road** on Tuesday, 11 June 1968, while, at the same time, John was experimenting with sound effects for *Revolution 9* in Studio Three. Paul's voice was double-tracked in parts. The song was said to have been inspired by a newspaper report which Paul had read concerning race riots in America.

Some sounds of blackbirds singing were also added to the track, taken from a sound effects recording, 'Volume Seven: Birds of a Feather'.

The number was also included on the compilation *The Beatles Ballads*.

Paul performed the number on his 1975/76 tour with Wings and it is also featured on his *Wings Over America* album.

● Blackboard Jungle, The

1955 film starring Glenn Ford as a teacher dealing with the problems of juvenile delinquency. The highlight of the film, as far as youngsters were concerned, was the soundtrack number by Bill Haley and the Comets, 'Rock Around The Clock', the first rock 'n' roll number introduced into a feature film.

The movie was said to have inspired the embryo members of the Beatles. John, at **Quarry Bank School**, was impressed by the film's main song, although it was never introduced into the repertoire of the **Quarry Men** when they formed in 1957.

A sixteen-year-old Paul and a fifteen-year-old George decided to see the film. George's mother **Louise** laughed when the pair said they were going as it had an Adults-Only certificate in Britain. George put dirt on his upper lip to form a moustache, and both boys gained entrance, although Paul said they only went to see it because they'd heard about the featured song.

● Black, Cilla

Born Priscilla Maria Veronica White on 27 May 1943, this Liverpool singer was the only female vocalist from the Mersey scene to achieve major success.

Cilla was a typist for a local cable company and at the age of seventeen, worked occasionally at the **Zodiac Coffee Club** in Duke Street, Liverpool in the evenings, usually in the company of her close friend Pat Davies, who was Ringo Starr's girlfriend. Cilla liked to sing and began performing one or two songs on stage with local bands such as **Rory Storm & the Hurricanes** and **Kingsize Taylor** & the Dominoes.

In the 6 July 1961 issue of ***Mersey Beat***, in an article headed 'Swinging Cilla', Bill Harry mistakenly wrote, 'Cilla Black is a Liverpool girl who is starting on the road to fame.' The name she'd always used was her own, Cilla White, but she liked the new name and adopted it.

In the **Blue Angel Club** one night Bill Harry arranged for Brian Epstein to listen to her singing **'Boys'** on stage and Brian arranged a meeting with her the next day and offered to sign her up.

Due to the huge media attention focused on Liverpool because of the Beatles' success, the papers were given the story that Cilla had been a **Cavern** cloakroom girl. This was not strictly the case – she had only helped out a friend there unofficially once or twice – but it sounded more newsworthy than her daytime job as a typist or her evening job at the Zodiac Club.

Brian arranged a contract for her with Parlophone Records and George Martin became her recording manager. She made her recording debut with the Lennon & McCartney number 'Love Of The Loved', which was released on 27 February 1963 on Parlophone R5065. It didn't achieve the anticipated success and only reached No. 35 in the charts. Brian then changed her image, dressed her in sophisticated clothes and achieved a No. 1

Cilla Black in her film debut as Betty Dorrick in *Work Is A Four Letter Word*. (Universal Films)

British hit with her second release, a cover of Bacharach and David's 'Anyone Who Had A Heart', which had been an American chart topper for Dionne Warwick. Issued on Parlophone R5101, it achieved its hit status in February 1964. Her second American cover, 'You're My World', issued on Parlophone R5133, also hit the top spot in Britain.

Next she recorded a Lennon & McCartney number, 'It's For You', which was released in Britain on Parlophone R5162 on 31 July 1964, where it reached the No. 7 position. It was issued in America on **Capitol** 5258 on 17 August 1964. John and Paul visited Cilla in the studio during the recording of this track on which Paul plays piano.

Cilla became an all-round entertainer appearing in variety shows, pantomimes and on summer seasons at seaside resorts. She also had her own BBC television series 'Cilla', which made its debut in 1968. The singer invited her old friend Ringo Starr to join her on the first programme, which was screened on Tuesday, 9 February. The two of them appeared in a comedy sketch and sang a duet, 'Do You Like Me Just A Little Bit'. Ringo also performed 'Act Naturally'. His fellow Beatles sent along a number of telegrams to the BBC studios where he was recording the show: 'Come home Jim. All is forgiven. Love. Your Buddies And Pals', 'We will be watching. Luv Herbert And Family' and 'Big Brothers are watching and wishing you well. Love from your Big Brothers'.

Paul McCartney had written Cilla a number called 'Step Inside Love', which was used as the signature tune for the series. The song was issued as a single in Britain on Parlophone R5674 on 8 March 1968, where it reached the No. 8 position. The American release on Bell 726 was issued on 6 May 1968.

Cilla appeared in a guest spot in the film *Ferry 'Cross The Mersey* and made her acting debut opposite David Warner in the movie *Work Is A Four Letter Word.*

George Harrison actually wrote a song specially for Cilla called 'I'll Still Love You'. Arrangements were made for her to record it during a hectic summer season at Blackpool and she travelled to London on a Sunday to record it, with George producing and Ringo playing drums. Unfortunately, Cilla had toothache and a swollen mouth at the time and the session didn't work out.

Throughout the seventies Cilla consolidated her position as an established all-round show-business celebrity and married her long-standing boyfriend Bobby Willis. During the early eighties she reduced her appearances while she reared her sons, but from the middle of the decade she became an even more established television star when she was signed by London Weekend Television to host their shows 'Blind Date' and 'Surprise, Surprise'.

On Paul McCartney's 40th birthday, Cilla sent him a telegram which read: 'Life begins at 40, what-the 'ell 'ave you been doing all these years?'

● *Black Dyke Mills Band, The*

A famous British brass band. Paul selected them to record his composition 'Thingumybob', the theme tune of London Weekend Television's comedy series starring Stanley Holloway which was first networked in Britain on 2 August 1968.

On Sunday afternoon, 30 April of that year, Paul travelled to Bradford in Yorkshire to record the single, which he also arranged. The band, conducted by Geoffrey Brand, also produced an instrumental version of 'Yellow Submarine' for the flip, which Paul produced. The single was issued in Britain on Apple 4 on 6 September 1968, but failed to register in the charts. In America, 'Yellow Submarine' became the 'A' side when the disc was issued on Apple 1800 on 26 August 1968.

Although the band never recorded for the Apple label again, Paul was to feature them on a Wings album over a decade later, in 1979, when they performed on 'Winter Rose' and 'Love Awake' for his *Back To The Egg* album.

● *Blackjacks, The*

When guitarist **Ken Brown** was sacked from the **Quarry Men** because **Mona Best** had paid him a share of the fee (despite the fact that he didn't perform because of a cold), he approached Mona's son, **Pete,** and suggested that they form a group, with Pete on drums. Pete Best had been considering becoming a drummer and took up the opportunity. With Pete on drums and Brown on rhythm guitar, the other members of the Blackjacks were **Charles Newby** on lead guitar and Bill Barlow on bass guitar. The band immediately began a residency at the **Casbah Club** playing a repertoire consisting mainly of numbers by **Jerry Lee Lewis**, **Carl Perkins**, **Little Richard** and **Chuck Berry**, rock 'n' roll classics such as **'Twenty Flight Rock'**, 'Whole Lotta Shakin' Goin' On', **'Sweet**

Little Sixteen', **'Rock And Roll Music'**, **'Honey Don't'**, 'Tutti Frutti', **'Long Tall Sally'** and **'Memphis Tennessee'**.

On 6 August 1960, the Silver Beetles found that their gig at the **Grosvenor Ballroom** had been cancelled and they drifted over to the Casbah Club to see if there was any work. They watched the Blackjacks and were particularly impressed by Pete's brand-new drum kit.

Paul McCartney phoned Best with the offer to join them as drummer and go with them to Hamburg. As the Blackjacks were virtually on the point of disbanding, with Brown soon to move down to London and Newby still a chemistry student, Pete, who had now abandoned the idea of going to Teacher's Training College, accepted the offer.

Coincidentally, John Lennon's first name for his skiffle group had been the Black Jacks.

● Blacklers, *Great Charlotte Street, Liverpool L1*

Large department store in the city centre, situated opposite the former site of **NEMS** first record store, which had originally been managed by Brian Epstein.

When George Harrison left **Liverpool Institute** with no qualifications in 1959 and failed to obtain a job working for Liverpool Corporation, he went to the Youth Employment Centre in Dale Street and was told there was a position for a window dresser at Blacklers department store. When George went for the job it had already been taken, but he was told the maintenance department was looking for an apprentice electrician.

George was to comment, 'So I got a job cleaning all the lights with a paint brush, all those tubes to keep clean, and at Christmas I kept the Grotto clean.'

George began working at the store in 1960 and was paid £1.10s (£1.50) per week, but at the age of seventeen was able to tell his boss he was leaving – this was to go on tour in Scotland backing **Johnny Gentle**.

Mona Best bought her son **Pete** a drum kit at the store, which so impressed the Beatles when they saw him playing it that they invited him to join them.

The store closed in the eighties and was converted into smaller commercial units.

● Blair Hall, *Walton Road, Walton, Liverpool WA4*

One of the venues used as a jive hive by Walter Hill, who ran Peak Promotions under which he organized weekly jive dances at four venues, the others being **Holyoake Hall**, the **David Lewis Theatre** and Columba Hall, Widnes.

The Beatles made their first appearance for Hill on 5 February 1961 when they made their debut at Blair Hall. Their only other appearances were for a run of three consecutive Sundays on 16, 23 and 30 July 1961 and on Saturday, 29 July 1961.

● Blair, Lionel

British television personality, actor, choreographer, who met the Beatles socially at various events such as the parties at **Alma Cogan**'s house or in the **Ad Lib Club**. He also appeared with them on the **Mike and Bernie Winters** TV show 'Big Night Out'.

He says, 'One of the most exciting shows we did was with the Beatles, and later, when the show moved to Blackpool and changed its name to "Blackpool Night Out", they came on again and did their latest hit, which was "Help!" I invented a little kick movement which the Beatles could do with me on the show, and the day after the programme letters poured in asking how to do the kick.'

As a result, Brian Epstein asked him to develop the movement for a tour he was promoting, which Epstein nicknamed the 'kick tour'. The bill included the Everly Brothers, **Cilla Black** and **Billy J. Kramer**. Blair compered the show and performed a dance number involving the kick.

He also appeared with the Beatles at the **London Palladium** on the *Night Of A Hundred Stars*.

Blair was also engaged to provide choreography for *A Hard Day's Night*. He said, 'It was just like "Blackpool Night Out", when I had first worked with the Beatles, so it went off very easily. **Dick** [**Lester**] was one of those directors who thought I was a bit of a joke because I played the fool a bit during breaks.' Blair was also hired to choreograph the 'Hamlet' strip scene with Laurence Harvey in the **Peter Sellers**/Ringo Starr film ***The Magic Christian***.

● Blake, Peter

Prominent contemporary British artist who grew to become one of the country's most popular painters during the sixties.

He was awarded the CBE and his retrospective

exhibition at the Tate Gallery in 1983 was the most successful show ever held at the gallery for a living artist.

Born in Dartford, Kent, in June 1932, he had launched several exhibitions prior to the one at the Tate.

It was London gallery owner **Robert Fraser** who recommended that Blake design a new cover for the album *Sgt Pepper's Lonely Hearts Club Band* after he had dissuaded the Beatles from using a psychedelic design by the **Fool**.

The basic concept of the album had been evolved. Blake commented: 'They'd established that there would be another persona that they'd invented and I said well, perhaps we could pretend that you'd just done a concert and were posing for a photograph. So what we evolved was that we'd build it in the studio. It wasn't a collage, which not many people realize: there have been a great many rip-offs of it and they've always cut up photography and stuck it down. Well, we built the whole thing life-size and made a platform for them to stand on – and the flowers were all delivered and built – and then they came in and posed and the photographs were taken.

'I said (to the Beatles), each of you make a list [of people they wanted to appear on the cover]. John made a very comprehensive list. Paul did, too, and the lists were fascinating. George's list was all Indian gurus at that point and I think Ringo just sort of agreed with everything. I don't think he actually gave me a list. He said that what the others were doing was fine. I made a list too, and Robert Fraser did. On my list I'd put Leo Gorcey and Huntz Hall from the Bowery Boys and as it is, there's only Huntz Hall because Leo Gorcey must have been down on his luck because he wrote and said, "Could you pay me a fee?" and **EMI** weren't prepared to do that, so he had to come out.'

Michael Cooper, who was a business partner of **Robert Fraser**'s, was to take the photographs in his studio in Flood Street, Chelsea. Blake said: 'I worked in the studio for a fortnight constructing the set, fixing the top row to the back wall and putting the next about six inches in front and so on, so that we got a tiered effect.'

Blake was paid approximately £200 for the commission. His wife **Jann Howarth**, the sculptor, whom he married in 1963, also helped him on the project, co-designing the special Sgt Pepper cut-out figure contained

A lobby card for *Blindman*, a spaghetti western featuring Ringo Starr.

on a cardboard sheet enclosed with the album. She also made some cloth sculptures, which weren't used on the final tableau. The couple were separated in 1985.

Blake did a number of notable works which were inspired by the Beatles. They include *The Beatles (1963-68)*, a 48 x 36 in. acrylic on hardboard which was based on magazine photos and had a space left on it for autographs. He also painted an oil-on-canvas *Beatles (1963-67)*, which is in the collection of Colin St John Wilson and was used as the cover of George Melly's Penguin paperback *Revolt Into Style* in 1967.

Blake also created a collage in 1973 entitled *A Souvenir For John (Lennon)* which featured a drawing of a circus performer holding a barrel over his head while balancing another barrel with the words 'Mr Kite'. Underneath and in large letters was the message, 'For John'.

Blake also designed the famous poster for *Live Aid* in 1985.

● Blindman

Ringo Starr's third non-Beatles feature film. **Allen Klein** arranged for Ringo to appear in the movie and Klein himself makes a guest appearance, along with Beatles roadie **Mal Evans**.

The 'Spaghetti western', which received an X-certificate in Britain, was written by Tony Anthony who also played the lead, and direction was by Ferdinando Baldi. In the 1971 release, Ringo appeared as a 'baddie' called Candy.

The film's plot concerns a blind gunslinger who is hired to escort 50 beautiful girls to an equal number of miners from Texas who have marriage in mind. On his way to collect his charges he discovers that they have been hijacked by a ruthless Mexican bandit called Domingo. He sets off for the border, riding a horse who seems to know the way. He comes across an old man whose daughter, Pilar, has been ravished and kidnapped by Domingo's brother, Candy. The old man leads him to the bandit's camp. Domingo and his sadistic sister Sweet Mama have sold the girls to a group of Mexican soldiers; they then massacre the men before imprisoning their general. Blindman captures Candy and offers to barter him for the girls. He is tricked and ends up with 49 aged Mexicans and Sweet Mama, who captures him and puts him in a cell with Pilar and the general. Blindman escapes from jail with the general and later kills Candy. Domingo then arranges a bizarre funeral-marriage between Candy and Pilar. The general arrives with his troops and routs the bandits while Blindman kills Domingo. He discovers that the general has taken all the girls and sets off, once more, in pursuit.

The *Monthly Film Bulletin* commented, 'There are some nice ideas here and there, most notably the spectacle of the 50 girls twittering through the desert in their nighties and being rounded up like a herd of cattle, and of Ringo Starr tethered to a locomotive and hung with cowbells lest he move without alerting the Blindman.'

The Blue Angel Club – the Beatles were originally barred from the club by Allan Williams, but later became regulars.

● 1 Blomfield Road, Springwood, Garston, Liverpool L19

When **Julia Lennon** went to live with **John Dykins**, they moved into this house on the Springwood council estate. John lived only two miles away with his Aunt **Mimi**, but for some time wasn't aware that his mother lived so near. When he did find out he became a frequent visitor to the premises and began to establish a relationship with his mother.

He was also able to meet his two half-sisters Julia and Jacqueline and the **Quarry Men** sometimes rehearsed here.

John was visiting Blomfield Road the night his mother was killed and he was the person who opened the door to the policeman's knock.

● Blue Angel Club, 108 Seel Street, Liverpool L1

Nightclub opened by **Allan Williams** on 22 March 1961 on the premises of what had formerly been the **Wyvern Social Club**. The Silver Beetles had auditioned at the Wyvern on 10 May 1960 for impresario **Larry Parnes**. Williams had taken over the premises at the time and was planning his new club. On 12 August 1960, **Pete Best** auditioned for the Beatles at the club.

Williams called it the Blue Angel after the **Marlene Dietrich** film and had a large blow-up photograph of Dietrich in a scene from the film on the club wall.

On the club's opening night, cabaret artist Alma Warren appeared, backed by the Terry Francis Quartet. Allan intended the club to be a sophisticated night spot and, at first, didn't want members of the local groups to frequent the club. However, within a short time it became the main late-night watering hole for the Mersey Beat scene and presented beat music in the basement. There was a bar in the basement and one on the ground floor and the first floor had a casino run by Williams' brother-in-law Barry Chang.

The Beatles frequented the club on a regular basis, as did Brian Epstein and most members of the Mersey Beat scene. One evening Bill Harry asked Epstein if he would listen to a girl singer and arranged for **Cilla Black** to get on stage and sing 'Boys' with the group who were performing that night. He then introduced Cilla to Epstein who arranged to meet her at his office the next day and then signed her up.

The Beatles never performed at the club, although the **Rolling Stones** did. When they were performing at Southport, Bill Harry called them at their hotel and they drove into Liverpool and did a free show at the Angel for the members of various Mersey groups.

Allan Williams used the lid of a grand piano as a 'wall of fame', with signatures from the famous. Celebrities from around the world visited the club including **Bob Dylan**, **Allen Ginsburg** and **Judy Garland**.

● Blue Gardenia Club, The, Greek Street, London W1

A late-night club in London's Soho district which, in 1961, was being managed by **Brian Casser**, former leader of one of Liverpool's top bands, Cass & the Cassanovas.

When promoter **Sam Leach** had brought the Beatles down to perform at the **Palais Ballroom, Aldershot** on 9 December 1961, the gig hadn't lived up to expectations due to lack of advertising. After they'd finished performing and had had a number of drinks, Sam suggested they all drop in to the Blue Gardenia Club to see Cass.

They set out from Aldershot at 1.00 a.m. and when they reached the club, John, Paul and Pete got up on stage while George was having a chat with someone who'd recognized him.

● Blue Jay Way

Song penned by George. He wrote it in August 1967 soon after arriving in America with **Pattie**. They'd rented a house on a street called Blue Jay Way. **Derek** and Joan Taylor, who were living in Los Angeles at the time, were due to pop around to see them. Derek had phoned to say that because of the fog they'd been delayed and were having difficulty locating the house. George was tired from jet lag but decided he wanted to remain awake and see Derek and Joan, so he sat at a small Hammond organ and began to compose a song about the fact that he was waiting for Derek – and called it 'Blue Jay Way'. He completed the number back home in Esher and the number was recorded in September 1967 and included on the *Magical Mystery Tour* soundtrack album and EPs.

Of interest is the fact that a number of technical effects were added when the song was recorded at **Abbey Road** in September 1967, including the use of the ADT (Artificial Double Tracking) machine devised by **Ken Townsend**.

● Blue Moon Of Kentucky

Number penned by Bill Monroe and originally recorded by him in 1947. It was the version by **Elvis Presley**, recorded in 1954, which inspired the **Quarry Men** to use the number in their act, with Paul McCartney singing lead vocals.

● Blue Suede Shoes

Classic rock 'n' roll number penned by **Carl Perkins** in 1955. Perkins had a million-seller with the song and was only prevented from reaching No. 1 in the charts by **Elvis Presley**'s 'Heartbreak Hotel'. Elvis also recorded the number, although the version which inspired the **Quarry Men** was the original Perkins one. John Lennon was lead vocalist on the number, which remained in the repertoire when they became the Beatles, and they continued to perform it until late into 1961.

● Bond, Angela

A former BBC producer. When she was a disc jockey in Hong Kong, her radio show was the top show at the time and she was the first person to play a Beatles record in Hong Kong when she gave 'Please Please Me' a spin. She said, 'The reason my show was so popular was that I had a secret mole living at home in England in the shape of my eleven-year-old daughter, who used to listen to **Radio Luxembourg** under the bedsheets at night in school. She'd write me a weekly letter with the titles of the new records that she and her friends liked. I kept her letter about the Beatles because she said the kids called them "fantabulous". So I sent for "Please Please Me" by airmail. Being the first to play the Beatles in Hong Kong sounds a bit like being No. 1 in Lichtenstein or something, but I'm quite proud of the fact.'

When she returned to England she became a producer and recalls, 'One time I was producing a programme called "David Frost At The Phonogram" in 1966. I booked Brian Epstein as a guest and we'd just started rehearsals when we received a call from Brian saying his Doctor had called him and said he was not well enough to appear. I told him not to worry, that we'd manage. Five minutes later he rang again saying he was terribly worried he'd let us down and would try to get someone else for us. I said, "Look, Brian, don't worry, darling, you just get better." Five minutes later the phone rang again and Brian said "Will Paul McCartney do?" Well, you will recall in 1966 to try to get any Beatle was like drawing your back teeth, it was impossible to get interviews with them. So that was the first time I met Paul McCartney, he came along and did the show and I still have a contract that we issued and it says, "By arrangement with Brian Epstein, interview with Paul McCartney. Five guineas."'

● Bony Moronie

A hit for **Larry Williams**, who penned the number, in 1957. The **Quarry Men** immediately included it in their repertoire, with John Lennon on lead vocals. It was an indication of their musical direction, away from skiffle into rock 'n' roll, like so many other Liverpool groups, who also included the number in their act. The group continued to perform it when they became the Beatles, although it was dropped at the end of 1961.

● Bonzo Dog Doo Dah Band, The

One of the most eccentric British groups of the sixties, formed by a band of ex-art students in 1965.

The Beatles hired them to appear in *Magical Mystery Tour* and they can be seen performing in a sequence filmed at Raymond's Revue Bar, a Soho strip club.

They also played at the Beatles' celebration party at the **Royal Lancaster Hotel** at the end of filming, when they were joined by members of the **Beach Boys** and **Freddie Lennon**.

In 1968 the group were having problems recording a single called 'I'm The Urban Spaceman', penned by group member Neil Innes. They approached Paul to produce it for them and he agreed.

Roger Ruskin Spear, the group's saxophonist, commented: 'We really needed someone we would all respect to produce us, and Paul was asked if he could come down and help us out.'

Paul turned up for the session at Chappell's recording studio in Bond Street. He showed the bass player Joe Druckman what to play. Spear noted that: '. . . he wouldn't play the bass line on the record. In the end he did play some ukelele. He thrashed it along with Neil Innes and Viv Stanshall, out in the corridor, and you can hear it plucking in the background.'

It was decided that Paul should be credited with a pseudonym, Apollo C. Vermouth. Roger said, 'Of course, it was cleverly leaked to the press that it was really Paul McCartney. He was only with us for a day but it is extraordinary what he achieved.'

The record was issued in Britain in October 1968 and reached No. 5 in the charts, but it didn't make any impact when it was released in the States in December. When the album *Urban Spaceman*, which contained the track, was issued in America in June 1969, Paul's name had replaced the Apollo C. Vermouth credit.

The group's drummer Legs Larry Smith became a close friend to George Harrison and George wrote a song about him, 'Ladies And Gentleman His Name Is Legs', which appears on his 1975 album *Extra Texture – Read All About It*.

● Boone, Pat

Clean-cut American singing star who, between 1955 and 1962, had a staggering 27 major hits in the charts, including 'Ain't That A Shame', 'Long Tall Sally', 'Friendly Persuasion', 'April Love' and 'Speedy Gonzales'.

The Beatles included one of his numbers, 'Don't Forbid Me', in their repertoire and while the singer was touring in Britain he heard the Beatles' 'From Me To You' and decided to record it when he got back home to America – unfortunately, his record label, Dot Records, advised him against it.

The Beatles' sudden domination of the American charts in 1964 began to affect all sales by other acts and Boone commented, 'The Beatles were selling ALL the records, so the rest of us were twiddling our thumbs, saying, "What's going on here?"' An astute businessman, and noting the effect the Beatles were having on American youth, he obtained a merchandising licence to manufacture lithographs of oil paintings of the Beatles. He decided to promote them in a nationwide campaign by having each set numbered, allowing 30 numbers to be picked which would give 30 young Beatles fans tickets to attend the show at the Convention Centre, Las Vegas, on 20 August 1964.

The promotion was a big success and proved lucrative to Boone, who sold hundreds of thousands of the lithographs.

He turned up at the Las Vegas concert with his wife and daughters and was introduced to the Beatles backstage between shows. He showed them the lithographs and Paul noticed that one of the paintings, based on a photograph showing him holding a cigarette, no longer featured the cigarette. He pointed this out to Boone who mentioned that Leo Janssen, the artist, had anticipated that Boone wouldn't like to merchandise a product in which someone was smoking. Paul said, 'Well, Pat, you know, if we smoke, we smoke.'

● Bootlegs

A 'bootleg' recording is one which has been issued without permission and which does not provide royalties to those to whom royalties should be paid. Despite the fact that legislation has been passed in both the United States and Great Britain effectively making 'bootlegs' illegal, the practice has survived. In the case of the Beatles there is more bootleg material available than on any other act.

The material broadly derives from four main sources: their live appearances; club and concert shows; radio, film and TV performances, basically recorded from the radio or television; studio outtakes, recordings of material, some of it unreleased or not of a standard to be released, which have been illegally smuggled out of the recording studio. There are also various bootlegs of interviews.

There are so many hundreds of Beatles' bootlegs that to include a complete discography is outside the scope of this book. There are, in fact, several books and magazines which have specialized in documenting bootleg material, including *You Can't Do That! Beatles Bootlegs & Novelty Records, 1963-1980*, by Charles Reinhart, published by Pierian Press.

Among the sources from which radio bootlegs have been taken are: BBC radio shows such as **'Pop Go The Beatles'**, **'From Us To You'**, **'Saturday Club'**, 'The Alan Freeman Show' and **Radio Luxembourg** transmissions.

Recordings from television shows have included **'People and Places'**, 'Top Of The Pops', **'Around The Beatles'**, 'The Royal Variety Performance', 'Sunday Night At The London Palladium', 'The **David Frost** Show', 'Blackpool Night Out', **'Drop In'**, 'The **Ed Sullivan** Show', **'Shindig'**, **'Thank Your Lucky Stars'** and **'Our World'**. These also include individual appearances by Ringo Starr in **'Cilla'** and John Lennon in 'Rock And Roll Circus'.

Bootlegs have been issued of numerous live show appearances including the **Star Club**, Hamburg shows; a **Winter Gardens Theatre**, **Bournemouth** concert; an **Apollo, Ardwick** concert; a **Washington Coliseum** concert; a **Festival Hall**, **Melbourne** concert; a

Hollywood Bowl concert; an **Empire Stadium, Vancouver** concert; a **Palais des Sports**, Paris concert; a **Shea Stadium** concert, and a **Nippon Budokan Hall**, Japan concert.

Studio outtakes have included the **Decca audition** tapes; the Parlophone audition tapes; *Let It Be* outtakes and dozens of outtakes of particular numbers, such as 'Lucille', '**I Forgot To Remember To Forget**', 'I'll Be On My Way', 'Sure To Fall', 'Crying, Waiting, Hoping', '**A Shot Of Rhythm And Blues**', 'How Do You Do It', 'My Girl Is Red Hot', 'Dizzy Miss Lizzie', 'Keep Your Hands Off My Baby', 'Soldier Of Love', 'I Got A Woman', 'Little Child', 'Colliding Circles', 'What's The New Mary Jane', 'Annie', 'Not Unknown', 'India' and 'Stand By Me'.

There have also been bootlegs of soundtracks from *Yellow Submarine*, *Let It Be* and various promotional films, such as 'Strawberry Fields Forever' and 'Penny Lane'.

Another bootleg source has been that of the Beatles' interviews. Bootlegs in this vein have included material from *Ed Rudy's American Tour* album, **Murray the K** interviews, the *Hear The Beatles Tell All* album, an interview by disc jockey Tom Clay, a **Kenny Everett** interview and various interviews from **Brian Matthew**'s thirteen-part radio series **'The Beatles Story'**. There have even been such oddities as *I Apologize*, which was a bootleg recording of the press conference at the Astor Tower Hotel, Chicago, in which John Lennon apologized for his 'greater than Jesus' statement and a reading of excerpts from *A Cellarful Of Noise* by Brian Epstein.

The quality of bootleg recording varies, as does the production. Some albums are cheaply produced, others are as lavish as the professional releases. There are bootleg albums, EPs and singles and the individual titles run into the hundreds. Here are some examples of the titles of bootleg Beatles albums: *Abbey Road Revisited*, *ABC Manchester 1964*, *Alive At Last In Atlanta*, *Alpha Omega*, *And The Beatles Were Born*, *Around The Beatles*, *The Beatles By Royal Command*, *Beatles Happy Birthday*, *Beatles In Italy*, *The Beatles Introduce New Songs*, *Beatles Live In Washington DC*, *Christmas Message From Liverpool*, *Elvis Meets . . . The Beatles*, *Five Nights In A Judo Arena*, *Indian Rope Trick*, *The Last Beatle Record* and *Twickenham Jams*.

One of the most famous bootlegs was the anthology *Alpha Omega*, a four-volume collection issued in America by Audio Tape Inc on ATRBH 3583. When this was originally issued early in 1973 it was actually advertised on radio and television. There was quite a demand for the unauthorized recordings which contained virtually every number the Beatles ever recorded. As a result of this particular bootleg set, **EMI** decided to issue two double albums of Beatles material almost immediately and *The Beatles 1962–1966* and *The Beatles 1967–1970* were issued in both Britain and America in April 1973.

● Borashallen, Boras, Sweden

Fourth stop on the Beatles' first-ever foreign tour. They appeared at the Borashallen on 28 October 1963 when they gave one performance at 7.30 p.m. The group were booked to give nine concerts at five venues for a total fee of £2,000 during this very short Swedish tour.

They received an enthusiastic reception from the Swedish audience.

● Boston Gardens, Boston, Massachusetts

A sports arena which was the home of the Celtics and the Bruins. For the Beatles' appearance there on Saturday, 12 September 1964, the 13,909 tickets had sold out within a matter of hours.

There were intriguing little dramas taking place at most of the Beatles' American gigs and one of the stories here concerned a youth who escaped from reform school, held a male fan at knifepoint and stole his ticket. The police were able to apprehend the escapee because the fan remembered his seat number.

A black limousine with an escort of six motorcycles proved to be an effective decoy, while the Beatles sped away in a single car.

● Boyd, Jennie

One of Pattie Boyd's two younger sisters (the other is Paula). For a time Jennie was a model and then worked in the **Apple Boutique**. She joined the Beatles and party on their trip to Bangor to see the **Maharishi** and also went to Rishikesh with them. For a time she lived with **Alexis Mardas** and the two of them had been holidaying in Greece with **Cynthia Lennon** in May 1968 and were with her when she arrived at **Kenwood** and discovered John with **Yoko**.

Following the collapse of the Apple Boutique, she and Pattie went into the antique business with a stall called Juniper in Chelsea Market, but they closed it at the

Left: Pattie Boyd cuts George Harrison's hair in *A Hard Day's Night*. (©Walter Shenson Films/Apple)
Below: Pattie and Paul. (©Walter Shenson Films/Apple)

beginning of 1969 because it entailed getting up early in the morning.

Jennie became the inspiration for **Donovan**'s hit 'Jennifer Juniper'.

She married Mick Fleetwood, drummer with Fleetwood Mac, and went to live in America. They divorced, were reconciled, then split up again.

● Boyd, Pattie

Born Patricia Anne Boyd on 17 March 1944, Pattie first arrived in London with ambitions of becoming a model in 1962 and was brought to the attention of the British public when she appeared on a series of television commercials for Smith's Crisps. The commercials were produced by **Dick Lester** and when he was commissioned to direct the Beatles' debut movie *A Hard Day's Night*, he booked Pattie for the role of one of the schoolgirls who meet the Beatles on a train travelling from Liverpool to London.

George Harrison was enchanted by her and said she reminded him of his favourite film star, Brigitte Bardot. Their romance blossomed and she moved into his bungalow, **Kinfauns**, in Esher where he proposed to her on Christmas Day 1965. She was a popular figure with teenagers and wrote a column on the British rock scene for America's *16* Magazine called 'Pattie's Letter From London'.

The couple were wed at **Epsom Register Office**, Surrey, on 21 January 1966, with Paul McCartney in attendance, and spent their honeymoon in Barbados. When George was busy touring it was Pattie who became interested in spiritual matters (having decided to retire from her career as fashion model) and she was the first member of the Beatles' circle to join the **Maharishi Mahesh Yogi**'s Spiritual Regeneration movement and encouraged the others to attend his lecture at the **Hilton Hotel**, London, on 24 August 1967.

Her vivacity and beauty made headlines – she was an ideal Beatles bride in the eyes of the media, and proved to be the inspiration for several of George's songs, including 'Something', 'For You Blue' and 'It's All Too Much'. Over the years, however, the couple drifted apart. When they were ensconced at **Friar Park** in Henley-on-Thames, Pattie was not unaware of the interest George's best friend **Eric Clapton** showed in her. In an effort to revive George's interest, or to make him jealous, she began to flirt with Eric and soon Eric realized he had fallen in love with her.

He wrote a song declaring his love, which he based on a 1,000-year-old Persian book by Nizami called *Layla And Majnun*. The song 'Layla' was included on an album Eric made under the pseudonym Derek & the Dominoes and George was invited to play on it. The number entered the British Top Ten in 1972 and again in 1982.

Pattie was becoming bored living in isolation at Friar Park. After six years of marriage the couple still had no children and Pattie was restless and wanted to become a model again. At the end of 1973 she had a brief fling with Ronnie Wood and she also agreed to model at an Ossie Clark fashion show, against George's wishes. Eventually, Pattie left George to join Eric on his American tour but she and George were briefly reconciled before the final split when Pattie went to live with Clapton. George commented, 'I'd rather she was with him than some dope.'

Pattie was divorced from George in 1977 and married Eric on 27 March 1979 in Tucson, Arizona. On their return a wedding reception was held in the back garden of Clapton's home, Hurtwood Edge, in the village of Ewhurst. George and his second wife Olivia were among the many celebrity guests, who included Paul McCartney, Ringo Starr, Mick Jagger, **Elton John, Lonnie Donegan**, Jeff Beck and Ray Cooper. Clapton had hired workmen to erect a makeshift platform for a jam session and three of the Beatles shared the same stage once more!

Pattie and Eric were married for seven years but they broke up in 1986.

● Boyle, Bernard

A local fan of the Beatles during the days they were still playing in Liverpool. He formed a Beatles Fan Club in September 1961 prior to Brian Epstein managing the group and a few months before an official fan club was sanctioned.

In this first-ever Beatles Fan Club, Bernard was President, Jennifer Dawes Treasurer and Maureen O'Shea Secretary.

● Boys

A number penned by Luthor Dixon and Wes Farrell which was the flipside of the Shirelles single 'Will You Still Love Me Tomorrow?' when it was released in November 1960. Soon after, numerous Liverpool groups, including the Beatles, were performing the number, which provided a vocal vehicle for Ringo Starr when he was a member of **Rory Storm & the Hurricanes.** When **Cilla Black** used to sing occasionally with the Hurricanes, this was the number she wanted to perform, but she had to sing along with Ringo, both of them using the same mike. When the Beatles performed the number, it was drummer **Pete Best** who sang it.

When Ringo joined the Beatles, he also sang the number with them. Apart from the version on *The Beatles Live! At the Star Club In Hamburg, Germany: 1962* album, the group recorded the number on their *Please Please Me* album and on several BBC radio programmes, including **'Side By Side'**, **'Saturday Club'**, **'Pop Go The Beatles'** and **'From Us to You'**.

The number was included on the compilation *Rock 'n Roll Music* and a live version is found on *The Beatles At The Hollywood Bowl* album. American albums featuring the number include *Introducing The Beatles*, *The Beatles*

Wilfred Brambell, the character actor who appeared in the Beatles' debut film. (National Film Archive)

as *The Four Seasons*, *Songs, Pictures And Stories Of The Fabulous Beatles* and *The Early Beatles*.

A single of 'Boys' coupled with 'Kansas City/Hey! Hey! Hey!' was issued on **Capitol** Starline 6066 on 11 October 1965. The highest position it reached was No. 102 in the charts.

● BPI Jubilee Awards

In 1977, the year of the Queen's Silver Jubilee, the BPI (British Phonogram Industry) made some special awards covering the previous twenty-five years in the British music industry. The awards included:

Best British Pop Album, 1952–1977: *Sgt Pepper's Lonely Hearts Club Band*, the Beatles

Best British Pop Group, 1952–1977: the Beatles

Best British Record Producer, 1952–1977: George Martin

Best British Pop Single, 1952–1977: 'Bohemian Rhapsody', Queen (although the Beatles received a nomination for 'She Loves You').

● Brambell, Wilfred

A British character actor noted for his portrayal of the grizzled rag-and-bone man, Steptoe, in the long-running BBC TV series 'Steptoe And Son'.

He co-starred with the Beatles in *A Hard Day's Night* as John McCartney, Paul's eccentric grandfather, who travels down to London with them and causes chaos wherever he goes.

At the time of the filming he commented: 'I was worried about how someone like myself would fit in with these Beatles. I liked their music but I was no expert and I felt the whole thing could easily become a fiasco. Instead, they positively amazed me with their cool and professional approach.'

Wilfred travelled to Liverpool for the northern premiere of the film but refused to attend the opening as he claimed he had been slighted by officials at the civic reception.

He died of cancer on 18 January 1985 at the age of 72.

● Bramwell, Tony

A childhood friend of George Harrison, he became an office boy at NEMS in Liverpool after Brian Epstein signed the Beatles and was among the staff who moved to London when **NEMS Enterprises** decamped.

From office boy he graduated to handling various assignments and soon became one of those close friends the Beatles always had around who was also capable of doing a good job of work.

He travelled to America with them and wrote reports of their activities for various publications, including the *Beatles Monthly*.

Brian Epstein appointed him stage manager of the **Saville Theatre** and after Brian's death he was placed in charge of Apple promotion until 1970 and then ran Apple Music in Los Angeles for a year. He left in 1971 and became involved in the music for the James Bond films which led to him working on independent promotion for artists such as Paul McCartney and the **Moody Blues**. He became Head of Promotion for Polydor Records in the UK for a time at the beginning of the seventies, then an independent record plugger and later began to represent **Phil Spector**'s interests in Britain.

He was to say, 'I started in 1963 as the Beatles' roadie and toured the world with most of the Mersey Beat bands through to 1965. Then I became head of NEMS Presentations and Subafilms, Brian Epstein's production and film companies. This involved producing and directing promotional films and stage shows with the Beatles, the Who, Jimi Hendrix, the Bee Gees and Cream.'

Tony was also a dab hand with a camera and many of his photographs of Apple acts, such as **Mary Hopkin**, were syndicated throughout the world.

There were rumours abounding that Tony was 'the third virgin'. Although John and **Yoko** said that they took the nude photographs of each other for the *Two Virgins* album with a timer, it was generally known that there was a third person present. In **Ray Connolly**'s book *John Lennon 1940–1980* there is a photograph of John and Yoko in Tittenhurst Park and a large framed photograph can be seen in which there are three naked people at the *Two Virgins* session. The third is a bearded man who looks like Tony Bramwell.

During the late sixties the former NEMS office boy and 'gofor' became one of London's most eligible bachelors, dating an assortment of Miss Worlds and celebrities such as Christine Keeler, and he lived with Swedish actress Julie Ege for a number of years, before getting married and settling down.

● Bravo, Lizzie

A Brazilian girl, Lizzie was sixteen years old and a student living in Compayne Gardens, near to Abbey Road, when she waited outside the **Abbey Road Studios** on Sunday, 4 February 1968, hoping to catch a glimpse of the Beatles.

There were a number of other girls crowded outside the studio when Paul emerged looking for two fans to provide some falsetto harmonies on their current recording. He picked on Lizzie and another girl called Gayleen Pease and the two of them were asked inside to contribute some vocal harmonies to 'Across The Universe'. Lizzie and Gayleen were asked to sing the line 'Nothing's going to change my world' several times.

On the twentieth anniversary of the Beatles' recording career, a limited edition of 2,000 copies of a twelve-inch single was issued in Brazil with one side featuring Lizzie discussing her experiences in Portuguese. The 'B' side contained 'Love Me Do' and 'The Beatles Movie Medley'.

● Bresner, Sergeant Buddy

The policeman assigned to guard the Beatles when they arrived in Miami Beach. He took over as their personal police bodyguard on Friday, 14 February 1964, and also acted as their adviser and friend. Buddy had been chosen for the job because he had previously looked after celebrities in the district, and he was given two dozen officers to command.

That evening the Beatles accepted the offer of having dinner at his home, where they met his wife Dottie and his children Barry, Andy and Jeri. **Dezo Hoffman,** who was also present, was struck by how Paul seemed so completely at home with the children. 'The unbelievable patience he had with those kids was incredible,' Dezo said. 'They didn't let him alone for a moment. He sat there reading to them, in a way that was obviously not an inconvenience to him at all – he was completely at home.'

Buddy then took them back to the **Deauville Hotel** which had a couple of nightclubs. They went in to see comedian Don Rickells, who gagged: 'Look at this, a police sergeant guarding four Zulus when all over the city there's fighting and burglary going on.' After the show

Brian Poole – he beat the Beatles to a Decca recording contract. (Brian Poole)

John was tired and went to bed, but the others went to the second nightclub to see comedian Myron Cohen and singer/dancer Carol Lawrence. Comedian Cohen liked the Beatles and later commented, 'So long as they are still only TRYING to stamp out the Beatles in thirty years' time who cares?'

Part of Bresner's duties consisted of conducting bed checks every night to make sure there were no girls in their rooms – and no drugs. After they'd been to visit Cassius Clay (**Muhammad Ali**), Bresner took the lads to their very first drive-in movie, **Elvis Presley**'s *Fun In Acapulco*.

The Beatles loved Miami so much they decided to stay

n there for a few more days and Bresner arranged some ther outings, including a visit to Star Island.

Brian Poole & The Tremeloes

A group from Dagenham, Essex, who auditioned for **Decca Records** at their West Hampstead studios on 1 anuary 1962 on the same day as the Beatles had their ecording audition. As it turned out, Decca's **Dick Rowe** greed to take on one of the two groups recorded by **Mike mith** that day and it was eventually decided on the 'remeloes, presumably because they lived in closer roximity to London.

Brian Poole & the Tremeloes had no record success ntil after the Beatles had become a major British chart roup and, in fact, copied the style which was known as lersey Beat, initially covering 'Twist And Shout' four onths after the Beatles had included the number on their ebut album *Please Please Me* and they followed up with Do You Love Me', a number which had been released by nother Mersey Beat band, Faron's Flamingos – although e Flamingos' version was relegated to the 'B' side on the ecision of London executives. 'Twist And Shout' gave the remeloes a No. 4 position in the charts and 'Do You Love e' reached No. 1. Initially, the north/south divide was vident when northern fans were annoyed to see a group om the south achieve success by what they regarded as inching' the new sound from the north.

Brian Poole & the Tremeloes enjoyed some further hits ntil 1965: 'I Can Dance', 'Candy Man', 'Someone omeone', 'Twelve Steps To Love', 'Three Bells' and 'I 'ant Candy'. The Tremeloes went solo and, without Poole, hieved a further dozen chart entries.

The group comprised: Brian Poole, vocals; Rick West, ad guitar; Alan Blakely, rhythm guitar; Alan Howard, ss guitar; and Dave Munden, drums.

92 Broadway Avenue, Wallasey, Merseyside L45

e McCartney family lived in this house, situated across e Mersey from Liverpool, for almost two years in 1942 d 1943. **Jim** and **Mary McCartney** had moved into the all house with baby Paul, but decided to move back to verpool after **Mike McCartney** was born because the eet was close to the docks and suffered some of the rst air raids.

Broadwick Street, London W1

The gentlemen's lavatory, set in the centre of Broadwick Street, is one of the few subterranean toilets still left in the centre of the West End.

John Lennon filmed outside the toilet on 27 November 1966 as part of his sketch on the Peter Cook and Dudley Moore show, **'Not Only...But Also'**. The gentlemen's toilet was supposed to represent the entrance to a night-club and an additional sign, 'Members Only', was attached beneath the 'Gentlemen' sign. John was dressed as a commissionaire, in top hat and white gloves, wearing granny glasses. The programme, the comedy duo's Christmas show, was broadcast on 26 December 1966 and was repeated on 7 February 1967.

Brodax, Al

The head of the TV and Film section of America's King Features Syndicate in 1964 when he approached Brian Epstein for a licence to produce a series of animated Beatles cartoons featuring Beatles songs. The 35-year-old New Yorker agreed to a deal in which Epstein took 50 per cent of the fees. Brodax was both writer and producer of the series which became the highest rating Saturday morning show of its time when it was originally screened in America in 1965.

During his negotiations for the series, Brodax also expressed his desire to make an animated feature film of the Beatles. Epstein told him that if the television cartoon series was a success, he would agree to him making a feature film.

However, Brodax had difficulties in contacting Epstein to finalize a deal for the feature. This was in 1965 when Brian was rarely in his office, due to his increasing addiction to drugs. Several meetings were cancelled and at one time, Brodax had to hang around for ten days for an appointment. But he persevered with the project, which was called *Yellow Submarine*. He'd even paid major writers such as Joseph Heller, author of the best-seller *Catch 22*, to prepare ideas for the feature, but Epstein seemed uninterested. It was Wendy Hanson who finally bullied Epstein into a meeting, and he nearly sacked her because of it.

Epstein liked the title and agreed to Brodax going ahead with the film, promising that the Beatles would provide four original songs for it.

Brodax did not enjoy his meetings with Epstein who, he

claimed, treated him in a cavalier manner, but his persistence was rewarded with an animated film which became a classic of its kind.

● Brodziak, Kenn

The Australian promoter who took the Beatles down under to tour in June 1964.

Brodziak, who had previously brought major names such as **Marlene Dietrich** and Sophie Tucker to tour Australia, arrived in London in July 1963 to book acts. At a meeting at the booking office of agent Cyril Berlin he was offered the choice of six groups and he liked the sound of the Beatles best and decided to book them. On 5 July 1963 he made a verbal contract to promote the Beatles in Australia at £1,000 per week.

The Beatles' career then began to take off in a major way and the group could have demanded a considerably larger fee than the modest verbal deal. Brian Epstein sent a note to Berlin, 'You'll think me a very naughty boy, but I want £1,500 per week for Australia.'

Meanwhile, Brodziak was getting worried. He didn't have a contract and the fame of the Beatles was spreading to such an extent that there was great interest shown by rival promoters in bringing the group to Australia. In fact Epstein was offered a considerably increased sum for an Australian tour via **Tito Burns**, but decided to honour his verbal agreement. He sent a telegram to Brodziak, 'I made an agreement and I will stick to it. The Beatles will come to Australia'.

The contracts were finally signed on 10 January 1964.

Brodziak tied in with **Dick Lean**, managing director of Stadiums Limited, who controlled a number of venues, for the fourteen playing dates, with Lean handling the security and supports while Brodziak was in charge of the staging. A Melbourne rock singer, **Johnny Chester,** was booked at £125 a week, together with a four-piece band called the **Phantoms** and New Zealand rock singer **Johnny Devlin**

● Bron, Eleanor

British actress who first rose to fame on the 'satire boom' in the early sixties, appearing at London's first satirical nightclub, the Establishment, and as a resident performer on the TV series 'Not So Much A Programme . . . More A Way Of Life'.

She made her film debut in *Help!* in 1965 and the *Sun* newspaper ran a story headed 'The Beatles' First Leading

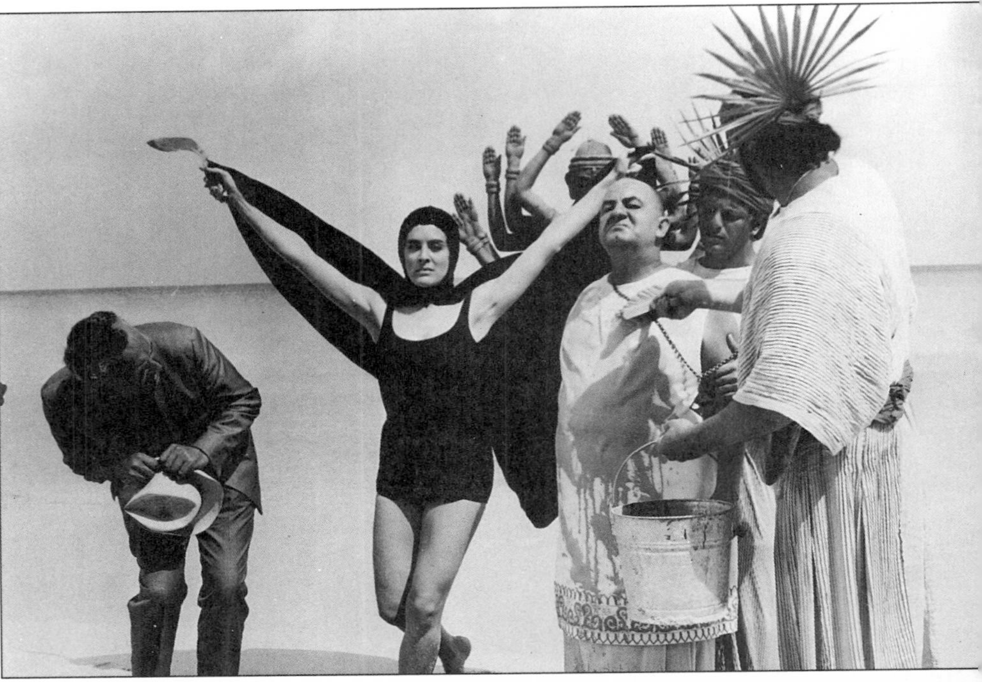

Eleanor Bron as the mysterious ally of the Beatles in *Help!* (©Apple/Walter Shenson Films)

Lady' in which they wrote: 'Miss Bron, who has made a name for herself with pitiless send-ups of upper-class English women, will herself be an upper-class woman of a type: a mysterious Eastern princess who wants to be loved by the Beatles. She will thus become the Beatles' first leading lady (the woman interest in *A Hard Day's Night*, the Beatles' first film, was minimal). But the film people are not anxious to push this point too hard: it might upset some of the Beatles' girl fans.'

Eleanor portrayed a mysterious princess called Ahme, who comes to the boys' rescue on several occasions when they are pursued by Clang, leader of a religious cult, and his gang of murderous thugs.

During the filming in the Bahamas, the press kept trying to talk her into posing for photographs in a bikini, but she refused. She was surprised to see a *Daily Mail* photo-story headed 'Bron The Beatle Tamer', with a photograph of Paul McCartney on a bike talking to a dark-haired girl in a bikini with her back to the camera. It wasn't her!

While she was filming, Eleanor struck up a friendship with John Lennon and they used to spend time together drinking in the hotel bars, discussing politics and philosophy. When the Beatles were staying in **Benedict Canyon** in Beverly Hills prior to their **Hollywood Bowl** concert, Eleanor visited John there and spent a few hours with him. John was later to claim that she had been one of his conquests, but Eleanor denies they were ever lovers, pointing out that John was married to **Cynthia** and she had a boyfriend at the time.

Eleanor's recollections of filming with the Beatles are to be found in *The Pillow Book Of Eleanor Bron*, published by Jonathan Cape in 1985.

Brook Brothers, The

A vocal duo from Southampton who were touted as Britain's answer to the Everly Brothers. They had several chart hits between 1961 and 1963: 'Warpaint', 'Ain't Gonna Wash For A Week', 'He's Old Enough To Know Better', 'Welcome Home Baby' and 'Trouble Is My Middle Name'.

They were booked to appear on the Beatles' autumn tour of Britain in November/December 1963.

Brookfield

A fifteenth-century, oak-beamed mansion in Elstead, near Guildford, Surrey. **Peter Sellers** bought the house and spent £50,000 on renovations. The house was set in several acres of ground and had its own lake, paddocks, walled gardens and barns. Sellers had a gymnasium, changing rooms, sauna and private cinema built into the barns.

When filming ***The Magic Christian***, Ringo Starr discovered that Peter was going to put the house on the market. He offered him £70,000 for it and Peter agreed. John Lennon also liked the house and offered him £150,000 for it, but Sellers decided to keep his word to Ringo. Ringo bought the house and later sold it to American singer Stephen Stills.

● Brooks, Elkie

One of Britain's major female vocalists.

Her real name was Elkie Brookbinder and she was a cabaret singer in Manchester before turning to rock music.

She appeared with the Beatles on 'Another Beatles' Christmas Show' at the **Odeon, Hammersmith** from 24 December 1964 to 16 January 1965. Elkie then changed her image from dance band singer to aggressive female rocker in the early seventies with Dada and Vinegar Joe. She was to enjoy success as a major concert performer and recording artist with over thirteen chart singles, including 'Pearl's A Singer', 'Lilac Wine', 'Fool If You Think It's Over' and 'No More The Fool'.

Her brother is Tony Mansfield, former drummer with **Billy J. Kramer** and the Dakotas.

● Brown, Bobbie

A Liverpool girl who launched the Beatles' first **Official Fan Club** in May 1962 (an unofficial club had been launched the year previously). Bobbie was a **Cavern** regular, began to advertise her club in ***Mersey Beat***, and was aided in her efforts by friends such as **Freda Kelly**. Bobbie passed over the running of the club to Freda when she became engaged to be married, early in 1963.

In December 1962 she wrote about the Beatles fan club in a letter to *Mersey Beat*:

> 'The Fan Club has now been operating since April last, and the amount of members accumulated during this time, which has risen tremendously to one thousand, has made our efforts seem well worthwhile. Our members come from all over the country, from such

places as Glasgow, Lancaster, Blackpool, Essex, Doncaster, Sussex, I.O.M., Northern Ireland – and even further afield from Hamburg, Belgium and Rhodesia. My daily post is fantastic, an average of thirty letters a day!

'Recently I visited the **Star Club** in Hamburg, with a number of fans, to see the Beatles. How pleased they were to see that they were appreciated there just as they had been by the numerous fans in this country. It is most rewarding to see after a hard struggle from the bottom that they have reached the top in their own special field of entertainment. It is the "get up and go" quality which these boys possess that makes the Fan Club well worth running. Early next year we're going to organize a "Fan Club Festival" in which the boys really "meet" their fans.'

● Brown, Joe

Popular, blond-haired singer/guitarist who was first spotted by TV producer Jack Good performing at a dance in Southend.

Good featured him on his shows such as 'Oh Boy!' and Brown was soon to become a well-established show-biz star.

Born in Lincolnshire on 13 May 1941, his family moved to London's East End when he was two years old.

Brown's string of hits began with '**Darktown Strutter's Ball**' in 1960 and he began appearing at live gigs backed by his band the Bruvvers.

In 1962 he was No. 3 in the charts with '**A Picture Of You**', when Brian Epstein booked him on behalf of **NEMS Enterprises** for two consecutive gigs, with the Beatles in support, part of Epstein's plan to present the group on bills with established acts. 'A Picture Of You' was one of Epstein's favourite records at the time which is presumably why the Beatles included it in their repertoire, with George on vocals, even though it was untypical of their style.

Their first gig with Brown was at the **Cambridge Hall** in Southport on 26 July 1962, followed by a **Tower Ballroom** appearance the next evening. On the 27 July show, apart from Brown and the Beatles, the other acts were the Statesmen, the Big Three, Steve Day & the Drifters and the Four Jays.

In 1967 Brown recorded **With A Little Help From My Friends**, which became a minor hit for him, reaching the position of No. 32 in the British charts in June of that year.

Brown was to marry Liverpool singer Vicki Haseman, former student at the **Junior Art School** and a member of the female vocal groups the **Vernon Girls** and the Breakaways.

Their daughter Samantha Brown was later to become a hit recording artist in her own right in the eighties.

Sadly, Vicki died of cancer on 16 June 1991.

● Brown, Ken

A guitarist who played with the **Les Stewart Quartet**, along with a sixteen-year-old George Harrison.

Ruth Morrison, George's first girlfriend, was a family friend of the Bests and when they were planning the **Casbah** and wondering how they would go about booking a group, Ruth mentioned that Ken had a group. He went to see the Bests and they agreed to book the group as resident band.

The group were due to appear at the Casbah on opening night, Saturday, 29 August 1959. However, Les Stewart and Ken had a big argument because Stewart was piqued that Ken had spent so much time fixing up the Casbah that he'd missed out on rehearsals at the **Lowlands Club**, and Stewart refused to play at the Casbah.

George was present at the flare-up and left with Ken. He told him he'd find two mates and turned up with John and Paul. The four of them played at the club that night, their only amplification being Ken's ten-watt amplifier, and secured the residency.

The local newspaper, The ***West Derby Reporter*** noted how Kenneth Brown, David Hughes and Dougla[s] Jenkins helped to decorate the club and make it shipshape and added: 'Kenneth Brown is also a member of a guita[r] group which entertains the club members on Saturda[y] nights. The other members of the group, who cal[l] themselves "The **Quarry Men**", travel from the south en[d] of the city to play.'

The group performed numbers such as 'Long Tall Sally' and 'Three Cool Cats' and received a payment of thre[e] pounds, which meant fifteen shillings for each of them. Ken played rhythm guitar with the band.

Ken's tenure lasted about six weeks due to a[n] unfortunate disagreement. One night Ken had a cold an[d] felt too ill to play with the band, so **Mona Best** suggeste[d] that he could collect the money at the door rather tha[n] play on stage. At the end of the night when it came to paying the band's fee, she divided it up as usual and paid Ken fifteen shillings. Ken noted that Paul objected saying that since he didn't play he shouldn't get paid and John and George backed him up. Mrs Best was adamant and the group boycotted the club for a time and also told Ken he was no longer a member of the Quarry Men.

Ken then suggested to **Pete Best** that they form their own group and Pete liked the idea, bought a drum kit and they replaced the Quarry Men as resident band with their new group which they called the **Blackjacks.** Ironically, this suggestion of Ken's led Pete to a career as a drummer which resulted in him joining the Beatles. Ken himself left Liverpool soon after.

While the Quarry Men were resident at the Casbah, George refused to take Ruth Morrison to the pictures one night and the incident led to their break-up.

She then moved to Birmingham where she became a nurse.

● Brown, Peter

One of Brian Epstein's close friends, Peter was born in Bebington in the Wirral, across the river from Liverpool. He worked for a time in Henderson's, one of Liverpool's large department stores, before becoming the manager of the record department in another store, Lewis's, which was quite close to the **NEMS** branch in Great Charlotte Street.

When Epstein went on to run the new NEMS store in Whitechapel he talked the 22-year-old Brown into taking his place as manager of the Great Charlotte Street shop.

In 1965, when he'd settled in London, Brian asked Brown to move to the capital as his personal assistant. Brown worked from offices in Stafford Street and dealt with a variety of matters relating to the Beatles, ranging from contractual dealings to arranging social events.

Brown was invited to spend the weekend with Brian and **Geoffrey Ellis** at Epstein's country house at **Kingsley Hill** over the Bank Holiday weekend in August 1967. Epstein decided to leave them and returned to London. Brown later received a call – Brian had been found dead.

In the power vacuum left by the death of the Beatles' manager, several people tried to hustle their way into taking Brian's place. Brown, similar to Brian in so many ways, looked after their affairs for a while and became General Manager of Beatles & Co and then became an executive at **Apple Corps** in Savile Row. In his book *The Longest Cocktail Party*, author **Richard DiLello** describes Brown as 'The impeccable Signor Suave of the Apple diplomatic corps and personal assistant and social co-ordinator to the Beatles'.

It was Peter Brown who accompanied John and **Yoko** to Gibraltar and acted as best man at their wedding. John mentions Peter by name on his single 'The Ballad Of John And Yoko'.

When **Allen Klein** moved in he found it very easy to get rid of the majority of the Apple staff, some of whom had been associated with the Beatles since the early Liverpool days. However, he found it more difficult to sack Brown or **Neil Aspinall**. At Apple the directors resigned each year and then were automatically reappointed. Klein made sure that when Brown's resignation came in, his directorship was not renewed.

In 1970 Peter left Apple to join **Robert Stigwood**'s organization and then moved to America.

In the eyes of Beatle fans, his copy book was blotted when he began to write what was to become known as a 'kiss-and-tell' book. He'd been approached by writer Stephen Gaines and the two were to receive a substantial advance payment for a book on the Beatles. As an 'insider', Peter would have access to the surviving members of the band and their relatives and friends. He told them that he was writing a book about the period of the sixties in general. When *The Love You Make: An Insider's Story Of The Beatles* was first published in America in January 1963 by McGraw-Hill, it infuriated Peter's former colleagues who had co-operated by discussing their memories, because the book did not portray the Beatles in a sympathetic light, was written like an exposé, suggested that Yoko Ono was responsible for the Beatles' break-up and intimated that she turned John into a heroin addict. It also revived some of the inaccurate stories that had appeared in previous books such as *Shout!* – in particular, the suggestion that Brian Epstein fell in love with John Lennon the moment he saw him, which became his main reason for signing up the Beatles. This unsubstantiated tale, which was originally told to Philip Norman by a gay friend of Epstein's in Liverpool, is false. Epstein was genuinely excited by what was happening on the Mersey scene and saw it as providing him with an exciting challenge to his creative talents.

● Browne, Tara

A close friend of the individual members of the Beatles and John and Paul in particular. He visited Paul at the McCartney home **Rembrandt** in the Wirral and became a good friend of **Mike McCartney**, too. His other friends included **Brian Jones** of the **Rolling Stones** and Spencer Davis of the Spencer Davis group and he visited the London 'in' clubs such as **Sibylla's** and the Bag O' Nails regularly.

Tara was married to Noreen, daughter of an Irish farmer, and they had two children, Dorian and Julian. However, he was estranged from his wife and dating a nineteen-year-old model Suki Potier when he was involved in a fatal car crash. The 21-year-old Tara, a member of the Guinness family and heir to one million pounds, which he was to receive on his 25th birthday, died on 18 December 1966. He was driving his Lotus Elan sports car when he crashed into the back of a van in South Kensington. He was killed, but Suki escaped with bruises and shock, saying that Tara had swerved the car to protect her. Her father, Gilbert Potier said, 'I am certain Mr Browne saved my daughter. It was very courageous.'

When John Lennon read about the accident in the *Daily Mail* newspaper he included a reference to it in his song 'A Day In The Life', which was featured on the *Sgt Pepper's Lonely Hearts Club Band* album.

Another item from the *Daily Mail*, regarding holes in the road in Lancashire, was also included in the words of the song.

● Bryan, Dora

British actress/comedienne who recorded what is arguably the first novelty record about the Beatles, 'All I Want For Christmas Is A Beatle'.

The single, issued on Fontana 427, entered the British charts in December 1963 and reached the position of No. 22, with a chart life of six weeks.

Dora was also to appear in a West End revue in which there was a parody of the Beatles called the Cockroaches, a four-girl group dressed in Beatles-style suits and wigs. Paul McCartney and **Jane Asher** went to see her in the show and thoroughly enjoyed the sketch.

● Bryce Hanmer Ltd

A firm based in London's Albemarle Street which was engaged to supervise the financial affairs of **Apple Corps**. Harry Pinsler was the head of the company and when John and **Yoko** appeared nude on the cover of the *Two Virgins* album, Pinsler and four other directors of Apple Corps resigned.

● Bryce, Leslie

Photographer who became the official photographer for **Sean O'Mahoney**'s *The Beatles Book* (later to become the *Beatles Monthly*), which gained him an access to the Beatles which was denied other photographers. As a result he took many exclusive picture sessions and travelled around the world with the group, taking literally thousands of photographs.

Leslie had previously worked under renowned photographers such as Baron and Lord Snowdon and passed on many tips to the Beatles who were genuinely interested in photography, particularly Ringo.

Because he was present with the Beatles on numerous occasions, he was one of the many people who were given the tag **'the Fifth Beatle'**.

● Bumblers, The

A spoof supergroup, who got together to perform a Beatles parody during the height of **Beatlemania** in America in 1964.

They comprised Frank Sinatra, Bing Crosby, Samm[y] Davis Jr and Dean Martin.

● Burns, Tito

A leading British impresario of the sixties. The former accordionist/bandleader had become a prominent manager and agent, representing acts such as **Cliff Richard**. He had the foresight to phone Brian Epstein in Liverpool following the release of 'Love Me Do' to enquire about the Beatles' availability for live shows.

Epstein wrote to him offering the Beatles to perform for £250 per week during January and February 1963 although Burns didn't take up the offer, merely filing the letter.

In the autumn of 1963 he phoned Epstein in Liverpool again on behalf of an Australian promoter, Harry Miller whom he represented. Burns knew that Epstein had discussed an Australian tour with another promoter, but had only been offered £2,000.

Burns offered Epstein £7,000 if the Beatles would agree to tour Australia for Miller. Although Epstein hadn signed any contract with the other promoter, he felt that he'd given his word and therefore refused the offer from Burns.

However, the two became friends. Burns had begun building a powerful show-business company and represented a number of artists ranging from Liverpool's the **Searchers** to **Dusty Springfield**.

At one time the two discussed the possibility of uniting their respective organizations and becoming partners. However, Brian couldn't come to terms with the idea that Tito should be able to close any deals in which the Beatles were involved and the merger didn't take place.

● Byrds, The

A group from California who comprised Roger McGuinn (guitar/vocals), Chris Hillman (bass/vocals), Gene Clark (vocals), Dave Crosby (guitar/vocals) and Michael Clarke (drums).

Following their first hit 'Mr Tambourine Man', in 1965 :hey were said to be America's answer to the Beatles and George Harrison once called them, 'The American Beatles'.

Former Beatles PR man **Derek Taylor** became their publicist when he opened offices in Los Angeles and the group met the Beatles socially on a number of occasions. On 2 August 1965 Paul and **Jane Asher** joined three members of the group for a night out at the London nightspot the Scotch of St James. A few weeks later Paul and George attended the Byrds' recording session for the Bob Dylan song 'The Times They Are A Changing' on the morning of 27 August 1965, the day of heir historic meeting some hours later with **Elvis Presley**.

● Byrne, Nicky

Prior to the Beatles' first trip to America, enquiries for licences for Beatles merchandising had increased to such an extent that Brian Epstein thought it was becoming too big for **NEMS** to cope with and asked his solicitor **David Jacobs** to find someone to handle the merchandising. Jacobs met Byrne at a party and considered he would be an ideal person to approach on the matter. Byrne's wife Kiki had recently designed a range of leather ski-wear in partnership with Lord Snowdon and Byrne was the son of a country squire, a former horse-guard trooper and amateur racing driver.

After the cocktail party Jacobs proposed the Nick Byrne take over the merchandising for the Beatles, although Byrne was reluctant at first.

Jacobs informed Epstein, who agreed to the deal, and Byrne gathered several partners, including John Fenton, Mark Warman, Simon Miller-Munday, Lord Peregrine Eliot and **Malcolm Evans** (not to be confused with the Beatles' road manager). He set up a European company called **Stramscact** and an American one called **Seltaeb** (Beatles in reverse).

Byrne flew to New York, booked into the Drake Hotel, set up offices on Fifth Avenue and found out what a goldmine he'd been given. Within a week **Capitol Records** offered to buy him out for $500,000 with the money being paid into the Bahamas for him and also allowing him to retain a half interest in the company. He turned them down.

With the success of the Beatles in February 1964, the offers began to pour in and Byrne was making millions. When he realized the full extent of the deal, with the Beatles only receiving 10 per cent of the vast merchandising goldmine, Brian Epstein was horrified. By August 1964 Jacobs had renegotiated the deal, raising the Beatles' royalty to 46 per cent, but by that time Epstein had instructed NEMS to begin negotiating with US firms directly.

The situation caused a number of major firms, including Woolworths, to back out of negotiations and it was assessed that $100 million of possible Beatles merchandising deals were lost.

Lord Peregrine Eliot and Malcolm Evans instigated court proceedings against Byrne claiming he'd spent $150,000 on his own comfort and benefit and had failed to pass on the Beatles' royalties. NEMS also began a lawsuit against Seltaeb for non-payment of $55,000 of merchandising royalties. Byrne countersuied for breach of contract dealings.

There was some confusion in the NEMS camp when Epstein was not informed he had to be present in court in New York. His failure to turn up went against him. The law suits took three years to unravel, at the end of which NEMS settled with Byrne for a substantial cash payment. He bought a yacht on the proceeds and went to live in the Bahamas.

● Cabana Motor Hotel, *Dallas, Texas*

The hotel where the Beatles stayed on Friday, 18 September 1964, prior to their appearance at the **Dallas Memorial Coliseum**. On their way to the hotel from the airport they passed the area where President John F. Kennedy had been shot and John Lennon asked, 'Is it safe?'

The group and their entourage filled the entire ninth floor of the hotel, which was under siege from hundreds of fans. Many were hiding in the building and armed police stalked the hotel searching them out. **Mal Evans** brought three members of the Dallas Beatle Fan Club to meet the group – Yolanda Hernandez, Marie Leggett and Stephanie Pinter who spent a few hours with the members of the group.

During the crush of fans outside the hotel, a plate glass window was smashed and three fans were hospitalized. Paul McCartney rang them up and talked to them at the nearby Methodist Hospital.

● Cabaret Club, *28 Duke Street, Liverpool*

One of the main Merseyside cabaret night spots in its time. A club totally unsuited to the proponents of the Mersey sound – the club catered for an older age group who preferred cabaret performers such as Lita Roza at the venue.

For some reason, Brian Epstein attempted to introduce the Beatles into the cabaret circuit and his influence resulted in a booking at the club on 25 July 1962. It was a total disaster.

● Caird Hall, *City Square, Dundee, Scotland*

Venue where the Beatles appeared on the final date of a three-day mini-tour of Scotland on 7 October 1963. They were to return to the venue for the second and last time on 20 October 1964.

● Calder, Tony

Calder worked in the Decca Press Office in the same room as **Tony Barrow**, who wrote the sleeve notes for the Beatles' Decca albums. He left Decca to set up his own PR firm in partnership with **Andrew Loog Oldham**. When Brian Epstein offered the job of Beatles Press Officer to Barrow, he turned it down and Epstein offered it to Oldham, whom he met at **'Thank Your Lucky Stars'.**

Epstein had asked Barrow's advice on promotion and when Barrow pointed out that new records needed a press release, Epstein commissioned him to provide one for the Beatles' 'Love Me Do'. As he was still working for Decca, Barrow arranged for Calder and Oldham to post out all the releases to the relevant newspapers.

● Caldwell, Iris

Blonde sister of the late Liverpool Beat group leader **Rory Storm**. Her first boyfriend was George Harrison in the days before he was interested in music. Iris was only twelve at the time, George was fourteen. Her mother V said, 'George used to come and watch TV three times a week. He and Iris used to sit there holding hands. It was the first time either of them had ever taken any interest in someone of the opposite sex. At Iris' fourteenth birthday party, I remember George turned up in a brand new Italian-style suit covered with buttons. As in most teenage parties, they kept on playing kissing games and somehow or other, George and Iris always ended up together.'

When she was seventeen her boyfriend was Paul McCartney and she claimed that 'Love Me Do' was a song Paul had written for her.

Her romance with Paul lasted for twelve months, and for at least six months they were serious enough about each other to be what Northerners would call 'going steady'. She commented, 'Epstein was not very pleased that I was going out with Paul and I wasn't allowed to go anywhere with the group in case any of their fans saw me. But every night after they'd appeared at the **Cavern**, Paul would come round to our house – and when they were away to Hamburg he used to write me the most fantastic letters.'

The romance came to an end when **Jane Asher** entered the picture. Iris was to say, 'I'm quite sure there were many other girls around at that time . . . and then when he came back from London once and said that he had met Jane Asher I didn't want to go out with him anymore, though we remained good friends and kept a good relationship.'

Iris married singer **Shane Fenton** in 1964 and they went on the road as a double act. In the seventies Shane was to change his name to Alvin Stardust and had the chart success which had eluded him in the sixties. The couple had two children, but divorced several years later and Iris remarried in 1983.

● Caleb

Long-haired Tarot card reader who was hired by the Beatles to work at **Apple**. No one seemed to know his surname, so he was always referred to, simply, as Caleb.

He was given the power to authorize or approve all Apple business dealings, which he would do using the Tarot cards, an ancient method of divination. Caleb was also an I Ching diviner and would regularly visit the various members of Apple staff and use three coins to advise on various decisions. He also used to compile daily in-house horoscopes.

He eventually became bored with people asking him to predict the positions of records in the charts and left.

● Cambridge Hall, Lord Street, Southport, Lancashire

Venue in the main thoroughfare of a smart seaside town, close to Liverpool.

On Thursday, 26 July 1962, **NEMS Enterprises** promoted a concert at the venue starring **Joe Brown** & his Bruvvers, who were No. 3 in the British charts at the time with **'A Picture Of You'**. It was one of two bookings by NEMS Enterprises of the blond-haired cockney guitarist who first rose to fame in Britain after his appearances on the TV programme 'Six Five Special'. He was a popular recording artist at the time and had an engaging personality. His chart hits included **'Dark town Strutters Ball'**, 'Shine' and 'What A Crazy World We're Living In'. At the time of this engagement he was No. 3 in the charts with 'A Picture Of You', a number which the Beatles had recently featured in their act, with George Harrison on vocals.

The Beatles were second on the bill to Joe Brown on this occasion.

● Canadian Broadcasting Company, The

On Saturday, 19 December 1969, the Canadian Broadcasting Company screened a 45-minute discussion programme between John Lennon and Marshall McLuhan from the University of Toronto. McLuhan was a noted intellectual, author of the best-seller *The Medium Is The Message* and head of the University's Department of Culture and Technology.

During the discussion, John mentioned that his initial interest in becoming a musician had been sparked off by hearing **Elvis Presley**. McLuhan pointed out that John's way of approaching music was by forming a band and that the English were more team-orientated than the Americans. McLuhan then went into a detailed theory of the growth and decline of pop festivals. The conversation touched on a few other topics and John mentioned that the Beatles had had to change because there was a danger in remaining the same, and that they had to avoid getting in a rut.

● Candie Auditorium, The, Candie Gardens, St Peter Port, Guernsey, Channel Isles

The Beatles travelled the 30-mile distance between Jersey and Guernsey in a twelve-seater plane for this concert promoted by Baron Pontin, the holiday camp millionaire. The group performed nine numbers at the sell-out show.

● Candlestick Park, San Francisco, California

The Beatles' final public concert performance took place at this venue on Monday, 29 August 1966.

A temporary stage had been erected in the middle of the baseball park, surrounded by a 6 ft fence, and over 200 police were on patrol to supervise the 25,000-strong audience, with 20,000 seats unsold.

The show began at 8 o'clock and support acts included the **Cyrkle**, the **Ronettes** (without Ronnie Spector), Bobby Hebb and the Remains. The master of ceremonies was Gene Nelson, one of the leading DJs of KYA-AM.

Paul had asked PR man **Tony Barrow** to record the

concert for him and Tony used a Philips cassette recorder with a Beyer microphone.

The group, wearing dark green double-breasted suits, began their performance at 9.27 p.m. with 'Rock And Roll Music' and then went straight into 'She's A Woman'. Paul then said, 'Thank you very much everybody and hello, good evening. We'd like to carry on with a song, not surprisingly, written by George, and this was on our *Rubber Soul* LP and the song is called "If I Needed Someone".'

George took over lead vocals on the song and John then said, 'Thank you everybody. We'd like to carry on now, carry on together, one together and all for one, with another number which used to be a single record back in, er, er, a long time ago and this one's about the naughty lady called "Day Tripper".'

They then performed the number and went straight into 'Baby's In Black', after which George announced, 'We'd like to carry on with something very old indeed and this one was recorded about 1959! It's called "I Feel Fine".'

George then said, 'Thank you. Like to carry on with a song from *Yesterday And Today*, and this one was a single as well, and it features Paul singing a very nice song called "Yesterday".'

Paul then said, 'It's a bit chilly', referring to the fact that a cold wind was blowing in from the north California coast, and continued, 'We'd like to do the next number now which is a request for all the wonderful backroom boys on this tour. The song is called "I Want To Be Your Man". To sing it . . . Ringo!'

After the number the boys thanked Ringo and he thanked them and John shouted out, 'Lovely working with you, Ringo!' before continuing with the introduction, 'We'd like to do another song from our BBC album, and this one's called "He's A Real Nowhere Man, Sitting In His Nowhere Land", oh yes!'

When the song finished, Paul had noticed a fan running across the field towards the stage. 'We'd like to carry on, certainly, definitely, but shall we just watch this for a bit. Just watch,' he said. After the police had caught the girl fan, Paul said, 'The next song is called "Paperback Writer", one . . . two . . . three . . . four!'

After the number he thanked the audience and commented, 'We'd like to say it's been wonderful being here in this wonderful sea air! Sorry about the weather, and we'd like to ask you to join in and clap, sing, talk, do anything. Anyway, the song is . . .' He was in the middle of saying, 'Good night', then realized he shouldn't be tipping the audience that it was the last number. The group performed 'Long Tall Sally', then rushed into the armoured van which had been waiting behind the stage with the engine running. They had finished their performance at 10.00 p.m.

If only the promoters Tom Donahue and Bobby Mitchell, who were disc jockeys at KYA-AM, had known that it was to be the Beatles' final concert, they would have ensured that the 20,000 empty seats were filled.

When the Beatles flew out of San Francisco following their final American concert, George Harrison remarked, 'Well, that's it, I'm not a Beatle any more.'

Tony Barrow auctioned off his tape at Sotheby's in London in 1988 and it was subsequently turned into a bootleg album. The official photographer for the show was Jim Marshall and his photographs were later to be featured in a special book of the concert by Eric Lefcowitz called *Tomorrow Never Knows: The Beatles' Last Concert*.

● Candy

Ringo Starr's first non-Beatles film role. The 1968 movie was scripted by Buck Henry from the comic novel by Terry Southern and Mason Hoffenberg. It was an Italian/French co-production, filmed in Italy by producer Robert Haggiag and director Christian Marquand.

In the X-rated movie, Ringo played the part of Emmanuel, a Mexican gardener who attempts to seduce Candy Christian. The comparatively unknown Swedish actress Ewa Aulin starred in the title role. It was her movie debut and she provided Ringo with his first screen kiss. Richard Burton portrayed Professor McPhisto, a college lecturer, first in a line of would-be seducers. Italian actress Elsa Martinelli appeared as Candy's Aunt Livia and Marlon Brando played a randy Eastern guru.

In the film McPhisto attempts to seduce Candy after she has attended his lecture and tries again while driving her home. When she arrives she finds that he has spilled whisky on her dress so she takes it off and begins to sponge it. Emmanuel the gardener enters the room and grabs her, attempting to make love to her on a pool table. Her father (played by John Astin) arrives and the gardener is thrown out. His pride hurt, Emmanuel complains to his relatives and this ill-assorted group of Mexicans pursues Candy and her father to the airport on motorbikes. One o

Emmanuel's kinfolk hurls a bolas, which splits open the head of Candy's father.

Apart from a brief appearance at the end of the movie, Ringo takes no further part in the film. Though much publicized, his part was little more than a cameo role with only a few lines of dialogue of the 'Dis no good' variety – wearing a suitably lustful leer on his moustachioed face as he tries to seduce Candy.

Ringo Starr in his first solo movie role in *Candy*. (Cinerama International)

Cannibal & The Headhunters

An American band who appeared on the bill of the Beatles' US tour of 1965. At the time Cannibal & the Headhunters had a Top Ten hit in the charts with 'Land Of 1000 Dances'.

Can't Buy Me Love

Advance sales for this single reached one million in Britain and 2,100,000 in America, the highest advance sales for a single ever recorded at the time. It was issued in Britain on 20 March 1964 on Parlophone R5114 and went straight to No. 1 in the charts, remaining in that position for four weeks. It was issued in the US on 16 March on **Capitol** 5150 and became the first record ever to go straight to No. 1 simultaneously in both Britain and the United States. When it reached No. 1 in the *Billboard* charts on 4 April 1964 the chart for that week was: 1. 'Can't Buy Me Love' 2. 'Twist And Shout' 3. 'She Loves You' 4. 'I Want To Hold Your Hand' 5. 'Please Please Me'. It was the biggest domination of the Top Five ever – and the group also had a fantastic domination of the Hot 100 in general as, when 'Can't Buy Me Love' celebrated its second week at No. 1, the Beatles had no less than fourteen singles in the charts. They were: 1. 'Can't Buy Me Love' 2. 'Twist And Shout' 4. 'She Loves You' 7. 'I Want To Hold Your Hand' 9. 'Please Please Me' 14. 'Do You Want To Know A Secret' 38. 'I Saw Her Standing There' 48. 'You Can't Do that' 50. 'All My Loving' 52. 'From Me To You' 61. 'Thank You Girl' 74. 'There's A Place' 78. 'Roll Over Beethoven' 81. 'Love Me Do'.

The single also created a record by giving the Beatles the most consecutive No. 1 singles in the *Billboard* chart. It immediately followed 'She Loves You' on the No. 1 spot, which had directly followed 'I Want To Hold Your Hand' at the top. The number was included on the *A Hard Day's Night* album, the 1965 compilation EP *The Beatles Million Sellers*, the 1966 album *A Collection Of Beatles Oldies (But Goldies)*, the 1973 compilation *The Beatles 1962–1966*, the 1979 *Hey Jude* album, the 1980 *Beatles Box* and various other compilations. The group also performed it on one **'Saturday Club'** and two **'From Us To You'** BBC radio programmes.

The flipside was 'You Can't Do That'.

Paul wrote 'Can't Buy Me Love' when the Beatles were in Miami, Florida, on their first American trip during 1964. John gave him a hand, but it was mainly Paul's work, which is why he was upset when critics assumed that the title was referring to 'love for sale'. He commented: 'Personally, I think you can put any interpretation you want to anything, but when someone says "Can't Buy Me Love" is about a prostitute, I draw the line. That's going too far.'

Several weeks after the Beatles single was released, jazz singer Ella Fitzgerald issued her version, which reached No. 30 in the British charts. Ella's was the most famous version, apart from the Beatles' own, but there have actually been about 70 different versions of the song by artists such as **Mary Wells**, Brenda Lee, Gerry Mulligan and the Supremes.

● Capitol Cinema, *Dock Street, Cardiff, Wales*

The Beatles made their first appearance at this cinema in Wales on 27 May 1963 as part of their tour with **Roy Orbison**. They headlined their own show when they appeared at the venue for the second time on 7 November 1964. Their third and final appearance at the Capitol was also the last date of a British tour when they performed there on 12 December 1965.

● Capitol Records

An American label founded in Los Angeles in the forties by Glen Wallichs and lyric writer Johnny Mercer. The company is based at Capitol Tower on Hollywood and Vine, a 13-storey building shaped like a stack of records.

In the fifties **EMI Records** in Britain began to experience a number of problems. In 1952 the American Columbia label left EMI to place its roster of artists, who included Doris Day, Johnnie Ray, Frankie Laine and Guy Mitchell, with Phillips Records. Then EMI also lost their contract with RCA-Victor. As American products were vitally important for the British and European market, in 1955 **Sir Joseph Lockwood**, with great foresight, decided to buy an American label outright and purchased Capitol Records for nine million dollars.

Although they owned Capitol, they did not want to pressure the label into accepting British artists, but gave Capitol the right of first and second refusal on British recordings.

With the success in Britain of 'Please Please Me', EMI decided to offer the record to Capitol. 'They wouldn't take it at any price,' said Sir Joe.

As **Beatlemania** grew in Britain and Europe, and following the success of 'From Me To You', George Martin offered Capitol the British chart topper. They refused it. Capitol President **Alan Livingston** was to send a memo, 'We don't think the Beatles will do anything in this market'. With their third massive No. 1 hit in the UK, 'She Loves You', George Martin tried again and in August 1963 told Capitol, 'For God's sake, do something about this. These boys are breaking it, and they're going to be fantastic throughout the world. So for heaven's sake, latch on to them.' For the third time Capitol said they considered that the Beatles had no prospects in America.

EMI were frustrated that their own American branch refused to handle their biggest British and European act, so they contacted another of their American subsidiaries, Transglobal. Transglobal usually made special deals with other American labels for EMI products which had been rejected by Capitol. Transglobal's Paul Marshall arranged for the small label **Vee Jay Records** to issue the singles 'Please Please Me' and 'From Me To You' and the album *Introducing The Beatles*. But they had no success and dropped their option. Marshall then placed 'She Loves You' with Swan Records. This was also unsuccessful.

Up to this time, EMI had exerted no major pressure from its chief executives, but Brian Epstein was becoming annoyed at the negative response from Capitol and told EMI to use their clout. He also phoned Alan Livingston personally and told him, 'Mr Livingston, we just don't understand it. The Beatles are doing very well in England, why don't you release them over there?' Livingston told him that he would listen to their records again and call him back. By this time, word was beginning to filter through to America that the Beatles were becoming a phenomenon in Europe. EMI's Senior Executive L. G. Wood had called Capitol's Lloyd Dunn, who was Vice-President in charge of Merchandising and Sales, to use his muscle. EMI's **Tony Palmer** had also put pressure on **Dave Dexter Jr.**, Capitol's A&R man, who said that he would agree to release the next Beatles record. Epstein had also got in touch with Brown Meggs, Director of Eastern Operations for Capitol. Livingston got back to Epstein and said he'd agree to release a single and an album by the group. Brian told him, 'I'm not going to give them to you unless you agree to spend $40,000 promoting this song.' He was referring to 'I Want To Hold Your Hand'. This was a vast amount of money for promotion as the largest amount the company had ever spent on the promotion of a record up to that time was $5,000. Livingston decided to take the gamble and it became the biggest single promotional campaign in the history of the record industry and included a crash publicity programme with posters and window stickers and the manufacture of five million 'The Beatles are coming' badges.

Although Capitol were literally forced to take what became the biggest-selling recording artists in history they didn't seem to learn their lesson. Following the success of the Beatles in America, EMI's Columbia label then offered Capitol the **Dave Clark Five**. Capitol rejected them and they went on to have 24 American hits. Capitol also turned down the Animals, who were to have fourteen US hits; Herman's Hermits, who were to have eighteen; the **Hollies**, who were to have twelve; Manfred Mann, who were to have four; **Gerry & the Pacemakers**, who were to have seven; Lulu, who had four, including the chart topper 'To Sir With Love'; and the **Yardbirds**, who had six – among others.

On 11 November 1963, Brian Epstein met Brown Meggs in New York to discuss the release of 'I Want To Hold Your Hand', on 26 December 1963. The commitment from Capitol at the time still wasn't one hundred percent and even the publishing rights to 'I Want To Hold Your Hand' had been given to MCA at a nominal fee and Capitol had to contact them for clearance on the publishing rights. Meggs and his colleagues had been uneasy about the record and, in particular, their promise that they would press 200,000 copies. As it happened, due to a growing demand, the orders outstripped that figure and during December three production plants – Capitol's, CBS's and RCA's – were all at work in an effort to press a million copies by the New Year.

The 14 December issue of *Cash Box* headlined their lead story: 'Capitol Gets The Beatles For US', and mentioned that Brown Meggs had announced that the first album *Meet The Beatles* would now be issued in January instead of February. In the 28 December issue of *Cash Box*, another Capitol story on the Beatles read: 'It was in one of Hamburg's rowdy and raucous strip joints, the **Indra Club**, that they were discovered by a young English talent agent and promoter, Brian Epstein.' A Capitol press release at the time called 'National Record News' had such innacurate information as: 'In those days they called themselves a variety of things – the **Quarry Men**, Moon Dogs or Moonshiners. It was early 1958 and they spent most of their time playing in the cellar of a friend's home in Liverpool for kicks.' The press release also referred to Paul as 'Paul McCatney'.

Capitol's first Beatles release, 'I Want To Hold Your Hand', became the company's fastest-selling record up to that time and their biggest seller, eventually achieving sales of over five million copies.

When George Martin accompanied the Beatles on their first trip to America, he was irked at how Capitol had implied that they had literally discovered the group. In his autobiography *All You Need Is Ears* he commented that when he arrived in America with the group, Capitol were embarrassed at his presence because they had been implying that the Beatles were their. He observed, 'At the Beatles' first press conference in New York, Alan Livingston ran the whole show. He kept me away from the press, which I must admit seemed a mite peculiar. To top it all, he introduced the Beatles as the Capitol recording artists – words which came ill from the lips of the man who had turned them down three times!'

It was ironic that the company which had been rejecting the Beatles for a year suddenly switched around to the extent that by April 1964 the Capitol Records' switchboard was answering calls with the message, 'Good morning: Capitol Records, home of the Beatles!'

Capitol distributed the Beatles' records in America between 1964 and 1968 and then handled the American distribution for **Apple Records**.

A few days after the release of 'I Want To Hold Your Hand', the album *Meet The Beatles* was issued on 20 January 1964. Within its first week it sold 750,000 copies and by December 1966 American sales had reached five million. Capitol was originally to issue different albums from the British releases.

Because American record companies paid higher royalties if more than ten tracks were featured on an album, many Beatles tracks were cut from the Capitol releases and put out as singles in the US. *Meet The Beatles* was a twelve-track album which differed from the British *With The Beatles*, because it had had five tracks removed and replaced with three others.

Capitol's second Beatles single 'Can't Buy Me Love' achieved the biggest advance order for any previous single – two million, eventually selling over three million copies in America. When it entered the American charts on 28 March 1964, 'She Loves You' was No. 1, 'I Want To Hold Your Hand' No. 2, 'Twist And Shout' No. 3, 'Please Please Me' No. 4 and 'I Saw Her Standing There' No. 27.

When Capitol issued *The Beatles Second Album* they used five tracks from the *With The Beatles* album, four tracks from American singles and two previously unreleased tracks from the British EP *Long Tall Sally*. It became Capitol's fastest-selling album up to that time.

Capitol next tried the EP format by issuing *Four By The*

Beatles in May 1964, which included tracks from two Capitol albums, *Meet The Beatles* and *The Beatles Second Album*.

In the meantime, United Artists had originally signed the Beatles to a film contract in order to secure them for a soundtrack album which, when released, went to No. 1. Under the agreement with EMI/Capitol they could only feature eight of the songs from the film *A Hard Day's Night* and the rest of the tracks they padded out with instrumental versions of Beatles tunes. Capitol also had the right to release five of the official soundtrack songs and used a number of them as singles and then used all five tracks on *Something New*, an album issued a month after United Artists' *A Hard Day's Night*.

Capitol Records continued to achieve incredible record success with the Beatles products throughout the balance of the group's career.

● Carfax Assembly Rooms, *Oxford*

The Beatles only appeared at this venue once, on 16 February 1963. The engagement was the first booking they undertook for promoter **John Smith**.

● Carl Allen Awards, The

Annual awards presented in the sixties on behalf of the Mecca chain of dance halls in Britain. On 11 March 1964 it was announced that the Beatles had won the Carl Allen Awards for (1) Best Group and (2) Best Single of 1963, 'She Loves You'. The group were presented with the awards by the Duke of Edinburgh on 23 March.

● Carlton Theatre, *Arcade Halls, Sinclairtown, Kirkcaldy, Scotland*

The Beatles performed two concerts at this venue before a capacity audience of 1,500 at each of the shows on 6 October 1963. It was their only appearance in the town.

In the song 'Cry Baby Cry' there is mention of the 'Duchess of Kirkcaldy'.

● Carnegie Hall, *New York City*

On Wednesday, 12 February 1964, the Beatles became the first rock 'n' roll act to perform in concert at the famous Carnegie Hall. The booking had originally been arranged by promoter **Sid Bernstein** the previous year, who was promoting the two concerts independently under his Theatre Three Productions Company. **Norman Weiss** of G.A.C. had concluded the deal on Bernstein's behalf during a visit to Paris in January 1964.

Bernstein had set the date for Abraham Lincoln's birthday and it fortunately tied in with the Beatles' huge American success immediately following their sensational '**Ed Sullivan** Show' appearance and their single 'I Want To Hold Your Hand' topping the American charts.

As the 6,000 tickets had been sold out in advance, Bernstein requested extra seats on the stage itself. This was granted, although the management insisted that these seats be reserved for older customers only. Among the VIPs who shared the additional seats on stage were Lauren Bacall and Mrs Happy Rockefeller, although other celebrities were unable to be accommodated. Bernstein was to say, 'It's a status symbol for the kids to be here, just as it's a status symbol for the 300 adults here tonight. I had to turn down David Niven, William Zeckendorf and Shirley MacLaine for tickets, I just didn't have one left.'

The Beatles travelled by train for two hours from Washington and arrived at New York's Penn Station and took taxis to their hotel where they showered, changed and refreshed themselves before moving on to Carnegie Hall for the two 34-minute shows, which took place at 7.45 p.m. and 11.15 p.m. Among the other acts on the bill were a folk group called the Briarwoods. One of the Beatles' backstage visitors was British singer **Shirley Bassey**, who was appearing at Carnegie Hall the following week.

Each house had a 2,900 capacity and there were 362 policemen handling security around the hall.

Capitol Records had wanted to record the two shows but their attempts to do so had been blocked by the American Federation of Musicians.

Bernstein himself took to the stage to ask the audience to comport themselves in the presence of the foreign press. Also making on-stage announcements was disc jockey **Murray the K** who joked and told the audience not to leave their seats or throw things at the stage. 'We have people especially to deal with things like that – but I'm sure you won't let it happen,' he said.

For both shows, the Beatles grossed $9,335.78.

● Carnival Of Light

An avant-garde psychedelic event at the Roundhouse, London, which took place in January 1967. Paul McCartney had promised the organizers that he would prepare a sound effects tape for them and during some early *Sgt Pepper* sessions, on Thursday, 5 January 1967, the Beatles spent part of their evening session at **Abbey Road**'s Studio Two recording a bizarre series of sounds, which resulted in a tape of electronic noises lasting thirteen minutes and 48 seconds. Paul then took the tape along to the Roundhouse organizers.

No announcement was made when the tape was played at the 'Carnival Of Light' and the audience were unaware that they were listening to a Beatles tape. The unusual Beatles recording remains in the Abbey Road vaults under the description 'Untitled'.

Carol

A song written and recorded by **Chuck Berry** in 1958. The Beatles introduced it to their repertoire in 1960, with John taking lead vocals. They performed the number on their **'Pop Go The Beatles'** broadcast on 16 July 1963 but never recorded it for release on record.

Carteret, Anna

A British actress, noted for her starring role in the BBC Television series 'Juliet Bravo' in 1983.

Anna first met Ringo Starr when he was a member of **Rory Storm & the Hurricanes** at Butlins in Skegness. Over twenty years later she met up with him again at the Ebony White Ball at the Embassy Club in London in December 1983. They discussed old times and she said, 'He was so thin then, I used to cook scrambled eggs for him in my caravan.'

Casbah Club, The, *8 Haymans Green, West Derby, Liverpool*

A club situated in the basement area of a fifteen-room Victorian house which the Best family moved into after the war. They comprised John and **Mona Best** and their sons **Peter** and Rory.

As there were so many friends calling in to see her sons and as they wanted a meeting place of their own, Mo Best suggested that they could redecorate the cellars and turn them into a club. There was plenty of room as the basement comprised seven adjoining rooms. The idea developed and she began to have in mind something like the nearby **Lowlands** club, with live groups at the weekend, with the club open during the week as a coffee bar where the youngsters could dance to a jukebox.

Work began on the decoration with Mo, Peter, Rory and a number of friends, including a girl called Ruth Morrison. When Mo said they'd have to find a group, Ruth suggested the **Les Stewart Quartet** who played at the Lowlands club. **Ken Brown** and George Harrison came round to see Mo, although it was Ken who seemed most enthusiastic about the project. Ken began to spend his spare time helping to convert the cellars into a club and spent weekends working there, with the result that group leader Stewart argued with him about the amount of time he spent helping out there. Brown left the Les Stewart Quartet and George joined him.

Bench seats and a counter were fitted in and Mrs Best painted a dragon on the ceiling. There was a table in the foyer where Mo would issue the tickets and there were tables and a fireplace, espresso coffee machines and in a small room a bar which sold coffee, sweets, soft drinks, hot dogs and crisps.

George Harrison turned up with John Lennon and his girlfriend **Cynthia** Powell and they helped with painting the walls shortly before the official opening. John used gloss paint on the walls instead of putting on an undercoat and the paint was not completely dry on the opening night. The conversion of the basement rooms into the club took two months. Mona's favourite film at the time was *Algiers*, which starred Charles Boyer. People mimicked his saying, 'Come with me to the Casbah', whenever the film was mentioned, although that line of dialogue was never in the actual movie. Mona settled on calling the club the Casbah.

When the club officially opened on Saturday, 29 August 1959, the resident band was the **Quarry Men**. The doors opened at 7.30 p.m. and each Saturday the Quarry Men appeared on stage at 8.00 p.m. Membership was two shillings and sixpence (12½p) per annum and entrance at the door cost one shilling (5p). During the first year the club enrolled more than 1,000 members.

The group had, in fact, not been active since January 1959 and George Harrison had joined the Les Stewart Quartet that month. They only got together again to take up the residency at the new club. When Les Stewart refused to take up the residency following his argument with Brown, Mrs Best had wondered how she would find a replacement. George said he had two friends and brought Paul and John down.

The four-man line-up of John Lennon, Paul McCartney, George Harrison and Ken Brown played without a drummer, using Brown's ten-watt amplifier, and they initially received £3 a night between them. This line-up played at the club each Saturday on 29 August, 5, 12, 19 and 26 September, 3 and 10 October. On 10 October, Brown arrived at the club, but he had a bad cold. Mrs Best told him he could help out and paid him a quarter of the group's fee, even though he didn't play. John, Paul and George were furious and stalked out of the club, giving up their residency. Brown encouraged **Pete Best** to form a group with him and as the **Blackjacks**, they took over the residency and the club went from strength to strength, building up a loyal membership and booking various local bands such as **Rory Storm & the Hurricanes**.

John, Paul and George didn't return to the Casbah until 8 August 1960 when they dropped into the club after their booking at the **Grosvenor Ballroom**, Wallasey, had been cancelled. They were then called the Silver Beatles and had been booked for their Hamburg debut that month, although they still hadn't found a drummer. They noticed Pete playing with the Blackjacks and Paul McCartney phoned him to invite him to audition with them. He did – and was invited to join the Beatles.

The first date they played on their return from Hamburg was the Casbah Club on 17 December, when Pete arranged for them to have a temporary bass player, **Chas Newby**, as **Stuart Sutcliffe** was still in Germany.

Pete and Mona Best now took charge of all the Beatles' bookings and, in addition to the Casbah gigs, formed Casbah Promotions to run dances at **St John's Hall**, Tuebrook, and **Knotty Ash Village Hall**, where they booked the Beatles regularly.

Their 1961 Casbah appearances took place on 8, 15, 22 and 29 January; 12, 19 and 26 February; 5 and 19 March; 6, 13 and 27 August; 10 and 24 September; 22 October; 19 and 24 November; 3 and 17 December. Dates in 1962 were on 7, 14, 21 and 28 January; 4, 11, 18 and 25 February; 4, 11, 18 and 25 March; 1, 7 and 8 April; and 24 June. This date saw the Beatles' final appearance at the club which was closed down a few days later following a death in the Best family.

The Beatles gathered together on the Casbah premises on 10 December 1961 with Brian Epstein to discuss their management contract with him.

The Casbah Club played an important part in the career of the Beatles. If it had not opened, the Quarry Men would probably not have re-formed and there would never have been any Beatles. The club provided them with their first residency and a base with regular money when times were tight. In fact, the Bests prevented the Beatles from disbanding in their early days by providing a number of bookings, including their own promotions, which helped to keep them working full-time as a group. The Casbah also provided them with their first regular drummer, Pete Best – their first road manager, **Frank Garner** – and their regular road manager, **Neil Aspinall**. In some ways it could be called the first 'Home of the Beatles'.

● Casey, Howie

Howie Casey (right), with Gibson Kemp at the Blue Angel club.

A Liverpool saxophonist regarded as one of the prominent local musicians during the ***Mersey Beat*** years. He led Derry and the Seniors, the first Liverpool band to be booked into Hamburg. This was as a result of a cancellation of a tour for **Larry Parnes**, arranged by **Allan Williams**, which caused Casey to threaten Williams with the result that he took Casey's group down to the 2 I' in London, where they were seen by **Bruno Koschmider** and immediately booked to appear in Hamburg.

The group had also been present at the Parnes audition at the **Wyvern Club** when the Silver Beatles performed. Howie wasn't enamoured with the Silver Beatles and was to comment, 'Quite frankly, I wasn't too impressed and can't remember the group singing. I believe they played a lot of instrumentals and **Shadows** numbers.'

With a group name change to Howie Casey & the Seniors, the band were enjoying their season in Hamburg when Allan Williams informed them that he'd be sending over the Beatles.

Williams had actually wanted to get **Rory Storm & the Hurricanes**, but they were at Butlins and he'd offered the gig to **Gerry & the Pacemakers**, but they'd turned it down. Howie replied to Williams, complaining that they had a good scene going in Hamburg which would be ruined '. . . by sending that bum group, the Beatles'. He said that they'd be bad for the scene.

When they did arrive, Howie commented, 'They had very, very pointed shoes in grey crocodile. They had mauve jackets with half-belting at the back. The length of their hair caused a great stir around the area – it was thick at the back, almost coming over their collars.'

The two lead singers with Howie's band were Derry Wilkie and Freddie Starr and the group became the first Mersey band to be recognized in Britain when they signed with the Fontana label and set off on a British tour. They were also the first Merseyside band to have a single recorded and released in Britain.

They appeared at the prestigious Inn At The Top club in Ilford before celebrities such as film star Diana Dors, and they recorded an album, *Twist At The Top*, there. However, despite their initial success, the group disbanded.

Freddie Starr formed various groups such as Freddie and the Delmonts and Freddie Starr and the Midnighters before becoming one of Britain's leading comedians, and Derry formed several groups, including the Pressmen, but didn't achieve any success.

Howie joined **Kingsize Taylor** and the Dominoes and spent many years in Germany before returning to England and becoming a successful session man in London. Paul McCartney asked him to join Wings on their 1975 world tour and 1979 tour of Britain. he also played on a number of Wings recordings, including the albums *Band On The Run* and *Back To The Egg*.

● Casino Ballroom, *Lord Street, Leigh, Lancashire*

The Beatles appeared at this venue only once, during a break in their tour with **Helen Shapiro**, on 25 February 1963.

● Cassanova Club, *Fraser Street, Liverpool L3*

One of several clubs which opened on the premises of Samson & Barlow's, a Liverpool catering firm, who had spacious rooms to let on their premises in the city centre.

Typical leaflet advertising local Beatles performance.

Promoter **Sam Leach** opened his Cassanova Club here on 9 February 1961, and two days later, on 11 February, he booked the Beatles for the first time. A club of that name had originally been launched above the Temple restaurant in Dale Street by **Cass & the Cassanovas** and the Beatles played there on Sunday, 10 January 1960, in an afternoon interval break. Sam was to take over the venue and moved the club to Samson & Barlow's.

While it was called the Cassanova, the Beatles appeared there on 14, 16, 21 and 28 February and 7 and 12 March 1961. The Tuesday, 14 February appearance was a 'Valentine's Night Rock Ball' with tickets priced at 4/6d. The posters announced: 'Four Rockin' Bands starring the originators of "The Atom Beat", The Sensational Beatles; Rockin' the Sound Waves, The Cassanova Big Three; **Rory Storm & The Hurricanes** and Introducing Mark Peters & The Cyclones'. Mark Peters (real name Peter Fleming) was said to be Liverpool's first disc jockey when he became DJ at the Locarno Ballroom in 1959. The group appeared on a number of bills with the Beatles and Brian Epstein booked them several times. Mark later fronted Mark Peters and the Silhouettes and made some unsuccessful records. In the seventies he went to work in Sri Lanka.

The Cassanova was closed by the police soon after these appearances due to the noise of the groups. Leach reopened it as the Peppermint Lounge in March 1963, naming it after the famous club in New York. The Blott Brothers took over the venue and began to run it successfully. Until February 1963, following the demise of the Cassanova Club, the venue had been reopened as a nightclub, the New Compton.

The Blotts got the club on-stream and promoted bands there on Thursdays, Fridays, Saturdays, Sundays and Tuesdays. Capacity was 350 people and prices varied from four shillings on Tuesdays to eight shillings and sixpence on Saturdays. There were three groups each night, four on Saturdays and regulars included Earl Royce & the Olympics, the Blackwells, the Chessmen, the Karacters and the Kirkbys.

● Casser, Brian

Newcastle-born leader of one of Liverpool's top Mersey bands, Cass & the Cassanovas. He was also known as Casey Valance.

Although relatively short-lived, Cass & the Cassanovas were arguably Liverpool's No. 1 band during their brief span. The group made their debut at the Corinthian Club, Slater Street in 1959. Cass played lead/vocals, **Adrian Barber** was on guitar and **Johnny Hutchinson** on drums. Soon after their formation Hutch brought Johnny Gustafson to see the group and suggested he join. Johnny didn't have a guitar but Adrian converted a Hoyer acoustic and put bass guitar strings on it.

Of the Liverpool acts appearing on the **Gene Vincent** concert at the **Liverpool Stadium** on 3 May 1960, Cass & the Cassanovas received top billing.

Allan Williams allowed Cass to sleep overnight in the **Jacaranda Club** in Slater Street and Cass claimed that he'd been using the club phone at night to make long-distance calls to a Hamburg promoter. He was trying to fix up a booking in Hamburg for the Cassanovas and had been speaking to **Bruno Koschmider**. Cass claimed that Koschmider called the Jacaranda one afternoon when he wasn't there and Allan talked to him and told him he could supply him with as many groups as he needed.

Cass eventually left the Cassanovas and they became the Big Three. In late 1963 when he had a debut record issued on **EMI**'s Columbia label *One Way Ticket*, he wrote to ***Mersey Beat***: 'Since coming to London three years ago I have been doing a great deal of film work, but films were not really my ambition. When everything started to happen in Scouseland, I really felt left out. So I decided to return to the singing scene.' The line-up of his band Casey Jones & the Engineers, between August and October 1963, comprised Casey Jones (vocals), **Eric Clapton** (guitar), Tom McGuinness (guitar), Dave McCumisky (bass) and Ray Smith (drums). He later moved to Germany where he had several chart entries.

When he originally moved to London he was managing a Soho club, the **Blue Gardenia**, where the Beatles dropped in to see him on 9 December 1961. It was Cass who once suggested to John Lennon that the group should call themselves Long John & the Silver Men.

● Cast Iron Shore, Dingle, Liverpool

In his song 'Glass Onion', John mentions standing on the Cast Iron Shore. This is an area officially called the Dingle Shore, but more familiarly known to Liverpudlians as the Cast Iron Shore or the 'Cassie'.

One of the settings in Frankie Vaughan's 1958 film *These Dangerous Years* was the Cast Iron Shore.

In 1984 the area was transformed as part of the twenty-acre site for the Liverpool Garden Festival. The Cast Iron Shore was converted into a site where a special Yellow Submarine was constructed, submerged in a pool, near to a Beatle Maze designed by Adrian Fisher.

● Castro, Bernard

An American millionaire who offered the Beatles the facility of his luxury yacht on 14 February 1964 during the group's stay in Miami, Florida. Castro was president of the Castro Convertible Company.

● Catcall

A number by Paul McCartney which was recorded by Chris Barber & his Jazz Band. Paul had originally written the instrumental in the late fifties when he was a member of the **Quarry Men**, under its original title 'Catswalk'.

Just as the sixties were dominated by the three Bs: Bardot, the Beatles and Bond, so the traditional jazz boom in Britain in the late fifties was dominated by the three Bs: Chris Barber, **Acker Bilk** and Kenny Ball.

Barber's Jazz Band appeared in Liverpool regularly in the mid-fifties featuring **Lonnie Donegan**, who later had success with 'Rock Island Line' and helped popularize the British skiffle boom.

When Barber recorded 'Catcall' on 20 July 1967, Paul and **Jane Asher** attended the session and at the end of the recording added their voices to the finale. The single was issued on 20 October 1967 on Marmalade 598-005, but it wasn't a hit. The track was later included on Barber's album 'Battersea Rain Dance'.

Chris Barber (left), with two founder members of his band, pictured in 1949. (Chris Barber)

● *Cathy's Clown*

A chart topper for the Everly Brothers, Don and Phil, early in 1960 which was included in the Beatles' repertoire for a short time during that year.

● Cavern Club, The, *10 Mathew Street, Liverpool*

The most famous club in the world during the early to mid-sixties when it was known as 'The Home of the Beatles'.

Originally the premises comprised a small group of cellars below seven-storey warehouses which, during the war, had been used as air-raid shelters. For a while wines and spirits were stored there and in 1958, Alan Sytner, son of a local doctor, noticed that the premises were empty. Sytner had been running jazz nights at the nearby Temple restaurant. He'd recently been to Paris and was impressed by a jazz cellar he'd visited called Le Caveau Francais Jazz Club. He immediately took over the lease of the basement and the club opened officially as the Cavern on 16 January 1957, with a local jazz band, the Merseysippi, topping the bill. Over 1,000 people queued to get in, but only 600 were allowed entrance.

The club was reached by walking down eighteen stone steps. At the bottom of the steps was a table where admission was paid. There were three long arches with a stage at the end of the centre aisle, where rows of wooden seats were placed. Patrons danced in the outer aisles. Only soft drinks were served and initially just traditional jazz was presented at weekends. Then skiffle was presented each Wednesday and modern jazz each Thursday. By 1959 Sytner had got married and moved to London, leaving the running of the club to his father.

Financially, the Cavern wasn't faring well and Sytner decided to sell. He found a buyer close to home – **Ray McFall**, the Sytner family's accountant, who had been financial adviser to the Temple Jazz Club and acted as cashier twice a week at the Cavern. Ray purchased the club on 1 October 1959 for £2,750. Music had always been a leading interest in his life and his tastes ranged from the classics to all forms of pop music.

Yet the Cavern had been run strictly on the lines of a jazz club – with no rock 'n' roll polluting the atmosphere. The only bands apart from jazz bands to be employed were skiffle groups. When the **Quarry Men** had appeared at the club on 7 August 1957 and played some **Elvis Presley** numbers, Sytner had sent them a note: 'Cut out the bloody rock!' When **Rory Storm & the Hurricanes** appeared and performed 'Whole Lotta Shakin'' they were fined for playing a rock 'n' roll number.

However, the times were changing and McFall began to change the club's policy. In the early summer of 1960 a radical departure from previous jazz club policy appeared – rock 'n' roll. Ray decided to take a chance and pioneer lunchtime sessions. From Tuesday to Friday they featured one day of jazz and three days of rock 'n' roll. Although the sessions were successful, Tuesday jazz performances lacked the audiences of the other days. In January 1961 the Tuesday jazz was replaced by rock and the Tuesday lunchtimes picked up. In March 1961 the lunchtime sessions were extended to Monday.

Experiments in evening sessions had begun on Wednesday, 25 May 1960, when the first rock 'n' roll evening was presented with the two top local bands Cass &

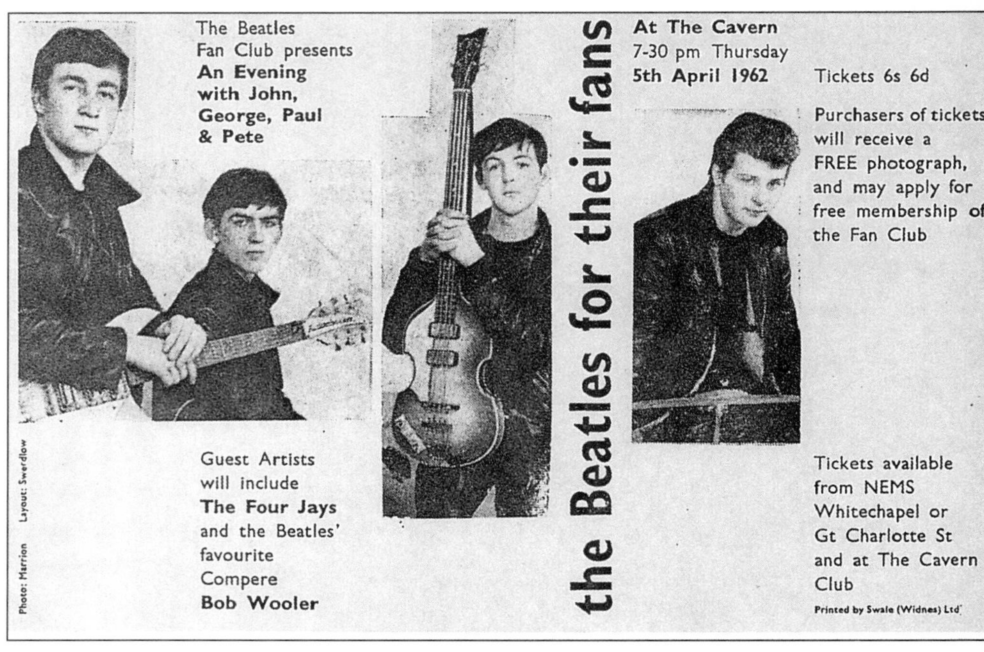

The Beatles
Fan Club presents
An Evening
with John,
George, Paul
& Pete
the Beatles for their fans
At The Cavern
7-30 pm Thursday
5th April 1962
Tickets 6s 6d
Purchasers of tickets
will receive a
FREE photograph,
and may apply for
free membership of
the Fan Club
Guest Artists
will include
The Four Jays
and the Beatles'
favourite
Compere
Bob Wooler
Tickets available
from NEMS
Whitechapel or
Gt Charlotte St
and at The Cavern
Club
Photo: Marrion
Layout: Swerdlow
Printed by Swale (Widnes) Ltd

The Beatles, dressed in black leather, perform at the Cavern. (Cavern Mecca/*Mersey Beat* Archives)

the Cassanovas and Rory Storm & the Hurricanes.

Ray was to tell **Tony Barrow** in 'On The Scene At The Cavern': 'A dozen or more suburban halls on the outskirts of Liverpool had been flourishing as a result of the increasing demand for beat groups. I decided to make the Cavern into Liverpool's first city-centre rock 'n' roll club. At the time I couldn't have dreamed of the destiny which lay ahead for many of the groups I began to use on Wednesdays. To me the introduction of a new rock 'n' roll night merely meant the drawing in of a separate crowd which wouldn't have visited the Cavern before. I knew that some of the jazz followers would give the Wednesday groups a try but I was equally interested in attracting the rockers who had been filling the ballrooms and club halls outside town.'

In February 1961 Tuesday became the Bluegenes guest night, in which they presented some of the top rock 'n' roll groups in the area, and their first 'guest night' on Tuesday, 21 March 1961, featured Dale Roberts & the Jay Walkers, the **Remo Four** and the Beatles. The Beatles were making their evening debut at the club and exactly one month prior, on 21 February, they had made their first appearance at a lunchtime session. In April, modern jazz

BEATLES at . . .

FRIDAY, 24th MARCH	WEDNESDAY, 28th MARCH
FRIDAY, 30th MARCH	WEDNESDAY, 4th APRIL

. . . the CAVERN

sessions, which had been tottering on the brink for some time, stopped.

The Beatles began a stream of appearances which included their 'Welcome Home' session on Friday, 14 July 1961, with Johnny Sandon and the Remo Four and the White Eagles Jazz Band. The Beatles began their own series of resident nights on Wednesday, 2 August 1961, and made a total of 292 appearances until their last one on 3 August 1963 for which they received a fee of £300.

There were too many Cavern appearances by the Beatles to list individually, but among their 1961 gigs were those on Tuesday, 25 July, when they appeared on another Bluegenes guest night, along with **Gerry & the Pacemakers** and the Remo Four; Friday, 1 September, when they were the only rock group, playing during the

The only entrance was down a narrow stone stairway. Top: The Beatles perform, having shed their black leather image. (©Apple/Peter Kaye Collection)

interval of a traditional jazz bill; and Saturday, 23 December, when they performed with Gerry & the Pacemakers and Johnny Sandon and the **Searchers** on an all-night session featuring several jazz bands. Their 1962 engagements at the club included acting as a support, along with Gerry & the Pacemakers, to the **Saints** Jazz Band from Manchester; Wednesday, 28 February, when they appeared with Gerry & the Pacemakers and Johnny Sandon and the Searchers; Thursday, 5 April, when they had their own fan club night, with the Four Jays also performing; Saturday, 7 April, when they performed a two-hour show in between two sets by the Saints Jazz Band; Saturday, 9 June, when they had their 'Welcome Home' evening following their Hamburg season; Sunday, 1 July, which saw the first Cavern evening which had no jazz content at all and featured the Beatles, the **Swinging**

Bluejeans, **Gene Vincent** and **Sounds Incorporated**; Wednesday, 1 August, with Gerry & the Pacemakers and the **Merseybeats**; Tuesday, 28 August, when they appeared on another Bluegenes guest night, along with Gerry Levene and the Avengers, the first group from Birmingham to appear at the Cavern; Sunday, 9 September, when they appeared with **Billy J. Kramer** and the Coasters and jazz singer Clinton Ford; Wednesday, 12 September, when **Simone Jackson**, a London singer, became 'the girl who sang with the Beatles', when the group backed her performance – also on the bill were Manchester's **Freddie & the Dreamers**; Friday, 12 October, when they appeared on a bill with their idol **Little Richard**; Wednesday, 5 December, when they shared the bill with Gerry & the Pacemakers; Sunday, 16 December, when they made their final appearance prior to their Hamburg season in December. Their 1963 shows at the Cavern included Sunday, 20 January, when they appeared with the Dennisons, the Swinging Bluejeans and the Merseybeats; Sunday, 3 February, was a 'rhythm and blues marathon' – appearing with the Beatles were Manchester's the **Hollies**, making their Cavern debut, and the Merseybeats, the **Fourmost**, the Swinging Bluejeans and **Kingsize Taylor** and the Dominoes; Friday, 12 April, a Good Friday session in which the Beatles topped the bill over seven other local groups, who included the Road Runners, Faron's Flamingos and the Dennisons; Saturday, 3 August, was a Bank Holiday special; the Beatles were supported by the Merseybeats, the Road Runners, Johnny Ringo and the Colts, the **Escorts** and the Sapphires.

Commenting on their 'Welcome Home' session on Saturday, 9 June 1962, which immediately followed their trip to Hamburg, **Bob Wooler** told Tony Barrow: 'You might have expected the Beatles to be tired after their strenuous Hamburg session. On the contrary they gave one of their finest-ever performances and seemed to draw extra inspiration from the feverish reaction they were getting from the one thousand fans who packed the place that evening. Although the national newspapers didn't invent the word **"Beatlemania"** until a year later, I would say that the Cavern reception given to John, Paul, George and Pete Best that Saturday was just as enthusiastic, just as genuine as the nationwide acclaim which was to follow. I would qualify this statement with one further observation. Cavern members didn't use the Beatles as an excuse for hooliganism. They cheered and screamed and showed their excitement in a dozen ways – but they were still an orderly audience with a respect for the club itself and its surroundings.'

As success began to spread across the Mersey scene, Ray undertook a policy of expansion and the Cavern soon became the most famous club in Britain. There was even a group called the Caverners (Kenny Smith (lead), Steve Roberts (bass), Mark Farrell (rhythm), Colin Roberts (drums)) and Beatles PR man Tony Barrow wrote a book *The Cavern*, which was published by Souvenir Press.

McFall organized a Cavern trip to Hamburg in which

Young revellers enjoy a night at the Cavern. (Cavern Mecca)

36 members of the club flew to the German city for two days to visit the **Star Club** and see the Kubas (formerly the **Koobas**) and Ricky Gleason and the Top Spots from Liverpool and **Tony Sheridan** backed by the Bobby Patrick Big Six. Ray was to forge a friendship with his counterpart at the Star Club, **Manfred Weissleder**. He carried a letter from the Lord Mayor of Liverpool to the Burgomeister of Hamburg which read: 'I have heard with interest that during the last few years groups of young Liverpool rock 'n' roll musicians have visited Hamburg. I feel confident that these visits will result in the formation

f friendships amongst members of the younger generation, happy augury for the future.'

The Cavern now had a Junior Cavern Club, membership of which cost 6d (3p) and admission cost members 2s (10p) and visitors 2s 6d (12½p). The sessions took place between 1.00 p.m. and 4.00 p.m. each Saturday and featured two groups and Top Twenty discs, was strictly for thirteen to sixteen-year-olds and began on 1 February 1964. A sign was displayed which read: 'Adults are not admitted unless accompanied by children!'

The club became the subject of worldwide media attention, with TV cameramen from America, France, Sweden and Germany focusing their cameras on the heady atmosphere; radio teams included several radio stations from India, the Russian news agency Tass, the **Canadian Broadcasting Company** – and a whole host of magazine journalists from American publications such as ***Time***, ***Life*** and ***Newsweek***. Celebrities from around the world took to dropping into the club, including film stars such as Anna Neagle, musicians such as Chet Atkins, classical conductor Arthur Feidler and dozens of others.

Ray continued his expansion plans and launched a management/agency called Cavern Artistes Ltd, representing a number of acts, including the Michael Allen Group, the Clayton Squares, the Excelles, the Hideaways, the Kubas, the Notions, Earl Preston's Realms and the St Louis Checks.

On 3 November 1963 he bought the premises next door to the Cavern, extended the width of the club and began building a recording studio, Cavern Sound, which opened on 15 October 1964 with £10,000 worth of equipment. The studio handled demonstration tapes, tape-to-disc transfers, master recordings, pressings, pressings for distribution to major labels and recordings for commercial radio. The first group to record there was the Clayton Squares and the studio was run by engineers Peter Hepworth and Nigel Greenburg. During alterations the old stage had to go and Ray had the idea of selling pieces of the original stage as 'Beatleboard' to Beatles fans who would like a souvenir of the stage on which the group had performed so many times. Beatleboard cost five shillings (25p) a piece, the proceeds being donated to Oxfam. There were so many requests from all over the world that it took four months to fulfil the orders.

On Saturday, 13 September 1964, there was a 'Caverncade', a parade through the streets of Liverpool by groups on decorated floats, the proceeds being donated to Oxfam.

There was even a weekly half-hour radio show which took place at the club. Called 'Sunday Night at the Cavern', it was broadcast on **Radio Luxembourg** each Sunday at 10.30 p.m. commencing on 15 March 1963. The show was hosted by Bob Wooler who played the latest chart records and introduced a group live from the Cavern stage each week.

Unfortunately, McFall had taken on too many enterprises and overextended his capital, with the result that, in February 1966, he had to declare himself bankrupt. The loyal troglodytes (one of the names by which the Cavern 'regulars' were known) wished to support McFall and keep the club open, but the bailiffs were called in. The irate Cavernites staged a sit-in. **Freda Kelly**, the Beatles fan club secretary, took part in the siege by blockading the stairway of the Cavern with chairs. On stage, moral support came from the music of the Hideaways. Eventually, the police entered the club and removed its struggling inhabitants. The cave dwellers continued their protests and a petition was sent to Prime Minister Harold Wilson at Lime Street Station as he arrived in Liverpool on a visit.

Following the bankruptcy proceedings, the club was acquired by Joe Davey, who ran Joe's Café, and Alf Geoghegan. It was officially reopened on 23 January 1966 by Harold Wilson, while **Ken Dodd** and local MP Bessie Braddock were also present. The first group to take the stage after the reopening were the Hideaways, who had been the last group to play at the club (the group also appeared at the Cavern more times than any other band, a total of 412 appearances). The Beatles were unable to attend, but sent a telegram.

The Cavern changed hands again and was taken over by another local club-owner, Roy Adams. Although he ran the club successfully, Roy couldn't fight the local bureaucracy. The corporation decided they needed to fit an extraction duct for the underground railway in the premises and Adams was given notice to quit. The club was forced to close on 27 March 1973 and the bulldozers razed the site. The Cavern itself was buried in rubble and when the railway work had been completed, the site was turned into a car park.

Adams obtained the premises directly opposite and opened the New Cavern Club. **Arthur Dooley** created a

Beatles sculpture for the outside wall. The premises were taken over by Roger Eagle who reopened the venue as Eric's in 1976 and a whole new generation of Mersey talent found an outlet – Elvis Costello, Frankie Goes To Hollywood, China Crisis, Orchestral Manoeuvres In The Dark, Echo and the Bunnymen, Teardrop Explodes, A Flock of Seagulls, the Lotus Eaters, Wah! and many more.

Following John Lennon's murder, Liverpool architect David Backhouse approached Royal Life Insurance Limited to develop the site. They were originally going to call it the Eleanor Centre, after 'Eleanor Rigby', but it was then dubbed Cavern Walks and £9 million was spent on the scheme. Backhouse designed the basic plans for the complex in only two days, producing an original design of a structure seven storeys high with an almost Victorian look to it. He also included provision for the restructuring of the original Cavern Club. The original bricks of the club were still buried below the car park in the packed earth and a number of the original bricks were used in the reconstruction. For some reason, the new Cavern was built parallel to Mathew Street, in contrast to the original, which had been built at a right angle to the street. As a result, instead of merely walking down eighteen steps into a club, a new entrance with a large spiral staircase had to be constructed.

The Cavern Walks complex was also to have a shopping centre, offices, an 'Abbey Road' pub, a restaurant, a Beatles museum, a central atrium where the shopping malls merged and an eye-catching statue of the Beatles.

Cynthia Lennon was asked to provide a design for the terracotta tiles that would face parts of the new building. On 25 April 1984 she unveiled a small commemorative plaque, placed on an outside wall, inscribed 'To John' and containing the lyrics to 'In My Life'.

In the centre of the atrium itself – which reaches up past the entire seven floors with a wall-climber lift, candy-pink lamp-posts, vaulted ceilings and hanging gardens of foliage – is the controversial £40,000 statue by John Doubleday, who says, 'It is the largest figurative group in bronze commissioned in Britain for 25 years, in fact since Epstein's Bowater House Group. It has been a considerable professional challenge. Above all, I have tried to capture the raw energy of the Beatles as they were when they were playing at the Cavern.'

At the time the local council ordered the destruction of the original Cavern to make way for the air vent, Liverpool bureaucrats spurned any efforts to promote the image of the Beatles in Liverpool, turning down requests for a statue and to name Liverpool streets after the Beatles. However, after the death of John Lennon, all that changed. Eventually even a series of streets was named after the group and further accolades were given to the Cavern. In April 1984, **EMI** issued a special sixteen-track album *Tribute To The Cavern*, to be sold exclusively at the club. All the tracks were recorded during the 1963/4 period, although none of them was actually recorded at the club. Among the artists represented were the Beatles, Billy J. Kramer & the Dakotas, the Fourmost, Gerry & the Pacemakers, the Swinging Bluejeans and **Cilla Black**.

However, there had been albums recorded at the Cavern in the past. George Martin had originally considered recording the Beatles during a live session at the Cavern, but decided that there were too many technical difficulties. The Big Three were recorded live at the club and an EP *The Big Three Live At The Cavern* issued on Decca DFE 8552 in July 1964. The group also recorded a number called 'The Cavern Stomp'. In March 1964 Decca issued an album on Decca LK 4597 which was recorded live at the club and called *Live At The Cavern*. Four of the acts were from Liverpool – the Big Three, **Beryl Marsden**, the Dennisons and **Lee Curtis**, while other acts featured were Dave Berry & the Cruisers, Bern Elliott & the Fenmen, the Fortunes and Heinz & the Marauders.

Abbey Road Studios also produced a 45-minute film, *Cavern Beat*, which was screened at the newly opened venue twice a day during the summer of 1984. The film was narrated by Terry Sylvester, former member of the Escorts and the Hollies, and included film of the Cavern's history and the groups who appeared there, with a soundtrack which included various Mersey groups and the Beatles tracks 'Penny Lane', 'Strawberry Fields Forever', 'A Hard Day's Night', 'I Feel Fine', 'Twist And Shout', 'She Loves You', 'Please Please Me', 'Love Me Do' and 'Some Other Guy'.

During 1984 there was also a musical play *Cavern Of Dreams*, presented at the Liverpool Playhouse.

● Caxton Hall, *London W1*

Originally Westminster Town Hall, the premises became Britain's most celebrated Register Office because it was the place where many celebrities were married, including

Elizabeth Taylor, Diana Dors, **Peter Sellers** and Roger Moore.

Mary (**Maureen**) Cox and Ringo were married at the hall on 11 February 1965. George and John were present at the ceremony while Paul was on holiday in Tunisia at the time.

The hall had a famous history and was the venue where the Suffragettes planned their campaign. Winston Churchill also made his wartime speeches from the hall.

Pattie Harrison attended a lecture on Transcendental meditation at the Caxton Hall in February 1967, which led her to encourage George, together with the other members of the Beatles, to attend the Maharishi's lecture at the **Hilton Hotel** a few months later.

In 1991 the Caxton Hall was set to be demolished to make way for an £18 million redevelopment programme.

CBS Studio, 50 Broadway & West 53rd Street, New York City

The former Maxine Elliott Theatre which became the CBS Studio base for the '**Ed Sullivan** Shows'.

It was quite a coup for Brian Epstein to have the Beatles booked for the show, particularly as bill toppers, for despite their fame in Europe, they were virtually unknown in America at the time of the booking.

Although **Ed Sullivan** believed the group were going to become major stars, he contested Epstein's insistence that they receive top billing as no British group had made it big in the States before. Brian Epstein got his way and the group were booked for three shows, although the $4,500 fee was very low – ten years previously Colonel Tom Parker had insisted on $50,000 for **Elvis Presley** to appear on three Sullivan shows (although some reports did say that the Beatles fee was $10,000 or $12,000). Another factor is that Sullivan Productions paid for the Beatles' air fares.

The theatre provided seating for an audience of 728 people and there was an unprecedented demand of over 50,000 ticket requests.

The Beatles had to become members of the AFRA trade union before they could begin rehearsing for the show. At the time, George Harrison was suffering from flu and remained behind at the **Plaza Hotel** while the group dropped into the studios on Saturday, 8 February 1964. **Neil Aspinall** stood in for George at the rehearsals and a concerned Ed Sullivan was assured that George would be present at the show itself. 'He'd better be or I'm putting on a wig myself,' Sullivan said.

On 9 February there was a dress rehearsal and the taping of another 'Ed Sullivan Show' to be broadcast on 23 February.

The show itself drew the biggest audience for an entertainment programme in the history of television. An estimated 73,000,000 viewers saw the performance and it was reported that the crime rate among teenagers throughout America dropped to virtually zero that night.

Conductor Leonard Bernstein had requested tickets for his two daughters and Wendy Hanson, Epstein's PA, arranged seats for them in the front row. She also escorted Bernstein to the Beatles' dressing room. After he'd left, John Lennon told her: 'Look, luv, could you keep **Sidney Bernstein**'s family out of this room.'

Brian Epstein had approached Sullivan with the request, 'I would like to know the exact wording of your introduction.' Sullivan replied, 'I would like you to get lost.'

The show went on the air at 8.00 p.m. and Sullivan opened with the words: 'Now, yesterday and today, our theatre's been jammed with newspapermen and hundreds of photographers from all over the nation, and these veterans agree with me that the city never has witnessed the excitement stirred by these youngsters from Liverpool, who call themselves the Beatles. Now, tonight, you'll twice be entertained by them – right now and in the second half of the show.' Sullivan also read out a congratulatory telegram from Elvis Presley (it had actually been sent by Colonel Parker) and the Beatles opened with Paul singing 'All My Loving'. This was followed by 'Till There Was You', also sung by Paul. During this number their christian names were flashed on the screen and when it was John's turn, there was also the comment, 'Sorry girls, he's married'. They ended the first part of their show with 'She Loves You'. Sullivan then announced that they would be back in the second half of the show and that the three numbers they'd played had been dedicated to Randy Parr (daughter of the TV host Jack Parr). When the Beatles returned they performed 'I Saw Her Standing There' and 'I Want To Hold Your Hand'. During the last number, one of the mikes went dead.

Other acts on the bill that evening included Frank Gorshin, the impressionist, comedian Charlie Brill, the Broadway cast of *Oliver*, with singer Georgia Brown, David

Jones (who would later become a member of the **Monkees**) and Tessie O'Shea.

The show's producer was **Bob Precht** and the musical director was Ray Bloch.

The Neilson ratings indicated that it was Sullivan's highest rating show with 45.3 per cent of all TV sets in America tuned to the programme.

The performance was widely reported in the American press the next day and the *Herald Tribune* was to comment that the Beatles were: '75% publicity, 20% haircut and 5% lilting lament', while *Newsweek* reported: 'Visually they are a nightmare: tight, dandified Edwardian beatnik suits and great pudding bowls of hair. Musically they are a near disaster, guitars and drums slamming out a merciless beat that does away with secondary rhythms, harmony an melody.'

Evangelist Billy Graham had decided to watc television on the Sabbath to see what all the fuss wa about, and later commented: 'They're a passing phase. A are symptoms of the uncertainty of the times and th confusion about us.'

Ed Sullivan died in 1974 and the studio is now know as the Ed Sullivan Theatre.

● Centennial Hall, *Adelaide, South Australia*

Adelaide had not been included on the initial plans for th Beatles' tour of Australia and the citizens of that cit

aunched a major campaign for Adelaide to be included on he itinerary. After promoter **Kenn Brodziak** received a etition with over 80,000 signatures he contacted London sking for an extension to the tour to include Adelaide and vas granted it.

The only venue in Adelaide where the concert could be eld was the Centennial Hall, which was run by the Royal Agricultural and Horticultural Society. Their usual ooking fee for the hall was £65, but they demanded £440 er night for the Beatles appearances. Brodziak elegrammed Adelaide disc jockey Bob Francis to tell him hat the bookings would be cancelled due to the exorbitant emands.

To add the further dates to the tour, Brodziak was equired to come up with a further £12,000, which was nore than he was paying the Beatles for the rest of the tour - and it would cost him all his profits from the four shows. ortunately some Adelaide businessmen, eager that the isit should take place, undertook to finance and promote t themselves.

The Adelaide concerts created a world record for ueues for Beatles tickets and thousands of applicants egan to take place in a massive queue and 250,000 eople came to watch the phenomenon as fans queued for 0 to 70 hours for their tickets. Several people in the ueue were hospitalized for exhaustion and all 12,000 ickets went within five hours.

When the Beatles arrived in the city there were 00,000 people lining the streets to watch the motorcade.

At that evening's show the Beatles performed the same et they had played in Denmark and Holland – and they vould repeat it throughout the Australian tour. It was: 'I aw Her Standing There', 'I Want To Hold Your Hand', You Can't Do That', 'All My Loving', 'She Loves You', Till There Was You', 'Roll Over Beethoven', 'Can't Buy Me Love', 'This Boy' and 'Long Tall Sally' or 'Twist And hout'.

The group appeared for two nights at the Centennial Hall on 12 and 13 June 1964.

Chains

A song penned by the busband and wife songwriting team Gerry Goffin and Carole King. It was issued as a single by he Cookies in November 1962 and rapidly became a opular number with Liverpool bands. George Harrison ook over on lead vocals for the Beatles version, which he recorded for the *Please Please Me* album. George also sang the number on the BBC radio shows **'Here We Go'**, **'Side By Side'** and **'Pop Go The Beatles'**.

The number was included on the British EP *The Beatles No. 1*, the compilation *The Beatles Collection* and the American albums *Introducing The Beatles*, *The Beatles vs The Four Seasons* and *The Early Beatles*.

● Chang, Barry

Chinese brother of Beryl Williams. Barry travelled with Beryl, his brother-in-law **Allan Williams**, the Beatles and **Lord Woodbine** to Hamburg in an Austin mini-van in August 1960. They travelled by sea ferry from Harwich to the Netherlands and overland to Germany. It was Barry who recorded the journey for posterity by taking photographs during the trip, including the famous shot in Arnhem Cemetery in front of a memorial inscribed 'Their Name Liveth For Evermore'.

Barry was later to run a casino on the first floor of Liverpool's **Blue Angel Club**.

● Channel, Bruce

Singer from Dallas, Texas, who had a major hit in 1962 with 'Hey Baby'.

Five weeks after the record entered the British Top Ten, Brian Epstein booked him to top the bill of a **NEMS Enterprises** promotion at the **Tower Ballroom**, New Brighton, on Thursday, 21 June 1962. This was part of Epstein's policy to place the Beatles as second on the bill to an established artist and thus give them prestige. He promoted the event with large advertisements in ***Mersey Beat***.

Channel was accompanied by his harmonica player Delbert McClinton, whose performance on the record added to its commercial appeal. John Lennon in particular, was struck by McClinton's harmonica sound, which became a big influence over the following two years and is particularly evident on the 'Love Me Do' recording.

Apart from McClinton, Channel was also backed by a group called the Barons, although they weren't the Liverpool group of that name.

The rest of the bill comprised Liverpool acts with the Beatles and **Howie Casey** & the Seniors advertised as recording artists. The show, which attracted an audience of 2,500, was compered by **Bob Wooler** and also featured the Big Three and the Four Jays.

● Chants, The

It was in 1960 that the Chants began life as the Shades, who began to rehearse and perform in Stanley House in Upper Parliament Street, Liverpool, a community centre for both blacks and whites.

The group developed their vocal sound and changed their name to the Chants. Apart from Joe, they comprised Edmond Ankrah, Nat Smeda, Alan Harding, Eddie Amoo and reserve singer Peter Ching.

They made their **Cavern** debut in November 1962 and being a vocal outfit they needed instrumental backing. This was provided for them on their early Cavern appearance by the Beatles. Brian Epstein attempted to prevent his prestigious local band backing a group of unknowns, but the Beatles insisted and the gig went ahead.

Epstein became their manager for a short time, but it didn't work out and they signed with a Manchester agent, Ted Ross, and made their recording debut on Pye Records in September 1963 with 'I Could Write A Book'. The Beatles voted it a hit on their **'Juke Box Jury'** appearance on 7 December 1963, but it wasn't to be. Several other releases followed, but they never enjoyed a chart hit and disbanded.

Incidentally, the group were the only local band invited to the Beatles' civic reception at **Liverpool Town Hall**.

● 24 Chapel Street, Belgravia, London SW1

Georgian brick house which Brian Epstein bought for £60,000 on 20 December 1964.

The five-storey building had a private garage, a small servants' quarters, a formal dining room and roof garden. Brian's staff included his chauffeur Brian Barratt, a Spanish couple – Antonio, the butler and his wife Marie, the cook. As Brian had ceased working at his Stafford Street office and now used Chapel Street as his base, his secretary **Joanne Newfield** travelled there each day from Edgware.

Brian liked to hold dinner parties at the lavishly decorated house and on 19 May 1967 held a special *Sgt Pepper* party for the press. His PA **Peter Brown** described the elite get-together as being 'for the ten most important representatives of the press to listen to the new album and enjoy a "family" dinner with one or two of the Beatles around the dining table'.

Press people included **Don Short** of the *Daily Mirror* and among the photographers was Linda Eastman. Fare included fine wines, caviar and poached salmon. Disc jockey guests included **Alan Freeman**, **Jimmy Savile** and **Kenny Everett**, and Everett was to observe that the Beatles were dressed in colourful clothes, with John wearing red trousers and a green shirt decorated with a yellow flower design.

The Chapel Street address was where Brian was found dead on 27 August 1967. He'd intended to spend the weekend at his country house in **Kingsley Hill** in Sussex with **Geoffrey Ellis** and Peter Brown as his guests. He'd arrived home to Chapel Street on the Friday with promises that he'd return. Peter Brown phoned his private number after midnight to see if he'd arrived safely and Antonio answered it, explaining that he was unable to contact Brian on the intercom.

Later, still unable to contact his employer, Antonio phoned Kingsley Hill but Geoffrey and Peter were out lunching at a local pub. He next called Joanne Newfield and **Alistair Taylor** who arrived at Chapel Street. They managed to contact Peter Brown on the phone, who suggested they get hold of his own GP, Dr John Gallway who lived nearby. When Dr Gallway arrived a decision was taken to break down the doors of Brian's bedroom. Antonio and Brian Barrett broke down the doors and Brian was found dead.

At the coroner's inquest the verdict was that he had died of an overdose of Carbitol.

● Chapman, Norman

The 6 foot 2 inch Chapman was a picture frame maker and restorer in July 1960 when he was discovered by the Beatles.

After **Tommy Moore** had left them the group were desperate to find a replacement. **Allan Williams** heard the sound of drums one evening coming from the block opposite his club the **Jacaranda**; he called the group, who were in the club, and they went in search of the drummer. The sound came from the windows above the National Cash Register office in Slater Street and the boys began shouting for whoever was playing the drums to come down.

Chapman emerged. He was an amateur drummer who practised after finishing work at night. They asked him to join them and he sat in for three Saturday night gigs at the **Grosvenor Ballroom** in July, but was then conscripted for National Service and posted to Kenya.

Charles, Tommy

lanager of WAQY, a C&W radio station in Birmingham, labama, who, on 31 July 1966, announced that the tation wouldn't play any more Beatles records and equested that his listeners burn records and photographs f the group because of John Lennon's alleged statement hat the Beatles were bigger than Jesus Christ. He resided over a publicized bonfire where Beatles records vere burned.

Other stations followed suit. One of them, radio KLUE, vhich had organized a public bonfire of Beatles records on 3 August, had their transmission tower struck by a bolt of ightning the very next morning which knocked their news irector unconscious and caused extensive damage to quipment!

Charts

Love Me Do' was the Beatles' very first chart entry, lthough it was not a massive hit in its first year of release. t reached its highest position of No. 17 in one London nusic paper for one week only, was No. 27 for one week in nother, but at least managed to make its presence felt in ll four London musical weeklies, reaching No. 24 in *Disc* nd No. 32 in *Record Mirror*, in addition to the *Melody laker* and ***New Musical Express*** placings.

However, as was to be expected, it reached No. 1 soon fter release in the North's only music paper: ***Mersey eat***. The full Top Twenty of the 18 October 1962 issue vas as follows:

1. 'Love Me Do', the Beatles
2. 'Telstar', the Tornadoes
3. 'The Locomotion', Little Eva
4. 'It Might As Well Rain Until September', Carole King
5. 'Sheila', Tommy Roe
6. 'Ramblin' Rose', Nat King Cole
7. 'She's Not You', Elvis Presley
8. 'Devil Woman', Marty Robbins
9. 'What Now My Love', Shirley Bassey
10. 'You Don't Know Me', Ray Charles
11. 'I Remember You', Frank Ifield
12. 'It'll Be Me', Cliff Richard
13. 'Let's Dance', Chris Montez
14. 'Reminiscing', Buddy Holly
15. 'Don't That Beat All', Adam Faith
16. 'Things', Bobby Darin
17. 'Venus In Blue Jeans', Mark Wynter
18. 'Speedy Gonzales', Pat Boone
19. 'Send Me The Pillow', Johnny Tillotson
20. 'It's Started All Over Again', Brenda Lee

The most prestigious British chart of the sixties was the *New Musical Express* chart. The *NME* was the music weekly with the largest circulation and had, in fact, been the publication which had run Britain's first-ever chart listing on 14 November 1952. The Beatles first entered the *New Musical Express* chart on Wednesday, 24 October 1962. To indicate the type of music popular at the time of the Beatles' record debut, the full Top Thirty of this date follows, with background details on the artists.

1. 'Telstar', The Tornadoes (**Decca**) – A group produced by the late Joe Meek, a major British record producer who committed suicide in 1967. This was the first million-seller by a British group in America. The most notable member of the Tornadoes was the blond-haired guitarist Heinz. He enjoyed brief fame as a solo artist, but never maintained his success and took on numerous jobs over the years before settling into a bakery in Eastleigh, Hants.

2. 'The Locomotion', Little Eva (London) – A Goffin-King composition, recorded by the couple's babysitter, Eva Boyd. Eva had one or two minor hits before settling down as a housewife.

3. 'Sheila', **Tommy Roe** (HMV) – American singer, born in Atlanta, Georgia, whose 'Sheila' didn't hit the British charts on its original release in 1960. The Beatles included this number in their repertoire and were to tour with Roe and another American singer, **Chris Montez**, in 1963. Tommy also appeared on the Beatles' first-ever American concert at the **Washington Coliseum** on 11 February 1964.

4. 'Ramblin' Rose', Nat King Cole (**Capitol**) – A fine balladeer who, sadly, died of lung cancer in 1965 at the age of 45. Several years later, his daughter Natalie Cole pursued a career as a singer.

5. 'It Might As Well Rain Until September', Carole King (London) – One half of the tremendously successful songwriting team of Goffin and King. In the late sixties, Carole maintained her career as a singer with a succession of hit albums.

6. 'Venus In Blue Jeans', Mark Wynter (Pye) – Handsome solo singer who covered American hits. First discovered singing in Peckham in 1959. After his spell as a British hitmaker he moved to Australia. Over the years he has turned to the stage and on his return to England he performed in pantomime and Shakespeare.

7. 'Let's Dance', Chris Montez (London) – This number and 'The More I See You' were the biggest hits by this American singer who toured Britain with Tommy Roe, billed above the Beatles. Apart from a minor revival of interest in the seventies for his early records, nothing much has been heard of him since.

8. 'Lovesick Blues' Frank Ifield (Columbia) – Coventry-born Ifield moved with his parents to Australia at the age of nine. When he returned to Britain he had a string of hit records, including four chart toppers.

9. 'You Don't Know Me', Ray Charles (HMV) – American singer who first rose to fame in 1959 with 'What'd I Say'. Born in Georgia, Charles became blind at the age of six due to an illness. He performed a distinctive style of rhythm and blues and had many hits before concentrating on music publishing and record promotion.

10. 'What Now My Love', **Shirley Bassey** (Columbia) – Born in the Tiger Bay area of Swansea in 1937, Shirley went on to become one of Britain's major international stars and was later to find her biggest recording successes with James Bond numbers such as 'Goldfinger' and 'Diamonds Are Forever'. She also had hits with George Harrison's 'Something' and Paul McCartney's 'Fool On The Hill'.

11. 'Swiss Maid', **Del Shannon** (London) – The song was written by Roger Miller and gave Michigan-born singer Shannon an international hit. He late became fabulously wealthy dealing in real estat and bought a large ranch in California. Tragically he died from a gunshot wound, presumably self inflicted.

12. 'Sherry', the Four Seasons (Stateside) – A majo American vocal group whose lead singer Franki Valli carved a successful solo career. Valli had a massive hit with the theme song from *Grease*. Th **Vee Jay** label in the States issued an album *Th Beatles vs The Four Seasons* in October 1964.

13. 'She's Not You', **Elvis Presley** (RCA) – One o popular music's legendary figures, who died i August 1977. The Beatles once had a privat meeting with Elvis at his home in California. At on time Paul wrote a number specially for Elvis, bu nothing came of it.

14. 'Devil Woman', Marty Robbins (CBS) – This wa one of a series of international hits by a countr singer who was a leading exponent of C&W music i Nashville.

15. 'It'll Be Me', Cliff Richard (Columbia) – Britain' most popular solo singer and the only recordin artist to have No. 1 hits in five different decades With his group the **Shadows** he was the majo British sensation until the Beatles made their bow.

16. 'She Taught Me How To Yodel', Frank Ifiel (Columbia) – Although he has settled in Hounslow London, Ifield is particularly popular in Australasi and the Far East, where he still tours.

17. 'I Remember You', Frank Ifield (Columbia) – Thre records in the Top Twenty for Frank – the sort c achievement which the Beatles were soon to enjo around the world.

18. 'Lonely', **Acker Bilk** (Columbia) – A survivor of th Traditional Jazz boom which hit Britain in the lat fifties and brought Acker his biggest hit 'Strange On The Shore'. The clarinettist/bandleader sti tours Europe regularly.

19. 'No One Can Make My Sunshine Smile', the Everly Brothers (Warner Bros) – Another classic act from the golden age of the fifties. The duo ceased performing together in 1973 and there were rumours of a feud between the brothers, but Don and Phil were reunited in 1984 and came to Britain. Paul McCartney was at their **Albert Hall** concert and penned 'On The Wings Of A Nightingale' for them, which gave the Evs their first hit in the singles chart for over a decade.

20. 'Don't That Beat All', Adam Faith (Parlophone) – Major British solo singer of the early sixties who found success in another sphere as an actor. His most notable TV series was 'Budgie' and he took over the role vacated by Ringo Starr in *Stardust*. He entered the field of management with Leo Sayer and still makes occasional TV appearances.

21. 'It Started All Over Again', Brenda Lee (Brunswick) – At one time this tiny Georgia-born singer was the top female vocalist in the world. She left the recording scene in 1967 to settle down in her home in Nashville and in the seventies turned to country music. A compilation of her original hits entered the British charts in 1980.

22. 'Send Me The Pillow You Dream On', Johnny Tillotson (London) – A spell in the army doing compulsory service seemed to end the career of this singer, whose biggest hit was 'Poetry In Motion'. He attempted several comebacks but never equalled his early success.

23. 'The Pay Off', Kenny Ball (Pye) – Another survivor from the Traditional Jazz scene of the fifties who continues to pursue a career on the club and cabaret circuit, making frequent television appearances. A regular at the **Cavern Club** at the time the Beatles began appearing there.

24. 'If A Man Answers', Bobby Darin (Capitol) – Sadly, this brilliant singer died of a heart attack in December 1973. He had eighteen chart singles and once even rivalled the popularity of Frank Sinatra himself.

25. 'Bobby's Girl', Susan Maugham (Philips) – Pretty, dark-haired singer from County Durham who made several records. This single was her only Top 30 entry. She pursued a career in pantomime and cabaret and still makes occasional appearances on television.

26. 'Because Of Love', **Billy Fury** (Decca) – At one time the closest rival to Cliff Richard in the pre-Beatle years. This late, lamented singer had to curtail a promising career due to ill health following 26 British chart hits. Born in Liverpool, he once shared the same class at school as Ringo Starr and the **Silver Beetles** auditioned to be his backing group in 1960.

27. 'Love Me Do', the Beatles (Parlophone) – The first chart entry of the most sensational group in the history of popular music.

28. 'Reminiscing', **Buddy Holly** (Coral) – A seminal influence on the Beatles, who recorded some of his songs. The name 'Beatles' was actually inspired by the name of Holly's backing group the Crickets. Paul McCartney was to become the publisher of Holly's songs. The singer died in an air crash in October 1959.

29. 'Roses Are Red', Ronnie Carroll (Philips) – One of several former danceband singers who had regular chart success in the fifties and early sixties. His last chart entry was 'Say Wonderful Things' in 1963.

30. 'The James Bond Theme', John Barry (Columbia) – Former leader of the John Barry Seven who became a major soundtrack composer following his association with the James Bond movies. Paul McCartney penned the theme tune for 'Live And Let Die'.

The first British charts were published on 14 November 1952 in the *New Musical Express*. The initial chart listed 12 records and was later enlarged to 20, then to 30. On 10 March 1960 the trade magazine *Record Retailer* inaugurated a Top 50 chart.

From 19 February 1969 the chart began to be

compiled for *Record Retailer* by the British Market Research Bureau. As the same chart was also used by the BBC, this became recognized as the major chart in Britain. *Record Retailer* later changed its name to *Music Week* and in 1983 the compilation of the charts was undertaken by Gallup.

However, during the sixties, the most important chart was still the one compiled by *New Musical Express*. The *NME* chart was also broadcast weekly on **Radio Luxembourg** and printed in national publications such as the *Daily Mail*. The *Record Retailer* chart was not really recognized by any major media outlet in the early sixties and it was not until later in the decade when it was compiled by the British Market Research Bureau that the BBC began to use it. The BBC had previously compiled its own chart based on the combined statistics of the *New Musical Express*, *Disc*, *Melody Maker* and *Record Mirror* and from this chart they chose the artists for 'Top Of The Pops'.

The positions reached by the Beatles in the *Record Retailer/Music Week* singles charts were:

'Love Me Do' reached No. 17.
'Please Please Me' reached No. 2.
'From Me To You' reached No. 1.
'She Loves You' reached No. 1.
'I Want To Hold Your Hand' reached No. 1.
'Can't Buy Me Love' reached No. 1.
'Ain't She Sweet' reached No. 29.
'A Hard Day's Night' reached No. 1.
'I Feel Fine' reached No. 1.
'Ticket To Ride' reached No. 1.
'Help!' reached No. 1.
'Day Tripper'/'We Can Work It Out' reached No. 1.
'Paperback Writer' reached No. 1.
'Yellow Submarine'/'Eleanor Rigby' reached No. 1.
'Penny Lane'/'Strawberry Fields Forever' reached No. 2.
'All You Need Is Love' reached No. 1.
'Hello Goodbye' reached No. 1.
'Magical Mystery Tour' reached No. 2.
'Lady Madonna' reached No. 1.
'Let It Be' reached No. 2.
'Yesterday' reached No. 8.

A number of Beatles singles were re-released in the seventies and eighties and these were their positions in the *Music Week* chart:

'Hey Jude' reached No. 12.
'Paperback Writer' reached No. 23.
'Strawberry Fields Forever' reached No. 32.
'Get Back' reached No. 28.
'Help!' reached No. 37.
'Back In The USSR' reached No. 19.
'Sgt Pepper's Lonely Hearts Club Band'/'With A Little Help From My Friends' reached No. 63.
'Beatles Movie Medley' reached No. 10.
'Love Me Do' reached No. 4.
'Please Please Me' reached No. 29.
'From Me To You' reached No. 40.
'She Loves You' reached No. 45.
'I Want To Hold Your Hand' reached No. 62.
'Can't Buy Me Love' reached No. 53.
'A Hard Day's Night' reached No. 52.
'I Feel Fine' reached No. 65.
'Ticket To Ride' reached No. 70.
'Eleanor Rigby'/'Yellow Submarine' reached No. 63.
'Penny Lane'/'Strawberry Fields Forever' reached No. 65.
'All You Need Is Love' reached No. 47.
'Hello Goodbye' reached No. 63.
'Lady Madonna' reached No. 67.
'Hey Jude' reached No. 52.

The album positions were:

Please Please Me reached No. 1.
With The Beatles reached No. 1.
A Hard Day's Night reached No. 1.
Beatles For Sale reached No. 1.
Help! reached No. 1.
Rubber Soul reached No. 1.
Revolver reached No. 1.
A Collection Of Beatles Oldies reached No. 7.
Sgt Pepper's Lonely Hearts Club Band reached No. 1.
Magical Mystery Tour, an import album, reached No. 31.
The Beatles reached No. 1.
Yellow Submarine reached No. 4.
Abbey Road reached No. 1.
Let It Be reached No. 1.

A Hard Day's Night, a reissue, reached No. 39.
Help!, a reissue, reached No. 33.
The Beatles 1962–1966 reached No. 3.
The Beatles 1967–1970 reached No. 2.
Rock 'n' Roll Music reached No. 11.
The Beatles Tapes reached No. 45.
The Beatles At The Hollywood Bowl reached No. 1.
Love Songs reached No. 7.
Rarities reached No. 71.
Beatles Ballads reached No. 17.
20 Greatest Hits reached No. 10.

The *Melody Maker* has been Britain's longest-running British music weekly. Here are the *Melody Maker* chart positions of the Beatles EPs and singles until the band broke up:

'Love Me Do' entered the charts on 27 November 1962 at No. 48, eventually reaching No. 21 with a chart life of sixteen weeks.

'Please Please Me' entered the charts on 19 January 1963 at No. 47 and eventually reached No. 1 for two weeks with a chart life of eighteen weeks.

'From Me To You' entered the charts on 20 April 1963 at No. 19 and eventually reached No. 1 for six weeks with a chart life of twenty weeks.

'My Bonnie' entered the charts on 15 June 1963 at No. 30, dropped to No. 46 the next week then left the charts.

Twist And Shout (EP) entered the charts on 27 July 1963 at No. 14 and eventually reached No. 2 with a chart life of 31 weeks.

'She Loves You' entered the charts on 31 August 1963 at No. 12 and eventually reached No. 1 for five weeks, with a chart life of 31 weeks.

The Beatles Hits (EP) entered the charts on 28 September 1963 at No. 44, eventually reaching No. 14 with a chart life of twelve weeks.

'I Want To Hold Your Hand' entered the charts on 7 December 1963 at No. 1 where it remained for four weeks with a chart life of eighteen weeks.

All My Loving (EP) entered the charts on 8 February 1964 at No. 42, eventually reaching No. 12 with a chart life of twelve weeks.

'Can't Buy Me Love' entered the charts on 28 March 1964 at No. 1 where it remained for three weeks with a chart life of fourteen weeks.

'Ain't She Sweet' entered the charts on 13 June 1964 at No. 36, eventually reaching No. 24 with a chart life of six weeks.

Long Tall Sally (EP) entered the charts on 4 July 1964 at No. 20, eventually reaching No. 14 with a chart life of thirteen weeks.

'A Hard Day's Night' entered the charts on 18 July 1964 at No. 1 where it remained for four weeks with a chart life of fifteen weeks.

A Hard Day's Night (EP) entered the charts on 28 November 1964 at No. 48, reaching No. 34 with a chart life of four weeks.

'I Feel Fine' entered the charts on 5 December 1964 at No. 1 where it remained for six weeks with a chart life of thirteen weeks.

'Ticket To Ride' entered the charts on 17 April 1965 at No. 1 where it remained for five weeks with a chart life of twelve weeks.

'Help!' entered the charts on 31 July 1965 at No. 1 where it remained for four weeks with a chart life of thirteen weeks.

'We Can Work It Out'/'Day Tripper' entered the charts on 18 June 1966 at No. 1 where it remained for four weeks with a chart life of ten weeks.

'Yellow Submarine'/'Eleanor Rigby' entered the charts on 13 August 1966 at No. 4, eventually reaching No. 1 for three weeks with a chart life of twelve weeks.

'Penny Lane'/'Strawberry Fields Forever' entered the charts on 25 February 1967 at No. 3, eventually reaching No. 1 for three weeks with a chart life of ten weeks.

'All You Need Is Love' entered the charts on 15 July 1967 at No. 3, eventually reaching No. 1 for three weeks with a chart life of eleven weeks.

'Hello Goodbye' entered the charts on 2 December 1967 at No. 3, reaching No. 1 where it remained for four weeks with a chart life of ten weeks.

Magical Mystery Tour (two EPs) entered the charts on 16 December 1967 at No. 17, eventually reaching No. 1 for one week with a chart life of ten weeks.

'Lady Madonna' entered the charts on 23 March 1968 at No. 3, eventually reaching No. 2 for two weeks with a chart life of seven weeks.

'Hey Jude' entered the charts on 7 September

1968 at No. 1 where it remained for four weeks with a chart life of thirteen weeks.

'Get Back' entered the charts on 26 April 1969 at No. 2, eventually reaching No. 1 for five weeks with a chart life of thirteen weeks.

'The Ballad Of John And Yoko' entered the charts on 7 June 1969 at No. 15, eventually reaching No. 1 for three weeks with a chart life of ten weeks.

'Something' entered the charts on 9 November 1969 at No. 26, eventually reaching No. 4 with a chart life of ten weeks.

'Let It Be' entered the charts on 14 March 1970 at No. 15, eventually reaching No. 3 with a chart life of eight weeks.

The Beatles releases in America during 1963 failed to chart. The situation changed the following year and recording history was made on 31 March 1964 when the first five places in the American Top Hundred singles chart were:

1. 'Twist And Shout', the Beatles
2. 'Can't Buy Me Love', the Beatles
3. 'She Loves You', the Beatles
4. 'I Want To Hold Your Hand', the Beatles
5. 'Please Please Me', the Beatles

A similar previously unprecedented chart blitz had also taken place in Australia when on 27 March 1964 the first six places in the Australian Top Twenty were:

1. 'I Saw Her Standing There', the Beatles
2. 'Love Me Do', the Beatles
3. 'Roll Over Beethoven', the Beatles
4. 'All My Loving', the Beatles
5. 'She Loves You', the Beatles
6. 'I Want To Hold Your Hand', the Beatles

The American trade publication *Billboard* runs a Hot 100 chart of the best-selling singles in America. The chart differs from the British chart, not only in the fact that it includes the hundred best-selling records of the week, but also because it includes chart placings for the flipside of discs, which is why the Beatles have 30 different titles among the singles chart entries for 1964 alone.

Here are the details of the Beatles' positions in the *Billboard* chart until the group's eventual break-up:

'I Want To Hold Your Hand' entered the chart on 18 January 1964 at No. 45 and was No. 1 fo seven weeks with a chart life of fifteen weeks.

'She Loves You' entered the charts on 25 Januar 1964 at No. 69 and was No. 1 for two weeks, with chart life of fifteen weeks.

'Please Please Me' entered the charts on February 1964 at No. 68 and eventually reached N 3 with a chart life of thirteen weeks.

'I Saw Her Standing There' entered the charts o 8 February 1964 at No. 68 and eventually reache No. 14 with a chart life of eleven weeks.

'My Bonnie' entered the charts on 15 Februar 1964 at No. 67 and eventually reached No. 26 wit a chart life of six weeks.

'From Me To You' entered the charts on 7 Marc 1964 at No. 86 and eventually reached No. 41 wi a chart life of six weeks.

'Twist And Shout' entered the charts on 1 March 1964 at No. 55 and eventually reached No. with a chart life of eleven weeks.

'Roll Over Beethoven' entered the charts on 2 March 1964 at No. 79 and eventually reached N 68 with a chart life of four weeks.

'All My Loving' entered the charts on 28 Mar 1964 at No. 71 and eventually reached No. 45 wi a chart life of six weeks.

'Do You Want To Know A Secret?' entered th charts on 28 March 1964 at No. 78 and eventual reached No. 2 with a chart life of eleven weeks.

'Can't Buy Me Love' entered the charts on March 1964 at No. 22 and eventually reached No. for five weeks with a chart life of ten weeks.

'You Can't Do That' entered the charts on 4 Ap 1964 at No. 65 and eventually reached No. 48 wi a chart life of four weeks.

'Thank You Girl' entered the charts on 4 Ap 1964 at No. 79 and eventually reached No. 35 wi a chart life of seven weeks.

'There's A Place' entered the charts on 11 Ap 1964 for one week only at No. 74.

'Love Me Do' entered the charts on 11 Ap 1964 at No. 81 and eventually reached No. 1 for o week with a chart life of fourteen weeks.

'Why?' entered the charts on 18 April 1964 at No. 88 for one week only.

'P.S. I Love You' entered the charts on 9 May 1964 at No. 64 and eventually reached No. 10 with a chart life of three weeks.

'Four By The Beatles' (EP) entered the charts on 13 June 1964 at No. 97 and eventually reached No. 92 with a chart life of three weeks.

'Sie Liebt Dich' entered the charts on 27 June 1964 for one week only at No. 97.

'A Hard Day's Night' entered the charts on 18 July 1964 at No. 21 and eventually reached No. 1 for two weeks with a chart life of thirteen weeks.

'Ain't She Sweet' entered the charts on 18 July 1964 at No. 90 and eventually reached No. 19 with a chart life of nine weeks.

'I Should Have Known Better' entered the charts on 25 July 1964 at No. 75 and eventually reached No. 53 with a chart life of four weeks.

'And I Love Her' entered the charts on 25 July 1964 at No. 80 and eventually reached No. 12 with a chart life of nine weeks.

'If I Fell' entered the charts on 1 August 1964 at No. 92 and eventually reached No. 53 with a chart life of nine weeks.

'I'll Cry Instead' entered the charts on 1 August 1964 at No. 62 and eventually reached No. 25 with a chart life of seven weeks.

'I'm Happy Just To Dance With You' entered the charts on 1 August 1964 for one week only at No. 95.

'Matchbox' entered the charts on 5 September 1964 at No. 81 and eventually reached No. 17 with a chart life of eight weeks.

'Slow Down' entered the charts on 5 September 1964 at No. 99 and eventually reached No. 25 with a chart life of seven weeks.

'I Feel Fine' entered the charts on 5 December 1964 at No. 22 and eventually reached No. 1 for three weeks with a chart life of eleven weeks.

'She's A Woman' entered the charts on 5 December 1964 at No. 46 eventually reaching No. 4 with a chart life of nine weeks.

'Eight Days A Week' entered the charts on 20 February 1965 at No. 53 and eventually reached No. 1 for two weeks with a chart life of ten weeks.

'I Don't Want To Spoil The Party' entered the charts on 20 February 1965 at No. 81 and eventually reached No. 39 with a chart life of six weeks.

Four By The Beatles (EP) entered the charts on 27 February 1965 at No. 81 and eventually reached No. 68 with a chart life of five weeks.

'Ticket To Ride' entered the charts on 24 April 1965 at No. 59 and eventually reached No. 1 for one week with a chart life of eleven weeks.

'Yes It Is' entered the charts on 1 May 1965 at No. 71 and eventually reached No. 46 with a chart life of four weeks.

'Help!' entered the charts on 7 August 1965 at No. 42 and eventually reached No. 1 for three weeks with a chart life of thirteen weeks.

'Yesterday' entered the charts on 25 September 1965 at No. 45 and eventually reached No. 1 for four weeks with a chart life of eleven weeks.

'Act Naturally' entered the charts on 25 September 1965 at No. 86 and eventually reached No. 47 with a chart life of seven weeks.

'We Can Work It Out' entered the charts on 18 December 1965 at No. 36 and eventually reached No. 1 for three weeks with a chart life of ten weeks.

'Day Tripper' entered the charts on 28 December 1965 at No. 56 and eventually reached No. 5 with a chart life of ten weeks.

'Nowhere Man' entered the charts on 5 March 1966 at No. 25 and eventually reached No. 3 with a chart life of nine weeks.

'What Goes On?' entered the charts on 12 March 1966 at No. 89, moved to No. 81 the following week, then dropped out.

'Paperback Writer' entered the charts on 11 June 1966 at No. 28 and eventually reached No. 1 for two weeks with a chart life of ten weeks.

'Rain' entered the charts on 11 June 1966 at No. 72 and eventually reached No. 23 with a chart life of seven weeks.

'Yellow Submarine' entered the charts on 20 August 1966 at No. 52 and eventually reached No. 2 with a chart life of nine weeks.

'Eleanor Rigby' entered the charts on 27 August 1966 at No. 65 and eventually reached No. 11 with a chart life of eight weeks.

'Penny Lane' entered the charts on 25 February 1967 at No. 85 and eventually reached No. 1 for one week with a chart life of ten weeks.

'Strawberry Fields Forever' entered the charts on 25 February 1967 at No. 83 and eventually reached No. 8 with a chart life of nine weeks.

'All You Need Is Love' entered the charts on 22 July 1967 at No. 71 and eventually reached No. 1 for one week with a chart life of eleven weeks.

'Baby You're A Rich Man' entered the charts on 29 July 1967 at No. 64 and eventually reached No. 34 with a chart life of five weeks.

'Hello Goodbye' entered the charts on 2 December 1967 at No. 45 and eventually reached No. 1 for three weeks with a chart life of eleven weeks.

'I Am The Walrus' entered the charts on 9 December 1967 at No. 64 and eventually reached No. 56 with a chart life of four weeks.

'Lady Madonna' entered the charts on 23 March 1968 at No. 23 and eventually reached No. 4 with a chart life of eleven weeks.

'The Inner Light' entered the charts on 30 March 1968 for one week only at No. 96.

'Hey Jude' entered the charts on 14 September 1968 at No. 10 and eventually reached No. 1 with a chart life of nineteen weeks.

'Revolution' entered the charts on 14 September 1968 at No. 38 and eventually reached No. 12 with a chart life of eleven weeks.

'Get Back' entered the charts on 10 May 1969 at No. 10 and eventually reached No. 1 for five weeks with a chart life of twelve weeks.

'Don't Let Me Down' entered the charts on 10 May 1969 at No. 40 and eventually reached No. 35 with a chart life of four weeks.

'The Ballad Of John And Yoko' entered the charts on 14 June 1969 at No. 71 and eventually reached No. 8 with a chart life of nine weeks.

'Come Together' entered the charts on 18 October 1969 at No. 23 and after six weeks, during which it reached No. 2, it was tied in with the 'Something' position for a further ten weeks, reaching No. 1 for one week.

'Something' entered the charts on 18 October 1969 at No. 20 and, after six weeks, during which it reached No. 3, it was tied in with the 'Come Together' position for a further ten weeks, reaching No. 1 for one week.

'Let It Be' entered the charts on 21 March 1970 at No. 6 and eventually reached No. 1 for two weeks with a chart life of fourteen weeks.

'For You Blue'/'The Long And Winding Road' entered the charts on 23 May 1970 at No. 35 and eventually reached No. 1 for two weeks with a chart life of ten weeks.

Here are the positions which the Beatles albums reached in the *Billboard* charts:

Meet The Beatles reached No. 1.

Introducing The Beatles reached No. 2.

The Beatles With Tony Sheridan And Their Guests reached No. 68.

Jolly What! The Beatles And Frank Ifield On Stage reached No. 104.

The Beatles Second Album reached No. 1.

The American Tour With Ed Rudy reached No. 20.

A Hard Day's Night reached No. 1.

Something New reached No. 2.

The Beatles vs the Four Seasons reached No. 142.

Songs, Pictures And Stories Of The Fabulous Beatles reached No. 63.

The Beatles Story reached No. 7.

The Beatles '65 reached No. 1.

The Early Beatles reached No. 43.

Beatles VI reached No. 1.

Help! reached No. 1.

Rubber Soul reached No. 1.

Yesterday . . . And Today reached No. 1.

Revolver reached No. 1.

Sgt Pepper's Lonely Hearts Club Band reached No. 1.

Magical Mystery Tour reached No. 1.

Unfinished Music No. 1 – Two Virgins, John Lennon and **Yoko Ono**, reached No. 124.

The Beatles reached No. 1.

Wonderwall Music, George Harrison, reached No. 49.

Yellow Submarine reached No. 2.

Unfinished Music No. 2 – Life With The Lions

John Lennon and Yoko Ono, reached No. 174.

Electronic Sounds, George Harrison, reached No. 191.

Abbey Road reached No. 1.

Wedding Album, John Lennon and Yoko Ono, reached No. 178.

Live Peace In Toronto, **Plastic Ono Band,** reached No. 10.

Hey Jude reached No. 2.

In The Beginning reached No. 117.

Let It Be reached No. 1.

The Beatles 1962–1966 reached No. 3.

The Beatles 1967–1970 reached No. 1.

Rock 'n' Roll Music reached No. 2.

The Beatles At The Hollywood Bowl reached No. 2.

Live! At The Star Club In Hamburg, Germany: 1962 reached No. 111.

Love Songs reached No. 24.

Rarities reached No. 21.

Reel Music reached No. 19.

here were three main trade music publications in merica during the sixties: *Billboard*, *Cash Box* and *ecord World*. The chart positions of the Beatles in *Record orld* were as follows:

'She Loves You' reached No. 1.

'Roll Over Beethoven' reached No. 35.

'I Want To Hold Your Hand' reached No. 1.

'My Bonnie' reached No. 31.

'Please Please Me' reached No. 5.

'All My Loving' reached No. 32.

'Twist And Shout' reached No. 1.

'Can't Buy Me Love' reached No. 1.

'Do You Want To Know A Secret' reached No. 3.

'Love Me Do' reached No. 1.

'Ain't She Sweet' reached No. 13.

'A Hard Day's Night' reached No. 1.

'I'll Cry Instead' reached No. 28.

'And I Love Her' reached No. 16.

'Matchbox' reached No. 22.

'I Feel Fine' reached No. 1.

'Eight Days A Week' reached No. 1.

'Ticket To Ride' reached No. 1.

'Help!' reached No. 1.

'Yesterday' reached No. 1.

'We Can Work It Out'/'Day Tripper' reached No. 1.

'Nowhere Man' reached No. 1.

'Paperback Writer' reached No. 1.

'Yellow Submarine'/'Eleanor Rigby' reached No. 1.

'Penny Lane'/'Strawberry Fields Forever' reached No. 1.

'All You Need Is Love' reached No. 1.

'Hello Goodbye' reached No. 1.

'Lady Madonna' reached No. 2.

'Hey Jude' reached No. 1.

'Get Back' reached No. 1.

'The Ballad Of John And Yoko' reached No. 7.

'Give Peace A Chance', Plastic Ono Band, reached No. 10.

'Something'/'Come Together' reached No. 1.

'Cold Turkey', Plastic Ono Band, reached No. 26.

'Instant Karma!', John Ono Lennon, reached No. 3.

'Let It Be' reached No. 1.

'The Long And Winding Road' reached No. 1.

'Got To Get You Into My Life' reached No. 9.

'Ob-La-Di, Ob-La-Da' reached No. 75.

'Sgt Pepper's Lonely Hearts Club Band'/'With A Little Help From My Friends' reached No. 103.

'The Beatles Movie Medley' reached No. 39.

Beatles album placings were:

Meet The Beatles reached No. 1.

Introducing The Beatles reached No. 1.

The Beatles Second Album reached No. 1.

The American Tour With Ed Rudy reached No. 32.

A Hard Day's Night reached No. 1.

Something New reached No. 2.

Songs, Pictures and Stories of the Fabulous Beatles reached No. 79.

The Beatles Story reached No. 13.

Beatles '65 reached No. 1.

The Early Beatles reached No. 29.

Beatles VI reached No. 1.

Help! reached No. 1.

Rubber Soul reached No. 1.

Yesterday . . . And Today reached No. 1.

Revolver reached No. 1.

Sgt Pepper's Lonely Hearts Club Band reached No. 1.

Magical Mystery Tour reached No. 1.

Unfinished Music No. 1 – Two Virgins, John Lennon and Yoko Ono, reached No. 56.

The Beatles reached No. 1.

Wonderwall Music, George Harrison, reached No. 33.

Yellow Submarine reached No. 2.

Unfinished Music No. 2 – Life With The Lions, John Lennon and Yoko Ono, reached No. 124.

Abbey Road reached No. 1.

Wedding Album, John Lennon and Yoko Ono, reached No. 108.

Live Peace In Toronto 1969, Plastic Ono Band, reached No. 18.

Hey Jude reached No. 1.

In The Beginning: The Beatles reached No. 139.

Let It Be reached No. 1.

The Beatles 1962–1966 reached No. 4.

The Beatles 1967–1970 reached No. 1.

Rock 'n' Roll Music reached No. 2.

The Beatles At The Hollywood Bowl reached No. 7.

The Beatles Live! At The Star Club In Hamburg, Germany: 1962 reached No. 165.

Love Songs reached No. 36.

Rarities reached No. 26.

Rock 'n' Roll Music – Volume One reached No. 134.

Rock 'n' Roll Music – Volume Two reached No. 137.

Reel Music entered the *Record World* chart at No. 90 on 10 April 1982 which saw the final issue of the publication.

The chart positions of the Beatles singles in *Cash Box* were as follows:

'She Loves You' reached No. 1.

'Roll Over Beethoven' reached No. 30.

'I Want To Hold Your Hand' reached No. 1.

'My Bonnie' reached No. 29.

'Please Please Me' reached No. 3.

'All My Loving' reached No. 31.

'Twist And Shout' reached No. 1.

'Can't Buy Me Love' reached No. 1.

'Do You Want To Know A Secret' reached No. 3.

'Love Me Do' reached No. 1.

Four By The Beatles EP reached No. 86.

'Ain't She Sweet' reached No. 14.

'A Hard Day's Night' reached No. 1.

'I'll Cry Instead' reached No. 22.

'And I Love Her' reached No. 14.

'Matchbox' reached No. 17.

'I Feel Fine' reached No. 1.

Four By The Beatles EP reached No. 68.

'Eight Days A Week' reached No. 1.

'Ticket To Ride' reached No. 1.

'Help!' reached No. 1.

'Yesterday' reached No. 1.

'Boys' reached No. 73.

'We Can Work It Out'/'Day Tripper' reached No. 1.

'Nowhere Man' reached No. 2.

'Paperback Writer' reached No. 1.

'Yellow Submarine'/'Eleanor Rigby' reached No. 1.

'Penny Lane'/'Strawberry Fields Forever' reached No. 1.

'All You Need Is Love' reached No. 1.

'Hello Goodbye' reached No. 1.

'Lady Madonna' reached No. 2.

'Hey Jude' reached No. 1.

'Get Back' reached No. 1.

'The Ballad Of John And Yoko' reached No. 10.

'Give Peace A Chance', Plastic Ono Band reached No. 11.

'Something'/'Come Together' reached No. 1.

'Cold Turkey', Plastic Ono Band, reached No. 32

'Instant Karma', John Ono Lennon, reached No. 3.

'Let It Be' reached No. 1.

'The Long And Winding Road' reached No. 1.

'Got To Get You Into My Life' reached No. 3.

'Ob-La-Di, Ob-La-Da' reached No. 47.

'Sgt Pepper's Lonely Hearts Club Band'/'With Little Help From My Friends' reached No. 92.

'The Beatles Movie Medley' reached No. 14.

'he positions of the Beatles albums in the *Cash Box* charts vere:

Meet The Beatles reached No. 1.
Introducing The Beatles reached No. 2.
The Beatles With Tony Sheridan And Their Guests reached No. 43.
Jolly What! The Beatles And Frank Ifield On Stage reached No. 73.
The Beatles Second Album reached No. 1.
The American Tour With Ed Rudy reached No. 55.
A Hard Day's Night reached No. 1.
Something New reached No. 2.
Songs, Pictures and Stories of the Fabulous Beatles reached No. 100.
The Beatles Story reached No. 7.
Beatles '65 reached No. 1.
The Early Beatles reached No. 24.
Beatles VI reached No. 1.
Help! reached No. 1.
Rubber Soul reached No. 1.
Yesterday . . . And Today reached No. 1.
Revolver reached No. 1.
Sgt Pepper's Lonely Hearts Club Band reached No. 1.
Magical Mystery Tour reached No. 1.
Unfinished Music No. 1 – Two Virgins, John Lennon and Yoko Ono, reached No. 82.
The Beatles reached No. 1.
Wonderwall Music, George Harrison, reached No. 39.
Yellow Submarine reached No. 3.
Unfinished Music No. 2. – Life With The Lions, John Lennon and Yoko Ono, reached No. 118.
Abbey Road reached No. 1.
Live Peace in Toronto 1969, Plastic Ono Band, reached No. 18.
Hey Jude reached No. 2.
In The Beginning: The Beatles reached No. 94.
Let It Be reached No. 1.
The Beatles 1962–1966 reached No. 1.
The Beatles 1967–1970 reached No. 2.
Rock 'n' Roll Music reached No. 4.
The Beatles At The Hollywood Bowl reached No. 3.
Live! At The Star Club, In Hamburg, Germany: 1962 reached No. 183.
Love Songs reached No. 28.
Rarities reached No. 20.
Reel Music reached No. 18.

The Beatles were a musical phenomenon on a global scale and their records also dominated the charts in non-English-speaking countries At one time it was believed that the Beatles would have to record in foreign languages in order to capitalize on the charts in some of the non-English-speaking countries and they actually recorded two of their numbers in German. However, despite the fact that *'Komm Gib Mir Diene Hand'/'Sie Liebt Dich'* topped the charts in West Germany, they never had to repeat the exercise as their records continued to be popular in the English language – the language of rock 'n' roll. Here are the West German singles chart positions as they appeared in the trade publication *Der Musikmarkt*:

'My Bonnie' reached No. 32.
'Twist And Shout' reached No. 10.
'She Loves You' reached No. 7.
'I Want To Hold Your Hand' reached No. 1.
'Misery' reached No. 37.
'Komm Gib Mir Diene Hand'/'Sie Liebt Dich' reached No. 1.
'All My Loving' reached No. 32.
'Please Please Me' reached No. 20.
'Can't Buy Me Love' reached No. 24.
'Do You Want To Know A Secret' reached No. 34.
'Long Tall Sally' reached No. 7.
'Please Mr Postman' reached No. 47.
'A Hard Day's Night' reached No. 2.
'If I Fell' reached No. 25.
'I Should Have Known Better' reached No. 6.
'I Feel Fine' reached No. 3.
'Rock 'n' Roll Music' reached No. 2.
'Eight Days A Week'/'No Reply' reached No. 7.
'Ticket To Ride' reached No. 2.
'Kansas City' reached No. 18.
'Help!' reached No. 2.
'Yesterday' reached No. 6.
'We Can Work It Out' reached No. 2.
'Michelle' reached No. 6.
'Nowhere Man' reached No. 3.

'Paperback Writer' reached No. 1.
'Yellow Submarine' reached No. 1.
'Penny Lane' reached No. 1.
'All You Need Is Love' reached No. 1.
'Hello Goodbye' reached No. 1.
'Lady Madonna' reached No. 2.
'Hey Jude' reached No. 1.
'Ob-La-Di, Ob-La-Da' reached No. 1.
'Get Back' reached No. 1.
'Ballad Of John And Yoko' reached No. 1.
'Something'/'Come Together' reached No. 3.
'Let It Be' reached No. 2.
'Long And Winding Road' reached No. 26.
'Got To Get You Into My Life' reached No. 22.

Chart placings for the Beatles albums were:

Beatles For Sale reached No. 1.
Something New reached No. 38.
Yeah Yeah Yeah (A Hard Day's Night) reached No. 5.
With The Beatles reached No. 34.
Beatles '65 reached No. 9.
Beatles VI reached No. 15.
Help! reached No. 1.
Rubber Soul reached No. 1.
Beatles Greatest reached No. 38.
Yesterday . . . And Today reached No. 13.
Revolver reached No. 1.
Sgt Pepper's Lonely Hearts Club Band reached No. 1.
Magical Mystery Tour reached No. 8.
The Beatles reached No. 1.
Yellow Submarine reached No. 5.
Abbey Road reached No. 1.
Let It Be reached No. 4.
The Beatles 1962–1966 reached No. 2.
The Beatles 1967–1970 reached No. 2.
Rock 'n' Roll Music reached No. 10.
Live! At The Star Club In Hamburg, Germany: 1962 reached No. 21.
The Beatles At The Hollywood Bowl reached No. 10.
20 Golden Hits reached No. 4.

● Chelsea Town Hall, *Kings Road, London SW3*

The venue chosen for the press reception to promote 'Give Peace A Chance', the first single from the **Plastic On Band**. Apart from John and **Yoko**, there were n confirmed members of their new musical concept at th time, so the Plastic Ono Band was to be represented b clear plastic robotic pieces of sculpture with bits o recording equipment attached. The robots were on displa on 3 July 1969, when the reception took place, but Joh and Yoko weren't. They'd been involved in a crash i Scotland on 1 July and had been detained in hospita Ringo Starr and his wife **Maureen** deputized for them.

● *Chester, Johnny*

A rock 'n' roll star from Melbourne who had been booke as support for numerous touring rock shows in Australia o the bill with the Everly Brothers, **Roy Orbison**, Conni Francis and Bobby Rydell. Chester had had nine chart hi and was compering his own TV show 'Teen Time' when h was offered a spot on the Beatles' Australian tour. H accepted a rather derisory fee of £125 a week, but wa upset when told he couldn't use his own backing band th Chessmen, but had to be backed by the **Phantoms**, wh had also been booked for the tour.

Following the Sydney appearances, writer Charle Higham wrote in the *Bulletin* newspaper: 'Excitement wa followed by bathos as Johnny Chester, wearing boots th colour of cherries with pointed toes, a pallid suit and cerise tie, sang "Fever" in the dark with luminous blu cuffs and a face that, because of some trick of lightin now matched both boots and tie.'

Chester continued to find success as an entertainer Australia for many years to come, although he changed h act and developed into a Country singer.

● *Chiffons, The*

An American girl vocal group of the early sixti comprising Patricia Bennett, Barbara Lee, Sylvia Peters and Judy Craig. The girls appeared with the Beatles on th bill of their very first major concert appearance in th States, at the **Washington Coliseum** on 11 Februa 1964, less than a year after the girls' biggest hit, 'He's Fine', a number penned by their manager Ronnie Mack.

In 1971 when George Harrison's first solo single 'M Sweet Lord' entered the charts, Bright Tunes, th American publisher of 'He's So Fine' instituted leg proceedings in March of that year claiming that 'My Swe Lord' was an unauthorized plagiarism of the Chiffons' h 'he court case dragged on until 1976 when it was finally esolved with George paying $587,000 to Bright Tunes – y that time, the publishing company was under the wnership of **Allen Klein**.

Child Of Nature

ne of the many songs John Lennon wrote during his stay t Rishikesh in India. He made a home demo disc of the umber during *The Beatles* white album sessions, but it as never recorded in a studio. Later, he completely wrote the number and retitled it 'Jealous Guy'.

Chipmunks, The

he brainchild of Ross Bagdasarian. Bagdasarian, rofessionally known as David Seville, was experimenting ith recording speeds until he hit on a novelty sound hich reminded him of chipmunks. This led him, in 1958, create the fictitious Chipmunks, who were named Alvin, heodore, Simon and Dave. Seville's productions of hipmunks records went on to sell over 30 million copies efore his death in 1972. The Chipmunks line-up omprised Theodore and Dave on guitars, Simon on drums nd Alvin on harmonica and drums!

One of his most interesting productions was the album *he Chipmunks Sing The Beatle Hits*, which was issued in merica on 24 August 1964 on Liberty LST 7388 and in ritain on 19 February 1965 on Liberty LBY 1218. The acks were: 'All My Loving', 'Do You Want To Know A ecret?', 'She Loves You', 'From Me To You', 'Love Me o', 'Twist And Shout', 'A Hard Day's Night', 'P.S. I Love ou', 'I Saw Her Standing There', 'Can't Buy Me Love', 'lease Please Me' and 'I Want To Hold Your Hand'.

Bagdasarian also created the Bedbugs, a novelty group ised on the Beatles, who appeared in a segment of the merican TV series 'F Troop'. The character Corporal garn decides to leave the army to manage the Bedbugs, ur young musicians from Boston who wear collarless iits and sport long hair. Four of his army buddies don't ant him to leave so they form another group, the ermites, wearing Beatle wigs. The show ends with the formation that the Bedbugs left for Liverpool, England, ecame a big hit and even performed before the Queen.

Chiswick House

country estate in Surrey whose grounds were used ıring the making of the promotional film of 'Paperback Writer'. The group had been filming at **EMI**'s No. 1 studio the previous day and completed their movie among the lawns, statues and lush gardens of the estate.

The Beatles, Director **Michael Lindsay-Hogg** and the crew paused for a luncheon break at three in the afternoon when food was brought over from **Twickenham Studios**, about half an hour's journey away. They all dug in to chops and veg, with red wine and rice pudding to follow – with the exception of Paul, who settled for cold meat and salad.

The film had its premiere on BBC TV's 'Top Of The Pops'.

● Cilla (TV Show)

Before he died, Brian Epstein negotiated with the BBC for **Cilla Black** to have her own peak time television show. This move was to provide her with a new career which continued when the recording side was on the wane.

The weekly 50-minute show made its debut on BBC 1 on 6 February 1968 and the series was to feature many top names, including Tom Jones, **Donovan**, Tony Bennett and Harry Secombe.

Paul McCartney specially wrote a theme song for the series called 'Step Inside Love', which provided Cilla with a Top Ten hit in Britain. Ringo Starr also agreed to be her guest on the first show, making him the first Beatle to appear solo on another artist's show.

Ringo said, 'Without John, Paul and George, I feel vulnerable – like a sultan with three hundred wives who, one day, goes out to buy an ice cream for himself.'

His fellow Beatles sent him a greetings telegram: 'From All Your Big Brothers'.

Ringo and Cilla performed a duet of an old 1920s number 'Do You Like Me Just A Little Bit', which had been suggested by Paul's father, **Jim McCartney**, who used to play the number when he had a jazz band. Ringo also appeared solo singing 'Act Naturally' and joined Cilla in a comedy sketch in which he was a ventriloquist and Cilla was his dummy.

● Cincinnati Gardens, Cincinnati, Ohio

This appearance was almost cancelled when the Musicians Union demanded that local groups should appear. The branch office was deluged with phone calls and surrounded by angry fans, and they withdrew their request – after all, the other acts on the bill were American.

The Beatles arrived at the former boxing ring at 6.00

a.m. and backstage they talked to **Elvis Presley** on the telephone for the first time. They then held a press conference in a private room. They appeared on stage at 9.35 p.m. before an audience of 14,000 people.

● Cinema Cyrano, *Versailles, France*

The venue where the Beatles made their first concert appearance in France on the evening of Wednesday, 15 January 1964. It was ten miles outside Paris and the show was, in effect, a dress rehearsal for their imminent three-week season at the **Olympia Theatre, Paris**, starring the same bill – **Trini Lopez**, **Sylvie Vartan** and the Beatles, with some variety acts.

The 2,000-seater cinema was sold out for the performance, which began at 9.00 p.m.

On their way to the theatre, the Beatles' Austin Princess had broken down and they completed their journey in a borrowed Cadillac, remaining in their dressing-room until it was time to go on stage. They were introduced shortly before midnight, then a juggling act came on stage. When they finally began their performance there was a mild reception. They didn't make any announcements in French as Trini Lopez had done earlier. A boy dressed up as French rock 'n' roll idol Johnny Hallyday came onto the stage and had to be carted off by **Mal Evans**. Eventually, when John broke into 'Twist And Shout', and Paul began to sing a **Little Richard** number, the audience came alive.

Among the celebrities in the audience were Francoise Hardy, Johnny Hallyday, Richard Anthony and Petula Clark.

When they returned to their hotel they received a call from New York informing them that 'I Want To Hold Your Hand' was No. 1 in the American charts.

● Circus-Krone-Bau, *Marsstrasse, Munich, Germany*

The Beatles flew to Munich from London Airport at 11.05 a.m. on Thursday, 23 June, 1966, on BEA flight BE 502, a Comet aircraft, and on landing ninety minutes later were picked up in a white Mercedes and driven to the **Bayerischer Hof Hotel**. While there they were presented with a trophy by *Bravo* magazine, which had sponsored the three-venue West German tour, which had been called the Bravo Blitztournee.

The following day, 24 June, they presented two shows at the Circus-Krone-Dau, which was basically a winte circus and during summer months was available for rock shows.

The first concert took place at 5.15 p.m. and the secon at 9.00 p.m. The show was opened by Cliff Bennett & th Rebel Rousers, followed by German band the Rattles an then **Peter & Gordon**. When the Beatles took the stag they wore bottle green suits with green collars an performed 'Rock 'n' Roll Music', 'She's A Woman', 'If Needed Someone', 'Day Tripper', 'Baby's In Black', 'I Fee Fine', 'Yesterday', 'I Wanna Be Your Man', 'Nowher Man', 'Paperback Writer' and 'I'm Down'.

Their second concert that evening was filmed by th German TV station ZDF.

● Cirkus, *Gothenberg, Sweden*

Third stop on the Beatles' brief tour of Sweden. Th group's appearance at the Cirkus on 27 October 196 proved to be one of the busiest of their tour dates as the gave no less than three performances at the venue that da – at 3.00 p.m., 5.00 p.m. and 8.00 p.m.

● City Barge, The, *No. 27 Strand-On-The Green, London W4*

Pleasant riverside pub which featured in a scene in *Help!*

The scene was filmed on 24 April 1965 and stuntme deputized for the Beatles as the script required them to b hurled through the pub windows!

● City Hall, *Northumberland Road, Newcastle-upon-Tyne, Tyne and Wear*

The Beatles made their debut at this venue on 23 Marc 1963. Their next appearance took place on 8 June 1963 a part of their tour with **Roy Orbison**. They headlined the own show when they next appeared at the hall on 2 November 1963 and their final appearance took place on December 1965.

● City Hall, *Fisherton Street, Salisbury, Wiltshire*

One of the promotions arranged by **John Fallon** for h Jaybee Clubs. The booking had been settled in April 196 for a fee of £300. Brian Epstein offered the promoter £20 if he would cancel the gig, but was refused and the grou appeared at the venue on 15 June. The hall was packed capacity and the local newspaper was to report, 'It was th first appearance in Salisbury of a group who shot to fame last year and have been called the most exciting group since the **Shadows** – the Beatles.

'Queuing for tickets began as early as 3.00 p.m. In all there were about 1,500 teenagers – the largest number ever to attend a personal appearance locally.'

● City Hall, *Barker's Pool, Sheffield, South Yorkshire*

The penultimate appearance of the **Helen Shapiro** tour took place at this venue on 2 March 1963. The Beatles soon returned to the hall as part of the **Roy Orbison** tour on 25 May 1963. They were bill-toppers in their own right when they appeared at the City Hall for the third time on 2 November 1963 and they made their final appearance at the venue on 9 November 1964.

● City Park Stadium, *New Orleans, Louisiana*

The Beatles appeared at this venue before an audience of 12,000 fans on Wednesday, 16 September 1964.

During their cavalcade from the airport, hundreds of fans lined the route and the group were taken to the Congress Inn, where they settled in Room 100, a three-room suite. Mayor Schiro had officially declared 16 September as 'Beatles Day' and he presented each of them with a key to the city and also a certificate of honorary citizenship. A local Councilman, Daniel Kelly, arrived at their rooms to present them with the proclamation regarding 'Beatles Day', but never got around to making the presentation.

For the first and only time on the tour, Brian Epstein allowed a newsreel cameraman to film the group's press interview. Among the questions and answers were:

Q: 'What do you think of topless bathing suits?'
George: 'We like them, we've been wearing them for years.'
Q: 'What do you expect to see when you visit Dallas?'
Paul: 'Oil wells.'
Q: 'You've experienced both – what's the difference between poverty and riches?'
John: 'Money.'
Q: 'Dave Brubeck told the *Dallas News* that America is reaping the harvest from the musical garbage it exported to England years ago. Comment?'
John: 'Quite true.'
Q: 'What is your chief gripe against the United States?'
Paul: 'The quality of your tea.'
Q: 'Will the draft break up your group?'
John: 'There is no draft in England anymore. We'll let you Yanks do the fighting.'
Q: 'Don't you think it's morally wrong to be influencing your fans with your atheist views?'
Paul: 'We're not atheists, we're agnostics. The story which said we're anti-Christ is not true. We simply don't know enough about it.'

After the press conference, much to their delight, the Beatles bumped into Fats Domino and had a long chat with him.

They began playing on stage at the stadium at 9.25 p.m. and within fifteen minutes several hundred fans rushed onto the field. Police and mounted policemen charged the fans, some wielding nightsticks, although no sticks actually hit any of the teenagers. Ringo said of it later, 'It was like watching the police play stickball with the kids.'

● Civic Arena, *Pittsburgh, Pennsylvania*

The Beatles appeared before an audience of 12,603 at the venue on Monday, 14 September 1964. There were 4,000 fans waiting for them at Greater Pittsburgh Airport and when they flew in their escort was far bigger than that given for a presidential visit. There were 120 policemen and deputies, twenty members of the Allied Detective Agency and fifteen members of the Allegheny County Mounted Police. There was a motorcade to the Civic Arena along streets lined with thousands of fans.

The group fielded questions at a press reception at 6.00 p.m. in the venue's conference room, dined and then performed.

They were due to be whisked away in a police car, but it was blocked by fans and they ran through an underground passage to a waiting limousine which sped them back to the airport.

● Civic Hall, *Whitby Road, Ellesmere Port, Wirral, Cheshire*

Although part of Merseyside and situated only nineteen miles from Liverpool's city centre, this industrial town was to be graced with only one Beatles appearance. This took place at the Civic Hall on 14 January 1963. The group appeared before an audience of 700 people. The dance was organized by the Wolverham Welfare Association.

● Clapton, Eric

One of the world's foremost rock guitarists, Eric was born in Ripley, Surrey, on 30 March 1945 and was raised by foster parents.

He took to the guitar at the age of seventeen and his first band was called the Roosters. In October 1963 he joined Casey Jones & the Engineers, but his stint with the band only lasted for seven gigs. The line-up comprised Casey Jones (**Brian Casser**), vocals; Eric Clapton, guitar; Tom McGuinness, guitar; Dave McCumisky, bass; and Ray Stock, drums. Casser had formerly been the leader of a popular Mersey Beat group Cass & the Cassanovas. Eric then joined the **Yardbirds** and they supported **Billy J. Kramer** on a 1964 tour before appearing on *The Beatles Christmas Show* at the **Odeon, Hammersmith**. It was during the Christmas show that Eric and George Harrison got to know each other and their long and enduring friendship began.

When Eric became a member of Cream, the group was booked to appear at Brian Epstein's **Saville Theatre** and was also, along with the Beatles, one of the stable of groups with **NEMS Enterprises** when Epstein brought **Robert Stigwood** and his discoveries into the company.

Eric's friendship with George Harrison had blossomed and he began to work with him quite closely. 'Badge' was a number he co-wrote with George for a Cream recording – and George played rhythm on the session and was credited as L'Angelo Misterioso. Eric joined George on the recording of **Jackie Lomax**'s 'Sour Milk Sea' and also played on the soundtrack for Harrison's *Wonderwall* album. George also brought him in to perform on the Beatles number 'While My Guitar Gently Weeps'. This created a precedent – bringing in another rock musician into a Beatles session. The event occurred on Friday, 6 September 1968. Eric was giving George a lift into town from Surrey, where they both lived, and on the spur of the moment suggested he join him in the studio to play a solo overdub on the track 'While My Guitar Gently Weeps'. Eric protested – it was unheard of for anyone else to play on a Beatles track, but George told him, 'It's my song!'

Following the break-up of Cream, Eric became part of another supergroup, Blind Faith – but the band only had a short career. His first public appearance after Blind Faith

Eric Clapton – the guitar virtuoso. (RSO Records)

was as a member of the **Plastic Ono Band** at the Toronto Rock 'n' Roll Revival Show in which he played with Lennon, **Klaus Voormann**, **Alan White** and **Yoko Ono**. Also on the bill were Bo Diddley, **Jerry Lee Lewis**, **Chuck Berry** and **Little Richard**. The group performed rock 'n' roll for half an hour and then Yoko joined them. Clapton said, 'A few people started to boo, but it turned into howling along with Yoko. Yoko has the same effect on people as a high-pitched whistle has on a dog. Her voice is spine-chilling. Very weird. John and I played some feed-back guitar while she was singing.'

Eric also played on 'Cold Turkey' and appeared at the Unicef Concert at the Lyceum, along with George, John and Yoko on 15 December 1969.

He joined George Harrison for recording sessions at **Olympic Studios**, along with Rich Grech, Denny Laine and Trevor Burton, but they proved abortive.

Eric became obsessed with George Harrison's wife **Pattie** and wrote a love song for her on his double album *Layla And Other Assorted Love Songs*. He said at the time, 'It was actually about an emotional experience, a woman that I felt deeply about and who turned me down, and I had to kind of pour it out in some way. It was the heaviest thing going at the time. I didn't consciously do it, though, it just happened that way. That was what I wanted to write about most of all.' Describing how the affair began, Eric Clapton said that George had, 'Once grabbed one of my chicks and so I thought I'd get even with him one day, on a petty level, and it grew from that, you know. She was trying to attract his attention, trying to make him jealous, so she used me, you see, and I fell madly in love with her.'

His emotional problems led to him becoming a heroin addict and when he travelled to New York to appear on the *Concert For Bangla Desh*, which was taking place in August 1971, he was too sick to attend rehearsals at **Nola Studios** and Jesse Ed Davis was brought in to play second lead to George. On the night before the concert, Eric didn't attend the last run through – but he did manage to turn up for the actual concert.

When Eric performed some solos on George's numbers, his record company didn't like it, so Ringo suggested he use the pseudonym 'Eddie Clayton', which was no doubt due to the fact that Ringo was once a member of the **Eddie Clayton Skiffle Group**. Eric was to appear on a number of George's albums, including *All Things Must Pass* and *The Concert For Bangla Desh*.

The two appeared on a European tour with Delaney and Bonnie and over the years teamed up on a number of occasions, including a concert at Guildford Civic Hall on 7 December 1978 and a *Prince's Trust Rock Gala* on 5 and 6 June 1987, along with Ringo. George also joined Eric on a twelve-show tour of Japan in December 1990.

Strangely enough, their friendship, although strained, didn't bust up when Eric wooed George's wife Pattie and eventually married her.

● Clarabella

A number popularized by American group the Jodimars in 1956, although it wasn't a hit. The Beatles introduced it into their repertoire and performed it during 1960, 1961 and 1962 with Paul McCartney on lead vocals.

● Clarendon Road, London W11

A street in the Notting Hill district of London where the Beatles filmed the police chase sequence from *A Hard Day's Night*. A building in the street had been disguised as a police station and the exterior scenes were filmed there. It is a popular street name and there are no less than twelve Clarendon Roads in London.

● Clark, Jimmy

The **Apple Corps**' doorman, hired to prevent unauthorized entry to the **Savile Row** headquarters of the Beatles' organization. A Cockney, Jimmy was hired by **Peter Brown** and wore a smart grey morning coat.

He also acted as Apple bouncer and whenever anyone needed an interloper removed from the offices, they contacted Jimmy.

● Cleveland Stadium, Cleveland, Ohio

The Beatles appeared at this massive baseball stadium, home of the Cleveland Indians, on Sunday, 14 August 1966. The stadium had a capacity of 50,000, but as parts of the rear-of-stage areas had a poor view, the tickets were limited to 30,000. Due to the size of the stadium there was only one show that evening, but crowds of fans poured onto the actual field and the appearances by support acts the **Cyrkle** and the **Ronettes** were delayed for half an hour while police tried to control the crowd. When the Beatles did appear the show was held up as 2,500 fans invaded the field while the group were playing 'Day Tripper'.

● Cliff Bennett & The Rebel Rousers

Originally formed in 1961, by Cliff Bennett from Slough, who got the group together primarily for German bookings. It was while they were in Germany that they made many friends among the Liverpool bands while appearing at the **Star Club**.

The group comprised Cliff Bennett (vocals), Dave Wendells (lead guitar), Maurice Groves (sax), Sid Phillips (sax), Roy Young (keyboards), Frank Allen (bass guitar) and Mike Burt (drums). When Frank Allen left the band in 1964 to join the **Searchers**, he was replaced by Bobby Thompson from **Kingsize Taylor** & the Dominoes. In one of his later bands, Cliff employed **Howie Casey**, Liverpool's famous sax player.

They were respected but remained unsuccessful until 1964 when they had a hit with 'One Way Love'. The Beatles had recommended the band to Brian Epstein who then signed them to **NEMS Enterprises** and Paul McCartney produced the group performing the *Revolver* album number 'Got To Get You Into My Life'. Issued on Parlophone 5489 on 5 August 1966 in Britain and on ABC 10842 in America on 29 August 1966. The record reached No. 6 in the British charts.

Cliff Bennett & The Rebel Rousers also joined the bill of the Beatles' tour of Germany and Japan in June 1966.

Paul next produced their *Got To Get You Into My Life* album, issued by Parlophone on PCS 7017 on 27 January 1967 in Britain. The group were never to achieve recording success again and disbanded in 1969.

Cliff went on to form a few more bands, including Toe Fat and Shanghai, before retiring from the music world for good.

● Clivedon, *Buckinghamshire*

The country house of Lord Astor, which doubled as Buckingham Palace during the filming of *Help!* in 1965. The scene in which the Beatles play cards was filmed in the luxurious Madame Pompadour room and Lord Astor himself treated the four to a cup of tea – poured from a grecian urn!

● C'mon Everybody

The last of three **Eddie Cochran** hits in the American charts. 'C'mon Everybody' reached No. 35 in the US in 1959, although it reached No. 6 in Britain the same year.

The **Quarry Men** introduced the song into their repertoire that year and continued to perform the numbe when they became the Beatles.

● Cochran, Eddie

Legendary American rock 'n' roll singer born in Oklahom in 1938. Cochran appeared in a few movies, including *Th Girl Can't Help It* and *Untamed Youth*, and had three char hits in America with 'Sittin' In The Balcony', 'Summertim Blues' and 'C'mon Everybody', although he wrote an recorded several other numbers which became roc classics.

Eddie Cochran – the legendary rock 'n' roller. (Rockstar Records)

Cochran was due to appear on a major show a Liverpool Stadium on 3 May 1960 with **Gene Vincen** but was killed in a road accident on 17 April 1960 i Wiltshire, England. In June, his 'Three Steps To Heave topped the British charts and became his biggest Britis hit, although it failed to make the charts in America.

The singer was one of the Beatles' early influences an they included four of his songs in their repertoire, 'Thre Steps To Heaven', 'Twenty Flight Rock', 'I Remembe and 'C'mon Everybody'.

Cocker, Joe

A Sheffield singer, born 20 May 1944. As lead singer with Vance Arnold & the Avengers he recorded the Lennon & McCartney number 'I'll Cry Instead' in 1963. His biggest hit was the ***Sgt Pepper*** number 'With A Little Help From My Friends', which was issued in Britain on Regal Zonophone RX 3013 on 19 October 1968 and reached the No. 1 spot in the UK charts. Cocker also recorded an album entitled *With A Little Help From My Friends*.

Alma Cogan – Britain's top female singer of the fifties, who became a personal friend of the Beatles. (EMI)

Cogan, Alma

Britain's top female singer of the fifties who had twenty records in the charts. She became such a close friend of Brian Epstein that there were even rumours that they would marry. Alma attended many parties with the Beatles and became a good friend of theirs. Immediately prior to their June 1964 tour they attended Alma's birthday party at her home at 4 Stafford Court, Kensington, where she lived with her mother, Faye. Other guests included Brian Epstein, **Noel Coward**, **Sir Joseph Lockwood**, George Martin, **Chuck Berry** and **Carl Perkins**.

Her last few records were covers of Lennon & McCartney songs. On 11 November 1965 her version of 'Yesterday' (Columbia DB 7757) was released and later in the month, on 28 November, her double 'A' side 'Eight Days A Week'/'Help!' (Columbia DB 7786) was issued. John and Paul attended her recording session for 'Eight Days A Week' on 9 October 1965.

Tragically, she died of cancer at the age of 34 on 26 October 1966.

Twenty years later when **EMI** released the double album *Alma Cogan: A Celebration*, there was a gatefold sleeve picturing Alma with the Beatles and a brief sleeve note penned by Paul McCartney.

Coleman, Bess

A former journalist from Leicester who joined **EMI Records** in London as a Press Officer, where she worked at the time of the early Beatles releases on the Parlophone label. She then moved to New York and when the Beatles achieved fame in the United States, was employed as their American press lady. Later in the sixties she returned to London and joined **Tony Barrow** in his new public relations company, Tony Barrow International.

Coleman, Ray

When Brian Epstein merged *Music Echo* with *Disc*, Ray Coleman became editor of *Disc & Music Echo*. Apart from his meetings with Epstein, he began to interview the Beatles regularly and continued to do so when he became editor-in-chief of *Melody Maker*. When John Lennon became disenchanted with the fortunes of Apple, he told Ray all about it for an interview which appeared in *Disc & Music Echo* on 18 January 1969. This was the interview in which John told him that Apple was losing money every week. John said, 'If it carries on like this, all of us will be broke in the next six months.' As a result of the article **Allen Klein** made his move to take over control of the Beatles. Paul McCartney was upset about the piece and when Ray dropped into the Apple office, told him, 'This is only a small company and you're trying to wreck it. You know John shoots his mouth off and doesn't mean it.'

Ray left the *Melody Maker* and became a full-time biographer. In 1984 he wrote the two-volume work *John Winston Lennon* and *John Ono Lennon*, with the co-operation of **Cynthia Lennon** and **Yoko Ono**. The following year *Survivor*, his authorized biography of **Eric Clapton**, was published. He also penned the first major autobiography of the Beatles' manager, *Brian Epstein: The Man Who Made the Beatles*, in 1969, with the co-operation of Epstein's family.

Ray Coleman during an interview with Billy J. Kramer.

● Coleman, Sid

Coleman was manager of **EMI**'s own publishing company Ardmore & Beechwood, when he played his part in the Beatles story in 1962.

In April of that year, Brian Epstein was in London seeking a recording contract for the group. He'd been turned down by a number of labels, but was now armed with the tapes of their Decca audition. He was passing EMI's HMV Shop in Oxford Street when he noticed a sign in the window offering the service of transferring tapes to disc. Epstein went into the store and made his way to the room where acetates were made. In his autobiography he mentions meeting Kenneth Boast, 'an exceedingly pleasant and interesting executive with the HMV Retail Store within the mighty EMI company'.

The man transferring the tapes to disc was engineer **Ted Huntley** who, noticing that a number of the songs were originals, commented: 'I don't think these are at all bad.' He told Boast, and Brian was asked if he'd be interested in meeting Coleman, who had an office on the top floor of the building. Brian, keen on any beneficial contacts, agreed and Boast phoned Coleman who asked Brian to come straight up.

He listened to the tapes and asked Brian if they had a recording contract. Together with his assistant **Kim Bennett** he believed that the group had something and offered to publish two of the songs, 'Love Of The Loved' and 'Hello Little Girl'. Brian demurred, saying he'd prefer to have a recording contract before agreeing to any publishing deal. Coleman considered the EMI A&R men – Norrie Paramor, Wally Ridley and Norman Newall – however, all had groups on their books, so he called George Martin's office. George's secretary Judy Lockhart Smith answered and a meeting was arranged for the following day.

There are some conflicting reports regarding the actual details of the initial contact. Bennett is reported to have said that Martin took some persuading, that he wasn't keen initially on the meeting with Epstein. Martin, on the other hand, in his autobiography says his response, on receiving the call from Coleman, was: 'Certainly, I'm willing to listen to anything. Ask him to come and see me.'

Martin did take the Beatles and they transformed the fortunes of EMI. Unfortunately, Ardmore & Beechwood did such a poor job promoting 'Love Me Do' that Brian decided not to sign with the company.

In his autobiography *All You Need Is Ears* Martin points out that on the release of 'Love Me Do': 'Ardmore & Beechwood, the EMI publishers, whose Sid Coleman had first put Brian Epstein on to me, did virtually nothing about getting the record played.' Yet Ted King, an ex-**Radio Luxembourg** DJ working for BBC radio at the time on 'Twelve O'Clock Spin', was one of the first people to play 'Love Me Do' because he said he was pressured to do so by Kim Bennett of Ardmore & Beechwood.

● Coliseum, Seattle, Washington

The Beatles concert on 21 August 1964 drew 14,045 fans and there were 50 police, 4 deputies, a fire chief and 1[illegible] firemen plus 100 navy volunteers to control them.

There was a backstage press conference and as the Beatles were walking back to their dressing room a girl fell 25 feet down an air vent onto the concrete floor in front of Ringo. When she came to he asked, 'Are you sure you're all right, luv?' and she ran away into the crowd. Among the visitors to their dressing room was Charmaine Smith, the current Miss Teenage America, who later commented, 'They're really nice. As soon as the kids find something new, the Beatles will be on the way out.'

The group went on stage at 9.30 p.m. and finished at 10.00 p.m., but it took them over an hour to leave the stadium. Their Cadillac, sent ahead on a dummy run, was swamped by fans who squashed the trunk, caved in the roof and ripped off the door handles. The group finally made their escape in a darkened ambulance.

The venue was also the site of one of the final appearances they made in America at the end of their last tour, on 25 August 1966. There were two performances with only 8,000 tickets sold for the matinee show, although the evening concert was sold out.

● A Collection Of Beatles Oldies (But Goldies)

EMI wanted to have a new Beatles album available for the Christmas market at the end of 1966, although *Revolver* had only been issued in August and was still gathering sales. The group's new album project *Sgt Pepper's Lonely Hearts Club Band* wouldn't be ready for some months, so the record company assembled this collection of tracks, compiling various previously released album and singles tracks. One of the tracks, 'Bad Boy', hadn't been available in Britain before, although it had been included on the American album release *Beatles VI*.

It was issued in Britain on Parlophone PCS 7016 on 9 December 1966 and reached No. 6 in the charts, becoming the first Beatles album not to hit the top spot.

The tracks were, Side One: 'She Loves You', 'From Me To You', 'We Can Work It Out', 'Help!', 'Michelle', 'Yesterday', 'I Feel Fine', 'Yellow Submarine'. Side Two: 'Can't Buy Me Love', 'Bad Boy', 'Day Tripper', 'A Hard Day's Night', 'Ticket To Ride', 'Paperback Writer', 'Eleanor Rigby', 'I Want To Hold Your Hand'.

The front cover was a painting designed by David Christian and the back cover featured a photograph of the Beatles by **Bob Whitaker**.

● Collingham, Anne

Fictitious head of the Beatles Fan Club in Britain. When **Tony Barrow** was involved in the organization of the Beatles Fan Club from offices in Monmouth Street in London he created the name Anne Collingham. The name was even used aside a regular column of fan club news in *Beatles Monthly* and a photograph of 'Anne Collingham' appeared in the publication. This was a picture of one of the several girls who worked full-time on the fan club from the Monmouth Street offices.

● Collins, Bill

The original manager of the Iveys, who were to become the popular Apple band, **Badfinger**.

Bill was a shipbuilder who became a pianist with a Liverpool jazz band in the thirties. After the war he worked in a garage. His son Lew worked with Paul McCartney's brother **Mike**, and Bill knew **Mal Evans**. In April 1966 Bill heard a semi-pro group called the Iveys playing at the Ammonford Ballroom in Swansea, South Wales. He introduced himself to them, kept in touch, then, in July 1966, arranged for them to become backing band to David Garrick, a Liverpool singer who'd had some minor hits. They turned professional and moved down to London with Collins who secured them a booking at the Marquee where Mal Evans brought **Peter Asher** to see them. Mal was a strong champion of the band and played their tapes to the Beatles, who then decided that the group should be signed to Apple.

Incidentally, Bill's son Lew was originally a member of a Liverpool band, the Eyes, before becoming an actor in television and movies. His most popular series was 'The Professionals' and he starred in films such as *Who Dares Wins*.

● Colston Hall, Bristol, Avon

The Beatles made their debut at this venue on 15 March, 1963 as part of the **Tommy Roe/Chris Montez** tour. Their second appearance took place during their autumn tour on 15 November 1963.

10 November 1964 saw the last gig of the Beatles' UK tour at the venue and the manager of the hall, Ken Cowley, was furious when an incident occurred as they finished 'If I Fell' and were about to begin their finale. Four local students had managed to gain access to the stage lighting gantries and they tipped bags of flour onto the Beatles' heads. However, the lads took it in good spirit, shook the flour from their guitars and carried on.

● Come And Get It

A number which Paul McCartney composed for the Ringo Starr film ***The Magic Christian***. Before the Beatles gathered for a recording session on Thursday 24 July 1969, Paul went into **Abbey Road**'s Number Two studio and cut a demo disc of the number.

It had been decided that Apple band **Badfinger** would sing the song over the titles of the movie and Paul produced their version of the song at Abbey Road on 2 April 1969.

The single was issued in Britain on 5 December 1969 on Apple 20 and reached No. 4 in the British charts. It was issued in America on Apple 1815 on 12 January 1970.

● Come Go With Me

A No. 4 hit in the American charts for the Dell Vikings, a quintet who formed while in the Air Force in Pittsburgh. The record reached the charts early in 1957 and it was included in the **Quarry Men** repertoire with John Lennon on lead vocals. It was one of the numbers the skiffle group performed when Paul McCartney heard them for the first time at **St Peter's Parish Church**, **Woolton**.

● Come Together

The song had its origins when **Timothy Leary** was planning a life in politics, intending to stand for the Governorship of California, and his wife asked John Lennon if he could write a campaign song. John began writing the number, but Leary's visions of a political career crumbled when he was imprisoned for his advocacy of drugs.

When John was initially composing the tune he said he was writing obscurely round an old **Chuck Berry** tune called 'You Can't Catch Me'. He added, 'I left the line in, "Here come old flat-top". It is nothing like the Chuck Berry song, but they took me to court because I admitted the influence once years ago.'

A settlement was made in which John agreed to include two Chuck Berry songs on an album, which resulted in 'You Can't Catch Me' and 'Sweet Little Sixteen' being featured on his 1975 album, *Rock 'n' Roll*.

The court action wasn't the only problem associated with the song. John had mentioned the words 'Coca Cola' and the BBC banned the number because it broke their code regarding advertising on TV.

'Come Together' was the last song recorded for the *Abbey Road* album and was the first track on the LP. The number was also used as the flipside of the single 'Something' and also included on the compilation album *The Beatles 1967–1970*.

It was one of the numbers John performed at the *One To One* concert in August 1972.

Aerosmith performed the song in the film *Sgt Pepper's Lonely Hearts Club Band* in 1978 and their single of the song reached No. 20 in the American charts that year.

● Comic Books

Over the years the Beatles have been the subject of several comic strips.

They appeared in the American Dell Comics' *Strange Tales*, No. 130, in March 1964. This issue featured a story entitled 'Human Torch and the Thing Meet the Beatles'. Dell also published a special Beatles comic in the autumn of 1964, named *The Beatles*. The comic was one of their 'Dell Giant' series and was a strip outlining the group's history to that date. There were also pin-up stories and some text on the individual members.

In September 1964 DC Comics featured a story, 'Red-headed Beatle of 1000 BC', in Issue 79 of their *Jimmy Olsen* comic. The group were also included in *Batman* No. 222 and were featured on the covers of a number of comics aimed at girls, including *Girls Romance* No. 109, *Heart Throbs* No. 101, *My Little Margie* No. 54 and *Summer Love* Nos. 46, 47 and 48. Issue 121 of *Mad*, published in September 1968, sported a cover with Alfred E. Neuman as the **Maharishi Mahesh Yogi** with caricatures of the Beatles.

In 1968 Gold Key Comics, published by the Western Publishing Company in the US, issued *Yellow Submarine*, which was the story of the film related in comic form.

The most interesting seventies comic book venture was the Marvel 'Super Special' edition of *The Beatles Story*, with visuals by George Perez and Klaus Jenson. Oddly, the illustrations seemed to evoke the atmosphere of the forties rather than the seventies – Brian Epstein is seen stalking off into a rainy night, dressed in trilby and raincoat, like some denizen of a film noir tale. Liverpool's tiny **Casbah Club** is depicted as a spacious nightclub, peopled by sophisticated couples sitting at tiny round tables. The Beatles themselves are shown using expensive equipment, whereas in those days they didn't even have mike stands.

The group are depicted as a bunch of Cockneys in the comic, continually calling each other 'Mate', and using words such as 'ruddy' and 'blooming'. At one point Paul says, 'This is ruddy insane, we're getting gongs!'; at another George says, 'Stress doesn't bother me like it did before, mates'; and Ringo comments, 'It'll tie in ruddy well with the TV taping, too.'

Published in 1978, *The Beatles Story* contains 39 pages of comic strip in colour, supplemented by several articles and photographs, including a pin-up poster, discography, filmography and group history.

The following year the Pendulum 'Illustrated Biography' series issued *Elvis Presley/The Beatles*, a comic book tracing the careers of both acts.

The most significant strip devoted to the Beatles appeared as a serial in the British teen paper *Look In* in 1981, under the name 'The Beatles Story'. The complete strip was published in April 1982 as a *TV Times/Look In Special*. The strip was padded out with thirteen photographs, three of which were in colour.

The strip's artist was Arthur Ranson and the text was written by Angus P. Allan. Ranson produced some exquisite black-and-white drawings, based on well-known Beatles photographs.

Unfortunately, the words that Allan put into the Beatles' mouths were not as accurately conceived as the illustrations, although their absurdity is, at times, extremely amusing.

Despite the passage of years which has elapsed since the Beatles disbanded, new books and magazines are published regularly – and the same applies to comic books. An eight-issue series called *The Beatles Experience* is a bi-monthly comic launched in March 1991 by Revolutionary Comics of San Diego, California. The text is by Todd Loven and the illustrations by Mike Sagara.

In November 1991, Personality Comics of New York issued a series of four comics entitled *Personality Comics Presents The Beatles*, each one devoted to an individual member of the group.

● Complete Beatles, The

The first major video documentary on the Beatles, which was later widely screened on television.

Originally made as promotional back-up to a book of the same name, it far exceeded expectations and became one of the biggest selling musical video cassettes on both sides of the Atlantic.

'The Complete Beatles' was produced by Stephanie Bennett and Patricia Montgomery (who also directed) for Delilah Films Inc. The group's history is related in chronological order and illustrated with hundreds of black-and-white photographs and movie and TV clips in colour and monochrome. The commentary, written by David Silver and spoken by Malcolm McDowell, is enlivened by interviews with several people associated with the Beatles.

The story opens with bleak images of the Liverpool docks shortly after World War II, with the dockers setting off to work in cloth caps and mufflers. McDowell begins his narration:

'Liverpool, two hundred miles to the north-west of London. Nothing ever comes from Liverpool but soccer teams and British comedians . . .' He sets the scene. Then, to the sound of rock 'n' roll, numerous fleeting pictures appear on the screen as the titles begin to roll; the Beatles introducing themselves to the American press; performing at **Shea Stadium** and on stage at the **Cavern**. McDowell then relates a brief history of rock 'n' roll with glimpses of Bill Haley, American teenagers, James Dean, **Little Richard**, Fats Domino, the Everly Brothers, **Eddie Cochran** and **Elvis Presley**. He then relates the rise of skiffle in Britain and **Lonnie Donegan** performs 'Jack of Diamonds'. This is followed by the background to John Lennon's early days in Liverpool. **Gerry Marsden** appears in a contemporary interview discussing the change from skiffle to rock in Liverpool, providing an example by playing the number 'Jambalaya'. We next have Paul McCartney's early life projected in words and photographs, culminating in his meeting with John.

We witness the arrival of Bill Haley in Britain, including newsreels of the riotous scenes at his concerts, then hear about the setbacks rock 'n' roll began to have in America; Elvis leaves the US for army duty in Germany; **Chuck Berry** is sent to prison for two years on an assault charge, and three legendary rock stars – **Buddy Holly**, Big Bopper and Ritchie Valens – are killed in a plane crash. Another nail is knocked into rock's coffin by the scandal surrounding **Jerry Lee Lewis**'s 'child bride'. American teenagers begin to turn to clean-cut idols such as Fabian, Dion and Rickie Nelson. Rock 'n' roll has been tamed.

Gerry Marsden remarks that by 1959 the British scene has followed a similar pattern, its biggest idol being the clean-cut Cliff Richard. Gerry begins to talk about rhythm and blues being played in Liverpool, then **Allan Williams** appears and makes an erroneous statement to the effect that groups all got their R&B records from seamen. This piece of romantic fiction crept into the Beatles history because it was mentioned in ***Mersey Beat*** that several members of local Country and Western groups got their records from relatives who were merchant seamen. The rock 'n' roll groups didn't have great difficulty purchasing rock 'n' roll records.

Following an early history of George Harrison and **Stuart Sutcliffe**, Bill Harry discusses the Beatles gigs at **Liverpool College of Art**. Allan Williams relates how the group went to Germany and **Howie Casey** of the Seniors wrote to him pleading with him not to send the Beatles to Hamburg because they were such a bad band and would ruin things for the rest of them. He describes Hamburg as the 'Las Vegas of Europe'. **Tony Sheridan**, glimpsed performing on a British TV show in 1959, then relates how the Beatles had to perform seven nights a week. **Horst Fascher** describes the awful condition of their German flat and how he became their bodyguard. Tony Sheridan and Gerry Marsden talk about their experiences in the city and how groups who appeared there returned to Liverpool vastly improved.

The *Mersey Beat* newspaper is launched and **Billy J. Kramer** talks about the first **Litherland Town Hall** gig. Allan Williams mentions it too, and we are treated to several advertisements from *Mersey Beat* showing how the Beatles were becoming major headliners all over Liverpool. Former postal clerk **Bob Wooler** becomes the disc jockey at the **Cavern** and reminisces while we see scenes from those early days. Bob mentions that he first recommended the number 'Hippy Hippy Shake' to the Beatles.

As John and Paul develop as songwriters, the group return to Hamburg in 1960. Tony Sheridan discusses the recording of 'My Bonnie', and Sutcliffe remains in Germany while Paul becomes the group's bass guitarist.

Bill Harry describes how London controls the British entertainment industry and Gerry Marsden mentions that groups never considered they could make a living from their music as professionals. Following a brief biography of Brian Epstein and archive film of him relating details of his first trip to the Cavern, Harry mentions how Brian smoothed out the group's image. George Martin tells of his first meeting with Brian. A brief history of George Harrison is followed by the story of how **Pete Best** came to be replaced by Ringo Starr. George Martin and Bill Harry both mention Best and there is a brief history of Ringo's days in Dingle and his spell with **Rory Storm & the Hurricanes.**

George Martin tells of the Beatles' first record and we hear how Brian Epstein bought 10,000 copies for his Liverpool shop to help boost it into the national charts. Martin comments that he wanted the Beatles to record 'How Do You Do It'. There is a clip of the Beatles' Royal Command Performance and various press interviews with examples of the Beatles' wit.

George comments that he thinks the group will last for four years and Ringo mentions his ambition to own a hairdressing salon. Prime Minister **Harold Wilson** presents them with Variety Club awards and impressive sales figures of their records are given. There are images of crowd scenes and details of how, now that they have conquered England, they are set to go to America. George Martin tells how their records were sent over to **Capitol Records** but were rejected on several occasions until 'I Want To Hold Your Hand'. The Beatles land in the US and hold a press conference. We see scenes of their American fans and **Ed Sullivan** introduces them on his show. After rare, brief scenes of their American concerts comes the news that they have secured the top five places in the American charts.

The railway station scene from *A Hard Day's Night* is shown, followed by the press reception scene from the same film. Scenes from their world tour (with Jimmy Nicol briefly substituting for Ringo), their US tour, and interviews with American fans follow. Then George Martin discusses the *Beatles For Sale* album, and John and Paul's songwriting activities and musical abilities.

Next come scenes from *Help!* and George Martin describes how 'Yesterday' was recorded. There are scenes at Buckingham Palace when the group receive their **MBEs**, then *Rubber Soul* is discussed. There are riots in the Philippines when it is suggested that the Beatles have insulted the First Lady. There is also a backlash in America because of the remarks John Lennon made about Christ in an interview and we see American DJs telling their listeners to burn Beatle records and boycott Beatle merchandise. John then appears, explaining his original remarks. McDowell tells how the group became disillusioned with touring.

George Martin relates how the group preferred to spend more time in the studio and American author **Nicholas**

Schaffner analyses the *Revolver* album. We are told how John experimented with drugs and how the group came up with the idea of 'a theme album about their childhood'. The results were the songs 'Strawberry Fields Forever' and 'Penny Lane' and parts of the promo films for both these records are shown. George Martin explains how a member of the London Symphony Orchestra played piccolo trumpet on 'Penny Lane' at the suggestion of Paul. It was also Paul who had the idea of using linking tracks on the *Sgt Pepper* album, according to George.

Other comments come from composer Milton Okum, Bruce Johnson of the **Beach Boys**, guitarist Lenny Kaye and music scholar Wilfred Mellers. The global television show, **'Our World'**, presents the Beatles performing 'All You Need Is Love', then their association with the **Maharishi** is related, with scenes of their trip to Bangor in Wales. **Marianne Faithfull** talks about the Maharishi and the death of Brian Epstein, and the group are also interviewed about his death. George Harrison mentions that he'd talked to Brian on the phone a few days previously and that he had told him that he would be coming up to join the Beatles at the weekend.

George Martin and Nicholas Schaffner discuss the group's 1967 releases and scenes from *Magical Mystery Tour*, the background to the TV film and its poor reception by British critics follow.

They record 'Hello Goodbye' at the **Saville Theatre** in Sgt Pepper uniforms and travel to India for a proposed three months at the Maharishi's ashram. Their sojourn is cut short, they break with their guru and then announce the formation of **Apple Corps**. George Martin mentions that the group were reluctant to do *Yellow Submarine*, but as the deal had been set up by Brian before he died, they agreed. Once they had seen the finished product they were delighted by it. We witness the **London Pavilion** premiere of the movie and then Marianne Faithfull talks about the recording of 'Hey Jude'. The boys perform the number and we next hear Nicholas Schaffner discussing the double LP *The Beatles*. We learn how Ringo walked out of the sessions, how George was unhappy about only usually getting two cuts on their albums, and the fact that **Yoko Ono** was present in the recording studios. We then learn further details about Yoko and Schaffner discusses 'Let It Be'.

Keyboards man **Billy Preston** relates that he knew the band back in their Hamburg days and that they asked him to play solo piano on 'Get Back'. There is mention that because Paul tried to get them organized, he sounded over-bossy to the others. George Martin describes the disenchantment of *Let It Be*, with its 100 songs and 30 hours of tape.

Lenny Kaye makes some comments, then there are scenes of John and Yoko and Paul and **Linda** getting married, shots of George and **Pattie** and Ringo and **Maureen** and comments about the 'pull' of domestic life affecting all four.

There is talk of Apple going sour. We see the appearance of **Allen Klein**. Paul protests. Klein brings in **Phil Spector** to deal with the tapes of the *Let It Be* album. Lenny Kaye makes some comments, then Billy Preston talks about the different interests of the four. George Martin comments about them wanting to live their own lives. The McCartney album is issued. Paul quits the group. We see the headlines in the papers. Then there is a full-screen picture of all four and, one by one, they each vanish until we are left with a blank screen.

'Let It Be' is released. People say it is 'the Beatles' swan song'. George Martin comments: 'I think that the great thing about the Beatles is that they were of their time. Their timing was right. They didn't choose it, someone chose it for them, but the timing was right and they left their mark on history because of that. I think they expressed the mood of the people, their own generation.'

There are scenes from the *Let It Be* film as the following information appears on the screen:

'Paul went on to form Wings with his wife Linda, and recorded many best selling albums.

'George continued to combine musical and spiritual interests. While maintaining his privacy.

'Ringo made several solo records and pursued an acting career in Hollywood.

'John collaborated with Yoko on music, humanitarian causes and raising a family. He was assassinated on 8 December 1980.'

● Concert For Bangla Desh, The

George Harrison's most ambitious project, coming almost a year after the Beatles had disbanded, led to speculation that the *Concert for Bangla Desh* in August 1971 would see the Beatles reunite on stage. It wasn't to be.

Ravi Shankar, distraught by the horrific events in his country, appealed to George for ideas on a way to help the refugee problem out there. The civil war in Pakistan, with the western sector fighting the eastern sector which had declared itself as the nation of Bangla Desh, had resulted in the exodus of ten million refugees into India. A million people had died from disease and starvation and there were countless orphaned children.

Ravi had in mind a modest concert, hoping to raise an amount in the region of $25,000. George once again proved his entrepreneurial skills, aiming for a brilliantly ambitious concert that would provide a souvenir three-album set, a television special and a cinema film. The project was destined to earn almost $15 million for the troubled country of Bangla Desh.

George immediately began contacting musician friends of his and spent the month of June and the early part o July 1971 phoning fellow musicians. On a visit t Disneyland with **Peter Sellers** and Ravi Shankar it wa suggested that Peter Sellers be compere of the event However, as he was involved in the post-production o *Being There*, George took on the task. Mick Jagger had jus settled in France and was unable to obtain a visa in time.

George decided to hold the concert at a venue where h could obtain maximum promotional exposure and chos Madison Square Garden in New York City. He set the dat for Sunday, 1 August 1971.

The Beatles had last made an appearance a **Candlestick Park** in San Francisco in 1966, and it wa just possible that George might have pulled off th

Bob Dylan was one of the superstar guests who accepted George Harrison's invitation to appear in the *Concert For Bangla Desh*. (National Film Archives)

ultimate coup and gathered them together again for the gig. Ringo Starr, who was filming ***Blindman*** in Spain, was one of the first people George called, and he immediately agreed to appear. John Lennon also agreed to appear but, when he arrived, the ever present **Yoko** was at his shoulder. She became quite furious when George quietly explained that he would only be requiring John's presence on stage and not hers. Yoko created such a scene with John that there was a violent argument, John's glasses were broken, he furiously left her and travelled to the airport for the first plane to Europe – and ended up in Paris. Yoko had dreamed of appearing at the concert and wanted to make New York their new home. Within a few days they had both cooled down and were reunited at Tittenhurst Park, only to leave England and settle in America for good the next month.

Paul felt that the Beatles had only recently split up and considered that it would be pointless if one of the first moves was to get back together again. He said he'd only agree if the other three would drop the legal action against him instigated because of his wishes for a legal dissolution of the Beatles. This was unacceptable to them at the time.

There were to be two performances that August evening at the 20,000 seater arena and both shows completely sold out within six hours of the box office opening.

The Bangla Desh Concert was **Eric Clapton**'s only appearance for a long time. He'd ceased appearing the previous year and was not to perform again until 1973. The problem was his addiction to hard drugs. When he arrived in New York, he sent his girlfriend Alice Ormsby-Gore, daughter of the former British Ambassador, out onto the streets trying to score heroin for him. Eric was terribly ill the night before the concert and didn't attend the rehearsals at the West 57th Street studios. Jesse Ed Davis was ready to take over as Clapton's stand-in. **Allen Klein** arranged for Dr William Zahm to treat him and on the day he was able to appear on stage.

The concert opened when George introduced Ravi Shankar who began a stirring set of Indian music – Ravi on sitar, backed by Ali Akbar Khan on sarod and Alla Rakha on tabla and Kamala Chakravarty on tamboura. A bearded George then appeared on stage in a white suit and orange shirt and opened with 'Wah-Wah'. Ringo Starr was on drums, Eric Clapton on guitar, Leon Russell on piano, **Billy Preston** on keyboards, Jesse Ed Davis on electric guitar, Jim Horn leading a brass section, Jim Keltner on drums, **Klaus Voormann** on bass, Claudia Linnear leading a nine-piece gospel chorale and three members of **Badfinger** playing acoustic guitars. The ensemble performed 'My Sweet Lord', 'Awaiting On You All', 'Beware Of Darkness', 'That's The Way God Planned It' (a Billy Preston showpiece), 'It Don't Come Easy' (Ringo's showpiece), 'Jumpin' Jack Flash'/'Young Blood' (Leon Russell's showpiece), 'While My Guitar Gently Weeps' (the genius of Eric Clapton), 'Something', 'Here Comes The Sun', the latter performed by George, who played six-string acoustic guitar, as did Peter Ham of **Badfinger**. George then introduced **Bob Dylan**, saying 'I'd like to bring on a friend of us all – Mister Bob Dylan.'

Dylan, now also sporting a beard, appeared dressed in jeans and a denim jacket and opened with 'A Hard Rain's Gonna Fall' and followed with 'Mr Tambourine Man', 'Blowin' In The Wind', 'It Takes A Lot To Laugh, It Takes A Train To Cry' and 'Just Like A Woman'. He was joined on the last number by George on slide guitar, Ringo on tambourine and Russell on bass. George finished the set with a performance of the number 'Bangla Desh'.

There was a party after the show and guests included the Who and Grand Funk Railroad.

CBS TV broadcast a version of the concert and a film was also made, directed by Saul Swimmer and distributed by 20th Century Fox. This was premiered the following year on 23 March 1972 in New York. George had worked with the director on the film, putting together the best excerpts from both shows, and Bob Dylan had also involved himself in the editing of the 4 hours of footage into 90 minutes of screen time. It was originally screened in thirteen major cities on 70mm film with six-track sound. There was also a version issued for general release in 35mm film with four-track sound. The movie was previewed at New York's DeMille Theatre and among the celebrity guests were John and Yoko, Jerry Rubin and Nino Tempo, although John left the cinema in the middle of Dylan's performance.

This, the first of the legendary rock-charity events, was soured by the intransigence of the income tax officials who insisted on their pound of flesh, despite the worthiness of the cause. Record companies had waived their royalties, but the British and American governments insisted on heavily taxing the event. George commented, 'The law and tax people do not help. They make it so that it is not worthwhile doing anything decent.' George lobbied in

Britain and even had a two-hour meeting with Patrick Jenkins, a governmental financial undersecretary, which had been arranged for him by MP **Jeffrey Archer**. No matter how sincerely George presented the case of the suffering innocents of Bangla Desh and how urgently they needed help, he was facing hard-nosed officialdom. Jenkins was unmoved, he refused to waive demands for tax. 'Perhaps you people would prefer it if I were to move out of England, like virtually every other major British pop star, and take my money with me?' said George. 'That, sir, would, of course, be entirely up to you,' said Jenkins. Naturally, sickened by this unyielding attitude, George personally paid a cheque for one million pounds to the tax authorities.

Difficulties arose with the triple album, with record dealers charging extra money for the package, and pocketing it. UNICEF was able to receive an early cheque for $243,418.50, the proceeds of the concert itself, but the rest of the urgently needed money took almost a decade to collect, with accusations being made against Allen Klein regarding the financial administration, which he took legal action against and then dropped.

● Concert Hall, *Argyle Street, Glasgow, Scotland*

The Beatles appeared at this venue only once. Their performance on 5 October 1963 was the opening night of a three-day tour of Scotland, promoted by Albert Bonici.

● Condon, Richard

American author of several best-sellers, including *The Manchurian Candidate*.

When a property for the Beatles' third film was being considered, United Artists' head of production **Bud Ornstein** suggested Condon's novel ***A Talent For Loving***. Condon was an old friend of his and he loved the book and suggested to Brian Epstein and the Beatles that they buy the film rights, which they did. The novel was a Western, set in 1871 and concerned a dramatic horse race set over distances of hundreds of miles.

A meeting was arranged between Condon and John Lennon in which the author discussed his ideas on the treatment of the film with John.

On 10 February 1965 it was announced in the press as their third movie, which was to be financed by Brian Epstein's Pickfair Films, a company he formed with Bud Ornstein on 21 December 1964. On 16 June 1965 it was announced that the film was postponed due to weather conditions in Spain, where it was to be filmed, and on 13 December it was announced that the project had been abandoned because the Beatles couldn't fit it into their heavy schedule.

In fact, the real reason seems to be that the Beatles weren't satisfied with Condon's script.

They decided to tell the author personally and arranged for him to fly to London where they gave him their reasons for not continuing with the project.

When Ornstein moved to Paramount he talked the studio into producing it and the film was made in 1968 with Richard Widmark and Topol. The Beatles still owned the property and had a share in the profits.

● Connolly, Ray

A Merseyside writer who was a student of social anthropology at the London School of Economics. He then became a journalist writing for the *Liverpool Daily Post* before graduating to Britain's largest evening newspaper, the *Evening Standard* in London. When he joined the paper in 1967 as a columnist specializing in the show-business field, he wrote about the Beatles on numerous occasions and interviewed them regularly.

Several of his Beatles interviews were collected in his book *Stardust Memories*, published in Britain by Pavilion in 1983. They included his first interview with Paul, which took place at the Cavendish Avenue house. Their conversation touched on a number of topics, ranging from the *Magical Mystery Tour* film to the group's forthcoming trip to India. An interview with Ringo was conducted in March 1968 and Connolly painted a happy picture of Ringo's home in Weybridge and his life with his wife **Maureen** and son **Zak**. His interview with **Yoko Ono** took place in October 1968 and began with a chat about the *Two Virgins* album and *Bottoms* film. The rest of the interview covered her childhood and years prior to meeting with John. Another interview with Paul took place in a Soho restaurant in April 1970 and was a detailed discussion of the Beatles' break-up. Later that year, Ray interviewed John at Tittenhurst Park. Yoko also joined in the conversation, which concentrated on John's solo career.

He became a confidant and learned many of their secrets, the biggest of which was the story of John's intention to leave the Beatles. Ray respected John's wishes that he keep the story on ice. Four months later, Paul was able to make his own announcement to the press and John regretted that he had asked Ray to withhold the story.

Ray also travelled to Toronto and stayed at Ronnie Hawkins' farm during John and Yoko's visit there. After John's period of being a househusband, Ray was one of the journalists invited to New York to interview John about his future plans. His interview was set for 9 December 1980. On 8 December Yoko called him to inform him of the tragedy.

Connolly is one of a handful of major freelance columnists in Britain and his writings frequently appear in publications ranging from the *Sunday Times* to the *Standard*. His books/film scripts include *That'll Be The Day* and *Stardust*, the latter winning him the Writers' Guild of Great Britain Award for the best original screenplay.

Among his published works is a biography of John entitled *John Lennon: 1940–1980*, published by Fontana in 1981. Among his unpublished works is a brilliant film screenplay on the life of John Lennon called *Working Class Hero*.

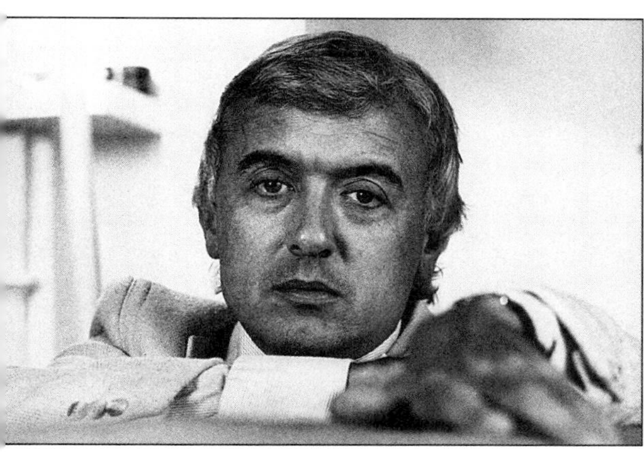

Ray Connolly – one of the writers given favoured treatment by the Beatles. (Ray Connolly)

● Continuing Story Of Bungalow Bill, The

A song which John wrote when he was at the **Maharishi**'s ashram in India. He commented that it 'was written about a guy in Maharishi's meditation camp who took a short break to go shoot a few poor tigers, and then came back to commune with God. There used to be a comic character called Jungle Jim, and I combined him with Buffalo Bill. It's a sort of teenage social comment song, and a bit of a joke.'

During the recording session on Tuesday, 8 October 1968 **Yoko Ono** spoke one line of the song and **Maureen Starkey** joined in on the chorus. Chris Thomas played mellotron on the track which was featured on *The Beatles* white album.

● Convention Centre, Philadelphia, Pennsylvania

Mersey Beat reader Sheila Dress of Pennsylvania wrote to the Liverpool-based newspaper about the Beatles' appearance here on 2 September 1964.

'Their concert in Philadelphia on 2 September was exactly the same (as the Atlantic City one) except that it started at 8 o'clock. One act, the **Righteous Brothers**, was replaced by Clarence 'Frogman' Henry. Unfortunately, we didn't have such good seats in Philadelphia as Atlantic City, so we couldn't see as well. We could hear them all right though.

'Philadelphia's Convention Hall is smaller than Atlantic City's, so there were only about 12,037 teenagers there. The kids were much noisier though and everyone had to stand on the back of their seats to see anything because the seats weren't elevated.

'Rose DeWolf, reporter for the *Inquirer*, wrote of the Philadelphia Press Conference: "The Beatles were asked, 'What's the best city you've ever played in?' They answered, 'Liverpool'."'

Another newspaper reported a question and answer session with the group:

Q (to Paul McCartney): 'Do you find any difference in teenagers of different countries you visit?'
A: 'Only in their accents.'
Q 'What do you think of serious music?'
A (Lennon): 'It's rock 'n' roll. Of course, all music is serious, it depends on who's listening to it.'
Q: 'What do you know of **Elvis Presley**?'
A (Ringo Starr): 'Some of his earlier stuff is good. Don't care for what he's been doing recently.'

Q: 'Where would you be with crew-cuts?'
A (Lennon): 'I don't think it would make any difference. Our sound was the original thing. The funny part came later.'

The police chief in Philadelphia spent two weeks preparing for the Beatles' appearance there and Ringo told him: 'You chaps gave us the safest and most protection we've had in any city.'

● Convention Hall, *Atlantic City, New Jersey*

George Hamid, who owned the Steel Pier in Atlantic City, had booked the Beatles to appear at the Convention Hall three days after the Democratic Party National Convention had been held there, on 30 August 1964.

Despite the fact that the population of Atlantic City was only 60,000, the concert was completely sold out in advance, with over 19,000 fans crammed into the hall.

Police were stationed outside the hall at 5.00 p.m. as there were already almost 1,000 fans gathered. When the Beatles' party arrived almost an hour later, the crowds surged forward. A fan jumped in between a radio car and the Beatles' limousine and had her legs jammed between the vehicles.

The police helped the group to get into the stage door and a press conference took place, supervised by **Derek Taylor**. There were various questions, one of which asked of all the cities they had been to, which one did they like most and Lennon answered, 'Liverpool.'

A 15 ft high platform had been specially erected in front of the stage and the group played on this, protected from the audience, who remained in their seats, by a line of eighteen policemen.

After the show, it seemed it would be impossible for them to leave the hall in the limousine. A marked laundry truck was requested and the Beatles climbed inside and made their escape.

Mersey Beat printed a report of the Beatles in Atlantic City and Philadelphia by reader Sheila Dress, who came from Philadelphia. She wrote: 'The **Fab Four** were in Atlantic City's Convention Hall on Sunday, 30 August, and their concert was scheduled to start at 8.30 p.m.

'My two sisters, a girlfriend and I went down to Atlantic City for the day (about 70 miles from Philadelphia) and walked on the Broadwalk (promenade). Atlantic City is the

Mark and Carol Lapidos with their guest Alistair Taylor at one of the three Beatlefests, which they produce annually. (Mark and Carol Lapidos)

nost popular seaside resort in New Jersey and is much ike Blackpool.

'At 7.00 p.m. we went down to Convention Hall to get n and the waiting line was blocks long on either side of the hall. We didn't get in until 8.20. Fortunately, all tickets had been sold months before, so that problem was eliminated.

'Convention Hall is a huge place and 20,000 kids were on hand to see the Beatles. The master of ceremonies gave everyone a strict lecture about sitting down in their seats, but that wasn't observed too well. Four other acts: the **Bill Black Combo**, the Exciters, the **Righteous Brothers** and **Jackie De Shannon** preceded the Beatles. Everything was pandemonium when they finally came on! We had seats in the eleventh row centre orchestra, so we could see and hear pretty well. My youngest sister and I took pictures, but none of them came out. To sum up their performance, they were absolutely FAB! They were only on for 30 minutes and sang 11 songs, but it was still great.'

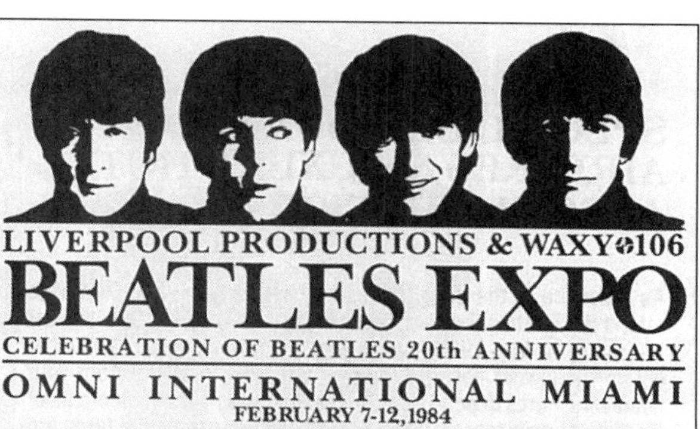

RELIVE THE LEGENDARY BEATLEMANIA!

- Beatles look-and-sound alike band
- Beatles memorabilia trade fair
- Beatles rare video
- Beatles look-a-like contest
- Beatles museum exhibition
- Personalities connected with The Beatles' legendary success and much, much more

FREE ADMISSION

● Conventions

Beatles conventions are held regularly in various countries throughout the world. Their origin dates back to 1974 when Joe Pope, who edited the popular Beatles fanzine *Strawberry Fields Forever*, decided to organize a Beatles party featuring a Beatles sound-alike group, Tasty Legs. Word got around and the response was so big that the event was moved to a larger venue – the ballroom of a big hotel in Boston. Beatles films were added to the bill, then a flea-market and when the event took place over the 26 July 1974 weekend, the Beatles convention had been born.

Later that year, Mark Lapidos organized a Beatlefest in New York. Lapidos was to prove the most successful of all Beatles convention organizers and his events have taken place in several US cities each year, ever since. Mark organizes the events with his wife Carol and they include a series of Beatles films and videos – sometimes as many as 50 different ones at a single convention; special guests including associates of the Beatles, musicians who have performed with them and authors of Beatles books; a giant Beatles flea-market and Beatles auctions; a Beatles museum and art contest and music by sound-alike bands.

The first real Beatles convention in Britain took place in London at **Alexandra Palace** on the weekend of 18–19 December 1976. Former **Cavern** DJ **Bob Wooler** was master of ceremonies and other DJs included Tony Prince, Roger Scott and Paul Gambaccini. Special guest was **Allan Williams** and groups included **Gerry & the Pacemakers**, Faron's Flamingos and Abbey Road. There was an exhibition of **Stuart Sutcliffe**'s works, a Beatles flea-market and several other events, but low attendance figures ensured the event was not repeated.

However, the following year, Allan Williams and Bob Wooler ran Liverpool's first Beatles convention, with the financial help of **Ron Jones.** It took place at Mr Pickwick's club in Fraser Street on the weekend of 8–9 October 1977 and was organized along similar lines to the London event. The next major conventions in Liverpool were organized by Liz and Jim Hughes who, at the time, ran Cavern Mecca, a Beatles museum. The first, called 'Mersey Beatle' (the title of a section of the ***Mersey Beat*** newspaper), was held at the **Adelphi Hotel**, Lime Street on Saturday, 29 August 1981, and was part-financed by sponsorship arranged by Ron Jones. The conventions are now annual affairs in Liverpool, generally taking place at the Adelphi on August bank holiday weekends, although arranged by different organizers.

The main annual conventions in Continental Europe are organized by the staff of Beatles Unlimited and began in 1976. They are generally one-day events held in various theatres in Holland and the first was held at the famous Paradiso Club in Amsterdam.

● Co-op Ballroom, Doncaster, Yorkshire

The Beatles appeared only once at this venue on the evening of 8 August 1962. They had been booked to appear at the **Cavern** that night but were allowed to cancel their appearance there for the Co-op Ballroom gig.

● Co-operative Hall, Market Street, Darwen, Lancashire

The Beatles appeared once at this venue on Friday, 25 January 1963. The dance was organized for the Baptist Youth Club by Mr T. Proudfoot.

Due to fog, the Beatles were five minutes late going on stage, but gave a performance which the local paper described as 'Fabulous!'

Naturally, the dance was a complete sell-out in advance and a number of local groups were booked as support acts – the Mustangs, the Electones and the Mike Taylor Combo.

● Co-operative Hall, Long Street, Middleton, Lancashire

The Beatles only appeared once at this venue, in Lancashire, on the evening of 11 April 1963.

● Cooper, Michael

The photographer who took the famous photograph of the *Sgt Pepper's Lonely Hearts Club Band* cover.

Michael was a prominent British photographer who worked closely with art gallery owner **Robert Fraser** and, as a result, photographed a number of the major painters of the time, including Duchamp, Magritte, Claus Oldenberg, Larry Rivers, Brigit Riley, Jim Dine and Rauchenberg. Fraser gave them all their first show in London and Michael was there to photograph them.

As a result of Fraser becoming an adviser for the *Pepper* sleeve, he hired Cooper to take the photographs and the special display was constructed in Cooper's studio in Chelsea. Cooper's four-year-old son Adam was present and years later he was to recall, 'There were lots of people milling around the studio at first, then when the shoot was about to commence, they cleared the studio.

'My grandparents were invited to the end-of-the-shoot party at my father's studio in Flood Street where the sessions took place. They were of that age group, middle-aged, middle-of-the-road, and I still don't think they've got over it to this day. They walked into this place and a whole cross-section of weird people were in there, from models from different agencies, to the Beatles, to **Robert Fraser**, Michael, **Peter Blake** and lots of people wearing colourful sixties gear. My grandparents walked into this scene and didn't know what was going on, but they were impressed by the whole set-up.'

Cooper also took many shots of the **Rolling Stones** and was responsible for the cover of *Her Satanic Majesties Request*. Michael devised the 3D effect, but **Allen Klein** decided that it was too expensive, so only a limited number of 3D copies were issued. Keith Richard remarked about how Cooper was proud of his record collection – with his own two covers at each end, one the *Sgt Pepper* cover, the other *Her Satanic Majesties Request*.

Michael Cooper took photographs of the Beatles during a concert performance and also took hundreds of shots of John and **Yoko** at their exhibition at Robert Fraser's gallery. A colleague commented: 'For the John and Yoko exhibition they had people walking up and down Oxford Street with signs promoting it, but people didn't believe John and Yoko would be there. Hardly anyone turned up at first and they were just closing down when suddenly hundreds and hundreds of people started turning up and the gallery became packed.'

In 1972 Cooper became depressed and committed suicide. He left behind over 17,000 photographs. He'd always planned to have a book of his work published which he intended to call *Blinds and Shutters*. Fourteen years after his death, *Blinds and Shutters* was finally published in a lavish limited edition of 5,000 copies by Genesis Publications. It had been put together by Cooper's son Adam, together with a friend, Perry Richardson, and the help of Bill Wyman.

● Corbett, Bill

A driver hired by John to become the chauffeur of his recently acquired £5,000 Rolls-Royce in 1964. Corbett had originally been an employee of a car hire firm which had assigned him to drive the Beatles around in an Aston Martin.

● Cordet, Louise

A teenage girl singer and **Decca** recording artist who was booked by **Arthur Howes** to appear on the **Roy Orbison**/Beatles British tour of May/June 1963.

Louise was promoting her new single 'Round And Around'. Her previous releases were 'I'm Just A Baby' and 'Who's Sorry Now?'. Her only chart hit was 'I'm Just A Baby', which had reached No. 13 in the British charts in May 1962.

In October 1963 the young French singer had her version of 'From Me To You' issued. A number which she sang in the French language.

● Cornell, Lyn

Blonde-haired member of the **Vernons Girls**, the all-female singing group from Liverpool. She was a member of the vocal outfit when they recorded 'We Love The Beatles'. Later she joined a group called the Carefrees with Betty Prescott, another former Vernons girl.

The other members were Barbara Kay, Johnny Evans, John Stevens and Don Riddell. The group recorded 'We Love You Beatles', which was issued in the US on London International 10614 in 1964 and reached No. 39 in the *Billboard* charts, with a chart life of five weeks, making it the most successful Beatles novelty single ever recorded.

As a solo singer, Lyn was booked to appear on the special all-British edition of the US TV series 'Shindig' on which the Beatles appeared. Lyn had lived quite close to Paul McCartney in Liverpool and during rehearsals at the Granville Theatre, Fulham, she was able to talk over old times with Paul.

Lyn was also married to **Andy White**, drummer on the recording sessions for 'Love Me Do' and 'P.S. I Love You'.

● Corn Exchange, *St Paul's Square, Bedford*

The Beatles appeared here only once, on the evening of 13 December 1962. **Joe Brown** & His Bruvvers had originally been booked to appear, but as they were unable to fulfil the engagement, the promoters sought an alternative and managed to book the Beatles, only days before the group left for their final season at the **Star Club**, Hamburg.

● Corrine, Corrina

A traditional song which the Beatles added to their repertoire in 1960. Joe Turner had recorded a version of the number in 1956 but the Beatles were probably influenced by the Ray Peterson version which reached No. 9 in the American charts in 1960. The Beatles dropped it from their repertoire at the end of 1961.

● Cott, Jonathan

An American author and journalist who conducted the first interview with John Lennon for *Rolling Stone* magazine on 23 November 1968. Jonathan was the magazine's European correspondent and the interview which took place in London was arranged by **Robert Fraser**, owner of the Fraser Gallery, where John was holding an exhibition.

Cott, who was an associate editor of *Rolling Stone* magazine from 1967, has penned several books. He co-wrote the text for *Get Back*, the lavish book issued in Britain with the original *Let It Be* album in 1970.

Several of Cott's articles about John were collected in the 1982 book *The Ballad of John and Yoko*, which he co-edited.

● Coventry Theatre, *Hales Street, Coventry, West Midlands*

The Beatles made only two appearances at this theatre, both in 1963. The first took place on 24 February 1963 as part of the **Helen Shapiro** tour. Their second appearance was part of their own autumn tour on 17 November.

● Coward, Noel

The late British playwright, composer and actor, who was knighted in 1970. The celebrated figure kept a diary and noted in his entry for Saturday, 6 June 1964, that he'd finished up at **Alma Cogan**'s London flat at 12.20 a.m. where he met two Beatles. They were John Lennon and Paul McCartney.

The following year, on Wednesday, 23 June 1965, he noted, 'The Beatles have all four been awarded MBE's, which has caused a considerable outcry. Furious war heroes are sending back their bravely-won medals by the bushel. It is, of course, a tactless and major blunder on the part of the Prime Minister, and also I don't think the Queen should have agreed. Some other decoration should have been selected to reward them for their talentless but considerable contributions to the Exchequer.'

● Cow Palace, San Francisco, California

Site of the first gig on their first American tour on 19 August 1964.

The entire stadium of 17,130 seats was sold out, bringing in receipts of $91,670 of which the Beatles' share was $47,600. The promoter was Paul Catalana.

The show began at 8.00 a.m. with the **Bill Black Combo**, followed by the **Righteous Brothers**, backed by the Exciters and then **Jackie De Shannon**.

Backstage, the boys were introduced to Joan Baez and **Derek Taylor** arranged a press conference at which there were a number of simplistic questions such as 'Do the Beatles have pillow fights?' Ringo was to make the plea, 'Please don't throw jelly beans – they're dangerous.'

A sheriff's deputy had spotted film star **Shirley Temple** in the audience and brought her backstage with her husband Charles Black and their eight-year-old daughter Lori. Brian Epstein had a ban on celebrity photos being taken at the time, but it was waived and the historic picture was taken by her husband.

The group took the stage at 9.20 a.m. Dressed in dark blue suits, they were on a stage surrounded by seats and were pelted by a hail of jelly beans, which mainly hit Ringo. Paul later commented, 'We'd step in them and they'd stick to our guitar leads and our shoes. The kids must've thought I was trying out new dance steps, but I was always just trying to get unstuck. And – we didn't even eat them!'

There was such a hail that the show was stopped twice while an announcer told the audience, 'You're hurting the Beatles!'

The group performed ten numbers in 30 minutes and then went backstage, planning to be driven to the airport and fly to Las Vegas. Their limousine driver didn't pull away quickly enough and the car was swamped by fans whose weight began to tell on the car roof. Security men pulled the Beatles out of the car and put them in an ambulance in which there were several drunken sailors who had been involved in a brawl at the show.

The Cow Palace opened their first American tour and it was also the venue where they finished their American tour in 1964 on 31 August. The group performed a matinee before 11,700 fans and an evening show before an audience of 17,000.

● Crawdaddy Club, *Station Hotel, Kew Road, Richmond, Surrey*

One of Britain's first R&B clubs, launched in 1962 by the slightly eccentric, but immensely talented Giorgio Gomelski, on a loan of five pounds he'd received. It was known as the Crawdaddy Blues Club.

Giorgio was the son of a Russian father and French mother, had been born in the Caucasus and had travelled widely. **Brian Jones** approached him about booking the **Rolling Stones** and he agreed. The deal was that they would split the takings 50-50, after the band had been paid a minimum guarantee of fifteen pounds per gig.

For the first few gigs, Giorgio earned no money at all but the audiences began to grow. Giorgio began to take over management responsibilities and Brian suggested he sign them to a contract, but Giorgio never got around to it.

When *Please Please Me* was at the peak of its success Giorgio managed to talk the Beatles into coming to the club to see the Stones and they arrived on the evening of 21 April 1963. It was the start of a long-lasting relationship between the two bands.

As a result of the Beatles' visit, George Harrison was able to recommend the Stones to A&R man **Dick Rowe** who signed them to **Decca**.

● Crittle, John

A clothes designer appointed to run Apple Tailoring. John Lennon was to say, 'We bought a few things from him and the next thing I knew, we owned the place.'

It became Apple's second boutique, was situated at 161

ew Kings Road and the large sign on the shop's facade bove the windows read: 'Civil And Theatrical Apple ailoring By John Crittle.'

A launch party and press reception was held to elebrate the opening of the boutique on 22 May 1968 ith John and **Yoko,** and George and **Pattie Harrison** in ttendance. Crittle designed the costumes for the shop and aged a fashion show at the launch party.

It was a short-lived venture. A few months after the pening, the Beatles relinquished control of the shop and anded it back to Crittle on 31 July 1968.

● Crosley Field, Cincinnati, Ohio

he Beatles had been due to appear at this venue on aturday, 20 August 1966. A canopy used to protect the lectrical equipment from rain failed to do so and there as a possibility that members of the Beatles could be lectrocuted. There were backstage arguments between rian Epstein, the American agents and the local promoter ue to the fact that 35,000 fans were already in the arena.

Minutes before they were due to go on stage the Beatles nsisted that they had Brian Epstein's word that there was o danger from the wet equipment and, as he couldn't ssure them, they refused to go on. The gig was rearranged o take place at noon the next day, 21 August.

After they'd performed their lunchtime concert they ad a 350-mile journey to St Louis for their performance at usch Stadium that evening.

● Crown & Mitre Hotel, Carlisle, Cumberland

he hotel where the Beatles stayed following their ppearance at the **ABC Cinema, Carlisle** on 8 February 963.

The group were appearing on the bill of the **Helen hapiro** tour. After the show they were relaxing at the otel when Helen mentioned that someone had invited hem all to attend a Young Conservatives' dance being eld in the hotel ballroom on behalf of the Carlisle Golf lub, but she'd turned the offer down. Helen was later to ay that it was very cold, everyone was bored and the eatles said they would drop into the dance. Helen uickly went to her room to make up and joined the eatles and **Kenny Lynch** as they approached the private unction. They passed the entrance desk into the dance rea, but because the Beatles were wearing leather jackets they were asked to leave. They hadn't even entered the main ballroom, but they all left.

On 11 February, the event made front-page news in the *Daily Express*, which blew the incident out of all proportion, sympathized with Helen, but castigated the Beatles. Helen was later to mention it was not the organizers of the dance who objected to the Beatles' attire, but personnel from the hotel itself.

● Cruikshank, Robin

A designer who launched his own company, Robin Limited, in the sixties. He did some work for Apple, following which Ringo Starr commissioned him to furnish his home and was so pleased with the result that he went into partnership with Robin and the firm's name was changed to Ringo Or Robin Limited.

The company proved an ideal outlet for Ringo's latent design talent and he went to work himself on a variety of intriguing designs, one of the most famous being a Rolls-Royce grill table.

● Cry Baby Cry

Track on *The Beatles* double album, composed by John and full of his 'Alice in Wonderland' imagery. The song, with elements of nursery rhyme, is about the King of Marigold and his family, the Duke and Duchess of Kirkcaldy and a midnight seance.

Commenting on the number, John Lennon told Beatles biographer **Hunter Davies**, 'I've got another one here, a few words, I think I got them from an advert – "Cry baby cry, make your mother buy". I've been playing it over on the piano.'

John also played piano and organ on the track while George Martin added harmonium. During one of the recording sessions, on Tuesday, 16 July 1968, engineer **Geoff Emerick** decided that he could no longer work with the Beatles due to what he perceived as a deteriorating atmosphere between them.

● Cry For A Shadow

The first Beatles composition to appear on record.

The song was mainly composed by George Harrison, with John Lennon's approval, and was really a parody of the **Shadows**' 'Frightened City', which George had done as a spoof to fool **Rory Storm**. The number had gone under the working title 'Beatle Bop'.

When **Bert Kaempfert** recorded the Beatles as a backing band for **Tony Sheridan** in June 1961, they asked if they could cut some tracks of their own. John sang on 'Ain't She Sweet'. Kaempfert had asked them if they had any original compositions of their own. John and Paul did play a couple of their own compositions for Kaempfert, but he was unimpressed with their songs, although he felt George's cod-Shadows style on 'Cry For A Shadow' was suitable and suggested that they record it.

'Cry For A Shadow' was included on Tony Sheridan's German album ***My Bonnie*** in June 1962 earning itself the honour of being the first original composition by a Beatle to find itself on record.

The news of the recording was announced on the front page of issue No. 2 of ***Mersey Beat***.

● Crying, Waiting, Hoping

One of **Buddy Holly**'s lesser-known compositions, which was originally included on the flipside of 'Peggy Sue Got Married' in 1959. The Beatles included it in their repertoire in 1960, with George Harrison on lead vocals. It was one of the numbers they recorded at their **Decca audition**. The group also performed the number on their radio show **'Pop Go The Beatles'** on 6 August 1963.

● Cumberland Gap

Traditional folk number, typical of the material utilized during the British skiffle boom of the fifties. It provided **Lonnie Donegan** with a No. 1 chart hit in 1957 and the **Quarry Men**, like thousands of skiffle groups around the country, included it in their repertoire. John Lennon took over on lead vocals during the Quarry Men performances, although they had dropped the number from their act by the end of 1959.

● Curtis, Lee

The stage name of Peter Flannery, younger brother of **Joe Flannery**, who had been a close friend of Brian Epstein.

Lee originally appeared on the Liverpool scene in 1961 in a group called Lee Curtis & the Detours, which was managed by his brother. When **Pete Best** was fired from the Beatles, he joined Lee in a new band called Lee Curtis & the All Stars. According to Joe Flannery, Epstein, guilty about sacking Pete, had approached him to see if he could fix him up with a job. Joe was also to say

that Epstein wanted to manage Lee Curtis, but the Beatles talked him out of it.

Lee was the first member of the Mersey Beat scene to record a solo single and moved to Hamburg where he appeared for several years. He later moved to Manchester where he became manager of a club.

● Cyrkle, The

An American band discovered by **Nat Weiss**. Weiss was an attorney who worked for Brian Epstein and became one of Brian's closest friends. Epstein encouraged the former divorce lawyer to involve himself in show business and suggested that he consider artist management and promotion. Weiss spotted a group called the Rondells in Atlantic City and mentioned them to Epstein who advised Weiss to manage them, promising he would help out. When Epstein next arrived in New York, Weiss had arranged for the group to appear in a club in Greenwich Village. Epstein changed their name to the Cyrkle (it is suggested that John Lennon thought up the name) and when Weiss signed the group to Columbia Records he sent several acetates to Epstein. Brian suggested that they release a number called 'Red Rubber Ball' as it would sell a million. It was released on Columbia 43589 on 4 June 1966 and reached No. 2 in the *Billboard* charts selling, as Epstein had predicted, over a million copies. Epstein then formed a management company with Weiss called Nemperor Artists to handle Cyrkle and placed them on the Beatles' American tour of 1966. The group had one more hit, 'Turn Down Day', in August 1966.

• Dallas Memorial Coliseum, *Dallas, 'exas, USA*

he Beatles appeared at this venue on Friday, 18 eptember 1964, in a promotion by Super Shows Inc of 'ashington DC. Earlier that day there had been a lephone call reporting that a bomb had been planted in e arena. The police carried out a thorough search and no omb was found, although two fans were found hidden ader the bandstand and a further four in a washroom. The eatles arrived and before their 30 minute performance, articipated in a press conference at 7.00 p.m. It was to be eir last press conference in America that year.

There were 200 police present in the auditorium and aother 200 on stand-by. The police chief, Jess Curry, rived with his daughter and two grandchildren.

Dalrymple Hall, *Fraserborough, berdeenshire, Scotland*

ae Silver Beetles made the third appearance of their ven-venue tour of Scotland backing **Johnny Gentle** at is venue on 23 May 1960.

Dance In The Street

ımber recorded by **Gene Vincent** and his Blue Caps in '58 which the Beatles introduced into their repertoire in 60 and continued performing until late in 1962.

Darktown Strutters Ball

aditional song which the Beatles introduced into their ertoire in 1960 and continued to perform until late in 1962. The Beatles probably included the number in their stage act following the version by **Joe Brown** & the Bruvvers which reached No. 6 in the British charts in March 1960.

• Dave Clark Five

A group from Tottenham in London. When the Mersey sound began to dominate the British music scene, the status quo had been seriously breached. The agents, managers, recording studios and media were all in London. Until the emergence of the Beatles, London had a complete grip on the music scene.

There was a determined effort to bring control back into the hands of the top London entertainment agencies. The Dave Clark Five and **Brian Poole & the Tremeloes** both recorded 'Do You Love Me'. Originally a vocal number by the Contours on Motown, it had been adapted into a beat version by a popular Liverpool band, Faron's Flamingos, who included it in their stage act. They recorded it for a small London label, Oriole, who inexplicably placed it on the 'B' side of the record. The Dave Clark Five and Brian Poole & the Tremeloes immediately came out with a version very close to the Flamingos' sound and both entered the charts with it.

There was media saturation on the Dave Clark Five. Their next record, 'Glad All Over', hit the No. 1 spot and the media had a field day: 'Tottenham Sound Has Crushed The Beatles' were the headlines in the *Daily Express*; cartoons in the *Evening Standard* dismissed the Beatles as old-fashioned. Despite the fact that the media went all out to promote the Dave Clark Five as the group to take over from the Beatles, it never happened.

The Dave Clark Five did become a major hit band, particularly in America where the publicity drive was completely opposite to that in Britain. Rather than being pushed as London's answer to Liverpool, the group were promoted as if they were a Mersey Beat band. Since 'Glad All Over' had replaced 'I Want To Hold Your Hand' at the top of the British charts, the Americans believed that the Dave Clark Five was the next big group from Liverpool. Epic Records exploited this belief by advertising them in *Billboard* as having 'the Mersey sound with the Liverpool beat'. In fact, the Motown Museum in Detroit still displays a framed photograph of the Dave Clark Five and the Supremes with the caption 'Liverpool meets Detroit'.

The group comprised Dave Clark (drums), Mike Smith

A scene from the film *Catch Us If You Can*, starring the Dave Clark Five. (Anglo Amalgamated/ Bruton)

(keyboards/vocals), Rick Huxley (bass), Denis Payton (tenor sax/guitar) and Len Davidson (guitar). During the next ten years they were to have 22 hit records in Britain and 24 in America. They'd originally formed as an instrumental group and had made their debut with 'Chaquita' on the Ember label. They moved to Pye records, but were also unsuccessful with their releases. In 1963 they signed with Columbia and their first release, 'Mulberry Bush', was also a miss. They also recorded Mitch Murray's 'I Like It', but never released it and it became a chart topper for **Gerry & the Pacemakers**. Then came 'Do You Love Me', and the group never looked back.

Drummer Dave Clark proved to have an astute business sense and did much to steer the group to success, while the main musical asset was vocalist Mike Smith, who wrote most of the group's material.

In 1965 they made the film *Catch Us If You Can*, which was directed by John Boorman.

The group finally disbanded in August 1970.

● David & Jonathan

A vocal duo who enjoyed a six-week residency in t British charts with the Lennon & McCartney numb 'Michelle'. Issued on Columbia DB 7800 on 13 Janua 1966 it entered the charts on 29 January and reached N 11. They issued another Beatles cover, 'She's Leavi Home', in June 1967, but it didn't reach the charts. T two singers were actually a songwriting team, Roger Co and Roger Greenaway, who later had a number of hits their own right. Greenaway had originally been a meml of the **Kestrels**, a vocal group who had toured twice w the Beatles in 1963.

● David Lewis Theatre, The, *Great Geor Place, Liverpool L1*

An unusual architecturally interesting building compl which housed a large theatre and hotel. The ma local promoter to use the venue was Wally Hill w presented regular rock 'n' roll shows at the theatre w groups such as Carl Vincent & the Counts and K

Terry & the Cruisers.

The Beatles never actually appeared at the David Lewis Theatre. However, on 17 October 1961, a number of girls who attended the Cavern regularly had formed a Beatles fan club in September and had pooled their money to raise five pounds to hire a room at the David Lewis for their first (and only) fan club gathering. The Beatles agreed to come along.

They had no PA equipment with them and couldn't really perform properly, although Paul sang some ballads and **Pete Best** was coaxed to sing 'Matchbox', 'Peppermint Twist' and the **Elvis Presley** number 'A Rose Growing Wild In The Country'. Paul's father **Jim McCartney** was also in attendance.

The David Lewis was levelled by developers in the late eighties.

Davies, Hunter

The Beatles' official biographer.

Davies had been working on the *Sunday Times* since 1960 and was currently in charge of the Atticus column when he first interviewed Paul McCartney for an item published on 18 September 1966. Davies had penned a novel, *Here We Go Round The Mulberry Bush*, which was being filmed. The director, Clive Donner, suggested that Paul McCartney might be approached to provide the music, as he'd done for ***The Family Way***. Davies met Paul again and he seemed interested initially. Then, finally, he said 'no'. It was during his discussions with Paul that Davies asked if he could write a book about the Beatles. Paul suggested that he contact Brian Epstein and helped him to draft a letter. Davies then met Epstein at his **Chapel Street** home in January 1967 and Brian said he would ask the individual members of the group. At the meeting the following week there was a positive response and Davies suggested that the Beatles receive one-third of the book deal.

For almost eighteen months, Davies travelled around with the Beatles, interviewed their parents, other relatives and friends and compiled over 150,000 words in note form. His completed manuscript contained enough to fill two volumes. However, the agreement he'd arranged with the Beatles meant that the book could be subject to cuts made by the Beatles themselves or relatives such as John's aunt **Mimi** – and that is what happened, resulting in a book which, due to the censoring, left certain aspects of their story out. Davies didn't like having to smooth the rough edges, but had no choice.

During the time he spent with the Beatles, at **Abbey Road** recording sessions and at their homes, he managed to retrieve a number of items, with their permission, which they'd thrown away – these were mainly the scraps of paper on which they'd been composing songs. As a result, a few years later, when the Beatles became interested in their own history, Davies was able to give both Paul and George some of their original handwritten items. He was also able to save a number for posterity and loan them to the British Museum.

The book was first published on 14 September 1968 with a cover by Alan Aldridge and, since Brian Epstein had recently died, Hunter dedicated the book to him.

Hunter also wrote Brian's obituary for *The Times* and was commissioned to prewrite obituaries for each member of the group. John was the only member who asked him to show him his obituary.

Davies' authorized biography was reprinted in 1985 with a lengthy introduction, which is a fascinating account of the story behind the original edition.

● Davis, Rod

Banjo player with the **Quarry Men** skiffle group. The bespectacled youth was in **Quarry Bank**'s 4a class with John Lennon and as John knew that Rod's parents had just bought him a banjo, he invited him to join the group.

Although the Quarry Men generally travelled to their gigs by public transport, Rod's father occasionally drove them to appearances at local competitions in his car.

Musically, while John was becoming more interested in adding rock 'n' roll to their repertoire, Rod wanted them to play pure folk music.

When John left Quarry Bank, Rod continued into the sixth form and became too busy with his studies to remain a member.

Rod was a member of the Quarry Men from March 1957 until February 1958.

● Dawsons Music Shop, *Widnes, Lancashire*

A record store in Widnes, the town fifteen miles from Liverpool. The Beatles made a rare personal appearance at the shop on 6 October 1962, the day after 'Love Me Do' was released. The group were well known in the area and the store advertised regularly in ***Mersey Beat***. The Beatles autographed copies of their debut single for half an hour after their arrival at 4.00 p.m.

● Day By Day

A regional television programme produced by Southern TV. The Beatles were due to appear on the show on 12 November 1963, but their spot was cancelled when Paul McCartney came down with gastric flu.

● A Day In The Life

A John/Paul collaboration, but one in which they each wrote separate parts, John penning the beginning and end of the number and Paul composing the middle section. Paul had already written some of the lyrics for another song, but decided to incorporate them into the number that John had been writing.

There is a long chord at the end of the song which lasts for 42 seconds and it has been suggested that it was only intended to be heard by Martha, Paul's dog!

John's section was inspired by two separate items: the death in a car crash of Guinness heir **Tara Browne**, a friend of the Beatles; and a story that he'd read in the *Daily Mail* concerning holes in the roads in Blackburn, a town in Lancashire. John had a copy of the *Daily Mail* newspaper resting on the piano when writing the song and noticed the short news item. It appeared on page 7 of the 17 January 1967 issue, the lead item in the 'Far And Near' column, and read: 'There are 4,000 holes in the road in Blackburn, Lancashire, or one twenty-sixth of a hole per person, according to a council survey. If Blackburn is typical, there are two million holes in Britain's roads and 300,000 in London.'

Paul's rather cheery section, according to Steven Norris, a former schoolmate at the **Liverpool Institute** who became Conservative MP for Oxford East, was based on a bus journey they used to take to school together. In a *Daily Mail* interview in 1985, Norris commented: 'Everyone says that "A Day In The Life" was about drugs, but Paul always claimed it was about catching the bus to school. I agree. It's exactly what we used to do. Went upstairs and had a smoke, somebody spoke and I went into a dream. That's just how I remember it. Getting sleepily out of bed, dragging a comb across your head, then going out and catching the bus, upstairs to the top deck like we all did, still not properly awake and having an untipped Woodbine.'

In fact, it was only ever John's part of the song that was said to be about drugs. The BBC banned it nonetheless. It has never been clear why they thought the holes in the road referred to holes caused by a drug addict's hypodermic needle. Paul commented: 'It was banned on the basis of the line about how many holes does it take to fill the **Albert Hall**. Somebody got the idea it was how many holes there are in their arm. I think they heard it was something to do with drugs and that was the only part they could find that sounded like drugs.' The reference to the English army winning the war was inspired by John's appearance in the film *How I Won The War*.

There was originally a 24-bar gap when John and Paul's contributions were put together in the studio. At one of the sessions, on Friday, 10 February 1967, Paul told George Martin that he considered the best way to fill the gap was with a build-up by a 90-piece orchestra. Martin took on the technical task of putting the complex number together and hired 40 musicians from the Royal Philharmonic and London Symphony Orchestras. They were **Erich Gruenberg**, Granville Jones, Bill Monro, Jurgen Hess, Hans Geiger, D. Bradley, Lionel Bentley, David McCallum, Donald Weekes, Henry Datyner, Sidney Sax and Ernest Scott on violins; John Underwood, Gwynne Edwards, Bernard Davis and John Meek on violas; Francisco Gabarro, Dennis Vigay, Alan Dalziel and Alex Nifosi on cellos; Cyril MacArthur and Gordon Pearce on double-bass; Roger Lord on oboe; Clifford Seville and David Sandeman on flutes; David Mason, Monty Montgomery and Harold Jackson on trumpets; Raymond Brown, Raymond Premru and T. Moore on trombones; Michael Barnes on tuba; Basil Tschaikov and Jack Brymer on clarinets; N. Fawcett and Alfred Waters on horns; and Tristan Fry on percussion.

The Beatles had originally planned to film the *Sgt Pepper* sessions as a television movie and **Tony Bramwell** from **Apple Films** was in charge of shooting the 'A Day In The Life' session, but the plan for the TV film was dropped when the BBC banned the song. The promotional film remained in the archives until it was screened as part of the *Beatles At Abbey Road* exhibition in 1983.

The Beatles had insisted that the orchestra members

wear full evening dress and they gave them carnival novelties to wear – including red noses and funny hats, upside-down spectacles, false eyes and fake bald heads. The Beatles had also invited a host of friends to add to the party atmosphere, including **Pattie Harrison**, **Marianne Faithfull**, **Mick Jagger**, **Donovan**, **Keith Richard**, **the Fool**, Mike Nesmith of the **Monkees** and the staff of the **Apple Boutique**.

Apart from its appearance on the *Sgt Pepper* album, the number was also included on *The Beatles 1967–1970* compilation in 1973 and *The Beatles Box* in 1980.

● Day Tripper

A John Lennon composition. John commented, 'That was a drug-type song in a way because she was a day tripper. I just liked the word tripper.' At another time he was to say, 'Day trippers are people who go on a day trip, right? Usually on a ferryboat or something. But it was kind of, you know – you're just a weekend hippie.' In fact, John wasn't quite satisfied with the number because he felt that he'd rushed the song while he was working to a deadline.

'Day Tripper' was issued as the first of four eventual Beatles double 'A' sides. The other track was 'We Can Work It Out'. In America it was issued on **Capitol** 5555 on 6 December 1965, although the Americans preferred to promote the 'We Can Work It Out' side, which reached No. 1 in all three charts. 'Day Tripper' reached No. 5 in *Billboard*, No. 10 in *Cash Box* and No. 15 in *Record World*.

In Britain the single was issued on Parlophone R5389 on 3 December 1965 and became the group's tenth consecutive No. 1 and their third Christmas No. 1. The Beatles performed the number during tours in 1965/66 and on their 'The Music Of Lennon & McCartney' TV show. It was also included on *A Collection of Beatles Oldies (But Goldies)*, the American album *Yesterday And Today*, *The Beatles 1962–1966* and *20 Greatest Hits*, and they lip-synched both 'Day Tripper' and 'We Can Work It Out' for '**Hullabaloo**', the American TV show.

Otis Redding had a hit with the song in 1967 and reached No. 6 in the British charts with it.

● Dear Prudence

Prudence Farrow was actress **Mia Farrow**'s younger sister who had a playful personality. The sisters became friendly with the Beatles who interested Prudence in the **Maharishi Mahesh Yogi** and she, in turn, interested her sister in the teachings of the guru, resulting in the two sisters travelling to Boston in January 1968 to hear the Maharishi speak to Harvard law students. The sisters decided to study under the Maharishi at Rishikesh.

While there, Prudence became intensely serious and spent so much time meditating in her cottage that she rarely came out. The Beatles were aware of this and John was asked to contact her and make sure she came out more often and mixed with people. He was to say, 'She'd been locked in for three weeks and was trying to reach God quicker than anyone else.'

The incident inspired John to write 'Dear Prudence'. The Beatles began recording the number at the 8-track **Trident Recording Studio** in London on Wednesday, 28 August 1968, and it was included as a track on *The Beatles* double album.

● Deauville Hotel, *Miami, Florida*

The site of the Beatles' second live performance for the '**Ed Sullivan** Show'. The Beatles arrived in Miami on National Airlines Flight 11, with a pilot who wore a Beatle wig. When the plane touched down at Miami International Airport at 4.00 p.m. there were over 7,000 fans waiting. The group's arrival caused a riot in which glass windows were smashed and chairs were torn to pieces, resulting in over $2,000 worth of damage.

They arrived at their hotel, which had been nicknamed 'Beatle Central'. The suite had three bedrooms and John and **Cynthia** had one room and Paul and Ringo another. George was disgruntled to find he had to share a room with disc jockey **Murray the K**.

Local police sergeant Buddy Bresner was in charge of their safety and supervised a Beatle Patrol of two dozen officers.

Murray the K took them to the **Peppermint Lounge** to see Hank Ballard and they also watched the Coasters perform in the Mau Mau Lounge of the hotel.

On Saturday, 15 February, they rehearsed before a live audience, dressed in their grey suits with velvet collars, and later, after a trip to the swimming pool, rehearsed without an audience and dressed in their swimming trunks in the Napoleon Room of the hotel.

George Martin arrived at the Deauville and was able to tell them that the recordings he'd made at the **Carnegie Hall** concert had come out fine – although the album was never to be released. Then, on Sunday, 16 February, the group performed their television show before a live audience of 3,200 people. Their numbers were 'She Loves You', 'This Boy', 'All My Loving', 'I Saw Her Standing There', 'From Me To You' and 'I Want To Hold Your Hand'.

The Beatles were to remain at the Deauville for a week during which they took in more shows, including the Don Rickles show at the hotel, saw **Elvis Presley**'s *Fun In Acapulco* at a drive-in and visited Cassius Clay's (**Muhammad Ali**) training camp. A local millionaire, **Bernie Castro**, lent them his luxurious houseboat in his absence. It had a full staff, including butler and chef, and they were able to enjoy barbecued steaks on board. During their time off they were also able to write 'Can't Buy Me Love'.

The group finally flew out of Miami at 5.18 p.m. on 21 February 1964.

● Decca Audition, *Decca Studios, Hampstead Studio No. 3, 165 Broadhurst Gardens, London NW6*

In December 1961, the American music trade publication *Cash Box* carried the following story: 'One of the most constructive moves to be made by Decca for many months is the formation of a new production team to handle the company's pop single output. Spearheaded by A&R manager, **Dick Rowe**, who will be directly responsible to the chairman, Sir Edward Lewis, the team is completed by Dick Rowe, Rowe's assistant and co-producer **Mike Smith**, Peter Attwood, recording engineer of three years standing and **Tony Meehan**, former drummer for the **Shadows**. Rowe, who will act in an advisory capacity, feels that this youthful team with their fingers on the teenage pulse, will be more than capable of producing the kind of sound that makes for chart success.'

Such a story would seem to bode well for the Beatles who, nine days after the story appeared, turned up on New Year's Day, 1962, for their Decca recording audition. From an initial approach by Brian Epstein to **Tony Barrow**, who then put in a word, followed by Epstein's meetings with Decca executives such as Dick Rowe and **Beecher-Stevens**, to a Liverpool meeting where Epstein wined and dined Mike Smith, the road led to the West Hampstead studios of Decca on an icy cold New Year's morning.

On New Year's Eve, Brian Epstein caught the train down to London and stayed overnight with his Aunt Frida in Hampstead. The Beatles were to travel down by van with **Neil Aspinall**. Neil, a pal of **Pete Best**, had become their road manager and one of their staunchest champions. He bought a van for £80 to drive them to their gigs, initially charging them a fee of around five shillings a trip. For the London trek he borrowed a larger van, loaded in the boys and their equipment and set out on a journey that took ten hours because of lack of visibility in the snowy weather. They were lost in Wolverhampton and arrived in London at 10 o'clock at night.

The Beatles and Neil were booked into the Royal Hotel in Russell Square, but soon after arriving they went into the streets of the West End where they witnessed various capers, including the revellers in Trafalgar Square and some pot smokers who wanted to use their van.

The group arrived at the recording studios for their 11 a.m. appointment and met Brian, who was furious that Mike Smith was late.

Smith then rejected their amplifiers and told them to plug their guitars into the studio speakers.

Brian and the Beatles had discussed their repertoire. John wanted to perform a strong rock 'n' roll set, like they played at the **Cavern**, but Brian wanted them to play safe, telling them not to play numbers such as 'One After 909' and concentrate on standards such as 'Till There Was You'. He also suggested that they play as few of their own original compositions as possible. John and Paul weren't happy about this, but decided to take Brian's advice.

When the red light in the studio went on they began to perform and they were obviously nervous. Paul's voice began to crack and George was having trouble playing the guitar.

At one point Epstein began to criticize John's voice. John went mad and shouted at him. Everything stopped, the red light went off and Epstein rushed out of the room and didn't return for half an hour.

The group performed fifteen songs, with Paul taking lead on 'Like Dreamers Do', 'Till There Was You', 'Sure To Fall', 'Love Of The Loved', 'September In The Rain', 'Besame Mucho', and 'Searchin''. John was lead vocalist on 'Money', 'To Know Him Is To Love Him', 'Memphis' and 'Hello Little Girl'. George sang 'The Sheik of Araby', 'Take Good Care Of My Baby', 'Three Cool Cats' and 'Crying, Waiting, Hoping'.

The session finished around 2.00 p.m. and they

istened to the playback and all seemed pleased with the session.

Brian then took them all to a restaurant in Swiss Cottage to celebrate and the Beatles and Neil then drove back to Liverpool.

Tony Barrow contacted Mike Smith to ask him if he would be signing the group. Smith said he'd have to wait for Dick Rowe to return from America, but felt confident that the Beatles would get their contract.

As it turned out, Smith had recorded another band that afternoon, **Brian Poole & the Tremeloes**, and Decca decided to sign them up rather than the Beatles. The precise details regarding this decision have never been clearly laid out. It is suggested that Smith liked the Beatles and wanted to sign them, but was either vetoed or asked to choose one of the two groups. There was certainly a suggestion that the Tremeloes were on Decca's doorstep whereas the Beatles were located over 200 miles away and for the sake of communication, it would be easier to sign the Tremeloes.

Yet, if Rowe and Smith were as on-the-ball as the *Cash Box* item suggested, why didn't they at least see the potential in the Beatles' repertoire? A third of the songs performed at that session were to become chart hits. Three of the Beatles numbers, 'Love Of The Loved', 'Hello Little Girl' and 'Like Dreamers Do', provided hits for **Cilla Black**, the **Fourmost** and the **Applejacks** and two other numbers they performed, **Chuck Berry**'s 'Memphis' and Berry Gordy's 'Money', were to provide hits for Dave Berry and Bern Elliott & the Fenmen.

When the Decca rejection was finalized, Brian was given the Decca tapes to use in his attempts to secure the group a recording contract.

However, Decca retained the master tapes of the Beatles session in their vaults and in the late seventies and eighties, bootleg albums and singles of the session began to appear followed, later on, by releases of the packages by legitimate record companies, even though the actual legalities of the rights have never been put to the test in court. EMI did not claim any rights to products recorded before the group signed with the label, but Decca itself did not release any of the tracks on its own label and it is unclear who actually sold rights to various record labels.

Bootleg singles began to appear in America in 1977 on a label called Deccagone. They were 'Three Cool Cats' c/w 'Hello Little Girl' issued on Deccagone PRO 1100 in April 1977; 'The Sheik of Araby' c/w 'September In The Rain' issued on Deccagone PRO 1101 in August 1977; 'Memphis, Tennessee' c/w 'Love Of The Loved' issued on Deccagone PRO 1102 in November 1977; 'Searchin'' c/w 'Like Dreamers Do' issued on Deccagone PRO 1103 in November 1977; 'Sure To Fall' c/w 'Money' issued on Deccagone PRO 1104 in February 1978; 'Crying, Waiting, Hoping' c/w 'Till There Was You' issued on Deccagone PRO 1104 in October 1978 and 'To Know Him Is To Love Him' c/w 'Besame Mucho' on Deccagone PRO 1106 in February 1979. Following the release of the fourth single, an album *The Deccagone Sessions* was available to fans containing eight of the Decca tracks, plus some radio material. More singles followed and in December 1979 another album called *The Decca Tapes* was issued on Circuit Records LK 4438-I.

UDL (United Distributors Lyrics Ltd) began to package ten of the tracks in an album called *Dawn Of The Silver Beatles* (although the Beatles had dropped the name 'Silver' from their name before the Decca sessions), issued by PAC Records, a mail order firm in Phoenix, Arizona, on 16 April 1981 on PAC Records UDL 2333. Various other tracks were issued, coupled with material by other artists, and Backstage Records issued *Like Dreamers Do*, which was a three-album package containing Decca tracks, excerpts from press interviews and an interview with Pete Best, issued on Backstage Records BSR 1111 in May 1982. During the same year, a company called Audio Fidelity Enterprises issued twelve of the tracks on an album called *The Complete Silver Beatles*, on Audio Fidelity AFELP 1047 in September 1982 and on Audio Rarities AR 2452 in October 1982 and followed with two budget album releases, *The Silver Beatles Vol. 1* in October 1982 on Phoenix PHX 352 and *The Silver Beatles Vol. 2* in October 1982 on Phoenix PHXC 353. All of these albums were aimed specifically at the American market. In Britain, Breakaway Records issued *The Audition Tapes* (Breakaway BWY 72) in December 1983. Tracks from the sessions have also been mixed with **Star Club** recordings for other album packages.

● Decca Records

Along with **EMI**, Decca was one of the major record labels at the time Brian Epstein was seeking a recording contract for the Beatles. Over the years Decca has, rather unfairly, been dismissed as the record label which turned down the Beatles.

It was, in fact, the first label to be enthusiastic enough about the group to grant them a recording audition. EMI, on the other hand, saw all of its pop labels dismiss the group out of hand without even considering an audition. It was only by a fluke that George Martin, on EMI's non-pop label Parlophone, eventually did sign the Beatles up.

At a time when the British charts had been dominated by American artists, cover versions of American hits, solo singers, jazz bands and former singers with dance bands, Decca had decided to actively seek new British talent in the pop field and had briefed **Dick Rowe** and his assistants **Mike Smith** and **Tony Meehan** to do just that. This would have seemed an auspicious moment to sign the Beatles.

Epstein had experienced great difficulty in his efforts to obtain a recording contract for the Beatles. He'd approached Les Cox of Pye Records, but was refused even an audition for the group. Philips Records was also uninterested, together with the minor label Oriole. Epstein had even considered approaching Woolworths' Embassy label, but this was a label which only covered current hits on budget releases and didn't actually sign up any artists.

On Epstein's urging, EMI's marketing manager **Ron White** had approached all three recording managers who looked after EMI's pop music labels: Norrie Paramor, Walter Ridley and Norman Newell all expressed their disinterest in the Beatles. The fourth EMI house A&R man George Martin was on holiday at the time, so White didn't approach him. However, he was able to contact Epstein to tell him that EMI was not interested as Martin's label, Parlophone, wasn't really a pop label and Martin had been recording comedy artists such as **Peter Sellers** and the 'Beyond The Fringe' team. As it turned out, the Beatles were able to enter EMI through the back door, via the piece of luck which drew Brian Epstein to have acetates made at Oxford Street's HMV store.

Decca, on the other hand, sent Mike Smith up to Liverpool to see the group. He was enthusiastic and arranged an audition. The audition took place and a satisfied Smith would have signed them up, but was given the option of signing only one of the two groups he'd recorded that day. The decision came down in favour of **Brian Poole & the Tremeloes** because of their proximity to London. If the Tremeloes had come from Sheffield, Decca would no doubt have signed up the Beatles. But even leaving out the hypothetical situation Decca was the only company which directly expressed enough interest in the group to grant them a proper recording audition, prior to the set of circumstances in which fate drew Epstein and Martin together.

Decca was able to offset the stigma of 'turning down the Beatles when it signed up the **Rolling Stones** – ironically, on the recommendation of George Harrison. George just mentioned the group to Dick Rowe when both of them had been participating in the judging of a beat contest in Liverpool. It probably didn't enter George's head to formally recommend them to his own record company. If he had, EMI would surely have signed them up. Yet it was Decca who signed them up and the Rolling Stones benefited. Due to the success of the Beatles, the Stones were able to demand and get an equitable royalty on their records, more than the Beatles received from EMI, a situation which was to rankle the members of the Beatles when they realized that the Rolling Stones made far more money from selling less records than they did.

Decca was also to sign up the Beatles' former drummer **Pete Best**, and Ringo Starr's former group, **Rory Storm & the Hurricanes**, but didn't have success with either of them.

Epstein was also to deal with Decca and signed up the Big Three to them. Decca issued a number of records by other Mersey Beat acts, including Freddie Starr & the Midnighters, **Lee Curtis** and **Beryl Marsden**, but didn't have much success with them. It's interesting to note that the only non-Epstein group from Liverpool to reach No. 1 was the **Searchers**. The media were firmly locked in on Epstein and his stable, who received the lion's share of the media attention and promotion during the 1963–64 period.

● Dee Time

Also known as 'The Simon Dee Show'. Simon Dee, a tall fair-haired disc jockey who had made his name on pirate radio in the mid-sixties, had been given his own television chat show by the BBC. It was a great success but for some reason, once the series ended, Dee was unable to find any further work and, apart from one or two short-term jobs has remained unemployed ever since. His show was cheerful and the choice of guests well considered.

On 20 July 1968, **Jane Asher** appeared on the show; at that time her long romance with Paul McCartney had

imon Dee, host of 'Dee Time', with a beauty queen. *Mersey Beat* Archives)

ırgely overshadowed her career as an actress. She asually announced that her seven-month engagement and ve-year romance was over. It was a great shock to the any fans who had seen them as an ideal couple – the andsome Beatle and the beautiful and talented actress.

Paul's brother **Mike** appeared on 'Dee Time' on 4 ovember 1967 with his group the Scaffold, performing eir hit 'Thank U Very Much'.

When he was a disc jockey with Radio Caroline, Dee sited the Beatles on 6 April 1965 during the filming of *elp!* at **Twickenham Studios** and during a break in lming presented them with the Radio Caroline Bell ward.

● Defeat Of The Dog, The

'hen Paul began his romance with **Jane Asher**, his tistic and creative talents were stretched. The two ecame very interested in the arts and although John ennon is the Beatle most associated with experimenting ith avant-garde films, it was actually Paul who first perimented with this form of artistic expression.

In 1966 he made two avant-garde films, *The Defeat Of e Dog* and *The Next Spring Then*.

Paul screened the films for journalist Patrick Skene Catlin and they were mentioned in his article about Paul which appeared in *Punch* magazine on 23 November 1966.

Catlin commented: 'They were not like ordinary people's home movies. There were over-exposures, double exposures, blinding orange lights, quick cuts from professional wrestling to a crowded car-park to a close-up of a television weather map. There were long still shots of a grey cloudy sky and a wet, grey pavement, jumping Chinese ivory carvings and affectionate slow-motion studies of his sheepdog Martha and his cat. The accompanying music, on a record player and faultlessly synchronized, was by the **Modern Jazz Quartet** and Bach.'

● Delaney, Patrick

A former member of the Guards, Patrick, more familiarly known as 'Paddy', joined the Liverpool Parks Police and later became a doorman at the **Locarno** and **Grafton** ballrooms in West Derby Road, Liverpool. In 1959 he was asked if he would work on the **Cavern** door one night.

Pat Delaney, former Cavern doorman, talks to Virginia Harry.

Believing it to be a proper club, he turned up in a dinner-suit with matching tie and cummerbund. He then became the regular doorman at the Cavern until the venue closed, spending a total of seven years working for the club.

When **Ray McFall** originally engaged him he told Paddy that there were fights going on almost every night as a group of hooligans had virtually taken control of the club. Paddy agreed to take on the job for one pound per night if he could have some other men to help him. He soon cleaned up the place.

Paddy became a friend of the Beatles and often chatted with them at the door, following a few incidents in which he initially almost stopped them from entering because of their appearance. For a time he also worked for ***Mersey Beat***, helping to deliver copies locally.

His memories of the years he served at the Cavern, written in a manuscript 'The Best Of Cellars', remain unpublished.

● Delfont, Bernard

In the sixties, together with his brothers **Lew** and Leslie Grade, Delfont was part of the triumvirate which virtually controlled British show business. Among the ventures under Delfont's control was the annual Royal Variety Show. Delfont was to book the Beatles for the show on 4 November 1963, saying that his ten-year-old daughter had recommended the group. When he sent the list of artists, with the Beatles' name on it, to Buckingham Palace for approval, there was no objection.

Delfont also ran a large management and agency group and Brian Epstein had several meetings with him, some of them in the South of France, to discuss Delfont purchasing **NEMS** and the Beatles. Eventually, Delfont offered Brian £150,000 in exchange for 50 per cent of Brian's companies. Epstein seriously considered the offer but when he mentioned it to the Beatles, John Lennon wouldn't hear of it and said that the group would break up if he tried to sell them. Epstein later leased the **Saville Theatre** from Delfont.

For his services to charity, the entertainments industry and the Royal Variety Show, Delfont was given a peerage and became Lord Delfont. He also became Chairman of a vast entertainment group called First Leisure.

● De Montfort Hall, *Granville Road, Leicester*

The major concert venue in Leicester. The Beatles appeared there for the first time on the last date of their **Tommy Roe/Chris Montez** tour on 31 March 1963. Their second appearance took place there on 1 December 1963 during the group's autumn tour of the UK. Their third and final appearance at the De Montfort Hall was the second date of their winter tour of Britain on 10 October 1964.

● Denver, Karl

Leader of the Karl Denver Trio, who were the resident group on the BBC radio series **'Side By Side'**. Denver had the Beatles as his guests on the programme on three occasions in 1963. The theme tune 'Side By Side' was recorded by the Beatles and the Karl Denver Trio together and used as the programme's signature tune.

Denver was born in Scotland in 1934 and his real name was Angus Mackenzie. He lived in Nashville for three years before returning to Britain, where he was discovered by Jack Good and had a series of eleven chart hits between 1961 and 1964, including 'Marcheta', 'Wimoweh' and 'Still'. Jack Good also booked the Karl Denver Trio to appear on the special Beatles edition of **'Shindig'**.

● Desert Island Discs

This radio show became virtually a British institution and proved to be one of the most durable BBC radio programmes; it is still running today. It was conceived by Roy Plomley in 1941. Plomley died in 1985, aged 71 having celebrated over 40 years of a programme he'd originally thought would run as a series of six.

The basic idea of the programme presented a 'castaway who was marooned in the BBC studio with Mr Plomley and selected eight record choices and one book, plus a single luxury which they would take with them on a desert island.

To be a guest on the programme was considered quite prestigious, although there were one or two refusals, most notably George Bernard Shaw and Lord Olivier – and also the Beatles. Plomley wanted all four members of the Beatles to appear on a special edition of Desert Island Discs, but Brian Epstein turned him down.

Almost twenty years later, Plomley did collar himself Beatle when he invited Paul McCartney to be the star of the programme's 40th anniversary on Saturday, 30 January 1982. Paul was the 1,629th castaway.

The early years rarely featured popular records. The emergence of the Beatles naturally changed this state of affairs and, although the majority of selections remained classical, a regular stream of popular discs were played due to the pioneering breakthrough of the **Fab Four.** In fact, since the Beatles made their 'Desert Island' debut on 25 May 1964 with 'She Loves You', a selection by disc jockey **David Jacobs**, they became the most popular choice outside the circle of classical music.

The top five most popular Beatles numbers over th

years in which Plomley hosted the programme have been: (1) 'Yesterday'/'Penny Lane' (both selected on seven occasions) (3) 'Eleanor Rigby' (4) 'Help!' (5) 'When I'm Sixty-Four'.

Although Epstein refused to allow an all-Beatles edition of 'Desert Island Discs', he did appear on the programme himself on 30 November 1964.

Epstein's selections were: 'All My Loving', performed by the George Martin Orchestra; Bach, Brandenburg Concerto No. 5 in D Major by the Stuttgart Chamber Orchestra conducted by Mumchiner; 'Kilimanjaro' by the Quartette Tres Bien; 'She's A Woman' by the Beatles; Symphony No. 2 by Sibelius performed by the Orchestre de la Suisse; Romande, conducted by Ansermet; 'Odun De! Odun De!' (Happy New Year) performed by the Michael Olatunji Ensemble; Bruch's Violin Concerto No. 1 in G Minor by the Philadelphia Orchestra; and Fiesta de Jerex by Carmen Amaya. Brian's book selection was Thomas Mestron's *Elected Silence* and his luxury: painting equipment.

Brian had been preceded on the programme by his protégé **Cilla Black** on 24 August of that year and her first selection was 'My Yiddishe Momme' by Sophie Tucker. She also picked Rita Moreno and George Chakiris performing 'America' from Bernstein and Sondheim's *West Side Story* musical. Her other choices included her own version of 'Anyone Who Had A Heart'; 'Love Me Do' by the Beatles; 'Priscilla' by Frankie Vaughan; Dinah Washington singing 'September In The Rain'; the Henry Mancini Orchestra and Chorus performing 'Fugue in D Minor' by Bach. Cilla's book choice was Lewis Carroll's *Alice In Wonderland* and her luxury: Leonardo Da Vinci's 'Mona Lisa'.

Film-maker **Richard Lester** was a castaway on 30 September 1969 and he opened with 'The Knack', the theme from the film soundtrack of his first critically acclaimed feature. His classical choices were: Satie, 'Three Gymnopedies (No. 1)' by the Concert Arts Orchestra conducted by Golschmann; Ravel's Piano Concerto in G, performed by Leonard Bernstein on piano and also conducting the Columbia Symphony Orchestra; Doina Oltului (Dubre Constantin Pan Pipes) by the United Folk Orchestra and Copland's Symphony No. 3 performed by the Minneapolis Symphony Orchestra, conducted by Dorati. On a more popular note were Ray Charles' version of 'Yesterday', Dylan's 'The Times They Are A-Changing' and 'Son Of Suzy Creamcheese' by the Mothers of Invention. His book selection was *The Guinness Book Of Records* and his luxury: a harp.

Surprisingly, George Martin didn't become a castaway until 31 July 1982.

Martin opened with Judy Garland and Mickey Rooney performing Rodgers & Hart's 'Good Morning' from the film *Babes In Arms*. His classical choices were: 'Prélude à l'après-midi d'un faune' performed by Peter Lloyd on flute and the London Symphony Orchestra conducted by Andre Previn; Cimarosa's 'Concerto in C Minor for Oboe and Strings'; Heinz Holliger's 'Bamberg Symphony'; and Bach's 'St Matthew Passion' performed by the Berlin Philharmonic Orchestra conducted by Herbert von Karajan. He also picked Michael Flanders and Donald Swann (who were originally one of his recording acts) performing 'A Song Of Patriotic Prejudice' from the revue *At The Drop Of A Hat* and the Beatles with 'Here, There and Everywhere'. His desert island book was *A Manual on Practical Engineering* and his luxury: a clavichord.

Following the David Jacobs appearance, here is a list of the castaways from July 1964 to February 1983 who selected numbers composed (and recorded – unless indicated otherwise) by the Beatles. The list is in chronological order but omits the guests already mentioned above.

DAVID WYNNE. The sculptor who was to create a series of bronze busts of the Beatles. 20 July 1964. 'I Saw Her Standing There'.

LAVINIA YOUNG. At the time she was Matron of Westminster Hospital. 21 December 1964. 'She Loves You'.

RITA TUSHINGHAM. Liverpool actress. 20 September 1965. 'Help!'

ROBERT CARRIER. Gourmet. 4 October 1965. 'Help!'

ADELE LEIGH. Singer. 11 October 1965. 'Help!'

TOMMY SIMPSON. The World Cycling Champion at the time. 31 January 1966. 'Yesterday' (sung by Matt Munro).

G. O. NICKALLS. The oarsman. 21 March 1966. 'All My Loving'.

HENRY COOPER. Boxing celebrity. 16 May 1966. 'Help!'

MORECAMBE & WISE. Renowned comedy duo who had the Beatles as their guests on some of their shows. 29 August 1966. 'Yesterday'.

DAVID HICKS. Interior decorator. 5 September 1966. 'A Hard Day's Night' (sung by Keely Smith).

ARNOLD WESKER. Playwright. 7 November 1966. 'Eleanor Rigby'.

BARRY BRIGGS. World Speedway Champion. 13 March 1967. 'And I Love Him' (sung by Esther Phillips, who was to appear on Granada TV's 'The Music of Lennon & McCartney').

DICK FRANCIS. Thriller writer. 27 March 1967. 'I Want To Hold Your Hand' (the Boston Pops Orchestra, conducted by Arthur Fiedler).

DEREK NIMMO. Liverpool-born comedy actor. 8 May 1967. 'Penny Lane'.

RICHARD BRIERS. Comedy actor. 21 August 1967. 'Within You, Without You' (the programme wrongly credited the number as a Lennon & McCartney composition – it had actually been written by George Harrison).

JOHN OGDON. Concert pianist. 4 September 1967. 'Lucy In The Sky With Diamonds'.

IRENE WORTH. The comedy actress who, during her appearance on 18 November 1967, didn't pick a Beatles number, but for her luxury settled for 'The Beatles' new television show'.

ANN MALLALIEU. First woman President of the Cambridge Union. 30 December 1967. 'Twist And Shout'.

ROSALIND FULLER. Actress. 2 March 1968. 'Fool On The Hill'.

MARGARET DRABBLE. Novelist. 6 May 1968. 'With A Little Help From My Friends'.

TREVOR NUNN. Theatre director, and at the time the artistic director of the Royal Shakespeare Company. 20 May 1968. 'Penny Lane'.

BARBARA MURRAY. Actress. 21 October 1968. 'If I Fell'.

ARTHUR ASKEY. Liverpool comedian who met the Beatles on several occasions and who made three 'Desert Island Discs' appearances. 23 December 1968. 'All My Loving'.

NICOLAI GEDDA. Tenor. 21 May 1969. 'Sgt Pepper's Lonely Hearts Club Band'.

KENNETH MORE. Actor. 30 June 1969. 'And I Love Him' (sung by Esther Phillips).

RACHEL HAYHOE. Then captain of the English women's test cricket team. 28 July 1969. 'Hey Jude'.

HERMIONE GINGOLD. Comedy actress. 18 August 1969. 'Eleanor Rigby'.

OLIVIA MANNING. Novelist. 25 August 1969. 'Penny Lane'.

ANTHONY GREY. Foreign correspondent. 1 November 1969. 'She's Leaving Home'.

FYFE ROBERTSON. TV reporter. 3 February 1970. 'Come Together'.

ROBIN KNOX-JOHNSON. Solo round-the-world yachtsman 4 July 1970. 'All You Need Is Love'.

DICK EMERY. Television comedian. 29 August 1970 'And I Love Her' (the Boston Pops Orchestra conducted by Arthur Fiedler).

LYNN REDGRAVE. Actress. 10 October 1970. 'Penny Lane'.

LAURIE LEE. Author. 30 January 1971. 'Isn't It A Pity (by George Harrison).

HARVEY SMITH. Showjumper. 13 February 1971. 'The Fool On The Hill' (by Shirley Bassey).

RAVI SHANKAR. Sitar player who became associated with George Harrison. 27 January 1971. 'My Sweet Lord' (by George Harrison).

CLODAGH ROGERS. Singer. 27 March 1971. 'Martha My Dear'.

GEOFF BOYCOTT. Cricketer. 10 April 1971. 'Yesterday'.

CLIVE DUNN. Comedy actor. 19 June 1971. 'Something'.

KENNETH ALLSOP. Broadcaster. 18 September 1971 'Hey Jude'.

MOLLIE LEE. 'Woman's Hour' broadcaster. 2. September 1971. 'Eleanor Rigby'.

IVY BENSON. Danceband leader. 16 October 1971 'Can't Buy Me Love'.

NICOLETTE MILNES-WALKER. Solo sailor. 13 November 1971. 'With A Little Help From My Friends'.

DAVID STOREY. Novelist. 11 March 1972. 'A Day In The Life' (the Beatles) and 'God' (John Lennon).

JOAN BAKEWELL. TV interviewer. 13 May 1972. 'Here Comes The Sun'.

JIMMY TARBUCK. Liverpool comedian and a friend of the group. 26 August 1972. 'This Boy' (the Beatles) and 'My Sweet Lord' (George Harrison).

LESLIE THOMAS. Novelist. 24 February 1973. 'Penny Lane'.

GEORGE MELLY. Liverpool-born jazz singer. 17 March 1973. 'Sgt Pepper's Lonely Hearts Club Band'.

JOHN HUSTON. Film director. 12 May 1973. 'Yellow Submarine'.

JOE BUGNER. Boxer. 9 June 1973. 'The Long And Winding Road'.

GARETH EDWARDS. At the time the captain of the Welsh

rugby team. 9 December 1973. 'Paperback Writer'.

MAUREEN O'SULLIVAN. Actress mother of Mia and Prudence Farrow. 2 March 1974. 'Dear Prudence'.

DODIE SMITH. Playwright. 17 August 1974. 'Being For The Benefit Of Mr Kite'.

GRAHAM HILL. Racing driver. 7 September 1974. 'Penny Lane'.

BRUCE TULLOH. Long-distance runner. 23 November 1974. 'Penny Lane'.

JOHN CONTEH. Liverpool boxer who was World Light Heavyweight Champion at the time. He also appeared on the cover of the *Band On The Run* album. 1 March 1975. 'Band On The Run' (Paul McCartney) and 'A Day In The Life' (the Beatles).

PATRICIA HAYES. Actress. 19 April 1975. 'Eleanor Rigby'.

SAMMY CAHN. American songwriter. 14 June 1975. 'Here, There and Everywhere' (Petula Clark).

LYNN SEYMOUR. Ballerina. 7 February 1976. 'A Day In The Life'.

CHARLOTTE RAMPLING. Actress. 3 April 1976. 'A Day In The Life'.

DR CHRISTIAN BARNARD. Heart surgeon. 17 April 1976. 'When I'm Sixty-Four'.

DOUGLAS FAIRBANKS JR. Actor. 29 May 1976. 'Strawberry Fields Forever'.

ALAN PASCOE. Hurdler. 10 July 1976. 'Hey Jude' (the Beatles) and 'Lucy In The Sky With Diamonds' (Elton John).

MELVYN BRAGG. Broadcaster who was to present Paul McCartney twice on his 'South Bank' television programme. 7 August 1976. 'My Sweet Lord' (George Harrison).

JAMES GALWAY. Flautist. 14 August 1976. 'Octopus's Garden'.

PENELOPE KEITH. Actress. 21 August 1976. 'All You Need Is Love'.

DAVID WILKIE. Swimmer. 18 September 1976. 'Instant Karma' (the Plastic Ono Band).

FRANK MUIR. Comedy writer. 2 October 1976. 'Let It Be'.

MARY MARTIN. Singer. 26 March 1977. 'Let 'Em In' (Paul McCartney).

PEGGY LEE. Singer. 14 May 1977. 'The Long and Winding Road'.

MIRELLA FRENI. Soprano. 11 June 1977. 'Michelle'.

SHIRLEY CONRAN. Author. 16 July 1977. 'When I'm Sixty-Four'.

BILLY CONNOLLY. Scottish comedian. 'Imagine' (John Lennon) and 'Across The Universe' (the Beatles).

DEBORAH KERR. Actress. 20 August 1977. 'The Fool On The Hill' (Sergio Mendes and Brasil '77).

BARRY SHEENE. Motorcycle champion. 15 October 1977. 'Crackerbox Palace' (George Harrison).

WAYNE SLEEP. Dancer. 29 October 1977. 'All You Need Is Love'.

SPIKE MILLIGAN. Comedian. 4 February 1978. 'Yesterday'.

ITZHAK PERLMAN. Violinist. 29 April 1978. 'I'm Looking Through You'.

CHARLES AZNAVOUR. Singer. 6 May 1978. 'Eleanor Rigby'.

TENNESSEE WILLIAMS. Playwright. 9 September 1978. 'A Day In The Life'.

CATHY BERNERIAN. Singer. 16 September 1978. 'Eleanor Rigby'.

PETER BLAKE. The artist who designed the *Sgt Pepper* sleeve. 12 May 1979. 'Sgt Pepper's Lonely Hearts Club Band'.

EVAN HUNTER. Author of *The Blackboard Jungle*, more familiarly known by his pen name Ed McBain. 23 June 1979. 'Something'.

BARRY NORMAN. Broadcaster. 25 August 1979. 'When I'm Sixty-Four'.

MICHAEL PALIN. Actor and ex-Monty Python member. 17 November 1979. 'Things We Said Today'.

DONALD PLEASENCE. The actor, who also penned 'Scouse The Mouse'. 29 March 1980. 'A Day In The Life' (the Beatles) and 'Scouse The Mouse' (Ringo Starr).

NATALIE WOOD. Actress. 10 May 1980. 'Imagine' (John Lennon).

TRISTAN JONES. Nautical writer. 23 August 1980. 'Hello, Goodbye'.

RENATO SCOTTO. Soprano. 30 August 1980. 'Yesterday'.

ARTHUR ASKEY. Fourth appearance. 20 December 1980. 'Yesterday'.

JEFFREY ARCHER. Author. 31 January 1981. 'Help!'

GARY GLITTER. Rock star. 4 April 1981. 'Startin' Over' (John Lennon).

STEWART GRANGER. Actor. 25 April 1981. 'Yesterday'.

TERRY HANDS. Theatrical producer. 8 August 1981. 'Michelle'.

James Clavell. Author. 14 November 1981. 'A Hard Day's Night'.

Trevor Brooking. Soccer player. 2 January 1982. 'Let It Be'.

Jenny Agutter. Actress. 1 May 1982. 'Blackbird' (Paul McCartney).

Sir Anton Dolin. Choreographer. 12 June 1982. 'Ebony And Ivory' (Paul McCartney and Stevie Wonder).

Eric Newby. Travel writer. 18 June 1982. 'When I'm Sixty-Four'.

Tim Severin. Explorer. 29 January 1983. 'Mull Of Kintyre' (Paul McCartney).

Zandra Rhodes. Fashion designer. 12 February 1983. 'Strawberry Fields Forever'.

There was a certain amount of drama surrounding Paul's appearance. On his way to the broadcast he had a tussle with a photographer – and during the broadcast he made some comments relating to **Larry Parnes**, and the former impresario subsequently sued him.

Paul's selections were: 'Heartbreak Hotel', **Elvis Presley**; 'Sweet Little Sixteen', **Chuck Berry**; 'Courtly Dances From Gloriana', the Julian Bream Consort; 'Be-Bop-A-Lula', **Gene Vincent**; 'Searchin'', the Coasters; 'Tutti Frutti', **Little Richard**; 'Walking In The Park With Eloise', the Country Hams; and 'Beautiful Boy', John Lennon. His book was *Linda's Pictures* and his luxury: a guitar.

The castaways are also asked to identify the record they would choose if they were only allowed a single selection, and Paul plumped for John's 'Beautiful Boy'.

● DeShannon, Jackie

Kentucky-born singer-songwriter, real name Sharon Myers, who was booked as a support act on the Beatles' first tour of America in the autumn of 1964.

Jackie, who at the time had just charted with 'When You Walk In The Room', was engaged to appear on the concert tour for $1,250 per week.

Liverpool's the **Searchers** were to cover 'When You Walk In The Room', which brought them a No. 3 chart placing in Britain. Jackie herself never had a chart hit in Britain as a singer. In 1969 she had a million-seller in America with her song 'Put A Little Love In Your Heart'.

● Devil In Her Heart

Number, originally called '(There's A) Devil In Her Heart' by female vocal group the Donays in 1962. Penned by Richard B. Drapkin, the record wasn't a major hit for the Donays, but the Beatles adapted the number and included it in their stage act with George Harrison on lead vocals. They recorded the number on Thursday, 18 July 1963, and it was included on their *With The Beatles* album. It was also included on their American release *The Beatles' Second Album*.

● Devlin, Johnny

Singer who appeared with the Beatles on their tour of Australia and New Zealand. Devlin was a rock 'n' roller from New Zealand who had begun singing in 1958 and received the first domestic Gold Disc awarded in that country. He moved to Australia and settled in Sydney where he had seven hit records within a two-year period. Shortly before the Beatles tour he had a new chart hit 'Stomp The Tumbarumba'.

As an A&R man for RCA Records, Devlin had been trying to get another singer a place on the bill, but it was decided that he'd be an ideal attraction himself, being popular in both Australia and New Zealand. He managed to gain immediate press publicity by insuring himself against injury on tour – for £25,000!

After instrumental group the **Phantoms** opened the show, Devlin was next on the bill, with backing from the Phantoms. His repertoire consisted of fifties rock 'n' roll numbers and he bought himself a black leather suit for the tour which led one critic to describe him as 'an overstuffed suitcase'. Another commented that: 'He looked and behaved like a skin diver with St Vitus Dance.' Not all reviews were as ungallant. Charles Higham in the *Bulletin* newspaper wrote: 'Introduced by a flabby compere named **Alan Field**, Johnny Devlin looked fat, well past the dreaded bourne of 30, and far from the condition that once won him the title of Mr West Coast of New Zealand. Nevertheless he was, for my money, unquestionably the best performer of the evening. Clad in pitch-black leather from toe to tippet, he looked at first like an animated suitcase; then he unzipped, screamed, shook from head to toe and turned into a blackberry jelly with legs.'

Backstage at the **Sydney Stadium**, Devlin co-wrote a pop song with Paul McCartney called 'Won't You Be My Baby'. Paul insisted that Johnny take all the credit and it became his first single after the tour.

Devlin continued to perform successfully in Australia for many years after the amazing tour.

Devon, Keith

A Director of the **Bernard Delfont** Agency. In 1963 Devon was one of the organizers, along with Delfont, of the Royal Variety Show and the Beatles were booked to appear that year. During discussions, Devon had been given the opportunity of representing the Beatles. However, when Epstein discussed the deal with him in Devon's office, Brian told him that he wanted £1,000 a week for the group. Devon said, 'You must be crazy! I think you've got more nerve than I have. You'd better come and sit in my chair!' He sent Epstein away, passing up the opportunity of representing the Beatles.

Later, when Beatlemania grew even bigger, Devon said, 'You can't win them all!'

At least, these are the details related by Rita Grade Freeman, sister of **Bernard Delfont** and **Lew** and Leslie Grade, in her book *My Fabulous Brothers*.

A similar story, with variations, is to be found in Roy Moseley's autobiography *My Stars And Other Friends*. Moseley had originally met Brian Epstein when they had both worked at **Ashcroft and Daws** paperback bookshop in Charing Cross Road. A few years later, Moseley was working for Keith Devon at Bernard Delfont's office when they received a call regarding one of their clients, Jet Harris, who was currently touring with **Little Richard**. When the tour reached Liverpool, Harris complained that his act had been cut down to five minutes by a local man who had booked the show at the **Empire Theatre, Liverpool** and had placed his own group the Beatles on the bill.

Moseley contacted Brian and arranged for him to come to London for an appointment with his boss, Devon.

'They confronted each other across Keith Devon's imposing desk. "How much do you think you should get per week for this group, the Beatles?" said Mr Devon. "About £600," Brian Epstein told him. "If you think you can get £600 a week for the Beatles, you should be sitting here, not me," Keith Devon said. And that's how the Delfont Organisation lost the Beatles.'

Dexter Jr, David

Dave Dexter was a **Capitol Records** A&R executive based in Hollywood. Each month he would receive a cardboard container with a selection of records issued by **EMI** in Britain. Dexter had once taken a chance by selecting a **Cliff Richard** record which, despite promotion, failed to make an impact on the American market and the general opinion was that British discs wouldn't be successful in the US. In 1962 one of the records included in the monthly box was 'Love Me Do'. Other Beatles singles were passed over to Dexter as they were released in the UK, but were turned down.

Dexter had formerly been a journalist on *Downbeat*, the jazz magazine, and a jazz producer.

EMI, embarrassed by their major act being constantly turned down by their American subsidiary, decided to pull some strings. L. G. Wood, an executive at the Manchester Square offices in London, contacted his Capitol counterpart Lloyd Dunn to plead the case for 'I Want To Hold Your Hand'. Dunn told Dexter to put it on their schedule. Dexter told him that he'd already decided to do so. He mentioned that while he'd been at the London offices of EMI during his annual visit there, the disc had been brought to his attention by **Tony Palmer** and he said that the first four bars of the record convinced him they had a hit.

Dexter was to process the Beatles' records for the American market and was also involved in compiling Beatles albums for Capitol, including the deluxe souvenir *Help!* album. He wrote a book, *Playback*, and Chapter 19 deals with his work for the Beatles.

He retired from Capitol Records in 1974 and died from a heart attack on 19 April 1991 in Sherman Oaks, California. He was 74 years old.

Dietrich, Marlene

The legendary Hollywood star who was born in Germany in 1904. Her many films included *The Blue Angel*, *Destry Rides Again*, *Stage Fright*, *No Highway*, *Rancho Notorious*, *Witness For The Prosecution* and *Judgement At Nuremberg*.

Dietrich embarked on a second career as an international cabaret star and on 4 November 1963 appeared on the Royal Variety Show with the Beatles. This took place at the **Prince of Wales Theatre** in London and was attended by the Queen Mother, Princess Margaret and Lord Snowdon.

When asked how she felt about the group, she said, 'The Beatles? I thought they were wonderful – who doesn't?'

In his book, *Dietrich: The Story Of A Star*, author Leslie Frewin pointed out that Dietrich was in great form when she rehearsed with the group and was philosophical in recognizing that the majority of those who had paid £50,000 to the Variety Artists Benevolent Fund largely wanted to see the Beatles. She didn't mind and lined up with them at rehearsals and agreed to be photographed.

While admitting that the Beatles stole the show, Frewin

The legendary Marlene Dietrich appeared with the Beatles on the Royal Variety Show. (National Film Archives)

pointed out the figures analysed from the television ratings when the show was screened on 10 November. It was discovered that when the Beatles were appearing 2,394,000 people in the London area were viewing, but when Dietrich appeared, the number shot up to 2,525,000, although it was pointed out that earlier viewers might hav been watching an Ingrid Bergman film on the othe channel while the Beatles were on, only to switch ove when the film ended.

The Beatles chose Marlene as one of the 68 figures o the cover of their *Sgt Pepper's Lonely Hearts Club Ban* album, where she is nicely positioned on the front right hand side, close to the Beatles themselves.

There was another anecdote concerning the Roya Variety Show which put a different slant on th relationship between Marlene and the Beatles. In the boo *My Fabulous Brothers* by Rita Grade Freeman it says ther were difficulties between the Beatles and Marlene durin rehearsals.

Comedian Dickie Henderson commented, 'That lady i without doubt one of the all-time great superstars, bu she's also one of the all-time great pains in the backside.'

Rita Freeman observed: 'She went on behavin petulantly and selfishly. Then when she had finished a long last, a group of photographers swept down to the fro stalls. "Not now, darlings!" she said to them, "come bac in an hour when I've got my make-up on." She then le the stage and four very unassuming young men began the rehearsal. They were playing guitars and singing, and a the cameras flashed them for the next 15 minutes. By th time Marlene returned, now resplendent in a sequine gown and wearing full make-up, there wasn't photographer in sight – those four young men who ha reaped all the publicity were the Beatles, invited to appe in their first Royal show!'

Marlene Dietrich died in Paris, May 1992.

● Dig A Pony

Track recorded at **Apple Studios** on 22 January 1969 part of the ill-fated 'Get Back' sessions. The John Lenno composition was first heard by the public when it wa included among the songs the Beatles sang at their Appl rooftop session on 30 January 1969. The track wa included on the *Let It Be* album and **Billy Preston** playe electric piano.

Phil Spector had worked on the tapes, deleting a introduction in which John and Paul say, 'All I want is . . In fact, the number was originally going to be called 'All Want Is You'.

John wasn't quite happy with the song and onc described it as 'another piece of garbage'.

Dig It

Number featured on the *Let It Be* album. The song credits read Lennon/McCartney/Harrison/Starr, but although all members contributed to the composition, it was mainly written by John, who sings lead vocals. Heard in the background is Paul's six-year-old stepdaughter **Heather** and the lyrics give namechecks to various people and institutions, including singers Doris Day and BB King, Manchester United soccer chief Matt Busby and the BBC and CIA.

The group recorded two versions of the number; the second, which was recorded on Sunday, 26 January, is the one used on the album, although in severely truncated form. One piece from the first version was tacked onto the end of the number, when John announces, 'That was "Can You Dig It" by Georgie Wood. Now we'd like to do "Hark The Angels Come".' Incidentally, 'Wee' Georgie Wood was a show business midget who appeared on variety bills, pantomimes and radio comedy shows.

DiLello, Richard

A New Yorker, born 28 September 1945, who became acquainted with **Derek Taylor** in San Francisco. He arrived in Britain in November 1967, then left for North Africa for four months before returning to London and asking Taylor for a job. Derek was able to provide him with a post as an assistant press officer to himself at Apple.

Richard became known as 'the House Hippie', and he took on the task of photographer and chronicler of the Apple days as he documented the day-to-day life in the **Savile Row** building.

He eventually rose to be Chief Press Officer, a post which lasted only a short time. Journalist **Anne Nightingale** ran a story describing a crumbling Apple empire, which provided **Allen Klein** with the ammunition he needed in order to sack him.

DiLello's amusing account of his Apple escapades was published in book form as *The Longest Cocktail Party* in 1973.

He is now a TV and movie scriptwriter in Los Angeles.

147 Dinas Lane, Huyton, Liverpool L36

Address of Paul McCartney's auntie Jin. On 18 June 1963 it was the site of Paul's eventful 21st birthday party.

It was decided to hold the party there because **Jim McCartney** felt that too many fans knew the **Forthlin Road** address and it would be impossible to hold the function there.

A marquee was erected in the back garden and the host of guests included Brian Epstein, **Mike McCartney**, John and **Cynthia**, Ringo and **Maureen**, George, the **Fourmost**, the Scaffold, the **Shadows**, **Billy J. Kramer** and disc jockey **Bob Wooler**.

John got drunk and took exception to a remark Wooler made to him relating to John's recent holiday in Spain with Brian Epstein, intimating that John was homosexual. John beat him so severely he had to be pulled off by Billy Kramer and members of the Fourmost. John then attacked a girl.

The next day when asked to apologize, John was unrepentent and said, 'He called me a queer.' An apology was sent on his behalf and a short item about the incident appeared on the back page of the *Daily Mirror*, written by **Don Short**.

Discs A-Go-Go

A local television pop programme produced by the regional TV station TWW. The Beatles appeared live on the programme, recorded at the company's Bristol studio, on 3 December 1962.

Dizzy Miss Lizzy

A song written and recorded by Larry Williams in 1958. It was a number very popular with Liverpool groups and the Beatles included it in their repertoire in 1960 while Mersey Beat band the **Escorts** issued it as a single in 1964.

John took over on solo vocal and the Beatles performed it on their last BBC radio recording, 'Ticket To Ride', in June 1965. The same year it was included on their *Help!* album and it later surfaced on *The Beatles Collection*, *Rock And Roll Music* and the American *Beatles V* album.

Dodd, Ken

Popular Liverpool comedian who was also a successful recording artist who had seventeen British chart hits between 1960 and 1975, including 'Love Is Like A Violin', 'Happiness' and 'Tears'.

The Beatles appeared on a charity show at the Albany Theatre, Maghull, with Dodd topping the bill on 15 October 1961, and reports suggest he wasn't too

Ken Dodd (centre) with the Beatles and Gay Byrne (far left) on Granada TV's 'Scene at 6.30'. (Granada TV)

enthusiastic about their appearance, although it's true that they were out-of-place on a bill of variety artists appearing before local councillors and civic dignitaries.

Fame began to come to both acts at around the same time and during an appearance on the Granada programme, **'Scene At 6.30'**, Ken Dodd joined the Beatles in a humorous dialogue, with Gay Byrne as the referee. They also appeared once on **'The Ken Dodd Show'**, a BBC radio programme, although Dodd's agent turned down the opportunity of booking the group twice as he didn't think they'd last.

When Dodd appeared in pantomime in 1964 he commented, 'When I found out I was doing pantomime in Liverpool, I knew I had to pick out at least one Beatle to do a little impersonation. I picked Ringo, got myself tight trousers and a wig and included it into the show. Fantastic reception! Fantastic! But then Liverpool lads have got to stick together, haven't they?'

● Dodd, Les

Dance promoter based in Wallasey, across the River Mersey from Liverpool on the Wirral, who ran dances for his own company, which he called Paramount Enterprises.

Dodd had been promoting 'strict tempo' ballroom dancing at two venues since 1936, the **Institute, Neston**, in Cheshire, and the **Grosvenor Ballroom, Birkenhead**, but eventually realized that the times were changing and he decided to book some Liverpool rock 'n' roll bands at his regular dances. Through **Allan Williams** he booked the **Silver Beetles** for a series of six Thursday night sessions at the Institute from 2 June 1960 and they also made their debut at his other venue the Grosvenor the same week, on Saturday 4 June. The Grosvenor, however, attracted the wilder teenage element and there were so many rowdy fights that Wallasey Corporation, who'd been leasing the venue to Dodd over the years, cancelled his lease and they last played there on 30 July 1960. They'd been booked for Saturday 6 August, which would have been their tenth appearance at the ballroom, but found that the booking had been cancelled and went to the **Casbah Club** that evening, where they saw **Pete Best** playing with the **Blackjacks**.

● Dodger Stadium, *Los Angeles, California*

The penultimate American concert appearance. It was the biggest single show of the Beatles' final US tour, attended by 45,000 fans at the mammoth baseball stadium on Sunday, 28 August 1966.

The Beatles had difficulty escaping from the arena after the show, but finally managed to get away in an armoured car. The local newspaper reported: 'As the quartet tried to leave by the main gates scores of delirious teenagers climbed over the limousine and it was forced to turn back.

'The Beatles then fled to offices under the grandstand as crowds charged the 151 foot high entrance gates.

'Time and again, police were forced to hit out with their clubs, to keep the fans off the gates.

'Youths then charged the gates with wooden barricades which had been set up to keep the crowds back.

'They hurled sticks and bottles at police until they were finally turned away with a shoulder-to-shoulder charge by officers who cleared a sort of no-man's-land between the crowds and the exit gates.

'Meanwhile, the Beatles, virtually imprisoned beneath the grandstand by fans stampeding from one spot to another in the vast outdoor stadium, made good their escape by armoured car at the opposite end of the field.'

● Doelen Hotel, *Amsterdam, Holland*

Hotel in Amsterdam where the Beatles stayed on the evening of 5 June 1964 during their brief visit to Holland on their world tour.

● Donegan, Lonnie

Arguably, the first major idol John Lennon, Paul McCartney and George Harrison had in common.

Donegan, who took his stage name Lonnie from the American blues singer Lonnie Johnson, virtually created the 'skiffle' phenomenon in Britain following a string of hits which began with 'Rock Island Line' and saw him with ten Top Ten chart entries within an eighteen-month period. The simple three-chord guitar sound, aided by tea-chest bass and washboard, was basic enough and cheap enough for thousands of youngsters throughout Britain to imitate – and it is estimated that at the height of the skiffle boom there were over 5,000 skiffle groups in the country.

Lonnie Donegan, leader of the skiffle boom and early influence on the Beatles. (National Film Archives)

When 'Rock Island Line' hit the charts in 1956, the sixteen-year-old John Lennon couldn't really afford to buy records, but he bought Donegan's 78 rpm disc which, after playing it until it was nearly worn, he sold to **Rod Davis**, who was to join him in the **Quarry Men**. When the group formed, their repertoire comprised a number of Donegan hits, including 'Rock Island Line', 'Midnight Special', 'Railroad Bill', 'The Cumberland Gap', and 'Worried Man Blues'.

When Lonnie Donegan appeared at the **Empire Theatre in Liverpool** a fourteen-year-old Paul McCartney took time off from school to wait outside the theatre one afternoon until he obtained Lonnie's autograph. A younger George Harrison was even more determined. He borrowed enough money from his parents to watch every one of Donegan's Empire shows. He then discovered where the singer was staying and went along to the house and knocked on the door until Lonnie came out and gave him his autograph.

George was to say, 'Lonnie Donegan was the first music star to make a big impression on me. Donegan and skiffle music just seemed made for me.'

Although the group were later to be influenced by a range of American rock 'n' roll stars such as **Carl Perkins**, **Elvis Presley**, **Buddy Holly**, **Chuck Berry**, **Little Richard** and **Gene Vincent**, it was really Donegan, a British musician, who set the ball rolling.

● Donovan

Scots folk singer, born Donovan Leitch on 10 May 1946. He became a friend of the Beatles and wrote a song in tribute to them called 'For John And Paul'. The name was changed to 'Sunshine Superman' when it was released and it reached No. 2 in the British charts in December 1966.

Donovan was also at Rishikesh with the Beatles and he composed 'Hurdy Gurdy Man' before the four Beatles, Beach Boy **Mike Love** and actress **Mia Farrow**. George Harrison immediately added a new verse to the song. Unfortunately, Donovan's record company Pye talked him out of including George's verse on the finished track as they wished releases of singles to be kept to a length of under three minutes. The record reached No. 4 in the British charts.

Paul and George attended Donovan's **Royal Albert Hall** appearance on 15 January 1967 and all four Beatles went to see him on the opening night of his week-long engagement at the **Saville Theatre**, on 24 April 1967.

George Harrison was to give Donovan his first lesson in playing the sitar in January 1967.

During 1968 Paul McCartney made a guest appearance on Donovan's 'Atlantis' single playing tambourine and providing some backing vocals. He'd also dropped into the studio during Donovan's recording of 'Mellow Yellow' and at one point sang the words 'Mellow Yellow'. A fifteen-minute session between the two artists, also from 1968, has been captured on an American bootleg album *No. 3 Abbey Road, NW8*. The interlude was taken from a studio warm-up between Donovan and Paul, and in their book, *The End Of The Beatles*, authors Castleman and Podrazik mention that the two stars sat down together with acoustic guitars and exchanged songs-in-the-works, with Paul offering 'Blackbird' and 'Heather' and Donovan selecting numbers from what eventually became *HMS Donovan*.

● Don't Bother Me

The first George Harrison composition to appear on a Beatles album.

When ***Mersey Beat*** editor Bill Harry met George in Liverpool clubs such as the **Blue Angel** and the Cabin, he pointed out that the first mention of an original Beatles song in *Mersey Beat* was 'Cry For A Shadow', in issue two. This was mainly a George Harrison composition and Harry kept mentioning that George should get down to writing songs himself and not leave everything to John and Paul. It got so that every time George went to a club Harry would ask him if he was writing a song. When George was about to go out one night he felt he might bump into Harry, so he started writing a number which he called 'Don't Bother Me'. In his book ***I. Me. Mine***, George says he completed it in a hotel in Bournemouth when on tour in 1963.

The Beatles began recording the number on Wednesday, 11 September 1963, and it was included on their *With The Beatles* album in November 1963 and on the American *Meet The Beatles* album in January 1964.

● Don't Ever Change

A Gerry Goffin and Carole King number issued as a single by the Crickets in June 1962. The Beatles immediately added it to their repertoire, with George performing the number on stage, although when they included it on their **'Pop Go The Beatles'** radio show on 27 August 1963, John and Paul shared the vocal honours. The group never performed the number for release on record.

● Don't Forbid Me

Pat Boone had a No. 1 hit in America with this song in 1956. The Beatles introduced it into their repertoire in 1960, but had dropped it by the beginning of 1962.

● Don't Let Me Down

Another composition written by John, which he dedicated to **Yoko**. Recordings began during the *Get Back* sessions and the number was issued as the flipside of the 'Get Back' single in April 1969.

Billy Preston played electric piano on the track and it

was one of the numbers performed on the Apple rooftop session and was included in the film *Let It Be*.

The track was included in the compilation albums *The Beatles 1967–1970* and *Hey Jude*.

● Don't Let The Sun Catch You Cryin'

A number which had been recorded by Ray Charles in 1960. The Beatles included the song in their stage repertoire the same year but had dropped the number by the following year. Paul McCartney sang lead vocal. It is a completely different number than 'Don't Let The Sun Catch You Crying', which Liverpool group **Gerry & the Pacemakers** took to No. 6 in the British charts in 1964.

● Don't Pass Me By

Ringo's first self-penned composition to appear on a Beatles album. Ringo had attempted to write numbers before, but his fellow Beatles had always commented that they sounded too much like other tunes. Ringo had been working on this number over a period of time and it became the second song to be recorded for *The Beatles* double album. When recording began, it was dubbed 'Ringo's Tune', then 'This Is Some Friendly' and finally, 'Don't Pass Me By'. Ringo's love of country music came to the fore in this tale of a girl who was late for a date because she was delayed in a minor crash.

Strangely enough, when he began writing the song in 1963 he revealed the fact to the ***New Musical Express***, saying, 'Every time I play it to the lads they just laugh.' But he also mentioned in the interview then that the title was 'Don't Pass Me By'.

He wrote the lyrics, then played the number to the other members of the group during a BBC recording session at the Paris Theatre. He'd hoped it would be an album track which Paul could sing. He was told that the tune was just like a particular 'B' side on a **Jerry Lee Lewis** record.

In addition to playing drums, Ringo played piano and to add to the country feel, violinist **Jack Fallon** was brought in to provide a country fiddle sound.

Commenting on his songwriting efforts to *Music Echo*, he said, 'I usually get a first verse and then I find it impossible to get anywhere else with the song. I can't say, "Now I'm going to write." I just have to be around a guitar or piano and it just comes. Usually, what I do if I'm in the mood is to put the tape on if I've got a tune, and then I play the same tune like a hundred times with different words. Then I take the tape off and get it all typed out and then I pick the lines out that I'll put together.'

● Dooley, Arthur

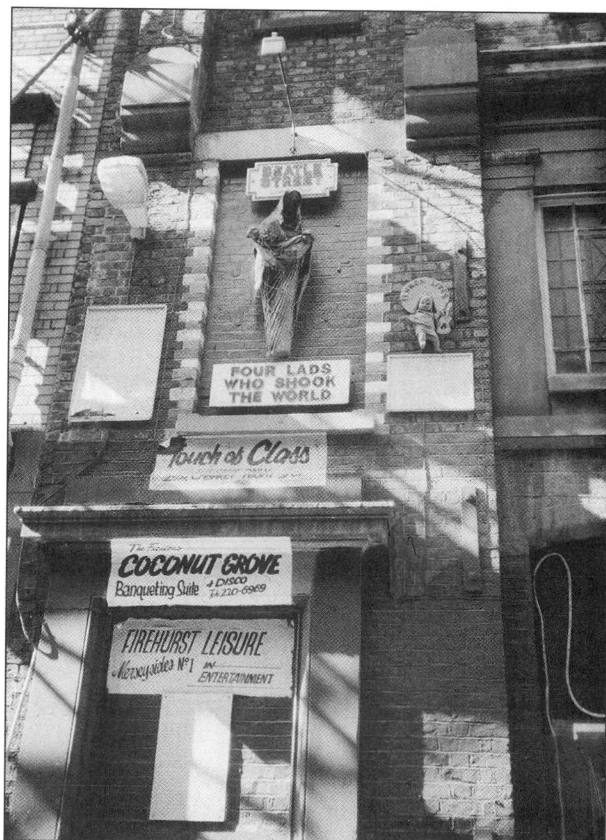

Arthur Dooley's 'Beatles Madonna' in Mathew Street, Liverpool.

A larger-than-life Liverpool sculptor who was the subject of a 'This Is Your Life' programme. **Alun Owen** also used him as the inspiration for a leading character in a TV play.

Arthur was a friend of the Beatles during the period when they all used to frequent clubs such as the **Jacaranda** and the **Blue Angel**.

Dooley created the statue dedicated to the Beatles which was erected in Mathew Street, Liverpool, opposite the site of the **Cavern**, in April 1974.

Disc jockey Peter Prince launched an appeal to raise

£500 to enable Arthur to work on his tribute. £1,300 was raised, the balance being donated to a Liverpool boys' club.

The completed work is fixed high on a wall in Mathew Street and depicts a Madonna holding three babies, a fourth is separated from the group and is flying away. The three represent John, George and Ringo and the solo babe is Paul. Five initials surround the piece: M.J.P.G.R. (the M standing for Madonna). Directly above the piece is a reproduction of a Liverpool street sign: 'Beatle Street, Liverpool 2'.

● Doran, Terry

A former Liverpool car dealer and good friend of Brian Epstein, whom he first met in a Liverpool pub in 1959.

In 1965 Brian decided that as his artists were buying so many cars, it might be a good idea to utilize Terry and the two went into business with Brydor (an abbreviation of their names) Auto, based in Hounslow, Middlesex.

Brian himself bought a silver Bentley convertible and a black Mini-Cooper. Among the other immediate customers were John Lennon, who bought a green Ferrari and a Mini Minor, Ringo Starr, who bought two Minis, a Land-Rover and a Facel Vega, and George Harrison, who bought a Maserati and an E Type Jaguar.

The business had problems when Brian kept borrowing money from the firm to use in his passion for gambling.

Terry was a close friend of the individual Beatles and John in particular and used to visit **Kenwood** regularly.

When Apple was launched, Terry was appointed Managing Director of Apple Music, which was situated in an office above the **Apple Boutique** in Paddington Street. Initially he was aided by **Mike Berry**, who formerly worked for Sparta Music, **Jack Oliver** was his personal assistant and there were two secretaries, Dee Meehan and Carol Paddon. Terry was also appointed manager of the music publishing company's first signing, **Grapefruit**. John Lennon thought up the group's name. In November 1968 Doran pulled the group away from Apple, commenting: 'I like the Beatles as friends, but not as bosses . . . there is too much driftwood at Apple.' Despite the reference to Beatles as bosses, he later became personal assistant to George Harrison for a number of years before returning to his original vocation as a car salesman in a London showroom. He is the 'man from the motor trade' in 'She's Leaving Home'.

● Dorchester Hotel, *Park Lane, London W1*

One of London's most famous and prestigious hotels. The Beatles were invited to the 12th Annual Variety Club Of Great Britain Awards, which took place at the hotel on 19 March 1964. The group received an award as Show Business Personalities of 1963, which was presented to them by Prime Minister Harold Wilson.

On 23 April 1964, the Foyle's Literary Luncheon was held at the hotel and John Lennon was guest of honour. The event paid tribute to his best-selling book *In His Own Write* and although John was expected to give a speech to the gathering of celebrity guests, all he could muster were the words, 'Thank you very much, and God bless you'.

Following the premiere of *A Hard Day's Night* at the **London Pavilion** on 6 July 1964, the Beatles were guests at a private party at the Dorchester. **Brian Jones** and Keith Richards of the **Rolling Stones** turned up, uninvited, but were warmly received by the Beatles, who greeted them with glasses of champagne. Princess Margaret and Lord Snowdon also attended the party.

The Dorchester was also the scene of the post-premier party for *Help!* on 29 July 1965.

On 1 December 1983, Paul, Ringo, George and **Yoko** met at the Dorchester Hotel to discuss the dissolution of Apple. After eleven hours of talk, Yoko told the press, 'We've just been having dinner and a chat with friends.'

● Dorinish

Island in Clew Bay in County Mayo in the West of Ireland. In 1968 John and **Yoko** were visiting Ireland and during their trip they viewed Achill Island with Robert Shaw, the late actor. They had dinner at the Amethyst Hotel in Keel. Then visited Dorinish Island in the company of Ronan O'Rahilly, former head of the pirate radio ship Radio Caroline, who had become a member of the Apple staff. The party stayed at the Great Southern Hotel.

John and Yoko bought the island, which became known as 'Beatle Island'.

Yoko said, 'It was a place where we thought we could escape the pressures and spend some undisturbed time together. We often discussed the idea of building a cottage there. It was so beautiful, so tranquil, yet so isolated it seemed a perfect place to get away from it all. But because of what happened our hopes never came to be.'

Although the couple bought Dorinish, they never

visited it again following their brief picnic. A year later, in November 1969, a group of hippies led by Sid Rawle were given permission by John to set up a commune on the island. However, although the picturesque island was a miniature paradise during the summer months, it underwent a transformation in winter. Icy cold weather and harsh gales from the Atlantic Ocean rendered it almost uninhabitable. The commune, unable to grow much of their own food on the sparsely vegetated island, just couldn't survive such chilling winters and left.

In November 1983, Yoko decided to sell the 25 acres of island with the proceeds going to an Irish orphanage. She commented: 'Putting Dorinish up for sale is an expression of the love we have for Ireland and its people. John would have wished the island to be returned to the Irish. John is still there in spirit. His grandfather was born in Dublin and John always thought of himself as Irish.

'I have been surveying which charity to donate the proceeds to. Children's orphanages have come to mind, but I do not know which one.

'John was always very concerned about the Irish cause. He thought a lot about the Irish people and always associated sympathetically with their suffering. He was aware of how severe the Irish plight was. For John, buying the island was a bit like Jewish people buying a bit of Jerusalem.'

● Dorn, Beno

Master tailor, famous on Merseyside due to his flair for publicity and the inclusion of his photograph in the numerous ads he took in the local papers under the slogan 'The master tailor for impeccable handmade clothes'.

When Brian Epstein decided to smarten up the Beatles' image in 1962 he took the group 'over the water' to Dorn's shop at Grange Road West in Birkenhead. Brian and the Beatles finally decided on the sort of suits which should be worn and Dorn made them grey tweed suits with matching ties for £40 each (but later discounted to £30) which they wore for the first time on stage at the **Heswall Jazz Club** on 24 March 1962 when they played for the Barnston Women's Institute. They also wore the suits for their 'new image' photo session with **Albert Marrion**.

● Dougall, Robert

A noted BBC Television newsreader who was awarded the **MBE** in 1965. In his autobiography *In And Out Of The Box*, published in 1973, he included a chapter called 'The Beatles and Buckingham Palace'.

On the day the Beatles were to be presented with their MBEs Dougall drove through the gates at Buckingham Palace at 10.15 a.m. and noticed that hundreds of youngsters were clinging to the railings and there were police barriers to hold back the crowds. Newspapers ran headlines proclaiming 'Beatlemania At Buck House' and when the group arrived in their black Rolls-Royce, pandemonium raged outside, but perfect decorum reigned inside. The groups for the investiture were then formed into the Orders of Knighthood, with the MBEs, the lowest, coming last. Other categories included CBEs and OBEs. There were 80 MBEs awarded that particular day and all participants were ushered into an anteroom for briefing.

Everyone in the room was obviously interested in the Beatles. Dougall was to comment in his autobiography: 'Four slim young men in dark lounge suits and dark ties. Nothing flamboyant about their dress although Ringo Starr's suit had eight buttons down the front and George Harrison's tailor had given him epaulettes and buttoned pockets. There they stood, all very well behaved, with their longish hair and pale green faces.'

Dougall joined the queue of fellow MBEs asking for autographs: 'They signed away as nice as pie.' Paul McCartney declared the Palace to be a 'keen pad' and John Lennon said he liked the carpets and especially the staff. He had expected them to be Dukes and things but, 'They are all just fellers.' They were all briefed by Lt. Col. Eric Penn, Comptroller from the Lord Chamberlain's office. They were to file into the ballroom in alphabetical order. Nearing the Queen they would come to a Naval officer. They would stop and wait by him until their name was called. They then walked forward, turned left, bowed in front of the Queen and took four steps to the dais where she was standing. They then shook hands with the Queen, engaged in a few words of conversation, took four steps back and then moved to the right.

The signal came for them all to leave the room and they were led down a long corridor with red carpet stretching into the distance. 'Cyril Lord could make a fortune in this place,' said Ringo.

The Beatles were together in a group and led the party because 'Beatles' was the first name in the alphabetical order of the list. As they shuffled down the corridor towards the ballroom, everyone seemed solemn. The

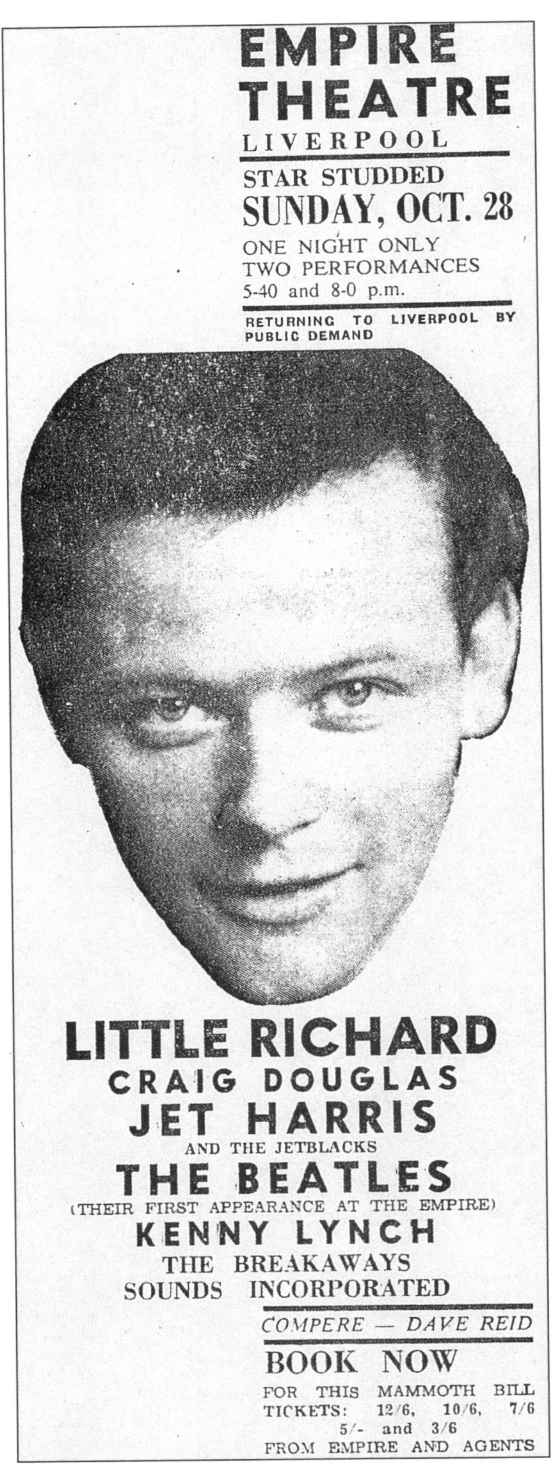

Beatles led the male MBEs and from another room, a host of middle-aged female MBEs emerged and walked ahead of the Beatles. As the Beatles were about to move forward to meet the Queen, together, a member of the party asked them if they were nervous. John replied, 'Yes, we are a bit, but we'll be all right when we go into our routine.'

● Douglas, Craig

British singer who enjoyed a string of chart hits from 1959 with 'A Teenager In Love' straight through to 1963 with 'Town Crier'. His eleven chart entries included the No. 1 hit 'Only Sixteen' plus 'The Heart Of A Teenage Girl' and 'When My Little Girl Is Smiling'. The former milk roundsman was born in Newport, Isle of Wight, in 1941 and made his film debut in *It's Trad, Dad*.

The wholesome singer appeared on the bill at the **Empire Theatre, Liverpool** on Sunday, 23 October 1962. Little Richard was the bill-topper and there were eight acts on the concert, presented by **NEMS Enterprises**.

Trailering the Empire show, ***Mersey Beat*** wrote: 'Recording, films and concerts are everyday parts of Craig Douglas' life, for this nineteen-year-old former tractor driver has several hits to his credit, and has the good looks which make him a natural choice for film parts – he has appeared in *Climb Up The Wall*, *The Painted Smile* and *It's Trad, Dad*.'

Douglas closed the first half of the show and the Beatles became his backing group for this performance which was billed as 'Their first appearance at the Empire'. It was a prestigious event for the Beatles, part of Brian Epstein's plan to build them up by presenting them on major venues on bills with star names. They'd only previously appeared at the Empire in talent competitions as the **Quarry Men**.

● Douglas-Home, Sir Alec

The British Prime Minister and leader of the Conservative Party when Beatlemania first blossomed. At a Conservative Party rally, Douglas-Home commented on the Beatles by describing them thus: 'The Beatles are now my secret weapon. If any country is in deficit with us, I only have to say the Beatles are coming.'

When the Beatles returned to England following their short Swedish tour on 29 October 1963, Heathrow was so crowded with fans that Sir Alec Douglas-Home, due to fly to Scotland, was held up in his car by the crowds. The Queen Mother was also due to arrive from Ireland and **Ed Sullivan**, puzzled by all the chaos, asked whether the crowds were gathered to meet the Queen Mother – and was told, for the first time, about the Beatles. The new Miss World was also at the airport – and was totally ignored.

Dovedale Road Primary School, *Dovedale Road, Liverpool 18*

The primary school which John Lennon attended between 1945 and 1951. One of his fellow pupils was Jimmy Tarbuck, who was to become one of Britain's leading comedians. George Harrison also attended the school between 1948 and 1950. As George was three years John's junior, it is doubtful whether the two ever met during their period at the school.

Do You Want To Know A Secret?

Number penned by John which was originally given to George Harrison to sing lead vocal on when the Beatles recorded it on 11 February 1963, during their marathon session for their *Please Please Me* album. This version was also included on the group's first EP *Twist And Shout*. It was also released in America on the **Vee Jay** label as the flipside of 'Thank You Girl' in 1964 and reached No. 2.

The Beatles performed the song on several of their BBC radio shows, including '**Here We Go**', '**On The Scene**', '**Side By Side**', '**Saturday Club**', and two '**Pop Go The Beatles**'.

The most successful version was by **Billy J. Kramer** & the Dakotas, the Beatles' stablemates in Brian Epstein's **NEMS Enterprises**. Kramer's version was issued in Britain on Parlophone R 5023 in April 1963 and topped the British charts. Later that year, in September it was issued in America on Liberty 55586.

John claimed his inspiration for the number came from a memory of a Walt Disney film he'd seen as a child.

Dream Baby

Number composed by Cindy Walker recorded by several prominent rock artists including **Roy Orbison**, **Del Shannon** and **Bruce Channel**. The Roy Orbison single had only been issued in Britain for a few weeks when the Beatles performed it on their first radio show '**Teenager's Turn**' on 8 March 1962. With Paul on lead vocal, it became the first song recorded on the radio by the Beatles.

Drive My Car

Number penned by Paul, although John helped him to tighten up the lyrics and both feature on lead vocals. It was recorded on Wednesday, 13 October 1965, and became the opening track on the *Revolver* album.

It was also included on their *Nowhere Man* EP, *The Beatles 1962–1966* and *Rock 'n' Roll Music* compilations and the American album *Yesterday and Today*.

Drop In

Title of the Swedish television show which the Beatles telerecorded before a live audience on 30 October 1963 at the close of their short Swedish tour. The group performed four numbers, 'I Saw Her Standing There', 'Twist and Shout', 'She Loves You' and 'Long Tall Sally'. The programme was transmitted in Sweden on 3 November 1963.

Dr Robert

Song featured on the *Revolver* album, with John singing lead. Penned by John, with help from Paul on the middle section of the song, it was also included on the American album *Yesterday . . . And Today*.

The Beatles began recording the number on Sunday, 17 April 1966.

It is the first direct reference they made to drugs on their records and was about a New York doctor, Charles Roberts, who had a practice on 49th Street. Paul McCartney commented, 'Well, he's like a joke. There's some fellow in New York, and in the States we'd hear people say: "You can get everything off him; any pills you want." It was a big racket, but a joke too, about this fellow who cured everyone of everything with all these pills and tranquillisers, injections for this and that; he just kept New York high. That's what "Dr Robert" is all about, just a pill doctor who sees you all right.'

Dykins, John

The man **Julia Lennon** went to live with after the birth of John and Elizabeth. Having placed John with his Aunt **Mimi** and given her second child up for adoption, Julia became John Dykins' common-law wife and they had two daughters, Julia and Jacquie.

Dykins was generally known as Bobby, although John Lennon sometimes referred to him as 'Twitchy'.

In 1963, Dykins became restaurant manager of the

Odd Spot Club in Liverpool's Bold Street, where the Beatles had appeared the previous year. He then went to work in a hotel on the Isle of Man. Eddie Porter, who worked with him at both places, observed, 'The reason John called him "Twitchy" was because of a habit he had. He would press his nose back because it was badly scarred and needed a new bridge built.'

Following Julia's death, Dykins married a waitress called Rona and in February 1966 they were both involved in a car crash on their return from a trip to Wales. Both were taken to **Sefton General Hospital** in Smithdown Road, Liverpool, where Julia had been pronounced dead after her car accident. Rona was treated for facial injuries and discharged. Dykins was admitted and died two weeks later. Rona later married a prison warder.

● *Dylan, Bob*

One of the most influential singer/songwriters to emerge in the sixties, he was born Robert Allen Zimmerman on 24 May 1941 in Duluth, Minnesota. He first adopted the name Dylan in 1959. It was suggested that this was in tribute to the Welsh poet Dylan Thomas – but this theory has been disputed.

The Beatles were first introduced to Dylan's music by American journalist Al Aronowitz who originally met the Beatles in 1963 while reporting for the *Saturday Evening Post*. While the group were appearing at the **Olympia Theatre**, Paris, in January 1964 they visited a radio station and picked up Dylan's two albums *Bob Dylan* and the *Freewheelin' Bob Dylan*, having only previously heard his hit single 'Blowin' In The Wind', and they played the albums continuously while in Paris.

When they arrived in New York the following month Aronowitz introduced them to Dylan.

When the group returned to America later in 1964 to tour, they were staying at the Delmonico Hotel in New York when Dylan visited them again. He'd been driven from his home in Woodstock by his friend and roadie Victor Mamoudas in company with Aronowitz and they were taken straight to the Beatles' room. When they began to talk, Dylan suggested that they smoke marijuana. The Beatles had been introduced to pills in Hamburg and now took them on prescription, but they'd been wary of trying marijuana which they regarded as a 'drug'. When they told him they hadn't smoked it before, Dylan was amazed and pointed out that on their number 'I Want To Hold Your Hand', which he thought was a drug song, they'd sung the words 'I get high'. John explained that the words were

Bob Dylan influenced the Beatles' lyrics, while the Beatles' music was to influence Dylan. (National Film Theatre)

actually 'I can't hide'. They bolted the doors, put towels around every cranny, pulled the blinds and drew the curtains while Dylan lit a joint and instructed them how to smoke it. Then he passed it on to John, who seemed scared and passed it straight to Ringo. Ringo finished the joint and Dylan rolled half a dozen more. Ringo was the first to start laughing and they all spent several hours together, chatting, giggling and laughing. Paul enjoyed the effects of the drug and said, 'I was thinking for the first time. Really thinking.' For the next few years they were able to compose songs under the influence of marijuana.

Over the years, Dylan and the Beatles were to meet on many occasions and become firm friends. Initially, John came under Dylan's influence and they met socially, but gradually the firmer ties were between Bob and George.

On 9 May 1965, all four members of the Beatles attended Dylan's concert at the **Royal Albert Hall** in London. This was the tour in which Dylan was receiving criticism from critics and fans alike because he had abandoned the acoustic guitar and 'gone electric'. During the concert, members of the audience began to boo and the Beatles shouted at the hecklers, 'Leave him alone – shut up!' George called the members of the audience who had walked out 'idiots' and commented, 'It was all still pure Dylan, and he has to find out his own directions. If he felt he wanted electrification, that's the way he had to do it.' He added, 'Who's laying down rules?' The Beatles' general comment on the show was, 'Great, just great.'

On 13 and 16 August 1965, Dylan visited them at the **Warwick Hotel** in New York and in May 1966 when he was in London, Paul and **Neil Aspinall** met him at Dolly's Club and went back to his room at the Mayfair to spend several hours chatting. In October 1968, George and **Pattie** spent two weeks at Dylan's home in Woodstock, New York. George and Ringo also visited Dylan in Nashville during the recording of 'Nashville Skyline'. George and Pattie, Ringo and **Maureen**, John and **Yoko** and Neil and Mal attended Dylan's concert at the Isle of Wight on 31 August 1969. After the concert he joined John, Yoko and George in a helicopter trip to Tittenhurst Park.

Early in 1970 George was again invited to Woodstock. This was over Thanksgiving and George was accompanied by **Mal Evans**. Dylan also presented George with a painting, which he displayed at home in his bungalow, **Kinfauns**. After the third day they got their guitars out. George said, 'Write me some words', and Bob said, 'Show me some chords, how do you get those tunes?' and the song 'I'd Have You Anytime' was born, with Dylan contributing the bridge. The number surfaced on a bootleg album in America called *20 x 4*. During 1970 Dylan also showed John and Yoko around Greenwich Village.

When George was making 'All Things Must Pass', Dylan recommended Peter Drake to play the pedal steel parts and George had Drake flown in from Nashville to appear on the album. George also included the number he'd co-written with Dylan, 'I'd Have You Anytime', together with the Dylan composition, 'If Not For You'.

One of their most successful teamings was at George's *Concert For Bangla Desh*, when Bob appeared for twenty minutes with a five-song set.

Bob Dylan also had a marked influence on John Lennon, particularly on the lyrics of John's own compositions. In 1964 John said, 'I was not too keen on lyrics in those days. I didn't think they counted. Dylan used to come out with his latest acetate and say "Listen to the words, man", and I'd say, "I don't listen to words."' It soon became obvious that Dylan inspired John, who began to wear a Huck Finn cap like Dylan and to pen songs such as 'I'm A Loser' and 'You've Got To Hide Your Love Away'.

At one time while Dylan was at John's Weybridge home for dinner, they played records and talked. John said, 'We swapped addresses and said we'd exchange ideas for songs, but it never happened. He said he sent me things, but he got the address wrong and it never arrived.'

Dylan liked John's 'Norwegian Wood' and took the tune and rewrote his own lyrics to it, resulting in 'Fourth Time Around'. John used Dylan's 'Masters Of War' as an inspiration for his 'Working Class Hero' and when John produced an album for **Nilsson** he included a new arrangement of 'Subterranean Homesick Blues'. In his song, 'Yer Blues', John wrote: 'Feel suicidal, just like Dylan's Mr Jones,' which was referring to a character in a Dylan song called 'Ballad Of A Thin Man'. Dylan, under his real name of Zimmerman, is also mentioned in the lyrics to John's composition 'God'.

Bob Dylan is one of only two contemporary music figures featured on the cover of the *Sgt Pepper's Lonely Hearts Club Band* album and the Beatles performed five Dylan songs during their *Let It Be* sessions.

In the mid-eighties George was to form a recording group called the Traveling Wilburys with Bob Dylan, **Roy Orbison**, Tom Petty and Jeff Lynne.

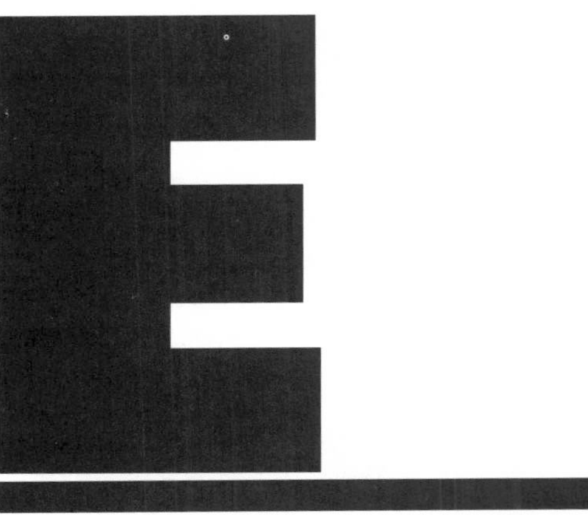

● Eamonn Andrews Show, The

The Beatles appeared on this television show, filmed live from Teddington Studios on 11 April 1965.

Andrews, a talk-show host, had worked for BBC Television for a number of years, but had decided to make a move to the commercial channel. His associate Tom Brennan thought it quite a coup to be able to secure the Beatles to appear on the new chat show, only a few weeks after its initial launch. Not only would the Beatles perform two of their latest hits live, but they would also be interviewed at length by Andrews. In fact, the entire show was devoted to the Beatles.

Both John and Paul were very amused to note that Andrews thought Ringo was George and vice versa and laughed when Andrews addressed Ringo as George.

On his forthcoming Easter Sunday show, Andrews had a family of boys from Merseyside as his guests and thought it would be a good idea to present them with an Easter egg with the Beatles' signatures in icing on it. When this suggestion was put to the Beatles management prior to the show, a message came back that they were not skilled in the art of writing in icing sugar and couldn't do it on the live show. Andrews told his producer, 'Sod them, we'll get somebody just to write their names on it with icing. Just John, Paul, Ringo and . . . ' 'George' his producer reminded him. Andrews said that they could forge the Beatles' signatures because the Beatles wouldn't admit that they refused to do such a thing for a bunch of kids and the kids themselves wouldn't know the difference.

Andrews had the egg made with the forged signatures and presented the youngest of the Merseyside boys with it on his Easter programme – and was proved right, there were no complaints forthcoming from the Beatles camp.

When Andrews was hosting a show called 'Today' for Thames Television, John and **Yoko** appeared on the programme on 1 April 1969 to discuss 'Bagism' and encouraged Andrews to climb into a large white bag with them.

● Early Beatles, The

A **Capitol** album issued in America on ST 2309 on 22 March 1965. This was material obtained by Capitol after **Vee Jay Records** ceased trading and mainly comprised material which had originally appeared on the *Introducing The Beatles* album and had been re-packaged several times since by Vee Jay. Despite the familiarity of the material and the fact that it had been issued for the fifth time, the album sold over a million copies and reached No. 24 in *Cash Box*, No. 29 in *Record World* and No. 43 in *Billboard*.

There were differences between this release and the original *Introducing The Beatles* album as Capitol took out 'I Saw Her Standing There', 'Misery' and 'There's A Place' and added 'Love Me Do' and 'P.S. I Love You'.

The track listing was, Side One: 'Love Me Do', 'Twist And Shout', 'Anna (Go To Him)', 'Chains', 'Boys' and 'Ask Me Why'. Side Two: 'Please Please Me', 'P.S. I Love You', 'Baby It's You', 'A Taste Of Honey' and 'Do You Want To Know A Secret'.

● Eastman, John

Linda McCartney's brother. He was a graduate of Stanford and NYU Law School and joined his father Lee's law firm in New York. When Paul McCartney asked **Lee Eastman** for advice on how to sort out the financial mess at **Apple Corps**, Eastman recommended John.

John Eastman flew to London and met the Beatles. John, George and Ringo were considering hiring **Allen Klein**, but decided that they could also hire Eastman, if only to placate Paul, and he was hired as General Counsel.

The first thing he suggested was that the Beatles buy **NEMS**. He started negotiations, but they fell through and the company was sold to Triumph Investments. Eastman blamed Klein and Klein blamed Eastman. The Beatles would have been satisfied retaining both men to look after their interests, but it was obvious that the two couldn't vork together, so Eastman was in the McCartney corner ınd Klein with Lennon, Harrison and Starr. Paul's ties vith Eastman became stronger when he married Linda and ohn became his brother-in-law. Paul refused to sign with Klein and retained Eastman as his representative. It was Eastman who advised him that he had no choice but to file vrits against John, George, Ringo and Apple in order to lissolve the Beatles partnership.

Eastman, Lee

Linda **McCartney**'s father. He was a graduate of Harvard Jniversity who changed his name from Epstein to Eastman. His wife Louise was killed in an air crash. Together with his son, John, he was set to represent the Beatles in their financial affairs in 1969 until **Allen Klein** ppeared on the scene with the same idea in mind. Klein von, although the Eastmans continued to represent Paul McCartney in various matters.

For over a quarter of a century, Eastman had pecialized in entertainment law with his son and, apart rom Paul, their clients included David Bowie, Billy Joel nd Andrew Lloyd Webber.

Lee died in New York of a stroke on 30 July 1991. He vas 81 years old.

Easy Beat

Sunday morning BBC radio programme broadcast etween 10.30-11.30 a.m. The show was presented by **Brian Matthew** and produced by Ron Belchier at the layhouse Theatre in London.

The Beatles appeared on four 'Easy Beat' shows, all of hich took place in 1963. The first was broadcast on 7 pril and the group performed 'Please Please Me', Misery' and 'From Me To You'. On their second ppearance on 23 June they performed 'Some Other Guy', A Taste Of Honey', 'Thank You Girl' and 'From Me To ou'. Their third performance on 21 July featured 'I Saw Her Standing There', 'A Shot Of Rhythm And Blues', There's A Place' and 'Twist And Shout'. Their final ppearance on 20 October saw them performing 'I Saw Her Standing There', 'Love Me Do', 'Please Please Me', From Me To You' and 'She Loves You'.

Eckhorn, Peter

t the age of 21, after returning home from sea, Peter ckhorn was presented with club premises at 136 Reeperbahn in Hamburg by his father. The premises had been called the Hippodrome and formerly hosted a topless circus. Eckhorn decided to open a rock 'n' roll club which he called the **Top Ten Club** and launched it in late October 1960.

Observing the success **Bruno Koschmider** was having in his Grosse Freiheit clubs with British rock 'n' roll bands, Eckhorn astutely hired **Horst Fascher**, the **Kaiserkeller**'s 'bouncer', who had developed a rapport with the bands. Through Fascher he was able to book **Tony Sheridan** & the **Jets** to open the Top Ten. As a follow-up band he wanted to book the Beatles. The Jets had completed their contract for Koschmider and were ready to go home, but Eckhorn managed to get some of them to stay and remain with Sheridan.

The Beatles made a few appearances at the club before Koschmider saw to it that they had to return to Liverpool. Members of the Jets remained for a further two months, but then left, although Sheridan had agreed to remain as the club's resident singer. **Gerry & the Pacemakers** were the next band to appear.

In the meantime, Eckhorn made arrangements for the Beatles to return and booked them for a short season from 1 April 1961. The group were so popular he renewed their contract twice and they appeared at the club until 1 July.

In 1962 Peter made a special visit to Liverpool to sign up the Beatles for another season at the club. This time he had to deal with their new manager, Brian Epstein. The money which Epstein demanded, 500 marks for each Beatle per week, was far higher than Eckhorn had intended to pay. He offered 450 marks each and Epstein said he'd let him know. Eckhorn was also unsuccessful in his bid to book Gerry & the Pacemakers again.

In the meantime a new club was being prepared in Hamburg – the **Star Club**. The owner, **Manfred Weissleder,** had done exactly what Eckhorn had done to Koschmider – he poached Horst Fascher. Three weeks after Eckhorn's visit to Epstein, Fascher arrived in Liverpool to book the Beatles and agreed to Epstein's demand of 500 marks. This ended the group's association with Eckhorn and the Top Ten Club.

Peter engaged **Iain Hines**, former member of the Jets, to become booking manager for the club, but its heyday had passed. Like Koschmider and Weissleder, Eckhorn died several years later.

● Eddie Clayton Skiffle Group, The

Skiffle group which Ringo Starr was a member of in 1957/1958. He was working as an apprentice engineer at H. Hunt & Sons at the time and had no thoughts of taking up drums as a career. He recalled, 'I remember my mum saying a neighbour was in a band and why didn't I have a go. I thought it was a jazz group – I was mad on jazz. When it turned out to be a silver band, playing in the park and sticking to the marches and all that, I chucked it in. I lasted just the one night.'

His stepfather had bought him a drum kit for ten pounds in London and brought it back by train. Ringo began playing during the lunchbreaks at work with Eddie Miles, a fellow apprentice joiner, when his grandfather lent him £50 to put down as a deposit for a brand new kit. The year was 1956.

His mother, **Elsie Starkey**, told ***Mersey Beat***: 'Richie joined the Eddie Clayton Skiffle Group with Ed Miles, the boy who lived next door, Roy Trafford and Johnny Dougherty – they all worked together in the same place. Eddie used to take his guitar to work every day. He was a smashing fellow – if ever a lad should have got somewhere he should have. I believe he's with Hank Walters & His Dusty Road Ramblers now.'

The group, who formed early in 1957, comprised Ed Miles (guitar/vocals), Ringo Starr (drums), Roy Trafford (tea-chest bass), John Dougherty (washboard) and Frank Walsh (guitar).

Their first gig was at the Labour Club in Peel Street and by that time they had three guitars, drums, washboard and bass. They attempted to look more professional by dressing in the same style of shirts with bootlace ties. They were to appear at skiffle contests such as the ones taking place at **St Luke's Hall** and also appeared regularly at meetings of the Boys' Club at the Florence Institute, near to their homes.

The group disbanded when Eddie Miles left to get married.

● Edelweiss Hotel, *Obertauern, Austria*

Alpine hotel where the Beatles stayed during the filming of *Help!* They occupied room numbers 501–507 during March 1965.

For the skiing scenes, four Austrian skiers were hired as doubles, each wearing identical clothes to their Beatle counterpart. Frank Bosensberger doubled for John, Herbert Lurzer for Paul, Gerhard Griens for George and Hans Pretscherer for Ringo.

The Beatles had been accompanied by **Cynthia**, **Maureen** and **Pattie** and one morning Maureen walked out of the Edelweiss, moved towards Ringo and gave him a kiss – then realized it was Ringo's double, Hans!

During their stay at the Edelweiss, the producers hired Gloria Makk, Miss Austria, 1964, to act as their contact, translator and ski coach.

After the Beatles vacated the hotel on Monday, 22 March, the rooms they stayed in were visited by numerous fans, who took towels and sheets as souvenirs.

● Edgewater Inn, *Seattle, Washington*

Hotel where the Beatles stayed on 21 August 1964 while appearing at the Seattle Center Coliseum.

The hotel manager, Don Wright, found his hands full with the consequences of Beatlemania. Fan mail and gifts of cakes and cookies were pouring into the hotel, security staff had to scour every nook and cranny – and four teenagers were found hiding in the toilets, three under a bed in one room and a further two under a bed in another, while 1,000 Beatles fans besieged the front of the hotel.

The Beatles had their own suite and were able to fish out of their windows which overlooked Elliott Bay.

When the Beatles left at lunchtime the next day, manager Wright heard that fans intended tearing up the Beatles' suite for souvenirs, so he sold the orange rug that had carpeted their room to MacDougall-Southwick, a company which intended to cut it up and sell the pieces as souvenirs. The Beatles had heard rumours that the hotel staff had planned to take their bedsheets and sell them, so they poured milk, orange juice and alcohol over them.

● Edison Award

A special award granted to the Beatles for their album *Beatles For Sale*. Brian Epstein accepted the Edison Award on behalf of the group at the Grand Gala du Disque at the Congresscentrum in Amsterdam on 2 October 1965. He was introduced as 'The Beatle with the shortest hair and the longest hand' and his acceptance speech comprised four words, 'Thank you very much'.

● 102 Edith Grove, *London SW10*

Street branching off the fashionable Kings Road in Chelsea where Mick Jagger, **Brian Jones** and Keith

Richard shared two rooms on the middle floor of this address in 1962.

In the building they had a two-room flat and had to walk up several flights of stairs to the grimy toilet. Wallpaper was hanging from the walls and the place was in disarray. It was to their flat that the Stones invited the Beatles on 21 April 1963, after the **Fab Four** had travelled to see the Stones at the **Crawdaddy Club** at the invitation of Giorgio Gomelski.

After the gig, the Beatles and Stones retired to Edith Grove where they chatted throughout the night. They got on well and became very good friends, although there were obvious differences in musical tastes at the time with the Stones not showing interest in the Beatles' enthusiasm for Chuck Jackson and the Beatles remaining indifferent to Mick Jagger's collection of rare Jimmy Reed albums.

● Eggermont, Jaap

A Dutch record producer, former drummer with the group Golden Earring, who devised the Beatles medley disc *Stars On 45* in 1981, which took Lennon & McCartney compositions to the top of the American charts for the first time since 1975 when **Elton John** had a No. 1 hit with 'Lucy In The Sky With Diamonds'.

The musicians who simulated the Beatles sound on the single, using the name Starsound, were: Bas Nuys (Lennon), Okki Huysdens (McCartney) and Hans Vermeulen (Harrison).

● Eight Days A Week

A John Lennon composition. When John was asked to recall the number in 1980 he said that he'd written the song quite quickly as it was considered as a title track for the Beatles' next film, which turned out to be called *Help!*

The group began to develop the number when they started recording it on Tuesday, 6 October 1964, and it ended up featuring what is probably the first fade-in to a pop record – as opposed to a record fading out.

The track was considered as a single, but found its way onto the *Beatles For Sale* album and the *Beatles For Sale* EP.

It was issued as a single in America on **Capitol** 5371 on 15 February 1965 with 'I Don't Want To Spoil The Party' on the flip and reached the No. 1 position in the charts.

The track was also included on the American *Beatles VI* album.

● Eleanor Rigby

Together with 'Yellow Submarine', this number was issued in Britain as the second double-A sided single by the Beatles on Parlophone R5493 on 5 August 1966 and in America on **Capitol** 5715 on 8 August. It became a No. 1 hit and the number was also featured on the *Revolver* album, issued in Britain on the same day. A few months later, in December, it resurfaced on *A Collection Of Beatles Oldies (But Goldies)* and also appeared on several other albums, including *The Beatles 1962–1966* in 1973, *The Beatles Box* in 1980 and *20 Greatest Hits* in 1982. It was re-released amongst a batch of singles to celebrate the group's twentieth anniversary in 1982.

From what Paul had said about the song in the sixties, it was assumed that Eleanor Rigby was a figment of his imagination, yet in 1984 stories in the press suggested that Eleanor Rigby had been a real person. This was because a tombstone for an Eleanor Rigby had been discovered in the graveyard of St Peter's Church in Liverpool, the same church where John and Paul had first met. She had died on 10 October 1939. Could he have seen the gravestone as a young man and held the name in his subconscious? Or is it just coincidence?

When the *Sun* newspaper ran a story about the song in 1984, it published a photograph of former dancehall compere Tom McKenzie posing at the side of the gravestone and commented that Tom was also the Father McKenzie referred to. Yet in Paul's version of the origin of the number, Father McKenzie was also fictitious.

Here is what Paul has said at various times to the press: '[It] started off with sitting down at the piano and getting the first line of the melody and playing around with words. I think it was "Miss Daisy Hawkins" originally; then it was her picking up the rice in a church after a wedding. That's how nearly all our songs start, with the first line just suggesting itself from books or newspapers.

'At first I thought it was a young Miss Daisy Hawkins, a bit like "Annabel Lee", but not so sexy; but then I saw I'd said she was picking up the rice in church so she had to be a cleaner; she had missed the wedding and she was suddenly lonely. In fact she had missed it all – she was the spinster type.

'**Jane** [**Asher**] was in a play in Bristol then, and I was walking round the streets waiting for her to finish. I didn't really like "Daisy Hawkins" – I wanted a name that was more real. The thought just came: "Eleanor Rigby picks

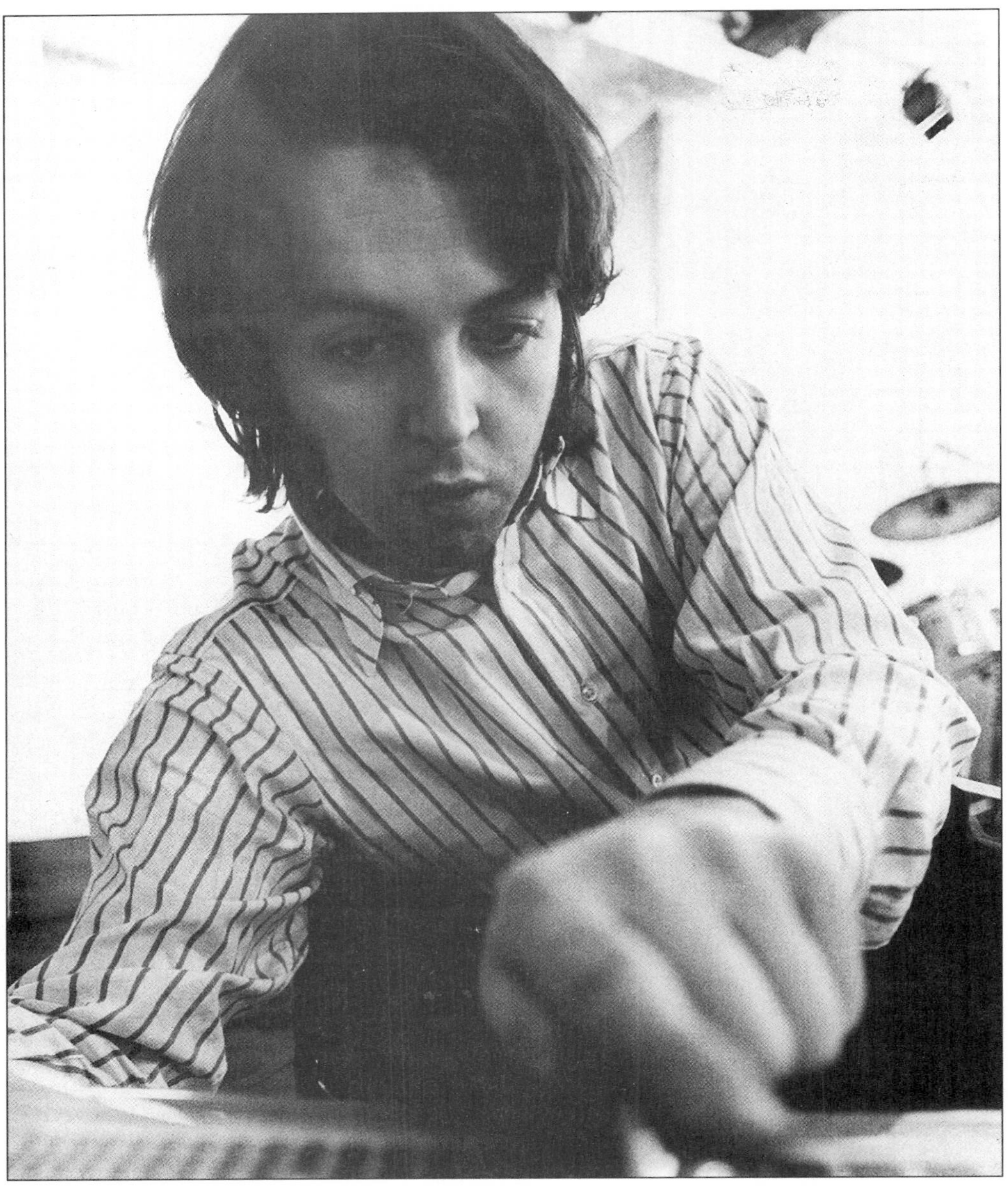

Eleanor Rigby – Paul's inspiration came during a trip to Bristol. (©Apple)

up the rice and lives in a dream" – so there she was.

'The next thing was Father McKenzie. It was going to be Father McCartney, but then I thought that was a bit of a hangup for my Dad, being in this lonely song. So we looked through the phone book. That's the beauty of working at random – it does come up perfectly, much better than if you try to think it with your intellect.

'Anyway, there was Father McKenzie, and he was jus as I had imagined him, lonely, darning his socks. W weren't sure if the song was going to go on. In the nex verse we thought of a bin man, an old feller going throug dustbins; but it got too involved – embarrassing. John an I wondered whether to have Eleanor Rigby and him havin a thing going, but we couldn't really see how. When played it to John, we decided to finish it.

'That was the point anyway. She didn't make it, she never made it with anyone, she didn't even look as if she was going to.'

The number was recorded in April 1966 and scored by George Martin who said he was inspired by the work of film composer Bernard Herrmann, particularly on his scoring of *Fahrenheit 451*. Paul sang lead with backing vocals from John and George. Apart from that, the Beatles weren't featured as the instrumental backing was provided by eight session men: Tony Gilbert, Sidney Sax, John Sharpe and Jurgen Hess on violins; Stephen Shingles and John Underwood on violas and Derek Simpson and Norman Jones on cellos.

The number has also become one of the most popular Beatles songs to be recorded by other acts with over 200 recorded versions, including those by Diana Ross & the Supremes, Paul Anka, Frankie Valli, the **Four Tops**, Johnny Mathis and Vanilla Fudge. The Ray Charles version reached No. 25 in the British charts in 1968 and Aretha Franklin's version reached No. 23 in the American charts.

Electronic Sounds

The second and final album to be released on Apple's specialist label **Zapple Records**. It was issued in America on Zapple ST 3358 on 26 May 1969 and reached No. 191 in the *Billboard* charts, although failing to find a place in either the *Cash Box* or *Record World* charts.

It was issued in Britain on Zapple 02 on 9 May 1969 and, like George's first solo album venture *Wonderwall*, failed to achieve a placing in the British charts.

The concept of Zapple was that it was to be an experimental label, which was certainly true in this case. George had recently acquired a Moog synthesizer and was experimenting with sounds on the new instrument when he decided to put them down on record – on what is probably the first album to consist entirely of synthesized sounds.

There were only two tracks on the LP, the first side was called 'Under The Mersey Wall', the second, 'No Time Or Space'. George recorded 'No Time Or Space' in California in November 1968 and recorded 'Under The Mersey Wall' in the studio at his home in Esher in February 1969. 'Under The Mersey Wall' was probably a reference to the *Liverpool Echo* column by journalist George Harrison.

George was to comment, 'All I did was get that very first Moog synthesizer with the big patch unit and keyboards you could never tune, and I put a microphone into a tape machine. Whatever came out when I fiddled with the knobs went on tape.'

When he'd been recording in California, George had hired an engineer for the session called Bernard Krause. Krause later told a magazine that he had created the music as a demonstration tape for the synthesizer and that George had taken his tapes. It seems unlikely as Krause didn't press the matter.

George also designed the album sleeve, using two paintings by himself and he also wrote sleeve notes, using the pseudonym Arthur Wax, in which he commented, 'There are a lot of people around, making a lot of noise, here's some more.'

● Elizabethan Ballroom, *Co-operative House, Parliament Street, Nottingham*

Brian Epstein approached Bill Harry for permission to use the ***Mersey Beat*** name in a showcase he'd wanted to promote on behalf of **NEMS Enterprises** which would be a package tour of Liverpool acts. Permission was given and Epstein called the series ***Mersey Beat Showcase***.

The first of them took place at the Elizabethan Ballroom on 7 March 1963 and the Beatles were bill-toppers with support from **Gerry & the Pacemakers**, the Big Three and **Billy J. Kramer** & the Dakotas. **Bob Wooler** compered the shows. For this debut, NEMS Enterprises hired two coaches and in addition to the groups, eighty fans were able to join the bands on the journey for a modest 25 shillings (£1.25), which included entrance to the show.

There were a total of six *Mersey Beat Showcase* packages, all in 1963, and the others took place on 19, 24 and 25 April and 14 and 16 June. Further presentations planned for 17, 18, 19, 20 and 23 June were cancelled by Epstein.

● Ellis, Geoffrey

One of Brian Epstein's closest friends. The two met as regulars at the Royal Court Theatre in Liverpool. Ellis, who was four years older than Brian, had studied for the bar at Oxford University. When Ellis became an executive for the Royal Life Insurance Company he was posted to New York in June 1958, but he and Brian corresponded on a regular basis. Ellis was later to work for **Walter Hofer**, a lawyer acting on Brian's behalf in America.

Brian asked Ellis to join his organization and he became a senior executive at **NEMS** in October 1964 and a director the following year. He ran the day-to-day office administration.

Brian invited Geoffrey and **Peter Brown** as his house guests to Kingsley Hill for the weekend on 25 August 1967. During the evening he left them to return to **Chapel Street** and was found dead on 27 August.

Ellis later worked for the **Dick James** Organization and John Reid Enterprises.

● Ellis, Royston

British author/poet who was an English exponent of the American 'Beat Generation' poetry. During a trip to Liverpool for a reading at Liverpool University in 1960 he met the Beatles who took him back to the **Gambier Terrace** flat. Ellis introduced them to benzedrine, which was obtained by opening up a Vick inhaler and chewing the strip inside. They were called 'spitballs'. The group also backed him at a Poetry-to-Beat session at the **Jacaranda Club**.

His books included *Jiving To Gyp, Driftin' With Cliff Richard* (co-authored with Jet Harris), *The Big Beat Scene* and a biography of the **Shadows**.

● El Rio Club, *El Rio Ballroom, Queen Victoria Street, Macclesfield, Cheshire*

A booking originally arranged for 19 January 1963 on a provisional basis, the booking was then confirmed and took place on 26 January 1963, with Wayne Fontana & the Jets in support.

Local boy Fontana, real name Glyn Ellis, was to find record success within the year. When he went into a Manchester studio to record his first single for the Fontana label, his backing group failed to turn up. Some session musicians were in the studio and backed him on record; they were Eric Stewart on guitar, Bob Land on bass and Rick Rothwell on drums. As the Mindbenders they became Fontana's backing group. Together they had ten chart hits between 1963 and 1966, including 'Hello Josephine', 'Um Um Um Um Um Um' and 'Game Of Love'. In 1966 the Mindbenders split with Fontana and had four hits, beginning with 'A Groovy Kind Of Love'.

Stewart went on to become a member of the highly successful group 10cc. and later recorded with Paul McCartney, beginning with the 'Tug Of War' album. He said, 'I meet Paul fairly often and we've known each other since way back when he was with the Beatles and I was with the Mindbenders. We used to play the **Cavern** together, we used to play the same kind of music, American R&B, and we're both from the North, we have the same accent, the same sense of humour. After I had a ca accident a while back, Paul phoned me up to see if I wa all right. I said I was, but in fact I was still rather messed up and still had to use drugs and all that. But Paul asked me if I felt like playing on his new LP so I said "Great!"'

Stewart also played on Mike McGear's solo album *McGear*.

● Embassy Theatre, *The Broadway, Peterborough, Northamptonshire*

The Beatles made their debut at this East Coast venue o 2 December 1962. Brian Epstein had managed to trace th telephone number of **Arthur Howes**, one of Britain' major tour promoters. Coincidentally, Howes lived i Peterborough. He related to Beatles biographer **Hunte Davies** the call he received one Saturday afternoon: 'H [Brian] said he had a great group, was there anything could fit them into? He told me their names, Beatles, and laughed . . . but I've never turned down a group witho first hearing them. I said there was a show at Peterboroug they could join.'

The Beatles cancelled a booking they had at th **Cavern** that evening, but didn't fare too well at the gi and, indeed, didn't even receive applause, which isn't to hard to understand as **Frank Ifield** topped the bill wit Julie Grant, Ted Taylor and Susan Cope as support act Howes was to comment: 'It was a Frank Ifield show so suppose it wasn't so surprising, they loved him so muc that the show was good enough to take ten minutes of bad group.'

Ifield had enjoyed spectacular success that yea reaching No. 1 in the charts with 'I Remember You' an remaining in the Top Twenty from 14 July until December. He followed up with another No. 1 hit November, 'Wayward Wind', and had several further hits

Journalist Lyndon Whittaker, writing in the loc newspaper, reported: 'The "exciting" Beatles rock grou quite frankly failed to excite me. The drummer apparent thought that his job was to lead, not to provide rhythm. H made far too much noise and in their final number, "Twi

And Shout", it sounded as though everyone was trying to nake more noise than the others. In a more mellow mood, heir "A Taste Of Honey" was much better and "Love Me Do" was tolerable.'

The group hadn't been paid a fee for the gig, just their xpenses from Liverpool, and Howes was prepared to take further chance with them, booking them on his next ationwide tour promotion which was headlined by **Helen hapiro**.

They were due to return to the Embassy again as part of tour on which they were bottom of the bill and only eceived £80 a week. The date was set for 10 February 963 but they had to travel to London for a recording ession and were excused from the gig and replaced by **Peter Jay & the Jaywalkers**.

However, only a short time was to pass before they ppeared at the Embassy again on their next tour, on a bill eadlined by American singers **Chris Montez** and **ommy Roe**. The Beatles made their second and final ppearance at the theatre on 17 March 1963.

Emerick, Geoff

young recording engineer when he joined **EMI**, Emerick as promoted to the position of George Martin's assistant nd won a **Grammy Award** for his work on the *Sgt epper's Lonely Hearts Club Band* album. He also won a rammy for his work on Paul McCartney's *Band On The un* album and worked on Paul's *Venus And Mars* and *ondon Town* LPs. Emerick also mixed the tapes for *The eatles At The Hollywood Bowl* album.

He was involved with a large number of Beatles cordings from the time he acted as tape operator on 20 ebruary 1963 for the recordings of 'Misery' and 'Baby It's ou'. Emerick replaced **Norman Smith** as engineer on e Beatles recordings on 6 April 1966. Formerly assistant Smith, he was only twenty years old when he began cording with the Beatles and had various fresh ideas.

Paul acted as his Best Man when Geoffrey was married January 1989.

EMI House, 20 Manchester Square, ondon W1

e headquarters of **EMI Records**. The Beatles posed in e stairwell of the building for the front cover picture of eir *Please Please Me* album. In 1969 they returned to the airwell to have a similar photo taken, intending it to be used on their projected 'Get Back' album. As 'Get Back' never came to fruition, the photograph was eventually used on their 1974 compilation, *The Beatles 1967–1970*, while the original pose was used in a companion compilation the same year, *The Beatles 1962–1966*.

Although the Beatles' recordings were made at EMI's studios in **Abbey Road**, the Beatles visited EMI House on a number of occasions. They recorded three radio programmes for **Radio Luxembourg**'s **'The Friday Spectacular'** show at EMI House early in 1963 and during succeeding years visited the headquarters for various meetings and award presentations.

● EMI Records

Over the years there has been too much emphasis placed on the fact that **Decca Records** turned down the Beatles. Decca Records at least took the trouble to arrange a studio audition and seriously considered signing the group. EMI, on the other hand, originally turned the Beatles down without even granting them an audition, and it was only by an unusual set of circumstances that they entered EMI by 'the back door', and transformed the fortunes of the company.

EMI originated in 1931 as the Gramophone Company, but changed its name to Electrical and Mechanical Industries. The company was involved in various activities, including the production of wooden cabinet TV sets, but when **Sir Joseph Lockwood** became Chairman in 1954 he ended the production of the cabinets and concentrated on the production of records. In 1955 he made the decision to buy an American record company, **Capitol**, for three million pounds.

EMI Records, who now described themselves as 'The greatest recording organization in the world', were actually the very first company Brian Epstein approached. Being a major record retailer he was able to set up a meeting in London with EMI marketing manager **Ron White**, who agreed to approach the company's four house producers: Norrie Paramor, Walter Ridley, Norman Newell and George Martin. Martin was on holiday at the time, but the other three A&R men told White they weren't interested. These A&R men handled EMI's pop labels, George Martin's Parlophone label was not strictly a pop label and therefore White wrote back to Epstein formally rejecting the Beatles on behalf of EMI.

Epstein went into the HMV shop to have acetates made

and was sent to see publisher **Sid Coleman**, who then arranged a meeting with George Martin, which led to the Beatles' signing with the Parlophone label. Even that set of circumstances is not straightforward. Epstein's assistant **Alistair Taylor** confirms that Parlophone began to play around with Epstein to the extent that he became frustrated and threatened to withdraw his business if EMI didn't give the Beatles a recording contract. Taylor was to tell writer **Ray Coleman**, 'EMI took them on sufferance because Brian was one of their top customers. I saw Brian in tears, literally, because Martin promised to phone back, and day after day went by and George Martin was never available, always 'in a meeting'. I saw Brian thumping the desk and in tears because George Martin hadn't phoned back.' According to Taylor, when Epstein finally got hold of Martin he told him that **NEMS** as a shop would jettison EMI's HMV, Parlophone and Columbia labels. The result was an offer of a recording test.

Parlophone was not one of EMI's pop-orientated labels and in the six years leading up to the signing of the Beatles had only had one Top Ten hit, 'Stop You're Driving Me Crazy', by the Temperance Seven. George Martin had once auditioned Tommy Steele, but had turned him down – and Steele became Britain's leading rock 'n' roll star. George had been recording stage revues and comedy records with artists such as **Peter Sellers**, Peter Ustinov and Flanders and Swann.

Martin admits that EMI had nothing to lose financially by taking on an unknown group such as the Beatles. He said, 'To say I was taking a gamble would be stretching it, because the deal I offered them was pretty awful.'

The contract offered them one penny in royalties per single – with no advance payments – and on overseas sales they would only get half of that. A twelve-track album would be regarded as six cuts. There were three one-year options with an increase of a quarter of a penny (a farthing) at the end of the first year and an increase of a halfpenny at the end of the second year. There was a new agreement in January 1967 which gave the Beatles 10 per cent of an album's wholesale price. Epstein dealt with Len Wood, EMI's Managing Director, who was to say, 'When we exercised the first option, and the royalty rate went up as a result, I asked George Martin to bring the royalty rate for the following option forward so that the Beatles got more rewards now . . . but at the same time get for EMI an extra year or two's option.' Brian couldn't give him an option beyond September 1967 because his management contract with the Beatles ended on that date.

EMI did, however, lose the Beatles' publishing. EMI's Chairman Sir Joseph Lockwood was justifiably frustrated not to have the Beatles' lucrative songwriting activities under the wing of EMI's own publishing company Ardmore & Beechwood, who had published the first two songs without a contract.

When the Beatles' contract with EMI expired in 1966 there were six months of negotiations before a deal was signed on 27 January 1967. Under the deal the Beatles received 10 per cent of the retail price of their records, which was double the normal royalty and the highest royalty given to an artist at the time. The contract was to last for nine years, which gave EMI the benefit of the individual recordings of John, Paul, George and Ringo for six years after the split in 1970.

The small Parlophone label benefited not only from the incredible success of the Beatles records, but also from the string of other acts Epstein placed with the label – **Cilla Black** (No. 1 with 'Anyone Who Had a Heart' and 'You're My World'); **Gerry & the Pacemakers** (No. 1 with 'How Do You Do It', 'I Like It' and 'You'll Never Walk Alone' and **Billy J. Kramer** (No. 1 with 'Bad To Me' and 'Little Children').

The Beatles' success also transformed the company's American arm, **Capitol Records**.

During the years the association between the Beatles and EMI worked very well, most particularly when the Beatles themselves were in the driving seat. When their nine-year contract ended on 6 February 1976 and EMI then had the right to issue any back catalogue material there were a few things the Beatles in their solo years weren't happy with (although they didn't have much say in the matter) – such as the choice of album covers and compilation selections. They hated the cover of *Rock 'n' Roll Music* and the company, unbelievably, turned down John Lennon's offer of designing the cover himself. George Harrison was also upset at their selection of tracks for *The Best Of George Harrison* compilation.

● Empire Pool, *Empire Way, Wembley, Middlesex*

Site of the prestigious ***New Musical Express*** **Poll** Winners Annual concerts in the mid-sixties.

The *New Musical Express* had the largest circulation

any music paper in Britain and had a powerful influence on the music business. The NME concerts comprised a bill of the main winners of their Readers' Polls and were filmed by ABC Television for screening on the commercial channel.

The Beatles made their debut on the show in front of an audience of eight thousand fans on the afternoon of 21 April 1963. On that occasion the bill toppers were Cliff Richard & the **Shadows**. The Beatles performed 'Please Please Me', 'From Me To You', 'Twist And Shout' and 'Long Tall Sally'. Paul introduced the last song with the words, 'Here's a song immortalized by that great gospel singer, Victor Sylvester!' The Beatles performed in the late second half of the bill, immediately before Cliff Richard & the Shadows. Other artists on the bill were **Joe Brown** & his Bruvvers, the Springfields, Adam Faith, **Mike Berry**, the **Brook Brothers**, the Tornadoes, Kenny Ball, **Gerry & the Pacemakers**, Jet Harris and **Tony Meehan**, **Frank Ifield**, Mark Wynter and Joe Loss & His Orchestra.

Their second appearance took place on 26 April 1964 and this time they topped the bill. They were introduced by **Murray the K** and then performed 'She Loves You', 'You Can't Do That', 'Twist And Shout', 'Long Tall Sally' and 'Can't Buy Me Love'. The ABC TV show was screened on 10 May as 'Big Beat '64' and repeated on 8 November.

The 11 April 1965 appearance found them performing 'I Feel Fine', 'She's A Woman', 'Baby's In Black', 'Ticket To Ride' and 'Long Tall Sally'. The ABC TV concert film was screened on 18 April. Other artists on the bill included the **Rolling Stones**, Dusty Springfield, the **Moody Blues**, Wayne Fontana and Tom Jones. The Beatles were presented with their awards by American singer Tony Bennett.

The Beatles' fourth and final Empire Pool appearance for the *New Musical Express* 1965–66 Annual Poll Winners All-Star Concert on 1 May 1966 was also the group's last live concert appearance in Britain. Due to contractual reasons, the Beatles' and the Rolling Stones' appearances on this particular concert were not filmed by ABC TV.

The four performed a fifteen-minute act comprising 'I Feel Fine', 'Nowhere Man', 'Day Tripper', 'If I Needed Someone' and 'I'm Down'. Paul McCartney commented: 'There's nothing like going on in front of a really big audience. It's like a little break coming after all those weeks locked away in the studios. We'd have gone on all night, honest!'

The huge bills on these concerts featured an average of fourteen live acts. Other artists appearing on the bill of their last concert were: the Spencer Davis Group, Dave Dee, Dozy, Beaky, Mick & Tich, the Fortunes, Herman's Hermits, **Roy Orbison**, the **Overlanders**, the Alan Price Set, Cliff Richard, the Rolling Stones, the Seekers, the Shadows, the Small Faces, **Sounds Incorporated**, Dusty Springfield, Crispian St Peters, the Walker Brothers, the Who and the **Yardbirds**.

● Empire Stadium, *Vancouver, Canada*

The Beatles' appearance in British Columbia was part of a fourteen-day fair, the Pacific National Exhibition, during which they were to give one performance at the Empire Stadium on 22 August 1964.

There was an audience of 20,261 inside the arena and thousands outside the stadium who couldn't get tickets. The 100 police found it difficult to control the crowds and crash barriers were buckled.

The Beatles appeared on stage at 9.23 p.m. and after their show were driven away in three limousines with a police motorcycle escort. One boy, in an attempt to stop the cars, threw his bicycle in front of the leading police motorbike, but the escort just swerved to the side and carried on.

● Empire Theatre, *Lime Street, Liverpool L1*

Liverpool's main theatre for live entertainment, situated in the heart of the city centre. The **Quarry Men** made their debut at the Empire at 3.00 p.m. on 9 June 1957 when they auditioned for Carroll Levis' *Search For The Stars* talent show. This was a talent show which was presented at the main theatres throughout the country, highlighting local talent. There were numerous heats, and the winners appeared on a short spot on Levis' television show. This particular heat was won by the Sunnyside Skiffle Group.

The Quarry Men's next appearance at the theatre, when they used the name **Johnny & the Moondogs**, was also as part of the Carroll Levis auditions. Levis held these auditions over three Sunday afternoons on 11, 18 and 25 October 1959. The winners were the Connaughts, a showgroup whose main member, Nicky Cuff, had previously been in the Sunnyside Skiffle Group. The Moondogs had also gained sufficient points to win them an appearance in the finals in Manchester.

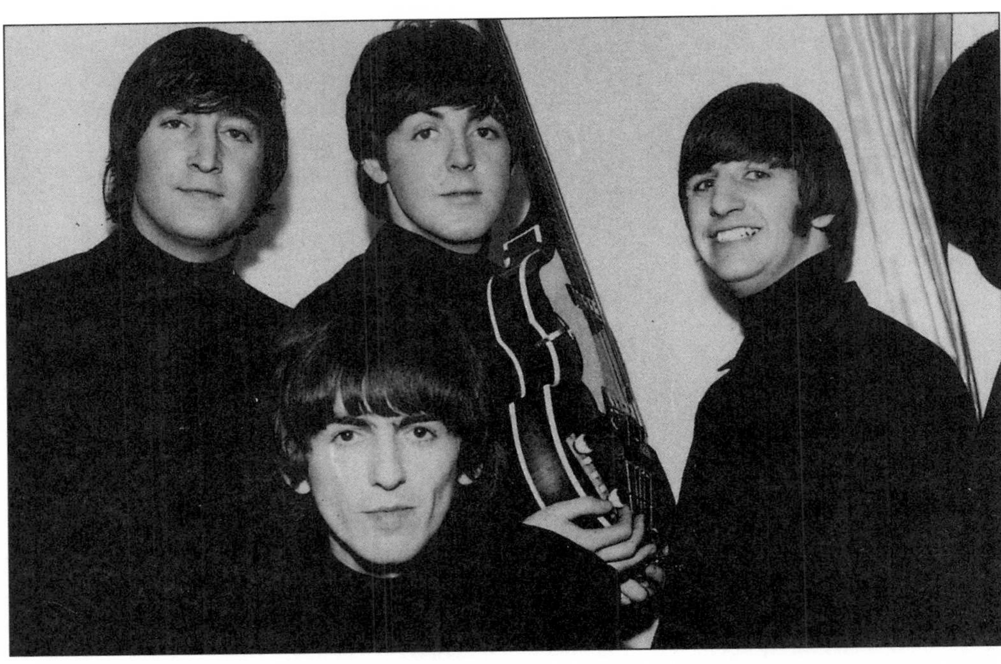

The Beatles backstage at their final performance in their home town, when they appeared at the Empire on 5 December 1965. (Graham Spencer/ *Mersey Beat* Archives)

The Beatles' first Empire appearance as part of the official bill took place on Sunday, 28 October 1962, on a co-production by Epstein's **NEMS Enterprises** and **Ray McFall** of the **Cavern Club**. There were eight acts on the bill, which was topped by **Little Richard** and included **Craig Douglas**, Jett Harris, **Kenny Lynch** and **Sounds Incorporated**. There were two houses that evening and the Beatles were the third act on stage, following the Breakaways. They performed four numbers and remained on stage to provide backing for singer **Craig Douglas**.

On 24 March 1963 they returned to the Empire as part of the bill of the **Chris Montez/Tommy Roe** tour and were back on 26 May 1963 on their **Roy Orbison** tour.

On the afternoon of 7 December 1963 they appeared on a special all-Beatle **'Juke Box Jury'**, filmed from the stage of the theatre as part of their special northern fan club convention and the live show for their fans later in the afternoon was also filmed by the BBC and screened later the same evening as **'It's The Beatles'**.

Their third Empire appearance in 1963 took place on 22 December when they previewed their first Christmas show.

It was almost a year later when they made their next appearance on 8 November 1964.

The Beatles' final concert at the Empire took place on 5 December 1965. It was also the last time they appeared in Liverpool. The demand was such that there were over 40,000 applications for tickets.

● Empire Theatre, *High Street, Sunderland, Tyne & Wear*

The Beatles made their debut at this venue during their **Helen Shapiro** tour on 9 February 1963. Their second and final appearance at the Empire took place on 30 November 1963.

● Empress, The, *High Park Street, Liverpool 8*

The public house on the corner of Admiral Grove, the street where Ringo was reared. The Dingle pub was immortalized on the cover of Ringo's debut album *Sentimental Journey* which was issued on 27 March 1970.

Ringo had decided to record an album of standards and consulted his family regarding the selection of the songs to be included. He then used a photograph of the pub on the album sleeve, with a picture of himself superimposed in the public house doorway and photographs of his relatives peering out from the four upstairs windows.

The Empress wasn't a pub which Ringo himself frequented as it was a drinking hole for a much older age roup and his mother had once worked behind the bar here. However, some years later, the brewers had the hristian names of the Beatles included as a feature above he pub's two doorways.

End, The

he penultimate track on the *Abbey Road* album. Actually, onsidering that there was a gap of twenty seconds ollowing this track and that the last track 'Her Majesty' as only 23 seconds long, in some ways it is considered to e the last song featured on the last recorded album by the eatles, making its title 'The End' quite appropriate.

Work first began on the number, under its working title The Ending', at **Abbey Road** on Wednesday, 23 July 969. Ringo performed a drum solo – his first recorded rum solo on a Beatles release – while there were guitar olos from John, Paul and George.

A 30-piece orchestra was overdubbed onto the track on riday, 15 August 1969, comprising one bass trombone, ne trombone, one string bass, three trumpets, four horns, ur cellos, four violas and twelve violins.

Ephgrave, Joseph

ritish fairground artist. In 1967 he was commissioned by **eter Blake** and the Beatles to paint an ornate drumskin be used in the kit in the centre of the *Sgt Pepper* sleeve bleau.

Ephgrave actually painted two skins, one was used on e sleeve and later went to John Lennon who had it splayed in his Dakota Building apartment in New York nd the alternative became part of Paul McCartney's llection of memorabilia.

EPs

Ps (Extended Players) were particularly popular in the xties and were mid-way between the single and the bum, generally comprising four tracks with a cardboard cture sleeve.

Prior to the release of the Beatles' first EP, the most ccessful EP release in Britain had been **Elvis Presley**'s *llow That Dream*, which had reached No. 11 in the ***New usical Express*** charts. *Twist And Shout*, issued on 12 ly 1963 on GEP 8882, comprised 'Twist And Shout', 'A Taste Of Honey', 'Do You Want To Know A Secret' and 'There's A Place'. It reached No. 4 in the *New Musical Express* chart.

Their next EP, *The Beatles Hits*, was issued on 6 September 1963 on GEP 8880 and comprised 'From Me To You', 'Thank You Girl', 'Please Please Me' and 'Love Me Do'. It reached No. 14 in the charts.

The Beatles (No. 1) was issued on 1 November 1963 on GEP 8883 and comprised 'I Saw Her Standing There', 'Misery', 'Anna (Go To Him)' and 'Chains'. It reached No. 24 in the charts.

All My Loving was issued on 7 February 1964 on GEP 8891 and comprised 'All My Loving', 'Ask Me Why', 'Money (That's What I Want)' and 'P.S. I Love You'. It reached No. 13 in the charts.

Long Tall Sally was issued on 19 June 1964 on GEP 8913 and comprised 'Long Tall Sally', 'I Call Your Name', 'Slow Down' and 'Matchbox'. This fifth EP release was the first to contain previously unreleased tracks and reached No. 11 in the charts. The chart positions quoted are those for the singles charts. There was also an EP chart and this record topped it.

Extracts From The Film A Hard Day's Night was issued on 6 November 1964 on GEP 8920 and comprised 'I Should Have Known Better', 'If I Fell', 'Tell Me Why' and 'And I Love Her'.

Extracts From The Album A Hard Day's Night was issued on 6 November 1964 on GEP 8924 and comprised 'Anytime At All', 'I'll Cry Instead', 'Things We Said Today' and 'When I Get Home'.

Beatles For Sale was issued on 6 April 1965 on GEP 8938 and comprised 'No Reply', 'I'm A Loser', 'Rock And Roll Music' and 'Eight Days A Week'.

Beatles For Sale No. 2 was issued on 4 June 1965 on GEP 8938 and comprised 'I'll Follow The Sun', 'Baby's In Black', 'Words Of Love' and 'I Don't Want To Spoil The Party'.

The Beatles Million Sellers was issued on 6 December 1965 on GEP 8946 and comprised 'She Loves You', 'I Want To Hold Your Hand', 'Can't Buy Me Love' and 'I Feel Fine'.

Yesterday was issued on 4 March 1966 on GEP 8948 and comprised 'Act Naturally', 'You Like Me Too Much', 'Yesterday' and 'It's Only Love'. Interestingly, a different member of the group takes lead vocal on each track.

Nowhere Man was issued on 8 July 1966 on GEP 8952

and comprised 'Nowhere Man', 'Drive My Car', 'Michelle' and 'You Won't See Me'.

Their thirteenth and final EP was *Magical Mystery Tour*, issued on 8 December 1967 on SMMT 1/2 as a set of two EPs comprising the tracks 'Magical Mystery Tour', 'Your Mother Should Know', 'I Am The Walrus', 'The Fool On The Hill', 'Flying' and 'Blue Jay Way'. The package came with a 24-page booklet and a gatefold sleeve.

Over a decade later Parlophone issued *The Beatles' EP Collection* on BEP 14 in December 1981, a boxed set containing all the above EPs, plus an extra bonus EP called *She's A Woman*, which comprised the tracks 'She's A Woman', 'Baby You're A Rich Man', 'This Boy' and 'The Inner Light'.

One other EP was issued in Britain during the sixties. This was *My Bonnie*, issued on Polydor NH 21-610 in July 1963 and contained the tracks 'My Bonnie', 'Why', 'Cry For A Shadow' and 'The Saints'. It made no impact on the charts.

Extended players weren't as common in America as they were in Britain.

On 23 March 1964 **Vee Jay** issued *Souvenir Of Their Visit To America (The Beatles)* on V JED 1-903 which contained four tracks from the *Introducing The Beatles* album: 'Misery', 'A Taste Of Honey', 'Ask Me Why' and 'Anna (Go To Him)'. The record failed to make a chart placing.

The first **Capitol** EP was *Four By The Beatles*, issued on 11 May 1964 on EAP 2121, and comprised two tracks each from the *Meet The Beatles* and *The Beatles Second Album* LPs. They were 'Roll Over Beethoven', 'All My Loving', 'This Boy' and 'Please Mr Postman'. The EP reached No. 92 in the *Billboard* charts and No. 86 in *Cash Box*, but didn't receive a placing in the *Record World* charts.

Capitol next issued *4 By The Beatles* on 1 February 1965 on R5365. This comprised tracks from the *Beatles '65* album: 'Honey Don't', 'I'm A Loser', 'Mr Moonlight' and 'Everybody's Trying To Be My Baby'. The EP reached No. 68 in both the *Cash Box* and *Billboard* charts. Capitol decided to abandon plans for any further Beatle releases in the EP format.

● Epsom Registry Office, Epsom, Surrey

Site of the marriage between George Harrison and **Pattie Boyd** on 21 January 1966. The honour of Best Man went to both Paul McCartney and Brian Epstein. John and Ringo weren't in attendance as they were on holiday i Trinidad at the time, but both sent flowers, greetings an presents. Brian Epstein, **Neil Aspinall** and **Mal Evan** were in attendance, together with the parents of the brid and groom. The wedding plans had been kept secret and short press conference was arranged after the event i which a member of the press asked, 'How on earth did yo manage to keep it a secret?' George replied, 'Simple. W didn't tell anyone.'

There was a reception afterwards at George's bungalo **Kinfauns** and Mrs Harrison told a friend: 'I felt as if I ha lost everything. Quite silly, really. As we were in the ca with them returning from the ceremony, George took m hand and said, "It doesn't mean because I'm married don't need you anymore, Mum. We need you more now. He's such a lovable son, and cares about how people feel.

George and Pattie then went off on honeymoon t Barbados.

● Epstein, Brian Samuel

The manager who steered the Beatles to success.

Brian was born on 19 September 1934 at a priva nursing home at 4 Rodney Street, Liverpool, to **Harry** an **Queenie Epstein**. His brother **Clive John** was born 2 months later.

The family moved to Prestatyn in North Wales for short time in 1939 at the onset of World War II and the spent three years in Southport where the five-year-old b attended Southport College. He was also educated Croxton Preparatory School and at the age of ten entere Liverpool College. He was not happy at this particul school and left after a year to attend Wellesley School Aigburth. His parents, however, feeling that there we elements of anti-semitism in the local schools sent him a Jewish boarding school, Beaconsfield School in Fra Sussex. He spent two years there, briefly attende Claysemore, near Taunton, and then Wrekin College. I left Wrekin in the summer of 1950 to begin work at branch of the family business, I. Epstein & Sons in Walt Road.

At the age of eighteen he was conscripted for Nation Service. His first choice was the Royal Air Force, but th rejected him and he began the two-year stint in the Ro Army Service Corps at Aldershot where he was medica discharged after ten months because he was deemed to emotionally and mentally unfit. On his return to the fam usiness he was put in charge of a branch of the family rm, Clarendon Furnishing in Hoylake, where he proved ery successful.

Brian had other aspirations than to spend his life orking in a family business and, due to his interest in the eatre and a friendship he had established with some ctors and actresses appearing at the **Playhouse 'heatre**, he decided he wanted to join RADA (Royal cademy of Dramatic Arts). Before doing so, he nburdened the fact that he was homosexual to his family. lis mother sympathized and his father and Clive were pset, although it was decided that Brian would be given e opportunity to study at RADA.

He passed the audition for RADA on 19 September 956, his 22nd birthday, but soon found he was not cut out be an actor and decided not to complete the RADA ourse and returned to the family business in 1957.

When Harry opened the premises of the new NEMS ore in Great Charlotte Street he placed Brian in charge of e ground floor record section while Clive ran the ectrical and domestic goods department on the first floor. nger Anne Shelton performed the opening ceremony.

The record department proved so successful that nother branch was opened at 12–14 Whitechapel, with rian in charge. His friend **Peter Brown**, from **Lewis's** cord department, replaced him in the record section at reat Charlotte Street. Singer Anthony Newley was ngaged to open the Whitechapel branch.

The first issue of a music publication called ***Mersey eat*** was issued on 6 July 1961 and Brian ordered a ozen copies. They sold out immediately and Brian dered more, which also sold out. He ordered twelve zen copies of Issue No. 2, published on 20 July 1961. ne cover was devoted to a story of the Beatles' recording nt for Polydor in Hamburg and the bold headline ran eatles Sign Recording Contract'. Epstein called up *ersey Beat*'s editor/owner Bill Harry to enquire about the cal scene which was being promoted in the paper. He is fascinated that so many customers came into the store buy *Mersey Beat* specifically and noticed how interested ey seemed in local groups. Harry told him that the scene Liverpool was unique, that there were more than 300 oups playing locally. Epstein's interest grew and he inted to know more about the group who seemed to be atured in each issue – the Beatles. He even asked if he uld contribute a record column and his first column appeared in the third issue, dated 3 August 1961. Harry told Epstein that his reviews were mainly of classical, jazz and middle-of-the-road records and that he should concentrate more on pop and rock 'n' roll, so Brian altered his direction and began to review records by artists such as **Elvis Presley**.

The *Mersey Beat* coverage of the Beatles continued and Epstein asked Harry if he could arrange for him to go down to the **Cavern** to see them, which he did. Accompanied by his personal assistant, **Alistair Taylor**, Brian arrived at the Cavern, which was only a short distance from his Whitechapel store, at 12.30 p.m. on 9 November 1961. He dropped into the bandroom and had a brief chat with the Beatles, discovering that they knew of him because of the record store, which they frequented. A month later he visited them again and left a message with George Harrison that he'd like to meet up with the group at NEMS. The meeting was arranged for 4.30 p.m. on Wednesday, 3 December 1961, and John Lennon asked local disc jockey **Bob Wooler** to accompany them, telling Epstein that Wooler was his father. John, George and Pete had arrived slightly late, which irked the punctilious Epstein, who was even more upset at the fact that Paul McCartney turned up 30 minutes later.

A further meeting at NEMS took place on Wednesday, 10 December 1961, with Alistair Taylor present. It was decided by all concerned that Brian would become the Beatles' manager. The first contract was to be for a five-year period from 1 February 1962, with the option that either side could end the agreement on three months' notice. Epstein's commission was to be 10 per cent of any income up to £1,500 per year and 15 per cent above that amount. A formal signing took place on 24 January 1962 at **Pete Best**'s home in Hayman's Green. All four signed, with Alistair Taylor as witness, although Epstein himself didn't sign the contract. A second management contract for five years was drawn up on 1 October 1962. By 1963 Brian's commission had been increased to 25 per cent.

Brian became utterly dedicated to the group and set about altering their image. Part of the contract, drawn up by the Epstein family solicitor Rex Makin, read that Brian would 'advise the artists on all matters concerning clothes, make-up and presentation and construction of the artists' act'. At the time the Beatles were a rough lot, smoking and chewing gum on stage, indulging in conversation with their fans during the act and were dressed in black leather.

Brian told them that they could no longer smoke or swea on stage, that they must become more professional an dress in smart stage suits. This delighted Paul McCartney although John Lennon wasn't happy about the new imag which Epstein was moulding for them. Brian even ha John visit Bill Harry to request the return of photograph of John in Hamburg – some of him reading a newspaper i his underpants, others of him on stage with a toilet sea around his neck. Smart mohair suits were made by Ben Dorn, new photo sessions were arranged, their hair wa styled by Brian's hairdresser at Horne Brothers.

Locally, Brian began to increase his advertising i *Mersey Beat*, upped the price of the Beatles appearance and decided to promote a series of concerts with majo names, placing the Beatles second on the bill, in an effort t build their name. As he still knew relatively little about th rock 'n' roll scene and the mechanics of promotion, h relied heavily on the advice of several experts, includin Bob Wooler, **Sam Leach**, **Joe Flannery** and Bill Harr Leach had been promoting large concerts at the **Towe Ballroom** and Epstein suggested that they go into busines

Above: Brian Epstein as a young schoolboy. (Clive Epstein)
Right: Backstage at the Empire Theatre, Liverpool, with Billy J. Kramer.

together with joint promotions at the venue. Leach refused because Brian wished his brother Clive to have a third interest and Sam didn't like the idea of only receiving a third when he'd practically built up the Tower Ballroom as a rock venue by his own efforts. Epstein then approached Bob Wooler and had him organize a number of the NEMS promotions, and he also organized some joint promotions with **Ray McFall** of the Cavern. The various events were held at local venues such as the Tower Ballroom, the **Empire Theatre** and the **Queens Hall, Widnes** with the Beatles supporting such artists as **Little Richard, Bruce**

Channel, Joe Brown and **Craig Douglas**.

Before this, Brian had realized that the ambition uppermost in the minds of the Beatles was to obtain a recording contract. His position in the family business gave him a certain amount of clout. The family now had nine record stores in Liverpool with a stock of half a million records. Brian had also organized the Liverpool branch of the Gramophone Record Retailers' Association. He contacted **Ron White** of **EMI** Records, but on 18 December 1961 was informed by White that EMI did not wish to sign the Beatles, who had been turned down by the A&R men in charge of their three main pop labels. His contacts with **Decca**, however, had resulted in an actual recording audition which was to take place on 1 January 1962 in London, supervised by **Mike Smith**.

Initially, it seemed that the audition had proved a success. Smith indicated to **Tony Barrow**, who wrote for the ***Liverpool Echo***, that Decca would be signing the group. However, at the last minute they were turned down in favour of **Brian Poole & the Tremeloes**. Brian was determined to plough ahead, although he was becoming despondent, realizing how important a record contract was to the band. On 8 May 1962 he went to London's HMV store to have some tapes transferred to acetates and was put in touch with **Sid Coleman** of EMI's music publishing company Ardmore & Beechwood. Coleman fixed up a meeting between Epstein and George Martin of the Parlophone label. Parlophone wasn't one of EMI's pop labels and had basically been a label for middle-of-the-road singers such as Matt Munro, comedy discs such as **Peter Sellers'** and Sophia Loren's 'Goodness Gracious Me' and the recording of revues such as *Beyond The Fringe* and *Flanders And Swann*. The meeting resulted in a recording audition and Brian was so convinced that they had passed it that he was to send telegrams to the Beatles and Bill Harry confirming that they had a recording contract with Parlophone. Paul sent him a return telegram: 'WATCH OUT ELVIS', while John's cable read: 'HOW SOON SHALL WE BE MILLIONAIRES'. Martin did make up his mind to sign them and following their initial recording test on 6 June 1962 they were booked to record their first disc on 4 September 1962. In the meantime, however, Brian received instructions from John, Paul and George that **Pete Best** had to go. Epstein was anguished over this decision, and sought to make the blow softer by offering Best other options. Epstein had now begun to sign various bands, such as **Gerry & the Pacemakers**, and was building a stable of acts. Best refused to remain under his management.

The Liverpool acts who were personally managed by Epstein grew to: the Beatles, Gerry & the Pacemakers, **Billy J. Kramer**, **Cilla Black**, the **Fourmost**, the Big Three, the **Remo Four** and **Tommy Quickly**.

The Beatles decided to offer Ringo Starr of **Rory Storm & the Hurricanes** the post as Best's replacement and the group's first British single 'Love Me Do' was issued on 5 October 1962. Rumours persisted in Liverpool that Brian had bought 10,000 copies of the disc. 'Love Me Do' had minor chart success and signalled the group's emergence on the national stage. They appeared on their first television show **'People And Places'** for Granada Television and were soon beginning to appear regularly on BBC radio programmes. Epstein next arranged for them to be placed on the bill of nationwide tours organized by **Arthur Howes**.

An event which was to prove controversial for many years took place on 28 April 1963. Brian Epstein and John Lennon flew out on a holiday together to Spain. This occurred less than three weeks after the birth of John's son, **Julian**. Although no one really knows what happened on this holiday as both parties are dead, it is generally believed that there was no sexual affair involved as John was heterosexual and **Cynthia** was to say that she was convinced that there were no sexual encounters between them. In 1992 there was even a film based on the holiday called *The Hours And Times*. At Paul McCartney's 21st birthday party Bob Wooler implied that there had been a sexual liaison between Epstein and Lennon which resulted in John beating him up.

Epstein's homosexuality did not affect his management of the Beatles. Suppositions, such as that in Philip Norman's book *Shout!*, that Epstein fell in love with Lennon as soon as he saw him at the Cavern, which is why he signed the Beatles, are false. Epstein went to the Cavern because he had discovered that there was a unique scene happening on Merseyside, with the Beatles at its core, and he wanted to be part of it. The people who were actually active on the local scene at the time and were friends of both the Beatles and Epstein, knew that his homosexuality had nothing to do with his signing of the group. It's true that he did once ask Pete Best to spend the night with him – and propositioned another musician, Paddy Chambers, but when they told him they were heterosexual, he made no further approaches. Brian's tastes were reputed to be for 'rough trade', and he was the object of blackmail on a few occasions.

As his **NEMS Enterprises** company was growing, he had to move to separate offices in Moorfields, Liverpool.

1963 was the year in which **Beatlemania** was born and the Beatles became a phenomenon in Britain, appearing regularly on TV and radio shows, they were the subject of the documentary **'The Mersey Sound'**, they appeared on top rating TV shows such as 'Sunday Night At the London Palladium' and appeared on the *Royal Variety Show*, ending the year with their own *Beatles Christmas Show*.

Over the next months and years, the Beatles were to grow into the most celebrated entertainers in history and Brian continued to guide them. He'd now moved to a prestigious suite of offices in London, but also involved himself in other activities, continuing to sign up furthe[r] acts – **Sounds Incorporated**, the **Rustiks**, the **Silkie**[,] **Michael Haslam** – and promoting shows of his own, suc[h] as *Pops Alive!* So much was happening with the Beatle[s] that their activities alone were enough to engage hi[s] continual attention. Colonel Tom Parker often wondere[d] why Epstein bothered with other acts when he had th[e]

Brian Epstein hosts the *Hullabaloo* TV show. (Clive Epstein)

Beatles. Perhaps this accounts for a number of slipshod decisions Epstein made during this period, such as demanding a petty percentage for the Beatles' first film *A Hard Day's Night*, when the producers were prepared to offer a much more substantial deal; also, giving away 90 per cent of the merchandising rights to an outside organization.

1964 was the year in which the Beatles conquered America. Brian had travelled to the States late in 1963 and negotiated their **'Ed Sullivan'** appearances and also arranged for **Capitol Records** to not only release the group's records, but to spend an unprecedented sum on the promotion of the band. The giant American and world tours followed.

Brian also wished to become a major personality in his own right. He appeared on numerous TV and radio shows, ranging from **'Juke Box Jury'** to **'Desert Island Discs'**, employed **Derek Taylor** to pen his biography, *A Cellarful Of Noise*, and even hosted an American TV show 'Hullabaloo'. In the meantime, many of the acts he signed proved unsuccessful – Quickly, Haslam, Silkie, the Rustiks and others all disappeared from the scene, as did new signings such as **Paddy, Klaus & Gibson**. His venture to establish a major rock venue/theatre at the **Saville Theatre** in London's West End was an expensive flop and he began to develop a passion for gambling.

By 1967 Epstein seemed to be losing interest in his own companies and was telling impresario **Robert Stigwood** that he wished to retire and live in Spain. He was to reveal to his friend **Larry Parnes** that he was afraid that the Beatles wouldn't re-sign with him when their contract lapsed. Brian had become heavily dependent on drugs and was now rarely seen at his offices.

On Friday, 25 August 1967, Brian decided to spend the weekend at his country home at **Kingsley Hill** with his friends **Geoffrey Ellis** and Peter Brown. When he arrived he phoned his mother in Liverpool to tell her that after the weekend he was going to join the Beatles at their Transcendental Meditation studies in Bangor, North Wales, after which he would visit her in Liverpool. During the course of the evening he became restless, due to the fact that a number of other friends he'd invited for the weekend hadn't arrived, so he drove back to London.

On Saturday morning his mother rang Kingsley Hill and spoke to Peter Brown and Geoffrey Ellis, who told her Brian had returned to London. She rang **Chapel Street** and Brian's butler Antonio told her Brian was still asleep, so she requested that he wasn't to be disturbed. On Sunday at noon, Antonio and his wife Maria attempted to contact Brian on the intercom. There was no reply, so they phoned Kingsley Hill, but Brown and Ellis were out, so Antonio got in touch with Brian's secretary **Joanne Newfield**, who called Alistair Taylor. Both of them arrived at Chapel Street and phoned Peter Brown, who had returned to Kingsley Hill. He advised them to contact his own GP, Doctor John Gallway, who lived nearby. When the doctor arrived a decision was taken to break down the doors to Brian's locked room. His body was found on the bed.

The coroner's decision was that Brian had died of an accidental overdose of Carbitol.

Brian Epstein was 32 years old at the time of his death and despite the coroner's verdict, writers have perpetuated the myth that he committed suicide. Philip Norman's *Shout!* hinted at a murder plot, as did Albert Goldman's *The Lives Of John Lennon*.

Brian's body was buried at the Jewish Cemetery in Long Lane, Aintree, Liverpool, in Section A, Grave H12.

● Epstein, Clive

Clive Epstein talks to Liz Hughes of Cavern Mecca.

Brian Epstein's brother, younger by 22 months. Clive's early years proved him a more successful and less troubled person than Brian. He excelled at Wrekin College and did well in the army, where be became a sergeant in the Royal Army Education Corps.

When the Epstein family opened their large NEMS store in Charlotte Street in Liverpool's city centre, Clive ran the electrical and domestic goods section while Brian handled the record department.

With Brian's discovery of the Beatles and the decision that he wished to manage them, the Epstein family agreed to the formation of **NEMS Enterprises**. The company was launched on 26 June 1962 with a share capital of £100. The brothers shared 50 per cent of the company equally and Clive was appointed Company Secretary.

On 27 April 1964 NEMS Enterprises increased its share capital to £10,000. Brian's share was increased to 5,000, Clive's to 4,000 and each member of the Beatles received 250 shares.

Clive was a scrupulously fair man, extremely popular with those he dealt with and, in some eyes, a more reliable person to deal with than Brian. Nevertheless, he always maintained a low profile. He didn't display the entrepreneurial skills of Brian, was slowly methodical in all of his dealings and was more at home working in Liverpool than in London. Paul once described him as a 'provincial furniture salesman'.

On Brian's death in August 1967, Clive was appointed Chairman of NEMS Enterprises. He realized that the Beatles and **Robert Stigwood** were not compatible and a deal was arranged which led to Stigwood leaving NEMS with his various acts such as the Bee Gees and Cream. A new company, NEMS Holdings, was formed with Clive as Chairman and **Vic Lewis** as Managing Director.

Although eternally suspicious of 'the men in suits', as Clive was a known and trusted friend, the Beatles appeared to accept him as Brian's successor until their NEMS contract expired.

It was Clive who first planted the seed which was to become **Apple Corps**. He realized that a vast proportion of their income, about two million pounds, would go to the taxman unless they diversified and he suggested that they should invest in retail outlets – shops. Paul was excited about the idea and initially visualized a department store in which everything would be white. Paul said, 'It would be great. We could have a department where they sell nothing but white clothes, another where you can buy white furniture – even a white grand piano – and still another where you can buy white pets.'

NEMS Holdings continued to act as agent for the Beatles, taking 25 per cent of their royalties, but was not really expanding or advising the group on their ventures such as *Magical Mystery Tour*. Clive didn't like the constant commuting to London from his Liverpool home.

He felt comfortable in Liverpool, had married Barbara Mattison and settled down. They had two children, a son Henry and a daughter Joanna. There were also the estate duties of half a million pounds hanging over the heads of the Epstein family following Brian's death.

When Clive was approached at the latter part of 1967 by a City merchant bank, Triumph Investment Trust, who wanted to buy NEMS, he gave it serious thought, but didn't immediately respond. He was approached again by Leonard Richenberg, representing Triumph, who made him a good offer, but he still demurred. Clive had felt that he was morally obliged to let the Beatles have first offer on buying NEMS and told Richenberg in January 1969 that he was going to sell NEMS to the Beatles' company Apple.

In the meantime, the Beatles' financial affairs were complicated. Paul had engaged **Linda**'s brother **John Eastman** to look after the Beatles' affairs, while the other three Beatles had decided on **Allen Klein**. There were mix-ups between the two. Klein met with Clive and asked him to defer a decision about selling NEMS until he examined the accounts. In February, Clive received a letter from Eastman, part of which read: 'As you know Mr Allen Klein is doing an audit of the Beatles' affairs vis-à-vis NEMS and Nemperor Holdings Ltd. When this has been completed I suggest we meet to discuss the results of Mr Klein's audit as well as the propriety of the negotiations surrounding the nine-year agreement between EMI, the Beatles and NEMS.'

Clive was furious and sent back a note: 'Before any meeting takes place, please be good enough to let me know precisely what you mean by the phrase "the propriety of the negotiations surrounding the nine-year agreement between EMI, the Beatles and NEMS".'

Six weeks after he had told Triumph he would be selling NEMS to Apple, Clive closed the deal with Richenberg.

Eastman blamed Klein and said that while he had been negotiating to obtain NEMS from Clive, Klein had turned up and told the Beatles, 'Forget it, I'll get you NEMS for nothing because the Epsteins owe you money.' However Clive maintained that it was Eastman who jaded him against selling NEMS to the Beatles.

Clive remained on Merseyside where he built up a successful furniture business. He later decided to return to show business and in the late seventies teamed up with **Joe Flannery** to manage a Liverpool band Motion Pictures. He was also intending to go into partnership with **Sid Bernstein**.

Tragically, Clive died of a heart attack during a skiing holiday with his wife Barbara, on 2 February 1988. His funeral took place on 5 February at Greenbank Drive Synagogue in Liverpool.

● Epstein, Harry

A Jewish furniture retailer from Liverpool. Harry's father Isaac was a penniless Polish immigrant who opened a furniture store, I. Epstein & Sons, in Walton Road, in 1901. Harry took over the running of the business. While on holiday in St Anne's-on-Sea he met Malka Hyman, daughter of a family who were also in the furniture business – they owned the Sheffield Cabinet Ltd. The couple were married in Sheffield in 1933 and immediately moved to 197 **Queens Drive** in Liverpool.

Harry and Malka (who was known as 'Queenie') had two sons, **Brian** and **Clive**. When Harry expanded his business he brought his two sons in as Directors.

The family also decided to support Brian in his plans to manage the Beatles, but insisted that Clive should join him to advise on business matters.

In 1966 Harry had a heart attack and was admitted to **Sefton General Hospital** in Liverpool. In 1967 Harry and **Queenie** moved to Bournemouth where he was to convalesce and recuperate. Queenie found him dead in bed on the morning of 17 July. He was 63 years old.

His son Brian died several weeks later.

● Epstein, Queenie

Although Jewish, Malka Hyman had been educated at a Catholic boarding school and had anglicized her first name, which, roughly translated in Yiddish, means Queen.

Her family owned the Sheffield Cabinet Company and at the age of eighteen she met and married 28-year-old **Harry Epstein**. A five-bedroom house in **Queen's Drive**, Childwall, Liverpool, was given to the couple as her dowry.

Queenie had two sons, **Brian** and **Clive**. When Brian revealed that he was homosexual, Queenie was supportive and always poured her love on her son.

When her husband died in July 1967, Queenie came to London to spend some time with Brian. She returned to Liverpool after ten days and three days later Brian was found dead. When she was told she collapsed and had to be sedated.

A concerned John Lennon said to her, 'Come to India with us and meditate.' Queenie apparently asked him what they actually did when they meditated. He said, 'Well, you think of something – like, say, a carrot.' Queenie told him, 'Whenever I think of a carrot, I think of tomorrow's lunch.'

A further blow was to come when her second son Clive died prematurely of a heart attack.

● Ernst Merck Halle, *Hamburg, Germany*

The Beatles arrived at Central Station at 6.00 a.m. on 26 June 1966 and were surprised to see an old friend waiting for them on the platform – Bettina Derlin, the buxom barmaid from the **Star Club**. They were then driven in a

Queenie Epstein with her son Clive and his family.

black Mercedes to the Schloss Hotel in Tremsbuttel, about 30 miles from Hamburg where they slept in until 1.30 p.m. and were then driven to the **Ernst Merck Halle** for their two final concerts in West Germany.

A number of old friends came to greet them backstage, including Bettina, Cattia, a former girlfriend of Paul's, Gibson Kemp, former drummer with bands such as **Rory Storm & the Hurricanes**, with his girlfriend **Astrid Kirchherr**, former fiancée of **Stuart Sutcliffe**, and **Bert Kaempfert** and his wife.

This was the Beatles' first visit to Hamburg since 1 January 1963.

Outside the hall the fans ran riot and 500 police were used to control them, with the aid of water cannons.

● Escorts, The

A popular Liverpool band who never quite achieved their potential.

They comprised Terry Sylvester (guitar), John Kinrade (guitar), Mike Gregory (bass) and Pete Clarke (drums), although an earlier member, when they first formed in 1961, was John Foster. John was Ringo Starr's cousin and Ringo arranged for the group to have a residency at the **Blue Angel Club**.

The group appeared on the bill with the Beatles at several **Cavern** appearances including the Beatles' very last gig there on 3 August 1963. Tickets went on sale almost two weeks prior to the gig and were sold out in half an hour. The Beatles were paid £300 for the appearance and although Brian Epstein told **Bob Wooler** that the group would be back, they never were.

Paul McCartney produced the Escorts single 'From Head To Toe' coupled with 'Night Time', issued on 18 November 1966 on Columbia DB 8061, but it fared no better than their previous releases.

Terry Sylvester was later to join the **Hollies**.

● Eubanks, Bob

The boss and also a disc jockey at the Hollywood radio station KRLA. It was Eubanks and the station who promoted the Beatles' **Hollywood Bowl** appearance on 23 August 1964.

When he booked the venue, Eubanks was told by the Hollywood Bowl officials that it would be physically impossible to sell out the show at the Bowl in one day. Three hours after the box office opened, every ticket had been sold.

Eubanks approached Epstein and tried to arrange a second show at the Bowl, but Epstein refused.

Eubanks was later to offer **Derek Taylor** a job when he left **NEMS Enterprises**. Taylor left England and settled in Hollywood as a member of Eubanks' Prestige Promotions. One of the tasks he had was to conduct interviews with the Beatles in the Bahamas during the filming of *Help!* This proved an embarrassment both to Derek and the Beatles, although the tapes were never aired.

● Euston Station, Euston, London NW1

The Beatles had decided to travel to the **Maharishi**'s weekend seminar at Bangor's Normal College and set off for Euston Station on 25 August 1967 to catch the 3.05 p.m. train. The press had found out all about it and the *Daily Mirror* had run a piece headed 'A Mystical Special'. When the group arrived at the station and set off for platform 8 there were thousands of sightseers milling about.

In the mêlée, a policeman forcibly held **Cynthia Lennon** back, thinking she was a fan. He prevented her catching the train and as it moved away, she burst into tears. She commented, 'Being an emotional female I burst into tears, I found it really very embarrassing. Brian's secretary put his arm around me in an effort to comfort me in my hour of need, telling me not to worry, that **Neil** [**Aspinall**] would drive me to Bangor and that we would probably get there before the train arrived.'

John, Paul, George, Ringo, **Pattie Harrison**, Mick Jagger, **Marianne Faithfull** and **Jennie Boyd** were all crammed into one first-class compartment. They were afraid even to go to the loo in case they were mobbed by fans. Eventually they went to see the Maharishi and had a chat with him in his compartment before moving off to the dining car for some tea. Although a section had been cordoned off for them a couple of teenagers had burst through. 'What are you going to Bangor for? Are you playing there?' they asked. 'That's right,' said Ringo. 'On the Pier Head at 8.30. Second House. See you.'

● Evans, Mal

The friend the Beatles called 'Big Mal'.

He was 26 years old and working as a telecommunications engineer at the Post Office building near to the **Cavern** when he decided to drop into the club one lunchtime. He became fascinated by the venue and began to attend regularly, becoming friendly with George Harrison, whom he asked back to his house one day to listen to his records. George suggested that he should ask for a job at the Cavern door where his 6ft 2in size would make him an ideal 'bouncer'. George introduced him to **Ray McFall** and Mal began to work the Cavern door in his spare time, together with fellow doormen Tony Buck, Sean Connelly and **Pat Delaney**.

He'd been working there for three months when, in 1963, Brian Epstein offered him the job as equipment road manager to the Beatles. This job was nicknamed 'the humper' and was the lowest in the pecking order of road managers, being the person who humps the gear around, unloading it from vans and setting it up – a position formerly occupied by **Neil Aspinall**, whose other duties precluded him from continuing with the job.

At the time Mal lived in Mossley Hill with his wife Lil and they'd just had a baby son. She advised him against taking the job, but he went ahead and joined the team as assistant to Neil. He travelled the world with the group and wrote of his adventures with the **Fab Four** in *Beatles Monthly*. He also appeared briefly as a long-distance swimmer in *Help!* and followed up with appearances in *Magical Mystery Tour* and *Let It Be*. He also had a cameo role in the spaghetti western ***Blindman***, in which Ringo appeared as a villain.

Since he was always at the Beatles' side in the recording studios, he was often asked to participate and played Hammond organ on 'You Won't See Me' on the *Rubber Soul* album; sang in the chorus of 'Yellow Submarine'; played bass harmonium on 'Being For The Benefit Of Mr Kite' and played one of the pianos on 'A Day In The Life' on the *Sgt Pepper* album; the tambourine on 'Dear Prudence' and trumpet on 'Helter Skelter' on *The Beatles* double album; the anvil on 'Maxwell's Silver Hammer' on the *Abbey Road* album and backing vocals on 'You Know My Name (Look Up The Number)'.

Following three years of globe-trotting with the Beatles he was given a job as one of their personal assistants when they ceased touring. In 1968 he was appointed an executive at Apple and took an interest in the recording activities there, discovering a group called the Iveys. He produced their record, 'No Matter What'. They later changed their name to **Badfinger**.

He also helped to co-produce a record by **Jackie Lomax**.

When Apple began to shed its staff in the wake of **Allen Klein**, Mal moved to America.

He'd become estranged from his wife and two children and found himself at a loose end, finding it difficult to cope with an uneventful existence after the intense excitement of the Beatles years.

He began to write a book of his experiences. At the time he was living in Los Angeles with a woman and her four-year-old daughter. When he seemed in a depressed and desperate state, she rang the police. Mal was locked in an adjoining room and had an air pistol. When two policemen burst into the room they saw the pistol and fired six shots into him, killing him instantly.

His ashes and the manuscript he'd been writing were sent to his wife in England, but it was rumoured that they were lost in the post. However, this seems to be just one of the many colourful stories associated with Beatles history. Mal had completed a book with John Hoernle called 'Living the Beatles Legend', which at one time seemed as if it would be published by Grosset and Dunlap, but the book remains unpublished.

● Evans, Malcolm

Not to be confused with the Beatles' road manager of that name.

Evans, a former junior executive of Rediffusion Television, was 25 years old when he was invited by **Nicky Byrne** to become one of the shareholders of the Beatles' merchandising company **Seltaeb** for a fee of £1,000.

Byrne made Evans Vice-President of the company and three weeks before the Beatles toured Australia, Evans flew there to visit Stephen, Jacques and Stephen, a Sydney law firm, to brief them on protecting the merchandising rights.

Following Evans' visit, a large amount of Seltaeb-approved merchandise began to flood the Australian stores – stockings, calendars, bracelets, wallpaper, plastic wigs, dolls, trays and posters. However, a large amount of the goods weren't sold as the Australians weren't as enthusiastic about merchandising souvenirs as the American fans.

● Evans, Mike

Born in Rhyl, North Wales, in 1941, Mike moved to Liverpool and became a member of the Clayton Squares, a popular group who were managed by Cavern Artistes.

Later he was to join the Liverpool scene and remained with the group until they disbanded in 1970. He joined various other bands before becoming Rock Organizer of the Musicians' Union.

Mike wrote *Nothing To Get Hung About*, a short Beatles book contained in the Liverpool Corporation package ***The Beatles Collection***. He also co-authored *In The Footsteps of the Beatles* with Ron Jones, which was published by Merseyside County Council in a limited edition of 5,000 copies in 1981.

Merseyside County Council asked him to conduct a feasibility study on a proposed major exhibition of art works inspired by the Beatles. The result was ***The Art Of The Beatles***, a major exhibition which was presented at Liverpool's Walker Art Gallery in 1984.

The exhibition was a tremendous success and Mike's book *The Art Of The Beatles* was published by Anthony Blond the same year. Later in the eighties Mike was to organize *Art Of The Beatles* exhibitions in Japan and Germany as well and he also helped to organize a travelling exhibition of **Stuart Sutcliffe**'s work while co-writing a book on Sutcliffe with Pauline Sutcliffe.

● Everett, Kenny

Liverpool-born disc jockey who first came to prominence while broadcasting from the pirate ship Radio London. In 1967 he joined BBC's Radio One, was later sacked over a controversial remark he made and went to Capital Radio. His 'The Kenny Everett Video Show' became a success on television and he was to return to work on both BBC radio and television. Everett became one of Brian Epstein's close friends. He interviewed the Beatles on a number of occasions and recorded a discussion with Paul which was aired on the BBC radio show **'Where It's At'** on 20 May 1967 when he also gave an exclusive preview of the *Sgt Pepper's Lonely Hearts Club Band* album. He interviewed John about *Magical Mystery Tour* for the 'Where It's At' programme on 25 November 1967. He also wrote occasional pieces for *Beatles Monthly*.

When the Beatles recorded their contributions to their Christmas records to fans separately in 1968 and 1969, it was Kenny who edited the parts together and he is credited on the sleeves as Producer.

In October 1982 his autobiography *The Custard Stops At Hatfield* was published and it contained many anecdotes relating to the Beatles and Brian Epstein.

● Everybody's Got Something To Hide Except Me And My Monkey

One of the longest titles of a Beatles track, this John Lennon number had no title when they began recording it in June/July 1968. A title 'Come On, Come On', the opening words to the song, was considered, but then John confirmed it was to be 'Everybody's Got Something To Hide Except Me And My Monkey' and commented, 'That was just sort of a nice line that I made into a song. It was about me and **Yoko**. Everybody seemed to be paranoid except for us two, who were in the glow of love.' It was included as a track on *The Beatles* double album.

● Everybody's Trying To Be My Baby

Number written and recorded by **Carl Perkins** in 1958. The Beatles began performing the song in 1961 with George on lead vocals. A live version is to be found on *The Beatles Live! At The Star Club In Hamburg, Germany: 1962* album and the group recorded it for their November 1964 album *Beatles For Sale*. It's also to be found on *The Beatles Collection*, *Rock 'n' Roll Music* and their **Capitol** EP *4 By The Beatles*. The group performed it twice on **'Saturday Club'** and also sang it on three other BBC radio shows, **'Pop Go The Beatles'**, **'Top Gear'** and **'Ticket To Ride'**.

● Every Little Thing

Track from the *Beatles For Sale* album. It's not clear as to who actually wrote it, although John credited it to Paul in a *Playboy* interview.

Recording began on Tuesday, 29 September 1964, and the number also appeared on the *Beatles For Sale* EP. It was included on the American album *Beatles VI* and the compilation *Love Songs*.

● Exhibition Hall (Veilinghal), Blokker, Holland

The Beatles performed two shows here on 6 June 1964. It was 35 miles from Amsterdam and the group travelled in two white Cadillacs, escorted by motorcycle police. Thousands of fans lined the streets, although for the matinee, the hall was only half full. This matinee had been added to the schedule at the last minute by Radio Veronica. The Beatles had a four-and-a-half-hour wait until the next show, unaware that a civic reception at a local restaurant and a tour of a Dutch village had been planned.

The evening show was a complete sell-out, with an audience of 7,000 fans who watched the 25-minute performance which included the numbers 'I Saw Her Standing There', 'You Can't Do that', 'All My Loving', 'She Loves You', 'Till There Was You', 'Roll Over Beethoven', 'Can't Buy Me Love', 'I Want To Hold Your Hand', 'This Boy' and 'Long Tall Sally'.

● Exhibitions

By 1992, with one exception, attempts to set up permanent Beatles museums or exhibitions had failed.

The one success was *The Beatles Story*, which opened its doors in the basement of the Britannia Pavilion in the Albert Dock, Liverpool, in April 1990. The project is run by Mike Byrne, who was originally the curator of 'Beatle City', the ill-fated Beatles exhibition in Liverpool's Seel Street, which had closed its doors a few years previously. One of the reasons put forward for the lack of success of 'Beatle City' was the fact that it was in an area not familiar to tourists.

The Albert Dock, however, has become one of the largest tourist attractions in the north of England, with more than five million visitors a year.

Mike formed his own Mersey band, Mike & the Thunderbirds, at the same time as the Beatles were rising to become Liverpool's top band. Over the years he appeared as disc jockey and compere for various clubs on Merseyside. His wife Bernadette, who aided him in the Beatles venture, was a **Cavern** regular, a former girlfriend of Paul McCartney and George Harrison and one of Liverpool's first official Beatle Guides.

'Beatle City' opened in April 1984 and was a bold and exciting venture, launched by Liverpool's commercial radio station Radio City. The 14,000 square feet area

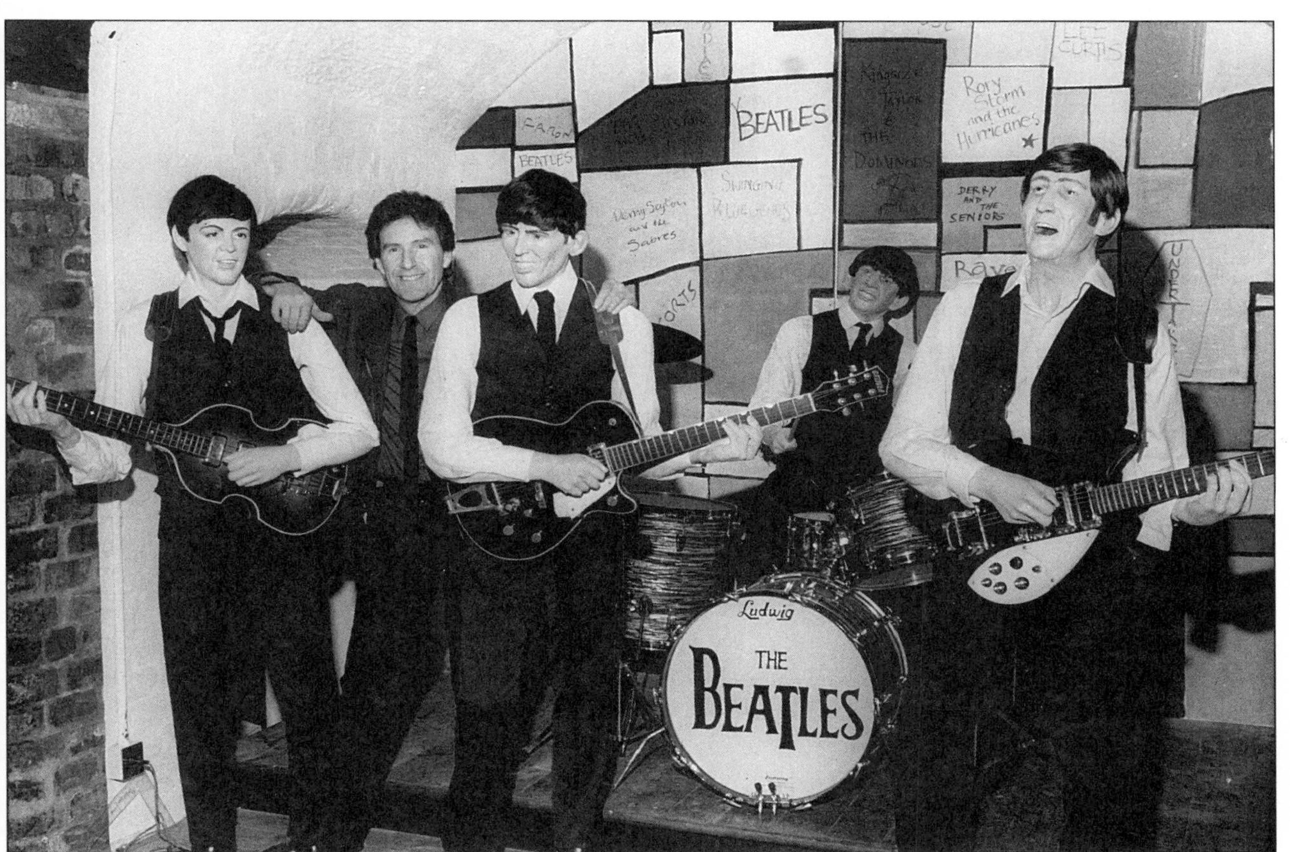

Mike Byrne of *The Beatles Story* exhibition poses with dummy figures of the Beatles in a Cavern setting. (Mike Byrne)

A display cabinet at the former 'Beatle City' exhibition.

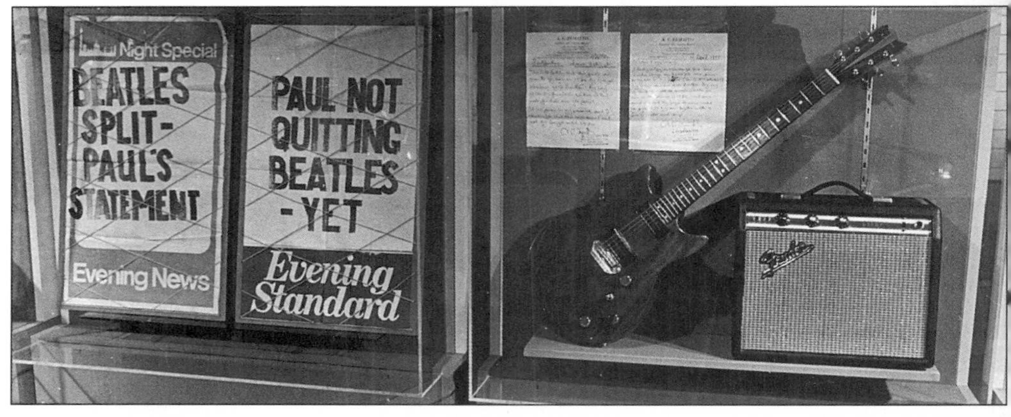

contained a treasure house of Beatles memorabilia and the museum was designed by award-winning architect Colin Milnes. On its opening, General Manager Roger White was to say, 'We have created here a living, moving, total experience which will enchant visitors of all ages. They will appreciate the intensely human story of how four youngsters who knew next to nothing of music made their own indelible mark on twentieth-century pop music – and in fact on the whole British social history scene from the late fifties right through to the seventies.'

Among the exhibits was a recreation of the Cavern Club, a recording studio and Brian Epstein's office.

When the exhibition was closed, the memorabilia were sold to an entrepreneur to launch one of the most ambitious Beatles museums of all – 'The Beatles Revolution' at the Trocadero in London's Piccadilly Circus in 1990. At a cost of over two million pounds the exhibition included re-creations of Hamburg streets, a yellow submarine, a recording studio and it displayed the vast amount of memorabilia once seen in 'Beatle City'. Unfortunately, despite its central position, the exhibition closed the following year.

Rock Circus, also in Piccadilly Circus, contains animated Beatles figures and its sister exhibition, **Madame Tussaud's**, still displays Beatles waxworks.

● Exis, The

The name the Beatles called the group of students who began to attend their gigs in Hamburg. They included **Klaus Voormann**, **Astrid Kirchherr**, Jurgen Vollmer, Detlev Birgfeld and Peter Markmann who were generally clad in black clothes, like the French Existentialists.

The Exis had their own nicknames for the Beatles. They called John 'the Sidie Man', George 'the Beautiful One' and Paul, 'the Baby'.

● Extracts From The Album A Hard Day's Night

Issued two days following the release of the Beatles' sixth EP, with a slightly different cover by **Bob Freeman**, the sales didn't warrant a Top 30 chart entry.

The EP was issued on Parlophone GEP 8924 on 6 November 1964 and contained the tracks 'Any Time At All', 'I'll Cry Instead', 'Things We Said Today' and 'When I Get Home'.

● Extracts From The Film A Hard Day's Night

The Beatles' sixth British EP. This was the first of the Beatles EPs not to enter the Top 30 – and no subsequent Beatles EP was to do so either. Their EP sales were never to equal those of the first five releases again, although the material was repackaged product which had already achieved fantastic sales when issued on albums and singles.

The cover featured the same **Bob Freeman** shot used on the album cover and the EP was issued on Parlophone GEP 8902 on 4 November 1964. The tracks were: 'I Should Have Known Better', 'If I Fell', 'Tell Me Why' and 'And I Love Her'.

Fab Four, The

One of the most frequently used of the nicknames given to the Beatles, along with 'the Moptops'.

The phrase began to be used by disc jockeys and other members of the media after the release of the *With The Beatles* album. In his sleeve notes, when writing about George Harrison's 'Don't Bother Me', **Tony Barrow** used the superlative 'The fabulous foursome', which then led the media to dub them 'The Fab Four'.

Fairfield Hall, *Park Lane, Croydon, Surrey*

The Beatles appeared at this venue on 25 April 1963 as part of the ***Mersey Beat Showcase*** with **Gerry & the Pacemakers**, the Big Three and **Billy J. Kramer**. Originally, as the Beatles and the other Liverpool bands weren't very well known in the south at the time, promoter **John Smith** booked them in January and he also booked singer John Leyton to top the bill. On the night of the concert, Leyton was unable to perform as he was ill.

The Beatles returned to the venue on 7 September 1963.

Faithfull, Marianne

Convent-educated girl, spotted by **Rolling Stone** manager **Andrew Loog Oldham**, who considered she had a 'virginal' appearance which would contrast with the Stones' image. He signed her up and she had immediate record success in 1964 with her debut disc 'As Tears Go By', penned by Mick Jagger and Keith Richard. She married John Dunbar, but left him to live with Mick Jagger.

She and Mick joined the Beatles on their trip to Bangor to see the **Maharishi**. She also appeared on **'The Music of Lennon & McCartney'** special, singing the second half of 'Yesterday', which had been begun by Paul.

Marianne was also among the group of celebrities at the Beatles' feet as they performed 'All You Need Is Love' on the **'Our World'** programme.

In February 1965, her mother Baroness Erisso approached Brian Epstein and asked him to manage Marianne, but he told her he would not manage another female singer as long as he had **Cilla Black**.

37 Falkner Street, *Liverpool 8*

A ground floor flat which Brian Epstein rented in 1961.

During John and **Cynthia**'s wedding lunch at **Reece's Restaurant** when they were married on 23 August 1962, Epstein told the couple that they could have the use of the flat for as long as they wished and gave them the key.

That evening the Beatles were appearing in Chester and Cynthia began moving her things into the flat. Their 'honeymoon' proved to be a strange one as John went on to

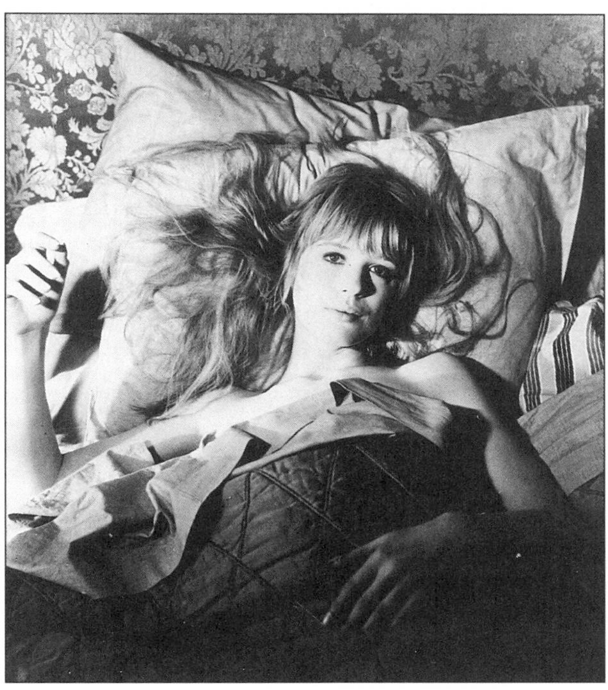

Marianne Faithfull – hit singer and girlfriend to Mick Jagger in the 60s. (National Film Archives)

London from Chester and began appearing at gigs in various cities.

When John eventually did manage to turn up at the flat, Cynthia told him that, as she was pregnant, she'd been afraid she might miscarry. Aunt **Mimi** insisted that John and Cynthia come back to live with her as she was concerned about Cynthia being left alone in the flat so often in her delicate state.

It was while John and Cynthia were residents in the flat that John wrote 'Do You Want To Know A Secret?' Later, John was to comment, 'I was in the first apartment I'd ever had that wasn't shared by fourteen other students – girls and guys at art school. I'd just married Cyn and Brian Epstein gave us his secret little apartment that he kept in Liverpool for his sexual liaisons separate from his home life. And he let Cyn and I have that apartment.'

● Falling In Love Again

A song which Paul performed during the early career of the Beatles in Liverpool and **Hamburg**. The number was originally sung by **Marlene Dietrich** in the classic German silent film *The Blue Angel*.

Paul sang the number at the **Star Club** when **Adrian Barber** was recording and this version can be heard on the **Star Club** recordings, first issued in June 1977 as a two-album set by Lingasong.

● Fallon, John

A Canadian-born musician, more commonly known as Jack. His early career, displaying his versatility on double-bass and violin, saw him performing with many major names, including Duke Ellington and Guy Lombardo. he also established himself in Britain as a session man.

In the early sixties he ran a prominent London booking agency, the Cana Variety Agency, in addition to organizing promotions under the name Jaybee Clubs.

Fallon booked the Beatles into their first venue in the south following their signing with Epstein (their only other southern appearance had been for **Sam Leach**), at the **Subscription Rooms, Stroud** on 31 March 1962. He also booked them into the Subscription Rooms on 1 September 1962; McIlroys Ballroom, Swindon, on 17 July 1962; the **Town Hall, Lydney** on 31 August 1962; and the **City Hall, Salisbury** on 15 June 1963.

Several years later, Fallon was approached by **Abbey Road Studios** in his capacity as session man and when he arrived at the studios on 12 July 1968 he found it was a Beatles recording session and he was to play country guitar on Ringo Starr's 'Don't Pass Me By'.

● Family Way, The

A British film which presented Paul McCartney with his first opportunity to compose film music. In 1967 he was asked to provide the score for *The Family Way*, which starred **Hayley Mills**, Hywel Bennett and John Mills.

A former lorry driver from Liverpool, Bill Naughton who had penned the highly successful *Alfie* in 1966, had written a play *All In Good Time*, on which the movie was based. On its release its theme of an unconsummated marriage earned it an 'X' certificate. Produced by the Boulting Brothers, it was set in Lancashire and concerned the newlywed Jenny (Hayley Mills) and Arthur (Hywel Bennett), who set off on their honeymoon only to discover that their travel agent has absconded with their money. The mental strain of living with Arthur's parents makes Arthur impotent. The film follows the further stresses this unfortunate problem brings, especially when parents and friends find out.

The Family Way was premiered at the Warner Theatre, London, on 18 December 1966, with Paul receiving his first screen credit as a solo composer. He produced 28 minutes of music for the film, arranged for him by George Martin. A soundtrack album (**Decca** SKL 4847) was released on 6 January 1967 and two singles, 'Love In The Open Air' coupled with 'Theme From The Family Way' (United Artists UP 1165) and 'Love In The Open Air' coupled with 'Bahama Sound' (United Artists UA 50148) were released on 23 December 1966 and 24 April 1967 respectively.

● Fan Clubs

The closure of the Official Beatles Fan Club in March 1972 didn't bring about the end of a Beatles fan club following, and a number of fan clubs and fan publications arose to fill the gap vacated by the official club.

Numerous Beatles fan clubs have been launched, only to close down a few years later, although a number of clubs have survived and continue to provide the facilities which fans seek.

Among the fan clubs still operating in 1991 were the following:

Beatles Beat, c/o Sandrea Langer, Lohweg 5 D-50120 Bergheim, Germany.

Beatles Information Centre, c/o Artillo Berhholt, Box 7481, S-10392, Stockholm, Sweden.

Beatles Information Centre, c/o Rainer Moers, Crackerbox Palace, Im Weidenbruch 4, D-5000 Koln 80, Germany.

London Beatles Fan Club, Richard Porter, 4 Oaklands, Constance Road, Whitton, Twickenham, Middlesex, England.

Yesterday: Beatles Fan Club of Austria, A 1080 Wein, Postfach 215, Austria.

The Beatles, 40 Hart Street, Droylsden, Manchester M35 7AW, England.

Beatle-Link, 293 Aylestone Road, Leicester LE2 7QJ, England.

Beatles Fan Club of Japan, c/o Box 6, Suginami, Tokyo 166, Japan.

Club Des 4 De Liverpool, c/o Jacques Volcouve, 43 bis Boulevard Henri IV, 75004, Paris, France.

Wings Fan Club, PO Box 4UP, London W1A 4UP.

The Beatles Fan Club of Poland, Krzysztof Jan Werner, ul, Kurantowa 4/129, 20-836, Lublin, Poland.

Club Beatles 4 Ever, c/o Wolfgang Brenner, Buchenring 21, 7513 Stutensee-2, Germany.

● Fans! Fans! Fans!

A British ATV documentary shown on 29 July 1964. The programme, on fan adulation and hysteria, was originally to have been called 'The Road To Beatlemania'.

The Beatles with two of their Liverpool fans. (Graham Spencer/*Mersey Beat* Archives)

● Fanzines

A source of delight to Beatle fans are the intriguing Beatle fanzines which have been produced, mainly since the seventies. They are limited circulation publications run by enthusiasts to circulate information, provide news and link up with people who share the same interests and are a unique form of communication.

Fanzines are different from mainstream publications because they are generally run at a loss and rarely at a profit and have different aims. They range from simple, duplicated news sheets to immaculately produced magazines.

Beatle fanzines come in all shapes and sizes, each one having a 'personality' of its own. They range from *Club Sandwich*, the glossy full-colour Paul McCartney publication produced by the Wings Fan Club, to the modest but informative, duplicated production, the *McCartney Observer*.

Although there were some fanzines in the sixties, the first major fanzine was produced in 1972. A 25-year-old Boston fan, Joe Pope, launched *Strawberry Fields Forever*, which has enjoyed the reputation of being one of the very best of the Beatle fanzines. Joe was to comment: 'At first, *Strawberry Fields Forever* was little more than a hobby. I figured if I could get the circulation up to twenty-eight, I'd break even.' In fact, by 1976 the fanzine had more than 3,000 subscribers. There was a gap for some years in the late eighties, but Joe resumed publication in 1992.

French fans are well served by the *Fab Four*, a publication edited by Jacques Volcouve. Jacques launched a Beatles fan club, Le Club des 4 de Liverpool, in the early seventies after the response he received when a French radio station broadcast a series called 'The Beatles Story'. He said, 'We received 13,000 letters and suddenly realized that the Beatles were more popular in France than when they were still together. I wanted to start something more important than a fan club: a kind of press agency and information centre dealing with the career of the Beatles and also their solo work. There were so many mistakes being printed about them that I started Le Club des 4 de Liverpool with the magazine the *Fab Four*. The aim: "To try to explain the social and musical impact of the Beatles as a group and individually."'

One of the most authoritative of the fanzines and also one of the most professionally presented, is *Beatlefan*, produced by Bill King and his wife Leslie. Bill is the music/radio editor of the *Atlanta Constitution*, a major morning daily newspaper, and Leslie is editor of a national magazine for sales people. The couple started *Beatlefan* in October 1978, with the first issue appearing in December 1978. They considered that most of the existing fanzines at the time 'were run by fan clubs, by amateurs with rather poor reproduction and articles consisting mainly of gushy accounts of near-miss encounters with the Fab Four and lots of unsubstantiated rumours'. Bill comments, 'Since in my capacity as a music editor I deal with all the major record companies, I had access to all the latest hard news about the group. And as a dedicated follower of the band since 1964 and a veteran collector, I had the background. Being professional journalists, we felt we could combine our interests – Beatles and publishing – into a Beatles fanzine like no other. We also determined it should be run like any professional publication – with display advertising (an innovation in Beatles fanzines) and with regular deadlines, an area in which the other fanzines were very weak. We have never missed an issue since we started and come out regularly every two months.

'We are the biggest US Beatle publication in terms of editorial volume. We run it as a business but it is, of course, not yet a profitable venture. We underwrite the expenses because we enjoy putting it out.'

Beatles Now is a glossy magazine, basically the same size as *Beatles Monthly*. The publication has authoritative articles, colour photographs and binders are available. It is published by Roger Akehurst, a printer by trade, who'd originally had the idea of producing a Beatle magazine on his return from a convention in Liverpool in the seventies. Aided by assistant editor David J. Smith and a team of writers who include Mark Wallgren, Mark Lewisohn, Steve Phillips, Stephen Baker and Ernie McGartland it is, like the other Beatles fanzines, available by direct subscription.

Club Sandwich is the official magazine issued by MPL Communications, Paul McCartney's company. Although aimed at fans, it is professionally produced in a giant-sized format with colour and black and white photographs reproduced on coated art paper. The magazine always contains exclusive stories and photographs of the McCartneys' world, including many shots from Linda and occasional news of the other ex-Beatles.

Good Day Sunshine is a publication issued by Liverpool Productions, a fan club run by enterprising Beatles-enthusiast Charles F. Rosenay. Charles took over the fanzine from Rosita Rodriguez, who originally launched the publication. He then expanded it and also absorbed the fanzine *Here, There and Everywhere*. The large-size issues are wrapped in tinted covers on semi-stiff card and are well illustrated. Some issues are quite unique as they are special audio issues: tapes with messages from personalities associated with the Beatles.

Instant Karma is a fanzine devoted to John Lennon and was launched in December 1981 by Marsha Ewing. Marsha comments: 'It was an effort on my part to get in touch with other John Lennon admirers who were as devastated by his death as I was. Also, after subscribing to a few other fanzines, I felt that there was a need for a magazine that shifted the emphasis from Paul to John and **Yoko**. I have always respected and admired Yoko and felt she was receiving very little respect from the more Beatle-orientated fanzines. With a background in writing and a huge stock of Beatle articles and photos from 1964 onwards, I decided that I could put together a decent fanzine for John and Yoko fans to enjoy.'

Beatles Unlimited is one of the most durable of all Beatle fanzines. Well produced with a fine selection of photographs and illustrations which add to its visual appeal, it has expertly compiled text.

The Dutch *Beatles Werk Group* was formed in 1971 and the magazine was originally conceived in 1973 by Koos Janssen and Aad van Zilt, who headed the Werk Group. They'd already published 50 issues of their 52-page magazine *Beatles Werk Group*, which was in the Dutch language, and wanted to produce a magazine in English. The magazine *Beatles Unlimited* was then launched in December 1974.

Addresses for these fanzines are as follows:

Beatlefan, The Goody Press, PO Box 33515, Decatur, GA 30033, United States of America.

Beatles Now, Roger Akehurst, 107 Endlebury Road, Chingford, London E14.

Beatles Unlimited, PO Box 602, 3430 AP Nieuwegein, The Netherlands.

Club Sandwich, PO Box 4UP, London W1A 4UP.

The Fab Four Publication, Le Club des 4 de Liverpool, 43 bis, Boulevard Henri IV, 75004, Paris, France.

Good Day Sunshine, Charles F. Rosenay, 397 Edgewood Avenue, New Haven, CT 06511, United States of America.

Strawberry Fields Forever, Joe Pope, 310 Franklin Street, No 117, Boston, Mass 02110, United States of America.

● Farrell, Bernadette

One of the Beatles' earliest **Cavern** fans. At one time the Beatles began dating their local fans and, as Bernadette was often given a lift home from the Cavern by the Beatles, she became George Harrison's girlfriend for a while. She was also dated by Paul McCartney.

Bernie, who was featured in the 'Face of Beauty' column in ***Mersey Beat***, went on to marry Mike Burns, a local musician and compere.

In the eighties she became one of Liverpool's first Official Beatles Guides and she also helped her husband open the 'Beatles Story' museum in the basement of the Britannia Pavilion at Liverpool's Albert Dock in April 1990.

● Farrow, Mia

At the age of 22, actress Mia Farrow, who had appeared in a hit TV series 'Peyton Place', married Frank Sinatra and starred in *Rosemary's Baby*, set out on a spiritual odyssey,

Actress Mia Farrow – sharing the Beatles' mystical search. (Cinema International Corp)

having studied alternative and Eastern philosophy which she regarded as 'a mathematical formula for mind expansion'.

It was her sister **Prudence** who introduced her to the

teachings of the **Maharishi Mahesh Yogi**, on the recommendation of the Beatles, who had become friendly with the two sisters shortly before Mia made *Rosemary's Baby*.

In January 1968, Mia and Prudence flew to Boston to see the Maharishi and decided to travel to Rishikesh and study under him for three months. Mia had been meditating for two hours a day at the ashram for nearly a month when she heard that the Beatles were to arrive. Aware of the media circus which surrounded them, she considered that the tranquillity she'd found would be compromised. 'I got into a panic,' she said. 'I had nightmares of armies of press invading.' As a result, after the Beatles had arrived, she decided to explore other parts of the country and set out on a three-week journey across India. She had decided that the Maharishi wasn't the teacher she was looking for and told the ***Ladies Home Journal***: 'Everyone made the mistake of trying to make a Christ figure out of him. He's a man. No religious man should try and become another pope-like figure. His edifices are bound to crumble.' However, she did acknowledge some value in his teachings and was to say, 'The Maharishi did do one thing right. He put meditation in terms that the Western world could understand. That was important.'

It has been reported in a number of books that John and George decided to confront the Maharishi and leave Rishikesh because they'd been told he'd made sexual advances to Mia Farrow. This is not true. The girl in question was a young meditator from California.

● Farrow, Prudence

One of actress **Mia Farrow**'s younger sisters. It was Prudence who first introduced Mia to the teachings of the **Maharishi Mahesh Yogi**. The two sisters had become close friends of the Beatles in London, particularly since both girls refused to be awed by them. It was the Beatles who first turned Prudence onto the Maharishi. The two sisters had been at Rishikesh for almost a month when they heard that the Beatles were coming to the ashram. Whilst there Prudence remained by herself in her room meditating for a long time and wouldn't come out to communicate with anyone, so John was picked as the person to persuade her to come out of her solitude and experience the reality of life. The task inspired him to write the song 'Dear Prudence'.

● Fascher, Horst

A former featherweight boxer who represented both Hamburg and West Germany, he was imprisoned for manslaughter following a street fight in which he accidentally killed a sailor.

He was employed as a bouncer by **Bruno Koschmider** at the **Kaiserkeller** club and soon gained a fiercesome reputation in the area, particularly as he employed some of his friends from the Hamburg Boxing Academy, who were soon known as 'Hoddel's Gang'.

Horst took an immediate liking to the Beatles – and subsequently the other Liverpool bands in **Hamburg**, and assured them of his protection in the tough area.

His efficiency in controlling trouble led to him being employed by **Peter Eckhorn** at the newly opened **Top Ten Club** and it was Horst who encouraged **Tony Sheridan** and the Beatles to play there.

Later, Horst moved to the **Star Club** – and the Beatles and the other Liverpool bands followed. His geniality and hospitality were legend among the bands and following the demise of the Star Club, he attempted to revive a similar venue in Hamburg for live groups to play. His new Star Club venture opened in the Grossneumark district of Hamburg on 15 December 1978 with Tony Sheridan as the headlining act. Both Ringo Starr and George Harrison turned up at the opening night.

Horst is a popular guest at Beatles conventions.

● Fawcett, Anthony

Born in Hillingdon Heath in 1948, Anthony studied art at Oxford and became an art critic for various magazines. He first met John Lennon and **Yoko Ono** in 1968 and became involved in organizing a number of artistic projects with them. As a result, John and Yoko invited him to work full-time for them as a personal assistant. He spent two years with the couple and his reminiscences of the period are documented in his 1976 book *One Day At A Time*.

● Fell, Ray

Apart from its group and football teams, Liverpool was also famous for its comedians – and the many successful funnymen from Liverpool included **Ken Dodd**, Tommy Handley, **Arthur Askey**, Ted Ray, Norman Vaughan and Jimmy Tarbuck.

Ray Fell was yet another Liverpool comedian and the

Beatles booked him to co-compere their second *Christmas Show* at the **Odeon, Hammersmith**. Unfortunately, Ray was one of the local comedians who never made the big time.

● Fenton, Shane

Born Bernard Jewry, he adopted the stage name Shane Fenton and led a group called the Fentones in the sixties, before changing his name to Alvin Stardust in the seventies and achieving fame with a series of chart hits.

He frequently appeared on Merseyside and was featured in ***Mersey Beat***. Shane became friendly with the Beatles and when they were appearing at the **Granada, Mansfield** in early 1963, a town where Shane's parents lived, he recalls: 'There were hundreds of girls blocking all the streets nearby – but being in the business I knew that if you went through the shop of the local chippie, through his back room, and then up over the roof of the cinema dressing-room and down a fire escape, you could get into the cinema backstage. I'd already worked with them a few times, so I went over the roof and found them trapped in their dressing-room. They said they were starving, because they hadn't been able to leave the cinema since they arrived there during the afternoon, so I went back home . . . and told my mother all about it and she made them up a picnic basket full of food, with containers full of hot soup and piles of salmon sandwiches, which I took to them backstage, again going over the roof, and they were absolutely knocked out.'

Shane Fenton – he eventually achieved success as Alvin Stardust. (Alvin Stardust)

He also appeared on a bill with them at the **Albert Hall** and on a promotion at the **Empire Theatre, Liverpool**. Backstage at the Empire, Brian Epstein offered Shane the number 'Do You Want To Know A Secret?' and said that he could record it if he would let Brian be his manager. Shane turned him down, saying he already had a manager.

Shane was to marry **Iris Caldwell**, sister of **Rory Storm** and former girlfriend of George Harrison and Paul McCartney. The two of them formed a double act and later opened a club on the outskirts of Liverpool. They had a couple of children, but were later divorced. Shane changed his name to Alvin Stardust and had thirteen British chart hits between 1973 and 1985, including 'My Coo-Ca-Choo' and 'Jealous Mind'. He married actress Liza Goddard, but that marriage also ended in divorce.

● Festival Hall, *Brisbane, Australia*

The Beatles made the final appearance of their Australian tour at this theatre on 29 and 30 June 1964, when they performed at four concerts, two shows per evening, to capacity audiences of 5,500 at each show.

When they arrived in the capital of Queensland they were pelted at the airport with missiles from a faction who later admitted they were students making a protest. As a result of the missile hurling, the Beatles restricted their public appearances. When they did go on stage at the Festival Hall, the faction was present and hurled numerous missiles on stage, including sweets, coins, food and drink. Two youths ran forward and tossed a metal biscuit tin onto the stage. A message of apology was later given and a meeting arranged between representatives of the protesters and the Beatles. Three protesters apologized to the Beatles at their hotel and said that their actions had been 'a protest against materialism'.

Between shows on the first night at the Festival Hall, the Beatles were visited backstage by Sir Henry Abel Smith and his wife Lady May Smith, who said that the Beatles were 'quite decent chaps'.

● Festival Hall, *Melbourne, Australia*

The Beatles appeared for a total of six concerts over three nights at this venue in the state of Victoria.

They appeared twice nightly on Monday, 15 June,

Tuesday, 16 June, and Wednesday, 17 June 1964, and drew capacity crowds, attracting audiences of 45,000 to the six appearances.

Ringo re-joined the group after an illness for the first of the shows. Their sixth show there was also recorded by the Nine Television network and broadcast under the title 'The Beatles Sing For Shell'.

● Field, Alan

A comedian from the north of England, whose main work took place in working men's clubs. He was hired to compere the Beatles' tour of Australia.

Unfortunately, his blunt, adult-orientated humour didn't go down well at the concerts, and his time on stage was cut back after every performance. One observer commented, 'He just died slowly every night.' Field appeared in every city on the tour with the exception of Adelaide, where **Bob Francis** took over the compering honours.

Field remained in Australia to become resident compere on a television show called 'The Go! Show', and later returned to England and the northern clubs.

● Fifth Beatle, The

'The Fifth Beatle' is a term which has been applied to several people, some close associates of the group, others with only a tenuous connection.

The first person looked upon as 'the fifth Beatle' was their original bass guitarist **Stuart Sutcliffe** who was, literally, the 'fifth Beatle' because he was the fifth member of the group. They became a quartet when he left.

Drummer **Pete Best** also has some claim to the title because there were four members of the group when he joined: John, Paul, George and Stuart, so he became the fifth member and remained with them during the formative days between August 1960 and August 1962.

Their original road manager **Neil Aspinall** has often been referred to as 'the fifth Beatle' and is possibly the most likely claimant to the title, having been associated with them longer than anyone else, someone whom they'd always trusted and relied upon, and who still administrates their Apple empire for them.

Manager Brian Epstein was also referred to as 'the fifth Beatle', but due to the age and class barriers between them, his title of Manager is more apt.

George Martin, their recording manager, was tagged 'the fifth Beatle' because of his contribution to their recorded sound. It was a symbiotic relationship because Martin's technical expertise and the **Fab Four**'s musical innovations provided a revolution in the sound of popular music in the sixties.

Jimmy Nicol, who deputized for Ringo Starr, who was ill, on the Beatles' European and Far Eastern tour in 1964 including some Australian dates, has also been referred to as 'the fifth Beatle'.

A self-styled 'fifth Beatle' was American disc jockey **Murray The K,** who bestowed the title on himself when he ingratiated himself with the Beatles on their arrival in New York in February 1964. Brian Epstein was furious and told him to stop doing so.

The most tenuous of all was American journalist **Ed Rudy**, who joined the entourage travelling with the Beatles on their American tour in 1964. He issued an album of his interviews with the group called *The Beatles American Tour With Ed Rudy*, in which the sleeve notes claimed: 'The Beatles call Ed Rudy "the fifth Beatle".'

The term was also applied to keyboards player **Billy Preston** who recorded with the Beatles on the 'Get Back' sessions. When the single was issued in April 1969, the record was credited to 'The Beatles with Billy Preston'.

● Films

The Beatles only appeared in three feature films as a group. A three-picture deal had been arranged with United Artists and the first two, *A Hard Day's Night* (1963) and *Help!* (1965), were produced by **Walter Shenson** and directed by **Richard Lester**.

There was great difficulty in finding a third project which the Beatles would agree to film. 'Shades Of A Personality', in which each member would portray a facet of one man's multiple personality, was rejected, as was Joe Orton's controversial 'Up Against It'. The rights to film the Western 'A Talent For Loving' was acquired by the group but they rejected it, also turning down a comedy version of 'The Three Musketeers' with their favourite film star Brigitte Bardot as Lady De Winter.

They agreed to the filming of the animated *Yellow Submarine*, believing this would fulfil the terms of their three-picture deal, but it didn't and they eventually decided to utilize their planned TV documentary on the making of an album, and turned it into the film *Let It Be*.

Before the group split up, individual members were

nvolved in a number of film ventures. Ringo appeared in *Candy*, ***The Magic Christian***, ***Blindman*** and ***200 Motels***, and in his solo career has appeared in numerous movies and TV specials including *Born To Boogie* (which

ingo Starr as the Pope in Ken Russell's outrageous *isztomania*. (Warner/VPS/Goodtimes)

e directed), *That'll Be The Day*, *Son Of Dracula*, *isztomania*, *Sextette*, *The Caveman* and others.

Paul made two avant-garde films in 1966, *The Next pring Then* and *The Defeat Of The Dog*, and composed e music for the 1967 film ***The Family Way***, starring hn and **Hayley Mills**. He was to score music for several ther films, including the 1973 James Bond movie *Live nd Let Die*, which was awarded a **Grammy** and ominated for an Oscar. He has been involved in many lm ventures in his solo career, including the feature film ased on his own script, *Give My Regards To Broad Street* 1984, which also featured Ringo.

John appeared in **Dick Lester**'s 1967 feature film *How Won The War* and began making avant-garde films with **Yoko** the same year. Over the years they included: *Two Virgins*, *Rape*, *Honeymoon*, *Self Portrait*, *Up Your Legs*, *Fly*, *Apotheosis*, *Erection*, *Ten For Two*, *The One To One Concert* and *Imagine*.

George composed the music for the feature film ***Wonderwall*** in 1969, and composed the soundtrack for the 1971 documentary on **Ravi Shankar**, ***Raga***. His main involvement in film began after the breakup of the Beatles when he founded Handmade Films.

● Fixing A Hole

A track from the *Sgt Pepper* album on which Paul sings lead. There has been some confusion regarding the harpsichord player **Neil Aspinall** claimed in *Beatles Monthly* that it was Paul, but others claim it was George Martin. George Harrison provides a guitar solo.

Commenting on the song, Paul has said, 'This song is just about the hole in the road where the rain gets in; a good old analogy – the hole in your make-up which lets the rain in and stops your mind from going where it will. It's you interfering with things; as when someone walks up to you and says, "I am the Son of God." And you say, "No, you're not; I'll crucify you," and you crucify him. Well, that's life, but it is not fixing a hole.'

There were the inevitable suggestions that fixing a hole referred to a drug 'fix'. Paul said, 'If you're a junky sitting in a room fixing a hole then that's what it will mean to you, but when I wrote it I meant if there's a crack or the room is uncolourful, then I'll paint it.'

When the Beatles began recording the number at Regent Sound Studios on Thursday, 9 February 1967, it was the first recording session they'd done for **EMI** in Britain outside the familiar **Abbey Road Studios** as the Abbey Road facilities were fully booked that night.

● Flannery, Agnes

Mother of Joe Flannery, one of Brian Epstein's Liverpool friends.

When Beatle City opened in Liverpool in 1985 the museum featured a photograph of Agnes, then 76, in her youth. It was accompanied by a notice that the photograph of her inspired the Beatle 'bob'.

Joe claimed that when the Beatles visited him at his flat early in their career they noticed a picture of his mother, when young. Apparently, John fell in love with it.

Agnes said: 'The picture that intrigued John was taken

at a studio in Bold Street, Liverpool, when I was just sixteen, two years before I married. I'm delighted to hear that the photograph is going on exhibition at "Beatle City" museum. I'm sure many folk will be thrilled to learn the true story of how the Beatles came by their distinctive hairstyle which, incidentally, I'd created for myself by washing and trimming my own hair in that particular fashion.'

● Flannery, Joe

A childhood friend of Brian Epstein, who was active on the Mersey scene in the early sixties, primarily to manage his brother **Lee Curtis** (Peter Flannery). Like Epstein, Joe had become enamoured of the scene, sold his lucrative grocery business and attempted to emulate Epstein by setting up an artist management and agency with his Carlton-Brooke Agency. At one time he managed the Mersey scene's most promising girl singer **Beryl Marsden** and he handled a number of the original bookings for the Beatles appearances outside Merseyside for **NEMS Enterprises**.

When the sacked **Pete Best** refused Epstein's offer of joining another of his bands, Epstein approached Flannery to offer Best a job with Lee Curtis & the All Stars. When Lee became a popular artist at the **Star Club**, Joe moved to Germany for several years to book groups into Hamburg. He returned to Liverpool in the late sixties.

In the early eighties he teamed up with **Clive Epstein** to launch a Liverpool-based management agency with acts such as Motion Pictures and Phil Boardman.

A few weeks before John Lennon's murder, Joe talked

Above: Agnes Flannery with her son Joe at the opening of Liverpool's 'Beatle City'.
Right: Joe Flannery, with Paul and Linda.
(Joe Flannery)

o him on the phone and John expressed his enthusiasm or a forthcoming British tour in which he would return to ,iverpool. Joe was so depressed by the news of the killing hat he wrote a poetic tribute to John, 'Much Missed Man'. 'his was put to music, recorded by Phil Boardman and ssued on Joe's own independent Mayfield label in 'ebruary 1982.

Floral Hall Ballroom, *The Promenade, Morecambe, Lancashire*

'he Beatles appeared twice at this ballroom, in a seaside esort in the north-west of England, quite close to Merseyside. Their first appearance took place on 29 August 1962 and their last on 18 January 1963.

● Floral Hall, The, *The Promenade, Southport, Lancashire*

'he Beatles played in the nearby seaside town of outhport on numerous occasions early in their career, and his venue was particularly impressive because it was a roper theatre, in contrast to the local jive hives they'd een appearing in.

They made their debut at the hall in a 'Rock 'n' Trad pectacular' on 20 February 1962, on a bill with several Mersey groups, including **Gerry & the Pacemakers** and **Rory Storm & the Hurricanes**, together with the jazz utfit the Chris Hamilton Jazzmen. Later that year, on 20 November, they appeared at the theatre again, performing wo shows in the course of the evening.

During 1963 they appeared at the venue twice, on 23 April and on 15 October.

Flying

An instrumental recording featured in the film and issued n the EP set and album of *Magical Mystery Tour*.

The Beatles considered they needed some instrumental ackground music to their film and began recording their rst instrumental number since 'Cry For A Shadow', which ey'd recorded in Hamburg for Polydor in 1961.

When they first began recording the number at **Abbey Road Studios** it went under the title 'Aerial Tour nstrumental'. All four members of the group contributed o the composition, which was credited to Harrison/Lennon/McCartney/Starkey.

The original recording was a lengthy nine minutes and irty-one seconds long; it was edited down to a more reasonable length of two minutes and fourteen seconds.

● Follow The Beatles

A 30-minute BBC television production. The documentary concerned the making of the Beatles' debut film *A Hard Day's Night* and also included footage of the Beatles recording in the **Abbey Road Studios**.

'Follow The Beatles' was screened on 3 August 1964.

● Fontaine, Dick

First television director to capture the Beatles on film. Fontaine worked for Granada Television, the station with the franchise to cover the north-west of England. **Mona Best** had originally written off to David Plowright of Granada, suggesting that the company use the Beatles on one of their programmes. A shoal of letters from Liverpool were organized to be sent to the station, resulting in Granada dispatching some scouts to watch the group perform at Southport's **Cambridge Hall** on 26 July and the **Cavern** on 1 August.

Filming was approved, and Fontaine moved in with his camera crew to film them performing at the Cavern during the lunchtime session on 22 August 1962. The idea was for them to film some live clips to be used on a programme called 'Know The North'. Fontaine filmed them performing 'Some Other Guy' and 'Kansas City/Hey, Hey, Hey', but the resulting film, due to the technical difficulties of filming inside the dank cellar, wasn't considered satisfactory and was scrapped.

Later, when the Beatles began to make their impact in Britain, Granada sought the original copy of the film, but only the clip of 'Some Other Guy' survived. They first broadcast it in 1963 and it has been aired several times since.

● Fool On The Hill, The

Paul McCartney composition which he wrote for the *Magical Mystery Tour* movie. The sequence was filmed in France. Three flautists were engaged – Christopher and Richard Taylor and Jack Ellery – with George and John adding harmonicas and George Martin playing piano. Before it was included on the *Magical Mystery Tour* double EP and album, it was pruned by 90 seconds. The number was also included on the compilations *The Beatles 1967–1970* and *The Beatles Ballads*.

Sergio Mendes and Brazil 666 reached No. 6 in the

American charts with their cover of the number in 1968 and **Shirley Bassey** had a minor hit with it in Britain in 1971.

● Fool, The

Josje Leeger and Marijke Koger were both born in Amsterdam in 1943. The two eventually met and teamed up as a design group, together with Marijke's boyfriend Simon Postuma, and for a while they ran a boutique in Amsterdam called The Trend.

In 1966 they moved to London, and while there they met Canadian-born Barry Finch (also born in 1943) and his partner Simon Hayes, who ran a public relations company handling artists for **Robert Stigwood** and the **Saville Theatre** for Brian Epstein. The work of the Dutch designers, who decided to call themselves the Fool, was shown to Epstein, who commissioned them to do some design work for the Saville.

Commenting on the origin of their name, Simon said, 'It represents Truth, Spiritual Meaning and the circle which expresses the Universal circumference in which gravitate all things.'

Barry Finch then joined the team and Simon Hayes was appointed their business manager. The group specialized in costumes, interior design and painting. They began to design clothes for the Beatles and their wives and girlfriends, including the outfits the group wore on their 'All You Need Is Love' segment of the **'Our World'** programme. They also painted the fireplace in George's bungalow, George's guitar and Mini, and John's Rolls-Royce, piano and caravan.

Another completed commission was a design for the centrespread of the *Sgt Pepper* sleeve, but it wasn't used.

The Fool interested the Beatles in funding them to design outfits for the **Apple Boutique** in Baker Street and a great deal of controversy was aroused by a large mural, designed by the Fool and executed by 40 art students, which covered the outer walls of the boutique. Local traders demanded its removal and it eventually had to be painted over with whitewash.

The shop opened on 7 December 1967, but lost so much money that the Beatles decided to close it down and offer the remaining stock free to all comers. By this time the Fool had made arrangements to move to America and were given a large amount of money to record an album for Mercury Records. The album, entitled *The Fool* and recorded by Graham Nash, was issued in 1968, but provec unsuccessful.

The group began designing theatres in America anc also opened a design company in Los Angeles called Th Chariot. Josje and Barry were married in July 1969 an later returned to Holland. They settled down i Amsterdam with their six children, Violet Dawn, Titu Blue, Scarlet Arrow, Jade Moon, Daniel Haze and Ambe Blue, and continued to design costumes and sets for po artists in succeeding years. Josje died in July 1991. Sh was 47 years old.

Simon and Marijke recorded some singles togethe produced by Graham Nash, which were released in 1972 under the name Seemon and Marijke. The couple finall split up in 1975 and Simon eventually returned to Hollan in the mid-eighties.

● For Arts Sake

Title of a magazine programme produced by Souther Television, one of Britain's regional TV stations. O Wednesday, 20 May 1964, Brian Epstein appeared on th show discussing his career.

● For No One

Composition by Paul, featured on the *Revolver* album. Joh Lennon was later to comment, 'That was one of m favourites of his.'

John and George didn't participate in the recording an after Paul and Ringo had recorded the number on Monda 9 May 1966, with Paul on piano and overdubbing o clavichord, and Ringo playing drums and overdubbin cymbals and maraca, a French horn solo was adde several days later on 19 May. George Martin contacte Alan Civil, principal horn player with the Roya Philharmonic Orchestra, and he was able to overdub th French horn obligato onto the song.

The number was included on the compilations *Lo Songs* and *The Beatles Ballads*, and **Cilla Black** als recorded it as a single, although it didn't bring her an chart success.

● For You Blue

A country blues number penned by George Harrison an first recorded on 25 January 1969 at **Apple Studios** i **Savile Row**, under the working title 'George's Blues'. Th working title was then changed to 'Because You're Swe nd Lovely', before it was eventually called 'For You lue'.

John Lennon added a bottleneck guitar solo to the ack, which George had described as a simple twelve-bar ues number.

George sang solo vocal on the number which was cluded on the *Let It Be* album in May 1970, and in the rics, George makes a passing reference to the bluesman lmore James: 'Elmore James got nothing on this, baby.' he number was also featured on *The Best Of George arrison* album.

In May 1970, 'For You Blue' was issued in America as double A side with 'The Long And Winding Road', on pple 2832, on 11 May 1970 where it reached No. 1 in e charts.

nile Ford in humorous pose with Pete Best and Paul :Cartney at the Tower Ballroom, New Brighton. (*Mersey Beat* :hives)

Both tracks had been subject to a production mix by **Phil Spector**, although, while Paul McCartney was upset at what Spector had done to 'The Long And Winding Road', George made no comment about Spector's work on his own track – but was obviously content and asked Spector to produce his solo album *All Things Must Pass*.

● Ford, Emile

A West Indian singer based in Britain who, with the Checkmates, had a No. 1 hit with 'What Do You Want To Make Those Eyes At Me For' in December 1959. He was born Emile Sweetnam in Nassau in 1937.

He continued to have chart hits until 1962: 'Slow Boat To China', 'You'll Never Know What You're Missing Till You Try', 'Them There Eyes', 'Counting Teardrops', 'What Am I Gonna Do', 'Half Of My Heart' and 'I Wonder Who's Kissing Her Now?'. Ford turned up at the **Tower Ballroom** on 24 November 1961 and got up to sing with **Rory Storm and the Hurricanes**. Backstage he was photographed with the Beatles by Dick Matthews and the picture was featured on the cover of ***Mersey Beat***.

● Ford, Gerry

Born in Athlone, Ireland, in 1943, Gerry moved to London and became a baker, also taking up a part-time job as compere and disc jockey at the **Majestic Ballroom, Finsbury Park**. He claimed that he introduced the Beatles on their first London gig, but their appearance there before an audience of two thousand on 24 April 1963 had followed several others. Gerry was later to become a professional Country singer, and made his debut at the Grand Ole Opry in Nashville in 1981.

● Forest Hills Tennis Stadium, *Queens, New York City*

Arena in New York where the Beatles appeared on 28 and 29 August 1964, performing a one-hour show on each occasion to a 16,000 capacity audience. Tickets had been sold out months in advance, and the shows had been promoted by **Sid Bernstein**. Their concert was taped and broadcast by the radio station WBOX.

On Friday, 28 August, officials at the stadium at first refused to allow the Beatles to arrive by helicopter, but the New York Police Department insisted it was necessary and they got their way.

Backstage, Benny Goodman, the legendary jazzman,

arrived with his two daughters, although the conversation proved to be strained, with Brian Epstein showing his annoyance at what he considered an intrusion.

When **Norman Weiss** realized the helicopter pilot had gone, he was annoyed. No one had told the pilot to wait, but Weiss refused to let the Beatles go on stage until the helicopter returned, and there was a delay. They eventually began their performance at 9.50 p.m. During the show a young girl rushed down the aisle, scaled a 15-foot-high fence and rushed straight for the Beatles. She was within six feet of them when she was eventually downed by two security guards and, in the struggle, a production man, Harry Hennessy, got knocked clean off the stage. The action of the girl had taken the 200 policemen on duty and the squad of Burns Security Guards completely by surprise.

The following night, Saturday 29 August, there were 150 policemen and 100 security guards, and almost 50 screaming youngsters were prevented from mobbing the stage. One girl got through and hugged George, before fainting. Another youth reached the stage, but was pulled off, knocking out a number of footlights. Over 50 girls fainted from hysteria.

The numbers performed were: 'A Hard Day's Night', 'All My Loving', 'Boys', 'Can't Buy Me Love', 'If I Fell', 'I Want To Hold Your Hand', 'Long Tall Sally', 'Roll Over Beethoven', 'She Loves You', 'Things We Said Today', 'Twist And Shout' and 'You Can't Do That'.

● 20 Forthlin Road, *Allerton, Liverpool 18*

A street in a Liverpool district which was a pleasanter area than Speke, where the McCartneys had previously lived. The McCartney family moved into Forthlin Road in 1955 and were to remain there until 1964, when Paul bought **Rembrandt** for his father. It was the seventh home Paul had lived in in Liverpool and was to be the last.

The house had a back garden which overlooked a police training field and **Jim McCartney** planted a black mountain ash beneath Paul's bedroom window. It was a three-bedroom house and Paul's bedroom was the smallest.

It was at Forthlin Road that **Mary McCartney** discovered she had cancer, from which she died in 1956.

One of the McCartneys' neighbours was Tom Gaul, who'd moved next door into No. 18 two years previously with his two sons. He enjoyed a friendly relationship wit Paul and when fans used to gather outside the front door No. 20, he'd let Paul clamber over the backyard fence an rush out the front of his house into a waiting car.

He has said that Paul told him that the essence of som of the lyrics of 'Yesterday' concerned the death of Paul mother.

Forthlin Road was where numerous Lennon McCartney songs were composed. As Jim McCartney wa out working at the Cotton Exchange during the day, Joh and Paul used to spend their time around Jim's piano the small front parlour, filling exercise books full of lyri to the songs they composed, which included 'The Or After 909', 'I Saw Her Standing There', 'Love Me Do' ar 'When I'm Sixty-Four'.

The McCartneys eventually moved from the house the spring of 1964, when Paul had bought a new home f his father – Rembrandt, 26 miles away in Heswall.

● Forum, *Montreal, Quebec, Canada*

Ringo had received a death threat from a fanatic Montreal who threatened to kill 'the English Jew'. Wh the Beatles arrived at Dorval Airport at 2.20 p.m. Tuesday, 8 September 1964, there were 5,000 fans at t airport awaiting them, but there was also a heavy poli presence from the Royal Canadian Mounted Police and t Dorval Municipal Police Force. Detectives accompani the group as they were driven straight to the Forum, whe they were to appear on two shows before an audience 21,000.

The death threat was taken seriously and when t Beatles took to the stage at 5.20 p.m. a detective crouch down behind Ringo's drums, and Ringo also crouched l while he played. He was to comment on the presence the detective behind him: 'God knows what he was tryi to do. I mean there's an assassin out there trying to get r and he's sitting next to me on stage as if someone in t back of a 12,000 seater is gonna go – Bang! – and h gonna catch the bullet?' He also remarked, 'No one w seeing much of me that day. It was the worst gig of r life.'

Between shows they posed for photographs and had press reception. When asked if any of them spoke Frenc Ringo replied *'Nein'*, and when asked who their lead was, Paul said 'It depends on who shouts the loudest.'

There were 75 Royal Mounted Police at the airp

when they returned and Ringo's detective escort had remained by his side from the moment of their arrival, until they finally boarded their plane to Florida. Once inside the plane, Ringo commented, 'I am English. But I'm not Jewish.'

4 By The Beatles

The second EP to be issued by **Capitol** in the States. *4 By The Beatles* was released on 1 February 1965 on Capitol R 5365. The four tracks were taken from the American album *Beatles '65* and were: 'Honey Don't', 'I'm A Loser', 'Mr Moonlight' and 'Everybody's Trying To Be My Baby'.

This was Capitol's second attempt at utilizing the EP (Extended Play) format with the Beatles, although it was not a popular format in America. Once again, it wasn't a totally successful venture, even though it reached No. 68 in the *Cash Box* and *Billboard* charts, and Capitol didn't repeat the experiment again.

Four By The Beatles

The EP (Extended Player) format was not an established format in America, but **Capitol Records** decided to try an experiment and issued an EP by the Beatles, probably inspired by the fact that **Vee Jay Records** had recently attempted such an experiment a few weeks earlier with *Souvenir Of Their Visit To America: The Beatles*.

They combined two of the most successful of the Canadian import singles on the EP, although the tracks were also available on albums – two on the *Meet The Beatles* album and two on *The Beatles Second Album*. *Four By The Beatles* was issued on Capitol EAP 2121 on 11 May 1964 with the tracks being: 'Roll Over Beethoven', 'All My Loving', 'This Boy' and 'Please Mr Postman'.

Compared to the sales of Beatles singles and albums, it wasn't a success, reaching only No. 92 in *Billboard* and No. 86 in *Cash Box*.

Capitol only tried the experiment one further time, the following year, with the similarly titled *4 By The Beatles* which was also deemed unsuccessful.

Fourmost, The

A Liverpool group who started life in 1959 as the Four Jays, and comprised Brian Redman (drums), Joey Bowers (vocals/rhythm guitar), Billy Hatton (vocals/bass guitar) and Brian O'Hara (vocals/lead guitar). They played rock, jazz and included comedy in their act and by 1962 they had called themselves the Four Mosts and their line-up was Brian O'Hara and Billy Hatton with Mike Millward (rhythm guitar) and Dave Lovelady (drums). They played R&B, C&W, jazz and standards and were interested in the cabaret circuit. Brian Epstein signed them up on 30 June 1963 and shortened their name to the Fourmost.

They made their recording debut with the Lennon & McCartney number 'Hello Little Girl' c/w 'Just In Case', which was issued in Britain on 23 August 1963 on Parlophone R5055 where it reached No. 9 in the charts with a seventeen-week chart life. It was released in the US on Swan 4152 on 16 September.

Shortly before the record's release, Billy Hatton commented, 'We were appearing with the Beatles at the Queen's Theatre, Blackpool, and we had been told previously that they had a number for us to record.

'We arranged to go to John Lennon's house, and they gave us a copy of the words. We hadn't heard the number before, and George and John gave us a rough idea of it by taping the tune. We received the tape at 4 o'clock on Monday morning.

'As we had to record on the following Wednesday, we had two days in which to make an arrangement good enough to put on disc. As a matter of fact, when we were recording, we were just learning the song as we went along and were tremendously encouraged by A&R man George Martin.'

The group, whose records were produced by George Martin, recorded another Lennon & McCartney song, which had been written especially for them: 'I'm In Love' coupled with 'Respectable' on Parlophone R5078, released on 15 November 1963. It was issued in the States on ATCO 6285 on 10 February 1964. This reached No. 17 in Britain with a chart life of twelve weeks. Their EP *The Fourmost Sound* containing the four tracks was issued on Parlophone GEP 8892 on 14 February 1964.

Their biggest hit was not a Lennon & McCartney number but a song called 'A Little Loving', which reached No. 6 in the British charts. This was during their peak year of 1964 when they also appeared in the film *Ferry 'Cross The Mersey* and starred on a series of **London Palladium** concerts with **Cilla Black**. They had several further chart hits, although these were minor ones, with 'How Can I Tell Her', 'Baby, I Need Your Loving' and 'Girls, Girls, Girls'.

The Fourmost appeared on *The Beatles Christmas Show*

at the **Finsbury Park Astoria** in December 1962. They performed 'Hello Little Girl', then Brian O'Hara sang 'White Christmas' during which he did impressions of Gracie Fields, **Elvis**, Dean Martin, Adam Faith and the Beatles. Mike Millward died in April 1966 after a long illness and there were various replacements from Liverpool bands, including George Peckham, Frank Bowen and Ian Edwards, until the group settled on the return of a founder-member, Joey Bowers, who had originally left to get married.

In 1969, Paul McCartney produced their single 'Rosetta', a number which he had found and thought would be suitable for the band. It was issued on CBS 4041 on 21 February but failed to make any impact on the charts. Drummer Dave Lovelady commented, 'Paul liked the way we could mimic instruments with our voices, our "mouth music", if you like. Brian O'Hara was a trumpet and we were the trombones. We used it on "Rosetta" and the Beatles did the same thing on "Lady Madonna". There were proper instruments on our record as well. I was playing piano at the session, but Brian O'Hara told me to play it badly. I soon found out why. Paul said, "Look, I'll do the piano bit," and so he ended up playing on the record.'

● Four Nights In Moscow

Another Beatles mystery. The song was reputed to have been a number which John Lennon wrote for Ringo to record as a solo single. Various Beatles books have suggested that the Beatles recorded the number in June 1969, but didn't release it.

However, the Beatles didn't visit the recording studios that month. John and **Yoko** were in Canada and on their return took **Julian** and Kyoko on a motoring trip to Scotland. George and **Pattie** were on holiday in Sardinia, Paul and **Linda** in Corfu and Ringo and **Maureen** in the south of France.

Another story purports that 'Four Nights In Moscow' was the title of a track on a lost Beatles album. This resulted from a fake story in a British music weekly at the beginning of the seventies which reported that the group had recorded an album, the master tapes of which were stolen in the summer of 1969. The group were said to have paid a huge ransom for its return, but were cheated by the thieves and never retrieved it.

Perhaps this made-up tale inspired Paul in his screenplay for *Give My Regards To Broad Street*, which concerned the loss of the master tapes of an album he'd made.

The Fourmost – part of Brian Epstein's stable of Liverpool acts. (EMI/Parlophone)

● Four Tops, The

A Motown group of four vocalists comprising Levi Stubbs, Abdul Fakir, Renaldo Benson and Lawrence Payton. Their hits included 'I Can't Help Myself', 'It's The Same Old Song' and 'Reach Out, I'll Be There'.

In October 1966, while in Detroit, Epstein negotiated with Motown to bring the Four Tops to the **Saville Theatre**. The quartet had already been set to tour Britain from January 1967 for **NEMS** in a deal negotiated by **Vic Lewis**. Vic, as managing director of NEMS, had worked out a contract which would make the tour profitable for NEMS if there were reasonable audiences on the ABC and Odeon cinema circuits. He had also made sure that even if there was a poor response, the tour would break even. Epstein rearranged the contract in Detroit, magnanimously offering the group bonuses and first-class air fares. He also agreed to pay the group's taxes. As a result, NEMS lost £10,000 on the tour. One of the dates on the NEMS 1967 tour was an appearance at the **Royal Albert Hall** on 28 January, which Paul McCartney and George Harrison attended.

Brian also lost money when he brought the group to Britain to appear at the Saville Theatre on 13 November. The backdrop to their stage act had been designed by Paul McCartney, who couldn't attend because he was holidaying in Kenya at the time with **Jane Asher**. John Lennon and George Harrison attended. They were also guests at a special party Epstein threw for the Four Tops at his **Chapel Street** house. Also at the celebration were Mick Jagger, Keith Richard and Charlie Watts of the **Rolling Stones**, Georgie Fame, **Donovan**, Eric Burdon and Hilton Valentine of the Animals and Chris Curtis, drummer with the **Searchers**.

● Fox And Hounds, The, *Gosbrook Road, Caversham, Berkshire*

A pub which had recently been taken over by Paul McCartney's cousin Elizabeth and her husband **Mike Robbins**. Paul and John took a break there during April 1960, during which they worked behind the bar for a week. They also made an appearance singing and playing acoustic guitars while calling themselves the Nerk Twins on 23 April.

● Francis, Bob

A disc jockey at the Adelaide radio station 5AD who orchestrated the 'Bring The Beatles To Adelaide' campaign. He was rewarded for his efforts by being

The Four Tops – one of the Motown acts admired by the Beatles. (Steve Rapport/Arista Records)

present with the Beatles for almost all of the time they were in Adelaide, joining them on the balcony of the town hall for their first public appearance and conducting various interviews with them. He was also selected to compere their Adelaide shows.

He later became station manager at 5AD.

● Fraser, Robert

Fraser, who died of AIDS in 1986, was one of the leading figures in the British art world of the sixties. In addition to promoting Pop Art and various new painters and sculptors at his prestigious Robert Fraser Gallery at 69 Duke Street, he was a friend and adviser to both the Beatles and the **Rolling Stones** in the field of art.

Fraser dissuaded the Beatles from using a psychedelic design by the Fool for their *Sgt Pepper* album. Although the Fool design had been completed, Fraser advised the Beatles that it would date rapidly. He also joined Brian Epstein in a meeting with **Sir Joseph Lockwood** to champion the idea of the famous *Pepper* tableau. Fraser became an adviser and was eventually paid £1,500 by **EMI**. He recommended that artist **Peter Blake** be brought in to design the sleeve, and also hired his regular photographer **Michael Cooper** to take the pictures.

Along with Blake and the Beatles, Fraser also made a list of characters to be included on the actual sleeve and was present at the construction of the tableau and the shoot of the final photo session.

Fraser was busted, along with Mick Jagger and Keith Richards, for possessing heroin, but while both Jagger and Richards were freed, Fraser was sentenced to six months.

On 1 July 1968, John Lennon held his first art exhibition 'You Are Here' at Fraser's gallery. The main focus of the exhibition was a huge circular white canvas with the words 'You Are Here'. There were lots of charity collection boxes on display and the students of Hornsey Art College sent along a rusty bike with the message: 'This exhibit was inadvertently left out.' John immediately placed it in the exhibition.

● Freddie & The Dreamers

A Manchester group who appeared on *Another Beatles Christmas Show*, which played for three weeks, twice-nightly at the **Odeon, Hammersmith**, London, over Christmas 1964. Freddie & the Dreamers appeared on stage immediately after the Beatles had performed a sketch as four Arctic explorers coming across the Abominable Snowman (a costumed **Jimmy Savile**).

Freddie & the Dreamers were a popular group whose hit records spanned two years from 1963-1965 and were: 'If You Gotta Make A Fool Of Somebody', 'I'm Telling You Now', 'You Were Made For Me', 'Over You', 'I Love You Baby', 'Just For You', 'I Understand', 'A Little You' and 'Thou Shalt Not Steal'.

The group successfully promoted a comedy-rock act and comprised Freddie Garritty (vocals), Roy Crewsdon (rhythm guitar), Pete Birrell (bass guitar) and Bernie Dwyer (drums).

● Freeman, Alan A.

The A&R (Artistes and Repertoire) Manager at Pye Records in London whose hit artists included **Lonnie Donegan**, Petula Clark and Kenny Ball. Brian Epstein arranged a meeting with him soon after the Beatles were rejected by Decca. Epstein played Freeman the Beatles' **Decca audition** tapes, but the recording manager was not impressed, and became another 'man who turned down the Beatles'.

● Freeman, Robert

A photographer who, between 1963-1965 acted in a semi-official capacity to the Beatles. In 1963 he requested a photo session with the Beatles and wrote a request to Brian Epstein, who asked him to submit samples of his work. Freeman sent a series of photographs he had taken of jazz musicians, which resulted in Epstein inviting him to take photographs of the Beatles in Bournemouth. During the photo assignment the group mentioned their forthcoming album and said they needed a cover. Freeman suggested it be in black and white and took photographs of them wearing black turtleneck sweaters, which resulted in the cover for *With The Beatles* (in America, *Meet The Beatles*), although **EMI** initially resisted the idea of a mono cover.

When John was looking for a London flat for himself, **Cynthia** and **Julian**, Freeman suggested the apartment below him in Emperor's Gate. When he accompanied the Beatles on a five-day trip to Sweden, he shared a room with John, and he also travelled to Paris with them in January 1964 and on their first trip to America. He was asked to design both John's books *In His Own Write* and *A Spaniard In The Works*, and also took colour and black and white shots when commissioned to provide the cover

›r the soundtrack to *A Hard Day's Night*. He also esigned the film's opening titles. The other album covers e designed and photographed were *Beatles For Sale*, *elp!* and *Rubber Soul*.

Robert was commissioned to photograph the marriage ' Ringo and **Maureen**, and another of his photographs ·ovided the cover to the *Long Tall Sally* EP.

Between 1963 and 1965 he had taken hundreds of ıots of the group in various settings, from outdoor cations in Austria and the Bahamas to backstage shots in ·essing rooms and sessions at **Abbey Road**. His final ıportant assignment with them came when he took the ıotographs for *Rubber Soul* in John's back garden at 'eybridge.

Several collections of his Beatle photographs have been ıblished in book form, including *Beatles Ltd*, George ewnes (1964); *Yesterday: Photographs Of The Beatles*, 'eidenfeld & Nicolson (1983) and *The Beatles*, Octopus .990). Paul McCartney wrote the introduction to *·sterday*, in which he described Freeman's large, grainy ·ints as 'artistic without being pretentious' and ›mmented, 'I have a feeling that Robert Freeman's photos ere amongst the best ever taken of the Beatles.'

Freight Train

umber included in the **Quarry Men**'s repertoire. The ng was performed by the group in 1957. The number ıs a No. 5 chart hit in Britain on the Oriole label for the ›pular Chas McDevitt Skiffle Group, with Nancy hiskey, in April 1957.

'Freight Train' was a traditional American folk song ıd John was lead vocalist when the Quarry Men ·rformed it.

Fresco, Monty

veteran Fleet Street photographer, born in London's East ıd, who had been providing photographic news on mera for the national press since 1930.

Monty had become acquainted with the Beatles at the set of **Beatlemania** in 1963 and, in his book *Pictures e My Life*, mentions that he had '. . . taken private ctures of them and, in fact, took the very last picture of em all together, just before they broke up'.

At one time Monty suggested to washing-machine :oon John Bloom that he invite the Beatles along to a ırty he was holding. The party was in full swing, already brimming with celebrities of the ilk of Adam Faith, **Shirley Bassey** and Max Bygraves, so Bloom sent the invitations to the theatre where the Beatles were appearing.

Monty was leaving the party at 1.30 in the morning, wondering what had happened to the Beatles, when he found them engaged in an argument with the doorman, who refused them entrance. Monty told the man who they were and confirmed that they'd been invited to the party, but he still refused to let them pass. Eventually, Monty phoned up to Bloom, who came down and arranged their safe passage to the party.

'I don't care a bugger who you are, you're not coming in dressed like that,' was one of the sentences Monty had heard the doorman utter, which affords an insight into the attitudes of a section of the older generation to the Beatles in 1963.

Monty relates some further stories about the Beatles in his book, which includes a photograph of Ringo at the John Bloom party, jokingly dancing with Max Bygraves; a picture of Paul taking a delayed action shot of himself, and **Linda** in hospital with their first child; a shot of the group holding their **MBE**s and a picture of Paul, Linda, Ringo, John and **Yoko** walking in the grounds of Tittenhurst Park.

● Friar Park, *Paradise Road, Henley-on-Thames, Oxfordshire*

Ornate Victorian mansion with 120 rooms, bought by George Harrison for $350,000, in February 1969. The building had originally been built for Sir Frank Crisp, a City of London solicitor, in 1889 and was erected on the site of a thirteenth century Friary.

The spired and turreted building, with a red brick and yellow low-stone exterior, had been owned by nuns of the Order of St John Bosco for over a decade and since they could no longer afford the upkeep, the building was about to be knocked down.

It was in quite a state of disrepair when George bought it and he and **Pattie** initially lived in the labourer's cottage on the grounds while the main building was restored.

He had a suite of two bedrooms, bathroom and dressing-room turned into a recording studio, and installed a cinema.

He paid tribute to the original owner with 'The Ballad

Of Sir Francis Crisp' on his *All Things Must Pass* album.

George had his brother **Harold** take over the task of managing Friar Park from a gatehouse office. His brother Peter was engaged to oversee the team of full-time gardeners attending the large grounds, which were spread over forty acres, with gardens, fields, hedges and caves.

He then had a sign placed outside the gates, stating 'absolutely no admittance' in ten languages.

● Friday Spectacular

A **Radio Luxembourg** show in which artists mimed to their records in front of an invited audience. The Beatles appeared on a series of 'Friday Spectacular' performances. They recorded a show at **EMI House** in London on 8 October 1962 which was transmitted on 12 October. The following month they appeared on the show on 16 November and it was transmitted on 23 November. For their show recorded on 21 January 1963, which was transmitted on 25 January, they actually performed live on the show for the first time, playing 'Please Please Me', 'Carol' and 'Lend Me Your Comb'. Their final appearance took place on 11 March 1963, for transmission on 15 March. The presenter was **Muriel Young**.

● From A Window

Billy J. Kramer's fourth single with a Lennon & McCartney songwriting credit. The number had been penned by Paul McCartney, and John and Paul cut an acetate of the song for Kramer and George Martin to listen to. The Beatles never recorded the number themselves, and Kramer's version was issued in Britain on Parlophone R 5156 on 17 July 1964, and in America on Imperial 66061 on 12 August 1964. It reached No. 13 in the British charts and No. 23 in the American.

● From Me To You

The Beatles' third single, which John and Paul wrote on 28 February 1963, while travelling by coach between York and Shrewsbury on a leg of their **Helen Shapiro** tour. Their inspiration had been the title of the letters column in the ***New Musical Express***, which was called 'From You To Us'. John commented, 'We nearly didn't record it because we thought it was too bluesy at first, but when we'd finished it and George Martin had scored it with harmonica it was all right.'

The song became their most performed number on their series of BBC radio shows and they featured it fiftee times – three times on **'Easy Beat'**, once on **'Swingin Sound '63'**, three times on **'Side By Side'**, twice o **'Saturday Club'**, once on **'Steppin' Out'**, four times o **'Pop Go The Beatles'** and once on **'Beat Show'**. The also adopted the number for their **'From Us To You** radio series.

The single was issued on Parlophone R 5015 in Britai on 11 April 1963 and became a No. 1 hit, with 'Thank Yo Girl' on the flip. It was issued in America by **Vee Ja Records** on VJ 522 on 27 May 1963, but failed to mak the charts. They reissued it in America on VJ 581 on 3 January 1964 coupled with 'Please Please Me'. The 'Fro Me To You' side reached No. 41 in the charts.

The number was included on their second British E *The Beatles Hits*, the compilations *A Collection Of Beatl Oldies (But Goldies)*, *The Beatles Hits 1962–66* and 2 *Greatest Hits*. It was in *The Beatles Box* set and Vee J included it on the album *Jolly What! The Beatles an Frank Ifield On Stage*. In Britain, **EMI** issued a pre release to go with the single, which read:

> 'Vocally and instrumentally this new dec matches the high spirits of PLEASE PLEASE ME wi John, Paul and George chanting and harmonisi expertly. BUT don't get the idea that this is a carb copy of their last single – in fact it is the mo unusual number THE BEATLES have recorded to dat
>
> 'In defiance of the tiresome trend towards weep lost-love wailers, FROM ME TO YOU is a rip-rocki up tempo ballad which has a happy-go-luck romantic story-line.
>
> 'EAR-CATCHING HIGH SPOT: Those unexpect falsetto-voice high-kicks on the line "If there anything I can do".
>
> 'OFF-BEAT FINALE: Sudden switch of speed a rhythm for that end-of-the-track instrument climax.
>
> 'UNANIMOUS VERDICT: The sturdy beat plus t unique Beatle-blending of harmonica, guitars a voices plus the thoroughly infectious tune mak FROM ME TO YOU another dead-cert Number O chart-smasher!'

'From Me To You' was also reissued as a single yet aga by Vee Jay, as the flipside of 'Please Please Me' on C 151 Oldies 45, on 10 August 1964.

There have been numerous covers of the song and

ecame the very first Beatles number to be covered by an merican artist, when **Del Shannon** issued it in the US nd it provided a minor chart hit for him. Their publisher **ick James** also recorded the number and there have een several foreign language versions, including *'Lo endras Amor'* in Spanish, *'Meidan Yhteinen'* in Finnish nd *'Des Bises De Moi Pour Toi'* in French.

From Us To You

our BBC radio programmes broadcast during holiday eriods. The Beatles adapted their number 'From Me To ou' to become the show's theme 'From Us To You'.

Produced by Bryan Marriott, the first show was ansmitted on 26 December 1963. The two-hour show, hich was presented by **Rolf Harris**, had guest ppearances from **Joe Brown** and the Bruvvers, Susan aughan and **Kenny Lynch**. The Beatles performed rom Us To You', 'She Loves You', 'All My Loving', 'Roll ver Beethoven', 'Till There Was You', 'Boys', 'Money', 'I w Her Standing There', 'I Want To Hold Your Hand' d 'From Us To You'.

The second in the series, presented by **Alan Freeman** 30 March 1964 (Easter Monday), featured the group erforming 'From Us To You', 'You Can't Do That', 'Roll ver Beethoven', 'Till There Was You', 'I Wanna Be Your an', 'Please Mr Postman', 'All My Loving', 'This Boy', an't Buy Me Love' and 'From Us To You'. Their guests ere the **Swinging Bluejeans**, Vince Hill and **Acker ilk and his Paramount Jazz Band**.

Alan Freeman also presented the third show on 18 May 64 (Whitsun Bank Holiday). The group performed rom Us To You', 'I Saw Her Standing There', 'Kansas ty/Hey! Hey! Hey!', 'I Forgot To Remember To Forget', ou Can't Do That', 'Sure To Fall In Love (With You)', an't Buy Me Love', 'Matchbox', 'Honey Don't' and 'From s To You'.

Their final programme was presented by Don Wardell 3 August 1964 (August Bank Holiday Monday) and the eatles performed 'From Us To You', 'Long Tall Sally', 'If Fell', 'I'm Happy Just To Dance With You', 'Things We id Today', 'I Should Have Known Better', 'Boys', 'A ard Day's Night' and 'From Us To You'.

Frost, David

elevision celebrity who first found fame on BBC TV's tirical series 'That Was The Week That Was'. He was to emerge as one of the most renowned television interviewers on both sides of the Atlantic, hosting shows for the BBC and ITV in Britain, as well as having his own series in America.

John and George appeared on his 'The Frost Programme' during a break in their **Abbey Road** session on 29 September 1967. It was broadcast the following day. The two chatted about the **Maharishi** and his Transcendental Meditation and how it had affected them personally. John mentioned that he had stopped using drugs long before he met the Maharishi. He said that he thought of God as a huge amount of energy, like electricity. The discussion went so well that Frost invited them both back to his show on 4 October – an offer which they took up.

Paul McCartney appeared with Frost later that year, on 27 December, to discuss the critical bashing received by the screening of *Magical Mystery Tour* on television.

On 4 September 1968 Frost visited the Beatles at **Twickenham Studios** where they were filming a promotional performance of 'Hey Jude', which he introduced and broadcast on 8 September on 'Frost On Sunday'. A clip of this was used on American TV stations and has cropped up in various film compilations. 'Frost On Sunday' was the new title of his show as it had changed channels and was then screened by London Weekend Television.

John and **Yoko** also appeared on his show to discuss conceptual art. Frost was quite sceptical and made some disparaging comments about John's badge, which displayed the words 'You Are Here'. John made his attitude to art quite clear: 'Our bodies are art, everything around us is art, the world is a gallery.' He commented that the public would enjoy creating art of its own. For the purposes of demonstration, Yoko had brought along a nail board and members of the audience were invited to knock a nail in. They all said how much they had enjoyed the experience.

By the late sixties, Frost had become a regular transatlantic traveller, flying back and forth across the Atlantic to host shows in New York and London. On his American show on 23 February 1969 his guest was Paul McCartney, who introduced his new Apple protégée, **Mary Hopkin**. On 29 March 1970 Ringo Starr performed 'Sentimental Journey', accompanied by the George Martin Orchestra. Ringo made a further appearance on Frost's show that year, with his co-star of the film *The Magic Christian*, **Peter Sellers**. Clips from the movie were shown and the two stars duetted on 'Octopus's Garden'.

George guested on 3 December 1971; John and Yoko also put in an appearance in the New York studios on 13 January 1972. George Harrison and guitarist David Bromberg appeared in December 1972 playing together on the numbers 'Suffer To Sing The Blues', 'The Hold Up', and 'Bangla Desh' and George and **Ravi Shankar** played some Indian music together.

On 21 May 1975, David Frost hosted a special tribute to the Beatles in America. It was screened on ABC TV and entitled 'Salute To The Beatles'. He was to host a similar tribute in 1977.

Frost also had a radio programme on the BBC Light Programme, called 'David Frost At The Phonograph'. Paul McCartney recorded an interview with Frost on 1 August 1966 which was broadcast on the show on 6 August.

● Furlong, June

A former artist's model at the **Liverpool College of Art**. She often used to contend with problems caused by John Lennon during the classes, particularly when he kept getting the life class to break out in laughter whenever the teacher left the room. At one time, in the teacher's absence, he came from behind his easel and sat on her knee and began kissing her. On another occasion he handed teacher Terry Griffiths his drawing of June in the nude – which consisted solely of a sketch of her watch. June lent John some of her clothing for his appearance as an Ugly Sister in an Art College pantomime of *Cinderella* in 1959.

● Fury, Billy

Born Ronald Wycherley on 17 April 1941, Billy Fury became Liverpool's first-ever rock star.

He'd once shared the same class as Ringo Starr at Dingle Vale Secondary School.

Billy had a string of hits in the sixties, including 'Maybe Tomorrow', 'A Thousand Stars', 'Wondrous Place', 'Halfway To Paradise' and 'Letter Full of Tears'.

At one time Billy and his manager **Larry Parnes** auditioned the Silver Beatles in Liverpool as a possible choice for a backing group for him. Billy, himself, decided that he liked the Silver Beatles best, but Larry Parnes seemed concerned about the age of the drummer, **Tommy Moore**, and Cass & the Cassanovas ended up backin him on a tour.

All four Beatles went to the **Empire Theatre** on 2 October 1962 to see Billy perform at a show there.

Together with Ringo Starr, he appeared in the fil *That'll Be The Day*.

Billy had been plagued by illnesses since he was child, and rheumatic fever had left him with a damage

Billy Fury – the Beatles almost became his backing group. (National Film Archive)

heart. He said, 'One of the valves of my heart had clos up, and the only way for the blood to come out was throu my mouth. That was one of the very bad symptoms that had. So I had to quit.'

He'd been working late at night, recording a comeba album to release prior to a tour, when he experienced heart attack and died on 28 January 1982.

● Futurist Theatre, Foreshore Road, South Bay, Scarborough, Yorkshire

The Beatles first appeared at this venue in the Yorkshi seaside resort, during their autumn tour of the UK, on December 1963. Their second and final appearance to place on 9 August 1964.

● 3 Gambier Terrace, Liverpool 8

Less than 100 yards from the entrance to **Liverpool College of Art**, this Georgian terrace, directly opposite the Anglican Cathedral, was where art student **Rod Murray** managed to rent a first floor flat in 1960. He'd previously been dwelling in nearby **Percy Street**, where **Stuart Sutcliffe** had also been renting a flat.

The Gambier Terrace accommodation was more salubrious than Rod's previous place – and more expensive. He talked Stuart into sharing it with him and John Lennon became a third tenant, although he had some difficulty in persuading his Aunt **Mimi** to allow him to leave the comforts of her home in Menlove Avenue.

John liked the freedom of Gambier Terrace and his girlfriend **Cynthia** was able to stay overnight with him on several occasions, telling her mother she was spending the night at her friend **Phyllis MacKenzie**'s house. Rod Murray's girlfriend Margaret Dizley also slept there on a number of nights.

The flat's proximity to the college, **Liverpool Institute**, **Ye Cracke**, the Philharmonic pub and the Liverpool 8 area in general, proved advantageous to the young students and the Silver Beatles were also able to rehearse there. One night, after meeting poet **Royston Ellis** and backing him on a poetry to rock session at the **Jacaranda**, they brought him back to the flat and he introduced them to some soft drugs such as benzedrine.

Bill Harry and his girlfriend Virginia were also regular visitors and one night, after they'd been so involved in discussions that they missed the late night bus, John took them in the bathroom and provided blankets and pillows, suggesting they sleep in the bath, which they did.

The flat was spacious, with high ceilings, although it was very sparsely furnished as the impecunious art students couldn't afford much in the way of furniture.

During 1960 the *Sunday People* newspaper was 'exposing' Beatniks – the British youngsters, inspired by America's Beat Generation, who had 'dropped out of society'. Journalists usually used **Allan Williams**'s coffee bar as a meeting place and Allan had established friendly relations with the local press corps. When the reporters from the *Sunday People* asked him if he knew of a dirty flat where they could take photographs of Beatniks in filthy conditions, Allan said he'd fix something up for them.

He asked John, Stuart and Rod if the newspaper could take photographs in their flat and was able to talk the naïve youngsters into granting their permission. Of course, the flat was quite a nice-looking one, despite the lack of furniture, but it didn't take Williams long to set about making the place scruffy, placing empty beer bottles on the floor, rumpling up old newspapers and scattering them about, making the furniture askew and generally turning the flat into a messy place. The pictures were taken and were published in the *Sunday People* on 24 July, under the title 'The Beatnik Horror'.

Due to this staged event, Beatle chroniclers mistakenly write that the Gambier flat was a slum, which it wasn't. Another Gambier Terrace fable is that there was a coffin in it. The original rumours, which began after Stuart's death, implied that Stu had slept in a coffin. He didn't. He slept on a camp bed which his mother collected from the flat in 1961. Over twenty years later, writer Albert Goldman was suggesting that John Lennon slept in a coffin there, complete with silver lining – pure fantasy.

Once John and Stuart left for Hamburg, Rod was in a dilemma. He just couldn't afford to pay the rent himself. When they didn't return to the flat – with John going back to his Aunt Mimi's and Stuart remaining in Germany, Rod was in further trouble because of the back rent. He contacted Mrs Sutcliffe, who paid off Stuart's part of the debt and hired a mini-van to collect both Stuart's and John's possessions.

One or two items of John's were left in the flat, including some exercise books which Rod was able to auction off at Sotheby's in 1984 for £16,000.

Garland, Judy

Legendary singer and Hollywood star. When Judy was living in England, Brian Epstein was introduced to her by Lionel Bart while they were attending the Manchester premiere of the *Maggie May* musical. Judy was among the many guests at the special show party held at Liverpool's **Blue Angel Club** later that evening – although **Allan Williams** actually threw her out of the club!

The singer provided one of the highlights of **'The Night Of A Hundred Stars'** at the **London Palladium** on 23 July 1964 when she sang the song most associated with her – 'Over The Rainbow'. The Beatles were also on the bill.

Judy was among the celebrity guests, along with the Beatles, who attended a party at Epstein's Knightsbridge home on 12 August 1964. Paul McCartney spent a great deal of time talking to her that evening and there were later rumours that he would be writing a song specially for her.

The Beatles' press agent **Brian Somerville** formerly handled Judy's publicity and Epstein's solicitor **David Jacobs** also represented her.

In October 1964 Brian Epstein and Lionel Bart announced that they would be promoting a Judy Garland concert, but it never took place.

The singer/actress died in 1969.

Garner, Frank

First road manager for the Beatles, although he only worked for them for a couple of months. Garner was a 'bouncer' at the **Casbah Club** when **Mona Best** asked him if he could act as a driver for the Beatles.

Frank's first assignment was their **Litherland Town Hall** gig on 27 December 1960. In addition to driving the group, he also humped their kit. For this he was paid the same amount as the members of the group – one pound. Their fee for that evening was six pounds and there were five members in the band. **Stuart Sutcliffe** was still in Germany at the time and **Chas Newby** deputized on bass guitar.

Garner continued to act as roadie for the next few months but began to find that he couldn't do two jobs at once, particularly at weekends, and by the autumn of 1961 **Pete Best** asked **Neil Aspinall**, who was lodging in his house, if he could take over the job from Frank, which he did.

Gator Bowl, *Jackson, Florida*

At the time of the gig, Hurricane Dora had swept over Jacksonville causing terrible damage. President Johnson had arrived to inspect the damage and when the Beatles flew in on Friday, 11 September 1964, to appear at the Gator Bowl, their plane had to circle Imeson Airport until the President's plane had flown out. His police escort had remained to take the Beatles into town and they were driven to the George Washington Hotel in a cavalcade of police cars and motorbikes.

There was a press reception at the hotel with 150 attendees asking questions such as 'Does your hair require any special care?' and 'How do you all feel about you and the President coming to town on the same day?', to which John replied, 'Amazing.'

The Beatles had originally refused to appear at the venue until they were assured that the audience wouldn't be segregated. Winds of 40 mph were whipping through the stadium and due to the devastation caused by Dora, 9,000 of the 32,000 ticketholders didn't make it to the concert.

The show started at 8.30 p.m. but when the Beatles were due to appear, a camera team from LA had entrenched themselves backstage and refused to move. **Derek Taylor** faced the audience and told them: 'The Beatles are one hundred feet away. They came thousands of miles to be here and the only thing preventing their appearance are those nasty cine-cameramen.' He pointed to them and the boos began. 'Now if you want the Beatles to perform here tonight,' he said, 'tell the police to make the cameramen leave.'

The entire audience began chanting 'Out! Out! Out!' and police moved forward and hustled the eight-man team away.

The winds continued throughout the show unabated and Ringo's drums had been nailed down. At one time an attendant held Ringo down because he thought he'd be blown away!

Gaumont, *Westover Road, Bournemouth, Hampshire*

The Beatles appeared at this venue three times, making their debut there for a one week season with two shows per night for six nights from 19–24 August 1963. They were driven to the gigs in a Ford Zephyr and their outfits comprised black velvet jackets with white shirts, together with string ties and grey-striped trousers. Support acts were **Billy J. Kramer** & the Dakotas and **Tommy Quickly**. During one of the performances a fan threw a five-inch metal safety pin at the stage which narrowly missed Paul's face.

Their second appearance on 2 August 1964 had the Kinks, **Mike Berry** and Adrienne Posta in support and their final show at the Gaumont took place on 30 October 1964, with **Mary Wells**, Tommy Quickly, **Sounds Incorporated**, **Michael Haslam**, the **Remo Four**, the **Rustiks** and **Bob Bain** in support.

● Gaumont, *New Victoria Street, Bradford, Yorkshire*

The venue for the Beatles' first-ever Christmas stage show. The **Fab Four** previewed their Christmas show here for one evening, 21 December 1963. Their guest artists were **Billy J. Kramer** & the Dakotas. It was the first of two northern previews for 'The Beatles Christmas Show', without the costumes, sets or comedy sketches which were to be featured in the London season at the **Astoria**, **Finsbury Park**.

The Beatles also made their major theatre tour debut here on 2 February 1963 as part of the **Helen Shapiro** tour. There were two performances and Paul said, 'We went on that opening night with Helen looking like a gang of Red Indians with war paint. But it was fun, and it was a challenge.' John was to say, 'It really was a relief to get out of Liverpool and try something new. Back home we'd worked night after night on the same cramped stage. Bradford wasn't very far away, but at least it was different as a field. We'd all started feeling tired, jaded, tied down, with the club scenes. Touring, with a different venue every night, was a real lift.' Their first performance that night was recorded by ABC TV and a part of it was broadcast on '**Thank Your Lucky Stars**'. Among the numbers they performed were 'Chains', 'Keep Your Hands Off My Baby', 'A Taste Of Honey', and 'Please Please Me'. The actual order of billing ran: Helen Shapiro, **Danny Williams**, **Kenny Lynch**, the Beatles, the **Kestrels**, the Red Price Orchestra, the Honeys and compere **Dave Allen**.

Local journalist Gordon Sampson was to write: 'A great reception went to the colourfully dressed Beatles, who almost stole the show, for the audience repeatedly called for them while other artists were performing! Undoubtedly their best number was an unusual vocal treatment of "A Taste Of Honey", sung by left-handed bass guitarist Paul McCartney, with the others harmonising.

'Their current hit, "Please Please Me", with which they closed, was the most popular. They also sang their first success, "Love Me Do", "Beautiful Dreamer", "Chains" and "Keep Your Hands Off My Baby".'

Their longest British tour, their fourth, also commenced at this theatre. This time the Beatles were top of the bill when, on 9 October 1964, they appeared with Mary Wells, **Tommy Quickly** and the Remo Four, **Michael Haslam**, the **Rustiks**, **Sounds Incorporated** and compere **Bob Bain**. They performed 'Twist And Shout', 'Money', 'Can't Buy Me Love', 'Things We Said Today', 'I'm Happy Just To Dance With You', 'I Should Have Known Better', 'If I Fell', 'I Wanna Be Your Man', 'A Hard Day's Night' and 'Long Tall Sally', with Ringo gaining the biggest applause of the evening for his rendition of 'I Wanna Be Your Man'.

● Gaumont, *Hallgate, Doncaster, Yorkshire*

All three appearances by the Beatles at this cinema took place in 1963. Their debut occurred on 5 February as part of the **Helen Shapiro** tour, followed by a visit the following month on 22 March as part of the **Tommy Roe/Chris Montez** package and finally as bill toppers in their own right on 10 December.

● Gaumont, *Piccadilly, Hanley, Staffordshire*

Site of the Beatles' final date on the **Helen Shapiro** tour on 3 March 1963. The group had begun the tour in the opening spot and had gradually risen to the more prestigious position of being the last act in the first half – generally regarded as second on the bill. They returned for their second and last appearance at the cinema several weeks later on 19 May on their tour with **Roy Orbison**.

● Gaumont, *St Helen's Street, Ipswich, Suffolk*

The Beatles played here during their tour with **Roy Orbison** on 22 May 1963. Their second appearance there was on 31 October 1964.

● Gaumont, *Barker's Pool, Sheffield, South Yorkshire*

Their one and only appearance at this cinema was one of the very last concert dates the group performed in Britain.

The Beatles Show was presented at the Gaumont on 8 December 1965 during their final British concert tour.

● Gaumont, *Commercial Road, Southampton, Hampshire*

The Beatles first appeared at this cinema during their tour with **Roy Orbison** on 20 May 1963. They returned to the venue for the final date of their autumn tour on 13 December 1963 and their last appearance at the venue took place on 6 November 1964.

● Gaumont, *Corporation Street, Taunton, Somerset*

The Beatles first appeared at this cinema during their tour with **Helen Shapiro** on 26 February 1963. However, this was the first of two dates on which Helen didn't appear due to her having contracted a cold. Her stand-in that night was Billie Davis, who had a chart hit called 'Tell Him'.

Their next and final appearance at the venue took place later the same year on 5 September.

● Gaumont, *Snow Hill, Wolverhampton, West Midlands*

When the Beatles first appeared at this venue on 14 March 1963, as part of the **Tommy Roe/Chris Montez** tour John Lennon was ill and only Paul, George and Ringo appeared in the Beatles' spot.

They next appeared on Tuesday, 19 November 1963, as eadliners in their own right. During the evening **Sean)'Mahoney** and **Leslie Bryce** of *Beatles Monthly* visited ıe boys backstage. Mahoney had brought along ten hats of arious styles from Dunn of Regent Street for the boys to ose in.

Also backstage were journalist **Mike Hennessy** and **'ony Bramwell** of **NEMS**. The group wore black mohair uits with velvet collars and during their set a fan threw a 'hite bunny on stage, which John kept, presumably for ulian.

Gaumont, Foregate Street, Worcester

'he Beatles first appeared at this cinema on 28 May 1963 uring their tour with **Roy Orbison**. They returned to the enue on 4 September 1963 as the first of a series of four ookings by the promoter **John Smith**.

Gaumont State Cinema, Kilburn High ₹oad, London NW6

arge picture palace originally built in 1937 which finally losed in 1980.

During the fifties and sixties the venue presented many ımous live performers on stage, including Bill Haley, Ella itzgerald and Duke Ellington.

The Beatles made their debut appearance at the cinema n 9 April 1963 and also performed there on 23 October 964.

● Gentle, Johnny

iverpool-born singer, real name John Askew, who was gned to the **Larry Parnes** stable. As a result of the ilver Beetles' audition at the **Wyvern Club**, 10 May 960, Parnes booked the group as Gentle's backing band r a nine-day tour of Scotland.

Gentle, who was twenty at the time, was a former pprentice carpenter and merchant seaman.

When he met the group his first impressions weren't all ıat favourable. He said, 'When I first saw them I ondered what on earth Parnes had sent me.' In spite of ıat he decided to help them out, provided them with some age clothes and was later to talk the promoter out of ring them.

Despite the fact that they only had 30 minutes of hearsal time before they began touring, Gentle was so npressed by the band that he urged Parnes to sign them up, but Parnes specialized in handling solo singers and didn't relish the problems he might face managing a five-piece group. Parnes was to comment: 'Johnny used to phone me virtually every night and say "Come up to Scotland and see these boys. I've given them a spot in my act and they're doing better than I am." He was very honest. I always said that if I'd found the time to go up to Scotland he might have been the fifth Beatle. Who knows?'

Gentle and the Silver Beetles were driven to their gigs by Gerry Scott in a van. On 23 May 1960 on a journey between Inverness and Fraserburgh, Gentle decided to take over as driver – and accidentally smashed the van into a stationary Ford Poplar. The only injured person was drummer **Tommy Moore** who suffered concussion and had his front teeth knocked out.

During their Scottish tour with Gentle, three members of the group decided to use stage names. Paul became **Paul Ramon**, George became Carl Harrison and **Stuart** was billed as Stu De Stael.

When the group appeared at the **Grosvenor Ballroom, Wallasey**, on 2 July 1960, Gentle visited them and performed a few numbers on stage with the band.

Gentle was later to change his stage name to Darren Young.

He was to relate that during the tour with the Silver Beetles he was working on a song called 'I've Just Fallen For Someone' and played it to John Lennon as he was having difficulty with it. John helped with the middle eight and he was to issue the song as a single when he recorded for Parlophone under the Darren Young name.

● Gerry & The Pacemakers

Liverpool's nearest rivals to the Beatles.

Leader **Gerry Marsden** had joined his first skiffle group at the age of fourteen and named one of his skiffle bands the Mars Bars. In 1959 the group had become a rock 'n' roll band and Gerry was accompanied by his brother Freddie on drums, Les Chadwick on guitar and Les Maguire on piano.

Although the group were a rock 'n' roll band they didn't have the same hard edge as groups such as the Big Three, the **Dominoes** or the Beatles, but their music was infectious and they had a huge local following. Gerry had an astonishing repertoire of 250 songs and among the numbers performed regularly by the band were 'Jambalaya', 'Skinny Minnie', 'What'd I Say' and 'Will

Above and facing page: Gerry and the Pacemakers – Liverpool's second most popular band. (*Mersey Beat* Archives)
Right: The band on stage at the Cavern. (United Artists)

You Love Me Tomorrow?'

In his own personal Top Ten of local groups, published in the 5 October 1961 issue of ***Mersey Beat***, **Cavern** disc jockey **Bob Wooler** placed Gerry and the Pacemakers directly behind the Beatles at No. 2.

Mindful of the publicity the local groups were receiving in *Mersey Beat*, Brian Epstein began talking to Marsden when the singer was in the NEMS, Whitechapel, shop, looking at records. Epstein, aware of the youngsters who frequented his shop, began to ask Gerry about his selection of records.

Gerry, who was born on 24 September 1942, was nineteen at the time and an apprentice working for British

Rail. In January, Bob Wooler's personal preferences were reflected in the first official *Mersey Beat* Poll. The Beatles were at No. 1, Gerry & the Pacemakers at No. 2. As Epstein had already signed up the No. 1 group, it was only natural that he next sign up their closest rivals. Interestingly enough, the following year, soon after **Billy J. Kramer** was voted into the No. 3 position of the *Mersey Beat* Poll, Epstein signed him up. In fact, an analysis of the poll results will show that Epstein signed up the highest-placed acts in the poll who were not already committed to a manager, such as the **Fourmost**, the **Remo Four** and the **Merseybeats** (the latter didn't stay with him for long).

Gerry & the Pacemakers made their Cavern debut in October 1960 and appeared at most of the leading Mersey venues, often on the same bill as the Beatles – during their 19 October 1961 appearance at **Litherland Town Hall** the two groups joined as one and called themselves the Beatmakers! They also went to Germany where they had the opportunity of meeting some of their idols – Fats Domino, **Jerry Lee Lewis** and **Gene Vincent**.

Freddie Marsden was to tell broadcaster Spencer Leigh, 'The Beatles appealed to a different audience from us. They had more of a beatnik following. There was always friendly rivalry between us. Despite their rawness, Paul McCartney used to get a great reception for the sentimental songs like "Over The Rainbow" and we thought we'd have to get a song that would go over just as well. We tried "You'll Never Walk Alone" a few times and it went down excellently. We'd be playing rock 'n' roll and then all of a sudden we'd stop and do "You'll Never Walk Alone".'

Gerry was proud when, one day, after the number had been a No. 1 hit, he heard Liverpool supporters begin to sing the number at football matches. It soon became the main football anthem, not only in Liverpool, but throughout Britain. He was to re-record the number almost a quarter of a century later and see it reach No. 1 again – a record no other artist has achieved.

When George Martin visited Liverpool on 9 December 1962 to see the Beatles perform at the **Cavern** and assess the technical difficulties involved in recording them live at the club, Brian Epstein also took him across the River Mersey to see Gerry & the Pacemakers performing at the **Majestic Ballroom, Birkenhead**. Martin was impressed and signed them. He gave them the **Mitch Murray** number 'How Do You Do It?', which the Beatles had rejected, to record. They reached the No. 1 position with the single at the end of March 1963 and, because the *Record Retailer* chart was the official industry chart, Gerry & the Pacemakers reached the No. 1 spot before the Beatles. They also reached No. 1 with their next two releases, 'I Like It' and 'You'll Never Walk Alone'. It was a unique achievement – no other artist had ever scored a hat-trick of chart toppers with their first three recordings. It was a record which has never been topped, although it was equalled at the beginning of the eighties by another Liverpool band, Frankie Goes To Hollywood, who, ironically, had Gerry's 'Ferry 'Cross The Mersey' on the flipside of one of their chart toppers.

Just as they'd appeared on many local bills together,

the Beatles and Gerry & the Pacemakers found themselves sharing bills on nationwide concert appearances, including the Brian Epstein series of 'Mersey Beat Showcase' gigs which featured the Beatles, Gerry & the Pacemakers, the Big Three and Billy J. Kramer & the Dakotas. The two groups also topped the bill on a special **NEMS Enterprises** promotion at the **Tower Ballroom**, New Brighton, on Friday, 14 June 1963. They also toured with the Beatles and **Roy Orbison** in May and June 1963.

Epstein attempted to pattern the career of Gerry & the Pacemakers on the model of the Beatles' success. They were placed with the same recording manager, George Martin, had publicity photographs by **Dezo Hoffmann**, suits by **Dougie Millins**, and Epstein even talked **Sean O'Mahoney** into publishing a Gerry & the Pacemakers monthly magazine similar to the *Beatles Monthly*. Just as the Beatles had a Christmas show, Epstein had a similar one for Gerry, 'Gerry's Christmas Cracker' – and following the success of *A Hard Day's Night*, he also arranged for Gerry & the Pacemakers to appear in a black and white feature film, *Ferry 'Cross The Mersey*, scripted by Tony Warren, who'd created the northern soap opera 'Coronation Street'. Epstein also tried the same tack in America, arranging for Gerry to appear on 'The **Ed Sullivan** Show' and on tour over there.

Despite such a push, the career at the top was relatively short-lived for Gerry & the Pacemakers. Trying to fit them into the same pattern as the Beatles didn't work. They were different groups; the Pacemakers needed specific attention paid to their own individuality and style as an act. Brian Epstein didn't really have that much time to spend on them as his attention was fully directed on the Beatles' career. The Pacemakers had enjoyed three No. 1 hits in 1963 and three further hits in 1964: 'I'm The One', which reached No. 2, 'Don't Let The Sun Catch You Crying', which reached No. 6, and 'Ferry 'Cross The Mersey', which reached No. 8. They had their last hit, 'I'll Be There', in 1965, which reached No. 15. They disbanded soon afterwards and Gerry starred for some time in the West End musical *Charlie Girl*, before becoming a host on children's television programmes.

In the seventies he re-formed Gerry & the Pacemakers with different personnel and has been touring on and off ever since. In 1985 he issued his own tribute to the Beatles, an album *Lennon/McCartney Songbook* (K-Tel ONE 1274) with his personal rendition of Lennon & McCartney classics. Paul McCartney provided the sleeve notes, in which he commented, 'In Liverpool his group was probably the biggest competition to the Beatles and I remember all too well sweating the outcome of our local newspaper popularity poll, hoping that we could scrape together the necessary points to beat their band. That's how close it was!'

Get Back

The single that was credited to 'The Beatles with **Billy Preston**', making Preston the only musician to officially share label billing with the Beatles at their request.

The Beatles had first met Preston in Hamburg and when George Harrison went to the Royal Festival Hall to attend a Ray Charles concert, he saw Billy perform on stage. George renewed the acquaintanceship and took Billy along to the **Apple Studios** where the group were recording. They then invited him to spend the next two weeks recording and filming with them on their 'Get Back' project, with Preston playing electric organ. Billy was later to say, 'I didn't even know until the record was out that they had put my name on it. It was something that I could have never asked for or no manager could negotiate, just something they felt for me.' Billy was also presented with a Gold Disc for his contribution to the single.

The number was a Paul McCartney composition, but it had seen many changes and the song had been rehearsed at the Twickenham sessions, although in a different form. Paul had originally written it as a satire on the British immigration laws, with such controversial lines as 'Don't dig no Pakistanis taking all the people's jobs'. Although Paul was making a political comment, aimed at attitudes towards immigration from people such as Enoch Powell, the MP, and also mentioning political figures such as **Harold Wilson** and Edward Heath, he was not being 'racist' as the ***New Musical Express*** accused him of being several years later when they heard some of the various recordings of the song. Different versions of the number in its early stages have been called by several names, including 'Commonwealth', 'Commonwealth Song', 'White Power' or 'No Pakistanis', and have cropped up on numerous bootleg albums.

Recordings of the new version began on Thursday, 23 January 1969, at the Apple Studios in **Savile Row**, with Preston. Apart from producer George Martin, **Glyn Johns** acted as engineer and Alan Parsons became tape operator on a Beatles disc for the first time. Recordings continued on other days at Apple and the number was also included in the group's live performance on the roof of the Apple building.

The single was issued in Britain on 11 April 1969 on Apple R 5777 with 'Don't Let Me Down' as the flip. A slightly earlier release date had been planned, but the Beatles halted the release and re-mixed the track.

In America it was issued on 5 May 1969 on Apple 2490 and entered the charts at No. 10, equalling their feat with 'Hey Jude'. An advertisement in *Billboard* stated, 'It's the first Beatles record which is as live as can be, in this electronic age.'

Over 4½ million copies were sold worldwide and the single was No. 1 in Australia, New Zealand, Canada, Germany, France, Spain, Norway, Denmark, Holland, Belgium, Malaysia and Singapore.

Rod Stewart recorded a version of the number for the *All This And World War II* film soundtrack which, when issued as a single, reached No. 10 in the American charts.

The song was included on *The Beatles 1967-1970* compilation, **EMI**'s *A Monument To British Rock, Volume 1*, *Rock 'n' Roll Music* and *20 Greatest Hits*.

When 'Get Back' was originally recorded it was produced by George Martin and his version can be found on the single and on compilations such as *The Beatles 1967–1970* and *Rock 'n' Roll Music*. When the 'Get Back' project tapes were handed to Phil Spector to re-dub and edit, his version became the one that was featured on the *Let It Be* album.

● Getting Better

A track on the *Sgt Pepper* album which was penned by Paul with some aid from John on the lyrics of the middle eight. Most of John and Paul's collaborations had been written in their early days in Liverpool and by the mid-sixties and their 'studio years' they mainly wrote individually, and this is one of the few occasions during those times when they did some work on a song together. Beatles biographer **Hunter Davies** was present in the studio when John began to help Paul with one of the verses in the song.

The number had its origin when Paul had driven to Primrose Hill, near St John's Wood, in the spring of 1967 to take his dog Martha for a walk. It was a sunny day and Paul recalled a phrase often used by **Jimmy Nicol**, the drummer who deputized for Ringo during part of the Beatles' world tour in 1964. Jimmy's phrase was a piece of positive homespun philosophy: 'It's getting better.' Paul mentioned to John at their next meeting that 'It's Getting Better' sounded like a good title for a song.

Additional instruments on the track included George Harrison playing a large four-string Indian instrument called a tamboura and George Martin playing piano.

● Gibson, Bob

Artist originally commissioned by **Sean O'Mahoney** to provide illustrations of the Beatles, in caricature form, for *Beatles Monthly*. He was then asked to illustrate the first paperback biography of the group, *The True Story Of The Beatles*, by Billy Shepherd (**Peter Jones**).

The Beatles liked his work and commissioned him to illustrate the book *Magical Mystery Tour*, which was issued with the double-EP set in December 1967.

● Gibson, Wayne

Minor British singer who was in Hamburg in 1961 at the same time as the Beatles. Paul McCartney told him that he had a number of original songs which Gibson might be interested in recording. Gibson turned them down saying that the opportunity of his group making records seemed remote.

He was, in fact, to record for **Decca**, Pye and Columbia a few years later with his Group Wayne Gibson & the Dynamic Sounds and, ironically, was to cut some cover versions of Beatles hits.

● Ginsberg, Allen

An American Beat Generation poet and Gay Rights activist. He travelled to England in 1965 and began to involve himself in poetic activities in London, aided by **Barry Miles**, who was later to write a Ginsberg biography. On 10 May he attended the **Bob Dylan** concert at the **Royal Albert Hall** and was invited to the after-show party at the Savoy Hotel, held in the suite of Dylan's manager, Albert Grossman. In Dylan's suite, the Beatles and their wives and girlfriends were there with **Neil Aspinall** and **Mal Evans**, and Ginsberg was asked to join them.

The poet was particularly impressed with the Beatles and spent a week up in Liverpool. Of his experiences there, he was to say, 'Liverpool is at the present time the centre of the consciousness of the human universe.'

John and **Cynthia** and George and **Pattie** were invited to Ginsberg's birthday party in London. When they turned up they were startled to find a naked Ginsberg, with a pair of jockey shorts on his head and a 'Do Not Disturb' sign on his penis. They soon left, with Lennon commenting, 'You don't do that in front of the birds.'

● Girl

A John Lennon composition featured on the *Rubber Soul* album. John commented, 'This was about a dream girl. When Paul and I wrote lyrics in the old days we used to laugh about it like the Tin Pan Alley people would. And it was only later on that we tried to match the lyrics to the tune. I like this one. It was one of my best.' He was also to add later on that he eventually found the 'dream girl' – **Yoko**!

The track, which John had to write under a tight deadline for the album, was recorded in one day, 11 November 1965, and John said that he had Paul and George sing the word 'Tit' over and over on the backing vocals.

The number was also included on the *Beatles 1962–1966* and *Love Songs* compilations. Two groups, St Louis Union and Truth, had Top 20 hits in the British charts with the number.

● Give Peace A Chance

A number which John wrote as the first single for the **Plastic Ono Band**. Although **Yoko Ono** gave him a little help on the number, the song was credited to Lennon & McCartney due to a verbal agreement the two had to credit all their songs to the joint name.

When John was growing more politically aware, he'd always felt the desire to write a political anthem, like 'We Shall Overcome' had been used in the Civil Rights marches in America. 'Give Peace A Chance' became the anthem of the anti-Vietnam marches in America.

The song was recorded on portable equipment in Room 1742 of the Queen Elizabeth Hotel, Montreal, on 26 May 1969, during John and Yoko's eight-day bed-in there. They had a large number of friends visiting them during the stay and a number of them took part in the recording singing the chorus, including poet **Allen Ginsberg**, youth culture spokesman **Timothy Leary** and his wife Rosemary, comedian **Tommy Smothers**, **Derek Taylor**, the Canadian chapter of the Radha Krishna Temple, disc jockey **Murray The K**, comedian Dick Gregory, singer

(©Apple/Walter Shenson Films)

'etula Clark and a priest and a rabbi.

The song, credited to the Plastic Ono Band, was issued n Britain on Apple 13 on 4 July 1969 where it reached No. 2 in the charts. It was issued in America on Apple 809 on 7 July 1969 and reached No. 14 in the charts.

The number on the flipside was 'Remember Love'.

'Give Peace A Chance' was included on John's *Live 'eace In Toronto* and *Shaved Fish* albums and he erformed it at the Toronto Rock 'n' Roll Revival Concert, t a peace demonstration in New York in May 1972 and at e 'One To One' concert in 1972.

Its use as a peace anthem has been powerful, although ere may have been more controversy attached had it not een for some self-censoring on John's part. He was to omment, 'The real word I used on the record was masturbation", but I'd just got into trouble for "The allad Of John And Yoko" and I didn't want any more iss, so I put "mastication" in the written lyrics. It was a op-out, but the message about peace was more important me than having a little laugh about a word.'

Glad All Over

ot to be confused with the hit by the **Dave Clark Five**. his number was composed by Bennett/Tepper/Schroeder nd recorded by **Carl Perkins** in 1957. The Beatles dded it to their repertoire, with George taking over lead ocals, and they performed it on two of their BBC radio hows, **'Saturday Club'** and **'Pop Gear'**. The Beatles ever issued it as a record, although their Mersey Beat ates the **Searchers** recorded it in 1964.

Glass Onion

composition by John which was included on *The Beatles* ouble album. The song contained references to five other eatles compositions: 'Strawberry Fields Forever', 'I Am he Walrus', 'Lady Madonna', 'Fool On The Hill' and 'ixing A Hole'.

Paul McCartney was to comment, 'John wrote the tune Glass Onion", I mean he wrote it mainly, but I helped im on it, and when we were writing it we were thinking pecifically of this whole idea of all these kind people who rite in and say "Who was the walrus, John? Were you the alrus?" or "Is Paul the walrus?" So John, I mean, he appened to have a line go "Oh yeah, the walrus was aul" and we had a great giggle to say "Yeah, let's do at", let's put this line in 'cause everybody's gonna read into it and go crackers 'cause they all thought that John was the walrus – "I am the walrus" you know, and it goes kind of insane after a while. So eventually he said, "Let's do this joke tune 'Glass Onion' where all kinds of answers to the universe are," but we thought it was a joke. Now someone the other night told me he'd met this feller who chartered a yacht and was going out into the middle of the ocean 'cause he knew the spot where to go through the glass onion. Now this feller hasn't been seen since!'

John was to say, 'I was just having a laugh because there'd been so much gobbledegook about "Pepper", play it backwards and you stand on your head and all that. Even now, I just saw Mel Torme on TV the other day saying that "Lucy" was written to promote drugs and so was "A Little Help From My Friends" and none of them were at all – "A Little Help From My Friends" only says get high in it, it's really about a little help from my friends, it's a sincere message.'

In 1980, John was to add a further comment about 'Glass Onion': 'That was me just doing a throwaway. I threw the line in – "the walrus was Paul" – just to confuse everybody a bit more. It could've been "the Fox Terrier was Paul". It's just a piece of poetry!'

Glenn Campbell Goodtime Hour, The

An American television show, networked by CBS TV. Film clips of the Beatles were featured on the programme on 30 April 1969. The group were filmed on 30 January 1969 playing 'Get Back' and 'Don't Let Me Down' on the roof of the Apple building in **Savile Row**. The clips differed slightly from those included in the film *Let It Be*.

Glenpark Club, *Lord Street, Southport, Lancashire*

The Beatles appeared at this venue in November 1961.

Globe Cinema, *High Street, Stockton-on-Tees, Durham*

The Beatles made their first appearance at this venue on 22 November 1963 during their autumn tour and returned to the cinema for the last time on 15 October 1964.

Golden Slumbers/Carry That Weight

'Golden Slumbers' was originally an English hymn, based on a 400-year-old poem by Thomas Dekker. Paul's stepsister **Ruth** approached him one day when he was composing on the piano and showed him the sheet music of 'Golden Slumbers', asking if he could read music. He admitted he couldn't, but was intrigued by the number and composed his own lyrics to one of the verses. He then contributed some further additions and the finished song appeared on the *Abbey Road* album with another of Paul's songs, 'Carry That Weight'. They were both recorded as one number on Wednesday, 2 July 1969.

'Golden Slumbers/Carry That Weight' was recorded by Apple band Trash and reached No. 27 in the ***New Musical Express*** charts in Britain. Another version by Orange Bicycle was a flop.

● Goldmann, Peter

A Swedish director whom the Beatles employed when they decided to make videos of 'Strawberry Fields Forever' and 'Penny Lane'. They'd decided to make special filmed inserts for programmes such as 'Top Of The Pops'. John mentioned that they found great difficulty appearing on television programmes to promote their singles and a simpler solution would be to make a promotional film which could be used at home and abroad.

It was really the beginning of the pop promo as we know it, although Goldmann had come to the Beatles' attention because of some acclaimed promotional films he had made for the Troggs and **Donovan**.

The Beatles weren't actually shown performing the two numbers in the film because of a Musicians' Union ruling in Britain which had recently been introduced which prevented groups from miming to their records.

Filming took place in February 1967 and as they were involved in recording an album, they couldn't make it up to Liverpool, so a team went up to the Mersey port to produce some background scenes to be spliced into the film. The 'Penny Lane' film, with its intercut shots of Liverpool, had John wandering around some London streets, then featured the Beatles riding horses in Stratford, London, a sequence filmed on a Sunday morning. They rode into the countryside, which was actually Knole Park Estate, near Sevenoaks in Kent. Ringo's drums were set up near a large banqueting table, bedecked with a candelabra, and the four sipped champagne from teacups, before John overturned the table and the group began to play their instruments.

The 'Strawberry Fields' promo had a strange, surrealistic air as Goldmann had devised the image of a huge tree strung with wires like a giant piano, with th wires leading to a keyboard on the ground.

Goldmann was to say, 'I found that Ringo was very wel informed on camera and photographic techniques, an Paul was a most entertaining conversationalist. But th group had all informed me that I was the director and so must direct. I was amazed to find that there was a ban i Britain which prevented the Beatles from miming to thei disc – I cannot think that this serves any useful purpose.'

The two films were first screened on 'Top Of The Pops in Britain, but only in mono. The colour films made thei debut in America on the '**Ed Sullivan** Show'.

● Gone, Gone, Gone

A number written and recorded by **Carl Perkins** in 195 The Beatles performed the song in their stage act for short period of time in 1960. Perkins was a majo inspiration to the Beatles and during their career the performed no less than ten of his numbers on stage.

● Goodbye

A song which Paul McCartney wrote specially for hi protégée, **Mary Hopkin**. He made a demo disc of th number, but it was never considered as a composition f the Beatles.

Paul also produced Mary recording the number and was issued in Britain on Apple 10 on 28 March 1969 an in America on Apple 1806 on 7 April 1969. The numbe was Mary's second single and the follow-up to he international No. 1 record 'Those Were The Days', whic had sold over five million copies. 'Goodbye' reached No. in the British charts.

● Good Day Sunshine

Composition by Paul McCartney. When recording bega on Wednesday, 8 June 1966, the song's title was then ' Good Day's Sunshine'.

The song was included as a track on the *Revolver* albu and it was a number Paul was particularly proud of and h was to feature it in his film *Give My Regards To Broa Street*.

● Good Morning, Good Morning

A John Lennon composition featured on the *Sgt Pepper Lonely Hearts Club Band* album.

John felt that there should be some brass on th

number and the three saxophonists from **Sounds Incorporated** – Barrie Cameron, David Glyde and Alan Holmes – performed on the track, together with two trombonists and a French horn player. At a later session, John felt that the sounds of animals should be included. A bizarre set of effects was used which began with a cock crowing and ended with a hen clucking. All other animal noises were introduced in between, including sounds of lions, horses, sheep, elephants, dogs, cats and a cow. The sounds were taken from sound-effect tapes, 'Volume 35: Animals and Bees' and 'Volume 57: Fox-hunt'.

John had originally been inspired to write the number after listening to a television advertisement and commented, 'I often sit at the piano working on songs with the television on low in the background. If I'm a bit low and not getting much done then the words of the telly come through. That's when I heard "Good morning, good morning". It was a cornflake advertisement.'

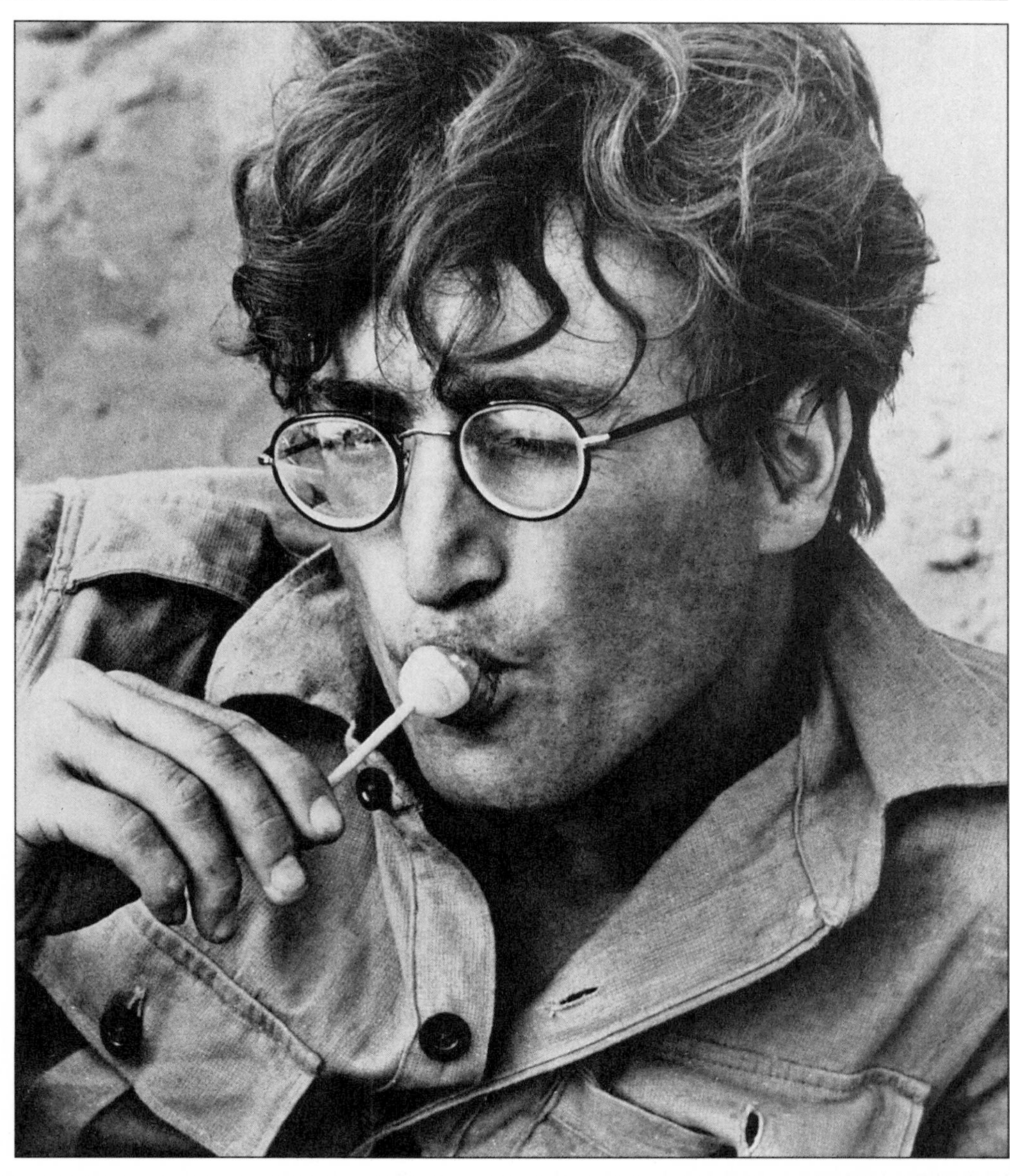

'Good Morning, Good Morning.' A cornflakes commercial inspired John to write this song. (National Film Archives)

● Goodnight

A children's lullaby which John had originally written for his five-year-old son, Julian. It was used as a vehicle for Ringo and featured as the final track on *The Beatles* double album.

At the initial recording session Ringo made some brief spoken invitations to children to settle into bed while he sang them the song. This was dropped from the final version of the number. Initially it was also considered to record the song in a simple way with John backing Ringo's vocal on acoustic guitar. George Martin eventually opted for a much more lavish production and conducted an orchestra of 26 musicians and also added a choir of eight voices. The members of the Mike Sammes Singers who provided the vocals were Ingrid Thomas, Pat Whitmore, Val Stockwell, Irene King, Ross Gilmour, Mike Redway, Ken Barrie and Fred Lucas.

● Got To Get You Into My Life

A song penned by Paul and featured on the *Revolver* album, issued on 5 August 1966. Paul sang a double-tracked solo vocal, with brass backing from Ian Hamer, Les Condon and Eddie Thornton on trumpet and Alan Branscome and Peter Coe on tenor saxophone. Both Thornton and Coe were members of Georgie Fame & the Blue Flames and when their names were mentioned in the press as having recorded with the Beatles, Thornton was booked for sessions with several acts, including the **Rolling Stones**, the Jimi Hendrix Experience, the Small Faces and **Sandie Shaw**.

On the same day that *Revolver* was released, Cliff Bennett & the Rebel Rousers issued 'Got To Get You Into My Life' as a single. Paul produced their version, which reached No. 6 in the British charts.

American band Earth, Wind & Fire recorded a version for the **Robert Stigwood** film, *Sgt Pepper's Lonely Hearts Club Band*, and this reached No. 4 in the US charts in August 1978, although it only reached No. 30 in Britain.

The Beatles' version was included on the compilations *The Beatles 1962–1966* and *Rock 'n' Roll Music*.

There was also an American single issued. This followed a revival of interest in *The Beatles* white album following an American television dramatization of the Charles Manson trial called 'Helter Skelter'. **Capitol** decided to rush-release a single of 'Helter Skelter', but at the last minute realized that the public might consider it in bad taste and then placed it on the flipside of 'Got To Get You Into My Life'. It was issued on Capitol 4274 on 31 May 1976 and rose to No. 3 in the charts.

The number remained one of Paul's favourite songs and he included it in his repertoire during the **Wings** British tour of 1979.

● Grade, Sir Lew

At the time of the emergence of **Beatlemania** in England, three brothers – Lew and Leslie Grade and **Bernard Delfont**, were the most prominent showbusiness impresarios in the country, with interests in television, theatres, agencies and management companies.

In 1964 it was rumoured that Sir Lew Grade had been approached by Brian Epstein, who said that he was ready to sell the Beatles. When he heard about it, John Lennon told him, 'If you do sell, we'll never play again. We'll disband.'

In November 1964, Brian Epstein had meetings with Lew Grade and a few days later made an announcement that he would never sell the Beatles.

Sir Lew was to acquire control of the Beatles' songwriting company, against their wishes. He was the head of ATV, who successfully took control of Northern Songs in March 1969 despite a fierce battle by the Beatles to prevent him gaining a foothold in their publishing company. Grade had already lost a similar battle in which he tried to take over Chappell's Music, but this time he was able to arrange a deal with **Dick James**, who sold his shares to Grade without informing the Beatles. When Grade had been an agent, James had been one of his clients.

The shares ATV bought from James enabled them to gain a stranglehold on Northern Songs and then obtain a controlling interest.

When Paul came to compose material for his first solo single, 'Another Day', the songwriting credits were attributed to Mr and Mrs McCartney, which caused a slight panic at ATV Music. Paul commented, 'Lew Grade suddenly saw his songwriting concession, which he'd just paid a lot of money for, virtually to get hold of John and I, he suddenly saw that I was claiming that I was writing half my stuff with **Linda**.'

ATV Music instigated legal action and the case actually went to court. Paul won the case, but to settle the matter with Sir Lew, he agreed to appear on a TV special, 'James

Paul McCartney' for ATV, which was described as '. . . a personal project of Sir Lew Grade, realized through the genius of Paul McCartney and the expertise of producer Gary Smith and director Dwight Hewison'.

The TV show was filmed in various places: on location in Scotland; in the Chelsea Reach pub in New Brighton where **Gerry Marsden**, former leader of **Gerry & the Pacemakers**, joined Paul and locals in a rousing singalong; and at ATV's Boreham Wood studios in front of a live audience, with Paul and Wings performing 'Big Red Barn', 'The Mess', 'Maybe I'm Amazed' and 'Long Tall Sally'.

Paul also performed a medley of 'Bluebird', 'Michelle', 'Heart Of The Country', 'Mary Had A Little Lamb' and 'Yesterday'. Finally, Paul ended the show singing 'Yesterday' to his own acoustic guitar accompaniment.

The show's major number was a Busby Berkeley-style spectacular to the tune of 'Gotta Sing, Gotta Dance', a number Paul had written for **Twiggy.** This featured a long-haired Paul, with moustache, in a white tail-suit, dancing with a host of showgirls whose costumes and make-up were half-male, half-female.

There were also scenes of Linda taking photographs of Paul and a clip from the James Bond movie *Live And Let Die*. Other numbers in the show were 'Little Woman Love', 'Uncle Albert', 'Another Day', 'Oh Woman Oh Why' and 'Hi Hi Hi'.

The programme was first screened in America on 16 April 1973 and in Britain on 7 June of the same year. Paul was to comment: 'You could say it's fulfilling an old ambition. Right at the start I fancied myself in a musical comedy. But that was before the Beatles. Don't get me wrong. I'm no Astaire or Gene Kelly and this doesn't mean the start of something big. I don't want to be an all-rounder. I'm sticking to what I am.'

Sir Lew also managed to arrange John Lennon's appearance on the television tribute 'Salute To Sir Lew Grade', which was screened on 13 June 1975. However, John produced a sardonic stunt by having the members of Etc, his backing group, wear masks with the large image of a face on the back of their heads.

This gave them the visual effect of having two faces and many people said that this was John's way of calling Sir Lew 'two-faced'. John and his band performed two numbers on the show, 'Slippin' And Slidin'' and 'Imagine'.

● Grafton Ballroom, *West Derby Road, Liverpool L6*

One of Liverpool's two major ballrooms, along with the **Locarno**, both situated next to each other in West Derby Road. Both venues were part of the Mecca ballroom chain and the **Quarry Men** appeared at the Grafton when skiffle contests were held at the venue.

The Beatles first appeared here as a band on 3 August 1962. A local promoter, Albert Kinder, who had previously specialized in jazz concerts, booked a bill of local rock 'n' roll groups, featuring the Beatles, **Gerry & the Pacemakers** and the **Big Three**.

Among the group's repertoire at the time were numbers such as 'Darktown Strutters Ball', 'Ain't She Sweet', 'Falling In Love Again', 'Some Other Guy', 'Hey Baby', 'Lay Down Your Arms', 'Don't Ever Change', 'A Picture Of You', 'Besame Mucho', 'Falling In Love Again', 'I Remember You', 'Shimmy Shimmy', 'A Shot Of Rhythm & Blues', 'Sharing You', 'Mr Moonlight', 'Red Hot', 'Please Mr Postman' and their own 'Love Me Do' and 'P.S. I Love You'.

GRAFTON BALLROOM
THURSDAY, JANUARY 10th
7-30——12-30
FIRST MERSEYSIDE APPEARANCE IN 1963 OF
THE BEATLES
with GERRY AND THE PACEMAKERS
SONNY WEBB AND THE CASCADES
THE JOHNNY HILTON SHOW BAND
THE BILLY ELLIS TRIO
M.C.: BOB WOOLER
TICKETS 7/- In Advance 6/-
FROM NEMS, RUSHWORTH'S, LEWIS'S, CRANE'S, HESSY'S AND THE GRAFTON

Their next appearance took place on 10 January 1963 when they topped a bill of five local groups. Their penultimate visit was at a special concert in aid of the National Society For the Prevention of Cruelty to Children on 12 June 1963 and they requested that Bill Harry introduce them on stage. Their final appearance at the venue took place on 2 August 1963.

● Grammy Awards, The

At an annual awards ceremony, the American National Academy of Recording Arts and Sciences present their 'Grammies'.

The awards received by the Beatles between the years 1964 and 1970 were:

1964 – Best New Artist. Best Vocal Performance By A Group.
1966 – Song Of The Year, 'Michelle'. Best Contemporary Vocal Performance, 'Michelle'. Best Album Cover, *Revolver*.
1967 – Best Album, *Sgt Pepper's Lonely Hearts Club Band*. Best Contemporary Album, *Sgt Pepper's Lonely Hearts Club Band*. Best Album Cover, *Sgt Pepper's Lonely Hearts Club Band*. Best Engineered Album, *Sgt Pepper's Lonely Hearts Club Band*.
1969 – Best Engineered Recording, *Abbey Road*.
1970 – Best Original Movie Score, *Let It Be*.

During the seventies there were several Grammies awarded to recordings by Paul McCartney and George Harrison and in 1975 the Beatles were bestowed with a special award: The Hall Of Fame.

● Granada Cinema, *St Peters Street, Bedford*

The group made their debut at this venue on 6 February 1963 during their tour with **Helen Shapiro**. They only made one further appearance at the Granada which took place the following month on 12 March as part of the **Tommy Roe/Chris Montez** tour. John had become the victim of a heavy cold and had to remain in bed. The three remaining Beatles went ahead with the show, although some of John's numbers had to be adapted for Paul or George to take over on lead vocals.

This was the group's first appearance at a Granada cinema and during their career they were to appear at a total of seven different Granada venues.

● Granada Cinema, *Barking Road, East Ham, London E6*

Traffic chaos resulted when 6,000 fans gathered outside the cinema on Saturday 9 November 1963, when the **Fab Four** were due to appear as part of the autumn tour.

At 3.50 p.m. the Beatles' car sped to the stage door and they began rehearsing and ate cheese sandwiches from the nearby Granada Cafe. The local newspaper reported: 'Souvenir-hunters mobbed 34-year-old John Perdoni when he left with the dirty cutlery and he had to be rescued by the police. He escaped more lightly when he took them their supper of steak and chips (for Ringo Starr and George Harrison) and egg salad (for Paul McCartney and John Lennon) later in the evening. Nobody noticed as he slipped in the front entrance.'

During the afternoon they were visited by four local office girls who had baked them a cake. They also had several other visitors to their dressing-room including George Martin who was able to tell them that 'I Want To Hold Your Hand' had pre-sales of a million copies – an unprecedented achievement in Britain. John Lennon commented, 'That's great, but how do we top that?' Other guests included **Alun Owen** in the first of several meetings he had with the boys to discuss the script for *A Hard Day's Night*, **Alistair Taylor** and the group's press man **Tony Barrow**.

Their last number came to an end at 11.08 p.m. and they made a dash for it down the stairs to the stage door, into their waiting limousine and sped away.

Paul dropped into the cinema on 27 November 1965 to watch the **Scaffold** make their first appearance on a nationwide tour with the Manfred Mann/**Yardbirds** package. Paul's brother **Mike** was a member of the **Scaffold**.

● Granada Cinema, *Mansfield, Nottinghamshire*

The Beatles only appeared twice at this venue, both times in 1963. They made their debut at the venue as part of the **Helen Shapiro** tour on 23 February and returned the next month as part of the **Tommy Roe/Chris Montez** tour on 26 March.

● Granada Cinema, *Castle Gates, Shrewsbury, Shropshire*

The Beatles appeared only once at this venue. It took place during their tour with **Helen Shapiro** on 28 February 1963.

● Granada Cinema, *Mitcham Road, Tooting, London SW17*

The Beatles only appeared once at this London venue, performing two shows on the evening of 1 June 1963. Prior

› their appearance they had spent eight hours in the :udio recording programmes for their radio series **'Pop ›o The Beatles'**.

Granada Cinema, *Hoe Street, Valthamstow, London E17*

nother London venue in the Granada chain where the eatles first appeared on 24 May 1963 during their tour ith **Roy Orbison**. They returned the following year on 4 October 1964.

On 28 March 1966, George and Ringo dropped by the nema to see a Roy Orbison concert performance.

Granada Cinema, *Powis Street, 'oolwich, London SE18*

he Beatles only made one appearance at this London enue, which took place on 3 June 1963.

Grandstand

BBC television sports programme. When the Beatles turned from America on the morning of 22 February)64, they held a press conference in the Kingsford-Smith iite at Heathrow Airport, which was filmed by BBC TV id included as an excerpt in the 'Grandstand' programme at afternoon.

Grant, Erkey

comedian who was booked to appear on the Beatles/**Roy rbison** British tour which commenced on 18 May 1963.

Grapefruit

hn Lennon thought up the name for this group, possibly cause *Grapefruit* was the name of a book by **Yoko Ono** perhaps because of the fruit association of the Apple ganization.

As **Apple Records** had not been formed when the atles took an interest in the group, they were signed by ›ple Publishing and publishing head Terry Doran came their manager.

They comprised George Alexander (bass guitar), John rry (lead guitar), Pete Swettenham (rhythm guitar), and off Swettenham (drums). Most members of the band had en in the line-up of Tony Rivers & the Castaways, who d been signed to **NEMS Enterprises**.

They had a minor hit with their first release 'Dear lilah' on RCA 1656, which reached No. 21 in the British charts in February 1968. On 17 January 1968, the day before the single was released, John, Paul and Ringo attended an RCA reception for the band. Paul McCartney directed a promotional film for Grapefruit's 'Elevator' single, filmed at the Albert Memorial on 26 May 1968. In August of that year they reached No. 25 in the British charts with 'C'mon Marianne', issued on RCA 1716.

Doran was eventually to obtain the group's release from Apple as he said the company wasn't doing enough for the band. They had no further chart success.

● Graves, Elsie

Richard 'Ringo' Starkey's mother. Her maiden name was Gleave and she married Richard Starkey in 1936. Both of them worked in a bakery at the time and after they were married they moved to No. 9 **Madryn Street**, Dingle, where their son Richard was born on 7 July 1940.

By the time Ringo was three his father had left the family home, although he continued to send a sum of money each week. But it wasn't enough and Mrs Starkey had to move to a smaller house in Admiral Grove and take on a job as a barmaid.

When Ringo was 11, a Romford-born painter and decorator, Harry Graves, who was working for Liverpool Corporation, entered their lives. Ringo took to him straight away and was quite pleased when, on 17 April 1953, Harry married his mother.

The relationship between the boy and his stepfather was very strong and it was Harry who bought Ringo his first drum kit.

● Green Street, *Mayfair, London W1*

The Beatles shared an apartment here in an area quite close to Marble Arch, from October 1963 until March 1964, but had to move as they were unable to renew the lease. They'd heard that a flat was available when Brian Epstein moved into **Whaddon House** in Knightsbridge and Ringo, George and Paul rented the floor below.

● Gretty, Jim

The former chief salesman at **Frank Hessy**'s music store in **Stanley Street**, Liverpool. He sold guitars to most of the Mersey Beatsters in the late fifties and early sixties.

It was Jim who sold a guitar to Mimi Smith when she dropped in one day in 1957 with her nephew John Lennon, and Jim was later to book the Beatles on some dates locally although they weren't on the rock 'n' roll bills the band were used to. They included the variety show at the **Albany**, Maghull and the **Pavilion Theatre** appearance with the Royal Waterford Showband.

Jim was also a performer and was quite well known as a country music singer/guitarist. He offered advice to all the groups and once built a 'wall of fame', a panorama of photographs of all the local bands, which stretched along Hessy's main showroom wall.

Jim Gretty, who sold the Beatles their musical instruments, was a performer in his own right. (*Mersey Beat* Archives)

● Griffiths, Eric

An original founder member of the **Quarry Men**. Eric lived in the same Woolton area where the band was formed by John Lennon and the main reasons he was asked to join the skiffle group were because he had a new guitar and was friendly with a boy who had a new set of drums and could also be enticed to join them – **Colin Hanton**.

Eric was the group's lead guitarist but once Paul McCartney joined the group it was a position Paul wanted to take for himself. He tried it once, at the Broadway Conservative Club, and it didn't work, but the rest of the group eventually decided to freeze Eric out. Manager **Nigel Whalley** was told to approach Hanton and tell him of their plans. Eric wasn't invited to Paul's house for the next rehearsal and when he phoned them during the practice session, he was told they didn't want him in the group anymore.

Griffiths was a member of the band from their formation in March 1957 and left the group in mid-1958.

● Grosvenor Ballroom, *Grosvenor Road, Liscard, Wallasey, Cheshire*

Venue run by promoter **Les Dodd**. When **Allan William** decided to take a hand in the Beatles' career, Les Dod was the man he initially arranged some dates with, firstl at the **Liverpool Institute**, Wirral, and then at th Grosvenor on Saturday, 4 June 1960. Williams said tha their pay was £10, of which he received £1. A further £ was paid to the bouncer and the balance to the fiv members of the group: John, Paul, George, **Stu Sutcliff** and drummer **Tommy Moore**.

The group were calling themselves the **Silver Beetle** at the time and two days later they appeared on a speci Monday session to celebrate the Whitsun Bank Holiday o a bill with **Gerry & the Pacemakers**. The gig ran fro 8.00 p.m. to midnight and admission was 3/- (15p).

Their next appearance on 11 June is described in deta in Allan Williams' book *The Man Who Gave The Beatl Away*. Tommy Moore had decided not to play with th group anymore due to his full-time job at the Garsto Bottle Works and the protestations of his common la wife. The group arrived at the Grosvenor without drummer, although their equipment, with Moore's drumki had been set up for them. John asked if anyone from th audience would like to join them on drums and a loc thug called Ronnie, leader of a gang, volunteere Unfortunately, he enjoyed the episode so much he want to become their permanent drummer. They were afraid turning him down in case his gang beat them up, so th phoned Allan Williams, who arrived at the ballroom a sorted the situation out.

Tommy Moore was to make one last appearance wi them at the Grosvenor.

Their 18 June appearance was on the occasion of Pa McCartney's 18th birthday and they returned to the ven on 25 June.

They appeared there several times in July. On their July gig they were joined on stage by Johnny Gentle, wh they'd recently backed on a tour of Scotland. Other dat included 9, 16, 23 and 30 July.

They were next due to appear on 6 August, but the g was cancelled. The Grosvenor had a bad reputati because of the rowdiness caused by some of the hooliga who attended the dances. The ballroom was owned by t local council and when residents of Grosvenor Stre presented a petition to the council complaining about t oise caused by the dances, they banned further rock essions from the hall.

The ban was only temporary. The Beatles next ppeared at the Grosvenor on 24 February 1961 and their 0 March gig there was the last booking arranged for them y Allan Williams.

Their final appearance there was on Friday, 15 eptember 1961. The evening session lasted from 7.15 .m.–11.00 p.m. and the support band was Cliff Roberts & ne Rockers, the resident band at the ballroom.

● Grosvenor Rooms, *Prince of Wales Road, Norwich*

he Beatles only appeared at this venue once, on 17 May 963 the day prior to the opening of their tour with **Roy rbison**.

● Gruenberg, Erich

oted European violinist who had been a former leader of ne London Symphony Orchestra and the Royal hilharmonic Orchestra. Gruenberg was engaged to lead a 0-piece orchestra on the *Sgt Pepper* track 'A Day In The ife'. The Beatles had requested that the orchestra wear vening dress and handed out carnival novelties which ncluded funny hats and red noses – this was because the ession was being filmed for a proposed TV documentary, hich was never completed.

Gruenberg performed wearing a giant gorilla's paw on is bow hand. He also led the musicians on 'She's Leaving ome' and was leader of the eight violinists who erformed on 'Within You, Without You'.

Gruenberg was to comment: 'The Beatles were very harming and musical, expressing their personalities like l truly successful people by being quite themselves. hey had a good spirit and in the studio there was a sense occasion and momentum . . . They sent me a copy of the cord which I still have.'

● Grugahalle, *Essen, Nordrhein-Vestfalen, Germany*

he Beatles left their hotel in Munich to travel in a otorcade in the early morning of 25 June 1966 to the ilway station where they boarded the special train which d been used by Queen Elizabeth the previous year on r royal trip to Germany. The group and their party, hich included Brian Epstein, **Neil Aspinall**, **Tony Barrow**, **Mal Evans** and **Alf Bicknell**, had a suite of rooms aboard the train comprising a large dining-room, lounge and four bedrooms and bathrooms.

The train arrived in Essen at 4.30 p.m. and among the crowd on the platform were three men dressed as barbers, wearing bald-topped wigs and carrying giant combs. The group were driven to the Grugenhalle in a white Mercedes, with a motorcade. They performed two shows and arrived back at the railway station at 12.30 a.m.

● Guildhall, *The Square, Portsmouth, Hampshire*

The Beatles first appeared at this venue on 30 March 1963 on their **Tommy Roe/Chris Montez** tour.

They were next due to appear at the venue during their autumn tour later the same year, on 12 November. However, Paul McCartney had contracted gastric flu and the concert was cancelled. The Beatles spent the evening at a hotel in Southsea where Paul was visited by a doctor and the group resumed their tour the following day after the Guildhall concert had been rescheduled for 3 December.

● Guitar Boogie

Composition by Arthur Smith, recorded by Arthur Smith & his Crackerjacks in 1946. The **Quarry Men** used the instrumental in their repertoire between 1957 and 1959.

● Gunther, Curt

A freelance photographer from Los Angeles, who began a career as a photojournalist in 1941, with his work appearing for over four decades in major American publications such as *Life*, *Look*, *Rolling Stone* and *Playboy*.

He met the Beatles in 1964 and received permission to travel with them on their American tour at his own expense. He supplemented his income by playing cards with the Beatles at night! During the tour he took a vast amount of photographs, including many exclusive sessions, arranged for him by Beatles PR man **Derek Taylor**, who became one of his closest friends.

150 previously unpublished Gunther photographs of that tour were eventually published in 1989 by Doubleday in America and Sidgwick and Jackson in Britain in *Beatles '64: A Hard Day's Night In America*, with text by A. J. S. Rayl.

Gunther died in New York in September 1991.

● Hague, Jonathan

A student at **Liverpool College of Art** who shared the lessons in 'Lettering', as part of an Intermediate course, with John Lennon, **Cynthia** Powell and **Phyllis MacKenzie**.

When Jonathan was 29, John and Paul McCartney sponsored an exhibition of his work. Jonathan said, 'One day I took my paintings to his (John's) house and we spread them all over his sitting-room. He liked them, hence the exhibition. He dragged Paul in on it, but I don't think Paul was very keen, although he didn't mind putting up the money.'

The exhibition took place at the Royal Institute Gallery in 1968 and there was a diverse selection of paintings whose subjects included the Beatles, Mick Jagger, Vincent Van Gogh and the funeral of Winston Churchill.

However, rather than boost Jonathan's career as a painter, it seemed to end it.

He said, 'After the exhibition I gave up. I'm not sure why. The newspapers, TV, etc . . . but I think I thought I was no good. So I drifted into antiques, which I still do for a living.'

Jonathan became an antiques dealer and lives in Leamington Spa in a house which John bought for him.

● Haig Dance Club, *Haig Avenue, Moreton, Wirral, Lancashire*

Venue 'over the water' from Liverpool, on the Wirral peninsula, where the **Quarry Men** appeared for a single performance one Friday night in November 1957.

● Hair Style

The hair style developed by the Beatles didn't raise an eyebrows on Merseyside, where it wasn't actually radicall different from the hair style of the other local groups. I barely raised attention in the British media onc **Beatlemania** began to sweep the country (although i their first national newspaper story in London's *Evening Standard*, Maureen Cleave mentioned their 'weird' hair 'French styling, with the fringe brushed forwards') but i caused a sensation in America when the Beatles arrive there in 1964. The affectionate term 'Moptops' was create and almost every comedian in the country cracked gag about the hair style. Hundreds of thousands of Beatle wigs were manufactured and it eventually led to th American youth growing their hair longer than had bee previously acceptable for the young male.

The hair style caused amusement in various countrie and in Sweden it was referred to as the 'Hamlet' cut whil in Germany it was described as a 'mushroom'.

It is generally acknowledged that the style was firs developed in 1961 by **Stuart Sutcliffe**'s girlfriend **Astri Kirchherr**. Mrs Millie Sutcliffe commented: 'As for th haircut, it started when Stuart's hair was falling down an sticking out. One night Astrid had been moaning about h hair and then took him into the bathroom and cut it.'

Hunter Davies, in his authorized biography of th Beatles, corroborates this version: 'It was at this tim [1960–1961] that Astrid got round to telling Stu that sh didn't like his greasy, **Teddy boy** hair style. She said h would suit the sort of style that **Klaus [Voormann]** an Jurgen [Vollmer] had. After a lot of persuading, Stu let h do a special style for him. She brushed it all dow snipped bits off and tidied it up.

'Stu turned up at the **Top Ten** that evening with h hair in the new style, and the others collapsed on the flo with hysterics. Half-way through he gave up and combe his hair high. But thanks to Astrid, he tried it again th next night. He was ridiculed again, but the night afte George turned up with the same style. Then Paul had a g though for a long time he was always changing it back the old style as John hadn't yet made up his mind. **Pet Best** ignored the whole craze. But the Beatle hair sty had been born.' Pete didn't adopt the style simply becau he didn't think it suited him. Years later he was to wond if this was one of the reasons why he was sacked.

Philip Norman, in his book *Shout!*, had this to say: 'S

[Astrid] did away with his Teddy boy hair style, cutting it short like hers, then shaping it to lie across the forehead in what was called the French cut, although high-class German boys had worn a similar style since the days of Bismarck.'

Ray Coleman, in his book *John Winston Lennon*, covers the incident in detail: 'Tired of the fast-scissored, traditional formula of Hamburg hairdressers and looking for something that would emulate her own sense of the eccentric, Astrid had cut Klaus's hair for years. She never combed his hair backwards, always out from the side, and it was always longer than the accepted length . . . Stuart, the first to have his hair cut and styled by Astrid, faced John's scorn when, one night, he arrived at the club for work with what later became known as the Beatle haircut . . . Paul, always more conscious than the others about his appearance, was the next to ask Astrid to style his hair . . . John was the last Beatle to succumb to the Beatle cut. Only Pete Best declined, retaining his quiff and Teddy boy aura that attracted the girls.'

Jurgen Vollmer, one of the students in Hamburg who befriended the Beatles, puts forward his own claim in his book *Rock 'n' Roll Times*: 'When I moved to Paris in late 1961, John and Paul visited me and decided to have their hair like mine. A lot of French youth wore it that way. I gave both of them their first "Beatles" haircut in my hotel room on the Left Bank.'

As a joke, George Harrison once told a reporter that it was the result of the way their hair fell after being in the local swimming baths. The story was taken as fact!

The Beatles never wore wigs, but Beatle wigs were manufactured in vast quantities in America – although they looked more like the hair style of Mo Howard of the Three Stooges than the Beatles style, and when the group first arrived in America photographers and journalists kept tugging their hair, asking them if they were wearing wigs.

The wigmania took off when the Beatles made their February 1964 visit to America. The media seemed obsessed with the hair style. New York radio station WMCA ran a competition for listeners to paint or draw someone in a Beatlewig – either celebrity pictures clipped from newspapers or photos of friends. The most popular subjects were: Nikita Krushchev, Mayor Wagner, Alfred E. Newman (of *Mad* magazine), Brigitte Bardot and the Jolly Green Giant.

Capitol Records instructed all their sales staff to wear Beatle wigs during the working day until further notice and issued a memo: 'Get these Beatle wigs around properly, and you'll find yourself helping to start the Beatle Hair-Do craze that should be sweeping the country soon.'

When the group held their first American press conference, they were asked questions such as 'Will you be getting a haircut?' and 'What's the greatest threat to your career – dandruff or nuclear warfare?' Such questions continued throughout the press conferences that year during their autumn tour: 'What excuse do you have for your collar-length hair?' 'What do you do with your long hair in the shower?' 'Do you have any plans for a haircut?' 'Does your hair require any special care?' and so on. When Paul was asked 'Do you ever go unnoticed?' he replied, 'When we take off our wigs.'

When they arrived in America in February, the *New York Herald Tribune* reported: 'The Beatles' hairstyle is a mop effect that covers the forehead, some of the ears and most of the back of the neck.'

An example of the way in which the Beatles altered the style and fashions of the sixties is provided by the fact that the male youth of America began to grow their hair long, in contrast to the almost military short back and sides of previous years.

● Hallelujah, I Love Her So

Number composed by Ray Charles and recorded by him in 1956. It was also recorded by **Eddie Cochran** in 1960 and he promoted it when he was in Britain in March of that year, shortly before his death. Ray Charles was popular among Liverpool bands and several of them included the number in their repertoire. The Beatles included it in their stage act, with Paul McCartney on lead vocals. However, when the number was recorded at the **Star Club** in December 1962, a friend of the Beatles, **Horst Fascher**, sang the lead vocal with them and it is this version which is to be found on the album *The Beatles Live! At The Star Club In Hamburg, Germany: 1962*.

● Hambleton Hall, *St David Road, Page Moss, Huyton, Liverpool 14*

Situated in the suburbs of Liverpool, this large hall was booked by freelance promoters to present local bands.

Wednesdays, Saturdays and, occasionally, Sundays were the main evenings on which dances took place. **Bob Wooler** ran a few freelance promotions of his own at the

GREAT VALUE ! A Special Reduced Admission of 2/- only will be allowed on all holders of this advertisement at HAMBLETON HALL on WEDNESDAY, 20th SEPTEMBER

DON'T MISS THIS OFFER — Cut out this advertisement and take it to

HAMBLETON HALL

PAGE MOSS · HUYTON

Bus routes 10, 40a, 92, 12, 12a, 8c, 8d, 97, 97a, 98

GREAT ROCK SHOW DANCES EVERY WEDNESDAY AND SATURDAY

THIS SUNDAY NIGHT'S SPECTACULAR

THE BEATLES — JOHNNY SANDON AND THE SEARCHERS — DEE AND THE DYNAMITES

WATCH OUT FOR THE SENSATIONAL EARL PRESTON AND THE T.T.'s

venue and remembers the time the Beatles told the audience to go out and buy their German single 'My Bonnie'.

Paul McCartney remembers it as a rough place. He commented, 'They used fire extinguishers on each other one night there. When we played "Hully Gully". That used to be one of the tunes which ended in fighting.'

Wally Hill and Vic Anton were two promoters who booked groups regularly at the venue and they booked the Beatles through the 1961 period. Billed as 'The Sensational Beatles', they made their debut at the hall on 25 January 1961 on a bill with Derry & the Seniors and Faron & the Tempest Tornadoes. Their subsequent appearances that year took place on 1, 8, 15 and 22 February; 8 and 20 March; 3 and 17 September; 15 and 29 October; 12 and 26 November; and 10 December. Their last appearance at the venue took place on 13 January 1962. Hambleton Hall later became a Probation Office.

● Hamburg, Germany

Interestingly enough, Hamburg, the largest city in West Germany, is on the same latitude as Liverpool – 53 degrees north. Like Liverpool it is a major seaport, and lies on the River Elbe.

Unlike Liverpool, Hamburg had no thriving music scene in 1960 when the Beatles first appeared there. The St Pauli district, a large red-light area of the city, was an area of sex and violence, with clubs catering for the sexual needs of visitors – strip joints, female mud wrestling, nude circuses and so on.

Through a set of circumstances **Bruno Koschmider**, who owned two strip clubs, the **Kaiserkeller** and the **Indra**, began booking groups into his clubs in 1960. The first group he booked following a visit to London was called the Jets, the other was Liverpool's Derry & the Seniors. Liverpool club owner **Allan Williams** arranged with Koschmider for the Beatles to appear at one of the Hamburg venues from August 1960. Believing they were appearing at the Kaiserkeller, they were disappointed to end up in a much smaller club called the Indra. They were the only rock 'n' roll group to perform at the former strip club, which was closed by the police at the beginning of October that year. The Beatles then appeared at the Kaiserkeller from 4 October until 30 November, second on the bill to another Liverpool band, **Rory Storm & the Hurricanes**, whose drummer was Ringo Starr. On 15 October, John, Paul and George, with Ringo on drums made a recording of the number 'Summertime' at the small **Akustik Studios**, near to Hamburg's main rail station.

Hamburg had no real competition to offer the Beatles as, unlike Liverpool, there were few rock 'n' roll musicians. The Jets, with their lead vocalist/guitarist **Tony Sheridan**, were the only non-Liverpool band they encountered and they were, to some extent, influenced by Sheridan. He was nicknamed 'the Teacher' by the Liverpool bands, who were impressed by his stage style.

The most important consequence of their appearance in Hamburg was that it completely transformed the group's stage show. Koschmider, with his constant appeals for them to 'make a show', and the extremely long hours of playing they were contracted to, led the Beatles to develop an act.

There were other bonuses resulting from their Hamburg

'isits. Their visual look changed. Their 'teddy boy' image was to be replaced with the 'rocker' image when they ought leather jackets and trousers in the Reeberbahn and heir 'teddy boy' hair styles were to be replaced by what vas to become their trademark hair style. A group of Iamburg students, including **Astrid Kirchherr**, **Klaus Voormann** and Jurgen Vollmer, became firm fans of the roup and bass guitarist **Stuart Sutcliffe** decided to emain in Hamburg, study art and marry Astrid. His days n the group were already numbered, though, as Paul McCartney wanted to take over his spot as bass guitarist.

The second Hamburg rock 'n' roll club, the **Top Ten**, pened in October 1960 and the Jets were the first band to e booked there. The owner, **Peter Eckhorn,** booked the Beatles to replace them immediately following their Kaiserkeller season. Koschmider discovered this and was ırious. His contract stated that the Beatles could not ppear at another venue within 40 miles of his clubs and e even made threats of physical violence to them. They idn't take much notice of this because **Horst Fascher**, ıe former 'minder' at the Kaiserkeller, had now moved to ıe Top Ten and they were under his protection.

Koschmider was revenged. The under-aged George Harrison was deported and **Pete Best** and Paul McCartney were also sent back to Liverpool for allegedly ying to 'burn down' Koschmider's cinema, the **Bambi ino**.

It was an indication of the fact that the Beatles were ill relatively unknown in their own home of Liverpool hen they were billed as 'direct from Hamburg' on a **itherland Town Hall** appearance on 27 December 960 – many of the girls in the audience thought they were German group and were impressed at their grasp of the nglish language! This particular gig proved to be a nsation, established them locally and was an indication just how well the long hours of playing in the German ty had improved their act.

Their second trip to Hamburg commenced with ppearances at the Top Ten Club from 1 April 1961. oschmider's brief flirtation with rock 'n' roll had ended. ıe Indra had reverted to a strip club when the Beatles ıd left the previous October and the Kaiserkeller was so to revert back to a strip club called the Colibri.

The appearances at the Top Ten were much more fun an the Kaiserkeller. The money and accommodation ere better, for a start, and Peter Eckhorn was much more sympathetic to the needs of the musicians than Koschmider. The group performed from 7.00 p.m. until 2.00 a.m. with a fifteen-minute break each hour. George Harrison comented, 'We performed like a gang of lunatics. It was all right once we got the hang of it all and it was great fun. The boss would send up cups of coffee on stage and we'd take turns to take a nap.' There was a curfew in the St Pauli district and after 10.00 p.m. no one under the age of eighteen was allowed in the area. Paul McCartney was to say, 'We'd try out my sort of numbers from the Top Twenty. In a way it was marvellous – simply because we could experiment. Tired? We were dead whacked but we got great kicks out of watching the audiences, seeing the way they reacted to different gear.'

Their Top Ten contract was extended twice and they performed there for 92 nights. During this time they built up a great following in Hamburg and also made their first recordings for an established recording company when they backed Tony Sheridan during some recording sessions with A&R man **Bert Kaempfert** in June 1961. They only received a session fee rather than royalties and the recordings have been released and re-released on a regular basis ever since. It was during this trip to Hamburg that Stuart officially left the group and his position was taken over by Paul.

Their third visit to Hamburg found them appearing at a third venue, the **Star Club**. By this time the group were under the management of Brian Epstein and despite Peter Eckhorn's attempts to book them for the Top Ten Club, the proprietor of the Star Club, **Manfred Weissleder**, was the one to agree to pay Epstein's demand for an increased fee. Weissleder's right hand man was once again Horst Fascher, who had been the Beatles' friend when he worked for Koschmider, then Eckhorn and then Weissleder. The Star Club was the best of the Hamburg venues, specially catering for the audiences who wanted the best in rock 'n' roll. Weissleder was prepared to pay what was needed to attract the best names and apart from booking all the major Liverpool bands, he also engaged the leading American names – **Little Richard**, the Everly brothers, **Gene Vincent**. For a brief time, the Star Club was the greatest rock 'n' roll venue in the world. The Beatles' first appearance there lasted for seven weeks from 13 April to 31 June 1961. During their appearances there they shared the bill with Little Richard and Gene Vincent.

The Beatles appeared for their second visit to the Star

Club later the same year, from 1 to 14 November 1962. It was a brief appearance as the band were now becoming a major name in Britain and they were to perform their third and final visit at the Star Club between 18 and 31 December 1962. It was during this visit that **Adrian Barber** recorded them on tape, resulting in albums of material of their performances at the Star Club being released for decades later – although Barber never received either acknowledgement or remuneration for his efforts.

Their club days in Hamburg were over, although the Hamburg scene was of less importance than their grounding in Liverpool. The Hamburg scene was not unique – merely three main clubs (ignoring the Indra), over a short period of time. The long hours in the clubs made the group a force to be reckoned with, it was their 'baptism of fire'. But it would have meant nothing if there hadn't been that vital scene in Liverpool with hundreds of groups performing in hundreds of venues from the mid-fifties.

The handful of Hamburg clubs glittered brightly for a few years in the sixties, providing work for dozens of British groups, mainly from Liverpool, but also including groups from various parts of Britain including **Cliff Bennett & the Rebel Rousers**, Alex Harvey, Dave Dee, the Fortunes, Bern Elliot and the Fenmen and others.

The only other appearance the Beatles were to make in Hamburg was at the **Ernst Merck Halle** on 26 June 1966 during a brief tour of West Germany, Japan and the Philippines. That evening, many old friends dropped by to see them.

Yet another dimension to the Hamburg experience was that the young men from a relatively inhibited environment were plunged into a situation in which there were no restrictions regarding drugs and sex. During their period in Hamburg the members of the group (with the exception of Pete Best) took pills such as Preludin and Captogen and indulged in sex almost nightly with a variety of females ranging from girl fans to prostitutes.

They also witnessed violence of a kind which was even more outlandish than in the violent city of Liverpool – muggings, gas guns, clients in the audience being beaten with clubs, and so on. This obviously had some effect on the band mentally.

A detailed account of their days in Hamburg is to be found in Pete Best's autobiography *Beatle!*.

● Hamilton, David

Well-established British disc jockey/compere who because of his diminutive size, was nicknamed 'Diddy' b **Ken Dodd**.

In 1963 Hamilton worked for ABC TV in Manchester whose area covered part of the north of England and the Midlands. The company was based in Didsbury Manchester, and Hamilton was a continuity announce when he was given the job of interviewing the Beatles for special edition of 'ABC At Large'. At the Didsbury Studio he interviewed Brian Epstein, the Beatles and **Gerry & the Pacemakers**. Also included in the programme was conversation he had with **Bob Wooler** which was filme during a visit to the **Cavern**. Kennedy Street Enterprise paid Hamilton 10 guineas (£10.50) to compere a Beatle show at Urmston on 5 August 1963.

In the eighties Hamilton began regular broadcastin with Capital Radio, London's major radio station, and h includes a special 'Beatle Break' in his show several time a week.

● Hamilton, Richard

An artist introduced to the Beatles by gallery owne **Robert Fraser**, the man who had recommended them t engage artist **Peter Blake** to design their *Sgt Pepper Lonely Hearts Club Band* sleeve.

The *Sgt Pepper* sleeve was a hard cover to follow an the Beatles had engaged several artists to come up wit ideas. Initially, they were going to call the album the were working on 'A Doll's House', but were informed th an album using that title had already been released. On designer suggested a transparent cover which revealed colour photograph each time the record was taken out the sleeve.

Fraser showed the Beatles a sample of Hamilton's wor – a collage he'd made of newspaper clippings concernin the **Rolling Stones** drug trial. Paul McCartne immediately suggested to Hamilton that he should d something similar as the cover of their new album. Instea Hamilton suggested that they should opt for star simplicity by having a plain white cover. He als suggested that each copy of the album be numbered produce the effect of a limited edition and that they shoul include a collage of the Beatles which would b autobiographical.

All his suggestions were taken up and the plain whi

sleeve had the name 'The Beatles' embossed on it and an individual serial number, which is why it became known as 'The White Album'. Inside the sleeve was the poster collage and four colour photographs of the individual Beatles, taken by John Kelly. The collage was as Hamilton had suggested and **Neil Aspinall** and **Mal Evans** collected a selection of old photographs which **Jeremy Banks** co-ordinated into the overall design. One of the photographs was a tiny shot of Paul in the nude, although he is discreetly posed behind a white column. This caused an outcry in the British press with headlines such as 'Paul goes nude'. **Derek Taylor** was furious and commented, 'All this work, all these tracks, all this talent – and all their dirty little minds focus on is one tiny picture.' Strangely, the press ignored a far larger picture in the collage of John in the nude.

● Hamp, Johnny

At the time the Beatles released their first British single, 'Love Me Do', Johnny Hamp was a producer at Granada Television, a station which was transmitted over a large area of Lancashire. He first booked the Beatles on his 'People And Places' programme on 17 December 1962 and used the group regularly.

A few years later he was to comment: 'I first saw the Beatles in a club in Hamburg. They were very scruffy characters but they had a beat in their music which I liked.'

Coincidentally, it was on 17 December (1965 this time) that Johnny produced his most ambitious Beatles enterprise, a major TV special called 'The Music Of Lennon & McCartney'.

In 1982, when he was Granada's Head of Light Entertainment, he intended to produce a show to tie in with the 20th anniversary of the 'Love Me Do' release. He found such a wealth of interesting material in the archives that the programme wasn't finished until 1983 and, under the title 'The Early Beatles', was first broadcast on 1 January 1984.

● Hanover Grand Banqueting Suite, *Mayfair, London W1*

Venue booked by the Beatles for a special Christmas party for forty of their fan club secretaries from all parts of

Johnny Hamp, Granada producer who featured the Beatles on several of his TV shows. (Granada TV)

Britain. The event took place on Sunday, 17 December 1967, and was attended by John and George who had just returned from Paris where they had been visiting the **Maharishi**. Ringo was on his way back from Rome where he'd been filming ***Candy*** and Paul was in Scotland. The fan club secretaries, apart from enjoying the company of John and George and special guests such as Spencer Davis, were treated to a preview screening of *Magical Mystery Tour* prior to its debut on BBC Television. As an added bonus they were also shown the film *The Beatles At Shea Stadium*.

● Hanson, Wendy

Personal assistant to Brian Epstein. Wendy was born in Huddersfield and was a cousin of financier Lord Hanson.

She was efficient, discreet, could type 90 words a minute and wrote 140 words a minute in shorthand. Her qualifications took her to New York at the age of eighteen where she worked as secretary to conductor Leopold Stokowski for two and a half years. She also acted as temporary secretary to President Kennedy.

It was while he was in America in 1964 that Epstein asked **Capitol Records** to provide him with an English secretary during his thirteen-day stay. Wendy was working for Gian-Carlo Menotti at the time, but agreed to take up the temporary post and joined Brian at the Plaza Hotel. She was approximately the same age as Brian and he was impressed with her authority and efficiency, with the result that when he needed a personal assistant the following year, he offered her the position.

Epstein often chastised members of his staff, depending on his mood. Some were able to take the insults, others weren't and, over a period of years, a number of his staff left following disagreements with him.

Brian had berated his personal assistant **Derek Taylor** in front of a number of friends over a trivial incident regarding a ride in a limousine. Taylor, feeling that this was one humiliating scene too many, resigned. This gave Epstein the opportunity to hire Hanson and he contacted her and offered her £2,000 a year to work for him. She accepted and returned from America to work in the Argyle Street offices of **NEMS** on 12 October 1964. On that same day Epstein had written a letter to Taylor which read, in part: 'I write now to advise you of the appointment of Miss Wendy Hanson as my personal assistant. Miss Hanson assumes her responsibilities in this capacity from today, Monday October 12th . . . at this stage I must advise you that I will appreciate your understanding it is necessary that you relinquish your duties as personal assistant, and at the same time I will be most grateful if you can give to Miss Hanson your co-operation and help, in order that she may smoothly settle in to this position.'

The reason why Wendy decided to join Epstein at this time was because of an ill-fated affair she'd had. A change of scene was needed.

However, just like Derek Taylor, **Brian Somerville** and so many other associates of Brian's, she found that his tantrums led him to insult his aides over often trivial items and she quit her post as personal assistant several times. On each occasion he refused to accept her letters of resignation, would take her out to dinner and then talk her out of it.

It was Wendy who suggested he move into his own office at Hille House in Stafford Street and, while there she also became personal assistant to the Beatles.

However, Brian's whims, moods and tantrums proved too much even for her to cope with. One evening he phoned her at 10.00 p.m. to say that he'd lost the address of a recording studio he was due to be at. Then he began shouting at her over the phone. She told him she wasn't his nanny and refused to put up with his attitude any longer. She sent in her letter of resignation the next day and went to work for film producer David Puttnam. This was in December 1966. She'd worked for Brian for three years. The Beatles sent her a farewell gift and Brian wrote her a letter and requested that they keep in touch. A few months later he phoned her and asked if she could get permission to use their images on the cover of the *Sgt Pepper* album. She did.

In 1991 she was injured falling down the stairs at her home in Cortona, Italy, and failed to regain consciousness. She died on 27 January. She was 56 years old.

● Hanton, Colin

An apprentice upholsterer in 1958 when he was asked to join the **Quarry Men**. The group only wanted him as a member because he'd bought a new drum kit for £38 on hire purchase from **Hessy's**. His father was manager of a co-operative shop and the group often practised at his house on Saturday afternoons.

Colin liked to drink Black Velvet (a mixture of Guinness and mild bitter) and although he was two years lder than the other members of the group he was so small nat he looked younger than he was and always carried his irth certificate around to enable him to drink in pubs.

Early in 1959 the group were booked by George Harrison's father to appear at the Picton Lane Busmen's ocial Club Saturday night dance in Wavertree. Mr Harrison, who was master of ceremonies for the evening, ad told them that the manager of a local cinema would be ropping in to watch them play with a view to giving them series of bookings in the intervals between films.

During the interval the boys went to the bar and had too many pints to drink, with the result that they gave a isastrous performance and heard no more from the inema manager. On the way home, the upset Hanton had furious argument with the others and decided he'd never lay with them again. He got off the bus with his drums efore he'd even reached his own stop and the other embers of the Quarry Men never saw him again.

● Happiness Is A Warm Gun

ohn Lennon composition which was Paul McCartney's vourite number on *The Beatles* double album.

George Martin showed John the cover of an American un magazine which had the caption 'Happiness is a warm un in your hand'. John thought it was an outrageous title. 'A warm gun means that you've just shot something,' he aid.

Originally, the song was put together from three nfinished songs John had worked on. Although the emes of the songs were completely different, he managed weld them together into this number.

When discussing the song he said, 'I think it's a eautiful song. I like all the different things that are appening in it. Like "God", I had put together some three ections of different songs, it was meant to be – it seemed run through all the different kinds of rock music.'

The song was banned by the BBC because they thought ere was sexual symbolism in the number. Members of e media speculated that the 'H' in happiness stood for eroin.

John said, 'It wasn't about "H" at all.'

● Harburg Friedrich Ebert Halle, Hamburg, Germany

fants' school where the Beatles recorded with **Tony heridan** in June 1961. Recording manager **Bert Kaempfert** arranged for mobile recording equipment to be installed on the stage of the school auditorium. When they began recording 'My Bonnie' there were coke bottles on the stage and George Harrison knocked one over. Bert told him, 'All coke bottles off the stage.'

The children were off school during the school holidays and the numbers recorded included: 'The Saints', 'Why', 'Nobody's Child', 'Ain't She Sweet' and 'Cry For A Shadow'. On the third day Sheridan took the lead again on 'If You Love Me Baby', which had also been referred to as 'Take Out Some Insurance On Me Baby'.

● Hard Day's Night, A *(Album)*

The soundtrack album for the Beatles' debut film *A Hard Day's Night* was issued in Britain on Parlophone PCS 3058 on 10 July 1964 and reached No. 1 in the charts.

The album contained thirteen new Lennon & McCartney numbers and was the only album to feature Lennon & McCartney songs exclusively. Several numbers which appeared on the actual film soundtrack weren't included on the album, including 'I Wanna Be Your Man', 'All My Loving', 'She Loves You' and George Harrison's 'Don't Bother Me'.

The album also contained some numbers which weren't featured in the film.

The track listing on the British release was, Side One: 'A Hard Day's Night', 'I Should Have Known Better', 'If I Fell', 'I'm Happy Just To Dance With You', 'And I Love Her', 'Tell Me Why' and 'Can't Buy Me Love'. Side Two: 'Any Time At All', 'I'll Cry Instead', 'Things We Said Today', 'When I Get Home', 'You Can't Do That' and 'I'll Be Back'.

In America the album was issued by United Artists on UAS 6366 on 26 June 1964. This version included only numbers which were featured in the actual film, together with a number of instrumental tracks by the George Martin Orchestra.

The track listing was, Side One: 'A Hard Day's Night', 'Tell Me Why', 'I'll Cry Instead', 'I Should Have Known Better' (George Martin Orchestra), 'I'm Happy Just To Dance With You' and 'And I Love Her' (George Martin Orchestra). Side Two: 'I Should Have Known Better', 'If I Fell', 'And I Love Her', 'Ringo's Theme' (George Martin Orchestra), 'Can't Buy Me Love', 'A Hard Day's Night' (George Martin Orchestra).

Capitol Records were to use three tracks from the

British *A Hard Day's Night* soundtrack on their *Something New* album: 'Things We Said Today', 'Any Time At All' and 'When I Get Home'.

● Hard Day's Night, A *(Film)*

In 1963 **Capitol Records** in America were still refusing to issue Beatles products. Noel Rodgers, the British representative for United Artists Records, was witnessing **Beatlemania** first-hand in London and was convinced that it would inevitably reach the States. He approached **Bud Ornstein**, the British production head of United Artists' film division, with the suggestion that they offer the Beatles a three-picture deal in order to obtain three Beatles soundtracks. They were both primarily interested in obtaining the Beatles on record for UA and didn't initially realize how big the films would be.

Because of this they opted for a cheap budget and approached **Walter Shenson** who'd been making low-budget films in Britain, asking him to produce. Shenson chose **Dick Lester** as his director.

When the meeting to discuss the deal was arranged with Brian Epstein, Ornstein and Shenson had agreed that they would be prepared to give the Beatles 25 per cent of the net profits. They were surprised when Epstein said, immediately, 'I wouldn't consider anything under 7.5 per cent.' Fortunately, when the final contracts came to be signed, the Beatles' lawyer David Jacobs had renegotiated the deal for 25 per cent, although it would have been more lucrative to have asked for a percentage of the gross as opposed to net, due to the reputation the film world had for creative accounting.

In an *Evening Standard* interview, Shenson commented: 'Now I've got the Beatles, do I need stars? Are they necessary, even playing bit parts? My guess is, no. It would be all wrong to have say Kenny Moore or Dirk Bogarde appearing with the boys, though maybe not Margaret Rutherford. I have a hunch the fans would love her. But say, just say, it was **Hayley Mills**, will they feel resentment of her?'

A teenage daughter of a friend then said to him, 'Oh Mr Shenson, I'm just praying there'll be no love interest in your Beatles film!' He took the girl's advice and decided not to include any romances for the Beatles. He also eschewed big name stars, giving the largest non-Beatles role to **Wilfred Brambell**, known for his leading role in the BBC TV sit-com 'Steptoe And Son'. Others in the cast included Liverpudlian actor **Norman Rossington** a Norm, the group's road manager (a role said to be based o **Neil Aspinall**, who was to marry Bud Ornstein's daughte several years later).

Rossington was to tell *Beatles Monthly*: 'I've neve before met a bunch of characters who are so obviousl interested in everything going on around them. Always smile for the lowlier characters on the film set. Always quick gag if there was any hold-up.'

Another Liverpool-born actor was Deryck Guyler, wh portrayed a police sergeant. Actor **John Junkin** portraye the group's second road manager, Shake, and Kennet Haigh, who played the part of Simon, an advertisin executive, didn't want his name in the film's credits Shenson explained, 'He's a Shakespearean actor and, lik a lot of established people back then, he didn't want to b associated with the Beatles. He got a lot of money for on day's work and we agreed not to use his name. But toda he lists *A Hard Day's Night* in his credits wherever h goes.'

Victor Spinetti was cast as a manic television directo and he was to appear in further Beatles projects. Ann Quayle appeared as Millie and a touch of glamour wa added with the casting of ex-Miss World, Rosemari Frankland, as a showgirl. Margaret Rutherford, who' appeared in both of Shenson's 'Mouse' movies, didn' appear in *A Hard Day's Night*, but visited the set and tol Shenson: 'I'm so glad you're making a film about th Beatles. They're my favourite group.' George Harrison wa to return the compliment when he told a 'Ready, Stead Go!' audience that Margaret Rutherford was his favourit actress.

George, in fact, benefited in many ways from this fir film. He'd always felt slightly awed by the talent of Joh and Paul and, added to the fact that he was the younge member of the group, had tended to stay in the backgroun at interviews; yet he proved to be a natural actor. Shenso said: 'George came along well with his acting, so I aske the writer for another short scene for him because I like his "shirt scene". He [the writer] came up with th "shaving scene". The art director put a bath tub in, so said to the director, "Why don't we put John in the bath?" He didn't have any dialogue, but the scene became John instead of George's.

George also met his future wife on the set. There we four schoolgirls featured in an early scene: **Pattie Boy** ina Williams, Pru Bury and Susan Whitman. Pattie was a odel who had appeared in a series of Smiths Crisps TV ls directed by Dick Lester, who had hired her for the eatles' movie. George seemed enchanted by her from the oment he met her and a real-life romance began which ore than made up for the one aspect the movie noticeably cked.

The film was budgeted at £200,000, the production mpany was Proscenium Films and Shenson's production sistant was **Denis O'Dell**. It was decided to film in ack and white and **Robert Freeman**, the group's otographer friend, was hired to create the title sequence, ile George Martin was appointed musical director. He ovided instrumental versions of 'This Boy', 'I Should ave Known Better', 'And I Love Her' and 'A Hard Day's ight'. The director of photography was Gilbert Taylor and e scriptwriter was **Alun Owen**.

Walter Shenson was to comment: 'I don't want to take ything from Dick [Lester] who did a terrific job, but I n't think enough credit has been given to Alun's script. veryone assumed we just got the Beatles together and nged it. Actually, the film was very tightly scripted and t improvised at all. So much of the idiom that became mous – like George's use of the word "grotty" for otesque – were Alun's inventions.'

The other major contributor to the film's success was, of urse, director Richard Lester, who had previously orked with Shenson on the pop film *It's Trad, Dad*, arring **Helen Shapiro**, whom the Beatles had backed on eir first major British tour.

The official announcement about the making of the film s given in December 1963. Shooting began on 2 March 64 and lasted for two months. **Twickenham Studios**, iddlesex, was the setting for the interior scenes and ation shooting took place at several sites in the London ea. The Beatles are shown at Marylebone Station at the ginning of the film where they are pursued by hordes of ns, causing them to make an ingenious escape by dging through the doors of taxis. St Margaret's Field in twick was used for the scene in which they engage in a of horseplay during a break in rehearsals for their TV ow. It was also where the final scene – in which the boys picked up by a helicopter – was filmed.

The **Scala Theatre** in Charlotte Street, London, was setting for their performance before an audience on the evision show. (In fact the group actually performed to rows of empty seats. The audience was admitted after the group had left the theatre and did all their screaming to a film of the Beatles' performance.)

The street scenes and police station sequences were filmed in Clarendon Road in Notting Hill Gate. The train sequences were filmed over six days, mainly on the route between London and Minehead; during this period the cast and crew travelled approximately 2,500 miles by train. The scenes of Ringo by himself were filmed in Kew and the pub scene was shot in an actual pub near Twickenham Studios, where most of the movie was filmed.

The guards-van scene in which the Beatles perform 'I Should Have Known Better' in front of four schoolgirls, was filmed in the studios, among crates of live chickens. It had been suggested at one time that the chickens should be let loose during the sequence, but it was felt that they might end up stealing the scene!

Among the many suggestions for a title were: *What Little Old Man?*, this is one of the first sentences uttered in the film; *Beatlemania*, a term which, by then, was gaining widespread usage; *On The Move; It's A Daft, Daft, Daft, Daft, Daft World; Travelling On; Moving On* and *Let's Go*. Reports at the time all claimed that the title *A Hard Day's Night* had come from Ringo. *Beatles Monthly*, for instance, wrote: 'Ringo hit on *A Hard Day's Night*. Earlier, he'd been asked if he'd had a haircut and said, "No, it's the same difference." He often comes out with strangely worded quotes. And after a long day's work, as the hands on the clock reached into the early hours, he said casually, "Boy, this has been a hard day's night".'

Walter Shenson also credited Ringo as the person who thought up the title. However, in John Lennon's first book *In His Own Write*, published on 23 March 1964, there is a story called 'Sad Michael' in which John wrote: 'He'd had a hard day's night that day, for Michael was a Cocky Watchtower.'

Although Alun Owen had tried to ensure that all four received an equal share of the action, it was Ringo's role which seemed to catch the critics' attention. George also had an interesting scene in an advertising agency. A sequence featuring Paul was cut from the finished film. He had appeared with a girl dressed as a Shakespearean actress, but it ended up on the cutting room floor because it was felt that Paul had been too self-conscious.

The scene occurred following George's adventure in the

advertising agency and his confrontation with the teenage model Susan Campey. Paul has set out in search of Ringo who has managed to get himself lost. Paul wanders around the Notting Hill area, coming across an old church hall that sports a sign 'TV Rehearsal Room'. A group of figures dressed in costume emerge and pass him. He enters and notices a girl moving about the huge room. She is dressed in theatrical costume and is quoting Shakespeare. After some moments, the girl notices Paul and pauses in her speech. He asks her to continue but she tells him to go away as he's spoiled her solitary rehearsal. He remains and begins to chat with her, although she tells him he'll be thrown out when the others return. She guesses he's from Liverpool and they then discuss acting, although Paul admits he's only done Shakespeare in a school play.

She tells him she likes acting for herself and he considers such an attitude to be selfish, telling her that actors and actresses should act for an audience. He tells her that he'd approach her part acting in the manner of a Liverpool scrubber. He points out that this is a clearer way of explaining the character of the role she has been rehearsing. Paul has to utter such lines as: 'I know yo sort – two Cokes and a packet of cheese and onion cris and suddenly it's love and we're stopping in an emp street doorway. Gerrout of it! Ah, you're lonely all righ you're smashin', but come round here and tell all that me Mum – you won't, will you? You're just after me bo and you can't have it, so there!' Paul remembers h mission to find Ringo and says his farewells. As he leav he hears the actress return to the rather artificial voi she'd been using when he first heard on her rehears Then she pauses and begins again, using a much mo naturalistic mode of speech, just as Paul had suggested.

The basic story of the film, as outlined in a synopsis United Artists at the time of the release, is as follows:

'Once upon a time there were four happy Liverpool la called Paul, John, George and Ringo and they played the music all over the country. Now, when they'd finish playing in one place they'd run to the nearest railw station and go on to a new place to play some more of the music, usually pursued by hundreds of young ladies.

'On the day of our story, John, George and Ringo get

The Beatles with beauty queen Rosemary Frankland in *A Hard Day's Night.* (©Walter Shenson Films/Apple)

e station and fight their way into the railway ompartment where they meet up with Paul, who has a ttle old man with him, a very dear little old man. Anyway, ho is he? The little old man is "mixing" John McCartney, aul's grandfather (Wilfred Brambell). Grandfather is edicated to the principle of divide and conquer. The mere ght of a nice friendly group of clean-cut lads like the eatles brings him out in a rash of counterplots.

'Norm (Norman Rossington), the boys' road manager, ho is conducting a war of nerves with John, the group's appy anarchist, collects Grandfather and together with hake (John Junkin), the general dogsbody, he retreats to e restaurant car for coffee, leaving the boys to settle in r their journey to London and a live television show. owever, a well-established first-class ticket holder Richard Vernon) drives the boys out of their carriage by eing pompously officious, so they go and join Norm, hake and Grandfather in the restaurant car.

'By this time Grandfather has managed to get Norm and hake at each other's throats and Paul warns the others at this could be only the beginning. Sure enough, randfather has started a campaign of dissension that ads to frightening schoolgirls, a proposal of marriage to a hance acquaintance and general chaos culminating with randfather being locked in the luggage van where he and e boys complete their journey making music.

'When the boys arrive in London, they go to their hotel here Norm leaves them to sort out their fan mail. owever, Grandfather has noticed that a certain amount of ood-humoured banter is directed at Ringo. Here, thinks randfather, is the weak link in the chain. Instead of aying in the hotel the four boys sneak out to enjoy emselves at a twist club and Grandfather, trading his othes for a waiter's suit, heads straight for a gambling ub, passing himself off as Lord John McCartney.

'Again the boys have to rescue him, much to the old an's indignation.

'The following day sees the boys plunged into the ustle of the television world. Press conferences, hearsals, make-up, running from place to place, being epherded by the harassed Norm and got at by the levision show's neurotic director (Victor Spinetti), and ways in the background is Grandfather, interfering, srupting and needling Ringo.

'Only for a moment are the boys free. They can enjoy emselves playing in a large, open field, but even that doesn't last. John, however, does make the most of every second; he is always for the here and now. Paul tries keeping things on an even keel and George has a blind doggedness that sees him through. But the strain begins to tell on Ringo.

'Grandfather, of course, plays on this, pointing out the barrenness of Ringo's life and finally goading him into walking out into the world, outside of the group.

'The other three boys go out searching for Ringo, leaving Norm to fume and the director to worry himself to near collapse at the possibility of no show.

'Meanwhile, Ringo has found the world outside not too friendly, and through a series of encounters and misunderstandings, gets himself arrested. He is taken to the station, where he meets up with Grandfather who has been taken into protective custody. Grandfather storms at the Police Sergeant (Deryck Guyler) and manages to escape, leaving Ringo behind in the police station.

'He gets back to the television theatre and tells the boys, who, pursued again, but this time by the police, go and rescue Ringo.

'Finally they are able to do their show in front of a live audience.

'The show does well but as soon as it is finished, again it is the mad dash on to the next plane for the next show. The past thirty-six hours have been a hard day's night. The next thirty-six hours will be the same.'

The Beatles' music obviously played a major part in the film and it was introduced in a refreshingly natural way, unlike the forced musical breaks in so many rock 'n' roll films. The movie featured 'A Hard Day's Night', 'I Should Have Known Better', 'If I Fell', 'I'm Happy Just To Dance With You', 'And I Love Her', 'Tell Me Why', 'Can't Buy Me Love', 'Any Time At All', 'I'll Cry Instead', 'Things We Said Today', 'When I Get Home', 'You Can't Do That' and 'I'll Be Back'.

The film was given a Royal World Premiere at the London Pavilion before HRH Princess Margaret and the Earl of Snowdon to aid the Dockland Settlements and the Variety Club Heart Fund on Monday, 6 July 1964, at 8.30 p.m.

Piccadilly Circus had to be closed to traffic as there were literally thousands of fans crowding the area. After the show the group went on to supper at the **Dorchester Hotel**. The northern premiere took place in **Liverpool** on 10 July at the **Odeon Cinema**, following a civic reception at the **Town Hall**. The film then went on general release in Britain on 2 August. It was premiered in America at the Beacon Theatre in New York on 12 August and opened in 500 cinemas throughout the country the next day.

Both British and American critics were, in the main, captivated by the film.

Leonard Mosley of the *Daily Express* wrote: 'It's a mad, mad, mad, mad film, man. Nothing like it since the Goons on radio and the Marx Brothers in the thirties', a feeling which was echoed by Cecil Wilson of the *Daily Mail*, who commented: 'As crazily inconsequential, as endearingly insolent, as infectiously pleased with themselves – as funny as the Marx Brothers.'

The Times was to observe: 'Mr Richard Lester has had a real go, and a lot of his bright ideas come off very wel the way, for instance, that several of the numbers a treated as contrapuntal soundtrack accompaniments screen action of quite another sort; the outbursts Goonish visual humour; the freshly observed Lond locations and the vivid glimpses of backstage (or in th case behind-the-screen) show business life.'

A most quotable comment came from Andrew Sarris the American magazine *Village Voice* who described t film as 'the "Citizen Kane" of jukebox movies'.

A Hard Day's Night proved to be an internation success, bringing in almost $14 million on its initi release. There were various foreign language versions; Italy it was known as *Tutti Per Uno*, in Germany as *Yea*

(©Walter Shenson Films/Apple)

'eah Yeah die Beatles, in France as *Quatre Garcons dans e Vent* and in Holland as *Yeah Yeah Yeah, Daar de Beatles.*

The film began to receive television screenings from uly 1968. Walter Shenson thought that it had not been ully exploited despite the fact that an unprecedented umber of prints had been released so that it could be ssued in 500 US theatres simultaneously. He felt that 'roscenium Films had underrated the movie, and failed to onsider the possibility that it might have a long life span s far as commercial cinema release was concerned.

He commented: 'I'm angry with United Artists. I don't hink they ever had the respect for the Beatles' films that hey deserve. They considered them exploitation films and et them go for stupid hundred dollar bookings and TV. 'hey should have held them back.'

Fifteen years after the release of ***A Hard Day's Night***, henson regained control of the film. He prepared it for re-elease in the US with a Dolby stereo soundtrack in 1981 nd licensed its release as a video cassette in America and 3ritain in 1984.

Hard Day's Night, A *(Single)*

)nce the title for their debut film had been confirmed, ohn and Paul were asked to come up with a song to match t. It was the first time they'd been specifically ommissioned to write a song and John was the first to roduce the completed number. This was perhaps ppropriate as, although all reports credited Ringo with oming up with the phrase, it had actually appeared in one f John's written sketches prior to this time.

Recording of the single began on Thursday 16 April 964, and George Martin added piano to the track.

The single was issued in Britain on Parlophone R 5160 n 10 July 1964 and became the Beatles' third single to each No. 1 one week after release. It was issued in merica on Capitol 5222 on 13 July 1964 and also eached No. 1 in the charts. The million-seller also rought the group a Grammy Award as 'Best Vocal Group 'erformance of 1964'.

The flipside was 'I Should Have Known Better'.

It was included as part of their repertoire on their merican tour in 1964, their **Finsbury Park Astoria** Christmas shows and on their European and American ours in 1965.

Apart from being the first track on the *A Hard Day's Night* album, the number was also used extensively on compilation albums, including *A Collection Of Beatles Oldies (But Goldies), The Beatles 1962–1966, The Beatles At The Hollywood Bowl, Reel Music* and *20 Greatest Hits*. It was also one of the numbers on the medley single *The Beatles Movie Medley* in 1982.

Peter Sellers recorded a version which reached No. 15 in the British charts in 1965 and the Ramsey Lewis Trio recorded an instrumental version which reached No. 29 in the *Billboard* charts in 1966.

● Harris, Rolf

Australian singer/comedian/cartoonist who had his first British chart hit in 1960 with 'Tie Me Kangaroo Down Sport'. Harris moved to Britain and in 1963 was asked by the BBC to interview the Beatles. Aware of their reputation for 'taking the mickey' out of interviewers, he broke the ice by asking, 'Ringo, what do you think of spaghetti?'

He was booked on the bill of their 1963 Christmas Show at the **Finsbury Park Astoria** and drew a cartoon souvenir of the show which was sent to UK members of the **Beatles Fan Club**.

An incident during the run of the show occurred when John and Paul used an off-stage mike to cut in on Rolf's act. He rushed backstage and lambasted them on their unprofessional conduct. He was to observe, 'I got more respect from that point but less friendship.'

● Harrison, Dhani

Dhani, son of **Olivia** and George Harrison. Dhani was born at Princess Christian Nursing Home in Windsor on 1 August 1978. George chose the name which, in Sanskrit, means 'wealthy'.

Four weeks after Dhani was born, George and Olivia got married.

● Harrison, George

George Harrison was born on 25 February 1943 at **12 Arnold Grove**, in the Wavertree area of Liverpool, to **Louise** and **Harold Harrison**. The new baby had two brothers, **Peter** and **Harry**, and a sister, **Louise**.

When George was five his family moved to Upton Green, Speke, and he attended Dovedale Primary School with his brother Peter. In September 1954 he became a pupil at the **Liverpool Institute**. His interest in music was aroused with the skiffle boom and he initially bought a guitar from a schoolmate, but it was damaged and difficult to play. His mother helped him to obtain a proper guitar and he formed a group called the **Rebels** with his brother Peter and best friend **Arthur Kelly**, although the skiffle group only appeared for a single gig at the local British Legion club.

When George left the Institute he was sent by the Youth Employment Centre to **Blackler**'s store to apply for the job as a window-dresser. That job had been taken, but he found employment at the department store as a trainee electrician. In the meantime, his interest in music continued, although he had failed an audition to join Alan Caldwell's Texans (who were to become **Rory Storm & the Hurricanes**). He did manage to find a place with the **Les Stewart Quartet**, who had a residency at Lowlands club in West Derby. George had also developed a friendship with another Institute boy whom he met while travelling to school on the No. 86 bus – Paul McCartney, and he attended a few of the gigs performed by the **Quarry Men**, the group Paul was a member of.

During the early part of 1959, the Quarry Men had virtually ceased to exist. When **Ken Brown**, a fellow member of the Les Stewart Quartet, had an argument with **Stewart**, George walked out with him and suggested he contact John and Paul to join them in a residency at the **Casbah Club**. The Quarry Men then re-formed on 29 August with John, Paul, George and Ken. A different argument ended with Brown leaving the group in October.

In 1960 the group had become the Beatles and, with new drummer **Pete Best**, set off for Germany in August. They appeared at the **Indra Club**, then at the **Kaiserkeller**. When an opportunity came to appear at the rival **Top Ten Club**, Kaiserkeller owner **Bruno Koschmider** revealed that George was under-age and would have to return home. George told Beatles biographer **Hunter Davies**, 'At all clubs they used to read out a notice every night saying that all people under eighteen had to leave. Someone eventually realized I was only seventeen, without a work permit or a resident permit. So I had to leave. I had to go home on my own. I felt terrible'.

When the newspaper ***Mersey Beat*** reported on the Beatles' recording activities in Hamburg, it mentioned that George had written the only Beatles original composition recorded – 'Cry For A Shadow'. George had also co-written with Paul a number called 'In Spite Of All The Danger', which was the first original song the group recorded when

George in 1963. (The Nevitsky Collection)

they made a demonstration record in Kensington, Liverpool, in 1958. Over the next few years of the Beatles' success, the main focus of attention was John and Paul, in particular because of their songwriting. George felt frustrated because he believed his work wasn't being taken seriously by the others. He eventually began writing seriously with 'Don't Bother Me' and began to emerge as a talented songwriter in his own right, although he still had to fight to have his numbers accepted on the group's albums. His compositions included: 'I Need You' and 'You Like Me Too Much' on the *Help!* album; 'Think For Yourself' and 'If I Needed Someone' on the *Rubber Soul* album; 'Taxman', 'Love You Too' and 'I Want To Tell You' on the *Revolver* album; 'Within You, Without You' on the *Sgt Pepper* album and 'Blue Jay Way' on the *Magical*

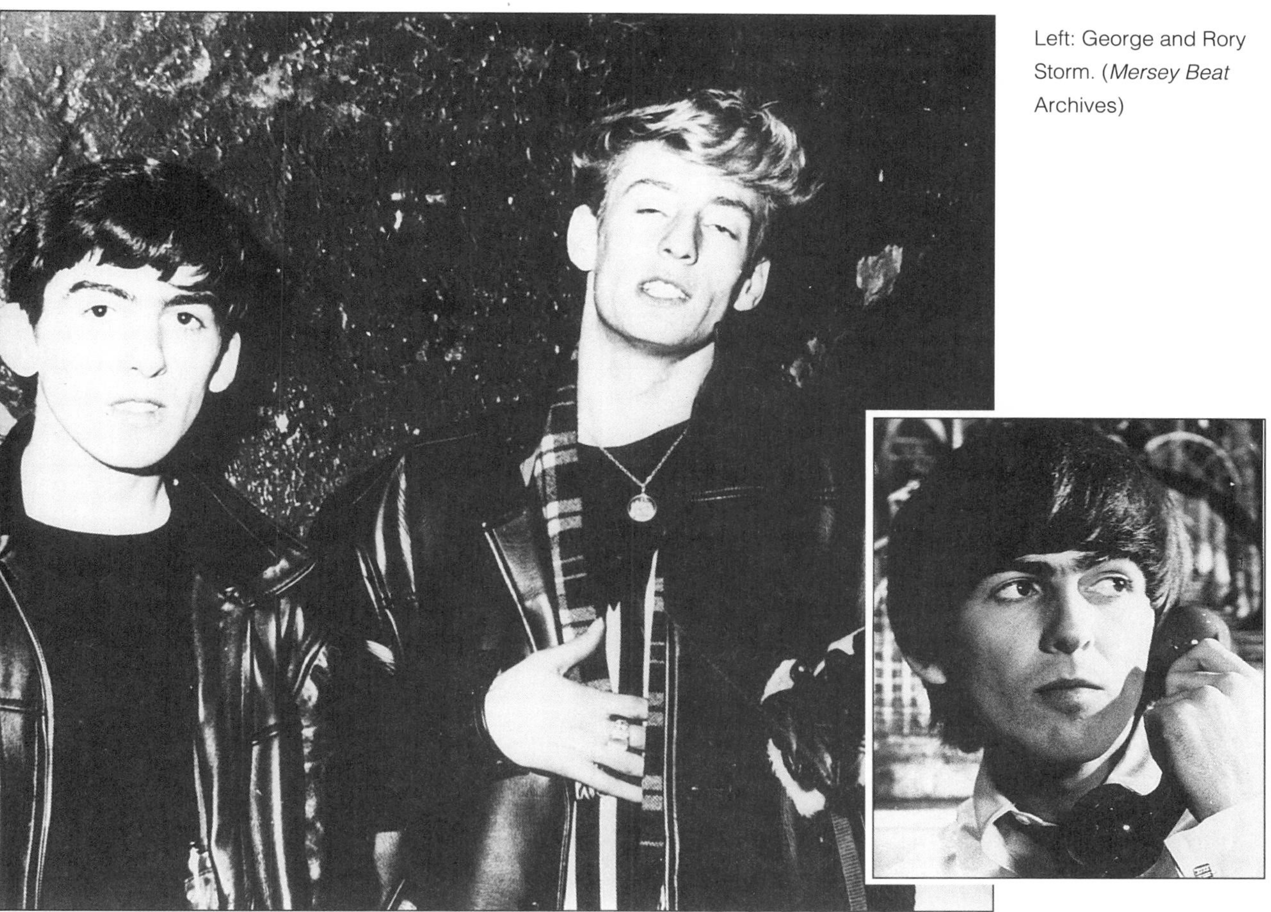

Left: George and Rory Storm. (*Mersey Beat* Archives)

Mystery Tour EP set. 'The Inner Light' became George's first song to be included on a single when it was issued as the flipside of 'Lady Madonna'. His compositions on *The Beatles* double album were 'While My Guitar Gently Weeps', 'Piggies', 'Long Long Long' and 'Savoy Truffle'. Other compositions by George included: 'Only A Northern Song' on the *Yellow Submarine* album; 'Old Brown Shoe', which became the flipside of the 'Ballad Of John And Yoko' single; and 'Something' and 'Here Comes The Sun' on *Abbey Road*. It was **Allen Klein** who finally made the decision to place a George Harrison song as the 'A' side of a Beatles single and this happened with 'Something'. On the Beatles' final album, *Let It Be*, George had two numbers, 'I. Me. Mine' and 'For You Blue'.

George did not have as large a profile in the Beatles' set-up as John or Paul, but he did attract the fans. Even in the Hamburg days the **Exis** referred to him as 'the Beautiful One'. During the filming of *A Hard Day's Night* he met and fell in love with teenage model **Pattie Boyd** and the two were married on 21 January 1966. The following two years proved to be a very important period for George. Apart from his marriage, he developed a close friendship with guitarist **Eric Clapton** and he met two men who were to alter the direction of his life. The first was Indian musician **Ravi Shankar**, whom George was introduced to in June at a party at the home of **Peter Sellers**, the other was the **Maharishi Mahesh Yogi**. These two 'Men from the East' were to have a profound effect on both George's musical and spiritual life, even though his association with the Maharishi was brief. From

Shankar he developed a love of Indian music, learned to play the sitar, and opened up his songwriting to new influences. Transcendental meditation was also to prove beneficial to him and he received inspiration from Indian philosophy and travelled to Bombay in January 1968 to record tracks for the album *Wonderwall* with Indian musicians.

With his new interests, George also began to develop confidence in his own abilities and was no longer prepared to take a back seat in the Beatles' activities. Following a dispute with Paul he walked off the set of the *Let It Be* film in January 1969. He returned, but he was determined never again to appear on stage with the Beatles, despite Paul's attempts to have the group appear in public again. Paul's urgings did, however, result in their last public appearance on the roof of the Apple building in **Savile Row.** During the year George and Pattie had been busted for drugs at their home and he vowed never to keep any drugs at his home again. He also became interested in the Hare Krsna movement and recorded the **Radha Krsna Temple** performing 'The Hare Krsna Mantra'. He also met his Divine Grace A. C. Bhakivedanta Swami Prabhupada.

The Beatles were, by now, effectively finished as a group and George recorded a solo triple album, *All Things Must Pass*, although, following *Wonderwall Music* and *Electronic Sound*, it was actually his third solo LP. Other solo albums included *The Concert For Bangla Desh, Living In The Material World, Dark Horse, Extra Texture (Read All About It), Thirty Three and 1/3, The Best Of George Harrison, George Harrison, Somewhere in England, Gone Troppo* and *Cloud Nine*. His singles have included 'My Sweet Lord', 'What Is Life', 'Bangla Desh', 'Give Me Love', 'Dark Horse', 'Ding Dong', 'You', 'This Guitar Can't Keep From Crying', 'This Song', 'Crackerbox Palace', 'True Love', 'It's What You Value', 'Blow Away', 'Love Comes To Everyone', 'All Those Years Ago', 'Teardrops', 'Wake Up My Love', 'Got My Mind Set On You' and 'When We Was Fab'. In 1975 George set up his own record label Dark Horse Records, which was distributed by Warner Brothers Records.

In April 1984, George announced that he had cut his

The Traveling Wilburys. From left: Bob Dylan, Jeff Lynne, Tom Petty, Roy Orbison and George. (Warner Bros)

last record, stating that he'd decided to retire from the music business to concentrate on film production. Fortunately, he changed his mind concerning recording, but he did channel most of his efforts into film-making when he founded HandMade Films in partnership with Denis O'Brien in 1978 and they salvaged two films from EMI, *The Life Of Brian* (1979) and *The Long Good Friday* (1981). Other films HandMade were involved with included *Time Bandits* (1981); *Monty Python Live at the Hollywood Bowl* (1982); *The Missionary* (1982); *Privates On Parade* (1982); *Scrubbers* (1982); *Bullshot* (1982); *A Private Function* (1984); *Water* (1984). *Shanghai Surprise* (1986); *Mona Lisa* (1986); *Withnail And I* (1987); *Track Twenty Nine* (1988); *The Lonely Passion Of Judith Hearne* (1989); *Pow Wow Highway* (1989); *Five Corners* (1989); *Checking Out* (1989); *How To Get Ahead In Advertising* (1989) and *Nuns On The Run* (1989).

George triumphed in August 1971 when he presented *The Concert For Bangla Desh* at Madison Square Garden, in which he was surrounded by a host of stars, including Ringo Starr, **Bob Dylan**, Eric Clapton, **Billy Preston**, **Badfinger** and Ravi Shankar.

In 1974 he went on the road again and performed 50 concerts in North America. His marriage with Pattie was breaking down and she became involved in a love affair with George's best friend, Eric Clapton. The couple were divorced on 9 June 1977. By that time George was in love with **Olivia** Arias and the couple were living together at George's palatial mansion, Friar Park in Henley. Olivia gave birth to their son **Dhani** on 1 August 1978 and the two were married the following month, on 2 September. In 1979 George had his autobiography *I. Me. Mine* published in a special limited edition.

During the eighties George began to make a number of appearances on stage and television, including a special TV tribute to the career of **Carl Perkins**. George was also to become part of a unique band called the Traveling Wilburys, which also included **Roy Orbison**, Bob Dylan, Tom Petty and Jeff Lynne, and they were instantly successful with their debut album *The Traveling Wilburys* in 1988.

● Harrison, George *(Journalist)*

A columnist with the *Liverpool Echo* at the time of the Beatles' rise to fame. When Brian Epstein took over management of the Beatles, ***Mersey Beat*** was the only publication reporting on the group's activities. Epstein particularly sought the prestige of *Liverpool Echo* coverage, although Harrison at first refused to print any items in his 'Over The Mersey Wall' column. Once the group began to achieve fame, he started to include items in his column and as their fame grew he became the main writer providing *Echo* coverage of the Beatles and he even travelled to America with them in 1964. Some of his reports were contained in *Around The World With The Beatles*, a souvenir book produced by the *Liverpool Echo* at Christmas 1964. Harrison had originally been a Fleet Street reporter who, later in life, had moved on to a provincial paper. With the phenomenon of the Beatles providing him with trips to America, it was a taste of the 'big time' once more, which he never thought he'd get to experience again.

His son Lee began work at the *Birkenhead News & Advertiser* in September 1964 and received a letter from **Derek Taylor** which read: 'I am at the moment in the middle of a game of poker with Ringo and your father, and John is tinkering about with a song he has in mind, George is making a call to London – and Pattie – and we don't know where Paul is.' It also included signatures from John and Ringo. Harrison retired in the late sixties and moved to a nursing home in the South.

● Harrison, Harold Hargreaves

George Harrison's father.

Born in Liverpool on 28 May 1909, Harold's parents were Henry Harrison and Jane Thomson. At the age of fourteen he became a delivery boy and then went to sea as a steward with the White Star line.

After marrying **Louise** he became a bus conductor, then driver and on the birth of George he described him as 'A tiny, squalling, miniature replica of myself'.

Harold and Louise spent a great deal of their social life at the Liverpool Corporation Centre for Conductors and Drivers and Harry became a Union official. He also became an MC at the Union's Saturday evening socials.

In 1965 Harold was earning ten pounds a week and George offered him five times that amount if he would retire – and he bought his parents a house for £10,000.

When Louise died, Harold began to visit **Friar Park** regularly and joined George on his Dark Horse tour in 1974. He died at his home in Cheshire in May 1978 of emphysema.

● Harrison, Harry

One of George Harrrison's elder brothers, known as Harry Junior. When Harry was called up for National Service, his girlfriend Irene McCann used to keep George company, taking him to shows, including the **Lonnie Donegan** shows at the Empire Theatre. She said that George was like a little brother and referred to him as 'our kid'. She married Harry after he'd completed his National Service and the **Quarry Men** played at their wedding reception on 20 December 1959.

Harry was a mechanic, but later in life he went to work for George at **Friar Park** as his estate manager.

● Harrison, Louise *(Mother)*

George's mother was born Louise French. She first met **Harry Harrison** on a street corner in Liverpool in 1929 and the couple were married on 20 May 1930, at Brownlow Hill register office. Louise worked at a local greengrocer's shop and gave up her job when her first child **Louise** was born in 1931, to be followed by **Harold** in 1943, **Peter** in 1940 and George in 1944. Her husband became a bus conductor and for ten years the two of them ran ballroom dancing lessons at the conductors' club.

Louise was supportive of George's interest in music and bought him an acoustic guitar for £3 when he was thirteen. When he joined the **Quarry Men** she let them rehearse in her drawing room, and she visited the **Cavern** to give support to the Beatles.

When the Beatles began to receive such a huge volume of fan mail she would go to the **Beatles Fan Club** office in Liverpool city centre and take home the letters to George, reading all of them, up to 2,000 a month between 1963 and 1966, and answering as many of them as she could, personally.

In 1965 George bought his parents a new house in Appleton, near Warrington. Tragically, Louise was only to spend five years there. She became terribly ill and suffered for twelve months before dying of a brain tumour on 7 July 1970.

A group of Beatle fans formed the Louise F. Harrison Memorial Cancer Fund.

● Harrison, Louise *(Sister)*

George Harrison's sister, now known as Louise Kane. George and Louise's first child, she was named after her mother when she was born in 1931. She studied at a training college in Liverpool before marrying an American, Gordon Caldwell, and the couple moved to America in July 1954.

George made his first trip to America in September 1963 when he went on a short holiday to St Louis, Illinois, to stay with Louise and her family. She'd been living in America for nine years and George, who was joined on the trip by his brother Peter, said, 'I've wanted to go there [America] for years, but I could never afford it before. Also, this may be my last chance for a while, 'cause it may be ages before the Beatles can get two weeks free again. We shall spend most of the time in St Louis and a few days in New York.'

In February 1964 when the Beatles arrived for their triumphant visit to America, George fell ill and a doctor was called to his room at the Plaza Hotel. Louise moved into the adjacent room and nursed him.

Louise became in demand for interviews on American radio shows and in 1965, Recar Records (2012) issued 'All About The Beatles', a compilation of her interviews with five American radio stations: WMEX Boston, WNDR Norfolk, WHK Cleveland, WKNR Detroit and KIMN Denver.

It was Louise who phoned George to inform him that John had been murdered.

● Harrison, Olivia

Born in Mexico in 1948, Olivia Trinidad Arias was educated in America and graduated at Hawthorne High School, California. She remained in Los Angeles and went to work at A&M Records as an assistant in the merchandizing department, where she met George Harrison in 1974. George was impressed by the serene, dark-haired beauty and engaged her to work as a secretary for his own Dark Horse records. The couple became close friends and when George fell ill following a number of problems relating to his marriage breakdown and a slump in his recording career, he suffered from serum hepatitis, but didn't respond to treatment. It was Olivia who recommended that he visit Dr Zion Yua, a noted Chinese acupuncturist, who cured him.

George realized he had found his soul mate and the two became inseparable on his travels around America. George also took her to visit Liverpool. They lived in splendour in Los Angeles for a while but it became apparent that Olivia was not particularly impressed by the lavish life style over there and the two of them moved to the tranquillity of the English countryside, to George's mansion, **Friar Park**, in Henley-on-Thames. The couple were not able to marry until George's divorce from **Pattie** came through, which took until 9 June 1977. They then planned to marry in May 1978, but the wedding had to be postponed because of the death of George's father. Their son **Dhani** was born on 1 August 1978 and George and Olivia were finally married by special licence at Henley Register Office on 7 September 1978, in a secret, ceremony at which the only guests were Olivia's parents, who had flown in from California. The couple then went on honeymoon to Tunisia.

● Harrison, Peter

One of George's elder brothers, who became a panel beater and welder before George asked him to move south with his family and oversee the gardeners at **Friar Park**.

Peter joined George in his short-lived band the **Rebels**, but Peter was basically uninterested in the guitar. He accompanied George on his first visit to America in September 1963.

● Harrods, Knightsbridge, London SW3

One of the world's most prestigious department stores.

On 25 November 1965, Harrods made a special arrangement for the Beatles to shop there one hour after the premises had closed. The Beatles were escorted around each department by salesgirls and were said to have spent an average of £2,000 each.

Among the items John bought was a 200-foot slide for Julian and he said he looked forward to bringing it into his garden in Weybridge. George bought furniture for his parents' new home in Liverpool.

● Harry Lime Theme, The

Instrumental number popularized in the 1949 film *The Third Man*. It was composed by Anton Karas who performed the number on a zither. Paul McCartney mentioned that the **Silver Beatles** played 'The Harry Lime Theme' when they backed **Janice the Stripper** at the **New Cabaret Artistes Club**.

● Haslam, Michael

A singer from Lancashire, who was 24 years old when he was signed to Brian Epstein in 1964.

Godfrey Winn, a leading show business writer for women's magazines, saw Haslam performing in a Bolton pub. A short time later he was dining with Brian Epstein and **Cilla Black** and raved over his discovery. Brian then set off for Bolton with Winn and arrived to witness a Sunday evening show by Haslam at the White Hart pub. Epstein was impressed and after the show told Haslam he would like to manage him and would put him on the next Beatles tour.

Epstein also arranged a Parlophone recording contract for the singer, who was to be recorded by George Martin. Haslam appeared on the Beatles' sell-out tour in October 1964 and also appeared on their Christmas show at the **Odeon, Hammersmith** in December of the same year. Despite the massive exposure, he had no record success. His first release was 'Gotta Get Hold Of Myself'. His second was the prophetic-sounding 'There Goes The Forgotten Man'. When his contract lapsed after two years, Epstein didn't bother renewing it.

Haslam's sister Annie later became a star in her own right in the seventies as lead singer with Renaissance.

● Hawaii

Kuppuqukua is the name of George Harrison's home in the tiny town of Huna on the island of Maui in Hawaii, an island which also harbours homes for a range of celebrities including Dolly Parton, Tom Selleck, Richard Pryor, Kris Kristofferson and Carol Burnett. The island is the subject of George's *Gone Troppo* album and his *George Harrison* album pays tribute to the town in 'Soft-Hearted Huna'.

George first travelled to Hawaii on 3 May 1964 when he arrived in Honolulu with **Pattie Boyd** and John and **Cynthia** Lennon. They arrived from Vancouver late on Saturday night, 2 May, and were booked into the Royal Hawaiian Hotel, overlooking the beach at Waikiki. Fans besieged the hotel and a local disc jockey tried to convince hotel security that he was Paul McCartney. Since it was unlikely that the four would have any peace from fans where they were, John McDermitt, advertising director of the hotel, phoned his wife to tell her he was bringing four guests home for dinner. Accompanied by her two daughters, nine-year-old Duffi and seven-year-old Kelli, she went shopping and returned to find the two Beatles plus their wives had arrived. They managed to spend three uninterrupted hours at the beach house, which was situated in Kailua, went swimming with the McDermitt daughters in a neighbour's swimming pool and had a dinner of steak, cold chicken and green salad. They flew off to Tahiti the next day.

In July 1964 Ringo, accompanied by Brian Epstein, was on his way to join the Beatles in Australia, following his throat infection, and stopped over in Honolulu for 85 minutes, signing autographs at the airport.

For his *George Harrison* album in 1979, George had written the lyrics to 'Love Comes To Everyone' in February 1978 whilst in Hawaii and, inspired by the local sunset, he also penned 'Here Comes The Moon'.

● Hawke, Jim

Former British soldier who remained in Germany after World War II. He married a German girl, Lilo, and at the beginning of 1960, together with their daughter Monica, they took over the running of the British Sailors' Society in Hamburg, known as the 'Mission'.

When the Beatles arrived in Hamburg, **Iain Hines** and **Tony Sheridan** of the Jets introduced them to the delights of the Mission, which were English breakfasts with lots of milk and cornflakes, and very cheap meals – steak, egg and chips.

Hawke made British musicians very welcome at the Mission and the Beatles would often arrive there at 11.00 a.m. and stay until 3.00 p.m. or 4.00 p.m. One of the rooms had a piano in it and John and Paul used it to compose songs on.

On one occasion John and Paul called on Tony and Iain to join them on their walk to the Mission, but the two members of the Jets refused to join them as they were embarrassed because the two were wearing German army forage caps and Tony and Iain told them they'd be 'lynched' walking around dressed like they were – particularly as the caps had a white swastika painted on them. John and Paul left and Tony and Iain trailed them ten minutes later. A man spat at them and a number of Germans began to follow them, so Tony and Iain broke into a run and fled to the Mission. They asked Jim Hawke why they had been picked on. He explained that they were wearing T-shirts – which they'd been given by some American sailors – with the initials D.D.R. on them. This meant D-Type Destroyer. However, in German eyes the initials meant Deutsche Democratic Republic – East Germany, which resulted in their hostile reception on the streets.

Jim Hawke became a kind friend to the Beatles and, aware of their financial hardships, ensured that they enjoyed hearty meals at a fraction of the price they'd have paid elsewhere in St Pauli.

● Hear The Beatles Tell All

An album originally issued in the United States in September 1964 on **Vee Jay** PROP 202. The record contained interviews with all four members of the group, conducted by **Dave Hull**, plus a John Lennon interview conducted by Jim Steck. The album was issued in Great Britain in March 1981 on Charly Records CRV 202.

● Hello Goodbye

Paul McCartney composition issued as a single with John's 'I Am The Walrus' as the flip. Released in Britain on Parlophone R 5655 on 24 November 1967, it was No. 1 for seven weeks. It was issued in America on Capitol 2056 on 27 November 1967 and also topped the charts.

John Lennon wasn't pleased that the number was chosen as the 'A' side of their single, with 'I Am The Walrus' as the 'B' side. He considered 'Walrus' a much better number and cynically referred to 'Hello Goodbye' as 'typical Paul'.

The song was included on the American album of *Magical Mystery Tour* in 1967, the 1973 double album *The Beatles 1967–1970* and the **EMI** album version of *Magical Mystery Tour*, issued in November 1976. It was also selected for their second twenty-track compilation *20 Greatest Hits* in 1982.

The promotional film of the number couldn't be screened in Britain due to a new musicians' union ruling which banned miming to records – on the supposition that it kept live musicians out of work! Its planned screening on BBC 2's 'Late Night Line-Up' on 23 November was scrapped and the film was replaced on **'Top Of The Pops'** with a film clip from *A Hard Day's Night*.

When the song was recorded in October 1967 it had the working title 'Hello Hello', and was recorded during the *Magical Mystery Tour* sessions. Paul was lead vocalist, with backing from John and George, and Paul also played piano, bongos and conga drums on the session while John played organ and lead guitar, George played lead and tambourine and Ringo played drums and maracas. Two viola players were brought in to play on the session – Leo Birnbaum and Ken Essex.

There was a reprise ending which the group referred to

as 'the Maori finale' and when the group were making their promotional film of the number at the **Saville Theatre**, they featured a number of girl dancers wearing grass skirts.

● Hello Little Girl

A number penned by John in his teens and included in the group's repertoire in 1958. John was to comment, 'This was one of the first songs I ever finished. I was then about 18 and we gave it to the **Fourmost.** I think it was the first song of my own that I ever attempted to do with the group.' John was also to say that he'd loosely based the song on a couple of old standards which his mother used to sing to him when he was a small child, and the song was an attempt to capture the mood of those songs written in the 1930s. The Beatles performed the number on their Decca and Parlophone recording auditions in 1962.

● Help! (American Album)

The American album of *Help!* was issued by **Capitol** on SMAS 2386 on 13 August 1965. It was the first album in history to have an advance order of over one million copies.

Unlike the version of the album which was issued in Britain and the rest of the world, the Capitol album only contained the seven Beatles songs from the movie. Capitol replaced the new Beatles tracks with seven soundtrack instrumentals from the film by the George Martin Orchestra.

Capitol advertised the package as a 'Special Movie Souvenir Package' but the Beatles were annoyed at the release containing only half of the Beatles numbers from the British version of the *Help!* album.

The track listing was, Side One: 'James Bond Theme', 'Help!', 'The Night Before', 'From Me To You Fantasy', 'You've Got To Hide Your Love Away', 'I Need You', 'In The Tyrol'. Side Two: 'The Bitter End/You Can't Do That', 'You're Going To Lose That Girl', 'The Chase', 'Another Girl', 'Another Hard Day's Night', 'Ticket To Ride'.

● Help! (British Album)

The soundtrack of the Beatles' second film, issued on PCF on 6 August 1965. The songs from the film were featured on Side One of the album which reached No. 1 in the British charts.

The tracks were, Side One: 'Help', 'The Night Before', 'You've Got To Hide Your Love Away', 'I Need You', 'Another Girl', 'You're Going To Lose That Girl', 'Ticket To Ride'. Side Two: 'Act Naturally', 'It's Only Love', 'You Like Me Too Much', 'Tell Me What You See', 'I've Just Seen A Face', 'Yesterday', 'Dizzy Miss Lizzy'.

● Help! (Film)

Work on the Beatles' second movie *Help!* started on 23 February 1965. It was decided that filming should begin in Nassau in the Bahamas and the cast and crew of 70 flew out on 22 February in a chartered Boeing 707. The temperature in the Bahamas was 90 degrees, but the Beatles couldn't afford to get a tan as they would next be filming a sequence in Austria that would be appearing prior to those shot in the Caribbean. Cast and crew left for Austria and the ski resort of Oberauern on 13 March. Producer **Walter Shenson** was to comment: '[*Help!*] is essentially a holiday picture. It was filmed in two totally contrasting holiday resorts. We travelled from calypso to yodel with a lot of yeah, yeah thrown in besides.'

A special wardrobe was made for the Beatles' Austrian scenes. All four wore black skin-tight trousers and ankle-length ski boots in black sealskin. John sported a black cape lined with white satin while Ringo wore a tight-fitting black sweater with white rings around the sleeves. George also wore a black sweater but with a white stripe down each sleeve while Paul had on a loosely cut ski jacket in lustrous sealskin.

Filming was completed on 11 May, the rest of the film's scenes having been shot in London, Salisbury Plain (with permission from the War Office) and **Twickenham Studios**. While *A Hard Day's Night* had cost only $500,000 to make, *Help!* (filmed in Eastmancolour) cost $1.5 million.

This Walter Shenson–Subafilms production was once again distributed by United Artists and directed by **Dick Lester**. The script was written by Marc Behm and Christopher Wood from a story by Behm. Behm didn't seem to capture the Beatles' humour in the same way as **Alun Owen** had in *A Hard Day's Night*, although there are touches of Scouse wit. While watching the belly-dancer Durra perform in a restaurant, the boys quip, 'Doesn't the blood rush to your stomach?' At another point in the movie, John picks up a season ticket out of his soup and says, 'I'd like a bit of seasoning.' When a Scotland Yard superintendent sarcastically remarks 'So you're the famous Beatles. How long do you think you'll last?' John

Above: The Beatles in disguise in *Help!* (©Apple/Walter Shenson Films) Facing page: South American poster for the film.

replies: 'And the Great Train Robbery – how do you think that's going?'

The film begins with the tribute: 'Respectfully dedicated to the memory of Elias Howe who in 1846 invented the sewing machine'. Title cards are used at various points in the film bearing such inscriptions as 'Intermission' and 'End of Intermission'; the scene in which Paul is miniaturized and dodges around the floor of

his flat is heralded by a card reading 'The Adventures of Paul on the Floor'.

By the time the cameras had started rolling, an official name still hadn't been confirmed. It was initially known as 'Beatles Two', and for a time was called 'Eight Arms To Hold You'.

John and Paul composed five numbers for the film: 'Ticket To Ride', 'Help!', 'You're Going To Lose That Girl', 'The Night Before' and 'You've Got To Hide Your Love Away'. George penned 'I Need You'.

Other members of the cast were Leo McKern as Clang, **Eleanor Bron** as Ahme, John Bluthal as Bhuta, Warren Mitchell as Abdul, Peter Copely as a jeweller and Dandy Nichols as a neighbour. Bruce Lacey plays Lawn Mower (he mows a lawn – situated in a drawing-room – with two pairs of false teeth) and **Mal Evans** pops up from time to time as a Channel swimmer who has lost his way.

The official synopsis outlined the story as follows:

> 'In the Eastern Temple of the Goddess Kaili a human sacrifice is about to be made. But the executioner, the High Priest Clang, is stopped by the beautiful Ahme, priestess of the cult who has discovered that the victim is not wearing the sacrificial ring essential for the ritual.
>
> 'On the other side of the world the Beatles are performing. Ringo sits on the stage playing the drums and amongst his many rings is – the ring – a present from an unknown fan of another continent.
>
> 'In the days that follow a series of mysterious events make no sense to the Beatles. At home, on the street, a strange force seems to be directed at Ringo. A gang of thugs descend upon the boys and attempt to amputate Ringo's entire hand – and the Beatles realize that it is Ringo's new ring they must have.
>
> 'After several more attempts, Clang and his gang nearly succeed in stealing Ringo's whole person, but just in time he is saved by Ahme.
>
> 'A few days later, while the boys are waiting for a meal in an Indian restaurant, the dreaded Clang and his henchman Bhuta appear disguised as waiters. They tell Ringo that since they cannot remove the ring from his finger he is to be sacrificed to the Goddess. The boys flee to the nearest jewellers and ask the man to cut off the offending ring. But the metal breaks the files and the cutting wheel.
>
> 'The boys call next at a science laboratory run by Professor Foot and his assistant Algernon who put Ringo through every machine they have – to no avail; the ring resists all the assaults known to science. Foot decides that the ring has properties which could give the owner the power to rule the world and he confides to Algernon that he must get the ring. So the Beatles have two more enemies who

will stop at nothing to retrieve the ring. Ahme once again comes to the rescue and they all flee from the laboratory – to the Alps!

'In no time the Beatles' winter sport activities are interrupted by the arrival of Foot and Algernon intent on mayhem to be joined almost at once by Clang and gang. After a frantic chase through snow and ice up mountains and down ski lifts the boys scramble to the nearest railway station and gasp to the ticket man, "London!"

'Back home they confide their troubles to a Superintendent of Scotland Yard and tell him they must have protection in order to record in peace.

'The next day the boys record two songs on Salisbury Plain, under the protection of the British Army, but Clang and his murderous thugs arrive and put the Beatles to flight. Ahme, in a tank, rescues them in the nick of time.

'Back in London the murder attempts increase and the Beatles decide to leave the country until the heat is off. Heavily disguised they fly off to the Bahamas. But, alas, the world is too small a place for the Beatles, Clang and his gang and the two power-drunk scientists. Soon, the whole fray is resumed. But Ringo learns the formula which releases him from the ring. The ring slips off and he hands it to Clang who hastily hands it on to Foot who tries to pass it on to Algernon and so on down the line.

'Ahme and the Beatles at last find peace and the dreaded Kaili will have no more victims.'

The film contains numerous clever touches and colourful scenes – the four terraced houses that are really a single, large luxurious flat; the emergence of animated snowmen on the slopes of the ski resort; the **Fab Four**'s appearance as members of a brass band in uniform (very Sgt Pepperish) and the giant idol rising from the sea. One of the best sequences was filmed in the cellar of a London pub and featured Ringo and a lion. In the film the animal, called Sheba, has been brought up on classical music at the Berlin Zoo. To calm the beast, the Beatles have to sing 'Ode to Joy' from Beethoven's Ninth. While the scene was being filmed, the film's insurance brokers insisted that the lion keeper stand close by armed with a safari gun.

The world premiere of *Help!* took place at the **London Pavilion** on 29 July. Crowds began to gather at 8.00 a.m. and by evening there were 10,000 people massed in Piccadilly. The statue of Eros was boarded up for its protection and 250 policemen were needed to handle the crowds. The area was so packed that John's Rolls-Royce was held up for twenty minutes.

The event was attended by Princess Margaret and Lord Snowdon. The Princess, when talking to Ringo about *A Hard Day's Night*, said, 'You were a trifle pessimistic about that one. I enjoyed it very much and I have been looking forward to this one. I've come with an open mind.' The premiere was sponsored by the Variety Club of Great Britain in aid of the Docklands settlement and the Variety Club's Heart Fund; £6,000 was raised for these two charities.

The film opened at 250 leading cinemas throughout the United States on 11 August and was the official British entry at the International Film Festival in Rio de Janeiro from 15–26 September, where it won first prize.

The critics weren't as universally enthusiastic about *Help!* as they had been about *A Hard Day's Night. The Spectator* noticed the slight stylistic influence of the Bond films (there were even a few bars of music on the soundtrack parodying the Bond music) and headed its review 'Beatles on the Bond Trail'. The reviewer commented: 'Ringo, the oddity and outsider, in so far as any one of them can be called that, is, as he was before both hero and victim, certainly the most individual character.

'*Help!* is almost consistently funny, sometimes almost confusingly fast, and above all a contrast to its predecessor. Its social satire is directed inwards as much as out . . . the Beatles put latchkeys into four identical front doors which, with carefully primitive exteriors, all open into a single opulent interior, a schoolboy millionaire's dream of gadgets and instant marvels – sunken beds, rising wurlitzers, orangeade-making machines and pigeon-holed sandwiches.'

Writing in the *Daily Express*, Clive Barnes commented 'These boys are the closest thing to the Marx Brothers since the Marx Brothers.'

Kenneth Tynan, in his *Observer* review, wrote: 'The Beatles themselves are not natural actors, nor are they exuberant extroverts. Their mode is dry and laconic, as befits the flat and sceptical Liverpool accent. Realizing this, Lester leaves it to his cameraman (David Watkin) to create the exuberance, confining the Beatles to dead-pan comments and never asking them to react to events with anything approaching emotion. He capitalizes on their wary, guarded detachment. "There's something been in this soup," says John, having calmly removed from the plate a season ticket and a pair of spectacles. "Not a bit like Cagney" is George's response when a CID Superintendent favours the group with a patronizing impersonation of Ringo.'

America's *Time* magazine commented: '*Help!*, in short, is a Beatle production rather than a Beatle movie. It must have cost, as the British say, a packet. It will certainly make, as the Americans say, a bundle.'

The film did go on to make a bundle and United Artists were obviously eager, along with Shenson and Lester, to make a third film with the group, but it never materialized. The Beatles were offered several scripts and ideas, but were unhappy with all of them. Perhaps *Help!* had been a disappointment to them.

Certainly, John never had anything positive to say about the film: '*Help!* was a drag, because we didn't know what was happening. In fact Lester was a bit ahead of his time with the Batman thing, but we were on pot by then and all the best stuff is on the cutting-room floor, with us breaking up and falling about all over the place.' Some years later he was blunt and dismissive about the film, describing it as 'Crap!'

Walter Shenson summarized his own and the Beatles' feelings as follows: 'The Beatles finally decided to discharge the third film in their contract by filming the *Let It Be* recording session. They financed it with UA (United Artists) and gave me a small piece of the profit.

'I think if we'd had a sensational script of a great idea, we might have made a third film. But it just wasn't in the cards.'

● Help! (Single)

Number written by John Lennon for the film *Help!* He was to describe it as one of his first 'message' songs, which was his own personal cry for help, and it became one of his particular favourites.

In 1970, John was to tell Jann Wenner in a *Rolling Stone* interview, 'The only true songs I ever wrote were "Help!" and "Strawberry Fields Forever". They were the ones I wrote from experience, not projecting myself into a situation and writing a nice story about it, which I always found phoney. On "Help!", the lyric is as good now as it was then. It was just me singing *help*, and I meant it.'

He told David Sheff during a *Playboy* magazine interview, 'It was my fat Elvis period. You see the movie; He-I-is very fat, very insecure, and he's completely lost himself. And I'm saying about when I was so much younger and all the rest, looking back at how easy it was.'

The song was issued in Britain on Parlophone R 5305 on 23 July 1965 and topped the charts for four weeks. It was issued in America on Capitol 5476 on 19 July 1965 where it also reached the No. 1 position. 'I'm Down' was the flip.

The number was also featured on the soundtrack album *Help!* and on several compilations, including *A Collection Of Beatles Oldies (But Goldies)*, *The Beatles 1962–1966*, *Reel Music*, *20 Greatest Hits* and the American *The Beatles Rarities*.

'Help!' was recorded on Tuesday, 13 April 1965. The Beatles' second film had used a working title and as soon as the name *Help!* was decided on, both John and Paul were asked to come up with a title song. As with *A Hard Day's Night*, John was the first to produce a number.

● Helter Skelter

Number penned by Paul and originally recorded on 18 July 1968, although that version was scrapped.

It was decided to record the number from scratch on Monday, 9 September 1968, and as George Martin was on holiday, the track was produced by Chris Thomas.

Various instruments were used on the backing and **Mal Evans** attempted to play a trumpet. The session was a long one and at the end of the recording, Ringo cried out, 'I've got blisters on my fingers!'

The song was featured on *The Beatles* double album, issued on November 1968.

A helter skelter is a spiral slide found at British fairgrounds, although an American hippie, **Charles Manson**, leader of a cult in Los Angeles, claimed there were hidden meanings in the song. Manson had created a bizarre sect who looked on him as a messianic figure. On hearing the Beatles album, Manson believed that the group were imparting a secret message heralding an armageddon. He believed that 'when the "Helter Skelter" came, the Black Panthers, led by "Rocky Raccoon", would rise and execute the "Piggies".'

He sent members of his sect out to commit murder and

among the victims was Sharon Tate, wife of film director Roman Polanski.

John Lennon was to comment on Manson's state of mind. 'Well, he's barmy. He's like any other Beatles kind of fan who reads mysticism into it. I mean, we used to have a laugh putting this, or the other in, in a light-hearted way. Some intellectual would read us, some symbolic youth generation wants it, but we also took seriously some part of the role . . . but, I don't know, what's "Helter Skelter" got to do with knifing somebody? I never listened to the words properly, it was just a noise.'

Manson was caught, put on trial in 1969 and jailed. A bestselling book called *Helter Skelter* by Vincent Bugliosi and Curt Gentry, the prosecuting attorneys at the trial, was filmed as a two-part television dramatization called 'Helter Skelter', featuring some of the white album tracks. This resulted in Capitol rush-releasing 'Helter Skelter' as a single on Capitol 4274 on 31 May 1976. However, although they'd sent a special single of 'Helter Skelter' to disc jockeys for promotion, when they released the single they placed it on the flipside of 'Got To Get You Into My Life', in case anyone accused them of exploiting the Manson case. The single reached No. 3 in the American charts.

'Helter Skelter' was also included in the 1976 compilation *Rock 'n' Roll Music* and the American 1980 compilation *The Beatles Rarities*.

● Her Majesty

At 23 seconds in length, the shortest Beatle track on record.

As Paul lived in St John's Wood, quite close to **Abbey Road Studios**, he often arrived far earlier than his fellow Beatles and sometimes began recording. This was one of his efforts which he recorded before the others arrived on Wednesday, 2 July 1969.

When the tracks for *Abbey Road* were being remixed on Wednesday, 30 July, second engineer John Kurlander played it to Paul who told him to throw it away. After Paul had left, Kurlander picked the small piece of tape off the floor and stuck it on the end of the edit tape. Eventually, Paul heard it again and decided it could be used on the album.

The number was the closing track on the *Abbey Road* album. Paul had composed the number in tribute to Queen Elizabeth II and copies of the LP were sent to Buckingham Palace.

Paul played acoustic guitar and sang solo on the number.

● Here Comes The Sun

A George Harrison composition which he wrote one day in Eric Clapton's garden. He'd become bored with the business problems of Apple and decided to take the day off, rather like 'sagging off school', and went to see Eric Clapton. It was while he was walking in the garden with one of Eric's acoustic guitars that he composed the number, which was featured as one of the tracks on the *Abbey Road* album.

It was recorded on Ringo's 29th birthday, 7 July 1969, and there were only three Beatles present at the session as John was indisposed with an injury.

George was gaining more confidence in himself as a musician and songwriter, after years under the Lennon and McCartney shadow, and was taking more control of how his own songs were recorded. In this instance he supervised most of the overdubbing sessions.

Some years later, in 1976, Steve Harley & Cockney Rebel had a hit with the number when they issued it as a single in Britain, where it reached No. 10 in the charts.

'Here Comes The Sun' is included in the compilations *The Beatles Ballads*, *The Beatles 1967–1970*, *The Best Of George Harrison* and on *The Concert For Bangla Desh* LP. In addition to performing it on *The Concert For Bangla Desh*, George also played the number on 'Saturday Night Live', with Paul Simon in November 1976.

● Here, There And Everywhere

One of Paul McCartney's compositions, which he regards as one of his favourite numbers. In 1980, John Lennon also said, 'That's one of my favourite songs of the Beatles.'

The number was recorded over three days in June 1966 for the *Revolver* album and it was suggested that Paul had been inspired to write it after listening to the **Beach Boys**' 'God Only Knows'.

When asked about the Lennon & McCartney songs and this title in particular, Paul commented, 'This one was pretty much mine, written sitting by John's pool. Often I would wait half an hour while he would do something – like get up. So I was sitting there tootling around in E on the guitar.' In addition to *Revolver*, the number surfaced on compilation albums such as *Love Songs* and *The Beatles*

Ballads. Paul was also to feature the number in his film *Give My Regards To Broad Street*.

In 1976 country music singer Emmylou Harris reached No. 30 in the British charts with her single of the song.

● Here We Go

A BBC radio show produced in Manchester by **Peter Pilbeam** and presented by Ray Peters. The Beatles made four appearances on the programme, recorded at the **Playhouse Theatre, Manchester**. The first was recorded on 11 June and transmitted on 15 June 1962 when they performed 'Ask Me Why', 'Besame Mucho' and 'A Picture Of You'.

The Beatles travelled to the gig by coach, which collected its passengers outside **Liverpool College of Art**. Apart from the Beatles there were members of their local fan club, Bill and Virginia Harry of ***Mersey Beat*** and Pete Mackey, a member of the Art College Students' Union. Pete had boarded the coach under false pretences, in the guise of a fan. His brief had been to recover the Students' Union amplifier which had been lent to the Beatles some years previously. When he did confront John Lennon and asked for its return, John told him quite bluntly that he'd sold it in Hamburg and if he had any problems he'd better discuss it with their manager, Brian Epstein. After the gig, there was hysteria outside the Playhouse and while John, Paul and George managed to board the coach, **Pete Best** wasn't so lucky and was trapped by hordes of Manchester girls. He found the ordeal terrifying as the girls tried to pull out tufts of his hair and almost ripped his mohair suit to pieces. He finally escaped, but **Jim McCartney**, Paul's father, who had also joined the coach trip, was annoyed at him and said, 'Why did you have to attract all the attention? Why didn't you call the other lads back?' Pete tried to explain that he'd been trapped and it hadn't been his fault, but Jim told him, 'I think that was very selfish of you.'

The Beatles' second appearance on the programme was recorded on 25 October and transmitted on 26 October and was the show in which Ringo Starr made his radio debut and they performed 'Love Me Do', 'A Taste Of Honey' and 'P.S. I Love You'. They also performed 'Sheila', the current chart hit by **Tommy Roe**, but their version wasn't transmitted. On 25 January 1963, a show recorded on 16 January, they performed 'Chains', 'Please Please Me' and 'Ask Me Why' although their performance of 'Three Cool Cats' wasn't transmitted.

On their final appearance on 12 March 1963, recorded on 6 March, they performed 'Misery', 'Do You Want To Know A Secret?' and 'Please Please Me'. Their version of 'I Saw Her Standing There' was not transmitted.

● Hessy, Frank

Frank Hessy's musical instrument store was where the Beatles and most of the Mersey Beat groups bought their equipment, mainly on hire purchase. Although there were other stores such as Rushworth & Dreaper and Crane's, it was mainly to Hessy's that the groups gravitated.

His first store was in Whitechapel and then he moved premises to Stanley Street, only fifty or so yards from both the **Cavern** and **NEMS'** Whitechapel shop.

Hessy's became a gathering place for musicians, with its walls displaying a range of guitars. Hessy's main salesman was **Jim Gretty**, a musician in his own right who appeared in local clubs and booked groups for promotions on the Liverpool clubland circuit. After the success of the Beatles, Hessy's began to build a 'wall of fame' of photographs of local bands.

The store is featured in a scene in the **Gerry & the Pacemakers** film *Ferry 'Cross The Mersey*.

In the mid-fifties, Frank Hessy funded a music magazine called *Frank Comments*, which was written and illustrated by Liverpool Art College student Bill Harry who also used to review local gigs and concerts in the magazine – a forerunner of ***Mersey Beat***.

Owner Frank Hessy's real name was Hesselberg and he

retired to Tel Aviv where he died in 1983, aged 74.

● Heswall Jazz Club, Barnston Women's Institute, Barnston Road, Heswall, Cheshire

The Beatles made their debut at this venue on the Wirral on Saturday, 24 March 1962. They topped the bill above the local jazz band, the Pasadena Jazzmen. Entrance was by ticket only at seven shillings and sixpence (37.5p) and the venue was open from 7.30 p.m. until 11.15 p.m. The Beatles were billed as 'Mersey Beat Poll Winners! Polydor Recording Artists! Prior to European Tour!' The European tour referred to their April visit to the **Star Club** in Hamburg.

It was a smart, new-look Beatles who appeared that night wearing their **Beno Dorn** suits for the first time.

Their next appearance at the venue took place on 30 June, headlining above the Big Three, when they were now advertised as Parlophone Recording Artistes and the last of their three appearances, all of them in 1962, took place on Tuesday, 25 September.

● Heubers, Erika and Bettina

A mother and daughter who spent a number of years involved in a legal battle with Paul McCartney concerning Erika's claim that Paul was the father of Bettina.

Erika worked in a Hamburg club and said that as a result of an affair with Paul she became pregnant. She also claimed that Paul encouraged her to have an abortion. Paul said that he didn't remember her or any affair they were reputed to have had in 1961.

Erika sued him in 1966 and although Paul didn't admit paternity, he paid up, commenting at a later date, 'It was 1966 and we were due to do a European tour. I was told that if the maintenance question wasn't settled we couldn't go to Germany. I wasn't going to sign a crazy document like this, so I didn't. Then we were actually on the plane leaving for the tour when they put the paper under my face and said if I didn't sign, the whole tour was off. They said the agreement would deny I was the father and it was a small amount anyway. I've actually seen the letter from Brian Epstein saying it would be cheaper to sign than not to go to Germany where we could make a lot of money.'

Paul paid up £2,700 and claimed that he was virtually tricked into paying for Erika's support until Bettina was eighteen. When Bettina came of age her mother instigated legal action.

From 1981 the publicity began to plague Paul because everyone acted as if the case against him had been proven – regular newspaper coverage about Bettina kept referring to her as 'Beatle Girl' and similar phrases. Paul commented, 'What I object to most is the effect on my children. It's not fair to them. Why should they suffer? She [Bettina] was on the cover of *Time* magazine in 1983 and there was a picture of her holding one of my record covers with the comment, "Dad says . . ." Not even "alleged" father. My kids had to read that. You have to put it down to life being tough at the top.'

The case was first heard at the District Court, Schoeneberg, Berlin, on 22 February 1983, and Paul appointed a German lawyer, Dr Klaus Wachs, to represent him. The Heubers were asking for maintenance of 1,500 marks per month (approximately £375) and an official declaration from Paul that he was the father. Under German law, if it were proven that Bettina was Paul's daughter, she would be entitled to inherit ten percent of any money he might leave. This would only be enforceable in Germany – but all German royalties could be frozen.

Paul had agreed to have blood and tissue samples taken and his first blood test was in February 1983. A blood test proves paternity with 90 per cent certainty. It identifies proteins and enzymes in the child which must be present in the mother's or father's blood. In March 1983, Paul was ordered to pay £180 a month interim maintenance by the German court who rejected the evidence of the blood test, which had indicated that Paul was not the father.

Paul said, 'It seems the girl's blood contains something that is not in mine or the mother's, so it must come from the third person and he is the real father.'

In April 1983 the German court finally awarded full maintenance. Paul commented, 'One thing I think is very unfair is that the judge is a woman and is pregnant herself. I am not going to ask for a different judge, I just want the whole thing settled.'

In June 1983, stories began to appear in the press with headlines such as 'Beatle Girl Strips To Raise Cash'. Bettina was then twenty and had posed naked for the sexy magazine *High Society*. There were eight pages of her wearing only leather gloves and carrying a glass guitar. It was disclosed that she received £600 for the session and said she was forced to do it because Paul refused to pay the maintenance that had been awarded by the court in pril. She'd worked as a kindergarten teacher until then nd had hoped to start in a new job in September. Her nother, now 39, commented, 'The pictures are very asteful . . . she did the session because she is broke and aul hasn't paid her any maintenance money yet.' In fact it eemed rather naïve of her to accept only £600 when the ictures were syndicated throughout the world and must ave generated tens of thousands of pounds in eproduction fees.

By the time Bettina was 22 and had settled in Berlin as hairdresser, she had lost two cases concerning her claim nd Paul had had a further blood test which once again ndicated that he was not her father. As Bettina had lost he case, she was liable to pay Paul's legal costs of 60,000. Dr Wachs advised Paul that he pay the money, ommenting: 'I advised Paul, and he agreed, for sychological reasons he should by no means enforce his ight for costs. It was my opinion that if he did, this would ive Miss Heubers another cause to make bad publicity for im.'

Hey, Bulldog

ecorded on Sunday, 11 February 1968, it was one of the ast songs the Beatles recorded before they left for India.

They hadn't originally intended to record that day as hey were in the studio to film a promo for 'Lady adonna', but decided that since they were in the studio hey might as well record a song. John has commented, Paul said we should do a real song in the studio, to save asting time. Could I whip one off? I had a few words at ome so I brought them in.'

It has also been said that there was originally no eference to 'Bulldog', but as they started recording, Paul tarted barking to make John laugh and they decided to all the number 'Hey, Bulldog'.

John had brought **Yoko** into the studio for the first time nd she said, 'I went to see the Beatles' sessions and in e beginning I thought, "Oh well". So I said to John, Why don't you do something more complex?"'. He noted, was doing "Bulldog", it was embarrassing.'

The song was included in the *Yellow Submarine* film, ut producer **Al Brodax** didn't like it and cut it from the merican prints.

The number was included on the *Yellow Submarine* oundtrack album and the *Rock 'n' Roll Music* ompilation.

Hey Good Lookin'

A number penned by country music's legendary Hank Williams and recorded by him in 1951.

The Beatles were probably influenced by the later version by their hero **Carl Perkins.** The Beatles performed the number in their stage act in 1960 and 1961, with John Lennon on lead vocals.

Hey Jude

This was the Beatles' longest single at seven minutes fifteen seconds and their first to be issued on the Apple label. It was released in America on 26 August 1968 and in Britain on 30 August, in the UK on Apple R522 and in the US on Apple 2276, with 'Revolution' on the flip.

It went to No. 1 on both sides of the Atlantic and in at least ten other countries around the world. In the UK it received the **Ivor Novello Award** for the highest number of record sales in Britain during 1968 and in America it had the longest spell of any Beatles single at No. 1 – a total of nine weeks. At over seven minutes it was the longest single to reach No. 1 up to that time. The single was re-released in 1982 as part of the batch of Beatles records celebrating their twentieth anniversary. It was also featured on *The Beatles 1967–1970* compilation and a *Hey Jude* album was issued in the States in 1970 and in Britain in 1979. The song has also been included on *The Beatles Ballads* compilation and *The Beatles Box* set in 1980.

During one of the recording sessions for the track, on Tuesday, 30 July, a film team from the National Music Council of Great Britain shot colour footage for their documentary *Music!* The 45-minute film, directed by Michael Tuchner and produced by James Archibald, was a documentary covering music in general, from classical to pop, and was shown as a second feature to *The Producers* at the Prince Charles Theatre, London, and then went on general release in Britain on 12 July 1971. The 'Hey Jude' sequence lasted for five minutes.

During a session on Tuesday, 1 August, which took place at **Trident Studios,** the orchestral accompaniment, using 36 instruments, was added.

Discussing the origin of the song, Paul says: 'It was going to be "Hey Jules" but it changed. I happened to be driving out to see Cynthia Lennon. I think it was just after John and she had broken up, and I was quite matey with Julian. He's a nice kid, Julian. And I was going out in me car just vaguely singing this song. I started to sing "Hey

Jules, don't make it bad", and then I changed it to "Hey Jude", you know, the way you do. It was just a name. It was just like "Hey Luke" or "Hey Max" or "Hey Abe" but "Hey Jude" was better.

'To one feller "Hey Jude" meant Jew, "Juden Raus – Jews Get Out". At the time we had the Apple shop, I went in one night and put whitewash on all the windows and rubbed out "Hey Jude" as a big ad. I thought it was a great thing, nothing happening in the shop, let's use the window as a big advertising thing for the record. So I did this "Hey Jude" right across the window and some feller from a little Jewish delicatessen rang up the office the next day. He said "If my sons vere vif me, I'd send von of them around to kill you. You are doing this terrible thing wif the Jewish name. What you want? Juden Raus, you trying to start the whole Nazi thing again?"'

Although Paul said that Julian Lennon was his inspiration, other people have thought it was inspired by them. Journalist Judith Simons of the *Daily Express* thought it referred to her. John Lennon believed that Paul had produced a subliminal message to him in which he blessed John's new relationship with Yoko. In September 1968, John told *Rolling Stone* magazine, 'Well when Paul first sang "Hey Jude" to me – or played me the little tape he'd made of it – I took it very personally. Ah, it's me! I said. It's me. He says, "No, it's me".' 'Hey Jude' is regarded as one of their major classics and has been recorded by hundreds of different artists, covering a wide musical spectrum, including Chet Atkins, Count Basie, Petula Clark, Bing Crosby, the Everly Brothers, Ella Fitzgerald, Stan Kenton, Joe Loss and His Orchestra, Wilson Pickett, **Elvis Presley** and Dionne Warwick.

The only version to reach the chart apart from the Beatles one was Pickett's.

'Hey Jude' received the American award for being 'The Most Performed Song' in 1968, 1969 and 1970.

● Hey Jude (The Beatles Again)

Capitol Records had been receiving orders for the proposed *Get Back* album when instructions came from Apple that the album would not be issued and all promo copies were to be recalled. Since they had received so many orders for a Beatles album, Capitol decided to produce their first collection of tracks not previously found on Beatles albums in the US. Initially the collection was called *The Beatles Again* and was given the catalogue number SO-385. Then it was decided to call the album *Hey Jude* and the photograph from the reverse of the album was placed on the cover and it was issued on Apple SW 385 on 26 February 1970. The album was a massive seller and reached No. 1 in *Record World* and No. 2 in *Cash Box* and *Billboard*.

The tracks were, Side One: 'Can't Buy Me Love', 'I Should Have Known Better', 'Paperback Writer', 'Rain' 'Lady Madonna', 'Revolution'. Side Two: 'Hey Jude', 'Old Brown Shoe', 'Don't Let Me Down' and 'The Ballad O John And Yoko'.

● Hey, Man

Title of a proposed stage musical based around the daily life in the Apple building. The idea had first been mooted by Mike Connor, head of the Apple office in Los Angeles.

It was agreed that George Harrison would write the music and **Derek Taylor** would provide the lyrics. Both George and John Lennon encouraged Derek in the project and there was talk of the musical opening at New York's Shubert Theatre.

Taylor told the music paper *Disc*: 'For everyone life is a mixture of fact and fiction – often this office is like *Alice In Wonderland* – and since Apple is constantly surrounded and involved in music, it seemed a natural subject to base a musical around.'

However, Derek found that he was unable to produce lyrics and the project was dropped.

● Highlight

A BBC Overseas Service radio programme. Pau McCartney was interviewed for the show on 14 July 196 and the interview was transmitted on 18 July. It was als transmitted on the BBC Home Service on 11 Septembe under the title 'A Beatle's Eye View'.

● High Park Farm, Nr Machrihanish, Argyllshire, Scotland

At the height of their romance, **Jane Asher** recommende to Paul that he invest in a farm which they could use as retreat and in June 1966 they went to view High Par Farm in Scotland.

Farmer's wife Janet Brown commented, 'Our farm ha been up for sale for a while now but what a surprise m husband and I had when we saw the famous pair – Pau told me that it had always been his ambition to own a far n Scotland.' Paul purchased the farm and Jane helped im furnish it. The farm comprised 183 acres near Iachrihanish, the nearest town being Campbeltown.

The affair with Jane over, Paul continued to enjoy elaxing at the faraway retreat, which was greeted with qual enthusiasm by **Linda** when the couple were married.

The area was too bleak and hilly for cows, so Paul ought sheep, almost 200 of them. However, he couldn't ear the thought of killing them and rarely sent any to arket, allowing them to breed. For some time Paul heared the sheep himself with some hand shears, ending the wool to the Wool Marketing Board. The ouple also grew lots of vegetables on the farm and abled horses with names such as Drake's Drum, Honor nd Cinnamon, along with ponies such as Coconut, ookie and Sugarfoot.

Paul took to farm life and Linda once bought him a actor as a Christmas present.

● Hilton Hotel, *Park Lane, London W1*

February 1967 **Pattie Harrison** had attended regular eetings of the Spiritual Regeneration Movement and had een given her own 'mantra', a secret word to chant. eorge was also beginning to show an interest in spiritual atters at the time. A girl friend told Pattie about ranscendental Meditation and she attended a lecture at **axton Hall**. The Maharishi wasn't at that particular eeting, but Pattie joined.

In August, George and Pattie noticed advertisements in e newspapers announcing that the **Maharishi Mahesh ogi** would be at the Hilton Hotel giving a lecture on TM. eorge suggested that they attend and also contacted the her members of the Beatles.

On Thursday evening, 24 August 1967, George, Pattie, ul, **Jane Asher** and John and **Cynthia** attended the cture which was held in the ballroom of the Hilton and st 35p entrance at the door. (Ringo was with **Maureen** Queen Charlotte's Hospital as she'd given birth to Jason e days previously.) Following the lecture, the Beatles ked for and received a private audience with the aharishi, during which he suggested that they all attend gathering he'd arranged at the University College of ngor during the coming weekend.

Hines, *Iain*

keyboards player who appeared with the **Jets**, the first British band to appear in Hamburg. Other members of the group included **Tony Sheridan** (guitar/vocals), Del Ward (vocals), Ricky Richards (rhythm), Colin Milander (bass), and Pete Wharton (rhythm).

Iain met **Bruno Koschmider** in the 2 I's coffee club in Soho, London, where the German promoter was seeking British rock 'n' roll bands. Although he didn't have a group at the time, Iain convinced Koschmider that he had and made a name up on the spot – the Jets. Koschmider immediately booked the group to appear in Hamburg and Iain gathered his musician friends who were present in the 2 I's to undertake the booking.

His reminiscences of those times were published in *Fiesta* magazine under the title 'Hamburg Rock' and included many stories concerning the Beatles. Iain and Paul regularly double-dated two German blondes. Paul's girlfriend was a barmaid called Liane who, Iain related, eventually ended up in the Herbertstrasse (the infamous 'street of windows').

Iain Hines contributed articles on the Beatles in Hamburg to the *Beatles Monthly* magazine in the sixties and seventies.

● Hippodrome Theatre, *Hurst Street, Birmingham*

The Beatles first appeared at the Hippodrome as part of the **Tommy Roe/Chris Montez** tour on 10 March 1963. After the show John came down with a heavy cold and had to miss the next three gigs, which went ahead with three Beatles only.

When the Beatles next appeared at the theatre on 10 November 1963 their popularity in Britain had increased to such an extent that plans had to be made to escort them in and out of the Hippodrome through the massive throng of fans.

'Operation Beatles' was the plan and the group were first taken to the local Digbeth Police Station where they drank hot cups of tea and signed autographs while a special van was prepared. They were driven to the theatre and the van drew up quickly outside the stage door. All four members of the Beatles were wearing police helmets and they jumped out of the van and briefly posed for photographers, standing among a group of policemen, before being smuggled into the theatre. John Lennon later quipped, 'Me in a copper's hat. No one will ever believe this.'

● Hippodrome Theatre, Middle Street, Brighton, Sussex

A hat-trick of appearances by the Beatles at this venue in the southern seaside resort. They made their debut there on 2 June 1963 during their tour with **Roy Orbison**.

Their second appearance was on 12 July 1964, the first British gig following their return from their Australian tour. Oddly enough, **Jimmy Nicol** and his group the Shubdubs were on the bill this night, although there was no reunion with the drummer who had recently deputized for Ringo.

The Beatles' third and final appearance at the theatre took place on 25 October 1964.

● Hippodrome Theatre, Hyde Road, Ardwick Green, Manchester

The theatre where Johnny & the Moondogs travelled to appear in the finals of the 'Star Search' talent contest, organized by Carroll Levis and offering the winners a brief spot on his television show.

The date was 15 November 1959 and this was the first time the group had ever travelled outside Merseyside for a performance and they didn't even have enough money to enable them to stay overnight in Manchester, resulting in them leaving the theatre before the end of the show in order to catch the last train back to Liverpool.

● Hippopotamus Club

Nightclub in New York where, on 20 December 1974, George Harrison hosted a party at the end of his American 'Dark Horse' tour. Among the guests were Ringo's wife **Maureen,** John and **Yoko** and Alice Cooper.

● Hippy Hippy Shake, The

Number composed and recorded by Chan Romero in 1959 which became very popular with Mersey Beat groups. The **Swinging Bluejeans** took their version to No. 2 in the British charts and No. 24 in the American.

Paul took lead vocals on the Beatles' version of the number which is captured on *The Beatles Live! At the Star Club In Hamburg: 1962* album. The group also recorded it on two BBC **'Saturday Club'** and three **'Pop Go The Beatles'** radio shows.

● Hofer, Walter

The Attorney who represented Brian Epstein and **NEMS** in America.

It was **Dick James** who recommended Hofer to Epstei and when Brian visited New York, Hofer invited him to hi offices in West 57th Street and also held a cocktail part in his honour. Brian hired Hofer, although he considere his fees to be extravagant.

It was Hofer's office which received notices that Bria was obliged to make an appearance in a New York court i the **Seltaeb** case.

In American civil cases the contesting parties have th right to examine each other, with sworn testimony before trial. Hofer mentioned the notices to Epstein, but didn stress their urgency. As a result, since Brian hadn responded to the legal notices to appear, the Suprem court granted a judgment against Epstein, the Beatles an NEMS for default. It cost Brian a great deal of money sort the problem out.

Hofer died in November 1984.

Hoffmann, Dezo

Slovakian-born photographer who began his career as cinematographer, covering Mussolini's invasion Abyssinia and the Spanish Civil War.

Dezo arrived in England in 1940 as a member of th Czech Army and became one of the first members of th Crown Unit with a brief to obtain footage in all maj theatres of war. During the Allied landings he wa wounded twice and eventually discharged from the army 1945.

Dezo Hoffman with Beatles publicist Tony Barrow.

He then moved to Leicester where he married. The ›ouple had two children before Dezo decided to move to ₋ondon where he established himself as a show business photographer, photographing stars such as Marilyn Monroe, Charlie Chaplin, **Marlene Dietrich**, Frank Sinatra and Louis Armstrong.

In 1955 he joined *Record Mirror*, the weekly show business newspaper. In 1962 he received a letter from a eader in Liverpool who waxed enthusiastically about a roup called the Beatles. Dezo became interested in this elatively unknown band and began taking photographs – which was to result in him taking more photographs of the Beatles than any other photographer. He photographed heir first **Abbey Road** audition with George Martin in June 1962, and travelled to Liverpool to take numerous xclusive shots in April 1963, including pictures of them t their homes, at the **Cavern,** in **Sefton Park** and at heir hairdressers. Until he had a dispute with John ennon on the set of *A Hard Day's Night* over a hotograph which had been printed in *Tit Bits* magazine, e was present covering almost every major event in their areer. Following the argument he continued taking shots f the Beatles, but not so frequently.

His collection of Beatles photographs are the most omplete visual/photographic documentation of their areer during 1963–1964 in existence, and the thousands f shots include them performing at Stowe School, the **iverpool Empire**, the **Albert Hall**, at BBC radio ecordings, television shows, during their trips to Paris and merica, appearances at **Twickenham Studios**, during heir Christmas Show at the **Hammersmith Odeon** and heir Royal Variety performance.

In addition to his photographs appearing in ublications throughout the world, there have also been a umber of books of his work printed. They include: *The eatles* (Shinko Music, 1975), *With The Beatles* (Omnibus ress, 1982), *The Beatles Conquer America* (Omnibus ress, 1984) and *John Lennon* (Columbus Books, 1985).

In the early seventies, Dezo and John met up at the **laza Hotel** in New York and settled their differences.

He died in 1986.

Holder, Owen

criptwriter whose most successful script was for the film, *Funny Thing Happened On The Way To The Forum.*

In 1966 he proposed a script for the Beatles' third film, which he called 'Shades Of A Personality'. Reporting on the story, the ***New Musical Express*** commented that it would: 'focus on one member of the group (yet to be chosen) who will supposedly have a split personality with four different sides to his character. Besides his real self he will imagine himself in turn as three other people. The three other Beatles.'

The film was to be shot in Malaga, Spain, in September 1967 with Michelangelo Antonioni directing. The *NME* was later to announce: 'John Lennon will play the part of the man himself, while the three other Beatles will portray each of the faces of his split personality – "the dreamer", the "human being" and the man as perceived by the outside world.'

Producer Walter Shenson regarded Holder's script as being dull and he passed it over to playwright **Joe Orton** to see if he could brighten it up. Orton commented: 'Basically it [the idea] is that there aren't four young men. Just four aspects of one man. Sounds dreary, but as I thought about it I realized what wonderful opportunities it would give.'

Orton developed the idea and came out eventually with a script which was totally different from the original, which he called 'Up Against It'.

Hold Me Tight

A Paul McCartney composition which the Beatles had first begun performing in 1961. The group recorded it for their *Please Please Me* album on Monday, 11 February 1963, but it was left off the album and that particular tape was lost. The group re-recorded the number on Thursday, 12 September 1963, and it was included on the *With The Beatles* album and the American release *Meet The Beatles*.

'Hold Me Tight' was the rare instance of a number being rejected for one Beatles album, but eventually placed on another.

● Hollies, The

A Manchester band who became one of the most popular groups in the beat boom and had 31 chart hits between the years 1963–1988, more hits than any other British band, including the Beatles.

It has been suggested that founder members Allan Clarke and Graham Nash, using the name Rikki & Dane, won the heat of the Carroll Levis 'Discoveries' show at the **Liverpool Empire** in October 1959 in which Johnny &

the Moondogs came third. Certainly, as a duo, Allan and Graham used several names, including the Two Tones and the Deltas, before linking with Tony Hicks (lead guitar), Eric Haydock (bass guitar) and Don Rathbone (drums) to form the vocal/harmony outfit, the Hollies.

They were at one time managed by **Shane Fenton** and Fenton's drummer Bobby Elliott replaced Rathbone. The group, like several other Manchester bands, began to travel to Liverpool to appear at the **Cavern** where they soon began to earn the tag 'Manchester's Beatles'. They were to comment to ***Mersey Beat*** about this at the time: 'Our sound is entirely different and the comparison has probably been made because we wear leather pants. The reason why we wear leather is because it's more serviceable and you can do anything with leather and it still stays the same. If you analyse the Beatles sound you will find it's entirely different from ours – and we hope people will stop associating our name with theirs.'

The group had their first hit in May 1963 with '(Ain't It) Just Like Me' and continued to have a stream of hits for several years, including 'Searchin'', 'Stay', 'Just One Look', 'Here I Go Again', 'Yes I Will', 'I'm Alive' and 'Look Through Any Window'.

The Hollies covered the George Harrison composition 'If I Needed Someone' from the *Rubber Soul* album. It was issued on Parlophone R5392 and entered the charts in December 1965. Unfortunately, George Harrison made uncomplimentary comments about the single and said it was 'rubbish'. He also said, 'They've spoilt it. The Hollies are alright musically, but the way they do their records they sound like session men who've just got together in a studio without ever seeing each other before.'

Graham Nash was furious and said, 'Not only do these comments disappoint and hurt us, but we are sick of everything the Beatles say or do being taken as law. The thing that hurt us most was George Harrison's knock at us as musicians. And I would like to ask this: If we have made such a disgusting mess of his brain child song, will he give all the royalties from our record to charity?'

George's comments seemed to have affected the record sales and the disc only reached No. 20 in the charts, their previous release 'Look Through Any Window' having reached No. 4 and their next single 'I Can't Let Go' reaching No. 2.

Graham was to leave the band and settle in America where he became part of the successful Crosby, Stills & Nash group. He was replaced in the Hollies b Liverpudlian Terry Sylvester, former member of th **Escorts** and **Swinging Bluejeans**.

The group continued to have hits during the seventie and embarked on an anniversary tour of Britain in 1986 and later returned to the top of the charts with a re-releas of one of their hits of 1969, 'He Ain't Heavy, He's M Brother'.

● Holly, Buddy

One of rock 'n' roll's greatest legends, who died in an ai crash, along with Ritchie Valens and the Big Bopper, on February 1959.

He was a seminal influence on the Beatles and th group played several of his numbers on their early gig and recorded his 'Words Of Love' and 'Crying, Waiting Hoping'. When they appeared on the Carroll Levis taler show in Liverpool during their early career they performe two of Holly's numbers, 'Think It Over' and 'It's So Easy'.

Although George Harrison was quoted as saying tha the name Beatles was inspired by the motorcycle gan 'The Beetles' led by Lee Marvin in *The Wild One*, it i

Buddy Holly – a great influence on the music of the Quarry Men. (MCA Records)

generally acknowledged that the group chose the title when seeking a similar name to that of Holly's backing group, the Crickets. **Stuart Sutcliffe** is said to have thought of the name Beetles and John Lennon replaced one of the 'e's' with an 'a'.

(Incidentally, *The Wild One* was banned in Britain for more than a decade after it was made, therefore the Beatles could not have seen it before choosing a name.)

Holly's manager, Norman Petty, was to present Paul McCartney with the cufflinks Holly was wearing at the time of his death.

Paul McCartney was the major Holly fan and his MPL Communications managed to purchase the Buddy Holly music catalogue of approximately 38 Holly compositions. From 1976 Paul began to run an annual 'Buddy Holly Week' on the anniversary of the singer's birth. Holly's widow, Maria Elana, commented: 'Paul told me that Buddy had more influence on his early songwriting than any other singer. Paul was very gracious and I appreciated what he had to say.'

John Lennon was to pay his own tribute to Holly on his 1975 album *Rock 'n' Roll*, which featured the track 'Peggy Sue'. When discussing his initial interest in music, John commented: 'I started off with a banjo at fifteen which my mother taught me to play. My first guitar cost ten pounds. It was one of those advertised in the paper you sent away for. **Julia** got it for me. I remember it had a label on the inside which said, "Guaranteed Not to Split". My mother used to say she could play any stringed instrument there was, and she really did teach me quite a lot. The first tune I ever learned to play was "That'll Be The Day" by Buddy Holly.'

Hollywood Bowl, The, *Los Angeles, California*

On Sunday, 23 August 1964, the Beatles became the first rock 'n' roll act to perform at the prestigious, open-air venue in the Hollywood hills which had previously been the setting for symphony concerts. All 18,700 seats were sold and thousands of fans roamed outside the Bowl in the hills, with further fans climbing onto trees.

Backstage the group were visited by Lauren Bacall and they went on stage at 9.30 p.m. for a 35-minute show, with John Lennon setting the scene by announcing, 'Welcome to you in the trees.'

There was an element of drama that night with the fervour of so many fans who couldn't get into the Bowl – and one fan gave birth to a son in the car-park.

Capitol Records recorded the show and the group rushed off stage at 10.05 p.m. and were spirited away in a limousine to a rented mansion where a private party had been arranged. Among the guests were Joan Baez and film starlet Peggy Lipton.

The Beatles returned to the Hollywood Bowl for two further concerts the following year, on 29 and 30 August. Their second concert was also recorded by Capitol Records. The album of the Hollywood Bowl concerts was not released until almost thirteen years later.

Holyoake Hall, *Smithdown Road, Liverpool L15*

A building originally erected on behalf of the Co-operative Society at the beginning of the century and situated only a few hundred yards away from Penny Lane. The entire first floor was used as a ballroom from the thirties. The **Quarry Men** made a few appearances here during 1957 and 1958 when the venue booked skiffle groups. The Beatles only appeared at the venue twice when promoter Wally Hill booked them on 15 July and 22 July 1961.

Many of the top Liverpool bands appeared regularly at the venue in the early sixties, where they reported that the large hall was ideal for dances, but the 'bouncers' proved to be over-zealous and groups were often arguing with them over their rough treatment of fans.

● Honey Don't

A **Carl Perkins** composition which was the flipside of his million-seller 'Blue Suede Shoes' in 1956. The Beatles included the number in their repertoire in 1962 with John on lead vocals. From August 1963 it provided a vocal spot for Ringo and he continued to perform it until late in 1964.

It was Ringo who sang the number when the Beatles recorded it on Monday, 26 October 1964, for the *Beatles For Sale* album. It was also included on the American *4 By The Beatles* EP and *Beatles '65* album.

● Honeymoon Song, The

A number composed by Greek musician Theodorakis and featured in the 1959 film *Honeymoon*.

There were several versions of the tune, the most notable being an instrumental by Manuel and the Music of the Mountains. There was also a French-language version by Petula Clark.

The Beatles began performing the song on stage in 1961 with Paul on lead vocals. They recorded it on the BBC radio show **'Pop Go The Beatles'** on 16 July and it was broadcast on 6 August 1963 and when **Apple Records** was launched several years later, Paul produced a version by **Mary Hopkin**.

● Honey Pie

Number penned by Paul which was included on *The Beatles* double album. Paul played piano and sang solo while John played electric guitar and George Harrison played bass. It was recorded at Trident Studios, London, on 1 October 1968 and a few days later George Martin recorded several musicians for a brass backing sound which he had scored. They were Dennis Walton, Ronald Chamberlain, Jim Chester, Rex Morris and Harry Klein on saxophones and Raymond Newman and David Smith on clarinets.

Commenting on the number in a **Radio Luxembourg** interview, Paul said, 'My Dad's always played fruity old songs like this, and I like them. I would have liked to have been a **1920s writer** because I like that top hat and tails thing.'

● Hopkin, Mary

A young, blonde folk singer, born in Pontardawe, Wales, on 3 May 1950, who came to the attention of Paul McCartney when **Twiggy** called him after spotting Mary on the popular TV talent show 'Opportunity Knocks', on which she appeared three times. Paul contacted Mary and signed her to Apple, deciding to produce her first single himself. He chose the song 'Those Were The Days', a number he had liked for several years and had once suggested that the **Moody Blues** record. It was among the first of the Apple releases and sold five million copies worldwide after being released in Britain on 30 August 1968 on Apple 2 and in America on 26 August on Apple 1801.

Mary also sang the number in Italian, French, Spanish and German. The hits on the Continent led to Paul recording her singing two more numbers in Italian, *'Quelli Erano Giorni'* and *'Lontano Dagli Occhi'*, and another song in French, *'Prince En Avignon'*.

'Those Were The Days' hit the No. 1 spot in Britain and reached No. 2 in America.

Paul participated in her early promotion and turned up with **Linda** at Mary's first press reception at London's Post Office Tower, where **Donovan** performed. Jimi Hendrix was also a guest. Paul also appeared in 'A Day In The Life Of Mary Hopkin', a special insert in 'Magpie', the ITV children's programme, which was filmed at the Apple office.

Mary's second Apple single 'Goodbye' was written and produced by Paul and reached No. 2 in Britain and No. 13 in America.

Paul also produced her album *Postcard*, which contained three songs by Donovan on which Paul played guitar. He also designed the cover of her album, which was released in Britain on 21 February 1969 on Apple Sapcor 5 and in America on 3 March 1969.

Paul also produced her version of *'Que Sera Sera'* issued in France on 19 September 1969 on Apple 16 and in America on 15 June 1970 on Apple 1823.

Dissatisfied with the managers offered to her by Apple, Mary chose her sister Carol to be her manager. Within a year her relations with Apple became strained and her Apple material was produced initially by Mickie Most and later by Tony Visconti, whom she married. The couple had a daughter, Jessica. Mary left Apple in 1972.

● Hot Chocolate

A popular British band who had a string of chart hits spreading over two decades and who became the only group to have had a hit in the British charts in every year of the seventies.

When singer Errol Brown teamed up with Tony Wilson the two of them decided they'd like to make their deb

Hot Chocolate. (Rak Records)

recording 'Give Peace A Chance'. Since they wanted to make some alterations to the lyrics they had to seek the permission of the songwriters and sent a tape to Apple.

John Lennon arranged to see them and suggested that Apple could release the disc. As they had no group name at the time, one of Apple's press officers, **Mavis Smith**, suggested they call themselves the Hot Chocolate Band. John Lennon recommended the name, although they cut it to Hot Chocolate after they made their recording debut with 'Give Peace A Chance', coupled with 'Living Without Tomorrow'. The single was issued in Britain on Apple 18 on 10 October 1969 and in America on Apple 1812 on 17 October, although it failed to make the charts.

Following that release they joined Mickie Most's Rak Records and have had a large number of hits, including 'Brother Louie', 'Emma', 'You Sexy Thing', 'Every One's A Winner' and 'No Doubt About It'.

● Hound Dog

An **Elvis Presley** chart topper of 1956. A Jerry Leiber/Mike Stoller song which the **Quarry Men** included in their repertoire in 1957 with John Lennon on vocals. It was also included in the Beatles' repertoire until 1961.

● How Do You Do It?

A number which songwriter **Mitch Murray** had originally written for singer Adam Faith. Faith didn't record the song and Murray took it along to George Martin's assistant, Ron Richards. Richards liked the number and called **Dick James,** who snapped up the publishing rights. Richards retained the acetate for a while but was unsure whom to place the song with. When George Martin was looking for material for the Beatles, Richards played him the acetate and Martin decided the Beatles should record the number and sent a copy up to Liverpool.

Martin was pleased with the number and claimed that it would turn the Beatles into a household name. He was therefore quite upset when John and Paul showed no interest in the song and said that they'd prefer to record their own material. Martin ticked them off and told them, 'When you can write material as good as this, then I'll record it. But right now we're going to record this.'

The session took place on Tuesday, 4 September 1962, and the Beatles didn't exactly put their heart into the recording. On the same day they recorded 'Love Me Do'. Martin wasn't pleased with the sound of that day's recording session and a new one was arranged for Tuesday, 11 September, although they didn't record 'How Do You Do It' this time.

Following 'Love Me Do', the Beatles played Martin their version of 'Please Please Me', which had been rearranged on Martin's advice, and it was decided to issue the number as their next single, with Martin acknowledging that, as far as the Beatles were concerned, it was a better choice for them.

His faith in 'How Do You Do It' was vindicated when he recorded Epstein's second Liverpool band, **Gerry & the Pacemakers**. Their version of 'How Do You Do It' was issued on Columbia DB 4987 on 14 March 1963 and was to reach the No. 1 position where it remained for four weeks.

Arguably, 'How Do You Do It' gave Gerry & the Pacemakers the honour of being the first Mersey Beat group to top the British charts. 'Please Please Me' had seen the Beatles reach No. 1 in the ***New Musical Express***, *Melody Maker* and *Disc* charts but they only reached No. 2 in the *Record Retailer/Record Mirror* charts. As the *Record Retailer* chart was to include Top 50 placings and because it was later changed to *Music Week* and carried the official chart compiled by the British Market Research Bureau, researchers generally use the Record Retailer chart placings in their statistics. To be quite fair, the most important British chart in 1963 was the *New Musical Express* chart, which was also printed in some national newspapers – and the chart placings in the BBC TV show **'Top Of The Pops'** were assembled from the placings in *New Musical Express, Melody Maker* and *Disc* – and 'Please Please Me' had topped all those charts.

● Howarth, Jann

An American sculptress who married the British painter **Peter Blake.** When Blake was commissioned to work on the *Sgt Pepper's Lonely Hearts Club Band* tableau, she worked on the project with him. The two artists also designed the special colour-card contained inside the sleeve which featured a set of army stripes, badges and a moustache, which could be used as cut-outs. The card also contained a painting of Sgt Pepper and a Beatles photograph. The couple separated in 1979.

● Howes, Arthur

One of the major British promoters of the sixties who was

the main tour operator for the Beatles between the years 1964 and 1966.

Howes was the biggest presenter of 'pop package shows', in which a handful of recording artists, with a current or recent hit in the charts, would appear on a countrywide tour, generally on the ABC, Gaumont or Odeon Cinema circuits.

In November 1962 Brian Epstein tracked down Howes' phone number and called him at his home in Peterborough one Saturday afternoon. Howes agreed to try out the Beatles to see how they would go down on a theatre tour and put them on a bill topped by **Frank Ifield** at the **Embassy Cinema, Peterborough** on 2 December. They cancelled a **Cavern** booking and set off for the Northamptonshire venue, but their appearance didn't receive a good response from the audience. To his credit, Howes saw potential in the band and agreed to book them as a support on the bill on his forthcoming **Helen Shapiro** tour for £80 per week. They received the same amount for the second tour he billed them on, with **Tommy Roe** and **Chris Montez**. Howes featured them on a third tour that year, but this time as bill toppers on an autumn tour which commenced on 1 November.

Apart from the **Roy Orbison** tour and some short mini-tours, all the Beatles' succeeding British tours were organized by Arthur Howes.

Howes became a group manager when he took over the management of **Rory Storm & the Hurricanes**, as a favour to Brian Epstein. Howes died in London on 12 February 1987 at the age of 63.

● Hullabaloo

An American coast-to-coast television series, produced by Jack Good, in which Brian Epstein had a five-minute spot as host and interviewer. During the Epstein segments of the shows, recorded at Shepperton Studios, Brian introduced and interviewed **Gerry & the Pacemakers**, **Marianne Faithfull**, **Freddie & the Dreamers** and **Andrew Oldham.**

● Hully Gully

A number recorded by the Olympics in 1959. The Beatles included it in their repertoire in 1960. The group never recorded the number and although there is a version of 'Hully Gully' on one of the later releases of the **Star Club** albums, the track is not by the Beatles.

● Hulme Hall, Bolton Road, Port Sunlight, Cheshire

A small hall with a capacity of 450, across the River Mersey from Liverpool in a pleasant town which Viscount Leverhulme had built for his employees in 1888.

The Beatles appeared at the venue four times in 1962. They were booked on their debut appearance there on 7 July for a local golf club dance. Their second appearance on 18 August saw Ringo make his first public appearance with the group, following two hours of rehearsal. They were booked for a dance promoted by the Horticultural Society and the society also booked them to appear on 6 October. Their final appearance at the hall took place on 27

Ringo Starr making his debut in Hulme Hall as a member of the Beatles. (*Mersey Beat* Archives)

)ctober at a dance organized by the Recreational)rganization. It was prior to their performance that they vere interviewed by **Monty Lister** for his radio shows roadcast at the Cleaver and Clatterbridge Hospitals. This vas the first radio interview the Beatles had and Lister was ccompanied by two friends, Malcolm Threadgill and 'eter Smethurst, who also took part in the interview, which vas broadcast to the Wirral hospitals the next day.

Huntley, Ted

A link in the chain of events leading to the Beatles' ecording contract in 1962.

Ted was working at the HMV shop in Oxford Street, ondon, in charge of cutting discs for customers. When Brian Epstein came into the shop to have acetates made of ome Beatles numbers, Ted, a former engineer at **EMI** tudios, was impressed by the group's sound: something hich several A&R men with different record companies ad not been. After a chat with Brian he discovered that ne group did not have a publishing contract so he phoned **id Coleman** of EMI's publishing company, Ardmore and Beechwood, who were in the same building, and ecommended that he meet Brian. Sid was also impressed ith the material and called George Martin's office to rrange a meeting between Epstein and the Parlophone &R man.

Huntley later left EMI to run a hotel in Jersey in the hannel Isles.

Hutchinson, Johnny

egarded as one of Liverpool's top drummers in the Mersey Beat era, the Maltese-born Johnny was a member f Cass & the Cassanovas, who became the Big Three hen Brian Casser left the group. Johnny sat in with the **ilver Beetles** at their **Larry Parnes** audition when their rummer **Tommy Moore** turned up late.

Johnny made his debut on drums at the age of 18 at the orinthian Club with Cass & the Cassanovas and also did e occasional gig with a modern jazz band. When the oup became the Big Three, Johnny turned down a two-ear contract with Johnny Kidd & the Pirates to remain ith them.

According to **Cilla Black,** when **Pete Best** was cked from the Beatles, Hutchinson was first choice as s replacement. Then the Beatles had second thoughts ecause of his belligerency and felt they needed a drummer with a more subordinate personality and chose Ringo. In the few dates between Best's departure and Ringo's joining, Hutchinson played drums with the band. It has also been suggested that Epstein, aware that Hutchinson was regarded as Liverpool's top drummer, offered him the Beatles seat, but he turned it down.

Epstein was to sign up his group, the Big Three, and they had some minor hits with 'Some Other Guy' and 'By The Way', but they disagreed with Brian's style of management and convinced him that he should release them from their contract. There were various line-up changes, with Hutchinson being the only consistent member, but the group disbanded in the mid-sixties.

Johnny Hutchinson – he preferred the drum seat with the Big Three to that with the Beatles. (Cavern Mecca)

● Huyton Parish Church Cemetery, *Stanley Road, Huyton, Liverpool L36*

Final resting place of the Beatles' original bass guitarist **Stuart Sutcliffe** whose grave is No. 552 in the 1939 section of the cemetery.

Stuart had died of a cerebral haemorrhage on 10 April 1962 and his body was flown back to Liverpool to be buried the same week as the Beatles went to Hamburg.

● I Am The Walrus

A bizarre yet fascinating surrealistic composition from John Lennon, featured in the *Magical Mystery Tour* film. The 'I Am The Walrus' sequence was shot in West Mallin, Kent, in September 1967.

Recording began on Tuesday, 5 September 1967, four days after the death of Brian Epstein. On Wednesday, 27 September, there were various overdubs onto the track using sixteen musicians and sixteen singers. The musicians were Sidney Sax, Jack Rothstein, Ralph Elman, Andrew McGee, Jack Greene, Louis Stevens, John Jezzard and Jack Richards. On cellos were Lionel Ross, Eldon Fox, Bram Martin and Terry Weil. Gordon Lewin played clarinet and Neil Sanders, Tony Tunstall and Morris Miller were on horns. The voices were provided by the Mike Sammes Singers: Peggie Allen, Wendy Horan, Pat Whitmore, Jill Utting, June Day, Sylvia King, Irene King, G. Mallen, Fred Lucas, Mike Redway, John O'Neill, F. Dachtler, Allan Grant, D. Griffiths, J. Smith and J. Fraser. On Friday, 29 September 1967, a radio was tuned in to the BBC's Third Programme and some lines from a production of *The Tragedy Of King Lear* were included on the track.

The number was included on the *Magical Mystery Tour* double EP release in Britain, the American album of *Magical Mystery Tour* and a later British album release of *Magical Mystery Tour*. It was also issued as the flipside of 'Hello Goodbye' in both Britain and America and was featured on the compilations *The Beatles 1967–1970*, *Reel Music* and the American *The Beatles Rarities*.

John was said to have been inspired to compose some of the verses after hearing the sound of a police siren in the distance while sitting at his home in Weybridge.

The song was banned by the BBC because John mentions 'knickers' in the lyrics, which caused him to comment: 'It always seems to happen now that people misinterpret what we write or say. We're happy with the words and I don't see how they can offend anyone.'

● I Call Your Name

A song written by John, who commented, 'I like this one. I wrote it very early on when I was in Liverpool, and added the middle eight when we came down to London.'

They gave the number to **Billy J. Kramer** who included it as the flipside of another Lennon & McCartney song, 'Bad To Me', on his second single. It was issued in Britain on Parlophone R5049 on 26 July 1963 where it reached No. 1, losing its place a few weeks later to the Beatles' 'She Loves You'. In America it was issued on Liberty 55626 on 23 September 1964 and rose to No. 9.

When the Beatles came under pressure to produce a number of songs for a new album, they dug out the number and recorded it themselves on 1 March 1964. As it turned out, it wasn't required for an album, but they included it on their EP *Long Tall Sally*, which was released in June 1964. The Beatles also performed the number on the radio show **'Saturday Club'** on 4 April 1964.

The Beatles version was included on their compilations *Rock 'n' Roll Music* and *Rarities* and in America on *The Beatles Second Album*. It was also used on the *Beatles Box* and *The Beatles Collection* sets.

● I Don't Want To See You Again

The third Paul McCartney composition to be recorded by **Peter & Gordon.** The Beatles never recorded the number, although a demo disc may have been prepared for the duo's recording manager Norman Newall.

This was the least successful of the Lennon & McCartney numbers to be given to Peter & Gordon and didn't provide them with a British chart hit, although it reached No. 16 in America. It was issued in Britain on Columbia DB 7356 on 11 September 1964 and in America on **Capitol** 5272 on 21 September 1964.

● I Don't Want To Spoil The Party

A John Lennon composition featured on the *Beatles For Sale* album which caused John to comment: 'That was ery personal one of mine. In the early days I wrote less aterial than Paul because he was more competent on uitar than I. He taught me quite a lot of guitar really.'

Recording began on Tuesday, 29 September 1964, and n addition to appearing on *Beatles For Sale*, the track was ncluded on the *Beatles For Sale (No. 2)* EP. In America it urfaced as the flipside of the single 'Eight Days A Week', ssued on 15 February 1965, and on **Capitol**'s *Beatles VI* lbum.

I Feel Fine

number which John penned during a recording session. he group performed the song on their radio shows **'Top ear'** and **'Saturday Club'** and it was issued as a single ith 'She's A Woman' on the flip. It was issued in Britain n Parlophone R5200 on 27 November 1964 and hit the o. 1 spot, where it remained for six weeks. It was issued America on **Capitol** 5327 on 23 November 1964 and so reached No. 1, selling a million copies within the first eek.

The Beatles used amplifier feedback on the number for e first time and it was a song they performed live on a umber of occasions, including their 1964 Christmas ows and on tours in 1964 and 1965.

John often experimented with tape recorders at his nall studio in **Kenwood** and may have developed the ea of the song's opening with a single note of feedback ere. Discussing the song with David Sheff in a *Playboy* terview, John told him, 'That's me, including the guitar k with the first feedback ever recorded. I defy anyone to nd an earlier record – unless it is some old blues number om the twenties – with feedback on it.'

'I Feel Fine' was the Beatles' sixth No. 1 hit in both ritain and America and the American radio plays began efore the official promotion was planned when KRLA in os Angeles began airing a copy it had obtained on 6 ovember, playing the song every hour. The station's ogramme director Reb Foster commented on his scoop to *llboard* magazine, saying, 'We've received calls from orida, New York, St Louis, Denver and Cleveland ations, offering us money and queries about where we cked up the single.'

The number was included on the compilations *A ollection Of Beatles Oldies (But Goldies)*, *The Beatles 962–1966* and *20 Greatest Hits*. It was also found on the merican album *Beatles '65* and the *Beatles Box* set.

● Ifield, Frank

Singer born in Coventry in 1937 who went to live in Australia from 1946 to 1959. When the Beatles first entered the charts with 'Love Me Do', Ifield's 'Wayward Wind' was in the Top Five. The singer had fifteen records in the British charts between 1960 and 1966, including 'I Remember You', 'Lovesick Blues' and 'Confessin''.

When promoter **Arthur Howes** agreed to give the Beatles a try-out, he placed them on a bill with Ifield at the Embassy Cinema, Peterborough, on 2 December 1962.

The reception to the Beatles was poor, obviously due to the type of audience attracted to top-of-the-bill singer Ifield. The report in the local newspaper read: 'It is easy to see why Frank Ifield has been so popular in this country. No pseudo American accent; no sulky Presley look. Frank Ifield is himself and he flashed many a happy smile as he breezed through a confident performance at the Embassy on Sunday.

'As expected his well-known songs "I Remember You", "Lovesick Blues" and "She Taught Me How To Yodel" were sung, in addition to "Lonesome Me" and "Lucky Devil".

'Ifield came well up to expectations, but the supporting artists failed to please, just as a year ago **Billy Fury,** Eden Kane, **Karl Denver,** the Allisons and Chas McDevitt all appeared on the same show. Since then there has been a gradual decline in the standard of supporting artists.

'"The exciting Beatles" rock group quite frankly failed to excite me. The drummer apparently thought that his job was to lead, not to provide rhythm. He made far too much noise and in their final number "Twist and Shout" it sounded as though everyone was trying to make more noise than the others. In a more mellow mood, their "A Taste Of Honey" was much better and "Love Me Do" was tolerable.'

In 1964, **Vee Jay Records** in America issued the album *Jolly What! The Beatles And Frank Ifield On Stage* on 26 February. The album was only a minor hit and the title was misleading as all tracks by both artists were studio recordings and were not taken from the one and only night they appeared on the same stage.

● I Forgot To Remember To Forget

A Stanley Kesler/Charlie Feathers composition which **Elvis Presley** recorded in 1956. The Beatles introduced the number into their repertoire in 1962, with George on lead vocals. They performed the song on their BBC radio show **'From Us To You'** on 18 May 1964.

● If I Fell

Number composed by John Lennon and included on the *A Hard Day's Night* album. It was also one of the tracks on the *Extracts From The Film 'A Hard Day's Night'* EP. The song was included on the *Love Songs* compilation and in America it was issued as the flipside of the single 'And I Love Her', which was issued in July 1964.

The Beatles included the number in the repertoire of their summer tour of America in 1964.

● If I Needed Someone

In his book *I. Me. Mine* George describes this song by saying that it is like a million other songs written around the D chord: 'If you move your finger about you get various little melodies.'

George performed the number on stage during the Beatles' British tour of 1965 and their world tour in 1966. Recording of the number began in October 1965 and the song was included on the *Rubber Soul* album. It was als featured on the American release, *Yesterday . . . An Today* and on *The Best Of George Harrison* album.

The **Hollies** recorded the number, but Georg criticized their version so much that it probably influence the record-buying public's attitude and the single didn sell as well as other Hollies records. The group hit back George for his criticism.

Freddie Garritty, who found success with 'If You Gotta Make A Fool Of Somebody'. (Freddie Garritty)

The Beatles at the Cavern. Their repertoire included cover versions such as 'I Got A Woman'. (Dick Matthews/*Mersey Beat* Archives)

● If You Gotta Make A Fool Of Somebody

'he one and only American hit by James Ray, who took it › No. 22 in the US charts in December 1961. The Beatles ıcluded it in their stage repertoire shortly afterwards with aul McCartney on lead vocals. The group included it in ıeir stage act and it was a popular number at the **Cavern.**

Manchester group **Freddie & the Dreamers** recorded ıe number and it became their first chart hit in May 1963 ıd reached No. 3 in the British charts.

● If You've Got Trouble

track which John and Paul composed specially for Ringo record for the *Help!* album. A fast rock number, it was ·corded on Thursday, 18 February 1965, and Ringo's ›ice was double-tracked. Ringo had been featured nging at least one song on each Beatle album and, as he dn't write songs himself at the time, he generally covered ımbers by other artists. John and Paul thought they'd ·ovide the vehicle for him this time, but the number was ›t deemed satisfactory; it was left off the album and mains one of the Beatles' unreleased tracks.

I Got A Woman

Ray Charles composition previously recorded by a large ımber of artists, including **Elvis Presley** and Bill Haley. ıe Beatles introduced it into their act in 1961, with John lead vocal. They performed the number on their BBC dio appearances on **'Pop Go The Beatles'** and **aturday Club'**.

I Got To Find My Baby

Chuck Berry composition which he recorded in 1960. ıe Beatles introduced it into their repertoire in 1961 with hn taking lead vocals. The group performed the number **'Pop Go The Beatles'** and **'Saturday Club'**.

I Just Don't Understand

chart hit for Ann-Margret in 1961 who took the song to ›. 17 in the American charts. The Beatles began rforming the number, with John Lennon on lead vocals, ring 1961 and 1962.

Ann-Margret, truncated from her full name of Ann-ırgret Olson, was once known as 'the female Presley' d had the potential to become a major female rock star. e appeared with **Elvis** in *Viva Las Vegas* and the two ·re romantically linked. Her name was also linked romantically with that of Ringo Starr and Ringo had to deny a romantic relationship several times during the conferences on the Beatles' first American tour.

● I'll Be Back

An early John Lennon composition. John said that he'd originally begun to write it while playing a **Del Shannon** number on his guitar. He just reworked the chords of the Shannon number and came up with a completely different song – 'I'll Be Back'.

It was one of the tracks used on the *A Hard Day's Night* album – an LP almost dominated by Lennon compositions. 'I'll Be Back' was also included on the American album *Beatles '65* and the compilation album *Love Songs*.

● I'll Be On My Way

A number penned by Paul McCartney which was used on the flipside of **Billy J. Kramer**'s debut single 'Do You Want To Know A Secret?' issued in April 1963.

The Beatles didn't record the number on record, but did tape a version of the song which was broadcast on the BBC radio show **'Side By Side'** on 24 June 1963.

● I'll Cry Instead

John Lennon was to comment: 'We were going to do this in *A Hard Day's Night* but the director **Dick Lester** didn't like it, so we put it on the flipside of the album. I like it.'

When recording was first begun on Monday, 1 June 1964, it was taped in two parts. As Dick Lester wasn't impressed by the number it was left off the film soundtrack and a short version was included on the British album *A Hard Day's Night*. The same version appeared on the British EP *Extracts From The Album 'A Hard Day's Night'*.

In America, **Capitol** wanted to issue it as a single and, due to the fact that it had been recorded in separate parts, they were able to extend its length and also repeated one of the verses in the editing, making the song longer. This is the version that was included on the American *A Hard Day's Night* album although the shorter version, from the British LP, was the one used on the American *Something New* album.

'I'll Cry Instead' was issued as a single in the States on Capitol 5234 on 20 July 1964, with 'I'm Happy Just To Dance With You' on the flip. It reached No. 25 in the charts.

In 1981, when **Walter Shenson** re-released the film *A*

The Beatles in 1964.
(EMI/Parlophone)

Hard Day's Night, the song was finally heard in the film – it was included at the beginning of the movie, over a montage of still photographs.

● I'll Follow The Sun

One of the many numbers that Paul wrote in the very early days of his songwriting career at his **Forthlin Road** home in Liverpool. Paul was sixteen at the time and was recovering from the flu. He was standing in the parlour with his guitar, looking out of the window through the lace curtains, when he began to write the song.

Recording of the number didn't begin until Sunday, 18 October 1964 as a result of the group needing material urgently for their *Beatles For Sale* album. The number was also included on the *Beatles For Sale (No. 2)* EP, the *Love Songs* compilation and the American *Beatles '65* album.

● I'll Get You

A John Lennon composition which, when the Beatl began recording it on Monday, 1 July 1963, had th working title 'Get You In The End'.

It originally surfaced as the flipside of 'She Loves You In America, the single was issued on the Swan label September 1963. In May 1964 Swan released *'Sie Lie Dich'* as a single, with 'I'll Get You' on the flip.

In the meantime, when **Capitol** acquired the track th included it on their release *The Beatles Second Album* April 1964. A version of the song was also included wi the *Rarities* album in the British *The Beatles Collection* se

● I'll Keep You Satisfied

Another Paul McCartney number for **Billy J. Krame** featured as the 'A' side of his third single. It was issued Britain on Parlophone R 5073 on 1 November 1963 a reached No. 4 in the charts. It was issued in America Liberty 55643 on 11 November 1963 and reached No. 3

The Beatles never recorded this number and didn even tape it during their numerous BBC radio session although it is likely they made a demo tape of the numb for George Martin and Billy J. Kramer to listen to prior the recording.

I Lost My Little Girl

Reputedly the first song that Paul McCartney ever wrote. He immediately introduced it into the **Quarry Men**'s repertoire when he joined the group, but the band dropped the number when they became the Beatles.

When Paul was unsuccessful in his attempt to become lead guitarist with the new group in the **New Clubmoor Hall**, Liverpool, on 18 October 1957 he is said to have attempted to recover his pride by playing John this number after the show. John was suitably impressed.

I'm A Loser

Number penned by John which the group performed on their **'Top Gear'**, **'Saturday Club'** and 'Ticket To Ride' radio appearances. They also featured it on their 1964 Christmas show, during their European tour in 1965 and on their January 1965 **'Shindig'** TV show appearance.

It was included on the *Beatles For Sale* album and within a short time **Marianne Faithfull** had included the song on her debut album.

'I'm A Loser' is also to be found on the American album *Beatles '65* and the EPs *Beatles For Sale* and *4 By The Beatles.*

John was said to be influenced by **Bob Dylan** when he wrote the semi-autobiographical number, which was originally considered for release as the Beatles' last single of 1964, along with 'No Reply' and 'Eight Days A Week'. Eventually, 'I Feel Fine' was chosen.

I'm Down

A Paul McCartney composition which the Beatles recorded on Monday, 14 June 1965. The track appeared as the flipside of the 'Help!' single and was also included on the compilation album *Rock 'n' Roll Music* and the British version of *Rarities.*

The group performed the number on stage during their world tours in 1965 and 1966 and also on their 'The **Ed Sullivan** Show' appearance in September 1965.

I'm Gonna Sit Right Down And Cry Over You

Originally written by Joe Thomas and Howard Biggs in the early fifties and recorded by Biggs. **Elvis Presley** recorded the number in 1956, but his single wasn't a hit. The Beatles added it to their repertoire in 1960 with Elvis ... John Lennon on lead vocals.

I'm Happy Just To Dance With You

John wrote this number specially for George to sing in *A Hard Day's Night*, in the days before George found the confidence to be a songwriter in his own right, although John was also to say, 'I would never have sung it myself.' Apart from being featured on the *A Hard Day's Night* soundtrack, it was issued as the flipside of the single 'I'll Cry Instead', which was released in America in July 1964. Due to the fact that 'B' sides received placings in the US charts, 'I'm Happy Just To Dance With You' reached No. 95. In the same month it was included on **Capitol**'s American album *Something New*. In 1982 the song was used as the flipside of 'The Beatles Movie Medley' single.

(©Walter Shenson Films/Apple)

The number was recorded on Sunday, 1 March 1964 – the first time the Beatles had been into a studio to record on a Sunday.

I'm In Love

Brian Epstein was conscious of the potential of using Lennon & McCartney numbers for his other acts and was to ask John and Paul for numbers for **Cilla Black, Billy J. Kramer**, the **Fourmost** and **Tommy Quickly** to record.

He was careful not to ask them for their best numbers and usually requested early songs that they'd written and didn't intend to record for themselves. One of these was a pre-Beatles composition by John Lennon called 'I'm In Love' which Brian obtained for the Fourmost as their follow-up to John's other early number, 'Hello Little Girl', which gave the group a Top Ten hit.

'I'm In Love' was issued on Parlophone R 5078 in Britain on 15 November 1963 where it reached No. 12 in the charts. It didn't fare so well in America, not charting at all when it was issued on Atco 6285 on 10 February 1964.

● I'm Looking Through You

One of the many songs inspired by **Jane Asher** – but not in such a loving frame of mind as most of the others. Paul was angry with her because she had gone to Bristol to appear in a play. He was to comment, 'My whole existence for so long centred around a bachelor life: I don't treat women as most people do. My life generally has always been very lazy and not normal. I knew I was selfish. It caused a few rows. Jane went off to Bristol to act. I said, "OK then, leave, I'll find someone else." It was shattering to be without her. That was when I wrote "I'm Looking Through You" – for Jane.'

The number first surfaced on the 1965 *Rubber Soul* album and has also been featured in the 1978 *The Beatles Collection* set.

● I'm Only Sleeping

A lazy atmosphere, a laid-back feeling prevails in the lyrics of John's song requesting he be left alone to sleep and dream. Some lengthy recording sessions took place to get this track down for the *Revolver* album, including the use of a 'backward guitar sound'. The number was also used on the American album *Yesterday . . . And Today*.

● I'm So Tired

Composition which John wrote during his stay at Rishikesh and which he later regarded as one of his favourite songs.

The introspective lyrics denote weariness, a desire for peace of mind after three weeks of virtual sleeplessness. There is also the mention of his addiction to cigarettes and a curse on Sir Walter Raleigh who is referred to as 'a stupid get'.

The number was included on *The Beatles* double album.

● I'm Talking About You

A **Chuck Berry** composition which he released as a single in June 1962. The Beatles introduced it into their repertoire the same year, with John on lead vocals. Th group performed it during their last season at Hamburg' **Star Club** and it's one of four Chuck Berry number contained on *The Beatles Live! At The Star Club I Hamburg, Germany: 1962* album. It became a popula number with British R&B bands and the Beatle performed the song on the BBC radio show **'Saturda Club'** on 16 March 1963.

● I. Me. Mine

A George Harrison composition. When discussing the son in his book *I. Me. Mine*, George wrote: 'Allen Klei thought it was an Italian song – you know, "Cara Mi Mine" – but it's about the ego: the eternal problem.'

When the song was recorded on 3 January 1970 ther were only three Beatles present in Studio Two at **Abbe Road** because John was on holiday in Denmark. Georg was able to give a short, amusing speech to the folk gathered in the studio: 'You all will have read that Dav Dee is no longer with us. But Micky and Tich and I woul

(©Apple/Walter Shenson Films)

just like to carry on the good work that's always been done in number two.'

A version of the song had originally been attempted at **Twickenham Film Studios**, but only 94 seconds of it had been recorded. As the excerpt was to be used in the *Let It Be* film it was decided to record the number for the soundtrack album with just George, Paul and Ringo.

This version lasted for 1 min. 34 secs., which is the length **Glyn Johns** let it remain when he mixed the tapes – only including a brief piece of dialogue at the beginning in which George says, 'Are you ready, Ringo?' and Ringo answers, 'Ready, George!' The Johns version was not used as **Allen Klein** gave the tapes to **Phil Spector** to whip into shape. Spector overdubbed a brass and strings section and made an extended re-mix of the number, lengthening it to 2 min. 25 secs. for the album. In the *Let It Be* film, John and **Yoko** are seen waltzing to the number.

● Imperial Ballroom, *Carr Road, Nelson, Lancashire*

Large ballroom situated in a town near to Merseyside. The Beatles first appeared here on 11 May 1963 before a capacity crowd of 2,000 and returned to a further capacity house on 31 July 1963.

● Indiana State Fair Coliseum And Grandstand, *Indianapolis, Indiana*

The Beatles performed two shows on Thursday, 3 September 1964, as part of the Indiana State Fair. The site was at the home of the famous Indianapolis 500 Racetrack. The first show took place at 5.00 p.m. in the Indiana State Fair Coliseum and the second at 9.30 p.m. at the Grandstand. There were approximately 30,000 people at the two shows.

In between the shows the Beatles took part in a press conference at the Radio Building. A phone call had reported that there was a bomb in the building, but a bomb squad discovered it was a hoax. Present at the conference was the obligatory beauty queen – Miss Indiana State Fair.

● Indica Gallery, *Masons Yard, London W1*

Gallery and specialist bookshop opened by **Peter Asher**, **Barry Miles** and John Dunbar in the sixties. Peter Asher was Jane's brother and Paul McCartney had designed the shop's wrapping paper, which he donated to them as a gift.

Barry Miles was a contributor to the fashionable 'underground' paper *International Times* and John Dunbar, a Cambridge graduate, was married to singer Marianne Faithfull.

It was Dunbar who invited John Lennon to 'Unfinished Paintings & Objects by **Yoko Ono**', an exhibition at the gallery, which ran from 9–12 November 1966.

Dunbar had told John, 'Some amazing things will be happening. Yoko sometimes puts people into bags to create a living, breathing work of art!' John thought the idea of the Japanese girl sticking people into bags was sexy and decided to attend the preview.

He was immediately struck by an apple on display. 'There was an apple on display there for two hundred quid. I thought that was fantastic.' He noticed a black canvas attached to the ceiling A tiny magnifying glass was dangling from its side by a chain and a step ladder was conveniently placed. He climbed up the ladder leading to the canvas, picked up the magnifying glass and peering through its lens read the tiny word 'Yes'.

'It was positive. I was relieved,' he said.

John Dunbar was eager to introduce John to Yoko and when he did, Yoko handed him a card on which the word 'Breathe' was printed. He panted on it.

John then noticed an exhibit called 'Hammer A Nail In' and asked if he could 'Bash a nail in'. Yoko, who claims she had not been particularly aware of the Beatles, that the only one she knew by name at the time was Ringo, was reluctant to allow John's request because the official opening didn't take place until the following day. Dunbar was anxious that John's wish be granted as he'd intended approaching him at some future date to sponsor exhibitions. 'He's a millionaire. He's one of the Beatles,' he impressed upon Yoko. So she said, 'OK. You can hammer a nail in if you pay me five shillings.' He paused, then offered to pay her an imaginary five shillings in exchange for knocking in an imaginary nail with an imaginary hammer.

'And that's when we really met,' said John. 'That's when we locked eyes and she got it and I got it.'

● Indra Club, *34 Grosse Freiheit, Hamburg, Germany*

The club where the Beatles played their first 200 hours of music in Hamburg and underwent their 'baptism of fire', transforming themselves from an average group into something special, due to the long hours, the frenetic shows caused by pills, booze and the insistent demands to 'make a show'.

Crammed into **Allan Williams**' mini-van in company with his wife Beryl, his brother-in-law Barry Chang, his friend **Lord Woodbine** and the German waiter **George Sterner**, the five Beatles finally arrived at the **Kaiserkeller** club in the Reeperbahn where they believed they would be playing. The group who were currently performing were **Howie Casey** & the Seniors and as the Beatles entered the club during one of the group's breaks, Casey told them that they wouldn't be playing there, but at a little strip club down the road. This was confirmed by the pugnacious little promoter **Bruno Koschmider** who took them down the Grosse Freiheit where, at the seedy end of the street, they found a tiny club with its neon sign shaped like an elephant.

Koschmider had decided to turn his small strip club into a rock 'n' roll venue. The Beatles were appalled at the narrow room with its low stage, jukebox, heavy curtains and thick carpet (which were to muffle the sound), as Koschmider hadn't bothered to alter it from its strip club decor. The acoustics were pathetic. The group were appalled still further when they were shown their awful lodgings in the adjacent **Bambi Kino**.

After their 36-hour journey the group went on stage at the club that very night, 17 August 1960, and played for four-and-a-half hours to an uninterested audience of half a dozen people.

Their contract called for them to perform four-and-a-half hours each evening during the week and six hours each Saturday and Sunday evening. For this they were paid DM30 (ten pounds) a week, which Bruno paid them each Thursday. Their contract also stipulated that they couldn't play any other venue within a radius of 40 kilometres without Koschmider's permission.

Initially disgruntled, they slowly began to change their act, urged on by Koschmider's pleas to 'make a show'. They began to take Preludin pills supplied by the toilet-frau **Rosa** (**Pete Best** didn't indulge), which made them dehydrated, causing them to swill back copious quantities of beer, usually sent up on stage for them by members of the audience. Their on-stage antics included mock fights amongst themselves, horse-play, John imitating a spastic and doing the goose-step, much to the frustration of Koschmider, who had formerly been in a Panzer division. In fact, John and Paul provided most of the on-stage action and John increased his verbal attacks on the audience, calling them 'krauts', 'nazis' and 'German spassies' (spastics). Strangely enough, members of the audience found this funny and more beer was ordered for the group on stage.

Although there was a little old lady living in a flat above the club, she was nearly deaf and Pete Best maintains she never complained about the noise they were creating. However, other nearby residents complained to the police – and although the area provided every variation of sex, a cornucopia of drugs and drinks around the clock, noise wasn't tolerated. The police kept warning Koschmider about the noise and they finally took action. The Beatles arrived at the Indra one night to find that the police had closed it down, 48 nights after it had been turned into a showplace for the group. During that time the Beatles had transformed their act, had increased the takings at the Indra and had begun to build a local following. Koschmider moved them to the Kaiserkeller for the duration of their contract.

● I Need You

One of the two George Harrison compositions featured on the *Help!* album. During recording, George introduced a wah-wah pedal for the first time on a Beatles session.

The number was also included on the *Love Songs* compilation.

● In My Life

A reflective, autobiographical composition by John which was featured on the *Rubber Soul* album and the compilations *The Beatles 1962–1966* and *Love Songs*.

John originally commented, 'I wrote that in **Kenwood**. I used to write upstairs where I had about ten Brunell tape recorders all linked up . . . I'd mastered them over the period of a year or two – I could never make a rock and roll record but I could make some far out stuff on it. I wrote it upstairs, that was one where I wrote the lyrics first and then sang it. That was usually the case with things like "In My Life" and "Universe" and some of the ones that stand out a bit.'

Interestingly enough, the concept of the song originally began as the story of a bus journey from John's home in Menlove Avenue to Liverpool city centre, mentioning every place on the way which John could remember. It included mentions of Penny Lane, Strawberry Fields and the Tram Sheds depot. 'In My Life' was written well before either 'Penny Lane' or 'Strawberry Fields' were composed by Paul and John respectively. John found that his original concept for the song turned out to be boring, so he rested, and then the lyrics of the song began to flow. He was to add, 'Now Paul helped write the middle eight melody. The whole lyrics were already written before Paul had even heard it. In the song, his contribution melodically was the harmony and the middle eight itself.'

The song was one of George Harrison's favourites and he rearranged the music and lyrics when he performed the number himself during his Dark Horse tour in 1974.

● *Inner Light, The*

The first of George Harrison's compositions to find its way onto a Beatles single. It was the flipside of the March 1968 release 'Lady Madonna'.

George had appeared on a '**David Frost** Show' with John Lennon, discussing meditation, and, as a result, received a letter from Juan Mascaro, a Sanskrit teacher at Cambridge University, who wrote to say how much he had enjoyed 'Within You, Without You'. Mascaro also enclosed a book called *Lamps Of Fire* in which there was a translation of a poem from the Tao Te Ching called 'The Inner Light'. George put the poem to music and wrote it specially for Mascaro.

George recorded the instrumental part of the number at the EMI Studios in Bombay, India, on 12 January 1968, using Indian musicians. He completed the vocals on 8 February at **Abbey Road**'s Studio One, with John and Paul adding their vocal harmonies the following day.

The track was also included on the *Rarities* compilation and the 1981 release *The Beatles EP Collection*.

Paul, perhaps not comprehending the importance of Indian music in George's mind, or the validity of its influence in the composition of his songs, commented, 'George wrote this. Forget the Indian music and listen to the melody. Don't you think it's a beautiful melody? It's really lovely.'

● *In Spite Of All The Danger*

One of Paul McCartney's earliest collaborations. He co-wrote the number with George Harrison when they were both members of the **Quarry Men** and it became one of two numbers they recorded at a recording studio in Kensington, in 1958. The other number was **Buddy Holly**'s 'That'll Be The Day', making 'In Spite Of All The Danger' the first song ever to be recorded by the group who were to become the Beatles and the first original song to be recorded by them.

The only member of the group to keep a copy of the acetate was **John Lowe** who, many years later, in 1981, attempted to sell it at auction. After some legal problems were ironed out, Paul McCartney bought the acetate.

● *Institute, The, Hinderton Road, Neston, Wirral, Cheshire*

Promoter **Les Dodd** had been running ballroom dancing events at this venue since the thirties, but had decided to present some jive dances.

Allan Williams secured the Silver Beatles a short residency at the hall and they made their debut there on Thursday, 2 June 1960. All their appearances took place during that year on consecutive Thursdays – on 9, 16, 23 and 30 June and 7 July.

On their 16 June appearance the support band was Keith Rowlands & the Deesiders.

● *International Amphitheatre, Chicago, Illinois*

The Beatles first appeared here during their debut American tour on 5 September 1964. Their limousines drove them from the Stockyards Inn where they had conducted a press conference and then their limousines drove them to the amphitheatre where the entire 15,000 tickets had sold out in a matter of hours. There were 4,000 frantic fans outside the stadium who hadn't been able to obtain tickets and several of them were threatening to commit suicide.

The Beatles ran onto the stage via a stairway draped in gold cloth at 9.20 p.m. and their performance went underway with Paul yelling, 'Why don't you join in? Clap your hands, stomp your feet, maybe even shout!' During the performance someone threw a raw steak at Ringo and Paul was hit in the face by a flashbulb.

To protect the Beatles, their fans and the amphitheatre, there were 320 policemen, firemen and private guards in attendance.

Immediately after the show had finished the group were herded off in limousines to the airport.

The Beatles began their final tour of America at this venue on 12 August 1966. They performed two concerts at the amphitheatre, which were virtual sell-outs, with 13,000 fans attending each of the shows.

● Interview Discs

Over the years there have been a number of discs which feature interviews with the Beatles. Such records have a more limited appeal and only a few have achieved chart positions. The handful of interview albums which have sold in any quantity are, in the main, the official releases – **Capitol**'s *The Beatles Story*, Columbia's *The McCartney Interview* and Polydor's *Heartbeat*, for instance, all entered the American charts.

The first interview album was *The American Tour With Ed Rudy*, issued on Radio Pulsebeat News Documentary No. 2 on 9 June 1964 which reached No. 20 in *Billboard*, No. 55 in *Cash Box* and No. 32 in *Record World*. Disc jockey Rudy made several interview discs, but this was the only one which charted. In 1965 he issued *Ed Rudy With New U.S. Tour (The Beatles Great American Tour)* on Radio Pulsebeat News L-1001/1002 (News Documentary No. 3). The third album was *The Great American Tour – 1965 Live Beatlemania Concert* issued on Lloyds ERMC Ltd Records. It wasn't really an interview album as the previous releases had been. Rudy had recorded Beatles concerts during their second American tour, then overdubbed a group called the Liverpool Lads and interviewed fans at the concerts and in the studio.

In September 1964 **Vee Jay Records** issued *Hear The Beatles Tell All* on Vee Jay PRO 202. Originally it was issued in a limited edition of 7,000 copies for promotional purposes to radio stations before it became available to the general public. Side One contained an interview with John Lennon by Jim Steck and Side Two featured Dave Hull interviewing all four Beatles. Vee Jay re-released it on Vee Jay PRO 202 on 18 January 1980. The following year it was issued in Britain on 23 January on Charly Records CRV 202.

The Beatles Story was a double album issued on Capitol STBO 2222 on 23 November 1964 and reached No. 7 in *Billboard*, No. 7 in *Cash Box* and No. 13 in *Record World*.

In November 1968 a seven-inch single was issued in Italy, '*Una Sensazionale Intervista Die Beatles*', on Apple DPR 108. This originally came with a package of three Apple singles, '*Quelli Erano Giorni*', 'Sour Milk Sea' and 'Maybe Tomorrow'. The Beatles interview had been conducted with disc jockey **Kenny Everett** during *The Beatles* white album recording sessions.

On 30 July 1976 *The Beatles Tapes From The David Wigg Interviews* was issued in Britain on Polydor 2683 068. These were taken from interviews *Daily Express* journalist **David Wigg** had conducted with individual members of the Beatles for the BBC programme 'Scene And Heard'. The album was issued in America on PBR International 7005/7006 two years later in 1978.

Beatle Talk: Ed Robinson Interviews The Beatles was issued in America on Great Northwest Music Co GWC 4007 on 15 November 1978 and included excerpts from Beatles' press conferences in Vancouver and Seattle. The album was repackaged and issued in Britain in June 1982 on Everest CBR 1008.

The McCartney Interview was issued in America on Columbia PC 36987 in December 1980. This was taken from a taped interview conducted by Vic Garbarini for the magazine *Musician: Player & Listener*. The interview was originally issued as a promotional package to American radio stations in a limited edition, but produced such interest that a commercial release limited to 57,000 copies was also issued.

Following the death of John Lennon, Silhouette Music issued a limited edition picture disc called *Timeless*. It was released on 1 March 1981 on Silhouette Music SM-10004. The edition was originally to have been limited to 10,000 copies, but due to a large demand from dealers, 25,000 copies were pressed. The album features four photographs of John on the 'A' side and a colour photograph of the Beatles dressed as matadors on the flip, but only two of the nine tracks on the album featured the Beatles. These were excerpts from their press conferences in Vancouver in 1964 and Chicago in 1966. The remaining tracks included a newscast about John Lennon and six tracks of tribute songs recorded by studio musicians.

The American Tour With Ed Rudy, originally issued in June 1964, was reissued in 1981 following John's death on INS Radio News Documentary No. 2.

In October 1982 Backstage Records issued a picture disc album *The Beatles Talk With Jerry G* on Backstage BSR 1165. These comprised recordings of interviews disc jockey Jerry G. Bishop had with the Beatles during 1964 and 1965. The company followed this up with *The Beatles Talk With Jerry G – Volume 2*, another picture disc album issued on Backstage BSR 1175 in August 1983.

Heart Play: Unfinished Dialogue was issued in America

on Polydor 817 238-1 Y-1 in December 1983 and in Britain at the same time on Polydor 817 238-I. Compiled with the cooperation of **Yoko Ono**, the album was subtitled 'A Spoken Word Documentary' and included excerpts from several John Lennon interviews.

● *Introducing The Beatles*

The first Beatles album to be released in America, issued on 22 July 1963, on VJLP 1062. It didn't make the charts. It was reissued with the same catalogue number (but not with the same tracks) on 27 January 1964 and reached No. 2 in the *Billboard* and *Cash Box* charts, and No. 1 in the *Record World* chart.

The tracks were, Side One: 'I Saw Her Standing There', 'Misery', 'Anna (Go To Him)', 'Chains', 'Boys', 'Ask Me Why'. Side Two: 'Do You Want To Know A Secret', 'A Taste Of Honey', 'There's A Place', 'Twist And Shout'.

● Invicta Ballroom, *High Street, Chatham, Kent*

The Beatles appeared here on 12 January 1963.

● I Remember

A number recorded by **Eddie Cochran** in 1959. The Beatles performed it during 1960 and 1961.

● I Remember You

A No. 1 hit for singer **Frank Ifield** in Britain in 1962 which the Beatles immediately included in their repertoire.

The group performed it during their **Star Club** set and it is included on *The Beatles Live! At The Star Club In Hamburg, Germany: 1962* album.

● Iron Door Club, The, *13 Temple Street, Liverpool L2*

A cellar club quite close to the **Cavern**, which began as a jazz club, called the Liverpool Jazz Society. The Beatles made their debut there on a special session promoted by **Sam Leach**.

The event took place on 11 March 1961. Sam had decided to feature twelve top local groups, who would replace each other on the hour, on a massive twelve-hour music marathon commencing at 8.00 p.m. on Saturday and finishing at 8.00 a.m. on Sunday.

The bill comprised the Beatles, **Kingsize Taylor** & the Dominoes, **Rory Storm & the Hurricanes**, **Gerry & the Pacemakers**, the **Big Three**, the **Searchers**, the Four Jays (later to become the **Fourmost**), the **Remo Four**, **Howie Casey** & the Seniors, Ian & the Zodiacs, Faron & the Flamingoes and Karl Terry & the Cruisers.

There was so much condensation dripping down the walls that the Beatles had to stand on their amplifier covers to avoid being electrocuted because they had American equipment which was wired differently. Paul said, 'The heat was "shocking!"'

Although the club only held 1,000 people, over 2,000 eventually saw the show. Queues continued until after midnight when the younger members of the audience left to catch their last bus home. Admission price was 6/6d (32½p) for members and 7/6d (37½p) for non-members.

The Beatles returned to the club for an appearance a few days later on 13 March and also on Wednesday, 15 March, on a five-hour afternoon session with Rory Storm & the Hurricanes and Gerry & the Pacemakers. Their final appearance at the venue that month was on 17 March.

When they next played the venue on 1 March 1962 it had undergone a name change to the Storyville Jazz Club. They also appeared there on 8 March.

They made their final appearance at the club on 15 March on a bill advertised as the 'Beatles' Farewell Party'.

The Iron Door Club
13 TEMPLE ST.
(off Dale Street)
Host Compere:
KEN LAURIE
JAZZ ★ ROCK ★ TWIST
You can enjoy yourself in the friendly happy atmosphere of this club in the heart of town.
New members are welcome—
IT COSTS ONLY 2/6.
SATURDAY, 17th NOVEMBER
CHARLIE GALBRAITH'S
ALL-STARS
T.V. RADIO and FILM PERSONALITIES

● I Saw Her Standing There

A song penned by Paul in the pre-Epstein days which the Beatles used to perform at their local Liverpool gigs. When the song had become a hit, Paul discussed it in an interview for the magazine *Beat Instrumental* as he described the genesis of the song. On the subject of learning to play an instrument, Paul advised that rather than use a tutor, aspiring musicians should learn to play by stealing bits and pieces from other guitarists they could listen to. He commented, 'Here's one example of a bit I pinched from someone: I used the bass riff from "Talkin' About You" by **Chuck Berry** in "I Saw Her Standing There". I played exactly the same notes as he did and it fitted our number perfectly. Even now, when I tell people about it, I find few of them believe me; therefore, I maintain that a bass riff hasn't got to be original.'

It first appeared as the initial track on the *Please Please Me* album in Britain and then on *The Beatles (No. 1)* EP. In the States it was included on the *Introducing The Beatles* and *Meet The Beatles* albums. The number also surfaced on *Rock 'n' Roll Music*.

The group had performed it as part of their repertoire during their **Star Club** season in Hamburg and this raw version is to be found on *The Beatles Live At The Star Club In Hamburg, Germany: 1962* albums.

Within weeks of 'Please Please Me' being released, Duffy Power issued a single of the number, but it failed to make an impact on the charts.

A version by John Lennon and Elton John is to be found on the flipside of Elton's 1975 single 'Philadelphia Freedom'. John had appeared on stage with Elton at Madison Square Garden in 1974 and this number was recorded at the concert. John had announced it as '. . . a song written by an old fiancé of mine called Paul'. The John/Lennon performance was also included on an EP issued by DJM Records in 1981, which reached No. 24 in the ***New Musical Express*** chart in Britain.

Originally, the working title of the song was 'Seventeen'.

● I Should Have Known Better

One of the several John Lennon compositions for *A Hard Day's Night*. John plays harmonica on the track and George played his twelve-string Rickenbacker guitar for the first time on record. A group called the Naturals covered the number and reached No. 26 in the British charts with it.

Apart from the album *A Hard Day's Night*, the number was used on the EP *Extracts From The Film 'A Hard Day's Night'* and was the flipside of the 'Yesterday' single, issued in Britain in March 1976. It was featured on the compilations albums *Hey Jude* in 1979 and *Reel Music* in 1982 and was one of the numbers included on 'The Beatles Movie Medley' single in 1982.

At the initial recording session on Tuesday, 25 February 1964, John kept laughing over his harmonica playing, causing the others to laugh, too. They re-recorded the number the following day.

● Israel

The Beatles never appeared in the country, although Brian Epstein attempted to arrange for them to perform there in 1964. The Israeli Government were against it as they regarded the Beatles' music as being harmful to the country's youth and they also commented that the extensive security measures required to protect them in the political climate would have been prohibitively expensive.

During the seventies the Beatles' records were broadcast on 'The Voice of Peace', an off-shore pirate station run by Abi Nathan, a venture advocating peace in the Middle East. John Lennon and **Yoko Ono** were later to offer financial aid to the station.

For a time there was a 'Beatles Hour' on the radio, sponsored by the Ha'Opalim Bank and also a two-hour show broadcast three times a week called '**The Beatles** Era'.

● It's All Too Much

A George Harrison composition which was called 'Too Much' when the Beatles first began recording it on Thursday, 25 May 1967, at De Lane Lea recording studios in Kingsway, London. George took lead vocals with John and Paul adding backing vocals and handclaps. At the session George sang a few bars from 'Sorrow', a hit single by the Merseys. When recording resumed on 2 June the title had been changed to 'It's All Too Much' and four trumpets and a bass clarinet were overdubbed onto the track.

At that time the number was more than eight minutes in length, but it was later edited down.

The song had been written for the *Yellow Submarine* movie and is one of the numbers featured on the film soundtrack. A shorter version, with one of the verses taken out, is to be found on the *Yellow Submarine* album, issued in January 1969, almost two years after George wrote it.

● It's For You

The majority of Lennon & McCartney songs given to other artists to record during the sixties were composed by Paul. This number, which he gave to **Cilla Black** for her fourth

British chart hit, reached the No. 8 position. It didn't fare too well in the States where Cilla only enjoyed one Top Forty chart placing in her entire career, although it did enter the lower regions of the charts.

Cilla recorded the number on 2 July 1964 and John and Paul attended the session, with Paul playing piano on the track.

The number was issued in Britain on Parlophone R 5162 on 31 July 1964 and in America on **Capitol** 5258 on 17 August 1964, with 'He Won't Ask Me' on the flip.

● It's Only Love

Composition by John, recorded on the afternoon of Tuesday, 15 June 1965, and featuring John on acoustic guitar and George on his tone pedal guitar. The number had the working title 'That's A Nice Hat'.

The number was included on the British *Help!* album and the *Yesterday* EP. It was also one of the two songs from *Help!* to be excluded from **Capitol**'s American version of the *Help!* album and was featured on the American *Rubber Soul* album. The song was also included on the *Love Songs* compilation.

Bryan Ferry performed the number on his hit British EP *Extended Play* in 1976 and, following John's death, it became a minor hit for Gary 'US' Bonds in 1981 – ironically, because John had said that he disliked it and described it as a 'lousy' song with 'abysmal lyrics'.

● It's So Easy

Number composed by **Buddy Holly** and Norman Petty. Holly was one of the major influences of the **Quarry Men** and they included this number, recorded by **Buddy Holly** & the Crickets, in their repertoire in 1958.

● It's The Beatles

A 30-minute BBC 1 TV show filmed at the **Empire Theatre, Liverpool** on 7 December 1963 and screened the same evening.

The Beatles had returned to their home town to appear at a special Northern Area Fan Club Convention before

(©Apple/Walter Shenson Films)

2,500 members of their fan club. In addition to the actual concert, they also filmed a **'Juke Box Jury'** show from the Empire stage that afternoon and after their fan club performance they rushed to the **Odeon** cinema, only 50 yards away, for yet another performance.

'It's The Beatles', filmed before the fan club members, was transmitted between 8.10 p.m. and 8.40 p.m. and the group performed 'From Me To You', 'I Saw Her Standing There', 'All My Loving', 'Roll Over Beethoven', 'Boys', 'Till There Was You', 'She Loves You', 'This Boy', 'I Want To Hold Your Hand', 'Money', 'Twist And Shout' and 'From Me To You'.

• It's The Beatles (Radio Luxembourg)

A weekly fifteen-minute series on Radio Luxembourg which was first broadcast on 23 December 1963. The second episode was aired on 30 December 1963.

• It Won't Be Long

Number penned by John which was included on the *With The Beatles* album, issued in November 1963 and which also appeared on the American *Meet The Beatles* album in January 1964.

It was recorded on Tuesday, 30 July 1963, and became the opening track on the album.

• I've Got A Feeling

A number composed by both John and Paul in which each sings his own verses. There was a version recorded in the studio and they also performed the number on their Apple rooftop session. When **Phil Spector** was given the tapes of the 'Get Back' sessions, he mixed two versions of this track, the studio track and the live track, and decided to use the live rooftop track for the release on the *Let It Be* album.

• I've Just Seen A Face

A folk-rock song which Paul composed for the *Help!* movie and on which he sings solo on the soundtrack recording. It was the first number he recorded on Monday, 14 June 1965, the same day he recorded 'I'm Down' and 'Yesterday'. The number was included on the *Help!* soundtrack album and also on the American version of the *Rubber Soul* album and the compilations *The Beatles Box* and *The Beatles Collection*.

When Paul was composing it the song became one of his Auntie Gin's favourites, so the working title of the song was 'Auntie Gin's Theme'. The George Martin Orchestra recorded an instrumental version of 'I've Just Seen A Face' under the title 'Auntie Gin's Theme'.

Paul performed it on the **Wings** world tour of 1975/6 and it became one of the tracks on the *Wings Over America* album.

• Ivor Novello Awards, The

Prestigious annual awards presented by the Songwriters' Guild of Great Britain and named in honour of the late, famous British composer Ivor Novello.

The Beatles received five awards on 25 October 1964. They were: 1. The most outstanding contribution to British music in 1963. 2. The most broadcast song, 'She Loves

The Beatles in 1964. (EMI/Parlophone)

You'. 3. The top-selling record, 'She Loves You'. 4. The second top-selling record, 'I Want To Hold Your Hand'. 5. The second most outstanding song of the year, 'All My Loving'.

On 25 March 1967 they received two awards for the year 1966. They were: 1. The most performed work, 'Michelle'. 2. The top-selling single, 'Yellow Submarine'.

In March 1968 they received three awards: 1. Best British song, musically and lyrically, 'She's Leaving Home'. 2. Best instrumental theme of the year, 'Love In The Open Air' (Paul's theme for the film *The Family Way*). 3. Second best-selling record of the year, 'Hello Goodbye'.

On 19 May 1969 they received an award for 1968: 1. The top-selling single in Britain, 'Hey Jude'.

On 10 May 1972 they were presented with two awards: 1. Best-selling British single, 'Get Back'. 2. Most requested song on the radio, 'Ob-La-Di, Ob-La-Da'.

They also received awards for 'Help!' and 'Yesterday'.

● I Wanna Be Your Man

A number penned by Paul McCartney and John Lennon.

On 10 September 1963 John and Paul had been present at a Variety Club lunch at the Savoy Hotel where they had received an award as Top Vocal Group of the Year.

They were in a taxi and went into the West End and in Jermyn Street bumped into **Andrew Loog Oldham**, co-manager of the **Rolling Stones**. He told them that he was on his way to visit the group at their rehearsals, but they were having difficulty finding material for their second single.

John and Paul said they had an unrecorded song which might be something suitable and went along with him to Ken Colyer's Studio 51 club in Soho.

While there they borrowed the Stones' instruments to play them part of a number they had been composing called 'I Wanna Be Your Man'. Bill Wyman was to recall his amazement that Paul played his bass guitar backwards. They had only played the first verse and chorus as the number was incomplete and the two asked if they could be excused for a few minutes and went into another room. After about ten minutes they returned and said that they had just finished the middle eight and last verse and played it to them.

The Stones recorded it at Kingsway Studios with their other co-manager Eric Easton producing. It was issued in Britain on 1 November 1963 and brought them their first Top Twenty hit. They also released it in America on 17 February 1964.

On Wednesday, 11 September 1963, the very next day after they'd given the number to the Rolling Stones, the Beatles recorded the song themselves at **Abbey Road Studios** as a vehicle for Ringo Starr. It was included on the *With The Beatles* album. It was also later included on the compilation album *Rock 'n' Roll Music*.

A group called the Rezillos had a minor hit with the song in the British charts in September 1979.

● I Want To Hold Your Hand

Possibly the most significant Beatles single of them all: the one that made the breakthrough in America and changed the direction of the charts irrevocably, eventually selling over fifteen million copies throughout the world, making it the biggest selling British single of all time.

John and Paul originally composed the song in the Harley Street house of **Jane Asher**'s parents and when they recorded it on Thursday, 17 October 1963, it was the first time they'd had the benefit of **EMI**'s new four-track machine.

Brian Epstein left for New York on 5 November 1963 with a copy of the disc and played it to Brown Meggs, Director of Eastern Operations for **Capitol Records**. The company had already turned down four of the Beatles' British chart records, but Meggs thought 'I Want To Hold Your Hand' would be suitable for the American market and a release date of 13 January 1964 was set with a pressing of 200,000 copies. Washington disc jockey **Carroll James** began to play a copy which his British air stewardess girlfriend had obtained for him and other radio stations took it up, resulting in Capitol advancing the release date to 26 December and increasing the pressing to one million copies.

The Beatles were at the George V Hotel in Paris when they were given the news that 'I Want To Hold Your Hand' was No. 1 in the American charts.

When they arrived for their triumphant first visit to America, part of the media loved them, another part treated them as a joke. Commenting on 'I Want To Hold Your Hand', William Williams of Radio WNEW in New York said, 'They want to hold your hand – a lot of people would like to hold their noses!'

More than fifteen years later a British vocal duo of

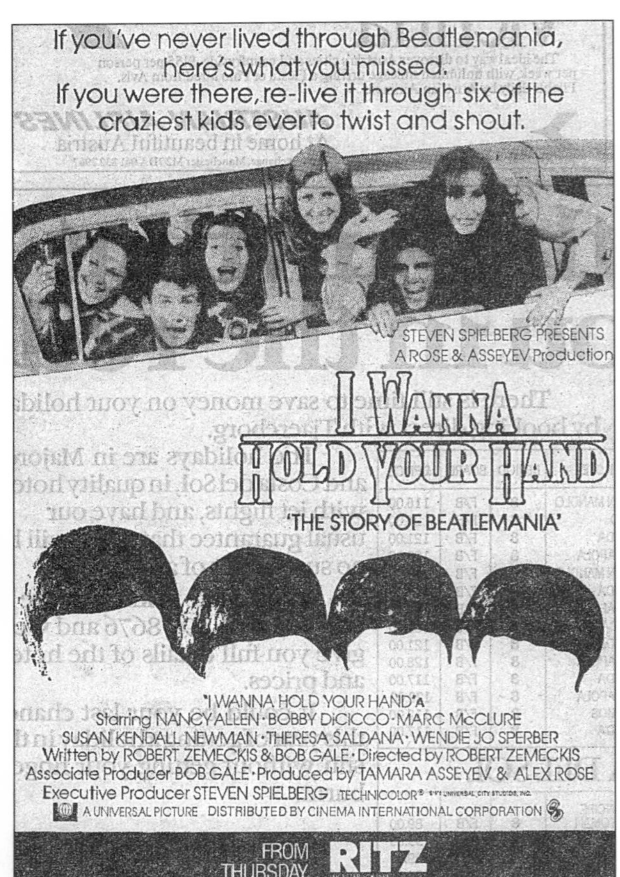

If you've never lived through Beatlemania, here's what you missed.
If you were there, re-live it through six of the craziest kids ever to twist and shout.
STEVEN SPIELBERG PRESENTS
A ROSE & ASSEYEV Production
I WANNA HOLD YOUR HAND
'THE STORY OF BEATLEMANIA'
'I WANNA HOLD YOUR HAND' A
Starring NANCY ALLEN · BOBBY DiCICCO · MARC McCLURE
SUSAN KENDALL NEWMAN · THERESA SALDANA · WENDIE JO SPERBER
Written by ROBERT ZEMECKIS & BOB GALE · Directed by ROBERT ZEMECKIS
Associate Producer BOB GALE · Produced by TAMARA ASSEYEV & ALEX ROSE
Executive Producer STEVEN SPIELBERG TECHNICOLOR®
A UNIVERSAL PICTURE DISTRIBUTED BY CINEMA INTERNATIONAL CORPORATION
FROM THURSDAY
RITZ

The Beatles' first major American hit was later to spawn a Steven Spielberg film.

David Van Day and Thereze Bazar, known as Dollar, recorded the number and reached No. 11 in the British charts with it in January 1980.

● I Want To Tell You

One of the three George Harrison compositions to find its way onto the *Revolver* album.

At the time, apparently, George had some difficulty in deciding on a title for his song. At the session on Thursday, 2 June 1966, George Martin asked George what the title of the number was. George had already come up with a song without a title which they were currently calling 'Granny Smith' (it became 'Love You To') and John Lennon, commenting to George that he never seemed to have a title for his songs, told him to call it: 'Granny Smith Part Friggin' Two!'

Engineer **Geoff Emerick** suggested that they call it 'Laxton's Superb', which was the name of another British apple, but by the next day the name had been changed to 'I Don't Know', before it eventually received its official name 'I Want To Tell You' on 6 June.

Emerick was later to comment that there seemed to be pressure to complete George's songs in as short a time as possible, while compositions by John and Paul took as long as was deemed necessary.

I Want You (She's So Heavy)

A John Lennon song, with **Yoko** as his inspiration. Rehearsals for the song began at Apple Recording Studios in January 1969 during the 'Get Back' sessions when it was called simply 'I Want You'. The next session was at **Trident Studios** in February when, on one of the takes, Paul McCartney sang lead vocal. Further recordings and overdubs took place at **Abbey Road Studios** in April and August of that year.

The track was included on the *Abbey Road* album and at seven minutes and 44 seconds in length, it was the longest number issued by the Beatles next to 'Revolution 9', which mainly consisted of tape loops put together by John.

● I Will

A love song which Paul dedicated to **Linda**. George wasn't present when the number was recorded in September 1968. It was included on *The Beatles* double album and later featured on the *Love Songs* compilation album.

● I Wish I Could Shimmy Like My Sister Kate

A number recorded by the Olympics in 1961, although it wasn't a chart hit. The Beatles must have appreciated this R&B group from Los Angeles, who only had two US chart hits – 'Western Movies' and 'The Bounce', as they included three of the group's numbers in their stage act: 'I Wish I Could Shimmy Like My Sister Kate', 'Hully Gully' and 'Baby . . . (Please Don't Go)'.

'I Wish I Could Shimmy Like My Sister Kate' was included in the Beatles' repertoire in 1961 and was popular at the **Cavern**. They continued performing it until late in 1962 with John Lennon on lead vocals.

● *Jacaranda* Club, *The*, *23 Slater Street, Liverpool L1*

The coffee bar which **Allan Williams** opened in September 1958. At the time, coffee bars were very fashionable and this particular area of Liverpool was honeycombed with them. Quite close to the 'Jac' was a coffee bar called the Studio, frequented by the models and students from **Liverpool College of Art**; local painter Yankiel Feather ran the Basement, directly to the rear of Mount Pleasant Registrer Office where John and **Cynthia** were married; 50 yards from the Jac, in Duke Street, were the **Zodiac** and Boomerang coffee bars; in Mount Pleasant was **Streates**, where poetry readings were held – and there were many more.

Allan saw an advertisement in the ***Liverpool Echo*** which read 'suitable premises for a club' and went to Slater Street. The premises to let were formerly occupied by Owens Watch Repair Shop and the lease was owned by a man in the sweetshop next door who demanded an extra £150 for 'goodwill and fittings'. Allan raised the money and managed to engage a group of West Indians to play in a steel band by offering them ten shillings (fifty pence) each.

Shortly before opening the club, Allan had been trying to think up a suitable name. He eventually decided he'd call it the Samurai, because he'd recently seen the film *The Seven Samurai*, when a friend, Bill Coward, who'd just read a book called *The Jacaranda Tree*, suggested Jacaranda.

The clientele was mixed – solicitors, doctors, art

The Jacaranda Club today – capitalising on its Beatles memories.

students, musicians – and two of the girls who served there as waitresses, Mary Larkin and Terry Shorrock, found themselves on the cover of the first issue of ***Mersey Beat*** after their photograph had been taken with rock 'n' roll star **Gene Vincent**.

The ground floor had a large glass window looking out onto Slater Street and there were small padded benches and coffee tables, a tiny kitchen, an outside loo for the Gents and steps leading to the tiny basement where the steel band played and steps leading upstairs to the Ladies loo.

Among the art students who went there were John Lennon, **Stuart Sutcliffe**, **Rod Murray** and Bill Harry and among the musicians George, Paul and Pete of the Beatles, **Gerry Marsden**, Cass & the Cassanovas and **Rory Storm**.

At one time Allan asked Stuart to paint some murals in the club, which he did, with the help of Rod Murray, although in later years Allan was to claim that John Lennon painted them with Stuart.

All appearances made by the Silver Beetles took place between May and August 1960, about a dozen appearances in all. Allan booked them mainly on Monday evenings when the **Royal Caribbean Steel Band** had a night off. They were crammed into a corner of the stone-floored basement and as there wasn't any room for equipment, their girlfriends had to sit opposite them on chairs holding broom handles to which the microphones were attached. Their first appearance at the Jac took place on 30 May and on 13 June **Tommy Moore** appeared with them for the last time. When the Silver Beetles asked **Pete Best** to join them, they held his audition at the **Wyvern**.

In later years the club was turned into a late night drinking club called the Maxie San Suzie then, following the death of John Lennon and the subsequent upsurge of interest in the Beatles, it reverted back to its original name, with a flamboyant giant placard above the club premises which featured a painting of the group in their 'Sgt Pepper' personae and the words 'The place the fab four first played'.

● Jack Paar Show, The

'The Jack Paar Show' broadcast a short clip of the Beatles performing 'She Loves You' on the evening of Friday, 3 January 1964. The highly rated NBC show screened the excerpt less than two weeks before 'I Want To Hold Your Hand' entered the American charts. The excerpt was likely to have been a clip filmed by Pathe News at the Manchester concert on 20 November 1963. There was also a fragment of a performance of 'From Me To You'.

Jack Paar may take the credit for being the first person to introduce the Beatles on a major American television entertainments show, but he marred the historic occasion by making snide remarks about their haircuts and the fans they attracted, with comments such as 'I understand scientists are working on a cure for this'.

News of the Beatles' impact in Europe had been filtering into the States and at the Beatles concert at the Winter Gardens, Bournemouth, on 16 November 1963 no less than three US camera teams were filming the group, including CBS and ABC. As a result, a clip from that show was screened on 7 December 1963 on 'The CBS Evening News with Walter Cronkite' which showed the screaming fans at the concert and clips of the **NEMS** staff tackling the huge Beatles mail sacks.

However, it is generally acknowledged that Paar was the first person to actually introduce them via a film on a major entertainment show.

When the Beatles appeared on the '**Ed Sullivan** Show' on 9 February 1964 their first three numbers were dedicated to Paar's daughter, Randy.

● Jackson, Simone

The Beatles provided backing for Simone Jackson at the **Cavern** on Wednesday, 12 September 1962.

The sixteen-year-old London singer was making a special appearance at the club and compere **Bob Wooler** was later to comment: 'She was one of the very few favoured people to be backed by the Beatles. In their earlier Hamburg days they had accompanied singer **Tony Sheridan** and they were sufficiently impressed by a Liverpool group of coloured singers called the Chants to play for them too. I can recall only two other occasions when the Beatles backed other people. Once was when they did their very first theatre date at a **Liverpool Empire** Sunday concert and accompanied Craig Douglas at the end of the first half. The other was when, as a novelty item, they backed **Ray McFall** himself at the Cavern for two numbers – Presley's "Can't Help Falling In Love" and Vic Damone's "Tender Is The Night". But Simone Jackson was something rather special. She had a superb voice with great soul and feeling in her delivery.

The Beatles thought a lot of her and so did the capacity crowd at the Cavern.'

Simone was represented by the Tito Burns agency and had only been singing professionally for five weeks.

Note: the Beatles did back other people, including Davy Jones.

Jacobs, David

A prominent show business lawyer whose clients included Diana Dors, **Judy Garland** and Laurence Harvey. He was an imposing figure, 6 ft 2 ins tall. What made him more striking was the fact that he was a homosexual who often wore stage make-up on his face. He used to hold lavish parties at his home at 2 Princes Crescent, Hove, where Ringo and **Maureen** were to spend their honeymoon.

Jacobs was responsible for the abortive merchandising deal with **Nicky Byrne**, which caused Brian Epstein so much frustration and lost the Beatles an estimated $100,000,000. Sixteen months after Brian's death, on 15 December 1968, Jacobs was found hanging in the garage of his Hove home. He'd suffered a nervous breakdown and hadn't been to his Pall Mall offices for a month.

Although the inquest rendered a verdict of suicide, there were many rumours surrounding the death of the 56-year-old lawyer, who had asked for police protection shortly before his death. John Merry, a private detective who had worked for Jacobs on numerous occasions, commented, 'I last heard from David two days before his death. He telephoned my secretary and told her it was urgent that I contact him. When I rang back he burst out, "It's no good John. I'm in terrible trouble. They're all after me." I asked who "they" were and he gave me six names – famous people in show business. I told him not to worry.'

Jacobs, David (DJ)

A British television personality who was the host of the popular BBC TV series **'Juke Box Jury'** throughout the sixties.

He travelled to Liverpool with the Beatles for their civic reception and the northern premiere of *A Hard Day's Night* and presented an all-Beatles edition of 'Juke Box Jury' from the stage of the **Empire Theatre, Liverpool**. Jacobs claimed that this edition of the programme gave them their biggest-ever audience. He said that around 24 million viewers watched it.

Brian Epstein, **Jane Asher** and the individual members of the Beatles also appeared on various editions of his show.

'Juke Box Jury' was revived by BBC 2 in the late eighties with Jools Holland as the host.

Jailhouse Rock

Another Jerry Leiber/Mike Stoller composition which **Elvis Presley** took to the top of the American charts in 1957. It was included in the **Quarry Men**'s repertoire sung by John Lennon. He continued performing it until late in 1960.

James, Carroll

The disc jockey credited with being the first person to play a Beatles record on the American airwaves.

James was a jock at WWDC-AM, the Washington DC radio station, when he received a letter from a listener, Marsha Albert, requesting that he play 'I Want To Hold Your Hand' by the Beatles. As the single hadn't been released in the States he asked his girlfriend, a stewardess with British Overseas Airways, to bring a copy of the record back from England. When he aired the single on 17 December 1963, he invited Marsha Albert into the studio to introduce it. He said, 'We played the record and I said to the radio audience, "We'd like to know what you think about the record. Don't call. Please write."' Despite that particular request, listeners began phoning straight away and the switchboard became jammed. James played the single again, an hour later.

Capitol Records had intended to issue 'I Want To Hold Your Hand' in America in late January 1964 as a build-up to the **Ed Sullivan** appearance, but the response in Washington was confusing them. It had proved to be so popular that it was being played every day, once an hour. Initially Capitol considered taking an injunction against the station for playing it when it hadn't been officially released, but decided to bring forward the release date and issued it on 27 December 1963. James had been playing it for ten days, calling it 'a WWDC exclusive'.

In an effort to take advantage of James' promotion, Capitol wanted to immediately ship hundreds of copies to Washington. They had to obtain publishing clearance first and contacted **Walter Hofer**, Brian Epstein's legal representative in New York. He told them that because of the lack of response by Capitol to Beatles products, the publishing rights to the number had been sold to MCA

Records for a nominal sum, simply to give them a foothold in America. In the meantime, one of James' friends had taped the number and sent it to a disc jockey in Chicago, who also began having an immediate response – and he sent a tape along to a disc jockey in St Louis. With all this going on, Capitol seemed to have little choice but to bring the release date forward.

When the Beatles appeared in their first American concert at the **Washington Coliseum** on 11 February 1964, James was able to introduce the group. During the same day he recorded a ten-minute interview with the Beatles, using as his theme the various questions which listeners had sent in to him. For example, what would Paul have been when he grew up if he hadn't joined the Beatles? Paul said that he might have become a teacher, but felt it was a good thing he had become a Beatle because 'I think I would have been a bad teacher'. He asked John whether he liked tea or coffee. John told him he preferred tea. 'How about tea bags?' asked James. 'I don't like them,' John answered, 'they get stuck in me teeth.'

The most perplexing part of the interview came from the conversation with George. When James asked him about what he would have become without the Beatles, George said, 'I wanna be a baggy sweeger.' James asked, 'A baggy sweeger?' 'Oh yeah,' said George, 'you know, in every town there's 25 baggy sweegers and every morning they get up and go to the airport and baggy sweeger all around.'

In 1984, 20 years after the event, James issued an album *The Carroll James Interview with the Beatles – February 11, 1964* on Carroll James CJEP-3301.

● James, Dick

The Beatles' music publisher, born Richard Leon Vapnick in London's East End in 1920. He left school when he was fourteen and became a professional singer at the age of seventeen in 1937 when he joined Al Berlin and his Band, who were resident at the Cricklewood Palais. Among the names he used were Isaac Vapnick and Lee Sheridan. During the war he joined the Medical Corps and continued to play in a band and in 1942 he made his first record with Primo Scala's Accordion Band. In 1945 he changed his name to Dick James. He appeared with various bands, including those run by Henry Hall, Stanley Black and Cyril Stapleton, but in the early fifties he lost his hair and became a song-plugger. He also began to record in the mid-fifties and his recording manager was George Martin, who produced James singing 'Tenderly' and 'Robin Hood'. Other chart hits for James were 'The Ballad Of Davy Crockett' and 'Garden Of Eden'. His biggest hit with Martin was 'Robin Hood', issued on the Parlophone label in 1955. The number became the theme tune for the TV series starring Richard Green and reached No. 9 in the charts. He ceased singing professionally in 1959 and worked as an assistant to Sidney Bron, the music publisher, until he formed his own music publishing company in September 1961. Incidentally, Bron was the brother of actress **Eleanor Bron**.

Dick James – the Beatles' music publisher. (Dick James)

Mitch Murray had brought along one of his songs to Ron Richards at **EMI.** Richards liked the acetate of 'How Do You Do It?' and phoned Dick James, who acquired the publishing rights to it. The song had been composed by Murray and Peter Callender and James approached Martin with the number and told him that it would be just right for a vocal group. Martin said that it might do for this new band from Liverpool. James laughed and said, 'Liverpool? A group from Liverpool – you gotta be kidding?' (That's the way James himself recalled it, although chroniclers have also written that he'd said, 'Liverpool? So what's from Liverpool?')

The Beatles did not like the song, but Martin insisted that they record it and they did, on Tuesday, 4 September 1962, along with 'Love Me Do' Martin was considering How Do You Do It?' as the Beatles' follow-up single, but John and Paul stressed that they wanted to record one of their own compositions and Martin agreed that a re-recorded version of 'Please Please Me' would be right for their second release. He was to comment, 'I still think the boys were too self-opinionated when they had that dispute, but they were right in the end.'

'Love Me Do' had been published by Ardmore and Beechwood, EMI's publishing arm, but Brian Epstein was dissatisfied with the promotion of the record and complained to George Martin that Ardmore and Beechwood hadn't pushed it. 'When the next one comes off I don't want to give the publishing to them.' Brian wanted to approach an American company, Hill and Range, and sign up with them because, 'They do all the **Elvis Presley** stuff.' He saw someone from Hill and Range, but Martin told him, 'They don't need you, they've already got Elvis. You need someone who's hungry.' He then suggested his former singer James, who he knew was having a struggle with his new company but who he considered was honest and would be dedicated.

Martin phoned James to tell him that they weren't issuing 'How Do You Do It?' as the Beatles' next single, but arranged a meeting between James and Epstein to discuss the plugging of 'Please Please Me'.

Brian Epstein had meetings arranged with various publishing representatives, including Alan Holmes of Robbins Music, David Platz of Essex Music and Dick James. On the day he was due to meet James for an 11.00 a.m. appointment, he had a prior meeting at 10.00 a.m. at Francis, Day and Hunter, another EMI subsidiary. The punctilious Epstein sat in the reception office at Francis, Day and Hunter's for 25 minutes. The man he was meeting hadn't turned up and it was suggested that he play the acetate to the office boy. Epstein stalked out and immediately went to the nearby James office at 132 Charing Cross Road, arriving half an hour early. James asked Brian if he could publish 'Please Please Me'. Brian asked him what he could do for the Beatles. James then picked up the phone and called **Philip Jones**, producer of the new television show **'Thank Your Lucky Stars'**. He told Jones about the record and asked him to listen. He put it on the record player and Jones listened over the phone and agreed to book them for the following show. James turned to Epstein and said, 'Now, can I publish the song?'

The 44-year-old James had asked his sixteen-year-old son, Stephen, the night before the meeting what he thought of the Beatles. Stephen told him the Beatles were great, which gave James the confidence to tell Epstein that 'Please Please Me' would be a No. 1 record. Impressed, Epstein told him that if he could make the record No. 1 he would have a long-term contract for Lennon & McCartney.

A deal was struck. James suggested that they form a company called Northern Songs, which would be administered by Dick James Music. James would have a half stake in the company and Brian and the Beatles the other half. The actual split would be 55 per cent for Dick James with John, Paul and Brian sharing the remaining 45 per cent.

Northern Songs was formed in January 1963 and during the next four years, John and Paul added more than 100 songs to the company's original catalogue of 59 songs, despite the fact that their contract demanded only a minimum of six songs per year. John and Paul were to have a company called Lenmac Enterprises which owned the rights on the first 59 songs, but this was acquired by Northern Songs before its flotation.

It was in 1965 that James persuaded Epstein that Northern Songs should go public on the Stock Exchange. John and Paul were reluctant to take that path, but they had no choice. Since the original formation the shares had altered slightly. James now owned 37.5 per cent, John and Paul owned 15 per cent each, Epstein owned 5 per cent, **NEMS** owned 7.5 per cent and Ringo and George each had 0.8 per cent. At the time of the company's flotation, with five million shares, John and Paul's percentage was worth £267,000 to each of them, George and Ringo had had their shares upped to 1.6 per cent which was worth £27,000 to each of them. Charles Silver, who was the accountant for Northern Songs, was made Chairman and together with the company's Managing Director, Dick James, he shared 37 per cent.

John and Paul had taken a lot of persuading to agree to

the flotation. Their misgivings were correct, from their point of view. Paul had said that they never owned their songs – and this proved to be true. Since their original deal with James, they were minor shareholders of their own compositions. They were never able to gain control of their songs, which were very personal to them, and over the years they were sold to various companies, and the Beatles were never able to gain possession of their work.

In December 1964, Dick James became a singer again and recorded a medley of Beatles hits, backed by a chorus of 100 voices. It was a party record for Christmas, called *Sing A Song Of Beatles* and released on 7 December on Parlophone R 5212. The number comprised a medley of 'From Me To You', 'I Want To Hold Your Hand', 'She Loves You', 'All My Loving', 'I Should Have Known Better' and 'Can't Buy Me Love'. Paul McCartney commented, 'Very good indeed – a lot of fun.'

The attitude of John and Paul to James appeared calm on the surface, but they regarded him as one of 'the men in suits', their term for the men who take control of the work of creative people and turn it into profit for themselves. They also resented the way he insisted on referring to them as 'the boys', a term they found patronizing.

Once, while they were editing ***Magical Mystery Tour*** in Old Compton Street, James dropped in and told them that Barbra Streisand wanted to record some of their songs for her new album. This was nothing new, Lennon & McCartney songs were being recorded by major artists all the time. James remained in the studio and when Paul asked him why he was still there, he said, 'Well, if you and John just write a few songs for her . . .' There was an atmospheric silence for a moment or two, then John told him to 'Fuck off!'

When **Allen Klein** moved into Apple, attempts were made to buy Northern Songs for the Beatles. James had already been approached by **Sir Lew Grade** in 1968, but told him that he didn't want to sell. Grade suggested that he should come back to him any time he wanted to make a deal. Then, in March 1969, James went to Grade and, together with Charles Silver, sold his Northern Songs shares to Associated Television Corporation. This was without the Beatles' knowledge. The first John heard about it was when he read it in the newspapers on 28 March. Paul was on honeymoon with **Linda** at the time.

According to **John Eastman**, James had decided to sell because he was afraid that Allen Klein would get control of Northern Songs and Klein had even threatened him with litigation. On top of that, the Beatles had refused to extend their contracts and the relationship between James and the Beatles was strained.

In mid-March the negotiations had begun with Silver, James and Jack Gill, the ATV Finance director. Then James told Grade that the deal was off, that there were too many complications surrounding it. A meeting was arranged between lawyers and representatives from the banks and James and Silver. Grade arrived at the meeting before the lawyers and put forward a proposition. Within five minutes they'd done a deal.

The Beatles attempted to buy Northern Songs but failed and it passed into the hands of Sir Lew Grade in 1969.

Dick James had become a multi-millionaire. From a small company which was teetering at the time he met Epstein, James was able to become fabulously rich on the songs penned by Lennon and McCartney. They felt he'd betrayed them by not allowing them a chance to buy control of the company from him which would have enabled them to buy their own songs.

James continued to thrive, becoming publisher to stars such as Elton John.

He died on 1 February 1986, aged 65.

● James, Ian

A classmate of Paul McCartney's at the **Liverpool Institute**. The two friends virtually taught each other to play guitar, passing tips, playing together.

They also used to wander round the visiting fun-fairs trying to pick girls up. They began to look and dress alike sharing the same hairstyle, the DA, and both wore white sports jackets and drainpipe trousers. Paul said they wore the jackets because of the song 'A White Sports Coat' and described his jacket as having 'speckles in it and a flap on the pockets'.

It was Ian who taught Paul the chords he played to John at their first meeting.

● Jamieson, Russell

One of the Beatles' most ardent Merseyside fans. Affectionately called 'Russell Beatle', he was four years old in 1963 when the press took numerous photographs of him dancing to Beatles records and wearing Beatle-type clothes. His devotion was such that he was made an Honorary Member of their official fan club.

Janice The Stripper

Fullsome figured striptease dancer from Manchester hired to appear at **Allan Williams' New Cabaret Artists Club**, which was managed on his behalf by **Lord Woodbine**.

Janice, surname unknown, refused to perform unless she had a backing band and Williams offered the Silver Beatles ten shillings each to back her. So, for one week early in June 1960 the four boys backed Janice's performance twice nightly at the seedy little shebeen.

She gave them printed sheet music of Beethoven and Khachaturian, which they couldn't read and they ended up playing their own versions of such standards as 'The Harry Lime Theme', 'September Song', 'Moonglow', 'Begin The Beguine' and 'It's a Long Way To Tipperary'.

Paul McCartney wrote about the experience in a letter to Bill Harry:

> John, George, **Stu** and I used to play at a Strip Club in Upper Parliament Street, backing Janice the Stripper. At the time we wore little lilac jackets . . . or purple jackets, or something. Well, we played behind Janice and naturally we looked at her, everybody looked at her, just sort of normal. At the end of the act she would turn round and . . . well, we were all young lads, we'd never seen anything like it before, and we all blushed . . . four blushing red-faced lads.
>
> Janice brought sheets of music for us to play all her arrangements. She gave us a bit of Beethoven and the Spanish Fire Dance. So in the end we said 'We can't read music, sorry, but instead of the Spanish Fire Dance we can play 'The Harry Lime Cha Cha', which we've arranged ourselves, and instead of Beethoven you can have 'Moonglow' or 'September Song', take your pick . . . and instead of the 'Sabre Dance' we'll give you 'Ramrod'. So that's what she got. She seemed quite satisfied anyway.
>
> The Strip Club wasn't an important chapter in our lives, but it was an interesting one.

Janov, Dr Arthur

One of John Lennon's friends, travelling through the States, came across a recently published book *The Primal Scream*, by the American psychiatrist Arthur Janov, who had theorized that all neuroses stemmed from a lack of parental love which resulted in a primal scene between the ages five and seven. His therapy was to encourage the patient to scream at his absent parents in an attempt to exorcise their ghosts.

The friend posted a copy to John at Tittenhurst Park. Both John and **Yoko** were so excited by the book that they wrote letters the same night to Janov, inviting him to try his therapy on them. Janov agreed to come if they faithfully followed his instructions and he included a list which directed that they stop smoking, drinking and taking drugs. Twenty-four hours before his arrival they were to isolate themselves in separate rooms and wait for him. There had to be no television, radio or telephone and nothing to read.

When Janov arrived he went straight to John's room, closed the curtain and made John lie spread-eagled on the floor while he told him to concentrate on unhappy childhood memories. 'Feel that, stay with it,' he kept repeating. After two hours he went into Yoko's room.

This particular system he called Pre-primal, the breaking down of reserves in order for the patient to be able to 'open up'. After a week he then instructed them that they must find themselves suites in different hotels. John moved into the Inn On The Park and Yoko into a nearby hotel and Janov visited them each day for a three-hour session.

John was to say, 'I was never really wanted when I was a child. The only reason I am a star is because of my repressions. The only reason I went for that goal is that I wanted to say: "Now, Mummy, will you love me?"'

After the sessions, which resulted in both John and Yoko crying for an entire two-week period, Janov returned to the States with the assurance that they would attend his Primal Therapy Institute and enrol for a proper course. They travelled to Los Angeles and stayed with **Phil Spector**, who lived near to the Institute. The two of them attended group therapy sessions for two half days per week over a period of four months.

After four months, although the therapy hadn't been completed, they both boarded a plane to London, feeling that they had benefited from the course. John was to say, 'Janov showed me how to feel my own fear and pain. Therefore I can handle it better than I could before, that's all.'

Therapy is generally an incredibly lengthy process, and four months is a very short time in which to expect results, yet the Primal Therapy was undoubtedly of immense benefit to John and led him to compose the numbers he recorded for his *John Lennon/Plastic Ono Band* album in 1970, which is often called 'The Primal Scream Album'.

● Jelly Babies

Small soft sweets, made by the confectionery firm Bassetts. They were in the shape of little babies and came in many colours. During their tour with **Roy Orbison**, fans began throwing jelly babies on stage because they'd heard that George liked them. This soon became a standard procedure at concerts and increased to an extent where it became dangerous with literally thousands of the sweets being hurled at the group during their shows.

The situation was far worse in America because they did not have the very soft jelly babies, but a hard-coated jelly bean.

George was to comment: 'They hurt. Some newspaper had dug out the old joke which we'd forgotten about, when John once said I'd eaten all his jelly babies. Everywhere we went I got them thrown at me. They don't have soft jelly babies in America but hard jelly beans like bullets.'

After their first American concert at the **Washington Coliseum**, Ringo commented, 'Some of them even threw jelly babies in bags and they hurt like hailstones.'

● Jessie's Dream

Actress Jessie Robins was featured as Ringo's Aunt Jessie in the *Magical Mystery Tour* film. Jessie, who is rather stout, has a nightmare in which she dreams of a waiter (played by John Lennon), who shovels lashings of spaghetti onto her dining-table by the spadeful. For this sequence, the Beatles worked out a piece of incidental music which they called 'Jessie's Dream'.

They recorded the incidental music privately, not in a recording studio, and it was credited to McCartney/Starkey/Harrison/Lennon.

● Jets, The

The first British band to perform in Hamburg. Some of the members were present in the 2 I's coffee bar in London when **Bruno Koschmider** arrived looking for bands for the **Kaiserkeller. Iain Hines** said he had a group and made up a name, the Jets, gathering individual musicians within 24 hours and rehearsing on the boat over to the Continent.

Their original line-up comprised Iain Hines (guitar), Colin Milander (bass), **Tony Sheridan** (vocals); Chas (guitar), Pete Wharton (second bass player), Rikki Richards (vocals) and Del Ward (drums).

After playing at the Kaiserkeller they were the group who opened the new **Top Ten Club** in the Reeperbahn in the latter part of 1960. During their season there, the Beatles occasionally joined them on stage for a jam and were due to take over the residency at the club when the Jets' season came to an end.

After the Jets had completed their contract at the Top Ten Club, Colin Milander wanted to remain in Hamburg because he was in love with a girl called Antje. He talked Iain Hines into remaining with him and they were able to get a gig as a duo at Fleurs Schanke, a tiny restaurant.

One night, when the Beatles played on stage at the Top Ten with Sheridan, Colin and Iain got up stage with them and the set included a 70-minute version of Ray Charles 'What'd I Say'.

When the Beatles were deported, **Peter Eckhorn** asked the Jets to remain at the Top Ten until he found a replacement group. Chas had already gone home, Pete Wharton, their second bass player, had also left, while Richards had gone to sing at US bases in Frankfurt.

The new line-up of the Jets which performed at the Top Ten comprised Iain on piano, Colin on bass, Sheridan on guitar and vocals and Del Ward on drums. They were also able to get an American musician to play with them later on. They remained at the Top Ten for a further two months until **Gerry & the Pacemakers** arrived from Liverpool.

The Jets then disbanded, with Tony Sheridan remaining in Hamburg as resident singer at the Top Ten. Colin and Iain returned home and joined the Echoes, backing various artists including **Gene Vincent**, Dickie Pride, Vince Eager and Ricky Valence. Later, Iain was to return to Hamburg and became booking manager at the Top Ten.

● Joe's Cafe, *139 Duke Street, Liverpool L1*

Late-night cafe popular with taxi drivers, prostitutes and members of the Mersey Beat groups. In the early sixties groups used to drop into Joe's in the early hours after a gig or following a few half-pints of beer at the nearby **Blue Angel**. There was a small ground floor, but the bands usually tumbled up the narrow stairway to the first floor where a few tables could be placed together and a party of several people could chat while they ordered a meal for a modest price from a limited menu.

Joe Davey, the bearded owner who also ran a taxi-hire

irm, was quite pleased with his musical clientele and)egan to build a 'wall of fame' with their photographs in he first floor rooms. In April 1966, Joe bought the **:avern Club** for £5,500, but retained it for only a short ime before re-selling. Commenting on the times when the 3eatles visited his cafe, he said, 'I used to give them tea ınd bread and butter free as they were earning so little.'

Even though Joe's Cafe closed down, its fame remained ınd a promising Liverpool band of the seventies was to all itself Eat At Joe's.

Almost opposite the cafe was the Pink Parrot Club, wenty-five yards away was the **Zodiac Coffee Club** and urther down the street, the Cabaret Club. The **Liverpool nstitute**, the Art College, the **Anglican Cathedral** and **;ambier Terrace** all branch off Duke Street.

Johanneshovs Isstadion, Stockholm, ;weden

'his massive ice-hockey stadium saw the appearance of ıe Beatles on their second and last visit to Sweden when, on 28 and 29 July 1964 they performed a total of four concerts, two per night.

During their first concert, John and Paul received mild electric shocks from an unearthed microphone.

The capacity of the arena was 8,500 although their audiences varied from 6,500 to 3,000.

● John, Elton

Born Reginald Kenneth Dwight in Pinner on 25 March 1947, he later became an office boy for a West End music publisher and wrote the debut single for a group called Bluesology. The lead singer was **Long John Baldry** and the saxophonist Elton Dean, so he borrowed their forenames and called himself Elton John, teaming up with Bernie Taupin and signing to **Dick James** Music in 1968.

Elton John went on to become an international superstar and met John Lennon in 1974. The two became close friends. Lennon was living in New York at the time and Elton recalled: 'When I was in New York getting off the SS *France* I saw him again and he said, "Come down to

:lton John, who)ecame godfather to 'ohn Lennon's son, ;ean. (Rocket Record :ompany)

my session," so I did, and ended up doing "Whatever Gets You Thru The Night" and "Surprise" from the album. And he was going back to LA to do a song for Ringo and I said, "On the way back why don't you come up to Caribou? 'Cos we're gonna do "Lucy In The Sky". And he said "Sure".' When Elton came to record John's 'Lucy In The Sky With Diamonds', John turned up and Elton asked if John could appear on the record with him and he agreed and John sang backing vocals and played guitar, using his Dr Winston O'Boogie pseudonym. It was the first single Elton had released which hadn't been written by himself and Bernie and it was issued in Britain on DJM DJS 340 on 15 November 1974 where it reached the No. 3 position and remained in the charts for ten weeks. The single, which featured the John Lennon composition 'One Day At A Time' on the flipside, was issued in America on 18 November 1974 on MCA 40344 and hit the No. 1 position for two weeks, remaining fourteen weeks in the charts.

In the meantime, when Elton had taken up John's invitation to visit him recording 'Whatever Gets You Thru The Night', he played piano and organ and sang backing vocals. He told John that the record would be a hit. John said it wouldn't be a No. 1 because he felt he was out of favour in America. Elton disagreed and said the record would be No. 1 – he also made a bargain with John and said that if the record reached No. 1, John should appear in concert with him.

Lennon agreed and turned up on 28 November for Elton John's Thanksgiving concert at Madison Square Garden in New York, unannounced. He turned down Elton's offer to perform 'Imagine', but played on three numbers with him: 'Whatever Gets You Thru The Night', 'Lucy In The Sky With Diamonds' and 'I Saw Her Standing There'. The concert had been recorded and 'I Saw Her Standing There' was issued as the flipside of Elton's 'Philadelphia Freedom', which became Elton's second No. 1 American hit in a row, following 'Lucy In The Sky With Diamonds'. The other two numbers which had been recorded were eventually issued on a twelve-inch single by DJM Records in Britain in 1981.

Elton's friendship with John continued and he became godfather to **Sean Lennon**. Together with Bernie Taupin, he also penned 'Snookeroo' for Ringo Starr to record.

In March 1976, he became the second rock artist since the Beatles to be the subject of a waxworks figure at Madame Tussaud's in London.

● *John F. Kennedy Airport, New York City*

Scenes of adulation greeted the Beatles when they flew in to John F. Kennedy Airport on Pan Am Flight 101 at 1.35 p.m. on 7 February 1964.

The group had flown out of Heathrow Airport ensconced in the first-class section of the plane. Among the other first-class passengers were **Cynthia** Lennon Brian Epstein, **Phil Spector** and **George Harrison** of the ***Liverpool Echo***. Also on the plane were photographer **Dezo Hoffmann** and **Cavern Club** boss **Ray McFall** who alighted wearing a fur hat he'd bought in Hamburg. Other seats in the plane were occupied by pressmen and businessmen who were trying to obtain Beatles merchandizing rights. The businessmen kept sending notes to Epstein, who ignored them. **Neil Aspinall** and **Mal Evans** spent a great deal of time forging the Beatles signatures on photographs.

There were 5,000 fans gathered at the airport, mainly on the balcony above the customs hall, waving banners with messages such as 'Welcome to Beatlesville USA' and singing 'We love you Beatles, Oh yes we do'.

As the passengers alighted, each was given a Beatle kit with the compliments of **Capitol Records**. This comprised a 'signed' photograph, an 'I like the Beatles' badge and a Beatles wig.

There was a 100-man police cordon holding back the crowds and escorting the Beatles to the customs hall and one policeman said, 'I think the world has gone mad' while another commented, 'Boy, can they use a haircut!'

All their luggage was thoroughly examined in the customs hall, while airport officials said that they had experienced nothing like it since General MacArthur had returned from Korea.

Brian Sommerville, the group's press agent, had arrived a few days earlier to co-ordinate the press and there were 200 press representatives waiting for them on the first floor of the main terminal.

The 200 journalists and photographers were almost impossible to control and they ignored Sommerville's request for order – until John Lennon shouted at them to 'Shut up!' This was greeted with applause, followed by a quiet spell during which Sommerville was able to introduce each member of the group and the question and answer session began.

Q: 'Are you in favour of lunacy?'

Paul: 'Yeah. It's healthy.'

Q: 'Will you be getting a haircut?'

All: 'No!'

George: 'We had one yesterday.'

Q: 'Will you sing something?'

John: 'No, we need money first.'

Q: 'Which one of you is really bald?'

Paul: 'I'm bald.'

John: 'We're all bald.'

Q: 'Is there any truth to the rumour that you're really st four **Elvis Presleys**?'

Ringo: 'No, nah, we're not.' (His voice mimicking vis.)

Q: 'What is the secret of your success?'

Ringo: 'We have a press agent.'

Q: 'What do you think of the campaign in Detroit to tamp out the Beatles"?'

John: 'We have a campaign to stamp out Detroit.'

Q: 'Are you part of a social rebellion against the older neration?'

Paul: 'No, it's a dirty lie.'

All: 'Yeah, a dirty lie.'

Q: 'Ringo, why do you wear two rings on each hand?'

Ringo: 'Because I can't fit them through my nose.'

Q: 'Do you think it's wrong to set such a bad example to nagers, smoking the way you do?'

Ringo: 'It's better than being alcoholics.'

Q: 'What do you think of the criticism that you are not ry good?'

George: 'We're not.'

Q: 'What do you believe is the reason you are the most pular singing group today?'

John: 'We've no idea. If we did we'd get four long-ired boys, put them together, and become their nagers.'

Q: 'What do you miss most now that your fame ohibits your freedom?'

Ringo: 'Going to the movies.'

George: 'Having nothing to do.'

John: 'School, because you don't have much to do re.'

Paul: 'Going on buses.'

Q: 'What do you do when you're cooped up in a hotel om between shows?'

George: 'We ice-skate.'

Q: 'How did you find America?'

Ringo: 'We went to Greenland and made a left turn.'

Q: 'Would you like to walk down the street without being recognized?'

John: 'We used to do that with no money in our pockets. There's no point in it.'

Q: 'How do you keep your psychic balance?'

Ringo: 'The important thing is not to get potty. There's four of us, so whenever one of us gets a little potty, the other three bring him back to earth.'

Q: 'Does all the adulation from teenage girls affect you?'

John: 'When I feel my head start to swell, I look at Ringo and know perfectly well we're not supermen.'

Q: 'How do you feel about the invasion of your privacy all the time?'

Ringo: 'The only time it bothers us is when they get us to the floor and really mangle us.'

Q: 'Do you speak French?'

Paul: '*Non*.'

Q: 'Do you have any special advice for teenagers?'

John: 'Don't get pimples.'

Q: 'What would you do if the fans got past the police lines?'

George: 'We'd die laughing.'

Q: 'What will you do when the bubble bursts?'

George: 'Take up ice-hockey.'

Paul: 'Play baseball.'

Q: 'Has success spoiled the Beatles?'

John: 'Well, you don't see us running out and buying bowler hats, do you? I think we've pretty well succeeded in remaining ourselves.'

Paul: 'The great thing about it is that you don't have big worries anymore when you've got where we have, only little ones – like whether the plane is going to crash.'

Q: 'What is the biggest threat to your careers, the atom bomb or dandruff?'

Ringo: 'The atom bomb. We've already got dandruff.'

After the press reception the Beatles made their way to the **Plaza Hotel**.

● John Fred & His Playboy Band

An American group who took a parody of 'Lucy In The Sky With Diamonds' to the top of the American charts in January 1968. The record was called 'Judy In Disguise (With Glasses)'. Group leader John Fred had bought a copy of the *Sgt Pepper* album and he was shaving when the track 'Lucy In The Sky With Diamonds' was playing. He'd never heard the number and recalled, 'When it came on, I thought he was saying "Lucy in disguise with diamonds". That's the first time it hit my mind, these Beatles were so clever! When I looked at the album it said "Lucy In The Sky . . ." and then I was totally disappointed.' However, the song remained on John's mind and when he noticed hundreds of girls on a beach in Florida wearing sunglasses, he came up with a song, 'Beverly In Disguise (With Glasses)', although he later changed the name to Judy. Ironically, the song knocked the Beatles' 'Hello Goodbye' from the No. 1 spot in the American charts.

● Johnny & The Moondogs

A stopgap name adopted by the **Quarry Men** when they entered the Carroll Levis talent competitions in 1959. They thought it would be a more suitable name as most successful groups at the time had the name of a lead singer in the title. John, Paul and George used the name when they performed at a couple of heats at the **Empire Theatre, Liverpool** in October 1959 and at the **Hippodrome Theatre, Manchester** in November.

George commented: 'For this we dreamed up a new name, Johnny & the Moondogs. There were just the three of us and I remember we were on a **Buddy Holly** & the Crickets kick at the time. So, of course, we sang "Think It Over" and "It's So Easy".'

Carroll Levis asked the boys what the name Moondog meant. They'd made it up, but told him that it referred to a Red Indian who banged tin cans!

The Liverpool heats were won by another band, but Johnny & the Moondogs had received enough applause to be booked into the special heat at Manchester's Hippodrome Theatre on 15 November. The winner of the Manchester show would be given the opportunity of appearing for two minutes on Levis' ATV television show 'Discoveries'.

It was the boys' first performance outside of Liverpool but they had to leave before the end of the show in order to catch the last train home. As all the acts appeared singly in a finale to receive audience applause, which determined the winner, Johnny & the Moondogs never had the opportunity of appearing on 'Discoveries'.

The name Johnny & the Moondogs was used from October 1959 until January 1960.

● Johnny B. Goode

A classic rock 'n' roll recording by **Chuck Berry** originally released in 1958, which became a standard item in the repertoire of most rock groups, including the Beatles, who began performing the number in the late fifties, before they had even decided on the name the Beatles. John was lead vocalist on the number, which the group performed on their BBC radio appearance on **'Saturday Club'** on 15 February 1964.

● Johns, Glyn

A leading British record producer/engineer who had worked with a number of top bands such as the **Rolling Stones** and the Who when he received a phone call from Paul McCartney in December 1968, inviting him to work with the Beatles as balance engineer on a current project. Paul explained that they were producing their own television show and intended making a documentary and an album from it. The project, then called 'Get Back' eventually turned into *Let It Be*.

The tapes which Glyn recorded, together with George Martin, were later given to **Phil Spector** to mix. Glen was to comment: 'I cannot bring myself to listen to the Phil Spector version of the album – I heard a few bars of it once, and was totally disgusted, and think it's an absolute load of garbage.'

Glyn's first association with the Beatles occurred when he acted as second engineer on Jack Good's television special **'Around the Beatles'** at IBC Studios on 19 April 1964.

As a vocalist, Glyn recorded 'I'll Follow The Sun' from the *Beatles For Sale* album. His single was issued on Pye 7N 15818 on 2 April 1965.

Paul later called Glyn, this time to work on the *Red Rose Speedway* sessions, but it was said that he felt Paul's work on the album was too slow and he walked out on the session.

John used to humorously refer to him as Glynis (an in joke referring to Glynis Johns, the British actress of fifties films).

● Jolly What!

Jolly What! England's Greatest Recording Stars The Beatles & Frank Ifield On Stage was an unusual album which has become a collector's item.

Issued by **Vee-Jay Records** in America on Vee-J.

085 on 26 February 1964, it reached No. 104 in the *illboard* charts and No. 73 in *Cash Box*. The reason for s poor showing was that most American Beatles fans lready had the few Beatles tracks on the album.

The Vee-Jay label had been given the opportunity of icking up some Beatles tracks for release in America in 963 after **Capitol Records** had turned the group down. nce the build-up began in 1964, Vee-Jay decided to take dvantage of the material. They'd released an album *ntroducing The Beatles* (the tracks from the British debut lbum *Please Please Me*) in July 1963 with no success. hey re-released the album in January 1964 and it eached No. 2 in *Cash Box* and *Billboard* and No. 1 in the *ecord World* charts. As the company was unable to obtain ny more Beatle cuts due to the fact that Capitol had now ealized the group's potential, Vee-Jay placed four of the acks from *Introducing The Beatles* – 'Please Please Me', 'rom Me To You', 'Ask Me Why' and 'Thank You Girl' – nto this album, which also contained eight **Frank Ifield** its – 'Any Time', 'Lovesick Blues', 'I'm Smiling Now', Nobody's Darling', 'I Remember You', 'The Wayward 'ind', 'Unchained Melody' and 'I Listen To My Heart'.

The cover blurb implied that the album had been corded live, which was untrue. All the tracks were studio its. By sheer coincidence, the Beatles and Frank Ifield ad once actually appeared on the same show in eterborough.

The original album sleeve was a rather bland affair porting a drawing of an Edwardian-type figure with a long oustache and spectacles, obviously illustrating the 'Jolly hat!' phrase. The album was re-pressed with a different over featuring a painting of the four in their collarless ckets.

The sleeve notes read:

he tremendous surging influence that has of recent onths been felt by the European Recording artists has ever been equalled as on this album. Without any uestion The Beatles and Frank Ifield are the most pular recording stars in Europe. The Beatles are nsidered a phenomenon on the American scene in that is is the first time that a European based recording act s so captivated the American public from both TV and cording standpoint.

'It is with a great deal of pride and pleasure that this pulation [sic] has been presented.'

● Jones, Brian

Blond, charismatic founder-member of the **Rolling Stones**, born in Cheltenham on 28 February 1942.

Giorgio Gomelsky, who acted as manager of the group for a time, invited the Beatles to see the Stones at the **Crawdaddy Club**, Richmond. They became friends and Brian, in particular, found the Beatles' music exciting and wanted the Stones to adopt Beatles-style harmonies.

In the early days of the group, Brian had been looked upon as their leader. However, the power in the band began to revolve increasingly around Mick Jagger and Keith Richard, primarily because they wrote the group's material. Although Brian had innovative ideas and was one of the first British musicians to be influenced by ethnic music, his role in the group continued to be eroded. This caused him to turn increasingly to drink. He was in love with Anita Pallenberg, but when she slept with both Keith Richard and Mick Jagger, he became depressed still further, took solace in drugs and was constantly depressed. John Lennon was to comment, 'From being brilliant he became the kind of person you dread ringing you up. He was in a lot of pain but I was going through so much myself that it seemed there was nothing I could do to help.'

Brian left the Stones in 1969, announcing on 9 June: 'The music of Mick Jagger and Keith Richard has, to my mind, progressed on a tangent as far as my own tastes are concerned.'

In May 1967 he had played saxophone with the Beatles on their track 'You Know My Name (Look Up The Number)', which wasn't released until March 1970 when it was used as the flipside of 'Let it Be'.

Brian had expressed his desire to join the Beatles and thought he might end up as the fifth member of the band.

He was found drowned in the swimming pool of his Sussex house on 3 July 1969. He was 27 years old.

● Jones, Davy

American singer who had appeared on several major US TV shows, including the **Ed Sullivan**, Walter Winchell, Arthur Godfrey and Alan Freed Shows, before moving to Britain in 1960 and signing with Pye Records.

In 1961, at the age of 22, he made several appearances in and around Liverpool, getting to know the local groups and promoters before moving on to the Continent. He'd first appeared in Liverpool on Tuesday, 3 May 1960, at

The Beatles provided backing for American singer Davy Jones at the Cavern. (*Mersey Beat* Archives)

Liverpool Stadium on the **Allan Williams** promotion headlined by **Gene Vincent**.

He made his debut with the Beatles on 24 November 1961 when he dropped by the **Tower Ballroom, New Brighton** where the group were appearing on a **Sam Leach** extravaganza. Jones got up on stage with the Beatles and they backed him on two numbers.

The Beatles became his backing group once again, this time on two occasions on the same day – 8 December 1961. During the day he joined the Beatles on stage at the **Cavern Club** for a lunchtime session and in the evening he topped the bill at the Tower Ballroom, and the Beatles also backed him on that occasion.

Jones later appeared at the **Star Club**, Hamburg.

● Jones, Peter

A prominent British music journalist who wrote the first-ever paperback book on the Beatles story, entitled *The True Story of the Beatles*, under the name Billy Shepher a pseudonym he was to use for his features on the Beatl in the *Beatles Book* magazine.

During his term as editor of *Record Mirror* he becan the first journalist on a national music paper to intervie the Beatles, in August 1962. An account of the interview given in the November 1978 issue of the *Beatles Boo* Peter, whose small office at *Record Mirror* was based 116 Shaftesbury Avenue, received a call fro photographer **Dezo Hoffmann**, whose studio was only few streets away. He'd just finished a photo session wi the Beatles and said, 'I have four boys from Liverpool would love you to meet.' He brought them around to me Peter, accompanied by Brian Epstein. There were on three chairs in the office. Epstein told him that the grou were probably the most popular vocal and instrument band in the North of England. Peter was to interview t group on numerous occasions.

He was later to become European representative of *illboard* magazine.

● Jones, Philip

roducer of the popular **'Thank Your Lucky Stars'** levision pop show of the sixties.

When Brian Epstein was meeting **Dick James** in his haring Cross Road office in January 1963 to discuss the ossibility of James promoting 'Please Please Me', James nmediately contacted Jones by phone in Epstein's resence. He asked Jones if he'd book the Beatles for the rogramme and Jones, although a friend of James, pointed ut that he had to listen to artists' records before he ecided on booking them. Undismayed, James nmediately put 'Please Please Me' on the record player nd Jones listened to the song on the phone. He then ooked them for the next available show.

The group travelled to Birmingham on 13 January 1963 record the show, which was transmitted on 19 January. s the show was networked, 'Thank Your Lucky Stars' ecame their first national TV appearance and Jones was book them for numerous further appearances.

Jones, Ron

ormer Tourist Development Officer of Merseyside, who as born in Liverpool in 1941. He joined a skiffle group nd attended the **Cavern** regularly. In 1972 he began romoting the Beatles on behalf of the Merseyside County ouncil and prepared the first-ever official souvenir of the roup, 10,000 copies of which were released in 1974. alled *The Beatles Collection*, it was packaged in a ouble-album sized folder, illustrated with fifteen Beatle bum covers. The items inside included a large fold-out ap of the 'Beatles Liverpool', a giant 'Back Track' poster llowing their lives and careers from 1955–1971, together ith further maps, a discography, postcards, a bookmark, n Official Beatles Fan Club release and a book, *Nothing o Get Hung About*.

Ron then arranged for funds to enable **Bob Wooler** nd **Allan Williams** to stage the first Liverpool Beatles onvention in 1977 and also secured funds for Jim and Liz ughes to launch two Beatle extravaganzas. He produced e first local Beatles postcard and conceived *In The ootsteps Of The Beatles*, a guidebook he wrote in ollaboration with **Mike Evans**. Ron also reintroduced uided Beatles tours of Liverpool and introduced Beatleguides, Mersey Beatle weekend holidays and devised the *Art of the Beatles* exhibition.

Since 1987 he has run his own marketing, public relations, tourism and photography practice and in 1991 published *The Beatles' Liverpool*.

● Joseph Williams Primary School, Naylorsfield Road, Belle Vale, Liverpool 25

The school where both Paul and **Mike McCartney** were moved when **Stockton Wood Road** became overcrowded. It was a half-hour bus ride from the McCartney home in Speke, but the two boys used to enjoy the journeys on the double-decker buses. It was the first school built in Liverpool after the war and it was situated in a conservation area.

Their headmaster John Gore, whom they called 'Pop', used to take them for nature walks, and they enjoyed their trips into the neighbouring countryside. However, for a period at the school, Paul was very unhappy because he'd put on weight and some of the pupils called him 'fatty'.

Paul was an apt pupil and came top in most subjects regularly. He did not have any difficulty in passing his 11-Plus examination and gaining entrance to the **Liverpool Institute**.

● Juke Box Jury

Popular BBC television programme in which a panel of four celebrities comment on a selection of the current week's record releases. The original series of the sixties was hosted by disc jockey **David Jacobs**. Early each Saturday evening Jacobs would introduce his panel who would listen to new releases, comment on them and predict whether each song in question would be a 'hit' or a 'miss'. One personality who made several appearances on the programme was **Jane Asher**.

John made his only solo appearance on the panel on 22 June 1963 for the programme which was transmitted on 29 June. He caused upset to **Elvis Presley** fans who wrote in several letters of complaint after he was critical of the latest Elvis release, 'Devil In Disguise' and referred to 'the King' as 'today's Bing Crosby', suggesting that he return to using rock 'n' roll material.

George made his only solo appearance when he guested 'live' on 25 July 1964. Ringo recorded a 'Juke Box Jury' appearance the same day for the following week's show, transmitted on 1 August. Ringo's fellow celebrities on the panel were actress Judy Cornwall, comedian Ray Martine and TV personality Katie Boyle. Compere David Jacobs introduced him by saying, 'A gentleman known in the trade as Ringo Starr'. Ringo was initially nervous and commented, 'I'm not worried about what records they'll play. I'm OK judging records – just as long as I don't get too carried away and get too outspoken.' One of the records he had to review was his friend **Cilla Black**'s 'It's For You'.

Brian Epstein was to make two appearances on the show, the first on 26 October 1963 and the second on 29 February 1964. The waxwork models of the Beatles, from Madame Tussauds, were displayed on the programme on 30 May 1964.

The outstanding highlight took place on 7 December 1963 when a special all-Beatles edition of the show was filmed from the stage of the **Empire Theatre, Liverpool**. It was broadcast the same day in the early evening to a television audience of 23 million viewers.

The records played to John, Paul, George and Ringo were:

1. 'I Could Write A Book', The Chants
2. 'Kiss Me Quick', Elvis Presley
3. 'Hippy Hippy Shake', The Swinging Bluejeans
4. 'Did You Have A Happy Birthday?', Paul Anka
5. 'The Nitty Gritty', Shirley Ellis
6. 'I Can't Stop Talking About You', Steve Lawrence and Edie Gorme
7. 'Do You Really Love Me', Billy Fury
8. 'There, I've Said It Again', Bobby Vinton
9. 'Love Hit Me', The Orchids
10. 'I Think Of You', The Merseybeats

The Beatles voted numbers 1, 2, 3, 6, 7 and 10 as hits. The records which actually charted were 2, 3, 7, 8 and 10. Four of the records – 2, 3, 7 and 10 – were by Liverpool artists.

When reviewing 'Hippy Hippy Shake', John Lennon said, 'I prefer Bill Harry's version.' This was an in-joke by John referring to the fact that ***Mersey Beat*** had been encouraging a Liverpool group to record the number. As a result, record stores throughout the land were inundated by requests from Beatle fans asking for Bill Harry's version of 'The Hippy Hippy Shake', a record which didn't exist!

The BBC were keen to present another all-Beatles panel on the programme and approached Brian Epstein in July 1964, but he turned the proposal down.

● *Julia*

John's song, named in honour of his mother. **Yoko** was said to have given him some small help with the lyric and she is herself mentioned in the song – as 'Ocean Child'.

This was the only completely solo John Lennon number recorded while he was a member of the Beatles. When he recorded the number at **Abbey Road** on Sunday, 13 October 1968, neither Paul, George or Ringo were in the studio and John sang the song himself, playing acoustic guitar.

'Julia' was included on *The Beatles* double album. **Capitol** also issued it as the flipside of the single 'Ob-La-Di, Ob-La-Da' in America on Capitol 4347 on 8 November 1976.

● Junior Art School, *Gambier Terrace, Liverpool L1*

School formerly situated in a large house in the Georgian terrace overlooking the **Anglican Cathedral**. Among its students were **Cynthia Powell**, later to become Cynthia Lennon; Bill Harry, founder of ***Mersey Beat***; Les Chadwick, photographer who took many of the early Beatles shots for **Peter Kaye**; and Vicky Haseman, who became a member of the **Vernons Girls** and later married **Joe Brown**.

● *Junk*

A song Paul wrote in India which had the original working title of 'Jubilee'. He'd originally recorded it for the *Abbey Road* album, but it wasn't used and he included it on his 1970 Apple album, *McCartney*.

● Junkin, John

A British comedian/actor who portrayed a road manager called Shake, loosely based on **Mal Evans**, in the film *A Hard Day's Night*.

Junkin had heard that the Beatles were only hiring Liverpool actors for the road manager roles, which seemed to be confirmed when **Norman Rossington** was employed to portray Norm. So Junkin affected a Liverpool accent and pretended to be a 'scouser'. Once the filming was underway he couldn't keep up the pretence, but the boys appreciated his nerve and were amused by it.

Kaempfert, Berthold

major German bandleader/composer, born in Hamburg, o was an A&R man at Polydor in 1961 when Alfred hacht of Aberbach Music approached him about cording an artist he'd seen in the **Top Ten Club**. hacht had visited the club, was impressed by **Tony eridan** and suggested that Kaempfert should record m. The 37-year-old recording manager/talent scout ited the Top Ten, agreed with his friend's assessment d signed Sheridan to a recording session. On Tony's ommendation, he hired the Beatles to back him on the ssions.

The Beatles began a three-day recording stint, backing ny Sheridan at the Harburg Friedrich Ebvert Halle, ich was in an infants' school, on 22 June 1961.

Kaempfert chose two numbers, 'My Bonnie Lies Over e Ocean' and 'When The Saints Go Marching In', and eridan also sang 'Why (Can't You Love Me Again)'. empfert had also decided to name the group the **Beat others** on the record release. The Beatles, who were id a flat fee of 300 marks (around £26) for the session d did not receive any royalties, asked Kaempfert if they uld record some other numbers. He asked them what ginal material they had, but they couldn't come up with ything original, apart from the George Harrison strumental 'Cry For A Shadow'. Kaempfert advised them start writing their own material if they intended to make ame for themselves. He also recorded them performing n't She Sweet'.

'Cry For A Shadow' was actually an instrumental George had composed (with a little help from John) on their previous Hamburg trip when **Rory Storm** asked him if he knew the **Shadows**' 'Frightened City'. It was a parody of the Shadows style which George had considered calling 'Beatle Bop'. On the third day in the studio they only managed to cut one number with Sheridan, 'If You Love Me, Baby'.

On 1 May 1961 the Beatles signed a recording contract with Bert Kaempfert Produktions for one year, but renewable for periods of one year, in which they agreed to record four songs per year.

When Brian Epstein took over the Beatles and was negotiating a British contract for them, he wrote to Kaempfert on 20 February 1962 asking him to release them. Kaempfert wrote, 'I do not want to spoil the chance

Bert Kaempfert – he supervised the Beatles' early recording sessions in Hamburg. (Polydor)

of the group to get recording contracts elsewhere, but I do think that we should have the chance to make recordings with the group for the Polydor label whilst they are in Hamburg.'

A few years later, Kaempfert told the British musical weekly, *Melody Maker*: 'One day Brian Epstein wrote to me asking under what conditions I'd release the Beatles. I said there's no conditions, you can take them. Polydor didn't want them, they were only interested in Sheridan.'

When the Beatles performed at the **Ernst Merck Halle**, Hamburg, on 26 June 1966, Bert was among the backstage visitors. As soon as they saw him, the Beatles began singing 'Strangers In The Night'.

Kaempfert became a major recording artist and composer in his own right and his first million seller was 'Wonderland By Night', which topped the American charts. In 1961 the Bert Kaempfert Orchestra was voted 'Number One Band of the Future' in a *Cash Box* poll. In 1965 Bert composed the music for the film *A Man Could Get Killed* and one of the numbers he composed was 'Strangers In The Night', which was to provide Frank Sinatra with his first No. 1 hit for several years. Other major hits by Kaempfert included 'Bye Bye Blues', 'A Swinging Safari', 'Spanish Eyes' and '*Danke Schön*'.

Kaempfert, who was married with two daughters, began his first British tour in 1980. In June of that year he died of a heart attack shortly after arriving in Spain.

● Kaiserkeller, 38 Grosse Freiheit, St Pauli, Hamburg, Germany

A large club in the notorious red-light district of Hamburg which was run by **Bruno Koschmider**. The events which led up to the Beatles appearing at the Kaiserkeller (King's Cellar) had their origins in the **Jacaranda Club**, Liverpool.

The main attraction at the Jacaranda was the **Royal Caribbean Steel Band**. One day **Allan Williams** arrived at the club to discover that the band had not turned up and they later contacted him to say that they were playing at a club in Hamburg and suggested that he come over and book some groups into the German city.

Williams decided to act on the tip and recorded a number of local acts on a tape recorder in the cellar of the Jac. They were the Silver Beatles, Cass & the Cassanovas, **Gerry & the Pacemakers**, folk group the Spinners and a jazz band, Noel Walker's Stompers. He then set off on a weekend trip to Germany, via Amsterdam, accompani by his friend **Lord Woodbine**.

Arriving in Hamburg they couldn't locate the cl where the steel band were playing and when Lo Woodbine went off with a stripper, Williams decided explore the red-light district. Someone mentioned t Kaiserkeller club to him and he took a cab there and w quite impressed by the size of the venue. He observed th the decor was in a nautical style with glass floats on t walls, fishing nets, a bar shaped like a ship and vario brass portholes on the walls.

The German band on the stage were making mus which was having no impact on the audience who ignor it and continued drinking and talking. When the band to a break and the jukebox began to blast out rock 'n' r records by **Elvis Presley** and others, he noticed complete change of atmosphere, with members of t audience crowding onto the dance floor.

He stopped a waiter and requested to see the manag and was eventually taken to Koschmider's offic Koschmider couldn't speak English and their discussi was held through an interpreter. Williams impressed Koschmider that he needed rock 'n' roll groups at the clu that the best rock 'n' roll groups came from Liverpool a that he managed a number of them. Williams then told hi about the tapes and they were put on a tape recorder, b all that came out was a racket, the tapes had become d magnetized during the trek from Liverpool to Hambu Koschmider suggested that he send him some more tapes

There is a slight variation to the story. **Brian Casse** of Cass & the Cassanovas, maintained that Willian allowed him to sleep overnight at the Jacaranda. Cass h heard from contacts that a German clubowner call Koschmider was looking for bands to book. Eager to fi work for his own band, Casser discovered Koschmide number and phoned him, using the Jacaranda telepho after the club had closed for the night. He says convinced Koschmider that he should book Liverpo groups. Casser then alleges that Koschmider rang the J during the day when he wasn't around and Allan Williar took the call and decided to act as agent instead. T explanation couldn't be as straightforward as this, becau Koschmider didn't speak English, therefore any call wou have had to be made by someone who could translate f him.

Following Williams' trip to Hamburg, he had problen

th a group called **Howie Casey** & the Seniors. As a sult of Williams arranging for them to tour with one of arry **Parnes'** acts, they'd turned professional, only to scover that the tour had been cancelled. Howie arrived Williams' **Blue Angel Club**, determined to take it out his hide and Williams escaped a physical beating by fering to take the group down to the 2 I's in London and t them work.

By an amazing coincidence, when they arrived at the 2 s, Bruno Koschmider was there. Intrigued by the idea of oking British rock 'n' roll clubs into the Kaiserkeller, d not knowing the difference between London and verpool, he'd arrived in England and had been directed the 2 I's. As a result he'd booked a group called the ts. Williams arranged for the Seniors to go on stage and oschmider agreed to book them at a fee of 30 deutsche arks per man per day. The group began playing at the aiserkeller on 31 July 1960.

Koschmider contacted Williams for more bands and the eatles eventually wended their way to Germany, only to booked into the **Indra Club**, a seedier venue at the ong end of the Grosse Freiheit.

The Seniors ended their season at the Kaiserkeller and 1 October, **Rory Storm & the Hurricanes** took over. 1 4 October they were joined by the Beatles and the two oups took split shifts at the venue. The Beatles appeared om 4 October–30 November, a total of 58 nights.

Both groups got up to high jinks at the club, with ennon taunting the customers with shouts of '*Sieg heil! eg heil!*'. One night he walked on stage clad only in a ir of swimming trunks and turned his back on the dience, pulling down his trunks to show his bare bottom. e Hurricanes and the Beatles also had a bet as to who uld break the stage, which was a flimsy affair supported crates. Nightly they'd become more energetic, jumping and down in an effort to crack the stage. Eventually it ppened when the Hurricanes were playing and a furious oschmider fined the group 65 deutsche marks. It was ile they were playing at the club that they were scovered by a German student, **Klaus Voormann**, who ought along his friends such as **Astrid Kirchherr** and rgen Vollmer, all of them to play their part in the Beatles ry. Also among the regulars were prostitutes from the erbertstrasse who continually ordered waiters to send inks to the group on stage.

As their season neared its end, they were determined to remain in Hamburg and move on to another club, the **Top Ten Club** in the Reeperbahn, where **Tony Sheridan** was appearing. When Koschmider heard about their plans he was furious and told them that their contract forbade them to play in any venue within 25 miles radius of his clubs without his permission. A number of incidents then occurred, which soon put paid to the Beatles' plans for appearing at the Top Ten.

A letter from Koschmider was handed to George Harrison, which read:

> 'I the undersigned, hereby give notice to Mr GEORGE HARRISON and to BEATLES' BAND to leave on 30 November 1960.
>
> 'The notice is given to the above by order of the Public Authorities who have discovered that Mr. GEORGE HARRISON is only 17 (seventeen) years of age.'

George was deported, but the others elected to stay. Then Koschmider reported to the police that **Pete Best** and Paul McCartney had tried to set fire to his **Bambi Kino** and they were both arrested and deported.

The Kaiserkeller wasn't able to compete with the groups playing at the Top Ten Club and by the time the **Star Club** opened on the premises opposite to the Kaiserkeller, Koschmider had reverted the club back to a cabaret/strip joint and given it a new name, the Colibri.

● Kane, Larry

An American newsman who travelled with the Beatles during their 1964 tour of the US. His voice is that of the interviewer on the ***Beatles At Shea*** film. He also began writing a book of reminiscences of the 1964 tour, with the tentative title 'Ticket To Ride'.

● Kansas City/Hey! Hey! Hey!

Two separate compositions combined, which, when the Beatles recorded them as one, resulted in royalties for both Leiber and Stoller and **Little Richard**. Jerry Leiber and Mike Stoller had originally written 'Kansas City', although it was called 'K.C. Loving' when the first version by Little Willie Littlefield was released in 1952. Richard, under his real name, Richard Penniman, composed 'Hey! Hey! Hey!'. He, in fact, recorded the two numbers separately in 1959, then recorded them as a medley later the same year

– and this is the version that the Beatles adopted in 1961, with Paul on lead vocals.

They performed it on stage during their last **Star Club** season and it appears on *The Beatles Live! At The Star Club In Hamburg, Germany: 1962* album. The group also performed it on BBC recordings for **'Pop Go The Beatles'**, **'From Us To You'**, and **'Saturday Club'**. The number was also featured on their 1964 album *Beatles For Sale* and is to be found on the collections *The Beatles Box* and *The Beatles Collection*, their compilation *Rock 'n' Roll Music* and the American album *Beatles VI*.

● Kass, Ron

When he was appointed Divisional Head of Apple Records, Kass was 33 years old and married to film star Joan Collins. He had headed the International Division of Liberty Records and the Beatles were looking for an experienced professional to head their record company.

Kass travelled regularly arranging the various deals for the label and also set up an Apple office in California.

His office was situated on the ground floor at **Savile Row**, with white walls, an expensive sound system, and two desks with Danish chrome and wood chairs. He shared his office with his secretary Carol Chapman.

However, by August 1968 he had gone, one of the victims of the wholesale sackings at Apple by **Allen Klein**, to be replaced by **Jack Oliver**, who had no experience of running a record company. Kass's office was then taken over by John and **Yoko.**

Kass became head of Warner Bros Records in London. When his wife went to America to star in 'Dynasty' in 1984, Ron had to make a decision about whether to move to the States permanently. However, the marriage broke down and the couple divorced.

Ron died of cancer in 1986, at the age of 51.

● Kaye, Peter

A name which began appearing under Beatles photographs in 1961 with the appearance of the ***Mersey Beat*** newspaper. Peter Kaye was not a person, it was the name of a studio launched in the late fifties by photographer Bill Connell, who set up a photographic studio/shop in Park Lane in Liverpool's Dingle area, a few blocks from where Ringo Starr lived. He hired Les Chadwick, a former pupil at the **Junior School of Art**, as his assistant.

When Bill Harry launched *Mersey Beat* he sought out Les as one of his main photographers and a deal w made: in exchange for advertisements and h recommending to local groups that they should use h services, 'Peter Kaye' would take photograph commissioned by *Mersey Beat*. This resulted in the studi mainly Les Chadwick, but occasionally Bill Connel taking literally hundreds of shots of the Beatles and loc groups on behalf of the publication.

In 1987 a book of the studio's work was publishe called *Beatles In Liverpool*. Sadly, it was the year in whi Bill Connell died.

● K. B. Hallen, *Copenhagen, Denmark*

The Beatles only made a single appearance in Denma throughout their career. This took place at the venue on June 1964 on the opening date of their 25-day world tou Ringo was ill in hospital at the time and drummer **Jimm Nicol** deputized.

The group performed two shows at the K. B. Hallen, t first at 6.00 p.m., the second at 9.30 p.m. At each of t performances there was a capacity audience of 4,400.

● Keep Your Hands Off My Baby

A Gerry Goffin/Carole King composition, recorded b Little Eva in 1962 and included in the Beatles' repertoi in 1963, with John taking lead vocals. The grou performed the song on their **'Saturday Club'** appearan for BBC radio on 26 January 1963.

● Kelly, Arthur

Childhood and school friend of George Harrison. Arthu George and **Peter Harrison** played guitars in t **Rebels**, a skiffle group supplemented by two other frien on washboard and tea-chest bass, who made a sing appearance at the British Legion Club in Speke. When t fourteen-year-old George began dating **Iris Caldwe** Arthur made it a foursome when he started dating Iris best friend. Mrs Vi Caldwell used to call the two bo Arthur and Martha.

When George made the transference from the **L Stewart Quartet** to the **Quarry Men**, the skiffle gro had been without a bass player since the departure of L Garry. John Lennon suggested that George become the bass player, but he didn't like the idea and told Arth that he could become bass player with the Quarry Men he could find the necessary £60 to buy a bass guita rthur couldn't – and possibly missed out on becoming a nember of the Beatles.

Arthur did become famous in his own right, as an actor, nainly in stage and television productions with Liverpool ubjects. He portrayed Bert in the West End stage roduction of 'John, Paul, George, Ringo . . . And Bert' and eorge came to see him in the play. Arthur was to appear n various productions, including the highly acclaimed elevision series 'The Boys From The Black Stuff'.

● Kelly, Brian

Merseyside promoter who booked numerous events at iverpool halls, which became known as 'jive hives'. His rst promotion took place at the Savoy Hall, Bath Street, Vaterloo, on 11 May 1959 and he gradually built up a tring of regular events around Merseyside at **Lathom Hall**, Seaforth; **Alexandra Hall**, Crosby; **Aintree nstitute** and **Litherland Town Hall**.

He booked the Silver Beatles to appear at his Lathom Iall promotion on 14 May 1960 and then booked them to ppear the following week on 21 May. They didn't turn up. 'hey joined the **Johnny Gentle** tour of Scotland without nforming Kelly, who didn't book them again for some me.

Bob Wooler, who occasionally appeared as compere t Kelly dances, phoned him to talk him into booking the roup again. They haggled and Kelly agreed to a fee of six ounds and booked them at Litherland Town Hall on 27 ecember 1960, where they made a tremendous impact, esulting in Kelly booking them for numerous other gigs.

They made their last appearance for Kelly at the intree Institute on 27 January 1962. Brian Epstein had ccompanied the group to the gig and had secured a fee of ighteen pounds from Kelly. However, when he met Kelly n the kitchen of the venue to collect the money, Kelly ffered it to him in small change, silver. Epstein was upset nat it wasn't offered 'in a civilized manner in pound otes', and stalked out, telling Kelly to pay him a cheque. Ie thought the offer of the bags of coins was an insult to ne Beatles and refused to let them appear at any further rian Kelly promotions.

In an article in ***Mersey Beat*** headed 'The Man Who iscovered The Beatles', Kelly revealed:

'I was organizing a dance at Litherland Town Hall to be eld on Boxing Day, 1960, but I was short of a group. On hristmas Day I received a phone call from Bob Wooler who said, "I've found a group for you at the **Jacaranda** and they're free. They want eight pounds. Will they do?" "Not at that price they won't," I said. "A group won't increase my attendance enough to warrant that" . . . we finally agreed to pay them six pounds.

'On their first appearance I was completely knocked out by them. They had a pounding, pulsating beat which I knew would be big box office. When they had finished playing, I posted some bouncers on the door of their dressing room to prevent other promoters who were in the hall entering. I went inside and booked them solidly for months ahead.

'I had a huge poster made with "The Beatles" written in large fluorescent lettering. The poster caused a certain amount of curiosity and I remember the first reaction to their name. "Beatles – you've spelt it wrong, mister." "Beatles – where've you dragged them from?" "Beatles – who are they?"

'The group went from strength to strength at Litherland, and built up a fantastic following. Even then, the song-writing talents of Lennon & McCartney were evident. On stage they'd say, "Here's a song we've just written – if you don't like it you needn't clap."

'The group went away to Germany. When they returned we did reasonable business with them, but they had lost Stuart and seemed downhearted and had temporarily lost their lustre.

'They were the first really noisy group to appear on Merseyside – and amplifiers were insufficient to cope with their sound. I worked on the amplification for them – and received a great deal of business for Alpha Sound. Groups on Merseyside seemed to play wilder and louder and more of them approached me to help with their amplification.'

● Kelly, Freda

The Beatles' longest-lasting fan club secretary. The first official **Beatles Fan Club** was originally formed in May 1962 and run by Bobbie Brown. Freda, who worked for Princes food firm, met Bobbie at the **Cavern** and began to help her with the club work. Due to the association, Freda was employed as a shorthand typist in the **NEMS Enterprises** management office, operating from Whitechapel, at six pounds ten shillings a week. When Bobbie became engaged to be married in 1963, Freda took over the running of the club, initially having to ask the Beatles to have a whip-round to pay for the postage. Brian

Freda Kelly, Beatles fan club secretary, is interviewed by Bob Azurdia of Radio Merseyside. (*Mersey Beat* Archives)

Epstein then agreed to pay the fan club's running costs and Freda shared a small office with Brian's secretary **Beryl Adams**.

Freda had been born in Ireland and arrived in Liverpool when she was thirteen; she worked in an office in the city centre and attended the Cavern regularly. Once officially in charge of the fan club she was pleased to find, on her first day at the job, that there were two fan letters, but as time passed she was receiving up to 400 letters a day. When NEMS Enterprises moved down to London, Freda's father refused to let her go, so she remained in Liverpool and moved into new offices in Hackins Hay which she shared with ***Mersey Beat.*** Soon the club boasted more than 16,000 members to whom she would send a membership card, a photograph, a quarterly newsletter and, eventually, a Christmas record. She was the only full-time member and was helped by some part-time workers including John Parry, John McCartney (Paul's cousin), Lynn Edwards, Elsa Breden, Lillian Boyle and Linda Shepherd. Officially, it was a 10 a.m.–5.30 p.m. job, but Freda willingly worked until late at night.

As the club grew and the HQ was moved to London, Freda continued to handle the Northern Area of the club and in October 1966 became Joint National Secretary.

Freda was one of those stout 'Cavernites' who went down fighting when the Cavern was due to be demolished and on 28 February 1966 was involved in the sit-in at the Cavern, entertained by the Hideaways group, who kept on playing when the barricades were torn down by the police.

On 4 April 1968, Freda married Brian Norris, forme member of the Realms and the Cryin' Shames. When th club was officially closed in March 1972, Freda ha already decided to spend her time rearing her first child.

• Kelly, George

A man hired by Paul McCartney as a butler in 1966. Hi departure from the McCartney payroll was not an amicabl one and he sold an exposé revealing stories of wild partie at Paul's house to a newspaper.

• Kelly, John

A photographer whose pictures were used in the *Magica Mystery Tour* booklet, enclosed with the *Magical Myster Tour* record package. Kelly also took a series of colou portraits of the Beatles, four of which were used as insert in *The Beatles* white album. Paul employed Kelly as th official photographer of his wedding to Linda in 1969.

• Ken Dodd Show, The

Liverpudlian comedian Ken Dodd had his own radio serie on BBC's Light Programme, produced by Bill Worsley This was broadcast on Sundays from 2.30 –3.00 p.m.

The show was recorded in front of a live audience an the Beatles recorded their single appearance on th programme on 9 October 1963 at the Playhouse Theatre London, for a transmission on 3 November, which wa repeated on 6 November. The group performed a singl number, 'She Loves You', but didn't participate in an comedy sketches with Dodd.

Dodd's agent had told him that he could have th Beatles for two appearances on his programme. 'I'm n sure, what do you think?' asked Dodd. 'I think we shoul just have them for one show because they're going to b one of these groups that fade overnight,' said the agent so only one appearance was booked.

• Kensington Recording Studio, 53 Kensington, Liverpool L7

A small studio in Liverpool situated in the back room of house belonging to Percy Phillips. Phillips owned th studio and there was also an outside sign which sporte his name.

It was Paul McCartney's idea that the **Quarry Me** should record here in the summer of 1958, at a time whe hey hadn't been appearing at gigs locally. When Paul had een the sign with Phillips' name on it he had mistakenly hought that it had something to do with the Philips record abel. He found that they could record a double-sided ingle for less than one pound and the group booked a ession.

Despite the fact that John and Paul had already begun o write songs together and had filled an exercise book vith their lyrics, they didn't record a Lennon & McCartney ong, but settled on **Buddy Holly**'s 'That'll Be The Day' nd another song. John commented: 'I didn't want to push ny songs on the group, but Paul had written one with George Harrison called 'In Spite Of All The Danger', and ve did that one for the other side.'

John sang lead vocal on 'That'll Be The Day' and Paul lid the honours on "In Spite Of All The Danger".

Performing at the session were John, Paul, George, **Colin Hanton** and **John Lowe**. The cost of the recording vas 17s.6d. and each of the boys contributed 3s.6d. They ouldn't afford to buy a copy each and John Lowe was to etain the acetate. John later went back to the studio to uy a copy, but Phillips never kept master tapes. 'It was oo late,' said John, 'our stuff had been wiped off by nother recording session by some Country and Western inger.'

Paul eventually bought the record back from Lowe in uly 1981.

● Kenwood, *St George's Hill, Weybridge, Surrey*

t was the Beatles' accountants **Bryce Hanmer** who dvised the four members that they should invest some of heir untaxed income in property – in other words, they hould all buy a house. A member of the firm lived in Weybridge, twenty miles southwest of London, and uggested it was a convenient place for them to settle.

John paid £40,000 for 'Kenwood', in July 1964. The nock Tudor house was on the side of St George's Hill and ohn spent a further £30,000 on renovations. He was later o park a painted caravan on one of the lawns.

● Kesey, Ken

American author and hero of the counter-culture in the ixties. The Oregon-born Kesey became a guinea pig for controlled experiments into lysergic acid diethylamine and n 1966 he bought an old 1939 yellow International Harvester schoolbus, fitted it out with a sound system to play rock music, aerosolled the bus with day-glo mandallas and set out on a celebrated 'acid trek' with a group of friends called the Merry Pranksters, who were all high on the hallucinogenic drug LSD. The main destinations of the Pranksters' bus were rock concerts – one of them being a Beatles show. Their exploits became the subject of Tom Wolfe's book *Electric Kool Aid Acid Test*.

The psychedelic bus trip also triggered Paul McCartney into developing the idea of *Magical Mystery Tour*.

Kesey's novels included *One Flew Over the Cuckoo's Nest* and *Sometimes A Great Notion*.

Peter Asher and **Derek Taylor** were considering Kesey as the first artist in a proposed Spoken Word series of albums from Apple, under the imprint Zapple, and when Kesey arrived in London they provided him with a small rear office in the Savile Row building and lent him a tape recorder and typewriter. After a few weeks there were enquiries about who he was and what he was doing and the project never got off the ground, with Kesey returning to California with a bad impression of the Beatles and their Apple organization.

● Kestrels, The

A West Country vocal group, whose members included Tony Burrows and Roger Greenaway.

The Kestrels first toured with the Beatles on the cinema tour headlined by **Helen Shapiro** which commenced on 22 February 1963. They also accompanied the Beatles on a six-week tour of England and Ireland later that year, commencing on 1 November.

The Kestrels issued a single of Lennon & McCartney's, 'There's A Place', and also recorded 'Please Please Me' as a track on their album, released on Pye's Piccadilly label.

Burrows was to join several other groups, including the Ivy League, the Flowerpot Men and Edison Lighthouse, while Roger Greenaway teamed up with Roger Cook to form **David and Jonathan**, who had a chart hit with 'Michelle', and he later achieved success as a songwriter.

● Kinfauns, *Claremont Drive, Esher, Surrey*

Luxury bungalow, set back from the road and hidden by trees and bushes in a wooded estate owned by the National Trust. Soon after meeting **Pattie Boyd**, George took her around with him to view the property as a place where they could live together.

The bungalow comprised two long wings separated by a rectangular courtyard in which there was a heated swimming pool. The curved floor-to-ceiling windows of the living-room looked out onto a landscaped yard and the bungalow was surrounded on three sides by a twelve-foot-high brick wall and on the fourth by a hedge of fir trees. Near the changing rooms at the pool was a reproduction of one of John's drawings in marble mosaic. George had his own music room, containing his guitars, Indian instruments and juke boxes. George bought the property in June 1964, but despite its isolation, he found he had to remove the sign 'Kinfauns', because fans still managed to find it. At one time they actually gained entrance to the bungalow, stole George's pyjamas and left a nasty note for Pattie.

● King Curtis

American rock 'n' roll saxophonist, whose King Curtis Band appeared on the Beatles' American tour in 1965. When 'Reminiscing', composed by Curtis, became a posthumous hit for **Buddy Holly** in 1962, the Beatles included it in their repertoire, with George Harrison on lead vocals. They performed it at the **Star Club** in Hamburg and it is included on the Star Club double album.

In 1971 John Lennon hired Curtis to play on his *Imagine* album sessions and Curtis appears on the tracks 'It's So Hard' and 'I Don't Want To Be A Soldier'.

Shortly after the *Imagine* sessions, on 13 August 1971, he was stabbed to death in Harlem.

● King's Hall, *Showgrounds, Balmoral, Belfast, Northern Ireland*

There was controversy surrounding this appearance because the boys had received an invitation to appear at the Royal Command Performance two weeks before the gig. John Lennon commented, 'There was never any intention to snub the Queen' and Paul McCartney said, 'We couldn't let the Belfast fans down.'

The show took place on 2 November 1964 and with an audience of 17,400 it was the largest audience the Beatles had ever appeared before in the United Kingdom.

There were hundreds of fans crowding Aldergrove Airport and the Beatles arrived an hour late, due to fog at Heathrow. Four fans managed to slip through the security net and as Ringo became the first Beatle to step on the tarmac, they hurried forward and all managed to obtain autographs. The group were taken straight from the airport to the King's Hall and sat around in a tiny back room for over three hours. They huddled in their black top coats around an electric fire and John Lennon was heard to comment, 'They told us that we were getting food about two hours ago but it hasn't come yet – we are all starving.'

The Belfast promoter who set the appearance up was Trevor Kane, although the official notice was: 'Brian Epstein and Arthur Howes in conjunction with George Connell and Trevor Kane presents . . .' Tickets could be reserved at 20/-, 15/- and 10/- and unreserved seats in the balcony were 7/6d.

Ian Starrett reviewed the event for ***Mersey Beat***:

'For the second time since they hit the top, Liverpool's fabulous Beatles flew into Northern Ireland recently for two fantastic performances in the King's Hall.

'Because of fog their aircraft was an hour later than was scheduled. When the Merseyside Four eventually did fly into Aldergrove Airport a tight security net fell around the group and they were immediately whisked off to Belfast.

'The strangest party of fans in the King's Hall was composed of soldiers of the 1st Battalion the King's Regiment – the Beatles' home town regiment. The group had hoped to visit the soldiers in Berlin earlier this year so instead they sent them 300 free tickets for the Belfast show. The regiment is now stationed at Ballykinlar, which is just outside Belfast.

'Pandemonium reigned inside the hall. The yells were deafening when John, Ringo, George and Paul took the stage, dressed in immaculate black suits. Frantic teenage girls stripped off their clothes, others fainted and had to be carried from the hall. It was fantastic, incredible and completely disproved the critics who predicted that the Beatles were finished.

'The fanatical 17,500 fans composed the biggest night's crowd known in Britain for any pop show – yet another record added to the boys' long list of achievements.

'No matter where they roam, the Beatle lads are always thinking about the Mersey scene. On arrival in Belfast they immediately sent a telegram ("Hope it's a right Royal rave") to their old colleague **Cilla Black** who appeared that night on the Royal Command Show.

'Typical of the fans in the hall that night were two 14-year-old youngsters Margaret Whiteside and Florence Magill from Lurgan.

'They travelled to the airport to greet the Beatles on heir arrival and then went to the King's Hall. Before the how dark-haired Margaret proudly showed me the utograph she had obtained at the airport.

'It was Paul McCartney's. When Paul appeared on tage she went frantic with joy. When the show was over he broke down and wept.

'As I left the hall she tried to say goodbye, but the vords didn't come. She slumped over her seat with tears unning down her face. Only one of 17,500 victims of **Beatlemania**.'

King's Hall, *Northgate, Blackburn, Lancashire*

'he town of 4,000 potholes! The Beatles made a single ppearance at this venue on 9 June 1963, which was also he last night of their tour with **Roy Orbison.**

King's Hall, *Stoke-on-Trent*

'he Beatles appeared on two bookings on the evening of '6 January 1963. The first was at the El Rio Club in Macclesfield and the second at this venue in Stoke-on-'rent, 21 miles away. The group returned to the venue on bill with fellow Liverpool groups on a ***Mersey Beat Showcase*** promotion on 19 April 1963.

Kingsley Hill, *Rushlake Green, Warbleton, Nr Heathfield, Sussex*

Georgian farmhouse which Brian Epstein bought in 1967 or £20,000 as a weekend retreat.

On five acres of ground, it had gardens, a pond, a paddock and an old oasthouse which Brian used as a staff ottage. There was also a garage which he turned into a iny film theatre.

He decorated the house with expensive antiques, silver nd Persian carpets. In his music room in the attic he had Mellotron machine. There was also a Star of David in eeds on display. Brian's PA James Ruston observed that vhen Brian showed John Lennon over the premises, he ommented, 'The room is great, Brian, but what did you ave to crap it up for with that Jewish star?'

● Kingsway Club, *The Promenade, Southport, Lancashire*

A club situated in the seaside town of Southport, nearby to Liverpool. Brian Epstein had obtained a series of bookings at the club for the Beatles in early 1962.

The club was licensed and, as they were unable to sell alcohol to under-eighteens, they placed the Beatles in an upstairs hall which had no bar.

The group made their debut there on 22 January and also appeared on 29 January, 5 February, 26 February, 5 March and 23 July.

THE

BEATLES

Come and meet

" PETE, PAUL, JOHN and GEORGE "

The Group Everyone has been asking for — Now they're here, at the

KINGSWAY

NEXT MONDAY — ONLY 2/6

Come and hear them play their latest record, It's Sensational

● King, Tony

A promotions man who, at one period, worked for Apple, promoting their product. King also acted as one of John Lennon's companions during his 'long weekend' in Los Angeles.

In the late eighties he acted as assistant to Mick Jagger.

● Kinnear, Roy

This short, stout, red-faced British character actor specialized in bumbling, cowardly, self-deprecating fat men roles and he appeared as the incompetent Algernon, the assistant to a mad scientist in *Help!* who attempts to cut a sacred ring from Ringo's finger.

Kinnear also appeared as Private Clapper, one of the motley crew of musketeers in the **Dick Lester** film *How I Won The War*, in which John Lennon made his solo debut.

Roy was also featured in Lester's series of films of the *Three Musketeers*, which the director had offered as a vehicle for the Beatles, who'd rejected the project. Kinnear died during the filming of the last movie in the trilogy, *The Return Of The Musketeers*.

● Kirchherr, Astrid

A pale-skinned, blonde girl of an ethereal beauty who became engaged to **Stuart Sutcliffe**.

Astrid was born in Hamburg in 1938 into a middle-class family in the respectable Altona suburb of Hamburg. Her father was an executive for the Ford Motor company.

From an early age she showed a flair for art and design and was enrolled at the Meister Schule to study dress design. It was here that she met a student from Berlin called **Klaus Voormann** who became her boyfriend. Rheinhardt Wolf, who ran a photographic course at the school, felt that Astrid had potential as a photographer and she changed her course from dress design to photography. When she completed her course, Wolf hired her as his assistant.

It was in October 1960 that Astrid and Klaus had a row which resulted in Klaus wandering around the St Pauli district and being lured into the **Kaiserkeller** by the sound of **Rory Storm & the Hurricanes**. That night he saw the Beatles and was so impressed he began telling Astrid and his friends. On his third visit to the club, Klaus was joined by Astrid and Jurgen Vollmer. She was reluctant to make the trip and was initially frightened when she arrived at the club, but the sight of the Beatles fascinated her and she noticed Stuart Sutcliffe immediately and was later to say, 'I fell in love with Stuart that very first night.'

With her ghostly pale skin and dark clothes, Astrid looked uniquely appealing to the Beatles and Stuart was immediately smitten. Her friends, who were nicknamed **'Exis'**, after existentialists, began to gather every night at tables near the stage to watch the Beatles.

After a week she gathered up the nerve to ask them if she could take photographs of them and the group agreed. Her first location shooting with them took place at a fairground in the local park, Der Dom. After the session she invited the group to tea at her home in Altona and all but **Pete Best** took up the offer, Pete only refusing because he had to buy some drumsticks to replace the ones he'd broken.

Astrid's mother was charmed by the group and also took a particular liking to Stuart.

Over the next few weeks Astrid began to take other photographs of the group and some of her later shots – portraits in which one half of the face was in shadow, was to pre-date the famous **Bob Freeman** *Around The Beatles* cover. Her mum was concerned about the terrible accommodation the group had at the **Bambi Kino** and invited Stuart to stay in the attic room of their house. Almost two months after they first met, in late November 1960, Stuart and Astrid became engaged and exchanged rings, in the German fashion.

When **Bruno Koschmider** caused the police to deport George, Astrid and Stuart drove him to the station. Paul and Pete were next bundled off unceremoniously to Liverpool by the police following the Bambi incident and then John left. He was later followed by Stuart who, because he had tonsilitis, was to take a more comfortable route home – by airplane, funded by Astrid. It was Astrid who helped to organize their next trip to Hamburg, in March 1961, when they appeared at the **Top Ten Club**.

Astrid was more mature than her young lover from Liverpool and began to influence him in many ways, particularly regarding his looks and dress. She initially changed his hair style, shaping it across his forehead in a style which was then currently popular in France. This was to become the basis for the famous Beatle 'moptop'. At first, the rest of the group ridiculed Stuart's new style. Then George agreed to try it and Astrid shaped his hair. Paul tried next and finally John agreed to have Astrid style his hair. Pete was the only Beatle who refused to try out the new style.

She next made a leather jerkin and trousers for Stuart, which resulted in the other members of the group buying some leather outfits from a Hamburg store. When Astrid made Stuart a black corduroy jacket without lapels, in a style then being popularized by Pierre Cardin in Paris, the other members initially ridiculed him – but the collarless style was later to feature in the Beatles' image.

The relationship between Stuart and Paul had been deteriorating, mainly because Paul wanted to take over on bass. One night he made a remark about Astrid and the two began to fight, with the stronger Paul beating up his smaller colleague. By that time Stuart had realized that art meant more to him than music and as he had been unable to return to **Liverpool College of Art**, he was encouraged by two friends, who were students at Hamburg State Art College, to apply there. He obtained a grant and left the group to study under **Eduardo Paolozzi**.

When the Beatles returned to Liverpool in July 1961 Stuart remained in Hamburg with Astrid and they planned to get married as soon as he finished his course.

A few months later, Stuart fell down the narrow steps leading from his attic studio and banged his head severely. Soon after, he began to experience terrible headaches and blackouts, although the only one who associated the fal with the headaches at the time was Stuart's mother in Liverpool.

The pain became so violent that Stuart remained in his attic, looked after by Astrid and her mother. A specialist was called in and X-rays were taken, but nothing showed up on them. Three doctors were consulted and all were equally puzzled. Stuart had to take special massages under water, which didn't seem to help, and one day, on returning from a massage, he told Astrid's mother he'd seen a white coffin and asked her if she'd buy it for him.

On 10 April 1961, Astrid was at work in the photographic studio when she received a call from her mother. Stuart was so bad that she was calling the hospital. Astrid rushed home and joined Stuart in the ambulance – but he died in her arms at 4.30 p.m. on the way to hospital.

The distraught Astrid met the Beatles at Hamburg airport to tell them the tragic news.

Astrid was later to marry Gibson Kemp, former drummer with Rory Storm & the Hurricanes. They were divorced and some years later she was reunited with her original sweetheart, Klaus Voorman.

● Klaatu

In 1973 rumours began to abound that the Beatles had re-formed to record under the assumed name of Klaatu. An album by Klaatu was issued on 3 August 1976 by **Capitol**, the Beatles' American label. Entitled *Klaatu*, it contained the tracks: 'Calling Occupants of Interplanetary Craft', 'California Jam', 'Anus of Uranus', 'Sub Rosa Subway', 'True Life Hero', 'Doctor Marvello', 'Sir Bodsworth Rugglesby III' and 'Little Mevtrino'.

Klaatu remained relatively unknown until disc jockey Charlie Parker of WDRC in Providence, Rhode Island, played one of the album tracks on his show. Hundreds of listeners phoned in to ask if Klaatu were actually the Beatles. Then an article by Steve Smith appeared in a newspaper in Providence, Rhode Island, claiming that Klaatu were the Beatles. In what became known as 'the Klaatu Konspiracy', numerous 'facts' were trotted out, in a similar way to the 'Paul is dead' affair, and over 150 alleged clues linking Klaatu to the Beatles were revealed, such as: 'At the University of Miami, voice prints of Klaatu and a recent McCartney album were made – and found to be the same . . . In Australia a disc jockey said that Klaatu was a missing Beatles album called "Sun". . . One of the tracks from the album, "Sub Rosa Subway", was played backwards at different speeds, using a vera-speed low-frequency oscillator, and the vocals were sharpened with a set of filters. This message was found: "It's us, it's the Beeeeeatles!"'

Various newspapers and disc jockeys took up the story and within an eight-week period over 300,000 copies of *Klaatu* were sold.

When questions were asked as to the group's identity – as no mention of group members was made on the album sleeve – Capitol Records commented that they had never actually seen the group. Frank Davies, the group's manager, had brought them the tape of the band – and had not told them anything about Klaatu. When he was asked directly if Klaatu were the Beatles, Davies refused to either confirm or deny.

Despite the fact that the group members were later identified as John Woloschuk (also known as L. M. Carpenter and Chip Dale), Terry Draper, David Long and Dino Tome, the fascination in the 'Klaatu are really the Beatles' craze persisted. In Australia, Beatles fan John Squires issued a 34-page booklet entitled *Under an Assumed Name: The Beatles Secret Re-Union*, gathering hundreds of tenuous associations in order to prove his theory, including the fact that Ringo Starr appears as the character Klaatu from *The Day The Earth Stood Still* on the cover of his *Goodnight Vienna* album.

The group released five albums before they eventually disbanded. Several years later, David Long became head programmer in a computer room at George Martin's AIR Studios.

● Klein, Allen

A controversial figure in the lives of the Beatles. Klein was born in Newark on 13 December 1931. His mother had died when he was two years old and his father, a Jewish butcher, felt he couldn't run his business and look after his family, so he placed Allen and two of his three sisters in the Hebrew Shelter Orphanage until Klein was ten. When his father remarried, Allen was sent to live with an aunt.

After a spell in the army he began to study accountancy at evening classes at Upsala College. This knowledge of accounting stood him in good stead when he entered show business. He set up music publishing companies, became manager of the Shirelles, and then took over management of Sam Cooke and **Bobby Vinton**. Klein specialized in discovering overlooked fees and royalties which were owed to performers due to negligence, dishonesty, or both. This was of tremendous advantage to artists who found that Klein could obtain substantial sums of money which were owed to them, much to the frustration of the record companies. He became known as the 'Robin Hood of Pop'. He also specialized in obtaining huge advances for artists against future royalties and managed to obtain a one million dollar advance for Sam Cooke, the highest record advance paid to an artist up to that time.

With his wife Betty, Klein was later to form ABKCO Industries, short for Allen and Betty Klein Co.

In 1965 **Andrew Oldham** hired him as business adviser to the **Rolling Stones** and one of the first things he did was to ease out their co-manager Eric Easton. He then flew over to Britain and renegotiated the Stones' contract with **Decca**, obtaining an advance of $1.5 million for them. This was to result in Oldham suing Klein over the whereabouts of the money. Klein then bought out the lawsuit by paying Oldham one million dollars and he then took over the Stones completely. Klein also began to represent other artists in 'the British Invasion' of America, including Herman's Hermits, the **Dave Clark Five**, **Donovan** and the Animals.

Following the Rolling Stones tour of America in 1966, Mick Jagger told the Beatles that the Stones were earning far more money than the Beatles despite selling less records. This upset the Beatles for a considerable time and led to Paul McCartney being the first member of the Beatles to suggest that Klein should act on their behalf, via **NEMS**. The news led to Klein boasting that he would have the Beatles before Christmas.

When the Beatles launched **Apple Corps** it was Jagger who suggested to John and Paul that Klein would be the ideal businessman to run their empire for them, but John Lennon couldn't be bothered replying to Klein's calls.

In January 1969, in an interview with Ray Coleman, editor of *Disc*, John Lennon said, 'If Apple goes on losing money, all of us will be broke in six months.' He bemoaned the fact that Apple was losing £20,000 a week and that personally he was down to his last £50,000.

This was the opportunity Klein had been waiting for and on 28 January 1969 John and **Yoko** met up with Klein in his suite at the **Dorchester Hotel**. None of the other Beatles had been told of the meeting. John saw a small, tubby man dressed in sweater and sneakers – completely different from the 'men in suits' image he hated. There were no lawyers or aides around and Klein soon put the nervous John at ease with his ability to discuss Beatles songs – and John's in particular – in detail and to display a knowledge of the problems experienced by Apple. John was also sympathetic to Klein's background, particularly when Allen told him how he'd been placed in an orphanage by his father and then farmed off to an aunt. John Lennon then sent a message to **Sir Joseph Lockwood** of **EMI Records**: 'Dear Sir Joe – from now on Allen Klein handles all my stuff.'

In the meantime, the Beatles also had **John Eastman** representing them. Paul had brought in the New York law firm of Eastman and Eastman to advise them and all four Beatles had authorized Eastman to act for them in contractual matters.

Following his meeting with John, Klein also saw George and Ringo and impressed them with his grasp of the mechanics of Apple Corps. They agreed to listen to him and a meeting was arranged – although Paul walked out of it soon after it began. John, George and Ringo then agreed that both John Eastman and Allen Klein should work as their advisers. Eastman was to look after their attempt to buy NEMS Enterprises and Klein could deal with EMI regarding the raising of a one million pound loan.

There was immediate conflict. Klein claimed that Eastman was blocking his deals. Eastman claimed that Klein was jeopardizing his negotiations with NEMS by claiming that he could get NEMS for nothing because of money owed to the Beatles in back payments.

There followed a number of complicated business moves, some of them overlapping. Triumph Investments managed to buy out NEMS, together with NEMS' 25 per cent claim on the Beatles' earnings. Klein visited Leonard Richenberg of Triumph offering him one million pounds for their stake in the Beatles. He was rejected. Klein then had the Beatles write to Sir Joseph Lockwood requesting that their royalties be sent directly to Apple and not to NEMS/Triumph. EMI were about to send out the latest royalty payment of £1.3 million but held up the amount while Triumph went to court. The judge decided not to take any action. Richenberg then agreed to relinquish the 25 per cent interest in exchange for £800,000 cash and a quarter of the suspended royalties.

Once freed of the NEMS problem, Klein attempted to

supervise the takeover of Northern Songs. The Beatles owned 31 percent of the company and Klein decided to offer £2 million for a further 20 per cent which would give the Beatles control. The balance of power lay with a consortium of city brokers who owned 14 per cent of the company – but they were suspicious of Klein following a number of detrimental newspaper articles about him. However, he managed to convince them to side with the Beatles and promised he wouldn't interfere with them. They agreed, but at the last minute John Lennon objected to the consortium's involvement and said, 'I'm sick of being fucked about by men in suits sitting on their fat arses in the city.' The consortium then sided with **Lew Grade** and ATV was able to take control of Northern Songs on 20 May 1969. On the same day ABKCO was officially appointed business manager to the Beatles. Only the names of John, George and Ringo were on the contract as Paul refused to sign.

Klein moved into **Savile Row** and immediately sacked all the executives. **Ron Kass**, **Dennis O'Dell**, **Peter Asher**, **Alistair Taylor** all went. Klein intended that there should be no one between himself and the Beatles: all people who had any influence with them had to go if he were to take complete control. He even attempted to get rid of **Neil Aspinall** and **Peter Brown**. Brown said, 'I gave Klein the perfect excuse. We were just coming up to the Annual General Meeting. I told him that all the directors had to resign as a formality and then be re-elected. Neil and I both resigned, but we weren't re-elected. We thought the Beatles wouldn't ditch us, but they did.' However, Apple couldn't function without them and they remained. Brown was to get his revenge over a decade later with his book *The Love You Make*.

Klein's three-year contract with John, George and Ringo only gave him 20 per cent of income which was generated directly as a result of his management, so he decided to approach the record companies. Together with the four members of the Beatles he turned up at Sir Joseph Lockwood's office and told him they were there to renegotiate the Beatles' nine-year contract with EMI. 'Providing both sides get some benefit, there's no harm in renegotiating,' said Sir Joe. Klein told him, 'No, you don't understand. You don't get anything. We get more.' Lockwood told them to get out. Klein rang him back in half an hour to apologize.

Klein then turned to Bob Gortikov, President of **Capitol**. In the meantime, John had expressed his desire to retire from the Beatles, but Klein asked him not to mention it until after he'd completed his deal with Gortikov. Gortikov was not like Sir Joseph and Klein was able to get the unheard-of royalty of 69 cents on each Beatles album in America. His dealings had been tough and Gortikov was to tell **Derek Taylor**, 'We would have done the deal anyway, but did he have to be so nasty about it?'

Klein's next move indirectly led to Paul McCartney's decision to break away from the Beatles. Klein commissioned **Phil Spector** to assemble an album out of the tapes from the 'Get Back' sessions. The result was the *Let It Be* album. Prior to release, Spector sent an acetate to each Beatle explaining the changes he'd made, but assuring them that they could make whatever changes they wished. Paul was furious with the alterations to his 'The Long And Winding Road'. He tried in vain to contact Spector, who was conveniently 'unobtainable'. He also wrote to Allen Klein demanding the restoration of the original version. His letter was ignored and the Spector version of 'The Long And Winding Road' was issued.

Paul then had no choice. He felt it was no use continuing with the Beatles. Whatever the 'men in suits did', they never screwed about with the Beatles' actual music. With Klein, Paul's very compositions were being altered and released against his direct wishes.

The Beatles were to break up and Klein finished his association with Apple Corps in 1973 and was paid £3 million.

● Knight, Terry

American musician who, with his group the Pack, had a minor hit in 1966 with 'I (Who Have Nothing)'. He was acting as Master of Ceremonies on an American promotional tour for **Twiggy** in 1967 when she decided to fly him to Britain to see Paul McCartney, who was looking for artists for Apple. Paul forgot all about the meeting and was in Scotland with Linda while Terry was waiting to see him in London. He eventually flew back to America without seeing Paul.

His group the Pack had broken up, then reformed as Grand Funk Railroad and he became their manager.

In 1969, under his own name, he recorded a single dealing with the 'Paul is dead' rumour called 'Saint Paul', issued on **Capitol** 2506.

● Knotty Ash Village Hall, Junction of Eaton Road and East Prescot Road, Knotty Ash, Liverpool L12

Mona Best, already booking the Beatles regularly into the **Casbah Club**, began a series of promotions over a six-month period at this local venue. The group made their debut there on 15 September 1961 and further bookings included 22 September, 20 October, 27 October, 10 November and 17 November.

The following year, on Saturday 17 March 1962, local promoter **Sam Leach** booked the Beatles and **Rory Storm & the Hurricanes** on a 'St Patrick's Night Gala'.

His main reason for the promotion was to raise some ready cash to pay for his engagement to Joan McEvoy, to be celebrated in style at her mother Dolly's house, nearby in Huyton. After the show, the Beatles and the Hurricanes attended the party which lasted until the following afternoon.

● Komm, Gib Mir Deine Hand

A German language version of 'I Want To Hold Your Hand'. The Beatles recorded the number at **EMI**'s Pathe Marconi Studios in Paris on Wednesday, 29 January 1964, at the request of Odeon, the West German outlet for EMI Records. George Martin came to Paris to record the group, together with engineer **Norman Smith**.

During the session they also recorded a German version of 'She Loves You' and both tracks were issued separately in Germany, where they were both Top Ten hits. The Beatles never repeated the exercise.

The track was included on the *Rarities* album and the American album *Something New*.

● Koobas, The

A Liverpool band who originally formed in April 1963 as the Kubas and performed at all the major Merseyside venues, appeared in Hamburg and were signed to Brian Epstein for a short time.

They also appeared in the film *Ferry 'Cross The Mersey* in 1965 and toured Britain with the Beatles from 3–12 December 1965. There were occasional changes in personnel, but the basic line-up was Keith Ellis (bass guitar), Stu Leithwood (rhythm guitar), Tony O'Rielly (drums) and Roy Morris (lead).

They later signed with **Tony Stratton-Smith**, who also represented Liverpool acts **Paddy, Klaus & Gibson** and **Beryl Marsden**, although they were to enjoy only minor record success.

Liverpool band the Koobas, who joined the Beatles on tour. (EMI)

Kosh, John

The designer of the book included with the *Let It Be* album. It was a lavish production, prepared by Kosh, written by **Jonathan Cott** and David Dalton, with photographs by **Ethan Russell** and **Mal Evans**. Kosh designed the entire package for the *Let It Be* album, including the cover design with the black background.

Kosh was later to design the covers for the Ringo Starr albums *Beaucoups Of Blues*, *Rotogravure* and *Bad Boy*.

Koschmider, Bruno

Small, pugnacious former circus clown, fire eater and acrobat who was the first club owner to book British rock 'n' roll groups into Hamburg.

He ran strip clubs in the Grosse Freiheit in the notorious St Pauli district, the large **Kaiserkeller** (King's Cellar) and the smaller **Indra Club**.

Stories regarding how he first booked the British bands into his clubs vary. **Iain Hines** says that Bruno came over to London looking for groups, was advised to seek them in the 2 I's. Hines found out what he was there for and immediately formed a group on the spot called the Jets. Koschmider booked them and they became the first band to play at the Kaiserkeller. **Allan Williams** says that he travelled to Hamburg to find his **Royal Caribbean Steel Band**. He stumbled into the Kaiserkeller and asked to see the owner, was introduced to Koschmider and convinced him he should book British rock 'n' roll groups. By a series of coincidences, he happened to be at the 2 I's club in London with the Liverpool band Derry Wilkie & the Seniors where he bumped into Koschmider again. As a result, the Seniors became the first Mersey group to be booked into Hamburg. Williams then booked the Beatles and travelled over with them, although Koschmider made them play at the smaller Indra Club. When the Indra was closed by order of the police, he had the Beatles fulfil their contract at the Kaiserkeller as second on the bill to another Mersey band, **Rory Storm & the Hurricanes**. For some reason, while he paid the Beatles a low fee and they had to rough it up in inadequate sleeping quarters at the **Bambi Kino**, he paid the Hurricanes more money and they were able to board at the Seamen's Mission.

Koschmider was strict in his dealings with the groups and laid down the law. His method of controlling them was by confrontation – unlike **Peter Eckhorn** and **Manfred Weissleder**, who offered incentives. Koschmider forbade them to appear anywhere else within a 40-mile radius of his club, fined groups if they infringed his stringent rules, and therefore never built up any loyalty between himself and the bands, which resulted in him having to revert his venues back to strip clubs while the **Top Ten** and the **Star Club** enjoyed success with the bands.

When he discovered the Beatles were going to play at the Top Ten, he arranged for George Harrison to be deported. Arguably, he was already aware of Harrison's age, but was able to have the 'protection' of booking him into his club with impunity. He withdrew that 'protection' and sent George the following letter dated 1 November 1960:

> 'I the undersigned, hereby give notice to Mr GEORGE HARRISON and to BEATLES' BAND to leave on November 30th 1960.
>
> 'The notice is given to the above by order of the Public Authorities who have discovered that Mr GEORGE HARRISON is only 17 (seventeen) years of age.
>
> BRUNO KOSCHMIDER'

Koschmider was a tough individual who dealt with customers in his club roughly. He made threats to the Beatles regarding their physical well-being, but didn't carry them out because the group were under the protection of **Horst Fascher**, who had moved to the Top Ten Club.

His revenge came when **Pete Best** and Paul McCartney returned to the Bambi Kino to collect their belongings and singed some walls when they gave themselves with some light. Koschmider informed the police that they had attempted arson and they were deported.

Kramer, Billy J.

Liverpool singer, real name William Ashton, who was originally a member of Billy Forde & the Phantoms. When his guitar was stolen he became lead singer and the group changed their name to Billy Kramer & the Coasters.

He saw many early Beatles gigs and recalls, 'The first time I heard of them was when they played at the **Litherland Town Hall**. I remember Cliff Roberts & the Rockers were on at the time, but the only group who knocked me out were **Kingsize Taylor** & the Dominoes. I was a group freak. **Bob Wooler** announced that the next

Billy J. Kramer enjoyed a series of chart hits with Lennon & McCartney songs. (Billy J. Kramer)

week they would be presenting a group just back from Hamburg – the Beatles. I stopped in my tracks. I thought, I must go and see them.

'The Beatles had **Stu** playing bass on that occasion, McCartney had a black and green Rosetti guitar, Lennon had a Rickenbacker and George had a Gretsch.

'When the Coasters had been given an audition by **Brian Kelly** at the **Aintree Institute**, the venue opposite the Coronation pub in Linacre Lane, we had to travel to the gig by 61 bus, me, the boys and all our gear. That was when I had my first meeting with Lennon. He was just lounging about in the dressing room and I asked him about his Rickenbacker guitar and he let me have a go of it. I'd seen the Fender guitar and the Gibson and the Gretsch, but I hadn't seen a Rickenbacker. The fact that he had one must have put him on the market. Paul was there with his Rosetti, unplugged and with strings missing.

'I also remember them on the Bluegenes night at the **Cavern**. They'd come back from Hamburg and Stu had left. I was freaked out by the whole band when I saw them at the Cavern. McCartney, Lennon, Harrison and **Pete Best**. McCartney was playing bass and they were into leather. It was a lot slicker, the space between numbers had tightened up a lot and the vocal backings and everything, the whole thing flowed better. They had a restricted repertoire but I realized that Lennon and McCartney had a character.'

Billy Kramer & the Coasters were voted No. 3 in the ***Mersey Beat*** Poll, following the Beatles and **Gerry & the Pacemakers**. Despite this, Billy was about to leave the group and take up a full-time post with British Rail at Rugby. He'd been down to Rugby to discuss his new job and his parents had agreed that he should take it up. His manager at that time was Ted Knibbs and he phoned Billy to arrange a meeting in Liverpool city centre. 'I had no idea what Ted had in mind,' says Billy. 'I was about to tell him I was packing it all in. He took me up to **NEMS**, introduced me to Brian Epstein and Brian said he wanted to manage me. I was so knocked out, I completely lost my appetite for remaining with British Rail. Shortly afterwards I was called in to a meeting with Brian at his office and John Lennon was there. Brian said to me, "John's come up with an idea. He thinks your name would sound much better if we added the initial 'J' to it. How does Billy J. Kramer sound?" I said, "That's OK by me, but what do I say to the press if they ask me what the 'J' stands for?" John said, "You can tell them it stands for Julian." To tell you the truth, I didn't like the name Julian and refused to use it. I didn't know at the time that John had a son and had named him Julian in memory of his mother.'

The Coasters refused to turn professional and Brian Epstein sought a new group to back him. He asked the **Remo Four** during a Cavern appearance. Their lead singer at the time was Johnny Sandon and they told Brian that they'd like him to manage them, but wouldn't back Billy as they were happy with Sandon. Epstein next approached Manchester's the Dakotas who initially turned him down. When he offered them the chance to record as the Dakotas in their own right, they took up the offer, shedding their lead singer Pete Maclaine. Epstein immediately sent Billy and the group to Hamburg for a **Star Club** season for them to work on their act. Group and singer never really got on well together.

The Dakotas comprised Mike Maxfield (lead guitar), Robin McDonald (rhythm guitar), Ray Jones (bass guitar) and Tony Mansfield (drums).

The group was featured on a number of Beatles gigs and their debut record was the Lennon & McCartney composition 'Do You Want To Know A Secret?' which George Harrison had sung on the *Please Please Me* album. It was issued on R 5023 by Parlophone in Britain on 26 April 1963 and reached No. 2 in the charts. It was issued on 55586 by Liberty in America on 10 June. The 'B' side of the record was 'I'll Be On My Way', which Paul McCartney had written specially for Billy.

Billy hadn't been Epstein's first choice to record 'Do You Want To Know A Secret?'. He'd originally offered it to **Shane Fenton** if the singer would be prepared to let Epstein manage him. Fenton told him he already had a manager and Epstein gave the number to Billy, who wasn't particularly keen on it.

His second single was 'Bad To Me', a number which John had written for him in Spain. It was issued on R 5049 by Parlophone on 26 July 1963 and topped the British charts. It was issued on 55626 by Liberty in America on 23 September, where it reached No. 9 in the charts. The flipside was 'I Call Your Name'.

The third Lennon & McCartney number Billy recorded was 'I'll Keep You Satisfied', which was issued on R 5073 by Parlophone on 1 November 1963 and on 55643 by Liberty in America. It reached No. 4 in Britain and No. 30 in the US.

His fourth and last Lennon & McCartney single was penned by Paul. 'From A Window' was issued on R 5156 Parlophone on 17 July 1964 and on 66061 by Imperial in America on 12 August. It reached No. 10 in the British charts and No. 23 in the US.

Billy's other hits included 'Little Children' and 'Trains And Boats And Planes'.

He asked Paul McCartney if he could provide him with another song and Paul offered him 'Yesterday'. Billy turned it down.

One Lennon & McCartney number which Billy recorded has never been released. It's called 'One And One Is Two'. It was mainly written by Paul. John and Paul worked together on the number in their suite at the George V Hotel in Paris after a show at the **Olympia Theatre**. They had to send a tape off the next day to **Dick James** for Billy J. Kramer to record. Paul sat at the piano while John sat at a table playing guitar. They had a microphone leading from the tape recorder strapped to a floor lamp. As they were singing 'One and one is two . . .' George popped his head round the door and suggested, 'Can't you take one of the "one and one is two's" out?' At another time he interjected, 'Can't you do something with "do" or "Jew"?' John said, 'I'm a lonely Jew. How's that?'

The song was duly sent to James and recorded by Billy, but John wasn't happy with the number and is said to have advised Billy, 'Release that and your career is over.' So it was never released, although a version by the **Strangers** with Mike Shannon was issued in 1964 and flopped.

● Kungliga Hallen, Stockholm, Sweden

The second date of the Beatles' short tour of Sweden. They performed two shows at the hall on 26 October 1963.

Due to the enthusiastic crowds, a cordon of 40 policemen, armed with truncheons, surrounded the stage. The force of the fans, however, overpowered them at first and George Harrison was knocked over. The police then restored order.

● Labour Club, *Peel Street, Liverpool L7*

Situated in the Dingle area, quite close to where Ringo spent his childhood. The Labour Club was one of the many scores of small working men's drinking clubs which booked local entertainers. It was the venue of the first gig by the **Eddie Clayton Skiffle Group** which included Ringo on drums, Roy Trafford on tea-chest bass, Eddie Miles on guitar and three other musicians. The full line-up comprised three guitars, drums, washboard and bass. Ringo was to comment in the *Beatles Book*, their monthly magazine, some years later: 'The organizer got a bit drunk and seemed to forget all about paying us. Whatever happened, we didn't get a penny.' The organizer threatened a law suit. However, Ringo stuck to his story and said he'd be prepared to go to court and swear to it. The club manager withdrew the action.

There was no such person as Eddie Clayton – although **Eric Clapton** was to use the name as a pseudonym on an album many years later.

● Labour Club, *Devonshire Road, High Park, Southport, Lancashire*

There were almost 350 clubs in the Merseyside Clubs Association. These clubs were for various union and political organizations and provided entertainment, generally with cabaret-style singers, comedians, speciality acts and Country music. Occasionally, such clubs featured local rock 'n' roll bands. The Beatles appeared at a handful of such clubs at the onset of their career and the group made one appearance at this venue early in 1961.

● Lady Madonna

In addition to writing the song, Paul also designed the press advertisements to promote it.

The single was issued in Britain on Parlophone R 5675 on 15 March 1968 and was the last Beatles single on that label. It was also the last American single to use the **Capitol** label.

The flipside was George Harrison's 'The Inner Light', his first song on a Beatles single.

The number topped the charts in Britain while in America it reached No. 2 in *Cash Box* and *Record World* and No. 4 in *Billboard*.

There is a brass section of four saxophones, with jazzman Ronnie Scott leading Harry Klein, Bill Povey and Bill Jackson.

The track was included on a number of compilations, including *The Beatles 1967–1970, Hey Jude* and *The Beatles Box*. A live version of the number is also included on *Wings Over The World*.

At the time of the original release, Paul mentioned that the arrangement of the number was based on an old song called 'Bad Penny Blues'. Coincidentally, that number had been a minor hit for Humphrey Lyttelton in 1956 on a single produced by George Martin.

● Lady Mitchell Hall, *Cambridge*

The event which took place at this venue on 2 March 1969 marked the first time that a member of the Beatles made a solo appearance without his fellow members of the group. John and **Yoko** appeared as part of an avant-garde jazz concert with saxophonist John Stevens. Yoko provided the high-pitched vocals and John performed on guitar. Their entire set was recorded and later issued as Side One of the *Unfinished Music No. 2: Life With The Lions* album.

● La Motta, Stephanie

Adopted daughter of ex-boxer Jake La Motta (his life story was filmed as *Raging Bull* with Robert De Niro). She moved to England and became a favourite of the gossip columnists, frequenting all the fashionable clubs such as Tramps and Stringfellows, and revealing details to the newspapers of her affairs with celebrities, such as Liverpool's former world champion boxer John Conte.

She had a well-publicized affair with Ringo Starr and in 1981 began taking **Julian Lennon** under her wing. She bought Julian a white horse for his nineteenth birthday which she presented to him at Stringfellows in March 1982, during a party at which models were photographed topless.

It was during a trip to Austria and Greece with Ringo Starr in 1981 that she contracted multiple sclerosis.

● Lancaster, Burt

A major Hollywood star whose films include *Gunfight At the OK Corral, From Here To Eternity, Elmer Gantry* and *Seven Days In May.*

The Beatles had originally met the star while they were staying at the George V Hotel in Paris and when the group were settling into a rented house in **Benedict Canyon** in California for a few days in August 1965, they were invited over to Burt's Bel Air house on the evening of Monday, 24 August.

Unfortunately, John Lennon couldn't attend because he was completing a song. Paul, George and Ringo arrived in company with **Neil Aspinall, Mal Evans, Derek Taylor** and Roy Gerber. They were shown around the house, then treated to dinner, followed by a screening of the new **Peter Sellers** Pink Panther comedy, *A Shot In The Dark.*

Ringo was particularly excited about the meeting with one of his screen heroes and Lancaster presented him with a sharpshooter, although it no longer worked. The gun was later confiscated by British customs. When Lancaster heard about it, he sent Ringo another gun.

Burt Lancaster, a major Hollywood star who played host to the Beatles. (National Film Archives)

● La Scala Ballroom, *Runcorn, Cheshire*

A regular venue for Mersey bands, situated only fourteen miles from Liverpool. The Beatles didn't make their debut there until 16 October 1962 and their only other appearance at the ballroom was on Tuesday, 11 December. The latter gig was a **NEMS Enterprises** promotion, organized by **Bob Wooler** and also featuring Johnny Sandon and the **Remo Four** and the **Merseybeats.**

● Las Vegas Convention Centre, *Las Vegas, Nevada*

The Beatles had stayed overnight, almost under siege, at the Sahara Hotel and a police escort surrounded them as they were driven to the convention centre at 3.00 p.m. on 20 August 1964. There were two shows at the venue that day, a matinee at 4.00 p.m. and an evening show at 8.00 p.m., both of which were advance sell-outs, with a total audience of around 16,000.

The ban against having celebrities backstage, which Brian Epstein had introduced, had been broken the day previously when **Shirley Temple** visited them, and when Liberace came backstage saying, 'I want to meet these young artists who are doing such amazing things', **Derek Taylor** realized it was a ban which it wouldn't be diplomatic to enforce and Liberace met the lads – as did **Pat Boone.**

There were the inevitable hails of jellybeans and during the evening show there was a bomb threat – but it was bogus.

● Lathom Hall, *Lathom Avenue, Seaforth, Liverpool L21*

One of several venues, including **Litherland Town Hall** and the **Aintree Institute,** promoted by **Brian Kelly**. It was standard practice in Liverpool to offer groups 'auditions', which would actually take place at a live show.

In other words, the promoter would regularly have groups playing for free with the enticement that he might book them.

Under the name the Silver Beats, the group auditioned for Kelly at Lathom Hall on 14 May 1960 on a bill which included established Liverpool bands **Kingsize Taylor** & the Dominoes, Cliff Roberts & the Rockers and the Deltones. As a result of their brief performance, Kelly booked them for the following week, on 21 May – but the group didn't turn up. They left for their tour of Scotland with **Johnny Gentle** without informing Kelly who, as a result, didn't book them again for several months until **Bob Wooler** talked him into it.

Drummer Cliff Roberts recalled the Silver Beats' appearance that first night and said they were a scruffy bunch whose drummer hadn't even brought his kit and

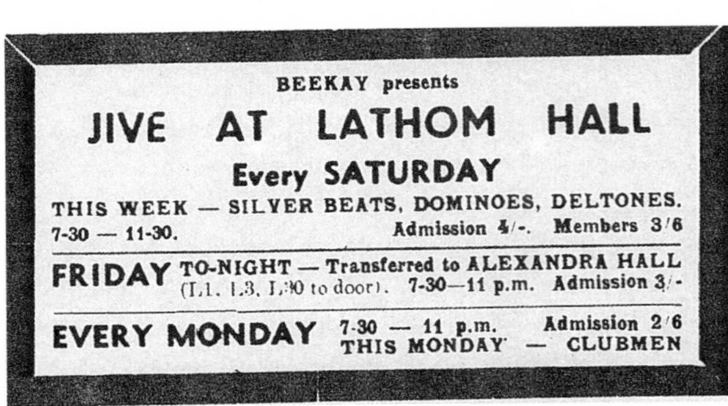

asked if he could borrow Cliff's. Roberts had a brand new Olympic kit which he hadn't even used on stage himself, so he naturally refused. However, he agreed to play with the Silver Beats and they performed six numbers together: 'four rock 'n' roll standards that all of the groups played, and two originals that they had to teach me'. He says that the group then disappeared and he didn't see them until eight months later when they appeared on the bill at the **Alexandra Hall, Crosby** on 19 January 1961, where, says Roberts, 'They wore black leather, had brand new instruments and played brilliantly.'

BEEKAY presents
JIVE AT LATHOM HALL
Every SATURDAY
THIS WEEK — SILVER BEATS, DOMINOES, DELTONES.
7-30 — 11-30. Admission 4/-. Members 3/6
FRIDAY TO-NIGHT — Transferred to ALEXANDRA HALL
7-30—11 p.m. Admission 3/-
EVERY MONDAY 7-30 — 11 p.m. Admission 2/6
THIS MONDAY — CLUBMEN

All their subsequent appearances at Lathom Hall took place during the first two months of 1961, by which time Kelly was paying them an average of eight pounds and tenpence a performance. Their appearances at the venue took place on 20, 21, 28 and 30 January and 4, 6, 10, 11 and 25 February. Their last performance on 25 February took place on George Harrison's eighteenth birthday.

It was at Lathom Hall on 14 May 1960, that an incident occurred with troublemakers. In 1966, **Neil Aspinall** recalled that the group were often a target for gangs who would shout insults at them because they were either looking for a fight or were annoyed that their girls fancied the foursome. For the sake of peace, the group ignored the taunts. 'But it wasn't always easy,' said Neil. 'At Lathom Hall . . . two troublemakers followed **Stu Sutcliffe** into the dressing-room muttering things like "Get your hair cut, girl!" John and Pete saw this and went after them. A fight broke out and John broke his little finger . . . It set crooked and never straightened.'

Stuart Sutcliffe was never injured at the time, but this is where another apocryphal Beatles story had its origins. In *The Man Who Gave The Beatles Away*, by **Allan Williams** and Bill Marshall, journalist Marshall admitted that he just took the bones of Williams' memories and elaborated on them, exaggerating the violence, swearing and sex. The book, published thirteen years after the Lathom Hall incident, contains a lot of inaccuracies regarding specific dates and events. One of them is the 14 May 1960 event which Allan had been told about, but he was unsure of the details and thought, many years later, that it had taken place at Litherland Town Hall. The text read, 'It was on such a night that Stuart Sutcliffe received the injuries which I believe hastened his death a couple of years later. Stuart was attacked outside Litherland Town Hall, where the Beatles played regularly, and was kicked in the head by a local thug. From then on he complained to me often of severe headaches.' This is hindsight presuming too much Stuart's headaches only began after he'd had a fall in Hamburg, according to his mother.

The Williams story was taken up and elaborated on still further by writers such as Philip Norman and the Lathom Hall incident eventually took on a life of its own. In Chet Flippo's book *McCartney: the Biography*, he writes, 'In the middle of a jive night at Lathom Hall in Seaforth . . . that was the night that Stu was attacked and kicked in the head by teds who didn't like the Silver Beats' looks.'

Pete Best, who was present at the Lathom Hall incident, confirms that John suffered a broken finger, but clearly states that Stuart was never kicked in the head.

Even more bizarre is Albert Goldman's accusation in *The Lives Of John Lennon* that John was responsible for

Stuart's death. 'He had gotten into a quarrel with Stu at Hamburg . . . suddenly John was seized by one of his fits of uncontrollable rage. He lashed out with hands and feet . . . when he came to his senses he looked down and saw Stu lying on the pavement.' Goldman says that, as a result, John felt completely responsible for Stu's death. Of such stuff, myths are made.

Lawdy Miss Clawdy

Composition written and recorded by Lloyd Price in 1952. As there were no record charts in existence at the time, there was no way to gauge record hits. When the charts came into being, Price had ten hit records. The **Quarry Men** included this number in their repertoire which was gradually moving away from skiffle music and veering towards rock 'n' roll.

Lawson Memorial Hospital, *Golspie, Inverness-shire, Scotland*

Hospital where John, **Yoko,** Kyoko and **Julian** were taken on 1 July 1969.

Following their Canadian trip, John and Yoko decided to go on a holiday in Scotland with their respective children, to enjoy some privacy after the recent hectic events of the previous months. John hadn't driven a car in years, being used to chauffeur-driven vehicles, but he nevertheless rented an Austin Mini and they set off on their trip. Unfortunately, he lost control of the car and it crashed into a ditch.

At the hospital John had to have seventeen stitches in his chin, while Yoko was suffering from concussion and a fractured back and had fourteen stitches. Kyoko had four stitches and Julian was suffering from shock.

They were all released from the hospital on 6 July and chartered a jet to return to London.

John and Yoko later bought their crashed Mini and had it erected on a concrete plinth in the grounds of Tittenhurst Park, for all the world like a piece of modern sculpture.

Leach, Sam

One of the most innovative of the local Liverpool promoters, who first began booking groups into the Mossway Jive Club at **Mossway Hall** in 1958 and later went on to run various clubs such as the **Cassanova Rock 'n' Swing Club** where he booked the Beatles for the first time in February 1961.

Promoting under 'The Leach Organisation', Sam began to launch bigger promotions on Merseyside than the other local impresarios and used the Beatles regularly. Another of his major gigs was the Rock Around The Clock twelve-hour session at the **Iron Door Club** (also called the Liverpool Jazz Society) in March 1961.

Another highlight took place on 10 November that year when Sam launched the first of his *Operation Big Beat* promotions at the **Tower Ballroom,** New Brighton, a venue which had a 5,000 capacity. He had the Beatles appearing on further *Operation Big Beat* shows at the Tower on 24 November and 8 December 1961. Hundreds of tickets for Sam's first *Operation Big Beat* show were on sale at Brian Epstein's branch of **NEMS** in Whitechapel, and the Beatles' name was very prominent in the tickets, posters and leaflets for the gig and it would have been almost impossible for Epstein not to have been aware of the event – if the stories of how interested he was in every detail are to be believed. Sam, himself, had desires of managing the Beatles and he also had ambitions of launching a record label, Troubadour Records, with the Beatles and **Gerry & the Pacemakers** as his initial releases. First in the studio were to be the Beatles recording 'Twist And Shout' and 'Stand By Me', but Sam couldn't raise the necessary capital to carry it off. In an effort to promote the group in the South, he booked the **Palais Ballroom** in Aldershot for four consecutive Saturday nights, with the Beatles appearing on the first of the shows on 9 December 1961.

Once Brian Epstein had become the Beatles' manager, he also began local promotions at venues such as the Tower Ballroom, which Sam had pioneered. Admittedly, he did approach Leach to run the gigs in partnership with himself, but Sam was unhappy about the proposed division of profits and declined. Basically, Brian wanted his brother Clive involved and suggested a three-way split which Sam, having established the Tower as a venue for beat music, didn't regard as a fair deal.

Sam held several parties, to which the Beatles were invited. They included his Iron Door celebration on 11 November to toast the success of *Operation Big Beat*. After one of his shows at **Knotty Ash Village Hall,** they attended his engagement party.

When the Beatles made such an impact in America, Sam published a magazine called *Beatles on Broadway*, which proved very lucrative for him. He also published a book in 1983 called *Follow The Merseybeat Road.*

● Lean, Dick

The Managing Director of Stadiums Limited, a company which organized Australian tours. Lean worked in association with **Kenn Brodziak** to promote the Beatles' tour of Australia and New Zealand. Lean was basically in charge of the venues where the group were to appear and he travelled with them throughout the tour.

● Leary, Timothy

An American intellectual and a leading figure in the use and exploration of psychedelic drugs in the sixties. His book *Psychedelic Experience*, which he co-wrote with Richard Alpert, based on *The Egyptian Book Of The Dead*, inspired John Lennon to write the number 'Tomorrow Never Knows'.

Leary visited John and **Yoko** at the Queen Elizabeth Hotel in Montreal and participated in the recording of 'Give Peace A Chance', which was recorded on a mobile recording unit which had been installed in the suite.

Commenting on the Beatles, Leary was to say: 'The Beatles are prototypes of a new race of laughing freemen: revolutionary agents sent by God, endowed with a mysterious power to create a new human species.'

● Leave My Kitten Alone

A number composed by John/Turner/McDougal which Little Willie John recorded in 1959. The Beatles included it in their repertoire in 1961, the same year that Johnny Preston's version was issued.

The group recorded it at **Abbey Road,** with John on lead vocals, on Friday, 14 August 1964, during their *Beatles For Sale* album sessions. It was intended for the album, but the group weren't satisfied with how it was turning out and abandoned it after five takes. It remains unreleased.

● Leigh, Janet

Blonde American film actress, former wife of Tony Curtis and mother of Jamie Lee Curtis, whose films include *Psycho, The Manchurian Candidate* and *Touch Of Evil.*

In January 1964, Janet participated in a Beatles publicity campaign. Hair stylist Gene Shacore was engaged by **Capitol Records** to design a female hairstyle based on the Beatles haircut. Janet became the first woman to wear the new style and a special press kit with photographs of her and her Beatles-style cut was sent to the beauty editors of all the daily newspapers in America.

● Lend Me Your Comb

Composition by Kay Twomey, Fred Wise and Ben Weisman, recorded by **Carl Perkins** in 1957 and included in the Beatles' repertoire in 1961 when John and Paul shared vocal honours.

It was part of the group's repertoire during their final **Star Club** season and is found on *The Beatles Live! At The Star Club In Hamburg, Germany: 1962* album. The group also recorded it for their BBC radio show **'Pop Go The Beatles'** on 16 July 1963.

● Lennon, Alfred

John's father, born in Liverpool on 14 December 1912. When his father Jack died of a liver disease in 1921 Alfred was nine years of age and was placed in the Bluecoat School, which took in orphans.

Alfred remained at the school until he was fifteen years old and then left to take up his first job as an office clerk. It was during this period, in 1927, that he met Julia Stanley, a fourteen-year-old girl, in **Sefton Park.** He chatted her up and asked her to sit with him, and she told him she would on condition he got rid of his silly bowler hat. He immediately threw it into the lake. The couple then began to date and continued doing so over a period of ten years, in between Alfred's voyages abroad as a merchant seaman.

In 1930, at the age of sixteen, Alfred was drawn to the sea and signed up as a ship's waiter. In between voyages he stayed at the Stanley house in **Newcastle Road,** Wavertree, and taught Julia how to play the banjo.

It was Julia who finally suggested that they should get married and they did, at Mount Pleasant Register Office on 3 December 1938. No member of their family was present and after the ceremony the couple went to the **Trocadero Cinema** where they spent their 'honeymoon'. Later that evening Julia went back home to Wavertree and Freddie went to his digs; he left the next day on a three month trip to the West Indies. He was also away at sea in October 1940 when John was born.

While at sea, Fred had arranged to pay sums of money to the company he worked for, which Julia could collect rom the branch in Liverpool. He was now a head waiter und as it was wartime and he was in New York city, was isked to report to a ship sailing to Britain. However, he vas to be an assistant steward on the voyage and not head vaiter and he bemoaned the fact to the Captain, who uggested that he get drunk and miss the boat, which he lid. He was then interned on Ellis Island until another hip, this time sailing for North Africa, was available. Vhen they reached North Africa he said that one of the ooks asked him to bring a bottle of vodka from his cabin nd while Fred was drinking from it a party of police rrived to investigate some thefts and arrested him for tealing the vodka. He was jailed for three months and his noney was stopped. Unable to provide Julia with any cash, e wrote her letters and suggested she enjoy herself by oing out with other men. He later regretted the suggestion ecause she took him up on it – and he lost her.

In 1945 she gave birth to another child and had the aby adopted by a Norwegian couple. She also began ving with **John Dykins** and placed her son John with her ister, **Mimi,** in Menlove Avenue.

Docking in Southampton in the summer of 1946, Fred honed Aunt Mimi and asked if he could take John to lackpool. Mimi felt she couldn't refuse this request from e boy's father and Fred picked up the five-year-old and ok him to stay in a friend's flat in Blackpool.

During the few weeks they were in the northern seaside sort, Fred told John of his desire to take him to New ealand. The idea appealed to Fred because his friend was migrating there and, at the time, Fred was earning money n the side through black market deals.

Julia arrived at the flat demanding that John be turned to her. Fred asked the boy whether he wanted to o to New Zealand with him or return to Liverpool with his other, and John opted for Fred's proposal. However, hen Julia left the house he changed his mind and ran ter her. Fred did not see his son again for twenty years. 'hen Julia returned to Liverpool she placed the boy into imi's care once again.

In 1964, Fred had finally abandoned life on the ocean ave and was working as a porter in the Greyhound Hotel, ampton, near London, for ten pounds a week. The *Daily xpress* newspaper traced him and wanted to set up a eeting between him and his now famous son.

Fred went along to the set of *A Hard Day's Night* and itered the dressing-room. John wouldn't talk to him but asked him to leave his address. John sent a letter to the Greyhound with a note to: 'Dear Alf, Fred, Dad, Pater, Father, Whatever', with £30 enclosed.

John began to send Fred a regular twelve pounds a week and the ex-seaman moved into a flat in Kew, basking in the limelight as a minor celebrity, having his life story printed in the weekly magazines and gracing the London nightspots. He even found himself with a manager, Tony Cartwright, who co-wrote a song with him called 'That's My Life', which was issued as a single in December 1965 by Pye Records on their Piccadilly label. The company issued a press handout which read:

'Fifty-three-year-old Freddie Lennon, father of John, has made his first record. It is entitled "That's My Life (My Love And My Home)".

'Mr Lennon has been an entertainer in an amateur capacity for most of his life. He comes from a musical family, for his father was one of the original Kentucky Minstrels, and taught him to sing when he was young.

'Most of Freddie's childhood was spent in an orphanage, for he was born into a large family and in those difficult times parents could not afford to feed so many children. At the orphanage, Freddie always took a major part in concerts, played his harmonica to the other children and generally showed an inclination towards the stage. He once sang at a theatre but the orphanage authorities were dismayed at the thought of one of their boys going on to the stage, so Freddie's early dreams were quickly dampened.

'After leaving the orphanage at the age of 15, Freddie worked in an office, but the call of the sea was strong, and he joined his first ship as bell boy at the age of 16. He stayed at sea for 25 years and travelled the world.

'Freddie was always connected with entertainment on board ship, and has acted as compere, produced numerous concerts, sang in New York clubs and even conducted an orchestra in Lisbon. He has many interesting stories to relate about his adventures at sea.

'At the age of 25 Freddie married, and his son John was born three years later. He was the only child.

'When he left sea 12 years ago, Freddie took a job as a waiter, and later worked in holiday camps at northern resorts. He came to live in London seven years ago. Over the years, Freddie was always interested in songwriting, but he never took it seriously. Six months ago he met Tony

Cartwright, who is now his manager. Together they wrote "That's My Life (My Love And My Home)" – a story about Freddie's life. The song was taken to a music publisher, accepted and recorded.'

By the close of 1967 Alfred and his son were reconciled and Fred often dropped around to John's house in **Kenwood.** At the time a romantic relationship began between Fred and a nineteen-year-old student called Pauline Jones. At 56, Fred was almost three times her age.

Fred proposed and Pauline's parents were furious and had her made a ward of court, but the two eloped to Scotland where they were married. They then went to live in Brighton with John paying the rent for their flat. When their first son David was born they took him to see John at Tittenhurst Park. John was in a foul mood and tossed them out, seemingly upset at the thought of seeing his half-brother, which may have set off painful memories.

Years later, when Fred was dying, John spoke to him by phone from America on several occasions, although Fred could hardly speak a word in return. When Fred died John offered to pay for his funeral, but Pauline rejected the offer.

● Lennon, Cynthia

Born Cynthia Powell in Blackpool on 10 September 1939. Her mother and two brothers, Tony and Charles, had been evacuated to the northern seaside town during World War II. The family then returned to Hoylake where Cynthia spent her childhood.

Cynthia Lennon. (Merseyside Tourism Office)

She sat an entrance examination which provided her with a place at the **Junior Art School** in **Gambier Terrace** and at the age of eighteen began her studies at **Liverpool College of Art** in September 1957.

Her close friend at the college was **Phyllis Mackenzie** and the two, like all beginners at the college, took part in the two-year Intermediate Course which provided them with the basic groundwork in the techniques of art. One of the various subjects which were part of the Intermediate Course was Lettering and joining Cynthia and Phyllis in the Lettering class were two other students, John Lennon and **Jonathan Hague.** As Hoylake on the Wirral was regarded as a 'posh' place, John began to make snide remarks to Cynthia.

Despite his apparent roughness, compared to the boyfriends she'd had, Cynthia found herself attracted to him and at one of the school parties he began dancing with her and asked her out. Embarrassed, she told him she was engaged to a chap in Hoylake. 'I didn't ask you to marry me, did I?' he snapped back. Yet Cynthia and Phyllis were invited to join John and his friends at **Ye Cracke** pub after the party and the two began to date regularly.

Completely besotted by John, Cynthia began to change her appearance to please him and allowed her blonde hair to grow long and began to wear tight black sweaters, very short, tight skirts, high-heeled shoes and black stockings and suspenders. This sort of blatant attire caused her some embarrassment at the times when she waited to meet up with John outside **Lewis's** store in Liverpool. The clothes belied the timid girl she really was. John liked Brigitte Bardot and therefore Cynthia tried to style herself on the looks of the French actress.

Cynthia began to travel with the Beatles to their local gigs, although she often had to stay in the background because of the possible hostile reaction she'd receive from the group's fans. She also became friendly with Paul McCartney's girl-friend **Dot Rhone.** When the Beatles appeared at the **Top Ten Club** in Hamburg from 27 March–2 July 1961, Cynthia and Dot were invited over to stay with them for a couple of weeks.

When Cynthia returned to Hoylake her mother revealed that Cynthia's cousin and his wife, who were emigrating to Canada, had invited her to travel with them and act as nanny to their children. She wanted to take up their offer, but was worried about Cynthia. Cynthia told her she would rent a room from John's Aunt **Mimi.** She tried to act like a daughter rather than a lodger, but found that the relationship with Mimi was strained and decided to move out. She eventually moved into a small flat and managed to persuade Dot Rhone to rent out the room next to her.

In 1962 a doctor confirmed that Cynthia was pregnant and when she told John, he said that they would have to get married. John's Aunt Mimi wasn't too pleased to hear the news and didn't attend the wedding. The ceremony itself was to be a hush-hush affair due to the increasing popularity of the Beatles nationwide and Brian Epstein suggested a special licence. On 23 August 1962 the couple were married at the Registry Office in Mount Pleasant, with her brother Tony and his wife, Paul McCartney, George Harrison and Brian Epstein in attendance. Brian was also to let the newly married couple have access to his private flat in Faulkner Street. On the wedding night, John left for a gig at the **Riverpark Ballroom, Chester** and was to spend most of the time over the next few months performing. The pregnant girl found herself very lonely during this period as John was on the road and hardly ever at the flat. A concerned Aunt Mimi requested that Cynthia move in with her.

On Monday, 8 April 1963 at 7.45 a.m., Cynthia gave birth to a baby boy, John Charles **Julian Lennon**, at **Sefton General Hospital.**

When Julian was six months old, Cynthia's mother returned from Canada and found a flat in Trinity Road, Hoylake, where Cynthia and Julian could join her. When John managed to take a break from touring, the couple were able to take a belated honeymoon in Paris, spending a week at the George V Hotel.

On Cynthia's return to Hoylake she was tracked down by the press who had heard rumours of the marriage and the story eventually broke in the newspapers. Now that the marriage was out in the open, John arranged for Cynthia and Julian to move down to London with him and a photographer friend, **Bob Freeman**, arranged for them to move into a flat in Emperor's Gate, Knightsbridge. The accommodation was not really suitable, as there were too many steps for Cynthia to negotiate with a child in a pram, and the address was known to Beatle fans who would gather outside.

However, on the Beatles' return from America, John bought a large house, **'Kenwood'**, in Weybridge, Surrey, and the family were able to move into their six-bedroomed home at the end of July 1964.

Cynthia travelled to America with the Beatles and the fans were not hostile to her – as they would later be to **Linda McCartney** and **Yoko Ono.** However, Cynthia never seemed to lose her timidity and was often unable to get back into hotels where she was staying with John and the Beatles. When they were staying at the **Deauville Hotel** in Miami, Cynthia was attempting to return to the hotel when a security guard refused to let her pass. She identified herself but he didn't believe her. It took a group of fans, who realized who she was, to talk in strong terms to the guard to allow him to let her back into the hotel.

She was able to settle down in Kenwood, more content in the role of a housewife than a celebrity, although enthusiasts even launched a Cynthia Lennon Fan Club. There were holidays and she enjoyed the socializing with other Beatles wives and girlfriends – **Pattie**, **Jane** and **Maureen**.

Inevitably perhaps, the idyll came to an end. Cynthia seemed to believe it was as a result of drugs and in her autobiography, *A Twist Of Lennon*, commented: 'As far as I was concerned the rot began to set in the moment cannabis and LSD seeped its unhealthy way into our lives.' She hated drugs herself and when someone slipped LSD into a drink of hers one day, she thought she was going insane.

Cynthia was also aware that when the Beatles were on tour, attractive model girls were among the many females who threw themselves at the group, and their constant tours abroad worried her. She began to lose confidence in her looks and in 1967 decided to have plastic surgery on her nose. When she was at the London Clinic, following the operation, John sent her a bouquet of red roses and a card which read: 'To Cyn, a nose by any other name. Love from John and Julian'.

However, Cynthia began to feel estranged from John and the Beatles circle because she shunned drugs, and she could see that the others were obviously influenced by the effects of LSD in the way a colourful world of psychedelia seemed to open up with the lyrics of the *Sgt Pepper* album, and John having his Rolls-Royce painted in psychedelic colours. She felt outside of things and decided that she'd have to get back on John's wavelength to save the marriage. John had been asking her to take LSD for some time and she agreed, while John helped her through the trip. She regarded it as hell on earth and hated every moment. John kept telling her that he loved her and would never leave her, but when she looked at him the hallucinations made her see an animal-type person wit razor sharp teeth, laughing at her. She realized that she would never be happy taking drugs.

By the time Cynthia joined the group at Rishikesh to study Transcendental Meditation, **Yoko Ono** had entered the picture, Brian Epstein had died and the Beatles had decided to launch **Apple Corps**. She enjoyed Rishikesh and believed that Transcendental Meditation had done John a lot of good, but she was sad that John and George severed their relationship with the guru so drastically.

The first time Cynthia had met Yoko was at a meditation session in London. She then began to notice the letters Yoko sent to John at Kenwood asking for his help in promoting her book *Grapefruit*. Dot, the Lennons housekeeper, had also told Cynthia that Yoko had been turning up at the house regularly trying to see if John wa at home.

When things began to get on top of Cynthia, Joh suggested she go on a holiday for two weeks during a time when he would be recording. **Donovan** and Gypsy Dav were travelling to Greece with Jennie Boyd and **Alexi Mardas** and John suggested she join them. When Cynthi arrived back at Kenwood, accompanied by Jennie an Alexis, she found John and Yoko in the house together Confused, she asked John if he'd come out to dinner. H refused. She'd noticed a pair of Japanese slippers place outside the guest bedroom door and asked Alexis an Jennie if she could stay with them for a few days and left.

The opinion of people who knew both John and Cynthi at the time was that Cynthia should have stood her groun and demanded Yoko be thrown out of the house. If she ha responded strongly as an outraged wife, then there was strong possibility that John might have remained wit Cynthia, perhaps taking Yoko on as a mistress. The fac that Cynthia capitulated proved to be her downfall.

That evening Cynthia and Alexis sat up drinking win together and she awoke the next morning to find herself i bed with him. She felt disgusted with herself. She returne to Kenwood to find that Yoko had gone, and there was reconciliation. John told Cynthia he was bored with Yok However, John left for New York a few days later, refusin to take Cynthia with him. Cynthia didn't want to remain a Kenwood by herself, so she took a brief holiday in Ital with Julian and her mother. One day Alexis Mard arrived to tell her that John was divorcing her and that h would testify to adultery on John's behalf. Cynthia becam erribly depressed and ill, having to remain in bed for several days. When she returned to London there was a divorce petition citing her adultery with Alexis Mardas.

However, it was decided that it would be better for all concerned if it was John who admitted to his adultery with Yoko, which is what happened when Cynthia was granted decree nisi on 8 November 1969.

The following year, on 31 July, Cynthia married Roberto Bassanini at Kensington Register Office. Roberto had been the son of the hotel owners at the resort where Cynthia had been on holiday the previous year. At the ceremony, Julian was a page boy and **Twiggy** and Justin de Villeneuve were present. However, the marriage wasn't to last and after her divorce from Bassanini she married businessman John Twist and the couple moved to Ireland for a short time with Julian, then settled down in Ruthin, North Wales. Her autobiography *A Twist Of Lennon* was published in paperback in April 1978. When her marriage to Twist ended in divorce and after John's death, Cynthia reverted to the name Cynthia Lennon. Despite all that had happened, Cynthia remained in love with John.

Julian left home to seek a career in showbusiness and Cynthia attempted to make a living as an artist – the settlement John had made her following their divorce hadn't been large in comparison to his earnings. There were several exhibitions of her paintings and she was also involved in a number of design commissions. For a time she was involved in the West End restaurant Lennon's, but settled in the Isle of Man, and in 1991 finally put all her personal memorabilia relating to John up for auction.

Lennon, John

John Winston Lennon was born at 6.30 p.m. on 9 October 1940 at **Oxford Street Maternity Hospital,** Liverpool, to **Julia** and **Alfred Lennon**. The seaport of Liverpool had been subject to heavy raids by the Luftwaffe that week, but on the night of John's birth, there was a lull in the bombing.

Fred Lennon was away at sea and rarely saw his son. His mother Julia liked to enjoy herself and didn't seem to relish the responsibility of rearing a child at that time with the result that the young boy was left in the care of his aunt Mary **'Mimi' Smith** and Uncle George in the pleasant Woolton area of Liverpool.

John seemed fated to be reared by his aunt when Julia decided to live with another man, **John Dykins,** and eventually bore him two daughters. She'd previously given birth to another daughter by a soldier of brief acquaintance but was forced by her father to put the baby up for adoption.

In 1946 Fred returned to Liverpool and took his son on a short holiday to the nearby seaside resort of Blackpool where he made plans to emigrate to New Zealand with John. Julia turned up and took her son back to Liverpool, returning him to Mimi's care.

John went to Dovedale Primary School where he began to betray the streak of rebelliousness which was to remain with him for the rest of his life. He also began to take an interest in drawing.

Tragedy struck in 1955 when his kindly Uncle George died, leaving the troubled young boy to internalize another grief. Despite the love his authoritarian aunt gave him, the fact that he was not reared by his own mother and father was a factor in his outlook on life.

John began attending **Quarry Bank Grammar School** in September 1952 and struck up a friendship with another young 'tearaway', **Peter Shotton.** The two friends became inseparable and were always getting into trouble at school for crazy pranks and insolence to teachers. Their academic work suffered. It was during this period when John began to display his creative abilities as a writer and artist with a series of exercise books containing his drawings and humorous stories, which he dubbed 'The Daily Howl'. As a youngster he loved books and would prefer them as presents. His favourites included the Lewis Carroll *Alice* books and Richmal Crompton's *Just William* novels – these stories of a scamp of a schoolboy probably influenced his behaviour and he possibly identified with the character.

When the skiffle boom spread throughout Britain, John was one of the many boys who decided to form a group of his own and in May 1955 he gathered his school friends into a band he called the **Quarry Men.**

There were various changes in personnel, but the most important event occurred at **Woolton Parish Church** Fete on 6 July 1957 when he met schoolboy Paul McCartney who was soon to become a member of the group.

John's own preference for rock 'n' roll and his love of **Elvis Presley** soon began to have its effect on the Quarry Men as they shed the traditional folksy numbers and developed into a rock 'n' roll group. Although John was the leader of the group, his musical relationship with McCartney grew to the extent that they became a songwriting team and developed a vocal-harmony style. There were many suggestions and pressures for them to adopt the current style of having a leader's name at the front of the group. Suggestions included Long John and the Silver Men. At one time they used the name **Johnny & the Moondogs** for a series of talent contests, but generally resisted efforts to make them into a group with a front line singer. This pressure continued until they signed with Parlophone. George Martin initially thought of changing their style and having Paul McCartney as the leader, but then changed his mind.

In September 1957, John enrolled at **Liverpool Art College.** He met **Cynthia** Powell, who was to become his first wife, **Stuart Sutcliffe,** who became his best friend and the **Fifth Beatle**, and Bill Harry who published his first works and promoted the Beatles' career locally.

In 1960 the Beatles travelled to Hamburg and many stories filtered back to Liverpool of John's escapades there. In July 1961 his first published work appeared in ***Mersey Beat*** and he contributed a column called 'Beatcomber'. Later the same year the group met Brian Epstein who became their manager and the following year they signed with Parlophone. In the meantime, John married Cynthia on 23 August 1962 and she gave birth to their son **Julian** on 8 April 1963. Within a few weeks John went on a brief holiday to Spain with Brian Epstein, and when local disc jockey **Bob Wooler** made a snide remark about the trip, John beat him up.

The Beatles were enjoying international success when John's first book *In His Own Write* was published on 23 March 1964 and became a best-seller. In January 1965 he appeared on the TV programme **'Not Only . . . But Also'**, reading his poetry, and on 24 June of that year his second book *A Spaniard In the Works* was published. During the same year his father Fred re-entered his life and the Beatles received their **MBEs.** In 1966 there was a degree of anti-Beatle fervour in America following comments John had made in an interview with Maureen Cleave, in which he said that the Beatles were more popular than Jesus, and he reluctantly made a public apology. At the end of the year the Beatles had decided to cease touring and in November John met the Japanese artist **Yoko Ono** at the **Indica Gallery** in London.

The Beatles had begun to experiment with various drugs, including LSD, and in August 1967 met th **Maharishi Mahesh Yogi**. During the same month the manager Brian Epstein was found dead from an accident drug overdose. John's ties with Yoko grew stronger and h sponsored an exhibition of her work called *Yoko And Me* the Lisson Arts Gallery in October. Later than month *Ho I Won The War*, in which he played his first solo featu film role, was premiered.

Following the Beatles' stay at the Maharishi's ashra

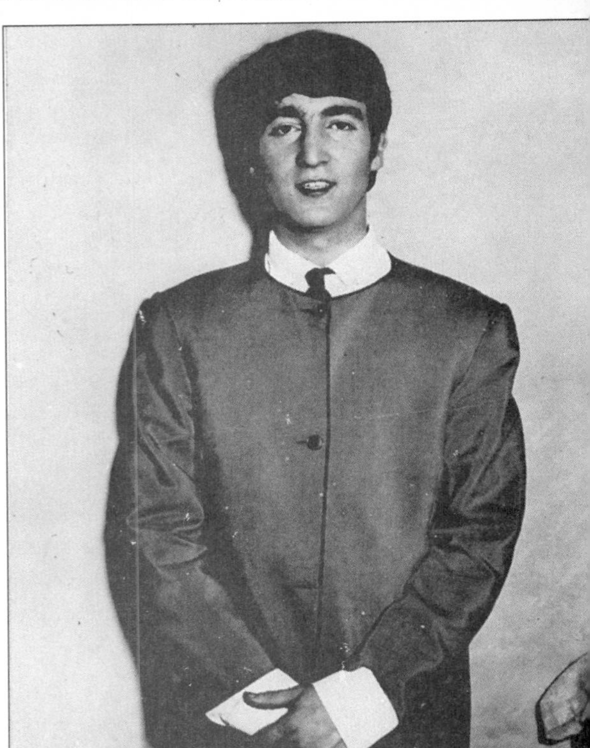

From the Nevitsky Collection.

in India, John and Cynthia split up and he began to li with Yoko. A play *In His Own Write*, based on Joh books, was staged at the National Theatre in June a John's first art exhibition, *You Are Here*, opened at t **Robert Fraser** Gallery. John and Yoko were raided the police while staying at Ringo's flat in **Montag Square** and John was fined for possession of cannab John and Yoko's album *Unfinished Music No. 1: T Virgins* was issued in November and created internatio controversy due to the cover, which showed the pair i

full frontal nude pose. John also appeared on the unshown *Rolling Stones Rock 'n' Roll Circus*.

In 1969, John was disillusioned with the Beatles' Apple empire and revealed as much to journalist **Ray Coleman.** As a result **Allen Klein** appeared on the scene and, with John's support, was able to take control of Apple. In the meantime Yoko's divorce from Anthony Cox came through in February and John and Yoko were married in Gibraltar on 20 March.

John and Yoko began making a series of avant garde films together, which included: *Apotheosis, Clock, Erection, Fly, Freedom Films, Imagine, Self Portrait, Smile* and *Up Your Legs Forever*. In May 1969 they bought an imposing mansion in Ascot called Tittenhurst Park and issued their second album *Unfinished Music No. 2: Life With Th Lions*. During the year they also travelled to Toronto whe they met Canadian Prime Minister Pierre Trudeau an they recorded the peace anthem 'Give Peace A Chance 1969 was also the year in which John introduced th **Plastic Ono Band** on record. In September he formed Plastic Ono Band for a live appearance at the *Rock 'n' Ro Revival Concert* in Toronto. In November the couple issue their *Wedding Album* and John returned his MBE to th Queen. At the year's end, John was featured in an IT documentary 'Man Of The Decade'.

An exhibition of John's erotic lithographs opened at th **London Arts Gallery** on 15 January 1970 which wa raided by the police. During the year there were furth lastic Ono Band releases, John and Yoko travelled to Los ngeles to undergo Primal Therapy under **Dr Arthur anov** and Cynthia Lennon remarried. In January 1971 *olling Stone* magazine published the first part of a ngthy interview with John in which he vented his spleen. y March a receiver had been appointed to wind up the eatles partnership and John and Yoko flew to New York. ley came to Britain for a short time before returning to merica in September, with John never to set foot in itain again. During 1972 John fought to obtain a Green ard and was involved in a number of political protests, d his album *Some Time In New York City* included a umber of songs based on the political causes he pported. During 1973 Ringo Starr bought Tittenhurst rk and John left Yoko to fly to Los Angeles with their

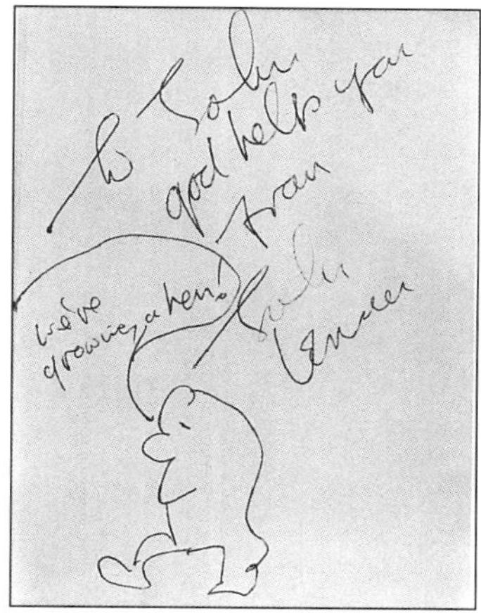

typical John Lennon ustration – it sold for ,210 at Sotheby's. otheby's)
ft: John in *Let It Be* Apple)

cretary May Pang, with whom he was having an affair. hat John called his 'long weekend' eventually ended and returned to live with Yoko in New York in January 75. Their son **Sean** was born in September of that year.

In 1976 John received his Green Card and at the end of e year decided to go into semi-retirement and rear Sean rsonally. He was to describe himself as a 'house sband' during this period. In late August 1980 he began cording his first album in six years and agreed to a mber of interviews prior to him becoming active in the isic scene once again. On 8 December he was shot dead tside the Dakota Building.

Among the non-Beatles albums made by John were: *finished Music No. 1 – Two Virgins*, issued in Britain on Apple SAPCOR 2 on 29 November 1968 and in America on Apple T 5001 on 11 November 1968; *Unfinished Music No. 2 – Life With The Lions*, issued in Britain on Zapple 01 on 9 May 1969 and in America on Zapple ST 3357 on 26 May 1969; *The Wedding Album*, issued in Britain on Apple SAPCOR 11 on 7 November 1969 and in America on Apple SMAX 3362 on 20 October 1969; *The Plastic Ono Band – Live Peace In Toronto 1969*, issued in Britain on Apple CORE 2001 on 12 December 1969 and in America on Apple SW 3362 on 12 December 1969; *John Lennon/Plastic Ono Band*, issued in Britain on Apple PCS 7124 on 11 December 1970 and in America on Apple SW 3372 on 11 December 1970; *Imagine*, issued in Britain on Apple PAS 10004 on 8 October 1971 and in America on Apple SW 3379 on 9 September 1971; *Some Time In New York City*, issued in Britain on Apple PCSP 716 on 15 September 1972 and in America on Apple SVBB 3392 on 12 June 1972; *Mind Games*, issued in Britain on Apple PCS 7165 on 16 November 1973 and in America on Apple SW 3414 on 2 November 1973; *Walls and Bridges*, issued in Britain on Apple PCTC 253 on 4 October 1974 and in America on Apple SW 3416 on 26 September 1974; *Rock 'n' Roll*, issued in Britain on Apple PCS 7169 on 21 February 1975 and in America on Apple SK 3419 on 17 February 1975; *Shaved Fish (Collectable Lennon)*, issued in Britain on Apple PCS 71173 on 24 October 1975 and in America on Apple SW 3421 on 24 October 1975; *Double Fantasy*, issued in Britain on Geffen Records K99131 on 17 November 1980 and in America on Geffen Records GHS 2001 on 17 November 1980. After John's death an album *The John Lennon Collection* was issued in Britain on Parlophone EMTV 37 on 8 November 1982 and in America on 10 November 1982.

John's singles included: 'Give Peace A Chance' c/w 'Remember Love', issued in Britain on Apple 13 on 4 July 1969 and in America on Apple 1809 on 7 July 1969; 'Cold Turkey' c/w 'Don't Worry Kyoko', issued in Britain on Apple 1001 on 24 October 1969 and in America on Apple 1813 on 20 October 1969; 'Instant Karma' c/w 'Who Has Seen The Wind', issued in Britain on Apple 1003 on 6 February 1970 and in America on Apple 1818 on 20 February 1970; 'Power To The People' c/w 'Open Your Box', issued in Britain on Apple R 5892 on 12 March 1971 and in America on Apple 1830 on 22 March 1971; 'God Save Us' c/w 'Do The Oz', issued in Britain on Apple 36 on 16 July 1971 and in America on Apple 1835 on 7 July 1971; 'Happy Xmas (War Is Over)' c/w 'Listen The Snow Is Falling', issued in Britain on Apple R 5970 on 24 November 1972 and in America on Apple 1842 on 1 December 1971; 'Mind Games' c/w 'Meat City', issued in Britain on Apple R 5994 on 16 November 1973 and in America on Apple 1868 on 29 October 1973; 'Whatever Gets You Thru The Night' c/w 'Beef Jerky', issued in Britain on Apple R 5998 on 4 October 1974 and in America on Apple 1874 on 23 September 1974; 'No. 9 Dream' c/w 'What You Got', issued in Britain on Apple R 6003 on 31 January 1975 and in America on Apple 1878 on 16 December 1974; 'Stand By Me' c/w 'Move Over Ms. L', issued in Britain on Apple R 6005 on 18 April 1975 and in America on Apple 1881 on 10 March 1975; 'Imagine' c/w 'Working Class Hero', issued in Britain on Apple R 6009 on 24 October 1975; 'Just Like Starting Over' c/w 'Kiss Kiss Kiss', issued in Britain on Geffen Records K79186 on 24 October 1980 and in America on Geffen Records GEF 49604 on 23 October 1980; 'Woman' c/w 'Beautiful Boy', issued in Britain on Geffen Records K79195 on 16 January 1981 and in America on Geffen Records 49644 on 12 January 1981; 'Watching The Wheels', c/w 'Yes I'm Your Angel', issued in Britain on Geffen Records K79207 on 27 March 1981 and in America on Geffen Records 49695 on 13 March 1981.

● Lennon, Julia (nee Stanley)

John's mother, a slim, auburn-haired woman of a decidedly unconventional nature. Julia was one of the five daughters of George and Annie Stanley and was born on 12 March 1914. Julia first met **Freddie Lennon** in **Sefton Park** when she was only fourteen. He was wearing a bowler hat at the time and when she told him it made him look silly, he threw the hat into the lake. Despite the disapproval of her father, Julia, known in the family as Juliet, married Freddie at Mount Pleasant Register Office on 3 December 1938, several years after they had first met. As a joke, she put down her profession as 'Cinema usherette' on the wedding certificate, because she loved going to the pictures so much. In fact, after the wedding, Freddie and Julia spent the evening at the Trocadero, her favourite cinema. Then she went back to her parents' home, he went back to his lodgings and the next day Freddie sailed to the West Indies as steward on a ship.

Their only child together was John Winston Lennon, born in October 1940. Julia became pregnant again in 1944 by a young Welsh soldier 'Taffy' Williams, b refused to divorce Freddie and marry him. In fact, she wa totally uninterested in the soldier and when he propose she told him to 'get lost!'

Her father was furious and gave her an ultimatum: sh had to have the baby adopted or leave the house. At first was suggested that her childless sister **Mimi** could rear th child, but Mimi did not want to have anything to do wi an illegitimate child. The baby, Victoria Elizabeth, wh had been born on 19 June 1945, was adopted by Norwegian Captain and his wife and never heard fro again.

Freddie spent almost the entire period of the war yea at sea and Julia, who worked for a time as a waitress at cafe in Penny Lane, moved in with one of her customer **John Dykins**. Mimi disapproved of the situation an insisted that Julia give John to her to rear. Eventuall Julia agreed to do so. When Freddie returned from sea the war's end he insisted on taking John on a holiday Blackpool. There he made plans to move to New Zeala with John. Then Julia turned up and demanded that h return her son to her. John at first said he wanted remain with his father, but then ran after his mother wh she began to leave. When Julia arrived back in Liverpo she returned John to Mimi's keeping.

Julia settled down with Dykins, although they we never married as Julia was never divorced from Freddi She gave birth to two daughters; Julia, born 5 March 194 and Jacqui, born 26 October 1949.

Over the years, John was able to visit his moth frequently and she obviously had a profound effect on hi She was very pretty, had an off-beat sense of humour, w musical and totally unconventional. For instance, she us to do the housework wearing a pair of old woollen knicke on her head. Sometimes she'd wear a pair of spectacl without lenses and when talking to someone wou suddenly put her fingers through the empty lens to scrat her eye.

Her new home was in Blomfield Road, close to whe John lived with his Aunt Mimi. Soon he'd bring along h friends to meet her and they were all charmed, particular **Pete Shotton,** who was delighted by her wacky humour.

She was also to influence John in his interest in mus Her grandfather, William Stanley, a part-time musicia had taught her to play banjo when she was a child. S used to sing to John and taught him how to play 'That'll ıe Day' on the banjo. John said, 'My mother could play ıy stringed instrument there was.' and Paul McCartney ıs to comment, 'Julia was lively and heaps of fun and ıy ahead of her time. Not too many blokes had mothers progressive as she was.'

On 15 July 1958 she was killed. She'd left her house at 00 p.m. to see Mimi. After her visit, Mimi told her, 'I n't walk you tonight, Julia. I'll see you tomorrow.' **Nigel halley,** who was managing John's group at the time, had opped by to see if John was in and witnessed the cident. Julia stepped off the pavement to cross to the ntral reservation on the dual carriageway when she was by a car which sent her spinning. She died instantly. er body was taken to **Sefton General Hospital**. The -duty policeman who had driven the vehicle was taken court, but was acquitted.

The tragedy was to affect John deeply, particularly as had a tendency to let things boil up inside him and not ow his emotions outwardly. His feelings were a mixed g of guilt, resentment of her for leaving him, frustration not having a normal family life and emotions which were ally to resolve themselves when he underwent 'Primal' erapy many years later. John named his young son **lian** after his mother and wrote a number of songs dicated to her: 'My Mummy's Dead', 'Mother' and lia'.

Lennon, Julian

hn's first son and the first child born to any member of Beatles. The group were currently promoting their new ıgle 'Please Please Me' and John's marriage to **Cynthia** d been kept secret from the world in general.

Accompanied only by her friend **Phyllis Mackenzie,** nthia was rushed to **Sefton General Hospital** in ıithdown Road, Liverpool, and gave birth to Julian at 45 p.m. on Monday, 8 April 1963. There was some fficulty at the actual birth as the umbilical cord was apped around the child's neck, but he proved to be a althy baby. Cynthia then requested a private room and ın visited her there a week later.

When Cynthia left hospital with Julian she returned to nlove Avenue where she had been staying with John's **nt Mimi.** When Cynthia's mother returned from nada six months later, they decided to return to Trinity ad, Hoylake, their previous home.

In November Julian was christened at Trinity Road parish church, although John was unable to attend. His full name is John Charles Julian Lennon. The first name was chosen in honour of John, the second in memory of Cynthia's father and the third in memory of John's mother.

News of the marriage and the birth of Julian eventually found its way into the press. The three were able to unite as a family at last and move into a flat in Emperor's Gate, Kensington, London. This proved inconvenient and they later moved to St George's Hill Estate in Weybridge, Surrey, where Julian attended the local prep school.

When Julian was four years old he brought home a picture of a school friend which he'd drawn and called it 'Lucy In The Sky With Diamonds'. This inspired John to write a song of the same name.

At one time there was a kidnapping threat and Julian was guarded day and night, both at home and at school.

When **Yoko Ono** entered the picture, John and Cynthia's marriage was doomed. **Alexis Mardas** conveyed a message to Cynthia that John was going to divorce her and take Julian away from her. Paul McCartney was particularly upset by the split and felt sorry for Julian, an emotion which led him to composing 'Hey Jude'.

After the divorce, John had access to Julian who joined his father and Yoko on numerous occasions, visiting the filming of the Rolling Stones' *Rock And Roll Circus* and joining them on a trip to Scotland with Yoko's daughter Kyoko in June 1967.

Later that same year another of his drawings was immortalized, this time as the sleeve of *Christmas Time Is Here Again*, the Beatles' Christmas record, issued in December.

In 1970 Cynthia married hotelier Roberto Bassanini, but the marriage was a brief one and they parted shortly afterwards. The divorce came through in 1973 and she married businessman John Twist in 1976. They settled in Ruthin, North Wales, where Julian attended the local school and Cynthia teamed up with Angie McCartney, ex-wife of Mike McGear, to open a venture called Oliver's Bistro.

During the remainder of the seventies, Julian led a more-or-less normal life, out of the limelight, attending the local school and making friends in Ruthin. Julian's life was shattered when John Twist had to tell him that his father had been murdered, and he lay on the floor in a state of shock for hours.

Yoko wanted him to come straight to New York, but

said that she didn't want Cynthia to come with him, so he was accompanied by one of his Ruthin friends, Justin.

Julian's life changed completely following the tragedy. Cynthia and John Twist became estranged, and she reverted to the name Cynthia Lennon and began to tour America with her paintings, also leaving North Wales for a new home in Wiltshire.

When he returned from America, Julian decided that the time had come for him to leave home and he moved to Chiswick in London. He became a favourite topic of the gossip columns, attracting escorts like moths to a flame. He'd had girlfriends in Ruthin such as Sally Hudson and a girl called Amanda, but the models who now pursued him in London were totally different.

He'd been befriended by an old Etonian Kim Kindersley who took him round all the fashionable clubs, from Tramps to Stringfellows. At Tramps he was approached by **Stephanie La Motta**, who became one of the series of girls he hit the headlines with.

He was given a nineteenth birthday party at Stringfellows, which received considerable press coverage, with models such as Sian Adley-Jones stripping to the waist for the photographers. For the next few years, models found that a date with Julian ensured them press coverage. Some examples include Kate Latto, featured in a *Daily Mirror* newspaper story in January 1982 under the heading 'Julian's Blonde'. Two months later the *Sunday Mirror* newspaper was featuring 'The New Girl For "So Shy" Julian' in a story which began: 'This beautiful blonde is the new girl in Julian Lennon's life. Model Jordana . . . has been wined and dined . . . by [Julian] since they met at a London nightclub.' The stories continued and a topless Debbie Boyland was featured in the *Sunday People* newspaper in April 1983 under the heading 'Love And Sun For Lennon' in a story beginning: 'Delicious Debbie Boyland and her lover Julian Lennon . . . are Barbados bound.' His club exploits caused controversy, such as the occasion when he was photographed with a blonde holding a gun to his head at L'Escargot club.

In the years immediately following John's death, Julian seemed only newsworthy for his partiality for blondes. His musical career seemed to be almost non-existent, despite the fact that he'd been signed up by Tariq Siddiqi.

When he was eighteen, Cynthia had said he could play the guitar better than his father. At one time he had a band called the Lennon Drops and in April 1982 the London

Left and facing page: Julian Lennon – following in his father's footsteps. (Virgin Records)

ening Standard in a story entitled 'Julian's Chilling ebut', wrote that Julian was about to 'astonish the world th the release of a chillingly brilliant debut record'. The mber was 'I Don't Wanna Feel It Any More', which John mself had actually recorded during the *Double Fantasy* ssions but had never released.

In March 1983, reports appeared in the British press at Julian had joined Quasar, a group led by Paul Inder, n of Lemmy of Motorhead. Paul was also managed by ddiqi. In May 1983 there was some controversy because ddiqi organized the group's appearance on the roof of the d Apple building in **Savile Row**. Even Paul Inder's other couldn't stomach this blatant use of Julian and id, 'The whole idea of using the memory of the Beatles d using John Lennon's son in this way is sick.'

In the years following John's death, there was always ntroversy regarding Julian's inheritance. Some papers scribed him as 'The heir to John's vast fortune – timated to be more than £50 million'. However, Julian gan to bemoan the fact that he was broke and began ering to tell his story to newspapers – for a price.

A series did appear in the *News Of the World* newspaper in January 1982 in which Julian talked to Polly Hepburn. The headline ran 'All You Need Is Love. The Beatles Said It, But I Wish Dad Had Shown Me Some'.

Julian claimed that John had offered him marijuana when he was only twelve years old, described his visits to John in America and said other boys often threatened to beat him up because he was the son of a Beatle, and other rather innocuous stories. Yoko granted him an allowance of 100 dollars a week, a sum which was criticized when the news leaked out. Julian said: 'Yoko decided to give me a hundred dollars a week some time ago, but it is not mine by right. The papers say I'm heir to a fortune worth millions, but Yoko has total control of everything. I will get half the trust fund cash, about two hundred thousand dollars, when I am 25. The other half goes to Sean.'

Yoko replied to the criticism by saying, 'Poor Julian is probably very confused. It all has to do with Cynthia. She is not getting any money from John's estate, rightly, and she is very hurt by this. It's hard for Julian to please his mother without saying bad things about me. John never gave him any allowance. Julian was complaining that he didn't have enough money to be able to buy beer so I said

“How much will cover that?” How much do most kids his age get? Should he grow up differently from other kids?’

Julian eventually succeeded as a musician in his own right, with tours and chart records. He moved to Los Angeles and settled in America.

● Lennon, Sean

The only offspring of John and **Yoko** was born on John’s 35th birthday, 9 October 1975, at New York Hospital. Yoko had had three miscarriages before the birth of their son, which was obviously one of the high points in their lives. John was to say, ‘I feel higher than the Empire State Building.’ At one time he considered calling his newborn son George Washington United States Of America Citizen Lennon.

The couple had almost given up hope of having a child together, but decided to try again on the advice of an acupuncturist. John said, ‘We went through all hell trying to have a baby, through many miscarriages and other problems. He is what they call a love child in truth. Doctors told us we could never have a child. We almost gave up. We were told something was wrong with my sperm, that I abused myself so much in my youth th there was no chance. Yoko was 43, and so they said way. But this Chinese acupuncturist in San Francisco sai “You behave yourself. No drugs, eat well, no drink. Y have a child in eighteen months.” We had Sean and se the acupuncturist a Polaroid of him before he died, G rest his soul.’

Having experienced a childhood without any dire parental care, and harbouring a guilt for letting his care take precedence over seeing his first son **Julian** grow u John decided that he would spend virtually his enti waking life in the company of Sean. He did this for period of time which lasted five years.

In the Dakota apartments, John became a hou husband, caring for Sean, feeding him, teaching him, a doting on him while Yoko went out to work, controlling t couple’s many business interests. For the first year Sean’s life, John took Polaroid shots of his son every sing day. When Sean began to draw, John had all the sketch framed. He was finding a satisfaction in life he had nev experienced before.

John’s life revolved around Sean’s meals. He would ri

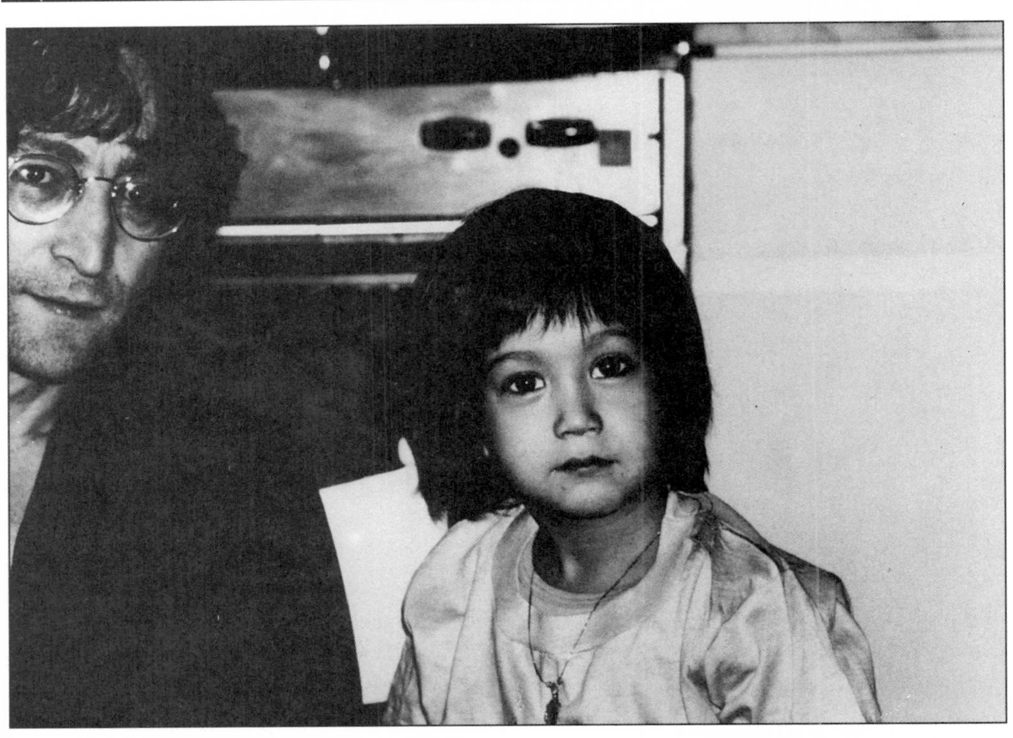

John with his son Sean in *Imagine*, the Warner Bros film released in 1988. (Warner Bros)

t six in the morning to plan breakfast. The two would ave this at around seven-thirty, when they would both ›ommunicate'.

Then at ten o'clock when Sean was involved in other ıings, John would be planning the next meal.

He didn't mind the role-reversal of having Yoko take are of business while he looked after the home. He'd nally ridden himself of that chauvinism so associated ith males from the north of England.

It was during his holiday in Bermuda with Sean that ›hn finally decided to resume a musical career. However, ıte tragically brought this to a chilling end.

Sean is left with memories, the treasure of five years of lose intimacy, rare between father and son. Nothing will ompensate him for his loss. Life must have seemed uzzling for such a child, growing up in a world in which e was forever surrounded by bodyguards.

Lennon & McCartney Songbook, The

n hour-long BBC radio show, transmitted on the Light rogramme on Bank Holiday Monday, 29 August 1966. he theme was cover versions of Lennon & McCartney ›ngs and both John and Paul were interviewed for the rogramme at Paul's Cavendish Avenue house on 6 August.

Only one Beatles number was played on the show, ›ood Day Sunshine' from their *Revolver* album, issued ırlier that month. All other music on the programme was y various artists who covered Lennon & McCartney ›ngs, including Ella Fitzgerald, the Mamas and Papas, **at Boone**, **Peter Sellers** and Nancy Sinatra.

Leonard, Barry

eonard worked as Brian Epstein's personal assistant in ondon for a short time. He quit when he said that the rain of managing the Beatles was too great. He then gave story to the *Daily Express* newspaper in which he said ıat Paul McCartney intended leaving the Beatles and was tempting to lose his Liverpool accent.

Les Ambassadeurs, Hamilton Place, ondon W1

ashionable club where the Beatles held a private party in ıne 1965 to celebrate the **MBE** awards they'd received. he club was also the setting for a special ***Magic hristian*** party hosted by Ringo and **Peter Sellers**.

On 24 October 1979, it was booked by *The Guinness Book Of Records* for a special party in honour of Paul McCartney.

Leslo

Name of the Greek island which the Beatles purchased in 1967, intending it to be an idyllic retreat where they would create their own community.

When the Beatles were in the recording studio one night, John suggested that they should find themselves a Greek island on which they could build houses, a studio and a school. He suggested that Julian could be taught there and they could invite **Bob Dylan**'s children to be educated on the island. **Alexis Mardas**, who was present in the studio with them, immediately said that he knew an island off the Greek mainland which could be bought quite cheaply. The following day **Peter Brown** sent Alexis and **Alistair Taylor** off to Greece to make the arrangements for the purchase. They located a tiny cluster of islands in the Aegean; the large main island of 100 acres contained four beaches and there were five smaller islands with sixteen acres of olive trees. The Beatles would be able to buy them all for £90,000.

When the group heard about it they all wanted to leave for Leslo at once. At the time Alexis didn't tell them about the political situation in Greece, which was under the control of a military junta that had banned both long hair and rock music.

Alexis, who was the son of a Greek military officer in the junta, contacted a Greek official and impressed on him the tremendous publicity value the Beatles would be for Greece. As a result, they struck a deal. As VIPs the Beatles and their party would not be searched at the airport. They would also pose for publicity photographs with the Minister of Tourism. The Beatles were unaware that such a move would mean that they were literally endorsing the junta.

Alexis warned John that he should not criticize the junta in the press. Despite the warning, John arrived dressed in army uniform and began saluting every soldier in sight. The Beatles were driven around for fourteen hours, having photographs taken all the time which were then sent all around the world by wire service.

When the Beatles saw the islands they loved them and immediately agreed to purchase them. They instructed their accountants, **Bryce Hanmer**, who then had to apply to the British government, due to the fact that they wished to buy foreign property. Because of the economic situation, the movement of capital outside the UK was severely restricted. Bryce Hanmer had to make the arrangements directly with James Callaghan, the Chancellor of the Exchequer. He wrote to them, allowing them the transfer of £95,000 outside the country, adding, 'But not a penny more – I wonder how you're going to furnish it?'

Bryce Hanmer were not happy about the deal. They advised the Beatles that they would have to pay the British government a premium of 25 per cent per pound on the £95,000, and that as the group only had funds of £137,000, it could prove disastrous for them.

The Beatles shunned the advice, deciding they were going to establish a community on Leslo with their families and John commented, 'It will be amazing. We'll be able to just lie naked in the sunshine together. There will be no hassles with the police because there won't be any police. The kids won't bother us because there won't be any kids. We can set a studio up and just make our albums, swim about in the Aegean and get stoned.'

They bought the islands, but the intricate financial hassles became too complicated for them and they lost interest. They sold the islands back to the Greek government, making a profit of £11,400.

● Les Stewart Quartet, The

A band formed in the West Derby area of Liverpool in January 1959. They were led by Les Stewart on guitar/vocals and included **Ken Brown** on guitar/vocals, George Harrison on guitar/vocals and Geoff Skinner on drums.

George had joined the group because the **Quarry Men** had ceased performing and had, to all intents and purposes, disbanded.

The Les Stewart Quartet had a residency at the **Lowlands Club** in Haymans Green, West Derby. Late that same year, **Mona Best** began to convert the cellars of her home in Haymans Green into a club and Ken Brown began to help out, with the assurance that the Les Stewart Quartet would be the resident band.

Stewart was upset at the amount of time Brown spent on the **Casbah** conversion, because it interfered with rehearsals, and this resulted in an argument between the two during which Stewart refused to take up the Casbah residency and Brown stormed out. Harrison joined him and said he'd contact two of his friends, John and Paul, to join them. The Quarry Men reformed in August 1959 fo[r] the Casbah residency.

This effectively finished the Les Stewart Quartet an[d] Stewart was to join various other Liverpool band[s] including Lee Castle & the Barons, the Kansas City 5 an[d] the Long and the Short.

● Lester, Richard

An American film director who was born in Philadelph[ia] in 1932. As a musician, Lester had toured the worl[d] playing guitar and piano in various bars and clubs. Durin[g] his last year at university he formed a vocal group wh[ich] made regular appearances on local television stations [in] America. He became a stage hand at the studios an[d] eventually a director.

He then moved to Britain where he made his first fil[m] *The Running, Jumping And Standing Still Film*, wi[th] **Spike Milligan.** He made his first pop film, *It's Tra[d] Dad*, in 1962, which starred **Helen Shapiro**, and direct[ed] a number of television commercials, including ones f[or] Smith's Crisps, which featured **Pattie Boyd**.

When he was commissioned to direct the Beatles' fir[st] film, he helped to fashion a style using hand-held camera[s]. Discussing *A Hard Day's Night*, he says, 'I made it for [a] tiny salary. No share in the profits.' However, **Walte[r] Shenson** decided to give him one half of one per cent.

Lester worked with Walter Shenson on the Beatles' ne[xt] film, *Help!*, although he didn't want **Alun Owen** to wri[te] the script for the movie. He was lined up to direct th[e] Beatles' third film for Shenson, but it didn't happen. [At] one time he planned to feature them in a comedy remak[e] of the *Three Musketeers*, but they turned the project dow[n]. He was later to make three feature films based on th[e] Musketeer idea.

It was Lester who hired John Lennon for his solo fil[m] debut in 1966 in *How I Won The War*.

Twenty-five years after his first association with th[e] Beatles, Lester approached Paul McCartney to say he['d] like to direct a film of his 1989/90 world tour. The res[ult] was the 1991 release *Get Back: The Movie*. Lester becam[e] involved in the tour from its inception and made th[e] eleven-minute film which began each concert, played on [a] giant split screen behind the stage and cataloguing, wi[th] documentary archive and McCartney's home mov[ie] footage, Paul's rock 'n' roll career from the sixti[es] onwards.

Lester was to say, 'Paul's audience brings a lot of romantic and nostalgic baggage with it and with the use of twenty-five years of music, including classic Beatles songs and the extraordinary newsreel footage that we were able to obtain, we tried to recreate that feeling of romantic nostalgia that hopefully makes the film work well on an emotional, as well as a musical, level.'

● Let It Be (Album)

The Beatles' thirteenth album was also their last. *Let It Be* was issued in Britain on PX1 on 8 May 1970 as part of a special boxed package which also included the glossy book *The Beatles Get Back*. An album without the book was issued on PCS 7096 on 6 November 1970. When it was issued in America on AR 34001 on 18 May 1970, it had the highest advance sales on record for that time – a total of 3,700,000.

Let It Be was salvaged from an original project which was to be called 'Get Back'. An album of that name was to have been issued in August 1969, but the Beatles cancelled it. It was decided to tie in a book, film and album under the title of *Let It Be*, but the project had dragged on for a long time. The Beatles had asked **Glyn Johns** to edit their hours of tapes from the sessions and he did compile a 44-minute master tape, but **Allen Klein** decided to bring in **Phil Spector**. Spector's tone seemed to please John and George, but not Paul.

John Kosh designed the cover, which had a photograph of each member of the band on a black background.

The album tracks were, Side 1: 'Two Of Us', 'Across The Universe', 'I. Me. Mine', 'Dig It', 'Let It Be', 'Maggie May'. Side 2: 'I've Got A Feeling', 'One After 909', 'The Long And Winding Road', 'For You Blue' and 'Get Back'.

● Let It Be (Film)

The film originally started life as a proposed television documentary on the making of an album. Paul had suggested the project, John was also keen on the idea, while Ringo was content to go along with what the others wanted, although George was reluctant right from the start. The television special was conceived to promote their new album, which was to be called *Get Back*, and would be screened at the end of the month in which the album was released. It was then decided that another half-hour documentary would be made showing how the television special had been made.

Initial plans were for the Beatles to perform three shows at the Roundhouse in January 1969 and have them edited into a one-hour TV special which would be broadcast around the world.

The Beatles were by now having great difficulty maintaining a relationship as a team and the problem of their contract with United Artists for a third feature film remained. The group had mistakenly believed that *Yellow Submarine* had completed their three-film contract with United Artists, but it hadn't and it was decided to give United Artists the footage the group had been filming at their recording sessions at Twickenham and **Apple Studios.**

The Beatles had hated recording at the bleak **Twickenham Studios,** particularly as they weren't able to film in the evenings as they'd planned, but were told they had to record from early in the morning if they were to use the studio's facilities. John Lennon was to remark, 'You couldn't make music at eight o'clock in the morning or ten or whatever it was, in a strange place with people filming you and coloured lights.' Filming began at Twickenham Studios on 2 January 1969 under the project title of 'Get Back' and lasted until 17 January. The group then left Twickenham and resumed filming at Apple Studios for the remainder of the month, culminating with the famous rooftop session on 30 January.

By the time they had completed filming in January 1969, they had almost 30 hours of music and 96 hours of film in the can, and the movie took a full year to edit. Plans to edit it down into two one-hour television documentaries to be screened on consecutive nights were dropped.

When they were discussing ideas for the documentary, director **Michael Lindsay-Hogg** suggested that they go and film a sequence in a Roman amphitheatre he'd seen in Tunisia. George protested, pointing out the impracticality of it, due to the difficulties they would have in transporting all the personnel and equipment to Africa, not forgetting the cost. Other locations were put forward including an ocean liner, a Liverpool Cathedral and the Houses of Parliament. John succinctly commented, 'I'm warming up to the idea of an Asylum.' The location eventually became the rooftop of Apple's **Savile Row** building.

George's unhappiness and frustration was all too obvious and at one point, on 10 January, he walked out of the sessions, keeping away for a few days because he felt that Paul had been treating him as an inferior. Paul had, in fact, even been talking down to John, saying, 'Now look, son', but was far more patronizing in his attitude to George and at one point told him, 'I always seem to be annoying you.' When Paul began to make suggestions on how he should play, George said, 'All right, I'll play whatever you want me to play. Or I won't play at all if you don't want me to play.'

Another reason why George walked out concerned the fact that he did not want to make any further concert appearances with the Beatles, and was upset by talk of going to Africa or finding alternative venues. He was later to accept the idea of the Apple rooftop performance.

When George eventually returned he brought in **Billy Preston** to join them on the sessions on 22 January, hoping the presence of another musician would reduce the tension in the air.

United Artists' description of the film in their publicity releases read, 'The picture gives an intimate view of the Beatles as musical creators and performers and shows them rehearsing, reading, philosophising and relaxing. *Let It Be* is presented by Apple, an ABKCO-managed company and was produced by **Neil Aspinall** and directed by Michael Lindsay-Hogg.' Actually, **Dennis O'Dell** was also producer of the film.

The colour movie was 81 minutes in length, was given a 'U' certificate and won an Oscar in the 1970 Academy Awards for 'Best Original Song Score: Music & Lyrics by the Beatles'.

Lindsay-Hogg's style of direction was criticized and, in the case of a review by Michael Goodwin in *Rolling Stone* magazine, was literally savaged. Paul also seemed to have his own ideas on how *Let It Be* should have been filmed and was to remark, 'Get bright lights so you see everything, instead of moody lighting, that kind of thing. With everything here, it hardly needs scenery. Really, it should be about him and his drum kit, it really looks great, beautiful sitting there. Then John and his guitar and his amp, sitting there, actually showing it at that minute. The scenery would just be the other things around, like the scaffolding and other cameras.'

Lindsay-Hogg was able to present his own point of view in a *Rolling Stone* interview and regarding the rooftop session, mentioned that they'd had an idea of introducing an actor in a policeman's uniform who would come to interrupt the session and be quite rude to them. He said, 'But when we shot it honestly, and the real Bobbies arrived, it was so charming we didn't do that. They called in the Black Marias and all that, but they were quite nice. We thought it would be good to show how nice some policemen can be.'

(This and facing page ©Apple)

Critic Michael Goodwin once again found it hard to credit that actors weren't used as policemen and commented: 'In the last part of the film, a sequence where the Beatles play on the rooftop of the Apple building, there are these cops who come up to investigate the noise. We first see them outside, in the street, as they walk up to the

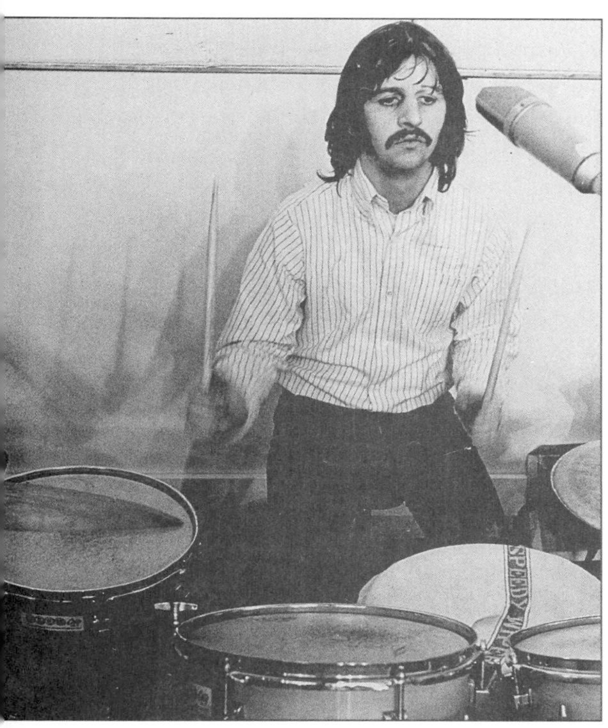

front door of the building. They open the door (this is shot from outside), and as they do so there is a cut to a reverse angle, in which we see them complete the action (opening the door) from the inside. Now this is a perfectly reasonable editing sequence for a film shot in a studio, with actors, but I find it a little hard to believe that such a perfect matching shot could have been made in a documentary situation. So the next logical question is: Were those cops or actors?'

There are 22 numbers featured in the film, most of them performed during the studio recording. The group are

seen playing, talking, eating, relaxing; the various people who appear in the film include Billy Preston, **Derek Taylor, Yoko Ono, Mal Evans,** Michael Lindsay-Hogg, **Heather McCartney** and George Martin. The Twickenham Studios setting is featured for approximately an hour's screen time and the film's most exciting moment is when the Beatles emerge onto the Apple roof, overlooking Burlington Gardens. There are edited sequences of the 40 minutes they spent there, including the entry of the police and comments from people below. One man, incapable of appreciating that fun in life needn't be restricted to outside business hours, comments: 'This kind of music is very good in its place, but it's a bit of an imposition when it disrupts all the business in the area.' The critics were generally unenthusiastic about the movie (although nowhere near as ferocious as the TV pundits who had savaged *Magical Mystery Tour*).

Nina Hibbin of the *Morning Star* wrote: 'For those who expected it to throw some light on the development of the Beatles phenomenon, it is disappointingly barren . . . Paul McCartney, now very much the guiding spirit of the team, comes over as a thorough-going professional who, one can imagine, may switch off his Beatle-self out of studio hours and change into a quite different person at home. George Harrison, with his strong-boned face and shut-in expression, looks as if he could fit into any tough and isolated position – as a shepherd in Bulgaria or the manager of a suburban sub-post office. John Lennon and Ringo Starr appear to be the true individualists, as far as the film allows us to glimpse their individuality, with Beatle eccentricities running through their veins.'

In the *Sunday Telegraph*, Tom Hutchinson wrote: 'It is only incidentally that one glimpses anything about their real characters – the way in which music now seems to be the only unifying force to hold them together: the way Paul McCartney chatters incessantly even when, it seems, none of the others is listening.'

Alexander Walker, in his *Evening Standard* column, wrote: 'Yoko passes by like Lady Macbeth sleepwalking. An aimless camera catches the others in inarticulate chit-chat; like most of us who consciously fool about for home movies they are dull and unfunny.

'A flicker of interest is provided by the folk standing out in the street when their comments – generally flattering – are caught in TV-style spot interviews.

'I'm told the film was made to complete the three-picture deal with United Artists made some years ago. If so, this explains why it looks like a chore. Let it pass.'

Dick Richards of the *Daily Mirror* wrote: 'Domestic touches are added by Paul McCartney's little stepdaughter frisking around the studio and by Yoko, who sits broodingly at her husband's elbow throughout, looking like an inscrutable miniature Mother Earth.

'This seems to inhibit John Lennon more than somewhat, especially when he and Yoko perform an ungainly waltz which will win them no Astaire-Rogers medals, and it is McCartney who comes over as the dominant figure and the musical boss.'

Despite the film's various shortcomings, there was no denying the excellence of the movie's soundtrack. Fans were treated to a host of numbers, which included: 'Don't Let Me Down', 'For You Blue', 'Maxwell's Silver Hammer', 'Besame Mucho', 'Two Of Us', 'Octopus's Garden', 'I've Got A Feeling', 'You've Really Got A Hold On Me', 'Oh Darling', 'The Long And Winding Road', 'One After 909', 'Shake Rattle And Roll', 'Jazz Piano Song', 'Kansas City', 'Across The Universe', 'Lawdy Miss Clawdy', 'Dig A Pony', 'Dig It', 'Suzy Parker', 'Let It Be', 'I. Me. Mine' and 'Get Back'.

Let It Be was premiered at the **London Pavilion** on 20 May 1970. A number of celebrities attended the occasion, such as **Jane Asher** and **Cynthia Lennon,** though none of the Beatles turned up for the film's launch, which perhaps gave some indication of their opinion of it. George, at least, had a good excuse – he was recording his *All Things Must Pass* album that evening with **Phil Spector.**

John was to comment: 'It was hell making the film. When it came out a lot of people complained about Yoko looking miserable in it. But even the biggest Beatle fan couldn't have sat through those six weeks of misery. It was the most miserable session on earth.'

● Lewis, Brian

A business consultant and legal adviser from Wallasey who, in 1968, at the age of 44, joined the Beatles' **Apple Corps** in **Savile Row.** He worked in the Accounts department on the third floor. Other members of the full-time staff who handled Beatles accounts included Brian Cappociama, Ronald Tolson and Allan Lewis.

After Allen Klein took over the Beatles' affairs, Lewis resigned.

Lewis, Jerry Lee

Major American rock star who was an early influence on the **Quarry Men,** who performed a number of his songs in their repertoire, including 'Whole Lotta Shakin' Goin' On', 'High School Confidential', 'Mean Woman Blues' and 'Fools Like Me'.

The blond-haired Louisiana-born singer/keyboard player first emerged internationally with two hits in 1957

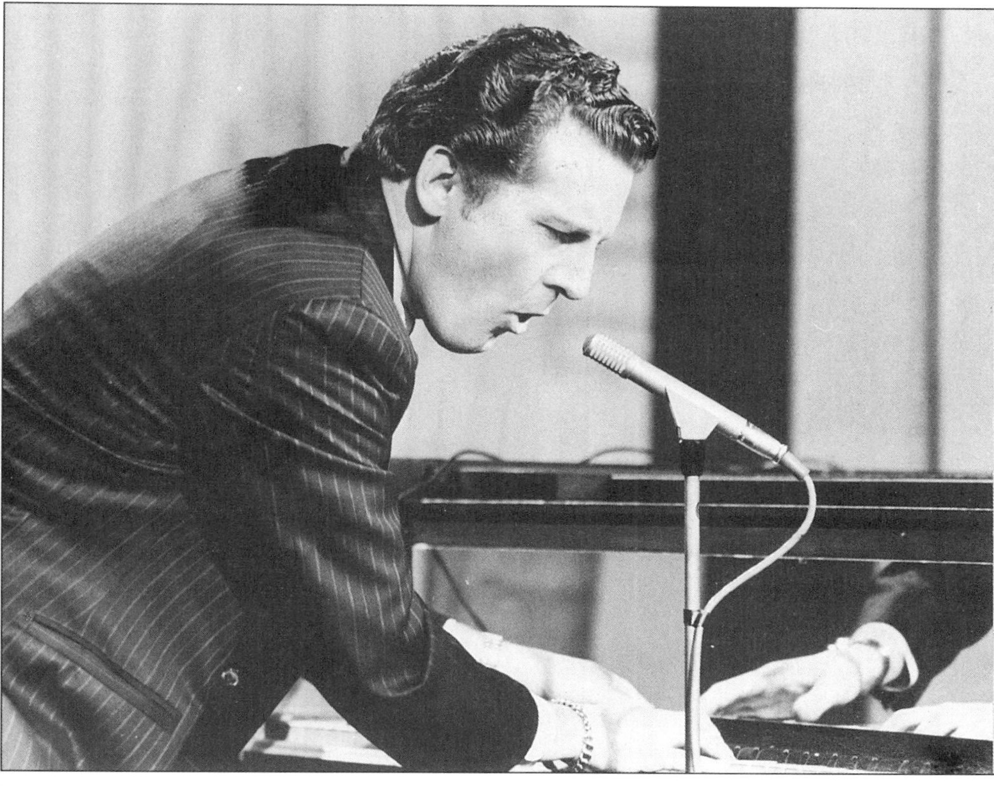

Jerry Lee Lewis – the Beatles helped to revive his rock 'n' roll career. (National Film Archives)

'Whole Lotta Shakin' Goin' On' and 'Great Balls Of Fire', followed by 'Breathless' and 'High School Confidential' in 1958.

Lewis's popularity had declined following a controversial tour in 1958 when it was revealed that his new bride, Myra, whom he brought to England with him, was only thirteen years old – and his cousin! Jerry Lee was 22 at the time.

As one of the original rock 'n' roll idols, Lewis was very popular on Merseyside and on Thursday, 17 May 1962, **Bob Wooler** presented him at the **Tower Ballroom**, New Brighton, where he topped the bill with ten local bands in support: the Big Three; the Pressmen; the Undertakers; the **Strangers;** Vince Earl & the Zeros; **Billy Kramer** with the Coasters; Lee Castle & the Barons; **Kingsize Taylor** & the Dominoes; Steve Day & the Drifters; and Rip Van Winkle & the Rip It Ups.

Lewis returned to England in 1963 when he'd been booked for a tour of Europe which included appearances at the **Star Club,** Hamburg and the **Olympia**, Paris. He was also to appear for a week in Scotland. Promoter Don Arden contacted Brian Epstein to suggest that the Beatles appear on the tour, but Brian said that apart from the fact that they were already booked for a tour supporting **Roy Orbison** at the same time, their days as a supporting band were over and they would be headlining their own tours in the future.

Almost a year later, when the Beatles were beginning to receive publicity in America, Jerry Lee was asked to comment on the group. Among the things he said were: 'These Beatles lack just one thing. Talent. I hate to say this, but I ain't afraid to say it. They're a great bunch of boys but they're just doing what **Elvis** started back in '56 . . . they've done well in the States because there've been no big rock 'n' roll groups in America for five years . . . the Beatles are limited.'

But the Beatles were responsible for a revival of interest in rock 'n' roll and, because they mentioned their influences in interviews, lots of the rock 'n' roll stars such as Jerry Lee found that they were back in favour with the public again, which was probably why Jerry Lee changed his tune. In the June 1964 issue of *Beatles Monthly*, there was a full-page feature on Lewis entitled 'Thank You Beatles' in which he praised them for reviving his career.

He said: 'I'd heard of the Beatles way back before they hit the big time – heard about them from friends who'd played in Germany. Reports were great and I felt real flattered when they mentioned me to those friends, or even told reporters about how they'd liked my original work.' He also added: 'I kinda feel an affinity with the boys. It's all too easy to drop your own principles if it means you're gonna earn more loot. But the fact that they kept on and on now means that there's a whole lotta interest in Beat music, played by white performers – and it stretches right around the world.'

Jerry Lee Lewis was invited to appear on the ***'Around The Beatles'*** TV special, but had to turn it down because of prior commitments.

In 1988 a feature film biopic was made called *Great Balls Of Fire*, with actor Dennis Quaid portraying Lewis.

● Lewis's, *Ranelagh Street, Liverpool L1*

Huge department store, situated in the centre of Liverpool. The corner entrance doors opposite the **Adelphi Hotel** were a favourite rendezvous for couples. This is where John would often arrange to meet **Cynthia** during the early days of their romance.

Rearing high above the doors was a controversial statue of a well-endowed naked man, by the eminent sculptor Jacob Epstein. Adding to Cynthia's embarrassment at having to stand beneath such a sculpture was the fact that, to please John, she used to dress quite sexily, often wearing short, tight skirts, fishnet stockings and high-heeled shoes. The Beatles also performed at a special event on the top floor of the store on 28 November 1962. The occasion was a staff dance for the 527 Club called 'Young Idea Dance'.

Peter Brown, who was later to become Brian Epstein's assistant, was also manager of Lewis's record department.

● Lewis, Vic

Former jazz musician and bandleader who became a major agent. Lewis was born in Brent, London, on 19 July 1919. After many years running his own band he formed a show business agency. With the success of the Beatles in Britain, Lewis contacted **Norman Weiss** of America's GAC and suggested he see the Beatles with a view to booking them in America. As GAC represented **Trini Lopez,** who was on the bill with the Beatles at the **Olympia**, Paris, Weiss saw them ahead of any other American agent and was able to make a deal.

Lewis didn't receive any commission from the contact, but he was repaid in kind in 1965 when Weiss suggested to Brian Epstein that he buy Lewis's agency and appoint him to the board of **NEMS Enterprises**. Epstein bought the Vic Lewis Organisation and made Lewis a director of his management/agency/show business company.

After Brian Epstein's death, **Clive and Queenie Epstein** asked Lewis to become Managing Director of NEMS. He was also approached by **Robert Stigwood** who wanted to place him in charge of the Stigwood Agency. Lewis decided to stay with NEMS, although he later declared that it was a mistake on his part. On 23 October 1969 he issued an orchestral album of covers of Beatles songs called *Beatles My Way* on the NEMS record label. NEMS was sold to Triumph Investments and Lewis remained. He also stayed for a while when the company was bought by an organization called Worldwide, but eventually quit in 1977.

In 1987 his biography *Music & Maiden Overs* (Chatto and Windus) was published, which Lewis had written in collaboration with former Beatles Press Officer **Tony Barrow.**

● Leyton Baths, *High Road, Leyton, London E10*

Indoor swimming pool in East London which had been converted to a dance hall and featured top groups live each Friday evening. The Beatles appeared here on 5 April 1963 after a presentation ceremony at **EMI Records** where they had been presented with their first-ever silver disc for the 'Please Please Me' single. They had also given a short performance for EMI executives.

At Leyton Baths they were on a bill with **Peter Jay & the Jaywalkers** and performed their forthcoming single 'From Me To You' and most of the songs contained on their *Please Please Me* album, to a capacity audience. They wore maroon mohair suits with velvet collars.

Disc jockey Norman Scott was working at the venue

hat night and offered to buy them some drinks backstage fter the show. He asked if he could take a photograph of he band and began a count from one to three. John houted out 'Three!' so loudly that he startled the other Beatles and Paul, who'd been holding a tube of toothpaste, queezed it so hard that a length of paste squirted down is trouser leg!

Peter Jay & the Jaywalkers were to join the Beatles tour ater that year, from 1 November until 13 December – and t was rumoured that a tape recording was made of the two ands having a jam session together. The group made everal singles but didn't achieve major success.

Like Dreamers Do

A Paul McCartney composition which the Beatles included mongst the thirteen numbers at their **Decca recording udition.** The song was later recorded by the **Applejacks** who reached No. 7 in the British charts with the number.

It was one of Paul's early compositions and was ncluded in the repertoire of the **Quarry Men** and was art of the Beatles' stage act until late in 1962.

Lime Street, *Liverpool L1*

Liverpool's most famous street, particularly in times past. Celebrated for the notoriety of its old reputation of rostitutes plying their trade with merchant seamen. It's lso mentioned in sea shanties and featured in the folk ong 'Maggie May', the legendary ballad about a Liverpool rostitute, which was used as the basis for a musical by **Alun Owen** and Lionel Bart, and was the name of a club wned by **Allan Williams**. The No. 1 hit 'Maggie May', which launched Rod Stewart's career in 1971, wasn't the riginal folk song.

Situated in the heart of Liverpool's city centre with the **Adelphi Hotel** at one end and the **Walker Art Gallery** t the other, Lime Street is the site of the main railway tation, some cinemas, a large hotel, St George's Hall, the **Empire Theatre** and St John's Precinct.

St John's Precinct, a modern shopping complex ontaining a Rank ballroom and pubs where local groups ppear, was erected in the mid-sixties. At the time of the Mersey scene there was a collection of grimy buildings ousing shops, hotels, the Press Club and Territorial Army eadquarters, with Liverpool's main market to the rear. The fronts of the main buildings were illuminated with arge commercial neon signs and were visually not unlike a section of Piccadilly Circus. Certainly, it was more picturesque than the modern precinct.

Fortunately, when the other buildings were levelled, the Royal Court Theatre and **Playhouse Theatre** were retained. A subway, built beneath the busy traffic-laden road between the station and St George's Hall, was originally to have been decorated with a Beatles motif.

The Crown public house in Lime Street with its ornate facade was a major haunt for seamen and tarts at the turn of the century. During the Mersey Beat days, promoter **Sam Leach** held his wedding reception at the pub, which was attended by Brian Epstein, Bill and Virginia Harry and other members of the local beat scene.

The Forum cinema, opposite the Crown, held the world premiere of *These Dangerous Years,* the first film musical to be set in Liverpool. It starred Frankie Vaughan.

Lindsay-Hogg, *Michael*

Director of the popular TV pop series, **'Ready, Steady, Go!'**, on which the Beatles appeared several times. Lindsay-Hogg was commissioned by the **Rolling Stones** to film their *Rock 'n' Roll Circus*, which included a performance by John Lennon, in 1968. It was not released.

The Beatles then engaged him to direct some of their promotional films, including 'Paperback Writer', 'Hey Jude' and 'Revolution'.

He also directed their third and final feature film, the documentary *Let It Be.* Michael Goodwin of *Rolling Stone* magazine was to comment: 'One of the delights of watching a movie made by a good director is that you can sit back and relax, knowing the film-maker has got everything under control. Here, you are constantly busy doing work that Lindsay-Hogg should have done, but didn't: cutting the bad stuff, rearranging the good stuff, placing the camera properly – really basic directorial responsibilities. You have to use so much energy doing his job for him that by the end of the film you've put in your hard day's night and ought to get paid.'

In an interview with *Rolling Stone* magazine, Lindsay-Hogg commented that it was lucky it was ever made: 'Even though half of them always were behind it, the trouble was it was never the same half.'

Lister, *Monty*

Wirral disc jockey who broadcast two regular shows, 'Music With Monty' and 'Sunday Spin', for the patients of

Cleaver and Clatterbridge hospitals on the Wirral, over the River Mersey from Liverpool.

Monty attended the Beatles gig at **Hulme Hall**, Port Sunlight, on 27 October 1962 and was able to record an interview with the Beatles. He'd brought along two friends, Malcolm Threadgill and Peter Smethurst, to help him out on the questioning, and the interview was broadcast to the two hospitals the following day.

During the seven-minute interview the Beatles mentioned their trips to Hamburg, their Polydor recording with **Tony Sheridan**, 'Love Me Do' and their forthcoming single. Ringo commented on being the newcomer and Paul said, 'John Lennon is the leader of the group.'

The interview, the Beatles' first-ever actual radio interview, was included as a free disc in Mark Lewisohn's book *The Beatles Live!* in 1986.

● Litherland Town Hall, *Hatton Hill Road, Litherland, Liverpool L21*

This was one of the venues used by local promoter **Brian Kelly**, who booked the Beatles for their debut appearance there on 27 December 1960. All their other appearances took place in 1961: 5 and 26 January; 2, 14, 16, 21 and 28 February; 2 March; 24 and 31 July; 7 August; 7, 14, 21 and 28 September; 19 and 31 October; 9 November.

Bob Wooler was the man who talked Kelly into booking the group, at a fee of six pounds. As it was a late booking, their names didn't appear in the local newspaper advertisements, which had already been placed, announcing the groups the **Searchers,** the Del Renas and the Deltones. Entrance to the gig was three shillings (fifteen pence). Kelly managed to place their name on some posters with the tag: 'Direct from Hamburg, The Beatles!' As they weren't all that well known in Liverpool at the time, this led to a number of members of the audience believing that they were a German group. Their line-up that night was John, Paul, George, **Pete** and **Chas Newby**.

Pete Best's brother Rory was also in the audience, along with accountancy student **Neil Aspinall**, a lodger at the Bests, who saw the Beatles for the first time.

This particular appearance transformed their local fortunes. Their experience in Hamburg had had an incredible effect on their performance and the audience were ecstatic.

Brian Kelly, impressed by the immense excitement the Beatles had generated, immediately booked them for a string of dates at all his main venues and Bob Wooler wa later to devote an entire page in ***Mersey Beat*** to them.

In the article, the only Beatle he mentioned by nam was Pete Best: 'Musically authoritative and physicall magnetic, example the mean, moody, magnificence o drummer Pete Best – a sort of teenage Jeff Chandler.' Thi was because, strangely enough, Best had become the mos popular Beatle with Liverpool audiences. So much so, i fact, that for their Valentine's night appearance a Litherland on 14 February 1961, Wooler talked the othe members into the unusual step of placing Pete Best an his drums to the forefront of the band. This stratager

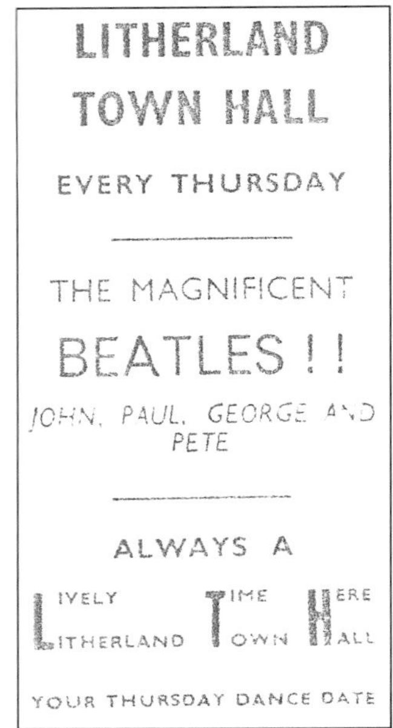

didn't work as the fans immediately surged forth an dragged Pete from the stage!

For the 7 August gig, the Litherland Town Ha classified advertisement in the ***Liverpool Echo*** carrie the message: 'Hear Pete Best Sing To-night'.

The 21 September appearance saw them share a bi with **Gerry & the Pacemakers** and **Rory Storm & th Hurricanes**.

On Thursday, 19 October, the Beatles and Gerry & th Pacemakers combined to make a single appearance as th **Beatmakers**.

● Little Child

Recorded over two sessions in September 1963 for the *With The Beatles* album, this track, composed by John Lennon, with a little help from Paul, was one of the songs on which John played harmonica. It was also included on the American *Meet The Beatles* album.

● Little Queenie

A **Chuck Berry** composition which Berry recorded in 1959. The Beatles included it in their repertoire in 1960, with Paul on lead vocals. They performed the number at Hamburg's **Star Club** and it is to be found on the various pressings of the Star Club recordings.

(ACE Records)

● Little Richard

One of the classic rock 'n' roll stars, born Richard Penniman in Macon, Georgia, in 1932.

Paul McCartney was a Richard fan and performed hits in the **Quarry Men** days. In fact, Paul was the Beatles Little Richard specialist and the numbers he performed which had been recorded by the star included 'Long Tall Sally', 'Lucille', 'Ooh! My Soul', 'Tutti Frutti', 'Good Golly, Miss Molly' and 'Kansas City/Hey Hey Hey'.

The Beatles finally met their idol when they appeared with him at the **Star Club** for a brief season in April/May 1962, during which they became friends, with Richard giving Paul tips on how to perform his numbers and George making the acquaintance of Richard's keyboards player, **Billy Preston.**

Brian Epstein booked Little Richard for a **NEMS Enterprises** presentation, *Little Richard At The Tower*. This was for a spectacular show at the **Tower Ballroom,** New Brighton, on 12 October 1962. It was a five-and-a-half-hour show, with entrance costing only ten shillings and sixpence (52.5p) with a support bill comprising the Beatles, **Billy Kramer** with the Coasters, the Dakotas with Pete MacLaine, the Four Jays, **Lee Curtis** & the All Stars, the **Merseybeats, Rory Storm & the Hurricanes** and the Undertakers. Little Richard also appeared at the **Cavern** that day when the Beatles appeared at a lunchtime session. Backstage at the Tower, Bill Harry had commissioned photographer Les Chadwick to cover the event on behalf of ***Mersey Beat*** and arranged a photograph of Richard and the Beatles together.

In an interview for *Mersey Beat* at the time, Little Richard said, 'Man, those Beatles are fabulous. If I hadn't seen them I'd never have dreamed they were white. They have a real authentic Negro sound.'

Epstein also booked Little Richard to top the bill at Liverpool's **Empire Theatre** later that month on 28 October. He tried to include Sam Cooke on the programme, but the singer was unavailable, so **Craig Douglas** was second on the bill and during his spot he was backed by the Beatles. Jet Harris, **Kenny Lynch** and **Sounds Incorporated** were also on the bill and the Beatles had their own spot.

In the book *The Life And Times Of Little Richard* (Charles Wood, Harmony Books, 1984), Richard claims that after the Beatles came off stage at the Empire, Brian Epstein approached him and said, 'Richard, I'll give you fifty per cent of the Beatles.' Richard commented, 'I couldn't accept 'cos I never thought they would make it.'

Richard also said that he developed a close relationship with Paul, 'but me and John couldn't make it. John had a nasty personality.' With Paul the obvious Richard enthusiast, the two were bound to get on together and Richard said, 'Paul is like my blood brother. I believe if I was hungry, Paul would feed me. We're that tight. Paul is a humanitarian.'

When **Apple Records** was launched and George

Little Richard and the Beatles – a shot taken backstage at the Tower Ballroom by Les Chadwick. (©Apple/Peter Kaye Collection)

Harrison began producing other acts, he said, 'Little Richard, that's who I'd love to record. He's a fantastic character with a fantastic voice – and whether he's singing rock or gospel, he's still great.'

● Little Theatre, The, *Houghton Street, Southport, Lancashire*

The Beatles made a special appearance at this small theatre on the morning of 27 August 1963. They gave a private live performance before an invited audience which was filmed for the BBC documentary **'The Mersey Sound'.**

● Liverpool

The city was founded by King John in 1207 when he discovered that the Mersey estuary was a suitable base for him to send his armies across to Ireland. A castle was built and a town began to grow around it. In the seventeenth century a Liver Bird was chosen to adorn the seal of the town.

Liverpool began its rise as one of the most important seaports in the world in 1760 when 69 Liverpool ships established a trade triangle trip to Africa. The slave trade ceased in 1807, but the city remained a major port although its influence began to wane with the building of the Manchester Ship Canal. This venture instigated by businessmen resulted in Manchester becoming the business centre of the North of England and Liverpool's influence slowly vanished.

Its prominence as a seaport had resulted in a cosmopolitan population, a large percentage of which came from Ireland, resulting in the city often being referred to as 'the capital of Ireland'. There were also a large number of Welsh immigrants and in addition, Liverpool accommodated one of the largest Chinese communities in Europe, over 8,000 gathering in the Chinatown area near the city centre. Ironically, the great houses built in what is now the Liverpool 8 area on the profits of the slave trade became the homes of the black community in a Liverpool harlem.

Stuck on the north-west coast of England, Liverpool was isolated from the main events. Manchester became the northern home of the media, housing the television and radio stations and the northern offices of the national press. News from the north generally emanated from Manchester and little was heard of the events on Merseyside.

Liverpudlians were called 'Scousers' (a name derived from a stew for seamen called lob scouse), had adenoidal accents, a self-deprecating wit and were noted for their comedians and football teams. If asked why so many comedians came from Liverpool, a scouser would reply, 'Because you have to be a comedian to live here', referring to the poverty, slums and general lack of work in the area. Liverpool comedians included **Arthur Askey**, Tommy Handley, Ted Ray, Norman Vaughan and **Ken Dodd**. Other entertainers who had risen to national prominence via the local clubland scene included Frankie Vaughan, Lita Roza, Michael Holliday and **Billy Fury**.

The music scene which grew and developed on Merseyside in the fifties was unique, although the skiffle boom which spawned it wasn't. In fact, the skiffle boom was a national phenomenon in Britain in 1956 following the success of **Lonnie Donegan** with 'Rock Island Line'. Skiffle groups sprang up throughout the country, but died away a few years later when the bubble burst. In Liverpool, however, the skiffle groups turned to rock 'n' roll and a number of circumstances resulted in an amazing scene in which music began to dominate the city, with literally hundreds of groups performing in clubs, cellars, private houses, ice rinks, synagogues, youth clubs, church halls, swimming baths, town halls, seaside piers, coffee bars, ballrooms, ferry boats, cinemas, social clubs, colleges, department stores and pubs. Among the skiffle groups who became rock 'n' roll bands were the James Boys (formed in 1956, later to develop into **Kingsize Taylor** & the Dominoes), the Ralph Ellis Skiffle Group (formed in 1957 and later to develop into the **Swinging Bluejeans**), the Raving Texans (formed in January 1957 and later to develop into **Rory Storm & the Hurricanes**), the **Eddie Clayton Skiffle Group** (formed in early 1957 with Richard Starkey on drums) and the **Quarry Men**, who were to become the Beatles. At the same time, there were groups who had been inspired directly by rock 'n' roll, such as the Bobby Bell Rockers, who formed in October 1956, probably Liverpool's first real rock 'n' roll band.

A number of independent promoters began running weekly dances at local venues which featured several groups per night. This resulted in a large range of venues across the Merseyside area which provided hundreds of local groups with regular work. The promoters included **Brian Kelly**, Charlie McBain, **Les Dodd**, Albert Kinder, Dave Forshaw, **Mona Best**, Doug Martin, **Sam Leach**, Wally Hill and Vic Anton. The venues were often called 'jive hives' and the music and promotions were referred to as either 'twist' or 'jive', and it is at such dances, in the local church and town halls, that the Liverpool music scene was nurtured and grew. In addition, there were regular venues such as the Mardi Gras (run by Jim Ireland) and various ballrooms including the **Locarno**, **Grafton**, **Plaza** and **La Scala**.

When the ***Mersey Beat*** newspaper was launched in July 1961, everyone was amazed to discover that there was so much activity on Merseyside. The coverage of the music scene had been virtually non-existent and the new publication revealed just how extensive the local scene was. An entertainments guide (later lampooned by John Lennon) provided details of jazz clubs, coffee clubs, cabaret shows and jive halls. Among the jive halls listed were: **Alexandra Hall**; **Aintree Institute**; **Blair Hall**; Bootle Town Hall; **Civic Hall**, Ellesmere Port; **David Lewis Theatre**; **Empress Club**; the **Grosvenor**; **Hambleton Hall**; La Mystere, Maghull; **Litherland Town Hall**; **La Scala**, Runcorn; **Lathom Hall**; **Mossway Hall**; Merrifield Old Swan; Orrell Park Ballroom; Quaintways, Chester; **St John's Hall**,

Right: The first of the Mersey Beat revivals, organized by Allan Williams.
Below right: The Beatles pose in front of the Liver Buildings. (©Apple/Peter Kaye Collection)

Tuebrook; **St Luke's Hall**, Crosby; Town Hall, Skelmersdale; Wavertree Town Hall and **Wilson Hall**, Garston. There were many more. The name Mersey Beat had been devised to describe an area rather than the beat of the music and the area covered included the whole of Merseyside, with Liverpool, Widnes, Warrington, St Helens, Skelmersdale, Crosby, Formby, Southport, the Wirral, Birkenhead, New Brighton, Chester and Ellesmere Port. Within the Merseyside conurbation at that time resided what was probably the greatest concentration of rock 'n' roll groups in the world, considerably more than 350 of them within that compact area. **Bob Wooler** and Bill Harry published a list of almost 300 groups in the 19 October 1961 issue of *Mersey Beat* and the humour and variety of the names was intriguing. They included Ahab & his Lot, Al Quentin & the Rock Pounders, Bennie & the Jumpin' Beans, Bruce & the Spiders, Dave & the Devil Horde, Eddie & the Phantoms, Foo Foo's Flashy Falcons, Hank's Hoppers, Johnny Apollo & the Spartans, Gerry Bach & the Beethovens, Vince Earl & the Zeros, Eddie Falcon & the Vampires, the G Men, the FBI, Ogi & the Flintstones, Pete Picasso & the Rock Sculptors, Johnny President & the Senators, Rikki & the Red Streaks, Rip Van Winkle & the Rip It Ups, Ray Satan & the Devils and Wump & his Werbles.

When the Beatles began to achieve success and the British media focused its attention on the Liverpool groups, they described the sound as 'Mersey Beat', taking the name from the newspaper and referring to a particular style, which also became known as the 'Liverpool Sound'. It referred to the Liverpool groups who were suddenly appearing in the charts – the Beatles, the **Searchers**, **Gerry & the Pacemakers** and the **Swinging Bluejeans**, who all had the four-man line-up of lead, rhythm and bass guitars, plus drums. However, the versatility and variety of the Mersey bands was far more extensive. There were line-ups featuring brass instruments, there were septets, quintets, trios and duos. There were also a large number of female artists who included all-girl rock bands such as the Liver Birds, the Blue Notes, the Demoiselles, the Fast Cats, the Rontons, the Three Bells, the Kandies and vocal groups such as the **Vernons Girls**, Collage, the Charmers and the Mystics. There were also many groups with female singers – Jenny & the Tall Boys, Three Hits & a Miss, Irene & the Santa Fe's, the Galaxies with Doreen, Joan and the Demons, Carol & the Corvettes, Vikki Lane & the Moonlighters and Tiffany's Dimensions. There were also a number of female solo vocalists – **Beryl Marsden**, **Cilla Black**, Barbara Harrison, Irene Carroll, Lorraine White, Rita Hughes, Rita Rodgers, Barbara Grounds, Karina, Barbara Dee, Christine Ching, Vickie Cheetham and Jacki Martin.

In the Liverpool 8 district there were a number of black vocal harmony groups, influenced by Tamla Motown and including the **Chants**, the Sobells, the Challengers and the Poppies. There was also a thriving folk music scene in Liverpool, due to its heritage as a seaport, and folk music was performed mainly in pubs. The most popular Liverpool folk artists were the Spinners, originally the Gin Mill Skiffle Group, and they were to become Britain's most popular folk group over a period of more than 25 years until they disbanded in the late eighties.

Growing alongside the rock 'n' roll scene, which was to become known as the Beat scene, was a healthy Country Music scene. There were over 40 Country bands playing at their own clubs such as the Black Cat Club and Wells Fargo and at many local clubs and factories. They even formed a Country Music Association and held a Grand Ole Opry annually at the Philharmonic Hall. They included the Hillsiders, Hank Walters & his Dusty Road Ramblers, the Boot Hill Billys, Phil Brady & his Ranchers, the Blue Mountain Boys, the Missouri Drifters, the Nashpool Four, the Country Four, Johnny Gold & the Country Cousins, the Miller Boys and the Foggy Mountain Ramblers.

A number of Country groups and rock bands also appeared on another thriving local entertainments scene – Clubland. There were over 330 clubs affiliated to the Merseyside Clubs Association. These social clubs were run by unions, local stores and factories. An example would be the Speke Bus Depot Social Club where George Harrison's father Harry was chairman. It was because of these clubs that Liverpool was able to develop so many comedians, and ones who grew popular during the Beatles' rise to fame in the early sixties included Ken Dodd, Jimmy Tarbuck, Johnny Hackett and **Ray Fell**.

Also active in Liverpool was a thriving poetry scene with **Streates** coffee bar in Mount Pleasant as the main venue for regular appearances by the local poets. Bill Harry also organized the North's very first Poetry-To-Jazz concert at the Crane Theatre. The Mersey poets who achieved national fame included Roger McGough, Brian Patten and Adrian Henri. At the same time, a number of writers were developing locally, including playwrights Willy Russell and Alan Bleasdale and horror specialists Clive Barker and Ramsey Campbell.

Such was the highly exciting and creative scene in which the Beatles developed. Competition between bands was strong, but amicable. Many Beatles scribes who were unaware of what really happened on the Mersey scene, have written that as soon as the Beatles achieved fame, everyone in Liverpool took up a guitar; the opposite was true, the scene was incredibly active long before the Beatles ever made a record.

The dimension of the Hamburg scene was added to the equation, with Liverpool groups gaining experience playing long hours at a stretch. However, with so many venues on Merseyside, groups such as the Beatles would be working three or four nights a week, often appearing at two and sometimes three different venues in a night – and also appearing at lunchtime sessions at places such as the **Cavern**. There was also a further area dominated by Liverpool bands, as from May 1962 – American bases in France, where the groups also played for long hours and developed their musical skills further.

By 1961 with so many venues, larger local promotions, the establishment of the *Mersey Beat* paper, the popularity of the Cavern (which had now turned exclusively to beat groups) and the interest taken in the Beatles by Brian Epstein, the Liverpool scene was ready to explode nationally.

Another apocryphal story is that groups derived their

repertoires from American records brought back by seamen. Beatles scribes who talk of 'Cunard Yanks' are perpetuating a falsity. When *Mersey Beat* featured a story 'Why Liverpool?' in which various members of the local scene gave their versions of why the scene happened locally, a member of a country music band mentioned that his repertoire was made up of songs brought back from America by seamen. While this may have been the case with a handful of country bands, it was not the case with the beat groups – as Paul McCartney has confirmed. The records by **Little Richard**, **Buddy Holly**, **Carl Perkins**, **Elvis Presley**, **Chuck Berry**, **Gene Vincent**, **Jerry Lee Lewis** and **Eddie Cochran**, which made up the backbone of local repertoires, were easily available. So were the Tamla Motown records at the onset of the sixties. Groups were able to listen to **Radio Luxembourg** and bands would raid the record bins at local stores to find lesser known rock records which they could include in their act – numbers by the Coasters and Ray Charles, songs such as 'The Hippy Hippy Shake' and 'Some Other Guy'. A study of the Beatles' repertoire prior to 1961 would find that the numbers by other artists which they performed were readily available on record in Britain – and not a single one obtained from a 'Cunard Yank'. Most Liverpool bands will confirm that the 'Cunard Yank' aspect is nonsense.

The Beatles' sense of humour which so endeared the media at press conferences was typical of the scouse wit; a prime example occurred when the Beatles held their first recordings with George Martin and he asked them if there was anything they didn't like. 'Well, I don't like your tie for a start,' said George Harrison. **Alun Owen** was able to capture this local humour effectively in the script of *A Hard Day's Night*. The Beatles also popularized a number of Liverpudlian phrases such as 'Fab', 'Wack' and 'Gear'.

Following the initial success of the Beatles, other Liverpool acts who reached the charts during the sixties included Gerry & the Pacemakers, **Billy J. Kramer**, Cilla Black, the **Big Three**, the Cryin' Shames, the Dennisons, the **Escorts**, the **Fourmost**, David Garrick, the Long & the Short, the **Merseybeats**, the Mojos, **Tommy Quickly**, the **Scaffold**, the **Searchers**, the Swinging Bluejeans, the Undertakers and Whistling Jack Smith.

The success of the Beatles also resulted in the huge beat boom in Britain and the British invasion of America. The British scene, controlled from London, later returned to its policy of running everything from London, which meant that bands had to travel to the capital as A&R men ceased talent-spotting in the provinces. The moguls also considered that Liverpool had been over-exposed and weren't really interested in discovering further new bands from the 'Pool. However, Liverpool continued to be a breeding ground for talent, always able to produce hit bands if the A&R people took the trouble to seek them out.

In 1976 there was talk of another Mersey Beat boom when Liverpool Express, the Real Thing and Supercharge entered the Top Twenty – then the Sex Pistols hit the scene and the entire media became dominated by the Punk Rock explosion. Liverpool continued to produce talent with groups such as Orchestral Manoeuvres in the Dark, Echo and the Bunnymen, Teardrop Explodes and Wah! and, amazingly, in the British charts of 28 January 1984 there were more Mersey acts in the Top Twenty than at any time since the original Mersey wave in 1963. The positions were:

1. 'Relax', Frankie Goes To Hollywood
2. 'Pipes Of Peace', Paul McCartney
3. 'That's Living Alright', Joe Fagin
6. 'Nobody Told Me', John Lennon
9. 'Wishful Thinking', China Crisis
17. 'The Killing Moon', Echo and the Bunnymen
19. 'Love Is A Wonderful Colour', Icicle Works

● Liverpool College Of Art, *Hope Street, Liverpool L1*

At the age of seventeen, John Lennon visited the college principal Mr Stevenson in June 1957 for an interview. **William Pobjoy**, headmaster of **Quarry Bank School** had set up the interview. John was accepted and began his first term at the college in September of that year.

The college itself was part of the same building as the **Liverpool Institute** where, coincidentally, John's fellow **Quarry Men** members Paul McCartney and George Harrison were pupils. They were able to get together for rehearsals at lunchtime in the college's 'life rooms' on the top floor of the building.

John soon made friends with a couple of boys in his class, Geoff Mohammed and Tony Carrick. He also went out with a couple of girls, including **Thelma Pickles** and Helen Anderson.

As with all new students, he was entered for the

Intermediate Course. One of the classes was to study 'Lettering' and he shared the lessons with **Jonathan Hague**, **Cynthia** Powell and **Phyllis Mackenzie**.

He also got to know Bill Harry, a student who had started an art college jazz magazine and was in charge of the college film society. Harry also encouraged the talents of other students. While at college he was selling his cartoons, using the pseudonym 'Kim' to professional publications such as *Time and Tide* magazine and the ***Liverpool Echo.*** He helped other students such as Mike Isaacson and Tony Ross to sell their cartoons to professional publications, too. Harry also co-edited Liverpool University's annual *Pantosphinx* magazine and contributed covers and poetry to the university monthly magazine *Sphinx*, in addition to helping to produce a music magazine for the local music store, **Frank Hessy's**. He became a close friend of **Stuart Sutcliffe** and, together with another student, **Rod Murray**, they became friends with John and used to meet frequently in the evening in local pubs and flats.

Both Bill and Stuart were members of the Students' Union Committee who ran the art college Saturday night dances and they booked John's group as a support at virtually all of the dances. Bill and Stuart proposed that the union buy PA equipment which the group could use.

John and Cynthia became lovers and eventually married. Stuart became a Beatle and Bill launched the ***Mersey Beat*** newspaper.

During his time at the college, John gained a reputation for causing trouble, although one of the tutors, **Arthur Ballard**, attempted to gain him a place in the new Graphic Design Department, without success.

John never returned to the college after the Silver Beatles toured Scotland with **Johnny Gentle**.

During the eighties the art college premises were changed to the Liverpool Polytechnic, Faculty of Art and Design.

Liverpool Echo, The

Merseyside's largest evening newspaper. Despite its dominance as the major Liverpool paper, the *Echo* didn't begin any extensive coverage of the Beatles until 1963.

Readers could only discover what was happening on the local rock 'n' roll scene in its pages by turning to the classified advertisements column, where local promoters advertised their gigs. These entries were placed under the heading 'Jazz', and despite pressure from the advertisers to have the heading changed to something more appropriate, the *Echo* refused to change it. Among their main rock 'n' roll advertisers were **Ray McFall** of the **Cavern** and **Sam Leach**, although **Bob Wooler** composed most of the advertisements for the local promoters in his own inimitable style. A typical example of one of Bob's classified advertisements would be:

> Bob Wooler's Married!!
> Yes cats Mr 'Big Beat' Bob
> Wooler has been married to
> the best rock sessions in
> Liverpool. See him only on
> Monday at
> HAMBLETON HALL
> Page Moss – Huyton
> 3 HOURS NON STOP ROCK
> BEATLES
> and the Ravin' Ravens
> On Friday and Saturday at
> AINTREE INSTITUTE
> And every lunch time session
> EXCLUSIVELY
> AT THE CAVERN
> Take Mr Big Beat's advice and go
> to only the best in ROCK!

The record review column in the *Echo* was credited to 'Disker', although it was written, at the time, by Liverpudlian **Tony Barrow** who was then working in the press office at **Decca Records** in London. Brian Epstein wrote to 'Disker' to request mention of the Beatles in his column and received a letter from Barrow explaining that he could only publicize groups who actually had a recording contract. Barrow was to help Epstein obtain a **Decca recording audition**, was then able to mention the group in his column and later became the Beatles' Press Officer.

Brian also attempted to gain publicity for the Beatles in the *Echo* by writing to **George Harrison**, who penned the popular column 'Over The Mersey Wall'. The veteran Harrison, a former Fleet Street journalist, was not interested in writing about an unknown local group and rejected Epstein's plea. However, once the Beatles began to find success in the charts, Harrison became their main

Echo contact and even travelled with the Beatles on the 1964 American tour.

The *Echo*'s coverage then became extensive and they published several pop 'specials', including *Around The World With The Beatles*, which was a souvenir magazine they produced at Christmas 1964. Priced at two shillings (ten pence), the 32-page publication included four colour photographs, stories of the group's trips abroad and a large selection of early black and white photographs. On the death of John Lennon, they were to produce *Lennon*, a 50-page book reproducing *Liverpool Echo* articles on the Beatles and John Lennon from 1963 onwards.

● Liverpool Institute, The, *Mount Street, Liverpool L1*

A high school for boys which was founded in 1825 as a Mechanics Institute, and was officially opened as a school on 15 September 1837. Charles Dickens lectured there in 1844 and famous pupils have included Sir Charles Lamb, Lord Mersey, Sir Henry Enfield and Sir Macalister of Tarbert.

In 1890 one half of the school became an Art College and brick walls were built to separate the two buildings internally. The Institute was changed from a fee-paying school to a grammar school in 1944, making it the oldest grammar school in Liverpool.

The school motto is *Non Nobis Solum Sed Toti Mundo Nati*, which means 'Not for ourselves alone but for the good of all the world'.

Paul McCartney entered the school when he passed his 11-plus examination. In the summer of 1957 he took two 'O' level exams and passed in Spanish, but failed in Latin. He took six further subjects in order to move up into the Sixth Form in 1958. He passed five and seemed to have a penchant for languages – apart from Spanish, he also has an 'O' level in German and French.

The boys nicknamed the school 'the Inny' and their headmaster, J. R. Edwards, 'the Baz'.

George Harrison was a year below Paul at the school. Other students included Paul's brother **Mike**; **Neil Aspinall**, who became the Beatles' road manager; Len Garry, a member of John Lennon's skiffle group the **Quarry Men**; **Ivan Vaughan**, who introduced Paul to John; Peter Sissons, who became a prominent TV celebrity in Britain; Les Chadwick, who was a member of **Gerry & the Pacemakers**; Colin Manley and Don Andrew, both members of the **Remo Four**; Bill Kenwright, who became an actor and later a leading West End theatre impresario; and Stu James who became a member of the Mojos.

'Dusty' Durband was Paul's Sixth Form teacher of English and Paul claimed he was the only teacher he liked and mentioned that Dusty told the boys about books such as *Lady Chatterley's Lover* and Chaucer's *The Miller's Tale*, pointing out that they weren't dirty books but examples of good literature.

One of Paul's classmates was Kenny Alpin, and Paul once used him as a scapegoat. He'd drawn a rather vulgar sketch of a naked woman for the amusement of his classmates, and had put it in his shirt pocket and forgotten about it. His mother discovered it there before washing the shirt and the embarrassed Paul told her that Kenny Alpin was the artistic culprit. His conscience got the better of him and two days later he confessed.

Paul and Mike used to catch the No. 86 bus to school and it was during these bus journeys that Paul first got to know George.

It had been anticipated that Paul would enter Teacher's Training College after leaving the Institute, but he took time off to tour Scotland with the Silver Beatles and then went off to Hamburg. He'd had a message from Mr Edwards asking him to visit the Head's office but he wrote back from Hamburg declaring that he'd resigned from the school: 'I said, "Dear Sir, I've got a great job in Germany and I'm earning fifteen pounds."'

Paul retained a fondness for the school and on Friday, 23 November 1979, arranged for **Wings** to give a special concert for the staff and students of the Liverpool Institute. The concert took place at the Royal Court Theatre, Liverpool, and Paul was to comment, 'It's my way of saying "Thank you" for some very happy years. Everyone seems to knock their schooldays but for me they have fond memories.'

● Liverpool Stadium, *Liverpool*

A large venue, close to Liverpool city centre and the Exchange Station, generally the centre for wrestling and boxing bouts. Although the Beatles never appeared at the venue, it does have some link with the Beatles story as it stimulated **Allan Williams**' interest in promoting local groups and led to **Larry Parnes** taking an interest in auditioning Liverpool bands.

Williams had decided to promote a rock 'n' rol

xtravaganza at the venue and contacted impresario Larry 'arnes to book the package tour starring **Eddie Cochran** nd **Gene Vincent**. The joint Parnes–Williams promotion eatured the American stars and some support acts and Villiams also added some Liverpool acts to the bill. It was take place on Tuesday, 3 May 1960. Then tragedy ruck when Cochran and Vincent were involved in a car ccident, which was fatal for Cochran. Parnes informed Villiams that although Vincent had been injured, he ould still honour the booking, although his own ggestion was that it be cancelled. Williams wanted to go head and the promotion proved to be a success.

The three-hour show started at 8.00 p.m. and starred ene Vincent, followed by **Davy Jones**, the black merican singer who would later be backed by the Beatles in 1961, Italian rock group Nero & his Gladiators and Lance Fortune, Dean Webb, the **Viscounts**, Julian X, Colin Green & the Beat Boys and Peter Wynne. Liverpool acts Cass & the Cassanovas, **Rory Storm & the Hurricanes**, **Gerry & the Pacemakers**, Mal Perry, Bob Evans & his Five Shillings and the Connaughts were added attractions.

Stuart Sutcliffe, John Lennon, Paul McCartney and George Harrison were in the audience, having recently changed their name from the **Quarry Men** to the Beatals. Williams had decided not to book the group for the event.

Parnes was impressed with the Liverpool acts and asked Allan Williams to arrange auditions for him to select local bands to back his artists on tour. This time Williams included the **Silver Beatles** on the list.

e Beatles in Liverpool's docklands in 1962. (©Apple/Peter Kaye Collection)

● Liverpool Town Hall, *Water Street, Liverpool L2*

Setting for the amazing civic reception of Friday, 10 July 1964.

When news of the Beatles' attendance at the Odeon, Liverpool, for the premiere of *A Hard Day's Night* was announced, Alderman John McMillan put forward the idea of a civic welcome and the wheels were set in motion.

Following their world tour, the Beatles flew into Speke Airport on a red and white Britannia belonging to British Eagle Airways. They touched down at 5.25 p.m. to be greeted by a reception balcony crammed with 1,500 fans, the maximum allowed. Emerging from the aircraft, they were presented with bouquets of flowers by the air hostesses and were led to a special room where they held a brief press conference.

The Beatles then rode in a limousine, preceded by the Chief Constable's car and two motorcycle outriders. Three other official cars followed, together with two other motorcycle policemen on a route which took them along Speke Road, Woolton Road, Mather Avenue, Allerton Road, Smithdown Road, Croxteth Road, Princess Street, Catherine Street, Hardman Street, Leece Street, Bold Street, Church Street, Lord Street and Castle Street.

A number of people had been present in their party, including the disc jockey **David Jacobs**, who had been their host on the various BBC TV '**Juke Box Jury**' programmes they had appeared on. **Wilfred Brambell**, the actor who starred as Paul's grandfather in *A Hard Day's Night*, had also arrived for the premiere and the group's movements were also covered by a travelling press corps which included **George Harrison** of the ***Liverpool Echo***.

Describing the scene, David Jacobs commented: 'We travelled from Liverpool Airport with a plane of one of the smaller airline companies and I sat in the back, and it was extraordinary to see how very nervous the boys were. They were absolutely petrified that they would not be bothered with in Liverpool. Liverpool, after all, they said was their home and had a lot of stars and they thought that nobody would turn out to meet them.

'When we got near the airport they were eagerly looking out of their windows and we eventually saw the airport at a distance, and it looked like an enormous black mass of insects. The place was covered absolutely from side to side with thousands of people except the runway was kept clear. And we eventually got off the plane and withi seconds the boys were surrounded by shouting fans. In thi crowd I was getting lost and then a very sweet thin happened. George Harrison noticed it and suddenl stopped and came to collect me so that I could be wit them. And then we went out for that nine-mile drive fro the airport to the centre of town where we were due t come out on the balcony with the Lord Mayor and the boy were to receive the "Freedom of the City".

'I was in the car behind them and the nine-mile driv took a very long time. We drove very slowly and every inc of the way on both sides was crowded with people and th strange thing was – in sitting at the back of the car behin them I saw the faces of the people after they had seen th Beatles and the look on their faces was almost as if Jesu Christ had just gone past.'

They were due to arrive at the Town Hall at 6.30 p. and leave for the Odeon Cinema at 8.30 p.m., but th crowds of almost 200,000 people lining the route we given a treat as the **Fab Four** took their journey slowly order to wave at their fans.

They actually arrived at the Town Hall at 6.55 p.m. be greeted in the doorway by the late Bessie Braddock, famous Liverpool MP of ample proportions, who al visited the band on one of their Liverpool **Empi Theatre** gigs. She had arranged for the **Chants** to atte the reception as they were one of the bands in her ov Exchange Ward and had once been backed by the Beatl on an early **Cavern** appearance. The Beatles were th taken to a private room to enjoy a cup of tea and a ch with the Lord Mayor, Alderman Louis Caplan, who was say, 'Liverpool is really proud of the Beatles. They a great ambassadors for the city and the inspiration th have given to youth clubs in Liverpool and througho Britain was magnificent.'

The group were then taken out onto the Town H balcony to greet the thousands of fans outside, packi Castle Street, Water Street and Dale Street. They made t appearances on the balcony and then changed into din jackets and appeared on the Minstrel Gallery in the To Hall ballroom, where they each said a personal 'Hell Paul then addressed the guests, saying, 'This has been best ever welcome and we would like to thank you all v much.'

There were exactly 714 guests, including Lord a Lady Derby, the Bishop of Liverpool and numerous C councillors and officials. There were only a handful of representatives from the local music scene who had been invited, apart from the Chants. They were **Ray McFall**, owner of the Cavern, **Bob Wooler**, the Cavern compere, and Bill Harry, editor of ***Mersey Beat***.

The Beatles were taken into a parlour where the Lady Mayoress showed them a large cake on which a map of the world in icing portrayed the message 'The City of Liverpool Honours the Beatles'. The cake was later presented to a local children's hospital.

The group then left the Town Hall and travelled up Dale Street and into William Brown Street where they entered London Road and reached the Odeon cinema where they attended the northern premiere of their debut film.

● Livingston, Alan

When George Martin first approached him to issue the Beatles records in the States, Alan Livingston was currently President of **Capitol Records**.

Capitol was actually owned by **EMI** and Martin naturally turned to them first, sending a copy of 'Please Please Me' to the company.

Livingston jotted down a memo: 'We don't think the Beatles will do anything in this market', and Martin began looking for another outlet and eventually had the single issued on **Vee Jay**.

He then offered Capitol 'From Me To You' and the company turned it down again. The single was issued on Vee Jay. When Martin tried a third time with 'She Loves You', Livingston told him that in Capitol's opinion the Beatles had no prospects in America and the single was issued on a New York label, Swan.

Livingston, who was married to film actress Nancy Olsen, eventually had to bow to the inevitable when Brown Meggs, Director of Eastern Operations for Capitol, was visited by Brian Epstein in New York who played him a demo of 'I Want To Hold Your Hand'. Meggs agreed to release it and a date was set for 13 January 1964.

Capitol reputedly spent 50 thousand dollars on an initial promotion when the Beatles first flew into New York in February 1964.

When the Beatles were touring California, Livingston held a party for them at his Hollywood home on 24 August 1964.

Guests included Edward G. Robinson, Jack Palance, Gary Lewis, Tony Bennett, Gene Barry, Jane Fonda, Richard Chamberlain, Rock Hudson, Groucho Marx, Dean Martin, **Hayley** and Juliet Mills, James Stewart, Lloyd Bridges and famed gossip columnist Hedda Hopper. Brian Epstein and **Derek Taylor** were at first prevented from entering the grounds by security officers because they weren't carrying their invitation cards, but a gatecrasher called Hal York managed to get them in!

The following year, on 29 August, Livingston presented the Beatles with a Gold record for the *Help!* album at an afternoon press conference.

● Locarno Ballroom, *West Derby Road, Liverpool L6*

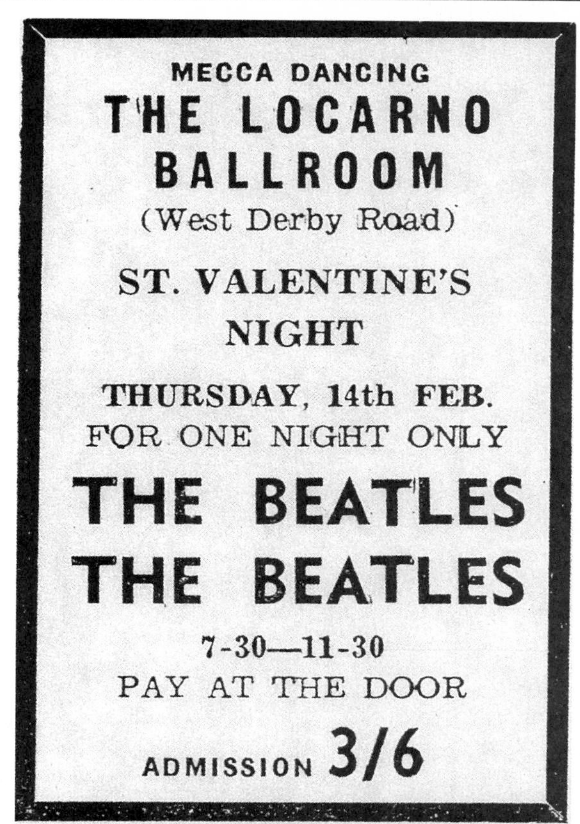

For many years the premier Mecca Ballroom in Liverpool. The venue mainly featured dance bands and rarely booked any of the Mersey Beat groups, preferring their own resident beat group the Delemeres who comprised Mac

McGibbon (bass), Dave Shipley (lead), Gordon Railton (rhythm) and Mike Wakefield (drums).

However, for a short time from 1963 they began to book some of the better known Liverpool names and presented the Beatles on a special Valentine's Night promotion on 14 February 1963. It was the only time the group appeared at the venue, although the **Quarry Men** had entered some talent contests there in the late fifties.

The Locarno regularly ran contests ranging from singing to beauty contests and during the skiffle boom, the Quarry Men entered a few of the talent contest heats at the ballroom.

In the seventies the ballroom was turned into a bingo hall and for a number of years, former **Cavern** DJ **Bob Wooler** acted as a bingo caller there.

● Lockwood, Sir Joseph

In their dealings at the top level of **EMI Records**, the Beatles were in contact with Sir Joseph Lockwood, who was Chairman of EMI from 1954 until 1974.

Sir Joseph had been an asset to the company, overseeing the purchase of the small American record label **Capitol Records**, which was later to become such a major giant. He also appointed a young George Martin as head of the Parlophone label.

The man the Beatles called 'Sir Joe' was always available to advise and help them in personal and financial matters. He was the one who vetoed Gandhi as a figure for the *Sgt Pepper* album cover lest it offend record buyers in India. When John and **Yoko** were photographed in the nude for the *Two Virgins* cover, they showed Sir Joe the photograph. He refused to allow EMI to distribute the record. John asked him if he were shocked. He told him that he wasn't, that they should have had better bodies on the cover. 'They're not very attractive,' he said, referring to the figures of John and Yoko, 'Paul McCartney would look better than you.' He agreed to press the record if Apple took over the distribution.

When John and Yoko were involved in a drug bust, Paul contacted Sir Joe who immediately rang Paddington Green police station to contact John and advise him how to conduct himself.

Sir Joseph died on 6 March 1991 at the age of 86.

● Lodge, Tom

A disc jockey for the pirate radio station Radio Caroline. When the Beatles were attending a photographic session for the cover of their American album *Yesterday . . . And Today* on 25 March 1966, Lodge interviewed the group. The interview was later included as a flexi-disc called 'Sound of the Stars' which was made available as a free gift to readers of the pop weekly *Disc and Music Echo*.

● Lomax, Jackie

The Undertakers were one of the most stylish Mersey Beat bands, whose image matched their name. They wore undertakers' dress – black top hats and mourning coats – and their amplifiers were shaped like coffins. They were voted twelfth most popular group in the ***Mersey Beat*** poll in 1961 (the year the group were formed) and had risen to the fifth position the following year.

Members were Jackie Lomax (a former wages clerk at the Mersey Docks and Harbour Board), Geoff Nugent, Chris Houston, Bugs Pemberton and **Brian Jones**. They played all the main Liverpool venues and appeared at the **Top Ten** and **Star Clubs** in Hamburg.

The group signed with Pye Records and recorded 'Mashed Potatoes', which they wanted as their debut single. Pye decided otherwise and relegated it to the 'B' side of 'Everybody Loves A Lover'.

For their second single they wanted to issue 'Money' but Pye ignored them once again and placed it on the 'B' side of 'What About Us'. Bern Elliott & the Fenmen then recorded 'Money' and had a chart hit with the number. Pye relented and allowed the Undertakers to pick their next 'A' side, which was 'Just A Little Bit', which became their first and only chart hit. Pye claimed that they didn't sell records because of their name and talked them into changing it to the 'Takers. Geoff Nugent believes that the name change contributed to their downfall. As the 'Takers they recorded 'If You Don't Come Back', but at the moment the record began to sell, the record company ceased plugging it.

Some members of the group travelled to America and Jackie and Bugs teamed up with two American musicians to form the Lomax Alliance.

Jackie met **Cilla Black** at a party in 1966 and she told him, 'Brian Epstein's looking for you.' He contacted Brian who told him he was looking for a solo singer. Jackie asked him to listen to his band and Epstein signed up the Lomax Alliance and booked them on his showplace, the **Saville Theatre** in London. They also recorded an album with ohn Simon, but like the Undertakers tracks 'Hold On, I'm -Comin'', 'My Babe', 'Watch Your Step' and 'What's So ood About Goodbye', it remains unreleased.

After Epstein's death the Lomax Alliance disbanded nd Jackie was signed to Apple. He had a voice with a emarkable range and George Harrison wanted to produce im. His debut single was one of Apple's first four releases n 26 August 1968 in America, on Apple 1802, and on 6 eptember in the UK on Apple 3. 'Sour Milk Sea' was also ritten by George and the flipside, 'The Eagle Laughs At ou', was written by Jackie. Paul McCartney joined in on ass, Nicky Hopkins on piano, **Eric Clapton** on lead uitar, Ringo on drums and George and Jackie on rhythm uitars. The 'supergroup' angle of the record wasn't omoted and the single wasn't a hit.

Lomax's debut album *Is This What You Want?* was leased in Britain on 21 March 1969 on Apple SAPCOR and in America on 19 May on Apple ST 3354. Eric lapton and Ringo played on the track 'You've Got Me inking', and George produced the album. George was terested in producing another record with Jackie, but omax wanted to record himself on a new song which he'd st finished called 'New Day'. This was issued in Britain 9 May 1969 on Apple 11, with 'I Fall Inside Your Eyes' the flip.

Paul McCartney had also been interested in Jackie and e night before he married **Linda**, Paul recorded Jackie nging 'Thumbin' A Ride' at a session in which George d **Billy Preston** also played. This appeared on the pside of 'New Day' when it was issued in America on 2 ne 1969 on Apple 1807. 'Thumbin' A Ride' was also atured as the flipside of Jackie's next British release, ow The Web Was Woven', which George produced. It s issued on 9 March 1970 on Apple 1819.

His final Apple single was a re-release. 'Sour Milk a', coupled with 'I Fall Inside Your Eyes', was issued on June 1971 in America on Apple 1834.

Like all of Jackie's previous releases, it failed to make e charts. This fact completely baffled the Beatles cause Jackie had one of those rare and distinctive voices ich have the potential of turning its owner into a perstar. The records were highly rated ones, and yet the blic didn't go for them.

Another track George produced with Jackie, 'Going ck To Liverpool', remains unreleased.

When **Allen Klein** entered the picture, Jackie was lost in the office intrigues. Three of his appointments with Klein were cancelled and he eventually went to Warner, where he released two albums, then signed up with **Capitol** and for a while appeared with a group called Badger.

When Jackie's wife was involved in a serious road accident which almost crippled her, he gave up his musical career for a time to devote himself to looking after her.

He now lives in Los Angeles and appears on the occasional gig, as well as producing some new up-and-coming bands.

● London Palladium, *8 Argyll Street, London W1*

Site of the live ATV variety shows 'Sunday Night At The London Palladium'.

The group's debut there on Sunday, 13 October 1963, saw the birth of **'Beatlemania'**. They were the bill toppers and performed before a television audience of fifteen million viewers with numbers such as 'From Me to You', 'I'll Get You', 'She Loves You', and 'Twist and Shout'. Comedian Bruce Forsyth compered a section of the show called 'Beat The Clock' and other acts included singer Brook Benton, Des O'Connor and Jack Parnell & His Orchestra.

The show started at 8.25 p.m. There were such huge crowds of fans gathered that the Fleet Street newspapers had a field day taking shots of what appeared in the headlines the following day as 'Beatlemania!'. There was such a horde outside the Marlborough Street stage door exit that it was decided that the Beatles should slip out the front entrance of the theatre in Argyll Street and into a waiting chauffeur-driven Austin Princess. A police chief thought the car would be conspicuous parked directly outside the front entrance, so he had it moved 40 yards further up Argyll Street. Press Officer **Tony Barrow** tipped off some pressmen about their escape route and when they dashed out they couldn't find their car and were then pursued by fans. The shots made impressive spreads in the major nationals the next day.

Their next appearance at the theatre was also for a spot on Val Parnell's 'Sunday Night At the London Palladium' on 12 January 1964 topping a bill which included **Alma Cogan** and **Dave Allen**.

Their third appearance at the Palladium took place on

Thursday, 23 July 1964, at a midnight performance of 'Night Of One Hundred Stars', a charity revue in aid of the Combined Theatrical Charities Appeals Council. During the first half of the show the group performed a sketch called 'I'm Flying' and in the second half they performed a musical set. Among the many other artists on the bill were Zsa Zsa Gabor, **Jane Asher**, Laurence Olivier, Harry Secombe, Frankie Vaughan, Max Bygraves, Frankie Howerd, Richard Attenborough, Millicent Martin, **Dora Bryan**, Miriam Karlin, Wendy Craig, Angela Douglas, Adrienne Corri, Peggy Cummins, Eunice Gayson, Marti Stevens, Elizabeth Welch, Eve Arden, **Hayley Mills**, Sylvia Sims, Chita Rivera, Susan Hampshire, Rita Moreno, Ronnie Corbett, **Wilfred Brambell**, Judy Garland, **Shirley Bassey**, **Marlene Dietrich** and Buddy Greco.

Backstage, Laurence Olivier, who was compere of the show, personally requested that he be introduced to the Beatles.

● London Pavilion, The, *Piccadilly Circus, London W1*

Site of the premieres for the Beatles films. The first event at the cinema was the premiere of *A Hard Day's Night* which took place on Monday, 6 July 1964, at 8.30 p.m. in the presence of Her Royal Highness The Princess Margaret and Lord Snowdon. The charity event was in aid of the Docklands Settlement and Variety Club Heart Fund. A crowd of 12,000 people gathered in Piccadilly Circus and they cheered and sang 'Happy Birthday, Ringo!' as it was Ringo's 24th birthday the following day. After the premiere, the group went off to the **Dorchester Hotel** for a special party, during which Paul gave his father a painting of Drake's Drum and told him he'd bought him the racehorse. Two surprise guests who turned up were **Brian Jones** and Keith Richard of the **Rolling Stones**.

At the premiere of *Help!* which took place on 29 July 1965 there were an estimated 10,000 people gathered in Piccadilly Circus. Once again, Princess Margaret and Lord Snowdon were in attendance. John arrived in his Rolls with **Cynthia**, Paul was accompanied by **Jane Asher** and Ringo by **Maureen**. Other guests included producer **Walter Shenson** with his wife Gerry and publisher **Dick James** with his son Steven. After the film there was a party in the Orchid Room of the Dorchester Hotel.

The premiere of *How I Won The War*, in which John had a cameo role, took place at the Pavilion on Wednesday, 18 October 1967. John and Cynthia, Ring and Maureen, Paul and Jane and **Pattie** and George we in attendance and guests included Jimi Hendrix, Anit Harris, **Cilla Black**, Mamma Cass Elliott, Davi Hemmings and Gayle Hunnicutt. After the film the Beatle attended a private party at Cilla Black's flat.

The *Yellow Submarine* premiere took place o Wednesday, 17 July 1968, and once again huge crowd poured into Piccadilly Circus. Paul was in attendance a were John and **Yoko**, Ringo and Maureen and George an Pattie. Guests included the Bee Gees, Ginger Bake **Twiggy** and **Grapefruit**. After the show there was a par at the Yellow Submarine discotheque at the **Roy Lancaster Hotel**.

The final Beatles movie premiere took place at th London Pavilion on 20 May 1970 for *Let It Be*. Not single member of the Beatles turned up, although tw former lovers did, Cynthia Lennon and Jane Asher.

The London Pavilion closed its doors for the last tin several years later and was redeveloped. It is now a entertainments complex which includes Rock Circus, museum of rock music which contains moving fibregla figures of the Beatles among its exhibits.

● Lonesome Tears In My Eyes

A number recorded by the Johnny Burnette Trio in 19 on an album issued by Coral (CRL 57080) in the States. was composed by Johnny Burnette, Dorsey Burnette, Pa Burlison and Al Mortiner. Johnny and his brother Dors were originally members of the Rock 'n' Roll Trio, Rockabilly band. Johnny drowned in 1964 and Dors died in 1979. Johnny's son Rocky became an artist in h own right and had a big hit with 'Tired Of Toein' the Line

The Beatles introduced this Burnette number into the repertoire, with John Lennon on lead vocals, ar performed it in their stage act during 1961 and 1962.

● Long And Winding Road, The *(Film)*

The projected official film documentary of the Beatle history.

Apple Managing Director **Neil Aspinall** was in char of the project as early as the late sixties and th documentary was originally to have been released duri December 1970, but was not completed at the time.

The plan had been to release the documenta simultaneously with a Beatles album containing previous unreleased tracks from the *Let It Be* sessions.

The documentary was to be a mixture of home movies, newsreel clips and promotional films and included live footage from concerts and film of the Beatles at Rishikesh with the **Maharishi Mahesh Yogi**.

For more than twenty years rumours have persisted about its imminent release.

● Long And Winding Road, The *(Single)*

A composition by Paul McCartney which the Beatles originally began recording at Apple on Friday, 31 January 1969, for the 'Get Back' sessions. The Beatles were becoming dissatisfied with the 'Get Back' project and **Glyn Johns** was handed the tapes to edit into album form. Johns' work was rejected and the following year **Allen Klein** brought in **Phil Spector**.

In April 1970, Spector altered 'The Long And Winding Road' substantially, introducing his own trademark, the 'Spector wall of sound', by utilizing no less than 50 musicians on the track. They included Ringo on drums, 2 guitarists, 3 trombonists, 3 trumpeters, a harp, 4 cellos, 4 violas, 18 violins and 14 vocalists.

Paul was furious at what Spector had done to his number and made his opinions vocal. His attitude about the post-production work on the *Let It Be* album differed from that of John and George. Paul felt that Spector had destroyed the documentary feel which had been the aim of the album. He was so incensed with the alterations Spector had made to his song that he wrote a letter to Allen Klein angrily demanding that he have the changes removed. Klein ignored him. Paul was later to comment how he didn't like the violins and the female voices on the track and how nobody minded but him.

Two versions of the number exist from the original recordings – one produced by George Martin, the other by Spector. Paul also performed it on tour with **Wings** and this version is to be found on the *Wings Over America* album.

The track was featured on the *Let It Be* album and has also been included on several compilations: *The Beatles 1967–1970*, *Love Songs*, *The Beatles Ballads*, *Reel Music* and *20 Greatest Hits*.

The number was released in America as a single on Apple 2832 on 11 May 1970 coupled with 'For You Blue'. The two soundtrack numbers from *Let It Be*, selected by Allen Klein as a double-'A' side release, topped the charts in *Billboard*, *Cash Box* and *Record World*.

This was to be the final Beatles single issued in America, apart from reissued material which began to be released from 1976. During a seven-year period the Beatles had achieved 20 No. 1 singles in *Billboard*, 22 in *Cash Box* and 23 in *Record World*.

● Long John Baldry

Influential British blues singer. A tall, blond figure, over six feet tall, Baldry first began singing in Soho pubs and coffee bars in the mid-fifties and later joined Blues Incorporated. While appearing at the **Cavern** in Liverpool, he became friends with Paul McCartney.

He was selected to be one of the guest artists on the Beatles' Rediffusion television special **'Around The Beatles'**.

● Long Long Long

A George Harrison composition which was included on *The Beatles* double album. John Lennon wasn't present at any of the recordings for this number. The love song isn't inspired by **Pattie**, as previous love songs were – George revealed that the 'you' mentioned in the number refers to 'God'.

Paul played Hammond organ on the song, which resulted in an interesting accident. There was a bottle of Blue Nun wine on the Leslie speaker and when Paul hit a particular note on the organ, the speaker vibrated and the sound of the bottle rattling can be heard at the end of the recording.

When recording began, the song had the working title 'It's Been A Long Long Long Time'.

● Long Tall Sally

The first number Paul ever sang on stage. While holidaying at Butlin's camp in Wales, Paul and his younger brother **Mike** were asked up on stage by **Mike Robbins**, their cousin-in-law, who was a Redcoat (official camp steward). The duo sang the Everly Brothers' hit 'Bye Bye Love' and then Paul went solo, singing Little Richard's hit 'Long Tall Sally'.

This was also a number Paul performed in history teacher Cliff Edge's classroom at the **Liverpool Institute**, along with George Harrison and Don Andrews, and it became part of the early Beatles repertoire.

It became the title of the Beatles' fifth EP release in

June 1964, which remained at No. 1 in the EP charts for seven weeks and reached No. 11 in the singles chart. It was included on the American release *The Beatles Second Album* in 1964, their *Rock 'n' Roll Music* compilation in 1976, *The Beatles Collection* in 1978 and *The Beatles Box* in 1980.

A live version of the number was featured on the *Live At Hollywood Bowl* album in May 1977 and it was also one of the tracks recorded at the **Star Club** in 1962, of which there have been various releases.

The number had been written by Little Richard under his real name Richard Penniman and Enotris Johnson and they'd originally called it 'The Thing', then 'Bald-Headed Sally' and finally 'Long Tall Sally'. The Little Richard version reached No. 3 in the British charts in 1956.

It was included in the repertoire in 1957 and became a highlight of the Beatles' early stage act. They performed it at the Star Club, Hamburg, and a version is to be found on *The Beatles Live! At The Star Club In Hamburg, Germany: 1962* album. The group also performed it on several of their BBC radio shows, including two **'Saturday Club'** broadcasts, **'Side By Side'**, **'Pop Go The Beatles'**, **'Top Gear'** and **'From Us To You'**.

● Long Tall Sally (EP)

The fifth Beatles British EP release. *Long Tall Sally* also became the first Beatles EP to contain previously unreleased tracks.

It was issued on Parlophone GEP 8913 on 19 June 1964 and reached No. 11 in the charts. It was very unusual for an EP to reach the singles charts, but the Beatles had managed it with every release. They had also popularized the EP, which resulted in a special EP chart and *Long Tall Sally* reached the No. 1 position in the EP charts and remained there for seven weeks.

The front cover photograph was taken by **Robert Freeman** and this time the sleeve notes were provided by **Derek Taylor**. The tracks were: 'Long Tall Sally', 'I Call Your Name', 'Slow Down' and 'Matchbox'.

● Lopez, Trini

Artist who shared the triple-headlining bill at the **Paris Olympia** from 16 January–4 February 1964. The 25-year-old singer from Dallas, Texas, had just had a million-selling hit with 'If I Had A Hammer'.

His manager **Norman Weiss** of the powerful American agency GAC came to Paris to see him and while he was there confirmed the New York **Carnegie Hall** date for the Beatles on behalf of **Sid Bernstein**. He was also able to arrange for GAC to represent the Beatles in America.

Lopez was to have a handful of hits in the sixties: 'Kansas City', 'I'm Comin' Home Cindy' and 'Gonna Get Along Without Ya Now'.

● Lord Of The Rings

A fantasy trilogy by an Oxford University professor, J. R. R. Tolkien. First published in three volumes (*The Fellowship Of The Ring*, *The Two Towers* and *The Return Of The King*) in the mid-fifties, it became a major cult in 1968 when the books appeared in a single volume as *Lord Of The Rings*.

The Beatles were quite keen on adapting the epic as their third film and John Lennon even arranged a meeting with director Stanley Kubrick to ask him to work on the project with them. He turned them down, but they managed to interest the Italian director Michelangelo Antonioni.

John had intended to portray the obsessive creature Gollum, George was to be the wizard Gandalf, Paul was to take the role of Bilbo Baggins, the Hobbit, and Ringo was to portray Bilbo's friend Gamgee. The four also asked **Twiggy** to appear in the movie with them.

Although some rumours purported that the author didn't like the idea of his book being turned into a vehicle for the Beatles, this is unlikely. **Pete Shotton**, in his autobiography ***In My Life***, says that when a Beatles representative approached Tolkien's agent, he discovered that the film rights had been snapped up only a few days previously.

● Love In The Open Air

When this instrumental was issued with the composer credit given solely to Paul McCartney, it was the first piece of music to be released using the name of only one member of the Lennon & McCartney songwriting team.

Paul had composed the theme tune and incidental music for the 1967 film ***The Family Way*** and passed the music over to George Martin for him to fine-tune, compose and record. The George Martin Orchestra then recorded the film's soundtrack album, issued by **Decca,** and also released 'Love In The Open Air' coupled with 'Bahama Sound' as a single on United Artists UA 50148 on 24 April 1967.

Lovely Rita

song by Paul which featured on the *Sgt Pepper* album.

Commenting on his inspiration for the song, Paul has id, 'I was bopping about on a piano in Liverpool when meone told me that in America they called parking eter women Meter Maids. I thought it was great and it got be "Rita, Meter Maid" and then "Lovely Rita, Meter aid" and I was thinking it should be a hate song, but en I thought it would be better to love her and if she was eaky too, like a military man, with a bag on her oulders. A foot stomper, but nice.'

In Paul's song, the narrator sees Rita filling in parking kets and notices that she has an almost military look th her cap and bag. He invites her out to tea, then takes r out to dinner – although Rita ends up paying the bill. then takes her home, but doesn't quite make it with her his two sisters are sharing the sofa.

Visually, artists interpret Rita as a very sexy woman. In e David Bailey colour photograph in *The Beatles ustrated Lyrics*, she is a sluttish figure, smoking a garette, her cap askew, face heavily made up and her left nd pulling aside her jacket to reveal an ample cleavage. e Robert Rankin illustration in *Behind The Beatles ngs* depicts her clothed only in a hat and black ckings.

Real life Meter Maid Meta Davis claimed to have been ul's inspiration. She retired after nineteen years as a affic Warden on Wednesday, 4 September 1985, when media gave her story major coverage. She appeared on th BBC and ITV news that evening, pictured walking oss the **Abbey Road** zebra crossing and discussing w she gave Paul his ticket (although she called him Paul cCarthy' in the interviews).

In 1967 Mrs Davis, who lives in St John's Wood, was ing Paul's car a ticket in Garden Road, when he turned . She commented: 'He saw that my name was Meta and laughed and said, "That would make a nice jingle, I ıld use that." We chatted for a few minutes and then he ve off. I didn't think any more of it, but later the song ne out and although I knew the record was about me I ver bought a copy.'

Paul didn't recognize her when, a few years later, she t him in the reception room of the local vet where she'd en her cat. Paul was there with his dog and Meta says, e chatted about animals and he didn't recognize me out ıniform and I didn't tell him who I was.'

When the record was originally released in Australia it included Meta's name in the lyrics, but this was changed to Rita in other versions.

The number has also been recorded by several other artists, including Fats Domino and Roy Wood.

● Love Me Do

A number Paul wrote one day when he was playing truant from school. John wrote the middle eight.

It became the Beatles' first single and was amongst the songs they recorded at their Parlophone recording audition on Wednesday, 6 June 1962, when **Pete Best** was a member of the group. Both George Martin and Ron Richards supervised the production of the session. When the group returned to **Abbey Road Studios** to record the number on Tuesday, 4 September 1962, Ron Richards rehearsed the group in Studio Three between 2.30 p.m. and 5.30 p.m. They then began recording with George Martin at 7.00 p.m. in Studio Three, initially recording 'How Do You Do It?' Next came 'Love Me Do', which took fifteen takes.

On their 6 June visit George Martin had commented that he wasn't happy with the drum sound. In fact, that was because he was used to a different style of drumming in the recording studios where producers had used show drummers rather than groups from rock 'n' roll bands. When the Beatles turned up with Ringo, Martin was unhappy with his drumming, too.

As he wasn't satisfied with the session, it was rearranged for the following Tuesday, 11 September. The Beatles told Martin that they thought Ringo was the best drummer in Liverpool, but Martin told them he'd be happier using Andy White as session drummer.

Ringo wasn't very happy when he arrived for his second recording session to find another drummer in place. He felt he would be kicked out of the group, just like Pete Best. The use of a session drummer, as it turned out, wasn't a reflection on either Pete Best or Ringo Starr – it was a common practice at the time. White was a show drummer who had appeared on many sessions and it was Ron Richards who had actually booked him, because he was used to working with him. Richards handled the recording session on 11 September in George Martin's absence. The first number recorded was 'P.S. I Love You' and an unhappy Ringo sat next to Ron Richards in the control box until the producer asked him to play maracas on the track. When they came to record 'Love Me Do', Richards asked Ringo to play tambourine.

Taking photographs at the session was **Dezo Hoffmann** and George tried to avoid the camera because he still had a black eye which a Pete Best fan had given him at the **Cavern**.

The record began with a distinctive harmonica solo by John. Discussing the harmonica, John had said, 'I can't remember why I took it up in the first place – I must have picked one up very cheap. I know we used to take in students and one of them had a mouth organ and said he'd buy me one if I could learn a tune by the next morning – so I learned about two. I was somewhere between eight and twelve at the time – in short pants anyway. Another time I was travelling to Edinburgh on me own to see me auntie and I played the mouth organ all the way up on the bus. The driver liked it and told me to meet him at a place in Edinburgh the next morning and he'd give me a good mouth organ. So I went, and he gave me a fantastic one – it really got me going.'

John had been particularly impressed by the distinctive harmonica opening by Delbert McClinton on the **Bruce Channel** hit 'Hey! Baby'. When the Beatles appeared on a bill with Channel at the **Tower Ballroom**, New Brighton, on Thursday, 21 June 1962, Lennon drifted over to McClinton and told him how much he liked the harmonica on the song and asked him how to play the intro. The two of them spent fifteen minutes together. John had actually performed 'Love Me Do' only two weeks previously at their Parlophone audition, but he was able to utilize the McClinton lesson when they recorded the number t following September.

'Love Me Do' coupled with 'P.S. I Love You' was issu on Parlophone R 4949 on 5 October 1962. The record h a red label which collectors can identify as the single wi Ringo on drums – after all the problems about having session drummer, the first single issued featured Rin after all. However, in April 1963, further pressings of t single on a black label featured the version with An White on drums.

The single reached its highest position of No. 17 in o London music paper for one week only, was No. 27 for o week in another, but at least managed to make its presen felt in all four London musical weeklies, reaching No. in *Disc* and No. 32 in *Record Mirror*, in addition to t *Melody Maker* and ***New Musical Express*** placings. went straight to No. 1 in the ***Mersey Beat*** chart.

The version with Ringo playing drums was included *The Beatles Box* set and on the American *Rarities* album.

The version with Andy White on drums appeared on t *Please Please Me* album, *The Beatles' Hits* EP, *The Beat 1962–1966* compilation, the American *Introducing t Beatles* album, the Tollie single, the Oldies single, t Capitol Starline single and *The Beatles Collection set*.

The 'Love Me Do' single had originally been availab in America as a Capitol of Canada import, but was issu on **Vee Jay**'s Tollie label on Tollie 9008 on 27 April 19 and reached No. 1 in the American charts, selling over million copies. Vee Jay reissued it again on their 'Oldi 45' series on OL 151 Oldies 45 on 10 August 1964. It a

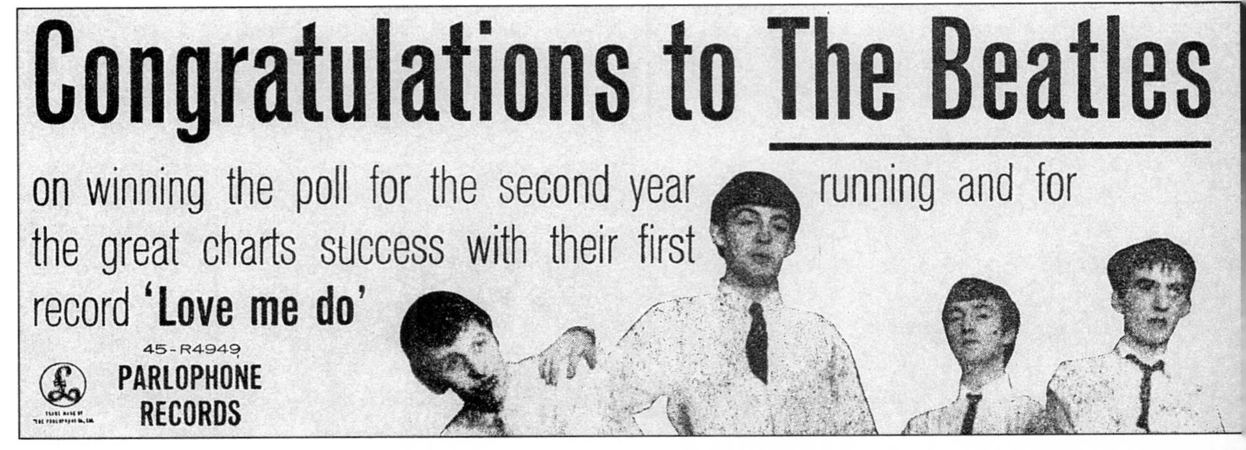

iled to chart when **Capitol** released it on their Starline ries on Capitol Starline 6063 on 11 October 1965.

To celebrate the twentieth anniversary of the Beatles' cording career in 1982, *20 Greatest Hits* was released d the compilation once again featured the Andy White rsion. It was discovered that the use of the White version er the past twenty years had been because the Ringo arr master had disappeared. The original masters were scovered at the time of the anniversary and both versions ere issued on one twelve-inch single on Parlophone 12R 49 on 1 November 1982. This followed the re-release of e single in a picture sleeve on Parlophone R 4949 on 4 ctober 1982 and the release of a picture disc on RP 4949 the same date.

Love Me Tender

n **Elvis Presley** number penned by Ken Darby and iginally based on an 1861 ballad called 'Aura Lee', itten by W. W. Fosdick and George R. Poulton. The mber became the title song of Elvis Presley's debut film. e Beatles included it in their repertoire as a showcase r **Stuart Sutcliffe** and it is one of the few songs that eir former bass guitarist sang while he was a member of e band.

Love, Mike

calist with the **Beach Boys**. Mike became interested in anscendental Meditation and was a student at Rishikesh en the Beatles went to study at the ashram. It was said at during the stay, Mike helped Paul to write 'Back In e USSR'. While they were there the Beatles taped a ng live as a birthday present for Mike which they called piritual Regeneration', although it has also been called ranscendental Meditation'.

Love Of The Loved

e of the earliest of the Paul McCartney compositions d one which the **Quarry Men** included in their pertoire. It was also one of the handful of original songs ey performed at their **Decca Records audition**.

Although written by Paul, John Lennon once nsidered offering the song to Liverpool singer **Beryl arsden**, but Brian Epstein insisted on giving it to his est signing **Cilla Black** as her debut record. Paul was so present at Cilla's recording session. The single was eased on Parlophone R 5065 on 27 September 1963 but it wasn't a big hit for her and only reached the position of No. 30 in the British charts for a single week. Paul was later to write some other numbers specially for Cilla.

● Love Songs

A 25 track double-album, issued after the Beatles' **EMI** contract had ended, leaving the company with the rights to repackage any back-catalogue material.

Love Songs was issued in both Britain and America in 1977. The British release was issued on Parlophone 721 on 19 November and the **American double** album on **Capitol** SKBL 11711 on 21 October. It reached No. 12 in the British charts and No. 24 in America.

The Capitol package included a 28-page booklet featuring the lyrics of the songs.

Both British and American albums contained the same cover photograph, which was a shot by **Richard Avedon** which had originally been featured, in a slightly different form, on the cover of *Look* magazine in 1967.

The tracks were – Record One/Side One: 'Yesterday', 'I'll Follow The Sun', 'I Need You', 'Girl', 'In My Life', 'Words Of Love', 'Here There and Everywhere'. Record One/Side Two: 'Something', 'And I Love Her', 'If I Fell', 'I'll Be Back', 'Tell Me What You See', 'Yes It Is'. Record Two/Side One: 'Michelle', 'It's Only Love', 'You're Going To Lose That Girl', 'Every Little Thing', 'For No One', 'She's Leaving Home'. Record Two/Side Two: 'The Long and Winding Road', 'This Boy', 'Norwegian Wood (This Bird Has Flown)', 'You've Got To Hide Your Love Away', 'I Will' and 'P.S. I Love You'.

● Love You To

Although George Harrison used a sitar for the first time on record on 'Norwegian Wood', he says that playing the instrument on that particular track came about by accident. The first number which he specifically wrote with the sitar in mind was 'Love You To'. This was also the first of George's Indian influenced numbers to be recorded and, apart from playing the sitar himself, he hired Indian musician Anil Bhaqwat to play tabla.

The working title of the song was 'Granny Smith', named after the apple, as George seemed to complete his numbers before deciding on a title at this time.

'Love You To' was featured on the *Revolver* album, although for some reason the American release carried the misspelling 'Love You Too', a mistake which completely altered the meaning of the title.

George was evidently fighting for his share of songs on Beatles albums and wrote three of the tracks featured on *Revolver*.

● *Lowe, John*

Former member of the **Quarry Men**, who was pianist with the group from February 1958 until January 1959. He was nicknamed 'Duff' and was with the group when they recorded 'That'll Be The Day' and 'In Spite Of All The Danger' at the **Kensington Recording Studio** in Liverpool in 1958 and kept an acetate of the recording for many years. In 1981 he announced that he was going to auction the recording at Sotheby's, London, in October of that year. Paul McCartney didn't want the disc auctioned, particularly as 'In Spite Of All The Danger' was a song he'd co-penned which had not been released commercially. He offered Lowe £5,000 for it, but Lowe refused to sell, reckoning he'd receive twice as much at auction. Paul placed the matter in the hands of his solicitors who were able to obtain a court order banning sale of the disc. This was probably due to the fact that Paul's publishing company MPL had the copyright to **Buddy Holly**'s 'That'll Be The Day', and no one can issue a disc without the permission of the copyright holder.

A settlement was made, Lowe received an amount of money which satisfied him and Paul received one of the rarest discs in the Beatles history for his proposed museum.

Lowe settled in Ashton, near Bristol, where he works in the investment business.

● *Lowlands Club, Hayman's Green, West Derby, Liverpool L12*

One of the numerous small clubs in Liverpool which provided an outlet for local groups to play. The **Quarry Men** appeared at a Saturday night audition at Lowlands during the middle of 1958, but were unsuccessful in obtaining any bookings there.

The club was situated on the opposite side of the street, 50 yards down from the Bests' home, which was to become the **Casbah Club** in August 1959.

When the Quarry Men ceased appearing locally at the end of 1958, George Harrison joined the **Les Stewart Quartet** who appeared several times at Lowlands from January 1959.

● *Lucille*

A **Little Richard** number by Penniman/Collins, fir released in 1957. It was immediately adopted as part the repertoire of the **Quarry Men** after Paul had joine with Paul taking over lead vocals, as he did with all Litt Richard songs.

The Beatles featured the number on their BB recordings for **'Pop Go The Beatles'** and **'Saturda Club'**.

Paul also recorded it for the Concert for Kampuchea c 29 December 1979 and this version is to be found on tl 1981 double album *Concerts For Kampuchea*.

● *Lucy In The Sky With Diamonds*

The inspiration for the song came when the four-year-o **Julian Lennon** returned from nursery school with painting. When John asked him what the subject wa Julian told him, 'It's Lucy in the sky with diamonds.'

Purely because the initials of the song coincide wi those of the drug LSD, which John had admitted takin several radio stations banned the record, convinced it w a song advocating the taking of drugs.

The Beatles began rehearsing the song at **Abbey Roa** on Tuesday, 28 February 1967, and the group bega recording it the following day. In John's surrealistic lyri can be detected the influence of his early love of Lew Carroll's *Alice in Wonderland* books.

Paul McCartney was to comment: 'We did the who thing like an *Alice in Wonderland* idea, being in a boat the river, slowly drifting downstream and those gre cellophane flowers towering over your head. Every so oft it broke off and you saw "Lucy in the Sky with Diamond all over the sky. This Lucy was God, the big figure, tl white rabbit. You can just write a song with imagination words and that's what we like.'

John was never really satisfied with the Beatles' versi of the number, voicing his opinion that they didn't real play well on it. He preferred the version by **Elton Joh** When Elton recorded the number, John agreed to pl guitar and sing backing vocals and the record w advertised as 'Featuring Dr Winston O'Boogie and h Reggae Guitars'. John also performed the number on sta with Elton John at Madison Square Garden in New York.

The number was featured on the album *Sgt Peppe Lonely Hearts Club Band* and was included on tl compilation *The Beatles 1967–1970*.

Lynch, Kenny

opular British entertainer, born in London's East End, ho had eight entries in the British charts between 1960 ıd 1983. His most successful singles were 'Up On The oof', which reached No. 10 in 1962, and 'You Can Never :op Me Loving You', which reached the same position the llowing year.

Kenny first met the Beatles on 28 October 1962 when e appeared on a bill at the **Liverpool Empire**, promoted y Brian Epstein. The Beatles asked him if he'd like them provide backing for him, but he told them he'd already red a backing band.

Their association continued when they both appeared ı the **Helen Shapiro** tour, promoted by **Arthur Howes**, 1963. John and Paul had written a number called Iisery' for Helen, but apparently her record producer orrie Paramor didn't like it. Kenny says that he was tting next to John on the tour coach when Helen came to lk to them. John asked what Paramor thought about the ng. When Kenny heard that she wasn't going to record e number he immediately seized on the opportunity. He id, 'I was leaning on the seat and I said to John, "Can u let me hear it?" and he played it to me on his guitar. I as going to record the number "You Could Never Stop e Loving You" at the time, but I gave it to Johnny llotson and recorded "Misery" instead. Tillotson had a t with his. I didn't. But I was the first person to record a eatles number.'

'Misery' was released in Britain on 22 March 1963 on MV Pop 1136. Kenny first played the single to John and ıul in **Dick James**' office and John Lennon admitted king Kenny's rendition of the number but couldn't stand e guitar work. 'He gave me a bollocking because he dn't like the Bert Weedon guitar on it,' Kenny said, ferring to the veteran British guitar player.

Incidentally, when Kenny was on tour with the Beatles, omoter Arthur Howes asked him to introduce the group stage each night. He also appeared with the Beatles on May 1964 on 'Pops Alive' at the **Prince of Wales heatre, London.**

In 1973, Kenny was one of several personalities Paul cCartney picked to appear on the cover of his *Band On ie Run* album. Kenny commented: 'I travelled all the ay down from Scotland to appear on the cover of the bum and when I arrived at the session I said to Paul, You owe me one." He said, "Right, I owe you one, Kenny", so I'm hoping he'll come on the cover of one of my albums.'

Lyndon, John

A former theatrical director who was hired by Brian Epstein to be Production Director for **NEMS Enterprises**. Lyndon introduced some innovations into the package show when he produced *Star Scene '65*, which starred several NEMS acts. He also staged the Sunday concerts at the **Saville Theatre** and was in charge of all NEMS theatre and cabaret presentations.

When the Apple Retail division was undergoing difficulties, the Beatles asked him to replace **Pete Shotton** and administer the Apple shops.

Lyntone Records

The record company which produced all the Beatles Christmas Records. The idea for the special Christmas messages to fans originally came from press officer **Tony Barrow**. He co-ordinated the project and the first Christmas disc was issued on 6 December 1963. For this release 30,000 copies were pressed in the basic format of a 33 rpm seven-inch flexidisc. Barrow took the 24 minutes of tape which the Beatles had recorded to Lyntone and, together with the company's director Paul Lynton, snipped the tape with scissors until they'd edited it down to a five-minute recording. They didn't keep a master copy and the rest of the recording ended up in the waste bin.

The records issued by Lyntone were:

'The Beatles Christmas Record', LYN 492, 6 December 1963.

'Another Beatles Christmas Record', LYN 757, 18 December 1964.

'The Beatles Third Christmas Record', LYN 948, 17 December 1965.

'The Beatles Fourth Christmas Record – Pantomime: Everywhere It's Christmas', LYN 1145, 16 December 1966.

'The Beatles Fifth Christmas Record – Christmas Time (Is Here Again)', LYN 1360, 15 December 1967.

'The Beatles Sixth Christmas Record – Christmas 1968', LYN 1743/4, 20 December 1968.

'The Beatles Seventh Christmas Record – Happy Christmas 1969', LYN 1970/1, 19 December 1969.

'From Then To You – The Beatles Christmas Record 1970', Apple LYN 2154, 18 December 1970.

● M*acbeth*, D*avid*

British singer whose single chart hit was 'Mr Blue', which reached No. 18 in 1959. The former Newcastle footballer appeared in Liverpool several times during 1962 to promote his new release 'Roses Are Red', including the lunchtime pop sessions at the Crane Theatre and cabaret shows at the **Cabaret Club** and Speke Airport Cabaret Club.

He appeared on the Beatles/**Roy Orbison** tour, which commenced in May 1963.

● M*acdonna* H*all, Corner of Salisbury Avenue and Banks Road, West Kirby, Wirral, Cheshire*

Also known in Beatles annals as Thistle Cafe, because when the Beatles appeared here for the first and only time, the venue, a dance studio, was situated directly above the Thistle Cafe.

It was the group's first booking under Epstein's aegis and Brian advertised the event as the 'Grand opening of the Beatle Club'. Why he described it this way is not known, because they never appeared at the venue again. It was an unlikely place for a gig and situated ten miles outside of Liverpool.

Epstein was also able to secure eighteen pounds for the performance, a substantial sum for a small local venue at the time, and entrance cost four shillings and sixpence (22½p).

The support group were Steve Day & the Drifters.

Sam Leach claimed that on this evening John Lennon was ill and he was able to secure **Rory Storm** as replacement for the gig. This seems very unlikely as Ro couldn't even play a guitar – and both George Harris and **Neil Aspinall** denied such an occurrence.

The Thistle Cafe later became a restaurant calle What's Cooking?

● M*ackenzie*, P*hyllis*

A student at **Liverpool College of Art** who travelled the college each morning on the 72 bus from Woolton the same bus which John Lennon travelled on. He w careful about how he behaved on the bus as he kne Phyllis was **Cynthia** Powell's best friend. As part of t Intermediate Course at the college there were week classes in Lettering and John and **Jonathan Hagu** shared this lesson with Cynthia and Phyllis.

The two girls had been friends since the age of twel when they were both students at the **Junior School Art** in Gambier Terrace. In 1959, when Cynthia used stay overnight with John at the **Gambier Terrace** fl she used to tell her mother she was staying with Phyllis.

After her secret marriage to John and following t birth of Julian, the press began to pursue Cynthia discover whether she was married to the famous Beatle and she told them her name was Phyllis Mackenzie.

● M*acmillan*, I*ain*

The photographer who took the famous cover shot for t *Abbey Road* album. Macmillan was only given a brief tim to take the shots outside the **Abbey Road Studios** in John's Wood at 10.00 a.m. on 8 August 1969. A policem was able to hold up the traffic for a few minutes whi Macmillan balanced on a stepladder and took six shots the Beatles traversing the zebra crossing. Paul McCartn then picked the shot to be used from the six transparenci which Macmillan gave him. Paul had originally made rough sketch of the basic idea for the photograph a Macmillan planned it out in more detail.

● M*adame* T*ussauds, Marylebone Road, London NW1*

The most famous waxwork collection in the world.

The Beatles effigies were added to the collection March 1964, when they became the first rock 'n' roll sta to be so honoured.

The wax figures were made from photographs whi

e Beatles waxworks are still a popular feature at Madame
issauds.

easurements for hair and eye colour were supplied by *bulous* magazine. The suits for the figures were made by e group's personal tailor **Dougie Millings**. In 1967 mpletely new wax figures were made and fitted with new gs and moustaches and there have been several changes clothing since then.

● 9 Madryn Street, Liverpool 8

Birthplace of Richard Starkey. The house was a small Victorian terraced one in Liverpool's Dingle area and Ringo's parents paid ten shillings (50p) per week in rent, which was to rise to fourteen shillings and tenpence (74p) per week.

The baby was born one week late, at midnight on 7 July 1940, one month before the Luftwaffe began bombing the city. Baby Richard weighed 10 lbs and was delivered by forceps.

His mother Elsie was 26 at the time and his father Richard was 28.

The bombing began when Elsie was still in bed recovering from the birth of her son, whom the couple had nicknamed Richie.

When Elsie and her husband split up in 1943, Elsie took her son to live in the nearby street, Admiral Grove, swapping the house with a friend as she didn't want to bump into her husband, who had moved to No. 59 Madryn Street.

● Magazines

While not attempting to list every magazine published on the Beatles, this round-up affords a general guide to Beatles magazines, the majority of which appeared in the sixties, beginning in 1963.

World Distributors began a series of handsomely produced, special issues devoted to the Beat music scene in 1963. The general title of the series was '*Meet The . . .*' and the most popular edition was *Meet The Beatles*, which sold a million copies. This was written by the Beatles' Press Agent **Tony Barrow**. Others in the series included *Meet Billy J. Kramer* and *Meet Gerry & the Pacemakers*.

Another magazine published in 1963 was Pyx's *The Beatles*. This featured a number of colour shots of the group, taken by **Dezo Hoffmann**, with a text by Patrick Maugham.

In 1964 another series of magazines, in a similar format to the '*Meet the . . .* series appeared, entitled *On The Scene. . .* One of them, *On the Scene At the Cavern*, was credited to Alistair Griffin (a pseudonym for Tony Barrow). This was keenly sought after by collectors and was republished in April 1984 to coincide with the reopening of the **Cavern Club** in Liverpool.

In the mid-sixties, Daily Mirror Publications issued

some well-produced magazines, one of the first being *The Beatles By Royal Command*. The colour cover featured Princess Margaret meeting the Beatles just after their Royal Variety Show performance. It contained over 30 photographs and was the first publication to concentrate on a specific show – similar commemorative magazines were subsequently issued by a number of enterprising publishers. One example is *The Beatles At Carnegie Hall*, issued in 1964 by Panther Pictorial at two shillings and sixpence.

The text was written by Ralph Cosham and the publication contained 60 photographs of the Beatles' concert at the venue, taken by United Press and the International Candid Camera team. There were also photographs of their appearance on the '**Ed Sullivan** Show'.

Encouraged by the success of *The Beatles By Royal Command*, the *Daily Mirror* issued *The Beatles In America*. This was a pictorial souvenir of the group's American trip in 1964 with lots of black and white photographs by **Robert Freeman**. The front and back covers were in colour.

World Distributors issued a magazine with a similar layout called *The Beatles On Broadway*, which was also published in America (by the Whitman publishing company). It was written by **Sam Leach**, the Liverpool promoter who had booked the Beatles on numerous occasions. The cover of *The Beatles On Broadway* shows the heads of Ringo, George, John and Paul suspended above the Manhattan skyline. Photographs taken during the Beatles' American tour include shots of their arrival at **Kennedy Airport**; their press conference; the fans outside the **Plaza Hotel**; the boys in Central Park; appearing on the 'Ed Sullivan Show'; visiting the **Peppermint Lounge**; receiving Gold Discs; travelling by train to Washington; appearing at the **Washington Coliseum**; appearing at a masked ball at the British Embassy; appearing at **Carnegie Hall**; relaxing in Miami; visiting Cassius Clay (**Muhammad Ali**) at his training camp; and returning to Heathrow Airport. The magazine sold a million copies.

There were a series of Pop Pics Specials. One was called *Beatles Around The World* and featured colour shots of the Beatles in Paris and America, early in 1964. There were four other Pop Pics Specials: *John Lennon*, *Paul McCartney*, *George Harrison* and *Ringo Starr*, with each of the magazines including a selection of colour and black-and-white photographs, together with brief background biographies.

Fabulous was the title of a large-format teen magazine published by IPC which featured considerable Beatles coverage, some of which were collected together to produce special magazines. *FABULOUS Goes All Beatles* was a collection of Beatles material, together with interviews with Paul McCartney, Brian Epstein and **Pete Best**. *The Best Of The Beatles From FABULOUS* was another special presenting some of the best photos of the group which had appeared in the magazine. *FAB Goes Filming With The Beatles*, presented a selection of photographs from the filming of *A Hard Day's Night*, together with behind-the-scenes stories of the production.

World Distributors also covered the same subject in *The Beatles Starring In A HARD DAY'S NIGHT*, although this publication was the official United Artists souvenir booklet of the film, with exclusive pictures, behind-the-scenes stories and the background to how John and Paul wrote the songs for the film.

From time to time, British teen magazines produced special editions such as *The Beatles In Sweden* and *The Beatles In Paris* from *Boyfriend* magazine.

The ***Liverpool Echo*** also brought out a special souvenir magazine, *Around The World With The Beatles*, Christmas, 1964, penned by the paper's senior journalist **George Harrison**. This was a 32-page publication complete with four-colour photographs, stories of the group's trips abroad and a large selection of early black and white photographs.

It was America, however, which proved to be whe Beatles magazines flourished. Various teen magazines produced special issues about the group: *Datebook* with *All About The Beatles*; *Teen Screen* with *John, Paul, George and Ringo*; *Dig* magazine with *Beatles Movie* and *Beatle Talk*; *Sixteen* magazine with *Sixteen's Beatle Movie: Hard Day's Night*, *Sixteen's Beatle Movie: Help!*, *Sixteen's Beatles Complete Story From Birth To Now* and *Sixteen's Beatles Whole True Story*; *Teen Talk* with *Teen Talk: The Beatles* and *Teen Talk: Picture Packed Edition*.

Among the magazines published in America in 196 was *A Hard Day's Night*, billed as 'The Official United Artists' Pictorial Souvenir Book' – it included background stories relating to the making of the film, many behind-the-scenes photographs and a foreword by the Beatles

Best Of The Beatles, which featured a three-page colour pin-up and articles such as '63 Ways To Meet A Beatle', 'What It's Like To Love A Beatle', 'The Girl Who Stopped Paul's Marriage' and 'Is Ringo Taken By Ann-Margret?'. This was published by MacFadden Bartell, who also published the magazines *Beatles Are Back* and *The Beatles Are Here*.

Magnum Publications issued *Beatles Make A Movie* and other magazines included: *Beatles Around The World* Nos. 1 and 2 from Acme News Company; *Beatles Baby Family Album* from SMP Publishing; *Beatles USA* by Jamie Publications; *Beatles, Beatles, Beatles* by JLD Publishing; *Beatles: Fab Four Come Back* by Ideal Publications; *Beatles Meet Dave Clark 5* by Kahm Publications; *Beatles vs Dave Clark 5* by Tempest Publications; *Beatles Punch-Out Portraits* from Whitman Publishing; *Big Beatle Fun Kit* from Deirdre Publications; *Who Will Beat The Beatles?* by Magnum Publications; *Beatle Hair Dos and Setting Patterns* by Dell Publishing; *The Original Beatles Book* Nos. 1 and 2 by Peterson Publishing; a series on each individual Beatle from SMH Publications; *The Beatles Complete Life Stories* by Sunset Publications; *The Beatles Personality Annual* by Country Wide Publications; *The Fab Four Come Back* by Romance Publishing Corporation; and *Real True Beatles* by Fawcett Publications and a magazine version of Michael Braun's book *Love Me Do*.

The trend continued in 1965, with numerous Beatles titles being published, including *Star Time Presents The Beatles* by AAA Publishing; *HELP!* by *Help* magazine; and *The Beatles – Our Naughty Nights* by Reese Publishing.

During the rest of the decade fewer Beatles magazines were published. However, *Beatles Monthly* produced some special Christmas magazines and the *Yellow Submarine* movie led to various spin-offs including *The Official Yellow Submarine Magazine* from Pyramid Publications and *Teenset Yellow Submarine Special* – both in 1968.

Magazines continued to be published in the seventies, despite the group's demise. Magnum issued *Beatles From The Beginning* in 1970; an Australian magazine, *Beatle Revival*, was published in 1976 and *Beatles Yesterday and Today* was issued by Countrywide Publications in 1975. Charlton Publications issued *Beatlemania: the Beatles From Liverpool To Legend* in 1979 and in Britain, Rainbow issued the lavishly produced *The Beatles: A Giant Scrapbook*.

A magazine which underwent several reprints was *Beatles Forever*. First published in 1975, this was a glossy magazine with 150 photographs and a 40-page photo history, discography and filmography. Later editions included pieces on the stage revue *Beatlemania* and the film *Sgt Pepper's Lonely Hearts Club Band*. The magazine was revamped and rush-released immediately following John's murder.

Two particular magazines of interest were *Paul McCartney Is Dead: The Great Hoax*, issued by Countrywide Publications in 1969, and *National Lampoon*'s Beatles issue, published in October 1977.

The first was an issue completely devoted to the ridiculous rumours sparked off by an American disc jockey that Paul had been killed in a road accident and replaced by a double. The disc jockey sought to prove this by pointing out a number of 'clues' that, he alleged, had been included on Beatles records. The cover announced: 'Paul McCartney Dead: The Great Hoax. Born 1942. Died 1966?' The magazine included articles such as 'Why Did The Beatles Keep Paul's Death A Secret?'; 'Paul's Mysterious Double – Who Is He?'; 'The Death Clues, How The Public Found Out' and 'The Beatles Death Curse'.

The *National Lampoon* Beatles issue was a totally irreverent look at the group with a cover which showed them being flattened by a steamroller on the **Abbey Road** zebra crossing. There is a spoof item on the 'Paul Is Dead' theme, but the humour in general is of a sniggeringly sexual nature.

The publication of Beatles magazines over the years may be seen as having three peaks. The first following their initial American impact, the second was occasioned by John's death and the third commemorated the group's twentieth anniversary.

British magazines published on the twentieth anniversary in 1982 included *P.S. We Love You* by Tony Barrow, from Mirror Books, an insightful look at the group's early years, covering the 1962–1963 period, well illustrated with carefully chosen photographs. There are sixteen sections which cover the hectic days of the birth of **Beatlemania** in Britain, the group's rise in status from Liverpool's No. 1 band to Britain's biggest musical export. Tony interviewed a number of early associates such as **Freda Kelly**, the secretary of the **Beatles Fan Club**, in addition to including his own recollections of the time. Another twentieth anniversary magazine was *It Was 20 Years Ago Today* by Bill Harry, published by Colourgold, which featured lots of full colour photographs reproduced on gloss paper, with articles on the individual members, fan club activities, a bibliography and several other features.

The John Lennon magazines published in America included *The Beatles Forever* (reprinted with some updated information from Ed Naha); *Beatles Memory Book* and *John Lennon and the Beatles, A Special Tribute* from Harris Publications; *John Lennon: All You Need Is Love* from Charlton Publications; *A Tribute To John Lennon and the Beatles* from *US* magazine; *John Lennon 1940–1980* and *John Lennon: the Legend* from S.J. Publications; *John Lennon Tribute* from Woodhill Press; *John Lennon: A Memorial Album* from Friday Publishing Corporation; *The World of John Lennon and the Beatles* from Graybar Publications; *Lennon: A Memory* from David Zentner Publications; *John Lennon: A Man Who Cared* from Paradise Press; *Sixteen Magazine Presents John Lennon and the Beatles, A Loving Tribute*; *Teen Bag's Tribute To John Lennon*; and *Lennon Photo Special* from Sunshine Publications.

Anniversaries still provide the occasional magazine special and there were a number of magazines issued in December 1990, ten years after the death of John Lennon. *A Tribute To John Lennon* by Mick St Michael, published by Denis One Shots, is an example, which displays all the faults of these sorts of magazines: 'Full of rare archive material', states the cover lines, but the photographs are the same ones which have been used for decades. The story is a basic biography of rehashed material with the usual amount of inaccuracies.

● Maggie May

A traditional sea shanty based on a Liverpool prostitute called Maggie May. Liverpool's **Lime Street** had the reputation of being one of the most notorious streets in the world during the days of the sailing ships because it was full of pubs and prostitutes. Maggie May became a Liverpool legend and there was even a musical, *Maggie May*, penned by **Alun Owen** in the mid-sixties, and a Liverpool club of that name, run by **Allan Williams**.

The **Quarry Men** introduced 'Maggie May' into their earliest repertoire as the old sea shanty had recently been re-popularized during the skiffle boom by the Vipers Skiffle Group.

The Beatles recorded the number in January 1969 and the track was included on their *Let It Be* album. As the traditional song was out of copyright, the credits read: 'Trad. arr. Lennon/McCartney/Harrison/Starkey'.

● Maggie May Club, *Seel Street, Liverpool L1*

Situated about fifty yards from the **Blue Angel Club** on the opposite side of the street. It was a beat club opened in October 1964 by **Allan Williams**, thus fulfilling an ambition that had been thwarted in 1961 when the **Top Ten Club**, his first beat club, at which he had booked the Beatles for a short residential season, burnt down in Soho Street a week after opening.

The Maggie May, named after a famous Liverpool song, had a resident band, the Blues System. Admission prices ranged from one shilling to six shillings and members had to be at least eighteen years old as there was a licensed bar. Resident disc jockey was Dave Beattie and there was a once-weekly spot for up-and-coming bands called 'The Bill Harry Guest Night'.

● Magic Christian, The

Ringo Starr co-starred with **Peter Sellers** in this 1969 movie, adapted from **Terry Southern**'s novel of the same name. The 95-minute British film was directed by Joseph McGrath and produced by **Dennis O'Dell**, head of **Apple Films**. The movie's score was composed by Ken Thorne, while the theme song, 'Come and Get It', was written by Paul McCartney and performed by the Apple band **Badfinger**. Peter Sellers appeared as Sir Guy Grand, Ringo played Youngman Grand and guest stars in the movie were Richard Attenborough, Leonard Frey, Laurence Harvey, Christopher Lee, **Spike Milligan**, Roman Polanski and Raquel Welch.

Margaret Tarrant, in *Films And Filming*, wrote: 'The surreal world of the Goons and the picaresque fantasy world of the Beatles are combined in an essentially genial indictment of British capitalist society.' While another reviewer wrote: 'Ringo Starr continues to exploit the melancholy wanderer's role he made his own in *A Hard Day's Night*.

Ringo's part had been specially written for the film (the character he played wasn't in the original book), and his role was mainly that of an observer, watching the various stunts which Sellers sets up.

Ringo appears as Youngman Grand, the adopted son of

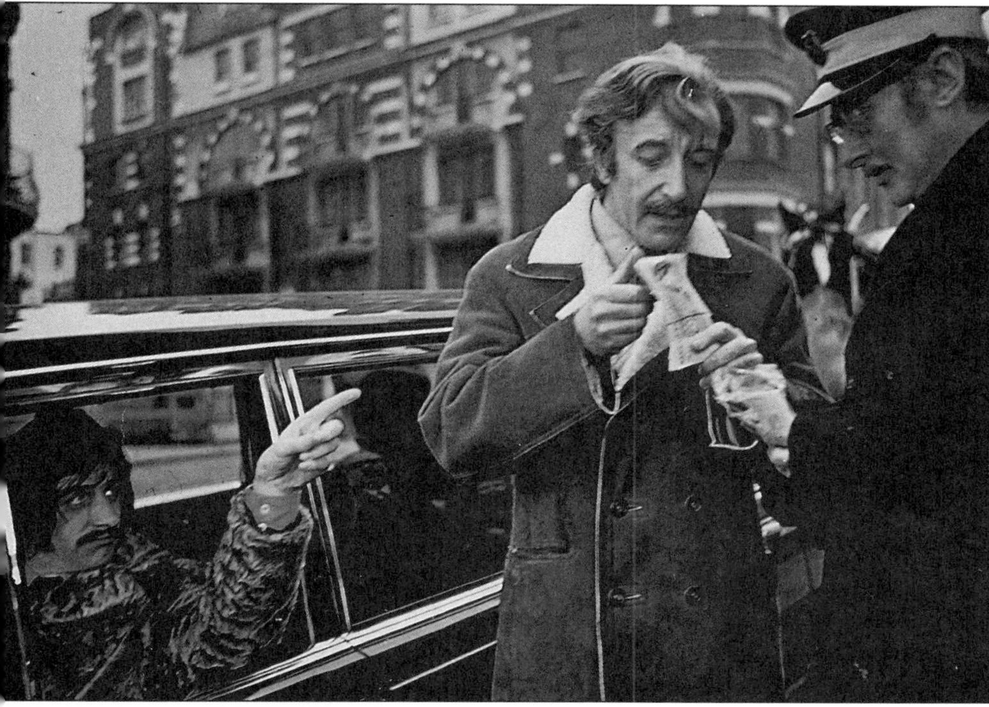

Ringo Starr, Peter Sellers and Spike Milligan in a scene from *The Magic Christian.* (Commonwealth United)

he world's richest man, Sir Guy Grand. Sir Guy resolves o show Youngman the extent to which people are obsessed y money and the ends they will go to obtain it. He seeks o prove that 'everyone has his price'. The lure of money ncourages a traffic warden (Spike Milligan) to eat his own icket and causes a snobby art gallery official (John leese) to sell him a Rembrandt. Before the man's orrified eyes, Sir Guy cuts out the nose in the painting, tating that he only collects Rembrandt's noses. He bribes he Oxford boat crew to lose the annual boat race against ambridge and entices two beefy boxers to embrace each ther in the ring during a bout. Money also persuades a amous Shakespearean actor (Laurence Harvey) to do a triptease in the middle of his soliloquy in *Hamlet*.

Sir Guy then takes Youngman on a cruise on the liner *lagic Christian*, where his education into man's greed ontinues. At one point he is shown over the engine room f the boat by a whip-wielding Raquel Welch, to discover hat it is in fact a galley with topless females at the oars.

The grand finale of the film occurs back on dry land in ondon where a giant vat has been filled with the most unspeakable detritus, including vomit, human excreta and pig's blood. Sprinkling it with money, Sir Guy stands back and watches as respectable, but desperately avaricious businessmen brawl amid the unsightly mess.

When filming was completed there was a special party held at **Les Ambassadeurs Club** in London. Among those in attendance were Ringo and **Maureen** and Paul and **Linda**. Ringo and Maureen and John and **Yoko** attended the Royal world premiere at the Odeon, Kensington, London, on 11 December 1969. The queues were taken aback by the sight of John and Yoko walking by them holding a banner proclaiming 'Britain Murdered Hanratty'.

● Magical Mystery Tour (Album)

The album of *Magical Mystery Tour* was issued in America by **Capitol Records** on SMAL 2835 on 27 November 1967 and had the biggest initial sale of any Capitol album to that time, notching up sales amounting to eight million dollars within three weeks and eventually selling over three million copies.

The No.1 album was packaged with a booklet of

photographs from the film and contained three tracks which had been released as singles in 1967.

The American track listing was – Side One: 'Magical Mystery Tour', 'The Fool On The Hill', 'Flying', 'Blue Jay Way', 'Your Mother Should Know' and 'I Am The Walrus'. Side Two: 'Hello Goodbye', 'Strawberry Fields Forever', 'Penny Lane', 'Baby You're A Rich Man' and 'All You Need Is Love'.

● Magical Mystery Tour (EP)

The soundtrack of *Magical Mystery Tour* was issued in Britain as a special double EP on Parlophone SMMT 1/2 on 8 December 1967. The package contained the two EPs and a special 24-page illustrated booklet of the film which had been edited by **Tony Barrow**, with a little help from **Neil Aspinall** and **Mal Evans.** It was lavishly illustrated with photographs by **John Kelly** and drawings by Bob Gibson. The tracks were – Record One: 'Magical Mystery Tour', 'Your Mother Should Know', 'I Am The Walrus'. Record Two: 'The Fool On The Hill', 'Flying', 'Blue Jay Way'. It was issued in America as an album, with the addition of three tracks previously issued as singles.

● Magical Mystery Tour (Film)

The Beatles' television film was conceived before Brian Epstein's death, discussed with him and became the group's first solo venture after Brian died.

The concept was Paul McCartney's and he had planned the venture on 11 April 1967 on a flight back to England from the US where he'd been visiting **Jane Asher** during her theatre tour. While there he'd been reading about the adventures of Ken Kesey (author of *One Flew Over the Cuckoo's Nest*) and his Merry Pranksters who had been travelling cross-country in a bus.

Paul's idea was for the Beatles to produce their own television spectacular, writing and producing it themselves, using the knowledge they had gleaned from **Dick Lester** and **Walter Shenson** while making their first two feature films. The Beatles reckoned that if *Magical Mystery Tour* proved a success on television, they would go on to produce their third feature film themselves. Press officer **Tony Barrow** has said that Paul was originally hoping that *Magical Mystery Tour* would be suitable for cinema release and was disappointed to be told that this was out of the question.

Magical Mystery Tour is now a popular video.

The hour-long special featured six numbers: 'Magical Mystery Tour', 'Your Mother Should Know', 'I Am The Walrus', 'Fool On The Hill', 'Flying', and 'Blue Jay Way'. Two other songs they wrote for the project were never recorded – 'Jessie's Dream' and 'Shirley's Wild Accordion'.

The idea was a surrealistic mystery trip in a gaily painted yellow and blue coach. The coach left London on 11 September 1967 and filming of the actual trip was completed on 15 September. Paul McCartney met up with the various *Mystery Tour* passengers at Allsop Place, near the London Planetarium. They picked up John, Ringo and

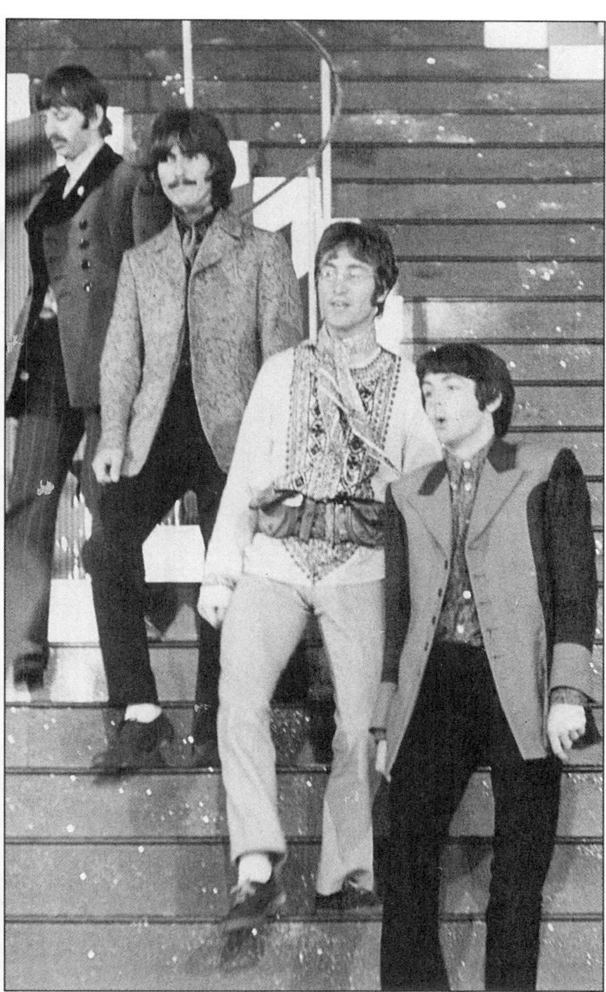

The Beatles in a scene from their television special – *Magical Mystery Tour.* (National Film Archives)

George at Virginia Water, which was close to Weybridge, where two of them lived at the time.

In all, there were 43 passengers. Apart from the Beatles and film crew (Ringo was billed as Director of Photography), they included four fan club secretaries, **Freda Kelly**, Barbara King, Sylvia Nightingale and Jeni Crowley; **Neil Aspinall** and **Mal Evans**; a small party of dwarfs; Luke Kelly; coach driver Alf Manders; Bill Wall; Linda Lawson; Pamela and Nicola Hale; Elizabeth and **Arthur Kelly**, Liz Harvey and Michael Gladden. There were also a number of actors and actresses for whom basic parts had been outlined on which they could improvise. They included Scottish actor/poet Ivor Cutler who portrayed Buster Bloodvessel, a passenger who travelled on all the mystery tours and who developed a passion for Ringo's Aunt Jessie, played by Jessie Robins; 'Rubber man' Nat Jackley, a music hall veteran who was filmed by John Lennon at the Atlantic Hotel joined by several swimsuited girls from around the hotel pool; Little George Claydon, a tiny actor who played the Amateur Photographer; Maggie Wright as Maggie the Lovely Starlet, Paul's mini-skirted girlfriend; Shirley Evans, a professional accordionist; Derek Royce as Jolly Jimmy Johnson, the Tour Courier; and Mandy Weet as the Tour Hostess. There were various other friends such as Paul's hairdresser Leslie Cavendish, Paul's brother **Mike** McGear and the Apple electronics wizard **Alexis Mardas**.

Travelling through Devon and Cornwall, they picked up a few extra passengers, such as Spencer Davis (leader of the Spencer Davis Group) with his wife Pauline and their children; the family had been holidaying near Newquay.

Most of the interior scenes had to be filmed at West Malling RAF Station, near Maidstone, Kent, as **Apple Films** were unable to book Shepperton Studios in time. One of the scenes had already been completed prior to the coach journey. This was the sequence in Paul Raymond's Revue Bar in Soho that featured the **Bonzo Dog Doo Dah Band** and stripper Jan Carson. Another scene was filmed after the coach trip, in Nice in November. This was the sequence where Paul sang 'Fool On The Hill'. He encountered difficulties when he flew to France, having forgotten not only his passport, but his wallet too. The French authorities wouldn't allow Paul any credit and filming was delayed while he arranged for money to be sent over from England.

During one sunny morning it was decided to take advantage of the good weather and Paul and Ringo took off to a nearby beach to film some scenes with one camera unit while John and George directed a scene in the hotel's swimming pool area. This was a comedy dream sequence featuring Nat Jackley. By all accounts this was a successful slapstick scene featuring girls in bikinis which, for some reason, was left out of the completed movie. The scene was included in the cartoon storybook of *Magical Mystery Tour* which accompanied the film's soundtrack album, as this was completed before filming took place.

The basic story concerns a coach trip that Ringo and

his Aunt Jessie have decided to take. They visit a tour office and are talked into going on the Mystery Tour by a young man (John Lennon) wearing a thick moustache. Meanwhile: 'Away in the sky, beyond the clouds, live four or five magicians. By casting wonderful spells they turn the Most Ordinary Coach Trip into a Magical Mystery Tour.' The magicians, of course, are played by the four Beatles and Mal Evans, dressed in long wizards' robes and pointed hats. We meet them several times during the course of the journey. The coach has started off to the tune of 'Magical Mystery Tour' and the second number we are treated to is 'Fool On The Hill'. At one point, Paul has a chat with five-year-old Nicola Hale, a touching scene which wasn't planned or rehearsed.

Many of the episodic scenes during the trip were surrealistic, the most visually intriguing being the one set in front of the high, concrete walls of the deserted West Malling Aerodrome (the walls were finally demolished in 1991). There, 'I Am The Walrus' was filmed, with the Beatles in their animal masks and with egg-headed spectators and swaying policemen on top of the wall. The Marathon Race was held on the same set, with Ringo driving the coach followed by a line of egg-heads, four midget wrestlers, racing motor cyclists, a rugby team, a dozen children, five clergymen and a host of passengers scrambling across the airfield.

For 'Blue Jay Way', the slightly mystical George Harrison song, a host of people find their way inside a tiny tent to watch George perform the number seated amid swirling smoke clouds. In another scene, Paul plays Major McCartney, with Victor Spinetti as the Recruiting Sergeant. Victor couldn't take up the invitation of accompanying the Beatles on the trip, but took time off from the film he was making to act out this scene, which is a variation on his *Oh, What A Lovely War* role.

One of the strongest sequences is Aunt Jessie's Nightmare, in which the overweight Jessie dreams of lashings of spaghetti while a greasy-haired waiter (John Lennon) heaps pasta on to her table by the spadeful.

In the climactic scene, to the tune of 'Your Mother Should Know', the **Fab Four** descend a grandiose staircase, dressed in white evening wear, to join a spectacular gathering of dancing couples and saluting girl cadets. Two hundred people were involved in this final scene.

The Beatles spent six weeks editing the film in a small office in Old Compton Street, Soho, London, and the 60-minute film was colourful, funny, mystical and musical. Unfortunately, it received almost universal condemnation from the critics after its initial screening in black and white on BBC 2 on Boxing Day, 1967, when it was watched by a reported viewing audience of between thirteen and fifteen million people. Negotiations had been taking place with CBS, NBC and ABC in America to buy the film for Stateside screening for $1 million (it cost $100,000 to make), but following the harsh criticism in the British press, the US TV networks lost interest.

The show was repeated on BBC 2 on 5 January 1968 in full colour. In the meantime, Paul had appeared on TV and radio shows in an attempt to reply to the hostile reaction from the critics. In 1968 *Magical Mystery Tour* was screened by Dutch television on 10 February and sold to Japanese TV in April. In May it was shown at special screenings at selected cinemas in America, mainly in Los Angeles and San Francisco. A few months later it was premiered at the Savoy Theatre, Boston, where it received positive reviews.

In the years since it was first screened, *Magical Mystery Tour* has been reappraised. Many have now agreed that the virulent criticism at the time of its initial screening was unjust and perhaps biased, affording critics their first opportunity of knocking the Beatles, who had been riding high for so many years.

● Magical Mystery Tour (Single)

The title song Paul wrote for his 'Magical Mystery Tour' concept. He also wanted to convey the sensation of excitement and jollity amid the car and coach noises as the trip got underway and another sound effects album from the **Abbey Road** archives was used, *Volume 36 Traffic Noise Stereo,* when the recording began on Tuesday 25 April 1967. Later, four trumpeters were hired to overdub a brass section: Roy Copestake, Elgar Howarth, David Mason and John Wilbraham.

The song was featured on the British double EP set of *Magical Mystery Tour*, the American album of the same name and also a British album of that title issued in 1976. The track was also featured on the *Reel Music* compilation.

● Magnus, David

Originally **Dezo Hoffmann**'s studio assistant. David became a popular photographer in his own right and he ɔok the last shots of the Beatles and Brian Epstein •gether in 1967, a shot in which they were blowing ·umpets.

Maguire, Mary

Liverpool girl who was like a sister to Richie (Ringo tarr) Starkey when he was growing up in the Dingle area f Liverpool. Mary, who was four years older than him, sed to look after the young child while his mother Elsie as working.

Maharishi Mahesh Yogi, The

or a brief time he was the Beatles' spiritual adviser.

Born Mahesh Prasad Varma in 1918, he graduated from ıe University of Allahabad with a physics degree and ıen spent thirteen years studying Sanscrit and the criptures under Guru Dev. He adopted the name Iaharishi, which means 'the great soul', and devised a ay of making an ancient form of meditation more alatable and marketable for the West in the shape of ranscendental Meditation. In 1959 he arrived in London establish the International Meditation Society. By 1967 ıe movement boasted 10,000 British members and was so known as the Spiritual Regeneration Movement. This as the year in which **Pattie** Harrison first came across ıe movement when she attended a lecture on Spiritual egeneration in February 1967 at **Caxton Hall**.

Pattie had plenty of time on her hands while George as involved in Beatle activities and she became intrigued ith the mysticism of India as presented by the Maharishi. is methods of meditation had been developed in India ıousands of years previously. What he did was re-ackage the goods, stamp them with a brand name, ranscendental Meditation, and sell them for consumption the West. The Maharishi believed that by popularizing M he could help bring peace to the world due to the fact ıat the meditation technique inhibits violence and calms e spirit.

Pattie interested George and the other members of the eatles in the movement and when notices began to ɔpear on the advertisement hoardings of London nderground mentioning a personal appearance by the aharishi at the Park Lane **Hilton**, all four Beatles ecided to attend. The event took place on Thursday 24 ugust 1967 and entrance was seven shillings and xpence (37½p) per head. His talk impressed the Beatles who requested a private audience with him following the lecture. When they spoke to him he invited them to join him at a ten-day course on TM at the University College, Bangor, which was to begin that weekend. They all agreed to go and they even asked Brian Epstein. Brian told them that he had made other plans for that weekend, but that he'd try to join them in Bangor at a later date. It was during the course that they learned of their manager's death.

They turned to the Maharishi as their guru and agreed to spend three months at his ashram in Rishikesh in India. Ringo and **Maureen** stood it for ten days before returning to England, Paul and **Jane Asher** left after ten weeks – and the loyal John and George then had a bust-up with the spiritual leader.

This began when John invited **Alexis** 'Magic Alex' **Mardas** to the ashram. Alex had a knowledge of spirituality and mysticism and firmly believed that the Beatles were under the spell of a clever man who was attempting to manipulate them. Alex could not accept a spiritual leader who, in his opinion, was so obsessed with material things. The Maharishi had come to be known as the 'Giggling Guru', because of his habit of giggling. He seemed to act as if he didn't understand business affairs, and always had an accountant present at his meetings. When travelling he stayed at the best hotels and his quarters in Rishikesh were luxurious by Indian standards. Although he said, 'I deal in wisdom, not money' money was still a consideration, as **Neil Aspinall** and **Peter Brown** discovered when they tried to negotiate for a film to be made of the Maharishi and the Beatles at Rishikesh; the Maharishi haggled for a larger percentage of the film's potential proceeds.

The Maharishi was aware of Alex's suspicions and attempted to coerce him by offering him the commission of building a radio station at Rishikesh. Alex was more interested in proving to the Beatles that the holy man was using them. His opportunity came when a young nurse from California alleged that the Maharishi had made sexual advances to her.

As a result, both John and George confronted the Maharishi and left the ashram.

John, in particular, was furious at his idol. TM had benefited him greatly. It had broken his drug addiction and opened his creative juices – resulting in a large number of songs being written in Rishikesh. The angry

John wrote a number called 'Maharishi', in which he intended to expose the holy man, but was persuaded into changing the title to 'Sexy Sadie' so as to avoid any possible legal suits.

The Beatles had obviously had too high aspirations regarding the abilities of the Maharishi. Neil Aspinall commented: 'John thought there was some sort of secret the Maharishi had to give you, and then you could just go home.' Paul said, 'We made a mistake. We thought there was more to him than there was. He's human. We thought at first that he wasn't.'

Despite the fact that the Beatles' association with him had been brief, the Maharishi's cause had blossomed with the international publicity. The money poured in as the converts grew and the Maharishi immediately began to buy property. In England alone he bought Mentmore Towers in Buckinghamshire, Roydon Hall in Maidstone, Swythamley Park in the Peak District and a Georgian rectory in Suffolk. He set up his headquarters in Switzerland and at one time he was reported to have an income of six million pounds per month, with two million followers worldwide, 90,000 of them in Britain.

● Mahon, Gene

Dublin-born graphic designer who was working for an advertising agency in London when he became involved in the design of the sleeve for the *Sgt Pepper's Lonely Hearts Club Band* album. He was art director of the back sleeve which featured the photograph of the Beatles with Paul turning his back to the camera, over which were printed the lyrics to the songs. While working on the assignment, Gene first came into contact with **Neil Aspinall** and in February 1968 it was Neil who phoned him and invited him over to the Apple offices in Wigmore Street to discuss a commission. Neil told him that he needed a photograph of an Apple to be used as an image for the Apple label. Gene said the inspiration came to him in a flash. He suggested that on the 'A' side they feature a complete apple with no writing on it whatsoever and on the 'B' side the picture of an apple sliced in half with the label copy on it. He suggested that to avoid confusion they should have 'This Side' written on the left-hand side of the sliced apple, with the song title, artist's name, running time, publishing credits and so on while on the other side would be the words 'Other Side' with the title and the copy for the 'A' side.

Unfortunately, this idea couldn't be used because of th legal requirements which obliged a record company t place details of the contents on both sides of a disc.

Gene had photographer Paul Castell take a number o photographs of apples, both red and green, sliced an unsliced, against a variety of coloured backgrounds. Th different two-and-a-quarter-inch transparencies wer shown to the four Beatles, Neil and **Ron Kass** at variou stages of development.

The design finally chosen was that of a green Grann Smith apple on a black background. Some final touche were added by Alan Aldridge on the actual lettering on th design.

From the initial commission to the final approval of th design, the project had taken six months to complete.

Mahon was also commissioned to work on other Appl record design projects.

● Mailman Blues

Another Lloyd Price composition which was included i the **Quarry Men**'s repertoire, along with 'Lawdy Mis Clawdy'. 'Mailman Blues' had been recorded in 1954 before the charts came into being. It was a popular numbe with other Liverpool bands such as **Rory Storm & th Hurricanes**.

● Majestic Ballroom, *Conway Street, Birkenhead L41*

When the Majestic Ballroom opened in 1962 it was 'luxury venue' compared to some of the cellar clubs an local halls the Mersey groups had been appearing in. was one of 28 ballrooms around Britain run by the To Rank organization.

When the Beatles made their debut there on Thursda 28 June 1962, it was their first ever appearance at a To Rank venue. The Majestic rapidly became one of the to Merseyside venues, open throughout the week an presenting several groups each evening – for instance, th Saturday, 15 December 1962, bill comprised the Beatle the **Fourmost** and Jenny & the Tall Boys.

The venue was managed by Bill Marsden and his offic became a meeting place for various members of th Mersey scene who would gather in Bill's office for a drin to chat about the business. Regulars at these meeting were Brian Epstein, **Bob Wooler**, Bill and Virgini Harry, **Joe Flannery** and Ted Knibbs. During one of th

TOP RANK

THE TOPS IN ENTERTAINMENT WISH EVERY CONTINUED SUCCESS TO THE TOP PROVINCIAL ENTERTAINMENTS PAPER

JIVE TO THE BEST
MERSEYSIDES ROCK GROUPS
7-30 p.m. EVERY
SUNDAY & MONDAY
Groups to be presented include
Gerry and The Pacemakers
Group One
Faron and The Flamingoes
Clay Ellis and The Raiders

★

DON'T FORGET WE PRESENT
THE BEATLES
ON THURSDAY NIGHTS

★

Top Rank Dancing
MAJESTIC BALLROOM
Conway Street, Birkenhead

Manager Bill Marsden says:
We at the Top Rank
MAJESTIC
BALLROOM CONWAY ST.
BIRKENHEAD (Tel. 6320)
Are proud to be associated with MERSEY BEAT in connection with our
FABULOUS
SATURDAY NIGHT
"MERSEY BEAT BALLS"
Variety with a Beat
STARRING
The Bluegenes
Billy Kramer
with The Coasters
Lee Curtiss
with The All Stars
The Spidermen
YOUR SATURDAY NIGHT OUT
7-30 to 11-30 p.m.

evenings Flannery tried a joke by putting in a call to the office and claiming it was Colonel Tom Parker trying to contact Brian Epstein.

The Beatles' complete appearances for 1962 were: 28 June, 5 July, 12 July, 28 July, 17 August, 24 August, 8 September, 22 September, 15 October, 22 November, 29 November, 15 December. The 1963 appearances were: 17 January, 31 January, 21 February and 10 April.

On their 17 August 1962 appearance their drummer was **Johnny Hutchinson**. Following their 15 December 1962 show there was a special ***Mersey Beat*** Awards party at which the Beatles were presented with their first-ever award by Bill Harry: the *Mersey Beat* Shield for being voted No. 1 group in *Mersey Beat*.

For their 17 January 1963 appearance all tickets had been sold out in advance and 500 angry fans queuing outside were unable to see the show as the hall only had a 900 capacity. As a result, for the next Beatles appearance, there was an innovation: two separate performances. Although it was common to have two performances at a theatre concert, it had never been done before in a ballroom.

The new shows took place at 8.00 p.m. and 11.00 p.m. to capacity audiences. The two performances on the 21 February 1963 appearances took place at 7.30 p.m. and 11.50 p.m.

In 1964 a new manager, John Glass, took over the running of the ballroom and he received a telegram from the Beatles for the second anniversary which congratulated the Majestic on 'its bi-centenary or something'.

● Majestic Ballroom, High Street, Crewe, Cheshire

The Beatles appeared at this Top Rank ballroom on two consecutive Monday nights in 1962, on 13 and 20 August.

A story in ***Mersey Beat*** newspaper headed 'All Change At Crewe' (referring to the fact that the Cheshire town contains one of Britain's main railway junctions) read: 'The Merseyside rock and roll scene has spread its wings to Crewe, due to the co-operation of two Top Rank managers, namely Bill Marsden of the Majestic Ballroom, Birkenhead, and Ron Ratty, his counterpart at the Majestic, Crewe.

'Bill, who has become well acquainted with Merseyside's top attractions, now books these groups for Crewe. The Beatles, **Lee Curtis** with the All Stars, **Billy Kramer** with the Coasters, the **Big Three** and Group One have all appeared at this exciting venue recently, and have been well received and enthusiastically welcomed by Crewe teenagers.'

For its rock 'n' roll nights, the ballroom used the slogan: 'The biggest rock since Blackpool rock!'

● Majestic Ballroom, Witham, Hull, Humberside

The Majestics were a group of ballrooms in various British cities, owned by Top Rank. After the Beatles had proved successful at the **Majestic Ballroom, Birkenhead**, this led to other bookings on the circuit. They appeared here on 20 October 1962 and performed at the ballroom for the second and last time on 13 February 1963.

● Majestic Ballroom, *Seven Sisters Road, London N7*

One of the largest venues in the Top Rank Majestic Ballroom chain. The Beatles appeared at the ballroom once, on 24 April 1963, headlining a ***Mersey Beat Showcase*** with **Gerry & the Pacemakers**, the **Big Three** and **Billy J. Kramer**. The occasion drew an audience of 2,000.

● Majestic Ballroom, *Mill Street, Luton, Bedfordshire*

Another in the Top Rank chain of ballrooms. The Beatles appeared at this venue only once, on 17 April 1963.

● Majestic Ballroom, *Westgate Road, Newcastle-upon-Tyne, Tyne & Wear*

The Beatles first appeared at this Top Rank ballroom on 28 January 1963. Their second and final appearance at the venue on 26 June 1963 was their last-ever appearance at a Top Rank Ballroom. After they'd finished the gig, back at their hotel, John and Paul composed 'She Loves You'.

● Majestic Theatre, *Christchurch, New Zealand*

The Beatles appeared at this theatre on the South Island on the final date of their brief tour of New Zealand, on 27 June 1964.

There were various incidents when the Beatles landed at Christchurch – at one point a thirteen-year-old girl threw herself on the Beatles' car and bounced into the road. Fortunately, she wasn't hurt and they took her into their hotel to have a cup of tea with them. When they went onto the balcony of their hotel to wave at the crowds they had to retreat when rotten eggs were hurled at them.

● Maltz, *Stephen*

An accountant from the firm of **Bryce Hanmer** whom the company placed as Staff Accountant at Apple. Maltz was appointed a member of the Board of Directors at Apple, but became increasingly disenchanted at what he considered the mismanagement and profligacy of the company. Finally, in November 1968 he tendered his resignation after warning the Beatles that their finances were in disarray and that they would encounter major problems unless something was done. He sent each member of the Beatles a letter: 'After six years' work, for the most part of which you have given pleasure to countless millions throughout every country where records are played, what have you got to show for it? . . . Your personal finances are a mess. Apple is a mess.'

The Beatles decided that they needed someone to manage their affairs properly and approached Lord Beeching, who had recently pruned British Rail to reduce its huge losses. He suggested they stick to making records, which they knew something about. The group approached other leading businessmen, including Lord Poole, chairman of Lazard's Bank. He offered to take the task on for nothing, but they never bothered to call him back or take advantage of the offer – an apathetic attitude which was possibly a reflection of what was wrong with Apple. Other businessmen such as Lord Goodman and Cecil King were considered and even Ronan O'Rahilly, the man who had launched the first British pirate radio station Radio Caroline – although talks broke down after Caleb, the Apple astrologer, told the Beatles that O'Rahilly didn't have the right 'vibes'.

Paul eventually decided on **Lee Eastman** and the other members of the Beatles turned to **Allen Klein**.

● Maney Hall, *Sutton Coldfield, West Midlands*

The Beatles only appeared once at this venue, on 1 February 1963. The same evening they also appeared at the **Assembly Rooms**, **Tamworth**, which was only eight miles away.

● Manila, *The Philippines*

Capital of the Philippines. The Beatles were due to perform their concerts at the Rizal Memorial Football Stadium, promoted by Cavalcade International, in July 1966.

When the Beatles arrived in the Philippines they found themselves attending a press conference three hours later at the Philippine Navy Headquarters. The site had been chosen by the promoter because it was near to a harbour where he had hired a luxury yacht for the Beatles to live on during their stay. However, Brian Epstein didn't like the yacht and insisted that they be moved into the Manila Hotel.

The promoter, Ramon Ramos, provided an itinerary in

which it was mentioned that prior to their arrival at the stadium at 4.00 p.m. they were to: 'Proceed to the Palace at 3.00 p.m. to call on the First Lady and from the Palace proceed to the stadium.' However, the itinerary stressed that the visit was dependent on 'approval of the Beatles and party'. Since the Beatles wanted to be at the stadium two hours before the show began, this wasn't practical, although the importance of the visit to the Palace wasn't stressed. Ramos, caught between the wishes of the Marcoses and those of the Beatles, decided to do nothing about it, neither telling the Palace that the Beatles couldn't make the appointment nor informing the Beatles that he hadn't let the Palace know they couldn't attend. A further complication was that although Ramos had mentioned a 3.00 p.m. meeting in the itinerary, the Palace had arranged the event for 11.00 a.m.

On 3 July, the *Manila Sunday Times* reported, 'President Marcos, the First Lady, and the three young Beatles fans in the family, have been invited as guests of honour at the concerts. The Beatles plan to personally follow up the invitation during a courtesy call on Mrs Imelda Marcos at Malacanana Palace tomorrow morning at 11 o'clock.'

At 11.00 a.m. the next morning representatives from the Palace arrived at the hotel to collect the Beatles. They were still asleep and Epstein refused to have them woken up. That afternoon they went to the stadium and performed a half-hour show before 30,000 people. At 6.30 p.m. they were back at their hotel. At 6.45 p.m. there was a television announcement that the Beatles had snubbed Mrs Imelda Marcos and Ferdinand Marcos, plus 200 children who had gathered for the meeting. 'The children began to arrive at ten,' said the commentator. 'They waited until after two. At first we were told that a mob at the yacht basin was delaying the scheduled arrival of the Beatles, but then we learned that the group was not even aboard. At noon the First Lady decided properly and wisely not to wait any longer. 'The children have all the time in the world, but we are busy people,' she said. Lunch had been planned for the President's family and the Beatles, but the place cards were removed when the group failed to show.'

Beatles PR man **Tony Barrow** watched the announcement with horror and then called the news director of the TV station, Channel Five, and said there had been a mistake and asked them to arrange for Brian Epstein to explain the situation on the channel. A statement was drafted, which read: 'It goes without saying that we did not receive any sort of invitation. No enquiry was received by me or my staff travelling with the Beatles as to whether we could approve any afternoon visit to the Palace before the first concert. The first we knew of the two hundred waiting children was on television tonight.'

The statement was read out on television, but there was deliberate interference in the transmission and the sound quality was so bad that it was almost unintelligible. Immediately the statement was finished, the static mysteriously disappeared. Tony Barrow was to comment, 'His [Brian's] voice was not dubbed out but intentionally scrambled.'

The Beatles' second show had taken place that evening, 4 July, at 8.30 p.m. before 50,000 fans. Other acts on the bill were the Reycard Duet, the Wing Duet, the Lemons Three, Eddie Rayes & the Downbeats, Dale Adriatico and Pilita Corrales with music by Carding Cruz and his Orchestra.

Promoter Ramos refused to pay the Beatles their share of the gate receipts at the time and when newspaper reports claimed that the Beatles would be held and refused permission to leave until a tax bill had been settled, the Beatles' representatives pointed this out and also explained that their contract with the promoter clearly stated that Ramos, not the Beatles, would be responsible for any tax payments. However, Misael Vera, a commissioner with the tax office, insisted that tax must be paid by the Beatles. Brian Epstein eventually decided that it would be simpler to just pay the money and arranged that the Beatles' fee, minus the tax, be sent directly to him in London by the promoter.

A hate campaign against the Beatles was growing and there were telephone death threats to the Manila Hotel and the British Embassy. All the security guards protecting the Beatles were removed and the group and their party were intimidated and jostled as they made their way to Manila International Airport. However, the reports in the *Manila Times* were exaggerated, particularly a paragraph which read: 'Drummer Ringo Starr was floored by an uppercut. As he crawled away the mob kicked him. George Harrison and John Lennon received kicks and blows as they ran to the customs zone. Paul McCartney was relatively unhurt as he sprinted ahead. Manager Brian Epstein received the brunt of the mob's ire. He was kicked and thrown to the floor. As a result he suffered a sprained ankle and had to be helped to the customs area.' The Beatles, although harassed, were protected by their entourage and weren't physically assaulted. Brian Epstein was punched in the face and kicked. **Mal Evans** was kicked several times and knocked to the floor and **Alf Bicknell**, the group's chauffeur, received injuries which resulted in a damaged spine and fractured rib.

They had to suffer a barrage of heckling and booing, with cries of '*Beatles Alis Diyan!*' (Beatles Go Home!). Guillermo Jurado, the airport manager, ordered all the escalators to be shut down, forcing the Beatles to carry their luggage up several flights of stairs with a baying mob of 200 Filipinos at their heels.

The party eventually boarded a KLM flight to New Delhi, but shortly before take-off Tony Barrow and Mal Evans were asked to return to the terminal where they were told that there had been no record of their arrival two days previously and therefore they were illegal immigrants and wouldn't be able to leave. It was a bureaucratic mess deliberately concocted to intimidate the Beatles still further. Eventually, after almost 50 minutes, they were finally allowed to return to the plane and departed.

Brian Epstein was violently sick and was attended by a doctor for the following four days, once they had arrived in Delhi, and the Beatles were so angry at what they regarded as a bad cock-up that they discussed the subject of touring in general and the fact that they were expected to embark on another world tour the following year, and came to the decision that they would stop touring completely after the next American tour.

● Mankowitz, Wolf

A playwright and screenwriter whose *A Kid For Two Farthings* had proved a successful film vehicle for Diana Dors. In April 1965 Mankowitz asked John Lennon and Paul McCartney to collaborate with him on a Broadway musical. They thanked him for the compliment but said they had to turn the offer down due to pressure of work.

● Mann, William

As music critic of *The Times* newspaper in London, on 27 December 1963 Mann wrote an in-depth article analysing the Beatles' music entitled 'What Songs The Beatles Sang', which was a prestigious feature which did much to enhance the Beatles' reputation as serious musicians. In describing their song 'Not A Second Time' from the *With The Beatles* album, he wrote: 'But harmonic interest is typical of their quicker songs too, and one gets the impression that they think simultaneously of harmony and melody, so firmly are the major tonic sevenths and ninths built into their tunes, and the flat submediant key switches, so natural in the Aeolian cadence at the end of "Not A Second Time" (the chord progression which ends Mahler's "Song Of The Earth").'

He also wrote a major analysis of *Sgt Pepper's Lonely Hearts Club Band* in an article entitled 'The Beatles Revive Hope Of Progress In Pop Music', published in *The Times* on 29 May 1967.

Pneumatic Jayne Mansfield, as she appeared in one of the Beatles' favourite films, *The Girl Can't Help It.* (National Film Archives)

He died at the age of 65 on 5 September 1989.

● Mansfield, Jayne

Pneumatic blonde, promoted by Hollywood as a rival to Marilyn Monroe and most famous among rock 'n' roll fans for her performance in *The Girl Can't Help It*.

May Mann, in her biography *Jayne Mansfield*, claimed that on the Beatles' first American tour John Lennon mentioned that the one film star he wanted to see was Jayne Mansfield. A rendezvous between the star and the group took place at the Whiskey A Go Go on Sunset Strip. Mann further claimed that John was annoyed when Jayne brought her husband along, commenting: 'I just wanted to be alone with Jayne. I've dreamed about it.'

Other sources suggest that it was Paul, not John, who made the original request, although Paul was the one member of the group who declined to attend the Whiskey rendezvous. The group had rented a house near Hollywood when the invitation to meet Jayne Mansfield came. They'd originally preferred a private meeting and didn't want to turn it into a publicity circus. John, George and Ringo agreed to go only if the meeting was kept secret from the press, which is what Mansfield's people promised. It was a promise that wasn't kept. When the three Beatles arrived, the club was swarming with hordes of fans and crammed with press reporters and photographers. They sat with Mansfield, but were continually hounded by the press. George threw a drink at one cameraman and an ice cube hit Mamie van Doren, another blonde bombshell actress.

A picture of George throwing the glass appeared in the papers the next day.

On another occasion, when the Beatles were staying in the Hollywood suburb of Bel Air in a private house on 25 August 1964, it was Jayne, dressed in a mauve catsuit, who dropped in to see them. John was the only member of the group present as Paul, Ringo and George had gone to **Burt Lancaster**'s house for a screening of the **Peter Sellers** film *A Shot In The Dark*.

Jayne tugged John's hair and squealed, 'Is this real?' to which John replied, dropping his eyes to her most famous features, 'Well, are those real?'

Other visitors who dropped in to see John that day were Bobby Darin and Sandra Dee.

● Manson, Charles

The leader of a bizarre cult whose members believed him to be some sort of satanic messiah. Like a Svengali he seemed to hold his 'family' in a mesmeric power.

Manson was obsessed by the Beatles' music and was convinced that their records contained mystical messages which he could interpret. He was certain that the Beatles were the four angels mentioned in the 'Book of Revelations'.

If *Sgt Pepper's Lonely Hearts Club Band* excited him, *The Beatles* white album sent him into paroxysms of delight because he felt he could translate the secret messages on that particular double album. 'Blackbird', 'Piggies', 'Happiness Is A Warm Gun' and 'Helter Skelter' were among the numbers which led him to believe that the Beatles had predicted a violent confrontation between the races, leading to a civil war in America.

He decided to provide the spark for the coming revolution and sent some of his crazed followers into Beverly Hills where they committed a number of grisly murders, leaving words from Beatles numbers scrawled in blood on the walls.

Manson is currently serving a life sentence.

● Maple Leaf Gardens, Toronto, Canada

The Beatles first appeared at this venue on Monday, 7 September 1964. There were over 10,000 fans awaiting their arrival at Toronto International and the group were whisked away to the King Edward Hotel, also besieged by fans. In fact, when the group arrived in their three-room suite they discovered a fourteen-year-old girl hiding in the linen closet.

The group appeared on two shows at the arena that night, drawing a total of 35,522 people, breaking the attendance record, held since 1946, for a Toronto–Montreal hockey match.

Disc jockey/compere Jungle Jay Nelson introduced the first act, the **Bill Black Combo**, who were followed by the Exciters and Clarence 'Frogman' Henry. The Bill Black Combo returned to play one song, then were joined by singer **Jackie DeShannon**, who sang five numbers. The Beatles appeared on stage at 5.30 p.m.

Between shows there was a press conference and the Beatles were introduced to the Mayor; Michele Finney – who was also Miss Canada and the President of the Beatles Fan Club of Canada. Officials from the Canadian branch of **Capitol Records** presented them with a Gold Disc.

The Beatles left the arena after their second show at 10.30 p.m.

The event had gone smoothly, much to the relief of the Montreal police who, earlier that day, had received a death threat against Ringo.

They returned to Maple Leaf Gardens the following year for two performances on 17 August 1965. The arena's full capacity was for 18,000 people and for the first time it was completely full at both houses.

When the Beatles returned the following year on 17 August 1966, they once again performed two shows. There was an audience of 15,000 at the afternoon show and 17,000 at the evening show.

● Mardas, John Alexis

When John Alexis Mardas first entered Britain on a student visa he was 21 years old, the son of a Greek military officer, said to be a member of the secret police for the junta who had recently come into power in Greece. He initially found work as a telephone repairman in Olympic Television before approaching John Dunbar of the **Indica Gallery**. He created some kinetic light sculptures and suggested that Dunbar become his agent. As a result the **Rolling Stones** bought a psychedelic light box he made and included it in their act. Brian Jones then introduced him to John Lennon, who dubbed him 'Magic Alex'.

The Beatles, and Lennon in particular, were completely fascinated by his electronic gadgetry, including the four tiny brooches he gave to each Beatle which bleeped and flashed at random. He was to come up with a number of electronic gizmos and suggestions of what he could create, given the money, which included a paint which glowed when connected to an electric current. He told them, 'One day it will replace conventional electric light as we know it.' He also constructed a tiny radio receiver which picked up and broadcast records being played on a special record player in another room; made a novel electric apple which trembled with light and music; and claimed he was working on a telephone which would automatically dial a number when you told it who you wanted to call.

Some of his other ideas seemed fantastical – an invisible curtain of ultrasonic vibrations which would screen the Beatles from their fans and an artificial sun which would illuminate the night sky by laser beams.

Alexis had been in Britain for some time and when the Beatles created a new branch of Apple for him – **Apple Electronics** – they also had to sort out the legalities which would allow him to remain in Britain. He'd only had a limited student visa and claimed that his passport had been stolen from his luggage. His visa had long since expired, so John asked **Peter Brown** to arrange Alexis' legal immigration to Britain through a solicitor.

Lennon was very gullible as far as Alexis was concerned, although he enjoyed the company of the young man who was now dubbed in the press as 'the Merlin of the Beatles Camelot'. When the Beatles were at Rishikesh, John missed him and summoned him over. Alexis had some experience of the search for spirituality and was appalled by what he found at the **Maharishi**'s camp: 'An ashram with four-poster beds? Masseurs, and servants bringing water, houses with facilities, an accountant – I never saw a holy man with a bookkeeper!' In fact, Alex was completely disgusted with the situation and became alarmed when he heard that the Maharishi expected the Beatles to donate 10–15 per cent of their annual income to a Swiss account in the Maharishi's name. Alex confronted the guru and told him that he was exploiting the Beatles. He claimed that the Maharishi then tried to bribe him by offering to pay him to build a radio station in the ashram grounds. Although wine was forbidden, Alexis began to bring wine in for the women of the ashram and began to win their confidence. A blonde nurse from California told him that the Maharishi invited her to private dinners in his quarters where they had chicken for dinner and he made sexual advances to her.

Armed with this information, he sat arguing with John and George, attempting to convince them of what he'd discovered. Initially, George didn't believe Alexis and John was in doubt. Alexis gathered further proof, which resulted in John and George's confrontation with the Maharishi.

Alexis helped them in their bid to find a Greek island retreat and he travelled with various members of the Beatles. He shared a mews flat in central London with **Pattie Boyd**'s sister **Jennie**, although their relationship was said to be platonic. He joined George, Pattie, Jennie and **Neil Aspinall** on their trip to the West Coast of the US in 1967.

He also holidayed in Greece with **Cynthia,** Jennie, **Donovan** and his friend Gypsy Dave. On their return to England, Cynthia, Alexis and Jennie arrived at **Kenwood** where they discovered John and **Yoko** together. They all left and Cynthia was invited to stay at the mews flat in Victoria. That evening she sat up drinking wine through most of the night with Alexis and they crawled into bed together. Cynthia was later to say that he practised black magic and hypnotized her into doing it.

While John and Cynthia were estranged, Cynthia and her mother Lil went on holiday to Italy. Alexis was sent over by John to give her an ultimatum. Alexis told her that John would be accusing her of adultery and that he had agreed to be the co-respondent and testify on John's behalf. As a result she would lose Julian. The ploy didn't work.

On Thursday, 11 July 1968, Alexis was married to Eufrosyne Doxiades at the Greek Orthodox Church in

Moscow Road, London. The Beatles attended the ceremony.

In January 1969 the Beatles became unhappy with the lack of atmosphere at **Twickenham Studios** and decided to record at Apple in **Savile Row**. Alexis had promised them a 78-track recording studio and had been working on it for months. When they arrived, they found a disastrous situation. Most of the material was not invented by Alexis, but was made by German manufacturers – and was still in the packing cases. Far from there being 78 tracks available, there were none and no recording machines had been installed. In addition, the heating and ventilation units of the building were installed in a corner of the studio creating a continuous noise, wheezing and humming all the time. Alexis had even forgotten to install an intercom system between the studio and the control booth. The group had to appeal to George Martin who immediately sent down a number of engineers, together with a mobile recording unit.

Despite the fact that Alexis had not come up with any of the amazing inventions he'd promised them, but had merely provided some electronic toys, he remained in their favour. However, when **Allen Klein** arrived on the scene Alexis was soon to fade out of the picture.

● Marietta, Hotel, *Obertauern, Austria*

Site of the Beatles' only live performance in Austria on 18 March 1965.

The occasion was the birthday of **Dick Lester**'s assistant, Mr Read, and the film crew threw a party for them at the hotel. The festivities lasted through the night, during which the Beatles performed for two hours with a repertoire comprising their hit songs and some standards such as 'Summertime'.

One old lady initially complained of the noise, but was invited to join in the party – and did so!

● Marine Hall Ballroom, *The Esplanade, Fleetwood, Lancashire*

Another venue where the Beatles only ever appeared once. It was a Lancashire fishing port and the gig took place on 15 August 1962.

● Marmalade

A Scottish band who covered the 'Ob-La-Di, Ob-La-Da' track from *The Beatles* double album. Their version of the song was issued on 4 December 1968 on CBS 3891, it entered the charts on 21 December and reached the No. 1 position. They spent two weeks at the top and a total of thirteen weeks in the charts. The group's line-up at the time was, Dean Ford (vocals), Junior Campbell (lead guitar), Pat Fairlie (rhythm guitar) and Raymond Duffy (drums).

A group called the Bedrocks also covered the number, but only reached No. 17 in the charts with it.

● Marrion, Albert

Photographer engaged by Brian Epstein to take the first official photographs of the Beatles.

Marrion and his partner Herbert Hughes had established their photographic business which specialized in portrait and wedding photographs. Marrion had been the official Liverpool photographer covering the Blitz for the city and, with his partner, had a studio at 19 Smithdown Place, on the corner of Penny Lane, and another across the Mersey in Wallasey.

Marrion had taken photographs of **Clive Epstein**'s wedding and Brian approached him to set up a photographic session with the Beatles. Marrion asked his partner to take the photographs, but Hughes refused. Marrion then handled the session himself at the studio at 268 Wallasey Village, Wallasey, on Sunday, 17 December 1961. Most of the thirty photographs taken that day weren't suitable because John Lennon kept horsing around and sticking his tongue out. Sixteen shots were selected and the main photo provided the front cover shot for Issue 13 of ***Mersey Beat*** which proclaimed 'Beatles Top Poll!'

● Marsden, Beryl

A Liverpool singer, real name Beryl Hogg, who initially began performing with local groups at the age of fourteen. Beryl was generally regarded as the best female vocalist on the Mersey Beat scene and at one time John Lennon recommended that she be given the Lennon & McCartney number 'Love Of The Loved' to record, but was vetoed by Brian Epstein, who gave it to **Cilla Black**.

Beryl was initially managed by **Joe Flannery**, Epstein's friend/rival, and she appeared on several pop TV shows such as **'Thank Your Lucky Stars'** promoting her early record releases such as 'I Know (You Don't Love Me No More)', her debut disc, released when she was sixteen, and 'When The Love Light Shines'. At the age of seventeen she was appearing on stage at the **Star Club** in Hamburg.

She was booked to appear with the Beatles on their last concert tour of Britain from 3–12 December 1965. Perhaps for the sake of nostalgia, the Beatles also had other Liverpool acts on the tour such as the **Koobas** and **Steve Aldo**.

Beryl moved to London and became a member of Shotgun Express with Rod Stewart and Peter Bardens, and later made some solo records while being managed by **Tony Stratton-Smith**. She returned to Liverpool, married and became a housewife. She then returned to her career as a vocalist in Liverpool in the seventies in a group she formed with Paddy Chambers called Sinbad, and finally settled in London where she became a Buddhist.

Beryl Marsden – regarded as Liverpool's best female vocalist, she was to join the Beatles on their last British tour.

● Marsh, Tony

The compere selected to present both the **Chris Montez/Tommy Roe** and the **Roy Orbison** tours in 1963 in which the Beatles were also on the bill. Tony was a popular comedian and compere and was booked to introduce many of the touring pop music shows before he was banned by a controversial incident.

During the Orbison tour on 23 May at the **Odeon, Nottingham**, the Beatles crawled into the orchestra pit and began making rude signs to Marsh as he was on stage, trying to upset his act. They were aware that Marsh was a practical joker. During that tour he told Roy Orbison that, as an American, he would need a passport to enter Scotland – and a worried Orbison believed him!

It was while he was compering a **Rolling Stones** tour that he got drunk and stood at the side of the stage and dropped his pants to distract **Brian Jones**. A woman who had brought her daughter to the show noticed this and complained to the management. As a result Marsh was taken to court and banned from all major touring circuits.

● Martha My Dear

Track penned by Paul which was included on *The Beatles* white album. The number was recorded at **Trident Studios** and it seems that the double-tracked McCartney is the only Beatle to appear on the recording. George Martin arranged the backing by fourteen musicians. Bernard Miller, Dennis McConnell, Lou Sofier, Les Maddox on violins; Leo Birnbaum, Henry Myerscough on violas; Reginald Kilbey, Frederick Alexander on cellos; Leon Calvert, Stanley Reynolds, Ronnie Hughes on trumpets; Tony Tunstall on French horn; Ted Barker on trombone; and Alf Reece on tuba.

The title was inspired by Paul's Old English sheepdog Martha, although the actual song is not about her.

Martha was born in 1966 and died of old age in the summer of 1982.

● Martin, George

The Beatles' recording manager.

Martin was born in London in 1926 and at the age of seventeen joined the Fleet Air Arm. When he was 21 he entered the Guildhall School of Music for training as a classical musician and was tutored on the oboe by Margaret Asher, who had recently given birth to a daughter, **Jane**, who was to become an actress. In 1948 during his three-year course at the school, he married his girlfriend, a former Wren, Sheena, and the couple were to have two children, Bundy and Gregory. On leaving the Guildhall, George worked in the BBC Music Library and in 1950 received an offer of a job by Oscar Preuss, head of **EMI**'s Parlophone label, who was seeking an assistant scar's secretary was Judy Lockhart-Smith, who became eorge's secretary when Preuss retired in 1955. When eorge and Sheena were divorced, he was to marry Judy in ugust 1967 and they were also to have two children, icy and Giles.

When he was appointed head of Parlophone, Martin ntinued other duties, acting as A&R man and also oducing recording sessions. He attended a revue in otting Hill, performed by the duo Michael Flanders and onald Swann, called *At The Drop Of A Hat*. He recorded album of it, together with other Flanders and Swann oductions, and also recorded another revue *Beyond The inge*. The artists Martin recorded were off-beat and like the artists on the pop labels of EMI – such as olumbia and HMV. He had success with **Peter Sellers** th *The Best Of Sellers* and also the singles 'Goodness acious Me' and 'Bangers and Mash' with Sellers and phia Loren. He recorded classical, jazz and comedy cords and among the artists he recorded were Sir alcolm Sargent, Sir Adrian Boult, Peter Ustinov, the oons, Cleo Laine, the Temperance Seven, Stan Getz, **irley Bassey**, Bernard Cribbins and Matt Munro.

At the time Brian Epstein approached EMI through **on White** regarding the Beatles, Martin was on holiday. hite contacted EMI's other A&R men who turned the oup down, but he didn't bother to contact Martin. By a ance accident, Epstein was put in touch with **Sid oleman** of Ardmore & Beechwood, who arranged the tial interview between Epstein and Martin. Although he tially wasn't impressed by the numbers the Beatles had corded on the **Decca audition** acetates which Epstein ayed him, Martin detected a rough sound which he liked d set up a recording audition for 6 June 1962 at **Abbey oad**'s Studio Three. He then confirmed to Epstein that rlophone would sign the group. The contract, however, s a tough one, initially for one year in which he aranteed to record four titles in exchange for the Beatles ceiving one penny per double-sided record. The options uld continue each year for four years, increasing their alties at the rate of one farthing per year. As the years ssed, these percentages would be altered, but it meant at the Beatles received paltry payment for their ording efforts compared with artists who were to follow em onto the recording scene, such as the **Rolling ones** – another example of the Beatles being pioneers d establishing a breakthrough in royalties for other recording artists.

The initial release was 'Love Me Do', which reached No. 17 in the charts. Both Martin and Epstein were disappointed in EMI's efforts to promote the record, which resulted in EMI's publishing arm Ardmore & Beechwood losing the publishing account. Martin still wasn't convinced of the Beatles' own songwriting abilities and elected to record them performing 'How Do You Do It' as their next single, a number penned by **Mitch Murray** which publisher **Dick James** had submitted. The Beatles didn't want to record it, feeling they had better material of their own. When they played him a rearranged version of 'Please Please Me', Martin had to agree. George did, in fact, realize that the Beatles had an uncanny instinct for commercial recordings and although he was to aid and advise, he was later to refrain from imposing his point of view on them. He did try it once in Paris in January 1964 when he insisted they record in the German language. They didn't want to do it, but he forced them to, and he realized that they were right, they had no need to record in a foreign language and never did so again.

Because of Epstein's disappointment with Ardmore & Beechwood, Martin suggested that they do a deal with Dick James. As a result, James offered Martin a share of the Northern Songs company, but he refused to accept on ethical grounds.

'Please Please Me' proved to be a No. 1 record and their next 11 releases also went to No. 1. Strangely enough, the record which Martin considered the best single of all, 'Penny Lane' c/w 'Strawberry Fields Forever', only reached No. 2 – although the Beatles returned to the No. 1 spot with subsequent discs.

In the first stage of their recording career, which Martin called the first era of recording, John and Paul would play their numbers on acoustic guitars and George would make his suggestions. This was called a 'head arrangement'. This changed at the next stage of their career, which occurred with 'Yesterday'. This number was the first one which used orchestrations, the first record on which he scored music for them, the first time that instruments other than those used by the Beatles were included. With 'Yesterday' Martin began to have a greater influence on the Beatles' music. As their records grew more sophisticated, his input became more important. He felt that with their earlier recordings prior to 'Yesterday', virtually any A&R man could have tackled the sessions, but in this new stage, his input had a valuable contribution to make to the increasingly complex productions.

Brian Epstein had placed some of his other artists, including **Cilla Black**, **Gerry & The Pacemakers** and **Billy J. Kramer**, with Martin and on 14 June 1963 George became the first A&R man ever to have achieved the top three places in the record charts with 'I Like It' by Gerry & the Pacemakers at No. 1, 'Do You Want To Know A Secret?' by Billy J. Kramer & the Dakotas at No. 2 and 'From Me To You' by the Beatles at No. 3. In fact, Martin had incredible chart success that year, with his productions being placed at No. 1 for 37 weeks. At the end of the year he didn't even receive a Christmas bonu[s]. When he asked why, he was told because he was on [a] salary of £3,000 per annum he was not entitled to a bonu[s]. When he discovered that the records he'd produced durin[g] 1963 had made a clear profit for EMI of £2,200,000 h[e] suggested that he should have some sort of bon[us] commission for the future, but EMI couldn't come [to] terms, so he left the company after fourteen years [to] launch AIR (Associated Independent Recording) wi[th] fellow EMI A&R men Ron Richards, John Burgess, Pet[er] Sullivan and their respective secretaries. In addition, mo[st] of the artists agreed to continue having their recor[ds]

George Martin, the Beatles' musical guru, with them during a March 1963 recording (EMI)

roduced by the new company. The artists included Adam 'aith, Manfred Mann, **Peter & Gordon**, the **Hollies**, **P. . Proby**, Billy J. Kramer, Cilla Black, the Beatles, Gerry & the Pacemakers and the **Fourmost.** A big loss for EMI who could have retained the loyal Martin for a modest alary increase or some commission. The artists remained with EMI, of course, but the independent producers now eceived a percentage commission on the recordings.

As George was now achieving recognition as the most uccessful A&R man in the world, offers poured in for him o use his expertise on orchestration for films – and he also ssued records in his own right with the George Martin rchestra. They included 'All My Loving' c/w 'I Saw Her tanding There', issued in Britain on Parlophone R 5135 n 8 May 1964; instrumental tracks on the album *A Hard ay's Night*; *Off The Beatle Track*, an album of Beatles umbers by Martin, using the title which was once onsidered for the Beatles' debut album – it was issued in ritain on 10 July 1964 on Parlophone PCS 3057 and in merica on United Artists UAS 6377 on 3 August 1964. he tracks were: 'All My Loving', 'Don't Bother Me', Can't Buy Me Love', 'All I've Got To Do', 'I Saw Her tanding There', 'She Loves You', 'From Me To You', here's A Place', 'This Boy', 'Please Please Me', 'Little hild', 'I Want To Hold Your Hand'. 'Ringo's Theme' c/w nd I Love Her' was issued in America on United Artists 43 on 31 July 1964 and in Britain on Parlophone R 5166 1 7 August 1964. 'I Should Have Known Better' c/w 'A ard Day's Night' was issued in America on United Artists 50 on 21 September 1964. A soundtrack release by nited Artists of *A Hard Day's Night* was issued in merica on UAS 6383 on 2 November 1964 which had strumental versions by Martin of 'I'll Cry Instead', ingo's Theme', 'If I Fell', 'I'm Happy Just To Dance ith You', 'A Hard Day's Night', 'I Should Have Known etter', 'I Want To Hold Your Hand', 'Can't Buy Me ve', 'She Loves You', 'And I Love Her', 'All My Loving', on't Bother Me' and 'Tell Me Why'. A British EP *Music om A Hard Day's Night* was issued in Britain on rlophone GEP 8930 on 19 February 1965 containing e tracks 'And I Love Her', 'Ringo's Theme', 'A Hard ay's Night' and 'If I Fell'. A single of 'I Feel Fine' c/w iagara Theme' was issued in Britain on Parlophone R 56 on 19 March 1965. An album *George Martin Scores strumental Versions Of The Hits* was issued in America 12 April 1965 on United Artists UAS 6420 and contained the tracks 'I Feel Fine', 'P.S. I Love You' and 'No Reply'. *Help!*, the original soundtrack album issued in America on Capitol SMAS 2386, contained instrumental tracks by Martin; they were: 'James Bond Theme', 'From Me To You Fantasy', 'In The Tyrol', 'Another Hard Day's Night', 'The Bitter End', 'You Can't Do That' and 'The Chase'. Another *Help!* soundtrack was issued in America on 6 September 1965 on United Artists UAS 6448 and in the UK on Columbia TWO 102 on 19 November 1965 and contained Martin's versions of 'Help!', 'Another Girl', 'You're Gonna Lose That Girl', 'I Need You', 'You've Got To Hide Your Love Away', 'The Night Before', 'Ticket To Ride', 'Bahama Sound', 'Auntie Jin's Theme', 'That's A Nice Hat', 'Tell Me What You See' and 'Scrambled Egg'. A single 'Yesterday' c/w 'Another Girl' was issued in Britain on Parlophone R 5375 on 12 November 1965. The next Martin album was *The Beatle Girls*, issued in America on United Artists UAS 6539 on 28 November 1966 and in Britain on United Artists SULP 1157 on 3 March 1967. It contained the tracks 'Girl', 'Eleanor Rigby', 'She Said She Said', 'I'm Only Sleeping', 'Anna', 'Michelle', 'Got To Get You Into My Life', 'Woman', 'Yellow Submarine', 'Here There And Everywhere', 'And Your Bird Can Sing', and 'Good Day Sunshine'. Martin had been brought in to help with the arrangement and conducting of the Paul McCartney compositions for the film ***The Family Way*** and a single was issued in Britain on United Artists UP 1165 on 23 December 1966 with the tracks 'Love In The Open Air' c/w 'Theme From The Family Way'. The track 'Love In The Open Air' was contained on the original soundtrack album of the film and a single was issued in America on United Artists UA 50148 on 24 April 1967 with the tracks 'Love In The Open Air' c/w 'Bahama Sound'. Martin contributed instrumental numbers to the original soundtrack album *Yellow Submarine* issued in America on 13 January 1969 on Apple SW 153 and in Britain on 17 January 1969 on Apple 7070. It contained the tracks 'Pepperland', 'Sea Of Time', 'Sea Of Holes', 'Sea Of Monsters', 'March Of The Meanies', 'Pepperland Laid Waste' and 'Yellow Submarine In Pepperland'. Martin's album *By George!* issued in Britain on Sunset SLS 50182 on 11 December 1970 included the tracks 'Sgt Pepper's Lonely Hearts Club Band' and 'I Am The Walrus'. Paul McCartney brought Martin into the James Bond *Live And Let Die* project and Martin was commissioned to score the soundtrack. It was issued in

America on 2 July 1973 on United Artists LA 100-G and in Britain on 6 July 1973 on United Artists UAS 29475.

One of the most creative periods of Martin's musical partnership with the Beatles came with the recording of *Sgt Pepper's Lonely Hearts Club Band* which had originally begun with the recording of 'Strawberry Fields Forever' which was left off the album and issued as a double 'A' side with 'Penny Lane'. In November 1976 Martin was approached by **Robert Stigwood** to compose the musical score for the film *Sgt Pepper's Lonely Hearts Club Band*. Initially he considered turning the offer down, but Judy pointed out to him that he'd never forgive himself if someone else did it and ruined it.

In December 1969 BBC Television began filming a documentary on Martin called 'A Little Help From My Friends'. Ringo made an appearance at a sequence filmed at London's Talk Of The Town club on 14 December and the programme was screened on 24 December.

In 1977 Martin was approached by Bhaskar Menon, president of **Capitol Records**, who asked him to listen to the tapes they had in their vaults of the recordings of the Beatles' **Hollywood Bowl** appearances in 1964 and 1965 which Martin had supervised. At the time they were not issued because the Beatles considered they were good enough. As so many technical advances had been made, Martin, with the aid of **Geoff Emerick**, worked on the tapes at AIR Studios, enhancing them for commercial release by transferring the three-track recording to multi-track tape and remixing and filtering until they had cleaned up the sound. They then edited together the best tracks from the two concerts and the album *The Beatles At The Hollywood Bowl* was issued in May 1977. In 1979, Martin's autobiography, written with Jeremy Hornsby, was published under the title *All You Need Is Ears*.

● Marylebone Magistrates Court, *181 Marylebone Road, London NW1*

On 18 October 1968 police raided Ringo Starr's **Montague Square** flat where John and **Yoko** were staying. They discovered some illegal substances and took the pair to Marylebone Police Station and charged them. John maintained that the drugs had been planted but decided to plead guilty in exchange for the charge against Yoko being dropped as she was pregnant at the time.

On 19 October the couple arrived at the Magistrates Court where a crowd of 300 people had gathered, some jeering and booing, although one woman called out, 'Yo are a holy man.'

As the crowds pressed against them, with lines of polic trying to keep the people back, John protectively put hi arms around Yoko and the photograph of that momen taken by a *Daily Mirror* photographer, was used on th back cover of their *Life With The Lions* album.

John was charged with possessing 219 grains o cannabis resin and was fined £150 with twenty guinea costs.

The guilty plea, however, was to have som repercussions a few years later when the immigratio officials in America sought to use it to deport John fro the country.

● Marylebone Registry Office, *Marylebon Road, London NW1*

Paul and **Linda** were married at Marylebone Regist Office on 12 March 1969, the day after the Apple Pre Office had issued a statement that they wouldn't be gettin married.

Linda had obtained the licence and Paul, who ha forgotten to buy a ring, had to persuade a jeweller to ope his shop and he bought one for twelve pounds.

Shortly after 9.30 a.m Paul arrived in a black Daimle Linda's daughter **Heather** acted as a flower girl, **M Evans** was in attendance and the only other Beatl associate present was **Peter Brown**. John and **Yoko** sa they couldn't attend because they were working on the *Life With The Lions* album. George said he'd be too bu working at **Savile Row** and Ringo and **Maureen** said th were involved with domestic matters at home.

The press turned its attention to some weeping **App Scruffs** and distraught fans, such as **Jill Pritchard**, hairdresser who'd heard the news on the radio and h rushed up to London, to stand outside the Register offi in the drizzling rain and weep.

Best Man was Paul's brother, **Mike McCartney**, w was late. The ceremony had been due to take place at 9. a.m. but the train bringing Mike from Liverpool had be delayed. Fortunately, there were no other marriag scheduled for that day and the Registrar was prepared wait.

Coming out of the Registry Office there was a scuff with the mass of press and weeping fans. One of the App Scruffs had been baby sitting and had brought her charg hom she nicknamed Bam Bam, with her. In the crush the aby cried out and Paul said, 'Is he all right, Margo?' As e Daimler drove away the press corps swooped on Margo sking, 'Whose kid is it anyway?' and photographs of her ith the 'mysterious child' appeared in the newspapers the ext day, along with shots of the tearstruck Jill Pritchard.

There was a blessing ceremony at St John's Wood hurch, a Roman Catholic church, after which the edding party drove to Cavendish Avenue for a ampagne toast. Angry McCartney fans forcibly pushed ide the gates and began to cram burning newspaper in e letterbox. The police had to be called. The party then ade their way to the Ritz Hotel for the reception.

Marylebone Registry Office was also the setting for the arriage between Ringo and **Barbara Bach** on 27 April 981. Wedding guests included George and **Olivia** arrison and Paul and Linda McCartney. Sixty guests and latives then celebrated at the London club, Rags. arbara wore a cream satin suit, made by the Emanuels, 10 had designed the famous wedding dress for Diana, incess of Wales.

Masked Marauders

group which never existed, with a name not unlike that one of **Jim McCartney**'s bands, the Masked Melody akers.

On 18 October 1969 in *Rolling Stone* magazine there s a fake review, placed as a joke by T. M. Christian, for album called *Masked Marauders*, which was allegedly corded by a supergroup comprising John Lennon, Paul cCartney, Mick Jagger and **Bob Dylan**.

There was immediate interest sparked off by the review, d Warner Bros rush released an album and single by asked Marauders on their Diety label with tracks to atch those in the *Rolling Stone* review.

The album and single were issued at the end of 1969 d entered the charts early in 1970 reaching No. 114, th a chart life of twelve weeks.

Titles on the album were: 'I Can't Get No Nookie', uke Of Earl', 'Cow Pie', 'I Am The Japanese Sandman', ie Book Of Love', 'Later', 'More Or Less Hudson's Bay ain', 'Season Of The Witch' and 'Saturday Night At The w Palace'.

Massey & Coggins

Liverpool firm of electrical engineers.

Following the Beatles' first trip to Hamburg in 1960, Paul, who had left school against the advice of his father, abandoning his idea of becoming a teacher, felt guilty about not getting a regular job and approached the Labour Exchange. Initially he worked temporarily for a parcels delivery service, being laid off after the Christmas rush. He was then sent to Massey & Coggins where he received a wage of seven pounds per week.

He admits he was not very good at the job which consisted of him winding electrical coils all day long. Whereas fellow labourers would complete between eight and 14 coils per working week, Paul confessed he was lucky if he managed one and a half.

One of his workmates called him 'Mantovani' because of his long hair, and his boredom with the job was such that after two months he didn't bother turning up one morning.

● Matchbox

Traditional blues number originally recorded in 1927 by artists such as Leadbelly and Blind Lemon Jefferson. **Carl Perkins** wrote his own version of the number and recorded it for Sun Records in 1957. It became part of the Beatles' repertoire in 1961 when it provided a vocal vehicle for drummer **Pete Best**. After Best left, the number was sung by Ringo, who performed it on the group's BBC radio shows **'Pop Go The Beatles'** and **'From Us To You'**.

Ringo's version of the song was recorded for their fifth EP *Long Tall Sally* and it appeared on the collections *The Beatles Box* and *The Beatles Collection*, the compilations *Rarities* and *Rock 'n' Roll Music* and the **Capitol** album *Something New*.

It was also released as a single in the States by Capitol with 'Slow Down' on the flip on 24 August 1964 and reached No. 17 in the charts.

A version sung by John is to be found on *The Beatles Live! At The Star Club In Hamburg, Germany: 1962* album.

● Mathew Street, Liverpool 2

A narrow, cobbled street in Liverpool's city centre which originally comprised a series of warehouses. The basement of No. 10, a fruit warehouse, was where the famous **Cavern Club** opened on 16 January 1957. When it changed from a jazz club to one which promoted the local rock 'n' roll bands, it became, for a time, the most famous club in the world.

Also in Mathew Street, on the opposite side, is the Grapes, a public house where the Beatles and many of the Liverpool bands used to drink. As the Cavern only sold soft drinks, the group members used to slip out the side entrance of the band room, which led to a narrow alley which was almost opposite the Grapes. As the band room at the Cavern was so tiny, and since there was no other room in the club where the members of groups could socialize between performances, they used the Grapes as their meeting place to talk to their managers and friends.

The Beatles statue in Cavern Walks. (Cavern Walks)

When **Pete Best** was sacked from the Beatles on 16 August 1962, he was joined by **Neil Aspinall** when he went to the Grapes to ponder the unexpected dismissal. Over the years it has continued to be frequented by former Beatle associates such as **Allan Williams** and **Bob Wooler** and has become a favourite watering hole for tourists visiting the Beatle sites.

When the warehouse buildings were razed to make way for an air vent for the underground railway system in 1973, the actual bulldozing of the warehouse left the cellar club below filled with rubble.

In 1974 local sculptor **Arthur Dooley** had his piece of Beatles sculpture placed on the wall opposite the former Cavern site and shortly after John Lennon's death, a local architect, David Backhouse, walked down Mathew Street, was shocked at the mess, and decided to design a building on the site as a tribute, something with character and style

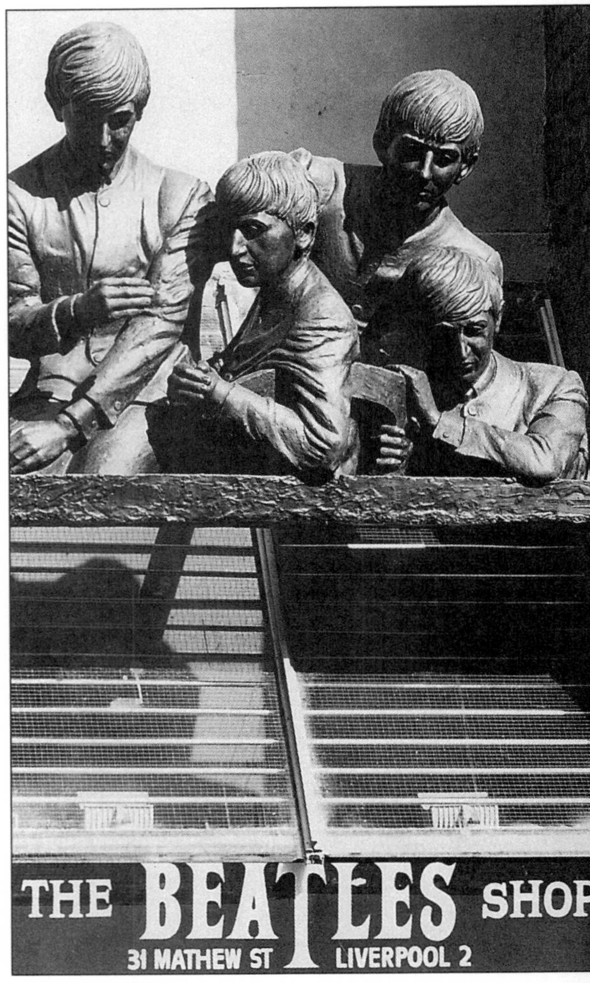

The statue erected above the Beatles Shop in Mathew Street. (Beatles Shop)

a fitting monument to the street's achievements during ıe sixties.

A main attraction of the new structure would be a esurrected Cavern Club, and when it came to rebuilding it as discovered that the original Cavern bricks were still ainly intact. So a number were sold off in aid of charity nd the remainder used to build several yards of wall in e new club.

Following John Lennon's death, the 'John Lennon /orldwide Memorial Club' opened at 23 Mathew Street, pposite Cavern Walks on the premises formerly known as e Left Bank Bistro.

Two brothers, Ian and Muir Wallace, opened the eatles Shop at 31 Mathew Street to coincide with the pening of Cavern Walks. Ian commented: 'To get it right e felt we had to have more Beatles gear than anyone else the world. We wanted people to walk down the stairs ıd be confronted by such a sight they'd say, "Wow, here did all this come from?"'

The shop also has a Beatles statue at the front of the ıilding, which was unveiled at a low-key ceremony on uesday, 2 April 1984. It was the work of Liverpool artist avid Hughes, RA, who actually trained at the same art ›llege as John Lennon before gaining entry to the Royal cademy.

• Matrix Hall, *Fletchamstead, Highway, oventry, West Midlands*

ıe Beatles only made one appearance at this hall, on 17 ovember 1962. It was the first time the group had ›peared in the Midlands.

• Matthew, Brian

BC radio host who worked with the Beatles more than y other radio personality in Britain. He presented **aturday Club'**, a prestigious radio show which was iginally launched in 1958 as a showcase for up-and-ming talent.

The Beatles made their debut on the programme on 16 arch 1963 and appeared on a total of ten 'Saturday Club' ows altogether, their last appearance taking place on 26 ecember 1964.

Matthew conducted various interviews with the group, scussing newsy topics such as their latest releases, the m *A Hard Day's Night*, their tours and so on. He also vered their American tour.

In addition to 'Saturday Club', Matthew also hosted **'Easy Beat'** and the Beatles made the first of four appearances on the show on 7 April 1963. On 14 July 1964 Brian launched another radio show, **'Top Gear'**, and the Beatles appeared on the first programme, which was broadcast two days later.

Matthew told **Kevin Howlett** in *The Beatles At The Beeb* book that although he worked with the Beatles so often, he wasn't very close to them on a personal level, although: 'I suppose it's fair to say that I was close to Brian Epstein – I did count him as a personal friend.'

In fact, both Brians went into business together when they launched a theatrical project in Farnborough, Kent. The two theatre lovers intended to create a new theatre, the Pilgrim Theatre, at a cost of £38,000, which would present a festival of new and classical productions which could later be transferred to the West End. The theatre would also stage musicals, jazz concerts and films. A host of stars agreed to donate their services in a series of concerts to raise funds for the venture. They included **Billy J. Kramer**, the **Searchers**, **Cilla Black**, **Gerry & the Pacemakers**, **Dusty Springfield** and Kenny Ball & His Jazzmen. The project was abandoned in July 1965 when planning permission was turned down by the Estates Committee of Bromley Borough Council.

In 1972 Matthew compiled a thirteen-part radio series 'The Beatles Story' for the BBC, during which he conducted interviews with a host of people, including John Lennon, Paul McCartney, George Harrison, Bill Harry, **Larry Parnes**, **Allan Williams**, **Bob Wooler**, **Tony Barrow**, **Peter Eckhorn**, **Gerry Marsden**, **Tony Sheridan**, Brian Epstein, **Alistair Taylor**, **Clive Epstein**, **George Harrison** of the ***Liverpool Echo***, **Queenie Epstein**, **Dick James**, **Norman Smith**, **David Jacobs**, Vi Caldwell, **Arthur Howes**, **Helen Shapiro**, **Tony Bramwell**, George Martin, **Hunter Davies**, **Freda Kelly**, **Brian Somerville**, **Jimmy Savile**, **Alf Bicknell**, Al Aronowitz, **Maharishi Mahesh Yogi**, **Joanne Newfield**, **Kenny Everett**, **Jane Asher**, **Derek Taylor**, **Allen Klein** and **Yoko Ono**.

● Maxwell's Silver Hammer

A Paul McCartney composition, featured on the *Abbey Road* album. Paul was to comment: 'This epitomizes the downfalls in life. Just when everything is going smoothly "bang bang", down comes Maxwell's silver hammer and ruins everything.'

Paul had written the number in 1968 and it was almost selected to be recorded for *The Beatles* double album. The group next rehearsed the number when they were at **Twickenham Film Studios** in January 1969 and a clip of them rehearsing the song is included in the *Let It Be* film.

Actual recording of the number began at **Abbey Road** on Wednesday, 9 July 1969. Backing vocals were provided by Paul, George and Ringo and an anvil was hired from a theatrical agency for Ringo to strike.

John Lennon didn't take much active participation in this recording as he made it plain that he didn't like the number and felt that Paul was pushing for it to be issued as a single.

In fact there were no less than four cover versions rush-released at the time of the *Abbey Road* album by Brownhill's Stamp Duty, Format, The Good Ship Lollipop and George Howe. None of them registered in the charts.

● Maysles, Albert And David

Two American filmmaking brothers who were noted for their early rock documentaries and, in particular, the 1963 documentary 'Yeah Yeah Yeah – The Beatles In New York', which they made for Granada Television.

David died on 3 January 1987. He was 54 years old.

● MBE

The initials stand for Member (of the Order of the) British Empire and refer to a prestigious award presented in the Honours List in Britain annually. The MBE is actually the lowest grade of civil award and was instituted in 1917 by King George IV.

The pop weekly *Melody Maker* had suggested in a March headline that the government: 'Honour The Beatles!'. **Harold Wilson**, then Prime Minister of a Labour Government, decided to put forward the names of the individual Beatles for MBE awards and 75 youngsters from Pennsylvania had already written to the Queen suggesting that the Beatles be given a knighthood.

The announcement that the group would be awarded the MBE was issued on 11 June 1965 and the Beatles held a press conference the following day at **Twickenham Film Studios** to discuss it. George was to comment: 'I didn't think you got that sort of thing, just for playing rock 'n' roll music.'

The following day the first of many awards by disgruntled previous recipients was returned to the palace. Over the next few days the irate former recipients making their protest included Hector Dupuis, a former Canadian MP; anti-aircraft expert James Berg; ex-Naval officer David Evans-Rees; another Canadian, Stanley Ellis; a Cyril Hearn; retired squadron leader Douglas Moffit – and a Colonel Frederick Wragg returned no less than twelve medals. Dupuis commented: 'The British House of Royalty had put me on the same level as a bunch of vulgar numbskulls.' Ex-RAF squadron leader Paul Pearson returned his award with the comment, 'Because it has become debased'. Author Richard Pape, on returning his MBE, wrote, 'If the Beatles and the like continue to debase the Royal Honours list, then Britain must fall deeper into international ridicule and contempt.'

On the other hand, hundreds wrote to Harold Wilson and the Queen expressing their approval. Lt General Sir William Oliver, retiring British High Commissioner to Australia, commented: 'I think the Beatles deserve their MBE.' Lord Netherthorpe echoed the sentiments, saying 'They thoroughly deserve the award.'

The Investiture took place in the Great Throne Room at Buckingham Palace at 11.10 a.m. on the morning of 26 October 1965 and there were a total of 182 people receiving medals from the Queen. Outside the Palace there was a crowd of 4,000 youngsters chanting, 'Long live the Queen, long live the Beatles.' When the group arrived John was accompanied by **Cynthia** and his Aunt **Mimi**, Paul by his father and **Jane Asher**; George by his father, mother and **Pattie Boyd**; and Ringo by his mother and stepfather. Brian Epstein was also in attendance.

Epstein had been suffering depression because he was not mentioned in the Honours list and felt that he wasn't put forward for an MBE because he was a homosexual and Jewish. It was apparent to many people that the fact that he wasn't given an honour was a snub. When he was dining at the Mirabelle with his friend **Geoffrey Ellis**, a noted actor sitting at the next table said, 'Look at that little boy over there – he couldn't get an MBE.'

However, the press was to print the quote that the MBE stood for 'Mister Brian Epstein', although different publications attributed it to Paul McCartney, George Harrison – and even Princess Margaret.

When the Queen presented the group with their silver medals, she said to Paul, 'How long have you been gether now?' He replied, 'Oh, for many years.' Ringo aid, 'Forty years.' The Queen then turned to Ringo and aid, 'Are you the one who started it?' He replied, 'No, I as the last to join. I'm the little fellow.' The Queen turned John and said, 'Have you been working hard lately?' nd he replied, 'No, we've been on holiday.'

After the Investiture the Beatles spoke with the press in e Palace courtyard. Paul said, 'We've played many alaces including Frisco's **Cow Palace**, but never this ne before. It's a keen pad and I liked the staff. Thought ey'd be Dukes and things but they were just fellas.' hen asked about the Queen, he replied, 'She's lovely, eat. She was very friendly. She was just like a Mum to s.' John, when asked if he was nervous, said, 'Not as uch as some of the other people in there.' When he was ked how the other recipients had acted towards them, hn replied, 'One formally dressed, middle-aged winner alked up to us after the ceremony and said, "I want your tograph for my daughter, but I don't know what she sees you." So we gave him our autographs.' John was then ked how they knew what to do for the ceremony. He plied, 'This big fellow drilled us. Every time he got to ingo he kept cracking up.' Paul was asked what they ould do with their medals and he said, 'What you rmally do with medals. Put them in a box.'

The group then went to the **Saville Theatre** for other press conference.

On 22 March 1970 *L'Express*, a French magazine, blished an interview with John Lennon in which he aimed that the Beatles smoked marijuana in the toilets at ickingham Palace. This was untrue, an example of hn's occasionally bizarre sense of humour.

However, John, who in some ways was anti-tablishment, had previously made it known that he had ver been entirely happy with receiving the award. When 'd originally seen the brown envelope with 'On Her ajesty's Service' written on it, he said he thought he was ing called up. When he discovered what it was he called that his first instinct was to turn it down. When ian Epstein phoned him to discuss it and he told him his elings Brian said that he had to accept the honour. John ew that if he spurned it, it would do incalculable mage to the group. Later, he was to comment, 'Taking e MBE was a sell-out for me.' Once he'd decided to mply with his manager's request, John began giving out s quotes to the press: 'I thought people got these things for driving tanks, winning wars.' When the protesters began sending their medals back to the Palace, John became annoyed and said that the Army officers got their awards for killing people. 'We got ours for entertaining. On balance, I'd say we deserve ours more.'

At Christmas he took it down to his Aunt Mimi's bungalow in Poole, Dorset, and told her she could keep it. She placed it on her sideboard beneath a picture of John taken by **Astrid Kirchherr**, but later placed it on top of her television set.

One day he sent his chauffeur, **Les Anthony**, to collect it from her. Anthony told Mimi, 'Mr Lennon said would you lend him the MBE medal for a while.' Mimi told him, 'Yes, but tell him, don't forget it's mine and I want it back.' John had it wrapped up in brown paper and sent to the Queen at Buckingham Palace with the message, 'I am returning this MBE in protest against Britain's involvement in the Nigeria-Biafra thing, against our support of America in Vietnam and against "Cold Turkey" slipping down the charts. With love. John Lennon. Bag Productions, 3 Savile Row, London W1.' He also sent similar letters to the Prime Minister and to the Secretary of the Central Chancery.

His Aunt Mimi was furious at the deception and told John in no uncertain terms, accusing him of insulting the Queen. 'He broke my heart over that,' she said, 'and also, he didn't tell me first why that medal was being taken away.'

John was later to regret that he'd added the facetious remark about 'Cold Turkey' in the letter, and despite the fact that he'd returned the medal, he still retained the honour as it could not be renounced once it had been accepted. Paul, George and Ringo, on the other hand, had no regrets in accepting their awards.

● McBean, Angus

Veteran British photographer, born in Newbridge, Monmouthshire, in 1904. His work was highly regarded and Lord Snowdon acted as his assistant at one point. His work for the British film industry and theatre was well known and he began to gain commissions from record companies to photograph artists for album covers.

Following his work with acts such as John Leyton, Johnny Kidd and Marty Wilde, McBean was commissioned to produce a cover pic for the Beatles' debut album. Paul McCartney had already worked on sketches for the cover of an album tentatively called 'Off The Beatles Track', but the title *Please Please Me* was agreed on and McBean took a photograph of the four looking down from a position on the staircase at **EMI House**, in London's Manchester Square. He was then commissioned to provide covers for beat groups such as **Freddie & the Dreamers** and **Billy J. Kramer** & the Dakotas.

In 1969, for the cover of the 'Get Back' session, the photograph was originally to be taken by **Dezo Hoffmann** on the steps of **Abbey Road Studio**s. John Lennon suggested that they return to the site of their first album sleeve, with a new McBean shot on the stairwell. It wasn't used on the 'Get Back' session, which became the *Let It Be* album, but the recreated scene was used on the 1970 retrospective album *The Beatles 1962–1966*.

McBean retired due to ill health and four-and-a-half tons of his glass negatives were purchased by Harvard University. In 1981 Quartet Books in Britain published a collection of his work entitled *Angus McBean*, which contained reproductions of the Beatles covers.

He died in Ipswich General Hospital on 9 June 1990. He was 86 years old.

● McCaffrey, Laurie

A Liverpool girl who, at the age of twenty, became switchboard girl and receptionist for Brian Epstein's **NEMS Enterprises** company when they moved from Whitechapel to new premises in Moorfields, Liverpool. Laurie had noticed an advertisement in the ***Liverpool Echo***, but instead of replying by mail, phoned **Clive Epstein** and was given an interview. There had been over 400 applications, but Laurie, who had been a regular **Cavern**-goer and Beatles fan since 1961, was given the job.

When NEMS moved premises to Argyle Street in London she moved down with them and after the death of Brian Epstein she left NEMS Enterprises to take up the Beatles' offer to join **Apple Corps**. After the Apple building in **Savile Row** was closed she later worked for Capital Radio.

● McCartney, Florence

Paul's paternal grandmother who was born in the Everton district of Liverpool at 131 Breck Road on 2 June 1874. On 17 May 1896, 21-year-old Florence, nee Clegg, married **Joseph McCartney** at Christ Church in Kensington, London. She was known as Florrie and ha seven children, two of whom died in early childhood. Sh died on VE day in 1944.

● McCartney, Heather

Linda McCartney's first child, born in Colorado on 3 December 1963.

During his early visits to Linda in America, Paul wa evidently charmed by Heather, who seems to have brough out his paternal instincts, and in 1969 when he marrie Linda, he formally adopted Heather.

When **Wings** began touring he asked her whether she' like to stay at home or join them on the road – sh plumped for the travelling life. However, in her early teen Paul allegedly became concerned about the crowd she wa mixing with in London to the extent that he decided move the family, lock, stock and barrel, out to Sussex.

In her late teens, Heather took an interest i photography, getting a job as a darkroom technician an in 1981, becoming Ilford's Young Printer Of the Year f printing up a photograph she called 'Waterfalls', whic was a snap she had taken of Carol and Steve Gadd i Montserrat, when Steve was session drummer on Paul *Tug Of War* recordings.

● McCartney, James (Father)

Paul's father, generally known as Jim. He was born at Fishguard Road, Everton, Liverpool, on 7 July 1902, t son of **Joe and Florence McCartney**.

He had two brothers and three sisters. A bad fall at t age of ten resulted in a broken eardrum, but this didn prevent him from learning to play the piano by ear. H started work at the age of fourteen as a sample boy at Hanney & Co, the cotton brokers of Chapel Stree Liverpool, where he received six shillings a week.

At the age of seventeen he began playing ragtime mus and his first public appearance with a band was at Catherine's Hall, Vine Street. Even in those day gimmicks were considered useful in the promotion bands, so they called themselves the Masked Melo Makers and wore black masks. But when they began sweat, the dye from the masks ran down their faces, whi put paid to that. Dressed in dinner jackets, they becan known as Jim Mac's Band and performed locally for abo five years, one of their notable appearances being at local cinema where the film *The Queen Of Sheba* w aying. Their brief was to provide musical background for e silent movie. It was during this period that Jim penned instrumental number called 'Eloise'.

At the age of 28 he was promoted to the post of lesman and his earnings rocketed to £250 per year. On April 1941, at the age of 39, he married **Mary** Mohin at Swithin's Roman Catholic church in the Gillmoss area West Derby in Liverpool and they moved into furnished oms in Anfield. The couple were to have two children, ul and **Michael**.

The cotton exchange was closed during the war years d Jim went to work at Napiers, an engineering firm ich produced engines for the Sabre plane. During the enings he was on call as a voluntary fire-fighter. At the d of the war he found work as an inspector for Liverpool rporation's Cleansing Department and later returned to s job at the cotton exchange.

His younger son **Michael** was to comment: 'We both e him a lot. He's a very good man, and he's a very bborn man . . . it would have been easy for him to have ne off with other birds when Mum died, or to have gone t getting drunk every night. But he didn't. He stayed me and looked after us.'

In 1964 Paul asked his father to retire. He was then rning ten pounds a week. Paul also suggested that he ove into a nice house 'over the water' and bought **mbrandt**, a detached house in Baskervyle Road, swall, Cheshire, for £8,750.

On Jim's 62nd birthday, the same year, Paul presented n with a horse called Drake's Drum. Two years later he oudly led the steed into the winner's enclosure at ntree after it had won the race immediately preceding Grand National.

Paul was also to delight his father when he put the rds to 'Eloise' and recorded the number in Nashville der the title 'Walking In The Park With Eloise'.

Jim was remarried on 24 November 1964 to a widow, **gela Williams**. Over the next ten years Jim became ppled by arthritis and had to move to a nearby ngalow. As a result, Paul bought **Rembrandt** back from n. He died on 18 March 1976. Paul was performing on a ropean tour with **Wings** at the time. Jim's second wife gela told Mike McCartney that just before he died, Jim d said, 'I'll be with Mary soon.' He was cremated at ndican Cemetery, near Heswall, on 22 March.

● McCartney, James Louis (Son)

Paul and **Linda**'s first son, born at the Avenue Clinic, St John's Wood, London, on 12 September 1977. His namesakes were Paul's father and Linda's mother.

● McCartney, Joe

Paul's paternal grandfather, who died before Paul was born.

Joe was born in Everton on 23 November 1866 and lived in the area all his life. He married Florence Clegg when he was 29 and worked throughout his life as a tobacco cutter at Cope's, a local tobacco firm. A keen amateur musician, his instrument was the big brass double-bass which he played in the line-up of two brass bands, one run by Cope's, the other by the local branch of the Territorial Army.

● McCartney, Linda

Linda was born Linda Louise Eastman on 24 September 1942. Her father, Lee V. Eastman, was an affluent lawyer, who had changed his name from Epstein and collected expensive works of art. Her father's speciality was copyright law in the showbusiness field and he once agreed to undertake legal work for songwriter Jack Lawrence in exchange for a song dedicated to his six-year-old daughter. Lawrence penned 'Linda' late in 1947 and in 1963 it was recorded by Jan & Dean.

Linda's mother, Louise Eastman, was the daughter of a rich Cleveland family, the Linders, who owned major department stores. The family home was in Scarsdale, Westchester County, in upstate New York. They also owned a house in East Hampton and a luxurious flat in Park Avenue.

During her formative years Linda was used to mixing with celebrity guests who were invited to dinner parties at the house, such as William Boyd (the screen's Hopalong Cassidy), Hoagy Carmichael and Tommy Dorsey.

Linda has said, 'All my teen years were spent with an ear to the radio.' She played truant from school to travel to shows at the **Paramount Theatre** in Brooklyn: 'They'd have twenty acts on, twenty-four hours a day. Alan Freed was the MC but sometimes they'd get Fabian or Bobby Darin to MC. I remember seeing **Chuck Berry** sing "School Days" for the first time.'

She was educated at Scarsdale High School, followed by the exclusive Sarah Lawrence School in Bronxville, near Scarsdale (where Yoko Ono had previously been a student).

At the age of eighteen, Linda's world fell to pieces when her mother died in a plane crash. Linda had gone to Princeton University to study History and Art. Her mother's death affected her so much that she rushed into marriage with a fellow student, Melvin See. Linda recalls, 'My mother died in a plane crash and I got married. It was a mistake.'

She realized things wouldn't work out: 'When he [Melvin] graduated he wanted to go to Africa. I said, "Look, if I don't get on with you here I'm not going to Africa with you. I won't get on with you there."'

They'd moved to Tucson, Arizona, and Linda had become pregnant. She gave birth to her first daughter Heather on 31 December 1963. See, who was a geophysicist, still hoped that Linda would follow him to Africa but she wrote him a letter telling him she was getting a divorce.

The marriage had only lasted a year, but while s lived in Arizona, Linda had studied Art History at t University of Arizona and had attended a short course photography given by Hazel Archer at Tucson Art Centr It was then that she first began taking photographs. S was to say, 'Arizona opened up my eyes to the wonder light and colour.'

Linda's break into the professional world photography had begun when she and Heather moved New York. Linda was holding down a job as receptioni for *Town & Country* magazine when an invitation to cover reception for the **Rolling Stones** on a boat on the Huds came in – she snapped it up, and found she was the on photographer on board! The photographs established h reputation, she secured an unpaid, but prestigious positi as the house photographer at the Fillmore East, a popul rock venue which featured major British and Americ

Linda McCartney and Virginia Harry at a 'Buddy Holly Week' party.

cts, and began to receive commissions to photograph ading bands such as the **Beach Boys**.

She photographed the Beatles in 1965 in Austria during e filming of *Help!*, but says that she first met them ficially at the **Shea Stadium** in 1966. She was to recall, t was John who interested me at the start. He was my eatle hero. But when I met him the fascination faded fast d I found it was Paul I liked.'

In 1967 she came to London to photograph British tists such as the Animals and Traffic. On 15 May she as taken to the Bag O' Nails club in Kingley Street by has Chandler, ex-bass player of the Animals, who troduced her to Paul. They had their first real nversation that night. A few days later on 19 May, she as one of the select band of fifteen photographers from ound the world who attended the private *Sgt Pepper* unch party at Brian Epstein's **Chapel Street** house. She anaged to receive an invitation through Epstein's aide **eter Brown** whom she'd provided with some otographs of the Rolling Stones.

In May 1969, Paul arrived in New York to promote pple and gave a number of press conferences. At one of em, Linda slipped him her telephone number and he got touch and spent a few days with her, meeting at **Nat eiss**'s flat. Paul became charmed by Heather to the tent that he baby-sat while Linda went out to take otographs at a rock gig.

He returned to London, then visited Los Angeles a onth later and called up Linda with an invitation to join m. They spent a week together before Paul left once ain. Linda returned to New York. In November she ceived an invitation from Paul to join him in London, st five months after he had split up with **Jane Asher**.

'I came over', she said, 'and we lived together for a hile, neither of us talked about marriage, we just loved ch other and lived together. We liked each other a lot, so ing conventional people, one day I thought: OK, let's get arried, we love each other, let's make it definite'.

And the occasion did seem to be hastily arranged. nda, four months pregnant with Mary, went to **arylebone Register Office** on 11 March 1969, to book for the next day at 9.45 a.m. Paul was in the studio cording **Jackie Lomax** singing 'Thumbin' A Ride' and, grossed as he was in his work, forgot to buy a wedding ng. As he had an early start the next day, he had to rsuade a local jeweller to open his shop after closing time. He bought a plain gold ring for twelve pounds.

On the morning of 12 March, determined fans, photographers and journalists, undaunted by the rain, gathered at Paul's Cavendish Avenue house from 6.00 a.m. onwards, hoping to catch a glimpse of the couple. **Mike McCartney** was best man, but his train from Liverpool was delayed and he arrived an hour late. He rushed into the Register Office saying, 'Forgive me, it wasn't my fault. Have you been done?' Fortunately there had been no other weddings booked for that morning, and Paul was able to answer: 'No, we've been waiting for you.' Linda's daughter Heather was bridesmaid and **Peter Brown** and **Mal Evans** were witnesses. None of the Beatles turned up as Paul had already started litigation to dissolve the group. The ceremony was conducted by Registrar Mr E. R. Sanders, and the marriage was blessed afterwards at the Anglican Church in St John's Wood by the Rev Noel Perry-Gore.

On the couple's return to Cavendish Avenue, the press were invited in and given champagne while Paul and Linda answered their questions. A rumour had spread that Linda was a rich heiress of the Kodak-Eastman family, but she quickly scotched it, saying that she had nothing to do with them. Paul quipped, 'What? I've been done. Where's the money?' Once the press had been satisfied, Paul and Linda went on to the wedding reception proper at the Ritz Hotel, Piccadilly. Later than evening Paul returned to the studios to complete the production of the Jackie Lomax single.

Unfortunately, around this time, Beatle fans who hung around Paul's house became quite nasty with Linda. While they had accepted Jane Asher as a suitable girlfriend and potential wife for Paul, they resented Linda and she received a degree of abuse from them.

One of the first songs which Paul wrote after the marriage was 'The Lovely Linda'. Paul officially adopted Heather as his daughter and the couple had three more children: Mary, Stella and James Louis.

Mary was born at 1.30 a.m. on Thursday, 29 August 1969, at the Avenue Clinic, St John's Wood, although an earlier announcement had said she was due in December. She weighed 6lbs 8ozs and arrived slightly less than six months after the couple had wed. Stella was born in London on 12 September 1971 and James Louis was born in London on 12 September 1977.

When Paul formed **Wings** he wanted Linda to tour with

him. There were initially some cruel jibes about her being in the band and she suggested dropping out, but Paul insisted and taught her to play keyboards. She continued to pursue her career as a photographer with some success, and also recorded in her own right, initially using the pseudonym Suzi & the Red Stripes for her record 'Seaside Woman'. She was also involved in two animation films, *The Oriental Nightfish* and *Seaside Woman*.

Linda was to stretch herself still further and, in addition to photographic exhibitions of her work in various galleries around the world and her growing authority as a musician in the various world tours undertaken with Paul, she appeared in a cameo role in the popular TV series 'Bread', set in Liverpool and scripted by Linda's friend Carla Lane. Linda also had a best-selling book on her vegetarian recipes and a range of Linda McCartney's vegetarian foods became a new line at major supermarkets.

Paul and Linda have remained close throughout their marriage and never been apart for longer than the nine days Paul spent in jail in Japan.

● McCartney, Mary *(Daughter)*

First child of Paul and **Linda** McCartney. She was born at 1.30 a.m. on Thursday, 29 August 1969, at the Avenue Clinic, St John's Wood, London, although an earlier announcement had said she was due in December.

She weighed 6lbs 8ozs and arrived slightly less than six months after the couple had wed. Two months after the birth Paul and Linda took their new baby up to Scotland with them. It was during this period that the 'Paul Is Dead' rumours first sprang up in America. In November they took Mary to America to show her to Linda's family.

● McCartney, Mary *(Mother)*

Paul's mother was born Mary Patricia Mohin on 29 September 1909 at No. 2 Third Avenue, Fazakerley, Liverpool. Her mother, Mary Theresa Dahner, was a Liverpudlian and her father, Owen Mohin, an Irishman. The couple had four children – Wilf, Mary, Agnes and Bill. Sadly, Agnes died at the age of two, and was followed by her mother who died giving birth to a fifth child, who also died, in 1919.

Mary was christened a Catholic and became a nurse at Alder Hey Hospital at the age of fourteen. She later moved to Walton Hospital, where she was promoted to Nursing Sister at the age of 24. She married Jim McCartney in 1941 when she was 31 and the couple moved to Anfiel When Paul was born at Walton Hospital, Mary gave up h position there to look after him. Her second son Micha was born eighteen months later. She became a heal visitor for a while and then a midwife, which meant th she was on call virtually 24 hours a day. The family w given accommodation on the various council estates whe she was on call to the residents.

Mary was concerned about both her sons making success in life and was supportive in their schoolwork. S also smoothed out Paul's scouse accent, instilling in hi the need to speak in as nice a way as possible. At the a of 45 she began to suffer from pains in her chest, b dismissed them as being part of the menopause. Howev they persisted and were so intense at times that she to Bisodal. When she eventually saw a specialist, diagnosed breast cancer. She underwent an operation, b it was too late – the cancer had spread, the operati exacerbated the condition and she died at the Northe Hospital on 31 October 1956, with rosary beads ti around her wrists. She'd said, 'I would have liked to ha seen the boys growing up.'

The fourteen-year-old Paul, on hearing the news of mother's death, said: 'What are we going to do without h money?' This initial reaction covered up his real gr which set in later; his brother Mike believed the trage caused Paul to lose himself in music, which became obsession.

Mary was buried at Yew Street Cemetery, Finch La Huyton, on 3 November 1956. Both sons were to p tribute to their mother: Mike by placing her photograph the cover of his first solo album and Paul by immortalizi her in 'Lady Madonna'.

Paul's first daughter Mary is also named after h mother.

● McCartney, Mike *(McGear)*

Paul's younger brother Peter Michael McCartney was b on 7 January 1944 at **Walton Hospital**, Liverpool, a his first home was in Roach Avenue. He was baptized Catholic, as was Paul, and he joined his brother at th first school, Stockton Wood Road Infants' School. Wh they moved to Ardwick Avenue in Speke, they shared same bedroom and began to attend **Joseph Willia Primary School** in Gateacre.

Mike attended the **Liverpool Institute**, but

mbition was to enter **Liverpool College of Art**. Jnfortunately, new rules made it mandatory for entrants to ave five GCE (General Certificate of Education) passes nd Mike was turned down. He was accepted for Birkenhead's Laird School of Art, but was unable to obtain grant from Liverpool Corporation, so at the age of eventeen, he began his first job at Jackson's the Tailors in Ranelagh Street. The following year he began an pprenticeship at Andrew Bernard, a ladies' hairdresser in he same street.

In 1962 he was asked if he'd take part in a sketch at he Merseyside Arts Festival with a Post Office engineer, ohn Gorman, and a young teacher, Roger McGough. Mike greed, but wanted to use a pseudonym. He suggested the ame Michael Blank, and he was so credited in the rogramme. The three decided to stick together as a

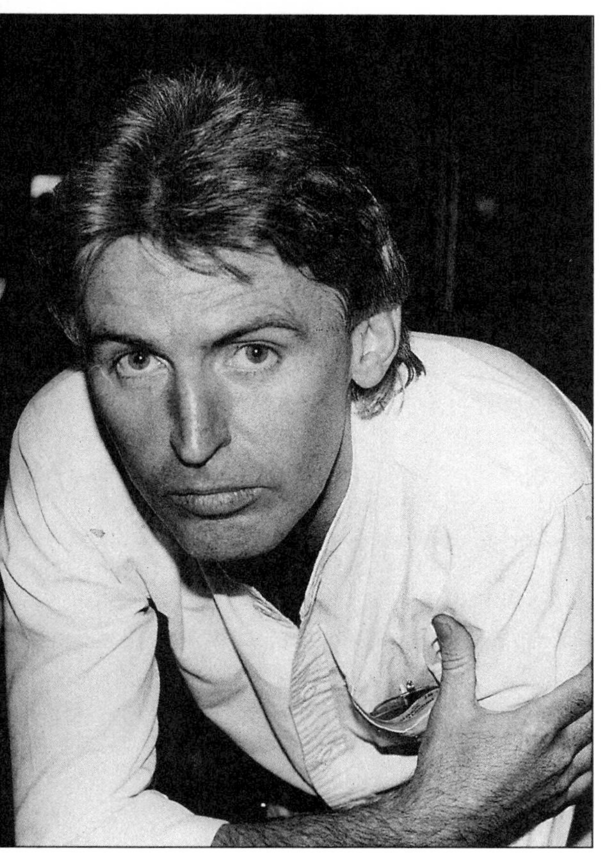

Iike McCartney – Paul's younger brother, an artist in his own ght.

satirical trio, performing songs and sketches, and called themselves the **Scaffold**. In 1963 they were asked to appear regularly on Granada Television's weekly magazine programme 'Gazette', so they all gave up their jobs to become professional members of Scaffold. Mike changed his name to Mike McGear as the Beatles were now achieving such incredible success that he didn't want to appear as if he were exploiting his family name. In any event, he was used to pseudonyms as his first published photographs had appeared in ***Mersey Beat*** under the name Francis Michael.

The Scaffold were to prove a tremendous success. In 1968 they were appearing regularly on a BBC satirical show and were also doing live gigs at prestigious venues such as the **London Palladium**. During the seventies the Scaffold line-up was regularly supplemented by Neil Innes and Viv Stanshall of the **Bonzo Dog Doo Dah Band** and Andy Roberts of the Liverpool Scene, using the collective name Grimms. The Scaffold performed their final live gig on the *All Fools Show*, a charity affair at the **Royal Albert Hall** on 1 April 1977. There was a further reunion, on Granada Television in 1979 when they teamed up on the programme 'What's On' to celebrate the 10th anniversary of their No. 1 hit 'Lily The Pink'.

Mike had married Angela Fishwick in 1968 in a country church ceremony in Caerog, North Wales, with Paul as Best Man, accompanied by **Jane Asher**. The marriage produced three daughters, but began to break down in the late seventies and the couple were divorced in 1979.

After the demise of Scaffold and the collapse of his first marriage, Mike began to write children's books. He then married Rowena Home, a 21-year-old dress designer at St Barnabas Church in Penny Lane, Liverpool, on 29 May 1982. Over 600 fans gathered outside the church in the morning and waited for Mike to arrive at 2.30 p.m. and Rowena about ten minutes later. Paul was dressed in casual style with grey jacket, blue trousers and white sneakers, and there were five bridesmaids: Mike's three daughters (Benna, thirteen, Theran, eleven, and Abbi, eight) and Rowena's two sisters. The Reverend Harrington, who conducted the ceremony, recalled when Paul was a choirboy at the church and commented: 'He used to sit up there in the choirbox, making some kind of noise.' After the ceremony the wedding party left the church and headed for Hoylake for the reception. Later Mike and

Rowena flew to Malta for their honeymoon.

The Scaffold enjoyed a successful recording career and their first single was produced by George Martin. It was '2 Days Monday', issued on Parlophone R5443 on 6 May 1966. John Burgess was the producer of their second single 'Goodbat Nightman', issued on 2 December of the same year on Parlophone R5548. They had a big chart hit with 'Thank U Very Much', produced by **Tony Palmer** and issued on Parlophone R5643 on 4 November 1967. Paul had bought Mike a Nikon camera and when Mike phoned him to thank him for the gift he chanted 'Thank you very much' on the phone. After the call the chant stayed in his head and he put it down on tape, then wrote 'Thank U Very Much'. Paul attended the recording session at **Abbey Road**, but told Mike the song was too oblique. When Mike pointed out that the entire song was oblique, Paul said, 'Have it your own way if you know so much'. The song became a spectacular hit and Paul phoned Mike and said, 'You were right . . . I was wrong.'

This was followed by 'Do You Remember', produced by Norrie Paramor and issued on Parlophone R5679 on 15 March 1968. Their next single '1-2-3' came out on 14 June 1968 on Parlophone R5703. Their biggest success, reaching the No. 1 spot in the British charts and proving to be the hit of the Christmas season, was 'Lily The Pink', issued on 18 October 1968 on Parlophone R5734. Other singles included 'Charity Bubbles', 'Gin Gan Goolie', 'All The Way Up', 'Busdreams', 'Liverpool Lou', 'Mummy Won't Be Home For Christmas', 'Leaving of Liverpool', 'Wouldn't It Be Funny If You Didn't Have A Nose?' and 'How Do You Do?'.

Paul's first involvement with his younger brother's recording career happened in 1968 when he produced the album *McGough & McGear*, released on Parlophone PCS 7047 on 17 May. He didn't produce the Scaffold's first album *The Scaffold*, but did produce their hit single 'Liverpool Lou', as well as Mike's solo album *McGear*, for which he wrote 'What Do We Really Know?' and 'Leave It' and co-wrote with Mike: 'Norton', 'Have You Got Problems?', 'Rainbow Lady', 'Simply Love You' and 'Givin' Grease A Ride'. He also co-wrote 'The Casket' and 'The Man Who Found God On The Moon', this time with Roger McGough.

At Island Records Mike recorded and released the single 'Woman' and an album of the same name in 1972. In 1973 Island issued the group Grimms' eponymous album, followed by a Scaffold album *Fresh Liver* an another Grimms LP *Rockin' Duck*. Mike then signed t Warners who issued *McGear* and *Sold Out* and a numb of his singles.

Mike's popularity engendered an American Mik McCartney Fan Club and a fanzine called *Gear Box*. In th eighties he issued the series *Mike Mac's Black & Whites*, collection of his photographs, which were also presented i a handsome range of postcards and posters. He began t tour American universities lecturing on his caree Liverpool and the Beatles and also completed a vide about Liverpool, in addition to furthering his career as photographer and recording various Liverpool bands – busy, creative life for a man with such a large family (h

Bill Harry and Mike McCartney on the Detroit chat show *Kelly & Co.*

and Rowena had three boys, in addition to the thre daughters from his previous marriage, who were reare with Mike), who has also penned his autobiography, *Than U Very Much: Mike McCartney's Family Album*, which w called *The Macs* in America.

● McCartney, Paul

Paul was born at **Walton Road Hospital** in Rice Lan Liverpool, on 18 June 1942, the first son of **Mary** an **James McCartney**. His brother **Michael** was bo eighteen months later.

Mary McCartney was a midwife and the family moved to various addresses in Liverpool before settling at **20 Forthlin Road** in 1955, where Mary died the following year of cancer of the breast.

When Paul passed his 11-Plus examination in 1957 he entered the **Liverpool Institute**, a popular high school near the city centre. While travelling to school on the bus he met with a younger student, George Harrison. Another Institute boy was **Ivan Vaughan** who invited Paul to a fete at **St Peter's Church in Woolton** where he introduced him to John Lennon, who was playing in a skiffle group he'd formed called the **Quarry Men**.

Paul had been interested in music due to the influence of his father, who had once led his own jazz band locally. Paul was able to play some songs to John and write down the lyrics which led to John inviting Paul to join the group.

The Quarry Men underwent changes and when the residency at the **Casbah Club** began they comprised John, Paul, George and **Ken Brown.** By that time they had introduced more rock 'n' roll numbers to their repertoire and Paul had been encouraging the group to perform their own original material. He began writing songs with John at Forthlin Road.

Although John was leader of the group, Paul was the one who seemed to have the greatest appetite for success and worked hard to achieve it. He developed a healthy respect for the media and became an ideal spokesman. He was also full of ideas which he was to continue to introduce to the group throughout the sixties, whether it was through his designs for album sleeves or scripts for a TV special such as *Magical Mystery Tour.* He was also the member who was most keen on public performances.

The left-handed Paul became the group's bass guitarist when **Stuart Sutcliffe** left the band in 1961. The majority of songs John and Paul wrote together were composed early on in their career, but once they became established, the two songwriters generally wrote their numbers individually, although they agreed to credit all songs as 'Lennon & McCartney' numbers. Paul, who had introduced numbers such as 'Till There Was You', 'Besame Mucho', and 'Falling In Love Again' to the early repertoire, veered toward romantic numbers and songs which indicated the influence of Hollywood musicals. Songs such as 'Yesterday', 'Michelle', 'When I'm Sixty-Four' and 'Lovely Rita' are typical of McCartney compositions, while Lennon opted for more biting compositions, harder, more experimental and rockier numbers than Paul. Paul's interest in the traditional musical was evident in the hour-long TV special 'James Paul McCartney', in 1973 when Paul performed numbers such as 'Gotta Sing, Gotta Dance'.

When the Beatles moved to London, Paul preferred to remain in the city centre, while his fellow Beatles opted for houses in the outer suburbs. Paul always seemed the 'culture vulture' of the quartet, attending the theatre and acquiring paintings by artists such as Magritte. His long-time girlfriend, **Jane Asher**, aided him in cultivating his artistic tastes. To the media they seemed the perfect couple, but their five-year romance came to an end because Paul continued to have affairs. Oddly enough, it was Paul rather than John who first began to experiment with avant-garde film-making.

After Brian Epstein was found dead in August 1967, Paul was determined to prevent the group from losing interest in their career and encouraged them to film *Magical Mystery Tour*; he even directed their promotional film for 'Hello Goodbye' that year.

Jane Asher suggested that he buy a farm in Scotland which could act as a retreat and he purchased property near Campbeltown. He'd also purchased a house in St John's Wood, quite close to **Abbey Road Studios**.

Paul was the first Beatle to become involved in a major solo venture when he composed the music for the feature film ***The Family Way*** in 1967. His interest in movies continued and he composed the title song for the James Bond film *Live And Let Die* in 1973. The following year he composed the theme for the TV series 'The Zoo Gang' and in 1983 composed the theme music for the Michael Caine film *The Honorary Consul*, while his biggest screen venture was the feature film *Give My Regards To Broad Street* in 1984.

In 1968 he began his affair with **Linda Eastman** and the couple were married in March 1969. Paul adopted Linda's daughter **Heather** and the couple had three children of their own, **Mary**, **Stella** and **James**.

During the filming and recording of the *Let It Be* project, tempers became frayed and George walked out of the project after an argument with Paul. He returned, but the Beatles were no longer the close team they used to be. A major split had developed between Paul and his three partners over the decision they made to appoint **Allen Klein** as manager, against Paul's wishes. Paul recorded a solo album *McCartney*, and had to argue with the other members and Allen Klein regarding its release date. It was finally issued in Britain on Apple PCS 7102 on 17 April 1970 and in America on Apple STAO 3363 on 20 April 1970. He was to form his own group called **Wings**, which had several changes of personnel, but whose line-up included his wife Linda on keyboards. His solo albums and those with Wings have included: *Ram*, issued in Britain on Apple PAS 10003 on 21 May 1971 and in America on Apple SMAS 3375 on 17 May 1971; *Wild Life*, issued in Britain on Apple PCS 7142 on 3 December 1971 and in America on Apple SW 3386 on 7 December 1971; *Red Rose Speedway*, issued in Britain on Apple PCTC 251 on 3 May 1973 and in America on Apple SMAL 3409 on 30 April 1973; *Band On The Run*, issued in Britain on Apple PAS 10007 on 30 November 1973 and in America on Apple 1873 on 8 April 1974; *Venus And Mars*, issued in Britain on Capitol PCTC 254 on 30 May 1975 and in America on Capitol SMAS 11419 on 27 May 1975; *Wings At the Speed Of Sound*, issued in Britain on Parlophone PAS 10010 on 26 March 1976 and in America on Capitol SW 11525 on 25 March 1976; *Wings Over America*, issued in Britain on Parlophone PCSP 720 on 10 December 1976 and in America on Capitol SWCO 11593 on 11 December 1976; *London Town*, issued in Britain on Parlophone PAS 10012 on 31 March 1978 and in America on Capitol SW 11777 on 31 March 1978; *Wings Greatest*, issued in Britain on Parlophone PCTC 256 on 1 December 1978 and in America on Capitol SOO 11905 on 22 November 1978; *Back To The Egg*, issued in Britain on Parlophone/MPL PCTC 257 on 8 June 1979 and in America on Columbia FC-36057 on 24 May 1979; *McCartney II*, issued in Britain on Parlophone PCTC 258 on 16 May 1980 and in America on Columbia FC-36511 on 21 May 1980; *Tug Of War* issued in Britain on Parlophone PCTC 259 on 26 April 1982 and in America on Columbia TC 37462 on 26 April 1982; *Pipes Of Peace*, issued in Britain on Parlophone PCTC 1652301 on 31 October 1983 and in America on Columbia QC 39149 on 31 October 1983. There have been several other releases, with Paul being the most active of all the ex-Beatles and the one with the most extensive discography.

His singles have included: 'Another Day' c/w 'Oh Woman Oh Why', issued in Britain on Apple R 5889 on 19 February 1971 and in America on Apple 1829 on 22 February 1971; 'The Back Seat Of My Car' c/w 'Heart Of The Country', issued in Britain on Apple R 5914 on 1[illegible] August 1971; 'Give Ireland Back To The Irish', issued in Britain on Apple R 5936 on 25 February 1972 and in America on Apple 1847 on 28 February 1972; 'Mary Ha[illegible] A Little Lamb' c/w 'Little Woman Love', issued in Britain on Apple R 5949 on 5 May 1972 and in America on Appl[illegible] 1851 on 29 May 1972; 'Hi Hi Hi' c/w 'C Moon', issued in Britain on Apple R 5973 on 1 December 1972 and in America on Apple 1857 on 4 December 1972; 'My Love

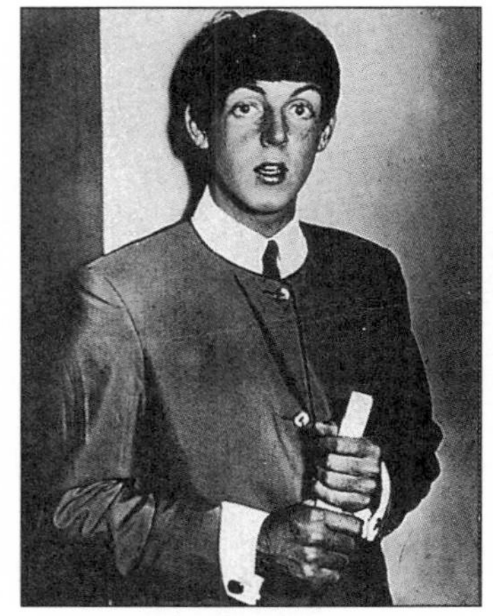

Above: Paul and John in the Cavern days. (*Mersey Beat* Archives)
Left: From the Nevitsky Collection.
Right: Paul in familiar left-handed guitar pose. (©Apple/Walter Shenson Films)

c/w 'The Mess' issued in Britain on Apple R 5985 on 23 March 1973 and in America on Apple 1861 on 9 April 1973; 'Live And Let Die' c/w 'I Lie Around', issued in Britain on Apple R 5987 on 1 June 1973 and in America on Apple 1863 on 18 June 1973; 'Helen Wheels' c/w 'Country Dreamer', issued in Britain on Apple R 5993 on 26 October 1973 and in America on Apple 1869 on 12 November 1973; 'Jet' c/w 'Let Me Roll It', issued in Britain on Apple R 5996 on 18 February 1974 and in America on Apple 1871 on 18 February 1974; 'Band On The Run' c/w 'Zoo Gang', issued in Britain on Apple R 5997 on 28 June 1974 and issued in America on Apple 1873 on 8 April 1974 with 'Nineteen Hundred And Eighty Five' replacing 'Zoo Gang' on the flip; 'Junior's Farm' c/w 'Sally G', issued in Britain on Apple R 5999 on 25 October 1974 and in America on Apple 1875 on 4 November 1974; 'Listen To What The Man Said' c/w 'Love In Song', issued in Britain on Capitol R 6006 on 16 May 1975 and in America on Capitol 4091 on 23 May 1975; 'Letting Go' c/w 'You Gave Me the Answer', issued in Britain on Capitol R 6008 on 5 September 1975 and in America on Capitol 4145 on 29 September 1975; 'Venus And Mars' c/w 'Magneto And Titanium Man', issued in Britain on Capitol R 6010 on 28 November 1975 and in America on Capitol 4175 on 27 October 1975; 'Silly Love Songs' c/w 'Cook Of The House', issued in Britain on Parlophone R 6014 on 30 April 1976 and in America on Capitol 4256 on 1 April 1976; 'Let 'Em In' c/w 'Bewar My Love' issued in Britain on Parlophone R 6015 on 2 July 1976 and in America on Capitol 4293 on 28 Jun 1976; 'Maybe I'm Amazed' c/w 'Soily', issued in Britai on Parlophone R 6017 on 4 February 1977 and i America on Capitol 4385 on 7 February 1977; 'Mull O Kintyre' c/w 'Girls School', issued in Britain on Capitol 6018 on 11 November 1977 and in America on Capito 4504 on 14 November 1977; 'With A Little Luck' c/ 'Backwards Traveller/Cuff Link', issued in Britain o Parlophone R 6019 on 23 March 1978 and in America o Capitol 4559 on 20 March 1978; 'I've Had Enough' c/ 'Deliver Your Children', issued on Britain on Parlophon R 6020 on 16 June 1978 and in America on Capitol 459 on 12 June 1978; 'London Town' c/w 'I'm Carrying' issued in Britain on Parlophone R 6021 on 15 Septembe 1978 and in America on Capitol 4625 on 21 August 1978 'Goodnight Tonight' c/w 'Daytime Nighttime Suffering' issued in Britain on Parlophone R 6023 on 23 March 197 and in America on Columbia 3-10939 on 15 March 1979 'Old Siam Sir' c/w 'Spin It On', issued in Britain o Parlophone R 6026 on 1 June 1979 – the releases i America differed; 'Gettin' Closer' c/w 'Baby's Request' issued in Britain on Parlophone R 6027 on 10 Augus 1979; 'Wonderful Christmastime' c/w 'Rudolph The Re Nosed Reggae', issued in Britain on Parlophone R 602 on 16 November 1979 and in America on Columbia 1

Ringo, Barbara, Paul and Linda in *Give My Regards To Broad Street.* (EMI)

11162 on 20 November 1979; 'Coming Up' c/w 'Coming Up', issued in Britain on Parlophone R 6035 on 11 April 1980 and in America on Columbia 1-11263 on 15 April 1980; 'Waterfalls' c/w 'Check My Machine', issued in Britain on Parlophone R 6037 on 14 June 1980 and in America on Columbia 1-11335 on 22 July 1980; 'Temporary Secretary' c/w 'Secret Friend', issued in Britain on Parlophone 12 R 6039 on 15 September 1980; 'Ebony & Ivory' recorded with Stevie Wonder, c/w 'Rainclouds', issued in Britain on Parlophone 12 R 6054 on 29 March 1982 and in America on Columbia 18-02860 on 2 April 1982; 'Take It Away' c/w 'I'll Give You A Ring', issued in Britain on Parlophone 12 R 6056 on 5 July 1982 and in America on Columbia 44-03019 on 16 July 1982; 'Tug Of War' c/w 'Get It', issued in Britain on Parlophone R 6057 on 20 September 1982 and in America on Columbia 38-03235 on 14 September 1982; 'This Girl Is Mine', recorded with Michael Jackson, c/w 'Can't Get Out Of The Rain', issued in Britain on Epic EPC A2729 on 29 November 1982 and in America on Epic 34-03288 on 3 October 1982; 'Say Say Say' recorded with Michael Jackson, c/w 'Ode To A Koala Bear', issued in Britain on Parlophone R 6062 on 3 October 1983 and in America on Columbia 38-04168 on 3 October 1983. Paul has had numerous singles issued since and in 1979 was awarded a rhodium-plated disc for his achievements which, by that time, had already brought him 43 songs which were million sellers and 60 Gold Discs. He had sold more records throughout the world than any other artist. Since then, Paul's achievements have continued and he has presented a unique classical piece called 'Liverpool Oratorio' in 1991, has continued to tour and runs one of the largest music publishing catalogues in the world.

● McCartney, Ruth

As Ruth Williams, she became a member of the McCartney clan at the age of five when, on 24 November 1964, her 34-year-old widowed mother Angela married 62-year-old Jim McCartney.

Ruth became Paul's stepsister, was given the McCartney surname and went to live in **Rembrandt**, the McCartneys' home in Hoylake on the Wirral. She recalls that Paul used to refer to her as 'Scabby' because she grazed her knees so often. After she'd broken her leg Paul bought her a pet dog which she called Hamish.

Jane Asher was a frequent companion of Paul's in the first three years of Ruth's life at Rembrandt and the young actress taught her to ride a bicycle. At school locally, Ruth came in for a fair amount of bullying from other children, jealous of her meeting the various famous guests who visited Rembrandt, such as Rod Stewart.

At the age of nine she was learning to play the piano and one day was attempting to play 'Golden Slumbers', a traditional hymn. She wasn't very successful, so Paul helped her out – and as a result he penned his own 'Golden Slumbers', which was included on the *Abbey Road* album. Ruth also recalls that Paul made up a song about her on the spur of the moment at a birthday party. As a young girl she observed the breakdown of Paul's romance with Jane Asher and the flowering of his relationship with **Linda**. Ruth, her mother and Jim were guests of Paul and Linda at the Campbeltown farm, where the conditions were very spartan, according to Ruth.

At fifteen, Ruth took an interest in choreography but claims that she didn't get much encouragement from Paul. Ruth spent twelve years in the McCartney family, but following Jim McCartney's death circumstances changed.

For a time Ruth led a dance trio called Talent, but didn't achieve much success. In 1981 she moved to Kings Lynn where she shared a flat with her mother and worked as a salesgirl at the local Debenham's store. But the McCartney name still brought her to the attention of the press. She returned to her love of dancing and in March 1982 entered a 'Claim To Fame' dance competition at the Embassy Club in Mayfair, London, in which she won a heat. Julian Lennon had a sponsorship link with the competition and as a result their names were romantically linked by the press. Eventually Ruth went to live in Los Angeles to pursue a career in show business.

● McCartney, Stella

Linda McCartney's third child and the second child of both Linda and Paul. Stella was born in King's College Hospital in London on 3 September 1971. As the child was delivered by Caesarean section, Paul was banned from the operating theatre. He said, 'I sat next door in my green apron praying like mad. The name **Wings** just came into my mind.' As a result he called his new band Wings.

● McFall, Ray

When Alan Sytner decided to sell the **Cavern Club** in Liverpool, he received an offer from Ray McFall, who worked on the accounts for the Cavern and another nearby jazz venue. Ray took over the operation from Sytner on 1 October 1959.

Ray was born in the Garston area of Liverpool on 14 November 1926 and during the war worked down the mines as a 'Bevan Boy'. He married and moved to London in 1952, but decided to return to Liverpool as an accountant two years later.

He began to work on accounts for the Sytner family and Alan asked him to handle the accounts of the Cavern Club. He also worked as a cashier on Sundays at the Temple Jazz Club and fulfilled the same function at the Cavern on Thursdays and Saturdays.

Once he'd taken control of the Cavern, Ray's new policies became an important factor in the development of the Liverpool sound. The Cavern had been primarily a jazz club and the local rock groups mainly played on the 'jive hive' circuit. After taking over the running of the club, McFall made a radical departure – he introduced rock 'n' roll. He also pioneered lunchtime sessions.

By the end of February 1961 he'd stopped the modern jazz nights as the musicians had failed to receive the support they'd deserved. The club was now almost exclusively presenting rock 'n' roll, with the **Swinging Bluejeans** running their customary guest night, during which the Beatles made their evening debut on 21 March 1961. This began a stream of appearances by the Beatles which included their 'Welcome Home' session on Friday, 14 July 1961, with Johnny Sandon and the **Remo Four** and the White Eagles Jazz Band.

The Beatles also began their own series of resident nights on Wednesday, 2 August 1961, and made a total of 274 appearances, their final one taking place on 3 August 1963.

As success began to spread across the Mersey scene, Ray undertook a policy of expansion and the Cavern soon became the most famous club in Britain.

McFall also launched a Junior Cavern Club, membership of which cost sixpence (2.5p) with admission at two shillings (10p) for members and two shillings and sixpence (12.5p) for visitors.

The sessions took place between 1.00 p.m. and 4.00 p.m. each Saturday and featured two groups and Top Twenty discs, was strictly for thirteen–sixteen-year-olds and began on 1 February 1964, with a guest appearance by **Billy J. Kramer** who was promoting his latest single, 'Little Children'.

Ray continued his expansion plans and launched a management/agency called Cavern Artists Ltd, and in November 1963 he bought the premises next door to the Cavern, extended the width of the club and began building a recording studio, Cavern Sound, which opened on 15 October 1964. During alterations the old stage had to go and Ray had the idea of selling pieces of the original stage as 'Beatleboard' to Beatle fans who would like a souvenir of the stage on which the group had performed so many times. Beatleboard cost five shillings (25p) a piece, the proceeds being donated to Oxfam. There were so many requests from all over the world that it took four months to fulfil the orders.

Ray McFall, owner of Liverpool's famous Cavern Club.

On Saturday, 12 September 1964, there was a 'Caverncade' – a parade through the streets of Liverpool by groups on decorated floats the proceeds again were donated to Oxfam.

There was even a regular half-hour weekly radio show which took place at the club. Called 'Sunday Night At The Cavern', it was broadcast on **Radio Luxembourg** each Sunday at 10.30 p.m. commencing 15 March 1963. The show was hosted by **Bob Wooler** who played the latest chart records and introduced a group live from the Cavern stage each week.

Unfortunately, Ray had taken on too many enterprises and stretched his capital too far, with the result that he had to declare himself bankrupt, and the Cavern was sold.

While the Cavern had become famous, Ray had become a minor celebrity and began to travel widely. He joined the Beatles on their first trip to America, but while he was away, things began to deteriorate at the club, particularly in relation to the cash which was collected at the door each session, much of which became unaccounted for. Unfortunately, Ray couldn't salvage the situation and the club was never the same after he left, and it was eventually torn down to make way for an air vent for an underground railway in 1973. A decade later, a new Cavern was rebuilt on the site of the old.

Ray moved down to London and resumed his career as an accountant.

● McKinnon, Duncan

An elderly chicken farmer from Dumfries who acted as **Larry Parnes'** intermediary for the **Johnny Gentle** tour of Scotland in May 1960, during which the Liverpool singer was backed by the Silver Beatles.

The tour was a short one covering Alloa, Inverness, Fraserburgh, Keith, Forres, Nairn and Peterhead.

McKinnon didn't like the appearance of the Silver Beatles and immediately phoned Larry Parnes to complain. He wanted to sack the band, but Gentle intervened on their behalf and arranged for them to have a more presentable 'look', wearing black shirts.

● McLemore Avenue

Title of an album by Booker T & the MG's which reached No. 76 in the American charts in June 1970. Their single, 'Something', taken from the *McLemore Avenue* album, also reached No. 76 in the American charts. The group had formed in 1962 in Memphis and had enjoyed several chart hits, including 'Green Onions'. They comprised Booker T. Jones (keyboards), Steve Cropper (guitar), Lewis Steinberg (bass), Donald Dunn (bass) and Al Jackson Jr. (drums).

The album was an instrumental interpretation of the *Abbey Road* album and the first album to 'cover' an entire Beatles LP. It was also released in Britain on Stax SXATS 1031 and reached No. 70 in the British charts in July 1970.

The group named the album after the street in Memphis where their own recording studios were located. They also had a photograph of the group walking across 'McLemore Avenue' on the album cover.

● Mean Mr Mustard

A number penned by John during his sojourn at Rishikesh in India. The number was included on Side Two of the *Abbey Road* album, which had some medley tracks.

'Mean Mr Mustard', about a peculiar chap who went around with a ten-shilling note stuck up his nose, was recorded as one song, not segued, with 'Sun King', although both tracks when originally recorded in July 1969 were recorded under the working title 'Here Comes The Sun King'.

● Mean Woman Blues

Composition by Claude DeMetrius which was featured by **Elvis Presley** in his movie *Loving You*, in 1957 and also recorded by **Jerry Lee Lewis. Roy Orbison** had a hit with the number in 1963.

The **Quarry Men** introduced the song into their early repertoire and, being popularized by Presley, it was probably sung by John Lennon.

● Meehan, Tony

Meehan was drummer with the **Shadows, Cliff Richard**'s backing group and the most successful British pop group prior to the Beatles. He left the Shadows in September 1961 to join Decca Records as a record producer, his final single with the Shadows being the hit 'Wonderful Land'. Guitarist Jet Harris also left the band shortly after 'Wonderful Land' entered the charts.

Under **Dick Rowe,** the **Decca** A&R department was intending to search for new talent for pop singles. After the Beatles had auditioned for Decca, the group were rejected. Brian Epstein tried to convince Decca that they should sign the group, but Dick Rowe merely suggested that he hire Tony Meehan to produce a session for him. Epstein felt insulted at being asked to pay £100 in advance for the hire of the studio and Meehan's time to record the Beatles, but he went along to the West Hampstead studio where he had to wait for half an hour before Meehan saw him. Epstein reported in his autobiography that Meehan seemed uninterested in the group, insisted that he and Rowe were busy men and that Brian should phone Meehan's secretary to make an appointment for the Beatles to make the record. Feeling insulted, Epstein wrote a letter to Rowe saying that he would not be taking up the offer of Meehan making a record with the Beatles.

Meehan's version of the story is different. He said he

talked briefly to Brian for five minutes, but their discussion had been friendly. Interestingly, Meehan teamed up with his former Shadow member Jet Harris to make records for Decca in 1963 and they had three chart records, including the chart topper 'Diamonds'.

Also of note is the fact that after leaving the Shadows, Harris made a couple of solo singles. One of them was 'Besame Mucho', one of the tracks the Beatles had recorded for Decca.

● Meet The Beatles

Finally, twelve months after **EMI** had been asking **Capitol** to issue Beatles products, the American label decided to issue their first Beatles album.

They took the British release *With The Beatles* and altered it slightly, changing the name to *Meet The Beatles*. They used the same, famous half-light portrait shots of **Robert Freeman**'s, although the actual cover design was slightly changed.

For the American release – as Capitol generally included less tracks on their albums than EMI – only nine of the original fourteen tracks from *With The Beatles* were used, together with 'I Saw Her Standing There', 'I Want To Hold Your Hand' and 'This Boy'.

The American LP was issued on Capitol 2047 on 20 January 1964, reached No. 1 in the charts and eventually sold over five million copies.

The full track listing is – Side One: 'I Want To Hold Your Hand', 'I Saw Her Standing There', 'This Boy', 'It Won't Be Long', 'All I've Got To Do', 'All My Loving'. Side Two: 'Don't Bother Me', 'Little Child', 'Till There Was You', 'Hold Me Tight', 'I Wanna Be Your Man', 'Not A Second Time'.

● Memorial Auditorium, Dallas, Texas

The Beatles appeared at this arena on Friday, 18 September 1964. The show had been promoted by Super Shows Inc and the entire 10,000 tickets had sold out within a day.

The group arrived in Dallas and drove to the **Cabana Motor Hotel.** There was a telephone call reporting that a bomb had been planted in the auditorium. The opening was delayed while police searched the arena – no bomb was found, but fans were discovered hiding in washrooms and under the stage. There were a total of 200 police in the auditorium and a further 200 were on stand-by. The Police Chief, Jesse Curry, brought along his daughter and two grandchildren. There was a press conference in the stadium at 7.00 p.m., the last one of the tour.

After the show, the Beatles were taken to the airport and flown to a ranch for a few days' holiday, while most members of their entourage remained at the hotel.

● Memorial Coliseum, Portland, Oregon

During their 1965 tour of America, the Beatles performed two shows at this arena before a total audience of 20,000 on Sunday, 22 August 1965.

Newspapers reported the drama as one of the engines on the plane which flew them into Portland caught fire and emitted smoke.

Among the Beatles' visitors backstage that evening were Carl Wilson and **Mike Love** of the **Beach Boys**.

● Memorial Hall, Chester Way, Northwich, Cheshire

Venue only 25 miles from Liverpool. The Beatles made their debut at the hall, also known as the Victory, on 2 June 1962. Other appearances took place on 1 September 1962, 1 December 1962, 27 April 1963, 6 July 1963 and 14 September 1963. Prior to their July 1963 appearance, the Beatles visited the Northwich Carnival where Paul McCartney crowned the Carnival Queen.

● Memphis, Tennessee

Chuck Berry composition which he recorded in 1959 although he didn't enter the British charts with the number until October 1963.

The Beatles included the number in their repertoire in 1961, when it was sung by John.

They featured the song on several of their BBC radio recordings, including two **'Saturday Club'** shows, two **'Pop Go The Beatles'** shows and **'Teenager's Turn'**.

The song also surfaced on *The Beatles Live! At The Star Club In Hamburg, Germany: 1962* album.

● Mendips, 251 Menlove Avenue, Liverpool 25

The semi-detached home where John Lennon was reared by his Aunt **Mimi** and Uncle George from the age of five. The house was named after the Welsh hills. John spent more of his life at this home than any other, almost 2[illegible] years, until he eventually moved down to London. From his bedroom above the front door, he learned to play his acoustic guitar, and he continued to practise in the small front porch.

Mendips is a pleasant home, with a large garden in an extremely nice area of Liverpool, so different from many people's idea of the slum which writers often believed the working class hero' came from.

● Mersey Beat

Title of the newspaper which gave the Liverpool sound its name.

Bill Harry was a student at **Liverpool College of Art** who'd worked on a music magazine for the local music store, **Frank Hessy's**. He was at one time considering launching a jazz magazine called 'Storyville/52nd Street', but due to his friendship with John Lennon and **Stuart Sutcliffe,** decided to produce a newspaper promoting the local rock 'n' roll scene.

A friend, Dick Mathews, who used to frequent the **Jacaranda** coffee club, knew that Bill was seeking finance to start the publication and introduced him to Jim Anderson, who provided the £50 needed to launch the magazine.

A small office was rented on the top floor of David Land, the wine merchant at 51 Renshaw Street and, as Bill was still studying at the art college, the only full-time member of staff was his girlfriend, Virginia.

Mendips – the house on Menlove Avenue where John Lennon was reared by his Aunt Mimi.

At that time the local groups were referred to as rock 'n' roll groups and most of the venues were called jive hives. The term 'beat' was seldom used. It was while Harry was sitting in the office late one night that he conceived the name. He was visualizing the area he would cover and defined it in his mind as reaching 'across the water' to the Wirral, extending out to the seaside resort of Southport and to nearby towns such as Widnes and Warrington. He pictured it as a policeman's beat across Merseyside and came up with the name *Mersey Beat*.

The first issue was published on 6 July 1961 and 5,000 copies were distributed through three wholesalers, Blackburn's, Conlan's and W. H. Smith, to 28 separate newsagents, to venues such as the **Cavern** and Mardi Gras and to all the record and musical instruments stores in the city centre, including Cranes, **Rushworths,** Cramer and Lea and **NEMS**. A particular interest was shown by the manager of NEMS in Whitechapel, Brian Epstein, who ordered twelve copies, then phoned for more when they immediately sold out. He ordered twelve dozen copies of issue No. 2 and wanted to know all about the phenomenon that seemed to be happening on his own doorstep – the local music scene he read about in the paper.

The entire edition sold out and orders continued to increase over succeeding issues. The Beatles were strongly featured from the very first issue and they used to drop into the *Mersey Beat* office to help Virginia out, answering the phone, typing – with John contributing a column.

Harry had asked John to come up with a biography of the Beatles and he submitted a piece which Harry called 'Being a Short Diversion On The Dubious Origins Of Beatles. Translated From The John Lennon'. John was so delighted with his piece being published in its entirety, that he brought a huge bundle of stories, poems and drawings, some of which were then published under the name Beatcomber, a pseudonym thought up by Harry in deference to the humorous Beachcomber column in the *Daily Express* newspaper. John Lennon also used to pay to take out classified advertisements.

The front page of issue No. 2, published on 20 July 1961, was devoted to the Polydor recordings with 'Beatles Sign Recording Contract!' as the headline illustrated by an **Astrid Kirchherr** photograph of the group in Hamburg. The Beatles were strongly featured in every issue and Harry also published letters which Paul McCartney sent him, together with photographs by **Mike McCartney.**

Left: Bill Harry presenting the Beatles with their first award ever – the Mersey Beat shield. (*Mersey Beat* archives.)
Below: Virginia Harry – originally the only full-time member of staff.

When the Beatles brought Harry photographs by Astrid Kirchherr and Jurgen Vollmer for him to publish, *Mersey Beat* began to take on a look totally unlike that of the music press, which was based in London. The photographic content, with the addition of the photographs taken by Dick Mathews, **Peter Kaye,** Graham Spencer and other local photographers, was innovative for its time.

Brian Epstein was impressed by the huge sales of *Mersey Beat* in his own store and asked if he could review records. His column was published as 'Stop The World – And Listen To Everything In It' and captioned 'Brian Epstein Of NEMS'.

Bob Wooler wrote a major feature on the Beatles in which he described them as a 'phenomenon' in the 31 August 1961 issue – an article which impressed Epstein even further with a group he had already begun to make enquiries about. Wooler also placed them No. 1 in his own personal Top Ten in the 5 October 1961 issue and they topped the *Mersey Beat* poll, announced in issue No. 13 on 4 January 1962.

Paul McCartney wondered whether the Beatles had altered the poll because they filled out a number of coupons for themselves – but most groups were doing this. Bill Harry and Virginia did the final count, eliminating the most obvious 'phoneys', and decided that the Beatles were definitely the winners and, after all, they'd been promote so heavily in every issue that it was almost a foregon conclusion. Local disc jockey Bob Wooler came to th *Mersey Beat* office and told Harry that it was causin resentment among the other groups who were now callir the paper 'The Mersey Beatle'. Harry then included special section called 'The Mersey Beatle'.

Once *Mersey Beat* had been published, th transformation in the local scene was enormous. What ha been 'underground' became 'overground' and peopl began to realize just how big the local scene was. Even received more promotion and advertising and the events became bigger.

The paper was now the unofficial HQ of the local scene, which now began to call itself the Mersey beat scene – and the groups had now started calling themselves beat groups instead of rock 'n' roll groups. The managers and group members visited the *Mersey Beat* offices daily and the paper's circulation was increasing to such an extent that larger offices had to be found, so the entire first floor of 51 Renshaw Street was taken over by the paper.

Harry needed more working capital to expand so he approached **Ray McFall** of the Cavern who agreed to provide finance, mainly guaranteed by large Cavern advertisements, and to act as a silent partner, with shares also going to Virginia and McFall's wife.

The publication continued to expand and introduced many innovations which were later adopted by the traditional music press – including the first gig guide, the first Top 100 chart, the first weekly listing of all the record releases and so on. The magazine had also expanded its coverage to take in the entire country, beginning with a section on the Manchester scene and one on the Birmingham scene, with coverage of groups from Sheffield, Newcastle, Glasgow and other provincial cities. By 1963 it had become the most imitated publication in the British Isles with no less than eighteen other publications based on it – including *Midland Beat* in Birmingham, *Western Scene* in Bristol, *Scottish Beat* covering the Scottish scene and so on.

In September 1964, due to the problems he was encountering at the Cavern, McFall asked Brian Epstein if he would buy his shares, which he agreed to do. Epstein's solicitor Rex Makin visited Harry to assure him of his editorial independence. He was told he would enjoy security with the publication, that Brian would be pouring a lot of money into it and that the copyright of all the previous issues would remain with Harry.

Mersey Beat became a full-colour weekly and initially continued to expand, becoming the first British music paper to be circulated in America. Epstein had requested a new name and Harry gave it the title *Music Echo*. Virginia had left several months earlier for a position in one of the major local booking agencies where she worked with Mike Chamberlain. She told Mike that Bill needed help with the publication and he became the Assistant Editor.

New offices were found in Hackins Hey, on the same floor as **Freda Kelly** and the Beatles Fan Club.

Epstein brought in a managing editor from London, Brian Harvey, and the paper soon began to change. Harry strongly disagreed with the alterations that stripped the paper of its innovative thrust and turned it into a carbon copy of the London music publications. Against Harry's wishes commissions were made for gossip columns from London, a fashion column and the type of features used in the other weeklies, e.g. 'A star at home', which were basically fan-style features and not the gutsy sort of features previously favoured by *Mersey Beat*.

Mersey Beat had also been innovative in its use of covers, giving acts like the **Rolling Stones** their first-ever cover and selecting groups on their quality rather than their current chart status. Epstein insisted that whoever was No. 1 in the charts had to be on the front cover. The first time this was done, the identical cover appeared on *Music Echo*, *Disc* and *Record Mirror* during the same week, a photograph of the Kinks. Harry resigned, even though the paper was in the black with a print order of 75,000 a week.

Epstein made an offer for Harry to work with him in London, but was turned down. Within a year, *Music Echo* was in trouble, unable to compete with the London weeklies on their terms. Epstein had no choice but to make a deal for it to merge with *Disc*.

● *Merseybeats,* The

A Liverpool band who were called the Mavericks. Due to the success of the ***Mersey Beat*** newspaper, they approached Bill Harry, who had the name Mersey Beat copyrighted, to ask his permission to use the name the Mersey Beats. He agreed and, under that name, they began to find success. At the time they comprised Tony Crane (lead/vocals), Billy Kinsley (bass/vocals), Aaron Williams (rhythm) and John Banks (drums).

The group began a Monday night residency at **St John's Hall**, Bootle, and one of their special guests was the Beatles.

After Brian Epstein had been forced to sack **Pete Best** on the instructions of the other members of the Beatles, he continued to feel guilty about the deed and requested another meeting with Pete. He told him, 'I have an idea that might work. I'm thinking of signing the Mersey Beats and I'd like you to join them.' Pete felt that after being in

Liverpool's top group it would be a retrograde step to join a new, young group who had not achieved any success and turned the offer down. Epstein decided not to sign them.

The group slightly altered their name from the Mersey Beats to the Merseybeats and became quite successful, with chart hits such as 'It's Love That Really Counts', 'I Think Of You', 'Don't Turn Around', 'Wishin' And Hopin'', 'Last Night', 'I Love You, Yes I Do' and 'I Stand Accused'.

The group appeared second on the bill to the Beatles at the Beatles' final appearance at the **Cavern Club** on 3 August 1963.

Billy Kinsley left the group, to be replaced by Johnny Gustafson, formerly of the **Big Three**. Gustafson approached Epstein to be their manager, but Epstein declined.

The Merseybeats, a Liverpool band who enjoyed several chart hits. (Edsel Records)

The group disbanded early in 1966 soon after Billy Kinsley rejoined. Billy and Tony teamed up as the duo the Merseys and had a hit with 'Sorrow' and were finally signed up by Epstein to **NEMS Enterprises**. George Harrison took a line from 'Sorrow', relating to a girl with 'long blonde hair and eyes of blue', and included it on his *Yellow Submarine* composition 'It's All Too Much', in tribute to his wife **Pattie.**

The Merseys split up and Tony Crane reformed the Merseybeats with different musicians and is still actively leading the group today.

Billy Kinsley returned to Liverpool and, ironically, became involved in a group with **Pete Best** and the two have since worked together on various recordings.

● Mersey Beat Showcase

In 1963 the stranglehold London had on the British pop world was finally smashed with the flood of hit groups emerging from Merseyside. The national tours that year, on which the Beatles appeared, contained bills with various chart acts from around the country. Epstein decided to take advantage of the growing interest in the Liverpool sound by promoting a package of his own acts. He approached Bill Harry, who held the copyright to the name 'Mersey Beat', for permission to call his package *Mersey Beat Showcase*. Harry agreed, and Brian launched the first of the *Mersey Beat Showcases* at the **Elizabethan Ballroom, Nottingham,** on 7 March 1963. Groups on the bill were the Beatles, **Gerry & the Pacemakers,** the **Big Three** and **Billy J. Kramer** & the Dakotas – with **Cavern** disc jockey **Bob Wooler** as compere.

During the next six months Brian promoted a further six *Mersey Beat Showcase* presentations which included the **King's Hall, Stoke-on-Trent** on 19 April; the **Majestic Ballroom, Finsbury Park** on 24 April; the **Fairfield Hall, Croydon** on 25 April; the **Tower Ballroom, New Brighton** on 14 June and the **Odeon, Romford** on 16 June. On the final *Mersey Beat Showcase* in Romford, three of the acts, the Beatles, Gerry & the Pacemakers and Billy J. Kramer & the Dakotas, occupied the top three positions in the British charts.

● Merseyside Civil Service Club, *Lower Castle Street, Liverpool L2*

The Beatles were booked for a series of four appearances at this small club near to Liverpool's Pier Head. All four gigs took place in November 1961. Their debut there took place on 7 November, followed by performances on 14, 2[illegible] and 28 November.

Mersey-Motown Sound, The

One of the major musical influences on the Liverpool groups in the early sixties was the Tamla Motown record label, created in Detroit by Berry Gordy Junior in 1959. Berry had originally derived the name Tamla from a Debbie Reynolds film *Tammy* and Motown was an abbreviation of the nickname or Detroit: Motor City. Berry actually used the name Tamla as a label in America in 1959 and Motown in 1961. The name Tamla Motown was used on the European releases.

In Britain in 1962, Tamla Motown was distributed by a small record label, Oriole, and the largest market for the records by the Detroit groups was on Merseyside.

At that time, the local music paper ***Mersey Beat*** began to feature Tamla Motown in each issue, profiling the artists and reviewing the latest releases. Oriole Records began to take half-page advertisements advertising Tamla Motown due to the interest aroused in the label in Liverpool.

When he received the latest Motown singles, *Mersey Beat* editor Bill Harry would take them down to the **Cavern**. When he took 'Fingertips' by Little Stevie Wonder, Ringo was there and requested it. Harry gave it to him. When Ringo later said it was his favourite, Harry told John Schroeder of Oriole who arranged for a complete Tamla Motown collection to be sent to Ringo.

The Tamla Motown numbers were included in the repertoire of the Liverpool bands. They adapted the songs to fit in with the developing Liverpool sound, the basic three guitars/drums/harmony line-up which produced a hybrid sound, known locally as 'the Mersey-Motown Sound'.

This particular sound found its way on record when a number of Mersey acts recorded their own versions of Motown numbers: Faron's Flamingoes with 'Do You Love Me' and 'Shake Sherry', Ian & the Zodiacs with 'Beechwood 45789', **Beryl Marsden** with 'When The Love Light Shines' and so on.

Differing from the Mersey-Motown sound was the straight Motown-sounding presentation of numbers by the local black vocal groups such as the **Chants**, who performed numbers made popular by acts such as the Miracles and the Marvellettes.

In 1963 the Motown distribution in Britain went to **EMI**'s Stateside label and the Motown artists soon began to have their first British hits, particularly since the Beatles had begun to mention the Motown artists in interviews.

1963 was also the year when the Beatles made their own Mersey-Motown recordings, with no less than three Motown numbers on their *With the Beatles* album: 'Please Mr Postman', 'You Really Got A Hold On Me' and 'Money (That's What I Want)'.

The Beatles also requested that **Mary Wells** be included on their autumn tour of Britain in 1964. Mary was later to pay her own tribute to the Beatles with an album of Lennon & McCartney songs.

Brian Epstein also became a fan of Motown artists and brought the **Four Tops** over to Britain to tour.

Paul McCartney was later to forge a close association with Motown artists, recording 'Ebony and Ivory' with Stevie Wonder and 'This Girl Is Mine', 'Say Say Say' and 'The Man' with Michael Jackson.

Ironically, the only reference to the Mersey-Motown Sound in the Motown Museum in Detroit is an inaccurate one. There is a picture of the **Dave Clark Five** with the Supremes which is captioned 'Liverpool Meets Detroit'.

Mersey Sound, The

The first major television documentary to concern itself with the Beatles and the Mersey sound. The programme, produced by Don Howarth, was first broadcast on BBC 1 on 9 October 1963 and was repeated on 13 November.

Howarth spent several weeks in Liverpool prior to the recording and filmed activities inside the ***Mersey Beat*** office: a conversation with a musician commenting on groups on the dole, a local promoter discussing protection rackets (there were none in Liverpool), scenes at the **Iron Door Club** with the Undertakers and Group One performing, and the Beatles commenting on their early careers, discussing fan letters, their home lives and their ambitions. There were scenes at **NEMS** record store, **Rushworths** music shop and outside Ringo's house in Admiral Grove. The group were televised performing on stage during their appearance at the **Odeon, Southport** and among the numbers they sang were 'Love Me Do', 'Twist & Shout' and 'She Loves You'.

Don Howarth told *Mersey Beat:* 'I visited Liverpool several months ago to see if the city was a good subject for a programme. I saw Bill Harry, Brian Epstein and several of the leading lights in the Beat scene, and visited several clubs including the **Cavern** and the Iron Door. Within two days I knew that there was such atmosphere and excitement on the Mersey Beat scene that I just had to use it in a programme. When I brought the production unit down in August I decided to let the people on Merseyside make their own comments on the scene and allowed the people who were interviewed to talk freely. In that way a truer picture of the scene could be formed.'

This is the documentary in which Ringo, dressed smartly in a suit, walks past a bank of hairdriers at a hairdresser's declaring that his ambition is to make enough money to open his own salon.

● Mersey View, Overton Hills, Frodsham, Warrington, Cheshire

Venue only twenty miles from Liverpool where Mersey groups played on a regular basis.

The Beatles only appeared at the venue once, on 20 April 1963. Entertainment is still provided at the venue, which is now known as the Mersey View Country Club.

● Michelle

Song penned by Paul which first appeared on the *Rubber Soul* album issued on 3 December 1965. Within a month of the album's release there were over twenty cover versions of the number. In Britain both the **Overlanders** and **David & Jonathan** found themselves with a major hit, the former reaching the No. 1 spot. There were a staggering number of versions recorded by almost 700 artists throughout the world, including Booker T and the MG's, the **Four Tops**, Jan & Dean, Jack Jones, Johnny Mathis, Diana Ross & the Supremes, George Shearing, Sarah Vaughan and Andy Williams.

The Beatles version was included on their EP *Nowhere Man*, issued in July 1966, and on several album compilations, including *A Collection of Beatles Oldies (But Goldies)* in 1966, *The Beatles 1966–1970* in 1973, *Love Songs* in 1977 and *The Beatles Ballads* and *The Beatles Box* in 1980.

Anthony Howard, who once worked for the Beatles organization, claimed that the song had been inspired by his daughter Michelle. He said, 'Michelle was a great friend of the Beatles and they loved her. They wrote a song called "Michelle" which was done for her.' In January 1981 Michelle Howard hit the headlines in the British press with stories such as 'Drugs Battle of Beatles Michelle', when, aged 23, she was charged with shoplifting and possession of drugs.

Despite the claim, when Paul was appearing on the London Weekend Television chat show 'Aspel And Company' in 1984, he discussed the inspiration behind his songs and said, 'I just kind of make it up. "Michelle" – I've never met her. I make it up, that's how I write'.

Soon after writing the song, Paul said, 'I just fancied writing some French words and I have a friend (**Ivan Vaughan**) whose wife taught French and we were sitting around and I just asked her, you know, what we could figure that was French. We got words that go together well. It was mainly because I always used to think the song always sounded like a French thing, and I can't speak French really, so we sorted out some actual words.'

● Mid-South Coliseum, Memphis, Tennessee

Site of the Beatles' first date in the American South following the controversial statement by John about the Beatles being bigger than Christ. The anti-Beatles protesters were strong in the Southern states and prior to their appearance at the **Mid-South Coliseum**, an anonymous phone call threatened that one or all of the Beatles would be shot on stage during one of the two concert appearances there.

Six members of the Ku Klux Klan picketed the venue, which had a capacity of 13,300 and which drew 10,000 to the afternoon show and 12,300 to the evening performance. During the evening performance a firecracker exploded and the Beatles thought it was a shot. Publicist **Tony Barrow** commented: 'Each Beatle just glanced at the others to see if one of them would drop. It says something for them that they didn't miss a note.'

● Mike Cotton Sound, The

When beat music became a force in 1963, Mike Cotton, who'd formerly led a jazz band, steered his band into playing R&B. The Mike Cotton Sound, as they were now known, were booked to appear on *Another Beatles Show* at the **Odeon, Hammersmith**, London, in December 1964/January 1965.

They comprised Mike Cotton (trumpet), Johnny Crocker (trombone), Stu Morrison (banjo), Dave Rowberry (keyboards), Derek Tearle (bass guitar) and Jim Garforth (drums). Rowberry later became a member of the Animals.

Miles, Barry

Jsually known simply as 'Miles', he co-owned the **Indica ;allery** where he became friendly with the Beatles, in articular with Paul and John. Miles was later involved in ne 'underground' newspaper *International Times* to which ohn donated £1,000.

Miles was a link between the Beatles and the worlds of ne arts and the avant-garde and at one time it was

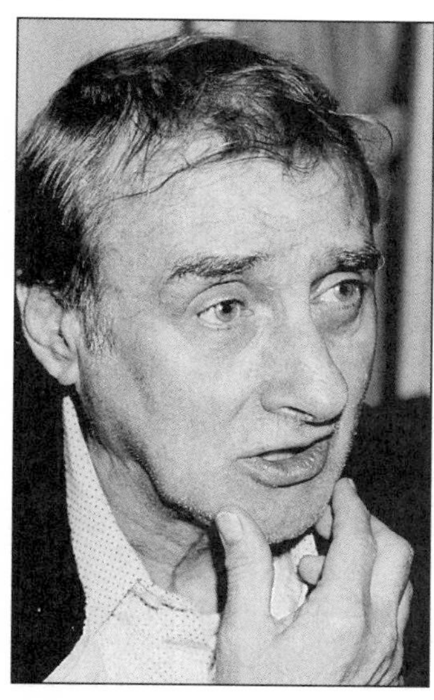

Spike Milligan, the ormer member of the Goons, held in high steem by the Beatles. Spike Milligan)

tended that he should organize a number of poets and thors to record for Apple's experimental label Zapple.

In 1978 he compiled the book *Beatles In Their Own ords* for Omnibus Press. Author of books on **Allen insberg**, he is also working on a biography of Paul cCartney and William S. Burroughs.

Milligan, Spike

zany British comedian, humorist and author, former ember of the Goons, who were very popular with the itish public in the fifties due to their anarchistic radio ries. Milligan was one of John Lennon's major literary fluences and he particularly enjoyed Spike's brand of mour.

John contributed a review of Spike's book *The Goon ow Scripts* to the 30 September 1973 issue of the *New rk Times*.

George Martin produced Spike's single 'Purple Aeroplane', issued on Parlophone R5513, which was a parody of 'Yellow Submarine'.

In 1981 Spike asked if Paul and George Harrison could contribute to a fund to set up a sanctuary for otters in Gloucestershire. They chipped in with £800 each.

Paul had once taken **Jane Asher** to see Spike in the West End stage production of *Son Of Oblomov* on 8 March 1964. Spike also inspired Paul to write 'Ebony And Ivory'. Paul has related how he was in Scotland, sitting at his piano, and he remembered a title he'd had in his head for some years after hearing Spike Milligan using the black and white notes on the piano as an analogy of harmonious race relations. The song 'Ebony And Ivory' developed from there.

● Millings, Dougie

Well-known show business tailor. From the late fifties he had built up a business specializing in clothing stars of the entertainment world and by the time Brian Epstein visited him in 1963 he had 80 show business clients, including **Cliff Richard** & the **Shadows**, Tommy Steele, **Billy Fury** and Marty Wilde. Brian dropped into Millings' shop at 63 Old Compton Street in Soho, London W1, with **Gerry Marsden** and discussed with Dougie the possibility of him becoming the tailor for his various acts.

Dougie and his son Gordon provided the Beatles with their stagewear for several years, during which they produced 500 garments for the group, including the famous collarless jacket. This was based on sketches of a steward's jacket after discussions with Brian and the Beatles.

Dougie charged £31 per suit at the time and established a rapport with the group, who called him 'Dad'. In fact, they got on with him so well that they insisted he be given a cameo role in *A Hard Day's Night*. The part of 'A Tailor' was introduced, although most of it ended on the cutting room floor. In the film Dougie had to wear a frown of frustration due to his unsuccessful attempts to measure the group, because they were never able to stand still.

Dougie also made the suits for the original **Madame Tussauds** waxworks figures of the Beatles.

He'd moved to Great Pulteney Street by the time the Beatles were set to make their first tour of America and the wardrobe which he and Gordon made from lightweight wool and mohair were in dark grey and dark blue, with velvet collars. Half a dozen of each suit were made for each member of the group.

● Mills, Hayley

Actress daughter of British actor John Mills. Producer **Walter Shenson** had considered engaging the 16-year-old Hayley for an appearance in *A Hard Day's Night* in a romantic sub plot between her and a member of the Beatles. However, he was advised that female Beatle fans might resent one of their idols being involved in a romance on screen and the idea was dropped. However, George was selected as Hayley's escort to a midnight charity performance of the film *Charade* at the Regal Cinema in Henley-on-Thames on 20 March 1964. Due to their one-off 'date', the press attempted to engineer a romance between the two, but George was already smitten by **Pattie Boyd**.

Paul McCartney was later to compose the film music for Hayley's film ***The Family Way***.

When George eventually went to live in Henley, he was once again to visit the Regal – this time to protest outside the cinema with a banner. The 740 seat cinema had originally opened in 1936, but due to the drop in audiences because of competition from video, the cinema was suffering a dearth in patronage fifty years later in 1986 when plans were put forward to level it and build a shopping mall on the site. George joined a number of celebrated Henley residents in a major protest against the plans.

● Milwaukee Arena, Milwaukee, Wisconsin

The Beatles made a single appearance at this venue on 4 September 1964.

When they flew into General Mitchell Field, there were over 1,000 fans at the airport, together with 65 policemen, 32 deputies and four airport police. Sheriff Michael Wolke had fire trucks ready to turn their hoses on the fans if they should break down the fence in the area they'd been herded into.

The Beatles' plane was then instructed to land on the opposite side of the field and the group left for their hotel without any of their fans seeing them.

A five-car motorcade took them to the Coach House Motor Inn where there was a press conference which John didn't attend as he had a sore throat. Most of the questions queried why the Beatles had avoided their fans at the airport – and they explained that it hadn't been their decision.

They took the stage at the **Milwaukee Arena** at 9.08 p.m., dressed in blue mohair suits. After the show they were driven back to their hotel and after dinner were each given antibiotic shots by the hotel doctor as all four were now suffering from colds.

● Misery

A song John and Paul collaborated on which they completed on their tour coach during their **Helen Shapiro** tour.

They'd written the song for Helen Shapiro, but her recording manager turned it down. **Kenny Lynch**, who was also touring with them, showed interest in the number and asked if he could record it. His version was issued by HMV on 22 March 1963, but it didn't have any effect on the charts.

The Beatles recorded it themselves during their marathon *Please Please Me* album session, with John and Paul sharing vocals.

Apart from on the *Please Please Me* album, the song appeared on the EP *The Beatles No. 1*.

Its most frequent use was in America. **Vee Jay** included it on their *Introducing The Beatles*, *The Beatles v The Four Seasons* and *Songs, Pictures and Stories Of The Fabulous Beatles* albums and on the EP *Souvenir Of Their Visit To America*. **Capitol** also issued it as the flipside of 'Roll Over Beethoven' on 11 October 1965 when it was released as part of the Capitol Starline series on Starline 6065. It was also used on the American release *The Beatles Rarities*.

● Modern Jazz Quartet, The

The Modern Jazz Quartet had been established for almost fifteen years when they signed a short-term deal with **Apple Records** in 1968.

The group comprised John Lewis (piano), Milt Jackson (vibes), Percy Heath (bass) and Connie Kay (drums).

The Beatles had long been admirers of the MJQ and when the quartet appeared at the Liverpool Philharmonic Hall in April 1964, John Lewis told ***Mersey Beat***: 'The Beatles are on record as saying they like our kind of music and I think you can say we appreciate their music, too. From the size and reaction of our audiences I'd say there is room enough for both styles in this city, though.'

They left Atlantic Records to sign with Apple, being the nly established act to sign with the label.

The group recorded two albums for Apple, *Under The ısmine Tree*, issued in Britain on 6 December 1968 and ı America on 17 February 1969, and *Space*, issued in ritain on 24 October 1969, and in America on 10 ovember 1969.

Mods And Rockers

ballet set to the Beatles' music which opened at the rince Charles Theatre in London on 18 December 1963. ıe modern ballet ran until 11 January 1964.

Money (That's What I Want)

ng penned by Berry Gordy and Janie Bradford, which ovided Barrett Strong with a hit in 1960. Gordy was to ıd great success building the Motown empire and this ımber is an example of the Motown influence on verpool groups which was called the '**Mersey-Motown ound**'.

The Beatles performed it at their **Decca audition** and is version has found itself onto various bootlegs and ecca audition outtake releases. The group also recorded for their *With The Beatles* album, issued in November 63. The Beatles performed the number on their 'Sunday ght At The London Palladium' appearance in October 63. It was included on their EP, *All My Loving*, the nerican *Beatles Second Album* and *Rock 'n' Roll Music*.

John sings lead vocal on the track and he also rformed it at the Toronto Rock 'n' Roll Revival Concert 1969 and this version appears on his *Live Peace In ronto* album.

A group from the south of England, Bern Elliott & the nmen, had a Top Twenty entry with the number shortly er the *With The Beatles* release, although they said that y first heard the **Searchers** performing it at the **Star ub**, Hamburg, and rushed straight back to England to ord it.

Monkees, The

e to the phenomenal success of the Beatles, NBC-TV cided, in 1966, to create a home-grown American group d attempt to make them as successful as the British artet. Originally they considered using the Lovin' oonful, then decided that a group of unknowns would ve a more interesting challenge. The concept was for the group to star in a major TV series, utilizing the style and techniques used in the Beatles film *A Hard Day's Night*. Producers Bert Schneider and Bob Rafelson advertised for: 'Folk and Rock Musicians – Singers for Acting Roles in new TV series – Running parts for four insane boys, age 17-21'. Hundreds of actors were auditioned and the final line-up of the group was: Mickey Dolenz, drums, vocals; Peter Tork, bass, vocals; Mike Nesmith, guitar, vocals; and Davy Jones, vocals. Jones was the only British member of the band, a native of Manchester, the nearest city to Liverpool, who had appeared as the Artful Dodger in the stage show of *Oliver* and had actually appeared on the same edition of the '**Ed Sullivan** Show' as the Beatles when they made their debut in America.

It was no secret that the group had been manufactured and that they were based on the Beatles, which didn't stop them from becoming a phenomenon and achieving ten gold records within two years with hits such as 'Last Train To Clarksville' and 'I'm A Believer'. American magazines hailed them as 'the new Beatles', and headlines described them as creating 'Monkeemania'.

Peter Tork of the Monkees. (Flying Music Co.)

Publisher Don Kirshner had been asked to find songs for their first recordings and he engaged Tommy Boyce and Bobby Hart to write them. Hart said that the idea for their debut single 'Last Train To Clarksville' came after he'd heard 'Paperback Writer'. He mistakenly thought the Beatles were singing about a 'last train', and developed the idea.

Peter Tork was unhappy with what he considered was manipulation of the group and left following their debut film, *Head*, which had been written by movie star Jack Nicholson.

The others continued as a trio for a short time, then disbanded, only to occasionally reform many years later for some reunion tours.

Musically, the Monkees weren't a challenge to the Beatles and they were aimed strictly at a teenybop audience. Despite this, the press continued to whip up a Beatles-Monkees rivalry, yet the two groups became good friends. Brian Epstein instructed **Vic Lewis** to negotiate for **NEMS Enterprises** to bring the Monkees to Britain and a deal was struck and NEMS presented the Monkees at the Empire Pool, Wembley, from 30 June–3 July 1967. After the final show a special party was held in their honour at the **Speakeasy Club**, Margaret Street, by NEMS, attended by the Beatles, the Bee Gees, Lulu and other British stars.

● 34 Montague Square, *Marylebone, London W1*

After the flat in Whaddon Street, which George and Ringo shared, was burgled in April 1964, the two moved to separate premises.

Ringo moved to a single-bedroom, ground-floor flat in a long Victorian block near the new Swiss Embassy. By Christmas of that year, **Maureen** Cox moved in with him.

After the couple were married and had moved into **Sunny Heights**, Ringo maintained the Montague Square flat and among the guests who stayed there were author William Burroughs and guitarist Jimi Hendrix.

John and **Yoko** were living at the flat on 18 October 1968 when six policemen, one policewoman and a sniffer dog raided the premises. They were led by Sergeant Norman Pilcher. John had been warned in advance of the raid and the flat had been thoroughly cleaned. The police found 1½oz of cannabis resin, which the couple seemed unaware was there, and they were taken to Paddington Green where they were also charged with obstructing the police in the execution of a search warrant.

John was still adamant that the cannabis was not his but because Yoko was pregnant and in order to have th charges against her dropped, he pleaded guilty to th charge on 28 November. He was fined £159 with twent guineas costs, although he was found not guilty o obstructing the police.

On 19 February 1969 Ringo was served with a wri from the landlords Bryman Estates for 'misuse of property The landlords said they had no grouse against th Starkeys, just some of their guests, and they took civi proceedings against Ringo to bar Lennon 'and othe undesirables' from the premises. Ringo was so upset h sold the leasehold to the premises on 28 February 1969.

● Montez, *Chris*

American singer who had his first chart hit with 'Let' Dance' in October 1962. As a result he was chosen b **Arthur Howes** to co-headline a British tour with fello American singer **Tommy Roe** in March 1963. Th Beatles were next on the bill and Montez commente 'Who are these guys the Beatles? I try to keep up to da with the British scene, but I don't know their work.'

'Let's Dance' was a British Top Ten hit once again i 1972 on its re-release and entered the charts for a thi time when it was reissued in 1979.

● Moody Blues, *The*

A group from Birmingham who formed in 1964 an comprised Denny Laine (guitar/vocals), Mike Pind (keyboards), Ray Thomas (horns/vocals), Clint Warwic (bass) and Graeme Edge (drums). Brian Epstei interviewed them for the **'Hullaballoo'** television show 1965 and in September of that year he signed them to management and agency contract. During 1965 they had major hit with 'Go Now', a million-seller which reache No. 1 in Britain and the Top Ten in America. In Decemb 1965 they joined the Beatles on their British tour.

Because of Epstein's initial enthusiasm, the group h believed that Brian would be managing them himself, b he appointed **Alistair Taylor**. By October 1966 they h become so discouraged that Laine and Warwick left, to replaced by Justin Hayward and John Lodge, althou their career seemed on the wane.

They were later to achieve success with best-selli albums such as *Days Of Future Passed*, *In Search Of T* ost Chord* and *On The Threshold Of A Dream*.

When Paul McCartney formed **Wings**, he brought enny Laine into the group and the two of them co-wrote e massive hit 'Mull Of Kintyre'.

● Moon, Keith

efore he died of a drug overdose in 1978 following one of aul McCartney's annual **Buddy Holly** promotions, Moon as known as 'Moon The Loon', one of the zaniest ersonalities of the British rock scene.

The drummer with the Who formed a close relationship ith Ringo Starr and they often went clubbing in each her's company and appeared in a number of films gether, including ***200 Motels***, *That'll Be The Day*, *The ids Are Alright*, *Born To Boogie* and *Sextette*. On Ringo's 5th birthday, Moon and Ringo caused so much damage uring a party that their Playboy membership cards were voked.

Moon also acted as an 'uncle' to **Zak Starkey** and was e favourite drummer of Ringo's son.

Keith, who was one of the personalities sitting at the eatles' feet during the 'All You Need Is Love' erformance on the '**Our World**' TV spectacular, made a lo recording of 'When I'm Sixty-Four'. Ringo played on s album *Two Sides Of The Moon* and when he became e of John Lennon's companions during his 'long eekend' in Los Angeles, Keith played on **Harry ilsson**'s *Pussycats* album, which John co-produced in 974. Moon also appeared with John on his appearance at e Lyceum Ballroom *Peace for Christmas* concert on 15 ecember 1969.

In 1975 he accepted the special 'Hall of Fame' **rammy Award** on behalf of the Beatles.

Moore, Tommy

ummer who played with the Silver Beatles for a short riod of time – May and June 1960. At 36 years of age he s almost twice as old as the other members of the group d he had a full time job at Garston Bottle Works.

When told by **Allan Williams** that the group were oking for a drummer, **Brian Casser**, leader of Cass & Cassanovas, recommended Tommy.

He turned up late for their **Larry Parnes** audition at **Wyvern Club**, but took time off work to join them on eir short tour of Scotland backing **Johnny Gentle**. On May Gentle was driving their van and crashed into a parked car in which there were two old ladies. The only injuries suffered were by Moore who was concussed and had his front teeth knocked out. He was taken to hospital. The promoter insisted on them having a drummer so they forced the injured Moore, still groggy from pain-killing drugs, to play with them that night.

Due to pressure from the woman he lived with, Moore decided to finish playing with the Beatles and didn't turn up to meet them at the **Jacaranda** where they were meeting prior to their appearance at the **Grosvenor Ballroom** on 11 June. Together with Williams, the group went to his works and interrupted him while he was operating a fork-lift truck to cajole him into joining them on the gig. He refused, although he did make his final appearance with them on 13 June at the Jacaranda.

Tommy died from a stroke in 1981, soon after joining a local jazz band.

● 24 Moorfields, Liverpool L2

Site of the **NEMS Enterprises** office which Brian Epstein relocated to this address from Whitechapel on 6 August 1963. Brian and three of his staff moved into the premises, above the Wizard's Den magic shop. Inside the building, directly opposite the NEMS office, was the studio of photographer Harry Watmough, one of the regular ***Mersey Beat*** photographers, who had been commissioned to take some early studio shots of the Beatles wearing suits, when **Pete Best** was still a member.

● Morecambe & Wise Show, The

Eric Morecambe and Ernie Wise were for many years regarded as Britain's top comedy duo and during the sixties and seventies their 'The Morecambe & Wise Show' was one of the highlights on British television.

The Beatles spent a day with the two comics recording at the ATV Studios, Boreham Wood, on 2 December 1963 for the networked ATV show which was not transmitted until 18 April 1964 and was repeated on 24 July. The Beatles performed three songs and appeared in a sketch with Eric and Ernie.

● Morgue Skiffle Club, The, 'Balgownie', 25 Oakhill Park, Broadgreen, Liverpool L13

A skiffle club set in the cellar of a Victorian house and,

during its brief existence, run by Alan Caldwell, leader of Al Caldwell's Texans. Caldwell was to change his name to **Rory Storm** and front the Hurricanes, whose drummer was Ringo Starr.

The **Quarry Men** were among the groups who appeared on the Morgue's opening night on 13 March 1958. The semi-occupied house was a former home for retired nurses. The club had walls painted black with white fluorescent skeletons dancing across them. The Morgue could accommodate an audience of 100 in cramped conditions, was open twice a week, on Tuesdays and Thursdays, but the Quarry Men only appeared a few times because the club was closed by the police on 22 April, presumably because it had no proper facilities.

Allegedly, at the 13 March gig, Paul McCartney was championing the cause of his young friend George Harrison, who played 'Raunchy' for them on his new Futurama guitar. John Lennon was impressed by the guitar, but not by George – although, as a result, George was allowed to sit in when regular lead guitarist Eric Griffiths didn't turn up and he soon became a full-time member.

● Mosspits Lane Infants' School, *Mosspits Lane, Wavertree, Liverpool 15*

The first school which John Lennon attended. His Aunt **Mimi** enrolled him there on 12 November 1945, although the Admission Book shows his address as 9 **Newcastle Road**. For some reason, not explained, Mimi withdrew John from the school six months later and he moved to Dovedale Primary School on 6 May 1946.

● Mossway Hall, *Mossway, Croxteth, Liverpool L11*

Small venue where the Beatles made a single appearance on 17 March 1961. It was their only booking for Ivamar Promotions, one of the handful of active local promoters. They were Jeff McIver and Doug Martin who promoted jive dances weekly at **St Luke's Hall**, Crosby, the Ivamar Club, Skelmersdale, and Mossway Hall.

● Mother Nature's Son

One of the songs Paul composed during his sojourn in India. Paul recorded it on Wednesday, 9 August 1968. The recording sessions had finished at 10.00 p.m. and the other members of the Beatles had gone home. Paul remained behind and recorded an acoustic version of the song. A brass overdub was added later.

Paul is the only member of the Beatles on the trac which was included on *The Beatles* double album, issue in November 1968.

● Mount Pleasant Registry Office, *64 Mount Pleasant, Liverpool L3*

On 3 December 1938 ***Freddie Lennon*** married Juli Stanley in this registry office. They retired to a nearb public house with one of Freddie's brothers and a friend Julia's and spent the evening at the **Trocadero** cinem before Julia returned to the Stanley home in Wavertre and Freddie spent the night in lodgings.

On 23 August 1963, John, Freddie and Julia's son, wa married in the same room of the same registry office. Hi bride was a pregnant Cynthia Powell and also present we Brian Epstein, Paul McCartney, George Harrison an Cynthia's brother Tony and his wife Margery. Ringo Star the new member of the Beatles, hadn't been invited. Pa signed the certificate as witness to the civil ceremon which had been so disrupted by nearby construction wo that Cynthia could hardly hear the words of the ceremony

The party then retired to Reece's restaurant for the wedding breakfast.

● Moynihan, Vyvienne

The Manager of Light Entertainment at Associate Rediffusion television in London in the autumn of 19 when Brian Epstein first contacted her. She was 38 yea old at the time and listened to Epstein's sales patter as tried to convince her to book the Beatles. She suggest that she arrange for someone to see them first, but insisted that he come down to London and discuss t matter with her personally. As a result the group we booked on Rediffusion's **'Tuesday Rendezvous'**.

Epstein was also involved with her when he beg negotiations for the **'Around The Beatles'** special a she was also involved in the production of a **Cilla Bla** TV show. He then offered her a job at **NEMS**, in charge all work associated with theatres. He set her up in her o office in Cork Street, but she moved on to work for t Central Office of Information.

● MPA Publicity

Liverpool firm which specialized in handpainted a silkscreen posters.

MPA Publicity, the Liverpool company which produced most of the Beatles' early publicity posters.

Most Liverpool promoters commissioned MPA to roduce posters for local gigs from their premises situated t 37-41 Seel Street, only several yards away from the **acaranda Club**.

In particular, the **Allan Williams** promotions, such as he **Gene Vincent** spectacular at the **Liverpool tadium**, the **Sam Leach** posters for events such as *peration Big Beat* and the various **NEMS Enterprises** romotions.

Most of the colourful day-glo posters for Beatles ppearances at the major venues in Liverpool were ndertaken by MPA.

The style and colour of such posters brightened the iverpool city centre in the early sixties.

The firm moved the premises to the nearby 22 Slater treet.

MPTE Social Club, *Finch Lane, iverpool L14*

ne of the various Merseyside social clubs for members of e Liverpool bus services. George Harrison's father **arold** was one of the social secretaries for the local union and organized various events at the different busmen's clubs.

Naturally, he took the opportunity of booking the group his son George was a member of – the **Quarry Men**.

On the skiffle group's appearance at the venue early in 1959, Mr Harrison told the boys that the manager of a local cinema was looking for a band to play in the intervals and would be watching their performance that evening. The Quarry Men had two spots and John and Paul got drunk during their break and the gig was a disaster, particularly with the two of them making fun of George, knowing that his father and mother were in the audience. Because of their unprofessionalism, drummer **Colin Hanton** left the band that night.

They never heard from the manager of the Pavilion, who booked the Darktown Skiffle Group instead – whose drummer was Ringo Starr.

Harold Harrison also booked the Quarry Men at social club gigs in Wavertree, Garston and Prescot.

The building housing the Social Club was later demolished.

● Mr Moonlight

A number penned by Roy Lee Jackson and recorded by Dr Feelgood & the Interns in 1962. Dr Feelgood didn't have a hit with the number, but it became part of the repertoire of the Beatles and several other Mersey bands that year.

John Lennon was lead vocalist on the number and it was included in their **Star Club** performance and is found on the various Star Club recordings. The group also recorded the song for their *Beatles For Sale* album and it was included on their American EP *4 By The Beatles*.

● Municipal Stadium, Cleveland, Ohio

Due to the large size of this baseball pitch, home ground of the Cleveland Indians, there was only one show. The ground had the capacity for 50,000, but only 30,000 tickets were on sale as most of the rear-seating area would have provided such a poor view of the concert.

Minutes before the concert was due to commence, thousands of fans poured on to the pitch and the appearances by opening acts the **Cyrkle** and the **Ronettes** was delayed for half an hour.

Because of the pitch invasion, extra security was taken for the Beatles and two black limousines, with their doors open and engines running, were positioned behind the stage throughout the Beatles' performance in the event that a quick escape might be necessary.

● Municipal Stadium, Kansas City, Missouri

Thursday, 17 September 1964, was originally scheduled as a rest day during their hectic American tour.

Charles O. Finley, owner of the baseball team the Kansas City Athletics, noticed that the Beatles weren't making an appearance in Kansas City during the tour and made a vow that he would bring them in. He went to see the group at the **Cow Palace, San Francisco** and then visited Brian Epstein. While the Beatles were playing cards in their dressing-room he offered Epstein $50,000 for them to appear at the Stadium. He didn't receive a reply, so he doubled the offer – and was told that several other promoters had offered to pay $100,000, so he then raised the sum to $150,000.

This was a world record price at the time and, realizing the publicity and prestige value of such a price, Epstein accepted.

The local police chief, on hearing that the deal had been done, commented, 'Personally, I would rather see an invasion from Mars than have to handle a Beatle concert', but he assigned 350 police to the stadium. The Bill Black Combo were followed by **Jackie De Shannon** and after the interval the Beatles came on and began with a medley of 'Kansas City'/'Hey Hey Hey'.

Hundreds of fans rushed forward and broke through the barriers and the show had to be stopped. **Derek Taylor** had to go on stage and tell the audience to settle down or else the police would have to cancel the rest of the performance. Although the stadium had 41,000 seats there were only 20,208 spectators – yet this was a record crowd for a concert.

Finley lost money on the deal but gained a vast amount of publicity. There was only $100,000 taken, but despite the loss, Finley's manager Pat Friday presented the local Children's Mercy Hospital with a cheque for $25,000.

On the reverse side of the ticket Finley had a photograph of himself in a Beatle wig, pointing to a picture of Ringo. Underneath were the words: 'Yeah! Yeah! Yeah! Today's Beatles Fans Are Tomorrow's Baseball Fans. Charles O. Finley, President'.

The group performed twelve songs during a 31-minute set and a report in the *Kansas City Times* the next day had a detailed report of the show, part of which read: 'But the event left some of the Beatle followers emotionally torn. As the crowds left the park, fully 10 minutes after all the shouting, there were groups of exhausted girls still seated in the playing field area and the stands.

'They were crying.

'Why?

'"Because they (the B's) just left and didn't say anything," a girl explained, rubbing her eyes. "Now they are gone forever."

'"Ah, they'll be back again," a policeman said.

'"What do you care?" the girl wept. "You were down in front there and you didn't care and I was way back here and I couldn't even get close to them."

'"Now wait a minute, honey," he said. "It's not my fault."

'Then he walked away.'

Two enterprising businessmen paid $1,000 for the hotel pillow-cases used by the Beatles. They then had them cut into 160,000 one-inch squares, advertised them for sale at $1 each and within a week had sold them all, making a profit of $159,000.

● Muni, Scott

One of the top three New York disc jockeys who covered the arrival of the Beatles at **J. F. Kennedy Airport** on 7 February 1964. Scott worked for WABC and that day they changed the station's name to W-A-Beatles-C. Scott began interviewing the Beatles on that first day and continued covering their activities right up until their break-up.

In 1965 he was interviewing Ringo in a New York hotel suite when Ringo fainted. Scott found that he was worried about a family heirloom, a St Christopher medal which had been given to him by an aunt and which he'd lost. Scott then broadcast a message over the radio, promising that whoever returned it would get a hug and a kiss from Ringo and tickets to the **Shea Stadium** concert. It was quickly returned.

Scott left the station to open a club in New York, presenting bands such as the Rascals, but returned to radio in 1966 when he joined WOR-FM, changing to WNEW-FM the following year.

When John moved to New York, Scott interviewed him several times and when a new radio series called 'Ticket To Ride' was launched in February 1985, Scott became its host. The show interviewed artists whose careers have been inspired by the Beatles, in addition to the many people who were closely associated with the group.

● Murphy, Paul

The man who bought the Beatles' Hamburg tapes from **Allan Williams** and **Kingsize Taylor**. He was head of Buk Records in London at the time and later gave distribution rights to Double H Licensing Corporation in America.

Murphy was originally a member of **Rory Storm**'s group the Raving Texans (using the stage name Paul Rogers), and performed with them at Liverpool's the **Morgue** club before joining another local band the Rhythm Quartet. He then began performing solo and was spotted at Liverpool's Latin Quarter club by comedians **Mike and Bernie Winters** who put him in touch with Walter Ridley of HMV. This resulted in his debut record 'Four And Twenty Thousand Kisses', which was voted a hit on '**Juke Box Jury**', but which flopped.

Murphy then moved over to Hamburg and became an A&R man for Polydor Records over there, recording several of the Mersey bands who went across to Hamburg to perform.

● Murray, Mitch

A British songwriter who penned the pop song 'How Do You Do It', which he gave to **Dick James** to publish. James presented it to George Martin who believed it would provide a hit for the Beatles. The Beatles didn't like the number, but Martin insisted that they record it – and they were later to admit that they didn't put their heart and soul into the performance. Martin challenged them to come up with a better song and they produced 'Please Please Me'.

Acknowledging they were right, Martin issued the Lennon & McCartney number, although he was still convinced of the commercial potential of 'How Do You Do It' and recorded it with **Gerry & the Pacemakers**, who topped the charts with the song.

Brian Epstein also sought a Mitch Murray number for the **Big Three** and he came up with 'By The Way'. This was totally unsuitable for one of Liverpool's top rock bands, but it provided them with a modest hit.

Murray teamed up with Peter Callender and continued to pen a string of pop hits including 'Bonnie And Clyde' and 'The Night Chicago Died', which resulted in his songs topping the 100 million sales mark.

Mitch Murray – hit composer of 'How Do You Do It.' (Mitch Murray)

He went into tax exile to Holland for a while and then moved to the Isle of Man, which also provided him with a tax haven. From that base he began to concentrate on composing radio jingles.

● Murray, Rod

Art school chum of John Lennon, who usually got together

with John, **Stu Sutcliffe** and Bill Harry at **Ye Cracke** pub or in students' flats. He rented a flat in **Percy Street**, near to the Liverpool Art College, and talked Stuart into renting a room in the building. Later, together with John and Stu, he rented a flat at No. 3 **Gambier Terrace**.

In the search to find a guitarist for the **Quarry Men**, John manipulated both of his friends. He told Stu and Rod separately that he would prefer them to join with him in his group, preferably as a bass guitarist. To do this, either would have to obtain a bass. Neither of them could afford to buy such an instrument. Believing that he was the only person asked, Rod began making a bass guitar, hand-carving the body himself. Then Stuart had a stroke of good luck when he won £65 for his painting in the John Moores exhibition at the **Walker Art Gallery**. In January 1960 he spent his entire prize on buying a Hofner President bass, and became a member of John's band, leaving a frustrated Rod wondering what had happened.

When the Beatles left for Germany, Rod was in a difficult situation. Three people sharing could just about manage to afford the flat, but Rod couldn't pay for it on his own. He contacted Stu's mother who came to Gambier Terrace, paid Rod for Stuart's share of the rent and took Stuart's belongings – and also a number of John's possessions.

Rod moved to another flat, taking with him a number of items John had left behind at Gambier Terrace. In 1962 Bill Harry found out that Rod had some copies of John's *Daily Howl* book which he knew John was looking for and contacted him. As a result Rod returned two *Daily Howl* books in exchange for payment of the money owing to him.

John had told him that he could keep any of his other possessions which he'd left behind at Gambier Terrace. These included the manuscript for a book titled 'A Treasury Of Art And Poetry', which began: 'This book contains only the work of J W Lennon, with additional work by J W Lennon, and a helping hand given by J W Lennon, not forgetting J W Lennon. Who is this J W Lennon?'

In the 1964 Rock And Roll Memorabilia auction at Sotheby's in London, Rod sold the book and received more than £16,000 for it, which must have been some consolation for the fact that he narrowly missed becoming a Beatle!

● Murray The K

Name by which disc jockey Murray Kaufmann was more popularly known. Murray worked for the New York radio station WINS and several days before the Beatles arrived for their '**Ed Sullivan** Show' appearance he announced on his station the airline, flight number and approximate time that the Beatles would be arriving.

He'd originally begun playing 'She Loves You' in October 1963 at the request of a listener on his weekly record contest show, but it had aroused no great interest.

When the group were booked into the **Plaza Hotel**, Kaufmann conducted a radio interview with them 'live' over the telephone. This tickled their interest and they didn't object when he turned up at the hotel.

He quickly weedled his way into their confidence and was soon almost running their social life, taking them to New York nightclubs such as the **Peppermint Lounge**, introducing them to starlets such as Stella Stevens and Tuesday Weld, taking them to the Playboy Club – and conducting interviews all the time.

When the group flew to Florida he joined them and he shared a room with George, much to George's personal frustration. During this time he began to call himself '*The Fifth Beatle*', which annoyed Brian Epstein so much that he threatened legal action. However, Brian was aware of the massive radio publicity he gave to the group and when the '**Around The Beatles**' show was being planned by Rediffusion Television in London, he insisted that Murray the K be the compere of the show. John Lennon, who considered Kaufmann a phony, talked Epstein out of it.

Over the years Murray kept in touch, visiting them in London where he interviewed them during the filming of *A Hard Day's Night*. He also travelled to the Queen Elizabeth Hotel, Montreal, some years later when John and **Yoko** had a ten-day bed-in and was one of the celebrities present, along with Petula Clark and **Timothy Leary**, who provided the background clapping on the 'Give Peace a Chance' recording.

Kaufmann's interviews from New York, Miami, London and Washington were contained on an EP, *The Beatles And Murray The K As It Happened* on Fairway 526, which also contained 'She Loves You' and 'Shout'. The interviews he recorded in 1965 are to be found on bootleg albums such as *Soldier Of Love* and *Murray The K Fan Club*.

In 1966 a book of his experiences called *Murray The K Tells It Like It Is, Baby* was published, with an introduction by George Harrison.

Kaufmann played himself in the film *I Want To Hold Your Hand*, released in 1978, which concerned the

Producer Johnny Hamp with the Beatles during the filming of Granada TV's 'The Music Of Lennon & McCartney' (Johnny Hamp)

dventures of a bunch of American youngsters attempting see the Beatles on their first American visit. He was also chnical adviser to the ***Beatlemania*** stage show and articipated in a major Beatles festival held in the alifornian town of Knotts in 1980.

He died of cancer on 2 February 1982.

Museum Hall, *Henderson Street, Bridge f Allan, Stirlingshire, Scotland*

enultimate show on the Beatles' five-day tour of Scotland, hich took place on Saturday, 5 January 1963, when the ritish Isles was experiencing its worst spate of bad eather for decades.

● Music Hall, *The Square, Shrewsbury, hropshire*

ewis Buckley was a promoter who booked the Beatles on imerous occasions, including the 14 December 1962 gig this venue. Buckley also booked them for their second id last appearance at the hall on 26 April 1963.

● Music *International*

A BBC 2 television show on which John Lennon was interviewed on 2 August 1965.

● Music *Of* Lennon & McCartney, The

The title of a music spectacular conceived by Johnny Hamp of Granada Television, the producer and station which had given the group their first TV airing. Hamp had been made Head of Light Entertainment for Granada and after deciding he wished to pay tribute to the songwriting talents of John and Paul he had discussions with them which resulted in 'The Music Of Lennon & McCartney', the biggest spectacular yet produced by Granada Television. The programme was produced by Johnny Hamp and directed by Phil Casson.

The 50-minute programme was filmed over a two-day period in one of Granada's largest studios, Studio 6, on specially constructed sets. The completed show was fully networked at 9.40 p.m. on Friday, 17 December 1965.

The Beatles had wanted Ella Fitzgerald to sing 'Can't

Buy Me Love', but she wasn't available. French singer Richard Anthony had been due to appear but was involved in a road accident shortly before the recordings and was replaced by Dick Rivers.

George Martin led a 25-piece orchestra in a rendition of 'I Feel Fine' and Paul introduced the American composer/pianist Henry Mancini with the words, 'Now we introduce our favourite composer, Henry Mancini, who is known to all his friends as Hank. Welcome to the Beatles' show, Henry.' Mancini played 'If I Fell' and **Peter And Gordon** performed their major hit 'World Without Love', with a dozen attractive female models decorating the background.

Esther Phillips flew in from America especially to perform 'And I Love Him' and Lulu, who had been driven up from London by Peter Noone of Herman's Hermits, belted out 'I Saw Him Standing There'. The Beatles closed the first half of the show with a rendition of 'Day Tripper'.

Six members of the Liverpool Philharmonic Orchestra appeared under the name Fritz Speigel's Barock And Roll Ensemble to perform 'She Loves You' in the style of Mozart. Peter Sellers, with a long wig and Shakespearean costume in the style of Richard III, rendered a theatrical interpretation of 'A Hard Day's Night'. **Billy J. Kramer** & the Dakotas performed their two hits 'Bad To Me' and 'Do You Want To Know A Secret'.

Cilla Black performed 'It's For You' and was followed by Paul McCartney who began singing 'Yesterday', and **Marianne Faithfull** appeared and completed the song. Organist Alan Haven performed another interpretation of 'A Hard Day's Night', with backing from drummer Tony Crombie, then the Beatles performed 'We Can Work It Out'. For the number, John Lennon played harmonium – it was the instrument used in 'Coronation Street' which was familiar to viewers of the soap opera as the harmonium in the corner of Ena Sharples' (Violet Carson) room. Incidentally, among the spectators who were witnessing the production were members of the 'Coronation Street' cast and disc jockey **Jimmy Savile**. Also appearing on the special was the Spanish dance star Antonio Vargas.

● My Bonnie

The number was composed by J. T. Woods and H. J. Fuller and first appeared in a songbook called *Student Songs Of 1881*.

Ray Charles recorded a rock version of the number in 1958 which probably led **Bert Kaempfert** and **Tony Sheridan** to include it among the songs recorded at the Harburg Friedrich Ebert Halle in May 1961, with the Beatles providing backing for Sheridan.

The record was issued in Germany in June 1961 where according to Kaempfert, it sold 100,000 copies. The single was credited to Tony Sheridan and the **Beat Brother** because Kaempfert decided that the Beatles' name sounded too like a German word for penis – peedles!

The Beatles brought copies of the single home with them to Liverpool in July 1961 and gave copies to **Bob Wooler** and Virginia Sowry. Wooler was currently dis jockey at venues such as **Hambleton Hall**, where he played the disc to his audiences, suggesting that they try to order it from record stores. The copy the Beatles brought round to Virginia in the Renshaw Street offices of ***Mersey Beat*** led to the front-page story on the 20 July issu headed 'Beatles Sign Recording Contract!' which s impressed Brian Epstein when 144 copies were delivered to his store.

Epstein then began to take an interest in the group and imported 200 copies of the record from Polydor in Hamburg, which had been issued under the catalogue number Polydor 24-673. When Polydor issued the singl in Britain on 5 January 1962 on Polydor NH 66-833, th credit now read Tony Sheridan & the Beatles. It wa reviewed in the *South Liverpool Weekly News* under th heading of 'They're Hoping For A Hit Record', and th review ended with the prophetic words, 'The boys hav always been full-time musicians ever since they left school, and are making quite a name for themselve locally. Who knows it might not be long before the achieve nationwide acclaim.'

The release, although not issued in America at the time led to their first mention in an American magazine whe an item appeared in the 13 January 1962 issue of *Cash Box*: 'A new rock 'n' roll team, Tony Sheridan and th Beatles, made their debut on the Polydor label with "M Bonnie". Sheridan was discovered by Polydor produce Bert Kaempfert while playing night spots in Hamburg' famous Reeperbahn.'

The number has been issued on various singles, EP and album compilations around the world ever since including the albums *The Beatles First*, *In The Beginnin* and *The Early Years*.

The 'B' side to the single was 'The Saints'.

● National Portrait Gallery, The, *Charing Cross Road, London WC2*

Situated at the extreme southern end of Charing Cross Road, where it meets St Martin's Place. The gallery was opened in the late 1830s because the Victorians were avid for heroes and sought a gallery to portray the worthies of British history. Over the years, the majority of paintings were by British artists and until the sixties, the trustees would allow no portrait to be hung unless the sitter had been dead for a minimum of ten years.

It was a situation which had to change and in 1980, the gallery also began commissioning paintings for the first time, of contemporary figures. At the time they decided to spend one tenth of their yearly grant on commissioning new works. This gave them a figure of £30,000 which meant they could commission an average of ten works per year.

In 1978 the gallery ran an exhibition called *The Great British*, which included photographic portraits of prominent British people taken by American photographer Arnold Newman. George Harrison was one of the subjects and his photograph is now part of the permanent collection. He was one of only eight people to be photographed in colour for the exhibition. George was photographed in front of a recording console in his studio at **Friar Park** in Henley.

A Beatle association next found display in the Norman Parkinson photographic exhibition, at which pride of place went to his famous portrait of the Beatles.

In 1983 a new gallery was opened, The 20th Century, a permanent gallery containing approximately 500 works including paintings, photographs and sculpture. On 2 February 1984, Humphrey Ocean's portrait of Paul McCartney was unveiled. *The Sunday Times* commented: 'The result shows a pale, thin McCartney as melancholy as an Elizabethan poet, and like such poets, emerging from a background of briar roses. It is ludicrously sensitive.'

Humphrey had won the 1982 Imperial Tobacco Portrait Award and when the painting was unveiled, there was a certain amount of controversy about the 33-year-old artist's portrayal of the ex-Beatle. A gallery spokesman said: 'This is a painting that puts the singer in a very unusual light. He looks nothing like he does on the record sleeves – it's bound to cause a few surprises.'

Ocean first met Paul in the mid-seventies and Paul commissioned him to join the 1976 American tour to record it for posterity in a visual journal. The result was *The Ocean View*, published several years later in 1982 by MPL Communications/Plexus Books, and containing Humphrey's paintings and drawings of the tour.

Humphrey coaxed Paul into sitting in the garden of his Sussex home. The portrait was completed in six sittings. 'The blood drained from [Paul's] face when I said I'd need him four hours a day,' said Humphrey, who also commented, 'He has seen the painting. He didn't say very much but I got the impression he liked it.'

● NEMS *Enterprises*

The company formed to direct the Beatles' careers.

Brian Epstein's family ran a furniture store in Walton Road, Liverpool, I. Epstein & Sons. The annexe to the furniture store sold pianos and sheet music and was called North End Music Stores (because it was in the North End of Liverpool). Eventually, just the initials N.E.M.S. were used. When the family decided to expand their business and launch a large store in the centre of Liverpool, they opened a branch of NEMS in Charlotte Street, run by Brian and his brother **Clive**. The family then opened a large record store at 12-14 Whitechapel and Brian was put in charge while his friend **Peter Brown** ran the record section at Charlotte Street.

When Brian wanted to become involved in the Mersey scene, initially signing the Beatles, his family agreed to support him, but his father **Harry** insisted that he should take advantage of his brother Clive's business acumen and Clive was appointed Company Secretary. NEMS

Enterprises Limited was registered on 26 June 1962 with its £100 shares divided equally between Brian and Clive, and over the next five years Brian was to register no less than 65 other different companies. NEMS Enterprises Limited was formed as a theatrical, concert and variety agency and as new acts were signed, such as **Gerry & the Pacemakers** and **Billy J. Kramer**, the company moved to new offices at 24 **Moorfields** on 6 August 1963. By that time the company had expanded to a staff of three. The share capital was increased to £10,000 on 27 April 1964 with Brian receiving 5,000 shares, Clive 4,000, and each of the Beatles 250. Eventually, by December 1965 the shares had been changed still further and Brian owned 7,000, Clive 2,000, and the individual Beatles 250 each.

A concert promotions division, NEMS Presentations, was formed on 12 July 1963.

On 9 March 1964 the organization moved to Sutherland House, Argyll Street, London, and the staff rose to fifteen. **Geoffrey Ellis** was appointed Executive Manager, Bernard Lee, who had formerly been with the Grade Organization, headed the NEMS Booking Agency, Peter Brown became Brian's Personal Assistant, **Tony Barrow** the NEMS Press Officer, **Alistair Taylor** became Office Manager and various other members of the NEMS Liverpool staff moved to London. By 1966 there were 80 members of staff in five different London offices.

Brian had the opportunity to merge with various other powerful music business figures over the next few years, including **Bernard Delfont** and **Tito Burns**, but, to the frustration of his associates, he decided to merge with the **Robert Stigwood** Organization and the merger took place on 13 January 1967. Epstein remained as Chairman and Robert Stigwood became joint Managing Director with **Vic Lewis**. Stigwood also had the option of buying 51 per cent of NEMS for £500,000 should Brian have wished to opt out of the business. When Brian died, Stigwood could have taken advantage of the option, but the Beatles told him that they would refuse to be associated with him and he never took the option up.

During the battle for Northern Songs and the entry of **Allen Klein** and the **Eastmans** into the picture, Clive Epstein had decided to let the Beatles buy NEMS. Due to a note which he received from Eastman suggesting that the NEMS contract with the Beatles had been improper, Clive sold his shares to Triumph Investments, who were able to take control of the company.

NEMS ENTERPRISES
PRESENT:—

MONDAY, SEPTEMBER 10th
QUEENS HALL, WIDNES
THE BEATLES
Rory Storm and the Hurricanes
Geoff Stacey and the Wanderers

MONDAY, SEPTEMBER 17th
QUEENS HALL, WIDNES
THE BEATLES
Billy Kramer with the Coasters
The Vikings

Tickets for these two exciting attractions must be purchased in advance from The Brazilian Coffee Bar, Widnes, The Music Shop, Widnes, El Cappucino, Runcorn and Dawsons, Widnes and Runcorn

FRIDAY, OCTOBER 12th
LITTLE RICHARD
AT
THE TOWER BALLROOM
NEW BRIGHTON
Tickets on sale at all usual agencies now in advance — 10/6

SUNDAY, OCTOBER 28th
EMPIRE THEATRE, Liverpool
This fabulous Bill will be headed by a great surprise Artiste—watch Press!
CRAIG DOUGLAS JET HARRIS
KENNY LYNCH THE BEATLES
SOUNDS INCORPORATED
A FANTASTIC LINE-UP!

THURSDAY, NOVEMBER 8th
THE TOWER BALLROOM
NEW BRIGHTON
KARL DENVER TRIO

● Newby, Chas

Stuart Sutcliffe remained in Hamburg when the Beatles returned to Liverpool in December 1960 and although he hadn't officially left the group, they needed the services of a bass player for their Liverpool gigs. **Pete Best** suggested **Ken Brown** who'd played with him in the **Blackjacks**, and now lived in London. John and Paul vetoed the idea, in case of any bad blood which may have remained when they threw him out of the **Quarry Men**. Paul wanted to play bass, but it was decided to try out another of Best's suggestions – Chas Newby, the former rhythm guitarist with the Blackjacks. Chas was on holiday from college where he was a chemistry student, but agreed to join them for a short time. He borrowed a leather jacket and bass guitar and played his first gig with them at the **Casbah Club** on 17 December 1960. He played a total of four gigs with the band, the others were at the **Grosvenor Ballroom** on 24 December, **Litherland Town Hall** on 27 December and the Casbah Club on 31 December.

He then returned to college. He mentioned that John had approached him to discuss going with them to Hamburg, but he wasn't interested – he was to comment years later that he had no regrets about what might have been.

● New Cabaret Artistes Club, *174a Upper Parliament Street, Liverpool 8*

The cellar of this Victorian house was used as a strip club by **Allan Williams** and **Lord Woodbine** for a short time in 1960. Strip clubs were illegal in Liverpool at the time by order of the local Watch Committee.

When Williams had booked a large-breasted model called **Janice**, she insisted on having live musicians provide backing for her. The only group Williams could find at the time who weren't working during the day were the Silver Beatles and Williams offered them ten shillings each for two twenty-minute spots a night.

● 9 Newcastle Road, *Wavertree, Liverpool L15*

The Stanley home, where John Lennon's grandparents George and Annie brought up their five daughters. **Julia** lived here during the years of her courtship with **Freddie Lennon** and on their wedding night, Julia returned to Newcastle Road while Freddie went into lodgings and then off to sea.

John Lennon's first home – at 9 Newcastle Road. (Les Chadwick)

John was reared at this address during the first five years of his life. It was suggested that as Julia liked going out and having a good time at night, the baby John was left alone in the dark on so many occasions that it traumatized him and left him in fear of the dark for the rest of his life.

John's Aunt **Mimi**, with no children of her own, wanted to rear John and eventually had her wish granted and took John away in 1945 to her home in Menlove Avenue.

● New Clubmoor Hall, *back of Broadway, Liverpool L11*

A Conservative Club where Paul McCartney made his debut with the **Quarry Men** on Friday, 18 October 1957. The group had been booked by local promoter Charlie McBain and entrance for members cost three shillings. The group wore matching outfits with long-sleeved cowboy shirts, black string ties and black trousers. John and Paul wore white sports coats.

The line-up that night comprised **Colin Hanton** on drums, Len Garry on tea chest bass, **Eric Griffiths** on guitar and John and Paul. On this occasion, Paul played lead guitar for the first and only time – and it was a disaster.

Paul played the old Arthur Smith hit 'Guitar Boogie', but ruined the guitar solo because he was playing his guitar upside down and backwards, as he still didn't know how to restring a guitar for a left-handed person.

After the show, aware that his debut as lead guitarist hadn't gone down too well, Paul tried to impress John by playing him an original number he'd written called 'I've Lost My Little Girl'. John responded by trying out a few tunes he'd written and sought Paul's opinion – the Lennon & McCartney songwriting team was soon to develop.

The group returned to the venue on 23 November 1957 and performed their third and last gig at the club on 10 January 1958.

● New Colony Club, *80 Berkley Street, Liverpool 8*

A run-down house in the black quarter of the Liverpool 8 district provided the premises for a cellar shebeen, run by **Lord Woodbine**, which he called the New Colony Club. The Beatles appeared here for a couple of informal afternoon sessions in 1960 to help out their friend 'Woodie'.

● Newfield, Joanne

Brian Epstein's personal secretary. She originally joined **NEMS Enterprises** as secretary to Wendy Hanson at the company's Stafford Street offices. She was 21 years old and the niece of dance band leader Joe Loss. Wendy had needed the services of an extra secretary at Hille House because in addition to her working as Brian's PA, she was also virtually PA for the Beatles. She was not pleased when Brian decided to make Joanne his own personal secretary at his Chapel Street base. Joanne was paid £15 per week and her working hours were from 10.00 a.m.–6.00 p.m., although she was to work late on many occasions due to Epstein's disinclination to rise before noon on various days as a result of his increasing reliance on drugs. She was devoted to him despite the occasional displays of bad temper and rudeness.

When Hanson left NEMS in 1966, Joanne inherited her job. As Brian began to work increasingly from his home she'd moved office into a small room at the top of the house at 24 Chapel Street. On Friday, 1 September 1967, when the servants couldn't wake Brian up in his bedroom, she phoned **Alistair Taylor** and it was soon confirmed that Brian had died.

Joanne then fulfilled the same functions for **Peter Brown** at Apple. In 1968 she was to marry Colin Peterson, former drummer with the Bee Gees, and moved to live in New South Wales, Australia, where Colin became a recording manager.

● Newley, Anthony

Major British singing star/actor. Using his contacts with **Decca**, Brian Epstein arranged for Newley to be the celebrity to open the new, large branch of **NEMS** in Whitechapel, Liverpool, in 1959.

Epstein was very impressed with the star's friendly and unassuming manner and in later years was to comment, 'This is how a real star should behave. In fact it is precisely the way my artistes behave, when they are permitted by press and public.'

Newley was the first new chart topper of the sixties in the British charts when his 'Why' replaced Neil Sedaka's 'Oh Carol' (which had held the top position from late December 1959). Newley, who had had three hits in 1959, had a further three in 1960: 'Do You Mind', 'If She Should Come To You' and 'Strawberry Fair'. In 1961 his hits were 'And The Heavens Cried', 'Pop Goes The Weasel' and 'What Kind Of Fool Am I?'. His final British hits were in 1962: 'D-Darling' and 'That Noise'.

Along with **Del Shannon**, Newley became the only artist to record a Lennon & McCartney number for the American market prior to their **'Ed Sullivan** Show' appearance. His version of 'I Saw Her Standing There' was issued on 28 October 1963 on London 5202.

George Harrison was the first member of the Beatles to visit America when he travelled there to stay with his sister Louise in St Louis in 1963. He said, 'I thought America was really great. I met Tony Newley over there. He'd never heard of any of our numbers so I played him some of our recordings. When I left he said he wanted to record "I Saw Her Standing There".'

● New London Synagogue, *Abbey Road, St John's Wood, London NW8*

Close to **Abbey Road Studios**, the synagogue where the

Memorial Service for Brian Epstein was held at 6.00 p.m. on 17 October 1967. A large crowd gathered and among the close friends attending and paying their respects were all four Beatles, George Martin, **Dick James**, **Cilla Black**, **Billy J. Kramer**, the **Fourmost**, Lulu, Lionel Bart and **Bernard Delfont**. The Beatles had originally meant to attend wearing their psychedelic clothes, but realized this might upset Brian's mother Queenie and they wore suits.

The service was conducted by Rabbi Dr Louis Jacobs B.A., assisted by Cantor George Rothschild. The choir was under the direction of Martin Lawrence and the order of service was: (1) Psalm 121 (2) Prayer (3) Psalm 23 (4) Scriptural Readings (5) Psalm 16 (6) Address (7) Memorial Prayer (8) Anthem (9) Alenu and (10) Adon Olam.

Rabbi Jacobs was to say, 'He encouraged young people to sing of love and peace rather than war and hatred.'

● New Musical Express

As ***Mersey Beat*** had built the Beatles' reputation in the North from 1961, the *New Musical Express* began heavily promoting the group from 1963. It was the British music weekly with the largest circulation and one of its writers, **Alan Smith**, had been contributing to *Mersey Beat* under the name George Jones. Another *Mersey Beat* writer, Roy Carr, went on to become one of the main *NME* journalists. The *NME*'s star writer was Chris Hutchins who, at one time, was about to take up Brian Epstein's offer of joining Bill Harry on *Mersey Beat* when the *NME* came up with a counter-offer.

It was Hutchins who was the main Beatles contact for *New Musical Express*, just as he was the paper's main contact for **Elvis Presley** and it was Hutchins, who travelled to America with the Beatles, who originally arranged their meeting with Elvis.

The *New Musical Express* featured a series of concerts in the sixties featuring artists who topped their annual popularity polls. The concerts, known as 'The Poll Winners' Concerts', were all held in Wembley and the Beatles appeared on the following dates: Empire Pool, Wembley, 21 April 1963; Wembley Stadium, 26 April 1964; Wembley Stadium, 11 April 1965; and Wembley Stadium, 1 May 1966. Their 1965 concert was screened on ABC TV and networked throughout the UK on 18 April of that year and their 1966 appearance was their last concert show in Britain.

From 1963–1976, places in the *NME* poll won by the Beatles both as a group and individually were:

Single Of The Year
1963 'She Loves You', the Beatles
1966 'Eleanor Rigby', the Beatles
1968 'Hey Jude', the Beatles
1970 'My Sweet Lord', George Harrison

Album Of The Year
1970 *Let It Be*, the Beatles

Bass Guitarist Of The Year
1972 Paul McCartney
1973 Paul McCartney
1974 Paul McCartney
1976 Paul McCartney

Vocal Personality Of The Year
1965 John Lennon

World Vocal Group	**UK Vocal Group**
1963 the Beatles	1963 the Beatles
1964 the Beatles	1964 the Beatles
1965 the Beatles	1965 the Beatles
1966 the Beatles	1966 the Beatles
1967 the Beatles	1967 the Beatles
1968 the Beatles	1968 the Beatles
1969 the Beatles	1969 the Beatles
	1970 the Beatles

● New Orleans

First hit for Gary 'US' Bonds, which reached No. 6 in the American charts in 1960. Bonds, real name Gary Anderson, followed up with a No. 1 hit 'Quarter To Three' and had a further seven chart entries.

The number was penned by F. Guida and J. Royster and the Beatles included it in their stage repertoire during 1961.

● Newsfront

An American television programme, produced by WNET-TV. John Lennon and Paul McCartney appeared on the show on 15 May 1968, promoting their launch of **Apple**

Records; they also discussed politics on the New York TV show. The programme was repeated the following week on 22 May.

Incidentally, on 15 May they also appeared on the networked '**Tonight**' show.

● New Springfield Ballroom, *Janvrin Road, St Saviour, Jersey, Channel Isles*

Ballroom in the town of St Helier on the island of Jersey, the largest of the Channel Isles. Although closer to France than to Britain, the Channel Isles (which comprises four large islands: Jersey, Guernsey, Alderney and Sark, together with a number of smaller isles) is a British dependency and has been since 1066. Jersey itself is a sunny holiday resort, much favoured by the British and French and both languages are in evidence in shop names, street signs and official notices.

The Beatles appeared at the **Springfield Ballroom**, before crowds of holidaymakers, as part of a five-day package promoted by **John Smith**, for which they were paid £1,000. They appeared at the Springfield on 6, 7, 9 and 10 August 1963.

● Nicol, *Jimmy*

A stand-in drummer for the Beatles for a short part of their 1964 world tour. On Wednesday, 3 June, Ringo collapsed during a photo session the group were having for the *Saturday Evening Post*, in Barnes, during the morning. He was then taken to University College Hospital where it was diagnosed he had tonsilitis and pharyngitis, with a temperature of 102 degrees.

Brian Epstein and George Martin began to discuss the possibility of a stand-in drummer and George Harrison, in particular, was averse to the idea. He said, 'If Ringo's not going then neither am I, you can find two replacements,' but Brian and George Martin talked him into accepting the situation.

Martin phoned Jimmy Nicol and asked him to attend a 3.00 p.m. session at **Abbey Road** with the Beatles. George had suggested Nicol because he had recently done session work on a **Tommy Quickly** record and he'd also become familiar with Beatles numbers from a session he'd done for an album *Beatlemania*, released on the Top Six budget label.

Jimmy had begun his career as a drum repairer for Boosey & Hawkes. For a time he'd been a member of the Swedish group, the Spotnicks, and had then joined Georgie Fame's Blue Flames for a while before forming his own band the Shubdubs, who had recently signed with Pye.

At the session Jimmy performed six numbers with the Beatles: 'I Want To Hold Your Hand', 'She Loves You', 'I Saw Her Standing There', 'This Boy', 'Can't Buy Me Love' and 'Long Tall Sally'. Journalist Dick Hughes, an Australian, was present at the rehearsals and says that Paul told him, 'This fellow is fine, but we just can't afford to be without Ringo at a real recording session because the kids would always know that a record was the one without him.'

Jimmy commented: 'I was having a bit of a lie down after lunch when the phone rang. It was EMI asking if I could come down to the studio to rehearse with the Beatles. Two hours after I got there I was told to pack my bags for Denmark.'

Confirming the decision to hire Jimmy, Brian Epstein commented: 'The difficulty was finding someone who looked like a Beatle and not an outcast.'

Jimmy's first live appearance with the band was at the KB Hallen, Copenhagen, on 4 June 1964. The group performed a ten-song set, cutting down from the planned eleven numbers because they decided not to do Ringo's spot with 'I Wanna Be Your Man'. After the show, George commented: 'Playing without Ringo is like driving a car on three wheels but Jimmy has grasped our rhythm very quickly.' Jimmy had to wear Ringo's stage suits, but the trousers were too short and Paul sent Ringo a telegram: 'Hurry up and get well Ringo, Jimmy is wearing out all your suits.'

Ringo was discharged from hospital on Thursday, 1 June. He teamed up with his fellow Beatles in Melbourne, Australia, and there was a single photo session in which all five were pictured together.

Jimmy left for Essendon Airport at 8.00 a.m. After packing his bags he was to comment: 'The boys were very kind but I felt like an intruder. They accepted me but you can't just get into a group like that – they have their own atmosphere, their own sense of humour. It's a little clique and outsiders just can't break in.'

He never said 'goodbye' to the Beatles. 'They were still asleep,' he said. 'I didn't think I should disturb them.'

Brian Epstein and tour manager Lloyd Ravenscroft accompanied him to the airport. Brian presented him with a cheque for £500 and a gold Eternamatic wrist watch inscribed: 'From the Beatles and Brian Epstein to Jimmy – with appreciation and gratitude.'

Jimmy had thought that his brief spell with the Beatles would boost his career and had said, during the Australian trip, 'When I get home I won't have to run a group on fifteen or twenty pounds a night anymore.'

Unfortunately, he didn't have much success on his return. His group issued 'Husky' c/w 'Don't Come Back', which failed to make the charts. They were also booked to replace the **Dave Clarke Five**, ironically because Dave Clarke was ill, in a short season at Blackpool. While he was there Jimmy received a bundle of 5,000 letters from fans in Australia, sent on by a local DJ. Jimmy sent his thanks with the message that he'd go and live in Australia permanently.

His group disbanded, he lived in South America for some time, then returned to Britain and moved on to Australia for a period.

At least he'd enjoyed, as Andy Warhol was to say, his 'fifteen minutes of fame'.

● Night Before, The

A number penned by Paul which was included on the *Help!* album and later surfaced on *Rock 'n' Roll Music.*

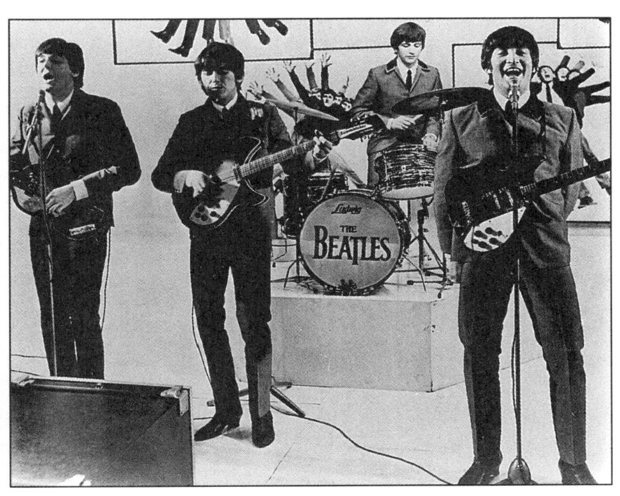

(©Walter Shenson Films/Apple)

● Nightingale, Anne

A blonde-haired British journalist/disc jockey who first began broadcasting in the mid-sixties when the Beat scene erupted in Britain. One of her earliest books was a collaboration with the **Hollies** on how to write a hit song.

Anne has broadcast for Radio One and other stations and hosted many TV shows, including 'The Old Grey Whistle Test'. She has also acted as music columnist for a number of newspapers ranging from the *Daily Sketch* to the *Daily Express*.

Her biography *Chase The Fade* included a chapter on the Beatles, together with several photographs of the group, mainly during the Apple days. She mentions how she interviewed **Yoko Ono** during a John Lennon recording session at **Abbey Road Studios** and Yoko told her that her worst fear was that of ending up as an old woman: '"shaking", living alone in a high-rise New York apartment'.

Anne mentioned that she was inadvertently responsible for **Richard DiLello** and Carol Paddon of the Apple Press Office getting the sack. This was due to a story she wrote which gave **Allen Klein** the excuse he wanted to prune them from the Apple payroll.

The story appeared in the *Daily Sketch* under the headline 'Apple Coming Apart At The Core' on Monday, 13 July 1970.

Richard and secretary Carole were used to Anne dropping in and had become friendly with her. They hadn't anticipated a conversation being turned into a sensational story which put their jobs at risk. DiLello immediately phoned his boss **Derek Taylor** and read the story to him over the phone, commenting: 'I don't know why the hell she did it. I mean, we were just talking, you know, casual conversation and it wasn't like we were giving her an interview or anything.' He added, 'She just came in here like always and we were sitting around dialoguing and she wasn't even taking notes! It was Anne Nightingale the Beatlemaniac, our friend, not William Randolph Nightingale the journalist. She didn't say she was writing a story about Apple, nothing!'

In her book, Anne also mentions a New Year's party she was invited to by **Peter Brown**. It was held at Ringo's North London flat on New Year's Eve, 1969. Among the other guests were George Harrison, **Klaus Voorman**, **Kenny Everett**, Michael Caine and Lulu. It was the night before the story appeared in the press about Paul leaving the Beatles.

Anne also attended the **Buddy Holly** Week party held by Paul at the **Peppermint Park**. It was the night before **Keith Moon** died and she was chatting with Keith, who'd asked her only a few days before if she would collaborate with him on his life story, which he wanted to call 'The Moon Papers'.

● Night Of A Hundred Stars, The

A midnight charity revue which took place at the **London Palladium** on Thursday, 23 July 1964.

The Beatles made an appearance, along with a host of stars, including Zsa Zsa Gabor, Laurence Olivier, Harry Secombe, Frankie Vaughan, Max Bygraves, Frankie Howerd, Richard Attenborough, Miriam Karlin, Millicent Martin, Barbara Windsor, **Dora Bryan**, Joyce Grenfell, Chita Rivera, Sylvia Syms, Susan Hampshire, Rita Moreno, **Hayley Mills**, Eve Arden, Elisabeth Welch, Marti Stevens, Peggy Cummins, Eunice Gayson, Adrienne Corri, Angela Douglas, Wendy Craig, **Jane Asher**, **Shirley Bassey** and Dame Edith Evans. John Lennon contributed a sketch for the cover of the programme.

John Lennon provided the illustration for the programme cover of the 'Night Of A Hundred Stars' charity event.

● Nilsson, Harry

An American singer/songwriter, born in New York on 15 June 1941. He moved to the West Coast in 1952.

In August 1967, Nilsson released an album, *Pandemonium Shadow Show* on RCA 3874, which contained the track of his single 'You Can't Do That', RCA 9298, whose lyrics included titles and lyrics from the Beatle songs 'I'm Down', 'Drive My Car', 'You're Gonna Lose That Girl', 'Good Day Sunshine', 'A Hard Day's Night', 'Rain', 'I Want To Hold Your Hand', 'Day Tripper', 'Paperback Writer', 'Do You Want To Know A Secret?', 'Yesterday' and 'Strawberry Fields Forever'.

The tribute came to the attention of **Derek Taylor**, who was also living on the West Coast at the time. He sent a copy of the album to Brian Epstein, calling Nilsson the best contemporary solo artist in the world, and added, 'He is the something the Beatles are.'

Harry's interpretation of their songs impressed John and Paul who, in an interview, said that he was their favourite singer.

He became a close friend of the individual Beatles and had a major hit with 'Without You', a number written by members of **Badfinger**, the Apple group.

George and Ringo performed on his album *Son of Schmilsson* and Derek Taylor produced *A Touch Of Schmilsson In The Night*. John Lennon produced his *Pussy Cats* album and he appeared with Ringo Starr in two films, *Son Of Dracula* and *Harry And Ringo's Night Out*, both produced in 1974.

● Nippon Budokan Hall, *Daikan-cho, Chiyoda-ku, Tokyo, Japan*

Promoter Tats Nagashima had booked the Beatles to appear on five shows at this impressive octagon-shaped hall, which could accommodate an audience of 11,000. Unfortunately, as it had been regarded by many Japanese as a sacred place because of the traditional and honourable martial arts exhibitions which were the main feature of the hall, a number of death threats were made against the Beatles by a Right Wing political group and as a result the police presence was considerable, with a total of 35,000 security men involved during the visit and 3,000 policemen mixing with the audience at each of the concerts.

The Beatles flew out from London to Tokyo, but because of the danger from a typhoon called KIT, they had to stop off at Anchorage, Alaska, for several hours. They eventually arrived at Tokyo International Airport at 3.40 a.m. on 29 June 1966. There were 1,500 fans at the airport and when the Beatles were driven to the Hilton Hotel in a fleet of Cadillacs, there were 15,000 uniformed policemen lining the route, drawn from all parts of Tokyo, and there were groups with banners stating 'Beatles Go Home'.

They performed a single concert on 30 June which was filmed in colour by the Japanese television channel NTV and screened on 1 July. On 1 and 2 July they performed two concerts each day at the hall where the dressing rooms had been specially decorated for their visit and stocked with food and drink. They were visited by many people, including Tetsusaburo Shimoya, the 50-year-old President of their Japanese Fan Club, who presented each of them with a transistor radio.

● *Nobody I Know*

The second number which Paul McCartney gave to **Peter & Gordon** to record, providing them with their second million-seller. The number was issued in Britain on Columbia DB 7292 on 29 May 1964 and reached No. 9 in the charts. It was issued in America on **Capitol** 5211 on 15 June 1964, but didn't chart.

● *Nobody's Child*

Peter & Gordon enjoyed a chart hit with the Paul McCartney composition, 'Nobody I Know'. (EMI)

This was one of the eight numbers recorded in Hamburg in May 1961 during the Polydor session in which the Beatles backed singer **Tony Sheridan**. The Beatles merely provided instrumental backing to Sheridan's interpretation of the number, which has since been released on various singles and albums.

● Nola Studios, *West 57th Street, New York City*

George Harrison rented the studios in July 1971 for the rehearsals for the **Concert For Bangla Desh**, which was to take place on 1 August at Madison Square Garden. Unfortunately, **Eric Clapton** was ill due to his addiction to heroin and never attended any of the **Nola Studios** rehearsals. His place as second lead to George Harrison was taken by Jesse Ed Davis. Clapton, did, however, turn up for the actual concert and performed at both shows.

● *Non Stop Pop*

A BBC radio programme. The Beatles were interviewed for the show by Phil Tate on 30 July 1963 and the programme was transmitted on 30 August 1963.

● *No One's Gonna Change Our World*

A charity album, originally compiled following a suggestion by comedian **Spike Milligan**, on behalf of the World Wildlife Fund. A number of major British artists contributed to the project, including the Beatles, who donated their recording of 'Across The Universe', from which the phrase 'No One's Gonna Change Our World' was taken. George Martin co-ordinated the production of the project and the album was issued in Britain on SRS 50143 on 12 December 1969.

● *No Other Baby*

The Vipers Skiffle Group were one of the handful of skiffle bands to make an impact on the British charts during skiffle's brief reign. Their hits were 'Don't You Rock Me Daddy-O', 'Cumberland Gap' and 'Streamline Train'.

One of the numbers they popularized and recorded in 1958 was 'No Other Baby', which the **Quarry Men** introduced into their repertoire, with John Lennon on lead vocals.

● *No Reply*

A composition by John Lennon which was considered for release as a single, until it was decided to issue 'I Feel Fine'. The track then appeared on the *Beatles For Sale* album. It is also found on the *Beatles For Sale* EP and the American *Beatles '65* album.

The track was recorded on 30 September 1964 and George Martin played piano on the session.

● Northern Meeting Hall, *Church Street, Inverness, Inverness-shire, Scotland*

Site of the second gig of the Silver Beetles' short tour of

Scotland backing **Johnny Gentle**. On Saturday, 21 May 1960, they appeared at this venue, which was divided into two halls, with the main hall on the ground floor where Lindsay Ross and his band performed. The Silver Beetles appeared in an upstairs hall on a bill with Ronnie Watt and the Chekkers Rock Dance Band.

● Norwegian Wood

Composition by John about a brief affair, possibly a one-night-stand. He wanted to describe his feelings regarding the affair without his wife **Cynthia** knowing. He commented, 'I was trying to write about an affair, so it was very gobbledegook. I was sort of writing from my experiences, girls' flats, things like that.

'I wrote it at **Kenwood**. George had just got the sitar and I said, "Could you play this piece?" We went through many different sort of versions of the song, it was never right and I was getting very angry about it, it wasn't coming out like I said. They said, "Well, just do it how you want to do it." And I said, "Well, I just want to do it like this." They let me go and I did the guitar very loudly into the mike and sang it at the same time and then George had the sitar and I asked him could he play the piece that I'd written, you know, dee diddly dee diddly dee, that bit, and he was not sure whether he could play it yet because he hadn't done much on the sitar but he was willing to have a go, as is his wont, and he learned the bit and dubbed it on after. I think we did it in sections.'

In fact, recording began on Tuesday, 12 October 1965, when the song was called 'This Bird Has Flown', but John was unsatisfied with the result and they began re-recording it on Thursday, 21 October.

It was the first time a sitar had been used on a pop single. Ringo also played tambourine, maraca and finger cymbals.

John then decided to include the words 'This Bird Has Flown' as a sub-title.

The track was featured on the *Rubber Soul* album and was included on the compilations *The Beatles 1962–1966*, *Love Songs* and *The Beatles Ballads*.

● Not A Second Time

A John Lennon composition recorded on Wednesday, 11 September 1963, for the *With The Beatles* album. George Martin played piano at the session.

The number was one of the Beatles songs mentioned by *The Times* music critic **William Mann** in his feature 'What Songs The Beatles Sang', '...but harmonic interest is typical of their quicker songs too, one gets the impression that they think simultaneously of harmony and melody, so firmly are the major tonic sevenths and ninths built into their tunes, and the flat submediant key switches, so natural is the Aeolian cadence at the end of "Not A Second Time" (the chord progression which ends Mahler's "Song Of The Earth").'

Commenting on the article, John said, 'Really it was just chords like any other chords. That was the first time anyone had written anything like that about us.'

● Not Guilty

A George Harrison composition, written in 1968, which the Beatles began recording for *The Beatles* double album. They recorded an incredible 101 takes of the number, more takes than they ever did on any other number, yet it still didn't find its way onto the album as originally planned.

George finally issued the song on his *George Harrison* album in 1979.

● Nothin' Shakin' But The Leaves On The Trees

A number penned by Cirino Colacrai, Eddie Fontaine, Dianne Lampert and Jack Cleveland which was recorded by Eddie Fontaine in 1958. The Beatles introduced it into their repertoire in 1960 with George Harrison on lead vocal. It was one of the numbers the group performed when they appeared at the **Star Club** and was one of the tracks recorded by **Adrian Barber** which has appeared on the various releases of the Star Club tapes.

● Not Only . . . But Also

BBC 2 comedy series featuring Peter Cook and Dudley Moore.

John Lennon was a friend of Cook's and they'd dined together a few times. On 9 January 1965, John appeared on the first edition of their new show reading excerpts from his book *In His Own Write*, alongside Dudley Moore and **Norman Rossington**. He also appeared in what was described as a 'surrealist sketch'.

His next appearance on the show took place on 26 December 1966 when he appeared in a sketch as a lavatory attendant. Dressed in a commissionaire's uniform ıd wearing 'granny' glasses, John was filmed outside a ›ntlemen's convenience in Broadwick Street, Soho, ɔndon W1. The word 'Gentlemen' remained above the •o, but a sign reading 'Members Only' was placed ɜneath it. The sketch, in which John appeared with Pete ıd Dud, concerned a 'Gentlemen's Club'.

Nowhere Man (EP)

ıe Beatles' twelfth British EP. All four tracks were taken ɔm their album *Rubber Soul*, which had been released e previous year.

The EP was issued on Parlophone GEP 8952 on 8 July ɔ66 and contained the tracks: 'Nowhere Man', 'Drive My ar', 'Michelle' and 'You Won't See Me'.

• Nowhere Man (Single)

number John penned at **Kenwood**. He was to say, 'I ıs just sitting, trying to think of a song, and I thought of yself sitting there, doing nothing and getting nowhere. ınce I'd thought of that, it was easy. It all came out. No, I member now, I'd actually stopped trying to think of mething. Nothing would come. I was cheesed off and ɜnt for a lie down, having given up. Then I thought of yself as "Nowhere Man" – sitting in his nowhere land.'

Recording began on Thursday, 21 October 1965, and e number was included on the *Rubber Soul* album and ıs also the title of the group's twelfth British EP. It was issued as a single in America on **Capitol** 5587 on 21 February 1966 with 'What Goes On' as the flip and reached No. 3 in the American charts. It was also featured on the American album *Yesterday . . . And Today* and the compilations *The Beatles 1962–1966* and *The Beatles Ballads*.

e Nowhere Man of John Lennon's song was brought to life as Jeremy Hilary Boob in the animated fantasy *Yellow ıbmarine*. (©Apple/King Features)

The Nowhere Man was brought to life in the film *Yellow Submarine* in the person of Hilary Boob, PhD.

A British vocal/instrumental group recorded 'Nowhere Man' and issued it as a single, reaching No. 47 in the British charts with it in March 1966.

• Nurk Twins, The

When the pre-teen Paul and **Mike McCartney** participated in the family entertainment, performing before their relatives, they invented the name the Nurk Twins.

During the Easter holidays in April 1960, John and Paul hitch-hiked down South and stopped off at the **Fox And Hounds**, Gosbrook Road, Caversham, Berkshire, where the new tenants were Mike and Elizabeth Robbins. 'Beth' was Paul's cousin and she and her husband had been Redcoats at Butlin's. The McCartneys had spent a holiday at their camp in 1957 and Mike had encouraged the fifteen-year-old Paul and his thirteen-year-old brother Mike to take the stage together in a talent contest.

When John and Paul turned up at the Fox and Hounds, Mike suggested that they give a show at the pub and he gave them the name The Nerk Twins (remembering the childhood Nurk Twins?). The boys had been helping behind the bar and Mike thought they'd like the idea of entertaining in the tap room, where they performed sitting on stools playing acoustic guitars on the evening of 23 April and during lunchtime on 24 April.

• Nya Aulan, Sundsta Laroverk, Karlstad, Sweden

Venue where the Beatles opened their Swedish tour on 25 October 1963. It was an unusual site for the group to be performing in as it was the hall of a secondary school. The Beatles performed twice that evening, at 7.00 p.m. and 9.00 p.m., to an audience of Swedish youngsters. Also on the bill were a group called the Phantoms.

The Beatles performed 'Long Tall Sally', 'Please Please Me', 'I Saw Her Standing There', 'From Me To You', 'A Taste Of Honey', 'Chains', 'Boys', 'She Loves You' and 'Twist And Shout'.

● Oasis Club, 45/47 Lloyd Street, Manchester

Touted as 'Manchester's Cavern', a cellar-club in the nearby city to Liverpool. The Beatles made their Manchester debut there on 2 February 1962 advertised as 'Polydor's Great Recording Stars', on a bill with the Allan Dent Jazz Band. The club was owned by Manchester promoters Kennedy Street Enterprises and managed by Tony Stuart, who also ran his own jazz band.

The Beatles also appeared at the venue on 29 September and 8 December 1962 and made their final appearance at the club on 22 February 1963.

● Obber, Horst

During their final season at the **Star Club** in December 1962 some of the Beatles' stage performances were recorded by **Adrian Barber**, including two songs on which someone sang lead vocals, with the Beatles backing. They were 'Be-Bob-A-Lula' and 'Hallelujah, I Love Her So'. Both were included on *The Beatles Live! At The Star Club In Hamburg, Germany:1962* album and the voice was credited to Horst Obber.

Horst Obber doesn't exist. The person who got on stage to sing the numbers with the Beatles was their old friend **Horst Fascher**. 'Obber' is simply a German term for 'waiter'.

● Ob-La-Di, Ob-La-Da

The Beatles began recording this number, penned by Paul, on 3 July 1968 and continued for several days. There were a number of changes over the various takes and at on time a number of session men were used, but tha recording was rejected.

The number was completed on Tuesday, 16 July, wit Paul on lead and John and George joining in on th chorus.

The lighthearted song had been inspired by regga music and the number was originally intended to be Beatles single, but John and George rejected it.

The song was recorded by both **Marmalade** and th Bedrocks in Britain and Marmalade topped the chart while the Bedrocks reached No.17 with their version.

'Ob-La-Di, Ob-La-Da' was featured on *The Beatle* double album and also the compilation *The Beatle 1967–1970*.

Ironically, it was issued as a Beatles single in Americ years later on 8 November 1976 on **Capitol** 4347.

Alistair Taylor recalls an anecdote concerning th number. Paul received a phone call on behalf of a regga musician called Scott who was in Brixton prison for failir to keep up with his wife's maintenance payment Apparently, Scott ran a band called Ob-la-di, Ob-la-d and suggested that Paul may have got the title after seein the name on the band's posters in South London. If Pa could deliver him £111 18s to have him released fro Brixton, he'd drop all claims to the title.

Paul couldn't remember whether he'd ever seen poster with that name on it, but he felt sorry for the gu and instructed Alistair to take the money to Brixton priso and arrange for Scott's release, which he did.

● Octopus's Garden

The second number penned by Ringo to appear as Beatles track. It's a children's song with a simil ambience to 'Yellow Submarine'.

During the recording of *The Beatles* double album, Pa made a comment to Ringo that he'd fluffed while playing tom-tom. Ringo walked out of the sessions threatening quit. He spent the next fortnight on a yacht in th Mediterranean owned by **Peter Sellers**. While on th yacht the ship's chef regaled him with stories of th creatures who lived on the bed of the sea, which inspire Ringo to write the song.

He returned to **Abbey Road** to find 'Welcome hom banners on his drum kit.

A scene in the *Let It Be* film reveals George goin

rough the number on a piano, working out the rangement with Ringo and making various helpful ggestions. George Martin joins them and then John also ters the scene and begins to play drums with them.

The Beatles recorded the song on Saturday, 26 April 69. George Martin was away at the time so the oduction was handled by Chris Thomas and the Beatles. Thursday, 17 July, various sound effects were added to eate an 'under sea' atmosphere. At Ringo's suggestion a ke was placed over him when he took a straw and began owing bubbles in a glass of water to simulate the sound being under water.

The number was included on *The Beatles* double um, it is seen in the *Let It Be* film, and was included on e *Beatles 1967–1970* compilation and Ringo featured it his 1978 TV special 'Ringo'.

Odd Spot Club, The, *89 Bold Street, verpool L1*

GRAND RE-OPENING ON SATURDAY, AUGUST 11th, OF THE
ODD SPOT CLUB
89 BOLD STREET, LIVERPOOL
DANCING FROM 7 O'CLOCK UNTIL 11 P.M. TO
THE BEATLES
FARON AND THE FLAMINGOS
JOHNNY TEMPLER AND THE HI-CATS with BARBARA

en the Odd Spot opened in Liverpool city centre on 9 cember 1961 the plan was to provide entertainment to a re affluent clientele than that which graced clubs such the **Cavern**. The owners of the Odd Spot hoped to act the middle-class patrons from the smarter areas of city such as Childwall, Woolton and Aigburth.

The ground floor of the club was a restaurant area and music was performed in the narrow basement. The atles made their debut here on 29 March 1962 and their ond and last appearance occurred a few months later on August.

For their 29 March appearance, Brian Epstein asked n Swerdlow, a former Liverpool Art College student, to e photographs of the Beatles' performance. The group e wearing their new suits, which they'd worn for the t time a few days previously at their Heswall Jazz Club gig. Swerdlow snapped a range of well-composed shots, although the only member of the Beatles he concentrated on taking solo shots of was **Pete Best** and one of the Best shots was used on the cover of ***Mersey Beat*** to announce their Parlophone recording deal.

John Dykins, who had lived with **Julia Lennon** before her death, worked in the Odd Spot restaurant for a time.

● O'Dell, Chris

Blonde-haired American girl from Tucson, Arizona. A friend heard that she wanted to travel to England and gave her a letter of introduction to Apple's Head of A&R, **Peter Asher**. She saw Asher and was given a job as Apple receptionist. She was 22 years old at the time. Within two weeks she had become Peter Asher's secretary.

Chris attended several of the Beatles recording sessions, and was later placed in charge of studio bookings for the **Apple Studios** and was also asked to handle album promotion campaigns. George paid tribute to her abilities with his 1973 Apple single 'Miss O'Dell'.

● O'Dell, Dennis

Irish-born film producer whose association with the Beatles first began when he was Associate Producer of their debut film *A Hard Day's Night*. O'Dell also worked on ***The Family Way***, for which Paul McCartney wrote the score, and ***The Magic Christian***, which starred Ringo and **Peter Sellers**. When **Apple Films** was originally formed in February 1968 he was appointed a director, together with all four Beatles and **Neil Aspinall**. He was also a director of Apple Publicity.

O'Dell became involved in the production of *Magical Mystery Tour*, *Let It Be*, and *The Concert For Bangla Desh*. The Beatles mention him by name in their song 'You Know My Name (Look Up The Number)'.

He was later to enter into partnership with George Harrison in the movie company Handmade Films.

● Odeon, *New Street, Birmingham*

The Beatles appeared at this venue twice, on 11 October 1964 and on 9 December 1965.

● Odeon, *Winchcombe Street, Cheltenham, Gloucestershire*

Venue where the Beatles opened their autumn tour of Britain in 1963. They appeared at the Odeon on 1

November with the **Brook Brothers** with the Rhythm & Blues Quartet, the **Vernons Girls**, **Peter Jay & the Jaywalkers** and the **Kestrels** in support. Introducing the show was Canadian compere Frank Berry.

The Beatles performed 'I Saw Her Standing There', 'From Me To You', 'All My Loving', 'You Really Got A Hold On Me', 'Roll Over Beethoven', 'Boys', 'Till There Was You', 'She Loves You', 'Money' and 'Twist And Shout'.

● Odeon, *Renfield Street, Glasgow, Scotland*

The Beatles first appeared at this venue on 7 June 1963. Their next appearance took place on 30 April 1964. Following this concert, the Beatles all went on a month's holiday to exotic climes. Their third appearance at the cinema took place on 21 October 1964 and their last concert there was the opening date of their final UK tour on 3 December 1965.

Their repertoire on their last British tour was: 'I Feel Fine', 'She's A Woman', 'If I Needed Someone', 'Act Naturally', 'Nowhere Man', 'Baby's In Black', 'Help!', 'We Can Work It Out', 'Yesterday', 'Day Tripper' and 'I'm Down'.

● Odeon, *Epsom Road, Guildford, Surrey*

The majority of appearances the Beatles made on the British cinema/theatre circuit were arranged by promoter **Arthur Howes**. However, there were a series of gigs at such venues arranged by other promoters.

Their appearance here on Friday, 21 June 1963, was presented by **John Smith**. Vic Sutcliffe was once again the compere, but after the Beatles were billed as headliners, the rest of the acts were listed under the slogan: 'The Jimmy Crawford Package Show' which comprised Lance Fortune, Jimmy Crawford, the Hayseeds, the Vampires, Rocking Henri, the Messengers and the Vikings with Michael London.

● Odeon, *Queen Caroline Street, Hammersmith, London W6*

Setting for the second of the Beatles' seasonal theatre specials, called 'Another Beatles Christmas Show'. Once again devised and produced by **Peter Yolland** it opened on 24 December 1964 and presented two shows a night for twenty nights, with the exception of 24 and 29 December when there was only a single show. Proceeds for the December appearance were in aid of the Brady Clubs a Settlement Charity.

The show opened with compere **Jimmy Savi** announcing the **Mike Cotton Sound**, who perform 'Yeh Yeh', a recent hit for Georgie Fame. They were th fronted by Brian Epstein's new discovery, singer **Mich Haslam**, who performed 'Scarlet Ribbons'. The next act appear was the **Yardbirds**.

The co-compere **Ray Fell**, a Liverpool comic, appea and told of four Arctic explorers in search of t Abominable Snowman. The Beatles, dressed in costum suited to Arctic weather, then appeared in a humor sketch. They were followed by **Freddie & T Dreamers** who performed 'Rip It Up', 'Bachelor Boy' a 'Cut Across Shorty'.

The second half of the show was opened by **El Brooks**, **Sounds Incorporated** and Ray Fell. Th Jimmy Savile reappeared to introduce the Beatles, w were dressed in midnight blue mohair shirts. Th performed 'Twist and Shout', 'I'm A Loser', 'Baby's Black', 'Everybody's Trying to Be My Baby', 'Can't B Me Love', 'Honey Don't' (a vocal for Ringo), 'I Feel Fi 'She's A Woman', 'A Hard Day's Night', 'Rock And R Music' and 'Long Tall Sally'.

They next appeared at the venue on 10 December 19 during their final British tour. The numbers th performed were 'I Feel Fine', 'She's A Woman', 'I Needed Someone', 'Act Naturally', 'Nowhere Man', 'Bab In Black', 'Help!', 'We Can Work It Out', 'Yesterda 'Day Tripper' and 'I'm Down'.

While at the Odeon the boys were visited by Canad DJ Dave Boxer of C.F.C.F. Radio who'd flown speci from Montreal with a petition from thousands of fa requesting that they visit the city on their next tour.

● Odeon, *The Headrow, Leeds, Yorkshire*

The Beatles appeared at this venue twice in 1963. Initi on 5 June on their second tour, with **Roy Orbison** a **Gerry & The Pacemakers**, and on 3 November as toppers with **Peter Jay & the Jaywalkers** and **Brook Brothers** in support. Part of this last performa was recorded, and part of the recording was used by Performing Rights Society in a court case.

The group returned to the Odeon on 22 October 19

eading a bill which also included **Mary Wells**, **Tommy Quickly**, the **Remo Four**, **Michael Haslam**, the **Rustiks** and **Bob Bain**.

● Odeon, Loampit Vale, Lewisham, London SE13

he Beatles made their debut at this London venue on 29 March 1963 as part of the **Tommy Roe/Chris Montez** our. Their second and final appearance at the cinema took lace on 8 December 1963.

● Odeon, London Road, Liverpool L3

he Beatles only made a single appearance at this major inema venue in their home town of Liverpool. The ccasion was on one of their busiest days since their ouring career began. It took place on 7 December 1963. arlier in the day the group appeared at the **Empire Theatre**, only 50 yards away, where they performed before embers of their fan club and filmed two BBC shows, '**Juke Box Jury**' and '**It's The Beatles**'. They then ushed down a heavily policed side street to the Odeon for eir concert, which had been specially added to their tour.

The Odeon was also the venue for the northern remiere of their film *A Hard Day's Night* on Friday, 10 uly 1964. It was the day of their famous Civic Reception nd after the group had left **Liverpool Town Hall** their ar, which had a police motor cycle escort, was halted four mes due to the massive crowds in the city centre. The roup eventually managed to slip into the cinema by a side oor in a side street.

The proceedings were opened by the Liverpool City olice Band who played 'Z Cars', the theme tune for a TV rama series about Merseyside police, followed by a eatles medley. When the curtain opened, disc jockey **David Jacobs** introduced several personalities from the lm, including **Norman Rossington** and **Lionel Blair**. here were also a number of star names in the audience, ncluding **Alma Cogan** and Tommy Steele. When the eatles returned there was an immense reception.

George walked forward and said 'Hello' to his parents nd relatives and John wondered where all his relatives ad got to. 'What happened to them at the Town Hall, I idn't get a chance to see them?' he said. Paul thanked veryone for the marvellous reception and Ringo entioned that people had said they were finished with as r as the Liverpool people were concerned – 'But we proved them wrong, didn't we kids,' he said.

The film was then screened, applauded after each song.

In 1984, the Odeon was the site for the northern premieres of Paul's feature film *Give My Regards To Broad Street* on 28 November. That day Paul was presented with the Freedom of the City at a special ceremony.

● Odeon, Llandudno, Caernarvonshire, Wales

The group were booked to appear at this venue for a week, heading a bill which also featured **Billy J. Kramer** and **Tommy Quickly**.

The short six-day season commenced on 12 August 1963 and finished on 17 August.

● Odeon, Dunstable Road, Luton, Bedfordshire

The Beatles only appeared at this venue once, on 6 September 1963.

● Odeon, Oxford Street, Manchester

The Beatles only appeared at this venue once, on 30 May 1963. The appearance was during their tour with **Roy Orbison** and **Gerry & the Pacemakers** and their repertoire comprised: 'Some Other Guy', 'Do You Want To Know A Secret?', 'Love Me Do', 'From Me To You', 'Please Please Me', 'I Saw Her Standing There' and 'Twist And Shout'.

Interestingly enough, it was the show at which **Derek Taylor** first reviewed a Beatles performance. Derek was to loom large in their lives, becoming personal assistant to Brian Epstein, Beatles press officer and, later, press officer for their Apple empire.

At the time of the Odeon concert he was a columnist with the Northern edition of the *Daily Express*, penning his own 'Taylor On Saturday' column, but also interviewing show business personalities.

There were no press tickets available for this particular show, but Derek phoned the cinema manager, Mr Bint, and bought two front stall tickets for the first house at one pound each. Accompanied by his wife Joan he watched the show, then retired to a nearby public house where he met the *Daily Express* photographer Bill Gregory who had been unable to get shots of the Beatles, but had taken photographs of Gerry & the Pacemakers.

Derek's review appeared in 'The Critics' section of the

Northern edition of the *Daily Express* the next morning. He described the concert '. . . as beneficial and invigorating as a week on a beach at the pierhead overlooking the Mersey'. He also wrote: 'I suppose there is not-yet-a-first-class musician among them. Last night's audience of screamers gave the ear little chance of picking up two consecutive notes.' Of their performance, he commented: 'Their stage manner has little polish but limitless energy, and they have in abundance the fundamental rough good humour of their native city', and he signed off with the words: 'It was marvellous, meaningless, impertinent, exhilarating stuff.'

● Odeon, Angel Row, Nottingham

The Beatles debuted at this cinema on 23 May 1963 as part of the **Roy Orbison** tour. They were headliners when they next appeared on 12 December 1963 and their final appearance took place on 5 November 1964.

● Odeon, South Street, Romford, Essex

The Beatles only ever made one appearance at this Essex cinema on Sunday, 16 June 1963. It was one of a handful of gigs promoted by John Smith, although billed as part of the '**Mersey Beat Showcase**' series of concerts. Supporting the Beatles were **Gerry & the Pacemakers**, **Billy J. Kramer** & the Dakotas and the Vikings with Michael London.

The occasion was quite unique considering that the three Mersey bands that week occupied the top three positions in the British charts. The Beatles with 'From Me To You', Gerry with 'I Like It' and Billy J. Kramer with 'Do You Want To Know A Secret'.

The compere was Vic Sutcliffe.

The programme blurb on the Vikings read: 'The average age of the group is 21, lead guitar being the baby at 20. The group as such have been together for about a year and are well known for their efficient support to several prominent recording stars. "The Vikings Show Combo", who feature clavioline, already have their latest attack on the charts "in the can", titled "Valhalla" which is shortly to be released; they are appearing in Jersey in early August.'

The piece on Michael London read, 'Michael is a coloured, very good looking boy, he is 23 years of age, and has many records to his credit, including "Stranger On The Shore". He was born in Trinidad where he is at the top of the Hit Parade.'

The programme was a well-designed souvenir an included several photographs of the Beatles, together wit articles on each of the acts appearing and a back pag blurb proclaiming: 'Goodnight folks! Hope you enjoyed th show. Thanks for coming.'

When the Beatles arrived for their two shows there wer over 2,000 teenagers outside the cinema and hundreds girls surrounded their car, trying to wrench open the door The car's radio aerial was ripped from its fixing and th doors and bonnet were badly dented.

Several girls climbed on the roof and the driv reversed the car through the crowd and sought refuge i Romford police station. The Beatles were then taken to th rear entrance of the Odeon in a van.

Six girls were selected to go backstage and meet th group and included the local Carnival Queen, eightee year-old Maureen Cox. The local paper, the *Romfor Recorder*, reported, 'During the two performances, gir pelted the stage with cards and gifts for Beatle Pa MacKenzie [sic] who was 21 last week.'

After the show, while Gerry & the Pacemakers an Billy J. Kramer struggled into the van at the stage door, th Beatles ran to the front of the cinema and into a waitir taxi. The crowd surged forth, traffic jammed and policeman was hit on the head and struck in the eye b pennies.

The Beatles finally got away by taxi and switched their own cars at the nearby Parkside Hotel.

Although Epstein had originally planned five mo 'Mersey Beat Showcase' productions for the rest of Jun he cancelled them.

● Odeon, High Street, Southend-on-Sea, Essex

The Beatles made their debut at this 2,100-seater ven on 31 May 1963 during their tour with **Roy Orbison**.

Their second and final appearance there took place Monday, 9 December 1963. Five hundred fans had queu all night before the box office opened (some had camp outside in sleeping bags for as long as 36 hours) and th tickets were all sold out within a single day. The show wa simply called *The Beatles Show* and the group arrived the Odeon at 2.30 p.m. Since they were unable to leave th theatre during the day, **Neil Aspinall** organized fo deliveries, mainly chicken for John, Paul and Georg hile Ringo opted for fish and chips. There was also a lection of Chinese foods.

The first half of the show comprised sets from **Peter y & the Jaywalkers** and the **Brook Brothers**. When e Beatles appeared they performed a one-hour show, aying sixteen numbers, including 'Love Me Do', 'Roll ver Beethoven', 'Please Please Me', 'From Me To You' d 'She Loves You'. After 'I Want To Hold Your Hand' ey left the stage, then returned for an encore during iich they played a blistering version of 'Twist And Shout'.

Odeon, Lord Street, Southport, ancashire

the nearby holiday resort to Liverpool, the Beatles first peared at the Odeon on 1 March 1963 as part of the **elen Shapiro** tour.

Their next appearance was for a week-long series of rformances for six nights from 26–31 August 1963.

Odeon, The Centre, Weston-super-Mare, omerset

e Beatles appeared at this seaside resort venue once, for run of six nights from 22–27 July 1963. Generally, aside resorts could present weekly bills rather than the ual one-nighters for package tours because of the large flux of holidaymakers who, being on holiday, sought tertainment every night, resulting in a higher proportion people attending theatrical shows than in the provincial ies.

During their appearance at the Odeon, photographer **ezo Hoffmann** arranged an afternoon session with the oup on the beach at Weston-super-Mare. This was the mous photo session in which the Beatles wore striped ctorian swimming outfits. The session was originally dertaken as an assignment for the Souvenir Press book ***eet The Beatles*** which was to retail for two shillings d sixpence. Dezo had also brought along his cine-mera and fifteen minutes of film was taken of the atles larking about on the beach and taking donkey les. The footage was in black and white and without und. Many years later, on Friday, 3 December 1982, on annel 4's pop show 'The Tube', ten minutes of Dezo's me movie was screened for the first time.

O'Donnell, Lucy

girl who was in the same class as **Julian Lennon** at Heath House infants' school in Weybridge in 1967 and indirectly proved to be the inspiration for the creation of John Lennon's classic *Sgt Pepper* track 'Lucy In The Sky With Diamonds'.

Julian drew a picture of Lucy, whom he used to invite to his birthday parties, and showed it to his parents. John asked him what the painting was supposed to represent and Julian answered, 'It's Lucy In The Sky With Diamonds'. John was struck by the title and wrote the song, but for many years people wouldn't believe the story as they were convinced it was a song about drugs because the initials of the song, L.S.D, were the same initials as those of the hallucinogenic drug which John had admitted taking. Lucy was the daughter of a journalist and later became a nursery nurse.

● O'Hara, Terry

A Liverpool designer, nicknamed 'Tex'. He is the younger brother of Brian O'Hara of the **Fourmost**, one of the

Tex O'Hara's abstract sculpture of the Beatles. (Merseyside Tourism Office)

groups in the Epstein stable who were also good friends of the Beatles.

Tex originally designed the Beatles' first drumskin 'logo', a design which featured a beetle's antennae on the letter 'B'. The Beatles must have provided a great deal of inspiration for him in those early days as he also completed a wooden sculpture of Ringo Starr in 1962. This work, in a 'cubist' style, is generally acknowledged as the very first piece of sculpture to be inspired by the Beatles.

These examples were later included in the ***Art Of The Beatles*** exhibition at the **Walker Art Gallery**, Liverpool, in 1984.

● Oh Darling

Track from the *Abbey Road* album, penned by Paul. The Beatles originally began the recording of this track at the **Apple Studios** in **Savile Row** on 27 January 1969. Then Paul recorded the vocals by himself at Abbey Road's No. 3 studio over 17, 18, 22 and 23 July. He commented: 'When we were recording this track I came into the studios early every day for a week to sing it by myself because at first my voice was too clear. I wanted it to sound as though I'd been performing it on stage all week.'

Robin Gibb of the Bee Gees sang the song in the film version of *Sgt Pepper's Lonely Hearts Club Band* and his single of the number reached No. 24 in the American charts in 1978.

● Old Brown Shoe

A George Harrison composition which he originally recorded by himself at **Abbey Road** on Tuesday, 25 February. It was George's 26th birthday and he treated himself to a session in the studios. Aided by engineer Ken Scott, George made demos of three of his numbers, including 'Old Brown Shoe'.

The number was recorded by the Beatles on Wednesday, 16 April, and Friday, 18 April 1969, and it was issued as the flipside of 'The Ballad Of John And Yoko'. It was also included on the compilation albums *The Beatles 1967–1970* and *Hey Jude*.

● Oldham, Andrew Loog

According to Ray Coleman's *Brian Epstein: The Man Who Made The Beatles*, Brian Epstein first met Andrew Loog Oldham, a young public relations man, during the Beatles' first recording for '**Thank Your Lucky Stars**' on 13 January 1963. Oldham was present with one of his client
the singer Mark Wynter, and he began to advise Brian
how he should present the Beatles' image to the pres
Brian was impressed and within a few days had hired hi
to be the Beatles' public relations representative.

According to **Tony Barrow**, the nineteen-year-o
Oldham had gone into partnership with **Tony Calder** a
was running a public relations office in Maddox Stre
near Bond Street, London. Epstein had hired Barrow
write a press release for 'Love Me Do', but as Barrow w
still working for **Decca**, he didn't have the facilities
post the releases to the relevant disc jockeys a
publications, or set up the interviews. As Calder was
former colleague at Decca he contacted him and ended
taking Oldham to lunch at the Aeolian Hall. A deal w
struck and Oldham and Calder were involved in t
promotion of the Beatles' debut record 'Love Me D
Epstein then offered Oldham the job as full-time Beat
Press Officer, but he turned it down.

In April 1963 journalist **Peter Jones** tipped Oldh
off about a talented new band called the **Rolling Ston**
He rushed to see them in Richmond, then contacted age
Eric Easton who agreed to co-manage the group with h
and provide the finance and back-up.

Almost a decade later, Oldham was to tell the ***N***
Musical Express that he remembered seeing the Beat
on an early concert bill: 'I sat there with a lump in
throat. In one night you knew they were going to be ve
big. It was just an instinctive thing. From that night on,
registered subconsciously that when they made it, anot
section of the public was going to want the opposite.'
created that opposite with the Rolling Stones' image
something that frustrated John Lennon for years. T
Beatles were portrayed as lovable moptops and the Roll
Stones had an aggressive 'bad boy' image. Lennon felt t
the Stones had taken the Beatles' real image. While
Stones were still living a civilized middle-class existen
in the home counties, the Beatles were raving it up in
red light district of Hamburg, playing rough rock 'n' r
and R&B and living a life which could have given th
the tag 'the savage young Beatles'.

Oldham and Epstein always remained on friendly ter
and the two of them agreed that they would ensure that
release dates of the Beatles and Rolling Stones reco
didn't conflict.

Oldham was one of the guests interviewed by Epst

r the **'Hullabaloo'** show, an American NBC television ries which Epstein recorded in London on 19 December)64.

Oliver, Jack

young Londoner who joined Apple as assistant to **Terry oran** of Apple Music. When the company moved to **vile Row**, he was one of seven people who shared space the Press Office. A few months later he moved to the cord Department on the first floor. When **Allen Klein** tered the picture and it was obvious that he was anoeuvring to oust **Ron Kass**, Oliver said he'd leave if ass was sacked. When Kass did get the sack, to the rprise of almost everyone, Oliver was made head of **pple Records** in his place, jumping from relative scurity to the head of the Beatles' record label within elve months.

Olympia Stadium, Detroit, Michigan

e Beatles first appeared at this venue on Sunday, 6 ptember 1964. There was the usual press conference, ce again attended by various Beauty Queens, including ss Michigan 1960, Miss Armed Forces and Miss rmont. There were two shows at the venue that evening d a number of fans had been thrown out for hurling jelly ans at the group. At the press conference earlier, one estion put to Paul was, 'Do you think girls should be own out of the show for throwing jelly beans?' Paul plied, 'No. It has become a bit of a trademark with our ows, but we'd prefer they throw nothing at all.'

The next time the group appeared at the stadium was Saturday, 13 August 1966, on their final tour, during ich almost 30,000 fans watched the two concerts.

Olympia Theatre, Boulevard des pucines, Paris, France

e Beatles were booked to appear at Paris's famous ympia Theatre for three weeks from 16 January 1964. ne reports claimed that they were only being paid £50 performance. There were ten acts on the bill and it was ver quite clear who was the actual bill-topper: the atles, **Trini Lopez** or **Sylvie Vartan**. The group peared at the Olympia for twenty days, with two, netimes three, performances a day. Their repertoire for theatre was: 'From Me To You', 'Roll Over Beethoven', e Loves You', 'This Boy', 'I Want To Hold Your Hand', 'Boys', 'Twist And Shout' and 'Long Tall Sally'.

During the afternoon on 16 January the Beatles performed before an audience of students. The evening performance seemed to draw from French Society and the audience were dressed in tuxedos and evening gowns. It was one of their toughest audiences and the Beatles didn't seem to appeal to the French as much as they did to audiences in the rest of the world. During the show their amplification broke down on three different occasions and George voiced his opinion on stage that the equipment had been sabotaged by photographers.

Trini Lopez had charmed the audience by speaking to them in French. The Beatles couldn't speak the language and made little attempt to do so, although at one point John said, '*Je me lève à sept heures*', which caused one woman in the front row to cry out, 'How barbaric!' When the Beatles left the theatre there were two dozen police at the stage door, helping to hold back the mass of photographers.

After their cool reception the group returned to the George V Hotel, only to receive a telegram which stated that they'd reached No. 1 in the American charts with 'I Want To Hold Your Hand', which made the reception at the Olympia seem of no importance.

The next day the reviews in the French papers were universally anti-Beatle. When asked at a press conference whether he'd read the French papers, Ringo said, 'I can't read French.'

On 19 January their show was recorded by ORTF Radio and on 22 January an ORTF TV camera crew filmed their performance.

● Olympic Sound Studios, 117 Church Road, Barnes, London SW13

The studio manager at the time was Keith Grant and he actively sought to have the Beatles record at the independent studio where the **Rolling Stones** were now recording regularly. The Beatles booked Studio One at Olympic and recorded 'Baby You're A Rich Man' there on Thursday, 11 May 1967. It was the first Beatles number to be fully recorded and mixed outside of **EMI**'s **Abbey Road Studios**.

The Beatles also recorded an early version of 'All You Need Is Love' at Olympic on Wednesday, 14 June 1967.

When the Beatles handed **Glyn Johns** the tapes of their 'Get Back' sessions and asked him to put the album together, he booked his favourite recording studios – Olympic Sound. Glyn began work on the album at Olympic on 10, 11 and 13 March and on 7 April 1969. He returned to Olympic with Steve Vaughan as his assistant on 5, 6, 7, 9 and 10 May when he completed his engineering of the tapes.

● O'Mahony, Sean

The publisher of the Beatles Book Monthly. Sean worked on a magazine called *Pop Weekly* at the beginning of the sixties, but was a songwriter at heart, although his work had been rejected by A&R men such as George Martin and **Dick James**. He first contacted Brian Epstein to request an advertisement for 'Love Me Do' for *Pop Weekly*. He later left the magazine to launch his own *Beat Monthly* and contacted Epstein to arrange a feature on the Beatles. In January 1963 Sean read that 500 fans had been turned away from a Beatles show. Intrigued, he phoned Epstein and arranged to meet him at the Westbury Hotel, London, where he proposed a magazine devoted entirely to the Beatles. Brian said he'd discuss it with 'the boys'. The Beatles wanted to meet Sean to discuss his ideas and he met up with them when they were broadcasting a BBC radio show **'Pop Go The Beatles'** on 1 June 1963. Later, Brian phoned him to tell him the deal was on. Epstein requested 50 per cent of the profits for the Beatles and it was eventually agreed that they would receive 33⅓ per cent.

80,000 copies of the first issue were printed and, at its height, the *Beatles Monthly* sold 350,000 copies per issue. The magazine continued for 77 issues over a six-and-a-half-year period and with issue 77, dated December 1969, Sean decided to cease publication. In a lengthy editorial entitled 'The End Of An Era', he put forward several reasons for his decision: the difficulty in obtaining photographs and gaining access to the Beatles; the fact that they were all approaching their thirties; their reluctance to maintain their group association; and preference for being interviewed or photographed individually.

The magazine's official photographer was **Leslie Bryce** who was afforded an access to the group denied other photographers with the result that he took literally thousands of photographs of them. There were cartoons and sketches contributed by artist Bob Gibson and a small core of regular feature writers.

The magazine was edited by 'Johnny Dean', a pseudonym that O'Mahony used. The Beatles' press offic **Tony Barrow** was also a regular contributor, although used the alias Frederick James, and **Peter Jones**, th editor of *Record Mirror*, contributed items under the na Billy Shepherd. From the Beatles' own camp there we regular reports and occasional columns from **N Aspinall** and **Mal Evans** and photographs from **To Bramwell.**

During the next six years, O'Mahony received considerable volume of mail from Beatle fans seeking ba issues; he noted that copies of *Beatles Monthly* w selling at outrageous prices to collectors, and decided reprint the entire run of issues. The publication w relaunched in May 1975 under the title the *Beat Appreciation Society Magazine Book*. George Harris objected to this and unsuccessfully attempted to prev publication. The entire rerun of issues continued u September 1982. By that time, interest in the Beatles v still growing and O'Mahony decided to begin a new se of magazines using entirely new material. He h presented 1,000 photographs in the original 77-issue r but still had over 4,000 photographs in his files. His n series, entitled the *Beatles Monthly Book*, was launched October 1982.

Beatles Monthly used various editors during the rer and new issues, including Lorna Read and Peter Dogg Many of its regular writers such as Tony Barrow, M Lewisohn and Bill Harry continued to contribute to new series.

O'Mahony was able to build a list of thriving magazi in his Beat Publications company, which included *Rec Collector* and *Book Collector*.

● One After 909, The

One of the very earliest of John Lennon's compositic which he first performed with the **Quarry Men** in the fifties. It was also included as part of the Beatles' st repertoire until late in 1962.

Incredibly, it was not released as a Beatles num until 1970 when it was included as a track on the *Let It* album. The song had first been recorded on Tuesday March 1963, but was finally included on an album a the Beatles performed the number on the rooftop sess on the Apple building.

The number 9 figured quite prominently in John's and he used it more than once in his songs.

One And One Is Two

song originally penned by Paul and John when they were :aying at the George V Hotel in Paris in January 1964. It as written under pressure as they had to get a tape to ondon quickly as the number was due to be recorded by **illy J. Kramer**. John Lennon wasn't too pleased with the umber and commented: 'Billy J's career is finished when e gets this song.' Kramer didn't like it and insisted he cord an American number he'd discovered himself called ittle Children'. 'Little Children' gave Billy J. another No. hit in Britain and his first Top Ten in the US. A British oup, the **Strangers** with Mike Shannon, recorded 'One nd One Is Two' and the single was issued by Philips on F 1355 on 8 May 1964, but it failed to chart.

Only A Northern Song

George Harrison composition, used in *Yellow ıbmarine*. Brian Epstein had promised the producers of e film four new titles. Some of them were tracks left over om the *Sgt Pepper* sessions, such as Paul McCartney's ll Together Now' and George Harrison's 'It's All Too uch' (which was cut for the *Yellow Submarine* undtrack because of its length). There was John's 'Hey ılldog' which producer **Al Brodax** didn't like and left t of the American prints of the film. The final number ıs 'Only A Northern Song'.

This number was also originally planned for the *Sgt pper* album when recording first began on Monday, 13 bruary 1967. As usual, George hadn't come up with a le, so it was tentatively called 'Not Known'. When it was cided to leave the number off the *Sgt Pepper* album, orge replaced it with 'Within You, Without You'.

The group continued recording the number, now known 'Only A Northern Song', on Thursday, 20 April 1967, d it was eventually issued on the *Yellow Submarine* oum on Friday, 17 January 1969. Another inaccurate ry became part of Beatle lore. It was said the Beatles re at **Abbey Road Studios** one night and *Yellow bmarine* producer Al Brodax said they were still short of e number for the soundtrack. George asked everyone to it and went into a room for an hour, returning with the mber saying, 'Here, Al, it's only a northern song.' ıbellishments on the story even have the London mphony Orchestra waiting while George wrote the mber.

Commenting on the song, George said, 'It was a joke relating to Liverpool, the Holy City in the North. The copyright belonged to Northern Songs Limited, which I didn't own, so "It doesn't really matter what chords I play, what words I say, or time of day it is, as it's only a northern song".' It was more of a comment about the Beatles song publishing company Northern Songs, which was mainly controlled by **Dick James**, whose percentage was more than those of John and Paul put together – George only received a nominal amount from the company, while at one time he was regarded as just a contract songwriter.

● Ono, Yoko

Yoko, whose name means 'Ocean Child', was born in Tokyo, Japan, at 8.30 p.m. on 18 February 1933. Her parents were Eisuke Ono and his wife Isako, both of whose families were prominent in the Japanese banking world. Yoko's brother Keisuke was born in December 1936 and her sister Setsuko in December 1941.

When Yoko was two and a half years old she was taken to America where her father had been placed in a prominent position in a bank. Isoko returned to her home country with her children when Japan invaded China, fearing the backlash of anti-Japanese feeling in America. She returned to San Francisco with her children for a short time and Yoko attended school there. The family then had to return to Tokyo in 1943 due to the impending war.

As her family were rich and influential, Yoko didn't suffer the hardships of many of the Japanese people during the war; she continued with her education, becoming fluent in English. After the war the family returned to America, settling in the high-class Scarsdale area outside New York where Yoko attended the Sarah Lawrence School in 1953.

The 19-year-old girl didn't like the school and left in her third year to live in Manhattan with a young Japanese composer and musician, Toshi Ichiyanagi, whom she married against the wishes of her parents. They lived for a few years in Greenwich Village, but Yoko was reportedly unfaithful and they were divorced after six years, although Yoko gave signs of the strength of character and leadership evident in her later life. She encouraged Toshi in his musical career and talked him into returning to Japan where he received a degree of acclaim. The couple were divorced in 1963.

Yoko continued living in Chambers Street in New York, becoming part of an artistic sect called Fluxus, composed

Left: Yoko and John in *Imagine*, the Warner Bros film of 1988. (Warner Bros)
Below: Yoko Ono, with members of the cast of the hit musical *Lennon*. (Maxine Barber Publicity)

of painters, musicians and writers. She began to hold concerts and art exhibitions of her own, gaining a reputation as a creative conceptual artist. She married a film producer, Tony Cox, and the two had a daughter whom they named Kyoko.

In September 1966 the family moved to London to further Yoko's career, after accepting an invitation to attend a symposium called 'The Destruction Of Art'. Even at this time it was very much a case of Yoko being the strong partner, advancing her career while her husband looked after the child.

Yoko began to involve herself in 'happenings' in London and gained attention when she appealed for volunteers to help her wrap up one of the stone lions in Trafalgar Square. She called this "happening', 'Trafalgar Square Wrapping Event'. She also gained notoriety in the media for her film *Bottoms*, which featured the bare backsides of a number of 'Swinging London' personalities; and a 'happening' called 'Snip Piece' in which members of the audience cut off all her clothes with a pair of scissors. She had also, by this time, had a small book of conceptual ideas called *Grapefruit* published in a limited edition [in] Japan and America.

It was during the preview of her exhibition at t[he] **Indica Gallery** on 9 November 1966 that the famo[us] meeting with John Lennon took place. Yoko claimed s[he] was relatively unaware of the phenomenon which t[he] Beatles had become and said she was initial[ly] unimpressed when the gallery's co-owner John Dunb[ar] urged her to speak to the 'millionaire'. The much report[ed] incident of hammering in the imaginary nail took pla[ce] and each realized that they had found a kindred spirit. [In] September 1967 John was to sponsor her *Half-Wind Sh[ow]* which was subtitled *Yoko Plus Me*.

Yoko began to pursue John with tenacity, writing h[im] endless notes, following him around, and he began to ta[ke] great interest in her conceptual ideas, keeping a copy book *Grapefruit* by his bedside, which he would ularly refer to.

It was in May 1968 when Tony Cox and Kyoko were in nce and **Cynthia** was on holiday that Yoko arrived on n's doorstep at **Kenwood** in Weybridge. He suggested t they go upstairs to his studio and make some erimental tapes – the ones which were to eventually be ed as *Two Virgins*. Yoko reported, 'It was midnight n we started and it was dawn when we finished and we made love.'

John's wife Cynthia arrived home, in company with xis **Mardas** and **Jennie Boyd**, to find Yoko conced in her home wearing a dressing-gown. It was ious what had occurred. Cynthia left.

There was a brief attempt at a reconciliation, but it n't work out and Cynthia was later to begin divorce eedings.

Yoko began involving John in her conceptual creations, inning with her acorn sculpture event at Coventry hedral in June 1968. The two made their involvement more public when they attended the play *In His Own e* on 18 June 1968. The couple were to move into go's **Montague Square** flat together.

The British press took an immediate dislike to Yoko, thus began the snide and hurtful comments which to continue over the succeeding months and years which were counted among the reasons which hed the couple's decision to live in New York.

n July 1968, John held an exhibition called *You Are – To Yoko From John, With Love*. Yoko was pregnant he time and when she was admitted to **Queen rlotte's Hospital** later that month, John took to ping on the floor next to her bed. Unfortunately, she a miscarriage – and was to have two more before she John a child. Before the year's end the couple had ed their *Two Virgins* album, telerecorded the **Rolling es'** *Rock & Roll Circus* and appeared at the **Royal rt Hall** in the *Alchemical Wedding*. The two were to inue to work jointly in the creative and business fields, ing records and films together, forming companies as Bag One and Lenono, with Yoko appearing on the ide of John's singles, on his albums and also recording albums in her own right.

1969 John and Yoko continued to dominate the lines, appearing on stage during a jazz concert in bridge and getting married in Gibraltar on 20 March – which they celebrated by holding their 'Bed-In For Peace' in Amsterdam. By May of that year John had officially changed his name to John Ono Lennon and the couple had moved into a large estate in Ascot called Tittenhurst Park. Following a trip to Montreal, the couple took John's son **Julian** and Kyoko on a visit to Scotland during which their car crashed. There were no serious injuries, although Yoko was later to attend Beatles sessions at **Abbey Road** resting in a double bed.

The vitriolic attacks in the media caused John a great deal of personal pain. He had made his choice, he loved Yoko and the two were inseparable. An attack on her was an attack on him. Why should outside people try to impose their preferences on him? He was aware that the other members of the Beatles did not like Yoko and this was more likely to have resulted in a breakdown between John and the other members of the group than Yoko's influence on John. He also resented the fact that certain people in Apple, whose security rested on the money he was putting into the company, also had an attitude towards her and talked about her behind her back.

It's also likely at the time that the British media couldn't come to terms with Yoko's independence, her determination to present her own ideas and to share them with John. Had a male been as 'pushy', no notice would have been taken. Yoko was perhaps ahead of her time in seeking equal rights with her man – and John was able to grasp this fact through reading books such as *The First Sex*. Although it may have seemed that, at times, Yoko was stifling John with her ideas – always at recording sessions, always wanting to take part in his stage appearances, wanting to write songs with him – at the same time she was stimulating him. John appreciated having his artistic horizons widened by someone else – just as had happened during his friendship with **Stuart Sutcliffe**.

But he could never understand why friends and foes alike all seemed to resent the woman he loved, and it was a constant source of frustration for him.

The Wedding Album, *Live Peace In Toronto* and 'The War Is Over' campaign occupied the remaining months of 1969, and in 1970, the year which the two christened 'Year One', they gained further notoriety when John's lithographs, some of them showing him in intimate sexual embrace with Yoko, were seized by the police. They also underwent Primal Therapy in America.

In 1971 Yoko and John appeared with **Frank Zappa** at

the Fillmore East in New York, and began their efforts to obtain custody of Kyoko. It was during their search for Yoko's daughter that they decided to remain in America, settling in New York and beginning a battle for John to obtain his Green Card.

John was later to feel ashamed at the way they pursued Kyoko and her father. When Cox and Yoko had been divorced, Kyoko had remained with her father, but Yoko always had access to the child. It was then suggested that Yoko had a sudden desire to take custody of Kyoko following her miscarriage of John's child. Over the next few years, a battle for custody began initially when John and Yoko attempted to take Kyoko away from Majorca where she had been attending a nursery. They were prevented from spiriting her away from the island by the Spanish authorities. John and Yoko were accused of kidnapping and had to appear in court. The court officials took Kyoko aside and asked her if she would prefer to go with her father or her mother (shades of a five-year-old John's tug of war in Blackpool). She opted for her father. A legal battle began in earnest, with John calling in **Allen Klein** to help them, and the Lennons spent six months in courts in Texas, New York and the Virgin Isles. Despite the Lennons' wealth, Cox managed to flee with Kyoko to an unknown destination in America. John and Yoko had to admit defeat and were unable to trace them.

John and Yoko settled in the Dakota Building in New York, and over the next few years were involved in the making of various avant-garde films.

The major event in their lives was the birth of **Sean Ono Lennon** on 9 October 1975. Sean had been born following their reunion after eighteen months during which John had left Yoko to live with their secretary, May Pang, who had been hired when John had turned 33 years of age and was perhaps experiencing a restlessness or 'seven year itch'. It was said that Yoko had encouraged the relationship. John suddenly fled to Los Angeles with May and for the period described as his 'Long Weekend', she became his mistress. She continued to act as his secretary and helped to organize some of his West Coast recording projects. When John returned to Yoko, May resettled in New York where she became a professional manager of United Artists Music and she was later to marry a record producer Tony Visconti and write a book called *Loving John – The Untold Story*.

John decided to spend the next five years looking after Sean while Yoko attended to the couple's business affa While John reared Sean in their apartment in the Dak Building, Yoko worked in the Lennon office on the gro floor of the building, turning their money into a v fortune, reported to be in excess of a hundred mill dollars – a figure which was to continue to increase o the years. She proved an astute businesswoman wh ventures included buying farms, real estate and breed cattle.

This was a time when her own recording activities addition to those of John, were put on hold. Apart from various recordings with John, she had become a recor artist in her own right, with her first solo album *Y Ono/Plastic Ono Band* issued in December 1970. This followed the next year by her single 'Mrs Lennon', t another album in December, *Fly*. Her other recordi included the 1972 single 'Mind Train', the 1973 al *Approximately Infinite Universe*, followed the same yea two singles 'Death of Samantha' and 'Run Run Run' another album *Feeling The Space*. She had no fur releases for the rest of the decade.

In 1980, after the horror of John's murder, Y remained at the Dakota, having to employ bodyguard look after Sean on a round-the-clock basis. administered the huge funds which were donated on Jo behalf to the Spirit Foundations, sending the mone various charities. She also began work on securir memorial to John in Central Park, called 'Strawb Fields'.

Yoko has done much to continue to perpetuate Jo memory, participating in both television and feature fi recordings and radio shows and publishing posthu books. In relation to the Beatles story she is still treate a hostile way by writers who are probably prejudi Taking a different point of view, they could just as concentrate on her considerable artistic ventures ove years, her courage and her incredible business acu which has made her one of the richest women in Am – and someone who has achieved success in what undoubtedly been a man's world.

● On The Scene

A BBC radio programme broadcast each Thursday 5.00 p.m–5.30 p.m. Produced by Brian Willey, 'On Scene' featured the Beatles performing 'Misery', 'Do Want To Know A Secret?' and 'Please Please Me' o arch 1963. They'd recorded the programme on 21 March the BBC studio in the Piccadilly Theatre, Denman reet. It was their only appearance on the show.

Ooh! My Soul

number written and recorded by **Little Richard**. The atles included it in their repertoire in 1961 with Paul on ad vocals and featured the number on their **'Pop Go e Beatles'** show on 27 August 1963.

Opera House, Church Street, lackpool, Lancashire

theatre in the main northern seaside resort. The Beatles ly appeared twice at the Opera House, both occasions parated by only a few weeks. They made their debut at theatre on 26 July 1964, immediately prior to their rt tour of Sweden, and it was the site of their last British on 16 August 1964, prior to their American tour.

Orbison, Roy

ger Roy Orbison was among several American artists o had been an early influence on the Beatles. In fact, very first song the Beatles broadcast on BBC radio was eam Baby', sung by Paul, which was broadcast on **enager's Turn'** on 8 March 1962, a month after the ison release.

John also claimed that it was Orbison's style which pired him to write 'Please Please Me'.

Kennedy Street Enterprises booked Orbison to tour tain from 18 May to 9 June 1963. They also booked the tles and **Gerry & the Pacemakers** as support acts. It the Beatles' third tour within a relatively short time they'd begun to build up such a large following that it felt they warranted topping a concert bill in their own t.

Roy had enjoyed nine chart hits and was currently ying success with 'In Dreams'. He was to comment: en I arrived in London to tour England in 1963 I wore glasses because I'd lost my clear glasses.' Those dark ses were soon to become something of a trademark.

Roy added: 'I arrived at a little theatre which had tles placards everywhere. There was very little of me. had three years of hit records in Britain. I said, "What Beatle anyway?" and John Lennon tapped me on the ulder and said, "I'm one." When he'd gone I asked n to take the placards down. I was earning three times their money. Then they approached me and said, "You're making the money, let us close the show."

'After their fourteenth or fifteenth encore, Paul and John grabbed me by the arm and said, "Yankee go home." They asked me how they could make it in the States and I told them: "Dress like you're doing, keep the hair, say you're British and get on a show like the **Ed Sullivan** Show."'

It was during this particular tour that the audience began pelting the Beatles with jelly babies for the first time as a result of a remark George had made in an interview.

The original billing for the tour had placed Roy's name above the Beatles, even though they actually closed the show. After one week, the billing was reversed. However, Roy continued to prove a major attraction. Reporting in a local paper on the tour's appearance at the **Rialto Theatre**, York, on 29 May, Stacey Brewer wrote: 'Roy Orbison got the biggest "hand" I've ever heard at the Rialto . . . Don McCallion, manager of the Mecca-Casino,

The Beatles eventually toured with one of their seminal influences – Roy Orbison.

must have felt glad he had Roy booked for a return date in York – on September 18 . . . Roy opened with "Only The Lonely" and followed with a selection including "Cryin', Fallin'", and, of course, his current chart entry, "In Dreams".'

Ringo Starr was to tell Beatles biographer **Hunter Davies**: 'It was terrible following him. He'd slay them and they'd scream for more. In Glasgow we were all backstage, listening to the tremendous applause he was getting. He was just standing there singing, not moving or anything. As it got near our turn, we would hide behind the curtain whispering to each other, "Guess who's next folks, it's your favourite rave."'

Roy became a good friend of the Beatles, although they were worried in June 1964 that they'd catch chicken pox from Roy's six-year-old son Roy Dewayne after Roy had brought the youngster to visit them – but they were given a clean bill of health by their doctor.

Roy underwent open heart surgery in 1979 but his career seemed to be given a new lease of life when he was invited by George to become part of the Traveling Wilburys and recorded a hit album with them. Two other Wilburys, Jeff Lynne and Tom Petty, produced a solo album by Roy, with George as guest – unfortunately, it was his last recording. Roy died of a heart attack in Nashville on 6 December 1988 at the age of 52.

● Ormsby-Gore, Sir David

The British Ambassador to America during the Beatles' first trip to the United States.

It was Beatles press officer **Brian Sommerville** who proposed that the Beatles attend a function at the British Embassy in Washington, after being approached by a former friend who was a naval attaché. Brian Epstein approved the suggestion, although John Lennon was reluctant.

The affair was to take place on the evening of 11 February 1964 following their appearance at the **Washington Coliseum**. The event was in aid of the National Association for the Prevention of Cruelty to Children and the Beatles had been asked to hand out the raffle prizes.

On their way to the reception, George Harrison asked Sommerville, 'Who is this Ormsby-Gore anyway?' 'Ormsby-Gore,' said Sommerville. 'Don't be daft, I know that, but is his name Ormsby or Gore?' said George. 'It's Sir David Ormsby-Gore,' Sommerville told him. 'Is he Lord?' George asked. 'No, he's a knight,' sa Sommerville. 'Was he gored when he was knighted?' ask George.

The meeting with Sir Ormsby-Gore proved cordi When Sir David, to confirm he would correctly ident them, asked John if he was John, 'No, I'm Fred. H John,' said John pointing to George. When Sir Dav began to address George as John, George pointed to Rin who said, 'No, I'm Charlie. He's John.' Then La Ormsby-Gore took the Beatles into the main hall a announced, 'Attention! Beatles are now approaching area. Please don't throw jelly beans!' Paul said, 'Thr peppermint creams instead. They're softer when they hit

The cordiality disappeared when they were surrounc by Foreign Office types, slightly drunk, snobbish and ru While John was signing an autograph, one of th remarked, 'Look, he can actually write.' There wa scramble for autographs with comments such as, 'Yo sign this and like it!' One woman in an evening dress t a small pair of scissors from her handbag and attempted cut off a piece of Ringo's hair. He dodged out of the w John was being manhandled and obviously becom angry. Ringo took him by the arm and said, 'Come on, l get it over with,' and they presented the prizes.

A furious Brian Epstein vowed they would never humiliated in such a way again and a policy was instiga that they would never attend any official governm functions.

The British press were also up in arms over treatment the group had received and Conservative Joan Quennell called on Foreign Secretary R. A. Butle investigate the manhandling of the Beatles. However, most diplomatic move of all had been made by Br Epstein who, wishing to play down the incident, written a polite note to Lady Ormsby-Gore thanking he the evening. Butler showed Quennell the note and noth more was said.

Sir David later became Lord Harlech and his daug Alice had a romance with **Eric Clapton** immediately a the beginning of Clapton's affair with **Pattie Harris** When John Lennon was fighting to obtain his green c Lord Harlech wrote a letter in John's defence to the Immigration and Naturalization Service on 4 July 1972

Lord Harlech died in a road accident on 26 Jan 1985.

Ornstein, Bud

ıe British production head of United Artists in Britain. e negotiated the three-picture deal with Brian Epstein, ·imarily because United Artists wanted to feature the eatles on a soundtrack album. They were prepared to fer the Beatles 25 per cent, although Brian Epstein pre-npted them by saying, 'I wouldn't consider anything ıder seven and a half percent.' Fortunately, lawyer **avid Jacobs** was able to finalize a deal in which the eatles did receive 25 per cent, although it would have en more sensible for him to have asked for it to be gross ther than net.

Dick Lester said that the concept of the movie *A Hard ıy's Night* came from a reply John made when asked out a trip they'd made to Sweden: 'Oh, it was a room and car, and a car and a room, and a room and a car,' he id.

On 18 December 1964 Ornstein quit United Artists to m Pickfair Films with Brian Epstein. They intended to oduce Beatles films, beginning with *A Talent For ving*, but nothing came of it.

Orton, Joe

ntroversial British playwright who was murdered on 9 gust 1967. Orton, who was a homosexual, had written ccessful plays such as *Entertaining Mr Sloane* and *Loot*. **Walter Shenson** contacted him in the hope that he ıld enliven a script called 'Shades Of A Personality'. wever, Orton's ideas grew to such an extent that he ded up with a completely different concept and penned ew screenplay called *Up Against It*.

He submitted a draft of his script to Brian Epstein and s invited to have dinner with Paul and Brian. Of his eting with Paul, Orton wrote, 'He was just as the otographs, only he'd grown a moustache. His hair was orter, too. He was playing the latest Beatles record, enny Lane". I liked it very much. Then he played the er side – Strawberry something. I didn't like this as ch.'

Brian Epstein gave him the go-ahead to continue, ıough his finished version of the screenplay didn't gain approval of the Beatles.

Orton sent his script to Shenson and a month later it s returned. Orton was to comment: 'No explanation why. criticism of the script. And apparently, Brian Epstein no comment to make, either. Fuck them.'

He rewrote the script and was about to discuss the filming of it with **Dick Lester** when his lover Kenneth Halliwell battered him to death in his flat, before committing suicide himself. The music chosen to be played at Orton's funeral was the Beatles' 'A Day In The Life'.

A film company immediately bought Orton's screenplay, but all attempts at making it into a movie failed. After his death, several other writers attempted to work on it, but it remains unfilmed. The script was published in book form in 1979 and it is fairly obvious why the Beatles turned it down. It is an anarchic comedy with sex, murder and politics in which the main characters end up killing a female British Prime Minister.

Osterreichischer Hof Hotel, Salzburg, Austria

Hotel at which the Beatles held their first Austrian press conference on 13 March 1965 during the filming of *Help!*

The group had landed at the Salzburg-Maxglahn Airport at 2.18 p.m. to be greeted by a large number of fans, with a small number wearing armbands stating 'Beatles Go Home'. They posed for a group of pressmen and then drove off to the Osterreichischer Hof Hotel, followed by the press corps, for the conference.

They then drove off to Obertauern, where they were filming, stopping on the way to eat lunch at a restaurant in the village of Werfen.

Our World

A spectacular television production that was transmitted live throughout the world by satellite on 25 June 1967 and lasted for six hours.

This unique event was the first time a worldwide satellite broadcast had been attempted and twenty-six different nations participated in the link-up which was to have the largest television audience ever, up to that time: 400,000,000 people.

The British contribution was a performance by the Beatles from the No. 1 studio at **EMI**'s **Abbey Road**. After the group had accepted the invitation to appear, John and Paul wrote the song 'All You Need Is Love' specially for the occasion and it was screened 'live' in a party atmosphere, complete with streamers, balloons and placards proclaiming 'All You Need Is Love' in several languages. The Beatles were backed by a thirteen-piece orchestra conducted by Mike Vickers which included Sidney Sax, Patrick Halling, Eric Bowie, Jack Holmes (violins); Rex Morris, Don Honeywell (tenor sax); Evan Watkins, Harry Spain, (trombones); Jack Emblow (accordion); and Stanley Woods, David Mason (trumpets).

The orchestra was dressed formally in evening suits while the Beatles and friends wore colourful flower-power gear. Among the friends sitting on the studio floor surrounding the group were Paul's brother **Mike**, **Jane Asher**, **Pattie Harrison**, **Mick Jagger** and **Marianne Faithfull**, **Eric Clapton**, **Keith Moon**, Keith Richard, Graham Nash and his wife Rose, Gary Leeds of the Walker Brothers and the group's official biographer **Hunter Davies**.

The group had recorded a backing track earlier, but they actually sang and played live when the show was broadcast and their song included excerpts from familiar tunes such as 'La Marseillaise', 'Greensleeves', 'In The Mood', and 'She Loves You'.

● Overlanders, The

A British folk trio comprising Paul Arnold, Laurie Mason and Peter Bartholomew. Within a month of the release of the *Rubber Soul* album, the 'Michelle' track had been covered by twenty artists around the world. The most successful British cover was by the Overlanders who topped the charts with it for one week after it had been issued on Pye 7N 17034 on 13 January 1966. It entered the charts on 22 January and remained there for ten weeks. It was their only hit. The trio also featured the number on an album and an EP.

● Owen, Alun

Born in Wales and reared in Liverpool from the age of eight, Owen became one of Britain's major television playwrights in the sixties, responsible for dramas such as 'No Trams To Lime Street', 'Ruffians' and 'The Strain'.

Paul McCartney suggested that Owen might be the one to write the script for their first film and Brian Epstein wrote him a letter. When Owen was in Liverpool for a performance of one of his plays he saw Brian in a coffee bar and joined him. They began to discuss the script and Epstein told him, 'Whatever you think, you must meet the boys. They're keen to see you – they admire your work.' He'd met George Harrison in Liverpool's **Blue Angel Club**, but he first got together with all four Beatles in October 1963 during the weekend following their 'Sund Night At The London Palladium' appearance.

He said, 'Getting to know them was remarkably eas They are immediate people and I knew from that that couldn't be a colour film. The boys are essentially bla and white people.'

When Owen was commissioned to write the script travelled to Ireland to spend two days with them duri their tour and **Walter Shenson** also took him to visit t group in Paris while they were staying at the George Hotel.

Owen began writing the script in November 1963 wi a 90-minute film in mind. He said, 'I write by the min not the page. I had a couple of false starts trying to writ fantasy film, but quickly realized that nothing cou compare with their own fantastic lives. They are always the move, usually from one box to another, hotels, ca dressing-rooms, but they know what they want. Where th are going.'

Alun pointed out that he was given complete freed with the script and nobody bothered him.

He further commented: 'In the film we see the boys i world which has no future and no past and I've tried incorporate into the script some of the fantastic a curious things which happen to the boys, the world th carry in them, by just being themselves. They haven't to act being themselves in the picture, by that I mean necessarily the way they see themselves. What I am doi is taking what I see in them and putting it down on pap In fact, they emerge as four very different people. I wan give them things they want to do. They have a terrific in being alive and there is a great sense of fantasy in th humour. There is a conflict in the script and there conflict in the way the boys send each other up. I'm s the film will do very well in America. Americans will fi the Liverpool accent easier to understand than, say Cockney one. Liverpool people hit their words when th talk, it's part of their aggressiveness.'

Although Owen travelled with the Beatles on a num of gigs to study their personalities and sense of humour, was already aware of their 'scouse wit', because this sor ready humour wasn't confined to the Beatles. Alun visi Liverpool regularly to remind himself of the spontane and often very funny dialogue of the average Liverpudli

Following the Beatles' enormous success at their air press conference in New York in February 1964, Ov 'as asked to include a scene that would give them an pportunity to sparkle in a similar way. He chose to :ature them at a press reception in a theatre lounge. This rovided the right setting, while his script was typical of ıe Beatles' off-the-cuff remarks.

A man asks John: 'What's your philosophy of life?' He :plies: 'I'm torn between Zen and I'm-all-right-Jack.'

Ringo is asked: 'Has success changed your life?' 'Yes' the simple reply.

'Do you like playing the guitar?' a voice snaps at eorge. 'Next to kissing girls, it's favourites,' he replies.

The Beatles liked the screenplay and John commented: Ie wrote the whole thing based on our characters then: e, witty; Ringo, dumb and cute; George, this; Paul that.'

Alun was nominated for an Oscar for his script for *A ard Day's Night*, one of the two Academy Award ominations the film received. Despite this, Owen wasn't .ked to script their second film. When Brian Epstein told m that **Richard Lester** had already engaged another ripwriter for *Help!*, Owen said, 'I don't get on very well ith John. Ringo is fine, but not the greatest intellectual in e world. We had trouble with one scene with Paul . . . ind you, I like George very much.'

An irate Epstein retorted, 'What would you say if I told u that the one person who doesn't want you to work on is film is George Harrison?' Furious, Owen's wife Mary .lled Epstein a liar.

The Mersey Beat scene continued to intrigue Owen and penned a stage musical with Lionel Bart called *Maggie ay*, which was premiered in Manchester in August 1964. was set in contemporary Liverpool and presented scenes the Pier Head, inside a beat club, on the Mersey ferry d at the docks. It starred Kenneth Haigh, who had fused to allow his name to be billed in *A Hard Day's ght*. Plans for a film version, to star **Peter Sellers**, fell rough.

Oxford Street Maternity Hospital, xford Street, Liverpool 7

the street continuing off Mount Pleasant, a few hundred rds from where both **Julia Lennon** and John Lennon :re married.

It is close to the city centre and at 6.30 p.m on the ening of 9 October 1940, Julia Lennon gave birth to a n. **Hunter Davies** in *The Beatles* wrote: 'He was born ring a heavy air raid' and Philip Norman in *Shout!* confirmed, 'John . . . was . . . born . . . during one of the fiercest night raids by Hitler's Luftwaffe on Liverpool.'

This particular story is to be found in most books documenting John's birth. They are all untrue. Archivist Helen Simpson consulted the local papers for that entire week and found that there was a lull in the bombing on the night of John's birth. Earlier in the week there had been some fierce attacks and the day after John was born saw one of the most destructive of the raids – but at the time of his birth, there was definitely no air raid. Other researchers have since found that the Luftwaffe gave Liverpool a miss on the night of John's birth.

Perhaps the only writer to include this fact in his book was David Stuart Ryan, author of *John Lennon's Secret*, who wrote, 'There were not – as he liked to imply – any bombs falling. There had been an unexpected interruption which was quickly shattered by the following evening when the docks were again hammered by German bombs.'

Within twenty minutes of the baby's birth, his Aunt **Mimi Smith** was at her sister's bedside. It was she who gave him the Christian name John and she also picked the middle name Winston, no doubt due to the feelings of patriotism rife at the time.

A notice of the birth appeared in the ***Liverpool Echo*** on Saturday 12 October.

LENNON – October 9, in hospital to JULIA (nee Stanley), wife of ALFRED LENNON, Merchant Navy (at sea), a son – 9 Newcastle Road.

Oxford Street Maternity Hospital – John Lennon's birthplace. (Les Chadwick)

● Paddy, Klaus & Gibson

A trio comprising Gibson Kemp (drums), **Klaus Voormann** (bass) and Paddy Chambers (lead guitar/vocals). Gibson was a Liverpool drummer who, at the age of sixteen, had replaced Ringo Starr in **Rory Storm & the Hurricanes** at the same time inheriting Ringo's pink stage suit. He was later to marry and divorce **Stuart Sutcliffe**'s fiancée **Astrid Kirchherr**. Paddy Chambers was a leading Liverpool guitarist/vocalist who was a former member of Faron's Flamingos and the **Big Three**. Klaus, who had always wanted to join a group from the moment he saw the Beatles in Hamburg, adopted the bass guitar, like Stuart Sutcliffe

The group were originally managed by **Tony Stratton-Smith**, a London-based journalist who had signed several Liverpool acts, including **Beryl Marsden** and the **Koobas**. Brian Epstein showed interest, on the Beatles' recommendation, so Tony reluctantly agreed to the management change and they signed with Epstein on 13 August 1965. As with almost every act signed by Brian following his initial handful of Liverpool successes, they vanished without trace. Paddy returned to Liverpool to manage some local clubs; Gibson became a prominent record executive and Klaus continued his association with the Beatles and appeared on many of their solo projects.

● Palace Theatre Club, *Turncoat Lane, Offerton, Stockport, Greater Manchester*

A totally untypical Beatles booking. On 13 June 1963 they were booked to appear at this cabaret venue and at another cabaret club ten miles distant. Although there was a flourishing variety club scene in the North of England Mersey Beat groups rarely played at such venues wher the adult audiences went to drink and watch specialit acts, comedians, strippers and solo singers. It is ironic tha the seventies saw the cabaret clubs becoming the mai places of work for the surviving groups of the sixties bea scene.

● Palais Ballroom, *Queens Road, Aldershot, Hampshire*

The scene of the Beatles' first performance in the South c England on Saturday, 9 December 1961. Enterprisin Liverpool promoter **Sam Leach**, who had high hopes c recording and managing the Beatles, decided that h would try to arouse interest in the group from prominer London impresarios: he'd book the Beatles to appear i London and invite several major agents, such as Tit Burns, to see them. Unfortunately, he booked them into venue in the out-of-the-way town of Aldershot, 37 mile from London. Naturally, no agents turned up.

Sam had contacted Bob Potter, who ran the hall, an booked the venue for five consecutive Saturdays beginning on 9 December 1961. He had leaflets printe announcing a 'Battle of the Bands'. It was to be 'Liverpo vs London' with the Beatles representing Liverpool an Ivor Jay & the Jaywalkers appearing for the South.

The party set off at 5.00 a.m. on Saturday morning, Sa accompanied by photographer friend Dick Matthews an the Beatles travelling with their equipment in a van drive by one of Sam's bouncers, Terry McCann. There was motorway at the time and the drive took nine hours. Whe they arrived Leach told the group that he'd promoted th gig in a big way and bought a copy of the *Aldershot New* expecting to see a large advertisement publicizing th event. There was nothing. Angrily he went to th newspaper office and discovered that the £10 advertisement didn't appear because he'd sent a chequ and only cash bookings were accepted from first-tim advertisers. It was also explained that he hadn't left a address, so the paper couldn't contact him about the rule.

With no promotion, things looked grim. They were eve grimmer when only four people turned up and Sam had go round local pubs and coffee bars pleading wi youngsters to come along. Eventually, eighteen peop witnessed the Beatles performing their London(!) deb d, due to the fact that the record player didn't work, they d to play an extended set. As some consolation, Sam ught four crates of brown ale and they sat drinking and ayed a football match on the dance floor with some bingo lls. The noise they were making had led to a neighbour oning the police to complain and when they emerged m the hall at 1.00 a.m. there were three police cars and ır police vans. They were told to leave Aldershot and not urn.

Leach suggested that they drive into London and they ived at the **Blue Gardenia Club** in Greek Street, Soho, ich was run by **Brian Casser**, former leader of one of erpool's top groups, Cass & the Cassanovas. The group k to the stage for a jam session and eventually set off ck to Liverpool at 5.00 a.m. on Sunday morning. Sam naged to place an advertisement in the *Aldershot News* the following week and a total of 210 youngsters paid 5/- (25p) entrance fee to see **Rory Storm & the ırricanes**. Despite this promising response, Sam ıcelled the three remaining dates.

n Leach, George Harrison, John Lennon and Dick Matthews r their Palais appearance. (Sam Leach)

● Palais Des Fetes, *Nice, France*

The Beatles made a final French appearance at this venue in the south of France during their fortnight tour of Europe in 1965. Slotted in between an Italian and Spanish concert on 30 June.

● Palais Des Sports, *Porte De Versailles, Paris, France*

The Beatles opened their short European tour at this venue on 20 June 1965. They appeared on two shows at the arena, the first at 3.00 p.m. and the second at 9.00 p.m. The event was broadcast by both French television and radio and the two houses were full to the 6,000 capacity – something which hadn't happened for several years.

Their repertoire comprised: 'Twist And Shout', 'She's A Woman', 'I'm A Loser', 'Can't Buy Me Love', 'Baby's In Black', 'I Wanna Be Your Man', 'A Hard Day's Night', 'Everybody's Trying To Be My Baby', 'Rock And Roll Music', 'I Feel Fine', 'Ticket To Ride' and 'Long Tall Sally'. The group received a tremendous reception after their final number, 'Long Tall Sally'. Ringo had had a solo spot with 'I Wanna Be Your Man' and George had sung lead on 'Everybody's Trying To Be My Baby'. There was enthusiastic applause for Paul when he tried to introduce several of the songs in French.

● Palais D'Hiver, *Boulevard De Stalingrad, Lyon, France*

The Beatles' second appearance in France during their two-week European tour in 1965. They performed two concerts at the venue on 22 June, with an audience of 3,500 at each show.

● Palazzo Dello Sport, *Piazza Kennedy, Genoa, Italy*

The Beatles performed two concerts at this arena on 25 June 1965 as part of their European tour. There were only three Italian venues visited throughout the entire career of the Beatles and not one sold out.

The Palazzo Dello Sport could accommodate an audience of 25,000, but only 5,000 turned up to see the first show that afternoon, with a larger audience for the evening performance. Audiences generally during the European tour were disappointing after the fever pitch receptions which the Beatles had received around the world in 1963 and 1964.

● Palmer, Tony

A former music journalist for the *Observer* newspaper. Palmer began producing a number of controversial rock music programmes for British television. The first was the 1968 documentary 'All My Loving', in which the Beatles were featured. His biggest success was the history-of-rock series 'All You Need Is Love', a seventeen-part television documentary first screened by London Weekend Television on 19 February 1978. Almost a million feet of film were shot as Palmer travelled throughout America, Europe and Africa, interviewing hundreds of people ranging from musicians and rock critics to managers and record producers.

There were many people who aided and encouraged the venture and Palmer commented: '. . . probably the films would not have been conceived without Aubrey Singer, now Head of BBC 2, but at the time of "All My Loving", Head of BBC features. It was Singer who devised a world-wide television programme called "Our World" on which the Beatles song "All You Need Is Love" was first broadcast'. Palmer also directed the movie ***200 Motels***, which starred Ringo Starr as **Frank Zappa**.

● Panorama

A BBC television current affairs programme. On Easter Monday, 30 March 1964, the entire programme was given over to the success story of Brian Epstein and the Beatles. Hosted by Richard Dimbleby, the special included an interview with Epstein, a short, filmed appearance by the Beatles shot during a break in the filming of *A Hard Day's Night*, and appearances by **Gerry & the Pacemakers**, **Tommy Quickly**, **Cilla Black** and **Sounds Incorporated**.

● Paolozzi, Eduardo

Internationally renowned Scots-born sculptor, who took **Stuart Sutcliffe** under his wing when Stu wished to remain in Hamburg and continue with his art studies. Paolozzi recognized Stu's potential, believed in his talent and not only arranged for him to become one of his students at Hamburg's State High School in June 1961, but also approached the Hamburg authorities to arrange for Stuart to receive a grant.

Paul McCartney bought one of Paolozzi's works, entitled *Solo*, and used another on the cover of his album *Red Rose Speedway*.

● Paperback Writer

Paul wrote this song, although John helped with one or tw words in the lyrics. Some sources claim it was written connection with John's two books, hence the mention nonsense writer Edward Lear in the fourth line.

A young man working for the *Daily Mail* wants become a paperback writer. It is also suggested that Pa even worked out the man's name, a character called I Iachimore, which he devised because it sounded like h own name after it had been played backwards on a ta loop.

The number was used quite successfully as the ther tune of a television book series in Britain called 'Read A About It'.

The single was issued in Britain on R5452 on 10 Ju 1966 and reached No. 1 in the charts – although it did go straight to the No. 1 position on release as several their other singles had. The flipside was 'Rain'. It al reached No. 1 in the States when it was issued on **Capit** 5651 in May 1966.

The number was featured on several compilatio including *A Collection Of Beatles Oldies (But Goldies)*, *T Beatles 1967–1970*, the 1979 *Hey Jude* album and *T Beatles Box*.

● Parade Of The Pops

A BBC Light Programme show on which the Beatles ma their first live radio performance on 20 February 196 The show was presented by Denny Piercy and produced John Kingdon and broadcast each Wednesday betwe 12.30 p.m.–1.30 p.m. The group performed 'Love M Do' and 'Please Please Me' at the Playhouse Theat London.

● Paramounts, The

A group from Southend comprising Gary Brook (keyboards/vocals), Robin Trower (guitar), Chris Coppi (bass) and Barrie Wilson (drums). They signed to t Parlophone label and the **Rolling Stones** described th as 'The best R&B band in Britain'. They had limit success and only one minor hit, 'Poison Ivy' in 1964. 1965 they were signed up by Brian Epstein's **NEM** organization and, as a result, were booked to appear on Beatles' last British tour in December of that year.

In 1967 Brooker formed Procol Harum and ove period of time brought all the original members of t ıramounts into the band.

Paramount Theatre, New York City

enue of the final appearance on the Beatles' first merican tour. The Beatles and several other artists peared at this special benefit in aid of the Retarded fants Service and Cerebral Palsy of New York.

Entitled *An Evening With The Beatles*, the charity show as held on Sunday, 20 September 1964, before an dience of 3,682 people who had paid from five to 100 llars a ticket. This resulted in an audience which was a range mix of teenage Beatle fans and bejewelled New ork elite, and when the fans began screaming for their roes, one onlooker commented, 'The kids were making ese people with diamonds very nervous.' Other acts on e bill were Steve Lawrence and Edie Gorme, Leslie ggams, the Tokens, Bobby Goldsboro, the Shangri-Las, e Brothers Four, **Jackie DeShannon** and Nancy Ames. e Beatles were due to go on at 10.45 p.m., but because e fans were screaming for the group continuously, the ne allotted to each of the other acts was cut drastically d the Beatles went on stage three-quarters of an hour ead of schedule to play ten songs in a 25-minute set.

Outside the crowds built up until there was a swell of ,000 people, with 240 policemen trying to control them. ckstage, the Beatles had a number of visitors, including **l Sullivan** and **Bob Dylan**. By 10.45 p.m. they were in imousine heading for the Idlewild Motel.

The occasion raised almost $25,000 for the charity and e Beatles were presented with an illuminated scroll ich read: 'To John, Paul, George and Ringo who, as the atles, have brought an excitement to the entertainment pitals of the world and who, as individuals, have given of eir time and talent to bring hope and help to the ndicapped children of America.' John said, 'We do ese shows whenever we can simply because we want to. e don't feel that it's any big deal on our part. We don't e talking about them because when you can give mething, even if it is only time, then you should do it.'

Paris, France

ench capital, which John Lennon and Paul McCartney re to visit in 1961. In September of that year, two weeks fore his 21st birthday, John's Aunt Elizabeth, who lived Sutherland, Scotland, sent John £40 as a coming-of-age esent. Together with Paul he planned to visit Paris and after the Beatles had completed a gig at **Knotty Ash Village Hall** on 29 September 1961, the group took a break while John and Paul left for their fifteen-day trip abroad. Some reports have suggested that the two of them left without informing George and **Pete**, who were disgusted by the action, which almost caused the group to break up and resulted in **Ray McFall** and **Bob Wooler** lecturing John and Paul about acting responsibly. This isn't actually so, John and Paul had planned the trip and no bookings were made for the period they were away.

Stuart Sutcliffe had informed John by post that Jurgen Vollmer, their friend from Hamburg, had moved to Paris, and he provided them with his address. During the trip they visited Jurgen who was to write about the visit and said that they wanted to have their hair cut in the same style as his. So he gave both of them their first 'Beatles' haircut in his hotel room on the Left Bank. They then went to the Flea Market and bought some mod-style clothes. Jurgen wore a corduroy jacket and a sweater with cut-off sleeves, which was collarless – and John wanted to dress like this. Jurgen wrote: 'At that time, the rage in Paris was bell bottoms. The Beatles always wore very tightly cuffed, or "pegged" pants with pointed shoes or very pointed boots. They were "Teddy Boys" in the English fashion and dressed in black leather and black jeans . . . John and Paul wanted to dress more in the Paris fashion, but they were afraid to look queer in their hometown of Liverpool.'

While in Paris, Paul sent a lengthy letter to Bill Harry in Liverpool in which he wrote, 'It was 10 O'clock, it was, when we were entering the Olympia in Paris to see the "Johnny Halliday Rock Show". The cheapest seats in "les theatre" (French) were seven and sixpence, so we followed the woman with the torch (English).

'When Johnny Halliday came, everybody went wild – and loud was the cheering and many the dancing in the aisles, too. But the man said "sit down", so we had to.

'The excitement rose, the audience rose to dance, like the many boys and girls dancing along the back rows. Also old men, which is stranger still, isn't it.

'Meanwhile, later the same week, we go to "Les Rock Festival" held in a club in Montmartre, with Danny et les Pirates and many more groups for your evening's entertainment. Topping the bill was Vince (Ron, my boy, Ron) Taylor, star of English screen and Two I's.

'The atmosphere is like many a night club, but the

teenagers stand round the dancing floor which you use as a stage. They jump on a woman with gold trousers and a hand microphone and then hit a man when he says "go away". A group follows, and so do others, playing "Apache" worse than many other bands. When the singer joins the band, the leather jacket fiends who are the audience, join in dancing and banging tables with chairs.

'The singers have to go one better than the audience, so they lie on the floor, or jump on a passing drummer, or kiss a guitar, and then hit the man playing it. The crowd enjoy this and many stand on chairs to see the fun, and soon the audience are all singing and shouting like one man, but he didn't mind.

'Vince (Ron, Ron) Taylor finally appeared and joined the fun, and in the end he has so much fun that he had to rest. But in spite of this it had been a wonderful show, lovely show . . . lovely'.

John and Paul stayed in Montmartre for a week and planned to travel on to Spain, but their money ran out. On their return to Liverpool they stopped off in London where they bought some Chelsea boots, which were later to become fashionable as 'Beatle boots'.

On 16 September 1963, John decided to take **Cynthia** on a belated honeymoon to Paris. The couple stayed at the luxurious George V Hotel and began to take in all the sights – the Eiffel Tower, the Arc de Triomphe, Montmartre – and John bought a movie camera. On their return to the hotel they found a note from **Astrid Kirchherr** which revealed that she was in Paris for a few days with a girlfriend. There was a phone number with the note and John and Cynthia contacted her and arranged to meet. The four of them had a night on the town, drinking rough red wine until dawn. They were so blotto they decided to go to Astrid's lodgings for coffee. After the coffee they drank another bottle of wine. John and Cynthia found they were in no state to return to the hotel and despite there being only a single bed, all four of them got into it and fell into a deep sleep. Brian Epstein had also arrived in Paris and John and Cynthia met up with him and all three returned to England together on 2 October.

The French market was a difficult one to break for an English-speaking act, but the Beatles were booked to appear at the **Olympia** in Paris for three weeks. John, Paul and George flew out on 14 January 1964 but Ringo remained in Liverpool and threatened not to go. He caught a plane and flew from Liverpool via London Airport the next day and the group appeared at the **Cinema Cyra[…]** in Versailles that night, opening at the Olympia on [1…] January. The group had a suite at the George V Hotel a[nd] on their opening night received a telegram informing the[m] that 'I Want To Hold Your Hand' had reached No. 1 in t[he] *Cash Box* charts in America. They then had a celebrati[on] dinner, hosted by Brian Epstein and George Martin.

They were appearing at the Olympia for £50 a day a[nd] the male dominated audiences weren't as fervent as t[he] group were used to. Vincent Mulchrone wrote in the *Dai[ly] Mail*: '**Beatlemania** is still, like Britain's entry into t[he] Common Market, a problem the French prefer to put off [for] a while.' The group finished their short season at t[he] Olympia on 4 February and flew back to London t[he] following day. They next returned to Paris in June 19[…] when they received a triumphant reception at the **Pal[ais] De Sport**.

● Parkinson, Michael

A British radio and television personality, born [in] Yorkshire. The ex-journalist became a household name [in] Britain with his BBC 1 chat show 'Parkinson', which r[an] for over a decade and ended when he accepted a lucrati[ve] offer to host the shows down-under as 'Parkinson [In] Australia'.

Ringo and his wife **Barbara** appeared on the show [on] 12 December 1981. The couple were featured [in] 'Parkinson In Australia' the following year on 8 Octob[er] although it had been recorded on 28 September.

'Parky' is also one of the characters featured on Pa[ul] McCarney's *Band On The Run* cover. Parkinson ask[ed] Paul to return the favour by appearing on one of his sho[ws] but he never did.

● Parkinson, Norman

Norman Parkinson, real name Ronald Parkinson Smi[th] was one of the major British photographers, particula[rly] famous for his exotic fashion photographs featured [in] magazines such as *Vogue*.

He took photographs of the Beatles at **Abbey Road** [in] September 1963. A selection of them were published [by] Hutchinson in *The Beatles Book* in 1964.

His photographs of the Beatles were also featured i[n a] special exhibition of Parkinson's work at the **Nation[al] Portrait Gallery** in London.

He died in Singapore on 14 February 1991, aged 76.

Parnes, Larry

ne of the most successful British pop impresarios of the te fifties and early sixties. Parnes, known as 'Mr Parnes iillings And Pence', because of his reputed tight-stedness in paying his artists, first discovered Tommy eele in 1956. He then began to build up a stable of pop ngers, known for the stage names he devised for them – **illy Fury**, Vince Eager, Marty Wilde, Duffy Power, **hnny Gentle**, Dickie Pride and Lance Fortune.

Epstein first met Parnes backstage at the **Liverpool npire**. Marty Wilde and Billy Fury were topping the bill d he was introduced to Parnes as a local record store anager. He told Parnes he was interested in the pop siness and they had drinks together and Parnes troduced him to Marty and Billy in their dressing rooms.

Allan Williams approached Parnes about co-omoting a bill in Liverpool starring **Eddie Cochran** and **ene Vincent**. He also arranged for groups to audition for rnes, who was seeking a backing group for Fury. At the **yvern Club**, Parnes and Fury watched several verpool groups, including the **Silver Beetles**. Reports ted that, because Parnes wanted them to play a number thout **Stuart Sutcliffe**, he was put off by Stu's lack of ill. Parnes denied this some years later, saying he ought the group were great, but had been put off by the ddle-aged drummer (**Tommy Moore**), who joined them lf-way through the session.

Parnes booked the Silver Beetles to appear on Johnny ntle's short tour of Scotland.

Williams also credited Parnes with inadvertently using him to meet **Bruno Koschmider** again. Parnes oned him to cancel a booking for **Howie Casey** & the niors in Blackpool. Casey came around to beat Williams , but Williams told him he'd drive them down to London d fix them up with a gig. He took them to the 2 I's and anged for them to appear on stage – Koschmider was in e audience and immediately booked them for the **iiserkeller**.

When Epstein signed up the Beatles, he phoned Parnes d asked him if he'd book the group for Sunday gigs at eat Yarmouth. Parnes remembered the band and offered 5. Epstein wanted £50. He then visited Parnes' Marble ch office and said that if Parnes would book the group thirteen dates he would come down to £45 and give n first option on a five-year contract to promote all of an's artists worldwide. Parnes upped his offer to £35. Brian phoned his office again, asking for £40 and Parnes offered £37 10s. Brian put the phone down on him.

In November 1962 Parnes wrote to Epstein offering the Beatles a tour. Brian asked for £230 a week. Parnes offered £140. Brian wrote back requesting £200 for a seven-day week. Parnes then suggested that if the follow-up to 'Love Me Do' entered the Top Ten he would pay £230 a week; if it entered the Top Three he would pay £300 a week.

The two never came to a deal, although they maintained good relations and Brian often approached him for advice and it was Parnes who recommended **Nat Weiss** as a New York attorney and **Dougie Millings** as a tailor for Brian's bands. It has also been suggested that Epstein offered Parnes a share in the Beatles, but was turned down.

In 1967 Brian Epstein became ill through drug abuse and entered a private clinic in Putney. Parnes went to visit him and Brian told him of his worries – that the Beatles' contract would be ending in four months' time and he was concerned that they wouldn't re-sign with him. Parnes commented, 'Brian was very ill. He told me that the contract was coming to an end and he understood the boys were going to leave him because another man was taking over. My answer to Brian was "I could never see the boys leaving you. Ever. I think you're depressed over nothing."'

In 1982, when Paul was appearing on the radio show 'Desert Island Discs', he jokingly said that the Beatles hadn't been paid for their early Parnes tour. Parnes sued him and Paul made a public apology on the radio two years later. Parnes died on 30 July 1989 aged 59.

Paul's Christmas Album

One of the rarest of the Beatle recordings. An album which Paul McCartney made. There were only four copies pressed and in December 1965 Paul gave a copy to each member of the Beatles.

Pavilion, North Parade, Bridge Road, Bath, Somerset

Venue where the Beatles appeared only once, on 10 June 1963 on the evening directly following the end of their **Roy Orbison** tour.

Pavilion Gardens Ballroom, St John's Road, Buxton, Derbyshire

The Beatles performed at this venue on Saturday, 6 April 1963. Their support act was a group called the Trixons.

Police struggled on the stage with fans as they attempted to prevent the youngsters from reaching the Beatles during their performance.

Their second and final appearance at the ballroom took place on 19 October 1963.

● Pavilion Theatre, *Lodge Lane, Liverpool 8*

PAVILION
LODGE LANE
PHONE ROYal 5931
ON STAGE FOR
ONE NIGHT ONLY
MONDAY, 2nd APRIL
COMMENCING 7-30 ——— DOORS OPEN 7 P.M.
FLYING VISIT OF "IRELAND'S PRIDE"!!
THE ROYAL SHOW BAND
(WATERFORD)
Winners of the Carl-Alan Award for the outstanding Showband of the year
ALSO—"MERSEYSIDE'S JOY"
THE BEATLES!!
LIVERPOOL'S OWN BEAT GROUP
All Seats bookable.
Prices from 3/6 to 7/6
Box Office open 10 a.m. to 5 p.m. Daily
A NIGHT YOU MUST NOT MISS

A former Music Hall which, in the fifties, was mainly the setting for weekly 'nude' revues such as *Bareway To The Stars*, which featured tableaux of nude girls who weren't allowed to move on stage by order of the Lord Chamberlain. As long as they were 'frozen', they could pose in the nude. In contrast, Chris Barber & his Band always drew capacity houses at the Pavilion and his show included a special solo spot for **Lonnie Donegan**. The Pavilion, when Lonnie Donegan had his own show there, at the time of his major hit 'Rock Island Line', was attended by members of several local skiffle bands, including Paul McCartney, and that particular Donegan concert was said to have inspired a lot of local musicians to keep on playing after the skiffle boom had died.

The Beatles appeared at the Pavilion on Monday, 2 April 1962, for one night only (they'd previously appeared as the **Quarry Men** in a skiffle contest at the theatre in the late fifties). The concert was promoted by **Jim Gretty** and the headliners were the Royal Showband from Waterford in Southern Ireland, winners of the **Carl Allen Award** as 'the Outstanding Showband of the year' and advertised as 'Ireland's Pride'. The Beatles, on the oth hand, were described as 'Merseyside's joy'.

The Pavilion was later turned into a snooker club.

● Peggy Sue

Buddy Holly's first major hit record, which took him No. 3 in the American charts and No. 6 in the Briti charts in 1957. The number became a rock classic a was included in the **Quarry Men**'s repertoire, with Jo Lennon on lead vocals.

● Penina

A song Paul had written while he was on holiday Portugal. 'Penina' was the name of the hotel at which was staying. Singer Carlos Mendes heard Paul singing t number and liked it so much that Paul allowed him to ha the song to record. That version was released in Portu on 18 July 1969 on Parlophone QMSP 16459. The flipsi was 'Wings Of Revenge'. The following year a Dutch ba Jotte Herre also recorded it. At the time, Paul h forgotten to inform Northern Songs about it.

● Pennebaker, D. A.

An American movie director who specialized in maki rock films. John Lennon appeared fleetingly Pennebaker's film of **Bob Dylan**'s 1966 British tour, *E The Document*, and John, **Yoko** and the **Plastic O Band** appeared in his film of the 1969 Peace Festi *Sweet Toronto*. Pennebaker was one of the personalit who allowed his legs to be filmed in John and Yoko's *Your Legs Forever*.

● Penner, Peter

A photographer friend of **Astrid Kirchherr**. When t Beatles were first in Hamburg in 1960, they got to kn Astrid and her friends, who used to visit them at t **Kaiserkeller** club.

At this time the Beatles wore typical 'Tony Curtis' st haircuts, which were popular in Liverpool then. Th noticed that Peter Penner, who was one of the group Astrid's friends who watched the Beatles' shows, ha special type of hair style. They discovered that Astrid h styled his hair for him. Later, she styled **Stuart Sutcliff** hair in the same way and the famous Beatle cut was bo A few years later, the Germans began to describe t Beatles' hair as 'Pilzenkopt' – mushroom shaped!

Penny Lane

ɔng penned by Paul in the autumn of 1966. The Beatles ɑd decided to make a concept album inspired by their ıildhood in Liverpool. Digging into their memories, Paul ːoduced 'Penny Lane' and John composed 'Strawberry ɩelds Forever'. When the time came for the song to be ·corded, Paul had the number completely finished and ɪd drafted out a rough arrangement for the brass section.

Paul was to comment: '"Penny Lane" is a bus ·undabout in Liverpool, and there is a barber's shop ɪowing photographs of every head he's had the pleasure know – no, that's not true, they're just photos of ıirstyles, but all the people who come and go/stop and ·y hello. There's a bank on the corner so we made up the ɫ about the banker in his motor car. It's part fact, part ɔstalgia for a place which is a great place, blue suburban :ies as we remember it, and it's still there.

'And we put in a joke or two: "Four of fish and finger pie". The women would never dare say that, except to themselves. Most people wouldn't hear it, but "finger pie" is just a nice little joke for the Liverpool lads who like a bit of smut.'

The track was recorded in January 1967 and among the musicians who were to perform on overdubs were flautists Ray Swinfield, P. Goody, Manny Winters and Dennis Walton; trumpeters Leon Calvert, Freddy Clayton, Bert Courtley and Duncan Campbell; oboists Dick Morgan and Mike Winfield; and bassist Frank Clarke.

Paul was still not satisfied with the track and he was sitting at home watching the BBC 2 TV show 'Masterworks' with David Mason performing Bach's Brandenburg Concerto No. 2 in F Major. He arranged for Mason to be hired to play trumpet on the 'Penny Lane' track and was satisfied with the finished result.

The number is one of the most uplifting and cheery of the Beatles songs and caused problems in Liverpool with fans stealing the actual Penny Lane street signs in a way they were later to repeat at **Abbey Road**, resulting in the Corporation ceasing to make street signs for Penny Lane, settling for painting the street name on buildings instead.

The number was issued as a double 'A' side with 'Strawberry Fields Forever' on Parlophone R5570 on 17 February 1967 where it became the first Beatles single since 'Love Me Do' not to hit the No. 1 spot. It was held at No. 2 by the Engelbert Humperdinck hit 'Release Me'. It

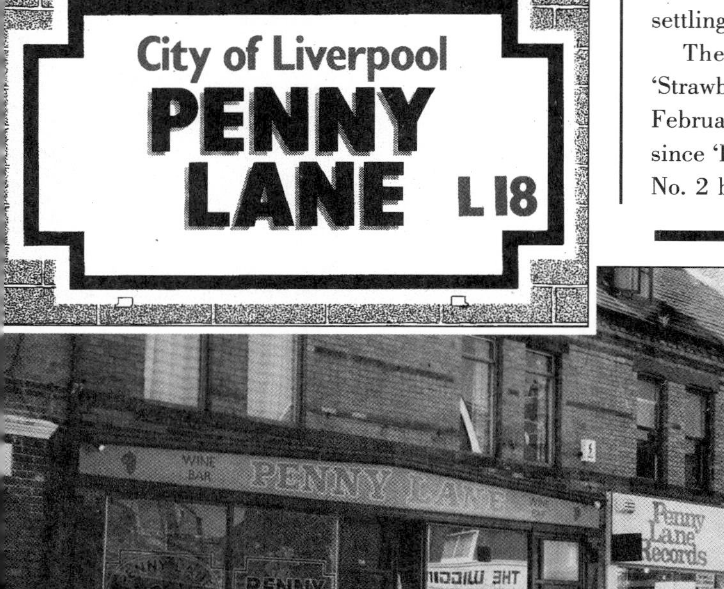

Above: The street sign for Penny Lane has become an object of desire for souvenir hunters. (Merseyside Tourism Office)

was issued in America on **Capitol** 5810 on 13 February 1967 with advance sales of over a million copies. This was a record in itself for Capitol with the highest quantity of a single ever pressed and shipped out in a three-day period. The number topped the charts.

The number was included on the *The Beatles 1967–1970* compilation, the American album *Magical Mystery Tour*, issued in the States in 1967 and then issued in Britain in 1976, and on the 1980 compilations *The Beatles Rarities* and *20 Greatest Hits*. The version on the American release *The Beatles Rarities* contains a trumpet flourish at the end of the song. Prior to the original release of the single a special promotional copy was sent out to American radio stations. At the last minute the Beatles decided to take the trumpet riff off the actual single. This was reinstated for *The Beatles Rarities* album.

● People And Places

A Granada television, early evening magazine programme, screened only in the north-west of England, which saw the Beatles' television debut on 17 October 1962 when the group performed 'Love Me Do' and 'Some Other Guy', for a fee of £35.

The Beatles travelled to the Manchester studio and were introduced by the show's host Gay Byrne. They were later to comment: 'Gay Byrne was the bloke who introduced us . . . made us feel at home and showed us round and generally took some of the fright out of the whole business.' Byrne was later to return to his nati Ireland where he became a major TV celebrity.

The Beatles making their television debut in *People and Places*, November 1962.

The programme was screened live at 6.35 p.m. and r for half an hour. It was to be produced by **Johnny Han** who filmed several Beatles shows over the years, includi the special 'The Music Of Lennon & McCartney' in 19 and the documentary 'The Early Beatles' in 1982.

Their planned appearance for 2 November w scrapped and they next performed on the programme on December 1962, promoting 'Love Me Do' again. 'Peo And Places' changed its name to **'Scene At 6.30'** duri 1963.

● Peppermint Lounge, The, *Miami, Florida*

A club where disc jockey **Murray the K** took the Beat on Thursday, 13 February 1964. Country singer Ha Ballard was on stage that evening and the Beat remained at the club for a couple of hours.

● Peppermint Lounge, The, *New York City*

The famous American nightclub of the sixties, home o noted band, Joey Dee & the Starliters. During their first t to America in 1964 three members of the Beatles visi the Peppermint Lounge on 9 February. George Harris had decided to return to the **Plaza Hotel** for a sleep af **Murray the K** had taken the group to visit the Playb Club. John, Paul and Ringo accompanied the New Y disc jockey to the lounge. Others in the party includ John's wife **Cynthia** and press agent **Brian Sommervil** The group declined to participate in the club's 'Tw Revue', but Ringo took to the dance floor to 'do the Tw with Peppermint Lounge Captain Marlene Klaire, who w to comment later: 'It was that exhausting that it felt lik Beatle was on me, and I had to shake it off.'

During the evening a group called the Seven Fabul Epics – featuring the Four Younger Brothers, alias American Beatles – played Beatle numbers, while wear Beatle wigs!

Incidentally, their old friend **Adrian Barber**, form member of the **Big Three** who had become stage mana at the **Star Club**, Hamburg, so impressed Joey Dee w the sound system that he had built at the Star Club that singer invited Adrian to New York to build a sound syst for the Peppermint Lounge.

● 7 Percy Street, *Liverpool 8*

The house at No. 7 was divided into flats. Art students **Stuart Sutcliffe** and **Rod Murray** rented rooms here.

Stuart's flat was on the ground floor rear (not a basement flat as some writers have stated), its solitary window overlooking a grimy backyard, surrounded by brick walls. Sparsely furnished, with a few high-back wooden chairs and a camp bed. Stuart was able to work in the flat during the long summer holidays as his mother agreed to support him financially. He also received tuition in the flat from art college lecturer **Arthur Ballard**.

Stuart carried on his work of painting and sketching at a prolific rate. He completed a portrait of Bill Harry, together with over two dozen sketches on pink foolscap paper, during a single afternoon. The painting was executed in a Van Gogh style, which Stuart had become quite adept at. It was in this single room that Bill and Stuart made plans to produce a book about Liverpool, projecting a positive image in visual and written terms. The book was never started as Stuart became involved with the Beatles as their bass guitarist.

When Stuart was about to be evicted from the Percy Street flat, he discussed the possibility of moving into **Gambier Terrace** where Rod Murray had recently found a flat, and John Lennon joined them.

Perkins, Carl

One of the original American rock 'n' roll legends, Carl was born on 9 April 1932 in Lake City, Tennessee. He signed with the legendary Sun Records, wrote and recorded the classic rocker 'Blue Suede Shoes' and a number of other rock 'n' roll standards. A serious car accident in 1956, in which his brother and manager were killed, left him hospitalized for a year. His career suffered a number of setbacks and he compounded his problems by drinking too much. He rose from the doldrums when **Chuck Berry** invited him to tour with him in Britain in 1964 and during the trip he met the Beatles for the first time. His career, personal life and finances were boosted when the Beatles recorded three of his numbers: 'Matchbox', 'Honey Don't' and 'Everybody's Trying To Be My Baby'. With the royalties he was able to buy his parents a farm.

The 1964 tour was the first time either Carl or Chuck Berry had been to England and Carl said that he was in total shock because the tour was sold out every night and: 'The kids were bopping in the aisles.' On the last night of the tour the promoter invited him to a party. Carl told him that he was tired and had a 9.00 a.m. flight to catch the next day. However, the promoter insisted he go to the party – and when he arrived he discovered that it was a party thrown by the Beatles in his honour. He told broadcaster **Scott Muni**: 'We wound up – John, Paul, George and Ringo – sitting on a couch and me sitting on a floor with a guitar.' The Beatles asked him what he was doing the next night and although he was due to fly out in the morning, he told them he had no plans, so they invited him to their recording session at **Abbey Road**. When he arrived at the studio, no one had told him that the Beatles were going to record some of his songs. He said, 'George Martin said, "Are we ready to go?" and Ringo cut out on "Honey Don't". It was a magic time . . . I was in the studio when they cut "Honey Don't", "Matchbox" and "Everybody's Trying To Be My Baby". And they did a version of "Blue Suede Shoes" which was never released.'

The Beatles had also recorded a number of Perkins songs on their various BBC radio appearances: 'Everybody's Trying To Be My Baby', 'Matchbox', 'Sure To Fall', 'Lend Me Your Comb' and 'Honey Don't'. George Harrison had also used the stage name Carl Harrison in his tribute to Perkins when the Silver Beetles had toured Scotland with **Johnny Gentle**.

Over the years Carl kept in touch with Paul, visiting him whenever he was in England. In 1981 Paul invited

Paul McCartney and Carl Perkins join forces. (Linda McCartney/ MPL Communications)

Carl to Montserrat to be one of his guests on the *Tug Of War* album. Carl was so delighted with the invitation that the night before he left for the island he sat down and composed a number, 'My Old Friend', in tribute to Paul. Paul composed the number 'Get It' for the two of them to record and during the sessions they had a jam in which they played a number of Perkins classics, including 'Honey Don't', 'Boppin' the Blues' and 'Lend Me Your Comb'. Paul recorded all the jam sessions, in addition to studio conversations for his personal collection.

Carl played Paul the number 'My Old Friend' on the day he was to leave Montserrat. Paul was so moved that he asked Carl if he had to leave that day and persuaded him to stay and record the number. Carl was to say that the song meant more to him than any other number he'd written, including 'Blue Suede Shoes'. On the track, Paul added backing vocals and played organ, rhythm guitar, drums and bass, but didn't use it on *Tug Of War*.

'Get It' was featured on the album and was also issued as the flipside of the 'Tug Of War' single.

Paul also produced Ringo performing Carl's number 'Sure To Fall' on the *Stop And Smell The Roses* album.

In October 1984, to celebrate the 30th anniversary of 'Blue Suede Shoes', Carl recorded a television special at Limehouse Studios in London called 'A Rockabilly Session – Carl Perkins And Friends'. Among the artists performing with him were George Harrison, Ringo Starr, **Eric Clapton**, Dave Edmunds, Rosanna Cash, Earl Slick, Slim Jim Phantom, Lee Rocker, Greg Perkins, John Davis, Mickey Gee, David Charles and Geraint Watkins.

Perkins is definitely one of the Beatles' major influences as can be seen from the fact that during their career they performed no less than ten of his compositions in their stage act: 'Blue Suede Shoes', 'Lend Me Your Comb', 'Sure To Fall', 'Tennessee', 'Your True Love', 'Glad All Over', 'Everybody's Trying To Be My Baby', 'Matchbox', 'Honey Don't' and 'Gone, Gone, Gone'.

● Peter & Gordon

Rumour has it that when Paul McCartney told the other members of the Beatles that he'd just written a song which began, 'Please lock me away . . .' they laughed. Probably untrue, but the song 'World Without Love' launched the career of a young duo called Peter & Gordon.

The two of them met at Westminster Boys' School, had mutual interests (both were sons of doctors) and decided to

Peter & Gordon – Paul McCartney provided them with several hits. (National Film Archives)

team up as a folk duo Gordon & Peter, performing at th various school events and in some Soho folk clubs. The swopped the name around purely because it sounde better and they were spotted playing at the Pickwick Clu by **EMI** A&R man Norman Newall in January 1964 whe the Beat scene had thoroughly transformed the musi industry to the extent that A&R men were continuously o the lookout for new talent (recording managers were calle A&R men in those days, the initials stood for 'artistes an repertoire').

Gordon Trueman Riviere **Waller** had been born i Braemer, Scotland, on 4 June 1945 and **Peter Asher** i London on 22 June 1944. One of Peter's sisters was **Jan** an actress, and as her current boyfriend was Pau McCartney, Peter decided to talk him into giving them song to record. They'd sent 63 demo tapes to recor companies before their signing to Columbia and had bee scheduled to record a song called 'If I Were You', bu Peter realized that a number written by a Beatle woul virtually assure them of a hit.

Paul decided to complete an unfinished song, 'Worl Without Love', and the duo saw their debut recor released in February 1964. Within two weeks it ha topped the charts, it eventually sold over 550,000 copie in Britain and became a million-seller worldwide. Pa ave them a second composition 'Nobody I Know', which as another million-seller. Peter & Gordon flew to the ates to appear at the New York World Fair and on the :d **Sullivan** Show' and became a major teen attraction.

'I Go To Pieces', a number given to them by **Del hannon**, didn't make much impact in the UK, although reached No. 9 in the States and they had a smash hit ith **Buddy Holly**'s 'True Love Ways', followed by 'To now You Is To Love You' and 'Baby I'm Yours'.

Paul then tried a little experiment. He'd wondered how ell a composition of his would fare if it didn't receive the dvantages of the Lennon & McCartney credit, so he enned a new song for Peter & Gordon, but insisted that e composer's credit should read **Bernard Webb**. The ong was called 'Woman' and reached No. 28 in the ritish charts, faring better in the States at No. 14.

They had one further British hit, 'Lady Godiva', and vo other singles, 'Sunday For Tea' and 'The Jokers', hich didn't reach the British charts but they received low acings in the American Top 100.

Late in 1967 Peter suggested to Gordon that they iould split due to the changing music scene. Gordon had veral solo releases, without much success, while Peter ined the Beatles' new Apple company as head of A&R. ne of his first moves was to sign up American singer **ames Taylor**. Asher later settled in the States as aylor's manager and also managed Linda Rondstadt.

Waller never found success in the recording field again ıd in 1973 appeared in the stage musical *Joseph and His mazing Technicolour Dreamcoat* at the Edinburgh estival, in London and in Australia. He later worked as a ılesman selling photocopiers before settling down in orthamptonshire and becoming a partner in a company aking radio commercials.

Peter Jay & The Jaywalkers

band from East Anglia who comprised Peter Jay rums), Pete Miller (lead guitar), Tony Webster (rhythm uitar), Mac McIntyre (tenor sax/flute), Lloyd Baker piano/baritone sax), Geoff Moss (acoustic bass) and ohnny Larke (bass guitar).

The group toured with the Beatles from 1 November ntil 13 December 1963. During their tour they had veral jam sessions with the Beatles and the **Brook rothers**, some of which were taped.

Peter Jay & the Jaywalkers disbanded in 1966.

● Phantoms, The

A four-piece instrumental group from Melbourne who were booked as one of the support acts on the Beatles' Australian tour in June 1964. The band had previously had two instrumental records in the Melbourne charts (there wasn't a national Australian chart at the time) and were booked for the series of Beatles concerts Down Under.

For their appearances the group wore electric blue suits and were first on stage. They remained on stage to back singer **Johnny Chester** and then singer **Johnny Devlin**.

After they completed the tour the group changed from their Shadows-style and recorded a Beatle-ish number 'I Want You' and by the following year had transformed themselves into a beat group with the new name, MPD Ltd, and became quite successful in Australia.

● Philadelphia Stadium, John F. Kennedy Memorial Park, Philadelphia

Slightly more than one third of this 60,000-seater stadium was gathered on the hot and humid evening on 16 August 1966 which saw constant streaks of lightning flashes throughout the show.

● Philharmonic Hall, The, Hope Street, Liverpool L1

Large concert hall which was primarily used for classical and jazz concerts. During the Mersey Beat days the local country music bands also ran an annual 'Grand Ole Opry' there.

On 10 May 1963 a special beat group contest was taking place at the venue with George Harrison and **Dick Rowe** among the judges.

The **Decca** A&R man sat next to George and while they were chatting, George said, 'We've seen a great band down in London called the **Rolling Stones** who are almost as good as our Roadrunners.' (He was referring to a popular Liverpool R&B group called the Roadrunners.)

Dick Rowe immediately left the hall, caught a train to London and went to see the Stones that evening, signing the group up for Decca and thus making up for the fact that he'd originally turned down the Beatles.

The contest in Liverpool was won by the **Escorts** – and they weren't signed up by Decca either, but eventually recorded for **EMI**'s Columbia label.

Phillips, Esther

Houston-born American singer who recorded the Lennon & McCartney composition 'And I Love Him', issued by Atlantic Records on 22 May 1967. Paul McCartney was so pleased with her rendition of the song at the time that he said it was the best cover version of any Beatles number. When John and Paul were involved in the making of **Johnny Hamp**'s 'The Music Of Lennon And McCartney' for Granada Television, they sent a cable to Esther, who was performing in cabaret in Bermuda, inviting her to appear on their show to sing 'And I Love Him'. She completed her engagement in the West Indies and flew to Manchester to appear in the television special.

She was thrilled that they'd contacted her and said, 'I wanted so much to meet the Beatles in the States but every time I hit a town on my own tour, they'd either just been or were coming the next week. I never met four young men before who are all in the genius class.'

Photographs

Due to their phenomenal domination of the sixties, the Beatles became the world's most photographed subject during the decade and there were literally tens of thousands of photographs taken of the group. However, if a photographic history of the Beatles were to be outlined, certain photographers would stand out.

Within three months of the formation of the **Quarry Men**, a friend, Charlie Roberts, took the famous pictures of them performing on the back of a lorry at the **Rosebury Street** party on 22 June 1957.

The next important image was a box brownie photograph by schoolboy Geoff Rhind, who was a pupil at **Quarry Bank School** and took the historic shot of the Quarry Men playing at the **Woolton Parish Church** Fete on 6 July 1957. Leslie Kearney took the shot of the Quarry Men appearing at **New Clubmoor Hall** on 23 November 1957 and David Hughes photographed the Quarry Men at the **Casbah Club** in September 1959. Ken Beaton took a photograph of the Silver Beetles performing with **Johnny Gentle** at the **Town Hall**, **Alloa**, Scotland, on Friday, 20 May 1960, although the most important set of pictures of this period were taken ten days earlier at the **Wyvern Club**, Seel Street, Liverpool, by Chenison Roland whose set of shots include the Silver Beatles performing with both **Johnny Hutchinson** and **Tommy Moore**, with reaction shots of **Larry Parnes** and **Billy Fury**. Another unique shot was taken at Arnhem Cemetery on the Beatles' first trip to Germany where **Stuart**, Paul, George and Pete together with **Allan** and Beryl Williams and **Lord Woodbine**, are posing before a memorial which states 'Their name liveth for evermore'.

Hamburg, of course, is when the first really sensational photographs of the Beatles were taken by **Astrid Kirchherr** and Jurgen Vollmer. Astrid had studied photography at the Meister Schule and had been taken on as assistant to her former photographic tutor. Once she had become a friend of the Beatles, she arranged her first photographic session with them, initially meeting them in the Reeperbahn and then taking them to Der Dom, the city park, where she took a series of shots. Over the next few weeks she took them to other locations, including the docks and the railway yards. Jurgen also took photographs of the group, his main action pictures taken at a single session when the group were on stage at the **Top Ten Club**. He also took photographs of George by the Hamburg lake and of Astrid and Stuart together.

The large, grainy prints were atmospheric and not unlike the shots **Bob Freeman** was eventually to take for the *With The Beatles* album cover.

Following their Hamburg trip, the Beatles brought the Kirchherr and Vollmer photographs to Bill Harry at ***Mersey Beat*** with a request to print them. The first used was the photograph which Astrid took of them posing at Der Dom, the Hamburg fair, which was used on the cover of Issue No. 2. The photograph dominated the front page, alerted Liverpool to the fact that the Beatles had made a record in Germany and intrigued Brian Epstein. When the Beatles began to enjoy major success in Britain in 1963 some Fleet Street journalists came to the *Mersey Beat* office asking if they could borrow some early photographs of the Beatles for publicity purposes. *Mersey Beat* lent the prints at no charge, hoping that they could provide further promotion for the band, unaware of such things as photo agencies and their practices. As a result, and without permission, Astrid's photograph of the Beatles at Der Dom not only began to appear in publications throughout the world, but copyright was claimed by a London newspaper – even though the print betrayed a slight tear across the photograph, as in the original *Mersey Beat* print.

With the publication of *Mersey Beat* in 1961, the most complete documentation of Beatle photographs began to be assembled. The first major *Mersey Beat* photographer was

Dick Matthews. Dick was a close friend of promoter **Sam Leach** and had once co-promoted dances with him at Mossway Jive Club in 1958. It was Dick who interested his friend Jim Anderson into lending Bill Harry £50 to launch *Mersey Beat*. Dick took some marvellous photographs for posterity, which were featured in the early issues, of the Beatles in their black leather image playing on stage at the **Cavern** and the **Tower Ballroom**. The atmosphere of the times is superbly captured in Dick's shots, especially the action ones on stage when it is obvious that the Beatles are enjoying themselves. He also took many informal shots of the Beatles with friends and at parties.

Another historic session took place on 17 December 1961 at Albert Mariott's studio in Wallasey. Thirty shots were taken and one of the photographs of the Beatles in black leather from this session was used on the cover of Issue 13, the January 1962 issue which announced 'Beatles Top Poll'. This has become one of the classic music paper covers of all.

Since *Mersey Beat* had changed their printers and were now handled by Swale's of Widnes who reproduced photographs from plastic blocks, the paper could now use more photographs. Les Chadwick, a former **Junior Art School** chum of Bill Harry, was working as a photographer for Peter Kaye Photography in Park Lane. This was a studio owned by Bill Connell. A deal was arranged in which *Mersey Beat* commissioned Peter Kaye Photography to take pictures specifically for *Mersey Beat* in exchange for classified and display advertisements, and the rights to sell photographs to readers, with *Mersey Beat* recommending groups to commission the studio to take their publicity shots. This same deal was hammered out with other local photographers such as Graham Spencer and Harry Watmough resulting in a stream of studio, location and stage shots of the Beatles.

The photographs in music papers at this time were basically static studio shots, formally posed. *Mersey Beat* changed all that with the artistic quality of the Kirchherr/Vollmer pictures, the exciting action of the Matthews pics and the location work of the Peter Kaye Studio. Les Chadwick and Bill Connell decided to try something different and get away from the studio setting, taking photographs of the Beatles and other bands on locations such as building sites and ferry boats. London photographers and publications were later to follow suit.

The majority of Beatles photographs commissioned by *Mersey Beat* from Peter Kaye Photography were taken by Les Chadwick, although a few assignments were

An innovative photograph in its time – the Beatles on a Liverpool bomb site, taken by Les Chadwick of Peter Kaye Photography. (©Apple/Peter Kaye Collection)

undertaken by Bill Connell. When Brian Epstein took over the management of the Beatles he initially had photographs taken by his family photographer Albert Marrion, and then commissioned a number of the *Mersey Beat* photographers to take publicity shots – including **Peter Kaye** and Harry Watmough.

Graham Spencer, who died in 1983, was a tall, pleasant, photographer with a quite distinctive personality and he documented the Beatles and Mersey Beat groups in a collection of hundreds of photographs in colour and black and white for the pages of *Mersey Beat*.

Harry Watmough was a photographer who specialized in cabaret artists' photographs and mainly took shots for the 'Clubland' section of *Mersey Beat*, although Brian Epstein, trying out each of the *Mersey Beat* photographers for publicity pic sessions, hired Watmough to take studio shots of them with their new mohair suits, looking very sartorial. This was in stark contrast to their previous wild, black leather image and while **Pete Best** was still a member of the band.

Due primarily to the Hamburg sessions of Kirchherr/Vollmer and *Mersey Beat* in Liverpool, the Beatles were in the unique position of having a wide range of photographic images available before they'd even secured a recording contract in Britain. A situation which few other groups, if any, could boast of.

Mersey Beat also provided **Mike McCartney** with his publishing debut by printing his photographs of Paul and the Beatles, using the pseudonym Francis Michael. A selection of Mike's work documenting the early Beatles has been collected in poster/postcard collections, exhibitions and the book *Mike Mac's White And Blacks* (Aurum Press, 1986).

Another important set of early photographs was taken at the **Odd Spot Club** in Bold Street, Liverpool, on 29 March 1962 by Alan Swerdlow, a friend of Epstein's, who was a former student at **Liverpool College of Art**. Swerdlow was on the panel of the Students' Union Committee, along with **Stuart Sutcliffe** and Bill Harry, when they requested Union funds for the Beatles' PA equipment.

The next major photographic figure in the Beatles' life was **Dezo Hoffmann**, who had been acting as staff photographer to the London-based music paper *Record Mirror* since 1955. In response to readers' enquiries, Dezo went to Liverpool in 1962 to take some photographs of the band. He took photographs of their **Abbey Road** auditions on 6 June 1962 and for the next three years had numerous studio sessions and travelled with the group regularly, taking thousands of shots of the band, many of which have become famous Beatle images. In April 1963 he visited them in Liverpool, taking shots of them in **Sefton Park** (one used on the cover of the EP *Twist and Shout*), at the Cavern and having their hair cut at Horne Brothers. His work has been collected together to form several books, including *With The Beatles* (Omnibus Press, 1982) and *The Beatles Conquer America* (Virgin Books, 1984). It was mainly Dezo's work which was featured in the initial promotion of the Beatles in America early in 1964.

Veteran photographer **Angus McBean** took the famous shot of the group on the **EMI** stairwell for their *Please Please Me* album and the next photographer associated with their album covers was **Robert Freeman**, who began taking shots of the group in 1963 and travelled with them as a photographer and friend, eventually handling design and photography for five of their album covers. His cover of the *With The Beatles* album, with its black and white portraits in half light, remains one of the famous early images and Freeman has had several collections of his Beatle photographs published, beginning with *Beatles Ltd* (George Newnes) in 1964.

Norman Parkinson, a leading fashion photographer, next took shots of the group at Abbey Road Studios and a collection of the photographs was published as *The Beatles* (Hutchinson) in 1964.

Once they had become established as international stars, hundreds of different photographers took thousands of shots of the group – at concerts, in hotels, at leisure, with girlfriends, on holiday – and photographers such as Dezo Hoffmann and Robert Freeman were still taking shots of the group on a regular basis. There were also photographers specially commissioned to take official shots of the group and also to document specific events in their personal life such as the wedding of Ringo and **Maureen Starkey**.

There were also the publicity photographs taken to promote their various film projects.

For a time, Epstein employed **Robert Whitaker** as official photographer and among the many unique images which Bob captured were those taken for the notorious 'butcher' cover, featuring the Beatles in butchers' smocks olding pieces of raw meat and parts of the bodies of dolls. Whitaker was to produce a book of his Beatle pics in 1991.

One of the major images of the mid-sixties were the hots of the Beatles in their colourful military costumes sed in the *Sgt Pepper* sessions, taken by photographer **Michael Cooper**, who documented the entire *Sgt Pepper* leeve sessions in his Flood Street studio. Many of the nages were published in his posthumous book *Blinds and hutters*.

John Kelly was the photographer who provided the set f colour portraits enclosed with *The Beatles* double album ackage and **Iain Macmillan** took the famous *Abbey Road* hots, the most famous being the front cover photograph on ne *Abbey Road* album, depicting the group walking across ne zebra crossing. The photographs for their final album *et It Be* were taken by **Ethan Russell**, who also provided ne shots for the special *Get Back* book which was ncluded in the package when the *Let It Be* album was riginally issued.

During their career, other notable photographs of the Beatles include those taken by American photographer **Richard Avedon** and, in particular, his psychedelic ortraits; the John and **Yoko** nude shots and the final live erformance on the roof of the Apple building.

Pickles, Thelma

When John Lennon was enrolling for his second year at **Liverpool College of Art** he noticed a new student, ixteen-year-old Thelma Pickles. They soon found they ad things in common, both were rebels in the way they ressed – he in his tight trousers, she in her black tockings – and both had been deserted by their fathers hen young.

The two began to date regularly for a period of six onths until the romance fizzled out of the relationship nd John set his cap at **Cynthia**.

Thelma observed that John had a cruel streak which anifested itself in verbal aggression. One night in **Ye Cracke** he began to verbally abuse her and she shut him p by saying, 'Don't blame me, just because your mother's ead.' She also noticed that he was scared of physical iolence and intimidated people more with his mouth than is fists.

During their time together he used to take her along to **Quarry Men** rehearsals at his Aunt **Mimi**'s house. It was uring this time that she met Paul, who was just starting in the Sixth Form at Liverpool Institute, next door to the college; he used to drop in and join them in the art college canteen, along with George Harrison.

Just before 'Love Me Do' came out, Paul began dating Thelma. Later, she married Roger McGough of the **Scaffold**, the group which had Paul's brother **Mike** as a member.

● Picture Of You, A

This Beveridge/Oakman composition was a British hit for **Joe Brown** & the Bruvvers in 1962. An odd choice for the Beatles' repertoire, although it was one of Brian Epstein's favourite records at the time. George sang the number and the group performed it on their BBC radio show **'Here We Go'** on 15 June 1962.

● Pigalle, Piccadilly, London W1

An unusual venue for a Beatles show. The Pigalle was a sophisticated nightclub in the heart of London's West End. The Beatles appeared here on the evening of 21 April 1963, following their appearance earlier that day at the ***New Musical Express*** poll winners' concert at Wembley.

The reason why Brian Epstein booked the group into this luxuriously decorated club with a wealthy middle-aged clientele was because he was seeking a West End showcase for the group, a place where he could invite the leading London booking agents and television producers to view the band.

The club was to undergo several transformations and name changes as times and tastes altered and in the eighties became the fashionable discotheque, Xenon's.

● Piggies

A George Harrison composition. When George was writing the number he needed a line to rhyme with 'backing' and 'lacking' and his mother came up with, 'What they need is a damn good whacking!'

He'd originally begun writing the number in 1966 but didn't finish it until 1968 when it was included on *The Beatles* double album.

Recording began on Thursday, 19 September 1968, and Chris Thomas was producer of the session and also played harpsichord on the track.

This was one of the numbers which **Charles Manson** believed was a special hidden message from the Beatles in which they called for a revolution.

● Pilbeam, Peter

The first BBC producer to book the Beatles for a radio show.

In 1962 he was holding auditions with new bands for the **'Teenager's Turn'** programme, based in Manchester, and was impressed by the Beatles. In his audition report he wrote: 'An unusual group, not as "rocky" as most, more country and western with a tendency to play music.'

Commenting on their first radio appearance to Kevin Howlett in *The Beatles At The Beeb* book, Peter said: 'We used to get some terrific audiences down at the **Playhouse** for the teenage shows that we did, and we'd have the Northern Dance Orchestra on stage trying to look like teenagers with their chunky jumpers on, which we kitted them out with. We used to have a group in each programme, a guest singer and a presenter and it was the usual style of show that we did in those days for half-an-hour. The Beatles came on and did a very good show. I was very impressed with them and I booked them straight away for another date after that first show.'

'Teenager's Turn', on which the Beatles made their radio debut, was broadcast on 8 March 1962. The programme underwent a name change to **'Here We Go'**, still produced by Pilbeam, who booked the Beatles for four appearances on the show, broadcast on 15 June and 26 October 1962 and 25 January and 12 March 1963.

● Pilchard

The title of a play which John and Paul tried to write in their early days together. Paul later described it as: '. . . a sort of precursor of *The Life of Brian*, about a working-class weirdo who was always upstairs playing. It was a down-market Second Coming. But we had to give it up because we couldn't actually work out how it went on, how you actually filled up all the pages.'

● Pinky And Perky

Two pig puppets which were very popular on British television in the sixties. When they sang songs their voices were doctored on tape in such a way as to make a peculiar singing sound – they were slightly similar to America's the **Chipmunks**.

As with most of the popular media in the sixties, they couldn't miss out on a tribute to the Beatles and on 8 March 1965 an EP by Pinky and Perky was issued on **EMI**'s Columbia label called *Beat Party*, which contained the tracks 'She Loves You', 'All My Loving', and 'Car Buy Me Love'.

● Pinwheel Twist

A number which Paul McCartney wrote for **Pete Best** perform on stage. Best told broadcaster Spencer Leig 'Paul wrote the song and asked me to do it. He coupled with Joey Dee's hit "The Peppermint Twist". I used to g up and do the twist on stage and Paul played my drums. was a little novelty act and it went down well with t fans.'

When the Beatles performed the number, Paul to over on drums, George played Paul's left-handed ba right-handed and Pete sang.

● Pittsburgh Civic Arena, *Pittsburgh, Pennsylvania*

This venue on Monday, 14 September 1964, drew maximum capacity of 12,603. There was a huge poli presence at the arena and a Beatles press conference w held at 6.00 p.m. in Conference Room A. After their sh there, the Beatles had intended to leave the arena police car, but the access was blocked by fans and th were smuggled out of another exit and left in a limousi heading straight for the airport.

● Plastic Ono Band, The

In 1969 when John Lennon was more interested cementing a creative partnership with **Yoko** th recording with the Beatles and soon after changing h name to John Ono Lennon, he created the name Plast Ono Band. The first record under this name, 'Give Pea A Chance', was issued on 4 July 1969 (7 July in the US John and Yoko had recorded the number at the Hotel Reine Elizabeth in Montreal, Canada, with a vario assortment of friends, including Tommy Smothers, Petu Clark, Rosemary and **Timothy Leary**, Rabbi Geinsbe **Allen Ginsberg** and members of the Canadian Chapter the **Radha Krsna Temple**.

The Plastic Ono Band was due to be promoted at 'Give Peace A Chance' press reception at the Chels Town Hall on 3 July 1969. As John and Yoko had be involved in a car accident, Ringo and **Maureen** deputiz for them – and as the Plastic Ono Band didn't exist as group, some plastic robots were used as substitutes.

The second Plastic Ono Band single was 'Cold Turke

issued on 24 October 1969 (20 October in the US). This time John and Yoko were accompanied by **Eric Clapton** on lead guitar, **Klaus Voormann** on bass and Ringo Starr on drums.

The Plastic Ono Band were not only a recording band, John formed a group of musicians using that name to accompany him to Canada for the *Toronto Rock 'n' Roll Revival Concert*. They were Eric Clapton on lead guitar, **Alan White** on drums and Klaus Voorman on bass guitar. Their performance was recorded and it was issued as an album on 12 December 1969 as *The Plastic Ono Band – Live Peace In Toronto 1969*. John also formed a Plastic Ono Supergroup who made a single appearance at the

John and Yoko – during the filming of *Let It Be*. (©Apple)

Lyceum Ballroom in London on 15 December 1969. Among the group of musicians John arranged to play with him was George Harrison.

The next single was 'Instant Karma', credited to Lennon/Ono with the Plastic Ono Band. This was issued on 6 February 1970 (20 February in the US). The other musicians were George Harrison on guitar and grand piano, Klaus Voorman on bass guitar and electric piano, Alan White on drums and grand piano and **Billy Preston** on organ. The next album was recorded after John and Yoko had experienced Primal Therapy and was simply called *John Lennon/Plastic Ono Band*. It was issued on 11 December 1970 and the musicians, apart from John and Yoko, were Ringo Starr on drums, Klaus Voorman on bass guitar and **Billy Preston** on piano.

A single, 'Mother', credited to John Lennon/Plastic Ono Band, was issued in America, but not in Britain, on 28 December 1970.

The following single, issued on 12 March 1971 (22 March in the US), was called 'Power To The People', credited to John Lennon and the Plastic Ono Band, while the flipside 'Open Your Box' was credited to Yoko Ono and the Plastic Ono Band. The musicians supplementing John and Yoko were Klaus Voorman on bass guitar and Jim Gordon on drums.

Imagine was the next album, issued on 8 October 1971 (9 September in the US) and credited to John Lennon and the Plastic Ono Band, with the Flux Fiddlers. There were various musicians on individual tracks and included Klaus Voorman on bass guitar and piano, Alan White on drums, Nicky Hopkins on piano, Steve Brendel on upright bass, George Harrison on dobro, Ted Turner on acoustic guitar, Rod Linton on acoustic guitar, John Tout on acoustic guitar, Jim Gordon on drums, John Barham on harmonium, **King Curtis** on saxophone, Joey Molland and Tom Evans of **Badfinger** on acoustic guitars and Andy Cresswell-Davis on acoustic guitar.

The next release was *Some Time In New York City*, a double-album set issued on 15 September 1972 (12 June in the US). The first album was credited to John and Yoko/Plastic Ono Band with Elephants Memory plus Invisible Strings, the second to the Plastic Ono Supergroup and the Plastic Ono Mothers (because part of it was recorded at a concert with the Mothers of Invention).

A single followed, 'Happy Xmas (War Is Over)', credited to John and Yoko/Plastic Ono Band with the Harlem Community Choir, issued on 24 November 1972 (1 December in the US). No more releases used the name Plastic Ono Band although the *Mind Games* album was credited to John Lennon with the Plastic U.F. Ono Band, the single 'Whatever Gets You Thru The Night' to John Lennon with the Plastic Ono Nuclear Band and the *Walls And Bridges* album to John Lennon with the Plastic Ono Nuclear Band.

● Playhouse Theatre, The, *St John's Road, Manchester*

Used by the BBC to record radio shows before live audiences in the sixties.

The Beatles appeared on their first radio session here on 7 March 1962. The show was called **'Teenager's Turn'** and it was broadcast on the BBC's Light Programme between 5.00 p.m. and 5.30 p.m. the next day.

The group performed 'Dream Baby', 'Memphis Tennessee' and 'Please Mr Postman' before a live audience. Resident musicians on the programme were the NDO (Northern Dance Orchestra). The group recorded another number at the session, 'Hello Little Girl', but it was not broadcast. The show was produced by **Peter Pilbeam**.

The group were to return to the Playhouse for four sessions of a programme called **'Here We Go'**, also produced by Pilbeam. Their first 'Here We Go' show was recorded on 10 June 1962 and transmitted on 15 June. The group were heard performing 'Ask Me Why', 'Besame Mucho' and 'A Picture Of You' and among the vocal supporters in the audience were members of their Liverpool fan club who had travelled to Manchester by coach. The Beatles next appeared on 'Here We Go' on 26 October, having recorded the show the day previously, affording Ringo his first BBC Radio session. They performed 'Love Me Do', 'A Taste Of Honey' and 'P.S. I Love You'. Another number, 'Sheila', was not broadcast. On 16 January 1963 they performed at the Playhouse once again with 'Chains', 'Please Please Me' and 'Ask Me Why', all transmitted several days later on 25 January. Another number recorded for 'Here We Go' but not transmitted was 'Three Cool Cats'.

They returned to the venue on 6 March 1963 to record 'Misery', 'Do You Want To Know A Secret?', 'Please Please Me' and 'I Saw Her Standing There', but the latter wasn't broadcast when 'Here We Go' was transmitted on 12 March.

● Plaza Ballroom, *Halesowen Road, Old Hill, Dudley, Staffordshire*

A Midlands booking which the Beatles undertook on 11 January 1963, during a severe winter in which there were fierce blizzards. That evening they had been engaged for a double-booking, but due to the nature of the weather they were unable to travel on to the Ritz Ballroom in Birmingham and the engagement there had to b rearranged.

They appeared at the Plaza for the second and last tim on 5 July 1963. Also on the bill were a Birmingham band Denny & the Diplomats, led by Denny Laine.

● Plaza Ballroom, *Queen Street, St Helens, Lancashire*

The ballroom opened in 1956 and began to feature loca groups in 1958 when the enterprising manager, Harr Bostock, held a rock 'n' roll group contest. It was also par of the company Whetstone Entertainments, which als promoted dances at the Orrell Park Ballroom in Liverpoo and the **Riverpark Ballroom** in Chester.

In 1959 the Plaza switched to a policy of exclusivel featuring groups and was open four nights a week: Friday

PLAZA BALLROOM DUKE STREET, ST. HELENS.

HARRY BOSTOCK PRESENTS HIS

" BIG BEAT BARGAIN NIGHTS "

MONDAYS 7-30—11 p.m. THE BEATLES PLUS ANOTHER TOP GROUP

First ever appearance of the North's No. 1 Recording Combo

COME EARLY ADMISSION ONLY 2/6

Saturdays 'MEET THE BIG BEAT' Jive to the North's Best Groups

Sundays BIG ROCK CLUB NIGHT NEW MEMBERS WECOME TOP GROUPS

Saturday, Sunday and Monday. There were usually thre groups per night and admission charges varied from 2s.6d to 3s.6d.

Most of the top Mersey groups appeared there including the Beatles, **Gerry & the Pacemakers**, th **Fourmost**, the **Swinging Bluejeans**, the **Merseybeat** and the **Searchers**.

The Beatles made their debut there on 25 June 1962 i a booking arranged by Brian Epstein for which the received £25. The Monday evening event was compered b **Bob Wooler**, entrance was two shillings and sixpenc and the support band was the **Big Three**. The even lasted from 7.30 p.m.–11.00 p.m. and it was the Beatles first appearance in St Helens and the first of a series c Monday night bookings. Promotional leaflets read: 'Harr

Bostock presents his *Big Beat Bargain Night* starring the North's No. 1 Rock combo THE BEATLES, Just back from their Sensational German Tour. Now Recording Exclusively for Parlophone. They're terrific . . . you must see them! FIRST EVER APPEARANCE IN ST HELENS.'

The group also appeared there on 2 July, 9 July and 16 July.

Their last appearance at the venue took place on 4 March 1963 and it was the first booking for which they received a three-figure sum – £100.

Ballroom manager Harry Bostock was a Mancunian who had previously led bands in Birmingham, Manchester, Folkestone and Liverpool. He could also play eight instruments, including piano, trumpet, saxophone, drums, violin and clarinet.

● Plaza De Toros De Madrid, Madrid, Spain

The Beatles' first appearance in Spain, which took place in the main bullring at Madrid on 2 July 1965 when the group appeared in a single concert at 8.30 p.m. Among the other acts on the bill were Freddie Davis, the Martin Brothers, Michel, the Modern 4, the **Rustiks** and the Trinidad Steel Band.

● Plaza De Toros Monumental, Barcelona, Spain

The final concert of the Beatles' fourteen-date European tour and the second and last appearance in Spain. The group appeared here on 3 July 1965.

● Plaza Hotel, West 58th Street, New York City

Famous conservative American hotel where the Beatles stayed when they first arrived in New York. After the group had held their press conference at **Kennedy Airport** on Friday, 7 February 1964, they were driven straight to the Plaza in air-conditioned Cadillac limousines.

As they arrived they discovered the hotel was surrounded by crowds of fans, held in check by 100 New York City cops with a squad of mounted police.

The management issued a statement that they wouldn't have accepted the bookings if they'd known who the Beatles were. They had assumed they were English businessmen. There has been some doubt cast upon this story as the hotel certainly knew who the Beatles were – and the hotel staff queued up for autographs.

The group were taken to the ten-room Presidential Suites (Suites 1209 to 1216) on the twelfth floor, which overlooked 58th Street. One of the corridors was sealed off by guards from the Burns Detective Agency and there were two guards on duty around the clock. The suites contained expensive modern furniture in creams, browns and turquoise. Fan mail was brought to them there, and there was also camera and radio equipment stored there by the various media who came for interviews. While the Beatles were sitting around they took a call from **Brian Matthew** in London for an interview on '**Saturday Club**'.

The next day, a Saturday, found George in bed with a throat problem. His sister **Louise** had arrived at the hotel and moved in to nurse him. The hotel doctor, Dr Gordon, told George, 'I'll have to get you fit, otherwise my young relatives will blunt all my needles.' He did, however, insist on a signed photo before starting treatment.

The rest of the group attended another press reception in the Plaza's Baroque Room during which one female reporter noticed Ringo smoking and told him that it set a bad example for teenagers. Ringo said, 'Who's a teenager? I'm 23,' and an angry John Lennon rounded on her, 'We're not here to set examples for teenagers.'

New York disc jockey **Murray the K** breezed into their suite with the **Ronettes**, still recording his show. 'We're what's happening, Babe. We're Murray the K and the Beatles, Babe on W-I-N-S'. The Beatles admired his nerve and he became one of their regular escorts over the following few days, taking them to various nightclubs and restaurants and introducing them to starlets such as Stella Stevens, Tuesday Weld and Jill Haworth.

A report in the *New York Herald Tribune* read: 'The Beatles are all short, slight kids from Liverpool who wear four-button coats, stovepipe pants, ankle-high black boots with cuban heels and droll looks on their faces. The Plaza, one of the most sedate hotels in New York was petrified. The reservations were accepted months ago before the Plaza knew it was for a rock and roll group.'

● Please Mr Postman

A number composed by Brian Holland, Robert Bateman and Berry Gordy which was recorded by the Marvelettes as their debut single and brought them a million-selling No. 1 entry in the States in December 1961. The Beatles included it in their repertoire in 1962 with John on lead vocal. They performed the number on their BBC radio shows **'Teenager's Turn'**, **'Pop Go The Beatles'** and **'From Us To You'**. They recorded it for their *With The Beatles* album. The track is also to be found on the American *Beatles Second Album* and *4 By the Beatles* EP and the collections *The Beatles Box* and *The Beatles Collection*.

● Please Please Me *(Album)*

The Beatles' debut album, recorded in one marathon session on Monday, 11 February 1963. Recording manager George Martin was amazed at the staying power of the group as they continued recording far longer than originally planned, including the time allotted for their lunch break. By the evening, when they did take a break in the canteen, he was able to tell them that they just needed one more number to complete the album – and they immediately decided on 'Twist And Shout'.

The group recorded eight of their own compositions and six other numbers which were then part of their stage repertoire. Paul had originally wanted to record 'Besame Mucho', but it was decided to include 'A Taste Of Honey', from the British stage play, instead.

'Please Please Me' was issued on Parlophone PCS 3042 on 22 March 1963 and reached No. 1 in the British charts, eventually selling over half a million copies.

The all-day session cost approximately £400 and was produced with George Martin, engineer **Norman Smith** and second engineer Richard Langham.

The tracks were – Side One: 'I Saw Her Standing There', 'Misery', 'Anna (Go To Him)', 'Chains', 'Boys', 'Ask Me Why', 'Please Please Me'. Side Two: 'Love Me Do', 'P.S. I Love You', 'Baby It's You', 'Do You Want To Know A Secret?', 'A Taste Of Honey', 'There's A Place', 'Twist And Shout'.

The American equivalent had a name change to *Introducing The Beatles* when it was issued by **Vee Jay** in July 1963.

● Please Please Me *(Single)*

The Beatles' second single, issued on Parlophone R 4983 on 11 January 1963. The group had originally hoped to use the number as the 'B' side of 'Love Me Do', but George Martin was unhappy about the arrangement and suggested they put it aside. Martin had wanted them to issue **Mitch Murray**'s 'How Do You Do It?' as a single, but acknowledged that the rearranged 'Please Please Me' was the right one. As soon as they'd completed recording on Monday, 26 November, Martin said to them, 'You've just made your first No. 1.' He was right, it went to No. 1 in most charts. The new arrangement owed something to Martin, as Paul commented: 'George Martin's contribution was a big one, actually. The first time he really ever showed that he could see beyond what we were offering him was "Please Please Me". It was originally conceived as a **Roy Orbison**-type thing, you know. George Martin said, "Well, we'll put the tempo up." He lifted the tempo and we all thought that was much better and that was a big hit.'

The number was penned by John who claimed that he'd thought of the idea when he remembered a Bing Crosby song which included the line, 'Please lend a little ear to my pleas'. The flipside of the single, which was originally issued on the red Parlophone label, was 'Ask Me Why'. Later the single was issued on the black label. It was included on their album *Please Please Me*, their EP *The Beatles Hits* and the compilation *The Beatles 1962–1966*. It was re-released in Britain in 1983 in different forms, one of them being a limited-edition picture disc.

In America it first surfaced as a **Vee Jay** single on VJ 498 with 'Ask Me Why' on the flip on 25 February 1963. It made no impact. It was re-released by Vee Jay on VJ 581 on 30 January 1964 with 'From Me To You' on the flip and reached No. 3 in the charts. Before Vee Jay closed as a company they reissued it as a single on OL 150 Oldies 45 on 10 August 1964, although it didn't chart and in October it was included on two Vee Jay albums, *The Beatles vs The Four Seasons* and *Songs, Pictures and Stories Of The Fabulous Beatles*. **Capitol** included it on their album *The Early Beatles* in March 1965.

Its release in Britain was greeted by enthusiastic reviews in the British press and it was also praised by radio disc jockeys. **Brian Matthew** said that the Beatles were 'Musically and visually the most accomplished group to emerge since the **Shadows**'.

'Please Please Me' provided a chart hit for David Cassidy in 1974.

● Pobjoy, William Ernest

When E. R. Taylor, the authoritarian headmaster of **Quarry Bank School**, retired in 1956, he was succeeded ɔy William Pobjoy who, a month after settling in, found ıimself having to apply the cane to the school's unruly ·ebel John Lennon.

Pobjoy realized that punishing Lennon had no real ·ffect and he had discussions with John's Aunt, **Mimi Smith**, and suggested that her nephew's talents for art ·ould be utilized. With her consent he arranged for John to ·nter the **Liverpool College of Art** without having to sit ·or an examination.

Polythene Pam

)ne of the songs which John had penned in India. The rack was featured on the *Abbey Road* album, although at ·ne time it had been considered for *The Beatles* white ılbum. John commented: 'I wrote this one in India and vhen I recorded it I used a thick Liverpool accent because t was supposed to be about a mythical Liverpool scrubber lressed up in her jackboots and kilt.' John later revealed hat it concerned a true incident when a friend of his ınsuccessfully tried to involve him in an orgy. On the ılbum the song ran straight into Paul's composition 'She Came In Through The Bathroom Window' and they were ·oth recorded as one song at **Abbey Road** sessions on 'riday, 25 July, and Monday, 28 July 1969. Extras ncluded John on maracas, Paul on cow bells and piano nd George on tambourine.

Pop Gear

ı 68-minute film, directed by Frederick Goode. Produced ·y Associated British-Pathe, the movie went on general elease throughout Britain on 18 April 1965.

Jimmy Savile hosted a string of groups in a format imilar to the TV show 'Top Of The Pops'. The Beatles ·ere shown singing 'She Loves You' and 'Twist And hout', although both performances had been edited from ıe Pathe News feature recorded at the **Apollo**, **Ardwick**, Ianchester, on 20 November 1963.

Other acts of interest in the movie included **Billy J. Kramer** & the Dakotas performing 'Little Children', **Peter & Gordon** with 'World Without Love', the **'ourmost** with 'A Little Loving' and **Tommy Quickly** erforming 'Humpty Dumpty'.

Pop Go The Beatles

. 1963 series of radio shows, hosted by the Beatles. The how's presenter was Terry Henebery and when discussions were taking place to decide what it should be called, Francis Line, a production secretary, suggested the title to Henebery. The Beatles began each show singing the title song 'Pop Go The Beatles', which was a variation of the traditional tune 'Pop Goes The Weasel'.

The first four shows were produced by Lee Peters and in each programme the Beatles featured a guest artist.

On the show's debut on 4 June 1963 which they had recorded on 24 May at the BBC's Studio 2 in Aeolian Hall in New Bond Street, London, the Beatles performed 'From Me To You', 'Everybody's Trying To Be My Baby', 'Do You Want To Know A Secret?', 'You Really Got A Hold On Me', 'Misery' and 'The Hippy Hippy Shake'. Their special guests were the Lorne Gibson Trio.

On the 11 June show, recorded at the BBC's Paris Studios on 1 June, they performed 'Too Much Monkey Business', 'I Got To Find My Baby', 'Young Blood', 'Baby It's You', 'Till There Was You' and 'Love Me Do'. Their guests were the Countrymen.

Their third show, transmitted on 18 June, Paul McCartney's 21st birthday, had also been recorded on 1 June, and the group performed 'A Shot Of Rhythm And Blues', 'Memphis Tennessee', 'A Taste Of Honey', 'Sure To Fall In Love (With You)', 'Money' and 'From Me To You'. Their guests were Carter Lewis and the Southerners, a group formed by John Carter and Ken Lewis. They had a minor hit in 1963 with 'Your Momma's Out Of Town', but by 1964 had changed their name to the Ivy League. Among the various members who passed through the Southerners' line-up were Jimmy Page (later to become leader of Led Zeppelin) and Viv Prince (later to become a member of the Pretty Things).

On the 25 June transmission, recorded at the BBC's No. 5 studio in Delaware Road, Maida Vale, on 17 June, they performed 'I Saw Her Standing There', 'Anna (Go To Him)', 'Boys', 'Chains', 'P.S. I Love You' and 'Twist And Shout'. A recording of 'A Taste Of Honey' was not transmitted. Their guests were the Bachelors, a popular Irish vocal trio who were to notch up thirteen chart hits between 1963 and 1967, including their No. 1 record 'Diane'. They comprised John Stokes, Con Cluskey and Dec Cluskey.

This was Peters' last stint as producer of the show, which had a break of three weeks to gauge the audience reaction, which proved positive. As a result, the programme returned on 16 July with a new producer,

Rodney Burke. The show was recorded on 2 July at Maida Vale and the Beatles performed 'That's All Right, Mama', 'There's A Place', 'Carol', 'Soldier Of Love', 'Lend Me Your Comb' and 'Clarabella'. Their guests were Duffy Power and the Graham Bond Quartet, who were to record the *Please Please Me* album track 'I Saw Her Standing There' as a single, released by Parlophone on 26 April 1963. Although they had the foresight to become one of the first artists to record Lennon & McCartney material, it wasn't a hit for them.

Three other numbers were recorded by the Beatles, but not transmitted – 'Three Cool Cats', 'Sweet Little Sixteen' and 'Ask Me Why'.

Their show on 23 July was recorded at the Aeolian Hall on 10 July and presented their performances of 'Sweet Little Sixteen', 'A Taste Of Honey', 'Nothin' Shakin' (But The Leaves On The Trees)', 'Love Me Do', 'Lonesome Tears In My Eyes' and 'So How Come (No One Loves Me)'. Their guests were Carter Lewis and the Southerners.

Their 30 July show had also been recorded on 10 July and the Beatles performed '**Memphis Tennessee**', 'Do You Want To Know A Secret?', 'Till There Was You', 'Matchbox', 'Please Mr Postman' and 'The Hippy Hippy Shake'. Their guests were the **Searchers**.

The show on 6 August had been recorded at the Paris Studio on 16 July and featured the Beatles performing 'I'm Gonna Sit Right Down And Cry (Over You)', 'Crying, Waiting, Hoping', 'Kansas City/Hey! Hey! Hey!', 'To Know Her Is To Love Her', 'The Honeymoon Song' and 'Twist And Shout'. Their guests were the **Swinging Bluejeans**.

The 13 August programme had been recorded on 16 July when, in fact, three complete shows had been put in the can at the same time. On this programme the group played 'Long Tall Sally', 'Please Please Me', 'She Loves You', 'You Really Got A Hold On Me', 'I'll Get You' and 'I Got A Woman'. Their guests were the **Hollies.**

The show on 20 August had the Beatles performing 'She Loves You', 'Words Of Love', 'Glad All Over', 'I Just Don't Understand', 'Devil In Her Heart' and 'Slow Down'. Their guests were Russ Sainty and the Nu-Notes.

On 1 August the next two shows were recorded at the **Playhouse Theatre**, **Manchester** due to the group's commitments in the North. On the 27 August show the group performed 'Oh! My Soul', 'Don't Ever Change', 'Twist And Shout', 'She Loves You', 'Anna (Go To Him)' and 'A Shot Of Rhythm And Blues'. Their guests were the Cyril Davies Rhythm And Blues All Stars with **Long John Baldry**. Davies was an innovative harmonica player who'd originally performed with Alexis Korner between 1957 and 1962. He formed the All Stars at the close of 1962 and Baldry joined him in January 1963. Tragically, Davies died in January 1964 and the band broke up.

The Beatles' 3 September show saw them performing 'From Me To You', 'I'll Get You', 'Money', 'There's A Place', 'Honey Don't' and 'Roll Over Beethoven'. They also recorded 'Lucille', 'Baby It's You' and 'She Loves You', but these tracks weren't transmitted. Their guests were **Brian Poole & the Tremeloes**.

10 September heralded their thirteenth show and was recorded at the Aeolian Hall on 3 September, when in a lengthy session lasting almost nine hours, they recorded the next three shows. The group performed 'Too Much Monkey Business', 'Till There Was You', 'Love Me Do', 'I'll Get You', 'A Taste Of Honey' and 'The Hippy Hippy Shake'. Their guests were Johnny Kidd & the Pirates.

Their penultimate show on 17 September had them performing 'Chains', 'You Really Got A Hold On Me', 'Misery', 'Lucille', 'From Me to You' and 'Boys'. A version of 'A Taste Of Honey' was not transmitted. Their guests were the Marauders, a group from Stoke-on-Trent who had a minor hit with 'That's What I Want' in 1963.

For their final show on 24 September the Beatles selected 'She Loves You', 'Ask Me Why', 'Devil In Her Heart', 'I Saw Her Standing There', 'Sure To Fall (In Love With You)' and 'Twist And Shout'. Their guests were Tony Rivers & the Castaways, a talented group from Dagenham noted for their vocal harmony, who were to cover the **Beach Boys**' 'God Only Knows' in 1966. At one time Geoff and Pete Swettenham and John Perry, who went on to form **Grapefruit**, were members.

● Pop Inn

A BBC radio progamme. The Beatles were interviewed live on the show on 9 April 1963.

● Pops And Lennie

The Beatles appeared before a live audience at the BBC Television Theatre, Shepherd's Bush Green, to record the children's show, 'Pops and Lennie', on 16 May 1963. The programme went out live at 5.00 p.m.

The Beatles were among the several guests of Lennie

he Lion, a puppet character, and performed 'From Me To You' and 'Please Please Me'. At the end of the show they oined Lennie and the other guests in a grand finale during which they sang the programme's signature tune, 'After You've Gone'.

Pop's Happening

A programme produced by the pirate radio station Radio Caroline. Paul McCartney pre-recorded an interview for he show which was broadcast on 26 December 1955.

Pop '63

A Swedish radio show. The Beatles recorded for the show uring their short Swedish tour on 24 October 1963. The roup recorded the programme at the Karlaplansstudio in tockholm. Among the numbers the group performed were: 'From Me To You', 'Roll Over Beethoven', 'Money', 'You Really Got A Hold On Me', 'She Loves You', 'Twist And hout' and 'I Saw Her Standing There'. There have been ootleg releases of this transmission, although they have een mistakenly attributed to another Swedish radio show ecorded a few days later, called **'Drop In'**.

Precht, Bob

roducer of 'The **Ed Sullivan** Show'. Precht, who was also ullivan's son-in-law, met Brian Epstein at his New York otel to discuss booking the Beatles on the show. Sullivan ad wanted to book the band after seeing **Beatlemania** in rce at Heathrow Airport. Precht wasn't really aware of eir appeal and had no idea how they'd suit American udiences and offered them a single appearance on the now. Brian insisted they be bill-toppers and after the iscussion, a deal was struck in which the Beatles would eadline two shows on consecutive Sundays, 9 and 16 ebruary 1964. For each show they would receive $3,500, ith Sullivan paying their air fares.

Presley, Elvis

he Beatles are the most famous group in popular music story and Elvis Presley is the most famous solo singer.

Born Elvis Aaron Presley on 8 January 1935 in East upelo, Mississippi, Elvis was to begin his phenomenal usic career in 1954, just two years before John Lennon unded the **Quarry Men**.

In the British charts Elvis was to share the same umber of No. 1 hits as the Beatles and remains the artist who has spent more weeks in the No. 1 position in the charts than anyone else. He's also spent more weeks in the charts than any other artist, had the largest number of hits and more Top Ten entries than any other artist. His chart success in America was also incredible, beginning with his No. 1 hit 'Hearbreak Hotel' in 1956 and stretching until 1981, a few years after his death at the age of 42 on 16 August 1977.

Elvis was a major influence on the Beatles and on John Lennon in particular. John once said, 'Nothing really affected me until I heard Elvis. If there hadn't been Elvis, there would not have been the Beatles.'

When the Quarry Men formed they began to introduce Elvis numbers into their repertoire, performed by either John or Paul, which included 'All Shook Up', 'Blue Moon Of Kentucky', 'Hound Dog', 'Jailhouse Rock', 'Mean Woman Blues', 'I Forgot To Remember To Forget', 'I'm Gonna Sit Right Down And Cry Over You', 'It's Now Or Never', 'That's All Right (Mama)' and 'Love Me Tender' (a showcase for **Stuart Sutcliffe**).

George Harrison was to comment, 'I remember at school there was all that thing about Elvis. When a record came along like "Heartbreak Hotel" it was so amazing. We know Elvis is great. He stopped being a rocker and they made him go into the army, and by the time he came out he was a clean, healthy American, doing clean, healthy songs and films. But basically he's got such a great bluesy voice.'

Paul McCartney was to say, 'Every time I felt low, I just put on an Elvis record and I'd feel great, beautiful.'

When Brian Epstein began touting the Beatles to the British record companies, he told them that the Beatles would become bigger than Elvis and when the Beatles eventually flew to America to appear on 'The **Ed Sullivan** Show', there was a congratulatory telegram from Elvis, which was read out on the air – although it was Colonel Tom Parker who had actually sent it.

During the group's first concert tour of America, when Brian Epstein arrived at the Hilton Hotel, San Francisco, he received a telegram from Parker offering to help as a friend and asking Brian to phone him up. Once the two were in touch with each other they became firm friends.

Journalist Chris Hutchins of the ***New Musical Express*** was travelling with the Beatles on their American tour in 1964 and on 30 August, when they were in Atlantic City, he passed on Elvis's private number, which Colonel

Parker had given him, to Paul McCartney, who phoned Elvis in Memphis. He apologized for the fact that the Beatles hadn't been able to take advantage of an invitation to visit Elvis at Graceland because of security reasons and said, 'How do you do. I want to tell you that we all think it's a drag that we weren't able to get together with you.' Elvis told Paul that he'd just got an electric bass guitar which he was learning to play. Paul asked if Elvis would be coming to Britain. 'Soon, I hope,' Elvis said, then asked if the Beatles would be making a film in Hollywood. Paul said that they'd continue to make their films in England.

Elvis Presley, the greatest rock 'n' roll singer of all, was to entertain the Beatles at his Hollywood home. (MGM)

Elvis said, 'Tell the other Beatles that I think they're doing a great job' and the two of them then discussed records. Elvis remarked that he liked the cover of the *With The Beatles* album, with their faces in half light, and said it reminded him of the faces in the British movie *Children Of The Damned*. The conversation ended with them agreeing that they'd try to get together as soon as possible.

That event happened on a sunny evening in California, on Friday, 27 August 1965.

Chris Hutchins was once again the mediator and the Beatles arrived at Elvis's home on 565 Perugia Way, Bel Air, at 10.00 p.m. from nearby 2850 **Benedict Canyon**, where they were staying. Elvis met them at the door and he was dressed in a red shirt and grey trousers. After greeting them, he took them into the living-room where there were members of his 'Memphis Mafia'. The Beatles were accompanied by Brian Epstein, **Neil Aspinall**, **Mal Evans** and **Tony Barrow**.

The main room was large and circular and Priscilla Presley was also there. Initially there was a degree of nervousness and, to break the ice, Elvis said, 'Look, guys, if you're just going to sit and stare at me, then I'm going to bed.' Everyone laughed. George squatted on the floor, Ringo began to look through Elvis's record collection and Brian and the Colonel began to chat.

Elvis suggested that they sing and play together and three guitars were brought over, including an electric bass, and plugged into amplifiers. John played rhythm and Elvis was on bass. 'Now here's how I play bass,' he told Paul. 'Not too good, but I'm practising!' Paul played piano and George played third guitar. Elvis turned to Ringo and said, 'Too bad we left the drums in Memphis.'

Paul said, 'Elvis, lad, you're coming along quite well there on the old bass. Keep up the rehearsals and me and Mr Epstein will make you a star.'

While they were playing 'You're My World', John said, 'This beats talking, doesn't it?'

The jam session lasted for an hour, during which Elvis drank 7-Up and the Beatles drank scotch and coke. Elvis didn't smoke.

John knew that Elvis liked **Peter Sellers**, so he imitated his voice, saying, 'Zis is ze way it should be; ze small homey gathering wiz a few friends and a leetle music.'

Paul was later to say that their jam session was captured on Elvis's tape machine, but George denied that there was ever a recording.

In the meantime Parker had escorted Epstein into the games room and unveiled a roulette table which had been disguised as a coffee table. The two gamblers began to play. Epstein asked the Colonel if Elvis would be touring in the future and Parker told him, 'We'd love to hit the ad, but we have to think of giving the maximum joyment to the maximum fans and the best way to do this by making films, which can be seen by millions.'

Elvis and the Beatles began to discuss various topics, cluding songwriting, films, tours and records.

John said, 'When the fans went for you, you were up ere all alone. With us, it's four against everybody and we n draw support from each other.'

When they were discussing life on the road, Elvis said, remember once in Vancouver. We'd only done a number two when some of the fans rushed the stage. It was lucky e guys and I got off in time. They tipped the whole damn strum over.'

He also told them, 'I once took off from Atlanta, orgia, in a small two-engined plane and one of the gines failed. Boy, was I scared! I really thought that my mber was up. We had to take everything out of our ckets that was sharp and rest our heads on pillows tween our knees. When we finally got down safely the ot was soaking in sweat, although there was snow on the ound outside.'

George then told him how the Beatles had been flying t from Liverpool when a window on the plane suddenly ung open.

Another topic was cars, with Elvis and John talking out their recently acquired Rolls-Royce Phantom Vs.

The meeting lasted for three hours and the Beatles left 2.00 a.m. As they departed, John said, 'Tanks for de sic, Elvis. Long live ze King.' Parker had given each of m a boxful of Elvis records. Epstein promised to send ker a Shetland pony and Parker said he'd give Brian a ktail cabinet. The Beatles invited Elvis to join them the owing evening at Benedict Canyon, but he didn't make - although some members of his entourage did.

Commenting on the meeting, Ringo said, 'Fantastic. He s just like one of us, none of the old Hollywood show-off ng.'

The Beatles as a group never met Elvis again. On the ath of Epstein, Elvis sent a message to the Beatles pressing: 'Deepest condolences on the loss of a good nd to you and all of us'. George managed to visit Elvis kstage at Madison Square Garden in June 1972 and ngo visited Elvis backstage at one of his Las Vegas ws.

Elvis was to record several Beatles compositions, luding 'Hey Jude', 'Yesterday' and 'Something'.

● Preston, Billy

Born in Houston, Texas, on 9 September 1946, Billy Preston began to carve a reputation for himself as a support musician in America. The Gospel-Rock keyboards player first met the Beatles in Hamburg's **Star Club** in 1962 when he was a member of **Little Richard**'s backing band. He was fifteen at the time and was befriended by George Harrison. He was also to back Sam Cooke and later became resident keyboards player on the '**Shindig**' TV show.

It was while he was touring Britain with Ray Charles that he met up with George again, who introduced him to the other members of the Beatles and they bought his contract from **Vee Jay Records** and signed him to Apple.

He also became the first musician to be credited on a Beatles record when he performed on the 'Get Back' single, which was released with the credit 'The Beatles with Billy Preston'. At one time, because he was doing so much recording work alongside the Beatles, he was dubbed '**The Fifth Beatle**'. It was said that the introduction of Preston at the sessions helped to soothe the tension between members of the group that had slowly been building up. Other Beatle tracks he performed on were: 'Let It Be', 'I. Me. Mine', 'I've Got A Feelin'', 'Dig A Pony', and 'One After 909'.

During his three years with Apple, Billy made two albums, *That's The Way God Planned It* and *Encouraging Words*, both co-produced by George. George also performed on Preston's later albums *I Wrote A Simple Song* and *It's My Pleasure*. During the sessions, George invited a number of friends to come to the studio, including **Klaus Voormann**, Keith Richard, Ginger Baker and **Eric Clapton**. Madeline Bell and **Doris Troy** also provided vocal backing on some tracks on Billy's first Apple album.

Among his Apple releases was a version of 'My Sweet Lord', the George Harrison number which he co-produced with George. It was issued in Britain on 4 September 1970 on Apple 29 and in the States on 3 December on Apple 1826.

The relationship with George continued and Preston performed on *The Concert For Bangla Desh* and on George's 1974 Dark Horse tour, in addition to the albums *All Things Must Pass, Extra Texture, Dark Horse* and *33 1/3*. He also appeared on John's *Sometime In New York City* album and on Ringo's *Ringo* and *Goodnight Vienna*.

Billy Preston, as he appeared in the film *Sgt Pepper's Lonely Hearts Club Band*. (Cinema International Corp)

He played piano on the 'God' track on the *John Lennon/Plastic Ono Band* album. Preston was also to feature in **Robert Stigwood**'s 1978 film, *Sgt Pepper's Lonely Hearts Club Band.*

● Prince Of Wales Theatre, *Coventry Street, London W1*

Site of the 1963 'Royal Variety Performance' in aid of the Entertainment Artistes' Benevolent Fund. The first royal show was held in 1912 and attended by King George V who said that he would attend such a variety show once a year provided the profits went to the fund. **Bernard Delfont** became involved in 1958.

The 1963 show took place on 4 November and was attended by Her Majesty Queen Elizabeth The Queen Mother, Princess Margaret and Lord Snowdon.

With the appearance of Britain's pop phenomenon, huge crowds of teenagers were anticipated and 500 policemen were in attendance to control the crowds.

The Beatles were seventh on a nineteen-act bill which comprised: the Billy Petch Dancers, the Clark Brothers, Max Bygraves, Luis Alberto Del Parana and Los Paraguayos, Susan Maughan, the Beatles, Dickie Henderson, Francis Brunn, Buddy Greco, Nadia Nerina and members of the cast from *Sleeping Beauty*, Joe Loss & His Orchestra with Rose Brennan, Ross McManus and Larry Gretton, 'Steptoe & Son' – **Wilfred Brambell** and Harry H. Corbett, Pinky & Perky and Company – Jan and Vlasta Dalibor, Eric Sykes and Hattie Jacques, Michael Flanders and Donald Swann, **Marlene Dietrich** with Bu Bacharach at the piano, Tommy Steele and members of th *Half a Sixpence* company, Harry Secombe and th *Pickwick* company.

The Beatles were to perform four numbers: 'She Lov You', 'Till There Was You', 'From Me To You' and 'Twi And Shout'.

Backstage, John Lennon was apprehensive about t reaction they'd receive from the audience and said that they were undemonstrative, 'I'll just tell them to ratt their fuckin' jewellery.'

They needn't have worried, the audience was ful behind them from the moment they walked on and Pa asked, 'How are yer – all right?' Between numbers cracked a joke about Sophie Tucker being their favouri group and when John announced their final number, 'Tw And Shout', he said, 'Will people in the cheaper seats cl your hands? All the rest of you, if you'll just rattle yo jewellery.'

This appearance was a major turning point in th career. The front-page headlines in the newspapers t next morning were ecstatic, with headlines such 'Beatles Rock Royals'. But the most significant headli was the one splashed across the cover of the *Daily Mirr* the biggest national of them all, with 6,000,000 readers **'Beatlemania!'** In a lengthy report it said: 'H refreshing to see these rumbustious young Beatles take middle-aged Royal Variety performance by the scruff their necks and have them Beatling like teenagers.'

'Beatlemania' had arrived! and was confirmed when show was televised to the nation on the ATV network on November 1963.

The group returned to the theatre on 31 May 1964. T occasion was a series of seven Sunday night pop conce promoted by Brian Epstein which he called 'Pops Aliv The Beatles were the fifth in the series and there were support acts: **Kenny Lynch**, **Cliff Bennett & the Re Rousers**, the **Vernons Girls**, the Lorne Gibson Trio, **Chants** and the Harlems.

The Beatles performed 'Can't Buy Me Love', 'All Loving', 'This Boy', 'Roll Over Beethoven', 'Till Th Was You', 'Twist And Shout' and 'Long Tall Sally'.

● Princess Theatre, *Kowloon, Hong Kon*

The Beatles performed two shows at this theatre on 9 J 1964, as part of their world tour. Ringo Starr was ill at me and drummer **Jimmy Nicol** was deputizing.

The group and their party flew into Kai Tak Airport, Hong Kong, where over 1,000 fans had gathered. They were taken to the President Hotel, Kowloon, where they were booked into the fifteenth floor. Paul McCartney and Neil **Aspinall** immediately put in an order for suits to be made for them within 24 hours – something which Hong Kong had been noted for.

The group were asked to judge a Miss Hong Kong pageant at the hotel, but were too tired to attend. There was some agitation as it was expected that the Beatles would be there. In order to smooth matters over, John Lennon turned up and the audience were happy.

When they heard that the promoters of the concerts at the 1,700-seater Princess Theatre had put a price of 75 Hong Kong dollars per seat on the tickets, they were highly critical of the huge charge, which amounted to the average weekly wage in the colony at the time.

There were 200 policemen outside the theatre to control the crowds, although the actual shows weren't fully booked due to the extravagant ticket prices.

The local newspaper *Sing Pao* didn't think too highly of the Beatles' performance and printed a review which commented: 'The incessant shrieking of fans was mental torture to those in the audience who came to appreciate music.' However, the other newspapers seemed more appreciative and the *Tin Tin Yat Po* said that 'Youth and its rhapsody had shaken Hong Kong'.

The *Hong Kong Standard* devoted the entire front page to the event, headlining: 'The Big Battle Of The Beatles'. The report contrasted the two shows at the theatre, the first before a mainly teenage audience who kept up such a wall of noise that the group couldn't be heard, and the more adult audience for the second concert who were actually able to hear the group perform.

The *Standard* reported: 'At the 7.30 show the predominantly teenage audience shrieked, screamed, applauded, stomped, cheered all through the 25 minutes of the Beatles' appearance.

'Despite the perfect sound system in the theatre – turned on full – the Beatles were singing a losing battle against the enthusiasm of the kids.

'At that show not a single number could be heard through. The Beatles were game though, and didn't appear to be disturbed by the din. They kept the show going and did their very best to out-shout the audience. But it was bigger than they.

'As the curtains drew closed on the last number, there was a dash by a vanguard of teenagers direct at the stage. But a flank of policemen blocked the way of the invading kids.'

The Beatles had originally planned to return to their hotel between shows to change and have a short rest, but they were advised by the police to remain in their dressing-room because of security problems.

The group performed ten numbers in each of their 25-minute appearances.

● *Princes Theatre, Torbay Road, Torquay, Devon*

The Beatles made a single appearance at this venue in the extreme south of England on 18 August 1963.

● *Pritchard, Jill*

One of the **Apple Scruffs**, the group of fans who waited patiently outside the Apple offices and various recording studios almost on a 24-hour basis. They even published their own journal called *Apple Scruffs*, which the Beatles read.

Jill was a hairdresser in Redditch who decided to nip down to London in March 1969 because she heard on the radio that Paul and **Linda** were getting married. While watching the couple on the steps of the **Marylebone Register Office** she got to chatting to one of the Apple Scruffs and decided to join them and remain in London.

She remembers the time when George Harrison paid his own tribute to the group of them who were waiting outside the recording studio when he was cutting an album. Jill recalled, 'It was about 6. o'clock one Sunday morning and we had been waiting outside all night. I'll always remember it. George took us into No. Three Studio and said, "This is for you" and switched on the song "Apple Scruffs". We all started to cry and then he played it again. It was just so emotional.' In 1979 Jill joined **Abbey Road Studios** as a receptionist.

● *Proby, P. J.*

A Texas-born singer whose real name was James Marcus Smith. Producer Jack Good brought him over to Britain to appear on the **'Around The Beatles'** television show and his subsequent success was meteoric. He began to tour and had a major hit with 'Hold Me'. He also recorded the

Lennon & McCartney number 'That Means A Lot' which was released in America on 5 July 1965 on Liberty 55806 with 'Let The Water Run Down' as the flip. The single was issued in Britain on 17 September on Liberty 10215 with 'My Prayer' as the flip. Proby's downfall was caused by the almost hysterical reaction in the media to the fact that his trousers split on stage.

American singer P. J. Proby – he almost became a superstar in Britain. (Liberty Records)

● Promotional Films

Promotional films, or 'promos', are now a staple ingredient of most record releases and are also known as 'pop videos'.

Such marketing tools weren't readily available in the early sixties and when clips were generally used on television shows they were basically clips from pop movies or from live concert footage.

The Beatles hired **Michael Lindsay-Hogg** in 1966 to film promotional movies of their numbers 'Paperback Writer' and 'Rain' for use on programmes such as 'Top Of The Pops'. The filming sessions took place at **Abbey Road** recording studios on 19 May 1966 and a colour clip was filmed specially for use on 'The **Ed Sullivan** Show' which was transmitted on 5 June. This also included a brief introduction, with Ringo apologizing for them not being there in person. They also filmed black and white clips for British television programmes. There were two films made of 'Paperback Writer' at Abbey Road, but the second version of 'Rain' was filmed at **Chiswick House**, West London, the following day. 'Top Of The Pops' featured both films on 2 June 1966.

In 1967 the Beatles engaged **Peter Goldmann** to direct the promotional films for 'Strawberry Fields Forever' and 'Penny Lane'. 'Strawberry Fields' was filmed at Sevenoaks, Kent, on Monday, 30 January, when night-tim sequences were shot. The following day they returned Sevenoaks to complete the daytime sequences. There we two different locations for 'Penny Lane'. A unit filme location shots in Liverpool of Penny Lane, the bus shelt and the barber's shop. The Beatles were filmed ridin horses in Stratford, East London, on 5 February and som of the additional scenes were shot in Angel Lane i Stratford. They returned to Sevenoaks on 7 February an filmed the sequences at the dinner table and with the larg tree. The tree remained standing throughout the seventi and displayed a plaque relating to its use in the film. T tree has since been cut down. The clips were aired America on ABC TV's 'Hollywood Palace' on 25 Februar on **'American Bandstand'** on 11 March, on Dick Clark 'Where The Action Is' on 14 March and an edited versi of 'Strawberry Fields Forever' was used on **'The Best O Record' Grammy Awards** special on 24 March.

Later in 1967 the Beatles had planned to make a fil surrounding the production of their *Sgt Pepper* album. Th didn't come about, although the 'A Day In The Lif sequence was filmed in which there was a par atmosphere with a number of celebrated friends and orchestra whose members wore funny noses and carniv masks. The film was banned by the BBC and never us as a promotional film, although it was shown in the speci *The Beatles At Abbey Road* exhibition in 1983.

The other promotional film of 1967 prov controversial. Paul directed the promo for 'Hell Goodbye' with the Beatles performing the number on sta at the **Saville Theatre**, London. There were three cli made on 10 November, one in which they are dressed Sgt Pepper uniforms, the other in casual clothes and t third which was made up of out-takes of the other tw **Neil Aspinall** flew to New York with copies for a numb of American shows, including the 'Ed Sullivan Show', b the clip didn't fare well in Britain. The Musicians' Uni still had their ban which prevented musicians miming their records. As a result, the BBC decided not to use t clip on 'Top Of The Pops' on 21 November as plann They attempted to make another clip themselves filming the Beatles editing *Magical Mystery Tour*, but t didn't work out. The BBC also dropped plans to screen o of the Saville Theatre clips of 'Hello, Goodbye' in colo on 'Late Night Line-Up' on 23 November.

The next Beatles promos were actually taken fr

avid Frost's London Weekend Television programme 'rost on Sunday', broadcast on 8 September 1968. They ere promotional films for 'Hey Jude' and 'Revolution' nd were filmed on 4 September at **Twickenham Film tudios**. David Frost was present at the filming as he ppeared in an introduction to 'Hey Jude' for use on his rogramme. At the same time, a video was made of the erformances for use on **'The Smothers Brothers omedy Hour'** in America. The 'Hey Jude' segment was ansmitted on the 'Smothers Brothers' show on 6 October nd the 'Revolution' clip on 13 October.

1969 was the final year in which the Beatles made omotional films, two for 'The Ballad Of John And Yoko' nd one for 'Something'. In March 1970 when the 'Let It e' single was issued, a promo was compiled from out-kes of the Twickenham Film Studios sessions.

There are, of course, many clips of the Beatles erforming various songs, including 'Help', 'I Feel Fine', ay Tripper', 'We Can Work It Out' and 'Ticket To Ride', ut these have come from clips of television appearances nd weren't specially made as promotional films.

Pseudonyms

e first time the Beatles used pseudonyms was in 1960 en, known as the Silver Beetles, they embarked on a ort tour of Scotland. Paul called himself **Paul Ramon**, cause he felt the name sounded exotic and romantic; orge called himself Carl Harrison in deference to **Carl rkins** and **Stuart Sutcliffe** adopted the name Stu De ijl, after the painter. Many years later some books ported that John called himself **Johnny Silver**, but he nied this, stating that he kept his own name for the tour, act which is backed by a press clipping of the time.

Incidentally, Paul was to use the name Paul Ramon ain many years later. On 3 February 1969 he dropped in see the Steve Miller Band who were recording 'My Dark ur' in a London studio – and he contributed to the track der the name Paul Ramon.

The Beatles rarely found the use of pseudonyms cessary during the sixties, although there were one or o examples, such as the time Paul called himself rnard Webb when he penned a number for **Peter & rdon**, but the aliases appeared later in their careers en they were recording or guesting on other artists' ords and when John began travelling.

John, in particular, loved pseudonyms, which is not surprising from the author of *In His Own Write*, which indicates a love of ridiculous names. Here are some of the pseudonyms used by the members of the Beatles.

JOHN LENNON Mel Torment, used when he recorded the number 'Scared'; John O'Cean, used when he appeared on **Yoko Ono**'s *'Feeling The Space* album – the moniker is obviously inspired by the Japanese meaning of Yoko's name 'Ocean Child'; Dr Winston O' Boogie, used on the *Mind Games* album – Winston was his real middle name and he used it on several pseudonyms; Mr Winston O'Reggae, used on his number 'Steel And Glass'; Dr Winston & Booker Table & The Maitre D's, used on his 'Beef Jerky' single, was obviously a pun inspired by Booker T & The MG's; Reverend Thumbs Ghurkin, used on his 'Old Dirt Road' song; Reverend Fred Ghurkin, one of the pseudonyms on the *Walls & Bridges* album, was also used when John travelled with Yoko and they booked into some hotels as the Reverend Fred and Ada Ghurkin; John Green, one of the pseudonyms John used when travelling.

PAUL MCCARTNEY Bernard Webb was the name he used when he penned the number 'Woman' for Peter & Gordon, as he was interested in seeing how well a number of his would be received without using the magic McCartney name – for the same number he also used the alias A. Smith. Apollo C. Vermouth was used when producing 'I'm An Urban Spaceman' for the **Bonzo Dog Doo Dah** Band. Apollo is obviously linked with Spaceman because of the American Apollo missions.

RINGO STARR Ringo, like Paul, was a person who used pseudonyms sparingly. The few he did use were not so far removed from his own name. R. S. were the initials he used for his appearance on David Hentschel's *Startling Music* album; Ritchie, used for his contribution to Stephen Stills' *Stills* album; Richie, the first name by which he is known to friends, this time without the 't', used on *The London Howling Wolf Sessions* album; Richie Snare, another thinly disguised alias, using his first name allied to 'snare', referring to drums, was used on the *Son Of Schmilsson* album; English Ritchie, another alias used on the *Stills* album; Ognir Rats, simply the name Ringo Starr (one 'r' missing) spelled in reverse, used in his 1978 TV show 'Ringo', which adapted the Mark Twain classic *The Prince and the Pauper* to a contemporary setting in which there are two identical men, one called Ringo Starr, the other Ognir Rats, who swop places.

GEORGE HARRISON Next to John, George seemed to enjoy hiding under an alias, although his pseudonyms were nowhere near as colourful as John's. Son Of Harry, used for his musical contribution to Dave Mason's album *It's Like You Never Left*; P. Roducer, used on the album *Splinter*, the group he produced; Hari Georgeson, used for his guest appearance on **Billy Preston**'s *It's My Pleasure* album; The George O'Hara-Smith Singers, used when his voice was overdubbed to produce the effect of several voices on his *All Things Must Pass* album; Jai Raj Harisein, was another of the pseudonyms on the *Splinter* album – a name with a touch of Eastern promise; George Harrysong was the alias he used for his appearance on the *Son Of Schmilsson* album and was similar to that of his early music publishing company, Harrisongs Ltd; George O'Hara-Smith, the Irish-sounding hyphenated name, appears once again – on Ashton, Gardner & Dyke's *I'm Your Spiritual Breadman* album (the group had evolved from Liverpool band the **Remo Four** and George had promised to return the compliment when the Remo Four recorded for him on the *Wonderwall* soundtrack); George O'Hara was a name he used thrice, as an alias on two of Garry Wright's albums, *Footprint* and *That Was Only Yesterday*, and also on the Nicky Hopkins LP *The Tin Man Was A Dreamer*; L'Angelo Mysterioso, used on Cream's 'Badge' single. This was a song he co-wrote with **Eric Clapton.** He also used the name on Jack Bruce's album *Songs For A Tailor*.

● P.S. I Love You

A number mainly written by Paul, with some help from John. The group originally recorded it as one of the tracks on their Parlophone recording audition on Wednesday, 6 June 1962, when **Pete Best** was a member of the band.

The Beatles next recorded it on Tuesday, 11 September, when Ringo was a member of the group. Ron Richards produced this session and he wasn't happy with the drumming on the original 'Love Me Do', so he hired drummer **Andy White** for the session. Ringo was in attendance but didn't play drums that evening. He sat quietly in the control box next to Richards and Richards asked him to play maracas on the 'P.S. I Love You' track.

The number was issued as the flipside of their British debut single 'Love Me Do' and was also included on th *Please Please Me* album and the *All My Loving* EP. Som years later it was selected for the *Love Songs* compilatio On the twentieth anniversary of its release Parlophor issued it as a picture disc and a month later it was als issued on a twelve-inch disc.

In America **Vee Jay** included it on the *Introducing Th Beatles* album. It was also issued on a single by Tollie ar was re-released on Vee Jay's 'Oldies' series later in 196 and on **Capitol**'s 'Starline' series in 1965 – in all cases the flipside of 'Love Me Do'. When the rights to the Ve Jay tracks were obtained by Capitol, they included 'P.S. Love You' on their *The Early Beatles* album.

● Public Auditorium, Cleveland, Ohio

The concert at this 12,000-seater venue took place on September 1964 and was promoted by the local rad station WHK. Tickets weren't on sale generally. There ha been so many ticket requests that the station decided computerize them and the machine then picked out t lucky 12,000 who had sent in postcards and would permitted to buy tickets, which cost an average of $3.50.

Acts on the bill included **Jackie DeShannon** and t **Bill Black Combo**. Following DeShannon's act, the D from WHK came on stage carrying boxes, to present t Beatles with gum chains which fans had sent to the stati as presents for the group.

During the show, fans began to rush towards the stag The Chief of Police went on stage and told the Beatles stop playing. They obviously didn't quite understand h and continued playing 'All My Loving' until the poli chief pushed George away from his mike.

The show stopped for almost ten minutes as the poli chief told the audience that if just one person stood up would stop the show for good.

● Public Ear, The

A BBC radio programme. The Beatles recorded interview for the show in between filming *A Hard Da Night* at **Twickenham Film Studios** on 18 March 196 The interview was transmitted on 22 March.

● Public Hall, Preston, Lancashire

The Beatles made their debut here on the evening of October 1962 and appeared at the venue for the seco and last time on 13 September 1963.

Quarry Bank High School, Harthill Road, Liverpool L18

Grammar School, founded in 1922. Its first headmaster was named George Harrison. Old boys from the school have included Labour Government Ministers William Rodgers and Peter Shore.

The school uniform was a black blazer with a red and gold stag's head badge which sported the motto *Ex Hoc Metallo Virtuten* which, translated, means 'From This Rough Metal We Forge Virtue'.

John Lennon became a pupil at the school in September 1952 and the twelve-year-old boy would cycle there each morning from his Menlove Avenue home one mile away, on his green Raleigh Lenton bicycle.

The school headmaster was E. R. Taylor, who found he had a couple of troublemakers on his hands in the form of Lennon and his mate **Pete Shotton**. The two were very disruptive, were always causing trouble at the school, were often disciplined by caning and were continually punished with detention. Academically, they were uninterested in studying and were both placed at the bottom of the 'C' stream where they remained for most of their school life. When John took his GCE 'O'-level examinations, he failed every subject.

In 1956 a new headmaster arrived at the school, the -year-old **William Ernest Pobjoy**. He was less of a disciplinarian than his predecessor and John was pleased and surprised when Pobjoy not only allowed the **Quarry Men** to play at the school (they performed at a Sixth Form dance in July 1957), but encouraged him in his interest in skiffle music. Pobjoy also spotted John's potential as an artist, contacted his Aunt **Mimi** and arranged for him to attend **Liverpool College of Art** when he left Quarry Bank School at the end of July 1957.

● Quarry Men, The

The skiffle group formed by John Lennon in March 1957, soon after his Aunt **Mimi** had bought him a guitar for £17. His friend and classmate **Pete Shotton** was engaged to play washboard and another Quarry Bank School classmate, Bill Smith, was brought in on tea chest bass. Smith was only with the group for a matter of weeks and the honours on tea chest bass until the middle of 1958 were shared between **Ivan Vaughan**, **Nigel Whalley** and **Len Garry**.

For one week John called the group the Black Jacks and then decided on the Quarry Men because of a line from the school song which read 'Quarry Men, old before our birth'. The other members were **Rod Davis** on banjo, **Eric Griffiths** on guitar and **Colin Hanton** on drums. Their initial repertoire comprised mainly popular skiffle

Quarry Bank school, where pupil John Lennon formed his first group, the Quarry Men.

hits of the time such as 'Lost John', 'Railroad Bill', 'Cumberland Gap', 'Freight Train', 'Midnight Special', 'No Other Baby', 'Rock Island Line', 'Worried Man Blues' and the Liverpool sea shanty 'Maggie May'.

The group appeared at various parties and entered several of the numerous skiffle group contests locally and a few months after their formation they took part in an afternoon audition at the **Empire Theatre** for the Carroll Levis Discovery competition, on 9 June, without success. Historically interesting 1957 gigs by the group included their appearance at the party in Roseberry Street on 22 June; their appearance at the Woolton Village Fête on 6 July, where John and Paul met for the first time; their **Cavern** debut on 7 August, sans Paul McCartney, where they were chided for performing rock 'n' roll numbers such as 'Hound Dog' and 'Blue Suede Shoes'; and their gig at the **New Clubmoor Hall** on 18 October where Paul unsuccessfully attempted to take over on lead guitar.

As was apparent from their Cavern engagement, John was increasingly interested in performing rock 'n' roll and moving away from skiffle music, which displeased music purist Rod Davis with the result that he left the group by February 1958. Rock numbers included in the early Quarry Men repertoire included 'All Shook Up', 'Be-Bop-A-Lula', 'Blue Moon Of Kentucky', 'Bony Moronie', 'Lawdy Miss Clawdy', 'Lend Me Your Comb', 'Mailman Blues', 'Mean Woman Blues', 'Roll Over Beethoven', 'Searchin'', 'Short Fat Fanny', 'Sure To Fall (In Love With You)', 'That's All Right, Mama' and 'Twenty Flight Rock'.

During the first two years of the group's existence, their repertoire developed. Paul's influence in the group brought in the **Little Richard** numbers 'Long Tall Sally' and 'Lucille', but one of their major influences was **Buddy Holly** and they performed several of his hits, including 'It's So Easy', 'Maybe Baby', 'Peggy Sue', 'That'll Be The Day', 'Think It Over' and 'Words Of Love'. John and Paul had also begun to write songs, individually and together, which were performed by the group and included 'Hello Little Girl', 'I Lost My Little Girl', 'Just Fun', 'Keep Looking That Way', 'Like Dreamers Do', 'Love Of The Loved', 'The One After 909', 'That's My Woman', 'Thinking Of Linking', 'Too Bad About Sorrow' and 'Years Roll By'. By February 1958, George Harrison was a member of the group and the songs he sang included 'Youngblood', 'Your True Love' and 'Three Cool Cats'. He also co-penned a number with Paul, 'In Spite Of All The Danger'. The group also performed some instrumentals including 'Guitar Boogie', 'Ramrod', 'Raunchy', the McCartney compositions 'Catswalk' and 'Hot As Sun' John's 'Winston's Walk' and the Lennon & McCartne instrumental 'Looking Glass'.

During 1958 the group made a recording at a smal studio in the Kensington area of Liverpool of the Budd Holly number 'That'll Be The Day' and the McCartney Harrison song 'In Spite Of All The Danger'.

In August 1959 they began a residency at the **Casbah Club** in the West Derby district of Liverpool, when th Quarry Men had pruned the line-up down to four: John Paul, George and **Ken Brown** on guitar/vocals. Th Casbah residency no doubt prevented the group fror disbanding. John and Paul had dispensed with the service of Eric Griffiths during 1958 and Len Garry had le around the same time. Colin Hanton became disenchante after an engagement arranged by George Harrison's fathe in which the band performed badly before a potenti booker – and he unceremoniously left. Pianist **John Low** also left in January 1959 and the group were in limbo f several months until the Casbah engagement came u George Harrison had, in the meantime, joined anothe band, the Les Stewart Quartet, between January an August 1959.

Following the Casbah series of engagements they we involved in the Carroll Levis auditions at the Empi Theatre, Liverpool, in October, which resulted in the appearance at the Hippodrome, Manchester, on 1 November. By this time Ken Brown had left over a dispu which occurred at the Casbah Club when he couldn appear one evening, but was paid for the gig, much to th anger of John, Paul and George. By this time they we already experimenting with new names and, as a tri called themselves Johnny & the Moondogs betwee October 1959 and January 1960. From January 1960 un April 1960 they called themselves the Beatals and h become a quartet, with the inclusion of **Stuart Sutclif** on bass. Between May and June they called themselves t Silver Beats and the Silver Beetles and had become quintet with the inclusion of **Tommy Moore** on drum Between June and July they became a quartet again, sa Moore, calling themselves the Silver Beatles and h **Norman Chapman** perform on drums for a couple gigs. In August 1960, when Pete Best was asked to jo them, they changed their name to the Beatles.

Queen Charlotte's Maternity Hospital, oldhawk Road, London W6

aureen Starkey was admitted to the hospital for the :th of her first child. **Zak** was born on 13 September 65. Two years later Maureen moved into the hospital ain, to Ward D in the west wing on the fourth floor. Her :ond son **Jason** was born at 3.35 p.m. on Saturday, 19 gust 1967, and weighed 8lbs 5½ozs. As Ringo had osen the name Zak, Maureen was in line for the choice a new name and suggested Jason.

Maureen returned to the hospital for a third time for the th of her daughter **Lee** on 17 November 1970.

Yoko Ono was admitted to the hospital in November 68. John insisted on being near her and slept in her m throughout the time she was there. Unfortunately, suffered a miscarriage on 21 November. The picture of n and Yoko together in the hospital was displayed on cover of their album *Unfinished Music No. 2: Life With Lions*.

197 Queen's Drive, Childwall, verpool 18

5-bedroom house which was the family home of the stein family for thirty years. Brian Epstein lived here h his mother and father and brother **Clive**. They had a ne-help and a live-in nanny. Soon after Brian signed Beatles, John became a regular visitor. The two of m would discuss plans in the morning room. A cocktail ty in Paul McCartney's honour was held at the house on June 1963 to celebrate Paul's 21st birthday. When the steins moved in the late sixties it became the home of Dean of Liverpool.

Queens Hall, Sovereign Street, Leeds, rkshire

arge venue which contained a capacity audience of 00 people on 28 June 1963 when the Beatles appeared a bill with **Acker Bilk** and his Paramount Jazz Band.

Queens Hall, The, Victoria Road, dnes, Cheshire

an Epstein, to enhance the local popularity of his ds, began to promote them on some of the larger ues in the Merseyside area. **NEMS Enterprises** ran a ng of promotions at the Queens Hall in Widnes, twelve es outside Liverpool.

The Beatles made their debut at the venue in a series of three Monday night gigs in 1962. On 3 and 10 September they were supported by **Rory Storm & the Hurricanes**, the group whose drummer they'd taken the previous month. They completed their trilogy of bookings on 16 September.

On 22 October 1962 they were back at the Queens Hall, this time with **Lee Curtis** & the All Stars on the bill. The All Stars had their new drummer **Pete Best** with them, but the Beatles never spoke to him.

Their final appearance at the venue, also promoted by NEMS Enterprises, was for two sell-out concerts on the evening of 18 February 1963.

● Queen's Hotel, The Promenade, Southport, Lancashire

A jazz club was situated on the ground floor of this hotel in the seaside resort close to Liverpool. It was called Club Django (after jazz violinist Django Reinhart) and mainly featured jazz bands. However, due to the increasing success of the Beatles locally, the organizers decided to book the Beatles and the group appeared at the club on 6 December 1962.

● Queens Theatre, Bank Hey Street, Blackpool, Lancashire

The Beatles only appeared at this venue twice – with only a few weeks between each of the bookings. They made their debut there on 21 July 1963 and their final appearance took place on 4 August 1963. On their second visit there were so many fans outside the theatre that the group had to gain access by climbing over the roof of the building and crawling through a trapdoor.

● Quickly, Tommy

Young Liverpool singer whom Brian Epstein attempted to turn into a star. Epstein first noticed the seventeen-year-old vocalist, when he performed with his group the Challengers, opening the show for the Beatles at the **Queens Hall, Widnes**. He was then called Tommy Quigley, lived in the West Derby area of Liverpool and was a telephone fitter by day.

Tommy Quickly – on stage at the Cavern.

Several months later Epstein decided to sign him up, got rid of his backing group and replaced them with the **Remo Four**. He changed his name to Quickly and he was signed to **Decca**, with Ray Horricks as his recording manager. Tommy was given 'No Reply' to record as it was believed that the number was hit song material. John and Paul attended the recording session, but Tommy couldn't sing it in key and after seventeen takes the session was abandoned.

Tommy made his recording debut on 30 July 1963 with another Lennon & McCartney composition, written by Paul, called 'Tip Of My Tongue', on Piccadilly 7N 35137. His major stage debut took place on 22 July 1963 when he appeared with the Beatles and **Gerry & the Pacemakers** for a week at the Odeon, Weston-super-Mare.

Epstein spent $30,000 on an American promotior tour for Quickly and in Britain placed him on three Bea tours, two **Billy J. Kramer** tours and a Gerry & t Pacemakers tour, but despite the vast amount of mon spent, the exposure on stage and the record play, he nev quite made it. When he appeared on the *Beatles Christm Show* in 1963 he performed 'Winter Wonderland' a 'Kiss Me Now'.

In February 1966 he left **NEMS Enterprises** to si with the George Cooper Organization, but was never find success.

In his 1984 autobiography, *Fifty Years Adrift*, **Der Taylor** wrote: 'It is painful to write about Tommy Quicl at this late stage, since I only heard this week that he di about fifteen years ago, one of the earliest victims of her among the sixties crowd of hopefuls.' Thankfully, De was wrong, Quickly still lived on Merseyside, although had suffered drug problems and was no longer a perform

● Quorum Restaurant, Denver, Colorado

Restaurant where **Jane Asher** held a special party o April 1967, to celebrate her 21st birthday. She was tour America at the time with the Old Vic Company a members of the cast were among the guests invited to party. Jane's extra-special guest was Paul McCart who'd flown over from England specially for the event.

Paul, accompanied by **Mal Evans**, arrived at Den Airport that Wednesday morning in a Lear Jet lent to th by Frank Sinatra and they were met by Bert Rosentl who lent Paul his house during his stay. Mal booked i the Driftwood Motel.

Rosenthal picked up Paul and Jane and took then the restaurant, within a hotel, where crowds of peo hovered outside. There were also a number of journal and photographers and among those who managed to into the party were writer Vic Davies and photograp Harry Benson of the *Daily Express* New York office.

The following day Mal drove Paul and Jane into Rockies. On Friday, 7 April, they attended an open Greek Theatre performance and on the Saturday, as J was appearing in both a matinee and evening performa Mal and Paul went exploring the local countrysi dropping into Paul's Cafe and having a drink in a called the Gilded Garter. The Old Vic Tour flew out on Sunday and Paul and Mal flew back to Los Angeles.

Radha Krsna Temple

e Radha Krsna Temple was founded in London in 1966 his Divine Grace A. C Bhakjtivedanta Swami abhupada. The Swami had originally travelled from lia to New York in September 1965 to bring the maha-ntra to the West; he was 70 years old at the time. The ntra was a repetition of Krsna's name, chanted as a m of meditation. George Harrison was to say, 'Silent ditation is rather dependent on concentration, but when chant, it's more of a direct connection with God.'

The Swami, with shaven head and distinctive robes, ived in Britain with a small following, members of om visited Apple and met up with George Harrison, who anged for them to meet the Beatles at **Kinfauns**. They had a vegetarian meal and after chanting began to talk, h John and George asking most of the questions. George n arranged for Apple to lease a building for them in ry Place, Holborn. However, there were complaints n local residents about the renovation work, which was n suspended while an independent inquiry took place. he meantime, John Lennon invited them to move into a servatory at Tittenhurst Park on a temporary basis.

In September 1969 his Divine Grace, author of over 80 ks on Vedic philosophy, moved into the annexe at enhurst Park with his followers, where he was to hold a eting with George and John. As problems with Bury ce continued, George helped to finance a 17-acre perty, Pickett's Manor in Hertfordshire, which was amed Bhakjtivedanta Manor in 1972.

George was impressed by the Swami who, with his self-inflicted poverty, presented a contrast to the Maharishi's commercial and material lifestyle. He advocated training in self-purification in which his followers did not eat meat, have illicit sex, gamble, take intoxicants such as drugs, alcohol, coffee or cigarettes. Unfortunately for George, he found he couldn't become a fully fledged devotee because he liked the occasional drink and smoke.

George decided to record the devotional chant and early sessions took place at George's bungalow with George on guitar and **Billy Preston** playing a synthesizer. Then a recording session took place at **Trident Studios** in London. This was more of a studio rehearsal and the final recording was made at **EMI**'s **Abbey Road Studios**. There were a group of devotees chanting the mantra, Paul and **Linda** McCartney were operating the control console and George played organ. George was to comment, 'While the words don't alter, the tune it is sung to doesn't matter. You could sing it to "Coming Round The Mountain" if you wanted. All I've done on this is is shorten it.'

The single 'Hare Krsna Mantra' by Hare Krsna Temple was issued in America on 22 August 1969 on Apple 1810 and in Britain on 29 August on Apple 25. The record entered the British Top 20, reaching the position of No.17. This was followed by 'Govinda', which was issued in Britain on 6 March 1970 on Apple 25 and in America on 24 March on Apple 1821. The record reached No. 23 in the British charts. This was followed by an album, also produced by George, called *The Radha Krsna Temple*, which was issued in America on 21 May 1971 on Apple SKAO 3376 and in Britain on 28 May on Apple SAPCOR 18.

The first single actually enjoyed international success, particularly in the European charts, and reached No. 1 in Germany and Czechoslovakia. It also reached the Top Ten in Japan.

Swami Prabhupada died on 17 November 1977 at the age of 81. Before he died he took a gold ring from his finger, passed it to a disciple and told him, 'Please give this to George Harrison. He was a good friend to us all. He loves Krsna sincerely and I love him. He was my archangel!'

● Radio Luxembourg

A commercial radio station which transmits its programmes to the UK from the Duchy of Luxembourg on the Continent. As the only alternative to BBC radio in the late fifties and early sixties, it promoted pop music and one of its most popular programmes was the weekly Top Twenty chart programme which played the twenty leading records in each week's ***New Musical Express*** chart listings. The station's signal was stronger in the north of England and it was more popular there than in the south. It was the station which the Beatles used to listen to when they first became interested in music and it played a wider variety of records to appeal to young people than the BBC and also gave more opportunities to new artists. **Rory Storm** became the first of the Mersey Beat artists to appear on the radio when he managed to get a booking for his group the Raving Texans on Luxembourg's 'Amateur Skiffle Club' programme on 30 April 1958 with the group performing 'Midnight Special'.

Radio Luxembourg also transmitted sponsored programmes. The one sponsored by **EMI Records** was called 'The Friday Spectacular' and the Beatles recorded three shows in the series, transmitted from **EMI House** in London. When they appeared on 'Friday Spectacular', hosted by Muriel Young on 16 November 1962, they mimed on stage before an audience at EMI House to 'Love Me Do'.

Radio Luxembourg also began broadcasting a Beatles special called '**This Is Their Life**' on 10 May 1964 and transmitted a second programme in the series on 17 May 1964.

From January 1965 Radio Luxembourg began running a fifteen-minute radio series devoted to Beatles records each Sunday evening at 8.45 p.m., introduced by Chris Denning.

In 1981 Radio Luxembourg ran a poll in which listeners voted for their all-time favourite Beatles number. They were:

1. 'Hey Jude'
2. 'She Loves You'
3. 'Yesterday'
4. 'Help!'
5. 'A Hard Day's Night'
6. 'Let It Be'
7. 'Can't Buy Me Love'
8. 'I Want To Hold Your Hand'
9. 'All My Loving'
10. 'Ticket To Ride'
11. 'Love Me Do'
12. 'Eleanor Rigby'
13. 'All You Need Is Love'
14. 'I Feel Fine'
15. 'Penny Lane'
16. 'Twist And Shout'
17. 'A Day In The Life'
18. 'Get Back'
19. 'Please Please Me'
20. 'Strawberry Fields Forever'

● Raga

A film, originally to be called 'Messenger Out Of T East', which was a documentary co-produced by Geo Harrison and **Ravi Shankar** and released by Apple 1971. The 96-minute documentary was based on Shank

George and Ravi held a press conference in I Angeles to announce that the film would focus Shankar's life and philosophy, taking in a general look Indian religions and traditions. George made a br appearance in the film taking a sitar lesson from R George also introduced Yehudi Menuhin, saying, '(friend Yehudi Menuhin, one of the great violinists, jo Shankar for an informal session while youthful Geo Harrison comes to the master to learn.' The film v produced and directed by Howard Worth, wit screenplay by Nancy Bacal.

George also produced the film's soundtrack alb *Raga*, which was issued on Apple SWAO 3384 o December 1971. The tracks were: 'Dawn To Dusk', 'Ve Hymns', 'Baba Teaching', 'Birth To Death', 'Vinus Hou 'Gurur Bramha', 'United Nations', 'Raga Parameshwa 'Rangeswhart', 'Banares Ghat', 'Bombay School', 'Kinn School', 'Frenzy and Distortion', and 'Raga Desh'.

● Railroad Bill

Traditional American railroad song popularized in Bri in 1957 by **Lonnie Donegan** & his Skiffle Group included in the repertoire of virtually every skiffle grou the country, including the **Quarry Men**, who performe in 1957 with John Lennon on lead vocals.

● Rain

John Lennon composition which was used as the flipsid the 'Paperback Writer' single in June 1966. There degree of experimentation on this record in which both music and the vocals have been slowed down technic in the recording studio. There is one sentence when J ıgs, 'Rain, when the rain comes they run and hide their ads', at the end of the record which is heard in reverse. hn claimed that he inadvertently played the tapes ckwards when he was at home and liked the effect so ıch he wanted it recreated on the record. George Martin ntradicts the claim and says that it was his idea. He cided to take the line of vocal by John off the four-track d put it on another spool and experiment with playing it ckwards.

The number is also found on the *Hey Jude* album and British *Rarities* compilation.

Ramon, Paul

eudonym Paul used when the Silver Beetles toured otland as backing band to **Johnny Gentle**. Paul uldn't remember why he chose that particular surname, t he thought it was rather glamorous. So much so, that was to use it again, many years later, when he recorded track with the Steve Miller Band, 'My Dark Hour' in '69. The American punk rock band the Ramones are puted to have taken their name from this alias of Paul's.

Ramrod

strumental hit for Duane Eddy in 1958. George Harrison gan to perform this number with the **Quarry Men** when band included it in their repertoire.

Rarities (American Album)

American album issued on **Capitol** SHAL 12060 on March 1980. This is a different compilation from the itish album *Rarities* which had originally been issued as rt of *The Beatles Collection* in 1971 and as a separate oum the following year.

Capitol had already stated that the American album *rities* would not be available in their limited-edition ease of *The Beatles Collection*, but announced that they uld be releasing *Rarities* as part of their Budget Line ries. There was some initial confusion over this, related to the fact that it was a different album from the itish one of the same name.

In 1979 it was rumoured that Capitol had decided to ue an album of rare Beatles tracks, which they called *llectors' Items*. The LP was given the catalogue number RO 9462 and the track listing was, Side One: 'Love Me ' (the recording featuring Ringo on drums), 'From Me You', 'Thank You Girl', 'All My Loving' (with the hi-hat introduction), 'This Boy' (which hadn't previously been released in stereo in the US), '*Sie Liebt Dich*', 'I Feel Fine', 'She's A Woman' (which had never been released in stereo in the US), 'Help!', 'I'm Down'. Side Two: 'Penny Lane' (the promotional copy version), 'Baby You're A Rich Man' (not previously available in stereo in the States), 'I Am The Walrus', 'The Inner Light', 'Across The Universe', 'You Know My Name (Look Up The Number)'.

The rumour then claimed that a decision was made to scrap *Collectors' Items*, with Capitol ordering that all copies were to be destroyed. The story further claimed that Capitol employees smuggled copies out of the pressing plant which then became, literally, 'collectors' items'.

This story is untrue. *Collectors' Items* was a bootleg release and the bootleggers concocted this story themselves. They carefully produced a professional-style album cover, duplicating the Capitol logo and even adding the message 'For Promotional Use Only'.

The *Rarities* issued by Capitol in March 1980 is the only genuine one. Capitol had decided to compile a different selection of rare tracks for its own version of *Rarities*, aimed specifically at the American market, as the original American releases had differed from the British ones. Randall Davis compiled the tracks and also contributed the detailed sleeve notes, aided by research from Ron Furmanek and Walter Podrazik. The album reached No. 21 in the *Billboard* charts. The tracks were, Side One: 'Love Me Do', 'Misery', 'There's A Place', '*Sie Liebt Dich*', 'And I Love Her', 'Help!', 'I'm Only Sleeping', 'I Am The Walrus'. Side Two: 'Penny Lane', 'Helter Skelter', 'Don't Pass Me By', 'The Inner Light', 'Across The Universe', 'You Know My Name (Look Up The Number)'. The album ended with a two-second burst of sound from the inner groove of the British *Sgt Pepper* album, which hadn't been included on the American release. It was called 'Sgt Pepper Inner Groove'.

● Rarities (British Album)

Originally, this album was a special bonus LP included in **EMI**'s *The Beatles Collection* boxed set of the Beatles' original twelve studio albums issued with the catalogue number BC 13 on 2 December 1978. The extra album, *Rarities*, had the catalogue number PSLP 261.

EMI had announced that this special gift album would only be obtainable with *The Beatles Collection* and would not be released as an album in its own right. Various record retailers actually took the album from the set and sold it separately at the inflated price of eight pounds, which resulted in EMI making the decision to release the album as a separate entity, which they did in October 1979 on PCM 1001. The sleeve design remained the same, except for the addition of a review of the album by Hugh Fielder of the weekly music paper *Sounds*.

The album had been compiled by EMI's Mike Heatley, who worked for the company's International Division. Initially, the tracks were to be a collection of EP tracks and the flipsides of singles which hadn't been available on previous Beatles albums issued in Britain. This wasn't actually the case as eight of the seventeen tracks had been available on albums issued in Britain.

The album's original sleeve notes had claimed that nine of the seventeen tracks were in stereo, but this wasn't the case – only four of them were in stereo, this error was pointed out on the notes to the 1979 release which stated that twelve of the seventeen tracks were in mono. Heatley admitted that this had been due to a mistake on EMI's part as they'd intended to include stereo versions of 'Rain', 'Long Tall Sally', 'I Call Your Name', 'Slow Down', 'Matchbox' and 'I'm Down', but due to an error, the mono versions were used.

The album tracks were, Side One: 'Across The Universe' (this had previously been issued on the charity album *No One's Gonna Change Our World*), 'Yes It Is' (originally the flipside of 'Ticket To Ride'), 'This Boy' (the flipside of 'I Want To Hold Your Hand'), 'The Inner Light' (first time on an album for the flipside of 'Lady Madonna', although only in a mono version), 'I'll Get You' (the flipside of 'She Loves You'), 'Thank You Girl' (first time on an album for the flipside of 'From Me To You', although only a mono version), '*Komm, Gib Mir Deine Hand*' (first British release of the German version of 'I Want To Hold Your Hand'), 'You Know My Name (Look Up The Number)' (first album release for the flipside of the 'Let It Be' single), '*Sie Leibt Dich*' (first British release for the German version of 'She Loves You'). Side Two: 'Rain' (mono version of the flipside of 'Paperback Writer'), 'She's A Woman' (originally issued as a double-'A' side with 'I Feel Fine'), 'Matchbox' (mono version of the track from the *Long Tall Sally* EP), 'I Call Your Name' (another track from the *Long Tall Sally* EP), 'Bad Boy', 'Slow Down' (another track from the *Long Tall Sally* EP), 'I'm Down' (the flipside of 'Help!'), 'Long Tall Sally'.

● Raunchy

The number which helped George Harrison to become member of the **Quarry Men**. Paul McCartney was comment, 'He could really play guitar, particularly t piece called "Raunchy", which we all used to love. Y see, if anyone could do something like that it was general enough to get them in the group. Of course, I knew Geor long before any of the others as they were all from Woolt and we hung out with the Allerton set. I can tell you both learned guitar from the same book, and that desp his tender years, we were chums.'

'Raunchy' had been a massive instrumental hit America in 1957 and Bill Justis and his Orchestra took t number to No. 2 in the charts. Justis had formerly be musical director of Sun Records in the fifties and died 1982. Eric Freeman also had a hit with the number t same year and reached No. 4 in the American charts, a the third version of the song to chart that year was by Bi Vaughan & his Orchestra, who took the number to No. 1

George began performing the instrumental with t Quarry Men and continued to play it with the Beatles u 1960.

● Ready, Steady, Go!

Influential weekly music show from Rediffusion Televisi which was networked on ITV between 1963 and 196 Cathy McGowan, Keith Fordyce and Michael Aldred w hosts of the show which was produced by **Micha Lindsay-Hogg** and screened early on Friday evenings was Britain's first live TV pop show.

The group made their debut ten weeks after t programme was launched, filming from Studio 9 Kingsway, London, on 4 October 1963. The show w repeated on 8 November.

The group appeared on 20 March 1964, once ag from the Kingsway studio and during the show they w presented with an award from *Billboard* magazine. Ke Fordyce announced: '. . . You've got a special aw coming to you and *Billboard* magazine in Ameri specially asked it be presented to you on this show a this is in recognition of the fact that two or three weeks you had in the American charts numbers one, two a three in their hit parade, all Beatles records, and that's outstanding achievement and you've got the award o type that's never been given before, for that. I might ad phoned the States just half an hour ago and they told

e Beatles during a 'Ready, Steady, Go!' appearance, with Keith Fordyce and Helen Shapiro. (Rediffusion)

s week that it's one, two, three and four of your records d once more you've got another six in the Top Hundred, king ten altogether, so all I suggest is don't keep on h this or there'll be a second War of Independance.'

John and George were interviewed by Cathy McGowan m the programme's new Wembley studios on 16 April 65 for a special edition called 'Ready Steady Goes e!'

On 23 November 1964 they recorded 'I Feel Fine' and e's A Woman' for transmission on 27 November.

The programme ceased, despite its huge popularity, nply because Rediffusion lost its TV franchise and was iged to amalgamate with ABC. Michael Lindsay-Hogg s later asked to direct some Beatles projects. The most nous personality created by the programme was Cathy Gowan, known as 'the Queen of the Mods', a pretty girl h long dark hair and a notable fringe which fell down onto her eyes. She married actor Hywel Bennett, although they were later divorced. For many years she shunned publicity, running her own successful clothing business although, in the late eighties, she returned to the media as a radio reporter.

● Rebels, The

A five-piece skiffle band formed by George Harrison which comprised George, his brother **Peter** and his best friend **Arthur Kelly** on guitars and two other friends on mouth organ and tea-chest bass. The bass had 'Rebels' painted in red across its front.

Their first and only gig was an audition at the nearby British Legion Club in Dam Wood Road, Speke. The group had been rehearsing at Arthur's house in Wavertree and in one of the bedrooms at the Harrisons' house. When the offer of the audition came up they trooped across to the

Legion Hall. Horror of horrors, they discovered that the band who'd been officially booked that night had failed to turn up and they immediately had to set up on stage and play a lengthy set. They enjoyed it tremendously, were given ten shillings for their trouble, but were never to play together again.

George was to comment: 'I remember the Rebels had a tea-chest with a lot of gnomes around it. One of my brothers had a five-shilling guitar, which had the back off. Apart from that it was all fine. Just my brother, some mates and me.'

● Red Hot

A number recorded by Ronnie Hawkins in 1959. Hawkins had a backing group called the Hawks who left him and changed their name to the Band. John and **Yoko** were to stay at Hawkins' farm in Canada during a visit to that country.

The Beatles included this number in their repertoire in 1961 with John Lennon on lead vocals.

● Red Rocks Amphitheatre, *Denver, Colorado*

The Beatles performed here on Wednesday 26 August 1964. The concert arena was twenty miles outside of Denver and there was no public transport, which was said to have accounted for the fact that only 5,000 of the 7,000 seats were taken. The concert was also considered to be expensive, with tickets costing $6.60 each.

The group were late on their arrival at the airport and stayed at the Brown Palace Hotel until the show. The Beatles performed for half an hour of the two-hour show, playing numbers such as 'If I Fell', 'Can't Buy Me Love' and 'A Hard Day's Night'. There were 250 policemen and reservists placed on concert detail and the altitude was such that the Beatles kept running out of breath during their performance, which began at 9.30 p.m., and had to regularly use some canisters of oxygen which had been provided on stage for them. As at other gigs, they were pelted with jelly beans.

Other artists on the bill were the **Righteous Brothers**, the **Bill Black Combo**, **Jackie De Shannon** and the Exciters.

● Red Sails In The Sunset

The Beatles included this number in their repertoire in 1960. The number was originally penned by Jimr Kennedy and Will Grosz and was first recorded by J Turner in 1959, although he didn't have a hit with it. T Beatles probably decided to perform the number aft hearing **Emile Ford** & the Checkmates version in 196 The song later became a minor hit in Britain for Fa Domino in 1963.

As part of their repertoire, the Beatles played it at t **Star Club** and it is one of the tracks on the vario releases of the Star Club recordings.

● Reece's Restaurant, *Corner of Parker Street and Leigh Street, Liverpool L1*

The building contained a food store at ground floor level restaurant on the first floor and also a dance hall. John a **Cynthia** had their modest wedding reception here on a c and rainy day, 23 August 1963. They all rushed down fr the register office as Brian Epstein had selected Reece considering that no one would recognize the couple. T restaurant was packed with lunchtime office workers milli about and as Brian hadn't booked a table, they had to w for twenty minutes before they could sit down.

Guests included Paul McCartney and George Harris There was a set lunch with soup as a starter, followed chicken as the main course and trifle as the sweet. Bri toasted the couple with a glass of water and paid the b which amounted to fifteen shillings (75p) per head.

● Reel Music

A compilation from **Capitol Records**, co-ordinated Randall Davis, who also penned the sleeve notes w Steve Meyer. The album contained tracks from the Beat five films and came with a twelve-page booklet featur an article and photographs from the films. The artwork the sleeve was by David McMacken.

Reel Music was issued in the States on Capitol S 12199 on 22 March 1982 and in Britain on PCS 7218 29 March 1982. In America the album reached No. 19 the charts, although it did not chart in Britain.

The tracks on the album were, Side One: 'A Hard Da Night', 'I Should Have Known Better', 'Can't Buy Love', 'And I Love Her', 'Help!', 'You've Got To H Your Love Away', 'Ticket To Ride', 'Magical Myst Tour'. Side Two: 'I Am The Walrus', 'Yellow Submari 'All You Need Is Love', 'Let It Be', 'Get Back', 'The L And Winding Road'.

● Regal Ballroom, Leopold Street, Nairn, Nairnshire, Scotland

Venue of the penultimate gig of the Silver Beetles' brief tour of Scotland as a backing band to singer **Johnny Gentle**.

● Regal Cinema, St Andrews Street, Cambridge

The Beatles made their first appearance at this venue on 19 March 1963 during their tour with **Tommy Roe/Chris Montez**. They returned to the cinema for the second and last time on 26 November 1963 during their own headlining autumn tour of the UK.

● Regal Cinema, St Aldgate Street, Gloucester

The Beatles only appeared at this venue once, on 18 March 1963 during their **Tommy Roe/Chris Montez** tour.

● Regal Cinema, Kirkgate, Wakefield, Yorkshire

The Beatles made a single appearance at this cinema during their tour with **Helen Shapiro**, on 7 February 1963.

● Regent Dansette, High Street, Rhyl, Flintshire, Wales

A ballroom situated above a branch of Burton's, the tailors, where the Beatles appeared on Saturday, 14 July 1962. It marked the group's very first gig in Wales. In common with most advertising of the time, the music was categorized 'Jive-Twist-Rock!', the reference to 'Beat music' and 'Beat groups' came after the establishment of the ***Mersey Beat*** newspaper. Entrance was five shillings (25p) and the dance took place from 8.00 p.m. to 11.30 p.m. and the Beatles were supported by another Mersey band, the **Strangers**.

● Remains, The

A group from Boston who appeared on the bill of the Beatles' last American tour in 1966. The group was formed by vocalist/guitarist Barry Tashian after he'd been on a visit to England in 1964 and fallen in love with the sounds of the British beat groups. He formed the Remains with Bill Briggs on keyboards, Vern Miller on bass guitar and Chip Damiani on drums. The group moved to New York where their new manager arranged for them to appear on the bill of the Beatles tour – although they had to get a new drummer as Chip quit the band prior to the tour.

● Rembrandt, Baskervyle Road, Heswall, Cheshire

Name of the house which Paul McCartney bought for his father in July 1964 for £8,750. Situated fifteen miles from Liverpool and overlooking the River Dee estuary, the five-bedroomed detached house even had its own wine cellar. A further £8,000 was spent on central heating, furnishing and decorations.

The removal of furniture from **Forthlin Road** took place at midnight to escape the fans gathered outside the house during the day. **Mike McCartney** was still living at home at the time and joined his father at Rembrandt. He was very impressed with the contrast between Forthlin Road and the new residence with its five bedrooms, wall-to-wall carpeting and three indoor bathrooms, although it seemed to be too much of a change for **Jim McCartney** who had lived his life on a relatively low income. Mike was to observe that the sudden contrast proved too much for him: 'Dad, a man of action who'd been striving for something "better" all his life, had suddenly been given it . . . on a plate.'

Jim was later to suffer from severe arthritis and found that he couldn't cope with Rembrandt, so Paul bought the house back off him and and Jim moved into a small bungalow nearby.

● Reminiscing

The Beatles introduced this **King Curtis** composition into their repertoire late in 1962, probably after hearing **Buddy Holly**'s version. Holly had a posthumous hit with the number, reaching the British Top Twenty in October 1962 and also climbing to No. 2 in the US charts.

It was one of the numbers the group performed at the **Star Club** over the Christmas season that year and it is included on the various recordings from **Adrian Barber**'s Star Club tapes.

George Harrison is lead vocalist on the song.

● Remo Four, The

A group who first formed as a vocal outfit, the Remo Quartet, in 1958, playing at social clubs and weddings before becoming known as 'Liverpool's Fendermen' because they were the first group on Merseyside to have a complete line-up of Fender guitars. They comprised Keith Stokes (vocals/rhythm), Colin Manley (guitar), Don Andrew (bass) and Harry Prytherch (drums).

The Remo Four had their own residency at the **Cavern** and became the backing band for Johnny Sandon, former lead singer with the **Searchers**. They made a few singles for Pye and there were various personnel changes with Phil Rogers (bass), Roy Dyke (drums) and Tony Ashton (keyboards) joining Colin.

Brian Epstein hired the group to provide backing for **Tommy Quickly** who made various tour appearances with the Beatles in 1963. The Remo Four also appeared on the Beatles' tour of Britain in the autumn of 1964.

George used the group as session musicians on his *Wonderwall* album and later reciprocated by producing an album for them.

When the group had undergone another change and slimming operation to emerge as Ashton, Gardner & Dyke, with Kim Gardner on bass, George Harrison played guitar on the 'I'm Your Spiritual Breadman' track on their *The Worst Of Ashton, Gardner & Dyke* album.

● 81a Renshaw Street, *Liverpool L1*

Address of the ***Mersey Beat*** office.

When Virginia Sowry moved in as the only full-time member of staff at the beginning of 1961, the office was originally situated on the top floor of the building in one small back room. Due to the rapid growth of the publication there was an internal move to take over the entire first floor, comprising two large rooms, the followin year. The offices were directly above David Land's, th wine merchants, and next door to the Renshaw Arm public house.

The offices became the meeting place for almos everyone on the Mersey Beat scene, ranging from th Beatles, Brian Epstein, **Bob Wooler** and includin groups, managers, agents and promoters.

During the first few months the office was opened, th Beatles used to be regular visitors, as they hung aroun local coffee bars. They dropped in and would often hel Virginia out by answering the phone. When they receive some copies of their first single they brought a copy roun to the *Mersey Beat* office to give to Virginia and personall signed it for her.

Virginia married *Mersey Beat* founder Bill Harry.

The local 'dole' office was also in Renshaw Street an when Ringo Starr went to collect his dole, he used to dro into *Mersey Beat*.

● Rescue Hall, *Peterhead, Aberdeenshire, Scotland*

The final date of the Silver Beetles' short Scottish tour, o which they backed singer **Johnny Gentle**, took place this venue on 28 May 1960.

The group arrived back in Liverpool the next day, whi Gentle remained in Scotland. They were under th impression that they'd be returning to Scotland to bac another **Parnes** singer, Dickie Pride, in July, on the sam circuit, but it never transpired.

● Revolution

John Lennon wrote 'Revolution' while he was in India. H had been feeling that it was time to start speaking u about the Vietnam War and decided he wanted to sa what he thought about revolution. It became a comple composition for him and there were several versions of th number.

About 'Revolution' itself, he says, 'There were tw versions of that song but the underground Left only picke up the one that said "Count me out". The original versio which ends up on the LP said "Count me in" too; I put i both because I wasn't sure. There was a third version th was just abstract, musique concrete, kinds of loops an that, people screaming. I thought I was painting in sound picture of revolution – but I made a mistake. You kno 'he mistake was that it was anti-revolution.' John pointed ut that on the single version he'd said, 'When you talk bout destruction you can count me out.'

On Thursday, 30 May 1968, the Beatles began ecording the first version of 'Revolution', called Revolution 1'. They were to do a second version which as called 'Revolution 9' and, in all, there were four ifferent versions of the number.

The fourth version of 'Revolution' was issued as the ipside of the Beatles' 'Hey Jude' single in August 1968 nd a slower version was issued on *The Beatles* White lbum – with John saying, 'Count me in', rather than, Count me out'.

There were many recording sessions for the versions of Revolution', including Friday, 31 May; Tuesday, 4 June; londay, 10 June; Tuesday, 11 June; Thursday, 20 June; riday, 21 June; Tuesday, 25 June; and Wednesday, 10 ıly 1968. During the session on 4 June, John sang the umber lying flat on the ground with the microphone ispended above him on a boom. On the 21 June session e had some other musicians added to the track – umpeters Derek Watkins and Freddy Clayton and ombonists Don Lang, Rex Morris, Bill Povey and J. ɔwer.

During one of the afternoon sessions, visitors to the udio while they were recording a version of 'Revolution' cluded Lulu, Davy Jones of the **Monkees** and **Twiggy**.

The number was over ten minutes in length, but was lited down to three minutes and twenty-two seconds for e single and four minutes and thirteen seconds for the bum.

The track was also featured on the compilation albums *ıe Beatles 1967–1970*, *Rock 'n' Roll Music* and *Hey Jude*. ıe Beatles were also seen performing the number on the V shows 'Frost On Sunday' and '**The Smothers rothers Comedy Hour**'.

Revolution 9

riginally a piece of avant-garde music created by John d **Yoko** which the other three members of the Beatles dn't wish to be included on *The Beatles* double album. ventually it was, together with 'Revolution', which is a fferent number.

John was to comment, 'All the thing was made with ops. I had about 30 loops going, fed them onto one basic ack. I was getting classical tapes, going upstairs and chopping them up, making it backwards and things like that, to get the sound effects.'

This was a Beatles track with no singing. There are muffled sounds of conversation, Paul is heard playing piano, a voice keeps repeating, 'Number 9, Number 9', and a range of other unusual sounds are heard. John said, 'One thing was an engineer's testing tape and it would come up with a voice saying, "This is **EMI** Test Series Number Nine." I just cut up whatever he said and I'd number nine it. Nine turned out to be my birthday and my lucky number and everything. I didn't realize it; it was just so funny the voice saying "Number nine", it was like a joke, bringing number nine into it all the time, that's all it was.'

When 'Revolution 9' appeared on *The Beatles* album, its length of eight minutes and fifteen seconds made it the longest track of any Beatles recording.

● Revolver

The Beatles' studio recordings were becoming more complex. Within a matter of weeks after the release of *Revolver*, the Beatles' touring days were over and their 'studio years' began – the type of music they were now experimenting with in the recording studio would have been difficult to present in their live stage performances.

The group originally intended to call the album 'Abracadabra', but discovered that there had already been an album released using that title. They had then considered 'Magic Circles' and 'Beatles On Safari'. Their use of the word 'Revolver' referred to the motion of a record turntable – and not to a handgun.

The tradition of other artists covering numbers from Beatles albums to coincide with their release had already been established, but the 'cover' versions tied to this album were far more than usual, with singles quickly issued covering eight of the tracks, by artists such as **Cilla Black**, **Cliff Bennett & the Rebel Rousers**, the **Tremeloes** and the **Fourmost**.

The album cover was designed by an old friend from their Hamburg days, **Klaus Voormann**. When he'd originally contacted the Beatles at the **Kaiserkeller** club, as a way of introduction he'd brought some designs of his, mentioning that he'd like to design record sleeves. This time he got his chance – and he was to receive a **Grammy Award** for his design, which comprised a collage of his drawings of the individual Beatles.

George Harrison had begun to emerge as a songwriter in his own right and was represented on the album by three compositions.

Revolver entered the British charts at No. 1 when it was issued on Parlophone PCS 7009 on 5 August 1966. The tracks were, Side One: 'Taxman', 'Eleanor Rigby', 'I'm Only Sleeping', 'Love You To', 'Here, There And Everywhere', 'Yellow Submarine', 'She Said, She Said'. Side Two: 'Good Day Sunshine', 'And Your Bird Can Sing', 'For No One', 'Dr Robert', 'I Want To Tell You', 'Got To Get You Into My Life', 'Tomorrow Never Knows'.

The **Capitol** *Revolver* album was issued on ST 2576 on 8 August 1966. The American album releases differed from the British ones, due to the American system of including fewer tracks on the LPs and also of including previously released singles on albums. While the British album featured fourteen tracks, the American version only had eleven. 'I'm Only Sleeping', 'And Your Bird Can Sing' and 'Dr Robert' were left off the US release, although *Revolver* became the final American album to contain different tracks from the original British release.

● Rhone, Dorothy

Paul McCartney's first serious girlfriend. Paul had many girlfriends in Liverpool and was particularly partial to blondes, but Dot was the girl he dated for several years from the end of the fifties until late in 1962.

Mike McCartney in his book *Thank U Very Much* states that Dot was Paul's first real sweetheart. He has a photograph of Paul holding her in his arms in the background of the **Forthlin Road** house and she's pictured again, with her arms around Paul's neck, in a photo taken at **Rory Storm**'s house.

Once the Beatles began to do the rounds in Liverpool and Hamburg she became friends with another regular Beatle girlfriend, **Cynthia** Powell.

Cynthia says that Dot lived with her parents and worked at a dispensing chemist's shop on the outskirts of Liverpool. Of their first meeting, Cynthia comments, 'Dot was lovely, seventeen years old, slim, short blonde hair (not out of a bottle), and the most attractive pixie face you have ever seen. Dot was such a gentle soul, she spoke almost in a whisper, blushed frequently and idolized Paul.'

When the Beatles set off for their **Top Ten Club** season in Hamburg in April 1961, they invited Cynthia and Dot to follow them over. Cynthia took time off from **Liverpool Art College** as it was the Easter holiday, but Dot had some difficulty in getting her parents' permission for her first trip outside Britain.

The couple set off from Liverpool's Lime Street Station travelling by boat train via the Hook of Holland. When they arrived at Hamburg station, they were met by a scruffy-looking reception committee, exhausted by the long hours of playing and the Hamburg night life.

Cynthia was to stay with **Astrid Kirchherr** at her home in Eims Butteler Strasse and Dot joined Paul on a barge on the river where Paul had been staying with **Tony Sheridan**. The 'houseboat' was owned by **Rosa**, the lavatory attendant at the Top Ten Club, who had become an almost maternal figure to the boys, having previously worked in **Bruno Koschmider**'s clubs where she had dispensed supplies of Preludin to the band.

Several months after that trip, Cynthia was living in a tiny room in a Liverpool house. When the room next to hers became vacant she persuaded Dot, who had now become her close friend, to move into it. It was in this boarding-house that Cynthia discovered she was pregnant.

One evening Dot had just washed her hair and had put it in rollers. She was dressed in an old sweater and a pair of her mother's bloomers when Paul arrived. He took her into her room and told her that their affair was over. Dot was heart-broken, she packed her bags and went back to her parents' home in Childwall.

In February 1984, in a special Beatles edition of *The Sunday Times Magazine*, another friend of Dot's called Sandra Hedges threw some light on what had happened to Paul's former sweetheart. She mentioned that within a year of the split with Paul, Dot emigrated to Canada and later married. According to Sandra, 'Dot with her husband and elder daughter Astrid were Rolls-Royced some years later to meet up with Paul when **Wings** played at Spring Gardens in Toronto. When she met Paul again the ghost was laid.'

Sandra also mentioned that Dot was the inspiration for Paul's song 'P.S. I Love You'.

In September 1984, Dot placed six items for sale in the auction at Sotheby's in London. They included her personal memorabilia from the Hamburg days, mainly photographs, including one of her and Paul sitting among a group of tourists on a river cruiser in Hamburg.

RIAA Awards, The

'he Recording Industry of America (RIAA) is an rganization which was launched on 15 March 1958 with he aim of auditing sales of million-selling singles in the Jnited States of America. It also audits the sales of albums vhich top the 500,000 mark. The RIAA present Gold)iscs to artists who have achieved these figures with sales f their singles and albums and the Beatles have won more RIAA awards than any other act – a total of 42.

Here is a list of the Gold Discs awarded to the Beatles, 'hich includes some awards achieved in the seventies, fter the break-up, but excludes details of awards to the ndividual members after the break-up. Singles are ıdicated by the sign (s).

3 February 1964	*Meet The Beatles*
	'I Want To Hold Your Hand'
31 March 1964	'Can't Buy Me Love' (s)
13 April 1964	*The Beatles Second Album*
24 August 1964	*Something New*
25 August 1964	'A Hard Day's Night' (s)
31 December 1964	*Beatles '65*
	The Beatles Story
	I Feel Fine
1 July 1965	*Beatles VI*
23 August 1965	*Help!*
2 September 1965	'Help!' (s)
16 September 1965	'Eight Days A Week' (s)
20 October 1965	'Yesterday' (s)
24 December 1965	*Rubber Soul*
6 January 1966	'We Can Work It Out' (s)
1 April 1966	'Nowhere Man' (s)
8 July 1966	*Yesterday And Today*
14 July 1966	'Paperback Writer' (s)
22 August 1966	*Revolver*
12 September 1966	'Yellow Submarine' (s)
20 March 1967	'Penny Lane' (s)
15 June 1967	*Sgt Pepper's Lonely Hearts Club Band*
11 September 1967	'All You Need Is Love' (s)
15 December 1967	*Magical Mystery Tour*
	'Hello Goodbye' (s)
8 April 1968	'Lady Madonna' (s)
13 September 1968	'Hey Jude' (s)
6 December 1968	*The Beatles*
5 February 1969	*Yellow Submarine*
19 May 1969	'Get Back' (s)
16 July 1969	'The Ballad Of John & Yoko' (s)
	The Beatles
27 October 1969	*Abbey Road*
6 March 1970	*Hey Jude*
17 March 1970	*Plastic Ono Band Live In Toronto*
	'Let It Be' (s)
30 April 1970	*McCartney*
26 May 1970	*Let It Be*
13 April 1973	*The Beatles 1962–1966*
	The Beatles 1966–1970
8 January 1974	*The Early Beatles*
14 June 1976	*Rock 'n' Roll Music*
5 May 1977	*The Beatles At The Hollywood Bowl*

The RIAA introduced Platinum Disc awards in 1976 and the Beatles have relatively few, despite the fact that combined sales since the original Gold Disc awards would doubtless have merited many. The RIAA refuses to grant Platinum Discs for records produced before 1976. On 14 June 1976 a Platinum Disc was awarded for *Rock 'n' Roll Music* and on 12 August 1977 another was awarded for *The Beatles At The Hollywood Bowl*.

● Rialto Ballroom, Upper Parliament Street, Liverpool L8

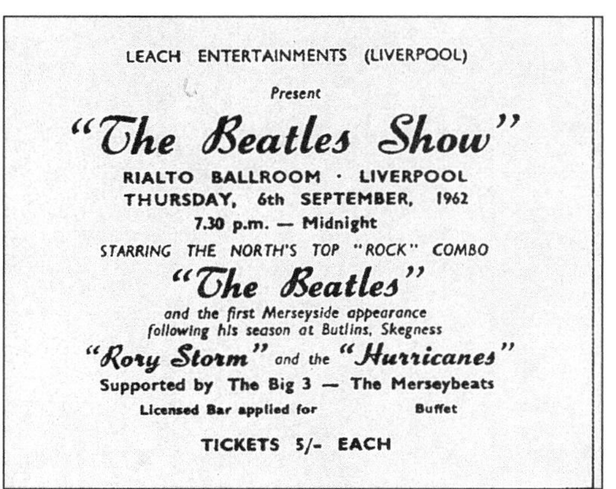

The **Quarry Men** made a couple of appearances here in 1957 but the Beatles didn't make their debut at the Top Rank venue until 6 September 1962 on a gig promoted by

Sam Leach, which also featured **Rory Storm & the Hurricanes**, the **Big Three** and the **Merseybeats**. Their next and final appearance took place on 11 October 1962 at an event promoted by Liverpool University Students' Union called 'Rock 'n' Twist Carnival'. Earlier that day they celebrated the news that 'Love Me Do' had entered the *Record Retailer* Top 50 chart at No. 49.

The Rialto was a cinema/ballroom complex and a mobile recording unit was used on the top floor of the cinema section for the recording of Oriole's two *This Is Mersey Beat* albums. The Rialto was burned to the ground in the Toxteth riots of 1981.

● Rialto Theatre, Fishergate, York

Each of the four appearances the Beatles made at this venue took place in 1963. Their first appearance took place on 7 February, when they were on the bill of the **Helen Shapiro** tour. However, due to illness, Shapiro didn't appear. It was while they were travelling by coach to the next gig that John and Paul were reading the ***New Musical Express*** and were inspired to write 'From Me To You'.

Their next appearance at the theatre found them on the bill of the **Tommy Roe/Chris Montez** tour on 13 March. This time it was John Lennon's turn to succumb to a severe cold and he was not able to appear that night.

Their 29 May appearance was on the bill of the **Roy Orbison** tour, but when they returned on 27 November they were bill toppers in their own right and the final gig was part of the Beatles' autumn tour.

● Righteous Brothers, The

One of the acts selected to support the Beatles on their first tour of America on 25 concerts in August and September 1964.

Vocalists Bill Medley and Bobby Hatfield weren't actually brothers and they'd just had a modest hit in America with 'Little Latin Lupe Lu'. They were among the list of potential acts who were available for the tour which GAC drew up for Brian Epstein's approval.

They received $750 a week during the tour. The following year they had their biggest hit, which became a pop classic, 'You've Lost That Loving Feeling', written by **Phil Spector**, Cynthia Weill and Barry Mann.

Cilla Black covered the song when it was issued in Britain, but the Righteous Brothers' version reached the No. 1 spot and Cilla's was right below at No. 2. Th Righteous Brothers version entered the British chart again in 1969 and 1977.

● Ringo's Theme

One of the four George Martin Orchestra instrumenta themes which were included on **Capitol**'s America release of the *A Hard Day's Night* soundtrack album. Th theme was used to provide atmosphere in Ringo's sol scenes where he was wandering along a canal bank an was actually just an instrumental version of 'This Boy'.

● Rink Ballroom, Park Lane, Sunderland, Tyne & Wear

Another of the British venues where the Beatles only mad a single appearance. This took place on 14 May 1963.

● Ritz Ballroom, York Road, King's Heath, Birmingham

The Beatles made their debut here on 15 February 1963 a they were unable to reach the ballroom on the date origir ally booked, 11 January, due to blizzards. The reschedule gig benefited the ballroom as the Beatles' latest singl 'Please Please Me' was then near the top of the charts.

● Ritz Ballroom, The Promenade, Rhyl, Wales

The Beatles appeared for two consecutive nights at thi ballroom, with both houses at the ballroom in the Wels seaside resort completely sold out. The dates were 19 an 20 July 1963.

● Ritz Cinema, Gordon Street, Luton, Bedfordshire

The Beatles only appeared at this venue once, on thei winter tour of the UK on 5 November 1964.

● Riverpark Ballroom, Off Love Street, Chester

Brian Epstein had secured four Thursday night booking for the Beatles at the venue, but had a problem. He' reluctantly been forced, on the urging of the othe members of the group, to sack **Pete Best**. Ringo Star who was currently in Skegness with **Rory Storm & th Hurricanes**, agreed to replace him. Although Pete ha said he'd appear with the group on their last few gig efore Ringo took over, he suddenly decided against it and rummer **Johnny Hutchinson** agreed to sit in with the roup for this appearance on 16 August 1962.

On the second of their appearances, on 23 August 962, it was John Lennon's wedding night. Their ther two bookings at the venue took place on 30 August

Vhen Pete Best failed to urn up for the gig at the Riverpark Ballroom, ohnny Hutchinson sat n with the Beatles.

nd 13 September.

Robbins, Mike

former Butlin's redcoat who married Paul and Mike's ousin Betty. In 1957 the McCartney family visited utlin's Holiday Camp in Filey. Mike and Betty were edcoats (official camp stewards). As Mike knew that the vo boys used to sing the Everly Brothers' 'Bye Bye Love' the family at home (calling themselves the **Nurk wins**), he entered them for a National Talent Contest, ganized by the Sunday newspaper the *People*, which was olding heats at the various Butlin's camps. He introduced em as the McCartney Brothers. They sang 'Bye Bye ove', then Paul sang a solo version of 'Long Tall Sally'. hey weren't eligible for any prizes as they were underge, but the thirteen-year-old **Mike McCartney** was too ervous to give a confident performance and was literally aking.

Mike and Betty gave up their jobs as redcoats to run a ub, the **Fox & Hounds** in Berkshire. In April 1960 Paul nd John visited the club and performed on a Saturday ght using the name the Nurk Twins.

The couple's children entered showbusiness and even had their own television series at one time. Their daughter **Kate Robbins** also became a recording artist in her own right and has occasionally guested as a backing vocalist on some of Paul's records. Paul took a hand early in her career and produced her recording 'Tomorrow', the song from the musical 'Annie', which was part of his own MPL publishing catalogue. The single was released in Britain on Anchor ANC 1054 on 30 June 1978, but didn't make the charts. Her biggest hit was 'More Than In Love', a song featured on the television soap opera 'Crossroads', which brought her to the No. 2 position in the British charts when the single was issued on RCA in May 1981.

Rock And Roll Music

A **Chuck Berry** rock standard which he took to No. 8 in the American charts in 1957. The Beatles included it in their repertoire in 1960 and it became one of the few non-Lennon & McCartney compositions to remain in their repertoire for several years – they were still playing it in 1966 when their touring days came to an end.

John sang lead vocals on both the stage and recorded versions. It was recorded by them on Sunday, 18 October 1964, for their *Beatles For Sale* album and also included on their *Beatles For Sale* EP. It was featured on their *Rock 'n' Roll Music* compilation and the American album *Beatles' '65*.

Rock 'n' Roll Music (Double Album)

When the nine-year recording contract which the Beatles had signed in 1967 expired on 6 February 1976, **EMI Records** had the rights to release any Beatles material from the back catalogue and *Rock 'n' Roll Music* became the first of several special compilations from EMI.

On being told about the album, John Lennon wrote to EMI offering to design the sleeve. Inexplicably, he was turned down, much to his annoyance when he saw the final album sleeve, illustrated by Ignacio Gomez, which he didn't like. John Lennon wasn't the only one who didn't like the *Rock 'n' Roll* package as it was widely criticized as being cheap-looking. Ringo Starr also criticized the cover as being unsuitable.

The 28-track double album was issued in Britain on PCSP 719 on 10 June 1976 and reached No. 10 in the ***New Musical Express*** chart.

George Martin, at the request of Bhaskar Menon,

President of **Capitol Records**, re-dubbed the tapes to enhance their quality – although he was never paid for his efforts, even though Capitol reportedly spent more money promoting this album than on any of their other Beatles releases. The only track not produced by George Martin was 'Get Back', which had been produced by **Phil Spector**.

The American release was issued on Capitol SKBO 11537 on 7 June 1976 and reached No. 2 in *Billboard*, No. 4 in *Cash Box* and No. 2 in *Record World*, prevented from reaching No. 1 by *Wings At The Speed Of Sound*.

The album tracks were, Side One: 'Twist And Shout', 'I Saw Her Standing There', 'You Can't Do That', 'I Wanna Be Your Man', 'I Call Your Name', 'Boys', 'Long Tall Sally'. Side Two: 'Rock And Roll Music', 'Slow Down', 'Kansas City/Hey Hey Hey', 'Money (That's What I Want)', 'Bad Boy', 'Matchbox', 'Roll Over Beethoven'. Side Three: 'Dizzy Miss Lizzy', 'Any Time At All', 'Drive My Car', 'Everybody's Trying To Be My Baby', 'The Night Before', 'I'm Down', 'Revolution'. Side Four: 'Back In The USSR', 'Helter Skelter', 'Taxman', 'Got To Get You Into My Life', 'Hey Bulldog', 'Birthday', 'Get Back'.

● Rock 'n' Roll Music Volume 2

The compilation *Rock 'n' Roll Music* was originally issued as a double album in Britain on 10 June 1976. The album was split into two separate LPs and reisssued on 27 October 1980 when it became the first Beatles album to be repackaged on a budget label. It was issued on Music For Pleasure, **EMI**'s budget label. *Rock 'n' Roll Music* was issued on MFP 50506 and *Rock 'n' Roll Music Volume 2* on MFP 50507.

The tracks on *Rock 'n' Roll Music Volume 2* comprised what were originally Sides Three and Four on the original double album. They were, Side One: 'Dizzy Miss Lizzy', 'Any Time At All', 'Drive My Car', 'Everybody's Trying To Be My Baby', 'The Night Before', 'I'm Down', 'Revolution'. Side Two: 'Back In The USSR', 'Helter Skelter', 'Taxman', 'Got To Get You Into My Life', 'Hey Bulldog', 'Birthday', 'Get Back'. It was issued in America in October 1980 by **Capitol Records** on SN 16021, together with the Volume 1 package on Capitol SN 16020.

Capitol had deleted the original double album and issued Beatles albums for the first time on its budget line shortly after the death of John Lennon. They sold well enough to warrant a minor chart placing with Volume 1 reaching No. 134 in the *Record World* chart and Volume reaching No. 137 in the *Record World* chart.

● Rocky Raccoon

A number penned by Paul when he was composing in Rishikesh. He had some help from both John Lennon and **Donovan** as he began writing it when the three of them were on the roof of one of the chalets at the ashram. He originally called it 'Rocky Sassoon'.

Recording began at **Abbey Road** on Thursday, 1 August 1968, and among the additional instrumen played were Paul on acoustic guitar and John on bass, wi George Martin on honky-tonk piano. The number was included on *The Beatles* double album.

● 4 Rodney Street, *Liverpool L1*

Site of a private nursing home where Brian Samuel Epste was born on 19 September 1934. Rodney Street Liverpool's equivalent of Harley Street and Brian was th first son of **Harry** and **Queenie Epstein**. Appropriatel he was born on Yom Kippur, the Jewish Day of Atonemen

● Roe, Tommy

American singer who had his first British hit, 'Sheila', September 1962, followed by 'Susie Darlin'' in Decemb 1962. As a result he was booked to co-headline a conce tour with **Chris Montez** which had been organized b **Arthur Howes**. The Beatles were next on the bill.

The Beatles had liked Roe's No. 3 hit so much th they'd included 'Sheila' in their repertoire, with George c lead vocals.

Tommy next appeared with them on their first-ev outdoor American concert at the **Coliseum, Washingto** DC on 11 February 1964, along with the **Chiffons** and th Caravelles.

Tommy's other hits in the sixties included 'The Fo Singer', 'Everybody', 'Dizzy' and 'Heather Honey'.

● Rolling Stones, The

The group who were regarded as second only to th Beatles in popularity.

Georgio Gomelski, who was unofficially managing th Rolling Stones and presenting them at the **Crawdad Club** in Richmond, went along to the recording of **'Than Your Lucky Stars'** at Twickenham, where the Beatl were performing 'From Me To You' on 14 April 1963 a invited them down to the Crawdaddy Club, which was only three miles away, to see the Stones. Later that night, dressed in leather overcoats, they arrived at the gig. George Harrison was to comment, 'It was a real rave. The audience shouted and screamed and danced on tables. They were doing a dance that no one had seen up till then, but we all know as the Shake. The beat the Stones laid down was so solid it shook off the walls and seemed to move inside your head. A great sound.' The Stones invited the Beatles back to their flat in **Edith Grove**, Chelsea, and they all went and spent a few hours chatting about music. The Beatles invited the Stones to come along to their **Albert Hall** show the following Thursday, 18 April, and **Brian**, Keith and Mick turned up.

The line-up of the Rolling Stones was Mick Jagger (vocals), Brian Jones (guitar, vocals), Keith Richard (guitar, vocals), Bill Wyman (bass) and Charlie Watts (drums).

When George Harrison was judging a beat group contest in Liverpool, he told fellow panellist **Dick Rowe** about the Rolling Stones and Rowe immediately set off for London and signed the group to **Decca Records**. By that time the Stones were being co-managed by **Andrew Loog Oldham** and Eric Easton and Oldham, who had turned down Epstein's offer of becoming press officer to the Beatles, had worked out an image for his group. The Beatles' tough image had been completely sanitized by Brian Epstein who had made them throw away their black leathers and dress smartly in mohair suits. This pleased Paul but enraged John Lennon. They were instructed not to swear or smoke on stage and the new image was obviously working, with the Beatles' clean-cut image appealing to all ages. Oldham wanted something in complete contrast to the 'lovable moptops', a rough, rebellious image, something to shock the establishment. He succeeded and one critic later commented: 'The Beatles became the kids who charmed a nation. The Stones were the louts who kicked it in the bollocks.' An American critic observed: 'If the Beatles are a wholesome lot, the Rolling Stones look like Neanderthal Teddy Bears.' John Lennon always considered that the Stones had stolen the original Beatles image. While the Stones were good little boys attending middle-class schools in the home counties, the black-leather Beatles were whoring in Hamburg, drinking and pill-taking and pounding out raw and savage R&B and rock 'n' roll music.

On 10 September 1963, John and Paul bumped into Andrew Oldham in Jermyn Street and he took them to the Stones' rehearsal at Studio 51, where they completed a song called 'I Wanna Be Your Man', which gave the Stones their first Top Ten hit. A few days later, on 15 September, the Rolling Stones opened *The Great Pop Prom* at the **Royal Albert Hall**, where the Beatles were bill toppers. The next month the Stones travelled from Manchester to Liverpool to pop into the **Cavern Club** to see the **Big Three** record. They were delighted to be mobbed by

The Rolling Stones – friends and rivals of the Beatles. (London Records)

Liverpool girls asking for their autographs.

There was friendship on a personal level between the two bands and they were often meeting socially at clubs such as the **Ad Lib** and Scotch of St James, laughing at the fact that the press painted them as bitter rivals.

Brian Epstein and Andrew Oldham had come to an

agreement that there would be no clash on release dates between the two groups. Oldham was later replaced as Stones' manager by **Allen Klein** and it was the Stones who recommended to the Beatles that they take him on board to run their Apple empire.

Following the success of the *Beatles Monthly*, publisher **Sean O'Mahoney** also launched a *Rolling Stones Monthly*, but it only lasted for 30 issues.

On 26 April 1964, both groups appeared on the ***New Musical Express*** poll winners concert at the **Empire Pool, Wembley**. On 8 July 1964, Keith Richard, Brian Jones and Bill Wyman turned up at the *A Hard Day's Night* party at the **Dorchester Hotel**. On 18 May 1967, while the Stones were recording at **Olympic Sound Studios** in Barnes, John and Paul turned up and added backing vocals to 'We Love You'. Mick Jagger was to send them a bunch of flowers by way of a thank you. The next month Paul McCartney invited Brian Jones to a Beatles session at **Abbey Road**. Paul commented, 'To our surprise he brought along a sax. I remember him turning up in this big Afghan coat at Abbey Road and he opened up a sax case and we said, "We've got a little track here", so he played sax on it. It was a crazy record, a sort of "B"-side, "You Know My Name (Look Up The Number)".' On 7 July 1967 Brian, Mick Jagger and **Marianne Faithfull** were among the guests at the live television transmission of 'All You Need Is Love' on the '**Our World**' television broadcast.

On 5 August 1967 Mick produced Marianne singing 'When I'm Sixty-Four' and later the same month, on 26 August, the two of them joined the Beatles at the **Maharishi Mahesh Yogi** seminar in Bangor, Wales.

On 15 October 1967 the *People* newspaper ran a story that the Beatles and Stones were going into business together. The story read, 'They are looking for new studios in London, probably to record unknown pop groups. And they may make films together. There is no question of the two pop groups merging.'

On 17 October Les Perrin, the Stones' publicist, issued a press release, 'Mr Jagger states that preparatory conversations of a purely exploratory nature were held between him and Mr Paul McCartney. These conversations have not been resolved and any assumption to the contrary should be considered premature.' The Beatles office had issued a statement, 'We look upon any merger as a fusion of nine people's business talents in a new and exciting project. Nothing has changed since Brian Epstein's death, but the prospect of some professional tie-in between the Beatles and the Stones is very intriguing. What the boys are contemplating is a separate business project for opening up a joint talent centre that will build up on other people's talents, produce and distribute their records.'

On 20 January 1968 Brian Jones was once again in the recording studios with Paul McCartney, this time playing sax on a track for the album *McGear*, by Paul's brother **Mike**.

On 12 December 1968 *The Rolling Stones' Rock 'n' Roll Circus* was shot at Intertel Studios in Wembley. Among the guests were black fashion model Donyale Luna, the Who, **Eric Clapton**, John Lennon, **Yoko Ono**, Mitch Mitchell, Marianne Faithfull and Jethro Tull.

During the career of both groups there were many occasions when they acknowledged each other. The Beatles had 'Welcome Rolling Stones' on the cover of their *Sgt Pepper* album and the Stones had a picture of the Beatles on their *Satanic Majesties Request* album. George Harrison also had Keith Richard play guitar on his production of 'That's The Way God Planned It'.

● Roll Over Beethoven

A number written and recorded by **Chuck Berry** in 1956, which provided him with his second American chart hit, although it only reached the position of No. 29 in June 1956. It was included in the Beatles' repertoire in the very early stages of their career, before they'd settled on their name. George was lead vocalist on their version of the number which they performed on three '**Saturday Club**' shows, two '**From Us To You**' shows and on their '**Pop Go The Beatles**' and '**Steppin' Out**' radio programmes. A live version of the number was recorded while they were at the **Star Club** and is included on *The Beatles Live! At the Star Club In Hamburg, Germany: 1962* album. The group recorded it for their *With The Beatles* album and the track is also to be found on *Rock 'n' Roll Music*, *The Beatles Second Album*, *The Beatles Box* and *The Beatles Collection*. Another live version was recorded at the **Hollywood Bowl** and issued on *The Beatles At The Hollywood Bowl* album. The number was also the opening track on their *Four By The Beatles* EP, issued by **Capitol** in May 1964.

A rock classic, the number was part of the standard repertoire of most Mersey groups, although it had never been a chart hit in Britain. 'Roll Over Beethoven' continued to be a favourite with the Beatles, who performed it on stage during their American tours in 1964.

● Ronettes, The

A trio of singers from New York who became a popular American singing group. They comprised Ronnie and Estelle Bennett and Nedra Talley. The group were discovered by **Phil Spector** who wrote and produced their first major hit, 'Be My Baby'. Other hits included 'Baby I Love You', 'Best Part Of Breaking Up' and 'Do I Love You'.

The Ronettes were among the first visitors the Beatles had at the **Plaza Hotel** in New York when they arrived for their first American visit in February 1964. The singing trio also appeared with the Beatles on their very last tour of America in August 1966.

Spector married Ronnie, who later sought a career as a solo singer under the name Ronnie Spector. George Harrison and Phil Spector got together to try to find a hit for Ronnie on the Apple label in 1971. They co-produced the single 'Try Some, Buy Some', which George had written. George also co-wrote the flipside, 'Tandoori Chicken', with Phil Spector. The single was issued in Britain on Apple 33 on 16 April 1971 and in America on 19 April on Apple 1832. Unfortunately, it only reached No. 77 in the American charts. George was later to use the backing track for 'Try Some, Buy Some', which he recorded over and used on his *Living In The Material World* album.

● Rory Storm & The Hurricanes

Rory Storm was one of the true legendary figures of the Mersey Beat scene. His real name was Alan Caldwell and he was an ex-cotton salesman when he first formed a skiffle group Al Caldwell's Texans. He changed the name to the Raving Texans in January 1957 and their line-up comprised Al Caldwell (guitar/vocals), Johnny Byrne (guitar/vocals), **Paul Murphy** (guitar/vocals), Reg Hales (washboard) and Jeff Truman (tea-chest bass). Spud Ward, former member of the **Swinging Bluejeans,** took over from Truman on bass guitar. The group continued as the Raving Texans until July 1959. For a short time in 1959 he changed the group's name, first to Al Storm & the Hurricanes, then Jett Storm & the Hurricanes and, finally, by the end of the year the group had become Rory Storm & the Hurricanes.

Alan had taken up the name Rory after appearing on a show with Rory Blackwell. Johnny Byrne also used the stage name Johnny Guitar. On 13 March 1959 Rory opened his own club, the **Morgue**, in Broadgreen. At the time the blond-haired, 6ft 2ins singer was eighteen years old. Ringo joined his band on 25 March 1959 at an appearance at the Mardi Gras Club, Mount Pleasant, and as Jett Storm & the Hurricanes they auditioned at the **Liverpool Empire** on 18 October for the Carroll Levis talent contest. It was during another contest earlier that year, the 6.5 Special, that Ringo and Rory first met. Ringo had left the **Eddie Clayton Skiffle Group** and was playing with the Darktown Skiffle Group. Rory told him he was short of a drummer and he decided to join him.

The line-up of Rory Storm & the Hurricanes was Rory Storm (vocals), Johnny Guitar (lead), Ty Brian (guitar), **Lu Walters** (bass/vocals) and Ringo Starr (drums). This line-up remained the same until August 1962 when Ringo joined the Beatles.

In May 1960 the group secured a summer season at Butlin's Holiday Camp in Pwllheli. The offer was for £25 per week, but it meant that the members would have to become professional. The reluctant one was Ringo Starr, who was actually known by his real name of Richie Starkey. He was an apprentice at Henry Hunt's, making school climbing frames, and didn't want to go to Butlin's. Rory decided to convince him. He was good at coining stage names and said, 'You can be Ringo Starr.' Richie said, 'No', he preferred his own name, but Rory talked him into it and said he could have his own spot, 'Ringo Starrtime', in which he would sing the number 'Boys'.

They were one of **Allan Williams**' main choices to fulfil the **Koschmider** booking at the **Indra Club**, but because they had taken up the Butlin's season, he finally offered it to the Beatles. The Butlin's gig found them performing for sixteen hours a week in the Rock & Calypso ballroom at the North Wales camp.

The Hurricanes were to team up with the Beatles in Hamburg later that year when they appeared for a season at the **Kaiserkeller** in October. They were billed above the Beatles and they alternated with them on the daily twelve-hour stretch which the groups had to play. So each band did 90 minutes on and 90 minutes off.

It was during this eight-week season, on Saturday 18 October 1960, that the recording session took place at the

Right: Rory Storm and the Hurricanes on stage. (Cavern Mecca)
Facing page, left: 'Mr Showmanship' – Rory Storm. (Cavern Mecca)
Facing page, right: Ringo and Rory with some fans. (*Mersey Beat* Archives)

Akustik Studio when two members of the Hurricanes, Lu Walters and Ringo, recorded with John, Paul and George. At the same session Lu sang 'Fever' and 'September Song' with Ty Brian and Johnny Guitar.

During 1961 the Hurricanes' reputation in Liverpool continued to grow and they appeared on all of the major venues, including many bills which they shared with the Beatles at places such as the **Cassanova Club**, the **Cavern**, **Litherland Town Hall**, **Lathom Hall**, **Hambleton Hall** and the Liverpool Jazz Society. They also had a second summer season at Butlin's, this time at Skegness in Lincolnshire, 161 miles from Liverpool. Incidentally, **Cilla Black** was to say, 'Rory Storm & the Hurricanes was the very first group I sang with.' When she appeared with them she sang Peggy Lee's 'Fever'. Drummer Dave Lovelady of the Dominoes has said, 'One night at **St Luke's Hall** was an absolute sensation. Rory Storm came in with Wally who had got the first bass in Liverpool. There was always a bass on American records, but we'd never seen one, and here was Wally with a Framus four-string bass guitar. The groups crowded round in amazement, and when they opened with 'Brand New Cadillac', this deep, booming sound was tremendous.'

On 30 December 1961 Ringo left the group to travel to Hamburg to act as drummer in **Tony Sheridan**'s band at the **Top Ten Club**, attracted by the fee and the use of a car and flat. In March 1962 he returned to the Hurricanes and they toured American Forces bases in France before returning to begin their third Butlin's season.

The big shock came later that year when the Beatles asked Ringo to join them. There are various reports on how the news was conveyed to Ringo. ***Mersey Beat*** reported how George Harrison went along to Admiral Grove to ask Mrs Starkey if she could let Ringo know they wanted him to join the Beatles – perhaps it was this report which resulted in **Pete Best** fans giving George a black eye at the Cavern! Another report says that John Lennon and then Brian Epstein put a message across the Butlin camp's public address system. Johnny Guitar says that John and Paul turned up at 10 o'clock one morning and knocked on their caravan door saying they wanted Ringo to join them. Rory told them that the Hurricanes couldn't work without a drummer and they hadn't finished their season. Paul told him that Brian Epstein said they could have Pete Best. Rory went to Liverpool, but Pete Best was too upset. Rory then returned to Skegness and used relief drummers.

Ringo had let it be known that he was becoming disenchanted as a drummer and was considering a full-time job. He'd also received a letter from **Kingsize Taylor** in Hamburg with the offer of a job. The Dominoes'

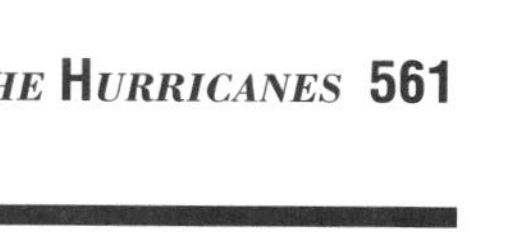

drummer Dave Lovelady was leaving and Taylor offered Ringo £20 a week. Ringo wrote to Taylor telling him he was joining the Beatles – who had offered him £25 a week.

Rory Storm & the Hurricanes never recovered from losing Ringo. They had a succession of very good drummers, including Gibson Kemp, Ainsley Dunbar, Keef Hartley and Trevor Morais, but they seemed to miss out on the nationwide boom in the Mersey sound.

In the 1961 *Mersey Beat* poll they were voted into the No. 4 position, although in the 1962 poll they had dropped to No. 19. Perhaps this was caused by their long absences from Liverpool at Butlin's, in Hamburg and at US bases in France. However, they were still regarded as one of Liverpool's top attractions and Rory was one of the biggest of the Mersey stars locally. Disc jockey **Bob Wooler** called him 'Mr Showmanship' and he was a favourite within the pages of *Mersey Beat* – there were photographs of him leaving hospital with nurses after breaking a limb at a gig, signing autographs for fans at the airport, leading the Mersey Beat XI soccer team, and so on. He was also known for his exuberant stage act. At the New Brighton swimming baths he stripped off to his bathing trunks during a number and climbed up the high diving board, diving off as he finished the song. At the **Majestic Ballroom, Birkenhead** he scaled one of the columns at the side of the stage during a number, and fell off the balcony, breaking his arm.

Rory also had a major impediment, a stutter, which was very apparent when he was conversing, but didn't seem to affect his performance on stage. He was so involved with his stage persona that he changed his name to Rory Storm by deed poll and called his house at 54 Broadgreen Road, 'Stormsville'.

Once the Mersey scene was underway nationally, A&R

Foreground: George Harrison, Rory, Ringo, Johnny Guitar and Ringo's girlfriend Pat Davies at a party. (*Mersey Beat* Archives)

men rushed up to Liverpool and signed up numerous bands – but not Rory Storm & the Hurricanes. They were featured in the Associated Rediffusion Television documentary 'Beat City', and were among the groups recorded in primitive conditions by an Oriole mobile recording unit at the **Rialto Ballroom** – but a contract with a major recording company eluded them. Rory even approached Brian Epstein and asked him to manage them, but he refused. Later, **Arthur Howes**, the promoter of the Beatles shows, took over as their manager.

Then, in 1964, Rory met Epstein in the **Blue Angel Club** one night and Epstein agreed to record the group personally. This was a coup and they travelled down to London where Brian was to record them at IBC Studios. They recorded 'America', the number from the musical *West Side Story*. Rory said, 'We first heard this number when we were playing in Spain. Everyone seemed to be playing it. We liked it a lot and when we came back to Liverpool we did our own arrangement and added it to our repertoire. We shortened it, used some of our own words, and it goes down a bomb!'

He told *Mersey Beat*, 'At the recording session we played one number after another to Brian Epstein. He kept saying "No" until we played this and then he gave an emphatic "Yes".'

The 'B' side was the old Everly Brothers number 'Since You Broke My Heart', which featured some painstaking guitar work – and the final note took two hours to perfect. 'America' was released on Parlophone R5197 on 20 December 1964, but didn't reach the charts. Epstein only ever recorded one other band – the **Rustiks**.

Rory had other chances to record, but didn't take them. Ringo had opened the door for him and said that he'd fix it for them to record whenever they wanted to, but Rory couldn't be bothered finding new material and seemed content with playing the rock 'n' roll standards. Perhaps he didn't really want to make the big time. His sister Iris said, 'He was happy to be the King of Liverpool; he was never keen on touring, he didn't want to give up running for the Pembroke Harriers . . . and he'd never miss a Liverpool football match!'

For a short time they were joined by Vince Earl, former leader of Liverpool bands such as the Zeros and the Talismen. Then, in 1967, Ty Brian collapsed on stage and was rushed to hospital. There were complications resulting from a recent appendicitis operation and he died at the age of 26. The group broke up for a short time and Rory and Johnny Guitar tried to revive it with three new members, but it didn't work out. After that, Rory became a disc jockey in Benidorm and Amsterdam – a strange profession for a man with a noticeable stutter.

In 1972 he was appearing in Amsterdam when news came that his father had died. He returned to Liverpool to console his mother, Vi, but neither recovered from the shock. Rory was suffering from a chest condition and took sleeping pills to ease it. On 28 September 1972 both Rory and his mother were found dead in 'Stormsville'. Their deaths remain a mystery, although Alvin Stardust, his brother-in-law at the time, commented, 'Rory became very ill. He had a chest condition which meant he couldn't breathe properly. He found it difficult to sleep so he'd take his pills with a drop of Scotch which doped him completely. At the post-mortem it was established that he hadn't taken enough pills to kill himself . . . It had been nothing more than a case of trying to get some kip, but because he was so weak, his body couldn't handle it. He died in the night and his mother found him. She must have felt that she'd lost everything. I think she took an overdose, but I'm convinced that Rory didn't. When you've known somebody long enough, you know whether they're going to do it or not. The whole thing was an accident.'

Johnny Guitar became an ambulance driver, Lu Walters a psychiatric nurse and Vince Earl a regular on the television soap opera 'Brookside'.

Rosa

The WC attendant at the **Indra Club** when the Beatles first appeared there in 1960. Her surname is not known. She was 67 years old when the Beatles first met her and she immediately set out to help them. They'd spent almost all of their money on their trip from Liverpool and were very hungry when they settled in on their first night in Hamburg, so Rosa gave them a few marks and sent them to the nearby Harold's Cafe for potato fritters, cornflakes and chicken soup. She used to provide them with soap and towels, washed their shirts and socks and gave them chocolate bars. She even allowed Paul to live in her bungalow in Dockland and said, 'I remember when young Paul used to practise guitar on the roof of my little place. We used to get crowds of burly old Hamburg dockers, just listening. They shouted out things in German, but Paul couldn't understand them.'

The Beatles called her 'Mutti', because she acted like a mother to them. She also had a large jar of prellies (Preludine) for sale in the Gents toilets and the group, with the exception of **Pete Best**, used to avail themselves of the pills to keep themselves awake.

When the Beatles moved to the **Top Ten Club**, she moved with them and when the Beatles appeared at the **Star Club**, they found that Rosa had become the toilettenfrau there, too.

● *Rosebery Street, Dingle, Liverpool L8*

Site of the first professional engagement of the **Quarry Men** on 22 June 1957. The group were no doubt booked because one of the main organizers was Mrs Marjorie Roberts and her son Charles was a friend of the skiffle group's drummer **Colin Hanton**.

The occasion was the granting of Liverpool's charter by King John and the 550th Anniversary of the event was celebrated throughout Liverpool. The Quarry Men performed on the flatbed of a stationary coal lorry belonging to the resident of No. 76, who also provided the group with a microphone. The event was a day-long party during which the Quarry Men performed twice.

Charles Roberts, who also took the famous photograph of the group performing in the street, related how two black boys from the neighbouring Hatherley Street began to heckle the group and threatened to beat up John. John jumped off the back of the truck and fled into No. 84, the Roberts' house, followed by the rest of the group. Mrs Roberts provided them with refreshments while a policeman was called and he escorted the boys to the bus stop where they caught a bus home to Woolton.

John's stepsister Julia Baird, in her book *John Lennon, My Brother*, says that she attended the gig with her sister Jacqui and their mother, **Julia Lennon**. She mentions that the group were called Johnny & the Rainbows because they all wore different coloured shirts (although, in Charlie Roberts' photographs, Colin Hanton's drums have 'The Quarry Men' written on them). She also observed that the group weren't paid for the gig.

● *Rossington, Norman*

Liverpool-born actor who appeared as the Beatles' road manager, Norm, in *A Hard Day's Night*. Norman was also one of the celebrities to be introduced to the audience at the northern premiere of *A Hard Day's Night* at the **Odeon, Liverpool**.

He also appeared with John on the TV programme '**Not Only . . . But Also**', reading from John's book *In His Own Write*.

As Norman also portrayed Arthur Babcock in *Double Trouble*, the **Elvis Presley** movie, he is the only actor to have appeared in films with both the Beatles and Elvis.

● Roundhouse, The, Camden, London NW1

A circular venue in Camden. On 6 November 1968 the Beatles decided that they would play some concerts there on 15 and 16 December with **Mary Hopkin** and **Jackie Lomax**. The idea was that the concerts would be filmed for a television special. Apple booked the venue between 14–23 December 1968, but the group then decided to drop the idea.

At one time, when the Beatles and the **Rolling Stones** considered going into business together, they were exploring the idea of turning the Roundhouse into a recording studio.

● Roundup

Children's programme, produced by STV (Scottish Television) from their Glasgow studios. During their brief tour of Scotland at the beginning of 1963, the Beatles appeared live on the show on Tuesday, 8 January, performing 'Please Please Me', prior to the record's release.

● Rowe, Dick

The **Decca** A&R (Artistes & Repertoire) man who, from 1962, had to live with the stigma of being 'the man who turned down the Beatles'. Although this label was attached to him for the rest of his life, it was perhaps an unfair one. According to Rowe, after his assistant **Mike Smith** had recorded the Beatles and **Brian Poole & the Tremeloes** at Decca's West Hampstead studios, Smith approached him and said he'd discovered two hit groups and would like to sign them both. Rowe asked him how long he'd been with the company. He said, 'Two years.' Rowe asked him how many hits he'd had in this time. He said, 'None.' 'And now you've discovered two hit bands on the same day,' said Rowe, sarcastically. But he told Smith he could pick one of the groups and Smith selected the Tremeloes simply because Dagenham was far closer to London than Liverpool.

The ball had originally been set rolling after Brian Epstein, in his capacity as a record retailer, had arranged a meeting with **Beecher-Stevens**, Decca's London Marketing Manager, and had then requested that Decca record the Beatles, offering to buy 5,000 copies of their record. Beecher-Stevens phoned Rowe, the head of A&R, and arranged a meeting at the company's executive club. Rowe then agreed to send Smith up to see them at the **Cavern**.

Once the decision had been made to reject the Beatles another meeting was arranged with Brian by Stevens and Rowe on 6 February 1962 in which Rowe told him, 'Not to mince words, Mr Epstein, we don't like your boys' sound. Groups are out: four-piece groups with guitars particularly are finished.'

Brian was upset at their decision and tried to convince them otherwise, but Rowe told him, 'The boys won't go, Mr Epstein. We know these things. You have a good record business in Liverpool. Stick to that.'

Rowe, not wishing to upset Epstein too much, suggested that they might have a solution. They could arrange for **Tony Meehan**, ex-member of the **Shadows**, who was now an A&R man with Decca, to record the group for a fee of £100. Brian went to see them at West Hampstead the next day, was kept waiting, then Meehan told him, 'Mr Epstein, Mr Rowe and I are very busy men. We know roughly what you require so will you fix a date for the tapes to be made of these Beatles? Telephone my secretary to make sure I am available.'

Brian was not too happy with the idea and, although he had no alternative record deal, sent off a letter:

> Dear Mr Rowe
>
> I am writing to thank you for your kind offer of co-operation in assisting me to put the Beatles on records. I am most grateful for your own and that of your colleagues' consideration of the Group and whilst I appreciate the offer of Mr Meehan's services I have decided not to accept.
>
> The principal reason for this change of mind is that since I saw you last the Group has received an offer of recording contract from another company.

Ironically, it was the Beatles who did much to rid Rowe o

e stigma of his turning them down. He was judging a
at contest at Liverpool's Philharmonic Hall and George
arrison was one of the fellow judges. George mentioned
him that the Beatles had been very impressed by an
known band they had seen in Richmond called the
olling Stones. Rowe rushed from the hall, caught the
ain to London and immediately signed the Rolling
ones.

Rowe was to say that he hadn't been informed that
stein had been willing to buy 5,000 copies of the
atles' first record and, if he had known this at the time,
would have signed them up.

Once, when asked about Dick Rowe, Paul said, 'He
st be kicking himself now', and John added, 'I hope he
ks himself to death.' Then Paul said, 'I don't blame him
turning us down.'

Rowe began writing his autobiography, called *The Man
o Turned Down The Beatles*, but died before it was
npleted. He had been suffering from diabetes for some
e and passed away on 6 June 1986 at the age of 64.

Royal Albert Hall, *Kensington Gore, ndon SW7*

erb Victorian building, erected in 1871 in honour of
Prince Consort and destined to become one of the
rld's most unique concert halls.

The Beatles made their Albert Hall debut on 18 April
63 in **'Swinging Sound '63'**, a radio concert broadcast
from the venue and featuring fifteen artists including
l Shannon, the Springfields, **Shane Fenton**, **Kenny
nch**, Susan Maughan, **Rolf Harris**, the **Vernons Girls**
Chris Barber's Jazzband.

The programme was produced by Terry Henebery and
n Belchier (confirmed on page 84 of Kevin Howlett's
k *The Beatles At The Beeb*), although Shane Fenton
ims (in the book *Alvin Stardust Story* by George
mlett) that the BBC producer on that occasion was
my Grant. He commented that the Beatles had a row
n the BBC production staff responsible for the sound
ipment. He heard the group arguing with them, John
ing, 'We can't play quiet', and the BBC staff men
ing them to turn their amplifiers down, which they
sed to do. Paul tried to placate John saying that they
have to do what they were told in case the BBC would
se to play any of their records. John said, 'Sod the
C', just as Jimmy Grant came onto the scene and he
asked, 'Are there any problems?' John said, 'I don't know who's supposed to be producing this show – but they're trying to get us to play quietly.' Grant told him to play normally, that everything was going to be all right.

The group spent the day rehearsing at the Albert Hall for the show, which was broadcast on the Light Programme, and they performed the numbers 'Twist And Shout' and 'From Me To You'.

There was a squabble when Del Shannon's British agent insisted on top billing for his artist, demanding that Shannon go on after the Beatles and close the show, which he did.

Shannon dropped in to see the band in America on 19 August 1965, the day after their spectacular **Shea Stadium** concert.

Jane Asher was in the audience at the Albert Hall that evening and posed for pictures for the *Radio Times* as an enthusiastic Beatles fan. She was introduced to the group later that evening and her five-year romance with Paul began.

Also in the audience were the **Rolling Stones**. The Beatles had rushed off after their appearance and **Brian Jones** was among a group of friends who helped to carry their guitars and amps out for them. Keith Richards was later to recall how impressed Brian had been with the Beatles' vocal harmonies and he tried to get the Rolling Stones to harmonize as a result, without success. 'After seeing the Beatles and this incredible show,' said Keith, 'which was at the height of English **Beatlemania** before America, he was completely overawed by them.'

The Beatles' second appearance at the Albert Hall took place on 15 September 1963 when they appeared on the bill of the *Great Pop Prom*, organized by Fleetway Publications and their magazines *Valentine*, *Marilyn* and *Roxy* and held on behalf of the Printers' Pension Corporation. There were ten other acts on the show, including the Rolling Stones, and the affair was hosted by disc jockey **Alan Freeman**.

On 29 February 1968, **Yoko Ono** recorded the number 'AOS' on stage at the Albert Hall and John played guitar. They were to return to the venue on 18 December 1968 to give the world a taste of 'bagism'. It was during the 'Alchemical Wedding', a huge Christmas party by London's alternative/underground scene. The couple appeared on stage inside a white bag.

On Monday, 13 December 1982, the Solid Rock

Foundation in association with Capital Radio presented *An Evening For Conservation* in the presence of Her Majesty The Queen and His Royal Highness Prince Philip, the Duke of Edinburgh. The proceeds of the charity presentation, which exceeded £30,000, were donated to the Royal Society for the Protection of Birds. Joan Collins and David Bellamy were the hosts while the Royal Philharmonic Orchestra and the Royal Choral Society, conducted by Louis Clark, with guest soloists Elena Duran and Honor Herrernam, performed 'The Music of the Beatles'.

Paul and **Linda McCartney** were in the audience and were given a standing ovation.

The programme was recorded and broadcast on Capital Radio. It was also to provide the material for a special album, issued in January 1983 by Evolution Records (SRFL 1001) entitled *The Royal Philharmonic Orchestra Plays The Beatles 20th Anniversary Concert*. The tracks were, Side One: 'All You Need Is Love', 'A Hard Day's Night', 'I Want To Hold Your Hand', 'Here, There And Everywhere/Norwegian Wood' (featuring Elena Duran), 'Fool On The Hill' and a Beatles medley. Side Two: 'Imagine' (featuring Joan Collins), 'Blackbird', 'Mull Of Kintyre' (featuring Roy Wood and the British Caledonian Airway Pipe and Drum Band), 'Happy Xmas (War Is Over)' and a *Sgt Pepper* medley.

● Royal Caribbean Steel Band, The

When **Allan Williams** first opened the **Jacaranda Club** in Slater Street, Liverpool, he turned the tiny brick cellar, with its stone floor, into a miniature club for dancing, with entertainment provided by **Lord Woodbine** and His All-Steel Caribbean Band. Steel bands were scarce in Britain at the time and they proved to be a popular attraction at the club.

When Lord Woodbine left the band to open a club of his own, the remaining quartet, Everett, Otto, Bones and Slim, began to call themselves the Royal Caribbean Steel Band. Williams was to comment, 'The boys were so black and the Jac basement dance floor so dark, that you couldn't see them until they smiled.'

One night Williams arrived at the club to discover that his star attraction hadn't turned up. They then wrote from Hamburg urging him to come over and book groups into the clubs there. Williams went to Hamburg with Lord Woodbine and established contact with **Bruno Koschmider**.

Casey Jones, leader of Cass & the Cassanovas, alwa[ys] maintained that he used the Jacaranda phone to mak[e] calles to Bruno Koschmider in Germany late at night, aft[er] the club had closed, and that Allan Williams answered th[e] phone one day and took over the contacts. If this were tru[e] it may explain how the Royal Caribbean Steel Band foun[d] themselves in the German port. Could they have answere[d] a call from Hamburg and found they had talke[d] themselves into a gig?

Williams urgently needed a band to fill the vacuum a[nd] he decided to book the **Silver Beetles**. John and **Stua[rt]** in particular, were regulars at the club and he was able [to] book them for a series of appearances, beginning on [3] May 1960 for a relatively low fee.

● Royal Hall, The, *Ripon Road, Harrogate, Yorkshire*

The Beatles only made a single appearance at th[e] Yorkshire venue, on 8 March 1963 on the eve of their to[ur] with **Tommy Roe/Chris Montez**.

● Royal Hotel, The, *Copenhagen, Denmark*

On Thursday, 4 June 1964, the Beatles booked into th[e] hotel. They were to appear at the K. B. Halle in the Tiv[oli] Gardens that evening, which was opposite the hotel.

Jimmy Nicol was with the group as Ringo was ill a[nd] had to remain in hospital in England. The suite which t[he] boys were given was the one which had been reserved [for] Russian Premier Nikita Krushchev the following fortnig[ht]. When told he was sleeping in the bed which Krushch[ev] would be using, George quipped, 'I'll be leaving a note [for] him under the pillow.'

● MV Royal Iris

A famous Mersey ferryboat which presented regu[lar] dances on board each week as it sailed up the Ri[ver] Mersey from the Pier Head. Independent promoters a[lso] ran events aboard and **Ray McFall**, owner of the **Cave Club**, rented the vessel for a series of 'Riverboat Shuffl[es]'. The Beatles were to appear on four of them.

They shared the bill twice with **Acker Bil[k's]** Paramount Jazz Band, on Friday, 25 August 1961, o[n a] three and a quarter hour cruise down the river and Friday, 10 August 1962. Their third cruise on Friday,

THE CAVERN PRESENTS
A RIVERBOAT SHUFFLE
FRIDAY, 25TH AUG. 1961.
ABOARD THE
" M.V. ROYAL IRIS "
WITH
MR. ACKER BILK'S
PARAMOUNT JAZZ BAND
And THE BEATLES
BOAT SAILS AT 7.45 P.M.
FROM LIVERPOOL LANDING STAGE
RETURNING AT 11.0 P.M.
Tickets
8/6

ıgust 1962, found them sharing the bill with the propriately named Johnny Kidd & the Pirates. Their ırth and final 'Riverboat Shuffle' took place on Friday, September 1962, when they topped the bill above other local Mersey Beat group, Lee Castle & the Barons.

Before being taken out of service in the late eighties, › *Royal Iris* sailed to London and held some special ıises down the Thames with entertainment provided by veral original Mersey Beat bands such as Faron's ımingoes.

Royal Lancaster Hotel, The, *Bayswater* ›*ad, London W2*

ting for a party for *Magical Mystery Tour* on Thursday, December 1967, which took place in the hotel's ›stbourne Suite.

The entire cast of *Magical Mystery Tour* were invited, together with the staff of **NEMS Enterprises** and Apple. Among the 200 guests were **Mike Love** and Bruce Johnson of the **Beach Boys**, **Billy J. Kramer**, **Peter Asher** and Mike McGear.

The fancy dress party saw **Cilla Black** dressed as Charlie Chaplin while her boyfriend Bobby Willis appeared as a nun. Singer Lulu was dressed as a Shirley Temple-like little girl. **Maureen Starkey** was kitted out as an Indian princess and Ringo as a Regency buck. Paul and **Jane Asher** appeared as a Pearly King and Queen. George was dressed as a Cavalier and **Pattie** as an Eastern Princess. **Cynthia** wore a lilac crinoline gown and feathered hat, while John was dressed in leather as a Rocker.

The company sat down to a traditional Christmas dinner with turkey and Christmas pudding and later there was music and dancing to the Chasers, the Symbols and the Dave Bartram Quintet. Actor Robert Morley appeared as Father Christmas and further entertainment was provided by Irish folk group the McPeake Family. There was also the showing of *Magical Mystery Tour* in colour on a large screen. A welcome addition to the entertainment was a performance by the **Bonzo Dog Doo Dah Band** and **Freddie Lennon** got up to sing.

John had had too much to drink and steamed up to Pattie, ignoring George, and turned on every iota of his charm to persuade her to join him between the sheets. It was an embarrassing moment, especially for Cynthia, until Lulu strode up and gave John a telling off, after which he returned to his wife.

The Beatles also attended a party at the hotel on 17 July 1968 following the premiere of *Yellow Submarine* at the **London Pavilion**. The hotel had opened a discotheque called 'The Yellow Submarine', based on the animated film, and the post-premiere reception was held there. The Rank Organization hosted the party for 200 guests from 11.00 p.m and apart from all four Beatles and Maureen, Pattie and **Yoko**, there were DJs Simon Dee, Tony Blackburn, **Kenny Everett** and Pete Brady, **Twiggy**, members of the Bee Gees, Ginger Baker and fan club secretary **Freda Kelly** and her husband.

● Royal Lido Ballroom, *Central Beach, Prestatyn, Flintshire, Wales*

Liverpool manager/agent **Joe Flannery** took over the task

of booking Mersey Beat bands into the Royal Lido, the first of them being the Beatles on 24 November 1962. Other Mersey bands he booked into the venue included **Lee Curtis** & the All Stars (with former Beatles drummer **Pete Best**), **Billy Kramer** with the Coasters and Johnny Templar & the Hi-Cats.

The Royal Lido was officially opened by HRH the Duke of Gloucester in June 1960. It was a prestigious ballroom with a maple dance floor, run by Prestatyn Urban Council and managed by F. E. Jackson.

Prestatyn was the town in North Wales where Beatles road manager **Neil Aspinall** was born. His family had evacuated from the area, moving from Liverpool during the war as the seaport was particularly hard hit. A large number of Merseyside families evacuated to North Wales during the Luftwaffe blitz. Brian Epstein's family also settled temporarily in Prestatyn in 1940.

● Royal Liverpool Children's Hospital, *Myrtle Street, Liverpool L7*

At the age of six, Ringo was rushed to the hospital after a burst appendix caused peritonitis. He'd had bad stomach pains and was taken by ambulance to the hospital where, '. . . this nurse started smashing me stomach. That's how it felt anyway. She probably just touched it.' He went into a coma for ten weeks following the operation and remained in the hospital for over a year.

When he was thirteen he returned to Myrtle Street with a lung infection caused by pleurisy, which had developed from a cold. He was later transferred to Heswall Children's Hospital. His stay in both hospitals lasted two years and he was fifteen before he was able to return to school.

It was while at the Royal Liverpool that he began playing drums with a makeshift band of fellow patients.

● Royalty

The Beatles touched every strata of British society and were even popular with the Royal Family. At one time Prince Charles wrote off requesting the Beatles' autographs – and received them. Unfortunately, they weren't genuine ones, but examples of the thousands of autographs signed on their behalf by **Neil Aspinall.**

The group's associations with royalty first began when they appeared at the Royal Variety Show at the **Prince of Wales Theatre** on 4 November 1963 in the presence of the Queen Mother, Princess Margaret and Lord Snowdon. This was the occasion when John Lennon made his famou remark to the audience, 'On this next number I want yo all to join in. Would those in the cheap seats clap the hands. The rest of you can rattle your jewellery.'

After the show the Beatles were presented to the Quee Mother in the Royal Lounge. She told them she'd enjoye the show and asked them where they would be performi next. They told her, 'Slough.' 'Ah,' she said, delighte 'that's near us.'

When she was asked to comment on the Beatles s said, 'They are so fresh and vital. I simply adore them.'

Prince Philip called them 'good chaps'. On 23 Mar 1964 he presented the Beatles with two Carl Allen Awar at the Empire Ballroom, Leicester Square, and chatt with John Lennon about books. Controversy was created October 1965 when the Queen and Prince Philip we touring Canada. The headlines in the newspapers quot the Prince as saying that the Beatles 'were on the wan The press made capital of this comment on the mo popular phenomenon and the *London Standard* ran a p in which five out of seven readers said that what Prin Philip had said wasn't true. In fact Prince Philip had made such a statement. He'd been misquoted. He se Brian Epstein a personal telegram in which he explain that he'd been asked about the Beatles and had replied, think the Beatles are away.'

The member of the Royal Family most associated w the Beatles is Princess Margaret. On 6 July 1964 t Princess and Lord Snowdon attended the premiere o *Hard Day's Night* at the **London Pavilion**. After premiere there was a private party at the **Dorchest Hotel** and the Princess and Lord Snowdon dropped This particularly pleased Paul McCartney who introduc his father to the Princess. The Princess and her entour seemed to be enjoying themselves when George Harris approached **Walter Shenson**, the film's producer, a said, 'When are we going to eat?' Shenson told him t they couldn't possibly eat until Princess Margaret a Lord Snowdon left. 'Just be patient,' he said. Af another fifteen minutes had elapsed, George walked up the Princess and said, 'Your Highness, we really hungry and Mr Shenson says we can't eat until you go.' 'I see,' said the Princess. 'Well, in that case, w better run.'

At the Carl Allen Awards on 8 March 1965, once ag held at the Empire Ballroom, Leicester Square, Princ argaret presented a Best Group Award to Brian Epstein behalf of the Beatles.

Princess Margaret and Lord Snowdon once again ended a Beatles premiere on 29 July 1965 when *Help!* s unveiled at the London Pavilion.

On Tuesday, 4 March 1969, Princess Margaret made an scheduled visit to **Twickenham Film Studios** to watch ngo Starr and **Peter Sellers** during the filming of ***The agic Christian***. She remained on the set from 11.00 n. until 5.00 p.m. Other visitors to the set that day were ul and **Linda** McCartney and **Mary Hopkin**. Paul and Princess spent most of the afternoon in conversation ether.

The Princess also attended the premiere of *The Magic ristian* at the Odeon, Kensington, on 11 December 69. Ringo and his wife were at the premiere, as were n and **Yoko** – who amused the crowds as they paraded ore them with a banner proclaiming 'Britain Murdered nratty'. Incidentally, in his books, John referred to the ncess as Priceless Margarine.

The Beatles all managed to view the inside of ckingham Palace when they were awarded the MBE at Investiture on 26 October 1965. Brian Epstein was not minated for any honour, which resulted in the 5 vember 1965 edition of the *Jewish Chronicle* quoting ncess Margaret as saying, 'I think the Beatles believe t MBE stands for Mister Brian Epstein.'

On 12 March 1969 Rory McEwan was throwing a ces party in Chelsea to which George and **Pattie** rrison had been invited. That same day there was a ice raid on their home, drugs were found and they were en to the police station for questioning. Their solicitor rtin Polden got them out and they arrived at the party t evening. Princess Margaret and Lord Snowdon were re.

George went up to them and told them that they'd just n busted.

Oh my, what a shame,' said the Princess.

Can you help us? Can you sort of use your influence to ninate the bad news?' George asked.

Princess Margaret seemed horrified at the suggestion. , I don't think so,' she said.

They were then joined by Pattie's youngest sister Paula, took a joint out of her purse and lit it. When she ced that everyone was staring at her she thought they e annoyed because she hadn't passed it round. She held it out to Princess Margaret and said, 'Here, do you want this?'

The Princess and Lord Snowdon fled the party.

● Royalty Theatre, City Road, Chester

Chester is a pleasant town across the River Mersey from Liverpool and the Beatles appeared there on a few occasions. They only appeared in the town's main theatre, the Royalty, once. The group performed at the venue on 15 May 1963.

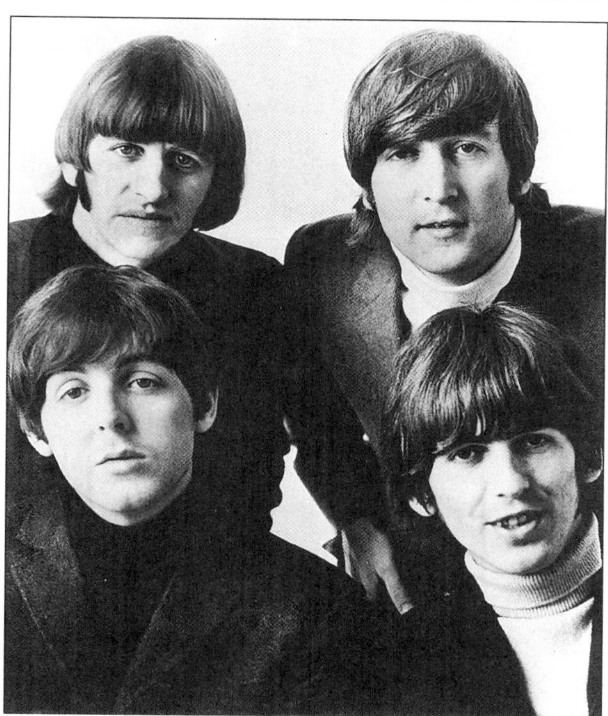

The Beatles in 1965. (©Apple)

● Rubber Soul

The Beatles' sixth British album release showed the group developing from their rock 'n' roll roots and becoming more adventurous in their musical outlook. George Martin was to comment, 'It was the first album to present a new, growing Beatles to the world.' Paul thought up the title – a humorous reference to white artists trying their hand at soul music: American soul music was very popular in Britain when the Beatles recorded the album between

October and November 1965.

It was issued on Parlophone PCS 3075 on 3 December 1965 and topped the charts less than one week after release. The tracks were, Side One: 'Drive My Car', 'Norwegian Wood (This Bird Has Flown)', 'You Won't See Me', 'Nowhere Man', 'Think For Yourself', 'The Word', 'Michelle'. Side Two: 'What Goes On', 'Girl', 'I'm Looking Through You', 'In My Life', 'Wait', 'If I Needed Someone', 'Run For Your Life'.

The American album was issued by **Capitol** on ST 2442 on 6 December 1965, containing only ten of the tracks on the British release. 'Drive My Car', 'Nowhere Man', 'What Goes On' and 'If I Needed Someone' were left off and, to bring the American album up to twelve tracks, two numbers from the British *Help!* album were included, 'I've Just Seen A Face' and 'It's Only Love'.

● Rudy, Ed

At the time of the Beatles' American debut, Rudy was a syndicated columnist and radio journalist. He first met Brian Epstein in New York late in 1963 through a friend, Bud Hellewell, who was promoting the non-Capitol Beatles material in the States for Epstein.

Rudy arranged to cover the Beatles' arrival and was at **John F. Kennedy Airport** on 7 February 1964, attending their famous first press conference in the US. He also travelled with them to Washington and Miami.

In an interview with Al Sussman and Bill King for the fan magazine *Beatlefan*, Rudy described their Miami trip: 'It was great fun. It was a happy time, magic time. We'd drive in my car, I had a station wagon and could get a lot of people in it, and there were reporters and Beatles and we'd tune in to WYNZ . . . Sometimes they tried to run away from the press, but it was nearly impossible. There was no place they could go that someone wouldn't tell us where they were. And sometimes they let some of us go along.'

Rudy also stated that he was the only reporter to join the Beatles on their summer tour of the US in 1964. He reported the events for 440 different American radio stations and issued a couple of albums containing interviews and background to the tours. The first of the albums was issued in June 1964 and reached No. 20 in the *Billboard* charts, No. 32 in *Record World* and No. 55 in *Cash Box*. Mark Wallgren, in his book *The Beatles On Record*, points out: 'He [Rudy] then ventured into a recording studio and re-recorded himself asking all th questions which had, in fact, been asked by a wide varie of reporters. The answers given by the Beatles we spliced in. The result was an entire album of Ed Ru "interviewing" the Beatles.'

In late 1980, Rudy decided to issue *The Americ Tour With Ed Rudy: News Documentary No. 2*. A blurb advertise the release read: 'This album was record during their American tour by the only Americ newsman/announcer to cover the complete tour, Rudy. The Beatles call Ed Rudy **"the Fifth Beatl** and after listening to these exclusive recordings, yo know why!'

In their *Beatlefan* feature, Sussman and King qu Rudy explaining his claim, thus: 'The Beatles called "The Fifth Beatle". It was good fun and I appreciated and they did that because I was covering for a lot stations. They knew that it would make me happy anc certainly did. That's not putting down **Murray the** Murray was "The Fifth Beatle" as much as anyone el The syndicators sold to the radio stations open-e portions of the Beatles introducing "The Fifth Beatle" a on the original tape it was me, John Lennon saying, "S tuned for the Fifth Beatle", and then local DJs would co in and they were "The Fifth Beatle!"'

● Run For Your Life

A composition which John Lennon didn't like because had to rush it. There was pressure for John and Paul come up with a lot of new songs for their recordings 1965. John even admitted to taking two lines from on his favourite **Elvis Presley** numbers, 'Baby Let's P House'. The song was recorded on Tuesday, 12 Octo 1965, and included on the *Rubber Soul* album.

● Rushworth's Music Store, *Whitechape Liverpool L1*

The largest musical instrument suppliers on Merseysi During the sixties it was also a record store a was situated quite close to the **NEMS** Whitecha branch.

In 1962 the manager of the store was musician Hobbs, who contributed a column to ***Mersey Be*** Following the band's success in the *Mersey Beat* p Rushworth's chairman James Rushworth presented J and George with a Gibson J45 guitar each. The guitars een flown in specially from Chicago. Unfortunately, ohn's guitar was stolen during their touring days.

Russell, Ethan

British photographer who produced the shots for the *Get ack* book, included in the limited-edition boxed resentation with the album *Let It Be*.

Ethan is featured in the first volume of *The Beatles llustrated Lyrics* with a double-page photograph of John nd **Yoko** illustrating 'Got To Get You Into My Life'.

Russell, Willie

ormer Liverpool schoolteacher, turned playwright, whose rst major stage show was *John, Paul, George, Ringo . . . nd Bert*, which was based on the Beatles and featured em with an imaginary fifth member who played with em on a few gigs. It was initially presented at Liverpool's veryman Theatre and then it moved to London's West nd where it won a special award from the London *vening Standard* as Comedy of the Year.

George attended the final Saturday matinee erformance and John sent a congratulatory telegram. Paul nly saw excerpts on television but was displeased at how e was being portrayed and prevented the show being staged in America. Willie eventually met up with Paul, who commissioned him to write a film script for a movie tentatively titled 'Band On the Run'. Willie completed the project, but the film was never made.

An album of the music featured in the play *John, Paul, George, Ringo . . . And Bert* was issued in Britain on 8 November 1974 on RSO 2394-141 by the original London cast, featuring Barbara Dickson. The tracks were: 'I Should Have Known Better', 'Your Mother Should Know', 'With A Little Help From My Friends', 'Penny Lane', 'Long And Winding Road', 'Help!', 'Lucy In The Sky With Diamonds', 'You Never Give Me Your Money', 'Carry That Weight', 'We Can Work It Out' and 'A Day In The Life'.

● Rustiks, The

A group from Paignton, Devon, who won a talent contest organized by Westward Television. Brian Epstein and **Decca**'s **Dick Rowe** were among the judges and when Brian presented their prize, he announced that they would be signed to **NEMS Enterprises**. He even produced the group's first single, 'What A Memory Can Do', issued by Decca in September 1964. The following month they appeared on the Beatles' autumn tour. When their contract lapsed, Epstein didn't renew it.

The Rutles – hilarious parody of the Beatles' story. (WEA)

● Rutles, The

The most successful of the Beatle parodies, which was originally conceived in the late seventies by Eric Idle, a former member of the hugely successful Monty Python.

In one episode he introduced the Rutles in a sketch which featured the Neil Innes number 'It Must Be Love'. The Rutles went down so well that Eric decided to plan a full-scale script and Neil set to work composing a series of songs parodying various Beatle numbers. The programme, under the title 'All You Need Is Cash', was first broadcast in America on NBC TV in mid-March 1978 and the British screening took place on BBC 2 on 27 March at 8.45 p.m.

The Rutles' career closely parallels that of the Beatles: a trip to Hamburg in which the Rutles play the Rat Keller and lose their fifth member, Leppo; their discovery in

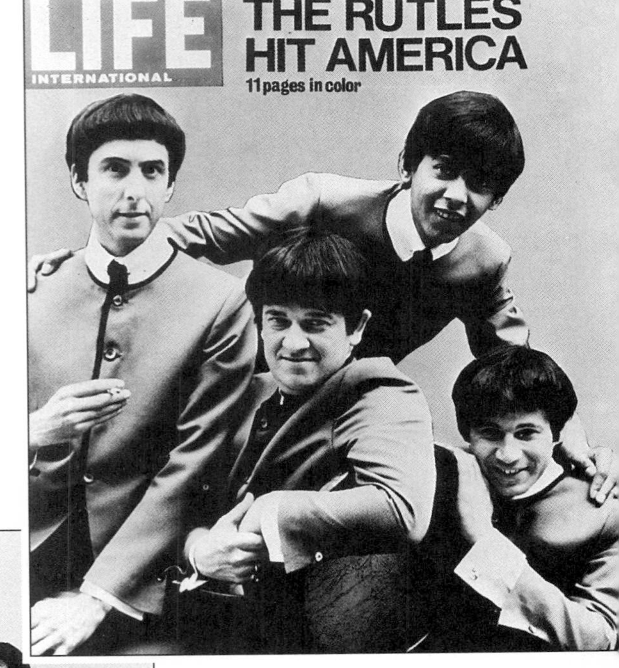

Cavern Rutland by Leggy Mountbatten; their appearance at Che Stadium and the Royal Variety Show; MBEs; press conferences; the launch of Rutles Corps; the Stig is Dead rumours; Nasty falling in love with an artist called Chastity; recollections of the Rutles from Mick Jagger and Paul Simon – and so on.

The film was made on location in Liverpool, London, New York and New Orleans and Eric Idle also took the roles of S. J. Krammerhead and the Commentator.

The Prefab Four were: Eric as Dirk McQuickly (th Paul figure), Neil Innes as Ron Nasty (the John figure John Halsey as Barry Wom (the Ringo figure) and Rik Fataar as Stig O'Hara (the George figure). The film w directed by Gary Weiss and Eric Idle.

George Harrison made an appearance as a interviewer, and, in addition to Mick Jagger and Pa

mon, other celebrities appeared. The cast included: anca Jagger (Martini); Gwen Taylor (Chastity); rinthia West (the Bigamy Sisters); Penelope Tree enelope); Terence Bayler (Leggy Mountbatten); chael Palin (Eric Manchester); Frank Williams (Archie caw); Barry Cryer (Dick Jaws); Robert Putt (roadie); n Ackroyd (Brian Thigh); John Belushi (Ron Decline); Franken and Tom David (Decline's henchmen); Jeanette Charles (HM The Queen); Ronnie Wood (I. J. Waxley, a Hell's Angel); Ollie Halsall (Leppo); Gilder Radnor (passer-by); Bill Murray (Bill Murray the K); Jerome Green (Blind Lemon Pye); Bob Gibson (Rambling Orange Peel); Pat Perkins (Mrs Peel); and Bunny May (journalist).

In addition to lovingly recreating all the major events in the Beatles' chequered career, the Rutles project was meticulous in its attention to detail.

In addition to composing the music and writing the lyrics, Innes produced the album and played guitar, keyboards and sang. The other musicians included Ollie Halsall (guitar/keyboards/vocals); Rikki Fataar (guitar/bass/vocals/sitar/tabla); John Halsey (percussion/vocals) and Andy Brown (bass).

The tracks on the album were: 'I Must Be In Love', 'Ouch', 'Living In Hope', 'Love Life', 'Nevertheless', 'Good Times Roll', 'Doubleback Alley', 'Cheese And Onions', 'Another Day', 'Piggy In The Middle' and 'Let's Be Natural', all of which were featured in the film.

In 1983, 'All You Need Is Cash' was issued as a video, under the title *The Rutles*.

● Saints, The

A traditional American number, more commonly known as 'The Saints Go Marching In', which was popularized by jazz bands. **Tony Sheridan** sang lead vocals on the song when the Beatles backed him at the Polydor recording session in Hamburg in May 1961. It was not an uncommon number for a rock 'n' roll band to play and Bill Haley & the Comets had actually reached No. 5 in the British charts with their version of the number, 'The Saints Rock 'n' Roll' in 1956.

This particular recording has been released on many singles and albums over the years, although it is generally issued as the flipside of 'My Bonnie'.

When Paul McCartney began learning to play the trumpet at the age of fourteen, it was the only number he actually managed to master before deciding to abandon the instrument, primarily because it develops a muscle on the lip and he said: 'I only got as far as learning "The Saints Go Marching In" before I got fed up with it. It used to hurt my lip and I didn't fancy the thought of walking around like a beat-up boxer, so I decided to buy myself a guitar.'

● Sam Houston Coliseum, Houston, Texas

The Beatles appeared at this arena on Thursday, 19 August 1965. The Coliseum had a 12,000 capacity and both shows that day were fully booked.

When the group arrived at Houston Airport at 2.00 a.m. there were huge crowds awaiting them. The vast numbers of fans turned into a mob and swarmed round the plane as it taxied to land. The situation was potentially dangerous and the Beatles were imprisoned in the aircraft. Togethe with Brian Epstein the Beatles were taken off the plane b a fork-lift and the rest of their entourage managed to joi them an hour later.

At the Coliseum there were no dressing-room facilitie for the group and they had to rush back to their hot between shows in an armoured van.

● Saturday Club

A unique BBC radio show because it was one of the fe radio shows of its time which presented current pop ac live and on record. The programme was launched in 195 by producer Jimmy Grant and its range of music include skiffle, trad jazz, pop and country music.

The show was so popular that at its height, during t period the Beatles were recording for the programme, had a Saturday morning audience of between 2 and million listeners and was broadcast each Saturday fro 10.00 a.m.–12 noon. Its co-producer was Bernie Andre and the show's host was **Brian Matthew**, who conduct more BBC radio sessions with the Beatles than anyo else.

The Beatles made their 'Saturday Club' debut on 2 January 1963, two weeks after the release of 'Plea Please Me', when they appeared live performing 'So Other Guy', 'Love Me Do', 'Please Please Me', 'Keep Yo Hands Off My Baby' and 'Beautiful Dreamer'. For the second appearance on 16 March 1963 they also appear live. Usually, the programme was pre-recorded on Tuesd afternoons and evenings at a three-and-a-half-ho recording session at the BBC's Playhouse Theatre London, during which three or four tracks were record for the following Saturday's show. However, on th occasion John Lennon had been suffering from a hea cold earlier in the week, which had also caused him miss the appearances at the **Granada, Bedford**; t **Rialto, York**; and the **Gaumont, Wolverhampto** They recorded at the BBC's Studio 3A which was actua used for talk shows and not really geared for recordi music. The group performed 'I Saw Her Standing Ther 'Misery', 'Too Much Monkey Business', 'I'm Talki About You', 'Please Please Me' and 'Hippy Hippy Shake

Their third performance was transmitted on 25 M 1963 and they performed 'I Saw Her Standing There', ' You Want To Know A Secret?', 'Boys' and 'Long T Sally'. On 29 June they performed 'I Got To Find aby', 'Memphis Tennessee', 'Money', 'Till There Was ou', 'From Me To You' and 'Roll Over Beethoven'. On 24 ugust 1963 they performed 'Long Tall Sally', 'She Loves ou', 'Glad All Over', 'Twist And Shout', 'You Really Got Hold On Me' and 'I'll Get You'. The programme on 5 ctober 1963 was a special fifth-birthday edition and the eatles sang a rendition of 'Happy Birthday Dear Saturday ub' for the occasion, in addition to performing 'I Saw er Standing There', 'Memphis, Tennessee', 'I'll Get You', he Loves You' and 'Lucille'. Their final 'Saturday Club' pearance of 1963 was on 21 December when they rformed 'All My Loving', 'This Boy', 'I Want To Hold our Hand', 'Till There Was You', 'Roll Over Beethoven' d 'She Loves You'.

Their first 'Saturday Club' in 1964 was transmitted on February and they performed 'All My Loving', 'Money', ippy Hippy Shake', 'I Want To Hold Your Hand', 'Roll ver Beethoven', 'Johnny B. Goode' and 'I Wanna Be our Man'. The next transmission was on 4 April during e week they had the top five positions in the American arts and 'Can't Buy Me Love' at No. 1 in the UK. They rformed 'Everybody's Trying To Be My Baby', 'I Call our Name', 'I Got A Woman', 'You Can't Do That', 'Can't y Me Love', 'Sure To Fall (In Love With You)' and ong Tall Sally'.

The Beatles' tenth and final appearance on the show s broadcast on 26 December 1964 when they performed ock And Roll Music', 'I'm A Loser', 'Everybody's Trying Be My Baby', 'I Feel Fine', 'Kansas City/Hey! Hey! ey!' and 'She's A Woman'.

Savarese, Louis

e driver who acted as the Beatles' chauffeur in New rk during their first tour in 1964. He drove them around a Cadillac limousine.

Savile, Jimmy

ne of Britain's most popular disc jockeys, who was rticularly prominent in the sixties with his trademarks of atinum blond hair and a big cigar.

The Beatles were booked twice at a club Jimmy co-ned in Manchester, the **Three Coins**, once in 1961 and other time in 1963.

Savile met the Beatles on numerous occasions and was e of the main presenters of 'Top Of The Pops'. He was vited to host their Christmas show at the **Odeon, Hammersmith**, which commenced on 24 December 1964. Apart from acting as a compere he appeared as the Abominable Snowman in their sketch 'The Search For The Abominable Snowman'.

Jimmy also hosted the 1965 film *Pop Gear*, which featured a clip of the Beatles performing the numbers 'She Loves You' and 'Twist And Shout' at the **Ardwick Apollo**.

On Saturday, 30 March 1984, while appearing on the popular radio series **'Desert Island Discs'**, Jimmy's third record choice was 'Paperback Writer' and he related a Beatles anecdote.

He mentioned that he was sitting in a dressing-room one Tuesday, ready to do a show with them, Paul was shaving and John was tying up his bootlaces. John turned to Paul and said, 'Don't forget Thursday, we're going into

Jimmy Savile, popular British disc jockey and one of the then hosts of 'Top Of The Pops'. (National Film Archives)

the studio and it's your turn to write the number.' Paul replied, 'Oh, don't worry, I'll get something done. One of my Aunties said not to write songs about love all the time.' Ringo was sitting in a chair reading a paperback. Paul looked at him and said, 'That's what I'll write a song about.'

● 3 Savile Row, London W1

The main headquarters of **Apple Corps**. The five-storey Georgian house had once been the Albany Club. The Beatles purchased it on 22 June 1968 for a reported £500,000. Its previous owner had been bandleader Jack Hylton.

The staff began to move into the building in July and the five floors were soon astir with the task of trying to translate the Beatles' dream of a benevolent business into reality. There were executives, accountants, secretaries – even a house astrologer and a doorman! Unfortunately, the business was beset by problems from the onset and the appearance of **Allen Klein** onto the scene brought mass sackings and resignations. By 1970 the top floor comprised Allen Klein's office, a press office and an office called 'the black room'. On the second floor were **Neil Aspinall**, Barbara Bennett and **Peter Brown**. On the ground floor were John and **Yoko**'s 'Bag Productions' and the **Apple Records** office. In the basement, which Jack Hylton had originally turned into a projection room, were **Apple Studios**.

On 23 December 1968 there was an Apple Christmas Party. The memo about the event mentioned: 'In the middle of the party we will be visited by Ernest Castro and April, entertainers to the Queen and Duke of Cornwall and the late Sir Winston Churchill, MacDonald Hobley and others. Mr Castro is a conjuror, ventriloquist and children's entertainer. April is his assistant and also his wife and she plays the guitar. So the idea is that all of us at Apple will bring our children and those of us who have no children are invited to bring a couple unless they can arrange to have one of their own in the meantime.'

There were over a hundred children at the party and John and Yoko, dressed as Mother and Father Christmas, handed out gifts, aided by **Mary Hopkin**.

One of the most potent images of Savile Row is that of the last performance by the Beatles on the rooftop of the building, which took place on the morning of 30 January 1969. Originally, the Beatles had considered performing at the Roundhouse in mid-December 1968 and had actually booked the venue. Then they decided they'd move it to 18 January 1969 and then changed their mind again. They only decided to perform on the rooftop of the Apple building the night before; the idea had come to them when they'd taken a breath of fresh air on the roof the previous Wednesday. The event was to be filmed and they wanted a helicopter shot of the Savile roof and the crowd in th street, but found that it was illegal to fly over London. was also too late to borrow a balloon and film the eve from that.

During the morning the equipment and film gear w set up. The performance was to last for 42 minutes wi the Beatles, plus **Billy Preston**, performing all new song including 'Get Back', 'Don't Let Me Down', 'I've Got Feeling', 'The One After 909' and 'Dig A Pony'.

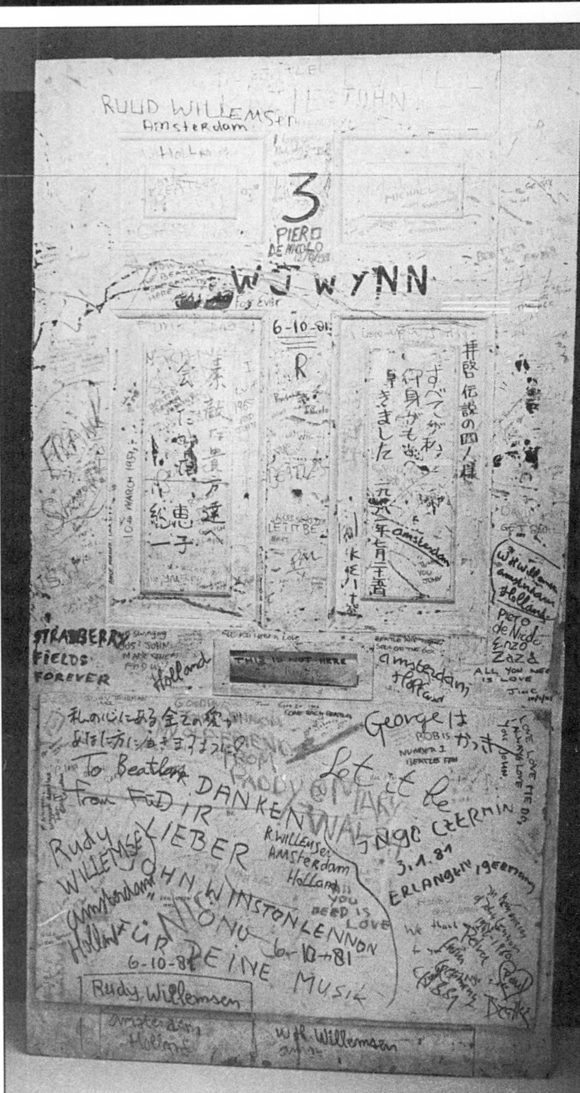

The door to the Beatles' Savile Row building was to end up a valuable auction lot. (Sotheby's)

The performance stopped the traffic, a man called obby Valentine phoned the police, but the event was ıptured for all time and included in the film *Let It Be*.

In 1972 it was discovered that the building was ıysically collapsing, which had been caused by the moval of beam supports when the basement studio had een reconditioned. Everyone moved out while the ıilding was being refurbished, but they never moved ıck in again and the building was sold in 1980.

Savile Row is a street famous for its tailors. The Beatles ıpported Tommy Nutter when he opened his 'House of utter' at 35a Savile Row on St Valentine's Day, 1969. utter made the suits for John, Paul and Ringo which are atured on the *Abbey Road* sleeve and he also made the edding suits for John and Yoko.

Saville Theatre, The, *haftesbury Avenue, London W1*

rian Epstein's love of the theatre had been a lifelong ıssion and with the wealth he was accumulating he ecided to involve himself in the West End theatre world. n 5 April 1965 his company Japspic Productions Limited, which he was controlling Director, acquired a three-year ase for the Saville Theatre from **Bernard Delfont**.

Brian intended to subsidize live theatre through rock ncerts which he would present on Sunday evenings. The ıville dream went sour, however, and at one time he was sing over £3,000 a week on the venture. Critics pointed ıt that it was at the wrong end of Shaftesbury Avenue – ıt it was the most central of all rock concert venues.

The theatre had an Art Deco frontage and inside there as a special box reserved for Brian and the Beatles which ıd its own private street entrance. The gilt-painted box ıd upholstered settees covered in leopard-skin prints, elvet curtains, and a private bar with a refrigerator which as always stocked with the best champagne.

Brian presented the West End premiere of James aldwin's *Amen Corner* at the theatre, but it is for the unday night rock concerts that the venue is most membered.

The Beatles held a press reception there after receiving eir MBE medals in 1965 and on 10 November 1967 erformed before a live audience during the filming of eir pop promo for 'Hello Goodbye', dressed in their *Sgt epper* uniforms.

The first major pop presentation was the **Four Tops** on 13 November 1966 and for the show Paul McCartney designed a special backcloth.

Members of the Beatles were able to enjoy watching shows there and the group joined Brian Epstein in the box on 29 January 1967 to watch *Soundarama*, a concert featuring the Who, the Jimi Hendrix Experience, the **Koobas** and the Thoughts. George and **Pattie** and Paul and **Jane Asher** were present at the 4 June 1967 concert which featured the Jimi Hendrix Experience, Denny Laine and his Electric String Band, Procol Harum and the **Chiffons,** and were impressed by Jimi's rendition of the 'Sgt Pepper's Lonely Hearts Club Band' song. Ringo Starr also went along to see the Jimi Hendrix Experience perform on 7 May 1967.

There was some controversy when Epstein presented **Chuck Berry** on 19 February 1967. When two fans climbed onto the stage during Berry's act, the house manager lowered the safety curtain while Berry still had two more numbers to perform. The audience rioted and were shouting up at the box where Epstein sat with Ringo and John. He sympathized with the audience's fury and sacked the house manager Michael Bullock. The National Association of Theatrical and Kine Employees threatened to strike unless he was reinstated – despite the fact that he wasn't even a member of the Union. They told Brian that his licence would be withdrawn. He said, 'If at any time my licence is withdrawn, I shall simply move the shows to another theatre.' He then presented Chuck Berry again on 26 February and, following the trouble-free concert, reinstated Bullock on 4 March.

Artists who appeared at the Saville during Brian's tenancy included **Del Shannon**, the Canadians, Hamilton & the Movement, Edwin Starr, Garnett Mimms, Lee Dorsey, the Impressions, Geno Washington & the Ram Jam Band, Georgie Fame, Fats Domino, **Gerry & the Pacemakers**, the Bee Gees, Cream, Lee Dorsey, Pink Floyd, Duane Eddy & the Wild Ones, Bo Diddley, Ben E. King, the Alan Bown Set, Denny Laine & His Electric String Band, Procol Harum, the Chiffons, Manfred Mann, the New Vaudeville Band, the Zombies, the **Yardbirds**, the Settlers, Jeff Beck and John Mayall's Bluesbreakers.

At the time of Brian's death, Tom Jones had been approached for a series of dates and appearances had been planned for Tim Buckley, Traffic, Stevie Wonder, **P. J. Proby**, Alan Price and **Long John Baldry**.

The theatre is now a multi-screen cinema.

● Savoy Ballroom, South Parade, Southsea, Portsmouth, Hampshire

The Beatles made a single appearance at this Hampshire venue on 7 April 1963.

● Savoy Truffle

George Harrison number included on *The Beatles* double album. George took his inspiration from the list of chocolates inside the cover of the lid of a box of Mackintosh's 'Good News' chocolates. It had reminded him of **Eric Clapton**'s insatiable appetite for chocolates, despite the fact that he had cavities and they gave him toothache.

Derek Taylor helped him out with some words in the bridges of the song.

John Lennon was not present at the recording sessions which took place at **Trident Studios** in October 1968.

● Scaffold, The

Not strictly a Mersey Beat group musically as they combined music with poetry and humour. They were part of the large cultural scene in Liverpool in the late fifties and early sixties which was to produce some of the leading British poets.

The members were Roger McGough, John Gorman and Mike McGear. The group had originally considered the ridiculous name: the Liverpool One Fat Lady All Electric Show, but settled on the Scaffold when they formed in 1962 after appearing together at the Merseyside Ar Festival.

Mike McGear was actually Paul McCartney's young brother **Mike McCartney** who had changed his nam because he did not want to cash in on the familial one. Th group soon had their own TV show and by 1964 ha turned professional and in 1966 began a five-ye association with the Beatles' label Parlophone, with the first record '2 Day's Monday' produced by George Marti This and their other novelty record 'Goodbat Nightma didn't fare too well. Then, in 1967, when Mike was on t phone thanking Paul for the present of a Nikon camera, got the idea for a number called 'Thank U Very Muc Paul attended the recording session and didn't believe would be a hit. When it reached No. 4 in the charts, Pa called Mike to admit he'd been wrong.

The group also had chart success with 'Do Y Remember', 'Lily The Pink', and 'Gin Gan Goolie', wi 'Lily The Pink' being their biggest hit and topping t British charts.

Paul expressed his interest in recording them and produced an album with Mike and Roger called *McGou and McGear*, which was to become a collector's item. Pa also produced Scaffold's last hit single, 'Liverpool Lo which reached No. 7 in the charts when it was issued Warner Brothers in 1974.

When the group split up, Mike continued to reco both with other artists and solo, he wrote books, produc

The Scaffold – Roger McGough, John Gorma Mike McGear. (Jan Olaffson)

ther acts on record and became a photographer. Roger McGough consolidated his success as one of Britain's major contemporary poets and John Gorman appeared in a number of children's television shows before retiring to France.

Scala Theatre, The, Charlotte Street, London W1

Theatre which was used as the setting for a number of scenes in *A Hard Day's Night*, including the television studio where the Beatles' live performance sequences were filmed.

When filming began in March 1964, the theatre had been abandoned for a time as it had ceased functioning as a theatre. Previously it had been noted as the theatre where the annual presentations of J. M. Barrie's *Peter Pan* had been staged. The theatre was later demolished and the offices of Channel Four television now stand on the site.

Scarfe, Gerald

Prominent British cartoonist with an international reputation whose caricatures are often wickedly grotesque in their representation of famous figures. Scarfe had originally created cartoons of the Beatles during the filming of *Help!* but his most famous Beatles representation was the one made for the front cover of *Time* magazine, published on 22 September 1967. For the commission Scarfe created four life-size models of the Beatles from fibreglass and papier-mâché, which were then photographed. The figures were particularly grotesque and in 1984 were featured in *The Art Of The Beatles* exhibition at Liverpool's **Walker Art Gallery**.

Scarfe was to marry actress **Jane Asher**, former girlfriend of Paul McCartney.

Scene At 6.30

Early evening programme covering events in the North-West of England, produced by Granada Television.

Granada executives had shown interest in the Beatles due to the large correspondence they received from viewers in mid-1962 and had sent representatives to watch the group on 28 July at the **Cambridge Hall**, **Southport** and on 1 August at the **Cavern Club**. As a result they sent a film crew to the Cavern on 22 August, led by **Dick Fontaine** who filmed the group performing 'Some Other Guy' and 'Kansas City/Hey Hey Hey'. This particular film wasn't shown until after the Beatles had become stars, although the 'Kansas City/Hey Hey Hey' sequence was lost.

However, Granada officials were sufficiently interested in the group to provide them with their television debut on **'People And Places'** on 17 October and 17 December 1962.

The programme's name was changed to **'Scene At 6.30'** and **Johnny Hamp** booked the group to appear on 16 April 1963. They made several other appearances on the show that year and were recorded on 14 August for a 19 August transmission. Their next appearance was on 18 October. A hilarious meeting between the Beatles and Liverpool comedian Ken Dodd was screened on 27 November and repeated on 27 December. When the group appeared on the programme on 20 December, they performed 'This Boy'.

Here is a transcript of the dialogue between host Gay Byrne, the Beatles and Ken Dodd:

BYRNE: 'We have always thought that it might be a good question to put to Mr Kenneth Dodd and members of the Beatles er, to what extent do they attribute their success to their hairstyles? And we'll start by asking the question now of Mr Dodd.'

DODD: 'We call it hair (*he pronounces it "hur"*) in Liverpool . . . you see we always have the judy with the fair (*he pronounces it "fur"*) hair. A fellow once went into a shop in Liverpool where they sell these minks and things and he said to the girl, "Give us one of those hairy coats." She said, "I beg your pardon, sir, what fur?" He said, "For the judy, who do you think?"'

BYRNE (*to the Beatles*): 'Do you think he owes a lot of his success to his hairstyle, fellas?'

JOHN: 'No. I don't think it helped at all.'

GEORGE: 'It might have been better if he was bald.'

DODD: 'Bald! . . . With the teeth and the hair, all the gimmicks, you know, I think you definitely have to have a gimmick. You've all got gimmicks, haven't you boys?'

BYRNE: 'What about the nose?'

DODD: 'The nose . . .' (*he looks at Ringo and points. Everybody laughs*). 'He's a Martian! We were writing this film script for the boys . . . you know the boys are making this new film and we've been writing the script and we've cast Ringo in the role of King Charles on account of the thing, you know, and he goes along to Nell Gwynne and picks her jaffas.'

BYRNE: 'Tell us more about this picture, we didn't know about this.'

DODD: 'Oh, yes, we've written the thing. I'm writing the script, yes, with Knotty Ash University . . . he's King Charles. John is a courtier and in this film he wears a long golden wig with all beautiful curls.'

JOHN (*camping it up*): 'Oh, very nice.'

DODD: '. . . And a blue velvet jacket and like, sort of knickerbockers, with lace round the bottom and buckled shoes with diamante clips on and he sort of walks round on the film set and there's a policeman standing at the side, says he'll pinch him when he comes off.'

BYRNE: 'And what's he supposed to be doing, though?'

DODD: 'Well, John, he's a peasant. He's an evil sort (*he points at George*).'

Commenting on the fact that Ken appears to have mistaken George for John, Paul and John say, 'He's Tom, Harry.'

DODD: 'Well, thingy. He's an evil smelly peasant.'

BYRNE: 'Why is he an evil smelly peasant?'

DODD: 'Come and stand where I am . . . and Paul is a jester, you see, and he's always making the King laugh. Every time he stands on his head the King laughs like anything – he wears a kilt!'

BYRNE: 'Getting back to this group, then, have you no ambitions to form a group yourself?'

DODD: 'Love to. With the boys? Kenny & the Cockroaches or Doddy & the Diddymen.'

BYRNE: 'What about yourself, would you . . .'

DODD: 'Or Ringo & the Layabouts.'

BYRNE: 'Would you not form one yourself, Ken?'

DODD: 'Yes, I'd like to. Yes, because, the only thing is, I'd have to change me name, you see. I'd have to have a name like Cliff or Rock, something earthy.'

PAUL: 'Or Cliff Dodd . . . Rock Dodd.'

DODD: 'Let's invite suggestions for an earthy name for me.'

JOHN: 'Sod!'

● Schaffner, Nicholas

An American musician/author, born in New York in 1953, who produced several articles about the Beatles for a number of US publications before writing *The Beatl Forever*, his first book, in 1977. The book was commercial and critical success and he followed up wit another book on the **Fab Four**, this time aimed at juvenil readers, called *The Boys From Liverpool* in 1980.

As a Beatles fan and collector of Beatles memorabili he contributed to publications such as *Beatlefan* and wa guest at Beatle Conventions.

1982 saw the publication of *The British Invasion*, collection of essays about the impact of British music o the American scene in the sixties. He teamed up with Joh Lennon's former school friend **Pete Shotton** to write *Joh Lennon, In My Life*, published in 1977. He also appeare in the film documentary **The Complete Beatles**.

Nicholas died of AIDS in New York on 28 Augu 1991. He was 38 years old.

● Schlact, Arthur

A German publisher based in Hamburg. In 1961 he wa associated with the German record label Deutsch Grammophon. The label specialized in classic recordings but had a pop subsidiary called Polydor, whos A&R man was the German bandleader and composer **Be Kaempfert**. It was Schlact who suggested that Kaempfe join him on a visit to the Reeperbahn to visit **Ton Sheridan** at the **Top Ten Club**, whom he thoug Kaempfert should record. The Beatles were backir Sheridan at the time and this led to their engagement Sheridan's backing band for the recording sessions.

● Schwartz, Francie

A Pennsylvanian-born, former advertising copywriter New York, Schwartz had watched John and Paul on th **'Tonight'** show inviting talented people to submit the ideas to Apple. She had written a ten-page treatment of movie script based on the life of a violinist who playe outside **Carnegie Hall**. She flew to Britain and took along to the Apple office in Wigmore Street. Paul notic the 24-year-old brunette in the reception area and ma contact. She gave Paul her Notting Hill Gate address a he came to see her one Monday morning. She was comment, 'He settled right into a chair with me on his la The kisses started.'

The affair began while Paul was engaged to **Jan Asher**, who was away touring. Paul fixed her up with a j at Apple and then had her move into Cavendish Aven with him. About three weeks into the arrangement, Jane turned up unexpectedly. Her tour of the provinces with the Old Vic had ended ahead of schedule.

Margot Stevens, one of the **Apple Scruffs** (the group of girls who hung around the Beatles' homes, offices and recording studios), spotted Jane arriving in her car and pressed the Entryphone, warning Paul of her arrival. He didn't believe her. Jane had a key, discovered what was going on and left.

Schwartz soon tired of the treatment she was receiving from Paul and decided to end the affair and wrote an exposé of it in the *News Of The World* entitled 'Memories Of An Apple Girl'. She then wrote a book called *Body Count* for *Rolling Stone* publishers, Straight Arrow, concerning her various love affairs. She devoted a full chapter to her short affair with Paul, whom she describes as: '. . . A little Medici prince, pampered and laid on a satin pillow at a very early age'.

● Searchers, The

The most successful Mersey Beat group not to be managed by Brian Epstein, although, ironically, Epstein did want to manage them. The group also thought that Brian Epstein could have made them an even more successful band, but they'd already committed themselves to a manager by the time he showed interest. Epstein did, however, give them an original Lennon & McCartney song to record, 'Things We Said Today'. However, due to their management problems they weren't able to record it and the Beatles used it as a 'B' side to 'A Hard Day's Night'.

The Searchers were a dynamic band, noted for their vocal harmony, and their Top Twenty hits between 1963 and 1965 were: 'Sweets For My Sweet', 'Sugar And Spice', 'Needles And Pins', 'Don't Throw Your Love Away', 'Someday We're Gonna Love Again', 'When You Walk In The Room', 'What Have They Done To The Rain?', 'Goodbye My Love', 'He's Got No Love' and 'Take Me For

The Searchers – one of the leading Mersey Beat groups.
(National Film Archives)

What I'm Worth'. They comprised Mike Pender (lead guitar), John McNally (rhythm guitar), Tony Jackson (bass guitar) and Chris Curtis (drums). When Jackson left, Mike became lead vocalist and Frank Allen, former member of **Cliff Bennett & the Rebel Rousers**, took over on bass guitar.

There are two groups called the Searchers currently performing; one is led by Mike Pender and the other by John McNally.

● *Searchin'*

A composition by Jerry Leiber and Mike Stoller which provided the Coasters with a million-selling hit in 1957. It was part of a double 'A' side with 'Youngblood', another number which the Beatles performed in their early stage act.

The Beatles were performing this song in 1958, with Paul on lead vocals, and they also played it at their **Decca audition**. It subsequently appeared on a number of bootleg albums of the Decca audition, prior to appearing on *The Silver Beatles*, an album issued by Audiofidelity Enterprises in Britain on 10 September 1982. Audiofidelity also issued 'Searchin'' on a three-track single, along with 'Money' and 'Till There Was You' on AFE AFSI on 29 October 1982.

Paul was to pick 'Searchin'' as one of his favourite songs on his **'Desert Island Discs'** appearance on 30 January 1982.

● *Sefton General Hospital, Smithdown Road, Liverpool L15*

When **Julia Lennon** was killed in a road accident in Menlove Avenue on 15 July 1958, her body was taken to Sefton General Hospital.

The 17-year-old John was at Julia's house in **Blomfield Road** at the time and a policeman knocked on the door to tell **John Dykins** and John that she had been involved in an accident. They caught a taxi to the hospital, only to be told the tragic news.

The hospital was where Julia had given birth to her daughters by Dykins, Julia and Jacqueline.

Dykins himself was also to die at Smithdown Road Hospital following a road accident in 1969.

Cynthia gave birth to **Julian** at the hospital on Monday, 8 April 1963. John was on tour at the time and when Julian was born the umbilical cord had wrapped itself around his neck. When John visited his wife and son at the hospital, he exclaimed, 'Who's going to be a famous little rocker like his dad, then?'

● *Sefton Park, Aigburth, Liverpool*

One of the several Liverpool parks. It was here that a sixteen-year-old **Freddie Lennon** first met **Julia** Stanley, a girl who caught his eye as she walked past the lake. Freddie, accompanied by a friend of his, was bold enough to engage her in flattering conversation. She told him he looked silly in the new bowler hat he was wearing, so he tossed it into the lake.

For many years Mr and Mrs Sutcliffe, **Stuart**'s parents, lived in a ground floor flat in Aigburth Drive, a road which skirted the main entrance to the park.

Photographer **Dezo Hoffmann** took the Beatles into Sefton Park for a photographic session in April 1963. Paul drove them all there in his Mark 1 Cortina and they noticed a cine camera among Dezo's possessions, so they asked if they could borrow it and filmed sequences of themselves in action. Dezo then began to take his photographs and had them jumping into the air for some shots. It was one of these photographs which appeared on the cover of their *Twist And Shout* EP.

● *Sellers, Peter*

The late Peter Sellers was one of Britain's major screen comedy stars, his most memorable character being the bungling Inspector Clouseau in the *Pink Panther* films.

He first rose to fame in Britain as a member of the Goons, an anarchic radio series in which he starred with **Spike Milligan**, Harry Secombe and Michael Bentine.

George Martin originally recorded Sellers, producing an album called *Songs For Swinging Sellers*, which proved to be a talking point when George Martin began recording the Beatles.

Sellers appeared as a guest of the Beatles on the Granada TV special **'The Music of Lennon & McCartney'** in which he dressed as Richard III and performed a cod Shakespearian rendition of 'A Hard Day's Night'. His single of the number was issued on Parlophone R 5393 and reached No. 14 in the British charts in December 1965.

Peter Sellers and Ringo Starr became close friends during the making of ***The Magic Christian*** and used to play practical jokes such as knotting together the belts of ats belonging to the film crew. When one of Ringo's iends visited the set he couldn't figure out why there ere so many sniggers, until he discovered that a variety of jects, including match boxes and empty cigarette ckets, had been taped to his back.

Sellers agreed to sell his house **Brookfield** to Ringo r £70,000, even though he'd recently spent £50,000 on novating it. John Lennon wanted to buy the house and fered him £150,000, but Sellers decided to keep his rd to Ringo.

While he was negotiating the sale at Brookfield, Ringo ticed a set of drums in the studio there and was told that ter had started out on his career as a drummer. The teenth-century oak-beamed house in Elstead, near

ter Sellers as spector Clouseau, his ost famous role. nited Artists)

uildford in Surrey, had several acres of ground, its own ke, paddocks, walled gardens and barns, a gymnasium, anging rooms, sauna and a private cinema. Ringo was er to sell it to Stephen Stills.

Michael Sellers, Peter's son, reminiscing in his book *S. I Love You* (Collins, 1981), mentioned that his father d once ordered a Beatle suit to be specially made for m. His father also revealed that he'd once been asked to vest in the Beatles' career before they became famous, t had decided that the £2,000 required was a sum he dn't want to risk at the time. However, he did agree to rm a property development business with George Harrison, as they both had Dennis O'Brien acting as their business manager. Sellers, however, lost interest in the company because things seemed to be taking so much time, so he resigned his directorship.

Peter presented the Beatles with a **Grammy Award** on the Tavern set of *Help!* for a television excerpt for America and, ironically, Sellers had originally been offered the script of *Help!* but turned it down.

Sellers used to visit George Harrison at **Friar Park** and had been introduced to **Ravi Shankar** by the Beatles. He was affected by George's philosophy for a time and began to wear kaftans, practise yoga, chant, burn incense and eat macrobiotic food.

Sellers had given Ravi Shankar financial support early in their relationship and became disenchanted when, on asking if Ravi could perform a recital for some friends, was quoted a huge fee for the short evening's entertainment.

In *The Magic Christian*, Ringo portrayed Sellers' adopted son, Youngman Grand. The two of them hosted a joint party at the fashionable **Les Ambassadeurs** in London and John and **Yoko** and Paul and **Linda** attended, along with a host of film stars, including George Peppard, Michael Caine, Roger Moore, Richard Harris, Sean Connery, Christopher Lee, Spike Milligan and Stanley Baker. This took place on 4 May 1969 and later that month Sellers joined Ringo, George and their respective wives on the *QE2*, heading for New York.

His version of 'She Loves You', originally recorded in 1965, was finally released in 1981.

Peter Sellers died of a heart attack in May 1980.

● Seltaeb

The word 'Beatles' spelt in reverse, which was used as the name of the American arm of **STRAMSACT**, the company which licensed Beatles merchandise in 1964.

It began when Brian Epstein asked his solicitor **David Jacobs** to find someone to handle the merchandising deals on behalf of the Beatles as there were too many enquiries for **NEMS** to cope with.

Jacobs felt that it could be dealt with by someone acting as agent for the merchandising and he decided to ask **Nicholas Byrne**, a young man whom he had met at parties and had surmised was young and ambitious enough to cope with such a task. Byrne decided to go into partnership with five of his friends: Lord Peregrine Eliot, Simon Miller-Munday, Mark Warman, John Fenton and

Malcolm Evans. Byrne took over the title of President of the company and asked each of his friends to invest £1,000, for which they were to receive a percentage of the shares.

Jacobs apparently had no yardstick by which to judge the percentages arising from such a deal, but he also seemed to lack a basic commonsense understanding of haggling: that as a rule of thumb someone looking for a deal expects you to bargain them down and will always start by throwing into the ring a percentage far higher than they would anticipate getting, on the presumption that it will be bargained down. Byrne said his company would take 90 per cent of the fees they received from licences, and grant NEMS and the Beatles a derisory ten per cent. To Byrne's surprise, Jacobs accepted immediately.

Byrne then went to America where firms were queuing up and clamouring for a share in the Beatles market. His team of reps found hundreds of firms willing to make bids, which turned Byrne and his partners into millionaires virtually overnight. The *Wall Street Journal* estimated that Beatles merchandising would make over $50,000,000 in the States in 1964 alone, but the sales of hundreds of ranges of goods were so successful that several sources have put the estimate at twice that figure.

One company which had a licence to manufacture Beatles clothes sold over two million T-shirts in a fortnight and also had healthy profits from sales of pants, hats, beach shirts, tennis shirts and other clothing. Another firm producing Beatle wigs could hardly cope with orders of over half a million when they were going all-out to produce 15,000 per day. The Reliant Shirt Corporation, which paid Seltaeb $100,000 for a licence to manufacture Beatle T-shirts, sold more than a million in only three days.

Byrne was licensing so many products – guitar-shaped brooches, cookies, Beatle nut-crunch popsicles, stationery, candies, toys, alarm clocks, scrapbooks, plates, lunch-boxes, loose-leaf books, pillows, purses, wallets, patches, wallpaper, belts, key-rings, pencil cases, commemorative medals, coathangers, dishcloths, dolls, play balls, scarves, toothbrushes, towels, aprons, balloons and so on – that he was living a lavish lifestyle in the best hotels, buying expensive cars and availing himself of an expensive account on which he personally ran up a bill of over $100,000.

The first inkling Brian Epstein had of the momentous blunder his British lawyer had committed by literally giving away the merchandising rights came when Byrn visited him on his arrival in the States with the Beatles an gave him a cheque for almost $10,000.

Brian realized that if Byrne could afford to give hi this amount Seltaeb must have already pocketed aroun $90,000 – and the merchandising sales were hard underway!

In June 1964 a new agreement was reached in whic NEMS were to receive 45 per cent from the deal, b things continued to go wrong. NEMS sued Byrne f refusing to return the agreed royalties and Byrne's partne also sued him for his profligacy in spending over $150,0(on personal expenses. Byrne discovered that NEMS ha begun granting licences to American firms behind h back and having the fees sent directly to the company Britain, so he in turn sued Brian for $5,000,000.

There was another mix-up when an American cou upheld his claim for the staggering amount because Bri Epstein had not turned up in court. He hadn't been tol American attorney **Nat Weiss** eventually sorted out t problem by having a lawyer explain the mix-up to t court and he then arranged for Brian to make a settleme of less than $100,000.

Because of the publicity surrounding the various co cases, a number of major American firms cancelled the orders and almost $100,000,000 was lost in potenti merchandising sales (Woolworth's and Penney's alone ha intended placing orders valued at $78,000,000). Th Beatles were to launch their own merchandising compan Maximum Enterprises, a few years later – but it was t late, the big merchandising boom had passed its 19(peak.

● September In The Rain

A number which Dinah Washington took to No. 23 in t American charts late in 1961. The Beatles then included in their repertoire, where it remained throughout 196 with Paul McCartney on lead vocals. Dinah, whose re name was Ruth Jones, was a leading American blu singer and died on 14 December 1963.

'September In The Rain' had been originally written Al Dubin and Harry Warren in 1937 for the film *Melo For Two* and over a decade later, in 1949, provided t George Shearing Quintet with a million-seller.

It was one of the numbers the Beatles recorded duri their **Decca audition** session.

Service House, 13 Monmouth Street, London WC2

Original London offices for the NEMS Press Division and also the Beatles Fan Club. **Tony Barrow**, who took up Brian Epstein's offer to head the new Press and Publicity Division of **NEMS Enterprises**, moved into Monmouth Street in May 1963.

He described it as: 'Consisting of two small first-floor rooms located above a dirty book shop – premises found for us by the ever-helpful **Dick James** who knew the place was being vacated by a man named Joe (Mr Piano) Henderson.'

Tony remained in Monmouth Street until 1964 when he moved into the Argyll Street offices of NEMS. The London office of the fan club was opened in June 1963 and Tony Barrow invented a secretary called **Anne Collingham**. The tasks of the fictitious fan club secretary were carried out by several office workers and the *Beatles Monthly* magazine ran a regular two-page fan club column using the name.

Sexy Sadie

John penned this song to rid himself of the frustration and bitterness he felt towards the **Maharishi Mahesh Yogi**, who he believed had betrayed him by his actions in Rishikesh. John had been benefiting from Transcendental Meditation and writing lots of songs during his weeks at Rishikesh. Then came the accusations that the Maharishi was making advances to one of the women in the ashram which led to John and George confronting him and John finding himself in the position of spokesman.

When John began writing the song he considered calling it 'Maharishi What Have You Done, You Made A Fool Of Everyone'. However, he was advised for legal reasons not to mention the Maharishi by name and altered the title to 'Sexy Sadie'.

The number was included on *The Beatles* double album.

Sgt Pepper's Lonely Hearts Club Band (Album)

Arguably, the most influential album of popular music ever released.

When the album was untitled and recording began, it was to have a theme of the Beatles' childhood memories of Liverpool. In December 1966, three tracks for the proposed album were recorded: 'When I'm Sixty-Four', 'Strawberry Fields Forever' and 'Penny Lane'. The last two tracks evoked the memories of Liverpool with John's 'Strawberry Fields Forever' and Paul's 'Penny Lane'. As it turned out, recording sessions were taking far longer than in the past and **EMI** needed a new Beatles single release, so it was decided to issue 'Penny Lane' and 'Strawberry Fields Forever' as a double-'A'-sided single in February 1967. The theme of Liverpool memories was then dropped.

The new theme concerned a mythical band which led to it being called the first 'concept' album. A Beatles associate, **Tony Bramwell**, said that at one time the group were considering calling the album 'One Down, Six To Go', in reference to the number of albums they had committed themselves to record under a new contract. This is likely to have just been an example of Beatles humour. The name 'Sgt Pepper's Lonely Hearts Club Band' was devised and the album took five months and almost 700 hours of studio time to record.

The original idea was said to have been thought up by Paul McCartney who'd said, 'Why don't we make the whole album as though the Pepper band really existed, as though Sgt Pepper was doing the record?' Paul at one time also suggested that the Beatles wear Salvation Army type uniforms to promote *Sgt Pepper*, but the others talked him out of it and the costumes they wore for the promotion were made by Maurice Burman's, the theatrical costumiers.

The music was so intricate, complex and innovative, that it staggered other artists who had been seeking to outdo the Beatles. Even more remarkable is the fact that this tour de force was recorded entirely on a four-track machine. George Martin was to comment: 'Technically, it was a bit of a nightmare. If I'd had eight- or sixteen-track recording facilities I could have done a much better job. I only had four tracks and I had to stretch it to the limits.'

Another innovation was to segue the tracks on the album. John Lennon said, 'It makes the whole album sound more like a continuous show. We've put everything in a sequence which is balanced just like a programme of stuff for a concert. It should be listened to all the way through so there's no point in having a silence every few minutes.' Brian Epstein disagreed and told the Beatles publicist **Tony Barrow**, 'People still want to drop the needle onto a favourite bit and play it more often than the rest of the album.'

The cover of *Sgt Pepper's Lonely Hearts Club Band* is

Left: The setting for the 'Sgt Pepper' shoot at Michael Cooper's studio. (EMI)
Below: Author Bill Harry in the 'Sgt Pepper' tableau in Abbey Road's Studio Two during the 20th anniversary party celebrating the album.

the most famous cover of any music album. The original idea of having a host of celebrities, living and dead, featured on the cover was, once again, Paul McCartney's. He said, 'We want all our heroes together here. If we believe this is a very special album for us, we should have a lot of people who are special to us on the sleeve with us.' Both EMI and Brian Epstein disagreed with Paul's idea for the sleeve as they felt it didn't give enough prominence to the Beatles themselves. In fact, Epstein hated the idea. When he was returning to London from New York by plane, he suddenly had a premonition that the aircraft would crash and he would be killed, so he wrote a note and gave it to his attorney **Nat Weiss**. The note read: 'Brown paper jackets for *Sgt Pepper's Lonely Hearts Club Band*.'

Robert Fraser, a prominent figure in the arts, was brought in to advise on the album package and he welcomed Paul's idea and, together with sleeve designe **Peter Blake**, sent the Beatles sheets of pape recommending that they write down their twelve mos popular heroes from throughout history.

A number of characters originally chosen didn' actually appear on the finished design. Two of Joh Lennon's selections, Adolph Hitler and Jesus Christ, wer vetoed as it was considered their appearance would offen people. When **Sir Joseph Lockwood** arrived at the se asked for the figure of Gandhi to be removed as he ought it would offend record buyers in India. In an early yout of the set, Gandhi had been placed behind the gure of Diana Dors.

There was also a figure of Bette Davis in her izabeth I costume behind Ringo and also an Albert hweitzer.

Since there were so many living figures featured on the ver, EMI insisted that permission be obtained from each the persons represented. This was an extremely complex d time-consuming job and Brian Epstein commissioned s former personal secretary Wendy Hanson to undertake e task.

A large set was assembled at photographer **Michael oper**'s studio in Flood Street, Chelsea, and the tableau as created by artist Peter Blake and photographed by oper.

Not every figure on the *Sgt Pepper* album cover has en identified. Some figures are almost obscured by other t-outs. The identifiable figures are:

SRI YUKTESWAR GIRI one of the Indian gurus, chosen by orge Harrison, who selected all of the holy men.

ALEISTER CROWLEY British Black Magician known as he Great Beast', once the subject of a novel by W. merset Maugham called *The Magician*. During his life was involved in many scandals and was referred to in e press as 'the most evil man in Britain'. He was a actitioner of 'Sex Magic' and wrote many books on the cult.

MAE WEST legendary Hollywood actress who, during orld War II, had a life-saving device named after her – inflatable rubber dinghy. Her films included *My Little ickadee* in which she starred with W. C. Fields, who is o featured on the cover. Ringo Starr appeared with Mae the film *Sextette* and Beatles aide **Derek Taylor** was ce employed to handle her publicity. When first proached for permission to use her image, Mae turned wn the request saying, 'What would I be doing in a ely hearts band?' but a personal letter from the Beatles nvinced her to change her mind.

LENNY BRUCE an American comedian who gained a cult lowing because of his abrasive comedy routine which ocked audiences with its liberal use of four-letter words. died of drug abuse and was the subject of a film graphy which starred Dustin Hoffman.

KARL HEINZ STOCKHAUSEN a contemporary German composer, born in 1928, who was noted for his use of electronic sounds.

W. C. FIELDS an eccentric American screen comedian, born Clarke William Duckenfield in 1880. His films included *Never Give A Sucker An Even Break* and *My Little Chickadee*. He was the subject of a film biography which starred Rod Steiger.

CARL GUSTAF JUNG a prominent psychiatrist, born in Switzerland, who studied dreams, the I Ching and various esoteric subjects. His theory of 'synchronicity' intrigued Sting of Police who named one of the group's albums after it. During the thirties Jung had a dream in which he claimed he saw the future. He was in Liverpool, which he called 'the city of light'.

EDGAR ALLEN POE an American author, creator of the modern detective novel and several classic horror tales, including *The Fall Of The House of Usher* and *The Pit And The Pendulum*. He died of a weak heart in 1849 caused by excessive drinking.

FRED ASTAIRE Hollywood's premier star of the dance musical. His films include *Top Hat* and *Funny Face*. He was featured in John Lennon's *Imagine* film.

RICHARD MERKIN a contemporary American painter, one of several featured on the sleeve, possibly one of Robert Fraser's choices.

BINNIE BARNES a London-born actress who came to prominence in the thirties in several Hollywood films, including *Barbary Coast* and *The Hour Before Dawn*.

THE VARGAS GIRL a pin-up by the artist Alberto Vargas.

HUNTZ HALL a member of a popular screen comedy gang, the Bowery Boys. Another member of the Bowery Boys, Leo Gorcey, was also selected to appear in the tableau and is, in fact, featured on some of the preliminary cover photographs. However, when he was approached for permission to use the cut-out, he insisted on receiving a fee for it, so his image was taken out.

SIMON RODIA a minor folk artist who was also a sculptor and designer. In 1954 he completed the famous Watts Tower, an unusual architectural structure of pottery and cement on a steel framework.

BOB DYLAN America's leading solo artist of the sixties and a friend of the Beatles. His real name was Robert Zimmerman.

AUBREY BEARDSLEY one of the most controversial artists of the Victorian age whose career was almost ruined by a scandal caused by his series of erotic drawings. He suffered from ill health from the age of six and died at the age of 25.

SIR ROBERT PEEL a former Prime Minister of Great Britain who originally formed the Conservative Party. Born in Bury, Lancashire, in 1788, he died in 1850. Apart from repealing the Corn Laws, he established the police force in Britain, hence early policemen were nicknamed 'peelers'.

ALDOUS HUXLEY a noted British author whose most famous work is the novel *Brave New World*. He explored the use of hallucinogenic drugs in his book *The Doors Of Perception*, a non-fiction work which influenced John Lennon and inspired Jim Morrison to call his group the Doors. Huxley died in 1963.

TERRY SOUTHERN American author of *Candy* and *The Magic Christian*, both of which were filmed and both saw Ringo Starr appearing as a guest actor. Southern was a friend of photographer Michael Cooper.

TONY CURTIS an American film star, born in Brooklyn, who became a teen idol in the fifties and later appeared in comedy roles. He was one of the guest stars in Mae West's *Sextette* film. Ringo Starr and Keith Moon also appeared in the bizarre comedy romp.

WALLACE BORMAN another contemporary American painter, based in Los Angeles.

TOMMY HANDLEY a Liverpool comedian who died in 1949. He became famous for his long-running radio series 'I.T.M.A.' ('It's That Man Again').

MARILYN MONROE Paul McCartney owns a sculpture of this famous Hollywood screen star who tragically died of an overdose of sleeping pills in 1962. Although regarded as one of the screen's 'sex goddesses', she was an under-rated comedienne and her films included *Some Like It Hot* and *The Misfits*.

WILLIAM BURROUGHS an American writer, born in 1914, whose novels gained a cult following, particularly in the sixties when several groups named themselves after the titles of his books, which included *The Soft Machine* and *Nova Express*.

SRI MAHAVATARA BABAJI another Indian guru.

RICHARD LINDNER a German-born artist who fled to America in 1941 to escape Nazi persecution. Originally a concert pianist, he took to painting the sordid low life of New York. He died in 1978.

OLIVER HARDY together with his screen partner, Stan Laurel, he created one of the classic film comedy duos – Laurel & Hardy. A song from their film *Way Out West*, 'Trail Of The Lonesome Pine', provided the pair with posthumous chart hit in the seventies. He died in 1957.

KARL HEINRICH MARX this German-born politic theorist developed a system of social philosophy based his experiences in London's East End. The pamphlet co-wrote with Friedrich Engels, 'The Communi Manifesto', had a profound effect on the course twentieth-century history.

H. G. WELLS the British novelist who created ma enduring science fiction classic novels such as *The War The Worlds*, *The Time Machine*, *The Invisible Man* and *T Island Of Dr Moreau*. His book *The War Of The Worl* was translated into a rock album by Jeff Wayne.

SRI PARAMAHANSA YOGANANDA another Indian guru.

STUART SUTCLIFFE the original **Fifth Member** of t Beatles who played bass guitar with the band. A student **Liverpool College of Art**, he remained in Hambu after the Beatles had performed there. Tragically, he di of a brain haemorrhage in 1962.

DYLAN THOMAS a Welsh poet who died in New York 1953. He was also a playwright and wrote works such *Under Milk Wood*.

DION an American teen singing idol whose hits includ 'Runaround Sue' and 'The Wanderer'. He originally front the Belmonts, who had a major international hit wi 'Teenager In Love'.

DR DAVID LIVINGSTONE a Scots missionary and explo who died in Africa in 1873.

STAN LAUREL the Lancashire-born comedian who mov to Hollywood and found fame in partnership with Oli Hardy. He died in 1965.

GEORGE BERNARD SHAW the Irish-born playwrig whose works included *Man And Superman*, *Pygmalion* a *Major Barbara*. Paul McCartney appeared as the inquisi in a school play production of Shaw's *St Joan* when he w attending the **Liverpool Institute**.

JULIA ADAMS an American actress who appeared beauty to the beast in the film *The Creature From T Black Lagoon*. She also appeared in several wester including *Where The River Bends*, *The Lawless Breed* a *The Man From The Alamo*.

MAX MILLER a controversial British music h comedian known as 'the Cheeky Chappie' because of risqué comedy routine.

LUCILLE BALL famous Hollywood comedienne. T drawing of the actress was said to be executed by Geo etty, an artist who, like Vargas, specialized in painting in-ups.

MARLON BRANDO the Hollywood superstar who studied ne 'Method' style of acting in films such as *A Streetcar amed Desire*. His other films ranged from *Julius Caesar Superman* and the controversial *Last Tango In Paris*.

TOM MIX one of the most famous western actors of the lent screen. A former working cowhand, he became a unt man and then a star.

OSCAR WILDE an Irish playwright noted for his witty oigrams. He was involved in a major scandal due to his omosexuality and served a jail sentence before dying in nominy in Paris in 1900.

TYRONE POWER a Hollywood leading man who appeared many swashbuckling roles. His films included *Captain om Castile, The Eddy Duchin Story* and *Son Of Fury*. He ed of a heart attack while filming *Solomon And Sheba*.

LARRY BELL a contemporary American artist, born in hicago in 1939. He based himself in Little Venice in alifornia and became a leading light in the Los Angeles t world. He began to concentrate on creating glass ulptures from 1964.

JOHNNY WEISSMULLER a prominent athlete who became e American swimming champion, winning five Gold edals in the Olympics. This led to offers from Hollywood d he became the screen's most popular Tarzan.

STEPHEN CRANE a talented American author who died om tuberculosis in 1900 at the age of 28. His novels cluded *The Red Badge Of Courage* and *The Outcasts Of ker Flat*.

ISSY BONN a noted British radio and music hall star of e forties and fifties.

ALBERT STUBBINS a famous Liverpool FC footballer.

ALBERT EINSTEIN the scientific genius, born in West ermany in 1879. He spent the last twenty years of his life the Institution for Advanced Studies at Princeton niversity in America. He revolutionized scientific inking with his Theory of Relativity.

HORACE CLIFFORD WESTERMANN a noted sculptor.

SRI LAHIRI MAHASAYA another Indian guru.

LEWIS CARROLL born Charles Lutwidge Dodgson in eshire, near Liverpool, in 1832. He was a teacher who s author of such classic works as *Alice In Wonderland* d *Through The Looking Glass*. John Lennon was spired by his works, as is evident from songs such as 'I n The Walrus'.

T. E. (THOMAS EDWARD) LAWRENCE he rose to fame during World War I when he united the Arab Nations and led the fight against the Turks. He became disillusioned when the British reneged on their promises to the Arabs and later enlisted anonymously in the RAF. He wrote several books, including *The Seven Pillars Of Wisdom*, and died in a motorcycle accident in 1935.

SONNY LISTON the American boxer who became Heavyweight Boxing Champion of the World when he knocked out Floyd Patterson in 1962. He died alone in 1970, his body being discovered a week after his death.

BOBBY BREEN the lead singer with a British dance band.

MARLENE DIETRICH the Berlin-born film star whose films included *The Blue Angel*, *Destry Rides Again* and *Shanghai Express*. One of the Beatles' drinking haunts in Liverpool was called the Blue Angel and Marlene appeared on the same bill as the Beatles at the Royal Variety Show on 4 November 1963. She died in May 1992.

DIANA DORS a British film actress who was touted as a screen sex star of the fifties. She became a popular character actress in British films and TV.

SHIRLEY TEMPLE the Californian actress who rose to fame as a child star in such films as *Wee Willie Winkie* and *The Little Princess*. She visited the Beatles in their dressing-room at the **Cow Palace** in San Francisco in 1964. When initially approached about permission to use her image she insisted on hearing the record first before she gave her approval.

The ornate drumskin in the centre of the album cover was conceived by Peter Blake and the Beatles, who commissioned a genuine fairground artist, **Joseph Ephgrave,** to paint it. Madame Tussauds lent a total of nine waxworks for the cover photograph – all four Beatles, Diana Dors, Lawrence of Arabia, George Bernard Shaw, Dr Livingstone and Sonny Liston.

Other interesting features on the cover include some stone statues from the gardens of the individual Beatles, a garden gnome, a flower display spelling out the name 'Beatles', flowers in the shape of a guitar, a cloth figure of **Shirley Temple** and a doll with a knitted jumper with the words 'Welcome The Rolling Stones' on it. Despite rumours, there are no marijuana plants on display.

Sgt Pepper's Lonely Hearts Club Band was also the first album to have a gatefold sleeve – and also the first one to include a full set of printed lyrics. It also came with a cardboard sheet of cut-outs of a moustache, a picture card, stripes and badges.

The Beatles were photographed in front of the tableau in their Sgt Pepper uniforms with Paul holding a cor anglais, Ringo holding a trumpet, John holding a French horn and George holding a flute.

The bizarre rumour that Paul McCartney had died, which sprang up in America in October 1969, led to fans seeking 'clues' in the Beatles songs and on album covers which could back up the theory. On the *Sgt Pepper* sleeve it is alleged that the hand raised above Paul's head was an Indian symbol of death and that the flowers represented a symbolic grave. In the centrefold of the album, Paul is wearing a badge with the initials OPP, which fans suggested meant 'Officially Pronounced Dead'. (A fold makes it appear OPD.) The patch on Paul's sleeve does sport such initials, but they stand for Ontario Provincial Police. Paul was given the official patch while the Beatles were appearing in Toronto on 17 August 1965. Incidentally, one of the members of the security force guarding the Beatles at the time was called Sergeant Pepper!

The back cover has George, John and Ringo with a back view of Paul. Fans said that this was because someone substituted for the dead Paul. This wasn't so, other pictures from the same session reveal that it was Paul in the photograph.

The first airing of the album on the radio took place at 5.00 p.m. on the evening of Friday, 12 May 1967, when the pirate station Radio London broadcast the tracks. Although American stations had broadcast tracks prior to this time, Radio London claimed a 'world exclusive' because they claimed to be the first to play the album in its entirety as 'Album Of The Week'.

A special press launch for the album was held at Brian Epstein's house in **Chapel Street**, Mayfair, on 19 May 1967.

When EMI released the album on Parlophone PCS 7027 on 1 June 1967 the reaction was staggering. It sold 250,000 copies in Britain during the first week and topped the half million mark within the month. It was issued in America on Capitol SMAS 2653 on 2 June 1967 with advance orders of over a million copies and it sold over two and a half million copies there within three months. It also topped the charts all over the world. The album was No. 1 in Britain for 27 weeks and topped the charts for nineteen weeks in America, remaining in the charts ther for a total of 113 weeks.

The album received four **Grammy Awards** during th year of release: (1) Best Album (2) Best Contemporar Album (3) Best Album Cover (4) Best Engineered Album In 1977 the British Phonogram Industry announced special award to celebrate 25 years of British music: Be British Pop Album 1952–1977. It went to *Sgt Pepper Lonely Hearts Club Band*.

The album tracks were, Side One: 'Sgt Pepper's Lone Hearts Club Band', 'With A Little Help From My Friends 'Lucy In The Sky With Diamonds', 'Getting Better 'Fixing A Hole', 'She's Leaving Home', 'Being For Th Benefit Of Mr Kite'. Side Two: 'Within You, Without You 'When I'm Sixty-Four', 'Lovely Rita', 'Good Mornin Good Morning', 'Sgt Pepper's Lonely Hearts Club Ban (reprise), 'A Day In The Life'.

● Sgt Pepper's Lonely Hearts Club Band (Film)

Robert Stigwood, erstwhile partner of Brian Epstein **NEMS Enterprises**, had hopes of becoming the Beatle manager in 1967. He was unable to carry off negotiatio successfully, but had quite a roster of major names on h own books, including the Bee Gees and Cream. He fou even greater success when he moved to America produci two hugely successful Hollywood musicals, *Saturd Night Fever* and *Grease!* He also discovered that produci an album to go with a successful film could pay va dividends, as was evident with the multi-million doll sales of the double album for *Saturday Night Fever*.

Stigwood wanted to complete a hat-trick of musica and poured $12 million into *Sgt Pepper's Lonely Hea Club Band*, in which the Beatles' mystical album conce was turned into a middle-of-the-road American fantas The ambitious film was a box-office flop, although t double album soundtrack was a multi-million seller. featured eleven of the thirteen songs on the Beatle original album. 'Within You, Without You' and 'Love Rita' were left off the album, but a further eighteen Beatl numbers were included.

The completed film was 111 minutes long, w produced by Stigwood and directed by Michael Schul The script was written by Harry Edwards from an idea co-developed with Stigwood. George Martin directed a arranged the music.

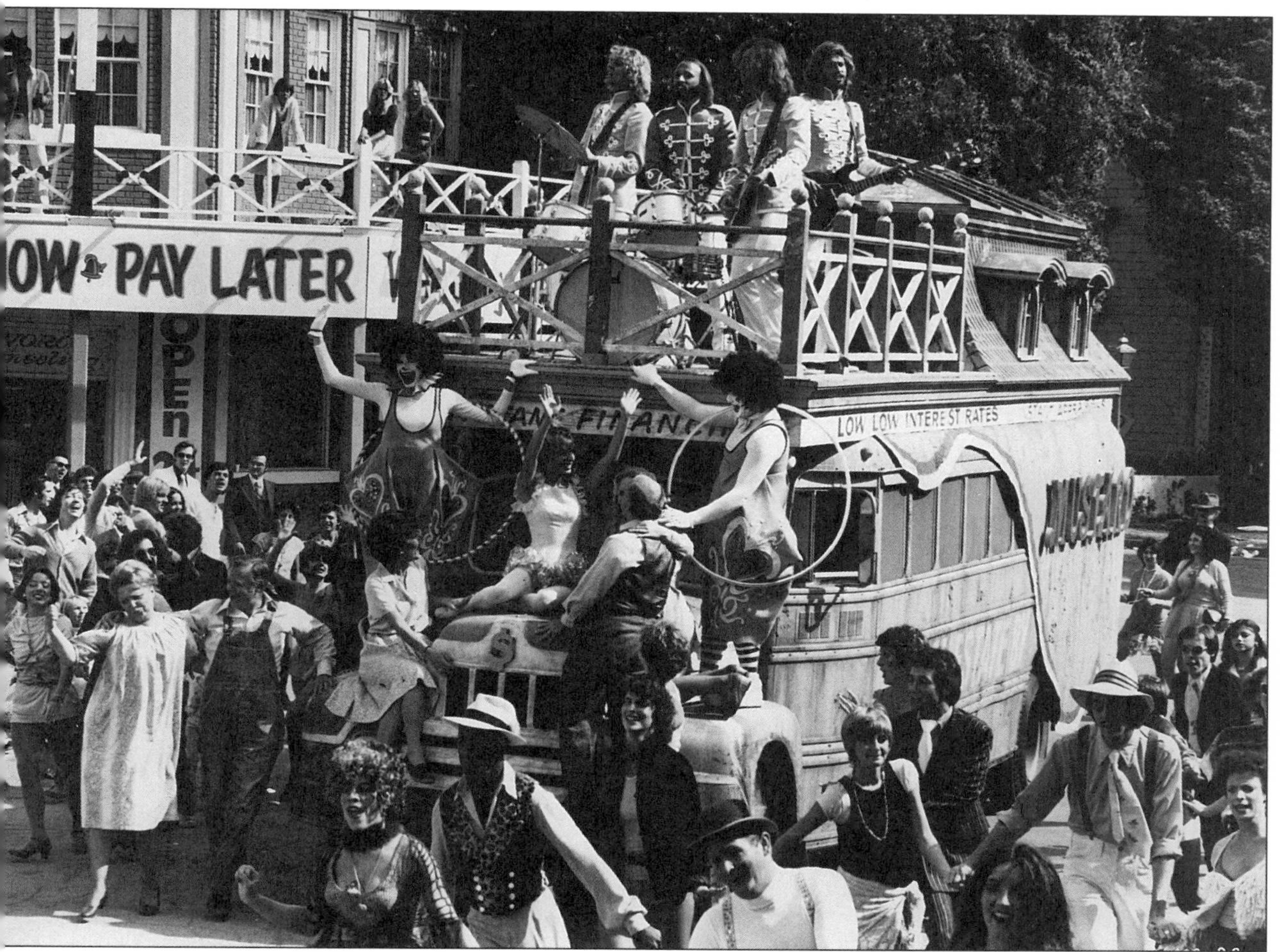

bove and following pages: Scenes from *Sgt Pepper's Lonely Hearts Club Band.* (Cinema International Corporation)

The synopsis read:

'For half a century, Sgt Pepper's Lonely Hearts Club Band has kept the music going and the people dancing. In the mid-fifties, Sgt Pepper's home town, Heartland, feels the time has come to honour its favourite son and a golden weather vane is erected at a celebratory dedication ceremony. Alas, at that moment, Sgt Pepper drops dead.

'When his will is read, it is discovered that the band's musical instruments have the magic power to make dreams come true. They must always be kept in Heartland or the town will fall to rack and ruin.

'Twenty years later, Sgt Pepper's grandson Billy Shears (Peter Frampton), with his friends Mark, Dave and Bob Henderson (Barry, Robin and Maurice Gibb), have formed a new Sgt Pepper's Lonely Hearts Club Band, and, in Heartland, are a huge success. Their manager is Billy's wicked half brother Dougie Shears (Paul Nicholas).

'Out of the blue, a telegram arrives asking them to send a tape to the biggest record company in the world, Big Deal Records. Mr Kite (George Burns), Mayor of Heartland and Custodian of the instruments, knows that if the band is successful, it will be Sgt Pepper's dream come true.

'However, evil is afoot in Heartland. An ugly yellow van arrives in town. It belongs to Mr Mustard (Frankie Howerd), an unscrupulous real estate broker who is accompanied by his bodyguard, the Brute (Carel Struycken) and his two female robots (Anna Rodzianko and Rose Aragon). Mustard is under orders from "FVB" to take over Heartland but the first thing to catch his eye is Billy's girlfriend, Strawberry Fields (Sandy Farina).

'The band's tape reaches Los Angeles where B. D. Brockhurst (Donald Pleasance), the greedy and lascivious chairman of Big Deal Records, loves it. So does his mistress, the trashy Lucy (Dianne Steinberg), leader of a female band, Lucy and Her Diamonds (Stargard).

'When Sgt Pepper's Lonely Hearts Club Band is summoned to Los Angeles to make their first record, Billy regretfully says goodbye to Strawberry and they leave town. In Los Angeles they are wined, dined, drugged and tricked by B. D. into signing a contract. They become an overnight success.

'Meanwhile, back in Heartland, Mustard has succeeded in stealing Sgt Pepper's instruments. The town of goodness and joy quickly goes to seed. Following FVB's orders, Mustard delivers one instrument to Dr Maxwell Edison (Steve Miller), another to Father Sun (Alice Cooper) and a third to FVB himself.

'In despair at what is happening to Heartland, Strawberry heads for Los Angeles and enlists the band's help in recovering the instruments. They steal Mr Mustard's van and, following the robot's instructions, they track the instruments.

'At Dr Maxwell's Institute of Youth, the power of a Sgt Pepper instrument is turning old, ugly, corrupt and greedy people into young, ugly, corrupt and greedy people. Dr Maxwell puts up a fierce struggle, but the instrument is retrieved.

'At Father Sun's Temple of Electronic Cosmology, the second instrument is recovered, but in the process, Billy suffers a violent electric shock. With the power of true love, Strawberry brings him back to his senses but, when the computer blows up, they have no way of finding the remaining instrument.

'A distraught B. D. Brockhurst, with the help of Dougie, is figuring out ways of getting his hands on the band once more and asks them to return to Heartland to perform a benefit for Mr Kite. The guest stars are to be Earth, Wind and Fire.

'During the concert, Lucy and Dougie steal all the money raised and store it in Mustard's van, but suddenly he reappears, kidnaps Strawberry and heads off in the van to take all the instruments to FVB, hotly pursued by Billy, Mark, Dave and Bob.

'FVB is the Future Villain Band (Aerosmith), the world's most vicious rock and roll band. Strawberry is offered up to them as a victim but suddenly the boys arrive and in a desperate struggle, overpower FVB, but Strawberry plunges to her death from the elevated stage.

'Back in Heartland, after Strawberry's funeral, a grieving Billy hurls himself from a window. As he falls, the Sgt Pepper weather vane (**Billy Preston**) comes to life and catches him in mid air. Strawberry is returned to life and the villains are suitably punished. Heartland finally celebrates its return to normality in a rousing musical finale.'

Stigwood gathered scores of stars to appear in a spectacular scene. They included Peter Noone, Wilson Pickett, Helen Reddy, Bonnie Raitt, Minnie Ripperton, George Benson, Keith Carradine, Barbara Dickson, Carol Channing, Jack Bruce, Rick Derringer, Bruce Johnson, Dr John, Etta James, Barry Humphries, Heart, Adrian Gurvitz, Leif Garrett, Jose Feliciano, Yvonne Elliman, **Donovan**, Randy Edelman, Hank Williams Jr, Gwen Verdon, Frankie Valli, Tina Turner, Al Stewart, John Stewart, **Del Shannon**, Seals and Croft, Connie Stevens, Sha Na Na, Johnny Rivers and Chita Rivera.

Stigwood had originally offered the part of Billy Shears to Paul McCartney, but he'd turned it down.

Sgt Pepper had made such an impression on Stigwood that four years prior to the movie, he had launched a stage musical, also called *Sgt Pepper's Lonely Hearts Club Band*, at the Beacon Theatre in New York. The show was directed by Tom O'Horgan and produced by Stigwood and the premiere on 14 November 1974 was attended by John Lennon.

● Sgt Pepper's Lonely Hearts Club Band *(Song)*

Paul composed this song when he was pushing forward his concept for the Beatles' ninth British album. He'd wanted a theme and also to give the appearance of a live band and felt that this song could fulfil that function, open the album and also be reprised near the end of the LP.

He had been fascinated by the colourful names of San Francisco bands such as the Electric Prunes, the Quicksilver Messenger Service and the Grateful Dead, which inspired him to come up with the name 'Sgt Pepper's Lonely Hearts Club Band'. However, there was the suggestion that he'd originally thought of 'Dr Pepper' but discovered that there was an American soft drink of that name, and another suggestion hinted that it was actually **Mal Evans** who had thought the name up.

Initial recording sessions began on 1 February 196[illegible] and resumed in March when four French horns were used, played by James W. Buck, John Burden, Tony Randall and Neil Sanders.

To provide the effect of a live band, with audience sounds and applause, the **Abbey Road** archives were consulted and extracts from sound effects albums were used – *Volume 6: Applause and Laughter* and *Volume 2[illegible] Audience Applause and Atmosphere, Royal Albert Hall and Queen Elizabeth Hall.*

Apart from its appearance on the *Sgt Pepper* album, the track was later used on the compilation *The Beatles 1967–1970.*

When the **Robert Stigwood** film *Sgt Pepper's Lonely Hearts Club Band* was released, **EMI** decided to take advantage of the publicity surrounding it and released 'Sgt Pepper's Lonely Hearts Club Band' as a single

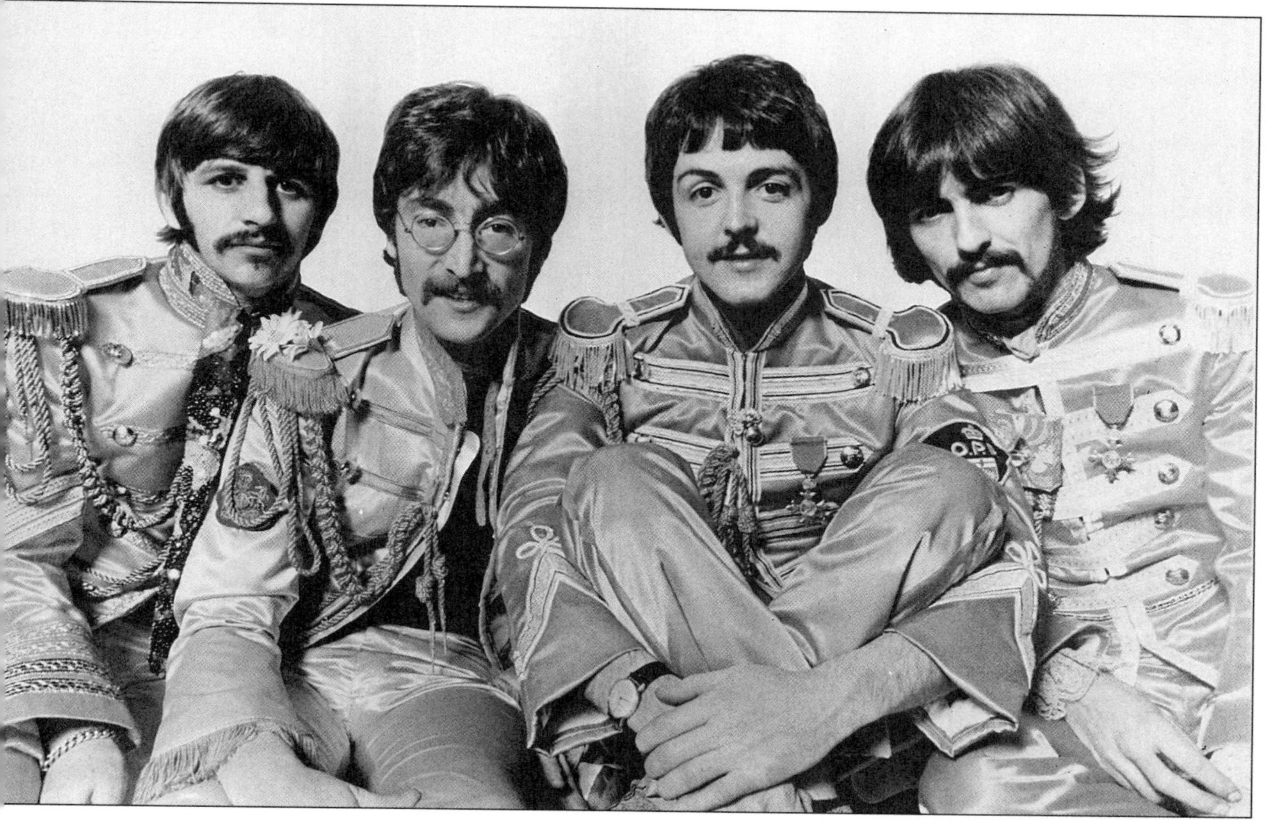
e Beatles wore bright military-style outfits designed by costumiers Maurice Berman's to promote the Sgt Pepper image. (EMI)

rlophone R 6022 on 30 September 1978 with the tracks ith a Little Help From My Friends' and 'A Day In The e'. It became the first Beatles British single to fail to er the charts.

Shades Of A Personality

other project touted as the Beatles' third movie.

At the beginning of 1967 producer **Walter Shenson** nounced to the press that the Beatles' third film would based on a script penned by a young playwright, **Owen lder**.

'Shades Of A Personality' was a tale of multiple sonality and each member of the Beatles would play the ne person, portraying different aspects of his sonality. John would be the main character, with the er three as alternative aspects of that character. They ld share the same girlfriend and the music would not be performed by the group, but would simply be used as background music on the soundtrack. In fact, only one of the Beatles would appear on the screen at any one time and there would be no mention of the Beatles in the film. Some time was set aside for the filming, but a suitable script was not available at the time and the project was eventually abandoned.

● Shadows, The

Prior to the emergence of the Beatles nationally, the Shadows, with their singer Cliff Richard, were Britain's most popular group. The Shadows themselves, together with Mike Read, discussed their brief association with the Beatles in their biography *The Story Of The Shadows* (Elm Tree Books, 1983).

The line-up of the group in 1963 comprised Hank Marvin (lead guitar), Bruce Welch (rhythm guitar), Cliff

Richard (guitar/vocals), and Brian Bennett (drums). During that year both the Shadows and the Beatles found themselves in Blackpool. The Shadows were appearing for a summer season at the **ABC** Theatre, but had Sundays off, and the Beatles were making a Sunday appearance at the venue. The Shadows decided it was a good time for them to get together with the band whose latest record, 'From Me To You', was at No. 1 in the charts and invited them to a party at a bungalow Hank Marvin had rented. Bruce was to point out that, 'The great thing was the lack of animosity or jealousy between the two groups and their mutual respect, both personal and musical.'

The Shadows – the most popular British band until the emergence of the Beatles. (EMI)

The Shadows were invited to Paul McCartney's 21st birthday party. Brian, Hank and Bruce travelled from Blackpool by car to meet up with Paul and **Jane Asher** at the **Empire Theatre, Liverpool**. They then travelled to Paul's Auntie Jin's house where the party was being held. They were pleased to meet various Mersey artists such as the **Fourmost** and **Billy J. Kramer** and noticed how drunk John Lennon had become during the course of th evening – which led to his incident with **Bob Wooler**.

The Shadows enjoyed themselves and Bruce was comment, 'In the future, though, the only brief encounte we had with the Beatles would be over a cup of tea and sandwich at **Abbey Road Studios** or a quick thumbs-u and odd word of greeting at the annual ***NME*** Poll Winne concert.'

Hank also pointed out that Brian Epstein had taken th Beatles to see the Shadows at the **Liverpool Empire**, the days before they had achieved success on recor Hank commented, 'He was obviously trying to impre upon John, Paul, George and Ringo that this was the wa they should present themselves: in neat looking suits an dickie bows!'

A Shadows single issued in November 1981 featured medley which included 'Imagine' and 'Woman'.

● Shakin' All Over

One of the few genuine British rock classics, penned Frederick Heath. Freddie began his career in a skif band, Freddie Heath & the Nutters. He changed his na to Johnny Kidd, led a group called the Pirates and had h first hit, 'Please Don't Touch', in 1959. They reached t No. 1 spot with 'Shakin' All Over' in 1960 and the Beatl included it in their repertoire and performed it until t following year.

Kidd had several hits, including 'A Shot Of Rhyth And Blues' and 'I'll Never Get Over You', but was kill in a road accident in October 1966.

● Shankar, Ravi

Noted Indian musician, born in Benares, India, on 7 Ap 1920. Ravi's family moved to Paris in 1931. He sa 'Paris was fantastic at that time, it was the art capital the world, very exciting.' At the age of thirteen he began learn to master the sitar. His guru was Baba. Ravi shav his hair, led a very frugal existence and made himsel sitar from a completely hollow gourd, which was ve fragile.

'How many hours a day did I practise?' he said. started eight hours at the beginning, some points fourte sometimes sixteen, but mainly twelve–fourteen.'

In his book *My Music, My Life* (Jonathan Cape, 196 Shankar mentions that what he calls the great si explosion happened in 1966. In June of that year he r orge Harrison and Paul McCartney at the home of a tual friend. George voiced his enthusiasm for learning play the sitar. Says Ravi, 'I carefully explained to him at one must undergo many long years of study and ctise of the basics before one can play even a single e properly. He understood all this perfectly and said he s prepared to go through the years of discipline.'

Ravi invited him to India to study, together with **ttie**, and George accepted. He invited Ravi to his Esher ngalow a few days before the sitarist was leaving gland and he played sitar for all four members of the atles. He recalled, 'I always feel inspired when I play a small, close group and especially for musicians – no tter what tradition or country they belong to. And that ning, as I was accompanied on the tabla by Alla Rakha, lt very happy with my music. And my little audience ponded very warmly as we played.'

On Ravi's return to India he received a letter from rge saying he'd be able to spend six weeks with him. y arrived at Bombay airport, George had taken Ravi's ice and cut his hair and sprouted a moustache. The ple weren't recognized at first. They registered in the Mahal Hotel under a false name, but within 24 hours ryone in Bombay knew and the hotel was besieged. i called a press reception to explain that George had e, not as a Beatle, but as his disciple and they needed e left in peace. They all then went to Kashmir and ares to begin the lessons.

Ravi commented: 'I had George practise all the correct tions of sitting and some of the basic exercises. This the most one could do in six weeks, considering that a iple usually spends years learning these basics.'

During his trip George met 200 of Shankar's students also observed a religious festival near the Ganges. Of lessons with Shankar, he commented: 'He sat down, great master giant of a man on the sitar, and showed scales, the first lesson.' The trip was to have a ound effect on George, who remarked: 'I went partly to n music and partly to see and learn as much as I could t India as possible. I'd always heard stories about men aves in the Himalayas, hundreds of years old, and le who can levitate and people who get buried under ground for six weeks and lots of what the West would mysticism.' George was later to involve himself in the a movement.

avi continued to give George lessons when he was in London and also on a trip to Hollywood in 1967. The contact with the Beatles obviously popularized him in a wider context than previously. He commented: 'The Beatles scene and the sitar explosion brought me immediately into a position of immense popularity with the young people, and I now find myself adored like a movie star or young singer.'

Following the trip, George performed on sitar for his track 'Within You, Without You' on the *Sgt Pepper* album, which was made with sitar and tabla accompaniment. In 1968 George wrote 'The Inner Light' using Indian musicians and by the summer of 1969 was recording several chant numbers with London's **Radha Krsna Temple**.

George arranged for Ravi to sign to the Beatles' Apple label and his first release was 'Joi Bangla'/'Oh Bhaugowan' c/w 'Raga Mishra'/'Jhinjhoti', issued in August 1971. The album *Raga* was issued in December 1971. This was the soundtrack album of the film *Raga*, a documentary. In one scene, George appears as Ravi's pupil.

Other Ravi Shankar records produced by George included *In Concert 1972*, recorded live at New York's Philharmonic Hall on 8 April 1972. This featured: Ravi Shankar (sitar), Ali Akbar Khan (sarad), Alla Rakha (tabla), Ashoka Susan (tambouras). The double album was issued in America on 22 January 1973. Another album produced by George was *Shankar Family And Friends*, issued in Britain on George's own Dark Horse label in September 1974 and in America the following month.

Ravi had been most concerned about the terrible conditions in Bangla Desh and considered the idea of holding a concert in order to raise money for the starving children of that unfortunate country. Initially, he had in mind a fairly modest amount of $25,000. While he was with George in California recording the soundtrack for the film *Raga*, he put the idea to George, who immediately took the situation in hand and contacted Ringo Starr and Leon Russell. Within a matter of weeks the concert had been organized, with several major musicians enthusiastic about supporting the charity event.

The concert took place before an audience of 40,000 at Madison Square Garden, New York, on 1 August 1971 and raised $243,418.50. A cheque for that amount was sent to the United Nations Children's Fund For Relief To Refugee Children Of Bangla Desh on 12 December of that year.

More money was raised from the film *The Concert For Bangla Desh*, released the following year. Ravi opened the actual concert and performed 'Bangla Dhun'.

● Shannon, Del

Major American singing star, born Charles Weedon Westover in Coopersville, Michigan, on 30 December 1939.

Shannon had a number of major hits, including 'Runaway', 'Little Town Flirt', 'Hats Off To Larry', 'Hey Little Girl' and 'Swiss Maid'.

He was one of the artists who appeared on BBC radio's **'Swinging Sound '63'** at the **Royal Albert Hall** on 18 April 1963. The Beatles were also on the bill and Shannon was impressed. He became the first American artist to record a Beatles song when he recorded the single 'From Me To You'. He told John Lennon he was going to record one of their songs and John seemed pleased. Then he changed his mind. Shannon told radio journalist Spencer Leigh, 'I think John had talked to Brian Epstein, who didn't want any American performer covering their songs. He wanted to invade America all by himself.'

However, Shannon recorded the number immediately in Britain, using British musicians, and it was a particular tribute because he did it before the Beatles became famous in America. 'From Me To You' c/w 'Two Silhouettes' was issued in the States on Big Top 3152 on 3 June 1963. It was a number the Beatles had performed on 'Swinging Sound '63' on which Del Shannon had topped the bill. Within a few days of release, Shannon's version entered the *Cash Box* chart at No. 86. The *Cash Box* review read, 'Shannon, who recently did chart business with "Two Kinds Of Teardrops", can do another big one in "From Me To You". It's an infectious thump-a-twist version of the tune that's currently riding in the number one slot in England – via the Beatles' stand (available here on VJ).' In fact, Shannon's version was issued in America exactly eight days before **Vee Jay** issued the Beatles version.

He also performed a duet of 'From Me To You' with Johnny Tillotson on stage at the **Empire Theatre, Liverpool**.

When Shannon appeared at the **Saville Theatre, London** on a bill with **Chuck Berry** on 19 February 1967, John and Ringo went along to see the show.

During 1987, Shannon made some recordings with George Harrison. The singer was found dead at his ho[me] in Santa Clarita, California, on 8 February 1990. He w[as] the victim of gunshot wounds, presumably self-inflicted.

● Shapiro, Helen

For a short time, Britain's most successful female sing[er] although her span of hits lasted only from 1961–19[6…] Born on 28 September 1946 in London's Bethnal Gre[en] area she was discovered by songwriter John Schroed[er] currently working for **EMI**, at a local singing school [in] 1961. He recommended her to EMI and she was signed [to] the Columbia label. Schroeder wrote 'Don't Treat Me Li[ke] A Child' for her and the debut record reached No. 3 in [the] British charts. This was followed-up by 'You Don't Kno[w]' which topped the British charts and became a milli[on] seller. At the time Helen was only fourteen and st[ill]

Helen Shapiro – billtopper of the Beatl[es'] first major British tour. (National Film Archive[)]

attending Clapton Girls' School; special permission ha[d to] be obtained for her to make radio and television dates.

The cinema documentary series 'Look At Life' featu[red] the young singer and she was voted 'No. 1 Female Bri[tish] Singer' in 1961 and 1962. Her other hits were 'Wal[king] Back To Happiness', 'Tell Me What He Said', 'Let's T[alk] About Love', 'Little Miss Lonely', 'Keep Away From O[ther] Girls', 'Queen For Tonight', 'Woe Is Me', 'Look Who I[t Is]' and 'Fever'.

Helen also starred in the film *It's Trad, Dad*, dire[cted] by **Richard Lester**, who introduced some of ınovations into that film which he was later to utilize in *A ɬard Day's Night*.

Helen first met the Beatles on the afternoon of 2 'ebruary 1963 at the **Gaumont Cinema, Bradford**, ·hich was the first date of the nationwide tour headed by ıe sixteen-year-old singer, on which the Beatles were ıaking their first package tour appearance. Although a pecial car had been arranged to take Helen to the various ities, she preferred to travel on the tour bus. When Helen aught flu she was unable to appear at the Taunton and 'ork gigs and was replaced by Billie Davis, whose current it was 'Tell Him'. In her absence, **Danny Williams** ›pped the bill. Following an appearance at the **ABC, ;arlisle**, there was an incident at the local hotel where ıembers of the tour were asked to leave a party for Young onservatives.

John and Paul began to write a song for Helen which ıey hoped she'd record in Nashville. Norrie Paramor, her &R man, was taking her to record in the American C&W entre and had suggested that the Beatles might come up ith a number for her. They wrote a number and Paul ommented, 'We've called it "Misery", but it isn't as slow s it sounds, it moves along at quite a steady pace and we ıink Helen will make a pretty good job of it. We've also one a number for Duffy Power, which he's going to ecord.' Paramor considered that the number wasn't ıitable for Helen and turned it down. They were iscussing it on the coach when **Kenny Lynch**, who was so appearing on the tour, asked them if he could record .

In an interview with ***Mersey Beat***, Helen told of how ıe became a big fan of the Beatles soon after they started ·uring together: 'John and Paul always used to be writing ımbers together on the coach. I remember them playing From Me To You" to me, and asking me what I thought of . I told them I thought it was terrific – and I'm glad to say was right!

'We used to have some great times together. Not many eople know it, but I've been playing the banjo for about ve years. I had it with me on the tour, and now and again would join the Beatles' line-up for an impromptu ession!'

Although Helen's success in the charts ended in 1963, ıe continued her career as a singer, developing into a fine zz stylist and at one time later in her career, she was anaged by **Tony Barrow**, the former Beatles publicist.

● *Shaw, Sandie*

One of Britain's leading female singers of the sixties, who appeared with the Beatles on the American TV show **'Shindig'**.

As a fan, Sandie saw the Beatles when they appeared at the **Odeon, Romford** on 16 June 1963. The week previously she'd sung there for free at the Saturday morning cinema show and the manager agreed to let her in backstage for the Beatles' show.

Sandie arrived with her friend Janet Llewellyn and they watched the show from the wings. As Paul passed, he kissed her on the cheek and said, 'This one's for you, la.' Sandie, at the time, was besotted by John Lennon.

In her autobiography *The World At My Feet* (Harper Collins), she recalled, 'Later, in the dressing-room, Ringo tried to put his hands up Janet's blouse, and we both marched out indignantly. It's a good job he didn't try that on with me or he would have discovered the cotton-wool padding in my otherwise empty bra.'

The second time she managed to get backstage was when the Beatles were at the **Albert Hall** on 15 September 1963. She phoned up the hall and said she was John's long-lost cousin Sandra – and John actually came and answered the phone, then arranged for her to come backstage.

Sandie Shaw with singer Adam Faith. (National Film Archives)

● Shears, Billy

A fictitious character created for the *Sgt Pepper's Lonely Hearts Club Band* concept. Ringo took the part of Shears and the character was later fleshed-out by the many wild stories in the 'Paul Is Dead' campaign of 1969.

One American Underground paper, *Rat Subterranean News*, ran a full-page story written by Lee Merrick which claimed that Shears had become a substitute for the dead Paul McCartney. The story was published on 29 October 1969 and had supposedly been rushed by cable from London the day before publication. Merrick began his 'exposé' with the words 'Paul McCartney is dead'. He then mentioned that he'd become very friendly with the Apple crowd during the previous six months and had seen the Beatles and 'Paul' around the offices. He went to a party with several Apple friends during the course of which he was given the story. He wrote, 'Billy Shears was a young London rock musician who did short gigs in London nightclubs and occasional tours, waiting for the chance to make it big.' At the beginning of the sixties Billy was on the Continent, presumably in Hamburg, when, 'In 1962 Shears played on the same nightclub bill as Paul McCartney. In fact, he was a dead ringer for Paul. Of course, you could tell the difference if they stood side by side. Billy had a somewhat oversized beak-shaped nose. But in photographs, or at a distance, they were absolutely indistinguishable.'

The article went on to relate how the two kept in touch as friends. Then: 'In November 1966, Paul McCartney was involved in an auto accident – a fatal accident. John, George and Ringo first wanted to stage a gigantic funeral in memory of Paul, but super-sharp manager, Brian Epstein, feared that Paul's death would destroy the Beatles mystique and managed almost entirely to suppress the news. Epstein's calculating mind had already devised a scheme for keeping the Beatles intact – at least for the public. With a minor nose job, Billy Shears would make a perfect replacement for Paul. Though hesitant at first, Shears soon accepted Epstein's offer. What musician could resist the opportunity to step into the shoes of one of the superstars of the rock world?'

Merrick then went on to state that because they knew the ruse wouldn't last, the Beatles began to scatter 'clues' on their albums.

He claimed that Shears had replaced Paul three years previously and that he had carried out a search for evidence to substantiate his story and finally tracked dow Philip Shears, Billy's father, in Chelsea. At first Shears father refused to discuss the well-kept secret, but finall agreed: '. . . the elderly Mr Shears relented and confirme the facts. "Mum and me always knew that it couldn't sta secret for ever. The Beatles are a bunch of wonderful la and have made a whole new world for us." But, he adde "It's high time our Billy received the credit he deserves."

In the 1978 feature film *Sgt Pepper's Lonely Heart Club Band*, Billy Shears was portrayed by Peter Frampton

● Shea Stadium, Flushing, Queens, New York City

Baseball stadium, home of the New York Mets. Th Beatles' first appearance there took place on Sunday, 1 August 1965. It was the first stage show of their 1965 to and support acts included Brenda Holloway, the **Ki Curtis Band** (introduced by New York DJ Scott Ross **Sounds Incorporated**, **Cannibal & the Headhunte** and a troupe of disco dancers.

It was promoter **Sid Bernstein**'s idea to use th 55,600-seater arena and the concert became the world biggest up to that time, attracting world record box offi receipts of $304,000, of which $160,000 was the Beatle share. Due to the vast cost of staging and, in particular, t cost of security, Bernstein himself only made a profit $6,500. The insurance from Lloyds of London for that o concert alone cost $25,000.

There was an overhead blimp decorated with Beat slogans and the boys were flown to a nearby point helicopter (the New York authorities refused to let t helicopter take them into the stadium itself), and th finished their journey in the back of a Wells Fargo secur van.

At the time, Bernstein had taken on management of American band called the Rascals and he alternated t flashing sign which said, 'Please stay in your seats for orderly concert', with 'The Rascals are coming'. A furio Brian Epstein told Bernstein to immediately stop t message else the Beatles would not perform.

Disc jockey **Murray The K** welcomed the crowd 'The biggest concert ever in history' and DJ Cousin Bru Morrow introduced **Ed Sullivan**, who said, 'Now, Ladi and Gentlemen, honoured by their country, decorated their Queen and loved here in America, HERE ARE T BEATLES!' The boys ran on stage, each shaking hands w llivan, and began their performance with 'Twist And out'. Their other numbers were 'Everybody's Trying To My Baby', 'Can't Buy Me Love', 'Baby's In Black', 'Act aturally' (Ringo's solo vocal), 'A Hard Day's Night', elp!' and 'I'm Down'. A white estate car was ready at the le of the stage and they were speedily driven away.

The show was filmed by Sullivan Productions Inc in sociation with Subafilm Ltd for a 50-minute colour evision special which was screened in Britain by the 3C on 1 March 1966.

The Beatles' final appearance at Shea Stadium took ace on 23 August 1966, although this didn't prove to be spectacular as the first, with 12,000 unsold seats. owever, the Beatles earned even more than their evious fee, receiving $189,000.

She Came In Through The Bathroom 'indow

nen the Beatles first tried to record this number at the **ple Studios** on Wednesday, 22 February 1969, the adio was in such an unfinished state that it proved possible to record there and George Martin had to make angements for equipment from **Abbey Road** to be pped down to **Savile Row**. Recording of the number s tried again at Abbey Road in July and the number was luded on the *Abbey Road* album.

Paul had originally composed the number with **Joe cker** in mind and Cocker actually recorded the song e the Beatles had cut their version.

The working title had been, simply, 'Bathroom Window' l it was based on a real-life experience. Some fans had ken into Paul's house, using the bathroom window, and l stolen a number of items including clothes and otographs.

Sheik Of Araby, The

vintage number penned by Harry Smith, Francis eeler and Ed Snyder. Various artists recorded it, luding Duke Ellington and **Joe Brown** & his Bruvvers, the Beatles were probably influenced by Fats mino's 1961 recording. They performed the song in ir stage act, with George Harrison on lead vocals, and orded it during their **Decca audition**.

Sheila

nber written by **Tommy Roe** which the singer issued in May 1962. It topped the American charts for him and when it was issued in Britain it reached the No. 3 position. The Beatles immediately included it in their repertoire as a vocal spot for George and the group performed it during their December 1962 season at Hamburg, resulting in the **Adrian Barber** recording. The following year the group toured Britain on a bill headed by Tommy Roe and **Chris Montez**.

● She Loves You

This number became Britain's biggest-selling record, until overtaken by sales of Paul McCartney's 'Mull of Kintyre' in 1978. It was also the Beatles' first million-seller.

John and Paul began writing the song on a coach during a British tour and completed it the same night, 26 June 1963, in a hotel room in Newcastle-upon-Tyne after their **Majestic Ballroom** appearance.

Paul commented, 'John and I wrote it together. I thought of it first and thought of doing it as one of those answering songs. You know, the sort of thing the American singing groups keep doing. A couple of us would sing "She Loves You" and the others would do the "yeah yeah yeah" ones. The one would be answering everything the other two sang. Then John and I agreed it was a pretty crummy idea as it stood and since we were borrowing an American thing, I suppose it was crummy. But at least we had the basic idea of writing the song. That night in Newcastle we just sat in the hotel for a few hours and wrote it.'

The group began recording the song at **Abbey Road** on Monday, 1 July. John and Paul had originally played the number to George Martin on acoustic guitars and he suggested that instead of going right into the first verse, they should start with the chorus of 'She loves you, yeah, yeah, yeah'. George Harrison also came up with the idea of having the sixth chord at the end of the song.

The number was released as their fourth single on Parlophone R 5055 on 23 August 1963 with 'I'll Get You' on the flip. It was also included on their tenth British EP *The Beatles Million Sellers* in 1965 and is found on the compilation albums *A Collection Of Beatles Oldies (But Goldies)*, *The Beatles 1962–1966*, and *20 Greatest Hits*. It was also the first track on *Savile's Time Travels – 20 Golden Hits of 1963* in 1981. It was included in *The Beatles Box* and *The Beatles Collection* sets. In America the single was issued by Swan Records on 16 September 1963 on Swan 4152. It was one of five new singles which

Murray The K played on the WINS radio station in New York and it came third in popularity with listeners. The record was not successful on its initial release.

The number received its first major airing when film footage of the Beatles performing it was screened on Jack Paar's networked TV show on 3 January 1964. With the huge Beatles promotion which ensued, Swan re-released the single and it immediately succeeded 'I Want To Hold Your Hand' in the No. 1 position in America, achieving the feat of being the first time that an artist had had two consecutive chart-toppers since Elvis Presley in 1956 when 'Love Me Tender' replaced 'Don't Be Cruel'/'Hound Dog' at the top of the charts. Capitol also issued it on *The Beatles Second Album* and a live version is to be found on *The Beatles At The Hollywood Bowl*.

The number was featured on numerous of their BBC radio shows – three times on '**Saturday Club**', five times on '**Pop Go The Beatles**' and one time each on '**Easy Beat**', '**The Ken Dodd Show**' and '**From Us To You**'.

There have been over sixty versions by other artists, including several foreign language recordings, and artists who have recorded it have ranged from the Chipmunks and Pinky & Perky to Vanilla Fudge and the Tottenham Hotspur Football Team. Peter Sellers also recorded two versions, one in the style of Dr Strangelove, the other in the style of an Irish dentist character.

The Beatles also entered the chart with a German language version of the number, '*Sie Liebt Dich*', although it only had a brief stay in the No. 97 position in *Billboard*.

● Shenson, Walter

San Francisco-born film producer who had been educated at Stanford University. For a time he was a Press Officer at Columbia Pictures and then moved to London, establishing it as his base for the making of a series of low-budget comedies, which included *The Mouse That Roared* with **Peter Sellers** and *The Mouse On The Moon*.

He was 45 years old in 1963 when United Artists approached him to produce a film about the Beatles, which they would fund. Before approaching Brian Epstein, United Artists and Shenson agreed that they would be willing to offer the Beatles 25 per cent of the profits of three films. When the meeting took place and the discussion about percentages was about to begin, Epstein said, 'I couldn't accept anything less than seven and a half per cent.'

It was Shenson's British accountant who suggested th there be a clause in his contract in which the rights to t films would revert back to him after a period of fifte years. United Artists agreed because they believed t Beatles would only be a passing fad. Shenson hir **Richard Lester**, who had worked with him on *The Mou On The Moon* as Director and says that **Alun Owen** w hired as Scriptwriter on Paul McCartney's suggestion.

Shenson brought in *A Hard Day's Night* on a budget £200,000, even though the film company were prepared spend up to double that figure.

After he'd produced *Help!* he found great difficulty persuading the Beatles to accept some of the oth projects, which included 'Shades of A Personality' and Talent For Loving'. He even suggested to John Lennon th he should write a script, but John turned it dow Altogether, Shenson received about 40 different scripts a third Beatles movie.

Eventually, the Beatles decided to make the third fi in their contract a documentary and *Let It Be* was fund by United Artists and Shenson was given a small share the profits.

Shenson remained in Britain filming a series of lo budget projects including *Thirty Is A Dangerous A Cynthia*; *Don't Raise the Bridge, Lower The River*; a *Digby, The Biggest Dog In The World*.

In 1973, after living in Britain for eighteen yea Shenson and his wife Gerry returned to America a settled in Bel-Air, California.

When the copyright of *A Hard Day's Night* and *He* reverted to him after the fifteen-year agreed term, Shens was able to re-record both films with a stereopho soundtrack using the Dolby system. He also added a tw minute prologue to *A Hard Day's Night*. Stills from film, allied to graphics and optical effects, were used the beginning of the film as a background to 'I'll (Instead', a song which had been originally written for movie but unused at the time of its initial release.

● Sheraton Motel Hotel, *Macleay Street, Sydney, Australia*

When the Beatles were to tour Australia, promoter **Ke Brodziak** initially had difficulty finding accommodat for them in Sydney. The four leading hotels had refusec accept a booking for them due to complaints from regu ıtrons and Brodziak was considering placing each Beatle a different hotel. However, Bert Dunn, who owned the latively small Sheraton Motel Hotel, agreed to commodate the group and their party when they arrived 11 June 1964.

The hotel manageress was former beauty queen argaret Walpole, who had been Miss Victoria 1950, and e took them to their penthouse, Suite 801, and troduced them to their two Spanish maids Maria Parra d Aurora Martinez.

Derek Taylor organized a press reception in the tel's conference room at 4.30 p.m. during which one urnalist asked: 'Paul, what do you expect to find in ıstralia?' 'Australians,' he answered.

Oddly enough, **Tony Sheridan** was staying at the eraton at the same time. The Beatles' former friend from eir Hamburg days was in Australia to tour with Billy orpe & the Aztecs and Digger Revell. However, he was and didn't make any attempt to contact them.

The Beatles returned to the Sheraton when they were pearing at **Sydney Stadium**. On 18 June a special rty had been organized in honour of Paul's birthday, ich had been tied up with a competition in the *Sunday rror* newspaper, with Derek Taylor and comedian **Dave len** among the judges who selected seventeen girls who uld attend the party at the hotel. The competition quired girls between the ages of sixteen and 22 to write a -word essay entitled 'Why I Would Like To Be A Guest A Beatles Birthday Party'. There were more than ,000 entrants. The party was quite a success and lasted til 2.00 a.m.

Sheridan, Tony

rn Anthony Esmond Sheridan McGinty in Cheltenham 1940, he was to become a musician who had a great luence on several Mersey bands.

While he was a pupil at Norwich Grammar School, ny joined a skiffle group called the Saints. The boys ran ay from home to audition at Chas McDevitt's Skiffle llar in Soho, London. Sheridan and the group's other itarist Kenny Packwood decided to stay behind and join rty Wilde's backing group. Later the same year, 1958, joined Vince Taylor's band, the Playboys. Tony then med his own trio with drummer Brian Bennett and bass itarist Brian Locking (who were both to become mbers of the **Shadows**). In 1959, at the age of nineteen, he made an impression on the TV show 'Oh Boy' where he performed four songs. This led to a booking for the TV show 'Boy Meets Girls'. However, Tony turned up late without his guitar and lost the gig – he was also unofficially banned from appearing on other British TV pop shows as he'd gained a reputation for unreliability. Over the years other musicians have found Tony's temperament frustrating and have suggested that it is the reason why he never made the big time. Even Ringo Starr got fed up backing him because Tony would suddenly perform songs he hadn't even mentioned he'd be playing.

He did manage to be included on a **Larry Parnes** bill when **Gene Vincent** toured Britain and was one of the artists who appeared on the Larry Parnes/**Allan Williams** concert at **Liverpool Stadium** on Tuesday, 3 May 1960.

By the following month, Tony had left for Hamburg. He'd been present at the 2 I's coffee bar in Soho when **Bruno Koschmider** came looking for a group for the **Kaiserkeller** club. **Iain Hines** quickly formed a group, they called themselves the Jets and set off for Hamburg.

After appearing at the Kaiserkeller for a month they got an offer of increased fees and better accommodation at the **Top Ten Club** and changed venues.

When the Beatles appeared in Hamburg they began to drop in to see the Jets and were particularly impressed by Sheridan. Over the next two years, most Liverpool groups were inspired by Sheridan and he was dubbed 'the Teacher'. John Lennon, **Gerry Marsden** and John McNally of the **Searchers** were three of the Liverpool musicians who copied Tony's high-chested guitar stance on stage – and the way he played with his legs astride. The Beatles even joined the Jets for some jam sessions on their first Hamburg trip and when they returned in 1961 they appeared at the Top Ten and backed Sheridan. This resulted in them being hired to provide backing for Sheridan on the Polydor recordings by **Bert Kaempfert**. When they went to the children's school to make their recording over the Whitsun holiday, Sheridan thought the equipment very primitive and said it looked like, 'A leftover relic of the British army occupation from some sort of radio station they had.'

In January 1962 Ringo Starr was enticed to leave **Rory Storm & the Hurricanes** in Liverpool and travel to Hamburg to back Tony at the Top Ten for a fee of £30 per week, a flat and the use of a car. However, he gave it up after three months as he couldn't stand Tony's habit of suddenly playing numbers on stage he hadn't even rehearsed with the band.

Sheridan remained in Hamburg, but the Top Ten couldn't survive the competition from the **Star Club** – and the Star Club itself was to close. Tony found himself playing jazz guitar in a Reeperbahn bar in 1964 when there was a flutter of interest in him due to the large sales (although no major chart placings) of some re-releases of his 1961 recordings with the Beatles. He was invited to appear as a guest star on a British tour with the Searchers and **Roy Orbison** and while in London he met up with the Beatles at **Whaddon House** to talk about old times during a break in the filming of *A Hard Day's Night*. Several months later he was in the same hotel in Australia as the Beatles, but they never met up.

Throughout the rest of his life, Sheridan was to experience momentary surges of interest in his career, but nothing ever came of the short 'revivals'.

Tony continued recording in Germany until 1967 and then left for Vietnam to perform for American troops. He was there for two years and one British music paper reported that he'd been killed over there, leaving many people to think he died in the sixties. He returned to Germany in 1969. A few years later **Horst Fascher** relaunched a new Star Club in Hamburg with Sheridan topping the bill and George Harrison and Ringo Starr visited him on opening night. This was another example of a revived interest in his career and at the same time **Klaus Voormann** had produced a new album, *World's End*, with him.

Sheridan did get on with the Beatles initially, due to their sense of humour, although he always made derogatory remarks about people from the north of England. He was one of those southerners with a stereotyped image of what he thought northerners were like. He supposedly turned anti-British in the seventies, applying for Irish citizenship because of what was happening in Northern Ireland – although some sources say he applied for citizenship because of the generous tax concessions offered to artists and musicians there.

He moved to America for a time where there was interest in recording and promoting him, but nothing happened. Most musicians who knew him felt that Sheridan had the potential to become a major artist. Why he didn't succeed may be due to pure bad luck or perhaps to Tony's own attitude towards success.

● She Said, She Said

A number written by John when he was under th influence of drugs. It was included as a track on th *Revolver* album.

John was to comment, 'I wrote it about an acid trip was on in Los Angeles. It was only the second trip we' had. We took it because we'd started hearing things abo it and we wanted to know what it was all about. Pet Fonda came over to us and started saying things like, " know what it's like to be dead, man", and we didn't real wanna know, but he kept going on and on.'

The Beatles recorded the number on Tuesday, 21 Jun When they began recording, John still hadn't given th number a title, but by the time they had finished it wa decided to call it 'She Said, She Said'.

● She's A Woman

A Paul McCartney composition which was recorded **Abbey Road**'s No. 2 studio on Thursday, 8 October 196 during the *Beatles For Sale* sessions. Paul actually wro the song in the studio on this day and Ringo Starr used percussion instrument called a chocalho for the first tin on this track, while Paul also added piano.

It was originally considered as a Beatles 'A' side b was eventually issued as the flipside of 'I Feel Fine' November 1964. It was also included on the *Rariti* compilation and the 1981 album *The Beatles E Collection*. In America it was included on the *Beatles '* album. A live version of the song can be heard on the 19 release *The Beatles At The Hollywood Bowl*. The Beatl performed the number on their Christmas show in 19 and on their subsequent tours.

● She's Leaving Home

Number composed by Paul which was featured on the S *Pepper's Lonely Hearts Club Band* album. The Beatles si but don't perform instrumentally on this track and Pa originally wanted George Martin to score it, but Geor had too much work on at the time and Paul asked Mi Leander to arrange it.

The musicians on the track included the first woman be specially engaged to perform on a Beatles track Sheila Bromberg on harp. The other musicians were E Gruenberg (leader), Derek Jacobs, Trevor Williams a Jose Luis Garcia (violins); John Underwood, Steph Shingles (violas); Dennis Vigay, Alan Dalziel (cellos); a rdon Pearce (double bass). The number was recorded March 1967 and it is a poignant song which George rtin confessed made him cry.

Paul was to comment, 'It's a much younger girl than leanor Rigby", but the same sort of loneliness. That was Daily Mirror story again – this girl left home and her her said: "We gave her everything, I don't know why left home." But he didn't give her that much, not what wanted when she left home.'

The number was also included on the *Love Songs* and *Beatles Ballads* compilations.

Shimmy Shimmy

bby Freeman took this number to No. 37 in the erican charts in 1960. The Beatles included it in their ertoire the same year with John and Paul duetting on song. The group dropped the number in 1963.

Shindig

American television music series, produced by Jack od, who had launched such early British TV rock 'n' shows as 'Oh Boy!'

Good decided to devote an entire show to British acts l began filming at the Granville Theatre, Waltham een, Fulham, which had previously been a variety atre, on 3 October 1964.

Among the audience of 1,000 were 150 winners of a *tles Monthly* magazine competition.

Acts on the bill included **Sounds Incorporated**, **ndie Shaw**, **P. J. Proby**, the Karl Denver Trio and erpool singers **Tommy Quickly** and **Lyn Cornell**. Beatles topped the bill and performed three numbers: nsas City', 'I'm A Loser' and 'Boys'. The show was eened in America on 20 January 1965.

Shiphol Airport, Holland

ch airport, close to Amsterdam. The Beatles arrived e on 5 June 1964 during their world tour. As Ringo suffering from laryngitis he had been temporarily laced by another drummer, **Jimmy Nicol**.

The airport was packed with fans and the group were cially greeted on alighting from their plane by a group Dutch girls dressed in traditional costume who sented them with flowers. They left the airport to travel earby Hillegom where they rehearsed for their vision appearance at **Treslong Studios**.

Ringo Starr arrived at the airport on 22 September 1975 with some friends, remaining there for only two and a half hours as they were flying off to Johannesburg, South Africa. While at the airport he met actor Rod Steiger, the Three Degrees and Dean Martin's son, Dino.

Paul McCartney & **Wings** arrived at the airport on 24 March 1976 from Germany. The group left on 26 March after their short trip to Holland.

● Shirley's Wild Accordion

An instrumental piece originally due to be featured in the *Magical Mystery Tour* movie. Accordionist Shirley Evans had been hired to appear in the film and John and Paul worked out an instrumental number for her to play. They hired songwriter Mike Leander to write down the music as they hummed it to him, to enable Shirley and her partner Reg Wale to play it at the recording session.

The number was recorded at De Lane Lea studios in London on Thursday, 12 October 1967, and John Lennon officially produced the session. Ringo added some drum sounds and Paul played a maraca.

As it turned out, the track wasn't issued on record and only appeared as a piece of incidental music in the film.

● Short, Don

'Beatle In Brawl – Sorry I Socked You', was the heading for a story about the Beatles on the back page of the *Daily Mirror* newspaper on 21 June 1963. It concerned the incident in which John Lennon beat up **Bob Wooler** at Paul's 21st birthday party and was the first Beatles story penned by Don Short, a show business journalist on the *Daily Mirror* which, at the time, had the largest circulation of any newspaper in the world.

Short was regarded as one of the most influential of journalists and was accorded VIP treatment from the Beatles camp. He was invited to special parties and events, given exclusives, and travelled extensively with the group. He is even mentioned by name in the title story in John Lennon's book *A Spaniard In The Works*: 'The honeymood was don short by a telephant . . .'

Short was to be found around the Beatles in clubs such as the **Ad Lib**, at parties such as the *Sgt Pepper* party at Epstein's Chapel Street home and at events such as the Bed-In at the Amsterdam Hilton. Brian Epstein often invited him for evening drinks at his home and used to personally phone him with exclusives about the Beatles. When Short managed to get the group splashed across the front page of the *Mirror*, Epstein would send him telegrams, such as: 'Great day today. The sun is shining. Congratulations on your front page lead. We will see you at lunch. Brian.'

Short maintained his special relationship with the Beatles, although his loyalty was to the *Mirror* and he wouldn't let sympathy interfere with his using a scoop, which is probably why **Derek Taylor** referred to him as 'A rogue's rogue but a man for a' that'.

When the Beatles were in Hollywood and took their second LSD trip at a party, John later commented, 'There was a reporter, Don Short. We were in the garden; it was only our second one [LSD trip] and we still didn't know anything about doing it in a nice place and keeping it cool.' When they saw Short they didn't know how to act. John said, 'We were terrified waiting for him to go, and he wondered why we couldn't come over. **Neil [Aspinall]**, who had never had acid either, had taken it and he would have to play road manager. We said, "Go get rid of Don Short," and he didn't know what to do.'

When the Beatles were planning the launch of Apple from their Wimpole Street office, John and **Yoko**, Paul and Neil Aspinall were in a room drinking coffee and checking the proofs of the Beatles biography when Short appeared in the doorway with his photographer.

John and Paul, both apparently horrified at the unannounced intrusion, muttered, 'Get him out.' Short said, 'Just a quick photo, boys', and his photographer clicked away. 'And what's all this big business you're getting into?' Short asked. John turned on him, 'Get out, we're not telling you anything.'

The very next day a full-page story appeared in the *Daily Mirror*, captioned 'The Big Business Beatles' and featuring a large by-line for Don Short.

A few days after John's death, a week-long series of articles on John began to appear in the *Sun* newspaper under the by-line: 'By Don Short – The man who shared his secrets'. The series was syndicated and a small excerpt entitled 'The Lighter Side Of John Lennon' was contained in the Proteus book *A Tribute To John Lennon 1940–1980*.

Short left the *Mirror* to run a literary agency providing, among other things, 'kiss-and-tell' stories to newspapers.

● Shot Of Rhythm And Blues, A

A number issued as a single by one of John's favourite artists **Arthur Alexander** in March 1962. The Beatles immediately included it in their repertoire, with John lead vocals, and performed it on two **'Pop Go T Beatles'** and an **'Easy Beat'** radio show. The numb was covered by British rock 'n' roll band Johnny Kidd the Pirates.

● Shotton, Pete

John Lennon's closest childhood friend, whose associati with John spanned thirty years. Blond-haired Pete lived Vale Street, quite close to John's home in Menlo Avenue. The two were at the same primary school, Sun school and also attended **Quarry Bank School** togeth Their first major encounter took place in an expanse ground called 'The Tip'. Shotton believed he'd fou John's weak spot – he was enraged when people call him 'Winnie' (from his middle name, Winston). Wh walking across the Tip, Shotton was ambushed by Lenn who pinned him to the ground and made him promise wouldn't call him Winnie any more. Shotton swore wouldn't and John let him go. As he walked away, Shot turned around and shouted 'Winnie, Winnie, Winn Winnie, Winnie!' They stared at one another, then J grinned and they became the best of friends.

Shotton became a member of John's gang and wh John formed the **Quarry Men**, he talked Pete into play

Pete Shotton – John Lennon's closest childhood friend.

shboard, even though he was not particularly interested music. One evening, at a party, John got drunk and ashed the washboard over Pete's head, bringing his reer as a musician to an end.

When John went to art college, Pete became a cadet at Police College. They kept in touch and once the atles had become successful, John wanted to provide ds for Pete to set himself up in business and arranged him to receive a cheque for £2,000. His initial business led, but in 1964 John offered to bankroll him again and otton found a supermarket in Hayling Island which was for sale for around £20,000. On 18 March 1965 a new npany was formed, Hayling Supermarkets Ltd, with n, George and Pete as directors. The Beatles funded venture.

When Apple was launched, John asked him to leave the ermarket in other hands and move to London to run the **ple Boutique**. This was in 1968. Unfortunately, the p didn't do too well and **John Lyndon** replaced Pete, o became John's personal assistant for a short time.

Shotton last visited Lennon in the Dakota Apartments. His years of friendship with John are documented in his k *John Lennon: In My Life*, first published in 1983 and tten in collaboration with **Nicholas Schaffner**.

Shout

mber written and performed by the Isley Brothers and orded by them in 1959.

The Beatles included the song in their repertoire in 50 with John, Paul and George producing a vocal mony interpretation of the number. In 1964 Lulu orded the song for her debut record and reached No. 7 he British charts with it.

Sibylla's Club, *Swallow Street, ndon W1*

ashionable club which first opened on 23 June 1966. night before the official opening there was a special ty at the club which was attended by the Beatles. The b was financed by celebrities, among them George rrison who had a ten per cent stake in the venture. orge was made a director of Kevin Macdonald ociated Ltd, the company which operated the club.

John and George attended a private reception at ylla's on 1 November 1966, in aid of the band Family, Paul often dropped into the club with **Jane Asher**.

● Side By Side

An early evening BBC Light Programme show broadcast from 5.00 p.m.–5.30 p.m. on each Monday. Presented by John Dunn and produced by Bryant Marriott, 'Side By Side' had a resident group, the Karl Denver Trio. The Beatles made three appearances on the show and on each occasion they opened and closed the programme singing 'Side By Side' with the Karl Denver Trio. In between, each group would alternate with a song. The title number 'Side By Side' was originally composed in 1927.

The Beatles' first broadcast took place on 22 April 1963, which had been recorded at Studio One in the Piccadilly Theatre, London, on 1 April. The group performed 'I Saw Her Standing There', 'Do You Want To Know A Secret?', 'Baby It's You', 'Please Please Me', 'From Me To You' and 'Misery'.

For their second appearance on 13 May 1963, also recorded on 1 April, they performed 'From Me To You', 'Long Tall Sally', 'A Taste Of Honey', 'Chains', 'Thank You Girl' and 'Boys'.

Their final appearance, recorded on 4 April, took place on 24 June 1963 when the group performed 'Too Much Monkey Business', 'Love Me Do', 'Boys', 'I'll Be On My Way' and 'From Me To You'.

● Sie Liebt Dich

One of two tracks the Beatles recorded in the German language. **EMI**'s German branch, Odeon, had appealed to both Brian Epstein and George Martin for the Beatles to record in the German language as their records hadn't been selling in Germany in the quantities they'd hoped. It was not an uncommon practice in the early sixties for British artists to record their latest hits in another language to boost sales in countries such as France, Germany or Spain.

The group knew a smattering of German from their Hamburg days, but were not fluent in the language and Odeon sent along a German translator to help them with the songs.

The group were currently appearing for a season at the **Olympia Theatre** in Paris, so George Martin booked the EMI Pathe Studios there on Wednesday, 29 January 1964.

Martin and engineer **Norman Smith** were waiting in the studios for the group, but they didn't turn up at the appointed time. Martin phoned the George V Hotel and asked **Neil Aspinall** why they weren't there. Neil told him that they weren't going to the studio that day and a furious Martin tore across to the hotel. He arrived to find the Beatles, together with Neil and **Mal**, being served tea by **Jane Asher**. He began shouting at them and they dived for cover behind settees and curtains. They apologized and accompanied him to the studios.

'Sie Liebt Dich' was the German version of 'She Loves You' and they also recorded *'Komm, Gib Mir Deine Hand'*.

The only version of *'Sie Liebt Dich'* to be issued outside Germany at the time was the one issued as a single by Swan on Swan 4182 on 21 May 1964 in the US, with 'I'll Get You' on the flip. It reached No. 97 in the American charts. The track was later issued on the compilation album *Rarities* in 1978.

● Silkie, The

A folk group, formed by students at Hull University. They comprised Sylvia Tatler (vocals), Mike Ramsden (guitar/vocals), Ivor Aylesbury (guitar/vocals) and Kevin Cunningham (double bass).

The group were managed by Brian Epstein and they made their recording debut in June 1965 on the Fontana label with 'Blood River' c/w 'Close The Door Gently'.

They entered the Top 30 with their second release, the Lennon/McCartney number 'You've Got To Hide Your Love Away' c/w 'City Winds', issued in October 1965 and actually produced by John Lennon with Paul McCartney on piano and George Harrison on tambourine. The track was featured on an album of the same name, released in America on 22 November 1965 on Fontana SRF 67548.

Their other releases were 'Keys To My Soul' c/w 'Leave Me To Cry', issued in February 1966, and 'Born To Be With You' c/w 'So Sorry Now', issued in June of the same year. They also issued an album in October 1965 entitled *The Silkie Sing The Songs Of Bob Dylan*.

● Silver, Johnny

The name John Lennon was purported to have used during a brief period when the Silver Beetles used pseudonyms in an attempt to smarten up their image, perhaps inspired by the **Larry Parnes** method of creating new names for each of his discoveries, such as **Johnny Gentle.**

During their short tour as backing musicians to Gentle, Paul called himself **Paul Ramon**, George was C[illegible] Harrison and **Stu Sutcliffe** adopted the name Stu [illegible] Stael.

In the Beatles' authorized biography, **Hunter Davi[illegible]** mentions that John denied he used the name **John[illegible] Silver**, although the other members of the gro[illegible] maintained that he did.

The controversy continued after the book *The Beatl[illegible] An Illustrated Record* mentioned the Johnny Silver nar[illegible] John took the trouble to send authors Roy Carr and T[illegible] Tyler a letter, together with clippings from a gig at t[illegible] **Neston Institute** on Merseyside immediately followi[illegible] their Johnny Gentle tour, which seems to bear out [illegible] contention. He wrote, 'I was never . . . repeat never kno[illegible] as Johnny Silver. I always preferred my own name.'

● Six O'Clock

A television programme produced by BBC Ulster. T[illegible] Beatles taped an interview and performed a number for [illegible] programme on 8 November 1963 when they w[illegible] appearing at the Ritz Cinema, Belfast. The excerpt v[illegible] screened the same evening.

● 6.25 Show, The

The Beatles made their BBC television debut on this ea[illegible] evening programme. The group recorded their spot on [illegible] show at BBC's Lime Grove Studios in London on 13 A[illegible] 1963 and it was broadcast on 16 April. The gro[illegible] performed 'From Me To You', 'Thank You Girl' a[illegible] 'Please Please Me'.

● Slice Of Life, A

A radio programme produced by the BBC's Home Servi[illegible] John Lennon was interviewed for the show on 31 Ma[illegible] 1964, discussing his recently published book *In His O[illegible] Write*. The interview was transmitted on 2 May 1964.

● Slow Down

A number written and recorded by Larry Williams in 1[illegible] and released on the same disc as 'Dizzy Miss Lizzy'. T[illegible] Beatles included it in their repertoire in 1960 with John[illegible] lead vocals. The group featured the number on their **'P[illegible] Go The Beatles'** radio show on 20 August 1963 and t[illegible] studio version was included on the *Long Tall Sally* EP[illegible] was issued as a single in America on **Capitol** 5255 on [illegible] August 1964 with 'Matchbox' and reached No. 25 in [illegible]

John performing the Larry Williams number 'Slow Down'. (©Apple)

charts. The track is also to be found on the *Rock 'n' ll Music* and *Rarities* albums, their American album *mething New*, *The Beatles Box* and *The Beatles llection* sets.

Smith, Alan

rseyside journalist who originally worked on the *kenhead News*. He based himself in London and joined **New Musical Express**, where he eventually became tor. In the early sixties he wrote for ***Mersey Beat*** der the pen name George Jones and interviewed the atles on a number of occasions on the paper's behalf. also interviewed them regularly for the *New Musical ress*.

He'd known **Derek Taylor** from his days on the *kenhead News* and when Derek became Press Officer at ple, Alan asked him if he could find a job for his wife **vis**, a former ballet dancer. When Derek met her he e her a job as his assistant in the Apple Press Office.

Alan was involved in an incident at the Apple ristmas party on 23 December 1968. A couple of Hell's gels from San Francisco were in attendance. One of them, Frisco Pete, became impatient waiting for the food to be served up and stalked over to John and **Yoko** and demanded to be fed. Alan Smith tried to smooth out the situation and Frisco Pete punched him and knocked him out.

● Smith, John

A leading London concert promoter who booked the Beatles on a number of concerts in 1963. His first booking of the group was on 16 February, for a gig at the **Carfax Assembly Rooms, Oxford.** He also booked some dates for Epstein's ***Mersey Beat Showcase***, featuring the Beatles, beginning with the **Fairfield Hall, Croydon** concert on 25 April.

Smith died of cancer on 25 April 1988 at the age of 75.

● Smith, Mavis

Dark-haired former dancer with the Ballet Rambert who was married to ***New Musical Express*** journalist **Alan Smith**. Mavis had given up her dancing career to work for pop PR man Les Perrin. She'd been working for Perrin for over a year when her husband began asking **Derek**

Taylor if he could find her a position at Apple. Derek met Mavis at a London concert and a week later invited her to join the Apple Press Office.

She worked on most of the accounts, ranging from **Mary Hopkin** to **Badfinger**, but when the artists began to leave and there wasn't much to do in the Press Office, she resigned. The action resulted in a small story in the trade publication Record Retailer on 20 June 1970:

> MAVIS SMITH LEAVES APPLE
> Mavis Smith has resigned from the Apple Press Office, which she left last weekend. Assistant to Derek Taylor for the past eighteen months, she previously worked with Leslie Perrin Associates.
>
> In the absence of Derek Taylor, now writing a book, Mrs Smith has been running the department together with **Richard DiLello**, who will now assume responsibility for press matters.

● Smith, Mike

In 1961 Mike Smith was a newly appointed assistant in the A&R division at **Decca Records**. After Brian Epstein had approached Decca asking them to sign up the Beatles, it was decided that his position as a prominent record retailer in the north warranted some attention, and Mike Smith was assigned to travel to Liverpool to see the group.

He arrived on 13 December and Brian took him out for a meal. They then went to the **Cavern** to watch the Beatles perform and Smith was impressed and immediately arranged for them to travel to London to take part in a record audition at Decca's West Hampstead studios on New Year's Day, 1 January 1962.

Brian and the Beatles arrived at 11.00 a.m. prompt, and Brian was peeved when Smith turned up late. The group performed fifteen numbers and Smith expressed such enthusiasm that Brian was convinced the group would receive a contract.

Tony Barrow, in his 'Disker' column in the ***Liverpool Echo***, wrote: 'Decca disc Producer Mike Smith tells me that he thinks the Beatles are great. He has a continuous tape of their audition performance which runs for over thirty minutes and he is convinced that his label will be able to put the Beatles to good use. I'll be keeping you posted.' However, Smith had to consult his boss, **Dick Rowe**. Rowe pointed out that another group had auditioned that day, **Brian Poole & the Tremeloes**. He said that Decca would only sign up one of the groups ar it was said, left the decision to Smith. Presumably, Sm felt that although he considered both bands to be good, would be more convenient to sign up the Tremelo because they came from nearby Dagenham. Ironically, was Dick Rowe and Mike Smith from Decca who signed **Pete Best** after he left the Beatles. **Mona Best** travell to London to see them with tapes of Pete's new band a Smith recorded the group's single 'I'm Gonna Knock Your Door'. Unfortunately, the disc wasn't a success a Decca dropped the band.

Smith also recorded the **Applejacks** with 'Li Dreamers Do', a Lennon & McCartney number which h originally recorded with the Beatles at the **Dec audition**.

● Smith, Mimi

Nee Stanley, Mary Elizabeth Smith was John Lenno aunt, one of **Julia Lennon**'s four sisters.

Like her other sisters, she was known by a pet nam Mimi. Mimi married a dairy farmer, George Smith, a eventually settled in Mendips, a pleasant semi-detach house in Menlove Avenue, Liverpool. She did not have a children of her own and doted on John from the moment was born.

When John was being reared by his mother Newcastle Road, Mimi was upset at what she regarded his neglect by Julia and insisted that she be allowed rear him. When Julia went to live with **John Dykins**, s agreed to leave John in the hands of her sister and Jo was five years old when he went to live in Mendips.

Mimi took her responsibilities seriously and broug John up with care, despite the times she despair because of his rebellious nature and poor school resu although teachers always impressed upon her that Jo had talent as an artist. At his junior school, when handi Mimi a bunch of John's drawings, the teacher comment 'The perspective is amazing for a boy of eleven.' Geo died when John was twelve and Mimi had to care for t strong-willed, stubborn boy single-handedly. He prov something of a handful and there was often fricti between them.

Mimi did not entirely approve of his interest in rock roll music and attempted to dissuade him, but on realizi that he was so determined, she bought him a guitar **Frank Hessy**'s music store for £18 when he w venteen. She later threatened to throw the instrument o the dustbin.

It was Mimi who took the advice of **Quarry Bank** eadmaster Mr **Pobjoy** and agreed to let John have an portunity of studying at **Liverpool College of Art**.

John's interest in the Beatles gained her disapproval as e felt that the group would draw him away from his idies. She went to see the group at the **Cavern** and ln't like them. She told John, 'The guitar's all right as a bby, but you'll never make a living out of it.' Much later, in had the phrase engraved on a silver plaque and esented it to her.

She was particularly upset when he left the art college d was disappointed in his determination to go to rmany. He returned broke, despite his assurances to her t he would make a lot of money, and she was able to e him an 'I told you so' speech.

His days at Mendips were coming to an end and John ared flats with fellow students and then married **nthia**. While John was on the road Cynthia stayed with mi for a while, but, by all accounts, preferred to return he company of her own mother.

When the Beatles' success in Britain grew, John was ermined to express his gratitude to Mimi for the love d dedication she had given to him in his formative years, d he bought her a home in Poole, overlooking the bour.

Mimi was proud to hear the news of the Beatles' **MBE** ard and John sent his medal to her because he knew she uld appreciate it. He later asked if he could borrow it m her and returned it to the Palace, much to Mimi's fury.

Mimi was 67 years old when John died. She was ldened and appalled by the various smears which pped up about John in subsequent books and articles, d decided to speak up on his behalf, to set the record aight, in a series of articles in the *Daily Star* newspaper February 1981. She mentioned that John had phoned the night before he died, that he had always asked for oks, rather than toys, on his birthdays; that he paid for tar lessons at five shillings a time out of his pocket ney and that he tithed a tenth of his income each year a charity for spastic children.

An insight was given into that magic moment when in charmed the media with his comments at the Royal riety Show. Apparently, John already had a ready wit en he attended pantomimes in Liverpool. When a fairy who was a bit older than the others appeared on the stage, the eleven-year-old John shouted out, 'She's a bit old for a fairy, isn't she?' and when the principal boy strode onto the stage, John shouted, 'Why, he's got my wellies on!'

Mimi remained in the bungalow at Harbour's Edge, 126 Panomaram Road, Sandbanks, Poole, Dorset, for the remainder of her life and died at the age of 88 on 6 December 1991, two days before the eleventh anniversary of John's murder, a tragedy from which she never recovered. Both of John's former wives, Cynthia and **Yoko**, were present with Mimi at the end. The funeral took place on 11 October and Yoko, **Sean** and Cynthia were among the mourners. Paul, George and Ringo sent wreaths. George's read, simply, 'From George Harrison and Family'; Paul's read, 'Dear Mimi, it was a great pleasure to know you in life – you were an exceptional woman and loved by many of us. God bless, Paul, Linda and children'; and Ringo's read, 'To Aunt Mimi, with our love, Ringo and Barbara'.

● *Smith, Norman*

The Beatles' original recording engineer. Norman was born in Edmonton, North London, and was a versatile musician, playing several instruments, until he served in the RAF. He left the Air Force in 1947 and, unable to make a career as a musician, eventually began working at **Abbey Road Studios** in 1959 as a tape engineer.

George Martin used him for the Beatles sessions, including their first-ever **EMI** recording stint, and he continued as their recording engineer right through to the *Rubber Soul* sessions in December 1965. In February 1966 he joined the A&R department at EMI as a fully fledged recording manager in his own right.

John used to call him 'Normal Smith' and Paul's pet name for him was 'Two D-C's Smith', referring to the time Norman told him to turn his amplifier down by a couple of decibels.

Norman also engineered sessions for various bands in the sixties, including **Billy J. Kramer** & the Dakotas, **Freddie & the Dreamers** and **Cliff Bennett & the Rebel Rousers**.

He was to find success in his own right as a recording artist, using the name Hurricane Smith, and even reached No. 1 in the American charts in 1972 with 'Oh Babe, What Would You Say?' After several hits he retired to the English countryside to breed horses.

● Smith, Rayston

One of the dwarfs featured in *Magical Mystery Tour*. He died in mysterious circumstances in 1989, shortly before his biography *Little Legs* was published. It was written by George Tremlett, author of *The John Lennon Story* and *The Paul McCartney Story*, and reveals that Smith was a hit-man who had killed several people and had served seven years in jail for manslaughter.

● Smothers Brothers Comedy Hour, The

The Smothers Brothers, Tom and Dick Smothers, were a popular comedy act with their own television show networked by CBS TV. A film of the Beatles performing 'Hey Jude' was featured on their programme on 6 October 1968. Later the same month, on 13 October 1968, the Smothers Brothers featured another Beatles promo clip, this time with the group performing 'Revolution'. The tape was one which had originally been screened on the British TV show 'Top Of The Pops' on 19 September 1968.

During the same year, on 17 November, George Harrison made a special appearance on the show in a small cameo with Tom and Dick.

Tommy Smothers was one of the voices on the chorus of 'Give Peace A Chance'. When CBS TV scrapped their show, there was much sympathy in America for the pair and they attempted a comeback by appearing at the Troubadour Club in Los Angeles in March 1974. Their show was interrupted by a drunken John Lennon who continually heckled their act. The incident received worldwide publicity.

● So How Come No One Loves Me?

Number composed by Felice and Boudleaux Bryant and recorded by the Everly Brothers in 1961. The Beatles included it in their repertoire the same year, with George on lead vocals. The group performed the song on their **'Pop Go The Beatles'** radio show on 23 July 1963.

● Soldier Of Love (Lay Down Your Arms)

A composition by Cason-Moon, recorded by **Arthur Alexander** and issued as a single in June 1962. The Beatles included it in their repertoire the same year, with John on lead vocals. The group performed the number on their BBC radio show **'Pop Go The Beatles'** on 16 July 1963.

● Some Other Guy

A Jerry Leiber, Mike Stoller, Ritchie Barrett compositic issued as a single by Ritchie Barrett in May 1962 a becoming an immediate favourite with Mersey Be groups, providing a minor hit for the **Big Three** Britain. The Beatles immediately began performing t number and were captured playing the song on stage at t **Cavern** by a Granada film crew. It was a number whi other local groups such as the **Searchers** also performe John was lead vocalist and the Beatles performed t number on their **'Saturday Club'**, **'The Talent Sp** and **'Easy Beat'** radio appearances.

● Something

George Harrison's most commercially successf composition. He wrote it on a piano during a break in t making of *The Beatles* double album. Paul was doi overdubs, so George went into an empty studio a composed it. It was too late to be included on *The Beat* album, so he gave the number to **Joe Cocker**.

However, he re-recorded it and twelve violas, fo violins, four cellos and one string bass were added. T number was then featured on the *Abbey Road* album ar at the insistence of **Allen Klein**, it became a single, givi George his first-ever Beatles 'A' side. It was issued, wi 'Come Together' on the flip, on 6 October 1969 in Ameri on Apple 2654 where it reached No. 3. In Britain it w issued on 1 October 1969 on Parlophone R 5814 where went to No. 5. The number was covered by **Shirl Bassey**, whose version did better than the Beatles reaching No. 4 in the British charts.

'Something' was included on the compilation albu *The Beatles 1967–1970*, *The Best Of George Harriso* *Love Songs* and *The Beatles Ballads*.

George was to say, 'When I wrote it, in my mind I hea Ray Charles singing it, and he did do it some years late Frank Sinatra called it, 'The greatest love song of the pa fifty years', and it was the most popular of George compositions with more than 150 cover versions. George favourite version was by James Brown and he also lik Smokey Robinson's cover of the song.

George was possibly influenced by a song written Apple recording artist **James Taylor**, which was includ on Taylor's debut Apple album *James Taylor*, issued December 1968. The song was called 'Something In T Way She Moves'.

Something New

he third Beatles album issued by **Capitol**.

It is interesting to note that although United rtists' original approach to the Beatles regarding a film as mainly because they wanted to secure Beatles ecordings on soundtrack albums, an agreement was ade between **EMI** and United Artists which allowed apitol to use material from the film soundtracks. his resulted in *Something New* including five songs from e official soundtrack of *A Hard Day's Night*, only a onth after United Artists had issued their movie undtrack.

Despite the fact that the material wasn't new, the album ached No. 2 in the *Billboard*, *Cash Box* and *Record World* arts. The album tracks were, Side One: 'I'll Cry Instead', hings We Said Today', 'Any Time At All', 'When I Get ome', 'Slow Down', 'Matchbox'. Side Two: 'Tell Me Why', nd I Love Her', 'I'm Happy Just To Dance With You', 'If Fell' and *'Komm, Gib Mir Deine Hand'*.

Sommerville, Brian

fter serving fourteen years in the Royal Navy, where he ecame a Lieutenant Commander, Brian Sommerville ecame a press agent, initially working for the Theo owan company handling clients such as **Peter Sellers** d **Judy Garland**.

Sommerville was 32 years old when he first met Brian pstein in a Liverpool pub. He was working in a public lations department at the time. The two became friends d when Epstein bought an apartment in Knightsbridge, ondon, he invited Sommerville around to dinner on a umber of occasions, during which he suggested that they ould work together.

Epstein then arranged for Beatles publicist **Tony arrow** to represent **Gerry & the Pacemakers**, **Billy Kramer**, **Cilla Black** and the **Fourmost** while he gaged Sommerville to represent the Beatles exclusively. e quite rightly felt that the authoritative figure and mmanding voice of Sommerville would be an advantage his handling of the press. It was, and it also came in eful when Sommerville began to travel to gigs with the eatles and was in daily contact with theatre managers d police officers who appreciated dealing with a person ho projected authority.

Sommerville did not become an employee of **NEMS**, it set up his own company, of which Epstein was a shareholder. As exclusive press representative to the Beatles, he received £100 a month.

Because of his receding hair, the Beatles called him 'old baldie'. He says that he got on with John, Paul and Ringo, but not with George and he had the impression that George resented him. There was one reported flare-up which occurred at the George V Hotel in Paris when George told Sommerville that a journalist would have to wait an additional hour before he'd consent to an interview. When Sommerville protested, George threw an orange juice at him and Sommerville clipped him over the ear.

It was Sommerville who arranged the publicity deal with British European Airways for which, with the Beatles sporting an inflight bag with the letters BEAtles, the group and their party would receive three weeks unlimited travel between London and Paris, which proved helpful during their **Olympia** season as their low fee for the gig didn't provide for air fares.

Sommerville also arranged the Beatles' unfortunate appearance at the British Embassy in Washington, via the Embassy's Naval Attaché, who was an old friend of his.

Relations between the two Brians deteriorated and Sommerville found that Epstein was jealous of anyone who became close to the Beatles and objected to a press officer making any statements on behalf of the group. He also quibbled about hotel bills and constantly embarrassed Sommerville by arguing in public.

Sommerville's term as Press Officer for the Beatles lasted ten months. The arrangement had been made on a gentleman's agreement, but Epstein now insisted on a watertight contract with some clauses which Sommerville disagreed with. They argued and Sommerville resigned. He then advertised in *The Times* newspaper: 'Ex-Beatles Publicity Manager looking for a job.' As a result he received enough clients to start his own public relations firm, representing artists such as the Kinks, the Who and Manfred Mann.

Years later he left the field of public relations and sought a career in Law, eventually becoming a stipendiary magistrate.

● Songs Lennon & McCartney Gave Away, The

A British album issued on **EMI** NUT 18 on 13 April 1979. This was a collection of twenty tracks by eleven different artists who had recorded Lennon & McCartney numbers. Although literally hundreds of other artists had 'covered' Beatles numbers throughout the sixties, there were a number of Lennon & McCartney compositions which were either not recorded or released by the Beatles themselves. These songs were recorded by other artists between the years 1963 and 1969. The album gathered most of these numbers on this special compilation – others not included, but which could have fit into the brief were, 'Thingumybob' by the **Black Dyke Mills Band**, 'Goodbye' by **Mary Hopkin**, 'Theme From The Family Way' by the George Martin Orchestra, 'Love In The Open Air' by the George Martin Orchestra and 'Come And Get It' by **Badfinger**. In some ways, the **Plastic Ono Band** tracks such as 'Give Peace A Chance' and 'Cold Turkey' would have been eligible.

Strangely enough, the one odd track was the opening track, 'I'm The Greatest' by Ringo Starr. This track featured Ringo on lead guitar and drums, with John Lennon on guitar and backing vocals, George Harrison on lead, **Klaus Voormann** on bass and **Billy Preston** on organ. It was a song which had been written by John Lennon specially for Ringo to sing on his 1973 album *Ringo*. The track listing was, Side One: 'I'm The Greatest', Ringo Starr; 'One And One Is Two', the **Strangers** with Mike Shannon; 'From A Window', **Billy J. Kramer** with the Dakotas; 'Nobody I Know', **Peter & Gordon**; 'Like Dreamers Do', the **Applejacks**; 'I'll Keep You Satisfied', Billy J. Kramer with the Dakotas; 'Love Of The Loved', **Cilla Black**; 'Woman', Peter & Gordon; 'Tip Of My Tongue', **Tommy Quickly**. Side Two: 'Hello Little Girl', the **Fourmost**; 'That Means A Lot', **P. J. Proby**; 'It's For You', Cilla Black; 'Penina', Carlos Mendes; 'Step Inside Love', Cilla Black; 'World Without Love', Peter & Gordon; 'Bad To Me', Billy J. Kramer with the Dakotas; 'I Don't Want To See You Again', Peter & Gordon; 'I'll Be On My Way', Billy J. Kramer with the Dakotas; 'Catcall', the Chris Barber Band.

The sleeve notes were penned by the Beatles' former Press Officer, **Tony Barrow**.

● Songs, Pictures And Stories Of The Fabulous Beatles

A repackaged version of *Introducing The Beatles*, issued by **Vee Jay Records** on VJLP 1092 on 12 October 1964. The album reached No. 63 in the *Billboard* charts. The copies of the record still had the number 1062 and th title *Introducing The Beatles* within the new packagin which introduced a special fold-out cover wit photographs and biographies. The tracks were, Side On 'I Saw Her Standing There', 'Misery', 'Anna (Go To Him)' 'Chains', 'Boys', 'Ask Me Why'. Side Two: 'Please Pleas Me', 'Baby It's You', 'Do You Want To Know A Secret?' 'A Taste Of Honey', 'There's A Place', 'Twist And Shout'.

● Sonny Webb & The Cascades

During the Mersey Beat days, Sonny Webb & th Cascades were one of the leading Liverpool C&W groups.

Leader Kenny Johnson claimed that Brian Epstei wanted to sign them up and gave them three songs, 'I You Want To Know A Secret?', 'Misery' and 'Tip Of M Tongue'. Then Brian gave 'Do You Want To Know Secret?' to **Billy J. Kramer**. The Cascades recorde 'Misery', then Beatles Fan Club secretary **Freda Kell** brought them a note from Epstein which said they couldn release 'Misery', but would they be willing to do 'Tip O My Tongue'? When they were prevented from recordin that they lost interest in **NEMS** and signed up with th Northern Variety Agency. They later changed their nam to the Hillsiders and had some success as a country mus group, and became the first British C&W act to eve appear on the Grand Ole Opry in Nashville.

● Sounds Incorporated

An instrumental group, formed in Kent in 1961. The backed several visiting American artists, such as **Littl Richard** and **Gene Vincent**, and first met the Beatles the **Star Club** in Hamburg. They came to the attention Brian Epstein, who signed them to a management contra in March 1964.

The group comprised Alan Holmes (flute, sax), Gri West (sax), John St John (guitar), Barrie Camero (keyboards), Wes Hunter (bass guitar) and Tony Newma (drums).

They appeared on the Beatles' autumn tour of Britain i October and November 1964, the *Beatles Christmas Sho* at the **Odeon, Hammersmith** and the Beatles' America tour in August 1965. They abbreviated their name Sounds Inc in 1967.

The group, whose signature tune was the 'William Te Overture', appeared in the film *Live It Up*. In March 196 three members of the group, Barrie Cameron, David Glyc ıd Alan Holmes, played saxophones on the 'Good orning, Good Morning' session for the *Sgt Pepper* album.

Sour Milk Sea

hn Lennon and Paul McCartney weren't the only ones ıo utilized the peaceful sojourn in Rishikesh to produce number of songs. While George Harrison was relaxing at e **Maharishi**'s ashram he also wrote some numbers, one which was called 'Sour Milk Sea'.

For some reason he didn't put the number forth as a ssible song to be recorded by the Beatles but kept it ıtil he had the opportunity of recording an old friend, verpool singer **Jackie Lomax**, who'd been signed to the ple label. 'Sour Milk Sea' became Jackie's solo single, ıich George produced, with a star-studded ensemble, ıich included himself and Jackie on rhythm guitars, **ric Clapton** on lead guitar, Ringo Starr on drums and cky Hopkins on piano.

The number was one of the first four Apple singles leased. It was issued in Britain on Apple 3 on 6 ptember 1968 and in America on Apple 1802 on 26 ıgust, but failed to register in the charts. A major sappointment as Lomax had the potential to become a ajor star.

South Africa

ıe Beatles always refused to tour South Africa because of artheid. Despite this, their records were hits there until 66. On 8 August of that year, following the controversy oused by John Lennon's quotes regarding Jesus Christ in s interview with Maureen Cleave, the South African oadcasting Corporation (SABC) announced that it was nning the airplay of all Beatles records. A ban on the les of Beatles records was also introduced. The ban ntinued until after the group split up, although it was ted on 3 March 1971 – but only on Beatles records. The n on John Lennon's songs and records continued.

Southern Sporting Club, *The Corona, irch Street, Hyde Road, Manchester*

hile Merseyside boasted scores of venues which omoted rock 'n' roll music, the nearby city of anchester was noted for its cabaret clubs, venues aimed the older audiences who drank alcohol, with middle-of-e-road music and entertainers. Brian Epstein had tried troducing the Beatles to the cabaret circuit before and tried again on 13 June 1963 with a double-booking for the evening at this cabaret club and the Palace Theatre Club in nearby Stockport.

● Southern, Terry

An American author whose risqué novel *Candy*, co-written with Mason Hoffenberg, was considered too sexually explicit to be published in America and was originally issued in Paris by the Olympia Press. When it was eventually published in the United States it became a best-seller and was filmed, providing Ringo Starr with his first solo screen role.

Southern also wrote ***The Magic Christian***, which provided Ringo with his second non-Beatle film role, in which he co-starred with **Peter Sellers**.

Appropriately, perhaps, Ringo had the words 'Buy a Terry Southern book' included in the sleeve notes of his *Goodbye Vienna* album.

Terry Southern was also one of the many characters selected by the Beatles to appear on the tableau of the *Sgt Pepper's Lonely Hearts Club Band* album cover.

● Speakeasy Club, The, *48 Margaret Street, London W1*

Fashionable members' club, part of the same group as the Revolution and Blaise's clubs. Overseer of all three was

The Beatles often dropped into the Speakeasy Club. (©Apple/Walter Shenson Films)

Jim Carter-Fea and manager at the Speakeasy was Roy Flynn.

The Beatles began attending the club in 1967, and it was a haunt for most of the big name British rock stars of the time and frequented by all the visiting American figures. There was live music, often by a name band, and a special restaurant section divided from the rest of the club by a glass wall.

The restaurant provided the setting on 3 July 1967 for a special party in honour of the **Monkees**, organized by **Vic Lewis** of **NEMS Enterprises** who had brought the Monkees to Britain.

Among the guests that night were the Monkees, *sans* Davy Jones, and the Beatles, *sans* Ringo Starr. Also present at the private function were the Who, Cream, Manfred Mann, Dusty Springfield, Lulu, **Klaus Voorman**, **Kenny Everett** and Jonathan King.

● Spector, Phil

The legendary record producer who was born Philip Harvey Spector in New York on 26 December 1940. He moved to California in the early fifties with his widowed mother.

Interestingly enough, the record which inspired him to become a musician was 'Rock Island Line' by the British performer **Lonnie Donegan**, who was a main inspiration of the Beatles. Spector bought a guitar and performed 'Rock Island Line' in a talent contest in 1957 and the same year formed a group called the Sleepwalkers, while still at high school, with Sandy Nelson, Bruce Johnson and Kim Fowley. When they broke up at the end of 1958 Spector formed the Teddy Bears and penned the number 'To Know Him Is To Love Him', which provided them with a No. 1 hit. He moved back to New York in 1960 and by 1961 had begun to produce records of new artists he discovered and launched the Phille label. Among his hits were songs such as 'He's A Rebel', 'Zip-A-Dee-Doo-Dah', 'And Then He Kissed Me' and 'Be My Baby' by artists such as the Crystals, Bob B. Soxx & the Bluejeans and Darlene Love, all of whom are featured in his 1963 album *Phil Spector's Christmas Album*. It was during this period that he developed his famous 'wall of sound', a distinctive system of multiple recording which produced a denser sound on record.

The Beatles sought Spector's advice on the American scene and he accompanied them on their first flight to New York in February 1964. Later that year he produced novelty single, 'I Love Ringo' c/w 'Beatle Blues' by Bonni Jo Mason, who later became successful as Cher.

Spector produced the **Righteous Brothers** performir 'You've Lost That Loving Feeling', but George Marti quickly recorded **Cilla Black**'s cover version in Britai and as she was popular there, her record overtook th Righteous Brothers in the British charts – and the **Andrew Loog Oldham** took out a newspape advertisement pointing out the superiority of the Righteou Brothers version, which then overtook Cilla's record an reached the No. 1 position. During the sixties, Spector success continued, although he was noted for hi production of singles, rather than albums.

When **Allen Klein** was brought in to handle th Beatles' affairs, one of the problems was the mess of th 'Get Back' product, a mass of tapes which George Marti and **Glyn Johns** had been trying to assemble into a album. Klein suggested that Spector be put in charge the project and allowed to assemble the tapes. Joh Lennon was not convinced and decided to try Spector o first on one of the **Plastic Ono** singles, so he had Ph produce 'Instant Karma'. The single became the first so Beatles record to sell a million in America, reaching No. in the charts – it also reached No. 5 in Britain. As th single didn't display the heavy Spector 'wall of sound', th producer was allowed to handle the 'Get Back' tape which were eventually released as the album *Let It Be*.

By all accounts, the Beatles were not too certain of th success of the Spector mixing on *Let It Be*, whic overloaded some tracks with the 'wall of sound'. Pa McCartney, in particular, was furious with what Spect had done to his 'The Long And Winding Road'. Spect had sent each member of the Beatles an acetate of h production work on *Let It Be*, together with a long lett explaining his reasons for the changes he had made. Pa McCartney felt sick about the over-production of 'Th Long And Winding Road', which he'd envisioned as simple production and which had now been overloade with celestial choirs and orchestral backing. Paul wrote Allen Klein demanding that the original version of hi number be used – but he was ignored. 'The Long An Winding Road' was issued in America where it became th Beatles' final No. 1 single, although it wasn't issued as single in Britain.

George and John, on the other hand, didn't seem

ave been upset by the hand of **Spector** on their work and eorge engaged him to participate in the production of his *ll Things Must Pass* album. Spector also worked with ennon on *John Lennon/Plastic Ono Band* and produced is single 'Power To The People'.

In the sixties Spector had married Ronnie Bennett of e **Ronettes** and, in an attempt to revive her solo cording career, produced her singing the George arrison composition 'Try Some, Buy Some'. He also roduced 'God Save Oz' by Bill Elliott and the Elastic Oz and for Lennon.

Apple Records issued his famous Christmas album nd he became A&R man for the company. His next roject was the John Lennon album *Imagine*, followed by is recording of the Madison Square Garden show for *The oncert For Bangla Desh* album. By this time Apple was rumbling and among the last productions he did for the ompany were 'Happy Christmas (War Is Over)' by John nd Yoko. He also worked with John and **Yoko** on their *ome Time In New York City* album.

In 1973 John had decided to record an album of rock ' roll records which he was going to call 'Oldies But oldies'. It was eventually released as *Rock 'n' Roll*. He rranged for Phil Spector to produce the album in Los ngeles, but the resultant sessions became chaotic and ere were disagreements between the two which caused a alt in the recordings, with Spector holding onto the tapes hich had been recorded. It was reported that he had been volved in a car accident at the time. Lennon found he as unable to contact Spector and when Spector eventually rned over the tapes for a reportedly large sum of money, ey were found to be virtually unusable.

Later in the seventies, Spector produced artists such as ion, Leonard Cohen and the Ramones and in 1981 co-roduced Yoko Ono's album *Season Of Glass* with Yoko at ew York's Hit Factory.

Speedy Prompt Delivery Service

hen the Beatles returned from their first trip to Hamburg ey were literally broke. Their proposed residency at the **op Ten Club** could no longer take place as the venue ad burnt down. Paul's father pressed him to apply for a b. 'It's time for you to get serious about life, to look for eal work, to make some real money, to get off your ehind,' **Jim** told him.

Paul went to the labour exchange and was given the job of package deliverer for the Speedy Prompt Delivery Service. He was laid off after a couple of weeks because he said he was, 'So buggered sometimes I fell asleep on the lorry when we went to places like Chester.'

● Spiegl, Fritz

A Liverpool-based author/musician who devised two of the earliest records, both EPs, placing Beatles music into a classic style, with the music being arranged by Harry Wild. The first, *Eine Kleine Beatlemusik*, was issued in Britain on HMV 7EG 8887 on 1 October 1965 and comprised, 'She Loves You', 'A Hard Day's Night', '**All My** Loving', 'Please Please Me', 'I Want To Hold Your Hand' and 'I'll Get You'. The second EP, *The Beatles Cracker Suite*, was issued a few week's later on 29 October and comprised, 'It's For You', 'Help!', 'She Loves You', 'From Me To You', 'Ticket To Ride' and 'All My Loving'.

Together with musicians from the Royal Liverpool Philharmonic Orchestra, he appeared on the Granada TV special **'The Music Of Lennon And McCartney'**.

● Spinetti, Victor

Actor, writer, director and producer, born in Abergavenny, Wales, who was the only person, apart from the **Fab Four** themselves, to appear in all three of their 'acting' films: *A Hard Day's Night*, *Help!* and *Magical Mystery Tour*. He also appeared with John in the film *How I Won The War*.

Discussing how his long association with the Beatles began, he explained: 'The lads saw the production I was in, *Oh What A Lovely War*, and they said, "We want you in our film", and that was it.'

He followed his *A Hard Day's Night* role as a panicky television director with the mad scientist character in *Help!* He was then asked to appear in *Magical Mystery Tour*, of which he said, 'They wanted me to play the courier on the bus in *Magical Mystery Tour* so I would be travelling with them all the time. But I couldn't because I was doing a show in London, so I could only join them from London and go back there to do the show. Otherwise I would have loved to have gone on that whole trip, it would have been marvellous.

'I had to write my own script. I've got a letter from John somewhere saying, "We want you to be in this," and I said, "What can I do?" and he said, "Well, write it yourself. You know, just do your own bits." I said, "Okay." So I did the drill-sergeant thing that I had done in *Oh*

What A Lovely War, where I was portraying the kind of establishment figure who was telling them to get their hair cut, pull themselves together and behave like responsible people. In other words, be killers!'

By that time Victor was a close friend of all four members of the band. He attended a number of their recording sessions and can be heard tap-dancing on their 1967 Christmas disc!

Victor next produced and co-authored a special stage version of John's two books. He said, 'A girl from Detroit called Adrienne Kennedy who wrote a play which was put on at the Royal Court Theatre came to see me when I was in London doing *The Odd Couple* and asked me to be in it. And I read it and said, "Well, you know, if you are going to put this on stage you will have to do more than you have done." And I told her what I felt about a person growing up and his own reactions to family situations, schools etc. Because it's very autobiographical, the whole thing.

'And so she said, "Come and tell Ken Tynan," and I told Ken Tynan and he said, "Come and tell Laurence Olivier," and I told Laurence Olivier, and he said, "My dear baby, direct it for us!" So then I said to Adrienne, "Have you had permission from John to do this, turn it into a play?" and she said, "No!"

'I said, "But you have to!" So I rang him up and asked him, and he said, "Yeah, OK. You got permission." And then he came to a rehearsal and became interested, and then we worked together on the script.

'At the rehearsal he in fact cried and said, "These were all the things that I was thinking about when I was sixteen," and he got involved in it and eventually we spent quite a bit of time together working on the script, writing out those little extra things that one needed for it.'

In His Own Write: The Lennon Play, credited to Victor, Adrienne and John, was published in 1968 by Jonathan Cape.

Incidentally, John had invited Victor to join himself and **Cynthia** on a six-day holiday in Casablanca in January 1968. Later that same year, John and **Yoko** had become inseparable. When John was staying with Yoko at **Queen Charlotte's Hospital** in November 1968 John asked Victor to pop in to see him each morning at 8.30 and sneak him a packet of Players Gold Leaf cigarettes.

● Sporthallen, *Eskilstuna, Sweden*

The Beatles made the final appearance of their short Swedish tour at this venue on 29 October 1963.

● Springfield Ballroom, *Janvrin Road, St Saviour, Jersey, Channel Islands*

One of the venues where the Beatles appeared during week-long engagement on the Channel Islands, booked b the promoter **John Smith**. The Beatles first appeared the venue for two nights, on 6 and 7 August 1963, an ended their Channel Islands appearances with anothe two-night engagement on 9 and 10 August 1963.

● Stanley Abattoir Social Club, *East Prescot Road, Old Swan, Liverpool L14*

The social club for the staff of Stanley Abattoir, the mai Liverpool slaughterhouse. The **Quarry Men** were booke to appear at the club for a single Saturday night dance o 16 November 1957, during which they played two sets.

● Stanley Street, *Liverpool L1*

City centre street leading off Whitechapel which contair **Frank Hessy**'s music store and Radio City, th independent radio station.

The street is also the home of Tommy Steele's sculptur of Eleanor Rigby.

The popular Cockney entertainer made the statue an presented it to the City of Liverpool. It was unveiled befor a gathering of 300 people on Friday, 3 December 198 and Tommy commented: 'Please enjoy her. It is m present to you and I hope you enjoy her as much as I do.'

The Eleanor Rigby statue is cleverly attached to a actual bench seat above which there is a plaque whic reads:

> ELEANOR RIGBY
> Donated to
> 'All The Lonely People'

'The statue was sculpted and donated to the City c Liverpool by Tommy Steele as a tribute to the Beatles. Th casting was sponsored by the ***Liverpool Echo***.'

December 1982.

● Star Club, The, *39 Grosse Freiheit, St Pauli, Hamburg, Germany*

The club was situated in a cobbled street crammed with bizarre mixture of clubs, pubs and tea shops, branching o from the Reeperbahn in Hamburg's notorious St Pau district.

Bill and Virginia Harry, Manfred Weissleder of the Star Club and Mr and Mrs Ray McFall of the Cavern, outside the Star Club in Hamburg. (*Mersey Beat* Archives)

It was formerly the site of the Stern Kino, a cinema, and nly minor conversions were made to turn it into a rock enue. Above the entrance was a huge star, the club's ademark, projecting out from the façade and illuminated t night to compete with all the other exciting neon ıvitations – Regina, Tabu, Salome, Spiel Casino – which t up the street. The Grosse Freiheit also contained many aptivating nighteries such as Gretel und Alfons, the eershop frequented by British bands; a club whose main ature was generously proportioned women wrestling in ud; another whose numbered tables were each fitted with n internal telephone – enabling clients to call up any of ıe lightly clad young hostesses disporting themselves round; a tiny tea shop run by two little old ladies; and pposite the Star Club a strip joint called the Colibri in the rmer premises of the **Kaiserkeller**, where the Beatles ppeared in 1960.

Right next to the Star Club itself was a church, and the lub shared its entrance with the Monica Biershop. Inside ıere was a large reception hall where, to the left, was a taircase leading to the Erotica Film-Night-Club on the ext floor, to the rear of the Star Club balcony. This was the setting for a non-stop Cinemascope film show consisting mainly of colour movies made by club-owner **Manfred Weissleder**. On each side of the screen giant-sized slides of nude females flickered and changed while a real stripper performed in front of the screen. The stairs continued to the next floor which housed Manfred's office and living quarters.

The ceiling of the entrance was covered in copies of ***Mersey Beat***, the Liverpool paper, and there were sets of doors leading to what were formerly the rear stalls. Through the doors was the long bar, with one of the barmaids, Bettina Derlin, displaying her own little gallery of photographs of her favourite groups.

The area which used to house the stalls had been stripped of all the cinema seats and fitted with settee-like seating and tables. On the stage was a huge backdrop depicting the Manhattan skyline.

Weissleder sent **Horst Fascher** and Roy Young to Liverpool in January 1962 to book the Beatles and as many other top Mersey bands as possible. Horst visited Brian Epstein at his office in Whitechapel and a contract was negotiated and signed on 22 January 1962. One of the clauses read: 'It is agreed that the band will not perform or accept other engagements in Germany from the date of this contract until the contract becomes effective.' **Peter Eckhorn** of Hamburg's **Top Ten Club** was also in Liverpool trying to book the Beatles and offered them 200 marks each per week. The Star Club upped this to 350 marks, but by the time Epstein had completed his negotiations for their first engagement to open the club from 13 April to 31 May, Manfred had upped his offer to 2,000 deutschmarks per week: 500 for each member!

For their debut, the posters displayed in Hamburg for several weeks prior to the engagement read:

> Die Not hat ein ENDE!
> Die Zeit der Dorfmusik ist vorbei!
> Am Freitag, dem 13 April, eroffnet
> STAR CLUB
> die Rock 'n' Twist Parade 1962
> mit The Beatles, Tex Roberg, Roy Young,
> The Graduates, The Bachelors.
> Zusatzlich ab Mai: Tony Sheridan Quartet
> und Gerry And The Pacemakers.
> Eine Ballung der Spitzenklasse Europas
> Hmb: St. Pauli, Gr. Freiheit 39.

It was most unfortunate that the tragic news of **Stuart Sutcliffe**'s death hit the Beatles immediately they arrived in April. But they had no alternative but to begin their first season at the club. During their seven-week stint they shared billing with two of their American rock 'n' roll heroes, **Little Richard** and **Gene Vincent**. The group were required to play for four hours on one evening, with an hour's break between each set, and three hours the following evening.

Their second engagement at the Star Club took place from 1 to 14 November later in 1962 and brought them 600 marks each per week and their third and final engagement, from 18–31 December, brought them 750 marks.

During their Christmas season, **Adrian Barber**, former member of Liverpool band the Big Three, who had become stage manager at the Star Club, experimented with a domestic tape recorder to check out the acoustics of the club. With a single mike fixed in the right spot he found he could get good results recording the Beatles on stage, complete with the dialogue between the group and the audience, the repartee, the jokes, and even a laugh and bit of a song from **Horst Fascher.**

Adrian completed his recordings on 31 Decemb[er] 1962, New Year's Eve. He was approached by Ted Taylo[r,] leader of **Kingsize Taylor** & the Dominoes, who aske[d] him what he was going to do with the tapes. As Adrian ha[d] only recorded them for test purposes he told Taylor h[e] could have them.

They were forgotten for many years until a Liverpo[ol] promotion in the mid-seventies in which Taylor wa[s] appearing. He mentioned the tapes to **Allan William[s],** who took them to Paul Rogers of Buk Records. As a resul[t,] fifteen years after Adrian's test recording, they emerged o[n] a double album *The Beatles Live! At The Star Club I[n] Hamburg, Germany: 1962*.

The Star Club had a number of flats in the Gross[e] Freiheit which Weissleder allowed the Beatles to live i[n] but told them, 'I always want you should enjoy yourselve[s] in the Star Club, but if you make shit I send you home[.'] There were so many Liverpool bands appearing at the clu[b] over the next two years that there were signs declarin[g] 'Uncle Manfred's Home For Lost Scousers'.

The original club closed down in June 1964, althoug[h] there have been several attempts to revive it, most notabl[y] by Horst Fascher in the early seventies.

● Starkey, Jason

The second son of Ringo and **Maureen** Starkey, born a[t] **Queen Charlotte's Hospital**, London, on 19 Augus[t] 1967.

● Starkey, Lee Parkin

Ringo and **Maureen**'s only daughter, born at **Quee[n] Charlotte's Hospital**, London, on 11 November 1970[.] The name Parkin was the reintroduction of a forme[r] Starkey family name.

In her teens Lee went to acting school, but didn't like i[t] and left. She next tried a make-up school, but although sh[e] received her diploma, said she didn't like it either. Sh[e] became co-owner of a boutique in Portobello Road. Whe[n] her mother Maureen married Isaac Tigrett and moved t[o] live in Los Angeles, Lee talked her partner Christian Pari[s] into relocating the shop in LA and they moved their Plane[t] Alice boutique there in 1991 when Lee was twenty. At th[e] official opening of the boutique, situated on Melros[e] Avenue, Maureen and Isaac and Ringo and Barbara (wh[o] ad also settled in LA) were in attendance.

The psychedelic boutique has clothes which are in the ixties style and reminiscent of clothes from the original pple **Boutique**. Lee commented: '[They are] '90s nterpretations of '60s styles. [I] didn't consciously do this ecause it's what the Beatles wore in their heyday, but it ust have something to do with it.'

Starkey, Maureen

Maureen was born Mary Cox on 4 August 1946. A onvent-educated Liverpool girl, she became a anicurist's assistant then joined Ashley Du Pre's airdressing salon as an assistant hairdresser.

A **Cavern** regular, she once went out with Johnny Guitar' Byrne of **Rory Storm & the Hurricanes**. Ringo vas drummer with the group. Three weeks after he joined the Beatles he dated Maureen. He spotted her queuing up outside the Cavern for a lunchtime session and started chatting to her, asking if she would come out with him after a Cavern gig the following night. She told him her parents insisted on her being at home by 11.50 p.m. at the latest, so they arranged to go for a day out together. They went to the park, the pictures, had some drinks in the Pink Parrot Club and then went to the **Blue Angel**.

The pregnant Maureen Starkey attending a reception with Ringo. (Cavern Mecca)

Although Maureen became his girl-friend, she saw little of him for the first six months, due to his hectic schedule.

By late 1964 with Ringo based in London and Maureen in Liverpool, Ringo was dating Vicki Hodge, the model. On 1 December he was taken to **University College Hospital** to have his tonsils out. Maureen decided to take matters into her own hands, caught the train to London and visited Ringo in hospital, taking him some ice cream. She then spent Christmas with him and by mid-January was pregnant. During a visit to the **Ad Lib Club** one evening, a slightly tipsy Ringo went down on his knees at 3.00 a.m. to propose. Maureen was eighteen years old and Ringo was 24.

The couple were married at **Caxton Hall**, Westminster, on 11 February 1965 at a simple ceremony which took place at 8.00 a.m. – the hall had opened two hours early to avoid the expected crowds. Brian Epstein acted as Best Man and in attendance were Ringo's mother and stepfather, Maureen's mother and father, John and **Cynthia** and George Harrison, who arrived on a bicycle. Paul was on holiday at the time. The wedding breakfast took place at Brian's house and he had also arranged for the couple to have a short honeymoon at 2 Princes Crescent, Hove, Sussex, the home of the Beatles' solicitor **David Jacobs**.

Ringo and Maureen moved into a **Montague Square** flat but when their first son **Zak** was born on 13 September 1965, Ringo bought a house, **Sunny Heights**, in Weybridge. Their second son **Jason** was born on 19 August 1967 and their daughter **Lee** on 17 November 1970.

The marriage had seemed a strong one until George and **Pattie** Harrison were invited to dinner one evening. George suddenly announced that he was madly in love with Maureen. A furious Ringo strode out, a tearful Pattie locked herself in the bathroom and a red-faced Maureen was lost for words. In the aftermath of this declaration it was rumoured that George and Maureen had a brief affair.

When George was asked, 'How could you, with your best friend's wife?' he replied, 'Incest, I guess.'

The marriage never survived the scandal and the couple gradually grew apart with Ringo drinking heavily and visiting nightclubs in the company of models. Eventually, they were divorced on 17 July 1975 with Ringo admitting to adultery with American actress Nancy Andrews.

Maureen and Ringo remained friends and Ringo was very generous, not only immediately settling £500,000 on her but later buying her a £250,000 house in Little Venice and continuing with financial support for many years to come.

On 27 May 1989, in Monte Carlo, Maureen eventually remarried. Her second husband was her long-time boyfriend, millionaire Isaac Tigrett of the famous Hard Rock Cafe. Among the wedding guests were Cynthia Lennon, Sting and Dan Ackroyd. The couple, who had been together for fourteen years and had a child, Augusta King, were married by Reverend Don Malloy, who had married **Elvis** and Priscilla Presley.

● Starkey, Richard

Father of Ringo Starr, originally a Liverpool dockworker and member of a large family. He had two brothers, Billy and Georgie, and three sisters, Angie, Lily and May. He later changed jobs and began to work in a bakery where he met **Elsie** Gleave. They were married in 1936 and initially moved in with Richard's parents who lived in the Dingle area of Liverpool. They then moved into a small two-storey terraced house in **Madryn Street** in the same area. Their son Richard, named after his father (a working class tradition of the time), was born in 1940.

Although Richard senior was called Dickie, it was decided to call Richard junior Richie. Dickie Starkey left the family home when Richie was three years old. There seemed to be no acrimony and the couple were divorced.

There were only a few brief occasions when Richie saw his father again, twice when he was a young child. Dickie had remained in Liverpool and still worked at the bakery and visited his son during one of his regular hospital confinements. He also met him at the Starkey parents' home in 1962.

Dickie remarried and moved from Liverpool to another town in the north-west of England. Little was heard of him until 1980 when the *Daily Express* ran him down and wrote a story on him. Now a window cleaner, he was to say about his son: 'He's done well, the lad, and good luck to him, but he owes me nothing.' Dickie also mentioned that the only item of Beatles memorabilia that he possessed was an autographed photograph.

● Starkey, Zak

The first child of **Maureen** and Ringo Starkey, born at **Queen Charlotte's Hospital**, Hammersmith, London, on 13 September 1965. Just in case they began to count the months between the marriage and the birth, journalists were told he was one month premature.

If a girl, the baby would have been called Lee. Ringo admitted that Zak was a name he'd always wished he'd been called when he was a boy. He said, 'It's a nice strong name and it can't be shortened – that was something I didn't want at all.'

When asked by the press if the baby would eventually follow in his father's footsteps, Ringo replied, 'I won't let Zak be a drummer!' However, Zak wanted to become a drummer, although Ringo wouldn't give him lessons because he'd been self-taught himself and advised Zak to simply listen to records and play along with them. He did, however, hire a piano teacher for his musically inclined son.

Zak's hero was **Keith Moon**, whom he called 'Uncle Keith', and Moon bought Zak a drum kit for his birthday. Zak was to comment, 'My old man's a good timekeeper but I've never thought of him as a great drummer.'

Twenty years later, Zak became a drummer in a rock band called the Next and continued to pursue a career in music with various bands over the succeeding years, including Nightfly and Ice. He was never in the press spotlight as much as John Lennon's son, **Julian**, but he was frustrated that press reports always concerned his conflicts with Ringo and never his drumming ability.

On 24 January 1985, at the age of nineteen, he married 25-year-old Sarah Menikides, but kept the wedding secret even from his parents. Ringo threw a celebration party for the couple at Tittenhurst Park the next day. Sarah gave birth to a girl, Tatia Jayne, making Ringo the first Beatle grandfather.

● Starline Club, *Windsor Street, Liverpool L8*

Premises of a former cinema, turned into a drinking club

hich had an extension of licence to sell alcohol during he afternoon. For a short period in 1961 the Beatles ropped into the club following some **Cavern** lunchtime essions, for additional rehearsals. They also appeared at he club for some evening sessions.

Starr, Ringo

ichard Starkey was born in the front room of 9 **Madryn treet** in Liverpool's Dingle area on 7 July 1940 to **Elsie** nd **Richard Starkey**. Father and son began to be eferred to as Big Richie and Little Richie, although the arriage was soon to break up and the couple were ivorced in 1943 when Elsie moved to nearby 10 Admiral rove with her son. Richie attended St Silas Infants' chool where he began to suffer the first of many illnesses hich seriously affected his education.

At the age of six he was taken to the Royal Children's nfirmary in Myrtle Street suffering from acute abdominal ains. A ruptured appendix was diagnosed and this led to n inflamed peritoneum and the first of several operations r the youth. He went into a coma for two months, during hich there were other operations, but he finally emerged om the coma, although he remained in hospital for everal further months.

He returned to St Silas where his classmates included **illy Fury** and Billy Hatton, then moved on to Dingle ale Secondary Modern.

Elsie met and married a painter and decorator from omford called Harry Graves, whom Richie referred to as is 'step ladder'.

In 1953, at the age of thirteen, Richie caught a cold hich turned into chronic pleurisy necessitating another ay at Myrtle Street hospital. The illness caused some ng complications which resulted in the youth being sent Heswall Children's Hospital in the Wirral, where he emained until 1955.

For a time he had a job as delivery boy for British Rail, hich lasted only a few months as he failed the medical. e next took on a job as barman on a ferry to New righton for a short time before becoming a trainee joiner Henry Hunt and Sons, along with his next door eighbour Eddie Miles. Early in 1957 Eddie and Richie rmed the **Eddie Clayton Skiffle Group** with three her employees from Hunt's, and they made their debut at eel Street Labour Club. Richie's stepfather Harry bought m a secondhand drum kit and the aspiring drummer soon changed outfits and became a member of the Darktown Skiffle Group, although he also sat in with other bands. In March 1959 he made his debut with Al Caldwell's Texans at the Mardi Gras Club in Mount Pleasant and decided to join the group, who were to change their name to **Rory Storm & the Hurricanes**. They secured a booking at the **Cavern**, which was strictly a jazz club at the time, using the name the Jazzmen, but were fined ten shillings by owner **Ray McFall** for playing 'Whole Lotta Shakin' Goin' On', because rock 'n' roll was not allowed to be played at the club at the time.

When the Hurricanes secured a summer season from July to September, at the Butlin's holiday camp in Pwllheli, Wales, performing in the Rock & Calypso Ballroom, they encouraged Richie to pack in his job at Hunt's. Rory Storm was a showman and he insisted that Richie add some colour to his act by renaming him Ringo Starr and introducing a solo spot called 'Ringo Starrtime', during which Richie, now named Ringo, sang numbers such as 'Boys' and 'You're Sixteen'.

The Hurricanes became one of the most popular groups on Merseyside and in October 1960 topped the bill at Hamburg's **Kaiserkeller** club, above the Beatles. They were also paid more money than the Beatles and could afford to stay at the Seamen's Mission. It was during their trip to Hamburg that the Beatles and members of Rory Storm & the Hurricanes recorded at the **Akustik Studios**, with a line-up comprising John Lennon, Paul McCartney, George Harrison, Ringo Starr and **Lu Walters**.

On their return to Liverpool the Hurricanes soon found that the Beatles, **Gerry & the Pacemakers** and other groups were now booked to headline over them. At one time, Ringo considered joining the Seniors, then decided to take up an offer to be part of **Tony Sheridan**'s backing group at the **Top Ten Club** in Hamburg and joined him there in January 1962. He returned to Liverpool to take up the drum spot with the Hurricanes once more, but began to feel at a loose end and even considered resuming his apprenticeship at Hunt's. He also wrote to the Chamber of Commerce in Houston, Texas, to enquire about the possibility of emigrating. He received the necessary forms, but couldn't be bothered filling them in. He also contemplated marriage to his girlfriend **Maureen** Cox.

While the Hurricanes were appearing for yet another summer season at Butlin's, this time in Skegness, Ringo received a letter from **Kingsize Taylor** offering him twenty pounds a week if he would join them as a replacement for Dave Lovelady, who was leaving the group to complete his studies. Ringo agreed to join him. Then, one day, John Lennon and Paul McCartney turned up at the camp and offered Ringo £25 a week if he'd join them. The extra five pounds sealed it and Ringo agreed to become a Beatle as from August 1962.

Much has been said about the musical prowess of the individual drummers. **Pete Best** was noted as a top drummer in Liverpool and the reasons for him being sacked are more likely to be based on the fact that John, Paul and George simply didn't want him in the band any more, rather than the oft-touted theory that he wasn't a good enough drummer. The reason they offered the job to Ringo is also more likely to be because they had played with him in Hamburg and had become friendly with him and felt he would fit in with the band. He certainly didn't have any major reputation as a drummer on Merseyside, as has been suggested. If anyone was reckoned to be Liverpool's top drummer, it was **Johnny Hutchinson** of the Big Three. Incidentally, Hutchinson considered Best to be an excellent drummer and **Billy Kramer** was also to comment, 'I didn't think the Beatles were any better with Ringo Starr. I never doubted his ability as a drummer but I thought they were a lot more raw and raucous with Pete.' Locally, fans were calling Ringo 'The luckiest man in the world'.

At the time, Ringo had a silver streak in his hair and a beard. These went and he adopted the Beatles-style haircut and image. When he arrived at **Abbey Road Studios** to record with the group for the first time, the same thing happened to him as had happened to Pete Best. George Martin said he'd prefer to engage a session drummer and the 32-year-old **Andy White** was hired for the session.

Ringo was given his own solo spot with the Beatles, the chance to sing one song, as he'd done in the 'Ringo Starrtime' spot with Rory Storm & the Hurricanes. Ringo was also to have his own vocal numbers on the Beatles albums. They included 'Boys' on *Please Please Me*, 'I Wanna Be Your Man' on *With The Beatles*, 'Honey Don't' on *Beatles For Sale*, 'Act Naturally' on *Help!*, 'What Goes On' on *Rubber Soul*, 'Yellow Submarine' on *Revolver*, 'With A Little Help From My Friends' on *Sgt Pepper's Lonely Hearts Club Band*, 'Don't Pass Me By' on *The Beatles*, and 'Octopus's Garden' on *Abbey Road*. There were only a handful of songs he performed on stage between 1962 and 1966: 'Boys', 'Honey Don't', 'I Wanna Be Your Man' and 'Act Naturally'.

As it turned out, Ringo was perfect for the Beatles and at one time was the most popular member of the group with American fans. He also proved to be more of a natural actor than any other members of the group and received favourable reviews for his performance in *A Hard Day's Night*. So much so, that he was put into the central position in their second film *Help!* Over the years, Ringo appeared in more films than any other member of the band. They included ***Candy*** (1968); ***The Magic Christian*** (1969); ***Blindman*** (1971); ***200 Motels*** (1971); *Born To Boogie* (1972); *Son Of Dracula* (1972); *That'll Be The Day* (1973); *Harry And Ringo's Night Out* (1974); *Lisztomania* (1975); *Sextette* (1978); *The Last Waltz* (1978); *The Kids Are Alright* (1979); *Caveman* (1981) and *Give My Regards to Broad Street* (1984).

Ringo married his long-time girlfriend **Maureen Cox** on 11 February 1965 and the couple were to have three children: **Zak**, **Jason** and **Lee**. The pair were eventually to divorce in July 1975 and Ringo was to marry **Barbara Bach**, his co-star in *Caveman*, on 27 April 1981.

Following the Beatles' break-up, Ringo had an initially successful solo recording career, although this faded slightly over the years. His solo recordings included the albums: *Sentimental Journey*, *Beaucoups Of Blues*, *Ringo*, *Goodnight Vienna*, *Blast From Your Past*, *Ringo's Rotogravure*, *Ringo The Fourth*, *Bad Boy* and *Stop And Smell The Roses*. His singles included 'It Don't Come Easy', 'Back Off Boogaloo', 'Photograph', 'You're Sixteen', 'Only You', 'Snookeroo', 'Oh My My', 'A Dose Of Rock 'n' Roll', 'Hey Baby', 'Drowning In The Sea Of Love', 'Lipstick Traces', 'Tonight' and 'Wrack My Brain'.

Ringo was also to appear in various TV shows, including his own special, 'Ringo', and a TV mini-series 'Princess Daisy', with his wife Barbara.

After a number of years out of the limelight, during which he did voice-overs for the children's TV series 'Thomas The Tank Engine' and experienced drink problems, which resulted in himself and Barbara attending a drying out clinic, he reappeared on the scene with an All-Starr Band to tour America and Japan in 1989. This

Left: Rory Storm and the Hurricanes. (Cavern Mecca)
Below: Ringo, their one-time drummer.

·oved to be so successful that he formed another All-Starr and in 1992, which began an American and European ur in June 1992. Members comprised his son Zak, uitarists Dave Edmunds, Nils Lofgren, Todd Rundgren d Joe Walsh, saxophonist Tim Cappello, bassist Timothy . Schmit and keyboards player Burton Cummings.

Steppin' Out

ne Beatles made a single appearance on this half-hour BC radio programme broadcast each Monday from 10.00 m. It was presented by Diz Disley and produced by Terry enebery.

The group appeared on 3 June 1963 and performed lease Please Me', 'I Saw Her Standing There', 'Roll Over eethoven', 'Thank You Girl' and 'From Me To You'. They

Ringo and his All-Starr Band. (EMI)

also recorded 'Twist And Shout', but it was not transmitted.

● St Barnabas Church Hall, *Penny Lane, Liverpool 18*

A church hall where the **Quarry Men** appeared early in their career.

The venue is now called Dovedale Towers.

● St James' Church Hall, *Gloucester Terrace, London W2*

The Beatles performed at a lunchtime audition for BBC Television at this venue on 23 November 1962.

It was an audition they failed.

● St James' Swimming Baths, *St James Street, Doncaster, Yorkshire*

The swimming baths in this Yorkshire town we occasionally used for dances, with the pool being cover over by boards. The Beatles made a single appearance the venue on 20 February 1963.

● St John's Hall, *Snaefell Avenue, Tuebrook, Liverpool L13*

After **Pete Best** joined the Beatles and following the return to Liverpool after their first Hamburg season, tl group were unofficially managed by Pete's mother, M **Mona Best**, who sought work for them at various loc enues, in addition to her own **Casbah Club**. She also romoted independently under the name Casbah Promotions and first presented the Beatles at St John's Hall on Friday, 17 February 1961, on a bill above Gene Day & the Jango Beats. For the engagement, she paid them a fee of twenty pounds, unusually high for a local roup at that time.

Following their season at the **Top Ten Club**, Hamburg, from 27 March–2 July, Mrs Best gave the group their first booking on their return, at this venue on 13 July 1961.

Other gigs at the hall took place on 20 July, 27 July also on the bill were the **Big Three**, with **Cilla Black**), 3 August, 10 August, 17 August (Johnny Gustafson of the Big Three performed with the Beatles on this occasion), 24 August, 31 August and 8 September 1961.

St Paul's Presbyterian Church Youth Hall, *North Road, Tranmere, Birkenhead, Liverpool L42*

The Beatles appeared at this venue twice. The initial gig took place on 10 February 1962 and they returned exactly a month later on Saturday, 10 March. Also on the bill of their second show at the hall were the Country Four with Brian Newman. The dance began at 7.30 p.m. and lasted until 11.30 p.m. Tickets were five shillings each.

St Peter's Parish Church, *Church Road, Woolton, Liverpool L25*

Site of the historic occasion on 6 July 1957 when John Lennon and Paul McCartney met for the first time.

The event was the annual summer fete and **Pete Shotton**'s mum had secured a booking at the event for the **Quarry Men**.

The leaflets read:

Woolton Parish Church
GARDEN FETE
and
Crowning of Rose Queen
Saturday, July 6th, 1957
To be opened at 3p.m. by Dr. Thelwall Jones
Procession At 2p.m.
Liverpool Police Dogs Display
Fancy Dress Parade
Sideshows Refreshments
Band Of The Cheshire Yeomanry
The Quarry Men Skiffle Group
Adults 6d. Children 3d. Or by Programme
GRAND DANCE
at 8p.m. in the Church Hall
GEORGE EDWARDS' BAND
THE QUARRY MEN SKIFFLE GROUP
Tickets 2/-

The procession through the Woolton streets saw a mixed group, with the band of the Cheshire Yeomanry leading and the Quarry Men, perched on the back of a coal merchant's lorry, bringing up the rear, with various floats containing Boy Scouts, Girl Guides and Brownies in between, together with the 13-year-old Rose Queen, Sally Wright.

The Quarry Men that day featured John Lennon, **Eric Griffiths**, **Colin Hanton**, **Rod Davis**, Pete Shotton and Len Garry while Geoff Rhind, a schoolboy with a Box Brownie, took a photograph of them for posterity.

As **Ivan Vaughan** wasn't playing tea-chest bass that day he'd invited along a friend from the **Liverpool Institute**, Paul McCartney, who cycled to the event.

During the Quarry Men's performance they played numbers such as 'Maggie May', 'Railroad Bill', 'Cumberland Gap' and 'Come Go With Me'. After they'd finished playing and took their gear over to the church hall

Woolton Parish Church
Garden Fete
and
Crowning of Rose Queen
Saturday, July 6th, 1957
To be opened at 3 p.m. by Dr. Thelwall Jones
PROCESSION AT 2 p.m.
LIVERPOOL POLICE DOGS DISPLAY
FANCY DRESS PARADE
SIDESHOWS REFRESHMENTS
BAND OF THE CHESHIRE YEOMANRY
THE QUARRY MEN SKIFFLE GROUP
ADULTS 6d. CHILDREN 3d. OR BY PROGRAMME
GRAND DANCE
at 8 p.m. in the Church Hall
GEORGE EDWARDS' BAND
THE QUARRY MEN SKIFFLE GROUP
Tickets 2/-

where they were performing that evening, Ivan took the fifteen-year-old Paul across to meet them.

The young lad made an impression because he showed them how to tune a guitar, which none of the band could do, and he particularly impressed John with his knowledge of the lyrics of rock 'n' roll songs and even wrote out the words of 'Twenty Flight Rock' and 'Be-Bop-A-Lula' for John. To cap it all, he borrowed a guitar and began to play some **Little Richard** numbers, including 'Long Tall Sally' and 'Tutti Frutti'.

Years later, Paul was to recall that John's breath smelled of beer, the result of several bottles of light ale he'd bought at a local off-licence.

● St Thomas' Hall, *Keith, Banffshire, Scotland*

One of the small venues where the Silver Beetles appeared during the short tour of Scotland promoted by **Larry Parnes**, on which they backed Liverpool singer **Johnny Gentle**. The group appeared at the hall on 25 May 1960.

● Step Inside Love

The third song penned by Paul McCartney which **Cilla Black** recorded. The others were 'Love Of The Loved' and 'It's For You'.

Paul composed the number for Cilla's 1968 television show **'Cilla'**, and recorded an acoustic version of the number as a demo for her. George Martin recorded the number and it was issued in Britain on Parlophone R 5674 on 8 May 1968 and in America on Bell 726 on 6 May. It reached No. 8 in the British charts but failed to make any impact in the States.

● Sterner, George

A German waiter who acted as **Bruno Koschmider**'s interpreter when the promoter came to England looking for bands. Sterner was to return to Germany to work for Koschmider in the **Kaiserkeller** and **Allan Williams** offered to give him a lift.

Sterner had been working at the Heaven and Hell coffee bar in London and he joined the minibus containing Allan and his wife Beryl, her brother Barry Chang, **Lord Woodbine** and John, Paul, George, Pete and **Stuart** on their journey to Hamburg.

The Beatles had considered him a friend, but discovered that he was Koschmider's 'spy' and reported on them. One day when they were rehearsing at the club an had two girl fans with them, Sterner was offensive to th girls and hit one of them. **Pete Best** knocked him to th floor. As a result Koschmider fined Pete five pounds fo hitting Sterner and also charged the others five pound each for allowing it to happen. It was also Sterner who tol Koschmider that the group were going to play at the riva **Top Ten Club**.

● Stigwood, Robert

An Australian impresario who arrived in Britain at th onset of the sixties and initially became successfu managing singers such as John Leyton and Mike Sarne. H also managed comedian Frankie Howerd and scriptwrite Ray Galton and Alan Simpson. He was to experienc financial difficulties and at one point decided to liquida his company. A few days before the liquidation h borrowed £10,000 from **EMI**. **Sir Joseph Lockwoo** considered that Stigwood knew that the money woul never be paid back and refused to allow EMI to do ar further business with him.

Stigwood then formed the Robert Stigwood Organizatic with David Shaw, a financial adviser.

Brian Epstein became acquainted with the 32-year-ol impresario at a Saturday night party held at the Waldc Court flat Stigwood shared with Chris Stamp. Epstein the began a series of discussions with him regarding a merg of their two companies.

Brian told Stigwood that he was becoming disenchante with the business, that he felt control slipping awa from him. He said that the pressure was becoming to much and he wanted to retire to Spain and manag bullfighters.

Initially, Stigwood wanted to buy **NEMS**, but Bria ended up buying the Robert Stigwood Organization in deal which made Stigwood Joint Managing Director NEMS, with **Vic Lewis**, while Epstein would remain Chairman, personally looking after the Beatles and **Cil Black**.

As far as Brian was concerned, Stigwood and Sha could have the rest. Brian had been offered twenty milli dollars only two years previously for his organizatic (although this included the Beatles and Cilla), yet offered Stigwood and Shaw a 51 per cent controlli interest in NEMS for only £500,000. He gave them deadline of raising the cash by May 1967. When the da ssed, there was a verbal agreement to extend the offer til September – by which time Brian had died. Although gotiations had been going on for three months, the erger was not officially announced until 13 January 967.

The announcement surprised a number of people as ostein had considered and rejected mergers with ernard **Delfont**, **Tito Burns** and Danny Betesh, all of iom had a bigger reputation in the industry than gwood and Shaw.

Stigwood moved into NEMS' Argyll Street offices and ere was immediate internecine warfare between the mps.

Vic Lewis' people didn't get on with Stigwood's, and ither did the original NEMS staff. **Geoffrey Ellis** mmented: 'He could be an absolute bastard. The longer tayed at NEMS, the less friendly I became with him.' ng-time members of NEMS such as **Alistair Taylor** nd themselves being given conflicting assignments by stein and Stigwood and the NEMS people regarded gwood as an autocrat.

Among the acts which Stigwood brought under the MS umbrella were Cream, the **Moody Blues**, Jimi ndrix, the Who, Screaming Lord Sutch, Crispian St ers and Oscar.

When he had settled in at NEMS, a group arrived at the ces to see Brian. They were referred to Stigwood, who s now responsible for signing new acts to the company. ey were called the Bee Gees and Stigwood immediately ned them. Soon, much to Brian's annoyance, he began claiming that they would be bigger than the Beatles. He k them to New York to launch them in America, renting acht for them for an all-day promotion. When Epstein rd of it, he cancelled it, saying, 'The Bee Gees can rter a yacht when they've earned a million dollars. til then they should be out playing.'

When Epstein died, Stigwood and Shaw began to plan ing the £500,000 to buy the option on NEMS, but the tles told him directly that they did not wish to have thing to do with their management. **Clive Epstein**, had now been appointed Chairman, also suggested Stigwood should split from NEMS with all his artists a substantial amount in severance pay (a figure of 5,000 has been quoted). Under the circumstances, gwood decided not to exercise his option, and on 8 cember 1967 Stigwood and Shaw resigned their directorships.

The Bee Gees went on to become a supergroup and Stigwood's empire became hugely successful. He was to employ former NEMS staffers such as **Peter Brown** and he moved to America and produced the hit movie musicals *Saturday Night Fever* and *Grease*.

He also produced a number of Beatles-associated ventures. In 1974 he produced a Broadway musical *Sgt Pepper's Lonely Hearts Club Band*, in 1975 he produced the West End stage musical *John, Paul, George, Ringo and Bert* and in 1978 he produced the movie musical *Sgt Pepper's Lonely Hearts Club Band*.

● Stinton, Roger

A London-based press agent who was asked to handle the press activities concerning the Beatles for a short period of time before becoming a personal representative of **Billy J. Kramer** on behalf of Brian Epstein.

● Stockton Wood Road Primary School, *Stockton Wood Road, Speke, Liverpool L24*

A large primary school built in the Speke area of Liverpool after World War II.

It was close to where Paul McCartney and his younger brother **Mike** lived at the time and was the first primary school they attended. Within a short time it had taken in so many pupils that, at over 1,500, it had the largest primary school enrolment in Britain. Due to the overcrowding, caused by the post-war 'baby boom', Paul and Mike were moved to the **Joseph Williams Primary School**.

● Stowe School, *Stowe, Buckinghamshire*

A British public school in Buckinghamshire which was the site of an unusual gig for the Beatles on 4 April 1963 – unusual because instead of performing before an audience of screaming teenage girls, the group took the stage before an all-male audience of schoolboys who sat politely in their seats and listened quietly to the music throughout the show.

In January a boy from Liverpool, David Moores, who was a pupil at the school, wrote to Brian Epstein with a booking request. Brian agreed to the Beatles' appearance there for a fee of £100 and travelled to the gig with them.

The group performed in the school's Roxburgh Hall and one of the students recorded the entire show on his domestic tape recorder.

● Strach, Doctor Walter

The man the Beatles called 'Uncle Walter'.

The Czech financial wizard worked in the offices of Bryce, Hanmer and Isherwood, a Liverpool firm of accountants who had offices in Albemarle Street, London. When Brian Epstein moved his organization to London he appointed the firm to handle the Beatles' finances and Strach was placed in charge of their account – initially he was given the task of finding the individual group members new premises to live in during 1963.

A senior partner in the firm, Strach immediately began to sort out the Beatles' tax difficulties and formed a limited company for them in which he was Treasurer and Secretary.

'Uncle Walter' lived in Weybridge and suggested it was an ideal place for the Beatles to live. John and Ringo settled there, but George bought a bungalow in Esher and Paul preferred to live in central London.

Walter advised them on their personal investments and when the four wanted to put money into John Bloom's washing machine company he talked them out of it. In 1965 he suggested that their profits from the film *Help!* be placed into Cavalcade Productions, a Bahamian company formed by the Beatles and **Walter Shenson** and administered by Strach. Unfortunately, it didn't make a profit for them. When sterling was devalued in 1967 it suffered an £8,000 loss.

Incidentally, Strach also had a home in the Bahamas where he invited George and **Pattie** to spend a holiday in December 1964.

● Stramscact

The name of the merchandising company, established in Britain late in 1963 by **Nicholas Byrne** and five partners to sell licences for Beatles product.

The deal, arranged by Brian Epstein's lawyer, did not prove advantageous to the Beatles and was to result in them losing what was probably the greatest merchandising opportunity of the sixties at the height of the American **Beatlemania** of 1964!

Merchandising was modest in Britain for Stramscact, compared to the vast profits to be made in the United States and the American arm of the company was call[ed] **Seltaeb**.

● Strangers, The

A popular Liverpool band who were placed No. 8 in t[he] first ***Mersey Beat*** popularity poll. They were also one [of] the groups featured on the front cover of *Mersey Beat*.

The group never made the big time and never ev[en] suceeded in cutting a record.

They appeared with the Beatles for the first time [at] **Aintree Institute** on one of the Friday night 'Battle [of] The Groups!' promotions. **Bob Wooler** advertised t[he] event in the ***Liverpool Echo***:

> 'Beatles Vs Strangers
> Referee: Bob Wooler
> Never before have these two great groups appeare[d] together.'

Both bands were to appear on further bills together [at] Mersey venues, but the Strangers' fame never spre[ad] outside the Merseyside area.

Lead singer Joe Fagin became a popular solo sin[ger] and reached No. 3 in the British charts in January 19[84] with 'That's Livin' Alright'.

He also charted with 'Back With The Boys Aga[in'] in 1986.

● Stratton Smith, Tony

A journalist and author whom Brian Epstein origina[lly] approached to ghost his biography *A Cellarful Of No[ise]*. Stratton spent a number of days in Holland discussing [the] project with Brian, but eventually turned it down.

His meetings with Epstein inspired him to becom[e a] pop group manager and in 1965 he signed up his first [act] – **Paddy, Klaus & Gibson**. This trio comprised [two] Liverpudlians and the Beatles' old friend from Hamb[urg] **Klaus Voormann**. They had been managed by Don Pa[ul], former member of the vocal group the **Viscounts**, [and] Tony took up a co-management deal and immediat[ely] booked the group a residency at London's fashiona[ble] Pickwick Club.

John Lennon and George Harrison pestered Epst[ein] into taking over the group and a reluctant Stratton Sm[ith] had to agree to the transfer, although he was later [to] observe, 'I had regrets because I think they should h[ave] ade it. They weren't a Top Twenty band but they had a arvellous live feel. I think the way I was handling them, ıilding them through the clubs and delaying a record ebut was, with hindsight, the best way.' He felt that EMS failed to develop the group.

His next signing was another Liverpool singer, **Beryl arsden**, who was to appear with the Beatles on tour. nfortunately, Beryl proved almost impossible to manage, iling to turn up to gigs and turning her back on portunities which would have furthered her career.

Stratton Smith also spent a great deal of time and effort the **Koobas**, another Liverpool band, who also peared on tour with the Beatles. They had minor ccess, but eventually disbanded.

For a time Stratton Smith returned to writing, but then tered the management field again with Nice, formed arisma Records and enjoyed tremendous success until s death from cancer in 1987. He was 53 years old.

Strawberry Fields Forever

song which, on several occasions, John Lennon pointed t as being his best Beatles song.

Strawberry Fields is a real place, a children's mmunity home run by the Salvation Army at aconsfield Road, Woolton, Liverpool L25 6LJ. It is very se to where John lived as a child and he often used to nder in Strawberry Fields and attended summer fetes in grounds.

The home now has a special unit called Lennon Court ich can accommodate four children.

In 1966 both John and Paul wrote songs about verpool for a proposed new album and 'Strawberry elds Forever' was the first number written for it. That ticular album project was abandoned in favour of *Sgt pper's Lonely Hearts Club Band* and the two Liverpool gs were issued as a single.

Recording began on Thursday, 24 November 1966, and umber of interesting recording techniques were used, luding vari-speed, tapes played backwards and the T (Artificial Double Tracking Device).

John had originally played the number to George rtin on an acoustic guitar. A week after the original ording sessions John approached Martin and said he'd e another crack at recording it. Martin suggested luding cellos and trumpets and on Thursday, 15 cember, he overdubbed the instruments, with Tony Fisher, Greg Bowen, Derek Watkins and Stanley Roderick on trumpets and John Hall, Derek Simpson and Norman Jones on cellos.

Further discussions revealed that John liked the two versions and he asked Martin to join up the beginning of the first one to the end of the second one. Initially, George thought it was virtually impossible as they were in different keys and tempos, but he was able to work it out to the satisfaction of all.

The number was issued in Britain as the flipside of Paul's 'Penny Lane' on Parlophone R5570 on 17 February 1967. It reached No. 2 in the charts, but was held off the top position by Engelbert Humperdinck's 'Release Me', becoming the first Beatles single since 'Love Me Do' not to reach the top of the British charts.

It was issued in America on **Capitol** 5810 on 13 February 1967 with advance orders of over a million copies – and it reached No. 1 in the US charts.

The number was included on *The Beatles 1967–1970* compilation and on the *Magical Mystery Tour* album.

● Streates Club, *Mount Pleasant, Liverpool L3*

A basement coffee club which was originally situated in Mount Pleasant, a street once crammed with small hotels. They were demolished in the late sixties to make way for a multi-storey car-park.

It was a gathering place for the Liverpool poets at the end of the fifties and early sixties and presented poetry readings by some of the talented writers who abounded in the area, including Phil Tasker, Roger McGough and Brian Patton.

Although the Beatles didn't actually perform in the club, which was too small to facilitate live groups, it is nevertheless important in the context of the general Mersey scene which spawned a number of famous Mersey Beat poets.

Satirizing the club's entry in ***Mersey Beat***'s entertainment guide, John Lennon wrote: 'The Sheates – The Bohernia of Liverpool'.

● Subscription Rooms, *Stroud, Gloucestershire*

The Beatles' first venture into the South of England under Epstein's management, which took place on Sunday, 31 March 1962.

The engagement was booked through the Cana Variety Agency and the group were advertised as 'Liverpool's top vocal and instrumental group – stars of Polydor Records – the sensational Beatles'. The **Rebel Rousers**, who had formed the previous year, were also on the same bill.

The Beatles returned to the venue for their second and final appearance there on 1 September 1962.

● Suffolk Downs Racecourse, Boston, Massachusetts

One of the most unusual venues the Beatles were to appear in during their 1966 tour of Northern America.

They appeared at the racecourse on Thursday, 18 August. 25,000 people were able to watch the group from the stands. A special stage had been constructed in the centre of the track and 100 labourers had worked throughout the day and night putting in 13,000 chairs.

● Sullivan, Ed

For over a quarter of a century Ed Sullivan hosted one of America's most popular TV entertainment shows and received his biggest-ever ratings when the Beatles made their debut.

In the 1920s Sullivan was sports editor of a New York newspaper called the *Evening Graphic*. In 1930 he was given the opportunity of hosting his own radio programme, for which he received $100 a week. By 1932 he was hosting a programme for CBS called 'Ed Sullivan Entertains'. At the same time he was acting as a Broadway columnist and as MC to dinners and shows.

One of these dinners, the Harvest Moon Ball, was televised on 3 September 1947. The show was seen by Worthington Miner, the Director of Programme Developments for CBS Television, and he thought that Sullivan would be an ideal host for a TV series. It was called 'The Toast Of The Town' and made its debut on 20 June 1948.

For the next 25 years, Sullivan hosted a prime-time Sunday evening show in which his guests included senators, variety acts, sports stars, astronauts, opera singers, Hollywood actors and rock stars. His show was considered so important that many star names made their actual television debut on it, including Bob Hope, Louis Armstrong, Humphrey Bogart, Walt Disney, Clark Gable, Grace Kelly, Fred Astaire, Margot Fonteyn, James Cagney, Julie Andrews, Lena Horne, Charles Laughton and Yul Brynner.

His biggest-rating show in the fifties took place in 19 when he booked **Elvis** for the programme. However, told his cameramen to photograph Elvis only from t waist up, commenting, 'We had a lot of Lutherans, a lot clergy and nuns in our viewing audience. It was a Sund night show.'

On 31 October 1963, Sullivan was at London Airport. was when the Beatles were returning from their Swedi tour and the roof of the Queens Building was packed wi screaming fans. Sullivan said, 'My wife Sylvia and I we in London, at Heathrow Airport. There was the bigg crowd I've ever seen in my life! I asked someone what w going on, and he said, "The Beatles." "Who the hell a the Beatles?" I asked. But I went back to my hotel, got name of their manager, and arranged for them to do th shows.

'When we got home, I found out that apparently Syl and I were the only people in the country who'd ev heard of the Beatles. I was very worried. But just one we before they arrived, their song "I Wanna Hold Your Han became a big hit, and on the night of their first show – February 1964 – they were so popular that people all o the country were having dinner parties to watch them.'

Brian Epstein arrived in New York and checked i the Regency Hotel on 11 November 1963 and met w Sullivan several times in his office at Suite 1102 in Delmonico Hotel.

He made a deal with **Bob Precht**, Sullivan's son- law and the show's producer. The usual payment for a s for one appearance on the show was $7,500. The deal the Beatles was for $10,000 for three shows; $3,500 e for two live shows and $3,000 for one taped show. Af the deal had been done, Precht was worried because group were unknown in America. He phoned Sullivan tell him of his reservations but Sullivan said, 'I th they're worth the investment.'

On the show itself, Sullivan read out a telegram fr Elvis, sent by Colonel Parker, and told the kids in audience to pay respectful attention to the ot performers, adding, 'And if you don't, I'll call a barber . After the first commercial break, Sullivan appeared ag and said, 'Our city – indeed the country – has never s anything like these four young men from Liverpool. Lad and gentlemen, the Beatles.'

The Beatles appeared on stage for a total of thirt

d a half minutes. Ray Block, musical director for the d Sullivan Show', was to comment, 'The only thing at's different is the hair, as far as I can see. I give them year.'

During that initial show on 9 February, they appeared the first half performing 'All My Loving', 'Till There as You' and 'She Loves You' and reappeared in the cond half to sing 'I Saw Her Standing There' and 'I Want Hold Your Hand'.

Their next Sullivan appearance was telecast from the **eauville Hotel**, Miami Beach, Florida, on 16 February 63.

During the first half they performed 'She Loves You', his Boy', 'All My Loving' and in the second half, 'I Saw r Standing There', 'From Me To You' and 'I Want To old Your Hand'.

Their third appearance was a segment they'd pre-corded before they left America and it was screened on February 1964. The group performed 'Twist And out', 'Please Please Me' and 'I Want To Hold Your and'.

Their appearance on 24 May 1964 was filmed in ndon during the making of *A Hard Day's Night*. They re in a special segment of the show and were seen rforming 'You Can't Do That'.

Their 23 February 1964 show was repeated on 23 gust 1964 and their 9 February 1964 show was peated on 20 September 1964.

The group taped another appearance before a live dience at the CBS Studios in New York on 14 August 65 and it was broadcast on 12 September 1965. The oup performed 'I Feel Fine', 'I'm Down', 'Help!', esterday', 'Act Naturally' and 'Ticket To Ride'.

On 5 June 1966 the promotional films of 'Rain' and aperback Writer' were screened on the show.

On 12 February 1967 'The Ed Sullivan Show' esented the two promotional films directed by **Peter ldmann**, 'Penny Lane' and 'Strawberry Fields Forever'.

Their performance of 'Hello Goodbye', which they'd ned on stage at the **Saville Theatre** in London, was eened on the programme on 26 November 1967 and on February 1970 there was a filmed segment of the group rforming 'Two Of Us', from the filming of *Let It Be*, ich had been taken from an hour-long TV special lute To The Beatles'.

Following the success of the Beatles' appearances, Sullivan continued to provide a showcase for rock acts. The British stars who appeared on 'The Ed Sullivan Show' included **Gerry & the Pacemakers**, the **Searchers**, **Billy J. Kramer** and the Dakotas, **Cilla Black**, the **Dave Clark Five**, the Animals, the **Rolling Stones**, the Bachelors, **Peter & Gordon**, **Freddie & the Dreamers** and Herman's Hermits.

Despite the fact that it still had high ratings, CBS cancelled 'The Ed Sullivan Show' because they wanted to modernize their schedule and it eventually went off the air on 6 June 1971. Sullivan died on 13 October 1974.

● *Summertime*

The famous George Gershwin standard. Several Liverpool bands played the number and various rock 'n' roll artists had turned to evergreen standards for inspiration, such as **Gene Vincent** with 'Over The Rainbow'. 'Summertime' had been recorded by Sam Cooke in 1957 and Ray Charles in 1958; either of the two is likely to have influenced the Beatles in their selection of the number, which was introduced into their repertoire in their **Quarry Men** days.

● Sun King

Number penned by John and included on the *Abbey Road* album.

His original title was *'Los Paranois'*, probably because of the pieces of nonsense in Spanish and Italian at the end of the song.

When the Beatles began recording the number on Thursday, 24 July 1969, the working title had been changed to 'Here Comes The Sun King', although *Abbey Road* also contains a George Harrison composition called 'Here Comes The Sun'. A variety of unusual sounds were used including cowbells.

● Sunny Heights, *St George's Road, Weybridge, Surrey*

The estate which Ringo bought following his marriage to Maureen in 1965 on the advice of **Walter Stracht**. The property cost £37,000 and Ringo spent a further £40,000 on improvements and additions to the Tudor-style mansion, which had large gardens overlooking St George's Hill golf course.

Situated in the stockbroker belt of Weybridge, which became known as the 'Beatle Belt', Sunny Heights was home to the Starrs for three years. It had no swimming pool, but there was a little bar called 'The Flying Cow' and a cowboy holster presented to Ringo by **Elvis Presley** was displayed there.

The garage housed three cars – a Mini Cooper, a Facel Voga and a Land-Rover – and in the gardens there was a playhouse in a tree.

The pets at Sunny Heights included two Airedale dogs, Daisy and Donovan, a white poodle called Tiger and nine cats!

When John Lennon eventually left for America, Ringo purchased Tittenhurst Park in Ascot from him for a reported fee of £2,000,000.

● Sure To Fall (In Love With You)

A number which **Carl Perkins** recorded for Sun Records in January 1956.

The **Quarry Men** included it in their repertoire, with Paul McCartney on lead vocals and continued to perform it when they became the Beatles, until late in 1962. It is also one of the numbers the group recorded during their audition for **Decca Records**.

● Sutcliffe, Millie

Scots-born mother of **Stuart Sutcliffe**. Her husband Charles was a merchant seaman who, as a second engineer, spent a great deal of time at sea. The couple had three children, Stuart and two daughters, Joyce and Pauline.

The family moved to Liverpool and settled at 37 **Aigburth Drive**. Millie worked as a teacher at a local school for the blind and helped to support Stuart when he was studying at **Liverpool College of Art**. She had a very close relationship with her son and a strong belief in his talent as an artist.

After Stuart had left the Beatles and settled in Hamburg, she received a call from **Rod Murray**, who had shared a flat in **Gambier Terrace** with Stuart and John Lennon. He told her that he could no longer afford the premises now that the other two had left and that they hadn't paid up their share of the rent. She paid Stuart's share to Rod and hired a van to collect his belongings, including a camp bed which he'd slept on.

She said that many people were to claim that Stuart had slept in a coffin – but that was nonsense, it was definitely a camp bed. She also took with her a chest of drawers full of Lennon's clothes, which she stored for a while in Aigbur until her husband returned home from sea and threw the all out.

She was in constant touch with Stuart in Germany a began to tell her friends that she was worried becau Stuart had fallen down the steps leading from the att where he lived in **Astrid Kirchherr**'s house. He'd stru his head and had begun to experience a series headaches which continued to worsen, at times inducing temporary blindness.

Prior to the fall there had been no instances of Stu suffering from headaches and until her death in 1985, M Sutcliffe was convinced that the fall down the attic ste was the cause of her son's death.

When Stuart died on 10 April Astrid sent Millie t telegrams, one saying that he was very ill, the other that had died. However, she received them out of sequen She flew to Hamburg and brought her son's body home Liverpool.

Aware of how close Stuart was to John, she w surprised that John never attended the funeral. She v even more disappointed when, after arranging fo posthumous exhibition of Stuart's work at the **Walker A Gallery** in Liverpool, none of the Beatles agreed to atte This was probably not a snub on their part as the booked holidays at the time.

She never heard from John again until Sunday November 1964. The Beatles were appearing at **Empire Theatre, Liverpool** and Bill and Virginia Ha were backstage and suggested to John that they drop in Millie Sutcliffe.

Together with **Pete Shotton** and his wife they all w up to Aigburth Drive and Millie was thrilled. She g John a clipping of one of their first-ever write-ups, hea '"Rock" group at Neston Institute', a book *How To Dr Horses* which John had won as a prize at school m years before and had lent to Stuart. She then took th round the rooms where Stuart's paintings were displa and John remembered a number of them. She then invi John and Bill Harry to take their pick of any work Stuart's they wanted. John picked a blue abstract painting and said, 'This will take pride of place in living room.'

Mrs Sutcliffe decided to devote the rest of her life promoting Stuart's work and arranged a further exhibi of his work in London. After the death of her husba hen her daughters had grown up and left home, she went live in Sevenoaks, Kent, where she died before iscovering the rising interest in her son's body of twork.

Sutcliffe, Stuart

ne original **'Fifth Beatle'** was born Stuart Fergusson ictor Sutcliffe in Edinburgh on 2 June 1940. His father, narles, was a seaman, his mother, **Millie,** a teacher and had two younger sisters, Joyce and Pauline.

When the family moved to Merseyside, settling at 37 gburth Drive, Stuart attended Prescot Grammar School d later attended **Liverpool College of Art**. He mediately displayed a talent which impressed teachers d students alike, with some tutors stating that he was the ost brilliant artist the college had produced.

Although on a different course, Bill Harry sought him t and they became friends. They also made friends with hn Lennon, from a different class from either of them d, together with other students such as **Rod Murray**, ey would spend a great deal of their spare time together the local pub **Ye Cracke** and at student flats in e area.

Stuart was slight, small and introvert. He and Harry ed to talk about literature, art, films and mystical ilosophy. Popular books at the time were Colin Wilson's *e Outsider* and J. D. Salinger's *The Catcher In The Rye*. ey also obtained copies of books by San Francisco Beat ets, published by the City Lights Bookshop, and copies books from the Olympia Press in Paris. Harry was in arge of the art college film society and he mostly booked eign films such as *L'Age d'Or* and *Un Chien Andalou*. drzej Wajda's films were also popular and a cult figure some of the students was Zbigniew Cybulski. He ticularly impressed Stuart, who tried to effect his look wearing dark-tinted glasses like the star who had come be called 'the Polish James Dean'.

In later years, Beatles biographers pointed out that art tried to look like James Dean. They were wrong. wasn't interested in Dean, the influence came m Cybulski. Stuart's knowledge of art was extensive l although his later work turned to the abstract, his tial college work was heavily under the influence of ncent Van Gogh, the most popular artist with the dents there.

At Stuart's flat in **Percy Street**, Harry and Stuart used to discuss the type of philosophy which seeks to explore the meaning of existence – mysticism, talking about what the future could hold and, in particular, how they could capture their own background and experience in their art. These were the sort of discussions they used to continue at Ye Cracke with John and Rod.

The college and the **Liverpool Institute** were one building and Paul McCartney and George Harrison were students at the Institute. During their breaks they'd frequent the college canteen or rehearse in the life rooms. John felt that his group needed a bass guitarist and he separately approached both Stuart and Rod offering them the job if they could get a bass guitar.

By this time John, Rod and Stuart were sharing a flat in **Gambier Terrace**. A painting by Stuart was entered into the John Moores Exhibition at the **Walker Art Gallery** and was bought by millionaire Moores himself, which enabled Stuart to buy a Hofner President bass guitar. But he didn't know how to play it. Another student at the college, David May, offered to teach him to play 'C'mon Everybody' if Stuart would let him measure his guitar, which would enable David to build one of his own.

As the group played at the Saturday evening dances in the college canteen, they were regarded as the college band. However, not having much money they couldn't afford a PA system. Stuart and Harry were both members of the Students' Union Committee and they proposed and seconded the motion that the Union should advance funds to the group to enable them to buy an amplifier which they could use, not only at the school dances, but wherever they played.

When Stuart joined John's group, Harry advised him against it because he applied the same dedicated enthusiasm to it that he had displayed towards his art and Harry thought that his art would suffer. John was often cruelly sarcastic to Stuart, even though he had become his closest friend, and he received general abuse from the band at this time, who didn't take him seriously. John referred to this by saying, 'We'd tell Stu he couldn't sit with us, or eat with us. We'd tell him to go away, and he did.' John and Paul generally made fun of Stuart on stage throughout his entire period with the band.

It was obvious that Stuart would never be as good a musician as he was an artist. He did, however, bring

Stuart Sutcliffe – the enigmatic fifth Beatle. (Pauline Sutcliffe)

something intangible to the group, a touch of style. Stuart had an artistic sense which also displayed itself in the way he looked and how he dressed. Despite his slight stature and the fact that he was an introvert, he drew people to him: **Arthur Ballard,** a college tutor, used to spend a great deal of time giving him extra tuition outside college hours; **Allan Williams**, who ran the coffee bar the **Jacaranda**, which they attended, was impressed by Stuart's quiet personality, intelligence and talent. He asked him to paint a mural in the club, which he did, with the help of Rod Murray. When Williams co-promoted the **Liverpool Stadium** concert headlined by **Ge Vincent**, it was Stuart who asked him why he had booked the group. Williams liked Stuart and short-lis them for the auditions to be held for **Larry Parnes** a **Billy Fury** at the **Wyvern Club**. At the auditions Stu is reputed to have played with his back to Parnes caus many writers to say that this prevented the group be booked as Billy Fury's backing band. Parnes hims disputes this and says he had no objections to Stuart - was the age and appearance of drummer **Tommy Mo** which put him off. The audition resulted in the band be booked to back **Johnny Gentle** on a tour of Scotland a Stuart chose to use the stage name Stu Da Stael deference to a Russian artist he admired.

you are invited to a private view
on Friday 24 August 6-8pm
STUART
SUTCLIFFE
1940-62
an exhibition of paintings and works on paper
Bluecoat Gallery
School Lane Liverpool L1 3BX
051 709 5689
exhibition 25 August - 29 September 1990
open Saturday 25, Sunday 26, Monday 27 August
12 noon - 5 pm, and thereafter Tuesday -
Saturday 10.30 am - 5 pm
This card also admits to
PETE FRAME
Merseybeat Rock Family Trees
Admit Two. Please bring this card with you
over: Stuart Sutcliffe, Hamburg: 1960-62
monotype with mixed media 33" x 23"
Bluecoat Arts Centre receives financial assistance from
Merseyside Arts, Liverpool City Council and the
Metropolitan Borough Councils of Sefton and Wirral
exhibition sponsored by
PILKINGTON
Royal
Insurance
CAVERN CITY TOURS
Merseyside Arts
LIVERPOOL
City Council

Stuart didn't have any real musical contribution make to the group, and his main spotlight was when took over on lead vocal on the **Elvis Presley** hit 'Love Tender'. Yet he gave the group an added dimension w his aura of mystery, brooding good looks and intelliger

was Stuart who suggested that they call themselves
etles, although John replaced one of the 'e's' with an 'a'.
was said that Stuart had thought of the name because it
s similar to that of **Buddy Holly**'s backing group the
ickets. His mother thought it was because he was often
lled a Beatnik, because he wore very tight jeans, winkle-
kers and at one time had a goatee beard. She was also
comment at one time, 'Stuart's influence on them has
en played down as if he was not a potent member of the
mation. At the time I was amazed that he was going
und with them and threatened to withdraw my financial
pport. I thought I was doing my duty, but he started
ying paints rather than food. Stuart went around like an
han of the storm. So I relented and agreed to come and
his group.

'John knew I was coming, the others didn't. Harrison
otted me and said, "Stuart, your Mum's here." They
ught I'd come to create a scene. But it was a pleasant
prise. I thought their music was out of this world.
erwards, Stuart said, "What did you think of it,
ther?" I couldn't express the feeling of pleasure the
sic gave me.'

Millie believed that Stuart's influence on their image
s an important one: the leather look, the original Beatle
rcut, even the collarless suit were all a product of
art's influence, she claims. 'I remember when Stuart
l the black leather suit and Astrid was wearing it
the time. In fact, Astrid liked it so much that Stuart
dly had a chance to wear it at all. As for the Cardin
t, Stuart had it on the very last time he came home.
vas a velvet Cardin suit. He took his sister Pauline
n to the **Cavern** to see John and the next day Pauline
l to me, "Those Beatles hate Stuart, especially Paul
Cartney."

'They were saying, "Oh, you're wearing your sister's
t, Stuart", mocking the suit the way they mocked
Beatle haircut. They always made Stuart out as a
ie, but it was the other way around. Stuart had a
ong character and in the important things John
led by what Stuart said. As for the haircut, it started
n Stuart's hair was falling down and sticking out.
e night Astrid had been moaning about his hair
then took him into the bathroom and cut it. He told
"They [the Beatles] laughed at it. I defied them and
t it that way."'

n May 1960 Williams started booking the group at the Jacaranda and then offered them the opportunity of performing in Germany.

After they arrived in Hamburg and were discovered by the young Hamburg students who included **Astrid Kirchherr**, Stuart's days with the group were numbered. For one thing, Paul wanted him out. He wanted to take over on bass guitar himself. This led to tension between them which manifested itself in a physical fight in which the more powerful Paul grappled with Stuart on stage at the **Top Ten Club**, much to the delight of the customers, who thought it was part of the show. The '**Exis**' were attracted more to Stuart than to any other member of the group – he had a particular charismatic appeal which drew them to him. Astrid fell in love with Stuart and she arranged for Stuart to lodge in the attic flat at her home in the Hamburg suburb of Altona.

When the Beatles returned to Liverpool in December 1961, Stuart remained in Hamburg. For a few gigs they had to get **Chas Newby** in as a replacement. When he left to return to college, John asked George to play bass. George refused and John asked Paul. Paul began to play his Lucky 7 upside down and backwards with piano strings on it. George wrote to Stuart: 'Come home sooner, as if we get a new bass player for the time being, it will be crumby, as he will have to learn everything. It's no good with Paul, playing bass, we've decided, that is if he had some kind of bass and amp to play on!'

Talking about Stuart, Astrid was to comment: 'If he wasn't painting, he was writing or playing the guitar. He used to spend hours writing letters to John in Liverpool. He'd put down all his feelings, all his experiences, even put in illustrations and pages of poetry. These letters used to run to twenty pages or so. And John's were just as long and deep.'

Stuart was to play some further gigs with the group when they returned to appear at the Top Ten Club in March 1961, but his days as a Beatle were drawing to a close. Paul now wanted to take over as bass guitarist and when they received an offer to back **Tony Sheridan** on record, he insisted that he play bass on the recordings.

Stuart had also returned to his first love, art, and had managed to secure a place at an art college in Hamburg. Two of his German friends, who were also artists, recommended that he seek a place at the State High School of Art Instruction in Hamburg. For a while he worked in Gustaf Seitz's Sculpture Department until the official authority came through for him to commence work under **Eduardo Paolozzi**, who had arranged for Stuart to receive a grant.

When discussing Stuart in the 1967 book *Art In A City*, Paolozzi said: 'He was a very perceptive and sensitive person and very restless.' He also said: 'There is that sort of marvellously desperate thing about the whole Liverpool business now. I always felt there was a desperate thing about Stuart in his life . . . I was afraid of it.'

It was around this time that his mother, Millie Sutcliffe, began telling Stuart's friends in Liverpool that she was concerned about her son because he was experiencing terrible headaches and blackouts after a fall down some stairs in Astrid's house. At Christmas 1961 he visited Liverpool with Astrid and his friends noticed how pale and ill he looked. **Mike McCartney** commented: 'When I met him in a jazz club when he was home on holiday a few weeks ago he said he had a feeling that something was going to happen to him when he went back to Hamburg. He was obviously worried and nervous.'

A letter from a reader in ***Mersey Beat*** pointed out that Stuart was no longer playing with the group and asked if the rumour were true that he'd died in Hamburg! It was a reflection of the mystique that Stuart radiated which caused people to create stories about him. There was a rumour that he slept in a coffin in Gambier Terrace – completely unfounded, just like the disputed tale that he was kicked in the head in a fight – it never happened.

Stuart announced that he was going to marry Astrid in June 1962 after he'd completed his course at college.

During his classes at college he began to suffer severe headaches and blackouts. Astrid said, 'For days at a time he would not come down from his attic studio to eat or sleep, and the headaches became violent, they seemed like fits.'

In February 1962 he was examined by a doctor, who could find nothing wrong. He fainted in class and had to be given pain killers, but although X-rays were taken, the doctors said they could find nothing wrong with him. He even suffered from temporary blindness.

On 10 April 1962 Astrid found Stuart unconscious in his bed. She called for an ambulance and while they were being driven to hospital, Stuart died in Astrid's arms. It was 4.30 p.m. He was 21 years old, Astrid was 23.

Astrid had sent two cables to Millie, who was 54 ye[ars] old at the time. The first read, 'My Stuart is dying', t[he] second, 'My Stuart is dead'. The second cable arriv[ed] before the first.

Charles Sutcliffe couldn't be contacted as he'd sail[ed] for South America and wouldn't be in touch for a furth[er] three weeks. Twenty-year-old Joyce Sutcliffe said, 'He h[as] a weak heart and we cannot radio his ship to tell him. [He] will be told when he reaches port.'

At the autopsy it was officially declared that the ca[use] of death was 'Cerebral paralysis due to bleeding into [the] right ventricle of the brain.'

Astrid met the Beatles at the airport the next day to [tell] them the dreadful news. John burst into hysterical laugh[ter] and couldn't stop. 'It was his way of not wanting to face [the] truth,' said Astrid.

Millie flew to Hamburg and brought her son's bo[dy] home to Liverpool. He was buried at **Huyton Pari[sh] Church Cemetery** in Stanley Road/Bluebell La[ne], Huyton. His resting place is number 552 in the 19[..] section.

His mother decided to devote her time to ga[ining] recognition for Stuart's work and a memorial exhibit[ion] was arranged at the Walker Art Gallery in Liverpool [in] 1964. Interest in Stuart seemed to fade away. When Mi[llie] arranged another exhibition of his work at a small gall[ery] in London, few people attended. When his painti[ngs] were offered up for sale at a Liverpool convention [in] the seventies for only £40 each, there were few taker[s for] the pieces.

Almost 25 years after his death a sudden burst [of] interest took flower and began to grow. *The Sunday Ti[mes]* included him in a feature on 'Smart Art', mentioning [that] his pictures were now fashionable among collectors. [His] work also commanded high prices at Sotheby's [..] auctions.

In the late eighties Pauline Sutcliffe worked o[n a] book about her brother's life and art in collaboration w[ith] **Mike Evans** and an exhibition of Stuart's work [was] launched in London and Liverpool. Granada Televis[ion] broadcast a documentary of his life in Hamburg an[d a] major feature film based on the Hamburg years [was] announced in 1992.

The Beatles selected Stuart as one of the figure[s to] appear on the cover of their *Sgt Pepper's Lonely He[arts] Club Band* album.

Suzy Parker

ng which the Beatles recorded at **Twickenham Film** **udios** during their filming of *Let It Be* in January 1969. ey are seen performing the number in the film and the nber was copyrighted in the name of all four members mbers of the group although the song has never peared on record.

Sweden

e Beatles toured Sweden from 24–31 October 1963. was their first foreign tour and the first time y had played outside Britain since their Hamburg s.

They appeared on Swedish radio and television and formed nine shows in five concerts, for which they eived a reported £2,000.

There were mob scenes in Sweden where the Beatles rcut was referred to as being in a 'Hamlet style'. e group opened their brief tour at the **Nya aulan** Karlastad on the 25th, followed by the **Kungliga llen** in Stockholm on the 26th, the **Borashallen** in as on the 28th and the **Sporthallen**, Eskilstuna, he 29th.

The Beatles returned to Sweden on 28 and 29 July for r concerts at the **Johanneshovs Isstadion** in ckholm.

Sweet Georgia Brown

of the numbers recorded at the May 1961 recording ion in Hamburg in which the Beatles were produced king **Tony Sheridan** by **Bert Kaempfert**.

The song was composed by Ben Bernie, Maceo Pinkard Kenneth Casey in the 1920s, but was open to temporary interpretations and had, in fact, been rded by the Coasters in 1957.

The American label ATCO issued it as a single on CO 6302 on 1 June 1964 with 'Take Out Some rance On Me Baby' on the flip. Although the label laimed 'The Beatles, featuring Tony Sheridan', it 't chart.

Sweet Little Sixteen

posed by **Chuck Berry** who had a million-seller with 1958. The song was included in the repertoire of the **rry Men**, with John on lead vocal. The Beatles ormed the number at the **Star Club** and it's to be found on *The Beatles Live! At The Star Club In Hamburg: 1962* album. They also recorded it for their BBC radio show **'Pop Go The Beatles'** on 23 July 1963. John also recorded 'Sweet Little Sixteen' for his *Rock 'n' Roll* album which he recorded in 1975.

● Swinging Bluejeans, The

Liverpool's longest-surviving group who still perform regularly throughout the world.

When they formed in 1957 they were a skiffle band known as the Swinging Bluegenes. They had their own guest night at the **Cavern Club**. In June 1961, when John Carter left the band to move to Canada, the line-up was: Ray Ennis (lead guitar), Ralph Ellis (solo), Les Braid (bass) and Paul Moss (banjo).

The group began to perform a three-quarters of an hour spot every Friday, Saturday and Sunday at the Cavern and opened their Tuesday evening guest nights in 1961.

On 21 March 1961 they welcomed the Beatles to their first-ever Cavern evening spot. Other Bluegenes guest nights on which the Beatles appeared included 25 July 1961 and 28 August 1962. The Beatles also appeared on the bill with the Bluegenes, **Gene Vincent** and **Sounds Incorporated** on Sunday, 1 July 1962, which was the first Sunday at the Cavern which wasn't headlined by a jazz band.

The Bluegenes were held in high regard in Liverpool and when **Bob Wooler** compiled a list of Top Ten Liverpool bands in the 5 October 1961 issue of ***Mersey Beat***, with the Beatles placed at No. 1, he qualified this by writing, 'My list of what I rate to be the ten most popular rock groups on Merseyside – excluding the Bluegenes, of course. They are beyond comparison. They are in a class of their own.'

With the growing popularity of groups and the death of the Trad Jazz boom, the group altered their name to the Swinging Bluejeans and began to play rock 'n' roll. Their line-up was: Ray Ennis (guitar), Ralph Ellis (guitar), Les Braid (bass guitar) and Norman Kuhlke (drums).

After the success of the Beatles, the Swinging Bluejeans made their recording debut with 'It's Too Late Now' c/w 'Think Of Me', released in June 1963.

They then released 'The Hippy Hippy Shake', which the Beatles voted a hit on their **'Juke Box Jury'** special on 7 December 1963. It became the Bluejeans' biggest hit.

The Bluejeans' success continued for some years. They appeared in a special film for Pathe Pictorial, had their own weekly **Radio Luxembourg** show 'Swingtime', appeared on the Christmas 1963 edition of TV's popular 'Z Cars', performing 'Hippy Hippy Shake', 'Angie' and 'Money'. They also appeared in the film *Circularama Cavalcade* which had its London premiere on 11 March 1964.

Their current line-up is: Ray Ennis (guitar), Les Braid (bass guitar), Colin Manley, ex-member of the **Remo Four** (guitar), and Ian McGee (drums).

● Swinging Sound '63

Title of a radio special broadcast live from the **Royal Albert Hall** on 18 April 1963. This was one of three special radio presentations by the BBC from the Albert Hall, but the only one on which the Beatles appeared.

The programme was produced by Terry Henebery and Ron Belchier. The Beatles were second on the bill to **Del Shannon** and among the other artists appearing were the Springfields, **Shane Fenton**, **Kenny Lynch**, Susan Maughan, **Rolf Harris**, the **Vernons Girls** and Chris Barber's Jazzband.

The Beatles performed 'Twist And Shout' and 'From Me To You'.

● Sydney Stadium, Sydney, Australia

The Beatles appeared at Sydney Stadium for six conce on 18, 19, 20 June 1964 with two concerts a night at 6. p.m. and 8.00 p.m., attracting over 12,000 people – biggest-ever audiences for a pop concert at the stadium to that time.

One newspaper hired a technician with a decibel me who registered 114 decibels when the Beatles appeared stage. As a Boeing 707 registered 90-100 decibels 2,000 feet, the newspaper headline read: 'Beatles F Sound Like A Jet In Flight.'

The show was compered by **Alan Field** and the f group on stage were the **Phantoms**.

They remained on stage to back **Johnny Devlin** then **Johnny Chester**. **Sounds Incorporated** t closed the first half and the Beatles appeared for the en second half of each show.

The *Sydney Sun* commented, 'Wanted: one new se drums, ear drums. Even today, more than twelve ho after the first Sydney concert, I've still got to tilt my h to hear properly. But I can't blame the Beatles, it's fans – they sounded like a very high-pitched swarm locusts descending on a ripening crop.' The *Sun Mirror* said: 'Beatles have thin legs and long h and would be very useful in a house for cleaning cobw off ceilings.'

The Swinging Bluejeans – the Beatles were their guests on early Cavern appearances. (EMI)

Take Good Care Of My Baby

Gerry Goffin, Carole King number which provided bby Vee with an American No. 4 hit in 1961. The atles included it in their repertoire that year with orge Harrison on lead vocals.

Take Out Some Insurance On Me Baby

mber composed by Charles Shingleton and Waldonese ll. The song was recorded by Jimmy Reed and issued as ingle in America on **Vee Jay Records** in April 1959. ny **Sheridan** included it in his repertoire and it was of the numbers he recorded with the Beatles in May 61.

The song was also known as 'If You Love Me, Baby' it was under this title that it appeared as the flipside 'Ain't She Sweet' when it was issued in Britain on ydor NH 52-317 on 29 May 1964. The single reached 24 in the ***New Musical Express*** charts. It was also d as the flipside of 'Sweet Georgia Brown' in America en it was issued on Atco 6302 on 1 June 1964, although title was now back to 'Take Out Some Insurance On Baby'. The record failed to gain a chart placing.

It next appeared on the British album *The Beatles First* une 1964 and has been used on various other releases.

Talent For Loving, A

novel by Richard Condon which was originally to have n the basis for the Beatles' third film. **Bud Ornstein**, ad of Production for United Artists, originally suggested property and Brian Epstein and the Beatles all liked Condon's book. Ornstein left United Artists to set up Pickfair Films in partnership with Brian Epstein, and it was officially announced to the press that 'A Talent For Loving' would be the Beatles' new film.

The story was a Western set in the year 1871 and concerned an epic 1,400-mile horse race between the Rio Grande and Mexico City, with a sub-plot about an American who arrives in Mexico to claim his land, only to find a Mexican has claimed the same land. The biggest part was to go to Ringo, who loved the idea of being in a Western. Filming was to have begun in 1965, but it was postponed, supposedly because of potentially bad weather in Spain, where locations were to be made.

As it turned out, the Beatles hated the first draft of the script they received and became disenchanted with the project. They decided to opt out. Later in 1965, John commented, '**Walter Shenson** thinks we're still considering that film, but as far as I'm concerned, it's scrapped. The original book was great, but the script they showed us turned out lousy.' Following a meeting between the Beatles and Shenson in December 1965, it was officially announced that they would no longer make the film.

A Talent For Loving was eventually made and released in 1969, with Richard Widmark, Genevieve Page, Topol and Cesar Romero.

● Talent Spot, The

BBC Light Programme radio show of the early sixties which spotlighted new talent. The half-hour programme was broadcast at 5.00 p.m. each Tuesday and was produced by Brian Willey and presented by Gary Marshal.

The Beatles made their London radio debut on the show on 4 December 1962, which was recorded at the BBC Paris Studio, Regent Street, on 27 November, and they performed 'Love Me Do', 'P.S. I Love You' and 'Twist And Shout'. Their second and final appearance on the programme was transmitted on 29 January 1963, following their recording at the Paris Studio on 22 January, when they performed 'Please Please Me', 'Ask Me Why' and 'Some Other Guy'. Their version of 'Three Cool Cats' was not transmitted.

● A Taste Of Honey

Composed by Ric Marlow and Bobby Scott for the play *A Taste Of Honey* in 1960, it was included in the Beatles' repertoire in 1962, with Paul on lead vocal. The group featured the song on several of their BBC radio shows including **'Here We Go'**, **'Side By Side'**, **'Easy Beat'**, **'The Beat Show'** and two of their **'Pop Go The Beatles'** shows. The group also recorded it for their *Please Please Me* album. It was one of the tracks included on their first British EP release *Twist And Shout*. In America **Vee Jay** issued it on the *Introducing The Beatles* and *Songs, Pictures And Stories Of The Fabulous Beatles* albums and the *Souvenir Of Their Visit To America (The Beatles)* EP while **Capitol** featured it on *The Early Beatles* album. It was also on *The Beatles Box* and *The Beatles Collection* sets.

● Taxman

A George Harrison number included on the *Revolver* album. George wrote the number following his frustration at the high taxes in Britain. It happened when he realized that if anyone actually started earning real money, then most of it would go to the government in taxes. In the song he mentions Harold Wilson and Ted Heath, who were the leaders of the Labour and Conservative parties.

One wonders if George remembered the song in July 1973 when he had to hand over a cheque for £1,000,000 to the Inland Revenue in taxes for the Bangla Desh concert and album. The Beatles were plagued with tax problems and it was in an attempt to alleviate them that they formed Apple. At one point Ringo commented, 'The government's taking over 90 per cent of all our money anyway – we're left with 1/9th in the pound.' In *I. Me. Mine*, George wrote, '"Taxman" was when I first realized that even though we had started earning money, we were actually giving most of it away in taxes; it was and still is typical. Why should this be so? Are we being punished for something we had forgotten to do?'

The number was recorded in April 1966 and John Lennon said, 'Many people have written in asking about how we sounded in the studio when we weren't actually recording a song. So at the beginning of "Taxman" there's a candid recording showing us just like that.' 'Taxman' was to resurface in 1976 on the *Rock 'n' Roll Music* and *The Best Of George Harrison* albums.

● Taylor, Alistair

The man who became known as Apple's 'Mr Fixit' originally joined the Whitechapel branch of **NEMS** as Brian Epstein's personal assistant. He accompanied Bri to the **Cavern** to see the Beatles for the first time and 13 December 1961 was a witness to the managem contract which Brian drew up for the group. Howev Brian didn't sign the contract, explaining to them tha would give them the freedom to opt out if they wishe but it was signed by all four Beatles and Alistair.

Soon after, Brian offered Alistair two and a half per c of the group, but Alistair turned him down, even though wasn't asked to invest any money in exchange for percentage.

Due to his wife Lesley's asthma problem, Alistair advised to move away from Liverpool and he took a jol Pye Records in London. In 1963 he bumped into Bri

Alistair Taylor– Apple's 'Mr Fixit'.

they had lunch together and Alistair was offered the jol General Manager of NEMS Enterprises at a salary £1,000 a year.

Alistair became involved in handling many tasks for Beatles and received the tag 'Mr Fixit' for his effo which ranged from attending an auction to buying island for John Lennon to surveying a farm in Scotland Paul.

On Sunday, 27 August 1967, Alistair received a from Joanne Newfield, Brian's secretary, asking him come over to **Chapel Street**. He rushed over and devastated to find Brian dead in his bedroom.

When the Beatles formed Apple, John Lennon pho Alistair to ask him to become Office Manager and du the next few years he played his 'Mr Fixit' role ag Early on, Paul had designed an advertisement for Ap and wanted Alistair to pose for the picture. It wa otograph of him wearing a suit and a bowler hat, posing a one-man band and it was featured in a poster mpaign and advertisements in the music press. The copy ich Paul wrote read: 'This man has talent. One day he ng his songs to a tape recorder (borrowed from the man xt door). In his neatest handwriting he wrote an planatory note (giving his name and address) and, nembering to enclose a picture of himself, sent the tape, ter and photograph to Apple Music, 94 Baker Street, ndon W1. If you were thinking of doing the same thing urself – do it now! This man now owns a Bentley!'

One day Alistair was having lunch with a client when received a call from **Peter Brown** insisting he return the office straight away. He arrived to see that Brown d been given a list of Apple personnel to be sacked and stair's name was top of the list. A victim of the **Allen ein**-inspired wholesale sackings at Apple.

Alistair attempted to call John and Paul, but was able to. Then he read a quote from Paul in the *Daily il* in which, when asked to comment on Alistair's king, he said, 'It isn't possible to be nice about giving neone the sack.'

He never saw any of the Beatles again and went to work a hotel. A number of years later he was 'discovered' by umber of Beatles fans and invited to appear at Beatle nventions to relate his stories.

His book *Yesterday: The Beatles Remembered*, which wrote with Martin Roberts, was published by Sidgwick Jackson in 1988. It was written in an unfortunate style a series of letters to an imaginary pen pal called chelle.

The book was completely rewritten in a straightforward hion in 1991.

Taylor, Derek

close associate of the Beatles from 1963, Derek was n in Liverpool on 7 May 1934. He became a journalist d initially worked on the *Hoylake and West Kirby vertiser* before graduating to the *Liverpool Daily Post* **Liverpool Echo**. In 1962 he was offered the post of wbusiness correspondent for the northern edition of the *ily Express*, based in Manchester.

On 30 May 1963 Derek attended the Beatles' concert at **Odeon, Manchester** and his review appeared in the *ily Express* the next day. He wrote: 'The Liverpool nd came to Manchester last night and I thought it was magnificent . . . Indecipherable, meaningless nonsense, of course, but as beneficial as a week on a beach at the pierhead overlooking the Mersey. The spectacle of these fresh, cheeky, sharp, young entertainers in apposition to the shiny-eyed teenage idolaters is as good as a rejuvenating drug for the jaded adult.'

He next travelled to Liverpool to interview Brian Epstein and the piece appeared in the *Daily Express* on 20 June 1963 under the banner 'Epstein, The Brain Behind The Beatles'. Then, at a preview of a BBC TV Beatles documentary, **'The Mersey Sound'**, he found out about the Beatles' seasons in Hamburg and flew to the German city to research their experiences there, which resulted in a week-long series in the *Express*. By that time he came to

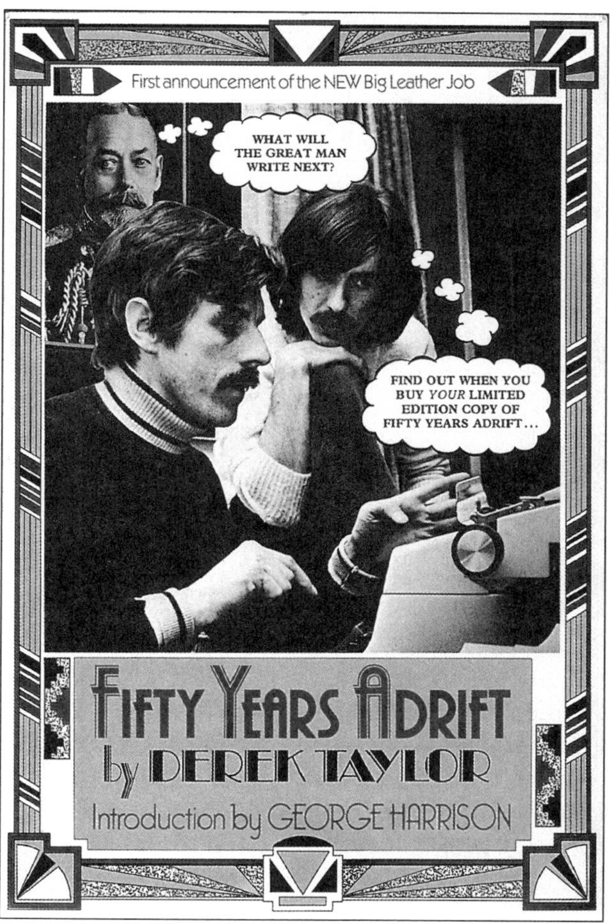

Promotional material for Derek Taylor's autobiography. (Genesis Fine Editions, photo ©Tom Hanley).

be known at the *Express* as 'the Beatles man' and later in 1963 he interviewed them backstage at the **Floral Hall, Southport** on 15 October and at the **Apollo, Ardwick** on 20 November. At the time he referred to them as, 'The gay quartet of grammar-school boys'.

Together with John Buchanan, the editor of the Manchester edition of the paper, Derek travelled to Liverpool once again to see Epstein and to suggest that a Beatle should contribute a weekly article to the *Express*, ghosted by Derek. Derek told Epstein that he had George in mind because he seemed nice and pleasant to talk to. Derek also visited all the Beatles' families and familiarized himself with their history and began to develop a close relationship between the group and his newspaper. On 14 January 1964 he flew with them to Paris where he ghosted George's column.

When Epstein's assistant **Barry Leonard** had a dispute with him and left his employ, Derek wrote to Brian requesting the job, but received no reply. He decided not to pursue it. A short time later, Epstein asked Derek to visit him in Liverpool and wondered whether he could recommend someone who could ghost his biography. Derek offered his services and the two of them stayed for five days at the Imperial Hotel, Torquay, while Derek taped Brian's memoirs, which were published as *A Cellarful Of Noise*. Brian then offered Derek the job as his personal assistant and he agreed to take up the post in April 1964.

In addition to becoming Epstein's Personal Assistant, Taylor also became his script writer and he travelled with the Beatles entourage on their world tour of Europe, the Far East and Australasia and also their American tour of 1964. However, the adventure was to last for only five months. At the end of the tour, when the group had embarked on a social night out, Epstein accused Derek of riding in a limousine meant for him, which Taylor denied. There was an argument and he resigned and in October was replace by Wendy Hanson.

Derek was then offered a job as press officer by Radio KRLA in Los Angeles and moved over to California with his family in February 1965 and remained there until April 1968. He became a public relations consultant for Prestige Promotions, based on Sunset Boulevard, and his first clients were the **Byrds**. He was also to represent groups such as the **Beach Boys** and helped to organize the Monterey International Pop Music Festival in 1967. At the same time he was contributing a regular column called 'Hollywood Calling' to *Disc & Music Echo*, a week British music paper, and continued to keep in touch wi the Beatles. When George Harrison came on a trip to L Angeles he arranged to meet Derek and while he w waiting, penned 'Blue Jay Way'. Derek had al introduced the Beatles to the work of **Harry Nilsson**.

When the Beatles decided to form **Apple Corps**, th invited Derek to join them as press officer and he return to England with his family. He was highly acti representing the Beatles once again, initially from offic at 95 Wigmore Street, then from the famous App

American singer James Taylor – Apple Records' first signing (CBS Records)

building at **3 Savile Row**. They were exhilarating tin for him and at one point there were plans for him to writ musical about Apple with George Harrison, but the proj was dropped when Derek admitted he couldn't writ script.

He departed from Apple on New Year's Day 1970 a went to work for Warner Bros Records as Director Special Projects. Since that time he has been involved various activities, a number of them involving the members of the Beatles. He is perhaps closest to Geo and helped him to compile his book *I. Me. Mine.* De also became the most reliable and informative of nsiders' who wrote books. They have included *As Time oes By* (Straight Arrow, 1973), *Fifty Years Adrift* (Genesis ublications, 1984) and *It Was Twenty Years Ago* (Bantam ress, 1987).

Taylor, James

merican singer/songwriter who was discovered by Apple &R man **Peter Asher** in 1968. He became one of the itital artists signed to the Apple label and when Asher egan producing Taylor's debut album, Paul McCartney ayed bass on the track 'Carolina In My Mind'. It's teresting to note that another song on the *James Taylor* bum was called 'Something In The Way She Moves', hich George Harrison used as the first line of his song omething' the following year.

Taylor was disturbed by what he considered was pple's lack of promotion of his records and he returned to merica and left the Apple label in 1969. Peter Asher mained as his producer when Taylor signed to the arner Brothers label. Ironically for Apple, Taylor mediately became a major hit with his first Warner bum, 'Sweet Baby James', and his million-seller single, ire And Rain'. Taylor was to enjoy chart success in nerica throughout the seventies.

It's likely that the rot set in when Paul McCartney ecame angry when **Jane Asher** announced that their gagement was over. A furious Paul wanted Peter Asher ed but **Ron Kass** talked him out of it. However, from at point Asher and the artists he looked after personally dn't receive the attention from Apple that they'd eviously enjoyed.

Taylor, Kingsize

ed Taylor was to become one of Liverpool's unsung roes. A singer with a unique voice and one of the very st of the Mersey bands, he missed out on the success of e Mersey boom, due mainly to the fact that he and his oup spent much of their time based in Hamburg.

Taylor first joined a skiffle group, the James Boys, in 56 and then teamed up with the Dominoes in 1958. By 60 the band had changed their name to Kingsize Taylor the Dominoes and began to build their local reputation. ey made their **Cavern** debut on 25 January 1961, with lla Black joining them for the gig as one of the lead calists. Cilla, who was Taylor's girlfriend for a time, ade several cameo appearances with the band.

The group were voted No. 6 in the first ***Mersey Beat*** poll and they made their Hamburg debut in 1962 and were so popular they were offered a residency. Drummer Dave Lovelady, who'd taken time off from his architectural studies for the Hamburg gig, couldn't remain, so Kingsize contacted Ringo Starr and asked if he'd be his replacement. Ringo agreed, but a few days later wrote back saying he'd received an offer from the Beatles which he'd decided to accept.

Brian Redman stepped in on drums and the group remained in Hamburg, appearing with a host of their idols, including Fats Domino, **Little Richard**, **Jerry Lee Lewis**, Joey Dee & the Starliters and Johnny & the Hurricanes. They also provided backing for singer **Davy Jones**, whom the Beatles had backed in Liverpool.

Redman left the group and the Dominoes contacted Gibson Kemp, who'd replaced Ringo Starr in the Hurricanes, and the seventeen-year-old obtained a special work permit and joined them. They were recorded on stage at the **Star Club** by **Adrian Barber**, former member of the Big Three and now stage manager at the club. He recorded most of the bands who appeared there and Taylor asked him if he could have the Beatles' tapes he'd recorded. The Dominoes also made numerous records for Phillips and Polydor in Hamburg although, recording for rival labels, they changed their name to the Shakers for the Polydor releases.

The group returned from Germany in 1964 to plug their first **Decca** single, 'Stupidity', appeared on '**Thank Your Lucky Stars**' and backed **Chuck Berry** on his British tour.

There were various members in the line-up of Taylor's group over the years and included saxophonist **Howie Casey**, Paddy Chambers of Faron's Flamingos and singer **Steve Aldo**.

Taylor returned to Germany in 1965, appearing in Hamburg and Frankfurt with his group Kingsize Taylor & His Band, but there were problems with gangsters involved in certain clubs, the group never got paid, they were repatriated back to Britain in 1965 where the band broke up and Taylor became a butcher.

Years later he was to dig up Adrian Barber's recordings of the Beatles and sold them.

Teatro Adriano, Rome, Italy

Venue where the Beatles appeared during their European

tour in 1965. They were due to make two appearances on 27 June at 4.30 p.m. and 9.30 p.m. An extra two appearances were added for the following day, although attendances on both days didn't reach capacity. The daily newspaper *Paese Sera* noted that the cinema was not air-conditioned and commented: 'Whoever succeeds in half-filling a cinema in mid-afternoon with the temperature at 37 [98 degrees Fahrenheit] can well be satisfied.'

The gig was recorded by **EMI** Italy and an album *Live In Italy* was issued later in the year featuring the tracks 'Twist And Shout', 'She's A Woman', 'I'm A Loser', 'Can't Buy Me Love', 'Baby's In Black', 'I Wanna Hold Your Hand', 'A Hard Day's Night', 'Everybody's Trying To Be My Baby', 'Rock And Roll Music', 'I Feel Fine', 'Ticket To Ride' and 'Long Tall Sally'.

Unfortunately, permission hadn't been obtained from the Beatles to release this album and it had to be withdrawn two weeks after release. A thousand copies of the album had already been sold and are obviously of great interest to collectors.

EMI Italy replaced it with an album *The Beatles In Italy*, but this consisted of studio tracks which hadn't previously been available on singles in that country.

Among the celebrities who attended the concerts in Rome were actor Marcello Mastroianni and actress Ursula Andress. The Rome newspaper *Il Messaggero* wrote: 'No more than four ugly faces, four long heads of hair, four sublime idiots, four barefoot bums – but they succeeded in creating a spectacle that one can only admire.'

● Technical College Hall, Borough Road, Birkenhead, Liverpool L41

A college 'over the water' from Liverpool where the Beatles were booked to appear for three consecutive Fridays in February 1962 on Fridays 9, 14 and 23.

● Teddy Boy

Number penned by Paul McCartney which the Beatles began recording at **Apple Studios** on Friday, 24 January 1969. They continued recording the number the following Wednesday, originally intending it to be included on the 'Get Back' album, which was scrapped.

When **Phil Spector** was mixing the 'Get Back' tapes to produce the *Let It Be* album, 'Teddy Boy' was one of the tracks he re-mixed, although it wasn't used on the album and the Beatles' version remains unreleased.

However, Paul recorded a solo version of the numbe which was included on his album *McCartney*, issued on 1 April 1970.

A 'Teddy Boy' was one of the youth cults of the lat fifties in Britain and was so called due to his use of a lon Edwardian style jacket with velvet collar.

● Teenage Heaven

A number recorded by **Eddie Cochran** in 1959 which th Beatles included in their repertoire in 1960.

● Teenager's Turn

Title of the BBC Light Programme radio show on which th Beatles made their radio debut. The show was broadca from the **Playhouse Theatre, Manchester** eac Thursday between 5.00 p.m. and 5.30 p.m., although was recorded the previous day. The resident band was th Northern Dance Orchestra.

Producer **Peter Pilbeam** thought the name 'Beatle was bizarre but decided to book them as a result of th audition tapes. They recorded the show on Wednesday, March 1962, and it was transmitted the following day.

The group organized a coach to take them fro Liverpool to Manchester in which they were joined b members of their Liverpool fan club, Mr **Jim McCartne** Bill and Virginia Harry and Peter Mackey, who was the President of the Students' Union at **Liverpool College Art.** Mackey had joined the coach, which departed fro Mount Street, at the side of the College of Art/Liverpo Institute, hoping to confront the Beatles about the P equipment which the Students' Union had purchased ar which the Beatles had never returned. He did manage confront John Lennon, and a nonplussed John told hi he'd been skint in Hamburg and had sold it.

The shows were recorded before a live audience an ***Mersey Beat*** reported: 'John, Paul and George mac their entrance on stage to cheers and applause, but whe Pete walked on – the fans went wild! The girls screame In Manchester his popularity was assured by his look alone.'

The group were mobbed as they left the theatre, b although John, Paul and George managed to reach th coach, Pete was prevented from doing so. Eventually h escaped, with his mohair suit ripped, to receive a tickin off from Mr McCartney who accused him of trying upstage the other members of the group.

The Beatles performed four numbers in the theatre, ıree of them sung by John: 'Hello Little Girl', 'Memphis ennessee' and 'Please Mr Postman'; and one sung by aul, 'Dream Baby'. 'Hello Little Girl' was not broadcast.

The show's presenter, Ray Peters, had the honour of eing the first person to announce the Beatles on the radio.

The name 'Teenager's Turn' was dropped by the time ıey returned for their second broadcast on 14 June (for ansmission the next day) and was then called '**Here We o**'.

Tell Me What You See

umber penned by Paul McCartney, although it is said at John aided him on the lyrics at the recording session, hich took place on Thursday, 18 February 1965. Paul ayed electric piano on the session and the group was so to feature a South American musical instrument alled a guiro. The number was included on their album *elp!* in August 1965 and on the American album *Beatles* in June 1965. It was later included on the *Love Songs* mpilation in 1977.

Tell Me Why

umber composed by John which was included on the *A ard Day's Night* album. The group recorded the number Thursday, 27 February 1964, and it was also included the British EP, *Extracts From The Film A Hard Day's ight*.

It was issued in America on United Artists' soundtrack bum of the film in June 1964 and the following month rned up on **Capitol**'s *Something New* album.

Temple, Shirley

ıe greatest child star of the movies. Born in California in 928, Shirley became one of the screen's most popular ars of the thirties and was voted Top Box Office Star ıen she was only seven years old, and Top Female Box ffice Attraction for the years 1935, 1936, 1937 and 938.

She retired from films while in her teens and was to arry John Agar and, later, Charles Black, an aide to ichard Nixon. As Shirley Temple Black she entered litics, unsuccessfully, but later became an American nbassador.

When the Beatles appeared at the **Cow Palace, San rancisco** on 19 August 1964, a sheriff's deputy spotted Temple, Black and their eight-year-old daughter Lori and escorted them backstage. The Beatles were in a partitioned section and were reluctant to come out and meet her. **Neil Aspinall** had to cajole them into going to meet her 'just for a few minutes'. George, however, was adamant: he wouldn't see her. Neil took the three Beatles into the other part of the room.

Charles Black, a major local political figure, had brought his camera and wanted to take a photograph. Brian Epstein had a rule against 'celebrity photographs', but Derek Taylor decided to waive it. He went behind the

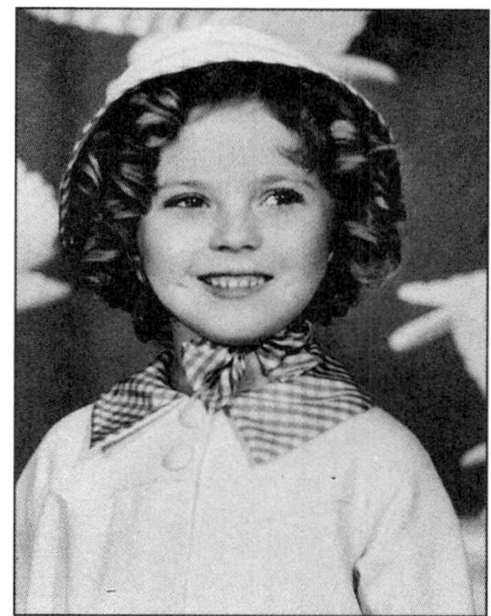

Shirley Temple – one of the numerous characters on the 'Sgt Pepper' album sleeve. (National Film Archive)

partition to talk George into joining the others. George raised his voice, 'I never liked her films, don't like her, don't want to meet her or have my picture taken.'

Derek pleaded with him and eventually he emerged. Meanwhile, the corps of press photographers outside were getting very angry as they wanted a photograph of the Beatles and Shirley Temple. They began banging on the door and Derek had to placate them by telling them he'd let them have Black's roll of film which they could pool together as long as they returned it after the show. He told Black about the arrangement and, although reluctant, he agreed. The film was given to the photographers and after the show, one of them, Curt Gunther, delivered a blank roll of film to Taylor. When Taylor asked what had happened he was told that they hadn't come out. An embarrassed Taylor had to explain this to an angry Charles Black.

Two days later, photographs of Shirley, Lori and the

Beatles began to appear in the newspapers. Hedda Hopper ran a story about the incident, chiding the Beatles and the photographers. Mysteriously, the film was then sent to Hopper, who was able to pass it over to the Blacks.

● Tennessee

A number written and recorded by **Carl Perkins** in 1956. The **Quarry Men** included it in their repertoire, with John Lennon on lead vocals, and continued to play the number when they became the Beatles until 1961.

● Terry Young Combo, The

A six-man instrumental group booked to appear on the **Roy Orbison**/Beatles British tour of May/June 1963. In addition to a short spot in which they played a couple of instrumentals, they provided backing for some of the solo artists, including **David Macbeth** and **Louise Cordet**.

● Thank You Girl

Looking back on his early collaborations with Paul, John Lennon was to comment, 'Paul and I wrote this as a 'B'-side for one of our first records. In the old days we used to write and write all the time, but nowadays I only do it if I'm particularly inspired.' The two of them penned the song while they were touring in 1963.

'Thank You Girl' was first issued in Britain as the flipside of 'From Me To You' in April 1963. In America, **Vee Jay** issued the single in May 1963, but it failed to register. Vee Jay then included the track on their *Jolly What! The Beatles And Frank Ifield On Stage* album in February 1964 and issued it as the flipside of 'Do You Want To Know A Secret' in March 1964 and the single reached No. 2 in the American charts.

In Britain it was included on *The Beatles Hits* EP in September 1963 and first appeared on an album when it was included on *Rarities*, included in *The Beatles Collection* boxed set in December 1978. The Beatles recorded the number on Tuesday, 5 March 1963, when it went under the working title 'Thank You Little Girl'.

● Thank Your Lucky Stars

First of the major networked TV pop shows of the sixties, produced by ABC TV from their Birmingham studios at Aston Road North, Aston, Birmingham. As a result of arranging for the Beatles to be booked on the show, **Dick James** was able to secure their music publishing rights.

'Thank Your Lucky Stars' producer, **Philip Jones**, w a friend of James' and when Brian Epstein was in t publisher's office discussing the promotion of 'Plea Please Me', James phoned Jones and asked him to bo the Beatles on the show. Jones said he couldn't do th until he heard the record. James played it to him over t phone and Jones said they could appear on the programn the following Saturday.

The Beatles made their debut on the programme wh they recorded 'Please Please Me' on 13 January 1963. was transmitted on 19 January. They also perform 'Please Please Me' on 17 February for a programn broadcast on 23 February.

For their third appearance they recorded 'From Me You' at ATV's Teddington Studios on 14 April, f transmission on 20 April. They also performed 'From M To You' on 12 May for transmission on 18 May on a sh which also featured the Countrymen, Dickie Pride, Hei Bruhl, **Peter Jay & the Jaywalkers**, Shani Wallis, Saxon and Jimmy Young.

Freddie Garritty holding Janice Nichols on the set of 'Thank Your Lucky Stars'. (National Film Archive)

The 23 June recording in Birmingham was a special vent – the 'All Merseyside' edition of the programme, roadcast on 29 June, and the other acts included **Gerry** **the Pacemakers**, **Billy J. Kramer** and the Dakotas, e Big Three and the **Vernons Girls**. The group's next ppearance was on 18 August, for a 24 August ansmission.

Another 'All Merseyside' edition took place on 15 ecember for transmission on 21 December and the group ere presented with two Gold Discs during the recording. hey performed 'I Want To Hold Your Hand', 'All My oving' and 'Twist And Shout'. Other artists on the bill cluded Billy J. Kramer and the Dakotas, **Cilla Black**, **ommy Quickly**, the **Searchers** and the Breakaways.

The Beatles appeared twice in 1964, both times cording at the Teddington studios, firstly on 11 July for ansmission on 18 July and finally on 14 November for ansmission on 21 November. In 1965 they made a single pearance at the Birmingham studios on 28 March for ansmission on 3 April. This was their last recording for e programme.

'Thank Your Lucky Stars', like '**Ready, Steady, Go!**', as a programme produced by a local television station d networked over the ITV system, but was also likely to a victim when the TV franchise ended, and eventually a w station took over the broadcasting for the area. This ppened with both 'Thank Your Lucky Stars' and 'Ready, eady, Go!'. 'Top Of The Pops', on the other hand, was a BC programme and therefore had its longevity aranteed. The final programme of 'Thank Your Lucky ars' was broadcast on 25 June 1966 when a promotional m for 'Paperback Writer' was screened.

That Means A Lot

nreleased Beatles song, mainly composed by Paul cCartney for the film *Help!* The Beatles recorded it on turday, 20 February, and Thursday, 30 March 1965, hn Lennon was to say, 'The song is a ballad which Paul d I wrote for the film but we found we just couldn't sing In fact, we made a hash of it, so we thought we'd better ve it to someone who could do it well.'

P. J. Proby recorded the song at **Abbey Road** on 7 oril 1965, but the record wasn't a hit for him.

That's All Right Mama

e Beatles used this number as part of their repertoire from the early **Quarry Men** days, with Paul on lead vocal. It was originally penned by Arthur 'Big Boy' Crudup and was **Elvis Presley**'s first record release. The Beatles performed the number on their BBC radio show **'Pop Go The Beatles'** on 16 July 1963.

● There's A Devil In Her Heart

A number which was originally recorded by female vocal group the Donays on the American Brent label in August 1962. The number wasn't a hit, but it appealed to the Beatles, who included it in their stage act, with George on lead vocal.

The actual title of the Donays' version, penned by Richard B. Drapkin, was '(There's A) Devil In His Heart'.

The Beatles recorded the number and it was included on their *With The Beatles* album. The song was also to surface on the **Capitol** release *The Beatles Second Album*.

● There's A Place

A number penned by John which was included in the Beatles' stage repertoire in 1963. It was recorded on the morning of Monday, 11 February 1963, during their marathon recording session for the *Please Please Me* album.

The evocative song was an early example of a reflective Lennon lyric and apart from the *Please Please Me* album it was used as one of the tracks on the *Twist And Shout* EP. In America it was featured on the **Vee Jay** albums *Introducing The Beatles*, *The Beatles vs The Four Seasons* and *Songs, Pictures And Stories Of The Fabulous Beatles*, and also surfaced as the flipside of the Tollie single 'Twist and Shout' in 1964. Later the same year the single was reissued in the **Capitol** 'Oldies' series. In 1980 it was included on Capitol's *The Beatles Rarities* album.

● Things We Said Today

Number penned by Paul which the Beatles recorded in June 1964 for their *A Hard Day's Night* album. It was also issued on the EP *Extracts From A Hard Day's Night* and on the American album *Something New*.

The Beatles included the number in the repertoire of their world tour and Paul also featured it on his own 1989/1990 world tour.

● Think For Yourself

One of the two George Harrison compositions featured on

the *Rubber Soul* album. A song about someone he'd parted the ways with, although he said he couldn't remember who the 'someone' was.

When the Beatles recorded the number on Monday, 8 November 1965, the working title of the song was 'Won't Be There With You'. There was a fuzzbox used at the recording, an electronic device which could control distortion. This was attached to Paul's bass guitar and it was said to be the first time a bass fuzz had been used on a record.

The track was also included on the album *The Best Of George Harrison*.

● Thirty Days

A number written and recorded by **Chuck Berry** in 1955. The Beatles included it in their stage act during 1961 with John Lennon on lead vocals.

● This Boy

A number penned by John on which he and Paul harmonize. They performed the song on their BBC radio appearances for '**Saturday Club**' and '**From Us T You**' and it was issued on the flipside of 'I Want To Ho Your Hand'.

'This Boy' – the orchestral version was called 'Ringo's Theme'. (©Apple/Walter Shenson Films)

'This Boy' was included on the *Love Songs* and *Rariti* compilations, *The Beatles Box* and *The Beatles Collectio* sets, the American album *Meet The Beatles* and th American EP *4 By The Beatles*. The group also performe the number on their 'Sunday Night At The Londo Palladium' appearance in October 1963, on their '**E Sullivan** Show' appearance in February 1964 and on the winter tour of America later the same year.

An instrumental version of the number, by the Geor Martin Orchestra, was featured in the film *A Hard Day Night* as incidental music in the background of the sce where Ringo wanders along a towpath. Martin intrumental version of the song was called 'Ringo's Them and the George Martin orchestra single was original released in Britain on 7 August 1964 with 'And I Lo Her' on the flipside, although it didn't make any impact the charts. When it was issued in America on 31 Ju 1964 it rose to No. 53 in the Top 100. It was also includ on Martin's Parlophone album *Off The Beatle Track* and an EP, *Music From A Hard Day's Night*, by the Geor Martin Orchestra, issued on 19 February 1965.

● This Is Their Life

An aural documentary produced by **Radio Luxembou** and originally broadcast in two parts. The first w transmitted on 10 May 1964 and the second on 17 May.

● Three Coins Club, Fountain Street, Manchester

A club which opened in October 1961. Being situated Fountain Street, it took its name from the film *Three Coi In The Fountain*. Jimmy Savile was a co-owner of the cl and recalls booking the Beatles there for the first time or Sunday in November 1961 for a fee of five pounds. I remembers it being a Sunday as the club only booked li groups on Sunday evenings. The Beatles appeared for second time at the club on 27 January 1963.

● Three Cool Cats

A Leiber/Stoller composition which provided an Americ hit for the Coasters in 1959. The **Quarry Men** included in their repertoire and performed it during their auditi for **Decca Records** on 1 January 1962, with George ad vocals and John and Paul harmonizing.

Three Steps To Heaven

posthumous No. 1 hit for **Eddie Cochran** in Britain, though it failed to reach the American charts. The eatles included it in their repertoire in 1960 and 1961.

Ticket To Ride

ne of John Lennon's favourite compositions which the eatles recorded on Monday, 15 February 1965, shortly fore leaving for the Bahamas to begin production of their cond feature film.

Paul McCartney also played lead guitar on the track – a ty usually handled by George Harrison. It's one of the w Beatles tracks on which Paul plays lead, but he peated the exercise on another *Help!* soundtrack mber, 'Another Girl'.

The single was issued in Britain on Parlophone R 5265 9 April 1965 where it reached No. 1 in the charts. It s issued in America with advance orders of 750,000 on **pitol** 5407 on 14 April 1965, where it also topped the charts. Of interest is the fact that the American label credits the song: 'From the United Artists release *Eight Arms To Hold You*'. The flipside was another John Lennon composition, 'Yes It Is'.

The Beatles performed the number on their various tours during 1965 and included it on their **'Ed Sullivan** Show' appearance in September of that year.

It was also included on the *Help!* album, *A Collection Of Beatles Oldies (But Goldies)*, *The Beatles 1962–1966*, *The Beatles At The Hollywood Bowl*, *Reel Music* and *20 Greatest Hits*, and 'The Beatles Movie Medley' single.

● Till There Was You

Song written by Meredith Willson for the Broadway musical *The Music Man*, which starred Robert Preston. It was also made into a big budget musical feature film.

Paul particularly liked the number after hearing Peggy Lee's 1961 version, and it was included in the Beatles act in 1962. Paul sang the song during the Beatles' **Decca audition** and it has resurfaced on various albums of Decca tapes, including *The Complete Silver Beatles*. He also

Paul in 1962, with Faron. (Cavern Mecca)

performed it on stage at the **Star Club**, Hamburg, and it became one of the many that **Adrian Barber** recorded live at that venue.

The Beatles featured it on two of their '**Pop Go The Beatles**' shows, two '**Saturday Club**' shows and two '**From Us To You**' shows for BBC radio.

The official studio version was recorded for the *With The Beatles* album issued in Britain in November 1963 and it also appeared on the *Meet The Beatles* compilation, released in America in January 1964.

It was said that during the recording of 'Till There Was You', Brian Epstein was in the studio and remarked to George Martin that he thought there was a flaw in Paul's voice. John spoke into the mike, 'We'll make the records. You just go on counting the percentages.'

● Tip Of My Tongue

Number penned by Paul McCartney and added to the Beatles' repertoire in 1962. The group recorded it on Monday, 26 November 1962, but George Martin considered that it wasn't suitable and it was left on the shelf. It was recorded by Brian Epstein's protégé **Tommy Quickly** and released in Britain on Piccadilly 7N 35137 on 30 July 1963, but failed to chart.

● To Know Her Is To Love Her

A number composed by **Phil Spector** who thought of the title after seeing the words 'To know him was to love him' on his father's grave. He recorded it with the Teddy Bears in 1968 as 'To Know Him Is To Love Him', but the Beatles changed the 'him' to 'her' when they included it in their repertoire in 1961, with John on lead vocal. A live version of the number is to be found on *The Beatles Live! At The Star Club in Hamburg, Germany: 1962* album and they also recorded it for their '**Pop Goes The Beatles**' radio show on 6 August 1963.

● Tomorrow Never Knows

The innovative closing track of *Revolver*, although it was the first number to be recorded for the album.

At the time John Lennon composed the song, **Dr Timothy Leary**'s version of *The Egyptian Book Of The Dead* was in vogue. It was a guide for young people seeking to gain spiritual enlightenment, particularly through the use of the drug LSD. It inspired John and he utilized one line from the book in his song.

When recording began on Wednesday, 6 April 196 John's various ideas had to be technically translated what could actually be achieved in the studio by Geor Martin and **Geoff Emerick**. John said, 'I want to sound though I'm the Dalai Lama singing from the highe mountain top. And yet I still want to hear the words I' singing.' This was achieved by putting his voice throu one of the Leslie speakers. John had said, 'Wi "Tomorrow Never Knows" I'd imagine in my head that the background you would hear thousands of mon chanting. That was impractical of course and we d something different. I should have tried to get my origin idea, the monks singing. I realize now that's what wanted.' Amazing results were achieved by the use of ta loops and playing several tape machines at various spee To achieve some birdlike sounds, a tape loop of Pa laughing was used.

'Mark 1', the working title, was obviously not a suitab name for the number and the title actually came from Ringo Starr remark – 'Tomorrow Never Knows', h version of 'Tomorrow Never Comes'.

● Tonight Show, The

Major American chat show. John and Paul appeared NBC's 'The Tonight Show' on 15 May 1968 to discu their launch of Apple. The usual host Johnny Carson w away at the time and the duo were interviewed by form baseball player Joe Garagiola. The former Hollywo actress Tallulah Bankhead was also a guest on the sh and her attitude towards John and Paul was qui antagonistic. Later, John was to comment that, 'She w pissed out of her head.'

During their discussion of Apple's philosophy, whi they described as a form of 'Western Communism', Pa said, 'We always had to go to the big men on our kne and touch our forelocks and say, "Please, can we do and so . . . ?" We're in the happy position of not needi any more money, so for the first time the bosses aren't in for a profit. If you come to me and say, "I've had such a such a dream", I'll say to you, "Go away and do it."'

John commented, 'The aim isn't just a stack of g teeth in the bank. We've done that bit. It's more of a tri to see if we can get artistic freedom within a busine structure – to see if we can create things and sell th without charging five times their cost.'

There was an audience of eleven million watching t

how that evening.

Too Bad About Sorrows

ne of the earliest of the Paul McCartney compositions. It as included as part of the **Quarry Men**'s repertoire in e late fifties, but was dropped when the group changed eir name to the Beatles and the song has never been corded.

Too Much Monkey Business

Chuck Berry composition from 1956 which the Beatles cluded in their repertoire in 1961, with John on lead ocals. The group featured it on two '**Pop Go The eatles**' shows and also a '**Saturday Club**' and a '**Side y Side**' radio recording.

Top Gear

BBC Light Programme radio show which made its debut 16 July 1964. It was a Thursday evening show ansmitted from 10.00 p.m. to midnight, was presented by **rian Matthew** and produced by Bernie Andrews. The eatles made an appearance on the first show, which they corded on 14 July at the BBC's Broadcasting House udios. The group performed 'Long Tall Sally', 'Things e Said Today', 'A Hard Day's Night', 'And I Love Her', Should Have Known Better', 'If I Fell' and 'You Can't o That'. Also on the bill were the Nashville Teens, Dusty ringfield and **Carl Perkins**.

Their second and final appearance took place on 26 ovember 1964, recorded at the **Playhouse Theatre, anchester** on 17 November. The group performed 'I'm Loser', 'Honey Don't', 'She's A Woman', 'Everybody's ying To Be My Baby', 'I'll Follow The Sun' and 'I Feel ne'.

Top Ten Club, *136 Reeperbahn, amburg, Germany*

hen 21-year-old **Peter Eckhorn** returned home from a, his father decided to pass over the Hippodrome emises on the Reeperbahn to him. It had previously en a topless circus. Eckhorn decided to convert the ace into a rock 'n' roll club and had a stage and dance or constructed and wooden booths, painted black, were ted in.

With premises which could accommodate 2,000 ople, Eckhorn decided to open it as the Top Ten Club in October 1960. Initially, he poached **Horst Fascher** from the **Kaiserkeller** club – and the poaching continued with the club securing **Tony Sheridan** & the Jets and even some barmaids and **Rosa**, the bierfrau from **Bruno Koschmider**'s employ. Eckhorn also tried to book Liverpool's Derry & the Seniors, but the group were broke, disenchanted with Hamburg and approached the British Embassy to provide them with an assisted passage home.

The Beatles, still at the Kaiserkeller, began drifting to the Top Ten during their breaks. Koschmider's 'spy' George Sterner informed him of this and he began to make threats to them. They ignored him and began to get on stage to jam with the Jets – on one session the two groups performed a 70-minute version of 'What'd I Say'.

Koschmider was furious and pointed out a clause in their contract which disallowed them to play at any other venue within a 45-mile radius of the Kaiserkeller. When they ignored him he threatened to take away their protection. They didn't worry unduly about this as they had Horst Fascher's protection in the area – but another kind of 'protection' disappeared, and the police swooped on George Harrison for being underage. In the St Pauli area there was a curfew for youngsters under the age of eighteen. The Beatles received a letter from Koschmider:

> I the undersigned, hereby give notice to Mr GEORGE HARRISON and to BEATLES BAND to leave on November 30th 1960.
>
> 'This notice is given to the above by order of the Public Authorities who have discovered that Mr GEORGE HARRISON is only 17 (seventeen) years of age.

The Beatles had, in fact, agreed to a residency at the Top Ten to replace the Jets. The group moved into the dormitory upstairs at the Top Ten Club, which had bunk beds and was much more comfortable than the accommodation at the **Bambi Kino**, even though the toilets were four floors below.

When George was deported, the Beatles then played a few sets at the Top Ten with John taking over on lead guitar, or even leaving out a lead guitar spot altogether and Paul played piano. They felt things were much better with 10 DM increase in pay per day. This didn't last for long. Paul and Pete had returned to the Bambi Kino for their gear and they were awakened from their sleep at the Top Ten 'dormitory' by the police, who put them in cells and deported them without allowing them to contact the British Embassy – for reportedly trying to set fire to the Bambi.

John returned to Liverpool several days later and **Stuart Sutcliffe** remained in Hamburg with **Astrid Kirchherr**.

The Jets were disbanding, but Eckhorn managed to get Tony Sheridan, **Iain Hines** and Colin Milander to stay and with Del Ward on drums and an American musician, they managed to remain for a further two months, until Eckhorn could find a replacement in the form of **Gerry & the Pacemakers**.

Although the Jets disbanded, Sheridan remained in Hamburg. Hines returned to England but was later to come back to the Top Ten and act as their booking manager.

Eckhorn parcelled up **Pete Best**'s drums and had them sent to Liverpool and agreed to book the group for April 1962 if they could resolve the deportation bans.

Pete Best had been making arrangements for their return to Hamburg and on 28 March 1961 he received a letter from the West German Immigration Office granting the group a one-year concession. It read: 'We should like to point out explicitly, that this decision is a special concession of the Foreign Dept., and you are expected to refrain from any more penalties in the future, and that you are to obey the German Laws and Provisions. In this way you are given the opportunity to fulfil the engagement contracted by you with Mr Eckhorn's firm, until 14.4.1961.'

Stu kept in touch with the rest of the group and in a letter to Pete Best, he added the P.S.: 'Everything has worked out fine. Paul will ring you or you ring Paul as soon as you have this. One thing I forgot to tell Paul, and that is that you both must pay Peter Eckhorn 79 DM, his cost of sending you home. The lifting of the deportation ban is only valid for one year, then you can have it reviewed. One thing they made clear, if you have any trouble with the Police, no matter how small, then you've had it forever.'

Once the Beatles had arrived and begun to play at the Top Ten on 27 March 1961, Eckhorn extended their contract twice and they played a total of fourteen weeks at the venue. They were required to play between 7.00 p.m. to 2.00 a.m. with a fifteen-minute break each hour. George Harrison commented, 'We performed like a gang of lunatics. It was all right once we got the hang of it all and it was great fun. The boss would send up cups of coffee on stage and we'd take turns to take a nip.' Paul McCartne said, 'We'd try out any sort of numbers from the To Twenty. In a way it was marvellous, simply because w could experiment. Tired? We were dead wacked but w got great kicks out of watching the audiences, seeing th way they reacted to different gear.'

The Beatles had built their own following in Hambur and among the regular crowd were the **'Exis'** with friend such as Astrid Kirchherr and **Klaus Voormann**. Durin the early evening they had crowds of youngsters and afte 10.00 p.m., when the curfew came into operation, the ag group would be between eighteen and 25 years old.

While they were at the Top Ten Stuart Sutcliffe left th group. There had been confrontations with Paul, wh wanted to take over the bass spot, and Stuart wa becoming involved in his art studies once again. Befor Stuart left, they encouraged him to write a letter to **Alla Williams** stating that they wouldn't be paying him an commission as they'd set up the deal with Eckhor themselves. Williams sent a letter to them at the Top Te dated 20 April 1961:

Dear All,

I am very distressed to hear you are contemplatin not paying my commission out of your pay, as w agreed in our Contract for your engagement at the To Ten Club.

May I remind you, seeing you are all appearing get more than a little swollen-headed, that you woul not even have smelled Hamburg if I had not made th contacts, and by Law it is illegal for any person und contract to make a contract through the first contract. would also point out that the only reason you are the is through work that I did and if you had trie yourselves to play at the Top Ten without a bona fi contract and working through a British Governme approved agency you would not be in Germany now.

Remember in your last contract under Koschmid you agreed not to play 30 weeks from terminating th contract. The only reason you managed to get out of th was, again, through myself. So far as you are concerne he kept the contract.

So you see lads, I'm very annoyed you should wel out of your agreed contract. If you decide not to pay promise that I shall have you out of Germany inside tw weeks through several legal ways and don't you thi

I'm bluffing.

I will also submit a full report of your behaviour to the Agency Members Association, of which I am a full member, and every Agent in England is a member, to protect Agents from Artistes who misbehave and welsh out on your contracts. Don't underestimate my ability to carry out what I have written . . .

My friend who has the Agency in London is bringing Ray Charles over to England in September and they plan to do a tour. I had thought of you going on tour with him, but unless you honour our agreement you can forget it. I will fix it for Rory Storm. This is no sprat, you check with your musical papers.

Look lads, I can do more for you than all the rest of Liverpool put together if I want to. Remember the others are only copying my original idea. In fact I told **Ray McFall** to put on Rock. So I think you are mad to try and make good with the Liverpool crowd who only want you to play for themselves.

I don't want to fall out with you but I can't abide anybody who does not honour their word or bond, and I could have sworn you were all decent lads, that is why I pushed you when nobody wanted to hear you.

Yours sincerely,
Allan.

he Beatles ignored him.

During their residency **Bert Kaempfert** arrived at the ub with a party of people. He had been advised to listen Tony Sheridan with a view to recording him for the eutsche Grammophon's pop label Polydor. While there e also booked the Beatles to back him and their cordings with Sheridan were made during this trip.

After the Beatles returned to Liverpool, Sheridan ontinued to play at the Top Ten with different rmutations of the Beat Brothers.

At one time Pete Eckhorn lured Ringo Starr away from **ory Storm & the Hurricanes** with promises of a car, a at and good weekly wages. Ringo backed Tony at the ub for six months.

When Eckhorn sought to rebook the Beatles during a ip to Liverpool, he was referred to their new manager ian Epstein. Epstein demanded 500 DM for each Beatle r week. Eckhorn offered 450. Brian wouldn't budge and entually negotiated a deal with the new St Pauli rock nue, the **Star Club**.

The Top Ten continued presenting rock 'n' roll until Eckhorn's death.

● Top Ten Club, *100 Soho Street, Liverpool L3*

Inspired by the clubs in Hamburg, **Allan Williams** decided to open a similar venture in Liverpool, the Top Ten Club. Unlike the 'jive hives', which were local halls booked on occasional days by amateur promoters, Williams intended having a permanent rock 'n' roll venue, open seven days a week. He also thought of it as a 'musical home' for the Beatles, who were to become the resident band on their return from Germany. He talked the 28-year-old **Bob Wooler** into giving up his job as an office clerk for the railway to become full-time compere and disc jockey at the Top Ten.

It was a long, barn-like structure, reached via a wooden stairway in one of Liverpool's tough areas close by the city centre. Opening night was Thursday, 1 December 1960, and Williams had booked singers such as Terry Dene and Garry Mills to appear during the first week, backed by local bands. The idea was to present singers such as **Davy Jones** and Danny Rivers who would be backed by Liverpool groups on a bill which would feature other Liverpool bands. The Beatles were to be the first group with a lengthy residency.

At 11.30 p.m. on Tuesday, 6 December 1960, the club was burned to the ground. Williams claimed that there was an electrical fault in the wiring, rumours around the scene in Liverpool at the time suggested it was arson. Derry Wilkie & the Seniors had all their guitars and amplifiers destroyed in the fire, Bob Wooler found himself out of a job and Williams didn't have the venture fully insured and only received £1,086 in compensation.

Relating the incident to ***Mersey Beat***, Williams commented, '. . . I was opening a new venture in Liverpool, namely the Top Ten Club. I had visions then of providing a club solely for beat music on Merseyside whilst others were still toying with the idea. Bob Wooler was to play a major part in it. I'd only met Bob briefly but was immediately captivated by his flair for this type of entertainment. I convinced him to give up his mundane office job and work professionally in a job for which he was more suited – that of providing entertainment for the starved population of Merseyside.

'Unfortunately, the club was severely damaged by fire

and I found myself in rather a difficult financial period as I was in the process of opening the **Blue Angel**. I remember, in my confused state of mind at the time, asking Bob Wooler if he could negotiate bookings for the Beatles who were shortly to arrive on the scene. Bob himself was confused, being left virtually unemployed, having burnt his boats behind him. He did, however, book the Beatles at **Litherland Town Hall**. I will always remember Bob raving to me on the reception that greeted the group on their first performance at one of the more established rock venues.'

● *Tours*

The Beatles' first experience of touring began on 20 May 1960 in the town of Alloa, Scotland, when they were booked to appear as **Johnny Gentle**'s backing group. They called themselves the Silver Beetles at the time, but were unbilled in the advertisements for the tour, which comprised seven gigs in Scotland, ending at Peterhead on 28 May. The tour was typical of the type organized by impresario **Larry Parnes** for his stable of acts, which included Marty Wilde, **Billy Fury**, Duffy Power and Dickie Pride. They were short tours of ballroom and town hall venues and the artists had to basically 'rough it', travelling in tiny vans and staying at cheap hotels. During this first tour, the group, with the exception of John, created stage names, although the Beatles weren't generally publicized and billing read: 'Johnny Gentle and his group'.

JOHNNY GENTLE SCOTTISH TOUR, 1960	
20 May	Town Hall, Alloa
21 May	Northern Meeting Ballroom, Inverness
23 May	Dalrymple Hall, Fraserburgh
25 May	St Thomas' Hall, Keith
26 May	Town Hall, Forres
27 May	Regal Ballroom, Nairn
28 May	Rescue Hall, Peterhead

The prestige tours in Britain at the time were those run by major London-based promoters such as **Arthur Howes** and **Tito Burns**. They comprised a bill topped by a star name who had a current or recent chart hit, supported by some lesser-known recording acts in a loose bill introduced by a compere/comedian. This type of package tour generally visited the cinema chains run by ABC Gaumont, Granada, Odeon and Regal, and there was a particular emphasis on Sunday concert presentations. Th other type of tour prevalent at the time was the ballroom tour, which visited chains such as the Rank or Mecca ballroom circuit.

At the beginning of 1963, the group were booked by th Cana Variety Agency to appear on a short Scottish tour Although the agency had secured the Beatles at th bargain price of £42 per show, they lost money on th event because of the atrocious weather which saw the firs of the shows, at the Longmore Hall, Keith, cancelled.

SCOTTISH TOUR, 1963	
3 Jan	Two Red Shoes Ballroom, Elgin
4 Jan	Town Hall, Dingwall
5 Jan	Museum Hall, Bridge of Allan
6 Jan	Beach Ballroom, Aberdeen

However, the Beatles enjoyed touring at the time and Joh Lennon commented, 'Touring was a relief. We wer beginning to feel stale and cramped. We'd get tired of or stage and be deciding to pack up when another stag would come up. We'd outlived the Hamburg stage an hated going back to Hamburg those last two times.'

Brian Epstein was determined to place the Beatles on theatre tour. Tito Burns made enquiries about the ban but didn't follow up and Larry Parnes wouldn't agree to th modest fee asked by Epstein for his protégés, so Bria contacted Arthur Howes who, despite the group's po reception at their 'trial' appearance at the **Embass Peterborough**, booked them to appear on the bill of th **Helen Shapiro** tour from 2 February–3 March 1963. Al on the bill were Danny Williams, **Kenny Lynch**, th Honeys, the **Kestrels**, the Red Price Band and compe Dave Allen. Despite various Beatle books mentioning th the group were virtually the bottom-of-the-bill act on th tour, Howes' advertisement for the tour appearing on th cover of the ***New Musical Express*** on 22 February 19 has them placed second on the bill to Helen Shapiro, wi their name printed bolder than the other acts.

The group were also able to travel in the tour bus wi the rest of the acts, instead of in the white van which Bri Epstein had bought for **Neil Aspinall** to drive them to gi in. This was the year in which travelling in a van with t enquipment ended.

The Beatles on the tarmac at Heathrow. (Granada TV)

HELEN SHAPIRO TOUR, 1963

2 Feb	Gaumont, Bradford
5 Feb	Gaumont, Doncaster
6 Feb	Granada, Bedford
7 Feb	Regal, Kirkgate
8 Feb	ABC, Carlisle
9 Feb	Empire, Sunderland
23 Feb	Granada, Mansfield
24 Feb	Coventry Theatre, Coventry
26 Feb	Gaumont, Taunton
27 Feb	Rialto, York
28 Feb	Granada, Shrewsbury
1 March	Odeon, Southport
2 March	City Hall, Sheffield
3 March	Gaumont, Hanley

p-of-the-bill acts were usually afforded special treatment and were generally driven to venues in private transport and not by tour coach – although Helen Shapiro preferred to travel on the bus with the rest of the company. Ringo also noticed the difference between top-of-the-bill performers and the support acts when he spotted a television in Helen's dressing-room while the rest of them had to make do with transistor radios!

Accommodation was not as rough as on their tour for Larry Parnes and they were generally booked into hotels of a comfortable standard.

During the Shapiro tour, Ringo was still feeling his way with the group and commented, 'I was still the odd one out, the new boy. But the togetherness of the tour helped a lot. It made me feel more part of a team. At first I worried about who I'd share with at our hotels, but mostly it was me in with Paul, and George with John sharing another room.'

John said, 'It really was a relief to get out of Liverpool

and try something new. Back home we'd worked night after night on the same cramped stage. Bradford wasn't very far away, but at least it was different as a field. We'd all started feeling tired, jaded, tied down with the club scenes. Touring, with a different venue each night, was a real lift.'

Howes became the man who was to promote most of their British tours and their success with Helen Shapiro caused him to immediately book them on the **Tommy Roe/Chris Montez** tour, only six days after the Shapiro tour had closed. Once again they were given billing immediately below the bill-toppers and in larger letters than the rest of the company. The other acts on the tour were the **Viscounts**, Debbie Lee, the **Terry Young Combo** and **Tony Marsh** and the dates were from 9–31 March 1963.

TOMMY ROE/CHRIS MONTEZ TOUR, 1963

9 March	Granada, East Ham
10 March	Hippodrome, Birmingham
12 March	Granada, Bedford
13 March	Rialto, York
14 March	Gaumont, Wolverhampton
15 March	Colston Hall, Bristol
16 March	City Hall, Sheffield
17 March	Embassy, Peterborough
18 March	Regal, Gloucester
19 March	Regal, Cambridge
20 March	ABC, Romford
21 March	ABC, Croydon
22 March	Gaumont, Doncaster
23 March	City Hall, Newcastle-upon-Tyne
24 March	Empire, Liverpool
26 March	Granada, Mansfield
27 March	ABC, Northampton
28 March	ABC, Exeter
29 March	Odeon, Lewisham
30 March	Guildhall, Portsmouth
31 March	De Montfort Hall, Leicester

Manchester-based agency Kennedy Street Enterprises had booked the Beatles to appear on a tour supporting an American artist in May. Originally the bill-topper was to be Duane Eddy, but this didn't work out and Ben E. King and then the Four Seasons were considered. Eventually, **Roy Orbison** was booked to headline. However, the Beatles' popularity was now so big in Britain that th American star was asked if he would allow the Beatles t be bill-toppers. The advertising was designed in such way that either Orbison or the Beatles could be taken a the bill-toppers, although the Beatles closed the show wit a 45-minute spot. Also on the bill were **Gerry & th Pacemakers**, **David Macbeth**, **Louise Cordet**, **Erke Grant**, Ian Crawford, the Terry Young Combo and Ton Marsh. The tour ran from 18 May–9 June 1963.

ROY ORBISON/BEATLES TOUR, 1963

18 May	Adelphi, Slough
19 May	Gaumont, Hanley
20 May	Gaumont, Southampton
22 May	Gaumont, Ipswich
23 May	Odeon, Nottingham
24 May	Granada, Walthamstow
25 May	City Hall, Sheffield
26 May	Empire, Liverpool
28 May	Gaumont, Worcester
29 May	Rialto, York
30 May	Odeon, Manchester
31 May	Odeon, Southend-on-Sea
1 June	Granada, Tooting
2 June	Hippodrome, Brighton
3 June	Granada, Woolwich
4 June	Town Hall, Birmingham
5 June	Odeon, Leeds
7 June	Odeon, Glasgow
8 June	City Hall, Newcastle-upon-Tyne
9 June	King George's Hall, Blackburn

It was during the Orbison tour that the fans started throwi jelly babies at them, due to a chance remark on televisi that George enjoyed the sweets. Another facet of t Beatles' tour appearances was that the female fa screamed so long and so hard throughout their show that became almost impossible to hear what the group sound like and their musical expertise on tour was never real called upon again. The group were now so popular that th could afford to be driven to gigs by car, usually a chauffeu driven luxury model as befitted their new status celebrities and stars. It was also the time when th freedom of movement was curtailed. No longer able to s out for a pint in a local pub during the long periods in t dressing-rooms, they also found it difficult to eat out ocal restaurants near the theatres where they were ppearing and generally food had to be brought in to them, sually by Neil Aspinall. They were now also playing for eriods of 25 minutes or half an hour, in contrast to the ng stints they used to perform in Hamburg and Liverpool.

Bill-toppers in their own right now, the Beatles next egan a mini-tour of Scotland with **Mike Berry** as ipport.

BEATLES MINI-TOUR OF SCOTLAND, 1963

5 Oct	Concert Hall, Glasgow
6 Oct	Carlton, Kirkcaldy
7 Oct	Caird Hall, Dundee

ike Berry also accompanied the band on their short tour Sweden between 25 and 29 October, where there was so support from local talent such as the **Phantoms**. It as the Beatles' first tour abroad – their appearances in amburg had been more in the nature of seasons at a rticular club rather than a proper tour.

BEATLES TOUR OF SWEDEN, 1963

25 Oct	Nya aulan, Karlstad
26 Oct	Kungliga Hallen, Stockholm
27 Oct	Cirkus, Goteborg
28 Oct	Borashallen, Boras
29 Oct	Sporthallen, Eskilstuna

e group immediately commenced their autumn tour of itain, their fourth British tour that year. Among the pport acts were **Peter Jay & the Jaywalkers**, the **ook Brothers** with the Rhythm and Blues Quartet, the **rnons Girls**, the **Kestrels** and compere/comedian ank Berry. The tour lasted from 1 November–13 cember.

BEATLES AUTUMN TOUR OF BRITAIN, 1963

1 Nov	Odeon, Cheltenham
2 Nov	City Hall, Sheffield
3 Nov	Odeon, Leeds
5 Nov	Adelphi, Slough
6 Nov	ABC, Northampton
7 Nov	Adelphi, Dublin
8 Nov	Ritz, Belfast
9 Nov	Granada, East Ham
10 Nov	Hippodrome, Birmingham
13 Nov	ABC, Plymouth
14 Nov	ABC, Exeter
15 Nov	Colston Hall, Bristol
16 Nov	Winter Gardens, Bournemouth
17 Nov	Coventry Theatre, Coventry
19 Nov	Gaumont, Wolverhampton
20 Nov	ABC, Ardwick
21 Nov	ABC, Carlisle
22 Nov	Globe, Stockton-on-Tees
23 Nov	City Hall, Newcastle-upon-Tyne
24 Nov	ABC, Hull
26 Nov	Regal, Cambridge
27 Nov	Rialto, York
28 Nov	ABC, Lincoln
29 Nov	ABC, Huddersfield
30 Nov	Empire, Sunderland
1 Dec	De Montfort Hall, Leicester
3 Dec	Guildhall, Portsmouth
7 Dec	Odeon, Liverpool
8 Dec	Odeon, Lewisham
9 Dec	Odeon, Southend-on-Sea
10 Dec	Gaumont, Doncaster
11 Dec	Futurist, Scarborough
12 Dec	Odeon, Nottingham
13 Dec	Gaumont, Southampton

1963 closed and 1964 opened with the Beatles' first Christmas Show taking place at the **Finsbury Park Astoria**, with **Cilla Black**, **Billy J. Kramer** with the Dakotas, the **Fourmost**, **Tommy Quickly** and the **Remo Four**, the **Barron Knights** with Duke D'Mond and **Rolf Harris** in support. The group then appeared for a short season at the **Paris Olympia** from 16 January–4 February 1964, and the French proved to be the most disappointing of all foreign audiences. Noticeably different was the fact that the audiences were mainly male – and the Beatles only brought them to life when they performed some rock 'n' roll classics.

It was when the group were booked to appear in America and their mammoth major tours before tens of thousands of fans began that the face of touring was to be completely revolutionized. Although those early tours of America by the Beatles seem crude by the standards of today's spectaculars, it was the Beatles who laid the groundwork for what was to come. As vast concerts of this type had never been organized on such a scale before, the

Beatles, more by design than choice, had to create some new rules. A ceiling was placed on ticket prices by Brian Epstein, contracts stipulated that security must be provided, together with the availability of a good hi-fi system and a sound engineer, as well as microphones and other equipment. Even details of the size of stages was worked out in advance. The promoters were to provide proper dressing-room facilities but also a TV set, clean towels, cots and mirrors, plus limousines with chauffeurs. They also included a clause for the southern states: 'Artists will not be required to perform before a segregated audience'.

The Beatles only made two concert appearances in America in February, at the **Coliseum, Washington** DC, on 11 February and at **Carnegie Hall**, New York, on 12 February. Their next major tour was their first world tour, which took place from 4 June to 29 June. For the initial part of the tour Ringo Starr was taken ill and drummer **Jimmy Nicol** deputized.

THE WORLD TOUR, 1964

4 June	Tivoli Gardens, Copenhagen, Denmark
6 June	Exhibition Hall, Blokker, Denmark
10 June	Princess Theatre, Hong Kong
12 June	Centennial Hall, Adelaide, Australia
13 June	Centennial Hall, Adelaide, Australia
15 June	Festival Hall, Melbourne, Australia
18 June	Sydney Stadium, Sydney, Australia
19 June	Sydney Stadium, Sydney, Australia
20 June	Sydney Stadium, Sydney, Australia
22 June	Town Hall, Wellington, New Zealand
23 June	Town Hall, Wellington, New Zealand
24 June	Town Hall, Auckland, New Zealand
25 June	Town Hall, Auckland, New Zealand
26 June	Town Hall, Dunedin, New Zealand
27 June	Majestic Theatre, Christchurch, New Zealand
29 June	Festival Hall, Brisbane, Australia
30 June	Festival Hall, Brisbane, Australia

On their return from Australia the group appeared at a small number of concert venues in Britain and then made a short trip to Sweden for two concerts before next creating history with their first tour of America, breaking audienc records as they appeared at major arenas throughout th States. Their tour lasted from 19 August to 28 Septemb

The Beatles on tour.

1964 and the other artists on the bill included **Jackie I Shannon**, the **Righteous Brothers**, the **Bill Bla Combo** and the Exciters.

THE BEATLES' FIRST AMERICAN TOUR, 1964

19 Aug	Cow Palace, San Francisco
20 Aug	Convention Hall, Las Vegas
21 Aug	Coliseum, Seattle
22 Aug	Empire Stadium, Vancouver
23 Aug	Hollywood Bowl, Los Angeles
26 Aug	Red Rock Stadium, Denver
27 Aug	The Gardens, Cincinnati
28 Aug	Forest Hills Stadium, New York
30 Aug	Convention Hall, Atlantic City
2 Sept	Convention Hall, Philadelphia
3 Sept	State Fair Coliseum, Indianapolis
4 Sept	Auditorium, Milwaukee
5 Sept	International Amphitheatre, Chica
6 Sept	Olympia Stadium, Detroit
7 Sept	Maple Leaf Gardens, Toronto
8 Sept	Forum, Montreal
11 Sept	Gator Bowl, Jacksonville
12 Sept	Boston Gardens, Boston
13 Sept	Civic Centre, Baltimore
14 Sept	Civic Arena, Pittsburgh

15 Sept	Public Auditorium, Cleveland
16 Sept	City Park Stadium, New Orleans
17 Sept	Municipal Stadium, Kansas City
18 Sept	Memorial Coliseum, Dallas
20 Sept	Paramount Theatre, New York

eir winter tour of Britain was once again promoted by thur Howes and began at the **Gaumont, Bradford**, site the first night of their Helen Shapiro tour. Support acts re **Mary Wells**, the **Rustiks**, **Michale Haslam**, **unds Incorporated** and Tommy Quickly and the mo Four. Compere was **Bob Bain**.

AUTUMN TOUR OF BRITAIN, 1964

9 Oct	Gaumont, Bradford
10 Oct	De Montfort Hall, Leicester
11 Oct	Odeon, Birmingham
13 Oct	ABC, Wigan
14 Oct	ABC, Manchester
15 Oct	Globe, Stockton-on-Tees
16 Oct	ABC, Hull
19 Oct	ABC, Edinburgh
20 Oct	Caird Hall, Dundee
21 Oct	Odeon, Glasgow
22 Oct	Odeon, Leeds
23 Oct	Gaumont State, Kilburn
24 Oct	Granada, Walthamstow
25 Oct	Hippodrome, Brighton
28 Oct	ABC, Exeter
29 Oct	ABC, Plymouth
30 Oct	Gaumont, Bournemouth
31 Oct	Gaumont, Ipswich
1 Nov	Astoria, Finsbury Park
2 Nov	King's Hall, Belfast
4 Nov	Ritz, Luton
5 Nov	Odeon, Nottingham
6 Nov	Gaumont, Southampton
7 Nov	Capitol, Cardiff
8 Nov	Empire, Liverpool
9 Nov	City Hall, Sheffield
10 Nov	Colston Hall, Bristol

e Beatles ended the year with *Another Beatles Christmas ow* at the **Odeon, Hammersmith**, London, nmencing 24 December 1964 and closing on 16 uary 1965 with the **Yardbirds**, the Mike Cotton Sound, Michael Haslam, **Freddie & the Dreamers**, Elkie Brooks, Sounds Incorporated, **Ray Fell** and **Jimmy Savile** in support.

The group next embarked on a two-week tour of Europe, taking in France, Italy and Spain.

EUROPEAN TOUR, 1965

20 June	Palais De Sports, Paris
22 June	Palais d'Hiver, Lyon
24 June	Velodromo, Milan
25 June	Palazzo dello Sport, Genoa
27 June	Teatro Adriano, Rome
28 June	Teatro Adriano, Rome
30 June	Palais des Fetes, Nice
2 July	Plaza de Toros de Madrid, Madrid
3 July	Plaza de Toros de Madrid, Madrid

Their next tour of America opened with the spectacular **Shea Stadium** appearance which, with an audience of 55,600, created a world record for a concert. Support acts on the tour were the **King Curtis** band, Brenda Holloway and Sounds Incorporated.

AMERICAN TOUR, 1965

15 Aug	Shea Stadium, New York
17 Aug	Maple Leaf Gardens, Toronto
18 Aug	Atlanta Stadium, Georgia
19 Aug	Sam Houston Coliseum, Houston
20 Aug	White Sox Park, Chicago
21 Aug	Metropolitan Stadium, Minneapolis
22 Aug	Memorial Coliseum, Portland
28 Aug	Balboa Stadium, San Diego
29 Aug	Hollywood Bowl, Los Angeles
30 Aug	Hollywood Bowl, Los Angeles
31 Aug	Cow Palace, San Francisco

Touring was now beginning to tell on the Beatles. Their equipment was not vast by today's standards and they appeared on stages with small Vox amplifiers, but as their music could hardly be heard through the piercing sounds of screaming fans, it didn't seem to be a problem, although the group were becoming bored. Their next tour of Britain was to be the last time they toured in the UK. They were supported by Birmingham band the **Moody Blues**, the **Paramounts** from Southampton and three Liverpool acts, the **Koobas**, **Beryl Marsden** and **Steve Aldo**. With only nine appearances, it became their shortest theatre tour of Britain. The group had also decided not to hold a third Christmas Show.

BRITISH TOUR, 1965

3 Dec	Odeon, Glasgow
4 Dec	City Hall, Newcastle
5 Dec	Empire, Liverpool
7 Dec	Apollo, Ardwick, Manchester
8 Dec	City Hall, Sheffield
9 Dec	Odeon, Birmingham
10 Dec	Odeon Hammersmith
11 Dec	Astoria, Finsbury Park
12 Dec	Capitol, Cardiff

1966 was the Beatles' last year as a touring group and it also saw the virtual end of their live appearances. They appeared at the ***New Musical Express*** Poll Winners' Concert on 1 May which, apart from their rooftop appearance on the Apple building, was their last live show in Britain. They next embarked on a short tour of Germany and Japan, supported by **Cliff Bennett & the Rebel Rousers** and **Peter & Gordon**.

TOUR OF GERMANY AND JAPAN, 1966

24 June	Circus Krone, Munich, Germany
25 June	Grugahalle, Essen, Germany
26 June	Ernst Merck Halle, Hamburg, Germany
30 June	Budokan Hall, Tokyo, Japan
1 July	Budokan Hall, Tokyo, Japan
2 July	Budokan Hall, Tokyo, Japan
4 July	Araneta Coliseum, Manila, Philippines

The most horrific incidents in their touring career occurred in Manila where they were manhandled and jeered at following a reported snub to the country's First Lady, Imelda Marcos. On the plane home, a shaken group decided that their touring days must soon be over. This was consolidated by their final American tour which was blighted by the uproar caused over John Lennon's quotes about Christ in an interview with Maureen Cleave. The American media exploited the quotes out of context and out of all proportion, resulting in the first wave of anti-Beatles feeling that had arisen in America. The love affair between America and the Beatles seemed to have soure[d]. A reluctant Lennon had to submit to a humiliating publ[ic] apology and there was still anti-Beatle feeling in t[he] southern states and middle-America, with various dea[th] threats. At some gigs the Beatles had to duck when th[ey] heard sharp noises, fearing them to be gunshots.

They decided that touring was no longer to be on t[he] agenda and George Harrison sighed with relief when flyi[ng] home after their final concert, saying, 'I'm not a Beatle a[ny] more.' In fact, the Beatles were about to move into t[he] most important phase of their career, their studio yea[rs] when they were able to develop their songwriting a[nd] musical abilities inside the recording studio – to an ext[ent] they would never have been able to do if they h[ad] continued touring.

Towards the end of their career, Paul McCartney w[as] anxious for the Beatles to take to the road again, even i[f it] meant appearing unannounced at colleges or small venu[es] or booking places such as London's Roundhouse. Gi[ven] time he might have persuaded Ringo and even John [to] embark on some further live gigs – but never Geor[ge].

A typical gathering of fans at Heathrow Airport. (Granada TV)

George had made his mind up that he would never [tour] again with the Beatles – and that is how it was.

Their final American tour saw them with acts suc[h as] the **Ronettes**, the **Cyrkle** and the **Remains** in support.

FINAL AMERICAN TOUR, 1966

12 Aug	International Amphitheatre, Chic[ago]

13 Aug	Olympia Stadium, Detroit
14 Aug	Municipal Stadium, Cleveland
15 Aug	Washington Stadium, Washington DC
16 Aug	Philadelphia Stadium, Philadelphia
17 Aug	Maple Leaf Gardens, Toronto
18 Aug	Suffolk Downs Racecourse, Boston
19 Aug	Memphis Coliseum, Memphis
20 Aug	Crosley Field, Cincinnati
21 Aug	Busch Stadium, St Louis
23 Aug	Shea Stadium, New York
24 Aug	Shea Stadium, New York
25 Aug	Seattle Coliseum, Seattle
28 Aug	Dodger Stadium, Los Angeles
30 Aug	Candlestick Park, San Francisco

Tower Ballroom, New Brighton, Wirral, erseyside L45

e of Merseyside's largest ballroom facilities, which was e to accommodate 5,000 people. When it was originally nstructed it sported the largest iron tower in Europe er the Eiffel Tower and was taller than Blackpool's nous Tower. The Tower itself was dismantled to provide tal for the war effort, but the material was never used the Tower was never rebuilt.

George Harrison's grandfather was once a nmissionaire at the ballroom.

Sam Leach was the promoter responsible for ognizing the ballroom's potential as a venue for ctacular dance promotions and on 10 November 1961 launched 'Operation Big Beat', which featured a nber of leading Liverpool bands.

The show opened at 7.30 p.m. and the Beatles peared at 8.00 p.m. They then fulfilled another agement at Knotty Ash Village Hall before returning their second Tower appearance that evening at 11.30 . Tickets for the event had been sold in advance at **MS'** Whitechapel store, which was managed by Brian tein, who must have been aware of the event, although re-dated the supposed enquiry from 'Raymond Jones'. event drew an audience of 3,000 people.

Operation Big Beat II' took place on the evening of lay, 24 November 1961, with the Beatles once again ping the bill. The other local groups who appeared were **ry Storm & the Hurricanes**, **Gerry & the emakers**, the **Remo Four**, Earl Preston & the Tempest Tornadoes and Faron & the Flamingos. Late-night transport had to be arranged with the various local authorities as the event took place between 7.30 p.m and 2.00 a.m. Tickets cost 6/- (30p). An added treat for the audience was the appearance of Emile Ford, who'd had several chart hits, including 'What Do You Want To Make Those Eyes At Me For' and 'Slow Boat To China'; he got up on stage and sang with Rory Storm & the Hurricanes and American singer **Davy Jones**, who joined the Beatles on stage and sang two numbers with them.

The Beatles returned to top the bill again on 1 December 1961 at a six-group extravaganza which attracted 2,000 people.

On 8 December 1961 Leach organized a further Tower promotion, adding South African singing star Danny Williams to the bill, whose current hit 'Moon River' was at No. 4 in the British charts. Leach also booked Davy Jones as headliner and he was once again backed by the Beatles – and they actually backed him earlier in the day at a **Cavern** lunchtime session.

Leach's final Tower promotion of the year took place on

15 December and featured five bands on a five-and-a-half-hour show. The Beatles topped the bill, which showed the appearance, for one night only, of a former top Liverpool band Cass & the Cassanovas. When **Brian Casser** had originally left the group, the remaining three members continued as the Big Three. On this evening's bill Casser joined the Big Three under their old name for a special reunion performance.

The first bill of the New Year was on Friday, 12 January 1962, on an extravaganza called 'Twist Around The Tower'. Leach advertised the bill as 'The Greatest Show on Merseyside, starring that horrible hairy Monster Screaming Lord Sutch (X certificate) and his horde of Savages, with Philips recording artists Mel (King of Twist) Turner and the Bandits. Also, ***Mersey Beat*** Poll Winners The Beatles (After 11.30 p.m.), Rory Storm & the Hurricanes, the Strangers. We introduced the Twist to Merseyside, Now we present another lead – a sensational Twist exhibition team, Mr Twist & the Twistettes'. Bill toppers Screaming Lord Sutch & the Savages failed to turn up.

The Beatles' next Tower appearance took place on 19 January, followed by a special Pre-Panto Ball on 15 February. Panto Day was an annual event in Liverpool, organized by students at Liverpool University. They would parade around the city on huge decorated floats, dressed in costumes, collecting for local charities. On the Panto Day evening, all students who had taken part in the event were invited to a special Panto Day Ball. Leach capitalized on the publicity by putting on this bill on the eve of Panto Day, with Terry Lightfoot and his New Orleans Jazz Band co-headlining with the Beatles. It drew an audience of 3,500 people. The Beatles then appeared at the Tower on a further Sam Leach bill the following night, 16 February. On 23 February they appeared at the ballroom twice, initially at 9.00 p.m., followed by a set at 10.45 p.m.

On 2 March they appeared at another Tower event, billed as the Mad March Rock Ball.

The Beatles' appearance on Friday, 6 April, was their last Tower appearance prior to their season at Hamburg's **Star Club**. The two headliners were Emile Ford & the Checkmates and the Beatles and the other bands were Gerry & the Pacemakers, **Howie Casey** & the Seniors, Rory Storm & the Hurricanes and the Big Three. Adding some novelty were the Original Kingtwisters.

Leach was the local promoter who had shown the foresight to gamble on promoting rock shows at the Tower. It was situated in an unfortunate location – near t[cut off] promenade of a fading holiday resort on the Wir[cut off] peninsula. However, Sam had solved this problem [cut off] organizing special late-night transport by bus and train [cut off] all areas of Liverpool and the Wirral. Once he'd got [cut off] system into place and had developed the Tower as[cut off] successful venue for promotion, other promoters obviou[cut off] considered taking advantage of its facilities.

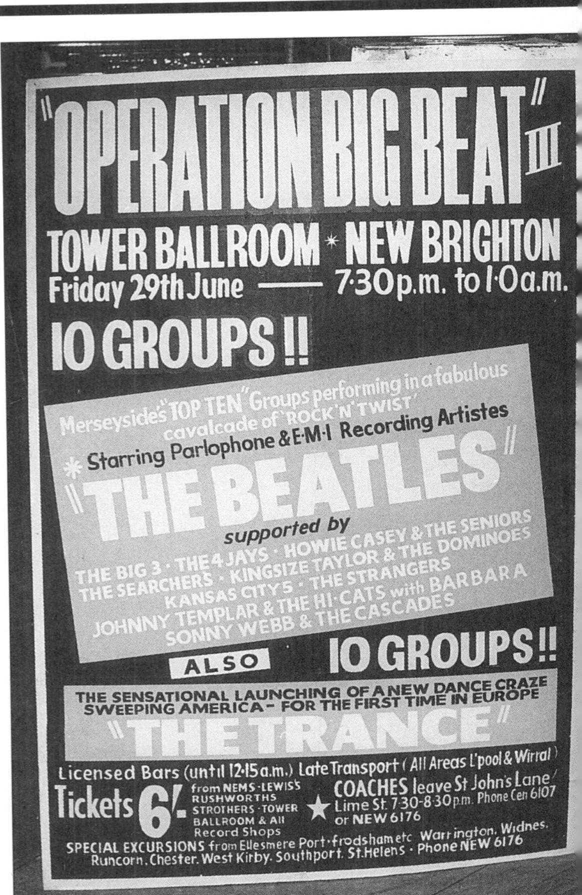

A poster advertising one of Sam Leach's 'Operation Big Be[cut off] promotions at the Tower Ballroom. (*Mersey Beat* Archives)

The next Beatles appearance there was on a prom[cut off] financed by Brian Epstein and organized and compere[cut off] **Bob Wooler**. It was the first of a series of pla[cut off] prestige gigs by Epstein to place the Beatles on a bill [cut off] name artists. For this appearance on Thursday 21 [cut off] 1962, the bill was topped by Bruce Channel. Channel d a massive hit with 'Hey Baby!' and he was backed by rmonica player Delbert McLinton & the Barons. The atles were advertised as 'Parlophone Recording Artistes d stars of the BBC's "Teenager's Turn"'. Bolton group Statesmen were next on the bill, followed by Mersey ups the Big Three and the **Four Jays**.

Sam Leach promoted his 'Operation Big Beat II' on 29 ne, topped by the Beatles and featuring ten local bands a five-and-a-half-hour spectacular.

The next Brian Epstein presentation at the Tower tured **Joe Brown** and his Bruvvers headlining over the atles on 27 July. The other acts on the bill were the tesmen, the Big Three, Steve Day & the Drifters and Four Jays.

For their appearance at the venue on 17 August, the atles had drummer **Johnny Hutchinson** sitting in with m as **Pete Best** had been ignominiously sacked a few s previously.

Sam Leach presented his 'Operation Big Beat V' on 14 tember, another five-and-a-half-hour marathon turing six local groups, headed by the Beatles. Later the ne month the Beatles appeared at the Tower on 21 tember with four other local bands – the occasion was lebration of Rory Storm's birthday.

The next event was another five-and-a-half-hour ravaganza, this time promoted by Brian Epstein and ring **Little Richard** on a 12-act bill. Sam Leach had ginally offered Richard £350 for a Tower Ballroom king and looked like securing the American star until was outbid by Epstein who paid £500 for Richard and money on the gig, although the Beatles' career was sted by the prestigious appearance.

t was another NEMS Enterprises presentation and Bob oler production and, apart from the Beatles, **Lee tis** & the All Stars appeared with their new drummer, Best. Other acts on the bill were the Big Three, **Billy Kramer** with the Coasters, the Dakotas with Pete Laine, the Four Jays, the **Merseybeats**, Rory Storm & Hurricanes and the Undertakers. Epstein was later to luce the Hurricanes on record and was also later to Billy J. Kramer and team him with Manchester's otas. He was also to sign the Big Three, whose nmer Johnny Hutchinson filled the stopgap when Best sacked. Epstein considered signing the Merseybeats eventually they became a NEMS band, and he signed Four Jays, who became the **Fourmost**. Jackie Lomax, lead singer with the Undertakers, later became an Apple artist, recorded by both Paul McCartney and George Harrison.

During the course of the evening, photographer Les Chadwick took the famous picture of Little Richard and the Beatles on behalf of *Mersey Beat*, the newspaper.

On 23 November the Beatles appeared on the bill of the 12th Annual Lancashire and Cheshire Arts Ball. Also appearing were Billy J. Kramer and the Coasters, the Llew Hird Jazz Band and the Clan McCleod Pipe Band.

Their last Tower appearance during 1962 was on 7 December when they topped the bill on a line-up of seven local bands.

The Beatles' final appearance at the Tower Ballroom took place on Friday, 14 June 1963, on a special NEMS Enterprises' presentation on their '**Mersey Beat Showcase**' series. the Beatles were supported by Gerry & the Pacemakers and five other groups.

The Tower was burned down in 1969, leaving only the foundations.

LATE NIGHT DANCE
BEAT BALLAD SHOW
Presenting
Star of TV and Decca Recording Fame—
JOHNNY GENTLE and HIS GROUP,
Supported by Scotland's Own Tommy Steele—
ALEX. HARVEY and HIS BEAT BAND,
With Ballad Singer—Babby Rankine.
To Entertain and Play For
DANCING
in the
TOWN HALL, ALLOA,
on
FRIDAY, 20th MAY,
9.30 — 1.30.
ADMISSION—Before 10 p.m., 4/-; after 10 p.m., 5/-.
Buses After Dance to the HILLFOOTS DISTRICT.
NEXT FRIDAY, 27th MAY — JOHNNY DOUGLAS and HIS NEW BEAT COMBO with Happy Jackie Benson and Andy Cook of S.T.V.

● Town Hall, *Alloa, Clackmannanshire, Scotland*

The first appearance by the Silver Beetles on their brief tour of Scotland with **Johnny Gentle** took place at this venue on Friday, 20 May 1960. The group and Gentle had never played together before and had a single rehearsal, lasting only thirty minutes, prior to their performance that evening. Gentle 'and his group' topped the bill and, announcing the support, the advertisements read, 'Supported by Scotland's own Tommy Steele – Alex Harvey & his beat band, with ballad singer – Bobby Rankine'. Harvey was to become a close friend of the Beatles during his appearances in Hamburg and he finally became a successful recording and concert artist in the seventies, a career curtailed by his early death.

● Town Hall, *Auckland, New Zealand*

The group appeared at this venue on New Zealand's North Island for four shows, over a period of two nights, which drew capacity audiences of over 10,000 people. The appearances took place on 14 and 25 June 1964. Initial there was some hostility from authorities in Aucklar although the concerts were very successful and brought t group enthusiastic reviews.

● Town Hall, *Congreve Street, Birmingham*

The Beatles appeared at this venue once, during their t with **Roy Orbison**, on 4 June 1963.

● Town Hall, *Dingwall, Ross and Cromarty, Scotland*

The beginning of 1963 saw the Beatles undertake a b tour of Scotland during hazardous weather conditions. (of the gigs was at the Town Hall in Dingwall where th appeared on 4 January 1963.

(©Apple/Walter Shenson Films)

Town Hall, Dunedin, New Zealand

ter appearing on the North Island of New Zealand, the ·atles flew to the South Island to appear in Dunedin and ıristchurch. They appeared for two shows on the evening 26 June 1964 at this venue with capacity audiences of)00.

The reception in the Town Hall was incredibly loud, hough the enthusiastic audience didn't leave their seats attempt to reach the group on stage as the raised ıtform was far too high. A line of policemen, their arms ked, stood between the audience and the stage and, cause the linked arms inhibited their movement, some ıyful fans knocked off their helmets and played football h them in the aisles.

Town Hall, Market Street, Earlestown, ewton-Le-Willows, Cheshire

nue where the Beatles made a single appearance on 30 vember 1962 in *The Big Beat Show No. 2*, a promotion the T & T Vicars Sports and Social Club. The civic lding is over a hundred years old and presented dances ularly until the mid-sixties.

Town Hall, Forres, Morayshire, otland

other venue on their short **Johnny Gentle** tour of)tland in 1960. The group backed Gentle here on ırsday, 26 May, but were not referred to by name in the ertising, which read, 'Johnny Gentle and his group'.

The dance ran from 9.00 p.m. to 1.00 a.m., cost five llings (25p) admittance and also featured Rikki Barnes ıis All Stars with Lena & Stevie.

The impecunious Silver Beetles were staying overnight he Royal Hotel in the town that night, but slipped away hout paying their bill.

Town Hall Chambers, Town Hall, dney, Gloucestershire

ingle appearance at this venue in Gloucestershire for Beatles, who performed at the venue on 31 August 2.

Town Hall, Wellington, New Zealand

Beatles opened their brief tour of New Zealand with shows at this theatre in Wellington, on the North nd. The group appeared at the Town Hall on 22 and 23 June 1964 and the 2,500-seater hall was fully booked.

At the first show on Monday, 22 June, the PA system was very primitive and the sound was inadequate. **Johnny Devlin** had to convince the man who owned the PA system that he could turn it up without it being destroyed and it proved to be fine for the second show. There were 50 police in the hall and they kept forcing the girls back into their seats. One young man managed to scramble on stage and almost knocked Ringo off his drum stool before he was bundled away. Incidentally, Ringo sang the number 'Boys' during the New Zealand gigs, instead of 'I Wanna Be Your Man', which he sang in Australia.

● Town Hall, Paul's Moss, Dodington, Whitchurch, Shropshire

The Beatles only made a single appearance at this Town Hall in Shropshire, on 19 January 1963.

● Townsend, Ken

The General Manager of **Abbey Road Studios** in London.

He joined the Abbey Road Studios in the mid-fifties as a tape engineer and was present assisting George Martin on the Beatles' first **EMI** recording audition on 6 June 1962. When he was chief technical engineer he worked closely with the Beatles and credits them with creating an atmosphere of experimentation which led to a revolution in recording methods.

In an attempt to facilitate some of the Beatles' experiments in the fields of double-tracking, he invented a machine which he called ADT (Artificial Double Tracking). He was driving home one night after a Beatles session in which they had spent the entire evening double-tracking when the idea came to him to develop a system of electronically putting one vocal onto another.

John Lennon persisted in calling the machine 'Ken's Flanger', with the result that 'flanging' has become a standard technical term used in recording studios throughout the world.

● Trash

A group from Glasgow, Scotland, originally known as the Pathfinders. They were discovered by **Tony Meehan**, ex-member of the **Shadows**.

They were signed to Apple and given the name White Trash by **Richard Di Lello** of the Press Office. This caused problems when they attempted to promote their debut single 'Road To Nowhere' because people found the name offensive, so it was shortened to Trash.

The group recorded the Beatles' medley number 'Golden Slumbers/Carry That Weight', which reached No. 35 in the British charts in September 1969. They had no further success and disbanded due to problems within the Apple company. Their album *White Trash*, although given the catalogue number SAPCOR 7, was never released.

Members of the group comprised: Ian Crawford-Clews (vocals), Fraser Watson (lead guitar), Ronald Leahy (organ), Colin Hunter-Morrison (bass guitar) and Tim Donald (drums).

● Trentham Gardens Ballroom, *Trentham Gardens, Trentham, Staffordshire*

The Beatles only made a single appearance at this ballroom in Staffordshire, immediately following their short tour of Scotland, on 11 October 1963.

● Treslong Studios, *Hillegom, Holland*

Dutch studios where the Beatles rehearsed for a television show soon after their arrival at Schiphol Airport on 5 June 1964.

The studios were situated in Hillegom, which was 26 miles from the capital, Amsterdam. Prior to their performance for the **Vara Broadcasting Corporation**, they were interviewed on videotape by Herman Stok and Berend Boudewijn in the bar of the studios. The interviewers asked them some rather bland questions regarding marriage, their opinion of Dutch girls, who mended their socks during their tours and such like. The Beatles then left the bar and walked into the studio where they performed before an audience.

The numbers they played were, 'She Loves You', 'Twist And Shout', 'All My Loving', 'Roll Over Beethoven', 'Long Tall Sally' and 'Can't Buy Me Love'.

The videotaped show was broadcast five days later on 10 June.

● Tribute Records

The Beatles have been the subject of scores of recordings by other artists. It is rare when a real person or a group of people themselves become the subject of a record, but in the case of the Beatles, their popularity ensured a large number of tributes, spoofs and novelty discs.

As in the case with most tribute records, few of th entered the charts. In Britain the comedienne **Do Bryan** reached No. 20 in the charts with 'All I Want F Christmas Is A Beatle' in 1963 and German instrumen group D.B.M. reached No. 45 in the charts with 'Beatl Discomania' in 1977.

Among other records inspired by the Beatles a 'Lennon Quickie' by Neil Innes, 'Lennon Song' by B Gaunt, 'Lennon & McCartney' by John Moreland, 'P McCartney' by Tony Hazzard, 'Beatles Are In Town' Norma Johnson, 'Beatle Boots' by Bruce Brand and Stev J. Hamper, 'Beatle Days' by Richard Jones and T Sebastian, 'Beatle Drive' by James Douglas and Jan Duncan, 'Beatle Express' by Heinz Kiessling, 'Bea Woman' by J. Fish, 'Beatle Man' by Chris Laidl 'Beatles and the MBE' by Leroy M. Emanuel, 'Beatles Home' by Dick Hyman, 'Beatles Got To Go' by Lee By and Llewellyn Vincent, 'Beatle Bug' by Long, Dav Wellbourne and Jay, 'Beatles-Go-West' by Leon Yo and 'Come Back Beatles' by Lipstick.

Some of the tributes were by well-known artists usin pseudonym. **Phil Spector**, for instance, produced 'I L Ringo' by Bonnie Jo Mason, who turned out to be Ch and Gene Cornish & the Unbeatables, who cut the albu *Wanna Be A Beatle*, later became famous as the Rascals

Ella Fitzgerald released 'Ringo Beat' and comed Rolf Harris came out with 'Ringo For President'. Ringo fact, seemed to be quite a popular subject for the trib disc and others include: 'Treat Him Tender, Maur (Now That Ringo Belongs To You)' by Angie and Chicklettes, 'I Want Ringo For Christmas' by the F Sisters, 'Ringo's Dog' by the Jack Dorsey Big Band, ' Can't Go Far Without A Guitar Unless You're Ringo St by Neil Sheppard, 'I Want To Kiss Ringo Goodbye' Penny Valentine, 'Santa, Bring Me Ringo For Christm by Christine Hunter, 'Ringo' by Weekend, 'Ringo' by Starlettes, 'Ringo' by Bob Dean, 'Ringo Part One/ Two' by Carl & the Haircuts, 'My Ringo' by the Rainbo 'Ringo Ringo' by Darlene Terri, 'Ringo, Dingo' coup with 'Here Comes Ringo' by the Tributes, 'R (Is Ringo)' by Tina Ferra, 'Ringo-Dear' by Gary Ferr 'Ringo Boy' by Dori Peyton, 'Ringo's Jerk' by Ron Ri 'Ringo's Walk' by Joey & the Classics, 'Like Ringo' Dick Lord, 'Go Go With Ringo' by the Whippets, 'Ri Did It' by Veronica Lee & the Moniques, 'Where Ringo Go?' by the Beatle Bugs, 'Ringo Comes To Town ug and Doug, 'Ringo, I Want To Know Your Secret' by Wynter, 'A Tribute to Ringo Starr (The Other Ringo)' Larry Finnegan, 'Ringo For President' by the Young orld Singers, 'What's Wrong With Ringo' by the nBugs (this girl group was later to re-emerge as the ngri Las with a huge hit, 'The Leader Of The Pack'), ngo Ringo' by Butler Daws (the man who provided the ce of the Huckleberry Hound character in the cartoons nd some copies of the single were actually credited to ckleberry Hound), 'Minuet For Ringo' by Viv Prince rmer drummer with the Pretty Things) and 'Ringo, go Little Starr' by Al and Lou Marks Fisher.

John also seemed to be singled out with: 'Get Back n' by Inner City Mission, 'John, You Went Too Far This e' by Rainbo (referring to John's interview in which ist was mentioned), 'Crazy John' by Tom Paxton and t John and Yoko Stay In The USA' by the Justice artment.

Rumours of Paul's death sparked off: 'Ballad Of Paul' the Mystery Tour, 'St Paul' by Terry Knight, 'Brother l' by Billy Shears & the All Americans and 'We're All Paul Bearers' by Zacharias & the Tree People.

There have been various tributes which include Beatle medleys such as 'You Can't Do That' by **Harry Nilsson**, 'Titles' by Barclay James Harvest, '*Eine Kleine Beatlemusik*' by Fritz Spiegel and 'The Beatles Cracker Suite' by Arthur Wilkinson and his Orchestra.

Spike Milligan issued a spoof version of 'Yellow Submarine' entitled 'Purple Aeroplane' and **Peter Sellers** gave thespian renditions of 'A Hard Day's Night', 'Help!' and 'She Loves You'.

The most popular Beatles single to be given the 'treatment' was 'I Want To Hold Your Hand' and the spoofs included 'I Don't Want To Hold Your Hand' by Rupert Holmes, 'I'll Let You Hold My Hand' by the Bootles, 'I Want To Hold Your Hair' by the Bagels, 'I Don't Want To Hold Your Hand' by Homer and Jethro, 'Yes, You Can Hold My Hand' by the Beatlettes, 'I Want To Bite Your Hand' by Gene Moss, 'You Can Hold My Hand' by Lafawn Paul, 'Just Hold My Hand' by Paul Perryman and 'Yes, You Can Hold My Hand' by the Teen Bugs.

There are many other records in this vein, including: 'We Love You Beatles' by the Carefrees (based on the tune 'We Love You Conrad' from the musical 'Bye Bye Birdie', it reached No. 39 in the *Billboard* charts), 'The Boy With The Beatle Hair' by the Swans, 'She Loves You' by the Haircuts, 'A Beatle I Want To Be' by Sonny Curtis, 'Bring Back The Beatles' by David Peel, 'My Beatle Haircut' by the Twilighters, 'Beatle Fan' by Zeke Mullins, 'Beatle Baby Walk' by the Al Martin Six, 'Beatle Song' by Dick Pillar and his Orchestra, 'To Kill A Beatle' by Johnny Garnier, 'I Ain't No Beatle' by Jerry Foster, 'Beatles, We Want Our Girls Back' by the Defenders, 'The Beatle Song' by the Twilighters, 'The Beatles Is Back (Yea, Yea, Yea)' by Lenore King and Tommy Anderson, 'The Beatles Song' by the Japanese Beatles, 'Beatle Walk' by David Hamilton, 'Beatle Crazy' by Bill Clifton, 'The Beatles' Flying Saucer' by Ed Solomon, 'The Beatles' by the Buddies, 'Beatlemania In The USA' by the Liverpools, 'Beatle Stomp' by the Exterminators, 'Let's Bug The Beatles' by the Insects, 'Beatle Beat' by Benny & the Bedbugs, 'Letter To The Beatles' by the Four Preps, 'Little Beatle Boy' by the Angels, 'Sgt Pepper's Epitaph' by Keith Green, 'I'm Better Than The Beatles' by Jekyll & Hyde, 'The Beatles Barber' by Scott Douglas, 'The Guy With The Long Liverpool Hair' by the Outsiders, 'Saga Of The Beatles' by Johnny & the Hurricanes, 'My Boyfriend Got A Beatle Haircut' by Donna Lynn (which reached No. 83 in the *Billboard* charts), 'We Love The Beatles' by the **Vernons Girls**, 'Beatle Fever' by the Bedbugs, 'John, Paul, George and Ringo' by the Bulldogs, 'Beatle Fever' by Brett & Terry and 'The Beatle Dance' by Ernie Maresca.

Satirist Allan Sherman issued 'Pop Hates The Beatles', sung to the tune of 'Pop Goes The Weasel', in which a father chastises his daughter over her Beatle fervour. He also recorded another number called 'I Hate The Beatles'.

Gary Usher and Roger Christian, who produced the documentary album *The Beatles Story* in 1964, came out with a record, 'The Beetle', which was a dance number. There were several attempts to create a dance craze around the Beatles, including 'The Beatle Beat' by Benny & the Bedbugs, 'Beatle Crawl' by the Del Ricos and 'The Beatles Dance' by Tommy Bee.

The subject of Beatles novelty discs has been exhaustively researched by Charles Reinhart in his book *You Can't Do That*, published by Pierian Press in 1981.

● Trident Studios, *Trident House, 17 St Anne's Court, London W1*

One of the numerous independent recording studios wh began to spread in Britain in the late sixties. During recording of *The Beatles* white album, the group decide try recording at Trident, which had the advantage of eight-track board. Unknown to them, **Abbey Road** received delivery of an eight-track deck, but it was currently in operation.

They began recording 'Hey Jude' at Trident Wednesday, 31 July, and hired Trident on 1, 2 an August 1968, before returning to Abbey Road. They w back at Trident for a six-day period from Tuesday October, during which they recorded 'Honey Pie', 'D Prudence', 'Savoy Truffle' and 'Martha My Dear'.

● Trocadero Cinema, The, *Camden Stre Liverpool L3*

Once a major city centre cinema, but it suffered the fat 95 per cent of Liverpool's cinemas – closure du shrinking audiences of the television age.

The 'Troc', as it was affectionately called, was **J Lennon**'s favourite cinema. When she and **Freddie** w married in 1938 they spent their honeymoon evenin the cinema and when the show ended for the night, J returned to her parents' home in Wavertree while Fre went back to his lodgings.

The cinema's name was changed to the **Gaumon** the 1950s and in 1964 was the setting for a receptio the film *Ferry 'Cross The Mersey*, which **Gerry Mars** attended as Guest of Honour. Pat Delaney, the **Cave** famous doorman, once mimed on stage there to ol Jolson records prior to a trailer for the film *Jolson S Again*.

● Troy, Doris

American R&B singer who had hits such as 'It's In Kiss' in the early sixties. After she joined **Billy Pre** for the recording of his first Apple album, she was si up to **Apple Records** herself and her single 'Ain't Cute' was produced by George Harrison, who also co-w the song with Doris. The flipside was 'Vaya Con Dios' the single was issued in Britain on Apple 24 o February 1970 and in America on Apple 1820 o March.

She only recorded one album for Apple, *Doris Troy*,

re were a number of prominent musicians who formed with her on the LP, including George Harrison, go Starr, **Jackie Lomax**, Steven Stills and **Klaus orman.** Of the numbers on the album, George arranged ob's Ladder' and co-wrote 'Gonna Get My Baby Back'. also played guitar on 'Vaya Con Dios'. George, Ringo Steven Stills penned the album tracks 'Give Me Joy ' and 'Gonna Get My Baby Back'.

Truth

ish duo comprising Steve Gold and Frank Aiello. The r were with **Dick James** in his office one day ussing the possibility of having a Beatles number for ir third single, following two unsuccessful record ases. Their manager, Jeff, was sitting in the outer office n Paul McCartney walked in and asked him for a light. considered this a good omen and when Truth issued l', a single taken from the *Rubber Soul* album, on 2 ruary 1966, it reached No. 18 in the charts, remaining he charts for a total of five weeks, providing the group their biggest hit.

Tuesday Rendezvous

e of a television programme produced by Associated-iffusion. The Beatles appeared live on the programme 4 December 1962, which was recorded at the pany's studios in Kingsway, London, during which promoted 'Love Me Do'.

hey appeared on another live performance of the gramme on 9 April 1963.

Twenty Flight Rock

umber which **Eddie Cochran** performed in the film *Girl Can't Help It*. This was the film that was to uence John, Paul and George. They included the ber in their repertoire.

20 Greatest Hits

had originally planned to bring out an extra special m to celebrate the twentieth anniversary of the les' recording career. This album was to be called *The les Greatest Hits* and it would feature 26 tracks – all f the Beatles' original singles, together with the tional four tracks from the double-'A' sided singles. ase was set for 11 October 1982 on EMTV 34 and the m was to be advertised on British television.

The company then changed its mind and issued a twenty-track album. This was the first of the Beatles compilation albums to feature their singles tracks only and on release it reached No. 9 in the British charts.

The sleeve was designed by Roy Kohara and Peter Shea and the inside of the gatefold sported a collage of photographs by Chuck Ames.

The tracks on the album were, Side One: 'Love Me Do', 'From Me To You', 'She Loves You', 'I Want To Hold Your Hand', 'Can't Buy Me Love', 'A Hard Day's Night', 'I Feel Fine', 'Ticket To Ride', 'Help!', 'Day Tripper', 'We Can Work It Out'. Side Two: 'Paperback Writer', 'Yellow Submarine', 'Eleanor Rigby', 'All You Need Is Love', 'Hello Goodbye', 'Lady Madonna', 'Hey Jude', 'Get Back' and 'The Ballad Of John And Yoko'.

Although maintaining the same sleeve design, the **Capitol** release of *20 Greatest Hits* had a different track listing. This was because the No. 1 singles in America differed slightly from the British ones – there were twenty No. 1 records in the States and only seventeen in Britain. Also, the American charts included chart entries for both sides of a single. The Capitol listing featured all twenty American No. 1 hits – all million sellers – and was issued on Capitol SV-12245 in October 1982. The tracks were, Side One: 'She Loves You', 'Love Me Do', 'I Want To Hold Your Hand', 'Can't Buy Me Love', 'A Hard Day's Night', 'I Feel Fine', 'Eight Days A Week', 'Ticket To Ride', 'Help!', 'Yesterday', 'We Can Work It Out', 'Paperback Writer'. Side Two: 'Penny Lane', 'All You Need Is Love', 'Hello Goodbye', 'Hey Jude', 'Get Back', 'Come Together', 'Let It Be' and 'The Long And Winding Road'.

● 21 Club, *New York City*

On Saturday, 8 February 1964, **Capitol Records** hosted a special dinner party for the Beatles at the prestigious 21 Club. George Harrison was absent due to his throat infection and Ringo quipped to one of the waiters, 'Do you have any vintage coke?' When asked at a press conference if they had enjoyed their dinner at the club, a journalist added, 'Did they feed you on pheasant and stuff?'

'Pheasant, you're joking! I had chops and chips,' was the reply.

● Twickenham Film Studios, *The Barons, Twickenham, Surrey*

Film facility on the outskirts of London which was used for

the filming of some interior scenes in *A Hard Day's Night* and *Help!* The promotional films for 'Hey Jude' and 'Revolution' were also made here.

The Beatles began filming *Let It Be* here from 2–17 January 1969. They weren't happy with the cold atmosphere of the place and were irked that they had to film from early in the morning when they would have preferred working in the early evening. George Harrison walked out for a time on 10 January and the group then decided to abandon the Twickenham location and complete their filming at the **Apple Studios** in **Savile Row**.

Ringo was back at Twickenham studios several weeks later when he began filming ***The Magic Christian*** with **Peter Sellers** at the beginning of March. Princess Margaret visited the set on 4 March and Paul and **Linda** were also there at the time.

● Twiggy

Born Lesley Hornby in London in September 1949, Twiggy was to become one of the leading fashion models of the Swinging Sixties. The first record she ever bought was 'Please Please Me' and she went to see the Beatles at **Finsbury Park Astoria** in 1963.

Once Twiggy was established as a model she sought to expand her career by becoming an actress. She and her manager, Justin De Villeneuve, thought that William Faulkner's *The Hanging Tree* would make a good film project for her and decided to approach the Beatles for backing. They met John and Paul in the Old Compton Street studio where they were editing *Magical Mystery Tour*.

Twiggy was to say: 'For me it was like meeting God. Paul was the one who was my hero; he was the one I'd stuck pictures of all over my desk at school and on my bedroom wall. At 13 it was him I'd screamed my head off for at the Finsbury Park Astoria. I was so excited to be meeting him at last, but trying to be cool. And he was lovely, just as I'd imagined, and he was the one I became most friends with. The Beatles did like the film idea, but we never managed to get it together.'

However, Paul suggested they contact Ken Russell, and Twiggy was later to star in his film *The Boyfriend*.

Twiggy commented in her autobiography *Twiggy*: 'I've stayed good friends with Paul and **Linda** McCartney. When Linda first came over here she didn't know anyone and I felt quite sorry for her and I'd take her shopping. We

Twiggy. (Arista)

:ame quite close.'

At one time the Beatles considered filming *Lord Of The* *gs* and intended giving Twiggy a prominent role.

In 1967, Twiggy toured America on behalf of Yardley metics. The master of ceremonies on her tour was Terry ight. Twiggy thought he was a talented singer and tarist and said, 'When we came back to England it was t the time when Paul McCartney was looking for neone to produce, and we'd earned a lot of money from tour so we paid Terry's air fare for him and we thought oring him over to Paul would be a nice break for him. : when he arrived here, imagine it, Paul and Linda had .e off to their Scottish hideaway and Paul had forgotten about the meeting. So poor Terry had to wait around a days, and then he got his flight back and that was the l of it.' Terry became a multimillionaire within two rs. He took over management of Grand Funk Railroad l later sent Twiggy back the cheque for the air flight.

In 1968 there were plans for Twiggy to tour Russia and nada Television intended making a documentary film he trip. Unfortunately, it fell through. Twiggy said, ul actually wrote a song for that trip to Russia that n't come off – and it was "Back In The USSR", which t on *The Beatles* white album. Justin was in Mr Chow's n Paul one night having dinner, and he said, "Hey, t about that song you were going to do for us when we e going to Russia?" and immediately Paul started ging it at the top of his voice.'

Twiggy, watching the talent contest 'Opportunity ocks' on television one night, noticed **Mary Hopkin** ging 'Turn, Turn, Turn'. Twiggy knew that Paul was cing for artists to promote. She said, 'It just happened that weekend we went to see Paul at his Dad's house Liverpool. He mentioned that he was looking for people ecord and I said, "Did you see that girl on 'Opportunity ocks?'" and Angie, his stepmother, said she'd seen it and we all hoped Mary would win or we wouldn't see the next week. So we all sat down and wrote cards for with our names – and we got about twenty people ied together to vote for her. She won easily. Paul ched the show, agreed she was wonderful and rang her immediately. She didn't believe it was him on the ne! But he sent a chauffeured car down to Wales for and then got together to make her name.'

After making *The Boyfriend*, Twiggy sought further s, and a film called *Gotta Sing, Gotta Dance* was planned. The name was inspired by the Gene Kelly song 'Broadway Melody', which contains the words 'Gotta Dance', and the story was to be set on a cruise liner in the thirties. But the film was never made. Paul wrote the title song for the film, which he never actually recorded. However, as the film project had been abandoned, Paul later used 'Gotta Sing, Gotta Dance' as the main dance spectacular in the 'James Paul McCartney' TV special.

● Twin Cities' Metropolitan Stadium, *Minneapolis, Minnesota*

The Beatles appeared before 25,000 people at this 45,000-seater auditorium during a single evening performance on Saturday, 21 August 1965.

The group had flown in from Chicago and their press conference that day was broadcast in its entirety by a local radio station. During the press reception George was presented with a brand new guitar, which he played during the evening's performance.

● Twist And Shout *(EP)*

The very first Beatles EP to be issued. Following the success of the Beatles' debut album and the first three singles, Parlophone decided to issue a release on the extended play format which comprised four tracks contained in a stiff picture sleeve cover.

On its release on Parlophone GEP 8882 on 2 July 1963 it reached No. 4 in the ***New Musical Express*** chart, the main British chart at the time, and became the very first EP ever to enter the Top Ten singles chart. It eventually sold over 800,000 copies in the UK and after slipping out of the charts after ten weeks, it reappeared in the charts for a further ten weeks. The tracks were: 'Twist And Shout', 'A Taste Of Honey', 'Do You Want To Know A Secret?' and 'There's A Place', all tracks from the *Please Please Me* album which was currently No. 1 in the album charts.

● Twist And Shout *(Single)*

At 10.00 p.m. on the evening of Monday, 11 February 1963, the marathon recording session for the *Please Please Me* album was nearly over, but they still needed one more song to complete the album. Everyone was gathered in the **Abbey Road** canteen discussing it, and 'Twist And Shout', which had been an American hit for the Isley Brothers in 1962 and included in the Beatles' repertoire the same year, was suggested. It had been written by Bert Berns, using a pseudonym Bert Russell, and Phil Medley.

As they'd been recording throughout the day their throats were sore, but John took some Zubes and ripped through the number in two takes, the first being selected as the album track.

Following the release of the album on 22 March 1963, **Brian Poole & the Tremeloes** released a single of 'Twist And Shout' on 28 June, which reached No. 4 in the charts. This was ironic considering that **Decca Records** had chosen to sign the Tremeloes rather than the Beatles and that the Tremeloes had been completely unsuccessful in the charts until they decided to cover this number from the Beatles album.

The Beatles' first EP release on GEP 8882, issued on 12 July 1963, was entitled *Twist And Shout*, and it also reached No. 4. It was the highest position ever reached by an EP in the British charts up to that date. The other tracks on the EP were 'A Taste Of Honey', 'Do You Want To Know A Secret' and 'There's A Place'.

The number was frequently featured on their BBC radio recordings and was included on four **'Pop Go The Beatles'** shows, plus **'The Talent Spot'**, **'Swinging Sound '63'**, **'The Beat Show'**, **'Easy Beat'** and **'Saturday Club'**.

A live version was included on *The Beatles At the Star Club* album and a further live recording was used on their *The Beatles At the Hollywood Bowl* album in 1976. It was also issued as the flipside of 'Back In The USSR' in June 1976 on a single to promote the release of the *Rock 'n' Roll Music* double album.

The number was also used as the powerful closing song at a number of their concert performances and they played it on their 'Sunday Night At The London Palladium' appearance in October 1963, their 'Royal Variety Show' performance in November 1963 and their **'Ed Sullivan Show'** television appearance in February 1964.

The song was also included on *Rock 'n' Roll* and *The Beatles Box* and *The Beatles Collection* sets.

In America **Vee Jay** included it on their *Introducing The Beatles* and *Songs, Pictures And Stories Of The Fabulous Beatles* albums. Vee Jay also issued it as a single on their Tollie label with 'There's A Place' on the flip. It was issued on Tollie 9001 on 2 March 1964 where it sped up the *Billboard* charts, reached the No. 2 position and sold a million copies within three weeks. **Capitol** also issued it with 'There's A Place' on the flip on Cap Starline 6061 on 11 October 1965, but it failed to chart.

• 200 Motels

Ringo Starr appeared in two roles, portraying both La the Dwarf and Frank Zappa in this 1971 movie, which described as a 'fantasy opera'. Produced by Jerry G and Herb Cohen, with a story and screenplay by **Fra Zappa**, it was directed by **Tony Palmer**, although it reported that he wasn't satisfied with the result and final credit read: 'Visuals directed by Tony Palmer'.

Ringo's chauffeur Martin Lickett also got a part in movie. He was told there were auditions for the role bass player. He attended, said he played bass and got part. Actor Theodore Bikel also appeared as the Rance Mohamets and **Keith Moon** played a nun overdoses on Mandrax.

The movie's 'band-on-the-road' theme was set i mythical town called Centreville. The Mothers of Invent arrive in Centreville and find it an extremely strange pl to be – at one end of town there is a concentration ca where an orchestra lives!

The movie was premiered in New York on 10 Novem 1971 but never received proper distribution in Britain.

• Two Of Us

A Paul McCartney composition, originally called 'On Way Home'. Recording of the number began on Friday January 1969, and the track was to open the *Let It* album.

It begins with John saying, '"I Dig A Pony" by Cha Hawtrey on the deaf aids. Phase one in which Doris her oats.' This is similar to remarks he made on one of versions of 'Dig It': 'That was "Can You Dig It" by Geo Wood, now we'd like to do "Hark The Angels Com (Charles Hawtrey was one of the 'Carry On' movie regu and Georgie Wood was a midget comedian.)

The number was recorded by a New York trio ca Mortimer (Guy Masson, Tony Van Benschoten and Smith) and intended for release as their debut single the **Apple Records** label. However, the Beatles wer confident about the record and it was never issued.

• Two Red Shoes Ballroom, *Elgin, Morayshire, Scotland*

The first date of the Beatles' second tour of Scotland

ursday, 3 January 1963. Originally, the tour was due to en on 2 January at the Longmore Hall, Keith, Banffre, but bad weather prevented the Beatles fulfilling the t booking and the tour had to be shortened to five days. e Scottish gigs had been booked by the Cana Variety Association in conjunction with Scottish promoter Albert Bonici. Due to the problems caused by extremely bad weather, the worst for decades, Brian Epstein offered Bonici the option of booking all future Beatles appearances in Scotland exclusively.

orge and John
ring the 'Let It Be'
ssions.
pple)

● University College Hospital, Gower Street, London WC1

Hospital to which Ringo Starr was admitted on 3 June 1964. Earlier that day he'd been taking part in a photographic session at a studio in Barnes. He collapsed and a local doctor examined him and found him to be suffering from tonsilitis and pharyngitis.

This was on the eve of the Beatles' world tour and a replacement had to be found. The drummer who deputized while Ringo was in hospital was **Jimmy Nicol**, 24-year-old former member of Georgie Fame & the Blue Flames. When he was discharged on Thursday, 11 June, Ringo joked, 'Everybody was just great to me. But don't tell John, Paul or George or they'll want to be ill too.'

Ringo returned to the hospital on 1 December that year to have his tonsils removed. He held an afternoon press conference at the hospital and the operation took place the next day. During his stay, he was visited by his Liverpool girl friend, **Maureen** Cox, and the couple were to marry a few months later.

Ringo was offered his tonsils as a souvenir, but declined.

George entered the same hospital for a tonsilectomy on 7 February 1969 and accepted their offer of the grisly souvenir, taking the tonsils home with him in a jar.

● 25 Upton Green, Speke, Liverpool L24

After eighteen years on the waiting list, the Harrison family moved in 1949 to a new council estate on the outskirts of Liverpool. With a bathroom and extra bedroom, it was a much superior dwelling to **Arno Grove** and on the first day there, George kept runni around the room in his excitement. It was situated at t end of a circular street, with a grass field in the cent Mrs **Louise Harrison**, however, particularly missed t friendliness of the Wavertree area and found t neighbours lacked the warmth of those at the previc address. Their stay here lasted exactly ten years.

● Van Gelder, Dick

The Dutch impresario who was responsible for bring the Beatles to the Netherlands. He'd originally contac Brian Epstein in 1963 seeking to book the band appearances in Holland, but Brian said that they had many commitments and the earliest they could app would be in June 1964 as part of their world tour. T contract was signed and just as the Beatles were due to out to Denmark on the first leg of the tour, Rir collapsed. The Beatles finally arrived on 5 June to app in two concerts at Blokker the next day.

● Vara Broadcasting Corporation

Dutch television company which filmed the Beatles dur their trip to Holland in 1964.

The group were signed to appear on the show by J Sims, the chief executive of the Vara Broadcast Company. They filmed the group at the **Treslo Studios**, Hillegom, 25 miles outside Amsterdam on evening of 5 June 1964, and the show was broadcast o June. The group performed 'She Loves You', 'Twist A Shout', 'All My Loving', 'Roll Over Beethoven', 'Long ' Sally' and 'Can't Buy Me Love'.

They stayed overnight at the **Doelen Hotel** in O Doelen Street in Amsterdam and later toured the red li district. In the morning they began a canal tour at 11 a.m. The event was covered by Vara and broadcast live the radio, with interviewer Herman Stok covering the tr

● Vartan, Sylvie

A blonde-haired French *chanteuse* of the sixties who married to France's rock 'n' roll idol Johnny Hollic Sylvie co-starred with the Beatles and **Trini Lopez** at **Olympia**, **Paris**, from 16 January–4 February 1964. ' predominantly male audience were as enthusiastic al the performance of the attractive young singer as they w about *Les Beatles*.

Vaughan, Ivan

boy from the Woolton area of Liverpool. He lived in Vale reet, along with **Pete Shotton** and **Nigel Whalley**, and e three of them became part of a small gang, together th John Lennon, who lived close by.

When he was six years old, Ivan attended Dovedale imary School, along with John. In 1952 he moved to the verpool Institute where he was in the same class as ul McCartney.

Ivan played tea-chest bass occasionally in the **Quarry en**, alternating with Len Garry. One day he asked Paul if 'd like to come along and watch the group at a church e. Paul wasn't particularly struck on the idea, but Ivan id that it would be a great place to pick up girls, so Paul cled along to the event that afternoon. The date was 6 ly 1957 and when Paul arrived at **St Peter's Church** rden Fete, Ivan took him into the church hall and roduced him to John.

Ivan kept in touch with his friends, particularly Paul, er the succeeding years. He became a teacher and idied Education Psychiatry. When Apple was launched, Beatles suggested that Ivan and his schoolteacher wife ad the proposed Apple School. Ivan was given an vance payment of £10,000 but it was decided that the ea was premature and the scheme was dropped. Ivan's fe helped Paul with the French section of 'Michelle'.

Tragically, during the seventies Ivan contracted a rrific ailment, Parkinson's Disease, for which there is no own cure. Ivan refused to accept the situation, bravely ttling against the disease by using himself as a guinea g for new drugs, mercilessly knocking his limbs against lid objects when they refused to respond. Jonathan ller heard of his remarkable and courageous struggle d produced a documentary, simply called 'Ivan', which s transmitted on BBC 2 TV on 3 December 1984 as part the 'Horizon' series. Paul had granted the use of his ng 'Blackbird' to be played at the beginning and end of e programme, free of charge, and an associate mmented: 'Paul was devastated by what has happened Ivan. They have known each other since they were kids. in was the lad who introduced Paul to John. He used to ly tea-chest bass in John's skiffle group the Quarry Men. went to America with them in the sixties.'

Paul invited Ivan to spend Christmas 1984 with the Cartneys at their home in Sussex.

Of the documentary, which centred on a day in his life, Ivan commented: 'I decided to make my illness my hobby. Not as something useful. Not to help thousands. Just selfishly, to find out all I could about it and its implications. I wanted to explore it, to play with it, and even to laugh about it.'

In 1986 his book *Ivan: Living With Parkinson's Disease* was published in Britain by Macmillan.

● Vee Jay Records

An independent American label which had enjoyed success in the States with the release of some British singles – the **Frank Ifield** hits 'I Remember You' and 'Lovesick Blues'. In 1963 Barbara Gardener, the head of the International division of the company, arrived in London to negotiate the release of albums by Chris Barber and the Alex Bradford Gospel Group.

While in London she was approached to release Beatles products in America due to the fact that **Capitol** had turned the opportunity down. On 21 January 1963 she signed a short-term agreement to release Beatles records in America on the Vee Jay label.

The first Beatles record to be issued was 'Please Please Me' coupled with 'Ask Me Why' on 25 February 1963. It didn't chart. They next issued 'From Me To You' coupled with 'Thank You Girl', but considered its highest placing, No. 116 in *Billboard*, to be unsuccessful. The single was also made 'Pick Of the Week' in *Cash Box* magazine.

The final Vee Jay release that year was the album *Introducing The Beatles*, which they issued on 22 July 1963. This also failed to register and Vee Jay were reputed to have turned down the opportunity of continuing issuing Beatles products and 'She Loves You' went to the Swan label. However, this was not strictly correct. A music licensing firm in New York called Trans-Global cancelled Vee Jay's right to release products on 8 August 1963 because they had not paid royalties for the first two Beatles releases. Trans-Global also informed Vee Jay that they no longer had licensing rights to the Beatles tracks for 'Love Me Do' and 'P.S. I Love You'. This caused problems for Vee Jay, who had already pressed the album *Introducing The Beatles*, which contained the two numbers. To have destroyed all the albums would have caused the company to go bankrupt, so they went ahead with the release, but did not list any of the tracks on the back cover of the album.

When the Beatles seemed set to become a major chart

act, Vee Jay set about re-releasing the limited Beatles products they had and used ingenuity in issuing a string of singles and albums, beginning with the *Introducing The Beatles* album on 27 January 1964, which reached No. 2 in the *Billboard* and *Cash Box* charts and No. 1 in the *Record World* chart. Three days later, on 30 January 1964 they issued the single 'Please Please Me' c/w 'From Me To You' which reached No. 3 in all three trade charts.

Vee Jay realized that to take advantage of the limited number of Beatles tracks they had, they needed to issue them in as many different formats as possible and next issued *Jolly What! The Beatles And Frank Ifield On Stage* on 26 February 1964. This was an album comprising a number of the **Frank Ifield** tracks on their catalogue with four Beatles tracks. The album only reached No. 104 in the charts. For their next release they took an unusual step. EPs weren't a popular format in America and were extremely rare. Vee Jay noticed how popular EPs were in Britain and decided to release four of the *Introducing The Beatles* tracks as an EP, with a special cardboard cover, which they called *Souvenir Of Their Visit To America: The Beatles*. Initially, the EP was issued in a cardboard sleeve at $1.29 on 23 March 1964. As this was an unusual price for a record they then issued it in an ordinary paper sleeve at the usual price of a single and claimed that they sold a million copies. This is quite possible, even though the EP didn't register in any of the main charts. Since EPs weren't generally issued in America, the trade magazines may not have included the EP in their chart figures.

Using the same cover picture as the *Souvenir* EP (paintings of the heads of Ringo, George, John and Paul), they issued the single 'Do You Want To Know A Secret' c\w 'Thank You Girl' on 23 March 1964, the same day as the EP, and the single went to No. 2 in *Billboard* and No. 3 in *Cash Box* and *Record World*.

On 10 August they issued four Beatles singles in a reissue series called 'Oldies 45', but none of them registered in the charts. They were 'Do You Want To Know A Secret?' c/w 'Thank You Girl', 'Please Please Me' c/w 'From Me To You', 'Love Me Do' c/w 'P.S. I Love You' and 'Twist And Shout' c/w 'There's A Place'.

Still utilizing their tracks from *Introducing the Beatles*, they repackaged them in a double album with tracks by the Four Seasons and issued *The Beatles vs The Four Seasons* on 1 October 1964. The album only reached No. 142 in the charts. Undaunted, within two weeks Vee Jay had issued yet another repackaging of the *Introducing T Beatles* tracks called *Songs, Pictures And Stories Of t Fabulous Beatles* on 12 October 1964. This reached N 100 in *Cash Box*, No. 79 in *Record World* and No. 63 *Billboard*. It was the final Vee Jay release. The compa had been plagued by problems since Capitol had realiz the potential of the Beatles and in January 1964, **EMI** music publishing company, Ardmore & Beechwood Musi attempted to obtain a court order restraining Vee J records from issuing 'Love Me Do' and 'P.S. I Love Yo on an album. They maintained that Trans-Global, wl were licensed to distribute EMI products in America, h cancelled the Vee Jay agreement on 8 August 19 because of the non-payment of royalties due from the fi two Beatles singles issued by Vee Jay. As a result, Tran Global relinquished its rights to their tracks to EMI a they were then acquired by Capitol Records.

A restraining order was placed on Vee Jay and i managing director Jay Lasker said that they had ceas shipping Beatles products because of it, but were to ta legal action as he considered they had a five-year contr with the Beatles and they were not in default for not payi the royalties. They took out a law suit against both Capi Records and Swan, who were also issuing Beatles produ at the time. The legal representatives of both Capitol a Vee Jay decided to settle the matter between themselv due to the complications which could arise from the le suits. It was agreed that *Introducing The Beatles* could reissued if the two Ardmore & Beechwood tracks we removed. Vee Jay replaced the two tracks with 'Plea Please Me' and 'Ask Me Why'.

However, the legal problems didn't go away. Capi considered that Vee Jay had violated their agreement altering and repackaging *Introducing The Beatles Songs, Pictures And Stories Of The Fabulous Beatles*. A result, a trial without jury took place on 15 July 1964 which Vee Jay pointed out that their 9 April 1964 licen did not mention that they could not repackage the Beatl product they had. Capitol disagreed, saying that Vee J had breached the agreement by presenting the album different packaging. On 23 July, Judge Mervyn A. Aggel announced:

'The court finds in favour of Vee Jay Records on all t issues raised in their cross-complaint.

'Vee Jay Records has the unqualified right to adverti and promote the covered masters in any cover, jacket ckage which Vee Jay Records, Inc., deems appropriate.

'Vee Jay has the unqualified right to advertise, sell and omote the long playing album in the type of jacket, a py of which is attached to Vee Jay Records complaint, arked as Exhibit C.

'Capitol Records and Beechwood Music, Inc., are rmanently restrained from declaring that promotion of e long playing record *Introducing The Beatles*, in the designed jacket, constitutes or will constitute a breach in ntracts, the License Agreement and Mechanical License th dated April 9 1965.'

As a result, Vee Jay were allowed to release Beatles cords they had masters of in any form until 15 October 64. After that time they no longer had the right to issue y Beatles product.

Vee Jay also had a subsidiary label called Tollie, on iich they issued some Beatles singles. The first Tollie lease was 'Twist And Shout' c/w 'There's A Place', sued on 2 March 1964. These tracks from the *troducing The Beatles* album went to No. 1 in *Cash Box* d *Record World* and No. 2 in *Billboard*. The second llie release was 'Love Me Do' c/w 'P.S. I Love You' on llie 9008 on 27 April 1964, which topped all three trade arts and was a million-seller.

Vee Jay Discography (In chronological order)

lease Please Me' c/w 'Ask Me Why', Vee Jay 498, 25 bruary 1963.

om Me To You' c/w 'Thank You Girl', Vee Jay 522, 27 ay 1963.

troducing The Beatles, Vee Jay 1062, 22 July 1963. acks: 'I Saw Her Standing There', 'Misery', 'Anna (Go Him)', 'Chains', 'Boys', 'Love Me Do', 'P.S. I Love u', 'Baby, It's You', 'Do You Want To Know A Secret?', Taste of Honey', 'There's A Place', 'Twist And Shout'.

troducing The Beatles, VJLP 1062, 27 January 1964. acks: 'I Saw Her Standing There', 'Misery', 'Anna (Go Him)', 'Chains', 'Boys', 'Ask Me Why', 'Please Please ', 'Baby, It's You', 'Do You Want To Know A Secret?', Taste Of Honey', 'There's A Place', 'Twist And Shout'.

ease Please Me' c/w 'From Me To You', VJ 581, 30 nuary 1964.

Jolly What! The Beatles And Frank Ifield On Stage, VJLP 1085, 26 February 1964.Beatles tracks: 'Please Please Me', 'From Me To You', 'Ask Me Why', 'Thank You Girl'.

'Twist And Shout', Tollie 9001, 2 March 1964.

Souvenir Of Their Visit To America: The Beatles. VJLP 1-902 Vee Jay, 23 March 1964. Tracks: 'Misery', 'A Taste Of Honey', 'Ask Me Why', 'Anna (Go To Him)'.

'Do You Want To Know A Secret?' c/w 'Thank You Girl', VJ 587 Vee Jay, 23 March 1964.

'Love Me Do' c/w 'P.S. I Love You', Tollie 9008, 27 April 1964.

'Do You Want To Know A Secret?' c/w 'Thank You Girl', OL 149 Oldies 45, 10 August 1964.

'Please Please Me' c/w 'From Me To You', OL 150 Oldies 45, 10 August 1964.

'Love Me Do' c/w 'P.S. I Love You', OL 151 Oldies 45, 10 August 1964.

'Twist And Shout' c/w 'There's A Place', OL 152 Oldies 45, 10 August 1964.

The Beatles vs The Four Seasons.VJDX 30 Vee Jay, 1 October 1964. Beatles tracks: 'I Saw Her Standing There', 'Misery', 'Anna (Go To Him)', 'Chains', 'Boys', 'Ask Me Why', 'Please Please Me', 'Baby, It's You', 'Do You Want To Know A Secret?', 'A Taste Of Honey', 'There's A Place', 'Twist And Shout'.

Songs, Pictures And Stories Of The Fabulous Beatles.VJLP 1092 Vee Jay, 12 October 1964. Beatles tracks: 'I Saw Her Standing There', 'Misery', 'Anna (Go To Him)', 'Chains', 'Boys', 'Ask Me Why', 'Please Please Me', 'Baby, It's You', 'Do You Want To Know A Secret?', 'A Taste Of Honey', 'There's A Place', 'Twist And Shout'.

● Velodromo, Vigorelli, Milan, Italy

The Beatles performed two shows at this venue on 24 June 1965. The appearances were part of their fourteen-day European tour and the first of only three Italian venues which the Beatles visited in their entire career. Despite the popularity of the group in the Italian charts, their live appearances didn't draw a fraction of the response they received in English-speaking countries and the Italian gigs didn't prove to be sell-outs.

Although there were 700 police and 400 guards to control the crowds at this open-air 22,000-seater stadium, only 7,000 people attended the afternoon show. There was a better response in the evening, with an audience of 20,000, although they still did not fill the stadium's capacity.

The repertoire was the same throughout their entire European fortnight: 'Twist And Shout', 'She's A Woman', 'I'm A Loser', 'Can't Buy Me Love', 'Baby's In Black', 'I Wanna Be Your Man', 'A Hard Day's Night', 'Everybody's Trying To Be My Baby', 'Rock And Roll Music', 'I Feel Fine', 'Ticket To Ride' and 'Long Tall Sally'.

● Vernons Girls, The

A female vocal group, originally formed in December 1961 and sponsored by the Liverpool Football Pools firm of Vernons. There were various personnel changes during the career of the group, whose major hit was 'Lover Please', which reached No. 16 in 1962. Other chart hits included 'You Know What I Mean', 'Loco Motion', 'Funny All Over' and 'Do The Bird'. The group survived as a trio for some years and appeared with the Beatles on a special Merseyside edition of the TV show **'Thank Your Lucky Stars'** on 21 December 1963 with fellow Liverpudlians **Cilla Black**, the **Searchers**, **Billy J. Kramer** and **Gerry & the Pacemakers**. The Vernons Girls also appeared on a five-week British tour with the Beatles and in 1964 issued a single called 'We Want The Beatles'.

● Vero, Diana

A secretary to Brian Epstein in the London offices of **NEMS Enterprises**. She first met the Beatles during a recording of **'Thank Your Lucky Stars'** and within a year was Brian's secretary. She travelled to America as part of the Beatles entourage during their 1964 tour.

● Victoria Hall, Village Road, Bebington, Wirral L63

A relatively isolated venue, which is probably why very few Mersey Beat bands ever played there. The Beatles only appeared at the hall once, on 4 August 1962.

● Veilinghal, Blokker, Holland

The Beatles only appeared in Holland once. The eve took place on 6 June 1964 on their second appearan during their 25-day world tour.

The group performed two shows at the 7,000-seat venue. The afternoon show was not fully attende although the evening show was completely sold out and t audience sang along with the Beatles.

● Village Hall, Thingwall Road, Irby, Heswall, Wirral L61

The Beatles appeared once at this venue on the Wir peninsula, which also housed the Newton Dancing Scho on 7 September 1962.

George joins Ringo on drums. (*Mersey Beat* Archives)

The legendary rock 'n' roller Gene Vincent, with his original band, the Blue Caps. (National Film Archives)

Vincent, Gene

ıe of the Beatles' favourite rock 'n' roll stars. Soon after ͽ **Quarry Men** formed they included Vincent's major 'Be-Bop-A-Lula' in their repertoire (Paul wrote out the ·rds to this song for John on their first meeting). His ance In The Street' was also a part of their early stage t and his haunting version of 'Somewhere Over The .inbow', which he performed on the 3 May 1960 concert **Liverpool Stadium**, attended by John, Paul, George d **Stuart**, was also incorporated into their repertoire.

Gene Vincent's 1956 rock interpretation of 'Ain't She eet' was also an inspiration and John began performing vith the Quarry Men.

When the Beatles first went to Hamburg, drummer **ːte Best** was to observe, 'John did his best to imitate ne Vincent, grabbing up the microphone as if he were ng to lay into the audience with it.'

Vincent was born Vincent Eugene Craddock in Norfolk, rginia, on 11 February 1935. In 1955 his leg was ıshed in a motorbike accident and the callipered leg ıtinued to pain him throughout his life. After a number of hits in America he was brought to Britain to appear on several TV shows and decided to make his home in England. He was touring with **Eddie Cochran** when they were both involved in a road accident in which Cochran died. Shortly afterwards, Vincent made his Liverpool Stadium appearance.

The Beatles met their idol in Hamburg in April 1962 when both acts appeared at the **Star Club** and they became friends. John even asked Vincent for his autograph. When later asked by **Sounds Incorporated** what Hamburg was like, Vincent told them, 'Oh, it's OK there. I had a nice band backing me up. They're called the Beatles.'

Gene also appeared with the Beatles at the **Cavern** on 1 July 1962, backed by Sounds Incorporated. **Mike McCartney** took a photograph of Vincent with John and Paul, in which all of them are wearing black leather jackets.

The American rock 'n' roll star appeared in Liverpool on a number of occasions and during a visit in 1964 he told ***Mersey Beat***, 'I sing rock 'n' roll because the kids always seem to have liked it – anyway, the stuff the Beatles sing is just rock 'n' roll, but a bit noisier.'

Vincent died of cardiac failure in 1971.

● Vinton, Bobby

The singer who was replaced at the top of the American charts by the Beatles' 'I Want To Hold Your Hand'. Prior to Vinton's hit there had only been five No. 1 records by non-American acts, after it the Beatles and the British Invasion changed it from a purely American dominated one, to an almost Anglo-American chart.

With the coming of the Beatles, the recording careers of many established American artists began to decline. Vinton, however, was one of the survivors and he was back in the No. 1 position in December 1964 with 'Mr Lonely'.

Commenting on the way that the emergence of the Beatles changed the nature of the charts, Vinton said, 'In a way, they may have helped me because they wiped out all of my competition. There were no more male singers in America.'

Vinton's manager was **Allen Klein** and Vinton recommended him to the English bands hence Klein began to represent the Animals and Herman's Hermits. Later he was to represent the Rolling Stones and eventually the Beatles themselves.

When Ringo Starr was a guest on '**Juke Box Jury**' he listened to Vinton's single 'There I've Said It Again' and described it as ideal, 'if you're sitting in one night and not alone'.

● Viscounts, The

A British male vocal group who were added to the bill of the **Chris Montez/Tommy Roe** tour promoted by **Arthur Howes** and featuring the Beatles, in 1963.

The vocal outfit had enjoyed two minor chart hits, 'Short'nin' Bread' in 1960 and 'Who Put The Bomp' in 1961.

● Voormann, Klaus

The son of a Berlin doctor, Klaus moved to Hamburg in 1956 to study art. His girlfriend was a pale, blonde-haired girl called **Astrid Kirchherr** and after having a minor argument with her one day, he walked along the Grosse Freiheit in St Pauli where he was attracted by the sound of rock 'n' roll music performed by **Rory Storm & the Hurricanes** at the **Kaiserkeller** club.

He went inside to listen and was even more intrigu by the next group to appear – the Beatles. In h excitement he talked Astrid into joining him and, despi her reluctance, brought her down to the seedy district listen to the group.

They both became wrapped up in the band and stru up a conversation with them, in spite of their poor Englis In one attempt to communicate, Klaus brought along so record covers he'd designed. Soon they encouraged oth students to join them and youngsters began to pour into Pauli to see 'der Peedles'.

Astrid left Klaus for the frail-looking bass guitar **Stuart Sutcliffe**, but this didn't alter Klaus's interest the group. He kept in touch with them, even travelling Liverpool to meet them on their home ground and wh they were based in London he went to live in Englar taking up the same instrument as Stu Sutcliffe – ba guitar.

He teamed up with two Liverpool musicians, Pad Chambers and Gibson Kemp, to form **Paddy, Klaus Gibson**, and they had their first single, 'I Wanna Kno issued by Pye on 9 July 1965. For a time Brian Epst managed the group, but they disbanded and Klaus join Manfred Mann.

In the meantime he continued producing artwork a was invited by the Beatles to design the cover of th *Revolver* album, for which he won a **Grammy Award.** also designed a number of lithographs illustrating songs the *Ringo* album and did the artwork for the cover George Harrison's *Wonderwall* album.

When Paul McCartney made the public announcem that he was leaving the Beatles, there were rumours t John, George and Ringo were going to replace him w Klaus and call themselves the Ladders. Klaus was invit to meet John, George and Ringo at the Apple offices on March 1971, a few days after the High Court had gran Paul victory in the first round of his battle to disband t Beatles. On 20 March a story appeared in the *Daily Mir* suggesting that Klaus was to be the new replacement Paul. On 26 March Apple issued a press stateme denying that the three were to continue as a group, w the addition of Klaus.

Over the years he performed on many recor supporting the Beatles on their solo projects and becam popular guest at Beatle conventions before returning Hamburg to become a recording manager.

W

Wait

[Nu]mber jointly written by John and Paul and featured on [th]e *Rubber Soul* album. The number was actually recorded [on] Thursday, 17 June 1965, during the *Help!* album [se]ssions.

Walker Art Gallery, The, *William Brown [St]reet, Liverpool L1*

[Liv]erpool's main, prestigious art gallery. In the late fifties [art] students such as John Lennon, **Cynthia** Powell, **Stuart [Su]tcliffe** and Bill Harry would regularly visit the Walker [to] view the paintings and also to study in the gallery's [lib]rary.

The major *John Moore's Exhibition* was held annually [at] the gallery and the 1959 event led to Stuart Sutcliffe [be]coming a member of the Beatles. John Lennon had [off]ered both Stuart and fellow art student **Rod Murray** [th]e chance of becoming bass guitarist for the group; [wh]oever won the position was dependent upon which of [the]m could come forward first with a bass guitar. One of [Stu]art's paintings was selected for the exhibition and it [wa]s bought by John Moores himself, the founder of the [fa]mous Littlewoods football pools. With the £65 he [rec]eived for the painting, Stuart bought his bass and [bec]ame a member of the group.

Following Stuart's death, his mother Millie organized a [po]sthumous exhibition at the gallery. It took place from [...]24 May 1964 and drew in more than 11,000 visitors. [Mr]s Sutcliffe was sad that no member of the Beatles could [att]end the exhibition although she wasn't to know at the time that they'd all left to go on their holidays on the day the exhibition opened. John and Cynthia, and George and **Pattie** to Honolulu and Paul and **Jane**, and Ringo and **Maureen** to the Virgin Islands.

The most successful exhibition at the gallery was *The Art Of The Beatles*, which was conceived by Ron Jones, organized by **Mike Evans** and presented by the Merseyside County Council. The exhibition ran from May to September 1984, and drew almost 50,000 visitors. The exhibition comprised a large selection of paintings, sculptures, photographs, drawings, record sleeves, posters and other material relating to the Beatles. Among the artists, photographers and sculptors contributing to the exhibition were: Stuart Sutcliffe, John Lennon, **Astrid Kirchherr**, Adrian Henri, **Peter Blake**, Alan Aldridge, Andy Warhol, John Bratby, David Oxtoby, **Cynthia Lennon**, **Dezo Hoffmann**, **Linda McCartney**, **Mike McCartney**, **Robert Freeman**, **Peter Kaye**, Graham Spencer and **Richard Avedon**.

The gallery owns a painting by Stuart Sutcliffe called *Hamburg Painting No. 2*, but it is not normally on display.

● Walletjes, *Amsterdam, Holland*

The red light district of Amsterdam, although a place not as notorious as Hamburg's St Pauli district. The Beatles visited Walletjes on the evening of 5 June 1964.

The area is in a picturesque setting alongside the city's canals and is crowded with brothels and sex shops. The Beatles had several drinks and decided to visit some. There was a photograph taken of John crawling out of the doorway of one of the brothels on his hands and knees. Commenting on the incident in the book *Lennon Remembers*, he says: 'There are photographs of me in which I am crawling on my knees through Amsterdam while I'm coming out of a brothel or something and people are saying, "Good morning, John!" and the police escorted us to those places and all that. They didn't want a scandal.'

● Walters, Lu

Lu, whose real name was Walter Eymond, was the bass guitarist/vocalist with **Rory Storm & the Hurricanes**, regarded as one of Liverpool's leading bands.

The bespectacled singer had been a member of the group since their formation at the end of the fifties as the Raving Texans. Their drummer was Ringo Starr.

In 1960 the Hurricanes were appearing at the

Lu Walters, member of Rory Storm & the Hurricanes – a man who sang with the Beatles.

Kaiserkeller in Hamburg at the same time as the Beatles. In fact, the Beatles had been appearing at the **Indra Club**, a smaller venue than the Kaiserkeller, but were then moved further up the Grosse Freiheit where the posters proclaimed: 'Original Rock 'n' Roll Bands. RORY STORM And His HURICAN und The Beatles. England. Liverpool.'

Earlier in the month Lu had visited the Indra to watch the Beatles and took to the stage to sing several numbers with them. **Allan Williams** was watching the show and was so impressed with Lu's singing that he arranged for him to make a record in a local studio with the Beatles backing him.

Reputedly, **Pete Best** was not feeling well at the time and the Hurricanes' drummer Ringo replaced him for the session which took place at the record-your-voice booth of **Akustik Studio** at 57 Kirchenalle, just behind Hamburg Central Station, on Saturday 15 October 1960.

Lu, together with John, George, Paul and Ringo, recorded 'Summertime'. It was the first time the quartet who were to be known as **'The Fab Four'** played together.

After the session the Beatles asked Williams if they could record a few numbers themselves with Ringo, but without Lu. Williams, who had paid ten pounds for the session, refused to spend any more money.

Several copies of the disc were made. Williams lost his copy over a decade later when he left it behind him in a London pub.

● Walton Hospital, *107 Rice Lane, Liverpool 9*

Paul McCartney was born here on 18 June 1942. H mother had previously been a nursing sister on t maternity ward there and, as a result, she was given private room.

When **Jim McCartney** first saw his newborn son thought that the baby looked terrible and commented, 'I had one eye open and he just squawked all the time. Th held him up and he looked like a horrible piece of r meat.'

● Warwick Hotel, *Corner of 6th Avenue and 54th Street, New York City*

The Beatles had originally resided at the **Plaza Ho** when visiting New York in 1964, but had changed to t Warwick in 1965. When the Beatles arrived in New Yo for their third American tour, **Cilla Black** was appeari at the Persian Room in the Plaza Hotel and oth celebrities who were staying there, such as Diana Do had expected the Beatles to return to the Plaza.

The group flew out from London on Friday, 13 Aug 1965, and were taken by limousine to the Warwick. 2.30 p.m. they took part in a press conference in the ho conference hall, which was attended by several hundr journalists. The reception went on for an hour: Paul w asked if he had been secretly married to **Jane Asher** a George was asked if he were marrying **Pattie**. When th were asked why they were staying at the Warwick inste of the Plaza, Ringo said, 'We can't afford those price John mentioned that he'd bought his Aunt **Mimi** bungalow in Poole and Ringo was presented with antique sword and a pikestaff in celebration of his rec birthday.

During their stay at the hotel they had many visito including **Bob Dylan**, the Supremes, the Crystals a **Del Shannon**. Dylan introduced them to marijua Among the media at the hotel was **Don Short** of the *Da Mirror*, music journalist Judy Sims, Chris Hutchins of t ***New Musical Express***, **Brian Matthew** of Radio C and disc jockeys **Larry Kane** and Jim Stagg.

The group had a suite on the 33rd floor and host members of the American Fan Club who had been broug along by **Bernice Young**, the Fan Club President. Dur their stay at the hotel the Beatles were also presented w a gold record for their *Beatles VI* album.

Washington Coliseum, Washington DC

sports stadium which became the venue for the Beatles' rst live outdoor concert appearance in America on 11 ebruary 1964. The concert had been booked by **Norman 'eiss** of General Artists Corporation and promoted by arry Lynn.

The group were due to fly down to Washington from ew York, but there was a snowstorm. The Beatles refused fly in a blizzard, remembering what had happened **Buddy Holly** a few years earlier, so arrangements ere made for them to travel down in a private train ach from Pennsylvania Station in New York to Union ation in Washington. When they arrived there ere 3,000 fans at the station, but they were prevented m approaching the Beatles by the twenty-foot platform tes.

The group were rushed to the Shoreham Hotel. The tire seventh floor had been booked for the group and eir entourage, but one family had refused to move out of eir room. While the Beatles were at the Coliseum the sistant manager cut off the family's light, heat and water d told them there had been a power failure on the venth floor. They agreed to be relocated to the ninth or.

The Beatles took to the stage at 8.31 p.m., following ts such as **Tommy Roe** and the **Chiffons**. They rformed from a rotating stage and the noise was so afening that they couldn't even hear themselves rform. They were pelted by jelly beans for the first time. ılike the soft British jelly babies, the beans were covered a hard shell and rained down on them like bullets.

They performed 'Roll Over Beethoven', 'From Me To u', 'I Saw Her Standing There', 'This Boy', 'All My ving', 'I Wanna Be Your Man', 'Please Please Me', 'Till ere Was You', 'She Loves You', 'I Want To Hold Your and', 'Twist And Shout' and 'Long Tall Sally'. mediately after they finished their act they rushed to eir dressing-rooms surrounded by a phalanx of twelve licemen. A happy Ringo exclaimed, 'They could have ped me apart and I couldn't have cared less. What an dience! I could have played for them all night.'

A camera team from CBS was present filming the ncert for a special closed circuit presentation to be reened at cinemas on 14 and 15 March. The film, titled *Live At The Washington Coliseum*, featured 'Roll er Beethoven', 'From Me To You', 'I Saw Her Standing There', 'This Boy', 'All My Loving' and 'I Wanna Be Your Man'. The ending came part way through a version of 'Twist And Shout' because the cameraman had run out of film!

Washington DC Stadium, 2001 E Capitol Street, Washington DC

The Beatles' final tour of America was fraught with tension due to the hostile atmosphere created by the reaction to the 'Beatles are bigger than Christ' interview. Outside the stadium, dressed in full robes, stalked the Imperial Wizard of the Maryland Clan and five klansmen from Prince George's County Ku Klux Klan.

The show began at 6.00 p.m. before an audience of 32,164 fans. Other acts on the bill were the **Cyrkle**, the **Ronettes**, the **Remains** and Bobby Webb.

Webb, Bernard

The pseudonym which Paul McCartney used when he wrote the number 'Woman' for **Peter & Gordon**. Bernard Webb was credited as songwriter on the actual record, but when it entered the charts a few weeks later, eventually reaching No. 21, Paul admitted that he'd written it but wanted to see if he could enter the charts without using the magical Lennon & McCartney name. Webb was said to be an aspiring songwriter and a student in Paris.

Paul also used the pseudonym A. Smith for the American release.

We Can Work It Out

It has been suggested that **Jane Asher** was once again Paul's inspiration when he wrote this song and, again, John helped him out with the song's middle section.

The number had the distinction of being the Beatles' very first double 'A' side, with 'Day Tripper', and was issued in Britain on 3 December 1965 on Parlophone R5389, leaping straight to the top of the charts. In America it came out on 6 December 1965, where it sold a million and also topped the charts.

It was included on *A Collection of Beatles Oldies (But Goldies)*, *The Beatles 1962–1966*, *The Beatles Box*, *20 Greatest Hits* and the American album *Yesterday And Today*.

This is also a number which has been recorded by dozens of different artists, including Dionne Warwick, George Burns, Petula Clark, Deep Purple, Humble Pie,

Johnny Mathis, Melanie, Johnny Nash, Sam & Dave and Caterine Valente. Stevie Wonder had the most successful version in 1971, when his single reached No. 9 in the States and No. 22 in Britain. The Beatles performed the song on their British tour in 1965.

● Wedding Album

The third of John and **Yoko**'s albums which could be considered part of their *Unfinished Music* series.

It took eight months in the preparation, had an extremely elaborate packaging set and was issued on Apple SAPCOR 11 on 7 November 1969.

The entire first side of the album, entitled 'John And Yoko', lasted 22 minutes and 38 seconds and comprised the duo calling out each other's names in numerous ways – cajoling, laughing, shouting, pleading, whispering, crying and so on. Side Two lasted for 24 minutes and 54 seconds and was called 'Amsterdam'. This side was recorded during the 'bed-in' while John and Yoko were honeymooning at the Amsterdam Hilton. Apart from the couple talking to reporters, there were four musical items: 'John, Let's Hope For Peace', 'Goodbye Amsterdam, Goodbye', 'Bed Peace' and 'Goodnight'.

The album was packaged in a box which contained a poster of the couple's wedding, a photograph of a piece of wedding cake, a cartoon strip of the wedding by John, a strip of 'passport' pictures and various photographs by Mlle Danlau, **Richard DiLello**, John Kelly, Nico Koster, David Nutter and John and Yoko. The packaging was designed by **John Kosh**.

The record failed to enter the charts, but there was an amusing story concerning the release. Advance review copies had been sent out comprising two single-sided test discs, with a factory test whistle on the reverse of each. The *Melody Maker* reviewer, Richard Williams, mistakenly believed he'd been sent a double album to review and consequently reviewed all 'four' sides, including the two sides with the **EMI** factory whistle. He described the blank sides as consisting 'entirely of single tones maintained throughout, presumably produced electronically'.

John and Yoko were amused and sent him a telegram from Bombay, where they were staying, which read: 'DEAR RICHARD THANK YOU FOR YOUR FANTASTIC REVIEW ON OUR WEDDING ALBUM INCLUDING C-AND-D SIDE STOP WE ARE CONSIDERING IT FOR OUR NEXT RELEASE STO MAYBE YOU ARE RIGHT IN SAYING THAT THE ARE THE BEST SIDES STOP WE BOTH FEEL THA THIS IS THE FIRST TIME A CRITIC TOPPED TH ARTIST STOP WE ARE NOT JOKING STOP LOVE AN PEACE STOP JOHN AND YOKO LENNON.'

● Weissleder, Manfred

Tall, blond-haired club owner who launched Germany legendary music venue, the **Star Club**, in April 1962 wi the Beatles topping the bill.

Once Liverpool groups had begun to attract their ow following in Hamburg from 1960 onwards, the way wa open for an enterprising promoter not only to book th bands but to provide exciting bills and specifically to ha a policy of encouraging the rock 'n' roll scene.

Manfred, who also owned a string of strip club secured a number of legendary American acts who we appearing at US bases in Germany. They included th Everly Brothers, **Little Richard** and Bo Diddley. H outbid the other clubs in booking British and Americ bands and continued to increase his bid for the Beatl until he had secured them for the Star Club opening.

He engaged **Horst Fascher**, a friend of the Beatl during his time at the **Kaiserkeller** and **Top Ten Club** and also **Rosa**, the lavatory attendant who had been friend of the Beatles at the **Indra** and Top Ten Clubs.

Manfred was more organized and imaginative than t other Hamburg promoters and arranged for the groups appear on short tours of Germany. He invited Bill Harry launch a German rock magazine, but when he was turn down, Manfred published *Star Club News*. He al engaged **Adrian Barber** to build a sound system in t club which could be used for recording the groups on sta and he began to promote home-grown Hamburg ban such as the Rattles. He also made various trips Liverpool, forging links with the **Cavern Club**.

During the sixties, a number of Liverpool ban appeared on extensive residencies at the Star Clu including **Kingsize Taylor** & the Dominoes, and Manfr hired various managers from Liverpool and London, su as **Joe Flannery** and Henry Henriod. He died in 1980.

● Weiss, Nat

Weiss was a divorce attorney in New York when he fi met Brian Epstein in 1964. A few years previously he h epresented **Larry Parnes** when the British impresario ad attempted to launch Tommy Steele in the States. arnes recommended Weiss to Epstein and suggested that e look him up. In fact, the two met at a party. They got hatting and Epstein took him on as an attorney. radually, Weiss turned from a divorce attorney to one pecializing in musicians and promotions and represented number of clients, including John McLaughlin, Cat evens, **Peter Asher**, **James Taylor** and Miles Davis. 'eiss and Epstein became friends and Weiss would meet m at the airport each time he arrived in New York. In 965 Brian asked him if he'd be interested in artist-anagement and Weiss said yes. Epstein said he'd help m and Weiss discovered a group playing in an Atlantic ity bar and signed them up. They were called the ondells, but Epstein changed their name to the **Cyrkle**. e then suggested that he and Weiss became partners and ey formed Nemperor Artists together and the Cyrkle re included on the Beatles' 1966 tour of America.

Epstein had been unhappy about the design of the *Sgt epper* cover and when Weiss took him to the airport, ian was convinced that the plane would crash and gave eiss a note with the message: 'Brown paper jackets for t Pepper's Lonely Hearts Club Band'.

A few months before he died, Epstein asked Weiss to come his manager.

Weiss, Norman

executive of the prestigious American agency General tists Corporation when the Beatles were becoming a ajor act in Europe. As Weiss dealt with European tivities, British agent **Vic Lewis** called him on behalf of ian Epstein and suggested that the time was right for the atles to tour America. The Beatles were appearing at the **lympia, Paris** on a bill with **Trini Lopez** in January '64 and Weiss, who represented Lopez, had arranged to sit him in Paris. He asked Lewis to set up a meeting with pstein and on his arrival he tied up a deal to book the atles for two shows at **Carnegie Hall** for promoter **Sid rnstein** and for them to make a live concert appearance the **Coliseum in Washington DC**.

Weiss organized the Beatles' first American tour on half of GAC and he advised Brian Epstein that he ould only accept bookings for large arenas such as adiums and should ask for $25,000 in advance, plus a rcentage of the gate receipts.

● Well . . . (Baby Please Don't Go)

A number recorded by the Olympics, an R&B quartet from Los Angeles, in 1958. They had two hits, but this wasn't one of them, although the Beatles included the song in their repertoire in 1960, 1961 and 1962 with John Lennon on lead vocals.

● Wells, Mary

Motown singer, born in Detroit, whose hits included the 1964 No. 1 record 'My Guy'.

After 'My Guy' entered the charts, the Beatles wanted her to appear on tour with them and she was booked to join their Autumn Tour, making her debut with them on the bill at the **Gaumont, Bradford** on 9 October. The tour lasted for four weeks. When it reached the **Apollo, Ardwick**, Manchester, Mary was interviewed backstage by Bill Harry for ***Mersey Beat*** and she told him, 'I first heard that I'd be touring with the Beatles in September and I thought it was wonderful. I admire them very much and as far as I'm concerned they're the best.' She added, 'I'd just love to record a number by John and Paul and I think I'll ask them about it.'

Harry talked to John Lennon that same night and John said, 'We've got a number which we think will really be suitable for her.' However, nothing transpired from it.

Mary also appeared on the television special '**Around The Beatles**'. She was also to pay tribute to the Beatles when she recorded the album *Love Songs To The Beatles*, which featured the tracks: 'He Loves You', 'All My Loving', 'Please Please Me', 'Do You Want To Know A Secret?', 'Can't Buy Me Love', 'I Should Have Known Better', 'Help!', 'Eight Days A Week', 'And I Love Him', 'Ticket To Ride', 'Yesterday' and 'I Saw Him Standing There'.

Mary died in August 1992.

● We Love You

A number recorded by the **Rolling Stones**. When the group were recording at **Olympic Studios** in Barnes, John Lennon and Paul McCartney dropped in to see them and ended up providing backing vocals on this song.

Bill Wyman recalled the event in his autobiography *Stone Alone* (Viking, 1990): 'We went into the Olympic Studios on 12 and 13 June [1967] to record "We Love You", produced by **Andrew [Oldham]**. In July John Lennon and Paul McCartney overdubbed back-up vocals as a gesture of support, and another sound-effect was added after the trial: the sound of a prison door being slammed.'

This reference was to the trial which took place after members of the Rolling Stones were arrested following a drug bust.

● 72 Western Avenue, *Speke, Liverpool 15*

The home of the McCartney family from 1947 until 1953. The house was situated on a large council estate and **Mary McCartney** was the local midwife.

When the family moved into the estate from their previous address in Sir Thomas White Gardens, Paul was four years old.

● 15 Whaddon House, *William Mews, London SW1*

When George and Ringo moved down to London in 1963 they lived together in Flat 7 of this residential building. Previously, they had used a small flat in **Green Street**. When they were unable to renew the Green Street lease they discovered that Brian Epstein had moved into Whaddon House where there was an available apartment on the next floor to him.

John, **Cynthia** and **Julian** moved to Emperor's Gate and although Paul was supposed to be sharing the flat with George and Ringo, he mainly stayed with **Jane Asher**'s family in **Wimpole Street**. Brian Epstein used his private flat, situated in the Knightsbridge area, to hold several lavish parties. The Whaddon House address was the one given on Ringo's wedding certificate in February 1965 as his home, but by that time he had moved to **Montague Square**.

● Whalley, Nigel

A playfriend of John Lennon's from the age of five, Nigel lived in Vale Road, close to John's home in Menlove Avenue. He became part of the small, close-knit group of friends cultivated by John, and was nicknamed 'Whalloggs'. When Nigel started at Bluecoat Grammar School, John formed his skiffle group the **Quarry Men** and Nigel was appointed tea-chest player, a task he divided between himself and **Ivan Vaughan**. One night when two tough Woolton teddy boys Rod and Willo threatened to beat them up as they alighted from a bus, the Quarry Men fled leaving the tea-chest bass in the roa
After that, Nigel became their manager and Len Garry too
over on tea-chest bass.

Nigel had cards printed:

COUNTRY. WESTERN. ROCK 'N' ROLL. SKIFFLE.
THE QUARRY MEN
OPEN FOR ENGAGEMENTS.

When he left school he became an apprentice go
professional at Lee Park Golf Club. He arranged for t
group to play there for free, but they got a slap-up me
and when the hat was passed round they ended up wi
twice as much as they'd have received for a paid bookin
At the club Nigel also played golf with Dr Sytner who
son Alan had just opened the **Cavern** as a jazz club. H
arranged for the Quarry Men to appear there and th
received a booking for 7 August 1957. Paul didn't pl
with them on this occasion as he was on holiday. Th
began with the Del Vikings number 'Come Go With M
then John launched into 'Hound Dog' and 'Blue Sue
Shoes'. Sytner immediately had a note delivered to the
on stage: 'Cut out the bloody Rock.'

The stint as manager didn't last very long as Pa
wasn't happy about Nigel receiving an equal split wi
them.

On 15 July 1958 Nigel dropped around to see if Jo
was at home in Mendips. He wasn't, but **Mimi** was talki
to **Julia Lennon** at the gate. Nigel walked with Julia
about 200 yards and then continued up Menlove Aven
while she crossed the road. He heard a squeal of brak
and turned to see Julia's body tossed into the air by a c
She was killed and the off-duty policeman who was drivi
was sent to trial, with Nigel as a witness. The man w
acquitted.

When he was eighteen Nigel left the area and he la
became a golf pro at Wrotham Heath Golf Club in Borou
Green, Kent.

His father was Chief Superintendent Harold Whall
head of City Police 'A' Division. The ***Liverpool Ec***
reported when he met John and Paul backstage af
they'd become famous: 'Mr Whalley first met the t
Beatles when they were part of a skiffle group which
son, Nigel, managed in 1957. "I used to worry about so
of the clubs and places they were performing at. I t
them that there was no future in that kind of thing a

dvised them to drop it. I told them a few times to get a aircut as well.'"

What Goes On

ne of the many numbers John Lennon wrote early in his reer, before the Beatles achieved fame, although the mber was never included in the group's stage repertoire. e band originally intended to record the song during eir recording session on Tuesday, 5 March 1963, but idio time ran out. The number wasn't revived until their cording session on Thursday, 4 November 1965, by ich time it had undergone a number of changes. The oup were under pressure for more tracks for the *Rubber ul* album deadline and also needed the customary Ringo arr vocal track.

Both Paul and Ringo participated in the final structure the song and Paul made a demo of the number as a ide to Ringo. Ringo was also given a co-composer credit, ich may explain the number's slight country music feel. was the first Beatles number on which Ringo received a ngwriting credit.

'What Goes On' was included on the British *Rubber ul* album, but was one of two numbers left off the nerican release. It was issued in the States as the side of the 'Nowhere Man' single in February 1966 and 'B'-side placing in the American charts saw it reach . 89, while the 'A' side reached No. 3. The song was o used on **Capitol**'s *Yesterday . . . And Today* album.

What's Happening: The Beatles In The SA

53-minute film, released in 1967. The documentary was de by brothers **Albert and David Maysles**, who were er responsible for the **Rolling Stones** documentary mme Shelter'.

What's Happening followed the Beatles on their first it to America in February 1964, covering their stay in w York, their train journey to Washington DC, their earance on the **'Ed Sullivan** Show' and several of their erviews. The two brothers had already used much of the terial for a TV special they had made called 'The tles in New York'.

Later that year, *What's Happening: The Beatles In The 4* was also featured in an hour-long CBS TV variety w hosted by Carol Burnett, called 'The Entertainers', er the title 'The Beatles in the USA'.

What's The New Mary Jane

Song which John composed and unsuccessfully tried to have included first on *The Beatles* double album and later as a **Plastic Ono Band** single. It remains unreleased.

In May 1969 John said, 'There was a mad thing I wrote half with our electronic genius, Alex. It was called "What A Shame Mary Jane Had A Pain At The Party" and it was meant for the last Beatles album. It was real madness, but we never released it. I'd like to do it again.'

The Beatles originally recorded it on Wednesday, 14 August 1968, for *The Beatles* album. At the last minute it was left off, officially because there was not enough room on the album, but it was also mooted that the other members of the group thought it was too bizarre to appear on the double album.

John sent producer Malcolm Davis into the studio to produce some stereo mixes of the song in September 1969 and John listened to them and decided to issue the track with another of his songs, 'You Know My Name (Look Up The Number)' as a Plastic Ono Band single. Together with **Yoko** he went into **Abbey Road Studios** on Wednesday, 26 November 1969, and they spent six hours working on both tracks, adding vocal and sound overdubs. Although 'You Know My Name (Look Up The Number)' finally surfaced as the flipside of the 'Let It Be' single, 'What's The New Mary Jane' was never issued.

'Mary Jane' is a slang name for marijuana. Some sources incorrectly refer to the number as 'What's The News Mary Jane'.

What You're Doing

Number by Paul which was used for the *Beatles For Sale* album when, once again, the Beatles were under pressure to adhere to a recording schedule. They first recorded the number on Tuesday and Wednesday, 29 and 30 September 1964, but weren't satisfied with that version and re-recorded it on Monday, 26 October. Apart from the *Beatles For Sale* album, the number also appeared on the American *Beatles VI* LP.

When I Get Home

Number penned by John Lennon which was included on the *A Hard Day's Night* album. The Beatles recorded the number on Tuesday, 2 June 1964, and it was also included on the American album *Something New* and the British EP *Extracts From The Album A Hard Day's Night*. The influence of some of John's favourite American girl groups such as the Shirelles is evident.

● When I'm Sixty-Four

Paul had written a version of this song when he was sixteen and the Beatles had sometimes played it at the **Cavern.** It's assumed that Paul revived and rewrote the number in 1966 as a tribute to his father who had reached the age of 64 in July of that year. Certainly, the influence of his own father's musical tastes are evident in the number. The track was recorded in December and was included on the *Sgt Pepper* album the following year, becoming the first *Sgt Pepper* track to be completed. It also featured three clarinettists – Robert Burns, Henry MacKenzie and Frank Reidy.

'When I'm Sixty-Four' has been recorded by over 40 different artists, including **Keith Moon**, Kenny Ball & His Jazzmen, Bernard Cribbins, Georgie Fame and Frankie Howerd.

The Beatles performing on a Granada special (Granada TV)

● Where Have You Been All My Life

A song which had been recorded by one of John Lennon's idols, **Arthur Alexander**, in May 1962. The number had been composed by Barry Mann and Cynthia Weil and John sang lead vocals on the number when it was included in the Beatles' stage act. They performed it at the **Star Club**, Hamburg, and it is one of the tracks on the Star Club double album.

● Where It's At

A BBC Radio One programme. John Lennon pre-recorde an interview for the show with **Kenny Everett** in whic he discussed the music for *Magical Mystery Tour*. Th interview was transmitted on 25 November 1967.

● While My Guitar Gently Weeps

George Harrison composition which appeared on *Th Beatles* double album.

George was visiting his parents' home near Merseysi when he first began writing the number. At the time he been consulting the *I Ching*, the Eastern 'Book Changes', which gave him the idea of writing a song bas upon the first thing he saw when opening a book. At h parents' home he just picked a book at random, opened and the first words he noticed were 'gently weeps'. He p the book down and began writing the song.

Recording of the number actually began on 25 Ju 1968, although there were to be several versions of t number, one in which George sings and plays to t accompaniment of an acoustic guitar and has added extra verse to the song.

The version that was issued on the album contained electric guitar solo from **Eric Clapton**, while George a John played acoustic guitars. The idea to include Clapt (one of George's closest friends) on the track came onl short time before the session when Eric was giving Geo a lift in his car. George suggested that Eric play on track. Initially, Eric was amazed at the suggesti because no other rock musician had been featured o Beatles recording before, but George assured him that number was his and he wanted Eric to play on it. E included his overdubs on the recording on Frida September 1968.

The track was also included on *The Beatles 1967–1* compilation and Harrison's *The Best Of George Harri* collection in 1976.

● Whitaker, Bob

The official Beatles photographer between the ye 1964–1966. The 23-year-old Whitaker was a professio photographer working on advertising, fashion and edito assignments in Melbourne, Australia, when the Bea toured there in 1964. During the tour Whitaker took sh of Brian Epstein, who liked the photographs so much visited Whitaker's studio to view some more of his w npressed, Epstein offered him a job at NEMS back in ngland where he would become the company's official notographer, taking shots of all the acts, in addition to ecoming NEMS' artistic director. Whitaker turned him own.

Three months later Epstein cabled Whitaker repeating s offer and this time the photographer accepted and flew London. He became official photographer to the Beatles om August 1964 to November 1966 and travelled tensively with them documenting their tours in America, ermany and Japan, in addition to arranging studio ssions.

In 1966, following a suggestion by John Lennon, hitaker took the notorious 'butcher' shots, which were ed in Beatles advertisements in Britain, but censored en one of the images was used in America as the cover the *Yesterday . . . And Today* album. The image of the eatles in butchers' smocks with decapitated dolls and eces of red meat caused panic among **Capitol Records** executives and the cover was replaced. Whitaker also took the photograph which became the replacement cover, an innocuous shot of the group posing around a travelling trunk. Bob's photographs for *Revolver* were passed over in favour of the award-winning **Klaus Voorman** design, although a Whitaker photograph was used on the back cover. Another Whitaker shot was used on the back cover of the *A Collection Of Beatles Oldies* album

Twenty-five years later a selection of Whitaker's photographs of the Beatles were published in a book, *The Unseen Beatles*, published by Collins, with text by Martin Harrison.

● White, Andy

A session drummer who performed on the second 'Love Me Do' recording. The original session had taken place on 4 September 1962 with Ringo on drums, but George Martin wasn't satisfied with the drum solo and another session was arranged for 11 September.

Bob Whitaker's famous 1966 photo session produced the controversial 'Butcher' album cover. (©Apple)

Martin wasn't present at the session and Ron Richards produced in his absence. Ron had used Alan White on several previous sessions and engaged him for the recording, asking Ringo to sit with him in the control box. He later had Ringo play tambourine on the track. He also re-recorded 'P.S. I Love You' with White on drums and Ringo playing maracas.

'Love Me Do' was completed in eighteen takes and for the session the 32-year-old White was paid £57s5d.

There has been some confusion as to which versions of the number were released. Initially, the 'Love Me Do' single released was the 4 September version with Ringo on drums, issued with a red label. The version with White was included on the *Please Please Me* album, then also as a single issued with a black label when it was re-pressed in April 1963.

White had previously been a member of **Vic Lewis**'s Orchestra and was married to **Lyn Cornell**, a member of the Liverpool group, the **Vernons Girls**. Alan White was later to join the BBC Radio Orchestra in Glasgow.

● White, Ron

The General Marketing Manager of **EMI Records** in London in 1961 when he was approached by Brian Epstein regarding the Beatles. As **NEMS** was a major record retailer, White agreed to meet him and Epstein played him the Polydor single 'My Bonnie', and showed him photographs of the group, suggesting that they would be an ideal band for EMI to sign. White pointed out that it was difficult to judge what the band were like from a record on which they were backing another singer, but he offered to take it round personally to all of EMI's four A&R (Artistes and Repertoire) managers and play it to them. In the meantime, Epstein arranged the **Decca audition**, then wrote to White on 8 December 1961. He expressed his disappointment that he hadn't heard from White and mentioned they would be seeing **Decca** A&R men. He wrote: 'These boys who are superb instrumentalists also produce some exciting and pulsating vocals. They play mostly their own compositions and one of the boys has written a song which I really believe to be the hottest material since "Livin' Doll".'

White's reply had actually crossed in the post and was dated 7 December. He told Epstein that he would be having the record carefully assessed by each of EMI's A&R men. White first played it to Norrie Paramor, whose artists included Cliff Richard and the **Shadows** a **Frank Ifield**. Paramor told him that they were a bit li the Shadows and as the Shadows were at the peak of th career, he didn't need a similar group. White th approached Walter Ridley who recorded artists such **Alma Cogan** and Frankie Vaughan. Ridley rejected th saying he wasn't particularly interested in their sou White then took the material to Norman Newall, w recorded artists such as Russ Conway, and he told Wh that he thought they sounded like the Shadows and wouldn't like to compete with Paramor, who recorded t Shadows.

EMI's fourth A&R man, George Martin, was on holid at the time, so White didn't offer it to him. He then repli to Epstein on 18 December, formally rejecting the ba writing, 'I am sorry that I have been so long in giving yo decision but I have now had an opportunity of playing record to each of our Artistes Managers. Whilst appreciate the talents of this group we feel that we h sufficient groups of this type at the present time un contract and that it would not be advisable for us to s any further contracts of this nature at present.'

Had George Martin not been on holiday at the time would have been approached by White and, in the ligh the Beatles being rejected by his three other colleagu the chances are that Martin would have rejected them, So EMI gave the Beatles the thumbs down, without e offering to audition them, while, at the same time, **De Records** was sufficiently interested to send **Mike Sm** up to Liverpool to see them and also to arrange for then perform a recording audition in London. Fate would h it that although Mike Smith wanted to sign the gro **Brian Poole & the Tremeloes** were signed instead the light of this, it seems unfair that Decca has b looked upon for so many years as the recording comp which turned down the Beatles when, in fact, E originally rejected them first.

When the white label of 'Love Me Do' was presente the EMI meeting to decide which records were worth release, the majority of sales-orientated EMI executi voted it a miss. White, however, decided he would b George Martin's judgement and release the single. The realized the name was familiar. Considering he formally rejected the group and then discovered that on his A&R men had accepted them, White decided to s another letter to Epstein and wrote, 'I was nonplussed newhat embarrassed to see details of a contract going ough for "The Beatles" especially in view of my letter to ı of 18 December 1961 when I told you that our Artistes nagers did not feel we could use them.' He mentioned v pleased he was that the contract was being negotiated l added, 'My only reason for writing is to endeavour to plain what must appear to you an anomaly in our anization. I can assure you that our Artistes Managers hear the record but I know you will appreciate that n Artistes Managers are human and can change their nd!'

At a later stage, White was to become Managing ector of EMI Records. He died on 18 September 1989, he age of 67, after a long illness.

White Star, *Rainford Gardens, erpool L2*

oublic house situated on the curve where **Mathew eet** veers towards Whitechapel. It's on a direct route n the former site of **NEMS** record store to the **Cavern**. e the Grapes in Mathew Street, it was a meeting place the Beatles and other Mersey groups and **Bob Wooler** **Ray McFall** often arranged meetings here with ern guests.

Why

umber penned by **Tony Sheridan** in 1958 in aboration with Bill Crompton. Its full title was 'Why n't You Love Me Again)'. The song was one of the ıbers selected when the Beatles backed Tony Sheridan ing a recording session with **Bert Kaempfert** in May 1, when they also provided the vocal harmony on the k.

Due to the success of the Beatles in Britain it was ed as one of the tracks on an EP, *My Bonnie*, released Polydor on H21 610 on 12 July 1963. A single of the ıber, with 'Cry For A Shadow' on the flip, was issued in erica on MGM K13227 on 27 March 1964 and it hed No. 88 on the *Billboard* chart. Its release in ain on Polydor NH 52 275 on 28 February 1964 didn't re a chart placing. It was also included on a Polydor pilation *Let's Do The Twist, Hully Gully, Slop, omotion, Monkey* on Polydor SLPHM 237 622 on 8 1964. It next appeared on the album *The Beatles* , issued in June 1964 and reissued in August 1967, on *The Early Years* compilation, issued by Contour in June 1971 (this album was issued in the States by Polydor under the title *The Beatles – Circa 1960 – In The Beginning*). It was included on the Charly Records album *The Savage Young Beatles* in 1982 and *First Movement*, issued by Phoenix in 1982.

• Why Don't We Do It In The Road?

On Wednesday, 9 October 1968, Paul McCartney took engineer **Ken Townsend** aside and they went into Studio Three of **Abbey Road** and recorded this number which Paul had written. Paul sang vocals, on which there was some double-tracking, and also played guitar, piano and bass.

The following day, together with Townsend and Ringo Starr, Paul went into Studio Three again and completed the number, with Ringo overdubbing drums and including further vocals, handclaps and another bass track. This was more or less a Paul McCartney solo effort. Some years later John Lennon was to say how disappointed he was to discover that Paul had gone ahead and done the track without consulting either himself or George or asking them to participate in the recording.

The number was included on *The Beatles* white album.

• Wigg, David

David has been a show business correspondent for Britain's *Daily Express* newspaper for a number of years and formerly produced a music column for the *London Evening News*. He interviewed the Beatles regularly in the sixties and early seventies and during 1969 conducted a series of radio interviews for the BBC series 'Scene And Heard'.

He first interviewed Ringo for the programme on 21 January and the show was transmitted on 25 January. He then interviewed George on 4 March, which was transmitted in two parts – on 8 March and 12 April. His interview with John and **Yoko** took place on 8 May and was also transmitted in two parts, on 11 May and 18 May. His interview with Paul was conducted on 19 September and transmitted on 21 and 28 September.

In 1970 he conducted a further interview for 'Scene And Heard' with John and Yoko on 6 February, which was transmitted on 15 February. Wigg recorded a final 'Scene And Heard' interview with John and Yoko in New York on 25 October 1971 which was transmitted in three parts on 13, 20 and 27 November.

David then compiled the interviews for a Polydor album

called *The Beatles Tapes from the David Wigg Interviews*, which was issued on Polydor 2683 068 on 30 July 1976. The double album set was released following a court case which had taken place because of an injunction on the record. The Beatles were unsuccessful in preventing its release. The set came complete with an eight-page booklet of photographs.

Wigg mentioned that his first interview with John and Yoko took place at the Apple offices, another 'was conducted at the Saint Regis Hotel, New York. John and Yoko were having breakfast in bed. It was 12.30 p.m. Yoko wore a black see-through negligee. John sat up in bed in a white T-shirt which carried the wording: "This Is Not Here".'

His interviews with Paul and George took place at the Apple offices. Wigg actually interviewed Ringo on three occasions, the first in December 1968, then in July 1970 and finally in December 1973. His first interview with Ringo was conducted from the back of a chauffeur-driven Mercedes en route from Ringo's home to London, where Ringo was to have a medical examination. He carried out his final interview with Ringo at Apple and commented, 'When I arrived . . . the notice on his office door at Apple read: "Dr Baron Frankenstein – Brain Specialist". Inside, a stuffed bat and skeleton head stared down from a coat hanger.' This was actually publicity material relating to Ringo's film with **Harry Nilsson**, *Son of Dracula*.

Among the topics discussed were the 'ticking off' John received from Paul for posing nude on the *Two Virgins* cover, the Beatles' split, Paul's solo album, George's difficulty in getting his songs on Beatles albums, meditation and Ringo's belief in reincarnation. When asked about **Beatlemania**, Ringo commented, 'It was the worst time and the best time of my life.'

• 95 Wigmore Street, London W1

Site of the first offices of the Beatles' **Apple Corps** company. Two office suites were rented in the building and the group and their friends and associates planned the growth of their Apple empire. During one discussion session they were interrupted by **Don Short** of the *Daily Mirror*, who revealed their plans in a full-page story.

Soon after moving into Wigmore Street Ringo, **Maureen**, **Peter Brown**, **Neil Aspinall** and **Mal Evans** were locked inside the building by the caretaker.

The offices were maintained for a period of time after all the main business had been transferred to **Savile R**
in the autumn of 1968.

• Wild Honey Pie

John, George and Ringo weren't around when P
recorded this brief number at **Abbey Road Studios**
20 August 1968. Paul sang, played guitar and bass dr
and also double-tracked. At only 53 seconds in length, i
the shortest cut on *The Beatles* double album.

Paul had originally penned the song in India but h
never really intended recording it. However, both **Ja**
Asher and **Pattie** Harrison liked it and encouraged him
record it. He commented, 'This was just a fragment of
instrumental which we weren't sure about, but Pattie li
it very much so we decided to leave it on the album.'

• Wild In The Country

The name of an **Elvis Presley** film. Elvis also recor
the title song which reached No. 26 in the Ameri
charts. It was penned by Hugo Peretti, Luigi Creatore
George Weiss. **Pete Best** performed the number whe
was included in the Beatles' repertoire in 1961.

• Williams, Allan

A Liverpool coffee bar owner who first became acquai
with John Lennon and **Stuart Sutcliffe** in 1959 w
they began to frequent his venue the **Jacaranda Co**
Club in Slater Street. Shortly after he'd promoted a s
at the **Liverpool Stadium** featuring **Gene Vincent**
leading Merseyside groups, he was approached
Sutcliffe who asked him if he'd do something for his gr
Williams asked him who they were and Stu told him a
John, Paul and George. Williams advised them to fi
drummer and **Brian Casser** of Cass & the Cassanovas
them onto one called **Tommy Moore**, who joined
group for a short time. Allan then agreed to get book
for the group and also arranged for them to audition
impresario **Larry Parnes**, who was looking for a bac
band for **Billy Fury**. This resulted in the group's s
tour of Scotland in May 1960 and Williams followed u
booking them at the Jacaranda and arranging some gig
them at the **Grosvenor Ballroom** in Wallasey. Du
the brief time Williams was booking them, he
arranged for them to provide backing for a stripper at
New Cabaret Artistes Club.

He was to tell ***Mersey Beat***: 'They appeared

n Williams at the door of the Blue Angel Club.

ous enterprises, and played at New Brighton Pier on rday afternoons. But they still could not break into the e regarding the **Cavern** or other well-known venues. en I tried to book them I was confronted with such culous statements as, "I will not have them as I have r seen them advertised in the ***Liverpool Echo***".'

'he major and most important move in the Williams-tles relationship was the visit to Hamburg which iams had arranged with **Bruno Koschmider**. He , 'I decided I would go over personally with the les, partly because they couldn't afford the fare and ot a minibus. So we embarked upon what was the most nturous trip the Beatles ever made . . . the hours that boys had to work in those days was from eight in the ing until two in the morning. This, I think, was a r contributing factor in making the group.'

is success in opening up the Hamburg market for rpool groups inspired Allan to further efforts. He was e process of opening a nightclub, the **Blue Angel**, but so decided to launch a rock 'n' roll club. He acquired ises in Soho Street and work began on the **Top Ten** . He'd intended making the Beatles the resident band s club, but the premises were gutted by fire. He said, 'The club was severely damaged by fire and I found myself in rather a difficult financial period as I was in the process of opening the Blue Angel.' He'd hired **Bob Wooler** to be compere at the Top Ten and Bob was now out on a limb. Allan asked him if he could try to get some bookings for the Beatles who were shortly to return from Hamburg. Bob arranged with **Brian Kelly** for the group to appear at **Litherland Town Hall** – and their local rise to fame began. This was also the beginning of the end of their relationship with Williams.

There was some disagreement regarding their season at the Top Ten Club in Hamburg during March/July 1961. Allan had insisted that he had arranged it and was due commission and the Beatles were adamant that they had concluded the deal directly with **Peter Eckhorn** via **Pete Best**. The group asked **Stuart Sutcliffe**, who had left the Beatles to resume his art studies in Hamburg, to write to Allan refusing to pay him a percentage. Williams commented: 'John Lennon was refusing to pay my commission. Stu, who was most unhappy about this attitude, said that Lennon complained they were having to pay income tax on their Top Ten earnings, whereas previously they hadn't.

'I was irked, no doubt about that! After all the trouble I'd taken on the Beatles' behalf Lennon's attack struck me as being completely unfair . . . I told Stuart to tell John that if they hadn't paid tax on their previous visit, the Beatles should consider themselves extremely lucky . . . I pointed out to the Beatles that while they had been paid for their first Hamburg tour, I hadn't received a single penny. In fact I'd run them at an absolute loss. Not only had I not received my commission from Koschmider, I'd also never been repaid the cost of my journey. The expenses for the minibus were to have been deducted from their wages, but nothing had ever reached me.'

The Beatles still refused to pay Williams his commission and he told them that he'd fix it so that they'd never work again. He even barred them from his Blue Angel Club, but later relented and they became regular visitors.

When Epstein was considering signing the Beatles, he asked Williams for his advice and was told – don't touch them with a barge pole!

Williams' biography, *The Man Who Gave The Beatles Away*, was co-written by Bill Marshall and published in 1975. It is an amusing but far from accurate account of

Williams' relationship with the group and a number of reported incidents, such as how Epstein came to sign **Cilla Black**, are pure fabrication.

The book reinforced the impression that Allan had been the Beatles' manager and had actually given the group up. In fact, he never managed the group at all, but acted as an unofficial agent. When he mentions that he has contracts signed by the Beatles which were charred in the Top Ten club fire, they are actually contracts for bookings with Bruno Koschmider and not management contracts as some people assume.

However, no one can deny the part he played in their early career and the series of circumstances which led to him booking Liverpool groups into Hamburg was an important step in the Beatles' career.

● Williams, Angela

Angela was a widow who was introduced to **Jim McCartney**, Paul's father, in 1964. On their third meeting Jim proposed and they were married on 24 November 1964.

Angie, as she was generally called, was more than twenty years younger than her new husband, who legally adopted her five-year-old daughter, Ruth. Paul McCartney was particularly fond of Ruth and the family ties we[re] quite strong until Jim's death in 1976.

Angie then tried to set up a rock group agency [on] Merseyside but Paul disapproved because he felt s[he] might be trading on the McCartney name. Relati[ons] between her and Paul cooled and she eventually rever[ted] to her first husband's name in 1981 following a series [of] articles, ghosted by **Tony Barrow** and very critical [of] Paul, which appeared in the *Sun* newspaper.

● Williams, Danny

South African singer who had enjoyed two recent ma[jor] British hits, 'Jeannie' and his No. 1 'Moon River', when [he] was booked on the bill of the **Helen Shapiro** tou[r in] February/March 1963. He had previously appeared w[ith] the Beatles at the **Tower Ballroom**, New Brighton, o[n 8] December 1961. He'd been appearing for a week at [the] **Cabaret Club**, Liverpool, when promoter **Sam Lea[ch]** booked him to appear on the Tower date. Williams' [last] chart hit was 'Dancin' Easy' in 1977.

● Williams, Larry

American artist who began his career as a session pia[nist] for Lloyd Price. He then began to record and compo[se]

South African singer Danny Williams, backstage at the Tow[er] Ballroom, New Brigh[ton] on 8 December 196[1]. From left to right: Mik[e] Millward (the Fourmo[st]), Williams, Brian O'Ha[ra] (the Fourmost), Davy Jones. (*Mersey Bea[t]* Archives)

mber of songs, two of which were Top Twenty hits in nerica – 'Short Fat Fanny' and 'Bony Moronie'.

Williams was a seminal influence on the Beatles and songs of his which they included in their repertoire re 'Bony Moronie', 'Short Fat Fanny', 'Bad Boy', 'Dizzy ss Lizzy' and 'Slow Down'.

Williams recorded for the Specialty label in the States d issued 'Bad Boy' in January 1959. The Beatles corded it during their *Help!* album sessions, with John on d vocals, and it was included on *A Collection Of atles' Oldies (But Goldies)*. 'Dizzy Miss Lizzy' was ued on a single by Williams in February 1958, with ow Down' on the flipside. The Beatles recorded 'Dizzy ss Lizzy', which was included on their *Help!* album, with in on lead vocals. John also sang the lead on 'Slow wn', which they included on their *Long Tall Sally* EP.

John Lennon was to record 'Bony Moronie' on his *Rock Roll* album.

Williams committed suicide on 2 January 1980.

Williams, Richard

eviewer for the British music weekly *Melody Maker* in sixties and early seventies. Williams achieved some oriety when he received acetates of John and **Yoko**'s *e Wedding Album*. He mistakenly thought that the ease was a double album and reviewed the two blank es, which he thought were Sides Two and Four of a ıble album, and wrote: 'Side Two and Four consist irely of single tones maintained throughout, presumably duced electronically.

'This might sound arid, to say the least, but in fact stant listening reveals a curious point: the pitch of the es alters frequently, but only by microtones or, at most, emitone. This oscillation produces an almost subliminal even "beat" which maintains interest.'

John and Yoko were tickled pink by the idea of lliams constantly listening to the two blank sides – and y sent him a telegram.

When reviewing George Harrison's solo album *All ings Must Pass*, Williams described it as: 'The rock ivalent of the shock felt by pre-war moviegoers when rbo first opened her mouth in a talkie: Garbo talks! rrison is free!'

Williams, who became a prominent journalist with *The ıes* newspaper in London, also penned the book, *Out Of Head: The Sound of Phil Spector*.

● Wilson Hall, *Speke Road, Garston, Liverpool 19*

A barrack-like, narrow, single-floored hall situated in Speke Road, opposite Garston Baths, which was also a venue for dances featuring local skiffle groups and rock bands in the late fifties. There were often quite violent gang fights around the hall, particularly on Saturday nights.

The **Quarry Men** were among the skiffle groups booked by promoter Charlie McBain and their appearances there included gigs on 7 November and 7 December 1957. Their 6 February 1958 appearance was when a fourteen-year-old George Harrison saw the band for the first time when he attended the gig at the invitation of Paul McCartney. McBain was a local promoter who ran Rhythm Nights every Thursday at the hall.

Garston is adjacent to Speke, where George lived at the time, and he has related how John Lennon was impressed with the guitarist of the **Ed Clayton Skiffle Group**, who were also on the bill. He told George that if he could play like Eddie Clayton (incidentally, Ringo Starr was once a member of the Ed Clayton Skiffle Group), he'd let him join the Quarry Men. So George played 'Raunchy' and got the job! – or so the story goes. Although accounts confirm that Wilson Hall was the probable site of the first meeting between George and the Quarry Men, the playing of 'Raunchy' is also alleged to have actually occurred at another venue called the Morgue.

George's father Harry was chairman of the Speke Bus Depot Social Club and he booked the Quarry Men to appear at Wilson Hall on a club Christmas function on the afternoon of 1 January 1959.

Wilson Hall, which was named after Francis Wilson, who built it, became a supermarket in the Lennons' chain in the seventies and a carpet warehouse in the eighties.

● Wilson, Sir Harold

British Prime Minister during the Beatles' rise to fame in the sixties. He was also the Member of Parliament for the Huyton district of Liverpool.

At the 12th Annual Variety Club of Great Britain Awards on 19 March 1964, he presented the Beatles with their award as 'Showbusiness Personalities of 1963'. When John Lennon got up to make his speech he began, 'Mr Chief Barker...' looked at Harold Wilson and continued, '. . . and Mr Dobson.' This was a joke referring to a famous

Merseyside sweet firm, Barker and Dobson.

Their award was a Silver Heart, which John referred to as a 'Purple Heart'.

On 14 October 1964, on the eve of the General Election, Brian Epstein, who had been a Labour voter all his life, sent Wilson a cable: 'Hope your group is as much a success.'

It was Wilson, whose favourite Beatles song was 'She Loves You', who put the Beatles down for their **MBE**s.

Harold Wilson also officially reopened the **Cavern Club** on 23 July 1966. The Beatles sent a telegram of support.

His wife Mary was to comment, 'I think they are lovely boys, and I've been dying to meet them. Harold and I are both tremendous fans of the Beatles and always listen to them and watch them on television. Harold and I met in Liverpool. Even in those days we used the word "gear", meaning fabulous or wonderful.'

● Wimbledon Palais, *High Street, Merton, Wimbledon, London SW19*

Site of 'The Beatles London Fan Club Convention' on 14 December 1963.

The South London ballroom comprised a massive shed-like structure with a long bar at the far end. All four members of the Beatles sat in the bar area behind tables while almost 3,000 fans passed by in a long queue to shake hands. There were several commissionaires and the Beatles were also accompanied by road managers **Neil Aspinall** and **Mal Evans**, newly appointed press officer **Brian Sommerville** and **NEMS** press agent **Tony Barrow**.

After the hand-shaking ceremony, the Beatles went on stage and performed several numbers, including 'Twist And Shout'. Unfortunately, the management of the Palais, fearing some sort of riot (which didn't happen with the well-behaved fans), had erected a cage-like structure in front of the stage, a physical barrier between the Beatles and their fans, which tended to inhibit the performance.

● 57 Wimpole Street, *London W1*

Address which Paul used as a London base between 1963 and late 1965. It was the home of the Ashers.

When Paul began dating **Jane Asher** he got to know her family and began to visit her at their home. Describing it at the time, Jane commented: 'Well, it's very, very tall. There's the ground floor and then the first, and second, t third, the fourth floor – four floors above the ground floor

Jane's room was on the second floor. It was a large ro which contained lots of her bits and pieces – a recc player and large collection of classical records, lots dolls, stuffed animals and teddy bears. The sitting-ro with the television was next door to Jane's room. H younger sister Clare lived on the third floor, which a contained the bathroom. There was also a bathroom on t fourth floor where Jane's elder brother **Peter** had l room, a large, L-shaped bedroom. Paul's room was on t same floor, was smaller and contained a large bro wardrobe.

Jane's mother Margaret was a music teacher and h in the past, taught George Martin how to play the ob Her husband was Dr Richard Asher, who was a specia in blood and mental diseases at Middlesex Hospital.

When Paul first began dating Jane, he'd return to home in Liverpool. One night, on missing his last tra Jane invited him to stay the night. Margaret Asl suggested that he could regard it as his permanent ho that he could stay whenever he was in London, thus sav himself the bother of hotels.

He lived there until the latter part of 1965 when bought his house in Cavendish Avenue.

● Winston's Walk

One of the earliest of the John Lennon compositions, instrumental which he introduced into the repertoire of **Quarry Men** in the late fifties. It's one of the very instrumentals John wrote and the number was a tribut Britain's wartime leader, Winston Churchill. Winston John's middle name, but one which he said always use embarrass him.

● Winter Gardens, *Exeter Road, Bournemouth, Hampshire*

Theatre in the fashionable coastal town of Bournemo When the Beatles appeared there on 16 November 19 no less than three American TV news teams covered event, in addition to reporters from *Life* magazine.

CBS News filmed at the concert and the group w interviewed in their dressing-room after the show by J Dansette. On 21 November 1962 CBS News, in an i narrated by correspondent Alexander Kendrick, concert clips were shown, along with part of the Dans erview. Excerpts were also screened in the US on 7 cember on 'CBS Evening News With Walter Cronkite'. ABC TV had screened its brief excerpt in the US on 19 vember 1963 and the NBC excerpt was featured on **he Jack Paar Show**' on 3 January 1964.

Winter Gardens, *Fort Crescent, argate, Kent*

ntish seaside town, popular with holidaymakers from ndon. The Beatles appeared for a short season of six nsecutive nights, with two performances per evening. eir repertoire for the week consisted of 'Roll Over ethoven', 'Thank You Girl', 'Chains', 'Please Please ', 'A Taste Of Honey', 'I Saw Her Standing There', aby It's You', 'From Me To You' and 'Twist And Shout'.

Winter Gardens Ballroom, *Heald Street, rston, Liverpool L19*

ballroom in the south end of Liverpool which featured k 'n' roll nights on Tuesday evenings. There were also ent competitions at the venue and the **Quarry Men** re one of the bands who appeared at the Winter rdens during 1958.

Winters, Mike & Bernie

e of the major British television comedy duos of the ties. The brothers eventually parted company with Mike ving permanently to America and Bernie pursuing a o career in Britain. Sadly, they were both to contract cer.

The Beatles appeared on a number of shows hosted by couple, including the 'Big Night Out' series and also ackpool Night Out'.

In their autobiography *Shake A Pagoda Tree*, Mike ated how they were appearing at the **London lladium** when Jack Murray called to see them in their ssing-room and showed Mike a magazine picture of four s. 'They're big up North,' he said. 'Their agent has a ord shop and doesn't know what to do with them. I've them for sixteen to twenty weeks, and I can have a manent share of their contract if I want to. Do you want come in with me?'

Mike told him, 'I'm not gambling any more, Jack. rnie and I are going to work on our act and try to make a of it. Thanks all the same.'

When the duo began hosting the series 'Big Night Out', the Beatles were booked on the fifth recording session and when the two comics arrived at Didsbury one day they saw huge mobs outside the studio and asked the doorman what was happening.

'The Beatles are on the show today, sir,' he said and, of course, they remembered the mop-tops who Jack Murray had said were big up in the North.

The group wandered in an hour late for rehearsal with **Jane Asher** carrying Paul's guitar, and John Lennon said, 'I'm sorry we're late, sir.' Mike told him OK, but not to make it a habit as it messed everyone else about. Then, in their act Bernie did a send-up of 'She Loves You' and the lads were very appreciative. John came round with the others afterwards and said, 'Thanks very much for all the plugs you've been giving us', which Bernie and Mike thought was rather touching.

The following Thursday, they all went to see the playback of the show at ATV House in London and when they were leaving, Brian Epstein got in the lift with Bernie, Mike and their agent, Joe Collins. Brian told them that he wanted to get his lads into London so they introduced him to Joe, who said, 'Certainly.' He fixed up two dates for the Beatles and Mike commented, 'And [he] made £10,000 in the ten seconds it took to go down two floors. Not a bad rate of pay.'

This particular story is obviously not accurately remembered as there would be no way an agent could make £10,000 out of his percentage for two bookings of the Beatles at that particular point in their career.

The special edition of 'Big Night Out' was filmed at Teddington Studios, London, on 23 February 1964. This was screened in Britain on 29 February and was also shown in America when it was networked by the New York station WOR TV on 3 October 1965. The show was repeated by WOR TV on 4 October. The numbers the Beatles performed were 'All My Loving', 'Till There Was You', 'I Wanna Be Your Man', 'Please Mr Postman' and 'I Want To Hold Your Hand'.

Of another Beatles appearance on 'Big Night Out' in 1964, Mike commented, 'They agreed to appear on the show immediately they returned (from their sensational tour of America). They landed at Heathrow Airport one day in February and nobody had ever before witnessed such an astounding, hysterical reception. Business ground to a halt as thousands of screaming girls took over the airport building. Then the fans streamed off to Teddington to besiege the studio, screaming and chanting, "We want the Beatles . . . we want the Beatles."' The fans were unaware that the boys were being brought down river by launch and Mike and Bernie welcomed them as it drew into the bank, a few yards from the back door of the studios. Mike observed, 'They were nice lads, and we got the impression they were a little bewildered by it all. At that age it must have been onerous to adjust to instant fame.'

The cameras followed the Beatles all day long, filming them rehearsing and relaxing and, from time to time, snippets were screened on TV so that people at home could see how they were getting on. It was quite unprecedented and the show was a resounding success. Mike and Bernie got on well with the group, who seemed to like the two comedians.

Bill and Virginia Harry went to visit the Beatles when they were rehearsing for 'Blackpool Night Out' at the **ABC Theatre, Blackpool** on 19 July 1964. Brian Epstein, **Neil Aspinall** and **Mal Evans** were there talking to Liverpool comedian Johnny Hackett. Jimmy Edwards and Frank Berry kept coming out with jokes that weren't in the script and John Lennon said, 'They'll use different jokes in the actual programme because they want to keep the musicians in the pit laughing.'

Apart from performing numbers such as 'A Hard Day's Night' and Long Tall Sally', the Beatles appeared in several sketches, joined by Mike and Bernie. In one, Ringo was a patient awaiting an operation and in another they were a crew of dustmen.

Bernie Winters died of cancer in May 1991.

● With A Little Help From My Friends (Song)

Paul wrote this song in March 1967 in the Cavendish Avenue work-room and received a bit of help from John with the lyrics. He'd used the working title 'Bad Finger Boogie' and was later to suggest **Badfinger** as a name for The Iveys. The song was included on the *Sgt Pepper* album and lead vocals were sung by Ringo.

Paul commented: 'Ringo's got a great sentimental thing. He likes soul music and always has, though we didn't see that scene for a long while till he showed us. I suppose that's why we write these sort of songs for him, with sentimental things in them, like "With A Little Help From My Friends".'

Young Idea covered the song and reached No. 29 in the charts with it in July 1967, but it was the **Joe Cock** version which was to top the British charts the followi year, in November 1968.

The number was included on *The Beatles 1966–19* album and Ringo sang it on his 'Ringo' TV special 1978.

There have been approximately 100 cover versions b variety of artists including Barbra Streisand, Count Bas Peter Frampton, Herb Alpert and Ike & Tina Turner.

● With A Little Help From My Friends (T Programme)

A BBC Television programme centred on George Mar which was filmed at London's Talk Of The Town Club 14 December 1969.

Ringo Starr was a guest on the show, which w transmitted on 24 December.

● Within You, Without You

Indian-sounding song, penned by George and included the *Sgt Pepper's Lonely Hearts Club Band* album.

The idea first came to George when he was invited dinner at **Klaus Voorman**'s Hampstead house. They la began to talk and George noticed a harmonium, instrument which he'd never played before. He began tinker on it and the idea for 'Within You, Without Y came to him then – and he completed the song when got home.

He was the only Beatle on the session when recorded the number on Wednesday, 15 March 19 There were a number of Indian instruments used duri the session. George himself played a swordmandel zither-like instrument) and a tamboura. An Indi musician acquaintance of George played the dilru (similar to a sitar) and tabla. Other Indian instrume were played by members of the Asian Music Circle fr Finchley, and **Neil Aspinall** played a tamboura.

'Within You, Without You' was the final song to completed for *Sgt Pepper's Lonely Hearts Club Band* and Monday, 3 April 1967, George Martin, who had writte score based on George's ideas, conducted a section strings to add to it, comprising eight violins and th cellos. The violinists were Erich Gruenberg, Alan Loved Julien Gaillard, Paul Scherman, Ralph Elman, Da Wolfsthal, Jack Rothstein and Jack Greene. The celli were Reginald Kilbey, Allen Ford and Peter Beaven.

With The Beatles

 group's second album, issued on Parlophone (PCS 5) on 22 November 1963. It went straight to the top of album charts on the day of its release, replacing ase Please Me', and remained in the No. 1 position for weeks, with a chart life of 40 weeks. During its first k of release it also entered the singles charts at No. 16 reached No. 11 the following week. It remained in the les charts for seven weeks.

ts American equivalent was *Meet The Beatles*, their album release on **Capitol Records** (ST 2047), issued 20 January 1964. This excluded five of the *With The tles* tracks: 'Please Mr Postman', 'Roll Over thoven', 'You've Really Got A Hold On Me', 'Devil In Heart', and 'Money', and included the tracks 'I Want Iold Your Hand' and 'I Saw Her Standing There'.

ith The Beatles included eight original compositions three Motown numbers. The album opened with two of 's compositions, 'It Won't Be Long' and 'All I've Got Do', followed by Paul's 'All My Loving'. George rison penned the next track 'Don't Bother Me', which followed by the Lennon & McCartney composition, le Child'. Paul takes over on lead vocal for 'Till There You', a number featured in the 1957 American ical *The Music Man* and a song which the Beatles had featuring in their stage act in Liverpool clubs.

Please Mr Postman' is the first of the Motown covers, a er hit in America for the Marvelettes. The **Chuck ry** rock classic 'Roll Over Beethoven' is sung by George Paul takes lead vocal on the following track, a Lennon IcCartney composition, 'Hold Me Tight'. Another wn hit, by 'Smokey' Robinson, was 'You Really Got A l On Me', an American hit for the Miracles.

 Wanna Be Your Man' was penned by Paul, with a help from John, and Ringo takes over on vocals. This e number which the Beatles gave to the **Rolling es** to record. 'Devil In Her Heart' had been recorded merica by female vocal group the Donays as 'Devil In Heart', but it hadn't been a hit. This was followed by A Second Time', a John Lennon composition which described by *The Times* music critic **William Mann** ich intricate detail that it helped to bring further ectability to the Beatles' music.

he final song on the album was the Motown hit 'Money t's What I Want)', which had been Barrett Strong's US chart success.

● Woman

A number which Paul McCartney wrote specially for **Peter & Gordon** and the fourth and last song he was to give them. It was the 'A' side of their single, issued in America in January 1966 and in Britain the following month. The flipside was 'Wrong From The Start'. The song was also the first track on the duo's album of the same name, issued in March of that year.

Paul used the pseudonym **Bernard Webb** when he wrote the song and that was the name credited as songwriter on the actual record in Britain, but when it entered the charts a few weeks later, Paul admitted that he'd written it but wanted to see if he could enter the charts without using the magical Lennon & McCartney name. Webb was said to be an aspiring songwriter and a student in Paris. Paul also used the pseudonym A. Smith for the single's American release.

There were three Beatles-related numbers with this same title. In 1972, Paul's brother **Mike** recorded a number called 'Woman' and it was also the title of John's single, issued from his *Double Fantasy* album.

● Wonderwall

Wonderwall was a film for which George Harrison composed the soundtrack. He wrote the musical parts for both the British musicians and the Indian ones, and produced the album himself. He went to Bombay to record it and commented: 'It was fantastic, really. The studio's on top of the offices but there's no soundproofing. So if you listen closely to some of the Indian tracks on the LP you can hear taxis going by. Every time the offices knocked off at 5.30 p.m. we had to stop recording because you could just hear everybody stomping down the steps. They only had a big old **EMI** mono machine. It was too incredible. I mixed everything as we did it. It was nice enough because you get spoiled working on eight- and sixteen-tracks.'

The *Wonderwall* soundtrack was the first album issued by **Apple Corps**. It was released in Britain on SAPCOR 1 on 1 November 1968 and in America on ST 3350 on 2 December 1968.

The 94-minute film was produced by Andrew Braunsberg from a screenplay by G. Cain. It was based on a story written by Gerard Brach. Jack McGowran starred as a professor who discovers he can peek into the flat of a young model, Jane Birkin, and the scenes he witnesses turn into psychedelic fantasies. The movie also starred

Irene Handl and Richard Wattis and received its London premiere on 20 January 1969.

Gordon Gow, writing in *Films and Filming*, commented: 'Unless you are jaded by too prolonged an explosure to the swinging half-myth, you might enjoy the blending of bright colours and Harrison music in ***Wonderwall*** . . . the Harrison music replaces dialogue, waxing almost vocal like a cinema organist from the silent days.'

● Wonderwall Music

The first solo Beatles album venture. *Wonderwall* was a film directed by Joe Mussot and starring Jack McGowran and Jane Birkin in a colourful psychedelic fantasy in which a man spies on a model through a chink in a wall. Mussot was a friend of George Harrison's and invited the Beatle to compose the film's soundtrack.

George recorded the album in two countries. Initially he recorded in London with Liverpool band the **Remo Four** who comprised Colin Manley on guitar/steel guitar, Tony Ashton on piano/organ, Roy Dyke on drums and Phil Rogers on bass. Other musicians included John Barham on piano/flugelhorn and Tommy Reilly on harmonica. **Eric Clapton** and Ringo Starr were also reported to have aided George at the sessions.

Further sessions took place in India at the **EMI** studios in Bombay. George hired a number of Indian musicians: Ashish Khan on sarod, Mahapurush Misra on tabla and pakavaj, Sharad and Hanuman Jadev on shanhais, Shambu-Das, Indril Bhattacharya and Shankar Ghosh on sitars, Chandra Shakher on surbahar, Shiv Kumar Shermar on santoor, S. R. Kenkare on flute, Vinaik Vora on thar-shanhai and Rij Ram Desad on harmonium and tablatarang.

Wonderwall Music was issued in Britain on Apple SAPCOR 1 on 1 November 1968 and in America on Apple ST 3350 on 2 December 1968. It reached No. 49 in the American charts but didn't chart in Britain.

The front cover illustration of the album was by Bob Gill and the tracks were, Side One: 'Microbes', 'Red Lady Too', 'Tabla And Pakavaj', 'In The Park', 'Drilling A Home', 'Guru Vandana', 'Greasy Legs', 'Ski-ing', 'Gat Kirwani', 'Dream Scene'. Side Two: 'Party Secombe', 'Love Scene', 'Crying', 'Cowboy Music', 'Fantasy Sequins', 'On The Bed', 'Glass Box', 'Wonderwall To Be Here', 'Singing Om'.

● Wong, Arthur

A dedicated fan of the **Quarry Men** skiffle group. In 1
he made some tapes of the group performing, as did
other fans of the band, Geraldine and Colette Da
However, none of the recordings exist as other items w
eventually taped over the Quarry Men numbers.

● Woodbine, Lord

This tall Trinidad-born, Liverpool-based characte
known only by this sobriquet. The 'Lord' is a grandi
title, self-bestowed in a West Indian fashion
'Woodbine' is taken from the brand of cigarettes
chainsmoked at the time. He is more familiarly know
'Woody'.

A well-known character in the Liverpool 8 dist
where he put his hand to everything from building
decorating to playing in a steel band and acting as barn
He opened his own club, the New Colony Club in Berl
Street, where the Silver Beetles appeared on one or
occasions. He also ran the **New Cabaret Artistes C**
for **Allan Williams**, a shebeen where the Silver Bee
backed a stripper known as **Janice**.

Lord Woodbine also joined Allan Williams, his
Beryl and her brother-in-law Barry Chang in the mini
with the Beatles on their first trip to Hamburg.

● Wooden Heart

A number featured in **Elvis Presley**'s 1960 film *GI Bl*
It was released as a single in Britain where it reached
1 and it remained in the charts for 27 weeks – the lon
chart life of any Elvis single in Britain.

The number was based on a German folk song '*Mi
Denn Zum Stadtele Hinaus*' and was adapted by **B
Kaempfert**, Kay Twomey, Fred Wise and Ben Weis
A single of the number by Elvis was issued in the State
1964 but it only 'bubbled under' the Hot Hundred at
107.

The Beatles included the song in their repertoire du
1961 and 1962 with Paul McCartney on lead vocals. It
a popular number at the **Cavern**, and also during
Beatles' Hamburg gigs due to the fact that part of
lyrics were in the German language.

● Wooler, Bob

Born in Liverpool on 19 January 1932, Bob becar
clerk in the local railway dock office in 1952, immedi

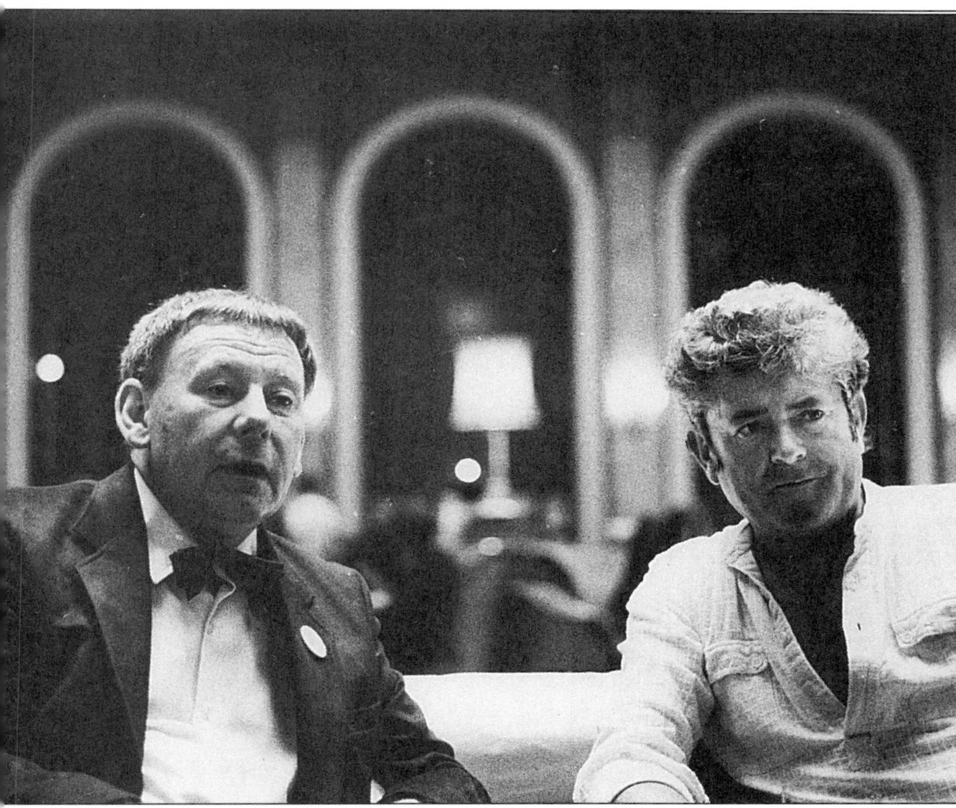

Bob Wooler and Allan Williams in Liverpool's Adelphi Hotel. (A Beatles fan)

owing his National Service. He was living in the ston area when, in 1957, he became involved in aging a skiffle group called the Kingstrums, who came n a notorious area of Garston called 'Under The lge'. He once entered them in a talent contest at the eacre Labour Club (which was won by the Mars Bars, later became **Gerry & the Pacemakers**) and lls, 'At that Labour Club I remember the Kingstrums ing into direct competition with John Lennon's skiffle ıp, the **Quarry Men**. Because they came from posh es like Woolton and Aigburth, the Quarry Men were sidered to be snobs "Under The Bridge"!' The gstrums disbanded in 1958 but the experience of king on the local rock 'n' roll scene convinced Bob that vas more suited to compering the shows put on at local hives and as a compere-cum-disc jockey he worked t-time for promoters such as Wally Hill of Peak motions, appearing at **Holyoake Hall** in Smithdown Road and similar venues. He also co-promoted his own shows at **Hambleton Hall** with Vic Anton.

When the Beatles arrived back from Germany with copies of their single 'My Bonnie', they gave a copy to Bob, who began playing it at Hambleton Hall, and another to Virginia Sowry at ***Mersey Beat***. The story of their recording session had already been featured on the front cover of Issue No. 2.

Bob's encyclopaedic knowledge of the local scene soon made him a sought-after figure by local promoters and his advice was regularly heeded. **Allan Williams** offered him a full-time job as compere/host at the **Top Ten Club**, but when it burned down eight days after the opening, Bob was without work, apart from his compering activities – which soon provided him with full-time employment when he was engaged as compere at the **Cavern Club**.

In the meantime, as Williams was involved with financial problems due to the Top Ten disaster, he suggested that Wooler become the Beatles' manager. Bob didn't want to involve himself in management again, but agreed to help them and talked promoter **Brian Kelly** into booking them.

Bob had a particularly pungent wit and he also created what were to become known as 'Woolerisms', a range of phrases he bestowed on local music personalities. They included 'The Nemperor' for Brian Epstein, 'Mr Showmanship' for **Rory Storm**, 'The Panda Footed Prince of Prance' for Faron, leader of Faron's Flamingos, 'The Sheik of Shake' for Karl Terry, leader of the Cruisers, and 'The Boswell of Beat' for Bill Harry, editor of *Mersey Beat*. Epstein was so flattered with the term 'The Nemperor' that he often used the phrase himself.

There was also a lot of good-natured banter between Bob and the Beatles during the Cavern introductions and John once told the Cavern audience that Bob was his long-last father, whom he hadn't seen for fifteen years – and they believed him!

Bill Harry invited Bob to write a column for *Mersey Beat* under the title 'The Roving I' and his contribution for the 31 August 1961 issue was full of praise for the Beatles:

> 'Why do you think the Beatles are so popular? Many people many times have asked me this question since that fantastic night (Tuesday, 27 December 1960) at **Litherland Town Hall**, when the impact of the act was first felt on this side of the river. I consider myself privileged to have been associated with the launching of the group on that exciting occasion, and grateful for the opportunities of presenting them to fever-pitch audiences at practically all of the group's subsequent appearances prior to their last Hamburg trip.
>
> 'Perhaps my close association with the group's activities, both earlier this year and since their recent re-appearance on the Merseyside scene, persuades people to think that I can produce a blueprint of the Beatles Success Story. It figures, I suppose, and if, in attempting to explain the popularity of their act, the following analysis is at variance with other people's views, well that's just one of those things. The question is nevertheless thought-provoking.
>
> 'Well, then how to answer it? First some obvious observations. The Beatles are the biggest thing to have hit the Liverpool rock 'n' roll set-up in years. They were, and still are, the hottest local property any R
> promoter is likely to encounter.
>
> 'I think the Beatles are No. 1 because t
> resurrected original style rock 'n' roll music, the ori
> of which are to be found in American negro sing
> They hit the scene when it had been emasculated
> figures like Cliff Richard and sounds like th
> electronic wonders, the **Shadows** and their m
> imitators. Gone was the drive that inflamed
> emotions. This was studio set jungle music purve
> skilfully in a chartwise direction by arrangement
> the A&R men.
>
> 'The Beatles, therefore, exploded on a jaded sc
> And to those people on the verge of quitting teendo
> those who had experienced during their m
> impressionable years the impact of rhythm 'n' b
> music (raw rock 'n' roll) – this was an experienc
> process of regaining and reliving a style of sounds
> associated feelings identifiable with their era.
>
> 'Here again in the Beatles was the stuff that scre
> are made of. Here was the excitement – both phys
> and aural – that symbolized the rebellion of yout
> the ennuied mid-fifties. This was the real thing. I
> they were, first five and then four human dyna
> generating a beat which was irresistible. Turning b
> the rock clock. Pounding out items from **Chuck Be**
> **Little Richard**, **Carl Perkins**, the Coasters and
> other great etceteras of the era. Here they w
> unmindful of uniformity of dress. Unkempt-like
> hair. Rugged yet romantic, appealing to both se
> With calculated naivety and an ingenuous, throw-a
> approach to their music. Effecting indifferenc
> audience response and yet always saying "Thank y
> Reviving interest in, and commanding, enthusiasm
> numbers which had descended the charts way b
> Popularizing (more than any other group) flipside i
> – example, "Boys". Compelling attention
> influencing, wittingly or unwittingly, other groups i
> style, choice and presentation of songs.
>
> 'Essentially a vocal act, hardly ever instrumenta
> least not in this country), here they w
> independently-minded, playing what they like
> kicks, kudos and cash. Privileged in having ga
> prestige and experience from a residency at
> Hamburg Top Ten Club, during the autumn and w
> of last year. Musically authoritative and physic

magnetic – example the mean, moody magnificence of drummer **Pete Best**, a sort of teenage Jeff Chandler. A remarkable variety of talented voices which song-wise sound distinctive, but when speaking, possess the same naivety of tone. Rhythmic revolutionaries. An act which from beginning to end is a succession of climaxes. A personality cult. Seemingly unambitious, yet fluctuating between the self-assured and the vulnerable. Truly a phenomenon – and also a predicament to promoters! Such are the fantastic Beatles. I don't think anything like them will happen again.'

sidering the piece was published in August 1961, it is zingly prophetic.

n Issue No. 7 of *Mersey Beat*, Bob listed his Top Ten sey groups:

'Well here it is then, my list of what I rate to be the en most popular rock groups on Merseyside – xcluding the Bluegenes, of course, they are beyond omparison. They are in a class of their own.

1. The Beatles
2. Gerry and the Pacemakers
3. Rory Storm and the Hurricanes
4. The Remo 4
5. The Strangers
6. Johnny Sandon and the Searchers
7. Karl Terry and the Cruisers
8. Mark Peters and the Cyclones
9. Ray and the Del Renas
10. The Big Three'

ddition to his writing activities for *Mersey Beat*, Bob posed most of the copy for the advertisements placed promoters both in *Mersey Beat* and the ***Liverpool o***. They were concise, lively and contained many .

When John Lennon paid for classified advertisements *ersey Beat* he would place notices such as 'HEAR BOB LER SING with the Beatles at **Aintree Institue**' and r BOB BEATLE at the Woolerstute'.

part from his compering duties, Bob advised groups tage presentation, discussed their musical repertoires them and often recommended numbers for them to n. Bob's collection of American singles, which he carried around with him to the venues in a portable record case, led to a lot of bands playing the numbers which Bob had searched for and selected himself.

Having sacrificed the security of a steady job to compere shows at the ill-fated Top Ten, he finally found what he was looking for when he became compere at the Cavern in 1960, a job which lasted for seven years. The audience loved his announcements: 'Hello, Cavern Dwellers, and welcome to the best of cellars!' During his years at the Cavern he was to introduce the Beatles on stage more times than anyone else in the world.

The fact that the Beatles looked to him for advice was indicated when they asked him to attend their meeting with Brian Epstein on Wednesday, 3 December 1961. It was half-day closing in Liverpool that day and Epstein had requested a meeting at his office in NEMS at 4.30 p.m. Bob, John, George and Pete went to a pub called the Bridge to discuss Brian prior to the meeting and arrived late. Paul was 30 minutes late. Brian was slightly irritated at their tardiness and wanted to know who Bob was. 'This is me Dad,' said John. Bob later discussed the meeting with them. He also began to meet Brian Epstein regularly and revealed to him that the group were, in fact, actively seeking a manager.

When Epstein began to promote shows on behalf of **NEMS Enterprises** in order to promote the Beatles and other groups he'd signed, he used Bob's expertise to organize, promote and run events at local venues such as the **Tower Ballroom**, **New Brighton** and the **Queen's Hall, Widnes**.

One of the most controversial situations regarding Wooler and the Beatles occurred at Paul McCartney's 21st birthday party on 18 June 1963. One of Bob's traits was to make cutting remarks, not intended maliciously, but rather out of his fondness for word-play. He made some reference to John's recent short holiday break in Spain with Brian Epstein, obviously couched in a way to contain a double-meaning. To a Lennon who'd drunk too many beers and wasn't interested in the subtle cleverness, it was like a red rag to a bull. He leapt onto Bob and battered him to the ground, giving him a black eye, bruised ribs and torn knuckles – which Bob sustained when he'd tried to protect his face from John's foot as he was being kicked. Members of the **Fourmost** pulled John off and Brian drove Bob to hospital. A small news item about the incident appeared in the *Daily Mirror* and John, initially refusing to apologize, saying 'He called me a queer so I battered his bloody ribs in', eventually allowed Epstein to smooth over the incident and Bob was paid a modest settlement of £200.

A few months later, Bob announced their final appearance at the Cavern. Their phenomenal success had taken him by surprise and for once he was lost for words, announcing them simply by saying, 'It's the Beatles!'

When the Beatles moved to London, Brian employed a number of his personal friends from Liverpool, causing an exodus of Merseyside people to the London offices of NEMS, but Bob wasn't among them. He remained at the Cavern until 1967. He became **Ray McFall**'s right-hand man, managed groups such as the Carrolls and, for a short time, was married to **Beryl Adams**, Brian Epstein's former secretary.

With the closing of the Cavern, Bob took on various jobs as disc jockey in the north and worked for a time as a bingo caller at the former **Locarno Ballroom**. In the seventies he presented an occasional promotion in Liverpool and worked on several projects with Allan Williams, primarily Beatle conventions. By the eighties he was escorting visitors to Liverpool on special Magical Mystery Tours of the Beatles' former haunts.

● Woolton Village Club, *Allerton Road, Woolton, Liverpool L25*

Small club in the area where John Lennon lived. The **Quarry Men** appeared at the venue only once, on a special Christmas party booking, during which they played a ten-minute spot on 24 January 1959.

● Word, The

Generally credited as a Lennon & McCartney collaboration, although it is believed to be a number written by John. It was included on *Rubber Soul* and as the deadline for the album was pressing it was rush-recorded in three takes on Wednesday, 10 November 1965, with additional instruments – Paul on piano and George Martin on harmonium.

The word in question was 'love'.

● Words Of Love

A **Buddy Holly** song which he recorded in 1957. It was a part of the early **Quarry Men** repertoire and originally John and George shared lead vocals on the number, although John and Paul were to take the vocal parts later on and were heard on their **'Pop Go The Beatles'** s on 20 August 1963 singing it, and it is also featured on *Beatles For Sale* album.

When they recorded the number on Sunday, 18 Octo 1964, at **Abbey Road** it was the first and only time recorded a Buddy Holly number in a recording stu apart from the time they performed 'Crying, Waiti Hoping' at their **Decca audition**.

The number is included on their ninth British *Beatles For Sale (No. 2)*, and their *Love Songs* compila and *The Beatles Collection* set. In America it was issued on the **Capitol** album *Beatles VI*.

● World Without Love, A

Composition by Paul and the first of four songs he w give to **Peter & Gordon**. The number established duo and took them to the top of the charts in both Bri and America, with world sales passing the million mar

Cynthia Lennon observes David Wynne's sculpture of the Beatles. (Merseyside Tourism Office)

s issued in Britain on Columbia DB 7225 on 28 bruary 1964 and in America on **Capitol** 5175 on 27 ril 1964.

The Beatles never recorded the number and it wasn't t of their repertoire. John Lennon was particularly used by the opening words to the song – 'Please lock away . . .'

Wynne, David

minent British sculptor, noted for his pieces on Yehudi nuhin and the Prince of Wales.

Wynne was the only sculptor the Beatles ever sat for. e group agreed to pose for the artist during their short son in Paris at the **Olympia Theatre** in January 1964. e result was a sculpture of four bronze masks in an tion of five and also four six-inch figures of the group ying their instruments.

Wyvern Social Club, 108 Seel Street, verpool L1

ıb where, on 10 May 1960, the Silver Beetles were ong the groups auditioning for impresario **Larry rnes** who was looking for a backing band for singer **lly Fury**, having been impressed by the Liverpool ups performing on the bill of the **Gene Vincent** cert at **Liverpool Stadium** on 3 May. Parnes told **an Williams** he'd like a couple of Mersey groups to k his artists on tour and Williams agreed to set up the dition. Mark Forster, one of Parnes' assistants, ıfirmed the arrangement in a letter in which he ntioned that they'd need backing bands for Duffy Power d **Johnny Gentle**. He added, 'We will make angements for Mr Parnes to come and audition your ups to select the most suitable. He will also bring Billy ry as Billy will want one of these four groups for his own sonal use. Incidentally, the idea of Billy wanting a up from his own home-town will provide several eresting press stories and publicity tie-ups.'

Williams had asked photographer Cheniston Roland to e photographs of the audition and a pictorial record of events that day were captured on film, showing the ups who auditioned, in sequence. They were Cass & the ssanovas, Derry & the Seniors, **Gerry & the cemakers**, Cliff Roberts & the Rockers and the Silver etles. Previous reports indicated that **Rory Storm & e Hurricanes** were also on the bill, although Chenison's photographs disprove this. The belief that they were on the bill probably stemmed from the fact that Rory was actually at the audition – but the publicity-conscious local singer was only there to press Billy Fury into posing in a photograph with him.

The Silver Beetles' drummer **Tommy Moore** was late for the audition and the group began their ten-minute spot with **Johnny Hutchinson** of the Cassanovas sitting in. Moore arrived halfway through the spot and took over.

Billy Fury plumped for the Silver Beetles and there are conflicting stories as to why they didn't become his backing band. Williams reports that Parnes quietly asked him if he could hear the Silver Beetles perform a number without **Stuart**. Stuart wasn't a very good musician and had his back turned to Parnes during the audition. When Williams asked them to play another number, but without Stu, John Lennon refused and the opportunity was lost. Parnes, however, although knowing straight away that Stuart wasn't a good bass player, alleges that he wasn't worried about him, he was more concerned about the drummer, whom he considered far too old to be a member of a rock 'n' roll band. At the time John, for instance, was nineteen, but Tommy Moore was 36. Such an age gap was all too apparent to Parnes. Apart from the drummer's age, he didn't dress in the same style as the other members of the group and Parnes didn't like the fact that he was not punctual. Parnes was later to say, 'The most distinctive thing I remember is that four of them had these special haircuts and wore black trousers. They stood out amongst the others in the room. Their dress impressed me tremendously. But one of them dressed differently. I liked their style and music, but I told them they needed a more powerful drummer, somebody to drive their music along.'

Although he liked the band, Parnes didn't want to cause disharmony and didn't press the matter. Williams persuaded Stuart to draw some sketches of Fury and Parnes and Lennon requested Fury's autograph. Parnes has also recalled that after the Silver Beetles had auditioned, Lennon later asked him if they could have some extra time to play some of their self-penned numbers and he gave them an extra ten minutes at the end of the afternoon. He praised them for their original material and made a note in his pad: 'Silver Beetles: Very Good; keep note for future work'.

Allan Williams was to transform the Wyvern into the **Blue Angel** nightclub.

● Yardbirds, The

London R&B group who formed in 1963 with the line-up of Keith Relf (vocals/harmonica), Andrew Topham (lead), Chris Dreja (rhythm), Paul Samwell-Smith (bass) and **Jim McCartney** (drums). Topham was soon replaced by **Eric Clapton** and the group took over the **Crawdaddy Club** residency from the **Rolling Stones** and were one of the various southern bands who made the pilgrimage up north to appear at the **Cavern** in Liverpool.

The group appeared on the *Beatles Christmas Show* at the **Odeon, Hammersmith** in 1964, during which they had a ten-minute spot. This was probably where George Harrison noticed the nineteen-year-old guitarist Clapton for the first time. The Yardbirds were also on the bill of the Beatles' final concert appearance in Britain on 1 May 1966 at the **Empire Pool, Wembley**.

They had a number of hits, including 'Good Morning Little Schoolgirl' and 'For Your Love' before disbanding in 1968. At that time Jimmy Page was a member of the band and formed the New Yardbirds, although he quickly changed the name to Led Zeppelin.

● Ye Cracke, *Rice Street, Liverpool L1*

The nearest public house to **Liverpool College of Art**. During a college party, John went across to **Cynthia** Powell and asked her for a dance. Cynthia, who had a crush on John, but was too nervous to admit it, panicked and said, 'I'm awfully sorry, but I'm engaged to a fellow in Hoylake.' Annoyed, John snapped, 'I didn't ask you to marry me.' When the dance was over, John invited Cynthia to Ye Cracke for a drink and later that evening he took to **Stu Sutcliffe**'s flat and they made love for the fi time.

Ye Cracke was the main after-hours haunt for some the art students. **Arthur Ballard**, one of the lectur used to tutor some of his pupils in 'The War Office', a t room in the pub, so named because it was where regul used to discuss the events of the Crimean War, as th occurred.

Once, when they were standing outside the pub lunchtime, drinks in hand, John and Cynthia spotted ac John Gregson (a Liverpool-born British film star wh most popular film was *Genevieve*). John desperately lool around for something unusual for the actor to sign. spotted an old boot and asked Gregson to autograph it. T

Ye Cracke – the watering hole for students of Liverpool Colle of Art in the sixties.

actor was amused by the gesture and signed it across stitching.

Painter Adrian Henri remembered one incident at Cracke where John was lying on the floor imitat swimming movements. A barmaid told him to stop and said, 'I can't stop, or I'll drown!'

John also used to have long conversations with St

ıtcliffe about art and artists, with Stu filling in the ıckground to art movements of the early twentieth ntury, such as the Dada school, to him.

Bill Harry and John also used to have long nversations together in their favourite seat, beneath an ching of 'The Death of Nelson'. This is where John owed Bill samples of his poetry, which led to Harry king him to contribute written work to ***Mersey Beat***. hen Lennon, Sutcliffe, **Rod Murray** and Harry used to at in the evenings, Harry suggested that the four of them ll themselves the Dissenters and attempt to make verpool famous: John with his music, Stu and Rod with eir painting and Harry with his writing.

Yellow Submarine (Album)

ıe soundtrack album of *Yellow Submarine* was issued veral months after the release of the actual animated m. It had been planned to issue it in December 1968, ıt it was finally issued in Britain on 17 January 1969 on ırlophone PCS 7070. There had been discussions about leasing a *Yellow Submarine* EP with four Beatles ımbers on it, but this plan was shelved.

The problem was that the LP couldn't strictly be garded as a new Beatles album as one half of it ntained music by the George Martin Orchestra, two of e Beatles numbers had already been available on evious releases some time before and the record buyer ıs left with only four new Beatles numbers.

The album became the second Beatles album not to top e British charts, reaching only the No. 2 position, though, ironically, the No. 1 position was occupied by *ıe Beatles* double album.

It was issued in America on **Capitol** SW 153 and also ached No. 2, once again being prevented from occupying e No. 1 spot by *The Beatles* double album. The track sting was, Side One: 'Yellow Submarine', 'Only A orthern Song', 'All Together Now', 'Hey Bulldog', 'It's l Too Much'. Side Two (All tracks by the George Martin rchestra): 'Pepperland', 'Sea Of Time', 'Sea Of Holes', ea Of Monsters', 'March Of The Meanies', 'Pepperland ıid Waste', 'Yellow Submarine In Pepperland'.

Tunes or parts of tunes heard on the film soundtrack ıt not included on the soundtrack album were 'Eleanor igby', an orchestral section of 'A Day In The Life', 'When n Sixty-Four', 'Nowhere Man', 'Lucy In The Sky With iamonds', 'Sgt Pepper's Lonely Hearts Club Band', 'With A Little Help From My Friends', 'All You Need Is Love' and 'Baby You're A Rich Man'.

● Yellow Submarine (Film)

The animated feature film *Yellow Submarine*, subtitled *Nothing Is Real*, originated in the series of Beatles cartoons made by TV Cartoons and financed by King Features.

Hungarian-born **Al Brodax** originally had the idea of using the Beatles in a 'Fantasia'-like full-length cartoon in 1966. He contacted George Dunning, a Canadian animator who had set up a studio in London in 1957 and who had been involved in the cartoon series, and director Charles Jenkins. They then hired a Czech-born artist, Heinz Edelmann, as designer.

The official screenplay credit reads: 'Written by Lee Minoff and Al Brodax, Jack Mendelsohn and Erich Segal, from an original story by Lee Minoff'. However, Heinz Edelmann commented: 'There was never one script. We had about twenty. Roger McGough (of the **Scaffold**) was responsible for much of it. But there were no strong opponents for the Beatles so I had to invent the Blue Meanies.'

Liverpool poet McGough was brought in to add a Liverpool flavour to the script and says he was paid £500, but wasn't credited – and he would have preferred the credit to the money.

Brodax was to say, 'We derived a lot from the *Sgt Pepper* album. We took the word "pepper", which is positive, spicy, and created a place called Pepperland which is full of colour and music. But in the hills around live Blue Meanies, who hate colour, hate everything positive.'

Brodax recalled that when he was working on the story with Erich Segal in a flat in London's Mayfair, John and Paul would ring up with script suggestions. Brodax recalls one particular call, made at 3.00 a.m. from John, in which he said: 'Wouldn't it be great if Ringo was followed down the street by a yellow submarine?' This somewhat bizarre notion found its way into the movie's opening scenes.

The writer who received the lion's share of press publicity was Erich Segal – largely because he was a university professor. One paper wrote: 'The script has been written by a Professor of Greek and Latin at Yale, Erich Segal, and the final draft of the film script was typed by the Dean's wife at Yale.' Brodax was responsible for

Yellow Submarine – an enchanting animated odyssey. (©Apple/King Features)

adding Segal to the project's team. 'Erich and I both have the same agent, you see,' he said. 'Erich is also writing the script for a new Richard Rodgers musical. Before that he used to do a lot of translating of foreign plays, but he's never done anything like a cartoon film before.'

Director George Dunning told David Rider of *Films And Filming*: 'We commissioned several artists to design the Beatles... in an effort to find out what the design ought to be. Fred Wolf worked mainly on animation, Dennis Rich dealt with a wide range of design and Bob Bals came over from Spain initially to do character design. W took some recorded conversations of the Beatles a animated against this to get the feel of their personalities

'The involvement of Heinz Edelmann was really a p between Charlie Jenkins and myself. We met him in t spring of 1967 to look at the trial film made, and discu the project. Then I showed Edelmann's work in t German magazine *Twen* to Al Brodax, the producer, a he was happy that Edelmann should be brought in.

'Edelmann was delighted to be exploring this n medium. After two weeks he presented me with fo drawings and that was enough – we knew we had worthwhile feature. Next, a two-minute pilot film was ma in colour with some of George Harrison's sitar music the soundtrack. Charlie Jenkins provided some sequenc using his polarization technique which was followed characters in backgrounds using some *Sgt Pepper* music.

Bob Balsar and Jack Stokes, as animation directors, c approximately half each, Eddie Radage did one sequen Charlie Jenkins took charge of "Eleanor Rigby "Northern Song", "It's All Too Much" and some ot parts. Heinz Edelmann controlled the overall desig developed the characters and initiated the Blue Mean when he pointed out that what was needed in the film w an enemy. This idea consolidated the film and gave i strong plot.'

There were many different approaches and styles us in the making of *Yellow Submarine*, one of which w rotoscoping, a method devised in the thirties by W. Disney Studios. This is a method where a live-acti sequence is filmed, then traced over, painted, and made appear like animation. This technique was subsequen used in the animation of ***Lord of the Rings***.

To match the movie's range of styles and techniques array of eccentric or fantastic characters were introduc such as Jeremy Hilary Boob, PhD, the Nowhere Man, w describes himself as a 'brilliant young physicist, classic botanist, essayist, satirist and artist'.

There were also the Hidden Persuaders, gangster-st figures with outsize boots that open to reveal guns; Ja the Nipper, who has hands like shark's teeth; the Ap Bonkers, tall, top-hatted blue-faced men who drop gi apples onto their victims' heads; the terrible Flying Glo a jet-propelled hand; the Butterfly Stomper; the Snappi Turtle Turks; and the Blue Meanies themselves, yello othed, red-lipped creatures with black masks, Mickey ouse-type ears, large boots and woolly blue bodies.

The Beatles were initially unenthusiastic about the nture, merely regarding it as a way of completing their nited Artists film deal. This was indicated by their titude to the movie's soundtrack. They provided four new ngs but, as George Martin pointed out in the case of ey Bulldog': 'John said, "We don't really need this in r album. Let's just give them that one."'

Incidentally, the 'Hey Bulldog' sequence was deleted om the American print of *Yellow Submarine*.

A popular, but untrue myth, is that as the London mphony Orchestra were recording the soundtrack in **MI** studios in the early hours of the morning, Brodax told e group that another song was needed. George Harrison ent a couple of hours writing, then came up with the umber 'Northern Song', saying to Brodax, 'Here, Al, it's ly a northern song.'

The third original number was 'All Together Now', the urth was 'It's All Too Much'. The other Beatles numbers sed were 'Yellow Submarine', 'Eleanor Rigby', a ortened version of 'A Day In The Life', 'When I'm Sixty-our', 'Lucy In The Sky With Diamonds', 'Sgt Pepper's nely Hearts Club Band' and 'All You Need Is Love'.

George Martin was musical director for the film; he mposed 'Pepperland', 'Sea of Holes', 'Sea of Monsters', larch of the Meanies', 'Pepperland Laid Waste' and ellow Submarine in Pepperland' which, performed by e LSO, took up one half of the soundtrack album.

The group also made a brief appearance at the end of e movie when they invite an international audience to in them in song. For the rest of the film the voices of the dividual Beatles were dubbed by actors. John Clive was e voice of John, Geoff Hughes was Paul, Peter Batten, eorge, and Paul Angelis, Ringo. Angelis also took the rt of the Chief Blue Meanie, Dick Emery provided the oices of Hilary Boob, the Lord Mayor and Max, and ance Percival that of Old Fred.

The synopsis of the plot is as follows:

'"Once upon a time – or maybe twice ... there was a ace called Pepperland." On a peaceful day in this happy ngdom, a concert by Sgt Pepper's Lonely Hearts Club and is interrupted by an anti-musical missile attack from e Blue Meanies. The chief Blue Meanie, his assistant ax, and their 99-numbered henchmen turn their splotch ns on the docile Pepperland populace, determined to rid the world of music, happiness and love ("A world without music is a Blue World!").

'Old Fred, conductor of the Band, flees to the Lord Mayor, who puts him into the Yellow Submarine for a last-minute escape. The sub surfaces in Liverpool where Ringo wanders aimlessly in boredom. The sub, radar-like, follows Ringo to his house. Fred enters Ringo's house, explains the situation and enlists his aid. They proceed to round up the others. John materializes out of a Frankenstein creature-like figure, Paul is found playing classical music, and George appears out of a haze of transcendental meditation. Armed with a battery of puns and four new songs, the Beatles board the Yellow Submarine and head for Pepperland. They are detoured through the Seas of Time, Science, Monsters, Consumer Products, Nowhere, Phrenology, Green and Holes.

'They undergo time warps, chase Lucy through her "sky of diamonds", climb clocks and soup cans, become ancient and infantile, molecularized, actually "disappear up their own existence" and almost drown in the avalanche of apples, among other adventures.

'Characters they encounter on their mad "Modyssey" include the US Cavalry, Father Mackenzie, assorted monsters (including a vacuum-flask monster), Cowboys, Indians, King Kong and several unidentifiable "things". Ringo takes a liking to the super-intellectual Boob (a poetic personification of the "Nowhere Man") and takes him along on the trip: in the Sea of Green he is captured by a giant blue hand.

'A Pepper-powered sneeze propels the Beatles through the Sea of Holes into occupied Pepperland, which has been almost completely drained of colour. The Lord Mayor is astonished at the resemblance between the Beatles and the original Sgt Pepper Band. Disguised as Apple Bonkers, they infiltrate the musical instrument compound. Then it's Beatles versus Meanies, with guitars against splotch guns, the ferocious Flying Glove, the Butterfly Stompers, the Hidden Persuaders with guns in their shoes, the snapping Turtle Turks with their mouths in their bellies and the Count Down Clown with his nose-cone nose. A battle is waged to the tune of "All You Need Is Love" and love becomes the overwhelming power. A surprise ending carries the fantastic fracas right into the theatre.'

The film was premiered at the **London Pavilion** on Wednesday, 17 July 1968. Apart from the Beatles, other celebrities who attended included **Donovan**, **Sandie**

Shaw, **P. J. Proby**, Mick Jagger, **Twiggy**, Simon Dee, Tony Blackburn and Alan Price.

Heinz Edelmann called the film: 'The first example of non-commercial, commercial entertainment.'

In his book *Full Length Animated Feature Films*, Bruno Edena commented: 'This production had the same explosive effect in the field of full-length animation that only *Hellzapoppin* had in the traditional cinema – getting far away from logical narrative structure. It is very close in atmosphere to the spirit of Lewis Carroll.

'The film is a masterpiece and it has opened up new and undreamed of horizons for animation. It bears seeing several times for its content to be fully appreciated, and it has given such an impetus to the full-length animated film and inspired the imagination of many film-makers, and original pieces of work are now being produced on animation benches all over the world.'

The critics seemed equally impressed. The *Daily Telegraph* commented: 'Not since Disney's *Snow White* or *Make Mine Music* has a full-length animated film cartoon come upon us with such surprising skill and charm and freshness as this little epic . . .

'It is more of a Beatles film than any of their others, partly because they do not come on themselves but also because the medium of a colour cartoon gives its creators closer control over every effect.

'The Beatles' spirit is here, if not in the flesh, their good-natured gusto, their kindly curiosity, their sympathy with their fellow men and their lack of pretentiousness are all summed up here with gaiety.'

The *Evening Standard* film critic, Alexander Walker, wrote: '*Yellow Submarine* is the key film of the Beatles era. It's a trip through the contemporary mythology that the quartet from Merseyside have helped create. It's a pop voyage – "mododyssey" is the word, I suppose – that sails under the psychedelic colours of Carnaby Street to the turned-on music of *Sgt Pepper's Lonely Hearts Club Band*. It combines sensory stimulation with the art of the now in a way that will appeal to teenage ravers and Tate Gallery-goers alike.

'Its inventiveness never flags. The influence of artists like Alan Aldridge and Andy Warhol is perceptible, but never plagiarized. And the richest bit of sociological cartooning owes more to writers like Marshall McLuhan and Vance Packard – I mean the regiment of Blue Meanies with their hidden arsenal of peremptory arrows and disembodied fists beating the Pepperland proles in stupefied obedience.'

The correspondent for *Variety*, the American shc business magazine, wrote: 'Unlike Disney, the film mak no concession to sentiment or the cuddly. The characte are motley, matter-of-fact, grotesque and tend to be har and angular and are introduced for their shock effec rather than any winsome qualities. They are modern pe art and surrealistic and eschew charm with determination

Unfortunately, *Yellow Submarine* was not given tl chance to be the financial success in Britain that it mig have been. Exactly three weeks after the London premier Judith Simonds, writing in the *Daily Express*, reported th the spokesman for Rank had said: 'Attendances at tl London Pavilion where the film opened on 17 July, did come up to expectations. As a result the film will not get full release. We have some two hundred cinem throughout the country and about half will show the film.'

Peter Brown of Apple commented: 'We are a puzzled. It's been doing capacity business at the Lond Pavilion, so we don't understand Rank's reaction.' Charl Berman of United Artists stated: 'We have do tremendous business during the three weeks *Yello Submarine* has been at the London Pavilion.'

The published box-office receipts for the Pavili proved that United Artists and Apple had been right a Rank wrong. But the damage had been done and Rank decision to withdraw the film from more than half of the cinemas drastically affected its potential box-office incon in Britain.

In America, where it opened a few months later, it w a great success, doing the same amount of business as tl other major box-office hit at the time, *Funny Girl*.

During 1978 *Yellow Submarine* was revived at thr film festivals: Locarno (where it received a Speci Mention), San Francisco and Cambridge.

● Yellow Submarine (Single)

Paul originally came up with the idea of writing children's song in 1966. For some reason, there was ta that 'Yellow Submarine' had some allusions to drug which was untrue.

Paul commented, 'I knew it would get connotations, b it really was a children's song. I just loved the idea of ki singing it. With "Yellow Submarine" the whole idea w "If someday I came across some kids singing it, that w it", so it's got to be very easy – there isn't a single big ›rd. Kids will understand it easier than adults... There's me stuff in Greece like icing sugar – you eat it. It's like sweet and you drop it into water. It's called submarine, had it on holiday.'

The number provided Ringo with his first vocal on the ' side of a Beatles single. When asked if there was any ference to drugs in the lyrics, he said, 'Nothing at all. s simply a children's song with no hidden meanings. any people have interpreted it to be a war song, that entually all the world would be living in yellow bmarines. That's not the case.'

John Lennon and **Donovan** were said to have aided ul with some of the lyrics. The recording began at **bbey Road Studios** on Thursday, 26 May 1966, and ednesday, 1 June, was the day when a number of special fects and a chorus were added. Among the helpers in the udio that day adding to the chorus and effects were **Mal vans** and **Neil Aspinall**, Rolling Stone **Brian Jones**, **arianne Faithfull**, **Pattie** Harrison, **George Martin** d members of the Abbey Road staff and engineers, cluding **Geoff Emerick**, John Skinner and Terry ndon. John Lennon blew bubbles through a straw in a cket of water and there was a 30-second introduction eech by Ringo which was cut from the final release.

It became the Beatles' second double-'A' sided single d was issued in Britain on Parlophone 5493 on 5 August 966 where it reached No. 1 in the charts. **Capitol** issued in America on Capitol 5715 on 8 August 1966 where it ached No. 2 in the charts. The single reached No. 1 in rious countries around the world, including Australia, anada, Germany, Holland, Norway, New Zealand and veden.

It was also included as a track on their new album *evolver*, issued on the same day. Later that year it was cluded on the December 1966 compilation *A Collection f Beatles Oldies (But Goldies)* and was also to be featured the *Yellow Submarine* soundtrack album in January 969, *The Beatles 1962–1966* compilation in April 1973 d the *Reel Music* compilation in March 1982.

Yer Blues

hn Lennon's parody of the British Blues boom of the xties recorded in August 1968, mainly in a small annexe ext to the control room of **Abbey Road**'s Studio Two. hn had originally penned the number at Rishikesh and the Beatles rendition of the song was included on *The Beatles* double album.

In 1968 he performed the number on the ill-fated 'The Rolling Stones Rock 'n' Roll Circus', a television project which still hasn't seen the light of day. John also performed it with the **Plastic Ono Band** at the Toronto Rock And Roll Revival concert in 1969.

Yes It Is

A number penned by John at the beginning of 1965. He wanted a three-part vocal harmony effect similar to 'This Boy'. It was recorded on Tuesday, 16 February 1965, and George Harrison was to use a guitar tone-pedal on a Beatles record for the first time. The song was issued on the flipside of 'Ticket To Ride' in April 1965.

Yesterday (EP)

The Beatles' eleventh British extended player, and the first EP to feature a different lead singer on each of the four tracks. It was issued on Parlophone GEP 8948 on 4 March 1966 and the tracks were: 'Yesterday', 'Act Naturally', 'You Like Me Too Much' and 'It's Only Love'.

Yesterday (Single)

Arguably, Paul McCartney's most famous Beatles song. It first appeared on the *Help!* soundtrack in August 1965 and was the title track on a 1966 EP. It resurfaced later in 1966 on *A Collection of Beatles Oldies (But Goldies)* and on the 1973 album *The Beatles 1962–1966*. It was finally released as a single in Britain on 8 March 1976 on Apple R6013 with 'I Should Have Known Better' on the flip. It was included on the 1977 *Love Songs* album and on the 1980 album *The Beatles Ballads* and *The Beatles Box*. In America it was issued as a single on **Capitol** 5498 on 13 September 1965 with 'Act Naturally' on the flip. It also appeared on the 1966 American album *Yesterday And Today*.

For such a classic love ballad, it had a very unromantic working title – 'Scrambled Eggs' is what Paul called the number during the first few days of the song's gestation period. He'd woken up one morning with the tune in his head and immediately began to put it down on the piano. He first played it to George Martin at the George V Hotel in Paris, while it was still under the working title 'Scrambled Eggs', and said he'd wanted a single word title. He mentioned he'd thought of 'Yesterday', but considered it might be too corny. Martin persuaded him it wasn't.

The recording took place on Monday, 14 June 1965, and it turned out to be something of a solo job as Paul's vocals were only accompanied by a guitar and a string quartet. John, George and Ringo don't appear on the track and it was George Martin's idea to include a classic string quartet – a first for a Beatles record. The musicians comprised Tony Gilbert and Sidney Sax on violins, Francisco Gabarro on cello and Kenneth Essex on viola.

Paul commented, 'First of all, I was just playing it through for everyone, saying: "How do you like this song?" I played it just on my acoustic and sang it and the rest of the Beatles said, "That's it, love it." So George Martin and I got together and sort of cooked up this idea. I wanted just a small string accompaniment and he said, "Well, how about your actual string quartet?" I said, "Great, it sounds great." We sat down at the piano and cooked that one up. I was so proud of it, I felt it was an original tune, it didn't copy off anything and it was a big tune, it was all there and nothing repeated. I got made fun of because of it, a bit. I remember George saying, "Blimey, he's always talking about 'Yesterday', you'd think he was Beethoven or somebody." But it's the one, I reckon that it's the most complete thing I've ever written.'

Paul has been quoted as saying that 'Yesterday' is his favourite self-penned number and he has continued to use it in his solo years, performing it on both the **Wings**' world tour in 1975–1976 and the British tour in 1977. It is also included on the *Wings Over America* album.

At one time Paul offered it to singer Chris Farlowe. He also offered it to **Billy J. Kramer**. Kramer had approached Paul in Blackpool and asked him if he had a song suitable to record. Paul played him 'Yesterday', but Billy said the song wasn't what he was looking for.

As it turned out, it became one of the most recorded songs of all time and within seven years of release there were 1,186 separate versions of the number on record.

A million-seller within ten days of release in the States, it received the 1966 **Ivor Novello Award** in Britain as the Outstanding Song of the Year and in America it was the most performed pop song for eight consecutive years, from 1965–1973.

Among the artists who have recorded 'Yesterday' on disc are **Cilla Black**, **Pat Boone**, Nat King Cole, Perry Como, **Marianne Faithfull**, Tom Jones, Otis Redding, Smokey Robinson & the Miracles and Frank Sinatra.

● Yesterday And Today

An American album issued on Capitol ST 2553 on 20 Ju 1966. **Capitol Records** were eager to rush out anoth Beatles album and compiled one containing tracks fr the British albums *Help!*, *Rubber Soul* and *Revolver* whi hadn't been used on the American releases of tho albums. They obtained an additional three tracks fro **EMI** which hadn't been available in the US, and decid on the title because 'Yesterday' was one of the featur tracks.

However, the album was to cause a great deal controversy. In Britain the Beatles had posed for photograph, taken by Robert Whitaker, in which they we dressed in white smocks. As props they had the heads a torsos of dolls and pieces of red meat, which were plac on their laps and shoulders. The picture had been used full-page advertisements in the British musical pre advertising 'Paperback Writer'. It also featured as a fro page colour cover in the music paper *Disc* on 11 Ju 1966.

This was the photograph originally used for the cover *Yesterday And Today*. Advance copies went out to DJs a the media and an immediate controversy was arouse Phone calls of complaint poured into the offices of Capi Records and an emergency meeting was held.

The picture had aroused no great alarm in Britain, ju as Maureen Cleave's article in which John talked abo the Beatles and Christ aroused no opposition in Britain yet the new album cover, which became known as t 'butcher' cover (because the picture was likened to t Beatles wearing butchers' smocks and being in abattoir), was greeted with horror in some quarters America.

Capitol apologized to the media and decided withdraw it and engaged Capitol staff to spend a weeke replacing the 750,000 covers with a different picture – bland shot of the group posing around a travelling tru They also had to destroy promotional material which h already been printed and the entire exercise cost the $200,000. Most employees just threw aside the old slee and replaced it with the new one. In a number instances, employees pasted the new cover over the o one – years later, when fans found they were able to pe off the top layer to reveal the original 'butcher' cover, t 'butcher' sleeves became collectors' items worth hundre of dollars.

The Beatles were perplexed by the American reaction d John Lennon said that the original cover was: '. . . as evant as Vietnam'.

At one time it was suggested that the Beatles had vised the photograph deliberately as a comment on the y Capitol 'butchered' their American albums. This was cause Capitol issued less tracks on American releases an their British equivalents, allowing Capitol to build up tra tracks which could provide material for additional 's.

The album reached No. 1 in the American charts, but pitol said that *Yesterday And Today* was the first and ly Beatles album to lose money – because of the costs sociated with altering the cover and replacing the omotional material.

The tracks were, Side One: 'Drive My Car', 'I'm Only eeping', 'Nowhere Man', 'Doctor Robert', 'Yesterday', ct Naturally'. Side Two: 'And Your Bird Can Sing', 'If I eded Someone', 'We Can Work It Out', 'What Goes ', 'Day Tripper'.

YMCA, *Birkenhead Road, Hoylake, irral L47*

arles Tranter was the organizer responsible for oking acts into the venue and had been an eager ***ersey Beat*** reader and keen to book the Beatles. spite this, when he eventually managed to engage the nd, he advertised them as 'the Beetles'.

Pete Best had been in charge of booking the group d Tranter first wrote to him on 19 August 1961:

'Dear Mr. Best,

'Will you let me have your terms for the services of the etles to play at Hoylake YMCA from 8.00 p.m. till 11.00 n., and if you are available on Friday, the 8th, Sept. xt.

'As I am going away from home in two days time, I uld appreciate it if you could let me have this ormation by return. You can get me on the phone at the ove no. on Monday or Tuesday mornings.

'We have other dates, but this is the present urgent one I wish to fix it before going away'.

No arrangement was made for the Beatles to appear ere on the September date, but the group made a single pearance at the venue on 24 February 1962, although ey were not very well received by the audience and were oed off stage.

● Yolland, Peter

The man who staged the two *Beatles Christmas Shows*.

Yolland had just completed a series of Intermediate French for Schools TV programmes when he was approached in October 1963 to produce the first *Beatles Christmas Show*. Yolland had produced pantomimes in provincial cities for the previous eight years and he received a phone call from agent Joe Collins who asked him whether he would be prepared to produce a show with the Beatles. He accepted the assignment, although he only had six weeks before the show was to open. He was commissioned to devise, produce and direct the Christmas show and stage it at the **Finsbury Park Astoria** in London. He immediately hired TV designer Andrew Drummond to design the sets and worked out that rather than simply present a series of pop acts, he would link the Beatles throughout the show by a series of sketches. He worked on a silent movie sketch and set off to the **Hippodrome, Birmingham** on 10 November, accompanied by a recording engineer to record the Beatles reading their dialogue, which was to be played over the sound system. The shows were a tremendous success with over 100,000 viewing them. They ran from Christmas Eve 1963 to 11 January 1964. As a result Yolland was hired to produce another *Beatles Christmas Show* the following year at the **Odeon, Hammersmith**, in addition to producing a similar show for **Gerry & the Pacemakers** called *Gerry's Christmas Cracker*.

Plans for a third *Beatles Christmas Show* were shelved.

● You Can't Do That

Number penned by John which the group recorded on 25 February 1964 as the flipside of 'Can't Buy Me Love'. It was also included as a track on the *A Hard Day's Night* album and the group performed it on their '**Saturday Club**' and '**From Us To You**' radio recordings. George Harrison played a twelve-string guitar on record for the first time on the number. He'd bought the guitar for $900 while in America and observed that it gave an extra depth to a group sound. Apart from their usual instruments, Paul played cowbells and Ringo played bongos.

'You Can't Do That' is also to be found on the *Rock 'n' Roll Music* compilation, the American *The Beatles Second Album* and *The Beatles Collection* set. They also performed it on the '**Ed Sullivan** Show' and on their summer tour of America in 1964.

● You Don't Understand Me

A number recorded by San Franciscan singer Bobby Freeman in 1960 and immediately included in the Beatles' repertoire, with John Lennon on lead vocals. The Beatles also performed Freeman's minor American hit (it reached No. 37 in the charts) 'Shimmy Shimmy' at the same time.

● You Know My Name (Look Up The Number)

A John Lennon number recorded during the *Sgt Pepper* sessions on Wednesday, 17 May 1967.

Several well-known musicians were rumoured to have guested on the track, including Rolling Stone **Brian Jones** on saxophone. Perhaps this was because the number was originally proposed as a **Plastic Ono Band** follow-up to 'Cold Turkey'. The track was eventually released as the flipside of 'Let It Be' in March 1970.

● You Like Me Too Much

A George Harrison composition recorded on Wednesday, 17 February 1965. George Martin plays a Steinway Grand piano on the track. The number first surfaced on t American album *Beatles VI*, issued in June 1965, and n appeared on the *Help!* album in August 1965. T following year it was included on the *Yesterday* EP March.

● You Never Give Me Your Money

Song penned by Paul and included on the 1969 alb *Abbey Road*. The financial crisis at Apple was t inspiration for this number, about which George Harris commented: 'It's very ironical in a way because you kno we've all got a big house and a car and an office but actually get the money that you've earned is virtua impossible, it's like, illegal to earn money, well, not earn it, it's illegal to keep the money you earn. "You ne give me your money, you only give me your funny paper. you know that's what we get, bits of paper saying h much is earned and what this and that is, but you ne actually get it in pounds, shillings and pence. But I thi it's another one of life's little problems that you ne actually solve.'

Recording of the number actually began at **Olymp**

'Young Blood' – one o the numbers the Beatl performed at the Cavern. (Cavern Mecca)

ound Studios on Tuesday, 6 May 1969, and continued uring July of that year at **Abbey Road**.

● Young, Bernice

young woman who worked for the Beatles' American wyer **Walter Hofer** in his New York office. When the eatles arrived for their American tour in 1966, she was ne of the several members of Hofer's staff who helped out the **Warwick Hotel** where the Beatles were staying.

Young also ran the American branch of the Beatles fficial Fan Club.

● Young Blood

Leiber/Stoller/Doc Pomus composition originally ecorded by the Coasters in 1957. it was added to the eatles' repertoire in 1959 with George performing it on age. When the group recorded it for their **'Pop Go The eatles'** radio show on 11 June 1963, Paul sang lead ocals.

● Young, Muriel

emale TV presenter and disc jockey, born in County urham in 1931, who became the first woman announcer n commercial television when she made her debut on ranada TV in 1955. Muriel then went on to host a umber of pop shows such as '5 o'Clock Club' and Arthur luckslow of **EMI** invited her to be the presenter of the aped shows sponsored by EMI records for **Radio uxembourg**. In 1961 she began to host a show called Monday Spectacular' from **EMI House** in Manchester quare before an audience of 100 people. Later she resented an EMI show from the building called 'Dance arty' and was also host on 'Friday Spectacular'.

When the Beatles appeared on 'Friday Spectacular' to romote 'Please Please Me', Muriel began to announce, And when I tell you that their names are John, Paul, eorge and Ringo . . .' and was then completely drowned n applause and screams.

Muriel was to say, 'The Beatles changed everything. efore them I used to do all my announcing in cocktail rocks and things, but after the Beatles you could wear any asual outfit you wanted. They got rid of all the stuffiness nd many, many years of dressing up. And of course after hem, groups like the **Hollies** and the Animals arrived, nd you looked absolutely potty in those formal clothes, ompletely wrong.'

● You Really Got A Hold On Me

A number penned by William 'Smokey' Robinson which provided the Miracles with their second million-selling single following its release in November 1962. It was included in the Beatles' repertoire the following year with

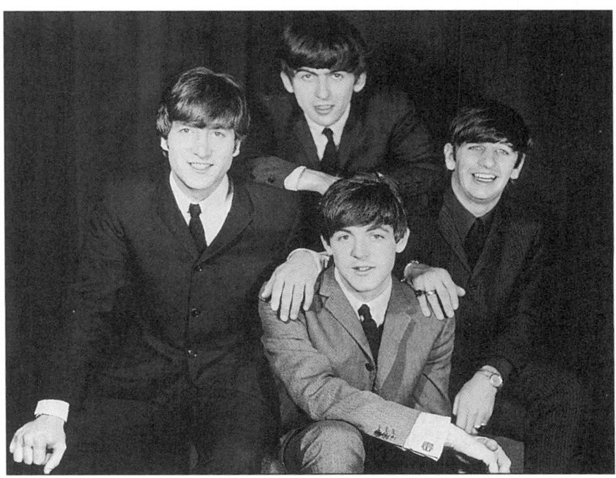

(EMI)

John on vocal, although he shares lead vocal with George on the version they recorded for the *With The Beatles* album. The number was the first track of the new album to be recorded and when they were in the studio on Thursday, 18 July 1963, they also cut another Tamla Motown number, 'Money (That's What I Want)'.

'You Really Got A Hold On Me' was included on the **Capitol** release *The Beatles Second Album* and is part of *The Beatles Collection* set.

The group performed the number on four of their **'Pop Go The Beatles'** radio shows, with John on lead vocal, and they performed the number in the *Let It Be* film, with **Billy Preston** playing organ.

● You're Going To Lose That Girl

A number written by John Lennon in an attempt to capture the spirit of the sound of one of his favourite girl groups, the Shirelles. The Beatles recorded the number on Friday, 19 February 1965.

It was composed for the film *Help!* and appears on the British and American soundtrack albums. It is also included on the 1977 compilation *Love Songs*. It is often wrongly called 'You're Gonna Lose That Girl'.

● *Your Feet's Too Big*

Song composed by Ada Benson and Fred Fisher, which the Beatles included in their repertoire in 1961, with Paul on lead vocal. The song was originally popularized by Fats Waller in 1939, but it's likely that the Beatles included it in their repertoire after hearing the Chubby Checker release in 1961. The Beatles performed it in Hamburg and it's to be found on *The Beatles Live! At The Star Club In Hamburg, Germany: 1962* album.

● *Your Mother Should Know*

A Paul McCartney composition in which he tried to capture some of the spirit of songs from the 1930s. He even mentions in the number: 'a song that was a hit before your mother was born'.

'Your Mother Should Know' was recorded at Chappell Recording Studios at 52 Maddox Street, London W1, on Tuesday and Wednesday 22 and 23 August 1967, due to the fact that the **Abbey Road Studios** were fully booked at the time.

It was also the last recording session undertaken by the Beatles prior to Brian Epstein's death and he actually popped into the Chappell studios on the Wednesday to hear the playbacks of the song. A few days later he was dead.

Further recordings of the song were made at Abbey Road, but Paul decided to use the version recorded at the Chappell Studios. The track appeared on the British *Magical Mystery Tour* soundtrack package of two EPs in December 1967, on the American album *Magical Mystery Tour* issued by **Capitol** in November 1967 and on the British released *Magical Mystery Tour* album issued in November 1976.

● *Your True Love*

A number written and recorded by **Carl Perkins** in 1957. The **Quarry Men** included it in their act with George Harrison on lead vocals and continued to perform it on stage when they became the Beatles.

● *You've Got To Hide Your Love Away*

Written by John at his home, **Kenwood**. He commented, 'This was written in my Dylan days for the film *Help!* When I was a teenager I used to write poetry, but was always trying to hide my real feelings . . . and it's one of those that you sort of sing a bit sadly to yourself.'

(©Apple/Walter Shenson Films)

John started to sing 'Here I stand, head in hand . . then began to think about his emotions and decided he' try to express himself like he'd done in his early writings.

The number was included on the *Help!* soundtrac released in August 1965. It was also included on *Th Beatles 1962–1966* compilation, the 1977 compilatio *Love Songs*, the 1978 *The Beatles Collection*, the 1980 *Th Beatles Ballads* and *Reel Music* in 1982.

Brian Epstein arranged for it to be recorded by th **Silkie**, a folk group he managed who were composed of ex students from Hull University. Their single was jointl produced by John and Paul with Paul playing guitar an George on tambourine. The Silkie single entered the ***Ne Musical Express*** chart for one week at No. 29.

● *You Win Again*

A country-style number written and recorded by th legendary Hank Williams in 1952. **Jerry Lee Lewi** recorded the song in 1958 and it was included in both th **Quarry Men**'s and the Beatles' repertoires, with Joh Lennon on lead vocals.

● *You Won't See Me*

A number penned by Paul, which was featured on th *Rubber Soul* album, issued in December 1965. It was on of three songs needed to complete the album and wa recorded during an extremely lengthy recording session o Thursday, 11 November 1965. The song was also include on the Beatles' twelfth British EP *Nowhere Man*, issued i July 1966.

● Zappa, Frank

altimore-born rock musician of some notoriety. He ›rmed the group the Mothers of Invention and although *gt Pepper's Lonely Hearts Club Band* is regarded as rock usic's first 'concept' album, the claim has also been ade of the Mothers of Invention's debut double album *reak Out*, issued the previous year in August 1966. In ct, Paul McCartney once cited *Freak Out* as a key ıspiration for *Sgt Pepper*. *Freak Out* was one of the first lbums to blend popular music with classical rrangements and its theme was a social commentary on ontemporary America.

Frank was preparing an album to be called 'Our Man In irvana' in 1967, but with the release of *Sgt Pepper* he crapped the plans, instead coming up with *We're Only In For The Money*. This was in reference to the Beatles aking money out of their new psychedelic/hippy image. uring a break in the recording of the album, Zappa and e Mothers visited Britain to appear at the **Albert Hall** nd during the trip Zappa phoned Paul McCartney to ask ermission to parody the *Sgt Pepper* album. Paul referred im to the Beatles management office because: 'He kept lking about "product", so it sounded like a business atter.' Paul was not amused by the Zappa album project, hich caused the LP to be delayed for a few months. appa hired a graphic artist, Calvin Schenkel, to make a arody of the sleeve in which the Sgt Pepper military niforms became dresses for transvestites, with Zappa ppearing in drag surrounded by a host of characters who ıcluded the Phantom Of The Opera and Liberace. The flowers on the *Pepper* sleeve were represented here by carrots and water melons.

In September 1967, Zappa came to the defence of John Lennon in an interview in the British music paper *Disc & Music Echo*, voicing his opinion that John was correct in his statement about the Beatles being more popular than Jesus in an interview with Maureen Cleave.

On 6 June 1971 when Zappa and the Mothers were appearing on a series of concerts at the Fillmore East, the last act to be booked at Bill Graham's famous rock venue which was closing down, John and **Yoko** joined him on stage. The concert was recorded and Zappa had intended using some of the tracks on his forthcoming album *Fillmore East*. **Allen Klein** refused to do a deal, so Zappa let him have the tapes. They turned up on John's double album *Sometime In New York City* and the illustration on the inner sleeve was a parody of Zappa's *Fillmore East* cover. John and Yoko had recorded four numbers with Zappa: 'Well... Baby Please Don't Go', 'Jamrag', 'Scumbag' and 'Au'. 'Scumbag' was a number jointly written by John, Yoko and Frank.

In 1971 Frank also teamed up with Ringo Starr after asking him to appear in his film ***200 Motels***. Ringo took on the roles of both Larry the Dwarf and Frank Zappa. When Zappa's bass guitarist Jeff Simmons left the group, Frank intended replacing him in the film with **Wilfred Brambell**, who'd appeared as Paul's grandfather in *A Hard Day's Night*. He couldn't get him and used Ringo's chauffeur Martin Lickert instead.

● Zapple

An experimental record label from Apple which was launched on 9 May 1969 with two albums, John and **Yoko**'s *Unfinished Music No. 2: Life With The Lions*, which was issued on Zapple 01, and George Harrison's experiments with a moog synthesizer called *Electronic Sound* on Zapple 02. John and Yoko's *Unfinished Music No. 1: Two Virgins*, released prior to the launch of the Zapple label, was issued on Apple, as was the November 1969 LP *The Wedding Album*.

Paul McCartney had originally designed a cover for the series of Zapple albums which featured a large apple-shaped cut-out on the front with a picture printed on the inner sleeve, but this was later dropped.

The label was to specialize in experimental and avant-garde music as well as presenting albums featuring contemporary writers and poets reciting from their works. **Barry Miles** of the Indica Bookshop had already begun to make arrangements on behalf of the label to record literary figures such as Lawrence Ferlinghetti, Michael McClure, Charles Bukowski, Ken Weaver, Charles Olsen, Kenneth Patchen and Richard Brautigan. There was also talk of issuing an album of recordings by Lenny Bruce.

Plans were set in motion to record *Listening to Richard Brautigan* as a third release on Zapple 03, to be issued in Britain on 23 May 1969. The album mainly consisted of author Brautigan reading excerpts from his works, such as *Trout Fishing In America*, *Revenge Of The Lawn*, *The Pill Versus The Springhill Mining Disaster* and *The Telephone Door That Leads Eventually to Some Love Poems*. In the wake of **Allen Klein**'s appearance at Apple, the Zapple label was abandoned before contracts could be exchanged on the Brautigan album and it was never released by Zapple, although the album did appear a year later when **Capitol** issued it on their Harvest label on Harvest ST-424 on 21 September 1970.

Brautigan was to write an introduction to a paperback book *The Beatles Illustrated Lyrics* in 1975.

With the presence of Klein at the helm of Apple, Zapple itself was scrapped after the first two releases, both of which failed to make the charts.

● Zec, Donald

At the time of the Beatles' early rise to fame in Britain, Zec was one of the country's most prestigious show business columnists and one of the *Daily Mirror* newspaper's leading writers. The *Mirror* was also part of the same publishing group as the music weekly, *Melody Maker*, and prior to the news being announced that the Beatles had topped the *Melody Maker* poll as No. 1 grou arrangements were made to boost the group's name with major *Mirror* interview.

Zec began the interview by attending their show at th Odeon, Luton, on 6 September 1963 and then invited th group to his home to complete the interview. While ther he recalled for them the numerous stars, such as Marily Monroe, whom he had interviewed in his flat.

The feature appeared as a double-page spread in th *Daily Mirror* on 10 September 1963 under the headin 'Four Frenzied Little Lord Fauntleroys Who Are Earnin £5,000 A Week'. The earnings were exaggerated as th group weren't pocketing that amount of money at the time Zec also referred to their hair as being 'A stone-age hai style'. Such a large feature in the newspaper with th world's largest circulation was a major boost to their career

● Zodiac Coffee Club, *Duke Street, Liverpool L1*

Small, narrow basement coffee club near Liverpool cit centre where Cilla White (later known as **Cilla Black** used to work part-time behind the counter and where sh met her future husband Bobby Willis. Various members c the local scene used to frequent the premises and on on night there was a lengthy jam session with differen members of local bands, including the Beatles, **Gerry & the Pacemakers**, the Big Three and **Rory Storm & th Hurricanes**.

The club only had one door which acted as bot entrance and exit and the Beatles and several othe musicians were under siege there one night when a loca gang attempted to break down the door and attack th customers.

5¢
THANK
YOU